THIRD EDITION

Life-Span Human Development

THIRD EDITION

Life-Span Human Development

CAROL K. SIGELMAN

THE GEORGE WASHINGTON UNIVERSITY

Brooks/Cole Publishing Company

ITP®An International Thomson Publishing Company

Pacific Grove • Albany • Belmont • Bonn • Boston • Cincinnati • Detroit • Johannesburg • London •
Madrid • Melbourne • Mexico City • New York • Paris • Singapore • Tokyo • Toronto • Washington

Sponsoring Editor: *Jim Brace-Thompson*
Marketing Team: *Lauren Harp, Aaron Eden, Jean Thompson*
Developmental Editor: *Penelope Sky*
Production Coordinator: *Mary Anne Shahidi*
Production: *Cecile Joyner, The Cooper Company*
Manuscript Editor: *Kevin Gleason*
Permissions Editor: *The Permissions Group*
Interior and Cover Design: *Terri Wright*
Cover Illustration: *Hamish MacEwan/SuperStock*

Interior Illustrations and Electronic Art: *Precision Graphics;*
  John and Judy Waller; Cyndie C. H. Wooley; Wayne Clark
Photo Researcher: *Terri Wright*
Indexer: *Do Mi Stauber*
Typesetting: *ColorType, San Diego*
Cover Printing: *Phoenix Color Corporation, Inc.*
Printing and Binding: *Courier Company*
(Credits continue on p. 675.)

For more information, contact:

BROOKS/COLE PUBLISHING COMPANY
511 Forest Lodge Road
Pacific Grove, CA 93950
USA

International Thomson Publishing Europe
Berkshire House 168-173
High Holborn
London WC1V 7AA
England

Thomas Nelson Australia
102 Dodds Street
South Melbourne 3205
Victoria, Australia

Nelson Canada
1120 Birchmount Road
Scarborough, Ontario
Canada M1K 5G4

International Thomson Editores
Seneca 53
Col. Polanco
11560 México, D.F. México

International Thomson Publishing GmbH
Königswinterer Strasse 418
53227 Bonn
Germany

International Thomson Publishing Asia
221 Henderson Road
#05-10 Henderson Building
Singapore 0315

International Thomson Publishing Japan
Hirakawacho Kyowa Building, 3F
2-2-1 Hirakawacho
Chiyoda-ku, Tokyo 102
Japan

Printed in the United States of America

10 9 8 7 6 5 4 3 2

Library of Congress Cataloging-in-Publication Data
Sigelman, Carol K.
    Life-span human development / Carol K. Sigelman. —3rd ed.
        p.   cm.
    Includes bibliographical references and index.
    ISBN 0-534-35442-4
    1. Developmental psychology.   I. Title.
BF713.S53   1999
155—dc21   98-17446
                                                         CIP

To the students who have inspired me

Brief Contents

1 Understanding Life-Span Human Development   1

2 Theories of Human Development   25

3 The Genetics of Life-Span Development   54

4 Early Environmental Influences on Life-Span Development   80

5 The Physical Self   109

6 Perception   142

7 Cognition and Language   170

8 Learning and Information Processing   205

9 Intelligence and Creativity   235

10 Self-Conceptions and Personality   267

11 Gender Roles and Sexuality   296

12 Social Cognition and Moral Development   328

13 Attachment and Social Relationships   360

14 The Family   395

15 Achievement   429

16 Psychological Disorders Throughout the Life Span   461

17 The Final Challenge: Death and Dying   494

Epilogue: Fitting the Pieces Together   522

Contents

CHAPTER 1
Understanding Life-Span Human Development   1

What Is Development?   2
    Developmental Processes   3
How Do People View the Life Span?   4
    Historical Changes in Life-Span Phases   5
        Childhood   5
        Adolescence   6
        Adulthood   6
    Cultural Differences   7
    Subcultural Differences   8
What Is the Science of Life-Span Development?   8
    Goals of Study   8
    Origins   9
    Today's Perspective   10
How Is Developmental Research Conducted?   11
    The Scientific Method   11
    Data Collection   11
        Self-Reports   12
        Behavioral Observations   12
    Developmental Research Designs   13
        Cross-Sectional and Longitudinal Designs   14
        Age, Cohort, and Time of
            Measurement Effects   14
        Strengths and Weaknesses of the
            Cross-Sectional Design   15
        Strengths and Weaknesses of the
            Longitudinal Design   16
        Sequential Designs: The Best of
            Both Worlds   16
    Explaining Development   17
        The Experimental Method   17
        The Correlational Method   18

What Problems Arise in Studying Development?   20
    Choosing Samples   20
    Protecting the Rights of Research Participants   21
SUMMARY POINTS   22
FOOD FOR THOUGHT   23
ON THE WEB   24
KEY TERMS   24

CHAPTER 2
Theories of Human Development   25

The Nature of Theories   26
Basic Issues in Human Development   28
    Assumptions about Human Nature   28
    Nature and Nurture   28
    Activity and Passivity   28
    Continuity and Discontinuity   28
    Universality and Context-Specificity   29
Freud: Psychoanalytic Theory   30
    Instincts and Unconscious Motives   30
    Id, Ego, and Superego   30
    Psychosexual Development   31
    Strengths and Weaknesses   33
Erikson: Neo-Freudian Psychoanalytic Theory   34
    Psychosocial Development   35
    Strengths and Weaknesses   36
Learning Theory   37
    Skinner: Operant Conditioning   37
    Bandura: Social Learning   38
    Strengths and Weaknesses   39

Cognitive-Developmental Theory 40
  Piaget: Intellectual Development 41
  Cognitive Development 41
  Strengths and Weaknesses 43
Contextual Theory 43
  Bronfenbrenner: Ecological Approach
    to Development 44
  Strengths and Weaknesses 46
Theories and World Views 47
  The Organismic World View 47
  The Mechanistic World View 47
  The Contextual World View 48
  Changing World Views 49
Applications: Developmental Theory and
Teenage Pregnancy 49
Clarifying Your Own
Theoretical Perspective 50
SUMMARY POINTS 51
FOOD FOR THOUGHT 52
ON THE WEB 53
KEY TERMS 53

CHAPTER 3

The Genetics of Life-Span Development 54

Species Heredity, Evolution, and
Human Development 55
  Darwin's Theory of Evolution 56
  Modern Evolutionary Perspectives 56
Individual Heredity 57
  The Genetic Code 57
    Genetic Uniqueness and Relatedness 58
    Determination of Sex 58
  Translation of the Genetic Code 59
  Mechanisms of Inheritance 60
    Single Gene-Pair Inheritance 60
    Sex-Linked Inheritance 62
    Polygenic Inheritance 62
  Mutations 63
  Chromosome Abnormalities 63
Studying Genetic and
Environmental Influences 64
  Experimental Breeding 65
  Twin and Adoption Studies 65
  Estimating Influences 65
Accounting for Individual Differences 67
  Intellectual Abilities 67
  Temperament and Personality 68
  Psychological Disorders 69
  Heritability of Traits 70

Heredity and Environment: A Closer Look 71
  Gene/Environment Interactions 71
  Gene/Environment Correlations 72
    Passive Correlations 72
    Evocative Correlations 72
    Active Correlations 72
    Genetic Influence on the Environment 73
Applications: Genetic Counseling
and Engineering 73
  Tay-Sachs Disease 73
  Huntington's Disease 74
  Prevention and Treatment 74
SUMMARY POINTS 77
FOOD FOR THOUGHT 78
ON THE WEB 78
KEY TERMS 79

CHAPTER 4

*Early Environmental Influences on
Life-Span Development* 80

Development in the
Prenatal Environment 82
  Prenatal Stages 82
    Conception and the Germinal Period 82
    The Embryonic Period 82
    The Fetal Period 84
  The Mother's State 88
    Age 88
    Emotional Condition 88
    Nutritional Condition 89
  Teratogens 89
    Diseases 89
    Drugs 91
    Environmental Hazards 94
    Summing Up 95
The Perinatal Environment 95
  Possible Hazards 95
    Anoxia 95
    Complicated Delivery 96
    Medications 97
    Identifying High-Risk Newborns 97
  The Mother's Experience 98
    Cultural Factors 98
    Early Bonding 98
    Postpartum Depression 99
  The Father's Experience 100
The Early Postnatal Environment 100
  Culture and Early Socialization 100
Risk and Resilience 102
  Low-Birth-Weight Babies 103

Applications: Getting Life off to a
Good Start   104
   Before Birth   104
   During Birth   105
   After Birth   105
SUMMARY POINTS   107
FOOD FOR THOUGHT   107
ON THE WEB   108
KEY TERMS   108

Applications: Optimizing
Healthy Development   136
   Nutrition   136
   Exercise   137
   Avoiding Known Health Risks   138
SUMMARY POINTS   139
FOOD FOR THOUGHT   140
ON THE WEB   140
KEY TERMS   141

CHAPTER 5
The Physical Self   109

The Endocrine System   110
The Nervous System   111
   Early Brain Development   112
      Proliferation   112
      Migration   112
      Differentiation   112
      Synaptogenesis   112
   Later Brain Development   114
   The Aging Brain   115
The Infant   116
   The Newborn   116
   Physical Growth   119
      Principles of Growth   119
   Physical Behavior   120
      Locomotor Development   120
      Manipulating Objects   122
      Nature, Nurture, and Motor Development   122
The Child   124
   Steady Growth   124
   Physical Behavior   124
The Adolescent   125
   Physical and Sexual Maturation   125
      The Growth Spurt   125
      Sexual Maturation   125
      Variations in Timing   126
      Psychological Implications   127
      Early versus Late Development   128
   Physical Behavior   128
The Adult   130
   Physical Appearance and Structure   130
   Functioning and Health   130
   The Reproductive System   131
      Menopause   132
      The Male Climacteric   133
   Physical Behavior   134
      Slowing Down   134
   Disease, Disuse, and Abuse   135

CHAPTER 6
Perception   142

Issues of Nature and Nurture   143
The Infant   144
   Assessing Perceptual Abilities   144
      Habituation   144
      Preferential Looking   144
      Operant Conditioning   144
   Vision   145
      Basic Capacities   145
      Pattern Perception   145
      Depth Perception   147
      Organizing a World of Objects   148
      The Infant as Intuitive Theorist   148
   Hearing   149
      Basic Capacities   149
      Perceiving Speech   149
   Taste and Smell   152
   Touch, Temperature, and Pain   153
   Integrating Sensory Information   153
   Influences on Early Perceptual Development   154
      Early Experience and the Brain   154
      The Infant's Active Role   155
      Cultural Variation   155
The Child   156
   The Development of Attention   156
      Longer Attention Span   156
      More Selective Attention   156
      More Systematic Attention   157
   Learning to Read   157
The Adolescent   159
The Adult   160
   Vision   160
      Basic Capacities   160
      Attention and Visual Search   161
   Hearing   162
      Basic Capacities   162
      Speech Perception   163
   Taste and Smell   163
   Touch, Temperature, and Pain   164
   The Adult in Perspective   165

CONTENTS   ix

Applications: Aiding People with
Hearing Impairments 165
SUMMARY POINTS 167
FOOD FOR THOUGHT 168
ON THE WEB 168
KEY TERMS 169

CHAPTER 7

Cognition and Language 170

Piaget's Approach to
Cognitive Development 171
  What Is Intelligence? 171
  How Does Intelligence Develop? 172
The Infant 172
  Substages of the Sensorimotor Stage 173
  The Development of Object Permanence 173
The Child 175
  The Preoperational Stage 175
    Lack of Conservation 175
    Egocentrism 177
    Difficulty with Classification 177
    Did Piaget Underestimate the
      Preschool Child? 177
  The Concrete Operations Stage 178
    Conservation 178
    Seriation and Transitivity 179
    Other Advances 179
The Adolescent 179
  The Formal Operations Stage 179
    Hypothetical and Abstract Thinking 179
    Problem Solving 180
    Progress toward Mastery 182
  Implications of Formal Thought 182
The Adult 183
  Limitations in Cognitive Performance 183
  Growth beyond Formal Operations? 184
  Aging and Cognitive Skills 186
Piaget in Perspective 187
  Piaget's Contributions 187
  Challenges to Piaget 187
Vygotsky's Sociocultural Perspective 188
  Culture and Thought 188
  Social Interaction and Thought 188
  Language and Thought 189
Mastering Language 190
  What Must Be Mastered 191
  The Course of Language Development 191
    Before the First Words 191
    The First Words 192
    Getting the Meaning 193
    Telegraphic Speech 193
    Mastering Grammatical Rules 194
    Later Language Development 195
    Language in Adulthood 195
  How Language Develops 196
    The Learning Perspective 196
    The Nativist Perspective 197
    The Interactionist Perspective 198
    A Critical Period for Language? 199
  Applications: Improving Cognitive Functioning 201
SUMMARY POINTS 202
FOOD FOR THOUGHT 203
ON THE WEB 203
KEY TERMS 204

CHAPTER 8

Learning and Information Processing 205

Basic Learning Processes 206
  Classical Conditioning 206
  Operant Conditioning 207
  Observational Learning 209
  Stability and Change in Learning 211
    Can Young Infants Learn? 211
    Developmental Changes 211
The Information-Processing Approach 212
The Infant 215
  Early Memory 215
  Infantile Amnesia 216
The Child 217
  Learning and Memory 217
    Do Basic Capacities Change? 217
    Do Memory Strategies Change? 218
    Does Knowledge about Memory Change? 219
    Does Knowledge of the World Change? 219
    A Summing Up 220
  Problem Solving 220
The Adolescent 222
The Adult 222
  Developing Expertise 223
  Learning, Memory, and Aging 224
    Areas of Strength and Weakness 224
    Explaining Declines in Old Age 225
  Problem Solving and Aging 228
  Applications: Improving Memory 230
SUMMARY POINTS 232
FOOD FOR THOUGHT 233
ON THE WEB 233
KEY TERMS 233

SUMMARY POINTS 264
FOOD FOR THOUGHT 265
ON THE WEB 266
KEY TERMS 266

CHAPTER 9
Intelligence and Creativity 235

What Is Intelligence? 236
  The Psychometric Approach 236
    A Single Attribute or Many Attributes? 236
    Fluid versus Crystallized Intelligence 238
  Gardner's Theory of Multiple Intelligences 238
  Sternberg's Triarchic Theory 239
    Contextual Component 239
    Experiential Component 240
    Information-Processing Component 240
How Is Intelligence Measured? 240
  The Stanford-Binet Test 240
  The Wechsler Scales 241
  The Distribution of IQ Scores 241
  Intelligence Testing Today 241
The Infant 242
  Developmental Quotients 242
  Infant Intelligence and Later Intelligence 243
The Child 244
  How Stable Are IQ Scores during Childhood? 244
  Causes of Gain and Loss 244
The Adolescent 245
  Continuity between Childhood and Adulthood 245
  IQ and School Achievement 245
The Adult 245
  IQ and Occupational Success 245
  Change in IQ with Age 245
  Predictors of Decline 248
  Potential for Wisdom 249
Factors That Influence IQ Scores 250
  Genes 250
  Home Environment 250
  Social Class Differences 252
  Racial and Ethnic Differences 252
    Culture Bias 253
    Motivational Factors 254
    Genetic Influences 254
    Environmental Influences 254
The Extremes of Intelligence 255
  Mental Retardation 255
  Giftedness 256
Creativity and Special Talents 258
  What Is Creativity? 258
  Creativity in Childhood and Adolescence 259
  Creative Achievement in Adulthood 260
Applications: Boosting Intellectual Performance across the Life Span 262
  Early Intervention for Preschool Children 262
  Enrichment for Low-IQ Adolescents 263
  IQ Training for Aging Adults 263

CHAPTER 10
Self-Conceptions and Personality 267

Conceptualizing the Self 268
  Theories of Personality Development 268
    Psychoanalytic Theory 268
    Psychometric Theory 269
    Social Learning Theory 270
The Infant 271
  The Emerging Self 271
  Temperament 272
    Emotionality, Activity, and Sociability 272
    Behavioral Inhibition 272
    Easy versus Difficult Temperament 273
    Goodness of Fit 274
The Child 274
  Elaborating on a Sense of Self 275
  Self-Esteem 276
  Influences on Self-Esteem 276
  The Personality Stabilizes 277
The Adolescent 278
  Self-Conceptions 278
  Self-Esteem 279
  Forming a Sense of Identity 280
    Developmental Trends 281
    Influences on Identity Formation 282
The Adult 284
  Self-Perceptions 285
  Continuity and Discontinuity in Personality 286
    Do People Retain Their Rankings? 286
    Do Personalities Change Systematically? 286
    Why Do People Change or Remain the Same? 287
  Psychosocial Growth 288
    Before Adulthood 288
    Early Adult Intimacy 289
    Middle-Age Generativity 290
    Old-Age Integrity 291
    A Summing Up 291
Applications: Boosting Self-Esteem 292
SUMMARY POINTS 293
FOOD FOR THOUGHT 294
ON THE WEB 294
KEY TERMS 295

CHAPTER 11
Gender Roles and Sexuality 296

Male and Female 297
Gender Norms and Stereotypes 298
Actual Gender Differences 299
The Infant 301
Differential Treatment 301
Early Learning 301
The Child 302
Acquiring Gender Stereotypes 302
Gender-Typed Behavior 303
The Adolescent 304
Adhering to Gender Roles 304
Theories of Gender-Role Development 305
Biosocial Theory 305
Psychoanalytic Theory 307
Social Learning Theory 308
Cognitive Theory 311
An Attempt at Integration 313
The Adult 314
Gender Roles 314
Masculinity, Femininity, and Androgyny 315
Changes with Age 315
Is Androgyny Advantageous? 316
Sexuality over the Life Span 317
Are Infants Sexual Beings? 317
Childhood Sexuality 317
Knowledge of Sex and Reproduction 317
Sexual Behavior 318
Child Sexual Abuse 319
Adolescent Sexuality 319
Sexual Orientation 320
Sexual Morality 321
Sexual Behavior 321
Adult Sexuality 322
Explanations for Declining Activity 323
Applications: Changing Gender-Role Attitudes and Behavior 325
SUMMARY POINTS 325
FOOD FOR THOUGHT 326
ON THE WEB 327
KEY TERMS 327

CHAPTER 12
Social Cognition and Moral Development 328

Social Cognition 329
Developing a Theory of Mind 329
Person Perception 332
Role-Taking Skills 332
Social-Cognitive Development in Adulthood 334
Perspectives on Moral Development 335
Moral Affect: Psychoanalytic Theory 335
Moral Reasoning:
Cognitive-Developmental Theory 336
Piaget's Theory 336
Kohlberg's Theory 336
Moral Behavior: Social Learning Theory 339
The Infant 339
Early Moral Training 340
Prosocial Behavior 341
The Child 341
Research on Kohlberg's View 341
Research on Piaget's View 342
Ignoring Intentions? 342
Viewing Rules as Sacred? 342
Moral Behavior 343
How Does One Raise Moral Children? 344
The Adolescent 345
Changes in Moral Reasoning 345
Antisocial Behavior 346
Dodge's Social-Information Processing Model 346
Contributors to Aggression 348
The Adult 349
Moral Development 349
Religion and Adult Life 350
Kohlberg's Theory in Perspective 350
Support for Kohlberg 350
Factors That Promote Moral Growth 351
Cognitive Growth 351
Relevant Social Experience 351
Is the Theory Biased? 352
Culture Bias? 352
Liberal Bias? 352
Gender Bias? 354
Is the Theory Incomplete? 354
Applications: Combating Youth Violence 355
Improving Moral Reasoning 355
Building Social Information-Processing Skills 356
Breaking Coercive Cycles 356
SUMMARY POINTS 357
FOOD FOR THOUGHT 358
ON THE WEB 358
KEY TERMS 359

CHAPTER 13
Attachment and Social Relationships   360

Perspectives on Relationships   361
  What Do We Gain from Relationships?   361
  Which Relationships Are Most Critical?   362
    Attachment Theory   362
    Peers and the Two Worlds of Childhood   363
The Infant   364
  Early Emotional Development   364
    Development of Specific Emotions   364
    Socialization of Emotions   364
    Emotion Regulation   365
  The First Relationship   366
    Caregiver's Attachment to Infant   366
    Infant's Attachment to Caregiver   367
    Attachment-Related Fears   367
    Exploratory Behavior   369
  Types of Attachment   369
    Influences on the Quality of
      Early Attachments   370
  *Early Attachment and
    Later Development*   372
    Effects of Social Deprivation   372
    Later Development of Securely and Insecurely
      Attached Infants   373
  First Peer Relations   376
The Child   377
  Parent/Child Attachments   377
  Peer Networks   378
  Play   378
    Play Becomes More Social   378
    Play Becomes More Imaginative   379
    Play Becomes More Rule-Governed   379
    What Good Is Play?   379
  Peer Acceptance and Popularity   380
  Friendships   382
  Contributions of Peers to Development   382
The Adolescent   382
  Attachments to Parents   383
  Friendships   383
  Changing Social Networks   384
    Cliques and Crowds   384
    Dating   385
  Parent and Peer Influence   385
The Adult   386
  Social Networks   386
  Romantic Relationships   387
    Partner Selection   387
    Attachment Styles   387
  Adult Friendships   389
  Adult Relationships and Adult Development   390

Applications: Building
Good Relationships   390
SUMMARY POINTS   392
FOOD FOR THOUGHT   393
ON THE WEB   393
KEY TERMS   394

CHAPTER 14
The Family   395

Understanding the Family   396
  The Family as a System   396
  The Family as a System within Other Systems   397
  The Family as a Changing System   397
  *A Changing Family System
    in a Changing World*   398
The Infant   399
  The Mother/Infant Relationship   399
  The Father/Infant Relationship   399
  *Mothers, Fathers, and Infants: The System
    at Work*   400
The Child   401
  Dimensions of Child Rearing   401
    Social Class, Economic Hardship,
      and Parenting   402
    Cultural and Ethnic Variation in Parenting   404
    Child Effects on Parents   405
  Sibling Relationships   406
    A New Baby Arrives   406
    Ambivalence in Sibling Relationships   406
    Contributions to Development   407
The Adolescent   408
  Parent/Child Closeness   408
  Renegotiating the Relationship   408
The Adult   409
  Establishing the Marriage   409
  New Parenthood   410
  The Child-Rearing Family   411
  The Empty Nest   412
  Grandparenthood   412
  Changing Family Relationships   414
    The Marital Relationship   414
    Sibling Relationships   415
    Parent/Child Relationships   415
Diversity in Family Life   417
  Singles   417
  Childless Married Couples   418
  Gay and Lesbian Families   418
  Families Experiencing Divorce   419
    Before the Divorce   419

After the Divorce: Crisis
and Reorganization 419
Remarriage and Reconstituted Families 421
Applications: Confronting the Problem of
Family Violence 422
Why Does Family Violence Occur? 423
The Abuser 423
The Abused 424
The Context 424
What Are the Effects of Abuse? 425
How Do We Solve the Problem? 425
SUMMARY POINTS 426
FOOD FOR THOUGHT 427
ON THE WEB 428
KEY TERMS 428

CHAPTER 15
Achievement 429

Achievement Motivation 431
Need for Achievement 431
The Value Placed on Achievement 431
Expectancies of Success 431
Attributions for Success and Failure 431
The Infant 432
Early Origins of Achievement Motivation 432
Influences on Effectance Motivation 433
Mastery through Play 433
The Child 434
Master-Oriented and Helpless
Achievement Styles 435
Age Differences 435
Parent Contributions 435
Schooling and School Achievement 436
Benefits of Preschool 436
Benefits of School 438
Effective Schools 438
Making Integration and Inclusion Work 440
The Adolescent 441
Declining Achievement Motivation 441
Cognitive Growth 441
Negative Feedback 441
Peer Pressures 442
Pubertal Changes 442
Poor Person/Environment Fit 442
Making Vocational Choices 443
Working after School 444
Pathways to Adulthood 445
The Adult 445
Achievement Motivation 446
Levinson's Conception of Adult Development 446

Career Paths during Adulthood 447
Exploration and Establishment 447
Midlife Crisis? 448
Aging Workers 449
Women, Work, and the Family 450
Sex Discrimination 450
Role Conflict and Overload 450
Implications for Children 451
Work and Adult Development 452
Retirement 452
Successful Aging 454
Applications: Improving the Quality
of Education 455
SUMMARY POINTS 457
FOOD FOR THOUGHT 459
ON THE WEB 459
KEY TERMS 460

CHAPTER 16
Psychological Disorders Throughout the Life Span 461

What Makes Development Abnormal? 462
Criteria for Diagnosing Psychological Disorders 462
Considering Social Norms 462
Considering Age Norms 463
Specific Diagnostic Criteria 463
Developmental Psychopathology 464
Psychopathology as Development,
Not Disease 464
Developmental Issues 465
The Infant 465
Infantile Autism 465
Suspected Causes 466
Developmental Outcomes 467
Depression 468
The Child 469
Attention-Deficit Hyperactivity Disorder 469
Developmental Course 470
Suspected Causes 471
Treatment 471
Depression 473
Nature, Nurture, and Childhood Disorders 474
Do Childhood Problems Persist? 475
The Adolescent 476
Is Adolescence Really a Period of Storm
and Stress? 476
Eating Disorders 477
Suspected Causes 477
Treatment 479
Drinking and Drug Use 479
Depression and Suicidal Behavior 480

The Adult   482
   Stress and Coping   482
      Age and Stressful Experiences   483
      Age and Coping Skills   483
      When Coping Fails   484
   Depression   484
      Age Differences   484
      Sex Differences   485
      Diathesis/Stress   485
   Aging and Dementia   486
      Alzheimer's Disease   486
      Other Causes of Cognitive Impairment   488
Applications: Treating Psychological Disorders   488
   Treating Children and Adolescents   489
   Treating Elderly Adults   490
Is Psychopathology Adaptive?   490
SUMMARY POINTS   491
FOOD FOR THOUGHT   492
ON THE WEB   492
KEY TERMS   493

CHAPTER 17
The Final Challenge: Death and Dying   494

Life and Death Issues   495
   What Is Death?   495
      Biological Definitions of Death   495
      Social Meanings of Death   496
   What Kills Us and When?   498
   Theories of Aging: But Why Do We Age and Die?   499
      Programmed Theories   500
      Damage Theories   501
      Nature and Nurture Conspiring   501
      Theories of Aging and Life Extension   502
The Experience of Dying   502
   Kübler-Ross's Stages of Dying   502
   Criticisms and Alternative Views   503
The Experience of Bereavement: An Attachment Model   504
The Infant   506
The Child   507
   Grasping the Concept of Death   507
   The Dying Child   508
   The Bereaved Child   509
The Adolescent   510
The Adult   511
   Death Anxiety   511
   Death and the Family Life Cycle   512
      The Loss of a Spouse   512

      The Loss of a Child   513
      The Loss of a Parent   515
   Who Copes and Who Succumbs?   515
      Defining Pathological Grief   515
      Personal Resources   517
      The Nature of the Loss   517
      The Context of Supports and Stressors   517
      Bereavement and Human Development   518
Applications: Lessening the Sting of Death   518
   For the Dying   518
   For the Bereaved   519
SUMMARY POINTS   520
FOOD FOR THOUGHT   521
ON THE WEB   521
KEY TERMS   521

Epilogue: Fitting the Pieces Together   522

Major Trends in Human Development   523
   1. Infants (Birth to Age 2)   523
   2. Preschool Children (Ages 2 through 5)   524
   3. School-Age Children (Ages 6 through 11)   524
   4. Adolescents (Ages 12 through 19)   526
   5. Young Adults (Ages 20 through 39)   526
   6. Middle-Aged Adults (Ages 40 through 64)   528
   7. Older Adults (Age 65 and Up)   528
Major Themes in Human Development   529
   1. We Are Whole Persons throughout the Life Span   529
   2. Development Proceeds in Multiple Directions   529
   3. There Is Both Continuity and Discontinuity in Development   529
   4. There Is Much Plasticity in Human Development   530
   5. Nature and Nurture Truly Interact in Development   531
   6. We Are Individuals, Becoming Even More Diverse with Age   532
   7. We Develop in a Cultural and Historical Context   532
   8. We Are Active in Our Own Development   533
   9. Development Is Best Viewed as a Lifelong Process   533
   10. Development Is Best Viewed from Multiple Perspectives   533

Glossary   535
References   551
Author Index   643
Subject Index   663

Preface

My purpose in writing this overview of life-span human development is to arouse students' curiosity about how and why human beings both change and remain the same from their beginnings as fertilized eggs to their last years of life. I share the best theories, research, and practical advice that developmentalists have to offer. I want students to understand that human development is an incredibly complex process that reflects transactions between a changing person and a changing world; I want them to appreciate that we do not stop developing at age 21. I hope to help them see that major theories of human development do not just guide researchers but can help anyone analyze the real-life issues we all face. I want them to believe as strongly as I do that the best advice about such matters as raising children, working with troubled adolescents, and easing the adjustment of new nursing home residents comes from research rather than from armchair speculation or the pronouncements of authorities.

Guided by these goals, I have included complex theoretical controversies such as the nature/nurture issue as well as the best classic and contemporary research from the several disciplines concerned with understanding developmental processes. But I also appreciate that solid scholarship is of little good to students unless they want to read it and can understand it. I have long believed that even the most complex issues in human development can be made clear through straightforward writing, apt use of examples and analogies, and highlighting the relevance of course concepts to students' lives and to the work of parents, teachers, psychologists, nurses, day-care workers, and other human service professionals. In short, I have aimed for a book that is both rigorous and readable, both research-oriented and "real."

An Integrated Topical and Chronological Approach

The large majority of life-span development textbooks are organized chronologically, carving the life span into age ranges and describing the prominent characteristic of individuals within each range. By contrast, I combine topical and chronological approaches within topics. Each chapter is focused on a domain of development such as physical growth, cognition, or personality, and developmental trends in the domain are traced from infancy to old age.

Why Topical?

Why have I bucked the tide? Like many other instructors, I have typically favored topically organized textbooks when teaching child, adolescent, or adult development courses. As a result, it seemed only natural to apply the same approach to the whole life span. Besides, chronological texts have to repeat themselves so we remember where development left off in an earlier period.

More important, a topical organization conveys the flow of development—the systematic and often truly dramatic transformations that take place in the course of human life, as well as the developmental continuities that maintain individual identity. The topical approach also lets us emphasize developmental *processes;* it helps us see how nature and nurture interact over the life span to bring about normal developmental changes as well as to create differences among individuals.

Finally, a predominantly topical approach is compatible with a *life-span perspective* on human development, which views events in the context of what comes before and what is yet to come. In chronologically organized textbooks, many topics are discussed only in terms of the age group to which they seem most relevant—for example, attachment in relation to infancy, play in relation to the preschool years, or sexuality in relation to adolescence and adulthood. Because this is a topical life-span text, I have repeatedly grappled with intriguing questions that I might otherwise not even have asked. Consider the topic of attachment: What do infants' attachments to their parents have in common with attachments between childhood friends or adult romantic partners? Do securely attached infants later have a greater capacity to form and sustain friendship or romantic partnerships than infants who lacked a close attachment early in life? Attachments are important throughout the life span, and a topical organization helps me make that clear.

Why Chronological?

Although I adopted a topical approach because I consider it the best way to introduce the how and why of human development, I also appreciate the strengths of the chronological approach, particularly its ability to portray the whole person in each period of the life span. For this reason, I have incorporated the age/stage approach within the topical framework, hoping to have the best of both worlds.

Each topical chapter contains major sections on infancy, childhood, adolescence, and adulthood. (Of course, I emphasize a particular period more or less depending on its significance to the topic under consideration.) These age/stage sections call attention to the distinctive qualities of each phase of life and make it easy for students to find material on a period of particular interest. Moreover, they allow instructors who wish to move toward an age/stage approach to cover infancy, childhood, and adolescence in the first portion of the course and save the material on adulthood for the end.

Throughout the text, I have also highlighted the intimate relationships among physical, cognitive, and psychosocial development at any age. In an epilogue, I summarize major developments in each of seven periods of the life span, as well as the broad themes in life-span development emphasized throughout the book. This integrative conclusion will be a handy reference for students who want "the big picture"; some instructors use it as a prologue at the start of the course as well as an epilogue at the end.

Organization

The book begins with an introduction to the scientific study of life-span development (Chapter 1) and to the central issues and theoretical perspectives that have dominated the field (Chapter 2). It continues with an in-depth examination of genetic influences (Chapter 3) and early environmental influences (Chapter 4) on development. In these chapters we'll see how genes contribute to maturational changes and individual differences throughout the life span and how people are also the products of a prenatal environment and of postnatal experiences that vary as a function of cultural context. If students gain nothing else from their study of human development, I hope they appreciate how many forces interact to create the developing person.

Chapters on the growth and aging of the body and nervous system (Chapter 5) and on the development of sensory and perceptual capacities (Chapter 6) launch our examination of basic human capacities. Chapter 7 covers Piaget's perspective on cognitive development, the quite different perspective offered by Lev Vygotsky, and how the development of language relates to the development of thought; in Chapter 8, learning, memory, and problem solving are examined from an information-processing perspective; and in Chapter 9 the psychometric approach to cognition is highlighted as we explore individual differences in intelligence and creativity.

The next three chapters are concerned with the development of the self—changes in self-conceptions and personality (Chapter 10), in gender roles and sexuality (Chapter 11), and in social cognition and morality (Chapter 12). The self is set more squarely in a social context as we trace life-span changes in attachments and other relationships (Chapter 13), in roles and relationships within the family (Chapter 14), and in life achievements in the context of play, school, and work (Chapter 15). Finally, I offer a life-span perspective on developmental problems and disorders (Chapter 16) and examine why people die and how we cope with death (Chapter 17).

Although links between chapters are noted throughout, instructors who teach short courses or who are otherwise pressed for time can omit a chapter here or there without disturbing the others. For example, a cognitively oriented course might omit one or more of Chapters 11, 14, 15, 16, and 17; a socially oriented course might omit some of the cognitive chapters (Chapters 6–9).

New Features

The basic structure of the book has not been changed. One goal of rewriting was to perfect the organization. For example, material on social cognition was moved from Chapter 13 to Chapter 12 to provide a context for the topic of moral development; meanwhile, material was exported from Chapter 12 to Chapter 15 to help create a new chapter on achievement motivation and achievement. Emotional development is integrated with material on attachment in Chapter 13, and sexuality is now covered at the end of Chapter 11, after the broader topic of gender-role development has been explored.

A second goal was to call even more attention to interactions of nature and nurture, giving serious attention to genes, hormones, and other biological forces while showing how development is affected by the individual's cultural and subcultural environment. The theme of goodness of fit between person and environment is now stronger. Finally, I have updated the book from start to finish with hundreds of new research reports. In pursuing these goals, I have added some exciting new topics and greatly expanded and updated coverage of other subjects. A sampling:

◆ Expanded survey of historical changes in the life span (Chapter 1)
◆ Bronfenbrenner's ecological approach highlighted as an example of a contextual theory of human development (Chapter 2)
◆ Latest breakthroughs in research on genetic diseases and disorders (Chapter 3)
◆ New reproductive technologies, from artificial insemination to cloning, and their implications (Chapter 4)
◆ New section on the development and aging of the brain, and coverage of the dynamic systems approach to studying motor development (Chapter 5)
◆ Examination of the notion that infants come equipped with intuitive theories of the physical world that guide their perceptions (Chapter 6)
◆ More on Lev Vygotsky's influential thinking about social influences on cognitive development and language (Chapter 7)
◆ New evidence demonstrating impressive memory skills in young infants (Chapter 8)
◆ New work explaining racial and ethnic differences in intellectual test performance (Chapter 9)
◆ More on infant temperament and on continuity and discontinuity over the life span in the key dimensions of personality known as "the big five" (Chapter 10)
◆ New evidence concerning how biology and gender-role socialization influence whether a child identifies as male or female (Chapter 11)
◆ Expanded coverage of how 3- and 4-year-olds develop a theory of mind that lets them understand why people behave as they do (Chapter 12)
◆ Applications of attachment theory to the infant's emotional development, the college student's anxiety upon leaving home for college, the lover's jealousy, and the willingness of adult children to care for their aging parents (Chapter 13)
◆ New research on the developmental implications of being a "latchkey child" after school (Chapter 14)
◆ The influence of views of ability and effort on children's achievement in school and an analysis of why Asian students outperform American students (Chapter 15)
◆ Intriguing arguments, growing out of evolutionary theory, that psychological disorders may serve adaptive functions (Chapter 16)
◆ Challenges to the assumption that people must work through their grief and sever their attachment in order to recover from the death of a loved one (Chapter 17)

Chapter Organization

Although not all these features will be found in the first four chapters, most chapters have a standard format.

◆ A *chapter outline* that orients students to what lies ahead
◆ *Introductory material* that stimulates interest, previews the chapter, and introduces key concepts and relevant theories and issues
◆ *Developmental sections* that describe important changes and continuities and the mechanisms underlying them during infancy, childhood, adolescence, and adulthood
◆ *Applications* that show how knowledge has optimized development in the given domain; for example, genetic counseling; innovations in care for premature babies; programs for improving health, intellectual functioning, self-esteem, and social relationships; and efforts to reduce youth violence and abusive family relationships
◆ *Summary points* to help students review the main themes
◆ *Food for Thought* questions that challenge students to apply the chapter material in new ways
◆ *On the Web,* a short list of sites on the World Wide Web that can provide further information on chapter topics and serve as the basis for student projects
◆ *Key Terms,* a list of the new terms introduced in the chapter, in order of appearance. (The terms are printed in boldface and defined when they are first presented and reappear alphabetically in the glossary at the end of the book.)

In addition, each chapter contains photographs, tables, and figures. Although some of these are intended to interest or to entertain, they have a serious educational purpose as well: summarizing stage theories, presenting revealing research data, or illustrating concepts discussed in the chapter.

Similarly, the boxes are integral to the text. They offer a closer look at selected topics, including ways of combating the infant's fear of strange babysitters, language acquisition among deaf children, misconceptions about hyperactivity, implications of early and late puberty, cultural differences in the experience of menopause, and interventions to increase the well-being of nursing home residents.

Finally, a word on referencing. In each chapter I cite the authors and dates of publication for a large number of books and articles, which are listed in full in the chapter-by-chapter bibliography at the end of the book. Although some students may find these citations distracting, they are included for good reasons: because I am committed to the value of systematic research, because I must give credit where credit is due, and because I want students and their professors to have the resources they need to pursue their interests in human development.

Supplementary Aids

The *Instructor's Manual* contains chapter outlines, learning objectives, graphics that can be converted to transparencies for use in class, and suggestions for class discussion, projects, films, videos, and additional readings. The test bank (available in print and on disk) offers multiple-choice, true–false, and essay questions for each chapter. Acetate transparencies and videotapes are also available.

The *Student Study Guide* is designed to promote active learning through a guided review of the important principles and concepts in the text. The study materials for each chapter include a comprehensive multiple-choice self-test and a number of applications, exercises that challenge students to think about and to apply what they have learned.

Brooks/Cole now has a *Web site* that supports this book in its on-line Psychology Study Center. As a leader in psychology publishing, Brooks/Cole is committed to bringing you the tools you need to teach or study psychology in new media. Study centers provide added instructional material in selected areas for both instructors and students. Features include chapter quizzes, discussion forums, links to related Internet resources, downloadable images, and more:

http://psychstudy.brookscole.com

Acknowledgments

A project of this magnitude cannot be carried out without the help of many people, all of whom deserve my deepest thanks. I am very grateful to the reviewers of the manuscript for their constructive criticism and useful suggestions. Reviewers of the first edition included Freda Blanchard-Fields of Louisiana State University, Janet Fritz of Colorado State University, John Klein of Castleton State College, Rosanne Lorden of Eastern Kentucky University, Robin Palkovitz of the University of Delaware, Suzanne Pasch of the University of Wisconsin at Milwaukee, and Katherine Van Giffen of California State University at Long Beach. Reviewers of the second edition were David Beach of the University of Wisconsin-Parkside, Charles Harris of James Madison University, Malia Huchendorf of Normandale Community College, Vivian Jenkins of the University of Southern Indiana, Nancy Macdonald of the University of South Carolina-Sumter, Jim O'Neill of Wayne State University, Marjorie Reed of Oregon State University, and Ruth Wilson of Idaho State University.

Reviewers of this edition were Bob Bornstein, Miami University-Oxford; Donna Brent, Hartwick College; Mary Ann Bush, Western Michigan University; Shelley Drazen, Binghamton University (SUNY); Suzanne Krinsky, University of Southern Colorado; Becky Loewy; Russell Miars, Portland State University; Elizabeth Rider, Elizabethtown College; Eileen Rogers, University of Texas-San Antonio; Timothy Shearon, Albertson College of Idaho; Polly Trnavsky, Appalachian State University; and Catherine Weir, Colorado College.

I would like to thank David Shaffer of the University of Georgia for everything he did to make the first and second editions of this book successful and for continuing our productive collaboration as we traded drafts and references. His outstanding developmental textbooks inspired me to write one myself.

For all that she did, so quietly and competently, to assist me during all phases of this project, from lugging books from the library and researching new topics to checking for missing references, Leokadia (Lodi) Lipien cannot be thanked enough; I truly could not have completed this edition without her, and I look forward to the time when she writes her own books on human development. Julie Relyea did a fine job of stepping in for Lodi when needed. Cathey Weir of Colorado College played a critical role in this edition, devoting many hours of her sabbatical leave to finding just the reference material I needed to respond to a reviewer's point or to update a section. I hope that she will enjoy teaching with this book more than ever.

Credit for excellent supplementary materials goes to Elizabeth Rider of Elizabethtown College, who is unrivaled in her ability to write thought-provoking material for study guides and instructor's manuals, and to Jennifer Kofkin, who joined Betty in preparing the instructor's manual this time around. I am delighted that Betty has chosen to stay with this book through all three of its editions.

Producing this book required the joint efforts of Brooks/Cole Publishing and The Cooper Company. I thank Jim Brace-Thompson and Penelope Sky of Brooks/Cole for overseeing the process; Cecile Joyner for her meticulous management of the book's production; Kevin Gleason for his capable copy editing; and Terri Wright for her creative work on the graphic design. These pros were a joy to work with, and the book is much better because of them.

I am also deeply indebted to the sponsoring editors who preceded Jim. I have not forgotten my debt to C. Deborah Laughton, who persuaded me to take on this project in the first place, or to Vicki Knight, who skillfully shepherded the first edition through its final stages and oversaw the second edition until placing the project in the capable hands of Jim. Finally, Lee Sigelman has coped superbly once again with a distracted and unamusing partner, and Andrew and Gooseberry Sigelman richly deserve more quality lap time with their mother.

Carol K. Sigelman

About the Author

Carol K. Sigelman is associate vice president for research and graduate studies and professor of psychology at The George Washington University. She has also taught at Texas Tech University, Eastern Kentucky University (where she won the Outstanding Teacher Award), and the University of Arizona. She has taught courses in child, adolescent, adult, and lifespan development for 25 years and has published extensively on such topics as the communication skills of individuals with developmental disabilities, peer reactions to children and adolescents who are different, and children's developing understanding of diseases and psychological disorders. Recently, through a grant from the National Institute of Child Health and Human Development, she studied children's intuitive theories of AIDS and developed and evaluated a curriculum to correct their misconceptions and teach them the basic facts of HIV infection. Now, through a grant from the National Institute on Drug Abuse, she and her colleagues are doing similar research on how well children of different ages understand the effects of alcohol and drugs on body, brain, and behavior.

CHAPTER 1

Understanding Life-Span Human Development

WHAT IS DEVELOPMENT?
Developmental Processes

HOW DO PEOPLE VIEW THE LIFE SPAN?
Historical Changes in Life-Span Phases
Cultural Differences
Subcultural Differences

WHAT IS THE SCIENCE OF LIFE-SPAN DEVELOPMENT?
Goals of Study
Origins
Today's Perspective

HOW IS DEVELOPMENTAL RESEARCH CONDUCTED?
The Scientific Method
Data Collection
Developmental Research Designs
Explaining Development

WHAT PROBLEMS ARISE IN STUDYING DEVELOPMENT?
Choosing Samples
Protecting the Rights of Research Participants

SUMMARY POINTS

FOOD FOR THOUGHT

ON THE WEB

KEY TERMS

When Robert Dole ran for President in 1996 at the age of 73, Ella Miller, nearing age 116, did not think he was too old. In fact, although she voted for Clinton, she figured age was an advantage for Dole: "I think he's just beginning to be a man. I've learned more since I've become old" (Tousignant, 1996, p. B5).

Mrs. Miller's developmental history is quite a saga. Born in Tennessee in 1880, 15 years after the Civil War and years before the automobile, she was the eldest daughter of former slaves. She had only two dresses as a child, and she recalls seeing her first airplane and thinking it was going to fall on her (Tousignant, 1995). She received no formal education. She married but had no children; her husband died when she was 40, and she then worked as a domestic helper for two elderly women until she retired (at age 107!). One of the nearly 60,000 **centenarians** (persons age 100 or older) in the United States, Mrs. Miller lives with her niece, remains active, and stocks up on candy and cookies whenever she goes grocery shopping. The secret to her longevity? She never worries: "I try to make life more jolly than sad" (Tousignant, 1996, p. B5).

Centenarian Ella Miller, daughter of former slaves, at age 115

This book is about human development from conception to death. Among the many, many questions it addresses are these: How in the world does a single fertilized egg cell evolve into an adult human being like Ella Miller? What does the world look like to newborn infants? Does the divorce of a child's parents have any lasting effects on the child's personality or later relationships with the other sex? Why do some college students have more trouble than others deciding on a major or committing themselves to a serious relationship? Do most adults really experience a midlife crisis in which they question what they have done with their lives? Is retirement good or bad for a person's sense of well-being?

Do any of these questions intrigue you? Probably so, for we are all developing persons who interact daily. What *are* we interested in, if not in ourselves and the people close to us? Most college students want to understand how they and those they know have been affected by their experiences, how they have changed over the years, and where they may be heading. Many students also have very practical motivations for learning about human development—for example, a desire to be a better parent or to work more effectively as a psychologist, nurse, teacher, or other human service professional.

This introductory chapter lays the groundwork for the remainder of the book by addressing some basic questions about the nature of life-span human development and describing ways to study it. Let's begin by asking what it means to say that people "develop" over the life span.

WHAT IS DEVELOPMENT?

We can define **development** as *systematic changes and continuities in the individual that occur between conception and death,* or "from womb to tomb." By describing changes as "systematic," we imply that they are orderly, patterned, and relatively enduring; temporary and unpredictable changes such as mood swings are therefore excluded. We are also interested in "continuities" in development, ways in which we remain the same or continue to reflect our pasts.

The systematic changes and continuities of interest to students of human development fall into three broad domains:

1. *Physical development:* the growth of the body and its organs during childhood; the functioning of physiological systems; the appearance of physical signs of aging during adulthood; gains, losses, and continuities in motor abilities; and so on.
2. *Cognitive development:* changes in perception, language, learning, memory, problem-solving, and other mental processes.

3. *Psychosocial development:* change and carryover in personal and interpersonal aspects of development, such as motives, emotions, personality traits, interpersonal skills and relationships, and roles played in the family and in the larger society.

Even though developmentalists often specialize in one or another of these three aspects of development, they appreciate that humans are *whole* beings and that changes in one area affect the others. The baby who develops the ability to crawl, for example, now has new opportunities to develop her mind by exploring the contents of shelves and cabinets and to hone her social skills by accompanying her parents from room to room.

How do you think humans typically change from birth to old age? Many people picture the life span this way: First there are tremendous positive gains in capacity from infancy to young adulthood; then there is little change at all during young adulthood and middle age; and finally there is only loss of capacities—a process of deterioration—in the later years. This stereotyped view of the life span is largely, although not entirely, false. It has some truth for biological and physical development. Traditionally, biologists have defined **growth** as the physical changes that occur from conception to maturity. We do indeed become biologically mature and physically competent during the early part of the life span. *Aging,* in a biological sense, is the deterioration of organisms (including human beings) that leads inevitably to their death. Biologically, then, development does involve growth in early life, stability in early adulthood, and the declines associated with aging in later life.

Most developmental scholars today have rejected this simple model of the life span, however. When they speak of *development,* they now mean more than positive changes that occur in infancy, childhood, and adolescence. They believe that developmental change consists of both gains and losses or may simply represent a difference between earlier and later behavior (as when a four-year-old who once feared loud noises comes to fear hairy monsters under the bed instead). Also, developmentalists today use the term **aging** to refer to a wide range of changes, both positive and negative, in the *mature* organism (Birren & Zarit, 1985). They maintain that both positive and negative changes—gains and losses—occur in every phase of the life span, and so we should not associate aging only with loss (Baltes, Smith, & Staudinger, 1992).

Consider this: From early childhood to young adulthood, although we certainly do gain many new abilities, we also experience negative changes such as increased rates of depression and suicide (Kagan, 1986). From our teenage years to our 40s, when we are supposedly not changing much, we are typically gaining self-confidence and other psychological strengths (Haan, 1981), and we are aging as well. And, although many elderly adults do find themselves becoming somewhat slower mentally, many are also still acquiring knowledge and expertise that young people lack (Baltes et al., 1992). In short, *development involves gains, losses, just plain changes, and samenesses in each phase of the life span.* Above all, we should abandon the idea that aging involves only deterioration and loss.

Developmental Processes

Two important processes underlie developmental change: maturation and learning. **Maturation** is the biological unfolding of the individual according to a plan contained in the *genes* (the hereditary material passed from parents to child at conception). Just as seeds systematically become mature plants (assuming that they receive the necessary nourishment from their environment), human beings "unfold" within the womb. Their genetic "program" then calls for them to walk and utter their first words at about 1 year of age, to achieve sexual maturity at age 12 to 14, and even to age and die. Since the child's brain also undergoes maturational alterations, there are cognitive changes such as increased memory skills and psychosocial changes such as increased understanding of other people's feelings. Genetically influenced maturational processes guide all of us through many of the same developmental changes at about the same points in our lives.

The second critical developmental process is **learning,** the process through which *experience* brings about relatively permanent changes in thoughts, feelings, or behavior. A certain degree of physical maturation is clearly necessary before a child can run, much less dribble a basketball at the same time. However, careful instruction and long, hard hours of practice are just as clearly required if the child is ever to excel in basketball. Many of our abilities and habits do not merely "mature" on their own as part of nature's plan; parents, teachers, and other important people show us how to behave in new ways, and we are changed by our experiences. We change in response to the **environment,** all the external physical and social conditions and events that can affect us, from crowded living quarters to stimulating social interactions. As we will see time and time again, developmental changes are generally the products of a complex interplay between "nature" (genetic endowment and maturation) and "nurture" (environmental influences and learning).

In summary, development is a multifaceted and complex process. It involves gains, losses, and just plain changes in physical, cognitive, and psychosocial functioning, brought about by both maturation and learning. As we shall now see, development also occurs in a historical and cultural context that influences how the life span and its phases are viewed.

HOW DO PEOPLE VIEW THE LIFE SPAN?

How would you divide up the life span into distinct periods? Table 1.1 lists the periods that many of today's developmentalists regard as distinct. You will want to keep them in mind as you read this book, for we will constantly be speaking of infants, preschoolers, school-age children, adolescents, and young, middle-aged, and older adults. Remember, though, that the given ages are only approximate because age is only a rough indicator of level of development: There are many differences among individuals of the same age.

It is generally more useful to focus on capacities and functioning than to consider only age. For example, 10-year-olds who have already experienced puberty might more appropriately be classified as adolescents than as children, and teenagers who are fully self-supporting with children of their own have more in common with young adults than with other adolescents. Similarly, some adults are physically and psychologically much "older" than others. This observation led Bernice Neugarten (1975) to distinguish two distinct subgroups within the aging population, the young-old and the old-old. The **young-old,** who are usually somewhere between 55 and 75 but can be older, are relatively healthy, active, and socially involved. They are the ones you see on the tennis courts and in the halls of Congress. The **old-old,** most of whom are 75 or older, often have chronic diseases and impairments, do not function as well as they once did, and may depend on others for care. According to Neugarten, these two groups have very different needs:

The young-old need meaningful roles in society, whereas the old-old need long-term medical care. Recently, as more people reach very advanced ages, developmentalists have even begun to talk of a third group, the **oldest old,** who are usually 85 and older and are often, but by no means always, extremely frail (Suzman, Willis, & Manton, 1992). Since some centenarians are swimming, cooking, or writing books rather than lying around in nursing homes, we must be careful not to stereotype adults on the basis of their age.

Table 1.1 represents only one view of the periods of the life span. Age, like gender, race, and other significant human characteristics, means different things in different societies. Each society has its own ways of dividing the life span and of treating the individuals who fall into different age groups. Each socially defined age group in a society—called an **age grade,** or age stratum—is assigned different status, roles, privileges, and responsibilities. We, for example, grant "adults" (18-year-olds, by law) a voting privilege that we do not grant to children, and we give retail discounts to older adults but not to young or middle-aged adults. Just as high schools have "elite" seniors and "lowly" freshmen, whole societies are layered into age grades.

Once it has established age grades, each society also defines what people should and should not be doing at different points in the life span. These expectations—called **age norms** (Neugarten, Moore, & Lowe, 1965)—are society's way of telling people how to act their age. In our culture, for example, most people agree that 10-year-olds are too young to date or drink beer, that 25-year-olds are at a prime age for

TABLE 1.1

An overview of periods of the life span

Period of Life	Approximate Age Range
Prenatal period	Conception to birth
Infancy	First 2 years of life
Preschool period	2 to 5 or 6 years (some prefer to describe as "toddlers" children who have begun to walk and are age 1 to 3)
Middle childhood	6 to 12 or so (until the onset of puberty)
Adolescence	12 or so to 20 or so (when the individual is relatively independent of parents and assumes adult roles)
Early adulthood	20 to 40 years
Middle adulthood	40 to 65 years
Late adulthood	65 years and older

marrying, and that 65-year-olds should think about retiring. In nonindustrialized countries, where people have children in their teens and tend to become ill and disabled in middle age, quite different age norms may prevail.

Why are age norms important? First, they influence people's decisions about how to lead their lives. They are the basis for what Neugarten (1968) termed the **social clock,** a sense of when things should be done and when one is ahead of or behind the schedule dictated by age norms. Prompted by the social clock, for example, an unmarried 25-year-old may feel that he should get married before it is too late or a childless 35-year-old might figure that she will miss her chance at parenthood unless she has a baby soon.

Second, age norms affect how easily people adjust to life transitions. Normal milestones such as having children typically affect us more negatively when they occur "off time" than when they occur "on time," at socially appropriate ages (McLanahan & Sorensen, 1985). It is challenging indeed to experience puberty as an 8- or 17-year-old girl or become a new parent at 13 or 48!

With this background, let us briefly examine how age grades and age norms have evolved through history and how they vary from culture to culture today.

Historical Changes in Life-Span Phases

Every human lives in a historical context: A developing person today may be quite different from a developing person in past eras. Moreover, the quick histor-

ical tour that we are about to take should convince you that the phases of the life span that we recognize today were not always perceived as distinct.

Childhood

Phillippe Ariès (1962) conducted an ambitious historical analysis and concluded that, before 1600 A.D., European societies had no concept of childhood as we know it. Until then, children were viewed as miniature adults. In medieval Europe (500–1500 A.D.), for example, 6-year-olds were dressed in miniature versions of adult clothing and expected to work alongside adults at home, in shops, or in the fields (Ariès, 1962). Moreover, a 10-year-old convicted of stealing could be hanged for it (Kean, 1937). It was not until the 12th century A.D. that the law in Christian Europe defined infanticide—the killing of children—as murder (deMause, 1974).

It is now clear that it is an exaggeration to say that pre-17th century adults held a "miniature adult" view of childhood (Cunningham, 1996). Parents throughout history seem to have recognized that children are different from adults. However, before the 17th and 18th centuries, people in Western societies *did* pressure children to grow up, adopt adult roles, and contribute economically to the family's survival as soon as possible. During the 17th and 18th centuries, our modern concept of childhood gradually came into being. Children came to be seen as more distinctly childlike—as innocent and somewhat fragile beings who should be protected, given a proper moral and religious education, and taught skills such as reading and writing so they would eventually become good workers (Ariès, 1962; Cunningham, 1996).

Some historians have also concluded that children were treated much more brutally in the past than now (deMause, 1974). Even as late as the 18th century, beatings were not uncommon. One mother in colonial America, for example, described struggling with her 4-month-old infant: "I whipped him til he was actually black and blue, and until I *could not* whip him any more, and he never gave up one single inch" (deMause, 1974, p. 41). Was this really brutality, though? Punishment that would be judged abusive from our modern perspective was often administered out of concern for the child's moral and social upbringing rather than to be cruel (Vinovskis, 1996). To the Puritans, for example, strict discipline that sometimes required breaking the child's will was thought to be the key to salvation.

Overall, then, it is inaccurate to conclude that, until the 17th century, parents regarded children as nothing but miniature adults and treated them with exceptional brutality. Yet the historical trend *has* been toward a greater appreciation of the uniqueness of childhood, the importance of parenting, and the need for greater protection of the rights and well-being of

Although medieval children were pressured to abandon their childish ways as soon as possible and were dressed like miniature adults, it is doubtful that they were viewed as nothing but miniature adults.

children. The historical context of child development continues to change. Although child abuse and neglect remain, modern technological and industrial societies treat children relatively well, moved by the belief that they are innocents who need guidance and protection in order to develop properly. In the 20th century, children came to be seen as "economically worthless but emotionally priceless" (Zelizer, cited in Remley, 1988).

Some observers claim that our society is reverting to the medieval view of childhood, by asking children to grow up very quickly with all too little help from their parents (Elkind, 1992, 1994). Think of it: Many of today's elementary schoolchildren have learned to converse intelligently about AIDS and condoms, "good" touches and "bad" touches, "crack" and "smack." They are expected to protect themselves from drug dealers and stray bullets and to let themselves into empty houses at the end of the day. Perhaps adults will once again step forward to protect children and relieve them of some of this pressure to grow up so quickly.

Adolescence

Because the modern concept of childhood arose only during the 17th and 18th centuries, it is not sur-

prising that adolescence did not come to be viewed as a distinct period of the life span in Western societies until the end of the 19th century (Kett, 1977). At first, developing industries in the United States and elsewhere needed cheap labor and could make do with children and, later, immigrants. But, as industry advanced, an *educated* labor force was needed, so laws were passed restricting child labor and making schooling compulsory. Now adolescents spent their days in school, separated from the adult world. They came to be regarded as distinct from adults, and they began to develop their own peer culture.

The adolescent experience has continued to change during the 20th century. For example, as adolescents began to attend college in large numbers after World War II, the age of entry into the adult world was even further postponed (Keniston, 1970). It seems, then, that our society's current age norms ask children to cease being helpless very quickly but to assume adult roles very slowly.

Adulthood

And how is adulthood today different from what it was in past eras? For one thing, more people are living longer. In ancient Rome, the average age at death was 20 to 30 years old; in the late 17th century, it was 35 to 40 years (Dublin & Lotka, 1936). True, these figures, which are *averages,* are low mainly because so many more infants died in the past. However, even those lucky enough to make it through early childhood still had relatively low odds, by modern standards, of living to be 65 or older.

The average life expectancy has continued to increase dramatically during this century. Around 1900, average life expectancy for a newborn in the United States was 49 years; by 1994, life expectancy had climbed to 80 for a white female, 74 for a black female, 73 for a white male, and 65 for a black male (U.S. Bureau of the Census, 1996a).

The makeup of the U.S. population has also changed significantly in this century. In 1900 about 4% of the population was 65 and older; today the figure is 12.5% (U.S. Bureau of the Census, 1996b). And we have not seen anything yet! Census takers are now watching the **baby boom generation**—the huge number of people born between 1945 and 1964—move into middle age. By 2030, when most baby boomers will have retired from work, an estimated 20% of the U.S. population—one in five Americans—will be 65 or older (U.S. Bureau of the Census, 1996b). No wonder the news media are discussing the "graying of America" and the challenges to society that an ever-aging population will present.

Has increased longevity brought changes in adulthood and aging? There does not seem to have been any simple historical trend toward a better and better (or worse and worse) experience of aging over the centuries

Each January 15 in Japan, 20-year-olds are officially pronounced adults in a national celebration. Young women receive kimonos, young men receive suits, and all are reminded of their responsibilities to society. Young adults also gain the right to drink, smoke, and vote. The modern ceremony grew out of an ancient one in which young samurai became recognized as warriors (Reid, 1993). The age-grading system in Japanese culture clearly marks the beginning of adulthood.

(Cole, 1992; Minois, 1987/1989). Historian Georges Minois (1987/1989) concludes that since ancient times most societies have held ambivalent attitudes toward aging and old people. On the one hand, the old have been devalued and mocked; on the other hand, they have often been idealized as sources of wisdom and put in positions of power. As Minois (1987/1989) puts it, old people have been ". . . respected or despised, honoured or put to death according to circumstance" (p. 11).

However, instead of viewing the adult portion of the life span as one long stretch with no age grades within it, as in the past, we now recognize that adulthood consists of distinct periods. In the 20th century, as more people lived long enough to see their children grow to adulthood and leave home, Western societies began to recognize *middle age* as a distinct period between the emptying of the nest and old age (Neugarten & Neugarten, 1986). The introduction of Social Security, Medicare, and other such programs for the elderly in this century has also changed the concept of old age (Cole, 1992). In earlier centuries, people who survived to old age literally worked until they dropped. Ella Miller, described at the start of the chapter, retired only at age 107, whereas now people retire in their 60s and consider old age the retirement phase of life. Today's elderly adults are also healthier and more active than the elderly adults of the past;

Kenneth Manton estimates that today's 85-year-old is about as healthy as a 65-year-old was just 25 years ago (Trafford, 1996).

In sum, age—whether it is 7, 17, or 70—has meant something quite different in each historical era. Most likely, the experience of being 7, 17, or 70 will be quite different in the 21st century from what it is now.

Cultural Differences

Just as the life span has been viewed differently in different historical eras, each society today has its own way of dividing it into socially meaningful periods, or age grades (Fry, 1996). In Western industrialized societies, the life span is often visualized as a straight line extending from birth to death. In some cultures, however, the recognized phases include a period before birth as well as an afterlife, or the life span may be pictured as a circle that includes reincarnation, or some other way of being "recycled" and born again (Fry, 1985). Anthropologist Jennie Keith (1985) reports that the St. Lawrence Eskimo simply distinguish between boys and men (or girls and women), whereas the Arusha people of East Africa have six socially meaningful ages for males: youths, junior warriors, senior warriors, junior elders, senior elders, and retired elders. The cultures Christine Fry (1996) has studied recognize anywhere from one to ten distinct stages of life, averaging five.

Consider, too, how societies define who is old and who is not. In our society age 65 is widely viewed as the beginning of old age and the retirement period. Most other cultures define old age in terms of *functional,* rather than chronological, age (Keith, 1985). Thus, among the !Kung hunter-gatherers of central Africa, one is old when one no longer bears or raises children (Biesele & Howell, 1981)—a good deal earlier than 65.

Subcultural Differences

The meaning of age also varies from subculture to subculture within a society. Our society is diverse socioeconomically, racially, and ethnically. African-American, Hispanic-American, Native-American, Asian-American, and European-American children are likely to differ in some of their developmental experiences. Within each of these broad racial and ethnic groups, of course, immense variations are also associated with such factors as specific national origin, length of time in North America, degree of integration into mainstream society, language usage, and socioeconomic status.

Although scholars who conduct cross-cultural research have long tried to avoid imposing their own cultural values on people from geographically distinct cultures, the same cannot be said of those who study racial and ethnic diversity within the United States and other industrialized countries. Too often, minority group children and adults have been judged according to white middle-class standards and found to be "deficient" (Helms, 1992; Ogbu, 1981). More and more researchers today appreciate the importance of understanding the distinctive contexts in which children from various racial and ethnic backgrounds develop.

Consider some possible implications of growing up as a female in a low-income, inner-city African-American community. Linda Burton (1996) found that, in one such community, it is considered appropriate for a young woman to become a mother at 16 and a grandmother at 34—earlier than in most middle-class communities, white or African-American. Teenage mothers in this community look to their own mothers and, especially, their grandmothers to help them care for their children. Much the same norms prevail among low-income whites in areas such as rural Appalachia. It may seem unusual from a middle-class perspective for children to be raised by someone other than their mothers and fathers. Yet it is not unusual at all in cultures around the world for child-care responsibilities to be shared like this with grandmothers and other relatives (Tronick, Morelli, & Ivey, 1992; Wilson, 1989), and there is no sign that grandmother care is damaging to development. After much dissecting of the "problems" of disadvantaged groups, devel-

opmentalists are now beginning to uncover some of the strengths of their cultural traditions.

The broader message is clear: We simply must view development in its historical, cultural, and subcultural context. We must bear in mind that each social group settles on its own definitions of the life span, the age grades within it, and the norms appropriate to each age range. As a result, human development differs from one historical, cultural, or subcultural context to another. We must also remember that most of the research reported in this textbook has been done with children and adults in 20th-century North America—mostly white, middle-class ones at that—and may not hold up in other societies. To be sure, many aspects of human development are universal; in many ways all humans develop along similar paths despite variations in their experiences. However, as Christine Fry (1985) puts it, "If you want your pet theory vetoed, ask an anthropologist" (p. 236), who will be able to find a society in which the theory does not apply.

WHAT IS THE SCIENCE OF LIFE-SPAN DEVELOPMENT?

If development consists of systematic changes from conception to death, the science of development consists of the study of those changes. In this section we consider the goals of the science of life-span development and the development of this science over time.

Goals of Study

Three broad goals guide the study of life-span development: the description, explanation, and optimization of human development (Baltes, Reese, & Lipsitt, 1980). To achieve the goal of *description,* developmentalists characterize the behavior of human beings of different ages and trace how it changes with age. Developmentalists attempt to describe both *normal development* and *individual differences,* or variations, in development. Although "average" trends in human development across the life span can be described, it is clear that no two of us (not even identical twins) develop along precisely the same pathways. Some babies are considerably more alert and active than others. Some 80-year-olds are out on the dance floor; others are home in bed.

Description is the starting point in any science, but ultimately scientists want to achieve their second goal, *explanation.* Developmentalists seek to understand (1) why humans develop as they typically do, and (2) why some individuals develop differently than others, so they attempt to answer important questions about the contributions of nature and nurture, genes and environment, to development.

The third goal is *optimization* of human development. How can human beings be helped to develop in positive directions? How can their capacities be enhanced, how can developmental difficulties be prevented, and how can any developmental problems that do emerge be overcome? The goal of optimizing development has involved such things as evaluating ways to stimulate intellectual growth in preschool programs, preventing alcohol abuse among college students, and supporting elderly adults after the death of a spouse. The goal of optimizing development often cannot be achieved, however, until researchers are able to describe development and explain how it comes about.

In summary, the scope of this book, like the scope of the science of human development, is large. We want to show you what developmentalists have learned about normal human development from conception to death and about individual differences in that development. Moreover, we will not be content merely describing development; we will also want to explain it and identify ways to optimize it.

G. Stanley Hall is widely recognized as the founder of the scientific study of human development.

Origins

Just as human development itself has changed through the ages, attempts to understand development have evolved over time. Philosophers have long expressed their views on the nature of human beings and the proper methods of raising children, but it was not until the late 19th century that scientific investigations of the developmental process were undertaken. A number of scholars began to carefully observe the growth and development of their own children and to publish their findings in the form of **baby biographies.** Perhaps the most influential of these baby biographers was Charles Darwin (1809–1882), who made daily records of his own son's development (Darwin, 1877; see also Charlesworth, 1992). Darwin's curiosity about child development stemmed from his theory of evolution. Quite simply, he believed that infants share many characteristics with their nonhuman ancestors and that the evolution of the individual child has much to tell us about the evolution of the entire species. Darwin inspired others of his era to study child development in the interest of gaining insights into our evolutionary history. His evolutionary perspective has strongly influenced early theories of human development (Parke, Ornstein, Rieser, & Zahn-Waxler, 1994).

Baby biographies left much to be desired as works of science. Because different baby biographers emphasized very different aspects of their children's behavior, baby biographies were difficult to compare. Then,

too, parents are not entirely objective observers of their own children, and early baby biographers may also have let their assumptions about evolution and development bias their observations. Finally, each baby biography was based on a single child—and often the child of a distinguished family, at that. Conclusions based on a single case may not hold true for other children.

We can give Charles Darwin and other eminent baby biographers much credit for making human development a legitimate topic of study and influencing early views of it. Still, the man who is most often cited as the founder of developmental psychology is G. Stanley Hall (1846–1924). Well aware of the shortcomings of baby biographies, Hall attempted to collect more objective data on large samples of individuals. He developed a now all-too-familiar research tool, the questionnaire, to explore "the contents of children's minds" (Hall, 1891). By asking children questions about every conceivable topic, he discovered that children's understanding of the world grows rapidly during childhood and that the "logic" of young children is often not very logical at all.

Hall went on to write an influential book entitled *Adolescence* (1904). Strongly influenced by Darwin's evolutionary theory, Hall drew parallels between adolescence and the turbulent period in history during which barbarism gave way to modern civilization. Adolescence, then, was a tempestuous period of the life span, a time of emotional ups and downs and rapid changes—a time of what Hall called **storm and stress.** Thus it is Hall we have to thank for the notion—a largely inaccurate notion, as it turns out—that most teenagers are half crazy! Later, this remarkable pioneer turned his attention to the end of the life span in his book *Senescence* (1922).

Today's Perspective

G. Stanley Hall viewed all phases of the life span as worthy of study. Unfortunately, however, the science of human development began to break up into age-group specialty areas during the 20th century. Some researchers focused on infant or child development, others specialized in adolescence, and still others formed the specialization called **gerontology,** the study of aging and old age.

Starting in the 1960s and 1970s, a true **life-span perspective** on human development began to re-emerge. Paul Baltes (1987) has laid out seven assumptions that are part of this perspective. These are the themes you will see echoed again and again throughout this book:

1. *Development is a lifelong process.* Today's developmentalists appreciate that human development is not just "kid stuff," that we change throughout the life span. They also believe that development in any one period of life is best seen in the context of the whole life span. For instance, our understanding of adolescent development is bound to be richer if we concern ourselves with what led up to it and where it is leading.

2. *Development is multidirectional.* In the past, development was viewed as a universal process leading toward more "mature" functioning. Today's developmentalists recognize that humans of any age can be experiencing growth in one set of capacities, decline in another set, and no change at all in still another. Moreover, the differences among us seem to become wider and wider as we progress along different pathways (Morse, 1993). As a result, you are likely to find a lot more diversity in a group of 80-year-olds than in a group of 8-month-olds.

3. *Development always involves both gain and loss.* As we noted earlier, development at every age involves both growth and decline. Gaining a capacity for logical thought as a school-age child may mean losing some of the capacity for fanciful, imaginative thinking one had as a preschooler, for example.

4. *Development is characterized by lifelong plasticity.* **Plasticity** refers to the capacity to change in response to positive or negative experiences. Developmentalists have long known that child development can be damaged by a deprived environment and optimized by an enriched one. For instance, highly aggressive children who are intensely disliked by their peers often improve their social status if they are taught the social skills that popular children display (Mize & Ladd, 1990). It is now understood that this plasticity continues into later life—that the aging process can be altered considerably depending on the individual's experiences. For example, elderly adults who have been losing intellectual abilities can, with the help of special training and practice, regain some of those abilities (Baltes et al., 1992).

5. *Development is shaped by its historical/cultural context.* A good example comes from research by Glen Elder and his colleagues, who have traced the impact of the Great Depression of the 1930s on the personality development of children growing up at the time (Elder, Liker, & Cross, 1984). This economic crisis caused some out-of-work fathers to become less affectionate and less consistent in administering discipline. Their children in turn displayed behavior problems and had low aspirations and poor records in school. As adults, the men had erratic careers and unstable marriages, and the women were seen by their own children as ill tempered. Clearly we can be affected for many years by the social context in which we grow up.

6. *Development is multiply influenced.* Early scholars believed that development is due to genetically programmed maturational processes. Others believed just as strongly that how we develop is the result of our unique learning experiences. Today we view human development as the product of ongoing interactions between a changing person and his or her changing world; a wide range of factors, both inside and outside the person, affect development.

7. *Understanding development requires multiple disciplines.* Because human development is influenced by everything from biochemical changes to historical events, it is impossible for any one discipline to have all the answers. A full understanding of human development will come only when many disciplines, each with its own perspectives and tools of study, join forces. Anthropologists, biologists, historians, psychologists, sociologists, and many others have something to contribute. Some universities have established interdisciplinary human development programs that attempt to bring members of different disciplines together in order to forge more integrated perspectives on development.

In summary, by adopting a life-span perspective on human development in this book, we will be assuming that development (1) occurs throughout the life span rather than just in childhood, (2) can take many different directions, (3) involves gains and losses at every age, (4) is characterized by plasticity at every age, (5) is affected by its historical and cultural context, (6) is influenced by multiple causal factors interacting with one another, and (7) can best be understood if scholars from multiple disciplines join forces to understand it.

HOW IS DEVELOPMENTAL RESEARCH CONDUCTED?

How can we gain understanding of this complex phenomenon called life-span development? Through the scientific method applied in any physical or social science. Let's review, briefly, some basic concepts of scientific research and then turn to certain research strategies devised specifically for describing, explaining, and optimizing development.

The Scientific Method

There is nothing mysterious about the **scientific method.** It is really more of an *attitude* than a method: a belief that investigators should allow their systematic observations (or *data*) to determine the merits of their thinking. For example, for every "expert" who believes that psychological differences between males and females are largely biological in origin, there is likely to be another expert who just as firmly insists that boys and girls differ because they are raised differently. Whom shall we believe? It is in the spirit of the scientific method to believe the data—that is, the findings of research. The scientist is willing to abandon a pet theory if the data contradict it. Ultimately, then, the scientific method can help the scientific community and society at large weed out flawed ideas.

The scientific method involves a process of generating ideas and testing them by making observations. Often, casual observations provide preliminary ideas that provide the basis for a **theory,** a set of concepts and propositions intended to describe and explain some aspect of experience. Sigmund Freud, for instance, carefully observed the psychologically disturbed adults whom he treated, began to believe that many of their problems stemmed from experiences in early childhood, and ultimately formulated his *psychoanalytic theory* of development.

Theories generate specific predictions, or **hypotheses,** regarding a particular set of observations. Consider, for example, a theory implying that psychological differences between the sexes are largely due to the fact that parents and other adults treat boys and girls differently. Working from this theory, a researcher might hypothesize that, if parents grant boys and girls the same freedoms, the two sexes will be similarly independent, whereas, if parents let boys do more things than they let girls do, boys will be more independent than girls. Suppose that the study designed to test this hypothesis indicates that boys are more independent than girls no matter how their parents treat them. Then the hypothesis would be disconfirmed by the findings, and the researcher would want to rethink this theory of sex-linked differences. If other hypotheses based on this theory were also inconsistent with the facts, the theory would have to be significantly revised or abandoned entirely in favor of a better theory.

This, then, is the heart of the scientific method: Theories generate hypotheses that are tested through observation of behavior, and new observations indicate which theories are worth keeping and which are not (see Figure 1.1). Now let's look at the more specific data-gathering methods and research designs researchers use to study human development.

Data Collection

No matter what aspect of human development we are interested in—whether it is the formation of bonds between infants and their parents, adolescent drug use, or memory skills in elderly adults—we must find an appropriate way to measure what interests us. Let's look briefly at some of the pros and cons of the two major methods of data collection used by developmental researchers: self-report measures and behavioral observations.

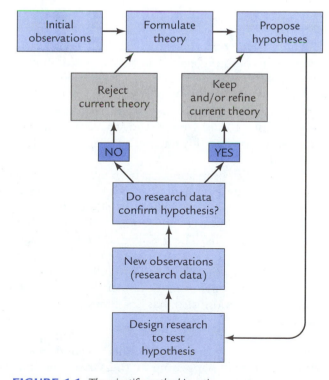

FIGURE 1.1 *The scientific method in action*

Self-Reports

Interviews, written questionnaires, and tests and scales designed to measure abilities or personality traits all involve asking people questions. These self-report measures are often *standardized,* meaning that they ask the same questions in precisely the same order for everyone so that the responses of different individuals can be directly compared.

Although self-report methods are widely used to study human development, they have their shortcomings. First, they typically cannot be used with infants, very young children, or other individuals who cannot read or understand speech very well. Second, because individuals of different ages may not understand questions in the same way, age differences in responses may reflect age differences in comprehension or interpretation rather than age differences in the quality of interest to the researcher. Developmental researchers always face the challenge of ensuring that their data-gathering tools measure the same thing at all ages they intend to study.

Third and finally, respondents may try to present themselves in a positive or socially desirable light. The interview findings in Figure 1.2, for example, suggest that older adults fear death less than younger adults do. But could it be that elderly adults were simply more reluctant to admit to a stranger that they were afraid? Might some other method of data collection have revealed a higher level of death anxiety among older adults than this single, direct question did? Very possibly.

Behavioral Observations

Naturalistic observation involves observing people in their common, everyday (that is, natural) surroundings (Pellegrini, 1996). Ongoing behavior is observed in homes, schools, playgrounds, workplaces, nursing homes, or wherever people are going about their lives. Box 1.1 describes a study that used naturalistic observation to study parents' attempts to control their toddlers.

Naturalistic observation has been used more often to study child development than adult development, largely because infants and young children often cannot be studied through self-report techniques that demand verbal skills. The greatest advantage of naturalistic observation is that it is the only technique that can tell us what children or adults actually do in everyday life (Willems & Alexander, 1982). Yet naturalistic observation also has its limitations. First, some behaviors (for example, heroic efforts to help other people) occur too infrequently and unexpectedly to be observed in this manner. Second, many events are usually happening at the same time in a natural setting, and any of them may be affecting people's behavior. This makes it difficult to pinpoint

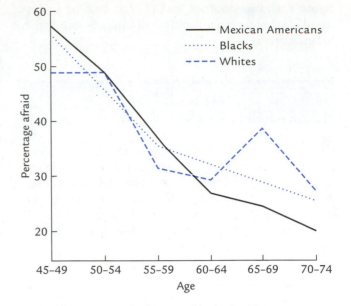

FIGURE 1.2 *How afraid are you of death? Would you say you are: not at all afraid?/somewhat afraid?/or very afraid? Vern Bengtson, Jose Cuellar, and Pauline Ragan (1977) asked this question in interviews with adults in Los Angeles. The graph shows the percentage of adults of each age who said they were "very afraid" or "somewhat afraid" of death.* (From Bengtson, Cuellar, & Ragan, 1977)

the causes of the behavior or of any developmental trends in the behavior. Finally, the mere presence of an observer can sometimes make people behave differently than they otherwise would. Children may "ham it up" when they have an audience; parents may be on their best behavior. For this reason, researchers sometimes videotape the proceedings from a hidden location or spend time in the setting before they collect their "real" data so that the individuals they are observing become used to their presence and behave more naturally.

Often, to achieve greater control over the conditions under which they gather behavioral data, researchers make use of the technique of **structured observation;** that is, they create special conditions designed to elicit the behavior of interest. Thus a researcher might bring children individually to a laboratory room and stage an emergency in which a loud crash and scream are heard from the adjoining room. The researcher might then observe whether each child intervenes and, if so, in what way and how quickly. Structured observation permits the study of behaviors that are rarely observable in natural settings. By exposing all research participants to the same stimuli, this approach also increases the investigator's ability to compare the effect of a stimulus on different individuals. Concerns about this method center on whether conclusions based on behavior in specially

BOX 1.1

Naturalistic observation of "terrible" two-year-olds and their parents

Parents who complain of the "terrible twos" know that toddlers can be extremely stubborn on occasion and often fail to comply with parents' requests and demands. Jay Belsky, Sharon Woodworth, and Keith Crnic (1996) conducted naturalistic observations of interactions between mothers, fathers, and toddlers in 69 families when the children were 15 months of age and then when they were 21 months of age. Each family was observed around dinnertime on two occasions. Interactions were audiotaped and observers later used their detailed notes and the tapes to construct a complete record of all the family interactions that occurred. Later still, coders read the narrative records and scored the frequency of each parent and child behavior of interest.

Each attempt by a parent to control the child's behavior (for example, "Put that cookie back") was categorized as either *negative control* (statements that expressed anger or irritation), *control* (straightforward requests and commands), or *control plus guidance* (attempts to tell the child what to do combined with an explanation, as in, "Get down before you hurt yourself"). The researchers also noted children's responses to parental control attempts, particularly those that reflected either *compliance* (doing what the parent asked) or *defiance* (protesting or doing the opposite of what the parent wanted). Different observers agreed on what happened, and different coders agreed about how behaviors should be scored, so the observation system was shown to produce reliable data.

By looking at patterns of parent and child behavior, the researchers were able to identify a subgroup of 31 families they described as "troubled." In these families, parents used control tactics frequently (but only rarely used "control plus guidance" techniques in which they explained the reasons behind their requests), children defied their parents a lot (about 21% of the time), and interactions often became more and more negative as they progressed. Several interesting differences between the troubled families and other families were detected. For example, both fathers and mothers in troubled families tended to be emotionally unstable and did not have many supportive social relationships. Toddlers in troubled families had more serious behavior problems than most toddlers and were more likely than most to have attended day care for 20 or more hours a week in their first year of life (see Chapter 13 on the pros and cons of day care).

As in other studies relying on naturalistic observation as a method of data gathering, it is difficult to determine which of many influences operating in the natural environment are actually causing behavior. We cannot be certain, for example, whether a parent's control tactics influence how compliant a child is or whether the child's level of cooperativeness influences how and how much the parent attempts to control the child. Most likely, parent and child influence one another.

designed settings will generalize to behavior in natural settings.

These, then, are the most commonly used techniques of collecting data about human development: self-report measures (interviews, questionnaires, and tests) and techniques of behavioral observation (both naturalistic and structured). Since each method has its limitations, our knowledge is advanced the most when *multiple* methods are used to study the same aspect of human development and these different methods lead to similar conclusions.

Developmental Research Designs

Once developmental researchers have figured out what they want to measure and how to measure it, they can turn their attention to the goal of describing developmental changes. Two developmental research designs have been relied on extensively to achieve the goal of describing development: the cross-sectional design and the longitudinal design. A third design, the sequential study, has come into use in an attempt to overcome the limitations of the other two techniques.

Let's first define the original two approaches and then explore their strengths and weaknesses.

Cross-Sectional and Longitudinal Designs

In a **cross-sectional design,** the performances of people of different age groups are compared. A researcher interested in the development of vocabulary might gather samples of speech from a number of 2-, 3-, and 4-year-olds; calculate the mean (or average) number of distinct words used per child for each age group; and compare these means to describe how the vocabulary sizes of children of ages 2, 3, and 4 differ. The cross-sectional study provides information about *age differences;* by seeing how different age groups differ, we can attempt to draw conclusions about how performance changes with age.

In a **longitudinal design,** the performance of one group of individuals is assessed repeatedly over time. The language development study just described would be longitudinal rather than cross-sectional if we identified a group of 2-year-olds, measured their vocabulary sizes, waited a year until they were age 3 and measured their vocabularies again, and did the same thing a year later when they were age 4, so that we can compare mean scores at the three ages. In any longitudinal study, whether it covers only a few months in infancy or 20 or 50 years, the same individuals are studied *as they develop*. Thus the longitudinal design provides information about *age changes* rather than age differences.

Now, what difference does it make whether we choose the cross-sectional or the longitudinal design to describe development? Suppose a team of researchers became interested in this question: How do attitudes about the roles of men and women in society typically change over the adult years? They devised a gender-role attitudes questionnaire that can characterize any adult as having traditional attitudes about gender roles or liberated attitudes that emphasize equality of the two sexes. They conducted a longitudinal study by administering the gender-role questionnaire three times to a group of men and women: in 1960 (when the men and women were 30), in 1980 (when they were 50), and in 2000 (when they were 70). But in 2000, another research team conducted a cross-sectional study of this same question, comparing the gender-role attitudes of adults 30, 50, and 70 years old. Figure 1.3 outlines these two alternative designs, and Figure 1.4 portrays hypothetical age trends that they might generate.

What is going on here? The cross-sectional study seems to indicate that, as people get older, their attitudes about gender roles become more traditional. The longitudinal study suggests precisely the opposite: As people get older, their attitudes about gender roles seem to become more liberated. How could a cross-sectional study and a longitudinal study on the same topic lead to totally different conclusions?

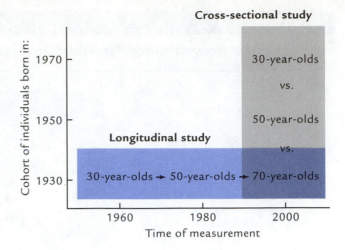

FIGURE 1.3 *Cross-sectional and longitudinal studies of development from age 30 to age 70*

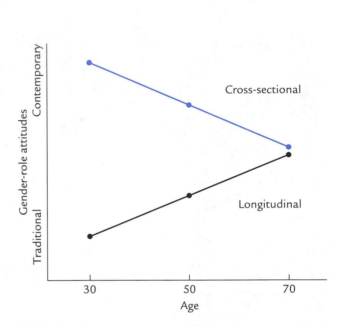

FIGURE 1.4 *Conflicting findings of hypothetical cross-sectional and longitudinal studies of gender-role attitudes*

Age, Cohort, and Time of Measurement Effects

To unravel this mystery, one must realize that the findings of developmental studies can be influenced by three factors: *age effects, cohort effects,* and *time of measurement effects.* **Age effects** are simply the effects of getting older; note that the whole purpose of our developmental study is to describe how attitudes about gender roles change as a function of *age* during adulthood. **Cohort effects** are the effects of being born in one particular historical context rather than another (for example, of being born during the Great Depression of the 1930s rather than in the 1920s). Any *cohort* is a group of people born at the same time, either in the same year or within a specified, limited span of years. People who are in their 70s today not only are older than people in their 30s, but they belong to a different cohort or generation and had different formative experiences. Finally, **time of measurement effects** in developmental research are the effects of historical events and trends occurring at the time when the data are being collected (for example, effects of the introduction of television or the World Wide Web). These effects are not unique to a particular cohort but can affect anyone alive at the time. Once one is aware that age, cohort, and time of measurement can all influence developmental research findings, one can appreciate that both the cross-sectional and the longitudinal designs have their problems.

Strengths and Weaknesses of the Cross-Sectional Design

In the cross-sectional study of gender attitudes, the three age groups being compared represent three different cohorts of people. The 70-year-olds were born in 1930, the 50-year-olds in 1950, and the 30-year-olds in 1970. Certainly these three groups had different formative experiences. The oldest group grew up in an era when traditional attitudes about gender roles were strongly held: Women were to stay at home and raise the children, men were to work and bring home the bacon. Possibly, then, older adults' unliberated responses to the questionnaire in 2000 reflect the traditional views they learned early in life and maintained for the rest of their lives. Perhaps their views did not actually become more traditional as they got older. And perhaps the 30-year-old cohort, which grew up when the women's movement was very influential, formed relatively liberated gender-role attitudes early in life and will retain those attitudes as they get older. Perhaps, then, what initially looked like a developmental trend toward greater traditionality (an age effect) is actually only a cohort effect.

The cross-sectional study *does* tell us how people of different ages (and cohorts) differ, and this can be useful information. But the cross-sectional technique does not necessarily tell us how people develop *as a function of age*. Do 70-year-olds have more conservative gender-role attitudes than 30-year-olds because they are older, or because they are members of a different cohort raised in a more traditional historical period? We cannot tell. *Age effects and cohort effects are hopelessly tangled.*

The problem of cohort effect, then, is the central problem in cross-sectional research, and it is a very real problem in studies designed to describe how adults develop over the years. As we shall see in Chap-

Children growing up earlier in the 20th century (for example, these children in a yarn mill in 1911) had different experiences from those of today's youth. Each cohort or generation develops somewhat differently as a result.

ter 9, cross-sectional studies of performance on intelligence tests once appeared to indicate that we lose our intellectual faculties starting in middle age. Yet the older adults in these studies grew up in a time when many people did not graduate from high school. Did these older people lose intellectual abilities in old age or did they merely perform less well than younger cohorts because they received less education? What cross-sectional studies often detect is a cohort effect, not a true developmental trend or age effect.

Despite this central problem, the cross-sectional design is still commonly used by developmentalists. Why? Because it has the great advantage of being quick and easy; we can go out this year, sample individuals of different ages, and be done with it. Moreover, this design should yield valid conclusions if the cohorts studied are likely to have had similar growing-up experiences—as when 3- and 4-year-olds rather than 30- and 40-year-olds are compared. It is when researchers attempt to make inferences about development over the span of many years that cohort effects are a serious problem.

The second major limitation of the cross-sectional design is this: It tells us nothing about the development of individuals. Because each person is observed at only one point in time, we learn nothing about how each person actually changes with age. We cannot, for example, see whether different people show divergent patterns of change in their gender-role attitudes over time, or whether individuals who are especially liberated in their attitudes as 30-year-olds are also especially liberated at 70. To address issues like these, we need longitudinal research.

Strengths and Weaknesses of the Longitudinal Design

Because the longitudinal design actually traces changes in individuals as they age, it can tell us whether most people change in the same direction or whether different individuals travel different developmental paths. It can indicate whether the characteristics and behaviors measured remain consistent over time—for example, whether the bright or aggressive or dependent young person retains those same traits in later life. And it can tell us whether experiences early in life predict traits and behaviors later in life. The cross-sectional design can do none of this.

What, then, are the limitations of the longitudinal design? In our longitudinal study of gender-role attitudes, adults were first assessed at age 30 and then reassessed at age 50 and age 70. The study centered on *one cohort* of individuals: people who were 30 years old in 1960, when they were first surveyed (and therefore were members of the 1930 birth cohort). These people were raised in a particular historical context and then experienced changes in their social environment as they aged. Thus we must focus attention on *time of measurement effects* on the gender-role attitudes they expressed.

In 1960 these adults' responses were undoubtedly influenced by the prevailing traditional views of that time. By the time they were interviewed in 2000, as 70-year-olds, the times had changed immensely because of the women's movement and other social changes. Why, then, are their responses in 2000 more liberal than their responses in 1960? It may not be because gender-role attitudes typically become more liberal as they get older but because society changed in a particular way from one time of measurement to the next during the time frame of our study. Perhaps we would obtain entirely different "developmental" trends if we did this longitudinal study in an era in which sexism suddenly became acceptable again!

In the longitudinal study, then, *age effects and time of measurement effects are tangled*. We cannot tell for sure whether the age-related changes observed are true developmental trends or whether they reflect historical events occurring during the study (either at a particular point of assessment or between assessments). The problem, then, is that we may not be able to generalize what we find in a longitudinal study to people developing in a different era. We can only generalize to the cohort studied.

There are still other disadvantages of the longitudinal design. One is fairly obvious: This approach is costly and time-consuming, particularly if it is used to trace development over a long span of time and at many points in time. Second, because knowledge is constantly changing, measures that seemed good at the start of the study may seem dated or incomplete by the end. Third, participants drop out of long-term studies; they may move, lose interest, or, in studies of aging, die during the course of the study. The result is a smaller and often less representative sample on which to base conclusions. Finally, researchers must be on guard for the effects of repeated testing; sometimes simply taking a test improves performance on that test the next time around.

Are both the cross-sectional and longitudinal designs hopelessly flawed, then? That would be overstating their weaknesses. As we have noted, cross-sectional studies are very efficient and informative, especially when the cohorts studied are not widely different in age or formative experiences. Meanwhile, longitudinal studies are extremely valuable for what they can reveal about the actual changes in performance that occur as individuals get older—even though it must be recognized that the cohort studied may not develop in precisely the same way that an earlier or later cohort does. However, in an attempt to overcome the limitations of both cross-sectional and longitudinal designs, developmentalists have devised a new and more powerful method of describing developmental change: the sequential design.

Sequential Designs: The Best of Both Worlds

Sequential designs combine the cross-sectional and longitudinal approaches in a single study (Schaie, 1994). Imagine, for example, a study of gender-role attitudes that involves comparing the attitudes of different age groups of adults (say 30-, 50-, and 70-year-olds), as in a cross-sectional design, and then repeatedly assessing the attitudes of the individuals in these different cohorts as they get older (say every 5 years), as in a longitudinal design. Sequential designs, by combining the cross-sectional and longitudinal approaches, improve on both. They can tell us (1) which age-related trends are truly developmental in nature and reflect how most people can be expected to change over time regardless of their cohort (*age effects*); (2) which age trends differ from cohort to cohort and suggest that each generation is affected by its distinct growing-up experiences (*cohort effects*); and (3) which trends suggest that historical events during a specific time period change most people alive at the time, regardless of their cohort (*time of measurement effects*). In short, sequential designs can at least begin to untangle the effects of age, cohort, and time of measurement and to indicate which age trends are truly developmental in nature. Yet they are extremely complex, expensive, and not always able to provide definitive answers. See Table 1.2 for a summary of the three basic developmental designs.

TABLE 1.2

Summary of the cross-sectional, longitudinal, and sequential development designs

	Cross-Sectional Method	Longitudinal Method	Sequential Method
PROCEDURE	Observe people of different ages (or cohorts) at one point in time	Observe people of one age group repeatedly over time	Combine cross-sectional and longitudinal approaches; observe different cohorts on multiple occasions
INFORMATION GAINED	Describes age differences	Describes age changes	Describes age differences *and* age changes
ADVANTAGES	Demonstrates age differences in behavior; hints at developmental trends Takes little time to conduct; is inexpensive	Actually indicates how individuals are alike and different in the way they change over time Can reveal links between early behavior or experiences and later behavior	Helps separate the effects of age, cohort, and time of measurement Indicates whether developmental changes experienced by one generation or cohort are similar to those experienced by other cohorts
DISADVANTAGES	Age trends may reflect cohort effects (differences between cohorts) rather than true developmental change Provides no information about change in individuals over time	Age trends may reflect historical (time of measurement) effects during the study rather than true developmental change Relatively time-consuming and expensive Measures devised may later prove inadequate Participants drop out Participants can be affected by repeated testing	Often complex and time-consuming Despite being the strongest method, may still leave questions about whether a developmental change is generalizable

Explaining Development

Researchers are not content to describe development through the use of cross-sectional, longitudinal, and sequential studies; they also want to achieve their goal of *explaining* it. We change with age but do not change *because* we get older. Instead, we change because we are affected by maturational processes and learning experiences that occur as we get older. So how can researchers identify the factors responsible for developmental change?

The most powerful method for explaining behavior and identifying the causes of developmental changes in behavior is the experiment. When experiments cannot be conducted, correlational research techniques may suggest answers to important "why" questions.

The Experimental Method

In an **experiment,** an investigator manipulates or alters some aspect of people's environment in order to see what effect this has on their behavior. Consider an experiment conducted by Lynette Friedrich and Aletha Stein (1973) to study the effects of different kinds of television programs on the behavior of preschool children. These researchers divided children in a nursery school into three groups: One group was exposed to violent cartoons like *Superman* and *Batman* (aggressive treatment condition), another group watched episodes of *Mister Rogers' Neighborhood* portraying many helpful and cooperative acts (prosocial treatment condition), and a third group saw programs featuring circuses and farm scenes with neither aggressive nor altruistic themes (neutral treatment condition).

The goal of an experiment is to see whether the different treatments that form the **independent variable**—the variable being manipulated so that its causal effects can be assessed—have differing effects on the behavior being studied: the **dependent variable** in the experiment. The independent variable in Friedrich and Stein's experiment was the type of television children watched (aggressive, prosocial, or neutral). One of the dependent variables that Friedrich and Stein chose to study, using a complicated observation system, was the number of aggressive behaviors children displayed toward other children in the nursery school. Behavior was observed before each child spent a month watching daily episodes of one of the three kinds of television programs and were recorded again after the period to see if they had changed.

And what were the findings? The children who watched violent programs became more aggressive than children who watched prosocial or neutral programs—although only if they were already relatively aggressive. Altruistic programs also had positive effects on dependent variables measuring prosocial behavior. Thus this experiment demonstrated clear cause-and-effect relationships between the kind of behavior children watched on television and their own subsequent behavior.

This study has the three critical features shared by any true experiment:

1. *Manipulation of an independent variable:* The investigator must arrange for different groups to have different experiences so that the effects of those experiences can be assessed. If children had been allowed to choose for themselves what kind of television programs they would watch, this study would not be an experiment.

2. *Random assignment of individuals to treatment conditions:* In **random assignment** the luck of the draw determines who ends up in each treatment condition in an experiment. Randomly assigning participants to experimental conditions is a way of ensuring that the treatment groups are similar (in previous tendencies to be aggressive or helpful, socioeconomic status, and all other individual characteristics that could affect their social behavior). Only if experimental groups are similar in all respects initially can we be confident that any differences among groups at the end of the experiment were caused by differences in the experimental treatments they received.

3. *Experimental control:* In a true experiment with proper **experimental control,** all other factors besides the independent variable must be controlled or held constant. Friedrich and Stein ensured that children in the three treatment conditions were treated similarly *except for* the type of television they watched. It would have ruined the experiment, for example, if the children exposed to violent programs had to watch them in a small, hot, crowded room where tempers might flare, while children in the other two groups watched in larger, more comfortable rooms. To establish that the independent variable, and not some uncontrolled other factor, caused any change in the dependent variable, it is essential to control extraneous aspects of the situation.

The greatest strength of the experimental method is its ability to establish unambiguously that one thing *causes* another—that manipulating the independent variable causes a change in the dependent variable. When experiments are properly conducted, they do indeed contribute to our ability to *explain* human development and sometimes help us to *optimize* it as well.

Does the experimental method have any limitations? Absolutely! First, the findings of laboratory experiments may not always hold true in the real world, because the situations created in laboratory experiments are sometimes quite artificial—unlike the situations that people encounter in everyday life. Urie Bronfenbrenner (1979), who has been critical of the fact that so many developmental studies are contrived experiments, once charged that developmental psychology had become "the science of the strange behavior of children in strange situations with strange adults" (p. 19). Experiments indicate what *can* cause development but not necessarily what actually *does* most strongly shape development in natural settings (McCall, 1977).

A second limitation of the experimental method is that for ethical reasons it cannot be used to address many significant questions about human development. Consider a ridiculous example: To conduct a true experiment to determine how older women are affected by their husbands' deaths, we would identify a sample of women aged 65 and older, randomly assign them to either the experimental group or the control group, and then manipulate the independent variable by leaving the control group participants alone but killing the husband of every woman in the experimental group! Ethical principles demand that developmentalists use methods other than true experimental ones to study many, many important questions about development.

Researchers sometimes study the effects of some program or intervention on development through a **quasi-experiment**—an experimentlike study that evaluates the effects of different treatments but does not randomly assign individuals to treatment groups. A gerontologist, for example, might conduct a quasi-experiment to compare the adjustment of widows who choose to participate in a support group for widows to those who do not. When individuals are not randomly assigned to treatment groups, though, uncontrolled differences between the groups studied could influence the results (for example, the widows who seek help might be more outgoing or socially skilled than those who do not). As a result, the researcher is not able to make strong statements about what caused what, as in a true experiment.

The Correlational Method

Most developmental research today is correlational rather than experimental (or quasi-experimental). The

correlational method generally involves determining whether two or more variables are related in some systematic way. The researcher does not randomly assign participants to treatment conditions, manipulate the independent variable, or control other factors, as in an experiment. Instead, the researcher takes people as he or she finds them and attempts to determine whether there are relationships between their experiences, characteristics, and developmental outcomes.

How would a correlational study of the effects of television programs on preschool children differ from Friedrich and Stein's experiment on this issue? Consider a project by Jerome and Dorothy Singer (1981). Parents completed detailed logs describing the TV viewing habits of their preschool children: how much they watched and what they watched during a year's time. On four occasions, observers rated how aggressive the children were in interactions with other children in their nursery schools. In this manner the researchers gathered data on the two variables of interest to them: amount of exposure to TV and level of aggression.

The Singers were then able to determine the strength of the relationship between these two variables by calculating a **correlation coefficient**—a measure of the extent to which individuals' scores on one variable are systematically associated with their scores on another variable. A correlation coefficient (symbolized r) can range in value from +1.00 to −1.00. A positive correlation between TV viewing and aggression would indicate that as the number of hours of TV a child watches increases, so does the number of aggressive acts he or she commits (see Figure 1.5). A large positive correlation (say $r = +.90$) indicates a stronger positive relationship than a smaller one (say $r = +.30$). A negative correlation would result if the heaviest TV viewers were quite consistently the *least* aggressive children and the lightest viewers were the *most* aggressive children. A correlation near .00 would be obtained if there were no relationship between the two variables—if it were impossible to predict how aggressive a child is from knowing his or her TV viewing habits.

Like many other researchers, Singer and Singer found a moderately strong positive correlation ($r = +.33$) between watching a lot of action and adventure programs and behaving aggressively in the nursery school. Does this correlational study firmly establish that watching action-packed programs *causes* children to become more aggressive? No, because there are alternative explanations for the correlation between TV watching and aggression. One possibility is that *the direction of the cause-effect relationship is reversed*. It may not be the case that exposure to violent TV causes aggressive children to be aggressive; instead, aggressive children may be more likely than other children to seek out blood and gore on TV.

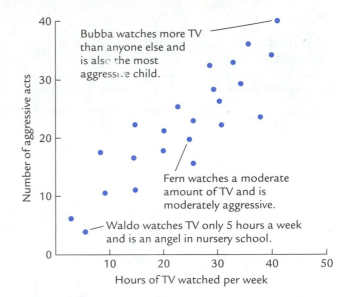

FIGURE 1.5 *Plot of a hypothetical correlation between the amount of TV children watch and the number of aggressive acts they display. Each dot represents a specific child who watches a particular amount of TV and commits a particular number of aggressive acts. Here the correlation is large and positive: The more TV a child watches, the more aggressive he or she is.*

A second possibility is that *the association between the two variables is actually due to some third variable*. An example of such a third variable might be parental rejection. Some children might have parents who are harsh and rejecting, and they might watch a lot more TV than most children simply to avoid their parents. They may also be aggressive because they are angry and upset about being rejected. If so, TV watching did not cause these children to become more aggressive than their peers; the treatment they received at home is the real cause of both their aggressive ways and their TV viewing habits.

Now that we have compared an experiment and a correlational study of the same topic, you can see that the correlational method has one major limitation: *It cannot unambiguously establish a causal relationship between one variable and another*. Correlational studies can *suggest* that a causal relationship exists, however. Indeed, Singer and Singer (1981) used complex statistical techniques to show that watching violent television probably did contribute to aggression in children and that several alternative explanations for the relationship between TV viewing and aggression could probably be ruled out. Nonetheless, they could not establish a definite cause-and-effect link.

Despite this important limitation, the correlational method is extremely valuable. First, as already noted, many problems can be addressed only through the correlational method (or with quasi-experiments)

TABLE 1.3

Comparison of the experimental method and the correlational method

Experimental Method	Correlational Method
Manipulation of an independent variable (investigator exposes participants to different experiences)	Studies people who have already had different experiences
Random assignment to treatment groups to ensure similarity of groups	Assignment by "nature" to groups (groups may not be similar in all respects)
Experimental control of extraneous variables	Lack of control over extraneous variables
Can establish a cause/effect relationship between independent variable and dependent variable	Can suggest but not firmly establish that one variable causes another
May not be possible for ethical reasons	Can be used to study issues that cannot be studied experimentally
May be artificial (findings from contrived experimental settings may not generalize well to the "real world")	Can be applied to data collected in natural settings (findings may generalize better to the "real world")

because it would be unethical to conduct certain experiments. Second, correlational studies often have a "real world" quality that laboratory experiments lack. The Singer and Singer (1981) study, for example, says something about relationships between children's actual, everyday TV viewing habits and their behavior. Overall, our ability to understand why humans develop as they do is advanced the most when the results of different kinds of studies *converge*—when experiments demonstrate a clear cause-and-effect relationship under controlled conditions *and* correlational studies reveal that this very same relationship seems to be operating in everyday life (see Table 1.3).

WHAT PROBLEMS ARISE IN STUDYING DEVELOPMENT?

Designing good developmental research is not easy. Researchers must first draw on theories and previous research to form a clear notion of what questions they want to answer and what hypotheses they want to test. They must then define the variables that interest them and decide how to measure them accurately.

And of course they must decide on a research design, choosing a cross-sectional, longitudinal, or sequential design if they are trying to describe age-related changes, and weighing the pros and cons of experimental or correlational methods if they wish to uncover possible influences on development. But there are many additional issues that researchers must grapple with. Here we will highlight just two: choosing the individuals to be studied and protecting their rights.

Choosing Samples

A research **sample** is simply a group of individuals chosen for study. Researchers study a sample and hope to generalize their findings to a larger **population**—a well-defined group such as American high school students or Canadian nursing-home residents. In many kinds of research, the ideal sample is a **random sample**—a sample formed by identifying all members of the larger population of interest and then, by a random means (such as drawing names blindly), selecting a portion of that population to participate in the study. Random sampling increases confidence that the sample studied is representative or typical of the larger population of interest and therefore that conclusions based on studying the sample will hold true of the whole population.

In actual practice, developmentalists often draw their samples—sometimes random, sometimes not—from their local communities. Thus a researcher might survey a random sample of students at a local high school about their drug use but then be unable to make statements about American teenagers in general if, for example, the school is in a high-income suburb where drug use patterns might be different from those in a low-income inner-city area. As a result, researchers must be careful to describe the characteristics of the sample they studied and to avoid overgeneralizing their findings to populations that might be socioeconomically or culturally different from their research sample.

When developmentalists conduct cross-sectional studies, one of their main challenges is to make sure that the age groups they study are similar to one another in all characteristics except age—that is, similar in average family income, intelligence, ethnic or racial background, and so on. But suppose we want to compare the memory abilities of 20-year-olds and 70-year-olds. If we randomly sample people in these age groups, we encounter a major problem: Older adults today typically have had less education than young adults today have had. We would have no trouble at all showing that elders do worse than young people on our memory tests, but we would not be justified in blaming that poor performance on the aging process. This age difference would most likely be due to a cohort ef-

Developmental findings established through the study of a sample of white children do not always hold true in a sample of African-American or Hispanic children. It is important to study development in a wide range of subcultural settings.

fect: age group differences in education (or in other characteristics besides age).

What is the solution? Many researchers cope with this problem by selecting younger and older adults with equivalent years of education—for example, college graduates only. Then any performance differences between the age groups would not be the result of differences in the amount of education they have received. But notice that the samples chosen are no longer representative of their age groups. Conclusions about college-educated older people might not hold true of the large number of older adults who did *not* graduate from college. Again, researchers need to describe their samples carefully and acknowledge that their findings might not generalize to different cultural or socioeconomic groups. What we learn about human development depends on whom we sample.

Protecting the Rights of Research Participants

Developmental researchers sometimes also face thorny issues centering on **research ethics,** the standards of conduct that investigators are ethically bound to honor in order to protect their research participants from physical or psychological harm. For example, is it ethical to deceive children by telling them that they performed poorly on a test in order to create in them a temporary sense of failure? Is it an invasion of a family's privacy to ask adolescents questions about conversations they have had with their parents about sex?

Such issues have led the American Psychological Association (1982), the Society for Research in Child Development (1990), the federal government (see Grodin & Glantz, 1994), and many other agencies to establish guidelines for ethical research with human beings. In addition, universities, research foundations, and government agencies that fund research have set up "human-subjects review committees" to determine whether proposed research projects conform to ethical standards. However, the ultimate responsibility for research ethics rests with the investigator; institutional committee approval is just one step. Deciding whether a proposed study is on safe ethical ground involves weighing the possible *benefits* of the research (gains in knowledge and potential benefits to humanity or to the participants themselves) against the potential *risks* to participants. If the potential benefits greatly outweigh the potential risks, and if there are no other, less risky, procedures that could produce these same benefits, the investigation will generally be viewed as ethical.

The investigator's responsibilities boil down to respecting the rights of research participants. This means (1) allowing them to make informed and uncoerced decisions about taking part in research, (2) debriefing them afterward, especially if they are not told everything in advance or are deceived, (3) protecting them from harm, and (4) treating any information they provide as confidential.

1. *Informed consent.* Researchers generally should inform potential participants of all aspects of the research that might affect their decision to participate so that they can make a voluntary decision based on knowledge of what the research involves. But are young children or mentally impaired children or adults capable of understanding what they are being asked to do

and of giving their *informed* consent? Probably not. Therefore researchers who study such "vulnerable" individuals should obtain informed consent both from the individual (if possible) and from someone who can act on the individual's behalf—for example, the parent or guardian of a child, or the legal representative of a nursing home resident. Investigators also must not pressure anyone to participate and must respect any participant's right to refuse to participate in the first place, to drop out at any point during the study, and to refuse to have his or her data used by the investigator.

2. *Debriefing.* Ideally, researchers are able to tell participants about the true purposes of the study in advance. However, in some cases doing so would ruin the study. If we told college students in advance that we were studying cheating and then gave them an opportunity to cheat on a test, do you think a single student would cheat? Instead, we might set up a situation in which students believe they can cheat without being detected and then *debrief* afterward, explaining the true purpose of the study. We would also have an obligation to make sure that participants do not leave feeling upset about the fact that they were caught cheating.

3. *Protection from harm.* Researchers are bound not to harm research participants either physically or psychologically. It is not always easy to predict whether participants might be upset by what they are asked to do in a study, but the investigator must try. The individual's developmental status may be one important consideration: Infants may cry if they are left in a room

with a stranger, adolescents may be embarrassed if they are asked personal questions (Koocher & Keith-Spiegel, 1994). If participants become upset or are harmed in any way, the researcher must try to undo the damage. If harm to the participants seems likely, another way of obtaining the information should be considered—or the research should be abandoned.

4. *Confidentiality.* Researchers also have an ethical responsibility to keep confidential the information they collect. It would be unacceptable, for example, to tell a child's teacher that the child performed poorly on an intelligence test or to tell an adult's employer that he or she revealed a drinking problem in an interview. Only if participants give explicit permission to have information about them shared with someone else would that information be passed on. However, there are a few circumstances in which researchers must violate confidentiality. For example, many states now have laws that prohibit an investigator from withholding the names of children who are believed to be the victims of abuse.

Clearly, developmental researchers have some serious issues to weigh if they want their research to be not only well-designed but ethically responsible. All things considered, understanding life-span human development is an incredibly complex undertaking. It would be downright impossible if researchers merely conducted study after study without any guiding ideas. *Theories* of human development provide those guiding ideas, and so we devote Chapter 2 to them.

◆ SUMMARY POINTS

1. Life-span human development consists of systematic changes and continuities occurring in the individual between conception and death. Developmental changes involve gains and losses, growth and aging. They are the result of nature and nurture—genetically programmed maturation as well as learning and other environmental influences.

2. Concepts of the life span and its distinctive periods (or age grades and their corresponding age norms and social clocks) have changed greatly over history and vary greatly from culture to culture today. Until the 17th and 18th centuries, children were expected to assume adult roles very early and were less often seen as innocents to be protected. In Western cultures, adolescence did not come to be viewed as a distinct phase of the life span until the late 19th century; also, a lengthening of the average life span and a decline in birth rates have led to a middle-aged "empty nest" phase and a period of old age in which people are retired.

3. The science of life-span development has three goals—the description, explanation, and optimization of development—and got its start at the end of the 19th century with the first baby biographies. Although many developmentalists have specialized

in studying one age group or another, today's developmentalists are increasingly adopting a life-span perspective that views development as (1) a lifelong, (2) multidirectional process that (3) involves gain and loss, (4) is characterized by considerable plasticity, (5) is shaped by its historical/cultural context, (6) has many causes, and (7) is best viewed from a multidisciplinary perspective.

4. The scientific method involves formulating theories based on observations, testing specific hypotheses (predictions based on theory) by collecting new observations in research investigations, and using the data to evaluate the worth of theories.

5. The most widely used data-collection techniques in studies of development are self-report measures (interviews, questionnaires, tests) and behavioral observation (either naturalistic or structured).

6. Developmental researchers rely principally on the cross-sectional and longitudinal research designs to describe development. The cross-sectional design, which compares different age groups (cohorts) at a single time of measurement, is easy to conduct but may be misleading if an age trend is actually due to differences in life experiences (cohort effects) rather than to true developmental change (age effects). In the longitudinal design, one group (cohort) is assessed repeatedly as its members develop. However, participants in a longitudinal study may change over the years, not as a function of age itself but in response to historical events (time of measurement effects). To counteract the limitations of cross-sectional and longitudinal designs, researchers have devised sequential designs that combine the two approaches.

7. To achieve the goal of explaining (and often of optimizing) development, researchers rely primarily on experiments. In an experiment an independent variable is manipulated to see what effects this manipulation has on a dependent variable, participants are randomly assigned to treatment groups, and extraneous factors are experimentally controlled. Properly conducted, an experiment can firmly establish that a cause-and-effect relationship exists, whereas a quasi-experiment, in which participants are not randomly assigned to treatment groups, cannot. The correlational method also cannot yield firm conclusions about cause and effect but is commonly used to study relationships among people's characteristics, experiences, and behavior and does not raise as many ethical issues as experimentation.

8. Developmentalists who want to conduct good research must decide whether to randomly sample the population of interest or use some other sampling approach and must ensure that the different age groups they compare in cross-sectional studies are similar in everything but age. They must also adhere to standards of ethical research practice, with attention to informed consent and debriefing, protection from harm, and confidentiality.

✳ FOOD FOR THOUGHT

1. "Children have never been better off than they are today." Do you agree or disagree with that statement? What evidence in this chapter supports the statement and what evidence refutes it?

2. You are interested in developmental changes, from age 12 to age 20, in adolescents' attitudes toward the use of condoms and other "safer sex" practices. Design both a cross-sectional and a longitudinal study of this topic, weigh the advantages and disadvantages of the two designs, and decide which one you will use.

3. What effect does nutrition during the first two years of life have on a child's performance on school readiness tests at age 5? Suggest both an experimental design and a correlational design to study this question. What features make the two designs different, and what are their pros and cons?

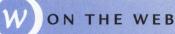

ON THE WEB

1. *Psychology Resources on the Web*   If you'd like an overview of psychology-related resources on the Web, try Psych Web's megalist of major sites in psychology. They range from the American Psychological Association's home page to "Internet Mental Health," an encyclopedia of mental health information. It's a bit overwhelming, though, so if you want to specialize in human development, read on.
   http://www.psych-web.com/resource/megalist.htm

2. *Life-Span Developmental Psychology Resources*   For a large menu of resources in life-span human development, try "Developmental Psychology Links." It links you to professional organizations and journals in the field, as well as to selected Web resources on infancy and childhood, adolescence, and aging.
   http://www.wesleyan.edu/spn/develop.htm#issues

3. *Child and Adolescent Development Resources*   For a list of Web resources on child and adolescent development, complete with "thumbs up" or "thumbs down" reviews, try "Mental Health Net." This site also describes mailing lists, or listservs, you can join on topics such as early childhood education and parent/child attachment.
   http://www.cmhc.com/guide/pro03.htm

4. *Gerontology Resources*   Mental Health Net can also help you find Web resources on aging, Alzheimer's disease and other forms of dementia, and death and dying.
   http://www.cmhc.com/guide/pro17.htm

KEY TERMS

centenarian	storm and stress	sequential design
development	gerontology	experiment
growth	life-span perspective	independent variable
aging	plasticity	dependent variable
maturation	scientific method	random assignment
learning	theory	experimental control
environment	hypothesis	quasi-experiment
young-old	naturalistic observation	correlational method
old-old	structured observation	correlation coefficient
oldest old	cross-sectional design	sample
age grades	longitudinal design	population
age norms	age effects	random sample
social clock	cohort effects	research ethics
baby boom generation	time of measurement	
baby biographies	effects	

CHAPTER 2

Theories of Human Development

THE NATURE OF THEORIES

BASIC ISSUES IN HUMAN DEVELOPMENT
Assumptions about Human Nature
Nature and Nurture
Activity and Passivity
Continuity and Discontinuity
Universality and Context-Specificity

FREUD: PSYCHOANALYTIC THEORY
Instincts and Unconscious Motives
Id, Ego, and Superego
Psychosexual Development
Strengths and Weaknesses

ERIKSON: NEO-FREUDIAN PSYCHOANALYTIC THEORY
Psychosocial Development
Strengths and Weaknesses

LEARNING THEORY
Skinner: Operant Conditioning
Bandura: Social Learning
Strengths and Weaknesses

COGNITIVE-DEVELOPMENTAL THEORY
Piaget: Intellectual Development
Cognitive Development
Strengths and Weaknesses

CONTEXTUAL THEORY
Bronfenbrenner: Ecological Approach to Development
Strengths and Weaknesses

THEORIES AND WORLD VIEWS
The Organismic World View
The Mechanistic World View
The Contextual World View
Changing World Views

APPLICATIONS: DEVELOPMENTAL THEORY AND TEENAGE PREGNANCY

CLARIFYING YOUR OWN THEORETICAL PERSPECTIVE

SUMMARY POINTS

FOOD FOR THOUGHT

ON THE WEB

KEY TERMS

Sheila is an attractive 15-year-old whose relationship with James has become the center of her life. She gets by in school, but most of what goes on in the classroom bores her. Her relationship with her parents has been a bit strained lately, partly because her mother does not want her to spend so much time with James and nags her about doing her homework and chores. James, age 16, is also struggling at school, juggling his part-time job, family responsibilities, and time with Sheila. And these two teenagers have a far more serious problem: Sheila is pregnant. The sex "just happened" one night after a party about five months ago and continued thereafter. Neither Sheila nor James wanted a baby.

Teenage pregnancy is one of the many facts about human development waiting to be explained by theories.

Here is a specific event in the lives of two developing individuals. How can we explain this unwanted teenage pregnancy? What is your theory? What explanations do the leading theories of human development offer? More practically, what can be done to reduce the high rate of teenage pregnancy in our society? Over 1 in 10 females aged 15 to 19 becomes pregnant each year, and about 60% of these pregnant teenagers give birth (Henshaw, 1997). The consequences may include an interrupted education, low income, and a difficult start for both new parent and new child (Brooks-Gunn & Furstenberg, 1989; Furstenberg, Lincoln, & Menken, 1981). Meanwhile, sexually transmitted diseases are epidemic among adolescents, more and more teenagers are becoming infected with the HIV virus that causes AIDS, and all too many continue to engage in risky sex (Hingson & Strunin, 1992). What practical solutions to the problems of unwanted teenage pregnancy and sexually transmitted disease might different theorists offer? I will attempt to answer those questions in this chapter to illustrate the fact that different theories of human development offer different lenses through which to view the same human development.

THE NATURE OF THEORIES

As noted in Chapter 1, a *theory* is a set of ideas proposed to describe and explain certain phenomena. Basically, then, a theory is a perspective on something (Kaplan, 1983). Theories of human development should give us insights into many developmental phenomena, including teenage pregnancy. Indeed, the beauty of theories is that they can organize our thinking about a wide range of specific facts or events.

In science it simply is not enough to catalog fact after fact without somehow organizing this information around some set of concepts and propositions. We would soon be swamped by unrelated facts, becoming trivia experts who lack a big picture. A theory of human development provides needed organization; it offers a lens through which we can interpret any number of specific facts or observations. A theory also guides the collection of new facts or observations, emphasizing what is particularly important to study, what can be hypothesized or predicted about it, and how it should be studied. Because different theorists often have very different views on these critical matters, what is learned in any science depends a good deal on which theoretical perspectives become dominant, which in turn depends a good deal on which theories best account for the facts.

Everyone, parent and nonparent alike, holds some basic beliefs about human development—for example, about the importance of good parenting to healthy development. Indeed, I hope that reading this chapter makes you more aware of your own assumptions about human development and how they compare to those of the major theorists. Scientific theories are expected to be more rigorous than our everyday theories, though. A good developmental theory should be

1. *Parsimonious:* as simple and concise as possible. A theory that can account for a large number of empirical observations or findings using only a few assumptions, concepts, and principles is generally more valuable than a theory that must introduce all kinds of assumptions and terms to explain the same phenomena.
2. *Internally consistent:* its different parts and propositions should be consistent with one another rather than contradictory.
3. *Falsifiable:* that is, capable of generating hypotheses or predictions that are precise, that can be tested through research, and that can then be disconfirmed. If a theory is vague or generates contradictory hypotheses about development, it cannot guide research, cannot be adequately evaluated, and therefore will not be very useful in advancing our knowledge.
4. *Supported:* the theory's predictions should be consistent with data gathered through research in which falsification is possible.

In short, a good theory should indeed help us better describe, predict, and explain human development. Theories that fail to meet these evaluation criteria—theories that are not parsimonious, internally consistent, falsifiable, and supported—need to be revised or, ultimately, discarded altogether.

In this chapter we examine four major theoretical viewpoints:

1. The *psychoanalytic* viewpoint, as developed by Sigmund Freud and revised by Erik Erikson and other followers
2. The *learning* perspective developed by B. F. Skinner, Albert Bandura, and others
3. The *cognitive-developmental* viewpoint associated with Jean Piaget
4. The *contextual* approach to human development across the life span, exemplified by Urie Bronfenbrenner

Each theory makes particular assumptions or statements about the nature of human development. To aid us in comparing theories, we'll first examine some of the basic developmental issues on which theorists—and people in general—often disagree.

BOX 2.1

Where do you stand on major developmental issues?

Choose one answer for each question, and write down the corresponding letter or fill it in at the end of the box. Compare your results with those in Box 2.7 at the end of this chapter.

1. Children are
   a. creatures whose basically negative or selfish impulses must be controlled.
   b. neither inherently good nor inherently bad.
   c. creatures who are born with many positive and few negative tendencies.
2. Biological influences (heredity, maturational forces) and environmental influences (culture, parenting styles, learning experiences) are thought to contribute to development. Overall,
   a. biological factors contribute far more than environmental factors.
   b. biological factors contribute somewhat more than environmental factors.

   c. biological and environmental factors are equally important.
   d. environmental factors contribute somewhat more than biological factors.
   e. environmental factors contribute far more than biological factors.
3. People are basically
   a. active beings who are the prime determiners of their own abilities and traits.
   b. passive beings whose characteristics are molded either by social influences (parents and other significant people, outside events) or by biological changes beyond their control.
4. Development proceeds
   a. through stages, so that the individual changes rather abruptly into a quite different kind of person from what he or she was in an earlier stage.
   b. in a variety of ways, some stagelike, some gradual or continuous.

   c. continuously—in small increments without abrupt changes or distinct stages.
5. When we compare the development of different individuals, we see
   a. many similarities; children and adults develop along universal paths and experience similar changes at similar ages.
   b. many differences; different people often undergo different sequences of change and have widely different timetables of development.

   Question
   1 2 3 4 5
   Your pattern of answers:

BASIC ISSUES IN HUMAN DEVELOPMENT

What are developing humans like? How does development come about? What courses does it follow? Let's look at five major developmental issues (see also Parke, Ornstein, Rieser, & Zahn-Waxler, 1994). I invite you to clarify your own stands on major developmental issues by completing the brief questionnaire in Box 2.1. At the end of the chapter, Box 2.7 indicates how the major developmental theorists might answer the questions in Box 2.1, so you can compare your own assumptions with theirs. In other boxes, I have taken the liberty of commenting for the theorists, whether they are dead or alive, imagining how each would view teenage pregnancy. You might want to anticipate what each theorist will say before you read each such box to see if you can successfully apply the theories to a specific problem. It is my hope that, as you grasp the major theories, you will be in a position to draw on their concepts and propositions to make sense of your own and other people's development.

Assumptions about Human Nature

Are people inherently good, inherently bad, or neither? Well before modern theories of human development were proposed, philosophers of the 17th and 18th centuries were taking stands on the nature of human beings. Thomas Hobbes (1588–1679), for one, portrayed children as inherently selfish and bad, believing that it was society's task to control their selfish and aggressive impulses and teach them to behave in positive ways. Jean Jacques Rousseau (1712–1778) took exactly the opposite stand, arguing that children were innately good, that they were born with an intuitive understanding of right and wrong, and that they would develop in positive directions as long as society did not interfere with their natural tendencies. In the middle was the English philosopher John Locke (1632–1704), who maintained that an infant is a **tabula rasa,** or "a blank slate" waiting to be written on by his or her experiences. Locke believed that children were neither innately good nor innately bad; they could develop in any number of directions depending on their experiences.

These different visions of human nature are all represented in one or more modern theories of development and have radically different implications for how one might best raise children. In teaching children to share and help others, for example, should one assume that the child's innate selfish tendencies must be combatted every step of the way, or that children are predisposed to be helpful and caring and will become so if they are simply allowed to grow in their own way, or that children have the potential to be-come either selfish beasts or selfless wonders depending on how they are brought up?

Nature and Nurture

Is development primarily the product of nature (biological forces) or nurture (environmental forces)? Perhaps no controversy in the study of human development has been more heated than the **nature/nurture issue.** On the nature side of the debate have been those who emphasize the influence of heredity, universal maturational processes guided by the genes, and biologically based predispositions. A strong believer in nature would claim that all normal children achieve the same developmental milestones at similar times because of maturational forces and that differences among children or adults are largely due to differences in their genetic makeups. On the nurture side of the debate have been those who emphasize *environment*—conditions and events outside the person. Nurture includes the influences of learning experiences, child-rearing methods, societal changes, and culture on development. A strong believer in nurture would argue, as John Locke did, that human development can take many different forms depending on which specific events the individual experiences over a lifetime.

Activity and Passivity

Are people active in their own development, or are they more passively shaped by forces outside themselves? With respect to this **activity/passivity issue,** some theorists believe that children are curious, active creatures who in a very real sense orchestrate their own development by exploring the world around them or by shaping their own environments. For example, a 4-year-old girl who asks her mother for clothes to play dress-up would be viewed as actively contributing to her own gender-role development.

Other theorists view humans as passive beings who are largely the products of forces beyond their control—usually environmental influences (but possibly strong biological forces). From this vantage point, children's academic failings might be blamed on the failure of their parents and teachers to provide them with the proper learning experiences, and the problems of socially isolated older adults might be traced to the effects of a society that devalues its elderly rather than to deficiencies within the individual. Theorists disagree about just how active individuals are in creating their own environments and, in the process, producing their own development.

Continuity and Discontinuity

Do you believe that humans change gradually, in ways that leave them not so different from what they were

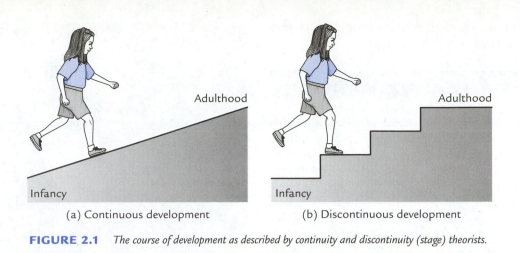

(a) Continuous development	(b) Discontinuous development

FIGURE 2.1 *The course of development as described by continuity and discontinuity (stage) theorists.*

before, or do you believe that human development takes dramatic turns that make people become very different from what they were earlier in life? One aspect of the **continuity/discontinuity issue** concerns whether the changes we undergo over the life span are gradual or abrupt. *Continuity* theorists view human development as a process that occurs in small steps, without sudden changes. In contrast, *discontinuity* theorists picture the course of development as more like a series of stairsteps, each of which elevates the individual to a new (and presumably more advanced) level of functioning (see Figure 2.1). When an adolescent rather rapidly gains six inches in height and achieves sexual maturity, the change may seem quite discontinuous.

A second aspect of the continuity/discontinuity issue concerns whether changes are *quantitative* or *qualitative* in nature. Quantitative changes are changes in *degree* and indicate continuity: A person becomes taller, or knows more vocabulary words, or interacts with friends more or less frequently. By contrast, qualitative changes are changes in *kind* and suggest discontinuity—changes that make the individual fundamentally different in some way from what he or she was before. The transformations of a caterpillar into a butterfly, of a nonverbal infant into a speaking toddler, or of a prepubertal child into a sexually mature adolescent are examples of qualitative changes. So, continuity theorists typically hold that developmental changes are gradual and quantitative, whereas discontinuity theorists hold that they are more abrupt and qualitative. Discontinuity theorists are the ones who often propose that we progress through **developmental stages,** each of which is a distinct phase of the life cycle characterized by a particular set of abilities, motives, emotions, or behaviors that form a coherent pattern. Each stage is perceived as qualitatively different from the stage before or the stage after. Thus the preschool child may be said to solve problems in an entirely different manner than the infant, adolescent, or adult.

Universality and Context-Specificity

Do we all follow the same developmental path, or do different people follow different paths? Developmental theorists often disagree on the **universality/context-specificity issue**—on the extent to which developmental changes are common to everyone (*universal*) or different from person to person (*context specific*). Stage theorists typically believe that the stages they propose are universal. For example, a stage theorist might claim that virtually all children enter a new stage in their intellectual development at about the time they start school, or that most adults, sometime around the age of 40, experience a "midlife crisis" in which they raise major questions about their lives. From this perspective, development proceeds in certain universal directions.

But other theorists believe that human development is far more varied than this. Paths of development followed in one culture may be very different from paths followed in another culture. For example, children in the United States give up their belief that dreams are real as they get older, but children raised in the Atayal culture of Taiwan, where dreams are viewed as real, come to view them as real (Kohlberg, 1966). Even within a single culture, sequences of developmental change may differ from subcultural group to subcultural group, from family to family, from individual to individual. One child in a family may become more studious with age, another may lose interest in school entirely.

These, then, are some of the major issues about human development that different theories resolve in different ways: goodness/badness of human nature/nurture, activity/passivity, continuity/discontinuity, and universality/context-specificity. For now, let's begin our survey of the theories, starting with Freud's psychoanalytic perspective.

FREUD: PSYCHOANALYTIC THEORY

It is difficult to think of a theorist who has had a greater impact on Western thought than Sigmund Freud, the Viennese physician who lived from 1856 to 1939. This revolutionary thinker challenged prevailing notions of human nature and human development by proposing that we are driven by motives and emotions of which we are largely unaware and that we are shaped by our earliest experiences in life (see Hall, 1954). His name is a household word, and his **psychoanalytic theory** continues to influence thinking about human development, even though it is far less influential today than it once was. We provide only a brief overview here and then turn to an example of a more modern psychoanalytic thinker, Erik Erikson.

Instincts and Unconscious Motives

Central to Freudian psychoanalytic theory is the notion that human beings have basic biological urges or drives that must be satisfied. What kinds of urges? Undesirable ones! Freud viewed the newborn as a "seething cauldron," an inherently selfish creature "driven" by two kinds of **instincts,** or inborn biological forces that motivate behavior. The *life instincts* aim for survival and direct life-sustaining activities such as breathing, eating, and having sex. The *death instincts* are destructive forces that motivate us to harm others and even ourselves. According to Freud, these biological instincts are the source of the psychic (or mental) energy that fuels human behavior and is channeled in new directions over the course of human development.

Freud strongly believed in **unconscious motivation,** in the power of instincts and other inner forces to influence behavior even though they are not known to us. A teenage boy, for example, may not realize that his devotion to body building could be a way of channeling his sexual or aggressive urges. As Freud developed his psychoanalytic therapy, he came to rely on such therapy methods as hypnosis, free association (a quick spilling out of ideas), and dream analysis because he believed that only these techniques would uncover underlying unconscious motives. So, we immediately see that Freud's theory is highly biological in nature: Biological instincts—forces that often provide an unconscious motivation for our actions—are said to guide human development.

Id, Ego, and Superego

According to Freud (1933), each individual has a fixed amount of psychic energy that can be used to satisfy

Sigmund Freud's psychoanalytic theory was one of the first, and certainly one of the most influential, theories of how the personality develops from childhood to adulthood.

basic urges or instincts and to grow psychologically. As the child develops, this psychic energy is divided among three components of the personality: the id, the ego, and the superego.

At birth all psychic energy resides in the **id.** The id is the impulsive, irrational part of the personality whose entire mission is to satisfy the instincts. It obeys the "pleasure principle," seeking immediate gratification, even when biological needs cannot be realistically or appropriately met. If you think about it, young infants do seem to be "all id" in many ways. When they are hungry or wet, they simply fuss and cry until their needs are met; they are not known for their patience.

The second component of the personality is the **ego,** the rational side of the individual that operates according to the "reality principle" and tries to find realistic ways of gratifying the instincts. According to Freud (1933), the ego begins to emerge during infancy when psychic energy is diverted from the id to energize important cognitive processes such as perception, learning, and problem solving. The hungry toddler may be able to do more than merely cry when she is hungry; she may be able to draw on the resources of the ego to hunt down Dad, lead him to the kitchen, and say "gookie." However, toddlers' egos are still relatively immature; they want what they want *now.* As the ego matures further, children become more and more able to postpone their pleasures until a more appropriate time and to devise logical and realistic plans for meeting their needs.

The third part of the Freudian personality is the **superego,** the individual's internalized moral standards. The superego develops from the ego and strives for *perfection* rather than for pleasure or realism (Freud, 1933). It begins to develop as 3- to 6-year-old children *internalize* (take on as their own) the moral standards and values of their parents. Typically, it grows stronger as children continue to absorb the values of adults. Once the superego emerges, children have a parental voice in their heads that tells them that it would be wrong to satisfy their ids by grabbing or stealing other children's snacks, and that voice makes them feel guilty or ashamed when they do violate society's rules and standards. The superego insists that we find socially acceptable or ethical outlets for the id's undesirable impulses.

Conflict among the id, ego, and superego is inevitable, Freud claimed. In the mature, healthy personality, a dynamic balance operates: The id communicates its basic needs, the ego restrains the impulsive id long enough to find realistic ways to satisfy these needs, and the superego decides whether the ego's problem-solving strategies are morally acceptable. The ego is clearly "in the middle"; it must somehow strike a balance between the opposing demands of the id and the superego, all the while accommodating to the realities of the external world.

According to Freud (1940/1964), psychological problems often arise when psychic energy is unevenly distributed among the id, the ego, and the superego. Because there is a fixed amount of psychic energy to be spent, too much energy devoted to one part of the personality inevitably means less to be channeled into the other parts. For example, people diagnosed as sociopaths, who routinely lie and cheat to get their way, may have very strong ids and normal egos, but very weak superegos, never having learned to respect the rights of other people. In contrast, the married woman who cannot undress in front of her husband may be controlled by an overly strong superego, perhaps because she was made to feel deeply ashamed about any interest she took in her body as a young girl. Analysis of the dynamics operating among the three parts of the personality provided Freud and his followers with an important means of describing and understanding individual differences in personality and the origins of psychological disorders.

Psychosexual Development

Freud (1940/1964) viewed the sex instinct as the most important of the life instincts because the psychological disturbances of his patients often revolved around childhood sexual conflicts. He maintained that, as the

The three parts of the personality proposed by Freud are inevitably in conflict.

child matures biologically, the sex instinct's psychic energy, which he called **libido,** shifts from one part of the body to another over the years, seeking to gratify different biological needs. In the process the child moves through five **psychosexual stages:** oral, anal, phallic, latency, and genital. These stages are outlined in Table 2.1.

Freud emphasized nature more than nurture. He believed that inborn biological instincts drive behavior and that biological maturation guides all children through the five psychosexual stages. Yet he also viewed nurture—especially early experiences within the family—as an important contributor to individual differences in adult personality.

At each psychosexual stage, the id's impulses and social demands come into conflict. Harsh child-rearing methods can heighten this conflict and the child's anxiety. To defend itself against anxiety, the ego, without being aware of it, adopts **defense mechanisms** (Freud, 1940/1964). We all use these coping devices, but some people become overdependent on them because of unfavorable experiences early in life. To illustrate, consider the defense mechanism of **fixation,** a kind of arrested development in which part of the libido remains tied to an early stage. A baby boy who was rarely allowed to linger at the breast, was screamed at for mouthing and chewing paychecks and other fascinating objects around the house, or was otherwise deprived of oral gratification might become fixated at the oral stage to satisfy unmet oral needs and to avoid the potentially even greater conflicts of the anal stage. He might display this oral fixation by becoming a chronic thumbsucker and, later in life, by

TABLE 2.1

The stage theories of Freud and Erikson

Freud's Psychosexual Theory		Erikson's Psychosexual Theory	
Stage/age range	*Description*	*Stage/age range*	*Description*
Oral stage (birth to 1 year)	Libido is focused on the mouth as a source of pleasure. Obtaining oral gratification from a mother figure is critical to later development.	*Trust versus mistrust* (birth to 1 year)	Infants must learn to trust their caregivers to meet their needs. Responsive parenting is critical.
Anal stage (1 to 3 years)	Libido is focused on the anus, and toilet training creates conflicts between the child's biological urges and society's demands.	*Autonomy versus shame and doubt* (1 to 3 years)	Children must learn to be autonomous—to assert their wills and do things for themselves—or they will doubt their abilities.
Phallic stage (3 to 6 years)	Libido centers on the genitals. Resolution of the Oedipus or Electra complex results in identification with the same-sex parent and development of the superego.	*Initiative versus guilt* (3 to 6 years)	Preschoolers develop initiative by devising and carrying out bold plans, but they must learn not to impinge on the rights of others.
Latency period (6 to 12 years)	Libido is quiet; psychic energy is invested in schoolwork and play with same-sex friends.	*Industry versus inferiority* (6 to 12 years)	Children must master important social and academic skills and keep up with their peers or they will feel inferior.
Genital stage (12 years and older)	Puberty reawakens the sexual instincts as youths seek to establish mature sexual relationships and pursue the biological goal of reproduction.	*Identity versus role confusion* (12 to 20 years)	Adolescents ask who they are and must establish social and vocational identities or else remain confused about the roles they should play as adults.
		Intimacy versus isolation (20 to 40 years)	Young adults seek to form a shared identity with another person but may fear intimacy and experience loneliness and isolation.
		Generativity versus stagnation (40 to 65 years)	Middle-aged adults must feel that they are producing something that will outlive them, either as parents or as workers, or they will become stagnant and self-centered.
		Integrity versus despair (65 and older)	Older adults must come to view their lives as meaningful in order to face death without worries and regrets.

chain-smoking, talking incessantly (as college professors are prone to do), or being overdependent on other people.

Similarly, the girl who is harshly punished for toilet training mistakes or forced to sit for hours on the potty seat may become fixated at the anal stage and become an inhibited or stingy adult. Or she may deal with her anxiety through another important defense mechanism, **regression,** which involves retreating to an earlier, less traumatic, stage of development. The three-year-old who has been punished for a toileting accident may revert to infantile behavior—gooing like a baby, demanding juice from a baby bottle, wanting to be held. Similarly, the man who has had a terrible day at work may want his wife to act like his mother and "baby" him. In this way, Freud argued, *early experiences may have long-term effects on personality development.*

Particularly treacherous for children, according to Freud, is the *phallic stage,* from age 3 to age 6, when children are said to develop a strong incestuous desire for the parent of the other sex. According to Freud, a 3- to 5-year-old boy develops an intense longing for his mother and begins to view his father as a rival for Mom's affection. Freud called this the **Oedipus complex** after Oedipus, the legendary King of Thebes who unwittingly killed his father and married his mother. Fearing that his father might castrate him as punishment, the preschool boy resolves his conflict by identifying with his father, taking on as his own the father's attitudes, attributes, and behaviors, in order to reduce the chances that his father will be angry with him. As a result, he learns his masculine sex role and develops a superego by internalizing his father's moral standards. If parents punish a young boy for being curious about male and female anatomy, Freud believed, the product may be a sexually inhibited man who is not quite sure how to relate to women.

Although Freud admitted that he was unsure about the development of preschool girls, he claimed that they experience an **Electra complex.** (Electra was the mythological Greek who avenged her father's murder by killing her mother.) Once a 4-year-old girl discovers that she lacks a penis, she blames her mother for this "castrated" condition, experiences *penis envy,* and hopes that the father she now idolizes will share with her the valued organ that she lacks. As a girl recognizes the impossibility of possessing her father, she identifies with her mother, who *does* possess her father. If development proceeds normally, then, girls resolve their conflicts by identifying with their mothers, thereby taking on a "feminine" role and developing a superego.

After the lull of the latency period (Table 2.1), during which sexual urges are tame and 6- to 12-year-olds invest energy in schoolwork and play, adolescents reaching puberty are said to enter the final stage of psychosexual development, the *genital stage.* During this phase, they may have difficulty accepting their new sexuality, may reexperience some of the conflicting feelings toward their parents that they felt as part of their Oedipus and Electra conflicts, and may distance themselves from their parents in order to defend against these anxiety-producing feelings. Although adults may develop a greater capacity to love and eventually satisfy the mature sex instinct by having children, Freud believed that psychosexual development stopped with adolescence and that the individual remains in the genital stage throughout adulthood.

In short, Freud insisted that the past lives on. Early childhood experiences may haunt us in later life and influence our adult personalities, interests, and behaviors. Parents significantly affect a child's success in passing through the biologically programmed psychosexual stages. They can err by overindulging the child's urges, but more commonly they create lasting and severe inner conflicts and anxieties by denying an infant oral gratification, using harsh toilet-training practices with a toddler, or punishing the preschooler who is fascinated by naked bodies. Heavy reliance on fixation, regression, and other defense mechanisms may then become necessary just to keep the ego intact and functioning. In Box 2.2, we hear what Freud might have said about the causes of teenage pregnancy and about the case of Sheila and James described at the start of the chapter.

Strengths and Weaknesses

Are we really driven by sexual and aggressive instincts? Could we really have experienced an Oedipus or Electra complex and simply repressed these traumatic events? Or could the sexual conflicts Freud thought so important merely have been reflections of the sexually repressive Victorian culture in which he and his patients lived? And are the lessons Freud learned from psychoanalyzing disturbed adults actually relevant to understanding *normal* development?

Many developmentalists fault Freud for proposing a theory that is difficult to pin down and test and therefore is not always falsifiable. Testing hypotheses that require studying unconscious motivations and the workings of the unseen id, ego, and superego has been challenging indeed. Freud himself offered little hard evidence to support his theory. Moreover, when the theory *has* been tested, many of its specific ideas have not been supported (Crews, 1996; Fisher & Greenberg, 1977). As a result, it has been judged "a theory in search of some facts" (Macmillan, 1991, p. 548). For example, many preschool children are quite ignorant of male and female anatomy (Bem, 1989; Katcher, 1955). How, then, could they experience castration anxiety or penis envy in the phallic stage? The whole idea that children experience Oedipus and Electra complexes has come under considerable attack. It seems that Freud initially uncovered evidence that many of his patients had been sexually or physically abused during childhood. Unable to believe that such abuse was as widespread as it appeared to be, Freud claimed instead that children wished for and fantasized about, but did not actually experience, seduction by their parents (Emde, 1992; Masson, 1984). Now, of course, we know that child sexual abuse not only is widespread but can contribute to lasting

Psychoanalytic theory applied: Freud on teenage pregnancy

I welcome this opportunity to return to life to comment on the problem of teenage pregnancy. As you know, I was always fascinated by sex! We must realize that teenagers experience intense conflicts during the genital stage of psychosexual development. Their new sexual urges are anxiety provoking and must somehow be managed. Moreover, the sexual conflicts of earlier psychosexual stages often reemerge during adolescence.

Of course, I would need to find out more about the early childhood experiences and psychic conflicts of Sheila and James to pinpoint the specific causes of their behavior, but I can of-fer a few suggestions. For example, Sheila and James may not have strong enough egos and superegos to keep their selfish ids in check.[1] Perhaps they sought immediate gratification of their sexual urges with no thought for future consequences or morality. It is also possible that these teenagers were motivated by inner conflicts that had their roots in infancy or the preschool years. For instance, many pregnant girls come from homes without fathers.[2] Perhaps Sheila never fully resolved the Electra complex of the phallic stage and was unconsciously seeking to possess her father by possessing James and having a baby. James, of course, might have been seeking to gratify his unconscious desire for his mother through Sheila. Teenagers often distance themselves from their parents as a defense against reawakened Oedipal feelings of love for the other-sex parent.

In short, teenage pregnancy is likely to result from difficulty managing sexual urges due to personality problems that are rooted in early childhood experiences.

[1] Babikian and Goldman, 1971; Hart and Hilton, 1988
[2] Hatcher, 1973

---

psychological difficulties (see Chapter 11). Many have also pointed out that Freud held sexist views by today's standards. For example, he believed, incorrectly, that girls do not progress as far in moral development as boys because the Oedipus conflict provides more motivation to identify with parents than the Electra complex.

Despite the fact that many of Freud's specific ideas have been difficult to test or have not been supported by research, many of his broad insights have stood up well and have profoundly influenced later theories of human development (Emde, 1992). First, Freud called attention to unconscious motivation, to the fact that much of our behavior is caused by forces of which we are not consciously aware. Second, Freud deserves credit for focusing attention on the importance of early experience in the family for later development. Third and finally, we can thank Freud for exploring the emotional side of human development: the loves, fears, anxieties, and other powerful emotions that play such an important role in our lives. Emotional development has often been slighted by developmentalists who focus intently on observable behavior or on rational thought processes.

ERIKSON: NEO-FREUDIAN PSYCHOANALYTIC THEORY

Still another sign of Freud's immense influence is the fact that he inspired so many disciples and descendants to contribute in their own right to our understanding of human development. Among these well-known *neo-Freudians* were Alfred Adler, who suggested that siblings (and rivalries between siblings) are significant in development; Carl Jung, who claimed that adults experience a kind of "midlife crisis" (see Chapter 15) and then become freer to express both the "masculine" and "feminine" sides of their personalities; Karen Horney, who challenged Freud's ideas about sex differences; Harry Stack Sullivan, who wrote extensively about how close friendships in childhood set the stage for intimate relationships later in life (see Chapter 13); and Freud's daughter Anna, who developed methods of psychoanalysis appropriate for children.

But the neo-Freudian who most influenced thinking about life-span development was Erik Erikson (1902–1994). Erikson studied with Freud's daughter, Anna, and emigrated from Germany to the United States when Hitler rose to power (see Hopkins, 1995, for a biography). Like Freud, Erikson (1963, 1968, 1982) concerned himself with the inner dynamics of personality and proposed that the personality evolves through systematic stages. Erikson's point of view differed from Freud's in the following ways:

1. Erikson placed less emphasis on sexual urges as the drivers of development and more emphasis on social influences such as peers, teachers, schools, and the broader culture.
2. Erikson placed less emphasis on the irrational, selfish id and more on the rational ego and its adaptive powers.
3. Erikson held a more positive view of human nature, seeing us as active in our development,

largely rational, and able to overcome the effects of harmful early experiences.

4. Erikson maintained that human development continues during adulthood.

Psychosocial Development

Erikson believed that human beings everywhere face eight major psychosocial crises, or conflicts, during their lives. (Erikson's stages are next to Freud's in Table 2.1.) Whether the conflict of a particular stage is successfully resolved or not, the individual is pushed by both biological maturation and social demands into the next stage. However, the unsuccessful resolution of a conflict will influence how subsequent stages play out.

The first conflict, **trust versus mistrust,** revolves around whether or not an infant becomes able to rely on other people to be responsive to his or her needs. To develop a sense of trust, infants must be able to count on their primary caregivers to feed them, relieve their discomfort, come when beckoned, and return their smiles and babbles. Whereas Freud focused on the significance of a caregiver's feeding practices, Erikson believed that the caregiver's *general responsiveness* was critical to later development. If caregivers neglect, reject, or respond inconsistently to the infant, he or she will mistrust others. A healthy balance between the terms of the conflict must be struck for development to proceed optimally. Trust should outweigh mistrust, but an element of skepticism is needed as well: An infant who is overindulged may become too trusting (a "sucker").

During the so-called "terrible twos," toddlers must learn to trust themselves enough to assert their wills. This is the psychosocial conflict of **autonomy versus shame and doubt.** Toddlers are determined to do things themselves to demonstrate their independence and their control over their parents. They say "me, me, me" and "no, no, no," loudly proclaiming that they have wills of their own. If their parents humiliate or punish them when they have toileting accidents or spill their milk, they may end up doubting their competence or even believing that they are fundamentally bad people.

Four- and five-year-olds who have achieved a sense of autonomy enter Erikson's stage of **initiative versus guilt,** in which they develop a sense of purpose by devising bold plans but must also learn not to step on other people in the process. In the preschool years of imaginative play, children acquire new motor skills, plot and plan to build sand castles or conquer the monsters in their fantasy play, and take great pride in accomplishing the goals they set. A sense of initiative, Erikson believed, paves the way for success in elementary school, when children face the conflict of **industry versus inferiority.** To gain a sense of industry,

Erik Erikson built on Freudian theory and proposed that people experience eight psychosexual crises over the life span.

children must master the important cognitive and social skills—reading, writing, cooperative teamwork, and so on—that are necessary to win the approval of both adults and peers.

Erikson (1968) is best known for characterizing adolescence as a time of "identity crisis," a critical period in the lifelong process of forming one's identity as a person. During this psychosocial stage of **identity versus role confusion,** adolescents attempt to define who they are (in terms of career, religion, sexual identity, and so on), where they are heading, and where they fit into society. They often change their minds and experiment with new looks, new majors, and new group memberships in the process.

Whereas Freud's stages stopped with adolescence, Erikson outlined three key psychosocial conflicts during the adult years. Young adulthood, Erikson believed, is a time for dealing with the psychosocial conflict of **intimacy versus isolation.** The young adult who has not resolved the issue of identity versus role confusion may be threatened by the idea of entering a committed, long-term relationship and being "tied down" or may become overdependent on a partner as a source of identity. In middle age, adults become concerned with the issue of **generativity versus stagnation.** They struggle to gain a sense that they have produced something that will outlive them, whether by raising happy, healthy children or by doing something meaningful through their work or volunteer activities. If all goes well, they will genuinely care about the welfare of future generations, as opposed to being "in a rut," absorbed with their own problems.

Finally, elderly adults confront the psychosocial conflict of **integrity versus despair.** They try to find a sense of meaning in their lives that will help them face the inevitability of death. If they are successful, they are able to look back over their lives and say that there is little they would change; if they are not, they may dwell on past injustices and paths not taken and have difficulty preparing for death.

Erikson clearly did not agree with Freud that the personality is essentially "set in stone" during early childhood. Yet he, like Freud and other psychoanalytic theorists, believed that people everywhere progress through systematic stages of development, undergoing similar personality changes at similar ages. As individuals successfully resolve the central conflict of each stage of psychosocial development, they gain new personality strengths (or "ego virtues")—for example, in infancy, trust of self and other people, and in middle adulthood, a greater concern for future generations. Individual differences in personality presumably reflect the different experiences individuals have as they struggle to cope with the challenges of each life stage. Both biological maturation and the demands of the social environment influence the individual's progress through Erikson's stage sequence, as illustrated in Box 2.3 by what he might have thought about teenage pregnancy.

Strengths and Weaknesses

Many people find Erikson's emphasis on our rational, adaptive nature and on an interaction of biological and social influences easier to accept than Freud's emphasis on unconscious, irrational motivations based in biological needs. Erikson seems to have captured some central developmental issues in his eight stages and has had a great impact on thinking about adolescent identity formation and changes in the self during adulthood (see Chapter 10). At the same time, Erikson's theory has many of the same shortcomings as Freud's. It is sometimes vague and difficult to test. And, while it provides a useful *description* of human personality development, it does not provide an adequate *explanation* of how this development comes about.

Important psychoanalytic theorists such as Erikson continue to shape our understanding of human development. However, many developmentalists have rejected the whole psychoanalytic perspective in favor of theories that are more precise and testable.

BOX 2.3

Erikson on teenage pregnancy

I am not quite as obsessed by sexual issues as my inspiration, Dr. Freud, but I can agree with him on some things. I agree that accepting one's self as a sexual being is an important task of adolescence. I also agree that early experience can affect later development. For example, if either James or Sheila had unresponsive caregivers when they were infants, they could have had difficulty resolving my psychosocial conflict of trust versus mistrust. Adolescents who never developed a strong sense of trust in other people may fear being abandoned and may try to use sex as a way to keep that from happening.

Ah, but why talk of infancy when we can simply view teenage sexual experimentation as part of the adolescent psychosocial conflict between identity and role confusion? Adolescents are changing rapidly, physically and cognitively, and they are being asked by society to establish who they are as individuals and as members of society. Many adolescents seek a sense of identity by experimenting with different roles and behaviors to see what suits them. They try drugs, dye their hair, join radical groups, change majors every semester, and so on—all to forge a firm sense of identity. Why, I should know: I was the tall, blond stepson of a Jewish doctor and wandered all over Europe after high school, trying out a career as an artist and a number of other possibilities before I ended up studying child psychoanalysis under Anna Freud and found my calling in life in my mid-20s.[1]

So, perhaps Sheila and James were simply searching for their identities when they began their sexual relationship. Or maybe they tried to find an easy resolution to their role confusion through each other—by becoming the other's boyfriend or girlfriend. Here's what I wrote in my book, *Identity*:[2]

For where an assured sense of identity is missing, even friendships and affairs become desperate attempts at determining the fuzzy outlines of identity by mutual narcissistic mirroring [sic]: to fall in love then often means to fall into one's mirror image, hurting oneself and damaging the mirror. [p. 167]

If Sheila and James are finding an identity prematurely through each other, I must be pessimistic about their future. I maintain—and research bears me out—that one must know oneself before one can love someone else—that is, that one must find one's true *identity* and end *role confusion* before one is ready to resolve the conflict between *intimacy* and *isolation*.[3]

---

[1] Hopkins, 1995
[2] Erikson, 1968
[3] Orlofsky, 1993

LEARNING THEORY

Give me a dozen healthy infants, well formed, and my own specified world to bring them up in and I'll guarantee to take any one at random and train him to become any type of specialist I might select—doctor, lawyer, artist, merchant, chief, and yes, even beggar-man and thief, regardless of his talents, penchants, tendencies, abilities, vocations, and race of his ancestors. [Watson, 1925, p. 82]

There is a bold statement! It reflects a belief that nurture is everything and nature, or hereditary endowment, counts for nothing. It was made by John B. Watson, a strong believer in the importance of learning in human development and the father of the school of thought in psychology called behaviorism.

A basic premise of Watson's (1913) **behaviorism** is that conclusions about human development and functioning should be based on observations of overt behavior rather than on speculations about unconscious motives or cognitive processes that remain unobservable. Moreover, said Watson, *learned* associations between external stimuli and observable responses are the building blocks of human development. Like John Locke, Watson believed that the infant is a *tabula rasa* to be written on by experience. Children have no inborn tendencies; how they turn out will depend entirely on the environment in which they grow up and the ways in which their parents and other significant people in their lives treat them. According to a behavioral perspective, then, it is a mistake to assume that children advance through a series of distinct stages partly programmed by biological maturation, as Freud, Erikson, and others have argued. Instead, development is viewed as nothing more than learning. It is a continuous process of behavior change that is particularistic and can differ enormously from person to person. Watson's basic view was advanced by the influential work of B. F. Skinner.

Skinner: Operant Conditioning

B. F. Skinner (1905–1990), whose name is as well known as that of any American psychologist, had a long, distinguished career at Harvard University. Through his research with animals, Skinner (1953) gained understanding of one very important form of learning. In **operant** (or instrumental) **conditioning,** a learner's behavior becomes either more or less probable depending on the consequences it produces. **Reinforcers** are consequences that increase the probability that a response will occur in the future. A boy may form a long-term habit of sharing toys with playmates if his parents reinforce his sharing with praise, or a

John B. Watson was the father of behaviorism.

computer saleswoman may work harder at making sales if she receives a commission for each sale. **Punishers,** on the other hand, are consequences that suppress a response and decrease the likelihood that it will occur in the future. A teenage girl whose car keys are confiscated every time she stays out beyond her curfew and a man who is criticized each time he interrupts people during meetings are likely to cut down on the responses that resulted in punishment. Very simply, we learn to keep doing the things that have positive consequences and to stop doing the things that have negative consequences.

Like Watson, then, Skinner believed that the course of human development depends on the individual's learning experiences. One boy's aggressive behavior may be reinforced over time because he gets his way with other children and his parents encourage his "macho" behavior. Another boy may quickly learn that aggression is prohibited and punished. The two may develop in entirely different directions based on their different histories of reinforcement and punishment. Skinner did acknowledge that evolution has provided us with a brain that allows us to learn from experience and that even influences what we can learn most easily and what we find most reinforcing. However, he believed that the essence of human development is the continual acquisition of new habits of behavior and that these learned behaviors are controlled by *external* stimuli (reinforcers and punishers).

From a learning theory perspective, even development that seems stagelike need not be caused by

B. F. Skinner, escorted by his daughter Julie Vargas, received an award for Outstanding Lifetime Contribution to Psychology from the American Psychological Association. He died shortly afterward at the age of 86.

biological maturation. Instead, age-related changes in the environment could produce age-related changes in behavior (Bijou & Baer, 1961). Six-year-olds starting school might change in response to a new system of reinforcements and punishments imposed by their teachers, or older adults might change when they are forced to retire and lose access to the reinforcers that employment brought them.

Most developmentalists appreciate that Skinner's operant-conditioning principles can help explain many aspects of human development. Yet some theorists believe that Skinner placed too much emphasis on a single type of learning and too little emphasis on the role of cognitive processes such as attention, memory, and reflection in learning. For this reason, today's developmental scholars are more attracted to Albert Bandura's cognitive social learning theory than to Skinner's learning theory.

Bandura: Social Learning

Albert Bandura's (1977, 1986, 1989) **social learning theory** claims that humans are cognitive beings whose active processing of information from the environment plays a major role in learning and human development. Bandura argues that human learning is very different from rat learning because humans have far more sophisticated cognitive capabilities. Bandura agrees with Skinner that operant conditioning is an important type of learning, but he notes that humans

think about the connections between their behavior and its consequences, anticipate what consequences are likely to follow from their future behavior, and often are more affected by what they *believe* will happen than by the consequences they actually encounter. For example, a woman may continue to pursue a medical degree despite many punishing hardships and few immediate rewards because she *anticipates* a greater reward when she completes her studies. We are not just passively shaped by the external consequences of our behavior; we actively think about past and present experiences and anticipate the future. We also reinforce or punish ourselves with mental pats on the back and self-criticism.

Nowhere is Bandura's cognitive emphasis clearer than in his highlighting of **observational learning** as the most important mechanism through which human behavior changes. Observational learning is simply learning that results from observing the behavior of other people (called *models*). It is the kind of learning involved when children learn patterns of aggression from watching TV, as we saw in Chapter 1. A teenager may pick up the latest dance, and a middle-aged executive may learn how to use a new computer program by observing other people. Such observational learning depends on cognitive processes. We must, for example, pay attention to the model, actively digest what we observe, and store this information in memory if we are to imitate at a later date what we have observed. Over the years we are exposed to hun-

Albert Bandura highlighted the role of cognition in human learning. He is on the faculty at Stanford University.

dreds of social models and have the opportunity to learn thousands of behavior patterns (some good, some bad) simply by observing others perform them. We need not be reinforced in order to learn this way. We do, however, take note of whether the model's behavior has positive or negative consequences and use this information to decide whether to imitate what we have observed.

Watson and Skinner may have believed that humans are passively shaped by the environment to become whatever those around them groom them to be, but Bandura does not. Because he views humans as active, cognitive beings, he holds that human development occurs through a continuous reciprocal interaction among the person, the person's behavior, and the environment—a perspective he called **reciprocal determinism.** Our personal characteristics and behaviors affect the people in our social environment, just as these individuals influence our personal characteristics and future behaviors.

Like Watson and Skinner, though, Bandura is skeptical of the idea of universal stages of human development. He maintains that development is context-specific and can proceed along many different paths. It is also continuous, occurring gradually through a lifetime of learning. Bandura does acknowledge that children's cognitive learning capacities mature over childhood, so that they can remember more about what they have seen and can imitate a greater variety of novel behaviors. Yet he also believes that children of the same age will not be much alike at all if their learning experiences have differed.

Obviously there is a fundamental disagreement between stage theorists like Freud and Erikson and learning theorists like Bandura. Learning theorists do not give us a general description of the normal course of human development, because they insist that there is no such description to give. Instead, they offer a rich account of the *mechanisms* through which behavior can change over time. They ask us to apply basic principles of learning to understand how each individual changes with age. To show how learning principles apply to the matter of teenage pregnancy, Bandura's point of view is summarized in Box 2.4.

Strengths and Weaknesses

Watson's and Skinner's behavioral learning theories and Bandura's more cognitively oriented social learning theory have contributed immensely to our understanding of development (see Gewirtz & Pelaez-Nogueras, 1992; Grusec, 1992). Learning theories are very precise and testable, and carefully controlled experiments have shown how we might learn everything from altruism to alcoholism. We will see the fruits of research on human learning throughout this text (especially in Chapter 8).

Moreover, the learning principles involved in operant conditioning, observational learning, and other forms of learning operate *across the entire life span;* learning theorists can go about trying to understand middle-aged or older adults in the same way that they attempt to understand infants. Finally, learning theories have very practical applications; they have been the basis for many highly effective techniques for optimizing development and treating developmental problems. Parents and teachers can certainly be more effective when they systematically reinforce the behavior they hope to instill in children and when they serve as role models of desirable behavior. And many

BOX 2.4

Bandura on teenage pregnancy

I would like to begin by building on the work of learning theorists who preceded me. B. F. Skinner would undoubtedly get right to the heart of it and say that teenagers have sex because sex is reinforcing and that they become pregnant because using contraception is not! One team of researchers put it well: "It is quite likely that if teenagers had to take a pill to become pregnant, early childbearing would quickly vanish as a social problem."[1]

This is true enough, but my social learning theory offers additional insights into teenage pregnancy. Sheila and James have been discovering a great deal about sexual behavior through observational learning. Today's adolescents live in a social world filled with messages about sex from their peers,

the media, and, to a lesser extent, their parents. They actively process this information for future use. If they learn that their friends are sexually active, and if they also think that their friends find sex more reinforcing than costly, they are likely to do what their friends are doing.[2] TV is a factor, too. Adolescents watch sex on TV all the time—often exploitive sex, with never a mention of birth control and rarely a mention of such consequences as HIV infection or the stresses of teenage parenthood. Soap operas are especially bad: Teenagers who watch them a lot seem to learn that single parenthood is a fulfilling experience that does little to hurt a young woman's chances in life.[3] Adolescents today have far more opportunities to learn sexually irresponsible

behavior than to learn sexually responsible behavior through observation.

Finally, let me emphasize that people's *expectations* about the consequences of their actions are often more important than the actual reinforcers and punishers operating in a situation. If James, for example, *believes* that using a condom will decrease his sexual enjoyment, or if Sheila *believes* that James will resent it if she asks him to use a condom, those beliefs will surely decrease the chances that they will use protection.

[1] Furstenberg et al., 1981
[2] Benda & DiBlasio, 1994
[3] Larson, 1996

---

psychotherapists today apply behavioral and cognitive learning techniques to treat psychological problems.

At the same time, learning theories, even Bandura's social learning theory, leave something to be desired as models of human development. Consider the following demonstration. Paul Weisberg (1963) reinforced 3-month-old infants with smiles and gentle rubs on the chin whenever they happened to babble. He found that these infants babbled more often than did infants who received the same social stimulation randomly rather than only after each babbling sound they made. But does this mean that infants normally begin to babble *because* babbling is reinforced by their caregivers? Not necessarily. All normal infants, even deaf ones, babble at about 4 months of age. Moreover, no matter what experiences we provide to a newborn, he or she will not be maturationally ready to begin babbling. We must suspect, then, that the maturation of the neural and muscular control required for babbling has more than a little to do with the onset of babbling during infancy.

This example really highlights two criticisms of learning theories as theories of human development. First, learning theorists rarely demonstrate that learning is actually responsible for commonly observed developmental changes; they show through their experiments only that learning *might have* resulted in developmental change. Some critics wish that learning theorists would provide a fuller account of normal changes across the life span. Second, early learning

theorists, and to a lesser extent Bandura, may have oversimplified their account of development by downplaying biological influences. Children simply cannot achieve certain developmental milestones or benefit from certain learning experiences until they are maturationally ready. And, although individuals differ from one another partly because they have different experiences in life, they also differ because they have different genetic endowments. After a number of years in which learning theories dominated the study of development, many scientists began to look for a theory that was more clearly "developmental," that showed how human beings change systematically as they get older. They found what they wanted in the remarkable work of Jean Piaget.

COGNITIVE-DEVELOPMENTAL THEORY

No theorist has contributed more to our understanding of children's minds than Jean Piaget (1896–1980), a Swiss scholar who began to study children's intellectual development during the 1920s. This remarkable man developed quickly himself, publishing his first scientific paper (a letter to the editor, really) in 1907, at the tender age of 11. Piaget wrote "An Albino Sparrow" primarily to persuade the curator of the Neuchâtel Museum of Natural History in Switzerland to allow him to work in the museum after hours (Gruber & Voneche, 1977). The paper testifies not only to his ambition and fascination with zoology but to the keen observational skills Piaget later applied in his studies of child development. Eventually, Piaget put his interest in zoology and the adaptation of animals to their environments together with his equally strong interest in philosophy by devoting his career to the study of how humans acquire knowledge and use it to adapt to their environments.

Piaget's lifelong interest in cognitive development emerged when he accepted a position in Paris at the Alfred Binet laboratories to work on the first standardized intelligence (IQ) test. In this approach to the study of mental ability, an estimate of a person's intelligence is based on the number and types of questions that he or she answers correctly. Piaget soon found that he was more interested in children's *incorrect* answers than in their correct ones. He noticed that children of about the same age were producing the same kinds of wrong answers. By questioning them to find out how they were thinking about the problems presented to them, he began to realize that young children do not simply know less than older children do; instead, they think in a qualitatively different way. Eventually Piaget developed a full-blown theory to account for changes in thinking from infancy to adolescence.

Swiss psychologist Jean Piaget revolutionized the field of human development with his theory of cognitive growth.

Piaget: Intellectual Development

Influenced by his background in biology, Piaget (1950) viewed intelligence as a process that helps an organism adapt to its environment. The infant who can grasp a cookie and bring it to her mouth is behaving adaptively, as is the adolescent who can solve algebra problems or fix a flat tire. As children mature, they acquire ever-more complex "cognitive structures," or organized patterns of thought or action, that aid them in adapting to their environments.

How do children develop more complex cognitive structures and increase their understanding of the world? Piaget insisted that children are not born with innate ideas about reality, as some philosophers have claimed. Nor are they simply filled with information by adults, as others have claimed. Instead, Piaget took a position called **constructivism,** claiming that children actively construct new understandings of the world based on their experiences. Some preschool children, for example, believe that the sun is alive because it moves across the sky, that children get diseases because they tell lies or otherwise misbehave, and that the new baby in the family came from the baby store. School-age children know better.

How do children construct more accurate understandings of the world? By being the curious and active explorers that they are: by watching what is going on around them, by seeing what happens when they experiment on the objects they encounter, and by recognizing instances in which their current understandings are inadequate to explain events. Children use their current understandings of the world to help them solve problems, but they also revise their understandings to make them fit the facts of reality better (Piaget, 1952). It is the *interaction* between biological maturation (most important, a developing brain) and experience (especially discrepancies between the child's understanding and reality) that is responsible for the child's progress from one stage of cognitive development to a new, qualitatively different, stage.

Cognitive Development

Piaget proposed four major periods of cognitive development: the *sensorimotor stage* (birth to age 2), the *preoperational stage* (ages 2 to 7), the *concrete operations stage* (ages 7 to 11 or later), and the *formal operations stage* (ages 11 to 12 or later). These stages form what Piaget called an *invariant sequence.* That is, all children progress through them in exactly the order in which

TABLE 2.2

Jean Piaget's four stages of cognitive development

Stage	Age Range	Features
Sensorimotor	Birth to 2	Infants use their senses and motor actions to explore and understand the world. At the start they have only innate reflexes, but they develop ever-more "intelligent" actions and, by the end, are capable of symbolic thought using images or words and can therefore plan solutions to problems mentally.
Preoperational	2 to 7	Preschoolers use their capacity for symbolic thought in developing language, engaging in pretend play, and solving problems. But their thinking is not yet logical; they are egocentric (unable to take others' perspectives) and easily fooled by perceptions.
Concrete operations	7 to 11 or later	School-age children acquire logical operations that allow them to mentally classify and otherwise act on concrete objects in their heads. They can solve practical, real-world problems through a trial-and-error approach.
Formal operations	11 or later	Adolescents can think about abstract concepts and purely hypothetical possibilities and can trace the long-range consequences of possible actions. With age and experience they can form hypotheses and systematically test them through the scientific method.

they are listed, with no skipping of stages, and no regression to earlier stages, either. The ages given are only guidelines.

The key features of each stage are summarized in Table 2.2. The big message is that humans of different ages think in very different ways. We will be exploring Piaget's theory in depth in Chapter 7, but for now let's look at an example of how children who are at different stages of cognitive development might approach the same problem. The problem is to figure out why some objects float and others do not, given objects such as a wooden board, a pebble, and a candle, along with a bucket of water. In presenting this problem, Barbel Inhelder and Jean Piaget (1958) first asked children to classify the objects according to whether they would float or not and to explain their classifications. Then they allowed children to experiment with the objects and try to formulate a general law to explain why some objects float and others do not.

What might the infant in the **sensorimotor stage** do in this problem-solving situation? Inhelder and Piaget were not foolish enough to try to find out! The problem is obviously far beyond the grasp of infants in the sensorimotor stage. They deal with the world directly through their *perceptions* (senses) and *actions* (motor abilities), but they are unable to use symbols (gestures, images, or words representing real objects and events) to help them mentally devise solutions to problems. Infants *will* use their eyes, ears, and hands to actively explore the fascinating materials placed before them. From the start, human beings are curious about the world; moreover, Piaget maintained, they learn about the world and acquire tools for solving problems through their sensory and motor experiences.

The preschooler who has entered the **preoperational stage** of cognitive development now has the capacity for symbolic thought but is not yet capable of logical problem solving. The 4- or 5-year-old can use words as symbols to talk about the task and can mentally imagine doing something before actually doing it. Preoperational children will take great interest in placing objects in the water to see what will happen. However, lacking the tools of logical thought, they must rely on their perceptions and as a result are easily fooled by appearances. For example, they tend to think that large objects will sink, even if they are light. According to Piaget, they are also egocentric thinkers who have some difficulty adopting perspectives other than their own. As a result, they may cling to incorrect ideas simply because they *want* them to be true.

School-age children who have advanced to the **concrete operations stage** seem much more logical than preschoolers in problem-solving situations, as long as they are asked to think about the "real" world of concrete objects. These children can perform a number of important logical actions, or *operations*, in their heads. For example, they can mentally form categorization schemes, which help them realize that either small or large objects can be heavy or light. They now begin to try to resolve contradictions such as the fact that a small object (a key) may sink while a large one (a plank) may float. They can also draw sound general conclusions from what they observe. But they have difficulty formulating an abstract, general rule to explain why some large objects float and some small objects sink; they must depend instead on a *trial-and-error approach* to problem solving using the concrete materials before them.

Adolescents who have reached the **formal operations stage** are able to think more abstractly and hypothetically than school-age children. They formulate hypotheses or predictions in their heads, plan in advance how to systematically test their ideas experimentally, and imagine the consequences of their tests. It often takes some years beyond age 11 or 12 before adolescents can adopt a thoroughly systematic and scientific method of solving problems and can think logically about the implications of purely hypothetical ideas. However, once this kind of abstract and hypothetical thought has developed, a teenager might be able to conduct experiments and formulate the general law of floating objects: An object will float if its *density* is less than that of water. This same adolescent might also be able to devise grand theories about what's wrong with the older generation or the school system or the federal government.

Obviously, children's cognitive capacities change dramatically between infancy and adolescence as they progress through Piaget's four stages of cognitive development. Young children simply do not think as we do. Adolescents also think somewhat differently, as illustrated in Box 2.5, where what Piaget might say about the issue of teenage pregnancy is presented.

Piaget believed that children are naturally curious explorers who try to make sense of their surroundings.

Strengths and Weaknesses

Like Freud, Piaget was a true pioneer whose work has left a deep and lasting imprint on thinking about human development (see Beilin, 1992). You will see his influence throughout this text, for the same mind that "constructs" understanding of the physical world also comes, with age, to understand sex differences, moral values, emotions, death, and a range of other important aspects of the human experience. Indeed, Piaget's cognitive-developmental perspective dominated the study of child development for two or three decades until the *information-processing approach* took command in the 1980s. This approach puts emphasis on the processes involved in human cognition such as attention, memory, decision making, and the like and will be the focus of Chapter 8.

The majority of developmentalists today accept Piaget's basic beliefs that thinking changes in qualitative ways during childhood, that children are active in their own development, and that development occurs through an interaction of nature and nurture. Piaget's description of intellectual development has been put to the test and has been largely supported. And, finally, Piaget's ideas have influenced education and child rearing by encouraging teachers and parents to aim their educational efforts at the child's level of understanding and to stimulate children to discover concepts through their firsthand experiences.

In spite of these many contributions, Piaget has come in for his share of criticism (Lourenco & Ma-chado, 1996; and see Chapter 7). For example, some theorists would fault Piaget for saying too little about the influences of motivation and emotion on thought processes. In addition, there is some question about whether Piaget's stages really hang together as coherent modes of thinking or whether children instead acquire distinct cognitive skills at different rates. Indeed, the more developmentalists tested Piaget's ideas, the more they began to question his assumption that all humans in every culture develop through the same stages, toward the same endpoints. They began to see, for example, that people often did not make it to the last of Piaget's stages unless they were exposed to formal education. As a result, developmentalists began to seek theoretical perspectives that allowed for more diversity in the pathways that human development could take, while still retaining Piaget's emphasis on the interaction of nature and nurture in development.

CONTEXTUAL THEORY

Contextual theories of development hold that changes over the life span arise from the ongoing interrelationships between a changing organism and a changing world (see, for example, Lerner & Kauffman, 1985; Riegel, 1979; Sameroff, 1983). Changes in the person produce changes in his or her environment; changes

You may be wondering what in the world I might have to say about teenage sexual behavior. After all, my main interest has been the development of the mind. Yet, don't you see, teenagers must *decide* whether or not to have sex and whether or not to use birth control. These decisions demand cognitive abilities.

Now you might think that an adolescent who has reached my stage of formal operations would be ready to consider all the possible consequences of his or her actions and make sound decisions. This is true. But different children achieve formal-operational thinking at different rates. I noticed that Sheila and James were not doing particularly well in school. Perhaps they are slow developers still functioning in the stage of concrete operations and do not yet have the cognitive skills required to consider all the implications of a decision to have sex without protection.

I also find that many adolescents who show the beginning signs of formal-operational thought have not yet developed the full capacity to plan solutions to problems in advance or to consider all possible alternatives. This sometimes takes a few years. Moreover, adolescents just entering the stage of formal operations often get carried away with their new cognitive powers. They sometimes begin to feel that they are unique and not subject to the laws of nature that affect others: "Other teenagers may get pregnant, but it won't happen to me." Studies show that many teenagers fail to anticipate that they will need contraception, act impulsively, misunderstand the risks of becoming pregnant, do not think about the future consequences of their behavior, and are seriously misinformed about sex and birth control.[1]

I conclude, then, that the cognitive limitations and knowledge gaps of many teenagers have quite a bit to do with today's high rate of teenage pregnancy. These adolescents are not necessarily in the throes of personality conflicts, as Dr. Freud would have you believe, or deprived of the proper learning experience, as Drs. Skinner and Bandura argue. They may simply be cognitively immature and uninformed.

---

[1] Cobliner, 1974; Finkel and Finkel, 1978; Gordon, 1990; and Morrison, 1985

---

in the environment produce changes in the person; and this interchange goes on continuously. According to this perspective, development can take a variety of forms depending on the individual and the historical, cultural, and social context in which he or she develops.

Bronfenbrenner: Ecological Approach to Development

American psychologist Urie Bronfenbrenner, early in his career, was disturbed that many developmentalists looked at human development out of context, expecting it to be universal and failing to appreciate how much it could vary from culture to culture, from neighborhood to neighborhood, and from home to home. Later in his career, after stimulating many developmentalists to study contextual influences on development, he complained that too many developmentalists now studied "context without development" (Bronfenbrenner, 1995). They had forgotten to look closely at biological and psychological changes in the individual interacting with his or her environment. What Bronfenbrenner really sought was a middle ground in which both biological and environmental influences on development are appreciated.

Gradually, Bronfenbrenner (1979, 1989, 1995) has formulated his own **ecological approach** to development; to leave no doubt about his emphasis on nature *and* nurture, he has begun to call his approach "bioecological" in recent years (Bronfenbrenner & Ceci, 1994). According to this model, the developing person is embedded in a series of environmental systems that interact with one another and with the individual to influence development. In Bronfenbrenner's view, people are not just lumps of clay molded by outside forces. They shape their physical and social environments and are, in turn, shaped by the environments they have helped create. In other words, the relationship between person and environment is one of *reciprocal influence;* person and environment form a dynamic, ever-changing system.

A woman, for example, may take cocaine during pregnancy, and this may make her newborn extraordinarily fussy. Environment has affected development. But a fussy baby is likely to affect the environment—for example, by irritating his mother. Mother now expresses her tenseness and irritability in her interactions with him, and this makes him all the more irritable and fussy, which of course aggravates his mother even more, which of course makes him even more cranky. Understanding the ongoing transactions between a changing person and a changing environment is quite a challenge, but Bronfenbrenner has offered a useful way of conceptualizing these transactions.

The developing person's environment consists of four systems. The environmental system closest to the individual is termed the **microsystem,** the immediate environment in which the person functions. The primary microsystem for a first-born infant is likely to be the family—perhaps infant, mother, and father inter-

Urie Bronfenbrenner developed an ecological approach to development, in which both biological and environmental influences are taken into account.

acting with each other. The infant may also experience other microsystems such as a day-care center or grandmother's house. Within any microsystem, infants contribute to their own development by affecting their companions, who in turn influence them in new ways. Indeed, even before they are born, infants can shape their future environment—for example, by causing their parents to break up or to marry. Thus a microsystem like the family is indeed a system in which each person influences and is influenced by every other person.

Understanding the complex reciprocal influences of infant, mother, and father is enough of a challenge, but Bronfenbrenner insists that we cannot understand human development or family relations unless we also understand the **mesosystem**—the interrelationships or linkages between microsystems. For example, a marital conflict in the family (one microsystem) could make a child withdraw from staff members and other children at the day-care center (another microsystem) so that his or her experience there becomes less intellectually stimulating. A loving home environment is likely to allow a child to benefit more from experiences in the day-care center, or later in school.

According to Bronfenbrenner, the environment also includes the **exosystem**—social settings that the individual never experiences directly but that can still influence his or her development. Thus, children can be affected by their parents' work experiences and social interactions outside the home. For example, mothers may have difficulty providing a stimulating home environment when they have few friends to turn to for information and support and when their husbands

work unusual shifts and are away from home a great deal (Cotterell, 1986). Similarly, children's experiences in school can be affected by their exosystem—by a racial integration plan adopted by the school board or by a plant closing in their community that results in a cut in the school system's budget.

Finally, we reach the broadest context in which development occurs—the **macrosystem**, or the larger subcultural and cultural contexts in which the microsystem, mesosystem, and exosystem are embedded. This broader social environment can indeed have important effects on development. The shared understandings that we call culture include views about the nature of human beings at different points in the life span, about what children need to be taught to function in society, and about how one should lead one's life as an adult. Because culture changes or evolves over time, and because people developing in particular historical periods are affected by societal events such as wars or technological breakthroughs, each generation (or *cohort*) of individuals in a particular society develops in a distinct social context. We cannot assume that development is the same in all cultures and historical periods.

The environmental systems proposed by Bronfenbrenner—each of them shaping and being shaped by the developing person—are sketched in Figure 2.2. Each of us functions in particular microsystems linked to one another through the mesosystem and embedded in

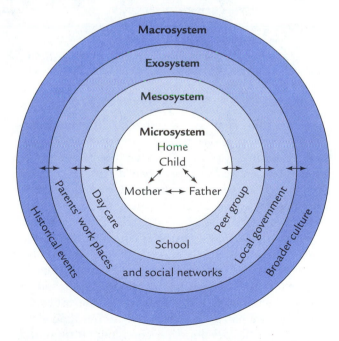

FIGURE 2.2 *Bronfenbrenner's ecological model of the environment as a series of nested structures. The microsystem refers to relations between the child and the immediate environment, the mesosystem to connections among the child's immediate settings, the exosystem to settings that affect but do not contain the child, and the macrosystem to the broader cultural context in which development takes place.* (Adapted from Kopp & Krakow, 1982)

BOX 2.6

Bronfenbrenner on teenage pregnancy

I believe that Sheila and James are faced with a pregnancy that resulted from the workings of multiple, interacting forces within themselves and within the environmental systems in which they are developing. According to my ecological theory, teenage pregnancy is unlikely to be rooted in just one simple cause such as a weak superego or limited cognitive development. We must analyze carefully the ongoing interactions between these changing young people and the changing world in which they are developing.

We know, of course, that Sheila and James, like other adolescents, are experiencing rapid physical, cognitive, and psychosocial growth—and that they are actively influencing those around them, including each other.[1] In turn, they are being influenced by the individuals in their *microsystems*. The microsystem of central interest here is the romantic relationship between the two of them. We know that an adolescent's sexual partner strongly influences his or her sexual behavior and use of contraceptives.[2] We should also learn more about the other microsystems that affect and are affected by these young

people—their families, peer groups, schools, churches, and so on. During adolescence, teenagers typically begin to spend less time with parents and more time with peers; as a result, parents often have less clout.

Consider too what I call the "mesosystem," those linkages between microsystems. Could troubles at home be causing Sheila and James to be overly dependent on each other for love and support? Might they be stressed by a clash between the values of the family microsystem and the peer microsystem?

We should also consider the possibility that James and Sheila have been influenced by the "exosystem," by forces within their community and neighborhood. Rates of teenage pregnancy tend to be high in low-income areas where educational and vocational opportunities are limited. In such areas, youths may not see much point in postponing parenthood in order to work toward long-term goals that look unattainable.[3] Perhaps the community in which Sheila and James live also provides very little in the way of family planning and contraception services.

Finally, consider the broadest of my four environmental systems, the "macrosystem." In some cultures, early childbearing is the norm, and teenage pregnancy is therefore not a "problem" at all. In our own society, it is a problem. The United States has undergone a number of important changes that have altered the adolescent experience—greater sexual permissiveness, more single-parent families and working mothers (and therefore less supervision of teenagers), the legalization of abortion, and more. Sheila and James have undoubtedly been influenced by these broad social changes, most of which, I think, have made the environments in which teenagers are developing chaotic.[4] If my ecological perspective on development seems complex, that's because human development is complex!

---

[1] Muuss, 1996
[2] Thompson and Spanier, 1978
[3] Hamburg, 1986
[4] Bronfenbrenner, 1995

the larger context of the exosystem and the macrosystem. We develop, and settings such as the family or the broader culture evolve and change too. Moreover, we move into new settings, as when a child progresses from preschool to elementary school to junior high school and becomes involved in new peer groups and social organizations. As our environments change and as we change them, we ourselves continue to change.

Contextual theorists such as Bronfenbrenner believe that person and environment form a system or unit, that both are in continual flux, and that changes in one inevitably produce changes in the other because they are part of a system. We cannot ignore the fact that people develop in a changing cultural and historical context—something that Piaget and other stage theorists tend to do. Nor can we focus all of our attention on environmental influences and ignore the ways in which human beings change and act upon their environments—something that Skinner and other behavioral theorists tend to do. A contextual perspective on teenage pregnancy is presented in Box 2.6.

Strengths and Weaknesses

Contextual perspectives on development began to emerge in response to some of the deficiencies of earlier stage theories and learning theories of development. Contextual perspectives are complex, but that is because life-span human development appears to be far more complex than it once appeared to be. We can applaud Bronfenbrenner and like-minded theorists for emphasizing some very important truths about human development. Development *does* occur in a context. People *do* change their environments and actively contribute to their own development, just as they are influenced by other people and by events in the world around them. And development takes different directions in different contexts; we cannot always predict where lives will turn unless we look more closely at the ongoing transactions between the person and the environment.

The life-span developmental perspective introduced in Chapter 1 is contextual in its orientation. It emphasizes that development grows out of interactions between person and environment and can be steered this way or that by social and historical forces. But perhaps you have noticed that the contextual perspective does not give us a very clear picture of the course of human development (Dixon & Lerner, 1992). Indeed, there is no full-blown contextual theory as yet. Up to this point, Bronfenbrenner and others have mainly alerted us to the need to examine how many personal and environmental factors interact over time to produce developmental change and given us some ways to think about it. We could, therefore, criticize contextual theory for being only partially formulated at this point.

But a more serious criticism can also be made: The contextual perspective may never provide any coherent developmental theory. Why? Suppose we really take seriously the idea that development can take a wide range of forms owing to the influence of a wide range of factors both within and outside the person. How can we ever state generalizations about development that will hold up for most people? Must we develop separate theories for different subgroups of people—one theory for black women born in 1920 and living in Kenya, another for white men born in 1960 and living in the southeastern United States, and so on? If change over a lifetime depends on the ongoing transactions between a unique person and a unique environment, is each life span unique?

Some theorists propose that we combine the contextual perspective with the best features of stage theories that propose universal developmental paths (Lerner & Kauffman, 1985). We might then see humans as moving in orderly directions in some aspects of their development, yet we could also try to understand how that developmental course differs in different social contexts. We might view developmental attainments such as formal-operational thinking not as inevitable achievements but as attainments that are more or less *probable* depending on the individual's life experiences.

THEORIES AND WORLD VIEWS

That completes our survey of some of the grand theories of human development. But these theories can be grouped into even grander categories, for each is grounded in a broader world view, or set of basic assumptions that guide scientific thought. By examining the assumptions that underlie different theories of development, we can better compare them and appreciate how deeply some of their disagreements run. We can also appreciate how perspectives on human development have evolved over the 20th century. Three broad models or world views can be delineated: the *organismic world view*, the *mechanistic world view*, and

the *contextual world view* (Pepper, 1942; Reese & Overton, 1970).

The Organismic World View

The **organismic world view** likens humans to plants and other living organisms. In this view, human beings are organized wholes or systems; they cannot be understood piece by piece, or behavior by behavior, because they are greater than the sum of their parts. In addition, humans are active in the developmental process; forces springing from within themselves, rather than environmental events, are primarily responsible for their development. True, just as plants need sun, rain, and soil in order to flourish, humans need a supportive environment in order to develop in healthy directions. However, they unfold, much as a rose unfolds, according to a master plan carried in their genes. Finally, the organismic model holds that humans evolve through distinct or discontinuous stages as they reorganize over time; these stages are universal and lead to the same final state of maturity.

Freud can be considered a subscriber to the organismic world view because of his emphasis on a biologically based sequence of development. And Jean Piaget, even though he rejected the position that biological maturation was *everything* in favor of an interactionist position on the nature/nurture issue, is a classic example of an organismic theorist. He described active individuals who move through distinct developmental stages. We might imagine parents who subscribe to this world view as supportive but not pushy in their efforts to enhance their children's development. They would tend to trust their children to seek out the learning opportunities they most need at a given stage in their growth. They would respond to their children's changing needs and interests but would not feel compelled to structure all their children's learning experiences for them.

The Mechanistic World View

The **mechanistic world view** likens human beings to machines. More specifically, this model assumes that humans (1) are a collection of parts (for example, they can be analyzed behavior by behavior, much as machines can be taken apart piece by piece); (2) are relatively passive in the developmental process, changing mainly in response to outside stimulation (much as machines depend on outside energy sources to operate); (3) change gradually or continuously as parts, or specific behavior patterns, are added or subtracted; and (4) can develop along a number of different paths, depending on environmental influences.

Learning theorists such as Watson and Skinner clearly held a mechanistic world view. They saw human beings as passively shaped by external stimuli, and analyzed human behavior response by response. Bandura's social learning theory is also primarily mechanistic. It focuses on specific behaviors and rejects the concept of stages, though it does claim, as organismic theories do, that humans are active beings who influence their environment. A mechanistic world view may be guiding parents who attempt to orchestrate every minute of their children's time from an early age—who insist that their children go to the "right" preschools, hear the "right" bedtime stories, and participate in the "right" recreational activities. Such parents may assume that their children will not develop at all (or at least will never be Harvard material) unless they are systematically exposed to the proper stimulation. A mechanistic world view also guides behavior modifiers who attempt to use learning principles to shape desirable behaviors and eliminate undesirable ones.

The Contextual World View

Finally, the **contextual world view** offers as a metaphor for human development an ongoing historical event or drama, an ever-changing interplay of forces. The focus is on the dynamic relationship between person and environment. Humans are active in the developmental process (as in the organismic world view), and the environment is active as well (as in the mechanistic world view). The potential exists for both qualitative and quantitative change, and development can proceed along many different paths depending on the intricate interplay of internal and external influences.

Parents who adopt a contextual model of development, such as Bronfenbrenner's ecological perspective, are likely to realize that their children are influencing them just as much as they are influencing their children. The mother of Carlos and Selena, for example, may notice that she often makes polite requests to cooperative Carlos but barks orders at stubborn Selena. Parents who fall in the contextual camp are likely to view themselves as *partners* with their children in the development process—not fans watching from the wings (as in the organismic world view) and not heavy-handed directors either (as in the mechanistic world view).

It is because different theories rest on different world views that they sometimes seem to offer such different pictures of human development and its causes (see Table 2.3). Each world view contains un-

TABLE 2.3

Organismic, mechanistic, and contextual models

	World View		
	Organismic	*Mechanistic*	*Contextual*
GUIDING METAPHOR FOR HUMANS	Plant	Machine	Historical event
NATURE OF HUMANS	Coherent, organized whole	Collection of "parts" (specific behaviors)	Part of changing person/ environment relationship
ROLE OF PERSON IN DEVELOPMENT	Active	Passive	Active
ROLE OF ENVIRONMENT IN DEVELOPMENT	Passive	Active	Active
FORM OF DEVELOPMENT	Discontinuous, stagelike	Continuous, gradual	Discontinuous and continuous
DIRECTION OF DEVELOPMENT	One universal direction of growth	Multidirectional	Multidirectional
EXAMPLES	Psychoanalytic theory:	Learning theories:	Ecological approach:
	Freud	Watson	Bronfenbrenner
	Erikson (Chap. 10)	Skinner	Sociocultural theory:
	Cognitive-developmental theory:	Bandura	Vygotsky (Chap. 7)
	Piaget		Life-span perspective: (Chap. 1)
	Kohlberg (Chap. 12)		
	Ethological theory: (Chaps. 3, 13)		

questioned assumptions that determine what facts are considered important and how they are interpreted. Consequently, theorists who view the world through different lenses are likely to continue disagreeing even when the same "facts" are set before them. This is the very nature of science.

Yet theorists with different world views agree on some matters, too. For example, Jean Piaget, an organismic theorist, and Albert Bandura, a mechanistic theorist, both appreciate that both nature and nurture, both maturation and experience, are involved in development, that children are very active in their own development, and that children's cognitive skills change as they get older. Similarly, Bandura and Bronfenbrenner (a contextual theorist) clearly agree about the importance of other people—the social environment—in development, and both expect children who grow up in different social contexts to develop along different paths. Sometimes we focus so much on the differences between theories that we lose sight of their similarities (Tudge & Winterhoff, 1993).

Changing World Views

Our understanding of human development has changed and will continue to change as one prevailing world view gives way to another. From the beginning of the study of human development at the turn of the century, through the heyday of Freud's psychoanalytic theory, the organismic world view prevailed (Parke et al., 1994). Learning theories, guided by mechanistic assumptions about development, came to the fore in the 1950s and 1960s. Then, with the rising influence of cognitive psychology and Jean Piaget's theory of cognitive development, the organismic world view regained influence in the late 1960s and 1970s.

And today? The stands on key developmental issues taken by contextual theorists such as Bronfenbrenner are the stands that most developmentalists have adopted. The field has moved beyond the extreme, black-or-white positions taken by many of its pioneers. We now appreciate that human beings have the potential to develop in good *and* bad directions, that human development is always the product of nature *and* nurture, that humans *and* their environments are active in the developmental process, that development is both continuous *and* discontinuous in form, and that development has both universal aspects *and* aspects particular to certain cultures, times, and individuals. In short, the world views and theories that guide the study of human development have become increasingly complex as the incredible complexity of human development has become more apparent. Perhaps as a result, "grand" theories of development, such as the ones discussed in this chapter, are not as influential today, and researchers are guided more by "minitheories" that are more specific in focus (Parke et al., 1994).

APPLICATIONS: DEVELOPMENTAL THEORY AND TEENAGE PREGNANCY

As we noted at the start of the chapter, one of the main functions of theories in any science is to guide attempts to gain knowledge through research. Thus Freud stimulated researchers to study inner personality conflicts, Skinner inspired them to analyze how behavior changes when its environmental consequences change, and Piaget inspired them to explore children's thinking about every imaginable topic. Different theories stimulate different kinds of research and yield different kinds of facts.

Theories also guide practice. As we have seen, each theory of human development represents a particular way of defining developmental issues and problems. Often how you define a problem determines how you attempt to solve it. To illustrate this point, let's take one last look at teenage pregnancy, which is clearly defined as a social problem in society today. As we have seen, different theorists hold radically different opinions about the causes of teenage pregnancy. How do you suppose each would go about trying to *reduce* the rate of teenage pregnancy?

Psychoanalytic theorists are likely to locate the problem within the person. Freud might want to identify teenagers who have especially strong ids and weak egos and superegos or are experiencing extremes of anxiety and strained relationships with their parents. Erikson might identify teenagers who are having significant problems resolving the crisis of identity versus role confusion. High-risk teenagers might then be treated through psychoanalysis; the aim would be to help them resolve the inner conflicts that might get them in trouble. This approach to solving the problem follows naturally from a psychoanalytic view of the causes of the problem. And it might well work with teenagers who are indeed emotionally disturbed. The only problem is that most pregnant girls are not psychologically disturbed; they are quite similar psychologically to girls who do not get pregnant (Furstenberg et al., 1981).

Adopting Piaget's cognitive-developmental perspective might make us pessimistic that young teenagers can learn to engage in long-term planning and rational decision making about sexual issues until they are solidly into the formal operations stage of cognitive development. However, if we could identify the kinds of faulty cognitive structures or misunderstandings that young adolescents have about their risks of pregnancy and about contraceptive methods, we could attempt to correct their mistaken ideas. The solution to teenage pregnancy, then, would be improved sex education courses—courses that provide teenagers with accurate information and help them think clearly about the long-term consequences of their sexual decisions. And, instead of just telling concrete-operational thinkers about the consequences of early pregnancy, we might make those consequences concrete for them, perhaps by having them talk to teenage mothers and fathers about their lives or tend infants in a day-care center.

Most researchers concerned about teenage sexuality and pregnancy do indeed agree that improved sex education is an important part of the solution. And yet, only if sex education programs are carefully designed do they succeed not only in imparting information but in persuading adolescents to use contraception and in reducing pregnancy rates (Franklin et al., 1997; Kirby et al., 1994). So perhaps we need to consider solutions that locate the problem in the environment rather than in the individual's psychological weaknesses or cognitive deficiencies.

Learning theorists strongly believe that changing the environment will change the person. In support of this belief, Douglas Kirby (1985) found that only one of the sex-education projects he studied resulted in an increase in birth-control use and a decrease in the rate of unintended pregnancies. It involved a major change in the school environment: the establishment of a health clinic where students who were already sexually active could, easily and in the strictest confidence, obtain specific guidance about how to use birth-control devices and where to obtain them. This program reflects a Skinnerian philosophy. In the face of the AIDS epidemic, more and more school systems are trying to encourage and reinforce abstinence and safer sex practices.

Albert Bandura's social learning theory gives us some additional ideas about how to change the environment. Parents might be taught how to be better role models of responsible sexual behavior and how to communicate with their children about sex. Peers might be mobilized to serve as models of the advantages of postponing sex or engaging in safer sex. Television programs might focus less on the joys of sex and more on its unwanted consequences. Through observational learning experiences, teenagers might develop more sexually responsible habits, especially if they come to believe that the consequences of more responsible sex will be to their liking (Balassone, 1991).

Contextual theorists such as Bronfenbrenner would insist that changing *both* the person and the environment—changing the whole ecological system—may be necessary. Quick fixes are unlikely to work. The solution may ultimately require changing the broader social context in which today's adolescents are developing. Teenage pregnancy in poverty areas may not be reduced significantly until poor parents face fewer stresses, schools are safe and stimulating, jobs are made available, and more disadvantaged young people gain hope that they can climb out of poverty if they pursue an education and postpone parenthood (Furstenberg, Brooks-Gunn, & Morgan, 1987). At the same time, adolescents can be helped to understand the pros and cons of different life choices and to appreciate that they have the power to contribute to their own development.

We see, then, that the theoretical position one takes has a tremendous impact on how one goes about attempting to optimize development. Yet, as we have also seen, each theory may have only a partial solution to the problem being addressed. In all likelihood, multiple approaches will be needed to make a serious dent in complex problems such as the high rate of teenage pregnancy—or to achieve the larger goal of understanding human development.

CLARIFYING YOUR OWN THEORETICAL PERSPECTIVE

Theories are not just useless ideas. Developmental researchers need theories to guide their work, and every parent, teacher, human service professional, and observer of human beings is also guided by some set of basic assumptions about how human beings develop and why they develop as they do. I hope that reading this chapter will stimulate you to clarify your own theories of human development. One way to start is by completing the exercise that appears in Box 2.7 and seeing which theorists' views are most compatible with your own.

You need not choose one theory and reject others. Indeed, because different theories often highlight different aspects of development, one may be more relevant to a particular issue or to a particular age group than another. Today many developmentalists are theoretical **eclectics**: individuals who rely on many theories, recognizing that none of the major theories of human development can explain everything but that each has something to contribute to our understanding. In many ways, the emerging contextual perspective on development is the broadest point of view yet proposed. There is no reason why many of the insights offered by Erikson, Piaget, Bandura, and others cannot be incorporated within this perspective to help us understand changing people in changing worlds.

In the remainder of this book, I take an eclectic and contextual approach to human development, borrowing from many theories in trying to draw a systematic and unified portrait of the developing person. I invite you to join me in examining not just the specific facts of development but also the broader perspectives that have generated those facts and that give them larger meaning.

BOX 2.7

Compare yourself with the theorists

Before you read this chapter, you were asked in Box 2.1 to indicate your positions on basic issues in human development by answering six questions. If you transcribe your answers below, you can compare your stands to those of the theorists described in this chapter (and also review the theories). With whom do you seem to agree the most?

Question
1   2   3   4   5

Your pattern of answers:

Psychoanalytic Theory: Freud's Version

a   b   b   a   a

Freud held that biologically based sexual instincts motivate behavior and steer development through five psychosexual stages. He believed that (1) the child's urges are basically selfish and aggressive; (2) biological changes are the driving force behind psychosexual stages (though he believed that parents influence how well these stages are negotiated); (3) children are passively influenced by forces beyond their control; (4) development is stagelike rather than continuous; and (5) the psychosexual stages are universal.

Psychoanalytic Theory: Erikson's Version

c   c   a   a   a

Erikson theorized that humans progress through eight psychosocial conflicts as they mature biologically and attempt to adapt to their social environment. He held that (1) we are born with basically good qualities, (2) nature and nurture are about equally important, (3) people are active in their own development, (4) development is stagelike, and (5) psychosocial stages are universal, though modified somewhat by culture.

Learning Theory: Skinner's Version

b   e   b   c   b

Skinner maintains that development is the result of learning from the consequences of one's behavior. In his view (1) children are inherently neither good nor bad; (2) nurture or environment is far more important than nature; (3) people are passively shaped by environmental events; (4) development is gradual and continuous, as habits increase or decrease in strength; and (5) development is context-specific and can proceed in many different directions and change directions depending on the individual's learning experiences.

Learning Theory: Bandura's Version

b   d   a   c   b

Bandura's social learning theory states that humans change through cognitive forms of learning, especially observational learning. He argues that (1) children are inherently neither good nor bad; (2) nurture is more important than nature; (3) people influence their environments and thus are active in their own development; (4) development is continuous rather than stagelike; and (5) development can proceed in many directions and change directions depending on life experiences.

Piaget's Cognitive-Developmental Theory

c   b   a   a   a

Piaget described four distinct stages in the development of intelligence that result as children attempt to make sense of their experience. He suggested that (1) we are born with positive tendencies such as curiosity; (2) maturation guides all children through the same sequence of stages, although experience is necessary as well and can influence the rate of development; (3) we are active in our own development as we "construct" more sophisticated understandings; (4) development is stagelike; and (5) everyone progresses through the same sequence of stages.

Contextual Theory

b   c   a   b   b

Bronfenbrenner and similar theorists believe that development results from the transactions between a changing person and a changing environment. These theorists appear to believe that (1) humans are inherently neither good nor bad; (2) nature and nurture, interacting continually, make us what we are; (3) people are active in their own development; (4) development probably involves some continuity and some discontinuity, some stagelike changes and some gradual ones; and (5) although some aspects of development may be universal, development also varies widely from individual to individual and can change directions depending on experience.

◆ SUMMARY POINTS

1. A theory is a set of ideas proposed to describe and explain certain phenomena; it provides a perspective that helps organize a wide range of facts and is valuable to the extent that it is parsimonious, internally consistent, falsifiable, and supported by data.

2. Theories of human development address issues concerning assumptions about human nature, nature/nurture, activity/passivity, continuity/discontinuity, and universality/context-specificity in development.

3. According to Freud's psychoanalytic theory, humans are driven by inborn instincts of which they are largely unconscious. The id, which is purely instinctual, rules the infant; the rational ego emerges during infancy; and the superego, or conscience, takes form in the preschool years. Five psychosexual stages—oral, anal, phallic, latency, and genital—unfold as the sex instinct matures; each is characterized by conflicts that create the need for ego defense mechanisms and have lasting effects on the personality.

4. According to Erikson's neo-Freudian version of psychoanalytic theory, development is a lifelong process involving eight psychosocial stages, beginning with trust versus mistrust in infancy and concluding with integrity versus despair in old age. Compared to Freud, Erikson emphasized biological urges less and social influences more; emphasized id less and ego more; held a more positive, optimistic view of human nature; and theorized about the entire life span.

5. Learning theorists hold that we change gradually through learning experiences and that we can develop in many different directions. Behaviorist John Watson advocated attention to overt behavior and environmental influences on development. B. F. Skinner advanced the behavioral perspective by demonstrating the importance of operant conditioning and reinforcement. Albert Bandura's social learning theory differs from behavioral learning theories in emphasizing cognitive processes, observational learning, and a reciprocal determinism of person and environment.

6. Jean Piaget's cognitive-developmental theory stresses universal, invariant stages in which children actively construct increasingly complex understandings by interacting with their environments. These stages are the sensorimotor, preoperational, concrete-operational, and formal-operational.

7. The emerging contextual perspective on development, illustrated by Bronfenbrenner's ecological theory, emphasizes the study of the relations between a changing person and a changing environment (the micro-, meso-, exo-, and macrosystems).

8. Theories can be grouped into families based on the broad world views that underlie them. The contextual world view differs from the mechanistic world view that guides learning theories and the organismic world view that underlies stage theories.

9. Theories of human development guide not only research but also practice; psychoanalytic, cognitive-developmental, learning, and contextual theorists would each propose different approaches to the problem of teenage pregnancy.

10. From an eclectic perspective, no single theoretical viewpoint offers a totally adequate account of human development, but each contributes in important ways to our understanding.

✸ FOOD FOR THOUGHT

1. Jasper, age 6, just started first grade and suddenly has a case of school phobia. Every morning he complains of headaches, tummy aches, and foot aches and begs his mother to let him stay home. His mother let him stay home almost all of last week and very much wants to understand why Jasper does not want to go to school. Help her out by indicating what psychoanalytic, learning, cognitive-developmental, and contextual/ecological theorists might propose as an explanation of school phobia.

2. Lee Harvey Oswald and John Hinckley both shot U.S. presidents, but their backgrounds differed considerably. Oswald came from a relatively poor home and had a string of stepfathers. He spent time in Russia, and his political views motivated him to shoot Kennedy. Hinckley is the middle child in a middle-class family. His motivation for shooting Reagan was to draw attention to himself so that he would be noticed by his movie-star idol, Jodie Foster. How could two of

the theories presented in this chapter contribute to a fuller understanding of why Oswald and Hinckley did what they did?

3. Play the role of Urie Bronfenbrenner, ecological theorist, commenting on the theories of Erik Erikson, Jean Piaget, and Albert Bandura. How would you assess the best contributions of each, and what is missing from or wrong with each perspective from an ecological point of view?

4. You have decided to become an eclectic and to take from each of the four major perspectives in this chapter (psychoanalytic, learning, cognitive-developmental, and contextual/ecological) only *one* truly great insight into human development. What four ideas would you choose and why?

 ON THE WEB

1. *Freud* The site of the Abraham A. Brill Library of the New York Psychoanalytic Institute (see especially its section, "Sigmund Freud on the Internet") offers biographical information and excerpts from a few of the writings of the founder of psychoanalytic theory.
http://plaza.interport.net/nypsan

2. *Piaget* The Jean Piaget Archives will give you a sense of the quantity and scope of Piaget's research and writing.
http://www.unige.ch/piaget/

3. *Bronfenbrenner* Although most of the theorists discussed in this chapter are no longer alive, you'll be interested to know that Urie Bronfenbrenner, emeritus professor at Cornell, has his own Web site, in which he outlines his current interest and lists his recent publications. His recent interests range from the "growing chaos" in children's environments today to developmental processes in middle adulthood and old age.
http://www.human.cornell.edu/HD/faculty/Bronfenbrenner.html

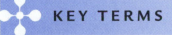 **KEY TERMS**

tabula rasa
nature/nurture issue
activity/passivity issue
continuity/discontinuity issue
developmental stage
universality/context-specificity issue
psychoanalytic theory
instinct
unconscious motivation
id
ego
superego
libido
psychosexual stages
defense mechanisms
fixation

regression
Oedipus complex
Electra complex
trust versus mistrust
autonomy versus shame and doubt
initiative versus guilt
industry versus inferiority
identity versus role confusion
intimacy versus isolation
generativity versus stagnation
integrity versus despair
behaviorism
operant conditioning
reinforcer
punisher
social learning theory

observational learning
reciprocal determinism
constructivism
sensorimotor stage
preoperational stage
concrete operations stage
formal operations stage
contextual theories
ecological approach
microsystem
mesosystem
exosystem
macrosystem
organismic world view
mechanistic world view
contextual world view
eclectic

CHAPTER 3

The Genetics of Life-Span Development

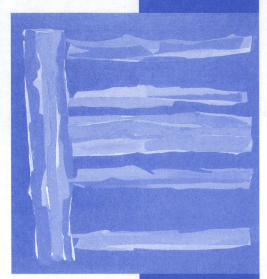

SPECIES HEREDITY, EVOLUTION, AND HUMAN DEVELOPMENT
Darwin's Theory of Evolution
Modern Evolutionary Perspectives

INDIVIDUAL HEREDITY
The Genetic Code
Translation of the Genetic Code
Mechanisms of Inheritance
Mutations
Chromosome Abnormalities

STUDYING GENETIC AND ENVIRONMENTAL INFLUENCES
Experimental Breeding
Twin and Adoption Studies
Estimating Influences

ACCOUNTING FOR INDIVIDUAL DIFFERENCES
Intellectual Abilities
Temperament and Personality
Psychological Disorders
Heritability of Traits

HEREDITY AND ENVIRONMENT: A CLOSER LOOK
Gene/Environment Interactions
Gene/Environment Correlations

APPLICATIONS: GENETIC COUNSELING AND ENGINEERING
Tay-Sachs Disease
Huntington's Disease
Prevention and Treatment

SUMMARY POINTS

FOOD FOR THOUGHT

ON THE WEB

KEY TERMS

Imagine meeting a long-lost identical twin face to face for the first time. This is a fantasy that many people have, but it has been a reality for many of the participants in a study of twins separated at birth being conducted at the University of Minnesota by Dr. Thomas Bouchard, Jr., and his associates (Bouchard, 1984; Bouchard et al., 1990). Although the research team expected to observe similarities in the ways twins responded to a 50-hour battery of tests, they probably were not prepared for the number of eerie coincidences that were revealed when these twins were reunited.

A newspaper story about Jim Lewis and Jim Springer inspired Bouchard to undertake his study in the first place (Wright, 1995). Together again after spending all but the first 4 weeks of their 39 years apart, these identical twins had both married women named Linda—and then women named Betty. They named their first sons James Alan and James Allan, had dogs named Toy, and liked Miller Lite beer and Salem cigarettes.

Barbara Herbert and Daphne Goodship, also reunited after 39 years apart, each wore a beige dress and a brown velvet jacket when they met for the first time in London. They shared a habit of "squidging" (pushing up their noses), had fallen down the stairs at age 15, laughed more than anyone they knew, and never voted. Oscar Stohr and Jack Yufe, one adopted by Catholic Czechoslovakians who had been loyal to the Nazis in World War II, the other raised in the Caribbean by his Jewish father and taught to despise Nazism, quickly discovered that they shared a passion for spicy food, a habit of flushing the toilet both before and after using it, a tendency to read magazines from back to front, and an enjoyment of sneezing loudly to scare people (Wright, 1995).

Perhaps the influence of genes on development must be taken seriously!

Jim Springer and Jim Lewis were unaware of each other's existence until they were reunited at age 39 as part of a study of identical twins reared apart.

What exactly are the roles of heredity and environment in shaping our many physical and psychological characteristics? That is the puzzle we grapple with in this chapter. Many people are environmentalists at heart, believing that there is no such thing as a "bad seed," that proper parenting and a stimulating environment can make any child develop well, and that most of the psychological differences between people reflect their experiences over a lifetime. Reading this chapter should increase your appreciation of genetic contributions to development without diminishing your belief in the importance of environmental influences.

We begin by considering some ways in which **genes** make human beings alike in their characteristics and in their development. We next turn to what we inherit at conception and at how this genetic endowment can influence our traits. Then we explore

how genes and environment make individuals different from one another in intelligence, personality, and other characteristics. Finally, we are able to draw some general conclusions about heredity and environment from a life-span perspective. Let's start by focusing on the characteristics that all humans share.

SPECIES HEREDITY, EVOLUTION, AND HUMAN DEVELOPMENT

Most discussions of heredity focus on its role in creating differences among people. Some individuals inherit blue eyes, others brown eyes; some inherit blood type O, others type A or B. But isn't it remarkable that just about every one of us has two eyes and that we all have blood coursing through our veins? And that virtually all of us develop in similar ways at similar ages—walking and talking at about 1 year, maturing sexually at 12 to 14, watching our skin wrinkle in our 40s and 50s? These similarities are not coincidental. They are due to **species heredity**—the genetic endowment that members of a particular species have in common, including genes that govern maturation and aging processes. Humans can feel guilty but cannot fly; birds can fly but cannot feel guilty. Humans and birds each have their own distinct species heredity. The fact that humans all over the world share both a human species heredity and a characteristically human environment explains why some patterns of development and aging are universal. Where did we get this common species heredity? That's a question evolutionary theory can help answer.

Darwin's Theory of Evolution

The theory of evolution proposed by Charles Darwin (1809–1882), and modified somewhat since, attempts to explain how the characteristics of any species change over time and how new species can evolve from earlier ones (Darwin, 1859). The main arguments are these:

1. *There is genetic variation in a species.* Some members of the species have different genes (and different genetically influenced characteristics and behaviors) from others'. If all members of the species were genetically identical, there would be no way for the genetic makeup of the species to change over time.

2. *Some genes aid in adaptation more than others do.* Suppose that some members of a species have genes that make them strong and intelligent, whereas others have genes that make them weak and dull. Surely those with the genes for strength and intelligence would be better able to adapt to their environment—for example, to win fights for survival or to figure out how to obtain food.

3. *Those genes that aid their bearers in adapting to the environment will be passed on to future generations more frequently than those genes that do not.* This is the principle of **natural selection**—the idea that nature "selects," or allows to survive and reproduce, those members of a species whose genes permit them to adapt to their environment. By contrast, those genes that somehow reduce the chances that an individual will survive and reproduce will become rarer and rarer over time because they will not be passed on to many offspring. Through natural selection, then, the genetic makeup of a whole species can slowly change over time.

Consider a classic example of speeded-up evolution. H. B. D. Kettlewell (1959) carefully studied moths in England. Genetic variation among moths makes some of them dark in color and others light in color. By placing light and dark moths in a number of different sites, Kettlewell found that in rural areas light moths were most likely to survive. Just the opposite was true in the industrial areas of Birmingham: Dark moths were most likely to survive. The explanation? In rural areas, light-colored moths blend in well with light-colored trees and are better protected from predators by camouflage. Natural selection favors them. However, in sooty industrial areas, light-colored moths are easy pickings against the darkened trees, whereas dark moths are well disguised. When industry came to England, the proportion of dark moths increased; as pollution was brought under control in some highly industrialized areas, the proportion of light-colored moths increased again (Bishop & Cooke, 1975).

Notice, then, that evolutionary theory is not just about genes. It is about the *interaction* between genes and environment. A particular genetic makeup may enhance survival in one kind of environment but prove maladaptive if the environment changes dramatically. Which genes are advantageous, and therefore become more common in future generations, depends on what traits the environment demands.

According to evolutionary theory, then, humans, like any other species, are as they are and develop as they do partly because they have a shared species heredity that has evolved through natural selection. Perhaps the most significant legacy of human evolution is a powerful brain that allows us to learn from our experiences and to master a complex language so that we can communicate almost anything to others. What could be more adaptive? Humans have not had to wait for biological evolution to give them furrier bodies as protection from the cold; they have been able to use their brains to invent better and better clothing and heating systems and to teach what they know to their children (Scarr & Kidd, 1983). Many of the changes we see over the course of history are due to this kind of *cultural* rather than to biological evolution. What evolutionary biologists teach us is that the ability to learn and the ability to teach others are themselves the products of biological evolution.

Modern Evolutionary Perspectives

Darwin's evolutionary theory was very influential when the scientific study of human development began and is appreciated anew today (Charlesworth, 1992). It has been the foundation for the work of ethologists, evolutionary psychologists, psychobiologists, and other scholars who attempt to understand relationships between biology and behavior.

Ethology is concerned with understanding the evolved behavior of various species in their natural environments (see Archer, 1992; Hinde, 1983). You may also have heard of sociobiology, the closely related discipline that asks how genetic self-interest helps explain such social phenomena as greater willingness to help kin than strangers (Walsh, 1995; Wilson, 1975). There are also scholars who call their work **evolutionary psychology** and test predictions about human behavior based on Darwinian theory. Research in all these areas has made developmentalists appreciate the importance of looking at human development from an evolutionary perspective and asking how what we do may be adaptive for us as for our evolutionary ancestors.

Noted ethologists Konrad Lorenz and Niko Tinbergen asked how many apparently innate animal behaviors might be adaptive in the sense that they contribute to species survival. Because behavior is adaptive only in relation to a particular environment, ethologists prefer naturalistic observation as a method of study. So, for example, they have recorded bird songs in the wild, analyzed their features carefully, explored how male birds learn the songs characteristic of their species, and attempted to understand how songs aid birds in reproducing and surviving.

Ethologists suggest that humans, too, display species-specific behaviors that are the products of our evolutionary history. In Chapter 13 we will encounter an influential ethological theory that views the tendency of human infants to form close attachments as a behavior that has evolved because it increases the odds that the young will survive: They cry for, cling to, and follow after their caregivers, like baby birds following behind their mothers. Other ethologists have observed that preschool children, like many other primates, form "dominance hierarchies," or pecking orders, in which each group member has a ranking. These social hierarchies have the adaptive function of reducing aggression; they make it clear when an individual should submit to a dominant member of the group rather than start what is likely to be a losing battle (Strayer, 1980).

From an evolutionary perspective, the most important goal in life, whether conscious or unconscious, is to ensure that a next generation is born and survives. Aspects of family life of interest to developmentalists such as mate selection, childbearing, and parenting behavior contribute to this goal. Evolutionary psychologists have shown how solutions to problems faced by our ancestors thousands of years ago may have become built into our species heredity and expressed in universal patterns of behavior.

Why is it, for example, that you see more couples with an older man and a younger woman than with an older woman and a younger man? David Buss (1989, 1994) has studied mate selection extensively. In the interests of ensuring the survival of her children, Buss predicted, a woman should prefer a man who can offer the resources necessary to support a family, a man who has good financial prospects. She should look for signs of earning potential such as ambition, intelligence, and, yes, age. In prehistorical days, older men probably had more hunting expertise and more accumulated resources than young men; today, older men have more money than younger men. Buss (1989) surveyed men and women in 37 countries, asking them to rate 18 characteristics of an ideal spouse. Consistent with his prediction, women in all 37 countries placed more emphasis than men did on a mate's earning capacity.

Meanwhile, evolutionary theory predicts that a man most wants a woman who will bear his children and pass on his genes. Since a woman's childbearing potential decreases starting in her 30s, evolutionary considerations may help explain a universal tendency for men to prefer younger women (Buss, 1994). We could, of course, offer explanations other than evolutionary ones to explain sex differences in mate preferences. Yet these and other findings generated by evolutionary psychologists point to the value of asking questions about the adaptive value of common patterns of human behavior and development.

Ethologists and other modern evolutionary theorists do not claim that humans are robots that simply act out instinctive behaviors dictated by their genes. Instead, they believe that humans have evolved in ways that allow them to learn which patterns of social behavior are most biologically adaptive in their culture, subculture, and particular circumstances (Archer, 1992; Belsky, Steinberg, & Draper, 1991). Indeed, it has become clear that innate, specieswide tendencies in both animals and humans can often be altered dramatically by early learning experiences. A growing number of developmental psychobiologists are studying how biological factors such as genes and hormones interact with experience to guide development, starting in the womb (see Gandelman, 1992; Gottlieb, 1996).

Consider, for example, that young mallard ducklings clearly prefer their mothers' vocal calls to those of other birds such as chickens—a behavior that appears to be innate and certainly has adaptive value for the species. Yet Gilbert Gottlieb (1991) has shown that duckling embryos that were exposed to chicken calls before hatching and then prevented from vocalizing at birth come to prefer the call of a chicken to that of a mallard mother! The ducklings' prenatal experiences apparently overrode their genetic predisposition. Genes do not *determine* anything, then; they are partners with the environment in directing individuals, including humans, along certain universal developmental pathways (Gandelman, 1992; Gottlieb, 1996). The message here is critical: *Even seemingly instinctive, inborn patterns of behavior will not emerge unless the individual has both (1) normal genes (species heredity) and (2) normal early experiences.*

Human beings are not only similar to one another but diverse. Let's now turn to the ways in which their different genetic makeups and environments contribute to differences among them.

INDIVIDUAL HEREDITY

To understand heredity, we must start at **conception,** the moment when an egg is fertilized by a sperm. Once we have established what is inherited at conception, we can examine how genes translate into traits.

The Genetic Code

A few hours after a sperm penetrates an ovum, the sperm cell begins to disintegrate, releasing its genetic material. The nucleus of the ovum releases its own genetic material, and a new cell nucleus is created from the genetic material provided by mother and father. This new cell, called a **zygote** and only the size of a pinhead, is the beginning of a human being. Conception has occurred.

The genetic material contained in the new zygote is 46 threadlike bodies called **chromosomes,** which function as 23 pairs. Both members of a chromosome pair influence the same characteristics. Each chromosome is made up of thousands of genes, the basic units of heredity. We have some 50,000 to 100,000 genes, few of whose functions are known specifically (Khoury and the Genetics Working Group, 1996). Genes are actually stretches of DNA, the "double helix" molecule that provides a chemical code for development. Like chromosomes, genes function as pairs, and the two members of each gene pair are located at the same sites on their corresponding chromosomes.

The sperm cell and the ovum each contribute 23 chromosomes to the zygote. Thus, of each chromosome pair—and of each pair of genes on corresponding chromosomes—one member came from the father and one from the mother. Sperm and ova each have only 23 chromosomes because they are produced through a specialized process of cell division called **meiosis.** A reproductive germ cell in the ovaries of a female and the testes of a male contains 46 chromosomes. It splits to form two 46-chromosome cells, and then these two cells split again to form four cells, each with 23 chromosomes. Each resulting sperm cell or ovum thus has only one member of each of the parent's 23 pairs of chromosomes.

The single-celled zygote formed at conception becomes a multiple-celled organism through the more usual process of cell division, **mitosis.** During mitosis a cell (and each of its 46 chromosomes) simply divides to produce two identical cells, each containing the same 46 chromosomes. As the zygote moves through the fallopian tube toward its prenatal home in the uterus, it first divides into two cells, and the two then become four, the four become eight, and so on. Except for sperm and ova, all our cells contain copies of the 46 chromosomes provided at conception. Mitosis continues throughout life, creating new cells that enable us to grow and replacing old cells that are damaged.

Genetic Uniqueness and Relatedness

To understand how we are both different from and like others genetically, consider more closely the 46 chromosomes that contain the blueprint for the development of a new individual. When a pair of parental chromosomes separates during meiosis, which of the two chromosomes will end up in a particular sperm or ovum is a matter of chance. And, because each chromosome pair separates independently of all other pairs, and since each reproductive cell contains 23 pairs of chromosomes, a single parent can produce 2^{23}—more than 8 million—different sperm or ova. Any couple could theoretically have 64 trillion babies without producing two children with identical genes!

In fact, the genetic uniqueness of children of the same parents is even greater than this because of a quirk of meiosis known as **crossing over.** When pairs of chromosomes line up before they separate, they cross each other and parts of them are exchanged, much as if you were to exchange a couple of fingers with a friend during a handshake. This crossing-over phenomenon increases still further the number of distinct sperm or ova that an individual can produce. In short, it is incredibly unlikely that there ever was or ever will be another human exactly like you genetically. The one exception is **identical twins** (or identical triplets, and so on), which result when one fertilized ovum divides to form two or more genetically identical individuals, as happens in about 1 of every 250 births (Plomin, 1990).

How genetically alike are parent and child, or brother and sister? You and either your mother or your father have 50% of your genes in common, because you received half of your chromosomes (and genes) from each parent. But if you have followed our mathematics you will see that siblings may have many genes in common or very few, depending on what happens during meiosis. Because siblings receive half of their genes from the same mother and half from the same father, their genetic resemblance to each other is 50%, the same genetic resemblance as that of parent and child. The critical difference is that they share half of their genes *on the average;* some siblings share more and others fewer. Indeed, we've all known some siblings who are almost like twins and others who could not be more different if they tried.

Fraternal twins result when two ova are released at approximately the same time and each is fertilized by a different sperm, as happens in about 1 of every 125 births. Fraternal twins are no more alike genetically than brothers and sisters born at different times and need not even be of the same sex. Grandparent and grandchild, as well as half-brothers and half-sisters, have 25% of their genes in common on the average. Thus everyone except an identical twin is genetically unique, but each of us also has genes in common with kin that contribute to family resemblances.

Determination of Sex

Of the 23 pairs of chromosomes that each individual inherits, 22 (called *autosomes*) are similar in males and females. The 23rd pair consists of the sex chromosomes. A male child has one long chromosome called an **X chromosome** because of its shape, and a short, stubby companion with fewer genes called a **Y chromosome.** Females have two X chromo-

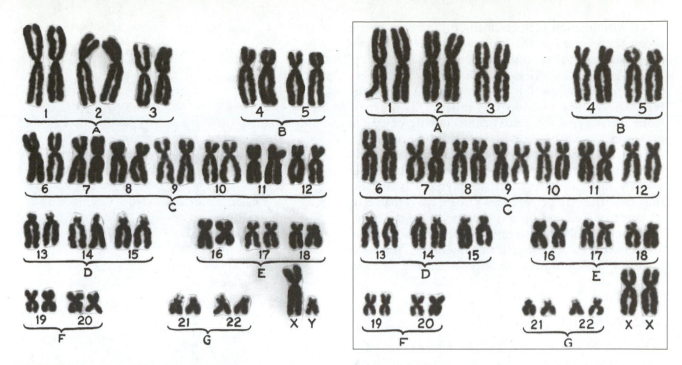

FIGURE 3.1 *The male karyotype (left) shows the 22 pairs of autosomal chromosomes and the 2 sex chromosomes—an elongated X and a shorter Y chromosome. The photographic arrangement of a female's chromosomes (right) shows two X chromosomes.*

somes. Figure 3.1 shows chromosomes that have been photographed through a powerful microscope and then arranged in pairs and rephotographed in a pattern called a **karyotype.**

Because the mother has only X chromosomes, and the father's sperm cell has either an X or a Y chromosome (depending on how chromosomes sort out during meiosis), it is the father who determines a child's gender. If an ovum with its one X chromosome is fertilized by a sperm bearing a Y chromosome, the product is an XY zygote, a genetic male. If a sperm carrying an X chromosome reaches the ovum first, the result is an XX zygote, a genetic female. Yet women throughout history have been criticized, tortured, divorced, and even beheaded for failing to bear male heirs.

So, a genetically unique boy or girl has 50,000 to 100,000 genes on 46 chromosomes. How do these genes influence the individual's characteristics and development? It is still a mystery, but we now have parts of the answer.

Translation of the Genetic Code

Genes provide instructions for development by calling for the production of chemical substances (see Aldridge, 1996; Plomin, 1990). Specifically, genes provide codes for the production of amino acids, which form proteins that form cells and other bodily tissues as well as essential substances such as hormones, neurotransmitters, and enzymes. For example, genes set

in motion a process that results in the laying down of a pigment called melanin in the iris of the eye. Some people's genes call for much of this pigment, and the result is brown eyes; other people's genes call for less of it, and the result is blue eyes. Genetically coded proteins also guide the formation of cells that become the brain, influencing potential intelligence in the process. Genes influence and in turn are influenced by the biochemical environment surrounding them during development (Aldridge, 1996; Gottlieb, 1996). For example, a particular cell can become part of an eyeball or part of a kneecap depending on what cells are next to it during embryonic development. No one, however, completely understands the remarkable process that transforms a single cell into millions of diverse cells—blood cells, nerve cells, skin cells, and so on—all organized into a living human being.

Nor does anyone fully understand how genes help bring about certain developments at certain points in the life span. Some genes clearly direct the production of proteins that are in turn responsible for how the body's organs are constructed and how they function. Other genes apparently have the task of *regulating* the first set of genes. Current thinking is that specific gene pairs with specific messages to send are turned on or off by regulator genes at different times (Plomin, DeFries, McClearn, & Rutter, 1997). Thus, regulator genes might activate genes responsible for the growth spurt we experience as adolescents and shut down the action in adulthood.

Environmental factors clearly influence how the messages specified by the genes are carried out. Consider the genes that influence height. Some people inherit genes calling for exceptional height and others inherit genes calling for a short stature. But **genotype,** the genetic makeup one inherits, is different from **phenotype,** the actual characteristic or trait a person eventually has (for example, a height of 5 feet 8 inches). An individual whose genotype calls for exceptional height may or may not be tall. A child who is severely malnourished from the prenatal period on may have the genetic potential to be a basketball center but may well end up too short to make the team. *So environmental influences combine with genetic influences to determine how a genotype is translated into a particular phenotype—the way a person actually looks, thinks, feels, and behaves.*

Mechanisms of Inheritance

Another way to approach the riddle of how genes influence us is to consider the major mechanisms of inheritance: how parents' genes influence their children's traits. There are three main mechanisms of inheritance: single gene-pair inheritance, sex-linked inheritance, and polygenic (or multiple-gene) inheritance.

Single Gene-Pair Inheritance

Through **single gene-pair inheritance,** some human characteristics are influenced by only one pair of genes: one from the mother, one from the father. Although he knew nothing of genes, a 19th-century monk named Gregor Mendel contributed greatly to our knowledge of single gene-pair inheritance by cross-breeding different strains of peas and watching the outcomes. He noticed a predictable pattern to the way in which two alternative characteristics would appear in the offspring of cross-breedings; for example, smooth seeds or wrinkled seeds, green pods or yellow pods. He called some characteristics (for example, smooth seeds) "dominant" because they appeared more often in later generations than their opposite traits, which he called "recessive."

As an illustration of the principles of Mendelian heredity, consider the remarkable fact that about three-fourths of us can curl our tongues upward into a tubelike shape, whereas one-fourth of us cannot. It happens that the gene associated with tongue curling is a **dominant gene.** A gene calling for the absence of tongue-curling ability is said to be a **recessive gene.** The person who inherits one "tongue-curl" gene and one "no-curl" gene would be able to curl his or her tongue (that is, would have a tongue-curling phenotype) because the tongue-curl gene overpowers the no-curl gene.

Let's label the dominant, tongue-curl gene uppercase T and the recessive, no-curl gene lowercase t. We

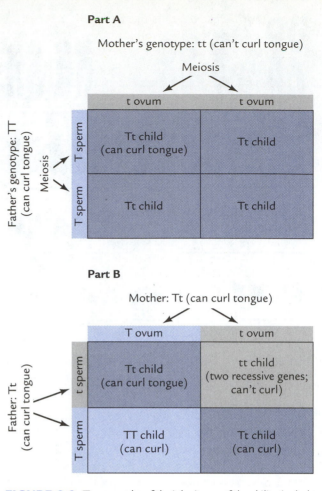

FIGURE 3.2 *Two examples of the inheritance of the ability (or lack of ability) to curl one's tongue*

can now calculate the odds that parents with different genotypes for tongue curling will have children who can or cannot curl their tongues. Figure 3.2 shows two examples. In each part we see that a father will contribute one or the other of his two genes to a sperm, and the mother will contribute one or the other of her two genes to an ovum. Each child inherits one of the mother's genes and one of the father's, so the four cells of each grid represent the four possible kinds of children that two parents, given their genotypes, could have.

Part A of Figure 3.2 shows that dominant genes triumph over recessive genes. If a father with the genotype TT (a tongue-curler) and a mother with the genotype tt (lacking the ability to curl her tongue) have children, each and every child they produce will necessarily have one gene for tongue curling and one for a lack of tongue curling (genotype Tt). Because the tongue-curl gene dominates, we can say that this couple has a 100% chance of having a tongue-curling child. Notice that two different genotypes—TT and Tt—both make for the same phenotype: an acrobatic tongue.

Part B of Figure 3.2 tells us that a tongue-curling man and a tongue-curling woman can surprise everyone and have a child who lacks this talent. These two parents both have the Tt genotype. If the father's recessive gene and the mother's recessive gene happen to unite in the zygote, they will have a non-tongue-curling child (with the genotype tt). The chances are 25%—one out of four—that this couple will have such a child. Of course, the laws of conception are very much like the laws of cards. This couple could either beat the odds and have a whole family of non-tongue-curling children or have no tt children at all. Since people who cannot curl their tongues must have the tt genotype, two non-tongue-curling parents will have only non-tongue-curling (tt) children.

Table 3.1 lists numerous examples of dominant and recessive traits associated with single gene-pair inheritance. In truth, some of the physical characteristics in this table (such as eye color and hair color and curliness) are influenced by more than a single pair of genes. However, it turns out that many genetically linked diseases and defects are entirely due to two recessive genes, one inherited from each parent. Consider an example of special significance to the African-American community: **sickle-cell disease.**

Individuals with this disease have sickle-shaped blood cells that tend to cluster together and distribute less oxygen through the circulatory system than normal cells do. People with sickle-cell disease have great difficulty breathing and exerting themselves, have painful swelling of their joints, and often die by adolescence from heart or kidney failure. About 9% of African-Americans in the United States have the genotype we'll call Ss; they carry one gene (S) that calls for round blood cells and one (s) that calls for sickle-shaped blood cells (Thompson, 1975). Such people are called **carriers** because, although they do not have the disease, they can transmit the gene for it to their children. The child who inherits two recessive sickle-cell genes (ss) has sickle-cell disease. As suggested by Part B of Figure 3.2, an Ss father and an Ss mother (two carriers) have a 25% chance of having a child with sickle-cell disease (ss). For this and other genetic problems traceable to a pair of recessive genes, a couple will not be at risk for having a child with the defect unless both are carriers of the trouble-making gene.

An important feature of the sickle-cell trait is that the dominant gene associated with round blood cells shows **incomplete dominance**—that is, it does not totally mask all the effects of the recessive sickle-cell gene. Thus carriers of the sickle-cell gene actually have many round blood cells and some sickle-shaped cells (see Figure 3.3). When they are at high altitudes, are given anesthesia, or are otherwise deprived of oxygen, carriers may experience symptoms of sickle-cell disease—very painful swelling of the joints and severe fatigue.

TABLE 3.1

Examples of dominant and recessive traits

Dominant Traits	Recessive Traits
Brown eyes	Gray, green, hazel, or blue eyes
Dark hair	Blond hair
Nonred hair	Red hair
Curly hair	Straight hair
Normal vision	Nearsightedness
Farsightedness	Normal vision
Roman nose	Straight nose
Broad lips	Thin lips
Extra digits	Five digits
Double-jointedness	Normal joints
Pigmented skin	Albinism
Type A blood	Type O blood
Type B blood	Type O blood
Normal hearing	Congenital deafness
Normal blood cells	Sickle-cell disease*
Huntington's disease*	Normal physiology
Normal physiology	Cystic fibrosis
Normal physiology	Phenylketonuria (PKU)*
Normal physiology	Tay-Sachs disease*

* This condition is discussed elsewhere in the chapter.
SOURCES: Data from Burns and Bottino (1989) and McKusick (1990)

FIGURE 3.3 *"Sickled" (elongated) and normal (round) blood cells from a carrier of the sickle-cell gene*

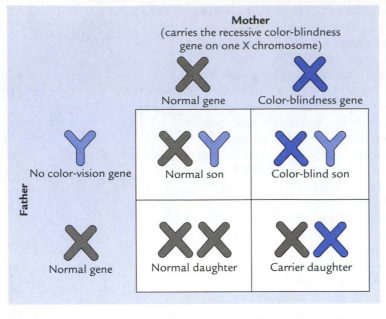

FIGURE 3.4 *The workings of sex-linked inheritance of red/green color blindness*

In still other cases of single gene-pair heredity, two genes influence a trait but neither dominates the other. This is called **codominance** because the phenotype of the person with two distinct genes in a pair is an exact compromise between the two genes. For example, an AB blood type is a blend of A and B blood types, and black/white interracial marriages often produce children with light-brown skin, a compromise between genes calling for heavily pigmented skin and genes calling for lightly pigmented skin. Single gene-pair inheritance is obviously a bit more complex than it looks at first glance.

Sex-Linked Inheritance

Some traits are called **sex-linked characteristics** because they are influenced by single genes located on the sex chromosomes rather than on the other 22 pairs of chromosomes. Indeed, we could say "X-linked" rather than "sex-linked" because the vast majority of these attributes are associated with genes located only on X chromosomes.

Why do far more males than females display red/green color blindness? The inability to distinguish red from green is caused by a recessive gene that appears only on X chromosomes. Recall that Y chromosomes are shorter than X chromosomes and have fewer genes. If a boy inherits the recessive color-blindness gene on his X chromosome, there is no color-vision gene on the Y chromosome that could dominate the color-blindness gene. He will be color blind. By contrast, a girl who inherits the gene usually has a normal color-vision gene on her other X chromosome that dominates the color-blindness gene (see Figure 3.4). She would have to inherit two of the recessive color blindness genes

(one from each parent) to be color blind herself. Which parent gives a boy who is color blind his color-blindness gene? Definitely his mother, for she is the source of his X chromosome. *Hemophilia,* a deficiency in the blood's ability to clot, is also far more common among males than females because it too is associated with a gene on X chromosomes. Other sex-linked traits include the Duchenne type of muscular dystrophy and certain forms of deafness and night blindness.

Polygenic Inheritance

So far we have considered only the influence of single genes or gene pairs on human traits. Every week, it seems, we read in the newspaper that researchers have identified "the gene" for cancer, bedwetting, happiness, or some other phenomenon. However, only rarely does one gene account for all or even most disorders or traits. Most important human characteristics are influenced by *multiple* pairs of genes (interacting with the environment, of course); that is, they are **polygenic traits.** Examples of polygenic traits include height and weight, intelligence, temperament, susceptibility to cancer and depression, and many others (Plomin, 1990). Suppose we know (we do not) that intelligence is influenced by three pairs of genes and that having the gene pairs AA, BB, and CC would result in genius, whereas having the genotype aa bb cc would result in extremely low intelligence. Without going into the mathematics, there are 27 distinct genotypes that could result if we calculated all possible children that one couple of average intelligence (each with an Aa Bb Cc genotype, for example) could produce. Gene combinations that call for average intelligence would be more likely to occur than combinations associated with either very high or very low intelligence. When a trait is influenced by multiple genes, we would therefore expect it to be distributed in a large population according to the familiar bell-shaped or normal curve. Many people would have scores near the mean, and few would be at the extremes. This is exactly the way intelligence and most other measurable human traits are distributed.

We have no idea exactly how many gene pairs influence intelligence or other polygenic traits. At this point all we can say is that unknown numbers and combinations of genes, interacting with environmental forces, create a wide range of individual differences in most important human traits.

Mutations

We have now surveyed the three major mechanisms by which the genes inherited at conception influence traits: single gene-pair, sex-linked, and polygenic inheritance. Occasionally, however, a new gene appears as if out of nowhere; it is not passed on by a parent. A **mutation** is a change in the structure or arrangement of one or more genes that produces a new phenotype. Experts believe that the recessive gene for the sex-linked disorder hemophilia was first introduced into the royal families of Europe by Queen Victoria. Since no cases of hemophilia could be found in the Queen's ancestry, the gene may have been a mutation that she passed on to her offspring (Massie & Massie, 1975). New cases of hemophilia, then, can be due either to spontaneous mutations or to sex-linked inheritance. The odds that mutations will occur are increased by environmental hazards such as radiation, toxic industrial waste, and agricultural chemicals in food (Burns & Bottino, 1989).

Some mutations have beneficial effects and become more and more common in a population through the process of natural selection. The sickle-cell gene is a good example. It probably arose originally as a mutation but became more prevalent in Africa, Central America, and other tropical areas over many generations because it protected those who had it from malaria and allowed them to live longer and produce more children than people without the protective gene. Unfortunately, the sickle-cell gene does more harm than good in environments where malaria is no longer a problem. Thus, mutations can be either beneficial or harmful depending on their nature and on the environment in which their bearers live.

Chromosome Abnormalities

Genetic endowment can also influence human characteristics through **chromosome abnormalities,** cases in which a child receives too many or too few chromosomes (or abnormal chromosomes) at conception.

Most such abnormalities are due to errors in chromosome division during meiosis. Through an accident of nature, an ovum or sperm cell may be produced with more or fewer than the usual 23 chromosomes. In most cases, a zygote with the wrong number of chromosomes is spontaneously aborted, but approximately 1 child in 200 is born with either more or, very rarely, fewer chromosomes than the normal 46 (Plomin, 1986).

One very familiar chromosome abnormality is **Down syndrome,** also known as *trisomy 21* because it is associated with three rather than two 21st chromosomes. Children with Down syndrome have distinctive eyelid folds, short stubby limbs, and thick tongues (see Figure 3.5). Their levels of intellectual functioning vary widely, but they are typically mentally retarded to some degree and therefore develop and learn at a slower pace than most children.

What determines who has a Down syndrome child and who does not? Sheer chance, partly. The errors in cell division responsible for Down syndrome can occur in anyone. However, the odds also increase dramatically as the age of the mother increases. The chances of having a baby with the syndrome are about 1 in 1000 for mothers under 30 but climb to about 7 in 1000 for mothers age 40 or older (see Figure 3.6). Mothers who have already borne one Down syndrome child have an even higher risk, presumably because they are more susceptible to producing defective eggs than most women are (Shafer & Kuller, 1996).

Why is the older woman at high risk for producing a child with chromosome abnormalities? First, ova begin to form during the prenatal period and age, as other cells age, over the years of a woman's life. DNA also deteriorates. Second, older women have had more opportunities to be exposed to environmental hazards

FIGURE 3.5 *Children with Down syndrome can live rich lives if they receive appropriate educational opportunities and support.*

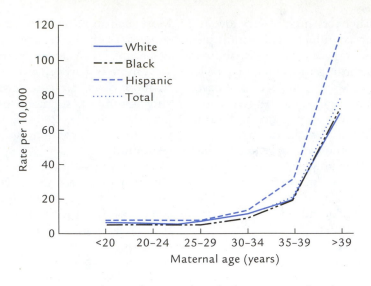

FIGURE 3.6 *The rate of Down syndrome births increases steeply as the mother's age increases.* (From Down Syndrome Prevalence at Birth, 1994)

that can damage ova, such as radiation, drugs, chemicals, and viruses (Strigini et al., 1990). A father's age also has some bearing on the odds of a Down syndrome birth, though not nearly as much as the mother's age. The risk is greater if the father has been exposed to environmental hazards that can damage his chromosomes—for example, radiation associated with repeated abdominal X rays (Strigini et al., 1990).

Most other chromosome abnormalities involve cases in which a child receives either too many or too few sex chromosomes. Like Down syndrome, these *sex chromosome abnormalities* can be attributed mainly to errors in meiosis that become increasingly likely in older parents and parents whose chromosomes have been damaged by environmental hazards. One well-known example is **Turner syndrome,** in which a female (about 1 in 3000) is born with a single X chromosome (XO) in each of her cells. These girls remain small and often have stubby fingers and toes, a "webbed" neck, a broad chest, and underdeveloped breasts. They are unable to reproduce and typically favor traditionally feminine activities. They tend to become emotionally stable and compliant women (Pasaro Mendez et al., 1993). Although they score about average on tests of verbal intelligence, their spatial and mathematical reasoning abilities are often lower than average and they tend to underachieve in school (Downey et al., 1991).

Another example is **Klinefelter syndrome,** in which a male (1 in 200) is born with one or more extra X chromosomes (XXY). Klinefelter males tend to be tall and generally masculine in appearance, but they are sterile and at puberty develop feminine sex characteristics such as enlarged breasts. Most have normal general intelligence test scores, but many are below average in language skills and school achievement (Mandoki et al., 1991).

We have now outlined the fundamentals of heredity. Each person has a unique genetic makeup, or genotype, contained in his or her 23 pairs of chromosomes. Combinations of the parents' genes are passed on at conception and influence people's traits (phenotypes) through the mechanisms of single gene-pair, sex-linked, and polygenic inheritance. A minority of individuals are also powerfully affected by genetic mutations or chromosome abnormalities. Now we are equipped to explore the extent to which important psychological differences among humans are influenced by their hereditary endowments and their experiences.

STUDYING GENETIC AND ENVIRONMENTAL INFLUENCES

Behavioral genetics is the scientific study of the extent to which genetic and environmental differences among people or animals are responsible for differences in their traits (Plomin et al., 1997). It is impossible to say that one person's intelligence test score is the result of, say, 80%, 50%, or 20% heredity and the rest environment. The individual would have no intelligence at all without *both* a genetic makeup and experiences. It *is* possible for behavioral geneticists to estimate the **heritability** of measured intelligence (IQ) and of other traits or behaviors—*the proportion of all the variability in the trait within a large group of people that can be linked to genetic differences among those individuals.* To say that measured intelligence is "heritable," then, is to say that differences among people in their tested IQ scores are to some degree attributable to the fact that these individuals have different genetic endowments.

It may seem from the name that behavioral geneticists tell us only about genetic contributions to development, but their work tells us about the contributions of experience as well. Behavioral genetics research is providing important evidence about the relative contributions of genetic and environmental factors to existing human differences. How is this evidence gathered?

Experimental Breeding

To study the influence of genes and environment on animal behavior, behavioral geneticists design breeding experiments. Deliberately manipulating the genetic makeup of animals to study genetic influences on behavior is much like what Gregor Mendel did to discover the workings of heredity in plants. One of the most commonly used breeding experiments is **selective breeding**—attempting to breed for a particular trait in animals. A classic example is R. C. Tryon's (1940) attempt to show that maze-learning ability in rats is a heritable or genetically influenced attribute. Tryon first tested a large number of rats for the ability to run a complex maze. Rats that made few errors were labeled "maze bright"; those that made many errors were termed "maze dull." Then, across several generations, Tryon mated bright rats with bright rats and dull rats with dull rats. If differences in experience rather than differences in genetic makeup had accounted for maze-performance differences in the first generation of rats studied, selective breeding would have had no impact. Instead, across generations the differences in learning performance between the maze-bright and maze-dull groups of rats increased. Tryon showed that maze-learning ability in rats is influenced by genetic makeup.

Selective-breeding studies have also shown that genes contribute to such attributes as activity level, emotionality, aggressiveness, and sex drive in rats, mice, and chickens (Plomin et al., 1997). Because people don't take kindly to the idea of being selectively bred by experimenters, such research cannot be done with humans. Research on genetic influence in humans relies instead on determining the extent to which people who are genetically similar are also psychologically similar.

Twin and Adoption Studies

Twins have long been recognized as very important sources of evidence about the effects of heredity. A simple type of twin study involves determining whether identical twins reared together are more similar to each other in traits of interest than fraternal twins reared together. If genes matter, identical twins should be more similar, for they have 100% of their genes in common, whereas fraternal twins share only 50% on the average. You might be thinking that identical twins are also treated more similarly than fraternal twins and thus share a more similar environment. True enough, and yet there is little relationship between how similarly twins are treated and how similar they are psychologically (Loehlin, 1992; Lytton, 1977). This suggests that the twin method of study is fundamentally sound.

Today, most sophisticated twin studies include not only identical and fraternal twin pairs raised together but also identical and fraternal twins reared apart—four groups in all, differing in both the extent to which they share the same genes and the extent to which they share the same home environment. Identical twins separated near birth and brought up in very different environments—like the twins introduced at the beginning of the chapter—are particularly fascinating and informative in their own right, of course, because any similarities between them cannot be attributed to common family experiences.

Much can also be learned about heredity and environment through adoption studies. Are children adopted early in life similar to their biological parents, whose genes they share, or are they similar to their adoptive parents, whose environment they share? If adopted children resemble their biological parents in intelligence or personality, even though those parents did not raise them, genes must be influential. If they resemble their adoptive parents, even though they are genetically unrelated to them, a good case can be made for environmental influence. Like the twin method, the adoption method is useful to researchers as a way to estimate the relative contributions of heredity and environment to individual differences.

Estimating Influences

Behavioral geneticists rely on mathematical calculations to tell them whether or not a trait is genetically influenced and to estimate the degree to which heredity and environment can account for individual differences in the trait. When they study traits that a person either has or does not have (for example, a smoking habit or diabetes), researchers calculate and compare **concordance rates**—the percentage of pairs of people (for example, identical twins or an adoptive parent and child) in which, if one member of a pair displays the trait of interest, the other does too. If concordance rates are higher for more genetically related than for less genetically related pairs of people, the trait is heritable.

Suppose we are interested in whether homosexuality is genetically influenced. We might locate gay men who have twins, either identical or fraternal, and then find their twin siblings and learn whether they too are gay. In one study of this type (Bailey & Pillard, 1991), the concordance rate for identical twins was 52% (29 of the 56 co-twins of gay men were also gay), whereas the concordance rate for fraternal twins was 22% (12 of 54 co-twins were also gay). This finding suggests that genetic makeup does contribute to a man's sexual orientation. Since identical twins are *not* perfectly concordant, however, their experiences must also affect their sexual orientations. After all, in 48% of the identical twin pairs, one twin was gay and the other was not, despite their identical genes. (Very similar evidence has been obtained for lesbian women, by the way; see Bailey et al., 1993.)

When a trait can be present in varying degrees, as is true of height or intelligence, *correlation coefficients* rather than concordance rates are calculated (see Chapter 1). In a behavioral genetics study of IQ scores, a correlation would indicate whether the IQ score of one twin is systematically related to the IQ score of the other, such that, if one twin is bright, the other is bright, and, if one is not so bright, the other is not so bright. The larger the correlation statistic for a group of twins, the closer the resemblance between members of each twin pair.

To better appreciate the logic of behavioral genetics studies, consider what Robert Plomin and his colleagues (1988) found when they assessed aspects of personality among twins in Sweden whose ages averaged 59. One of their measures assessed an aspect of emotionality—the tendency to be angry or quick-tempered. The scale was given to many pairs of identical twins and fraternal twins, some pairs raised together, others separated near birth and raised apart. Correlations reflecting the degree of similarity between twins are presented in Table 3.2. From such data, behavioral geneticists can estimate the contributions of three factors to individual differences in emotionality: genes, shared environmental influences, and nonshared environmental influences.

1. *Genes.* In our example, genetic influences are clearly evident, for identical twins are consistently more similar in emotionality than fraternal twins are. The correlation of +.33 for identical twins reared apart, in and of itself, also testifies to the importance of genetic makeup. If identical twins grow up in different families, any similarity in their psychological traits must be due to their genetic similarity. Thus these data suggest that emotionality is heritable; about one-third of the variation in emotionality in this sample can be linked to variations in genetic endowment.

2. *Shared environmental influences.* **Shared environmental influences** are experiences that individuals living in the same home environment share and that work to make them similar to one another—for example, a common parenting style or access to the same

TABLE 3.2

Correlations from a twin study of the heritability of angry emotionality

	Raised Together	Raised Apart
Identical twin pairs	.37	.33
Fraternal twin pairs	.17	.09

NOTE: An effect of *genes* is evident: .37 is greater than .17, and .33 is greater than .09. Only a small effect of *shared environment* is evident: .37 is greater than .33, and .17 is greater than .09. And a large effect of *nonshared environment* is evident: .37 is less than 1.00; if identical twins raised in the same home are not identical in emotionality, the differences between them must be due to their unique, nonshared experiences.
SOURCE: From Plomin et al., 1988

toys, playmates, books, and neighborhood. As you can see from the correlations in Table 3.2, both identical and fraternal twins are slightly more similar in emotionality if they are raised together (.37 exceeds .33, .17 exceeds .09) than if they are raised apart. However, these correlations tell us that shared environmental influences are weak: Twins are almost as similar when they grew up in different homes as when they grew up in the same home.

3. *Nonshared environmental influences.* **Nonshared environmental influences** are experiences that are unique to the individual, that are *not* shared by other members of the family. Whether they involve being treated differently by parents, having different friends, or undergoing different life crises, they make members of the same family different from one another (Rowe & Plomin, 1981; Rowe, 1994). Is there evidence of nonshared environmental influence in Table 3.2? Notice that identical twins raised together are not perfectly similar, even though they share 100% of their genes *and* the same family environment; a correlation of +.37 is much lower than a perfect correlation of +1.00. Differences between identical twins raised together must be due to differences in their unique experiences. Perhaps identical twins are treated differently somehow by their parents, friends, and teachers, or perhaps one twin seeks out or receives more social learning opportunities than the other, and this results in differences in their degrees of social sensitivity. Anyone who has a brother or sister can attest to the fact that different children in the same family are not always treated identically by their parents. They do not have the same experiences outside the home either (Manke et al., 1995).

Consider once more the four possible correlations in Table 3.2. If *genes* were all that mattered, the correlations for identical twins would be +1.00 (regardless of whether they were raised together or apart) and the correlations for fraternal twins would be .50 (because, on average, they share 50% of their genes). If shared environmental influences were all that mattered, we would see correlations of +1.00 for both identical and fraternal twins raised together but no similarity at all (correlations of .00) between twins raised in different environments. Finally, if nonshared environmental influences, or unique experiences, were all that mattered, members of twin pairs—whether identical or fraternal, raised together or apart—would be no more alike than strangers plucked at random from a street corner. Their characteristics would depend entirely on their idiosyncratic experiences in life, and all the correlations in the table would be .00. Keep these predictions in mind as we see what researchers have discovered about the actual contributions of genes, shared environment, and nonshared environment to the many similarities and differences among human beings.

ACCOUNTING FOR INDIVIDUAL DIFFERENCES

Information from twin and adoption studies has dramatically changed the way we think about human development. Our examples are drawn from behavioral genetics studies of intellectual abilities, temperament and personality, and psychological disorders (see Plomin et al., 1997; Rose, 1995; Rowe, 1994, for reviews).

Intellectual Abilities

How do genes and environment contribute to differences in intellectual functioning, and how do their relative contributions change over the life span? Consider the average correlations among the IQ scores of different types of relatives presented in Table 3.3. These averages are from a review by Thomas Bouchard and Matthew McGue (1981) of studies involving 526 correlations based on 113,942 pairs of children, adolescents, and adults. Clearly, these correlations rise when people are closely related genetically and are highest when they are identical twins. Overall, the heritability of IQ scores is about .50, meaning that genetic differences account for about 50% of the variation in IQ scores and environmental differences account for the other half of the variation (Plomin, 1990).

Can you also detect the workings of environment? Notice that (1) pairs of family members reared together are somewhat more similar in IQ than pairs reared apart; (2) fraternal twins, who should have especially similar family experiences because they grow up at the same time, are often more alike than siblings born at different times; and (3) the IQs of adopted children are related to those of their adoptive parents. All of these findings suggest that shared environmen-

TABLE 3.3

Average correlations between the intelligence scores of different pairs of individuals

	Raised Together	Raised Apart
Identical twins	.86	.72
Fraternal twins	.60	.52
Biological siblings	.47	.24
Biological parent and child	.42	.22
Half-siblings	.31	—
Adopted siblings	.34	—
Adoptive parent and adopted child	.19	—

NOTE: All but one of these averages were calculated by Bouchard and McGue (1981) from studies of both children and adults. The correlation for fraternal twins reared apart was based on data reported by Pedersen, McClearn, Plomin, and Friberg (1985).

tal influences tend to make individuals who live together more alike than if they lived separately. Notice too, though, that genetically identical twins reared together are not perfectly similar. This is evidence that their unique or nonshared experiences have made them different from each other.

Do the contributions of genes and environment to differences in intellectual ability change over the life span? Because the correlations in Table 3.3 are averages based on studies of children and adults, they do not tell us. Could genes be more important in explaining differences in intellectual performance early in life than later, after we have accumulated more experience? Sensible as that sounds, it does not seem to be the case. Genetic endowment actually appears to become more important with age as a source of individual differences in intellectual performance (McCartney, Harris, & Bernieri, 1990; McGue et al., 1993).

Consider a longitudinal study of the intellectual development of identical and fraternal twins from infancy to adolescence, conducted by Ronald Wilson (1978, 1983). Identical twins scored no more similarly than fraternal twins on a measure of infant mental development during the first year of life; thus, evidence of heritability was lacking. Generally, differences in neither genetic makeup nor experience account very well for the many behavioral and psychological differences among infants, perhaps because powerful maturational forces guide all infants along the same course of development (McCall, 1981).

However, in Wilson's study the influence of individual heredity began to show itself at about 18 months of age. Now the correlation of the mental development scores of siblings was higher for identical twins than for fraternal twins. Identical twins even experienced more similar spurts in intellectual development than fraternal twins. The identical twins in this study stayed highly similar throughout childhood and into adolescence. The correlation between their IQ scores averaged about .85. Meanwhile, fraternal twins were most similar in IQ at about age 3 and became less similar over the years, so that by age 15 the correlation between their IQ scores had dropped to .54. As a result, the heritability of IQ scores in this sample increased from the infant years to adolescence.

A similar message comes from adoption studies. The intellectual performance of adopted children is correlated with that of their biological parents *and* their adoptive parents, suggesting effects of genetic makeup and shared family environment. By adolescence the resemblance to biological parents remains evident, but adopted children's scores no longer correlate with their adoptive parents' scores (Scarr & Weinberg, 1978).

This is evidence that the heritability of intelligence test performance increases with age but that shared environmental influences on such performance become less significant as children grow older. Why? Very possibly, because children raised in the same home, especially if they are not genetically identical, increasingly go their own ways in life and therefore experience different influences on what they know and how they think. They may elicit different reactions from their parents, join different peer groups, encounter different teachers, and so on (Dunn & Plomin, 1990). These nonshared environmental influences on intellectual development (and other traits as well) become more and more significant from infancy to adolescence.

Do the relative contributions of genetic makeup and environment to individual differences in intellectual functioning change further in adulthood? Apparently not. Identical twins continue to perform more similarly on IQ tests than fraternal twins do even in old age (Plomin et al., 1994). What's more, if one identical twin experiences a major drop in intellectual performance in later life, the other twin often does too (Jarvik & Bank, 1983). Matt McGue and his colleagues (1993) conclude the following:

1. The estimated heritability of IQ scores increases from 50% in childhood to 80% in adulthood.
2. Variation due to shared environment decreases from 30% in childhood to near zero in adulthood because family members have fewer experiences in common.
3. The most important environmental influences in the long run appear to be *nonshared* and tend to make the IQ scores of brothers and sisters in the same family different from one another (see Figure 3.7).

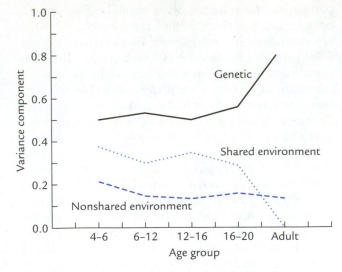

FIGURE 3.7 *Changes in the estimated contributions of genes, shared environment, and nonshared environment over the life span. Genes become more important as a source of differences in IQ from childhood to adulthood; shared environmental influences decrease as individuals who grew up in the same family become less and less alike; and unique experiences (nonshared environmental influences) remain important.* (From McGue et al. in Plomin & McClearn, 1993)

Some people interpret evidence of the heritability of IQ scores as proof that we cannot improve someone's intellectual development by enriching the environment. That's just not true! Yes, the IQs of adopted children are ultimately correlated more strongly with the IQs of their biological parents than with the IQs of their adoptive parents. However, the level of intellectual performance that these children reach can still increase dramatically (by 20 points on an IQ test) if they are adopted into more intellectually stimulating homes than those provided by their biological parents (Scarr & Weinberg, 1976, 1983; Weinberg, Scarr, & Waldman, 1992). Most likely, then, stimulating home environments help children realize more fully the genetically based potentials each of them has (Wilson, 1983). It is critical for parents, teachers, and others concerned with optimizing development to understand that qualities that are genetically influenced can still be altered.

Temperament and Personality

As parents well know, different babies have different personalities. In trying to describe infant personality, researchers have focused on aspects of **temperament:** a set of tendencies to respond in predictable ways such as sociability and emotional reactivity that serve as the building blocks of later personality (see Chapter 10 for a fuller discussion of temperament). Behavior genetics research indicates that genes do indeed contribute to individual differences in temperament in infancy and beyond (Plomin et al., 1997; Rowe, 1994).

For example, Arnold Buss and Robert Plomin (1984) reported average correlations of around .50 to .60 between the temperament scores of identical twins. The corresponding correlations for fraternal twins were not much greater than zero. Think about that: A zero correlation is what you would expect if they were strangers living in different homes rather than twins who, on average, share half their genes and the same home! It does not seem to matter whether we look at fraternal twin pairs or ordinary siblings or unrelated children adopted into the same family; living in the same home does little to make children similar in many aspects of personality (Dunn & Plomin, 1990).

Similar conclusions have been reached about the contributions of genes and environment to adult personality (see Chapter 10). Overall, it has been estimated that, of all the differences among adults in major dimensions of personality, about 40% of the variation may be due to genetic differences (Loehlin, 1985). Only 5% of the variation reflects the effects of shared family environment. Indeed, identical twins are about as similar in personality when they are raised apart as when they grow up in the same home (Bouchard et al., 1990). Finally, the remaining 55% of the variability in adult personalities is due largely to nonshared environmental influences.

The big question raised by behavioral genetics findings of this sort is this (Dunn & Plomin, 1990): *Why do fraternal twins and other siblings have such very different personalities despite sharing 50% of their genes on average and growing up in the same home?* It is increasingly clear that siblings simply do not have the same experiences. They are treated differently by their parents, they experience their relationships with one another differently, and they often have very different experiences with peers, teachers, and other people outside the home as well (Dunn & Plomin, 1990; Manke et al., 1995).

Herein lies a very significant message: The family environment is important in personality development, but not because it has a standard effect on all family members that makes them alike. True, there are some areas of socialization in which parents treat all their children similarly and that contribute to similarities among them (Hoffman, 1991). For example, parents may influence all their children to adopt moral, religious, and political values, attitudes, and interests similar to their own. Shared environment also makes adolescent siblings similar in the extent to which they smoke, drink, and commit delinquent acts (McGue, Shama, & Benson, 1996; Rowe, 1994). Indeed, siblings often do their mischief as a team. Yet behavior geneticists are discovering that the family environment often plays a more important role in creating differences among family members than in creating similarities (Rowe, 1994). When it comes to shaping many

basic personality traits, nonshared environmental influences interacting with genetic influences seem to be most significant.

Researchers are now trying to learn more about *how* differences in the experiences of brothers and sisters with parents, peers, and other people might contribute to differences in their traits. Denise Daniels (1986), for example, found that the sibling who received more fatherly affection had higher vocational aspirations than the sibling who experienced less paternal love. In another study (Baker & Daniels, 1990), a twin who reported greater maternal strictness was likely to be more depressed than his or her co-twin.

Although correlational studies of this sort cannot firmly establish that differences in experiences cause differences in personality, they do suggest that we should look more closely at the effects of experiences that are unique to each member of the family. This is a tremendously important insight. Developmentalists have long assumed that parents treat all their children much the same and steer them along similar developmental paths, so that shared environmental influences within the family matter most in the developmental process. Increasingly, it seems more useful to ask how differences in siblings' experiences inside and outside the home might explain differences in their development.

Psychological Disorders

Both genes and environment contribute to psychological disorders across the life span—to alcohol and drug abuse, depression, eating disorders, criminal behavior, and every other psychological disorder that has been studied (Plomin et al., 1997; Rowe, 1994). Consider just one example. **Schizophrenia** is a serious mental illness that involves disturbances in logical thinking, emotional expression, and social behavior and that typically emerges in late adolescence or early adulthood. The average concordance rate for identical twins is 48%; that is, if one twin has the disorder, the other does too in 48% of the pairs studied (Gottesman, 1991). By comparison, the concordance rate for fraternal twins is only 17%. In addition, children who have one or more biological parent who is schizophrenic have an increased risk of schizophrenia, even if they are adopted away early in life (Heston, 1970). The increased risk these children face has more to do with their genes than with being brought up by a schizophrenic adult.

But let's put this evidence in perspective. It is easy to conclude mistakenly that any child of a schizophrenic is doomed to become a schizophrenic. The rate of schizophrenia in the general population is about 1%. By comparison, about 13% of children who have a schizophrenic parent develop schizophrenic symptoms themselves (Gottesman, 1991). Although this figure

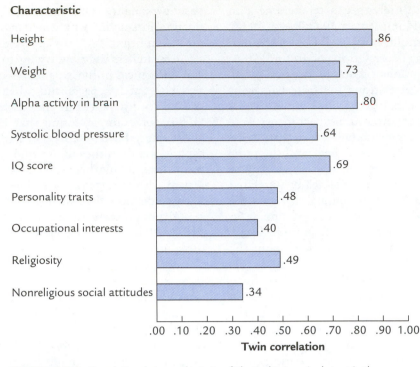

Characteristic

Height .86
Weight .73
Alpha activity in brain .80
Systolic blood pressure .64
IQ score .69
Personality traits .48
Occupational interests .40
Religiosity .49
Nonreligious social attitudes .34

.00 .10 .20 .30 .40 .50 .60 .70 .80 .90 1.00

Twin correlation

FIGURE 3.8 *Correlations between the traits of identical twins raised apart in the Minnesota Twin Study* (From Bouchard et al., 1990)

does indicate that children of schizophrenics are at greater risk for schizophrenia than other children, notice that about 87% of the children of one schizophrenic parent do not develop the disorder. Even if you are the child of two schizophrenics or an identical twin whose co-twin develops the disorder, the odds are only about 1 in 2 that you too will become schizophrenic!

Clearly, then, an individual's experiences also contribute significantly to this mental illness. People do not inherit psychological disorders; they inherit predispositions to develop disorders. Assuming that a person has inherited a genetic susceptibility to schizophrenia, it may take one or more stressful experiences (for example, hostile, rejecting parents; an abusive marriage) to trigger the illness. The same can be said for other psychological disorders that appear to have some genetic basis.

In short, we now know that children may inherit predispositions to develop a number of problems and disorders and that their experiences interact with their genetic makeup to determine how well-adjusted they turn out to be. One implication is clear: It is overly simple and often wrong to assume that any behavior problem a child displays must be the result of bad parenting.

Heritability of Traits

You may have the impression by now that individual differences in any human trait are significantly influenced by genes. Although there is truth to this, some traits are more heritable than others. Observable physical characteristics, from eye color to height, are very strongly associated with individual genetic endowment (Plomin, 1990). Even weight is heritable; adopted children resemble their biological parents but not their adoptive parents in weight (Grilo & Pogue-Geile, 1991). Certain aspects of physiology, such as measured brain activity and reactions to alcohol, are highly heritable, too (Lykken, Tellegen, & Iacono, 1982; Neale & Martin, 1989).

If physical and physiological characteristics are strongly heritable, general intelligence is moderately heritable. Somewhat less influenced by genes are aspects of temperament and personality and susceptibility to a number of psychological disorders. Finally, it has become clear that genetic endowment modestly influences even attitudes and interests (Rowe, 1994). Figure 3.8 presents some of the correlations obtained in the Minnesota Twin Study between the traits of identical twins raised apart and reunited later in life. Although this twin study has yielded higher estimates of heritability than some studies, it shows that heredity influences physical traits more than psychological ones, but that a broad range of psychological traits are heritable to some extent.

Is there any trait that is not influenced by heredity? From one perspective, we should answer "no." In the sense that all human traits depend on their influence, *both* a genotype and an environment are 100%

important (Hebb, 1970). Yet individual differences in some traits seem to have little relationship to genetic endowment. For example, identical twins are not much more alike than fraternal twins are with respect to how well or how poorly they perform on tests of creativity (Plomin, 1990; Reznikoff et al., 1973), and many social and political attitudes seem to be more heavily influenced by life experiences than by genetic makeup. Thus the balance of genetic and environmental contributions to human diversity differs for different traits.

HEREDITY AND ENVIRONMENT: A CLOSER LOOK

What should we conclude overall about the influences of genes and environment and about the ways in which these two great forces in development conspire to make us what we are?

Genes do not just orchestrate our growth before birth and then leave us alone. Instead, they are "turning on" and "turning off" in patterned ways throughout the life span, and they are partly responsible for attributes and behavior patterns that we carry with us through our lives. A shared species heredity makes us similar in the way we develop and age. Unique individual genetic makeups cause us to develop and age in our own ways. Genes even help explain why humans live no longer than about 120 years and why some people die earlier than others (see Chapter 17). Of course, we are also influenced by our environments from conception to death.

Increasingly, from infancy through childhood and adolescence, children's unique genetic blueprints show themselves more and more in their behavior; identical twins start similar and remain similar, but fraternal twins, like brothers and sisters generally, go their own ways and become more and more dissimilar. Shared environmental influences—the forces that make children in the same family alike—are stronger early in life than they are later in life (McCartney et al., 1990; McGue et al., 1993). Nonshared environmental influences—those unique experiences that make members of the family different—remain important throughout the life span. In short, as we move out of the home and into the larger world, we seem to become, more and more, products of our unique genes and our unique experiences. But genes and environment are also interrelated.

Gene/Environment Interactions

Behavioral genetics aims to establish how much of the variation we observe in human traits (such as intelligence) can be attributed to individual differences in genetic makeup and how much can be attributed to individual differences in experience. Useful as that research is, it does not take us very far in understanding the complex interplay between genetic and environmental influences over the life span. As Ann Anastasi (1958) asserted many years ago, instead of asking how much is due to genes and how much is due to environment, we should be asking *how* heredity and environment work together to make us what we are.

It is clear that genes do not determine anything; instead, they provide us with potentials that are realized or not depending on the quality of our experiences. Figure 3.9 illustrates this view. We see evidence that genetic endowment matters: Children with high genetic potential to be intelligent will generally outperform children with below-average potential on IQ tests. It is equally clear that environment matters: Regardless of their genetic potential, children generally obtain higher IQ scores if they are brought up in enriched, intellectually stimulating environments than if they are raised in restricted, intellectually impoverished ones.

The most important message in the figure, however, is embodied in the concept of **gene/environment interaction:** How our genotypes are expressed depends on what kind of environment we experience, and how we respond to the environment depends on what kind of genes we have. In Figure 3.9 we see that growing up in a deprived environment can make children with the genetic potential to be geniuses perform as poorly as children with far less genetic potential, even though this high-potential genotype will be expressed as highly intelligent behavior if children are brought up in more stimulating environments. Genes and environment also interact in the sense that children with high genetic potential are more able than children with low genetic potential to benefit from

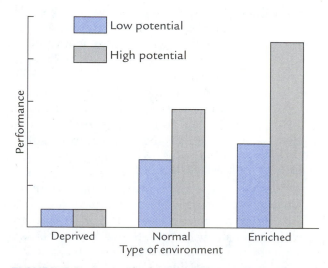

FIGURE 3.9 *An example of a gene/environment interaction*

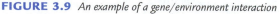

enriching experiences, although both groups of children benefit to some degree.

Gene/Environment Correlations

Appreciating that genes and environment interact is a good start, but heredity and environment are even more intimately intertwined than the concept of gene/environment interaction implies. Each person's genetic makeup influences the kinds of experiences that he or she seeks out and actually has, and these experiences then strengthen or weaken genetically based tendencies.

Sandra Scarr and Kathleen McCartney (1983), drawing on the theorizing of Plomin, DeFries, and Loehlin (1977), have proposed three kinds of **gene/environment correlations,** or ways in which one's genes and one's environment are systematically interrelated: passive, evocative, and active genotype/environment correlations. The concept of gene/environment *interactions* tells us that people with different genes react differently to the environments they encounter. The concept of gene/environment *correlations* says that people with different genes encounter different environments (Loehlin, 1992). As an illustration, let's imagine one child with a genetic potential to be highly sociable and a second child whose genes make for shyness and withdrawal.

Passive Correlations

The kind of home environment that parents provide for their children is influenced in part by the parents' own genotypes. And, since parents provide children not only with a home environment but with their genes, it turns out that the rearing environments to which children are exposed are correlated with (and are likely to suit) their genotypes.

For instance, sociable parents not only transmit their "sociable" genes to their children but also, because they have "sociable" genes, create a very social home environment, inviting their friends over frequently and taking their children to many social events. These children inherit genes for sociability, but they also receive an environment that matches their genes and that may make them even more sociable than they would otherwise be. By contrast, the child with shy parents is likely to receive genes for shyness *and* an environment without much social stimulation.

Evocative Correlations

A child's genotype also evokes certain kinds of reactions from other people. The smiley, sociable baby is likely to get more smiles and social stimulation than the withdrawn, shy baby does. Similarly, the sociable child may be sought out more often as a playmate by other children, the sociable adolescent may be invited to more parties, and the sociable adult may be given

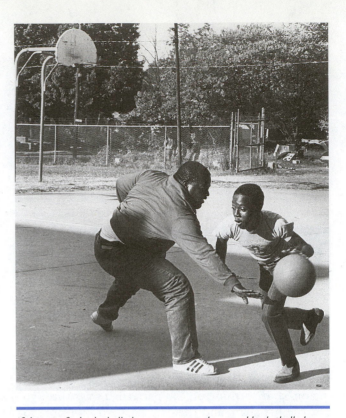

If the son of a basketball player turns out to be a good basketball player, is it due to genetic endowment or experience? We can't say because genes and environment are correlated. Through passive gene/environment correlation, the children of athletes not only inherit their parents' genes for athleticism but grow up in sports-oriented family environments.

more job assignments involving public relations. In short, genetic makeup may affect the reactions of other people to a child and, hence, the kind of social environment that the child will experience.

Active Correlations

Finally, a child's genotype influences what kinds of environments he or she actively *seeks*. The individual with a genetic predisposition to be extroverted is likely to seek out parties, invite friends to the house, join organizations, and otherwise build a "niche" that is highly socially stimulating. The child with genes for shyness may actively avoid large group activities and instead develop interests in activities that can be engaged in alone.

Scarr and McCartney suggest that the balance of passive, evocative, and active genotype/environment correlations shifts during development. Because infants are at home a good deal, their environment is largely influenced by their parents through passive genetic influences. Evocative influences continue to operate in much the same way throughout life; our characteristic traits consistently prompt characteristic reactions in other people. As children develop, however, they become increasingly able to build their own niches, so active gene influences become more important. Scarr and McCartney believe that this is one reason why fraternal twins, siblings, and adopted children in the same family become less alike as they get older. They share an early home environment, but, because they are genetically different, they increasingly build different niches (nonshared environments) as they get older and more independent. Identical twins, by contrast, may stay alike, even when separated, because their similar genes make them continue to seek out similar experiences.

Genetic Influence on the Environment

Is there any evidence supporting Scarr and McCartney's contention that one's genes are correlated with, and perhaps influence, one's experiences in life? Yes there is. Behavioral geneticists are discovering that measures of environment are themselves heritable! What this means is that identical twins are more similar than fraternal twins, and biological siblings are more similar than adoptive siblings, in the environments they experience (Plomin, Reiss, Hetherington, & Howe, 1994)—for example, in

◆ the degree of warmth their parents show toward them, though not so much *how* controlling their parents are (Kendler, 1996; Plomin & Bergeman, 1991);

◆ the time they spend watching television (Plomin, Corley, DeFries, & Fulker, 1990);

◆ the number of stressful life events they report experiencing as adults (Kendler et al., 1993), including the likelihood that they will divorce (Jockin, McGue, & Lykken, 1996).

If our genetically influenced personality traits affect how others treat us and what experiences we seek and have, these findings make perfect sense. However, such findings also challenge some of our most fundamental assumptions about human development. After all, what they really say is that what we regard as purely "environmental" influences on development may actually reflect, in part, the workings of heredity (Rowe, 1994). Robert Plomin (1990) offers a good example: Suppose we find that parents who read to their children have brighter children than parents who do not read to their children. In the not-so-distant past, most developmentalists would have interpreted this finding rather uncritically as evidence that parents make important contributions to their children's intellectual development. Without denying the importance of parents, suppose we offer this alternative interpretation: Parents and children whose genes predispose them to be highly intelligent are more likely to seek out opportunities to read stories than parents and children who are less intellectually inclined. If this is the case, can we be so sure that reading to children *causes* them to be brighter? Would we be able to show that reading to children is beneficial even when parents and children are genetically unrelated? The concept of gene/environment correlations reminds us that humans, partly guided by their genetically based predispositions, actively shape the environments that in turn influence them. As a result, genetic makeup may partly account for the relationships researchers find between experiences and developmental outcomes (Reiss, 1995).

In sum, both genes and environment are at work over the entire life span, although the relative contributions of these two forces change with age from infancy to adolescence. But we are missing the full story unless we appreciate both gene/environment interactions and gene/environment correlations. Environmental forces help determine whether we achieve our genetic potential, and genes determine how we respond to experiences—and, indeed, what experiences we have. Now you can understand why today's developmentalists regard it as foolish to ask whether nature *or* nurture is responsible for human development. We are shaped by an incredibly complex interplay of genetic and environmental influences from conception to death.

APPLICATIONS: GENETIC COUNSELING AND ENGINEERING

What use is genetic research to parents who run the risk of having a child with a genetically linked disorder? To set parents-to-be at ease, let's note that about 97% of babies will not have genetic defects (Shiloh, 1996). However, a couple of thousand genetic defects are associated with a single gene or gene pair, several kinds of chromosome disorders, and many polygenic susceptibilities to diseases and disorders such as schizophrenia. **Genetic counseling** is a service that offers relevant information to people who suspect that they or their unborn children are at risk for some genetically based problem. Today's genetic counselors have access to more information than ever about the nature, detection, and treatment of genetic defects (see Aldridge, 1996; Shiloh, 1996). To illustrate this, we will focus on two disorders: Tay-Sachs disease and Huntington's disease. We will also consider the prospects for preventing and treating genetic disorders.

Tay-Sachs Disease

Tay-Sachs disease causes degeneration of the nervous system and usually kills its victims in early childhood (Roche & Kuller, 1996). The problem is that a genetically caused metabolic defect results in an accumulation of fat in the child's brain. If a Jewish couple heard that Tay-Sachs strikes mainly Jewish children and sought the advice of a genetic counselor, the counselor might obtain a complete family history from each partner—one that includes information about the diseases and causes of death of relatives, any previous problems in childbearing, and the countries of origin of relatives (particularly since Tay-Sachs disease strikes most frequently among Jewish people of Eastern European ancestry and among French Canadians).

For some defects and disorders, especially those influenced by multiple gene pairs, family histories of this sort are the only basis for calculating the odds that a problem might occur. However, more and more tests are becoming available to determine conclusively whether prospective parents are carriers of genes associated with Tay-Sachs and many of the other 4000 or so known hereditary defects (Weiss, 1995). For example, simple blood tests can determine whether a prospective parent carries the recessive gene for Tay-Sachs disease, as well as sickle-cell disease, hemophilia, and countless other conditions.

Suppose our couple learns from a blood test that they are both carriers of the recessive gene for Tay-Sachs disease, which is inherited through single gene-pair inheritance. A genetic counselor would explain that there is a 1-in-4 chance that any child they conceive would inherit a recessive gene from each of them and have Tay-Sachs disease and a 2-in-4 chance that any child would, like the parents themselves, be a carrier. After providing the couple with this information, the genetic counselor would inform them about prenatal screening procedures that can detect many genetic abnormalities (including Tay-Sachs disease) in the fetus. Three widely used techniques—amniocentesis, chorionic villus biopsy, and ultrasound—are described in Box 3.1.

For the parents whose tests reveal a normal fetus, the anxiety of undergoing the tests and waiting for the results gives way to relief. For those who learn that their fetus has a serious defect, the experience can be agonizing, especially if their religious or personal beliefs argue against the option of abortion. In the case of Tay-Sachs disease, for example, the choice is between terminating the pregnancy and watching one's baby deteriorate and die, because no cure for this condition has yet been discovered. Better detection of carriers and affected fetuses has already resulted in a decreased number of Tay-Sachs babies (Mitchell et al., 1996).

Huntington's Disease

Occasionally a genetic defect is associated with a single dominant gene. **Huntington's disease** is a famous (and terrifying) example that typically strikes in middle age. The nervous systems of its victims steadily de-

teriorate. Among the effects are motor disturbances such as slurred speech, an erratic, seemingly drunken walk, grimaces, and jerky movements; personality changes involving increased moodiness and irritability; and dementia or loss of cognitive abilities (Bishop & Waldholz, 1990; Swavely & Falek, 1989). Any child of a parent with Huntington's disease will have the disease if he or she receives the dominant Huntington's gene rather than its normal counterpart gene at conception; the risk is therefore 1 out of 2, or 50%. Fortunately the gene is very rare; 5 to 10 people in 100,000 develop the disease (Gusella et al., 1983).

In 1983, James Gusella and his colleagues were able to apply a then-new technique of locating specific genes on the chromosomes to trace the gene for Huntington's disease to Chromosome 4. Nancy Wexler, a psychologist whose mother had developed Huntington's disease and who therefore stands a 50–50 chance of developing it herself, helped by assembling a team to collect blood samples from a large family in Venezuela in which Huntington's disease ran rampant (Bishop & Waldholz, 1990). Gusella and his team were then able to pinpoint how the genetic "fingerprints" of family members who had Huntington's differed from those of family members who did not.

The discovery of the location of the Huntington's gene led to the development of a test to enable the relatives of Huntington's victims to find out whether or not they had inherited the gene. Before the test became available, children of a Huntington's disease victim had to wonder about that for a good part of their lives. The slightest signs of clumsiness, mood swings, or personality changes aroused fear that the disease had struck (Bishop & Waldholz, 1990). Some sons and daughters of victims were afraid to marry or to have children in case they might later prove to have the Huntington's gene. Now that the test for the gene is available, not all individuals at risk for Huntington's want to take it, but many who do take it feel better knowing one way or the other what the future holds (Wiggins et al., 1992).

Prevention and Treatment

Ultimately, genetic researchers want to understand how genes associated with diseases and disorders work their damage and how their effects can be prevented, cured, or at least minimized. One of the greatest success stories in genetic research involves **phenylketonuria,** or **PKU,** a disorder caused by a pair of recessive genes. Affected children lack a critical enzyme needed to metabolize phenylalanine, a component of many foods (including milk) and the main ingredient in aspartame, the sweetener used in many diet foods and beverages. As phenylalanine accumulates in the body, it is converted to a harmful acid that

BOX 3.1

Prenatal detection of abnormalities

Today, pregnant women, especially those over 35 or 40, turn to a variety of medical techniques to tell them in advance whether their babies are likely to be normal (Kuller, Chescheir, & Cefalo, 1996). The easiest and most commonly used of these methods is **ultrasound,** the use of sound waves to scan the womb and create a visual image of the fetus on a monitor screen. Ultrasound can indicate how many fetuses are in the womb and whether they are alive, but it can detect only those genetic defects that produce visible physical abnormalities. Prospective parents often enjoy "meeting" their child and can find out (when the pregnancy is far enough along) whether their child is going to be a girl or a boy. Ultrasound is safer than X rays and generally very safe overall.

To detect chromosome abnormalities such as Down syndrome, **amniocentesis** might be used. Here a needle is inserted into the abdomen and a sample of amniotic fluid is withdrawn. Fetal cells that have been shed can be analyzed to determine the sex of the fetus and the presence of a wide range of chromosomal abnormalities and of many genetic defects. Despite complications and a risk of miscarriage in about 1 of 100 pregnancies, amniocentesis is considered quite safe and is commonly recommended for older mothers (Beardsley, 1997; Nightingale & Goodman, 1990). It is safer than it used to be because ultrasound is now used to guide the needle to a safe destination (Cabaniss, 1996). Because amniocentesis cannot be performed before the 14th to 16th week of pregnancy and involves a two-week wait for the results, however, it is often done too late for a couple who are fated to have a child with serious defects to consider abortion.

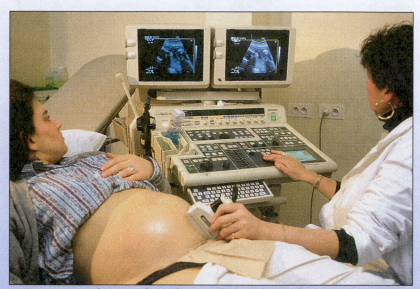

Having a sonogram done is painless and poses no known risk to the fetus.

Chorionic villus biopsy (CVS) involves inserting a catheter through the mother's vagina and cervix and into the membrane called the *chorion* that surrounds the fetus and then extracting tiny hair cells from the chorion that contain the genetic code of the fetus. Sample cells can then be analyzed for the same genetic defects that can be detected using amniocentesis. The difference is that chorionic villus biopsy can be performed as early as the 9th week, allowing parents more time to consider the pros and cons of continuing the pregnancy if an abnormality is detected. Most evidence suggests that CVS involves about the same risk of miscarriage as amniocentesis (Evans, 1994). However, use of CVS before the 11th week of pregnancy can be especially risky (Findlay et al., 1996), and one large study suggested that its use may increase the chances of certain rare

finger and toe abnormalities (Evans, 1994).

All prenatal diagnostic techniques should be used cautiously, then. Recently, researchers have been perfecting a technique that will allow them to extract from a maternal blood sample some of the small number of fetal cells that pass into the mother's blood, avoiding risk to the fetus entirely (Beardsley, 1997). Yet the small risks entailed should not keep women from agreeing to ultrasound, amniocentesis, or CVS when there is reason to suspect a problem. Moreover, techniques of prenatal diagnosis are becoming safer and safer. Most women find these procedures quite simple, and most couples can look forward to immense relief when they are told that their baby is just fine (Sjogren & Uddenberg, 1990).

attacks the nervous system and causes children to be mentally retarded and hyperactive.

In the mid-1950s, scientists developed a special diet low in phenylalanine, and in 1961, they developed a simple blood test that could detect PKU soon after birth, before any damage had been done. Today newborn infants are routinely screened for PKU, and af-

fected children are immediately placed on the special (and, unfortunately, quite distasteful) diet, which must be followed very strictly throughout childhood (Miller, 1995). Here, then, genetic research led to the prevention of one of the many causes of mental retardation. And here we also have a wonderful example of the interaction between genes and environment: A

child will develop the condition and become mentally retarded only if he or she inherits the PKU genes *and* eats a normal (rather than special) diet.

Ways of preventing and treating genetic conditions are not always easy to come by, however. Researchers are now experimenting with **genetic engineering**—therapies that involve substituting normal genes for the genes associated with a disease or disorder, or otherwise altering a person's genetic makeup (Aldridge, 1996). These techniques are being tested with certain single-gene pair disorders but have not yet proven effective (Begley, 1995). Preventing or curing polygenic disorders such as schizophrenia will be even harder, as it will require understanding how multiple genes *and* multiple environmental risk factors contribute to the disorder. No "quick fix" like the PKU diet will be possible.

In the meantime, many potentially devastating effects of genetic and chromosomal abnormalities can at least be minimized or controlled, if not cured (Khoury and the Genetics Working Group, 1996). For example, children with Turner syndrome or Klinefelter syndrome can be given sex hormones to make their appearance more gender-typical; individuals with sickle-cell disease can be given transfusions of blood containing the normal red blood cells they lack, and so on.

It is clear that society as a whole will have to grapple with the complex ethical issues that have arisen as geneticists have gained the capacity to identify the carriers and potential victims of diseases and disorders, to give parents information that might prompt them to decide on an abortion, and to experiment with techniques for altering the genetic code. Some observers are concerned that genetic testing will be used by insurance companies to deny coverage to individuals who are at risk for diseases and disorders—or by employers to discriminate against them. Others worry about **eugenics,** attempts to improve the human race by altering the genetic makeup of a population. The term arouses fear that the Nazis' crusade to breed a super race could happen again.

For these and other reasons, genetic research is controversial. Some respected researchers continue to question the validity of the kinds of studies that we have surveyed in this chapter. They doubt that the influences of genes and environment on individual differences can ever be cleanly separated, or they think that behavior genetics research does little to clarify how genotypes are translated into phenotypes (Bronfenbrenner & Ceci, 1994; Gottlieb, 1996). Then there are those who resist the messages that this research contains. They want to believe that all people are created equal in all respects. Or they don't want to think that they or others are doomed to resemble their parents or limited in their potential to achieve anything they choose.

Yet, it is quite possible to believe that people deserve equal rights and equal opportunities while still recognizing that they have different potentials sketched in their genetic codes. Indeed, it can be argued that society is richer when its members are diverse, when each has unique strengths to contribute. And, as we have stressed repeatedly, the fact that individual differences in behavior in a group of people are partly or even largely due to differences in their genetic makeups does not mean that those traits are un-alterable. Being born into a family of alcoholics hardly means that one must become an alcoholic or that one cannot be treated successfully if one does become an alcoholic. In fact, efforts to prevent alcoholism might well become more effective if we can identify individuals who are at risk and target preventive efforts at them. Of course, providing children with optimal experiences depends on knowing which kinds of environments stimulate growth and which kinds of environments do not. It is fitting, then, that our next chapter takes a closer look at early environmental influences on development.

◆ SUMMARY POINTS

1. As humans, we share a species heredity that is the product of natural selection and that makes some aspects of our development and aging universal. Ethologists and other modern evolutionary theorists believe that normal development must be understood as the product of both specieswide genes and experiential factors.

2. Each human also has an individual heredity provided at conception, when sperm and ovum, each having retained 23 chromosomes at meiosis, unite to form a single-cell zygote that contains 46 chromosomes (23 from each parent). The result is that each child of the same parents (other than identical twins) is genetically unique.

3. A child's sex is determined by the sex (X and Y) chromosomes; since genetic males have an X and a Y chromosome whereas genetic females have two X chromosomes, the father determines the child's sex.

4. The genetic basis for development is not completely understood, but we do know that genes provide an instructional "code" that influences how cells are formed and how they function and that regulator genes turn these genes "on" and "off" throughout the life span. Environmental factors influence how one's genotype (genetic makeup) is translated into a phenotype (actual traits).

5. There are three main mechanisms of inheritance: single gene-pair inheritance, sex-linked inheritance, and polygenic (multiple-gene) inheritance. Most important human traits are influenced by polygenic inheritance. Some children are also affected by noninherited changes in gene structure (mutations), and others, because of errors in meiosis, have chromosome abnormalities (such as Down syndrome) or sex chromosome abnormalities (such as Turner and Klinefelter syndromes).

6. Behavioral genetics is the study of genetic and environmental contributions to individual differences in psychological traits and behaviors. Human behavioral geneticists, by conducting twin and adoption studies, describe resemblances between pairs of people using concordance rates and correlation coefficients. They then estimate the heritability of traits (the proportion of variation in a trait in a group linked to genetic differences among those individuals), as well as the contributions of shared and nonshared environmental influences.

7. Performance on measures of intelligence is a heritable trait. Infant mental development is strongly influenced by a specieswide, genetically programmed, maturational plan, but, over the course of childhood and adolescence, individual differences in mental ability become more consistent and more strongly reflect both individual genetic makeup and environmental influences. Shared environmental influences that make members of the same family alike become less significant with age, whereas the effects of genes and nonshared or unique environmental influences remain evident throughout the adult years.

8. Aspects of temperament such as emotionality, sociability, and activity are also genetically influenced. Members of the same family often develop very different personalities owing to nonshared aspects of their experiences.

9. Many psychological disorders and problems, including schizophrenia, have some genetic basis, but environmental factors have a good deal of influence on whether or not a genetic predisposition to develop a problem is realized.

10. Overall, physical and physiological characteristics are more strongly influenced by individual genetic endowment than are intellectual abilities and, in turn, personality traits. Certain traits (creativity and some social attitudes) appear to be more strongly influenced by environmental factors than genetic ones.

11. Overall, both genes and shared and nonshared environmental influences are influential over the entire life span, although shared environmental influences are sometimes modest and become less important with age. Gene/environment interactions show that environment influences how genes are expressed, and genes influence how people react to the environment. Moreover, passive, evocative, and active gene/environment correlations suggest that we experience and seek out environments that match and further reinforce our genetic predispositions.

12. Genetic conditions such as Tay-Sachs disease, Huntington's disease, and PKU can have profound effects on development. Genetic counseling can help people calculate the risks that their unborn children may have a genetic disorder. Blood tests can identify the carriers of many single gene-pair disorders, and abnormalities in the fetus can be detected through amniocentesis, chorionic villus biopsy, and ultrasound. As knowledge of the genetic code increases, many more genetic disorders are likely to become predictable, detectable, and treatable, but applications of genetic engineering with humans have not yet been successful and raise serious ethical issues.

FOOD FOR THOUGHT

1. Hairy Ear Syndrome (I made it up) is caused by a single dominant gene, H. Using box diagrams like those in Figure 3.2, figure out the odds that Herb (who has the genotype Hh) and Harriet (who also has the genotype Hh) will have a child with Hairy Ear. Now repeat the exercise but assume that Hairy Ear is caused by a recessive gene, h, and that both parents again have an Hh genotype.

2. Suppose you are interested in physical aggression and want to find out how much genetic endowment influences how physically aggressive adolescents are. Sketch out two studies that could be conducted to answer this question and indicate what they would be able to tell us about the contributions of genes, shared environment, and nonshared environment to aggressive tendencies.

3. Researchers have found evidence that children who are physically punished by their parents tend to behave more aggressively around their peers than children who are not. What explanation for this finding might a social learning theorist like Albert Bandura propose? What alternative explanations does research on behavioral genetics, including work on gene/environment correlations, suggest?

4. Alan's biological mother developed schizophrenia and was placed in a mental hospital when he was only one. From then on he grew up with his father and stepmother (neither of whom had psychological disorders). On the basis of the material in this chapter, what would you tell Alan about his chances of becoming schizophrenic if you were a genetic counselor?

W ON THE WEB

1. *Charles Darwin*   This site has background material on Darwin and his theory of evolution, including the text of *The Origin of Species* (1859). Darwin's ideas have often been misunderstood, so you might enjoy seeing for yourself what he had to say and finding out whether it matches what you think he said.
http://www.stg.brown.edu/projects/hypertext/landow/victorian/darwin/darwinov.html

2. *The Human Genome Research Project*   The site of the National Human Genome Research Institute within the National Institutes of Health will orient you to the massive federal effort to map all the genes of the 46 human chromosomes. Good information about the latest efforts to understand the causes and prevention of genetic defects and diseases.
http://www.nhgri.nih.gov/

3. *Huntington's Disease*   For a closer look at this devastating and deadly disease caused by a single dominant gene, check a site created by Robert Laycock, who has Huntington's in his family. He will link you to research news as well as to personal stories of people who have lived with Huntington's disease.
http://www.interlog.com/~rlaycock/2nd.html

KEY TERMS

gene
species heredity
natural selection
ethology
evolutionary psychology
conception
zygote
chromosome
meiosis
mitosis
crossing over
identical twins
fraternal twins
X chromosome
Y chromosome
karyotype
genotype
phenotype
single gene-pair inheritance

dominant gene
recessive gene
sickle-cell disease
carrier
incomplete dominance
codominance
sex-linked characteristic
polygenic trait
mutation
chromosome abnormalities
Down syndrome
Turner syndrome
Klinefelter syndrome
behavioral genetics
heritability
selective breeding
concordance rate
shared environmental
   influences

nonshared environmental
   influences
temperament
schizophrenia
gene/environment
   interaction
gene/environment
   correlation
genetic counseling
Tay-Sachs disease
ultrasound
amniocentesis
chorionic villus biopsy
   (CVS)
Huntington's disease
phenylketonuria (PKU)
genetic engineering
eugenics

CHAPTER 4

Early Environmental Influences on Life-Span Development

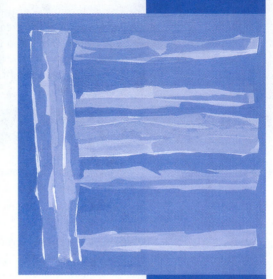

DEVELOPMENT IN THE PRENATAL ENVIRONMENT
Prenatal Stages
The Mother's State
Teratogens

THE PERINATAL ENVIRONMENT
Possible Hazards
The Mother's Experience
The Father's Experience

THE EARLY POSTNATAL ENVIRONMENT
Culture and Early Socialization

RISK AND RESILIENCE
Low-Birth-Weight Babies

APPLICATIONS: GETTING LIFE OFF TO A GOOD START
Before Birth
During Birth
After Birth

SUMMARY POINTS

FOOD FOR THOUGHT

ON THE WEB

KEY TERMS

In 1970, a severely neglected and abused child named Genie came to the attention of authorities in Los Angeles, California. Her incredible story is well known to developmentalists (see Curtiss, 1977; Rymer, 1993). Genie had been locked away in a back room as a toddler and remained in solitary confinement until she was rescued at age 13. During her captivity, she was tied into a potty chair during the day and caged at night in a crib covered with wire. Genie's mother, who was nearly blind, spent a few minutes with her every day as she fed the child. However, Genie's father, who apparently hated children, did not permit anyone to talk to her. (Nor did he tolerate television or other noisy appliances.) If Genie made a sound, her father allegedly beat her, while barking and growling like a wild dog.

We are affected by the physical as well as the social environments in which we develop.

What were the effects of this dreadful environment on Genie's development? About as disastrous as you might guess. Although when she was freed Genie showed some signs of having experienced puberty, she weighed less than 60 pounds, walked haltingly, and could not chew solid food. Her vision and hearing were normal, but her intellectual performance was at roughly the level of a normal 1-year-old. She understood only a few words and spoke only a couple of negatives, such as "stop it" and "no more" (Rymer, 1993). As you might expect, she was quite emotionally disturbed as well.

Now, what do you suppose happened once she was given a stimulating environment—special education classes, help from a speech therapist after school, and nurturance in a therapist's family? Genie surprised everyone with her progress. A mere eight months after her rescue she had a vocabulary of 200 words and was already putting together the two-word sentences that are typical of young language learners. Her intelligence test scores steadily climbed over the years. At the age of 19, she could use public transportation and was functioning quite well in both her foster home and her special classes at school.

And yet she was far from a normal young woman. Her speech was still less sophisticated than a normal 5-year-old's, as in such sentences as, "M. say not lift my leg in dentist chair" (Curtiss, 1977). And her intelligence test performance was still near the level associated with mental retardation. Moreover, she regressed after a series of foster placements, including an abusive one, and after enduring the loss of adults she had come to love (Rymer, 1993). At last report, she was living in a home for mentally retarded adults (Rymer, 1993).

Obviously, environmental influences on development—bad and good—demand our serious attention. In Chapter 3 we stressed that genes and environment interact throughout the life span to make us what we are. If a common genetic heritage can make different human beings alike in some respects, so can similar environments. If unique genes make one person different from another, so do unique experiences.

What is "environment," really? According to ecological theorists Urie Bronfenbrenner and Ann Crouter (1983): *environment* is "any event or condition outside the organism that is presumed to influence, or be influenced by, the person's development" (p. 359). The physical environment includes everything from the molecules that reach the fetus's bloodstream before birth to the architecture of one's home to the climate outside. The social environment includes all the people who can influence and be influenced by the developing person, as well as the broader culture. Early theorists tended to view the environment as a set of forces that shape the individual, as though a person were just a lump of clay to be molded. Now we understand that people shape their physical and social environments and are, in turn, affected by the environments they have helped create. In other words, the relationship is one of *reciprocal influence*.

For example, if a woman uses cocaine during pregnancy, her newborn may be extraordinarily fussy: Environment has affected development. But a fussy baby is likely to affect the environment by irritating his mother, who now expresses her tenseness in her interactions with him, which makes him all the fussier, which of course aggravates his mother even more, which of course makes him even crankier. These sorts of transactions between person and environment begin at the moment of conception (Smotherman & Robinson, 1996).

Environment, then, is (1) both physical and social, (2) at work prenatally and postnatally, and (3) involved in reciprocal transactions with the developing person. In this chapter, we examine some of the environmental factors that are critical to very early development: before birth, when a mother's condition, disease status, and drug exposure can be critical; during the period surrounding birth, when delivery techniques and opportunities to interact can be important; and in early infancy, when influences within the family and larger culture further shape development. We will, of course, consider environmental influences on development throughout this text. Our main mission in this chapter is to find out just how much early environmental influences, interacting with genetic influences, make or break later development.

DEVELOPMENT IN THE PRENATAL ENVIRONMENT

Perhaps at no time in the life span does development occur faster, or is the environment more important, than between conception and birth. To understand how the **prenatal environment,** the physical environment of the womb, can affect development, we must first understand the maturational milestones that normally occur before birth. Then it will be clearer why development can be thrown far off course by certain damaging influences at certain times.

Prenatal Stages

Conception and the Germinal Period

Midway in the menstrual cycle, every 28 days or so, females ovulate: an ovum (egg cell) ripens, leaves the ovary, and begins its journey through the fallopian tube to the uterus. Usually the egg disintegrates and leaves the body as part of the menstrual flow. However, if the woman has intercourse with a fertile man during ovulation, the 300 to 450 million sperm cells in his seminal fluid swim, tadpole-style, in all directions. Of the 5000 to 20,000 sperm that survive the long journey into the fallopian tubes, *one* may meet and penetrate the ovum on its descent from the ovary. A biochemical reaction occurs that repels other sperm and keeps them from penetrating the already fertilized egg. As explained in Chapter 3, *conception,* the beginning of life, occurs when the genetic material of the sperm and egg unite to form a single-celled *zygote.* The process may sound simple enough but, as we see in Box 4.1, many couples cannot conceive a child, much as they want to, and seek medical help.

The zygote contains the 46 chromosomes that are the genetic blueprint for the individual's development. It takes about 266 days (about 9 months) for the zygote to become a fetus of some 200 billion cells that is ready to be born. Prenatal development is divided into three periods: (1) the germinal period, (2) the period of the embryo, and (3) the period of the fetus.

The **germinal period** lasts 8 to 14 days. First the zygote divides many times through mitosis, forming the **blastula,** a hollow ball of cells about the size of the head of a pin. When the blastula reaches the uterus, it implants tendrils from its outer layer into the blood vessels of the uterine wall. This is quite an accomplishment, as only about half of all fertilized ova are successfully implanted in the uterus (Roberts & Lowe, 1975). In addition, as many as half of all implanted embryos are either abnormal or attached to a site incapable of sustaining them; they are miscarried (spontaneously aborted) and expelled (Adler & Carey, 1982). Apparently, only about 1 zygote in 4 survives the initial phases of prenatal development.

The Embryonic Period

The **period of the embryo** lasts from implantation, two weeks after conception, to the end of the eighth week of prenatal development. During this short time, every major organ takes shape in at least a primitive form, in a process called **organogenesis.**

Soon after implantation, the embryo secretes a hormone that prevents the mother from menstruating; this helps ensure its survival. (The presence of this hormone in a woman's urine is evidence of pregnancy in a common test.) Meanwhile, the layers of the embryo differentiate, forming structures that sustain development (Sadler, 1996). The outer layer becomes both the **amnion,** a watertight membrane that fills with fluid that cushions and protects the embryo, and the **chorion,** a membrane that surrounds the amnion and attaches rootlike extensions called villi to the uterine lining to gather nourishment for the embryo. The chorion eventually becomes the lining of the **placenta,** a tissue that is fed by blood vessels from the mother and is connected to the embryo by means of the **umbilical cord.** Through the placenta and umbilical cord, the embryo receives oxygen and nutrients from the mother and eliminates carbon dioxide and metabolic wastes into the mother's bloodstream. A membrane called the *placental barrier* allows these small molecules to pass through (as well as more dangerous substances, to be discussed shortly), but it prevents the quite large blood cells of embryo and mother from mingling (see Figure 4.1).

Meanwhile, the inner layers of the germinal cell mass are differentiating into an embryo. Influenced by both their genetic blueprint and their environment of neighboring cells, cells migrate to their appropriate locations, cluster into groups, take on specialized

BOX 4.1

Reproductive technologies: New conceptions of conception

Although many couples conceive children without intending to, many others have difficulty conceiving a child despite desperately wanting one. For example, adolescents and adults who have contracted sexually transmitted diseases may become infertile as a result (Steinberg, S., 1996). Difficulty conceiving is about as often traced to the man as to the woman; about 20% of the time, the source of the difficulty is unknown (Begley, 1995). "Assisted reproduction technologies" available through fertility clinics enable many couples who cannot conceive a child to do so. Some couples are helped in relatively simple ways. A man may be advised to wear looser pants and underwear (because an unusually high temperature in the testes interferes with sperm production). A woman may be asked to take her temperature in order to determine when she ovulates and is therefore most likely to become pregnant, or she may be prescribed fertility drugs to help her produce more eggs (drugs that therefore increase the odds of multiple births).

When simpler methods fail, some couples move on to more elaborate (and expensive) technologies. **Artificial insemination** has been used for years and involves injecting sperm, from a woman's partner or from a donor, into the uterus. In **in vitro fertilization (IVF)**, sperm fertilize eggs in a petri dish in the laboratory and then a few fertilized eggs are transferred to the woman's uterus in hopes that one will implant on the wall of the uterus. The first such "test-tube baby" was Baby Louise, born in England in 1978. Many variations of IVF are possible, depending on who provides the eggs and sperm. The couple wanting to have a child (the would-be biological mother and father) could donate both eggs and sperm. Or, at the other extreme, an infant conceived through IVF could wind up with five "parents": a sperm donor, an egg donor, a surrogate mother in whom the fertilized egg is implanted, and a caregiving mother and father (Beck, 1994)! Couples who seek IVF had better bring their checkbooks, as it costs at least $10,000 a try and is successful only about one time out of five (Begley, 1995).

What are the implications of using IVF and other reproductive technologies for the new family? Infertile couples may experience many heartbreaks in their quest for parenthood if try after try fails. But what if they succeed? To find out, Susan Golombok and her colleagues (1995) located families who had children through IVF using their own eggs and sperm, artificial insemination, egg donation, or both artificial insemination and egg donation and compared them with control families in which the children were conceived the usual way. The children were ages 4 to 8 at the time of the study, and the researchers looked at how involved parents were with their children as well as how the children were faring in terms of emotional adjustment, self-esteem, quality of relationships with parents and peers, and other developmental outcomes.

Importantly, there were no signs that parents cared less when their children were conceived with the help of someone else's sperm or egg and were therefore genetically unrelated to them than when their children were their biological offspring. In fact, parents who had conceived with the help of reproductive technology were warmer and more emotionally involved as parents than those who conceived naturally (see also van Balen, 1996). They were also less stressed by parenting. This may have been because they were older and because they had tried so hard and paid so much to become parents and undoubtedly wanted their children very much. Nonetheless, children in the four groups were equally well adjusted. Children conceived through today's reproductive technologies did not appear to be handicapped by their unique start in life, but they also did not seem to benefit from their parents' greater emotional involvement with them.

And what does the future hold for would-be parents who cannot conceive by any means? As always, they can adopt a child, but the day may also come when they can have a child through **cloning,** the process of converting a single cell from one animal into a new animal that is a duplicate of the original animal. In 1997, Keith Campbell, a Scottish cell biologist, reported that he had cloned a sheep from a single mammary cell obtained from an adult sheep named Rosie (Begley, 1997). Previous cloning experiments had been done with cells from embryos. Cloning adult cells had proven to be impossible because they have already become specialized to serve as brain cells, skin cells, or some other type of cell and could not be returned to their original undifferentiated state. Campbell and his colleagues were able to solve this problem by starving adult sheep cells of nutrients, thereby putting them into an inactive state in which genetic instructions that had been "turned off" when the cell became specialized could be "turned on again." An inactivated mammary cell from one ewe was inserted into another ewe's ovum (from which the nucleus had been removed), divided through mitosis, was implanted in a surrogate mother ewe, and ultimately became a cute and very normal lamb named Dolly.

Human cloning has not yet been performed, but experts believe that it will not be long. Would a cloned human really be identical in all ways to the person from whom he or she was cloned? If you internalized the message of Chapter 3, your answer should be, "No, because nature and nurture interact to make us what we are." Even though clones and their "parents" are genetically identical, they would be highly unlikely to have identical experiences throughout their lives. As a result, they would differ in many ways, just as identical twins do—a point that many people do not understand about cloning. Mainly, the prospect of human cloning horrifies many people: Will women be able to bear children without benefit of men—or even without benefit of sperm banks? Will Hitlers produce little Hitlers to carry on their evil work, as in the film *The Boys from Brazil*? Cloning may well join the roster of reproductive technologies available to infertile couples soon, and we as a society will have to make some critical decisions about whether and how this new technology should be used.

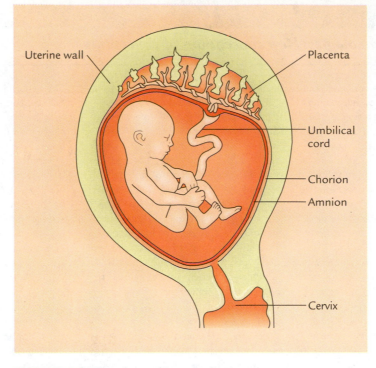

FIGURE 4.1 *The embryo and its prenatal environment*

functions, and become distinct organ systems (Aldridge, 1996). Development proceeds at a breathtaking pace. By only the fourth week after conception, a tiny heart has not only formed but has begun to beat. The eyes, ears, nose, and mouth rapidly take shape in the second month, and buds appear that will become arms and legs. During the second month, a very primitive nervous system also makes newly formed muscles contract. At only 60 days after conception, at the close of the period of the embryo, the organism is a little over an inch long and has a distinctly human appearance.

The important process of sexual differentiation begins during the seventh and eighth prenatal weeks. First, undifferentiated tissue becomes either male testes or female ovaries: If the embryo inherited a Y chromosome at conception, a gene on it calls for the construction of testes; in a genetic female with two X chromosomes, ovaries form instead. The testes of a male embryo secrete **testosterone,** the primary male sex hormone that stimulates the development of a male internal reproductive system, as well as another hormone that inhibits the development of a female internal reproductive system. In the absence of these hormones, the embryo develops the internal reproductive system of a female. Clearly, the period of the embryo is dramatic and highly important, a time when the structures that make us human evolve. Yet most pregnant women, either because they do not yet know they are pregnant or do not appreciate the value of early prenatal care, do not go to a doctor until *after* the 8th week of prenatal development, too late to prevent the damage that can be caused by an unhealthy lifestyle (Sadler, 1996).

The Fetal Period

The **period of the fetus** lasts from the ninth week of pregnancy until birth. Organ systems that formed during the period of the embryo continue to grow and begin to function. Harmful agents will no longer cause major malformations because organs have already formed, but they can stunt the growth of the fetus and interfere with the wiring of its rapidly developing nervous system.

In the third month of pregnancy, distinguishable external sex organs appear, the bones and muscles develop, and the fetus becomes quite frisky: By the end of the third month (that is, by the end of the first third of pregnancy, or trimester), it moves its arms, kicks its legs, makes fists, and even turns somersaults (Apgar & Beck, 1974). The fetus is only about three inches long, but it can swallow, digest food, and urinate. All this "behaving" contributes to the proper development of the nervous system, digestive system, and other systems of the body (Smotherman & Robinson, 1996).

During the *second trimester* (the fourth, fifth, and sixth months), more refined activities appear (including thumbsucking), and by the end of this period the sensory organs are functioning: Premature infants as young as 25 weeks respond to loud noises and bright lights (Allen & Capute, 1986).

At about 24 weeks of age, midway through the fifth month, the fetus reaches the **age of viability,** when survival outside the uterus is possible *if* the brain and respiratory system are well enough developed. The age of viability used to be older than 24 weeks, but medical techniques for keeping fragile babies alive have improved considerably over the past few decades.

During the *third trimester* (the seventh, eighth, and ninth months), the fetus gains weight at a tremendously rapid rate. This time is also critical in the development of the brain, as is the entire prenatal period (Spreen, Risser, & Edgell, 1995; Thompson, 1993; and see Chapter 5). Early in pregnancy, the basic architecture of the nervous system is laid down. During the second half of pregnancy, neurons not only multiply at an astonishing rate but also increase in size and develop an insulating cover, *myelin,* that improves their ability to transmit signals rapidly. Most importantly, guided by both a genetic blueprint and early sensory experience, neurons connect with one another and organize into working groups that control vision, memory, motor behavior, and other functions. For good reason, we should be very concerned about damage to the developing human during the first trimester, when the brain and other organs are forming. However, we should not overlook the significance of the second and third trimesters, which are critical to normal brain functioning and therefore to normal development (Diaz, 1997).

As the brain develops, the behavior of the fetus becomes more and more like the organized and adaptive behavior we see in the newborn. Recently, Janet DiPietro and her colleagues (1996b) repeatedly assessed heart rates, activity levels, and behavioral states such as sleeping and waking in 34 fetuses from the 20th week of pregnancy through the 39th week of pregnancy. During this period, fetal heart rates became more variable and more responsive to such stimuli as a vibrator placed on the mother's abdomen. Fetuses moved, on average, about once a minute and were active 20 to 30% of the time.

In addition, heart rate activity and movement became increasingly organized into the coherent patterns of waking and sleeping known as **infant states.** As Figure 4.3 shows, at 20 weeks of age, fetuses spent only about 17% of their time in one or another organized infant state such as quiet sleep, active sleep, or active waking. By the end of the prenatal period, they were in one distinct state or another at least 85% of the time. They spent most of their time sleeping, especially in active sleep. Whereas in the 20th week of pregnancy they were almost never active and awake, by the 32nd week they spent 11–16% of their time in an active, waking state (DiPietro et al., 1996b). The pat-

terns detected in this and other studies suggest that important changes in the nervous system occur 28 to 32 weeks after conception, when premature infants are typically well-equipped to survive. As the nervous system becomes more organized, so does behavior.

Interestingly, different fetuses displayed consistent differences in their patterns of heart rate and movement, and the researchers detected correlations between measures of fetal physiology and behavior and measures of infant temperament (DiPietro et al., 1996a). For example, active fetuses tended to be active, difficult, and unpredictable babies, and fetuses whose states were better organized were also better regulated at 3 months of age, as indicated by fewer wakings during the night. The message is clear: newborn behavior does not just spring from nowhere; it emerges long before birth. *There is a good deal of continuity between prenatal behavior and postnatal behavior.*

By the middle of the ninth month, the fetus is so large that its most comfortable position in cramped quarters is head down with limbs curled in (the "fetal position"). The mother's uterus contracts at irregular intervals during the last month of pregnancy. When these contractions are strong, frequent, and regular, the mother is in the first stage of labor and the prenatal period is drawing to a close. Under normal circumstances, birth will occur in a matter of hours.

The developing embryo-then-fetus is a vulnerable little creature. How can its development be optimized? What hazards does it face? A number of odd ideas about the effects of the prenatal physical environment on growth have been offered by "experts" throughout history. For example, it was once believed that pregnant women could enhance their chances of bearing sons if they exercised (thereby stimulating the muscle development of their fetuses!) and that sexual activity during pregnancy (now recommended until a couple of weeks before delivery) would cause the child to be sexually precocious (MacFarlane, 1977). And until the early 1940s, it was widely—and very wrongly—believed that the placenta was a marvelous screen that protected the embryo and fetus from nicotine, viruses, and all kinds of other hazards. Today, we understand that transactions between the organism and its environment begin at conception. When all is right, the prenatal environment provides just the stimulation and support needed for the fetus to mature physically and to develop a repertoire of behaviors that allow it to seek more stimulation, which in turn contributes to the development of still more sophisticated behavior (Smotherman & Robinson, 1996). When the prenatal environment is abnormal, development can be steered far off track, as we will now see by examining possible effects of a mother's physical and emotional condition, the diseases she has, the drugs she takes, and the environmental toxins she encounters.

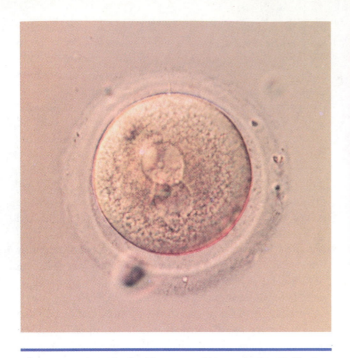

This egg is just being fertilized by a sperm during an in-vitro fertilization procedure. The fertilized egg is called a zygote.

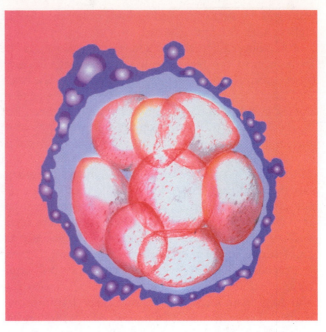

During the germinal period, through mitosis (cell division), the one-celled zygote becomes two cells, then four, then eight (as here), and so on.

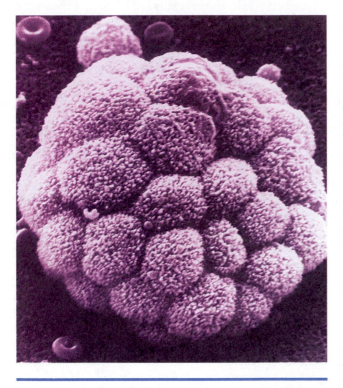

The cells form a hollow ball called the blastula that is ready to implant itself on the uterine wall.

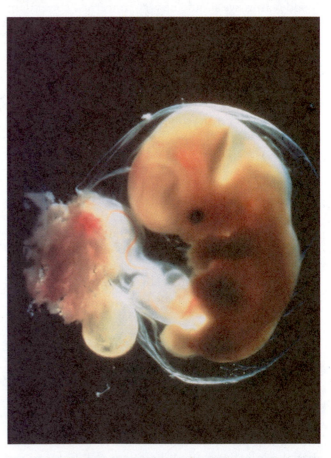

By 5 to 6 weeks after conception, head, torso, and limbs have formed, a tiny heart has begun to beat, and the umbilical cord (lower center) has taken shape to transport nutrients. By the end of the period of the embryo (8 weeks), all major organs have formed.

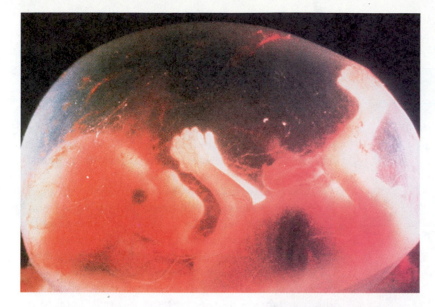

During the fetal period, growth is rapid. Here the fetus is approaching 4 months in the womb and has a distinctly human appearance.

As it nears the end of its nine months in the womb, the fetus shows many of the organized physiological states and many of the behaviors observed in newborns.

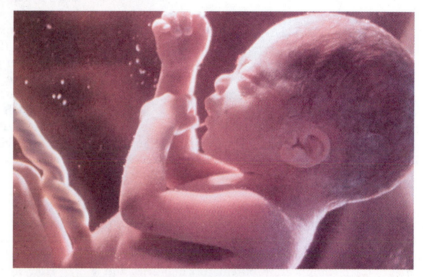

This photo shows a newborn super-imposed on a full-term mother's belly.

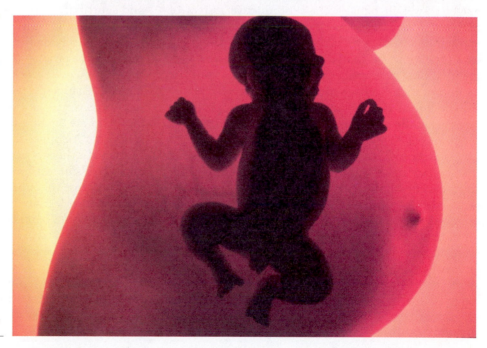

FIGURE 4.3 *Prenatal development*

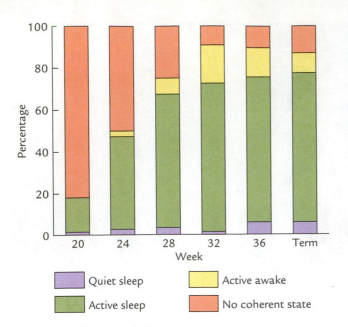

FIGURE 4.3 *Percentage of time the fetus spends in different states from the 20th week until the end of pregnancy. Time in one coherent state or another increases with age, and most time is spent in a state of active sleep.* (From DiPietro et al., 1996)

Legend:
- Quiet sleep
- Active sleep
- Active awake
- No coherent state

The Mother's State

The quality of the prenatal environment a mother provides is influenced by such factors as her age, emotional state, and nutritional status.

Age

The safest time to bear a child appears to be from about age 16 to age 35 (Amini et al., 1996; Dollberg et al., 1996). Young mothers have higher than normal rates of birth complications, premature deliveries, and low-birth-weight babies. The reproductive system of the very young teen may not be physically mature enough to sustain a fetus. However, the greater problem appears to be that teenagers often do not seek prenatal care, perhaps because they do not appreciate its importance. Teenage mothers and their babies are usually not at risk when they *do* receive appropriate care prenatally and during the birth process (Baker & Mednick, 1984).

As for mothers over 35 or so, they run a higher than average risk that their fetus will have chromosome abnormalities and may be spontaneously aborted as a result (see Chapter 3). The risks of birth complications, prematurity, and low birth weight are also higher for older women, even when the mother receives good prenatal care (Dollberg et al., 1996). Genetic defects in fetuses (which can be due to abnormalities in either sperm or ova) and a prenatal environment that is no longer nourishing may both contribute. Even so, the vast majority of older women have normal pregnancies and healthy babies (Leroy, 1988).

Emotional Condition

Does it matter how the mother feels about being pregnant or how her life is going while she is pregnant? Although most women are happy about conceiving a child, the fact remains that many pregnancies are unintended. Even mothers who want their babies are likely to experience some symptoms of anxiety and depression during their pregnancies. How might the fetus be affected by these negative emotions, as well as by more severe emotional stresses?

When a woman becomes emotionally aroused, her glands secrete powerful hormones such as adrenaline (also called epinephrine) that may cross the placental barrier and enter the fetus's bloodstream. At the very least, these hormones temporarily increase the fetus's motor activity. A temporarily stressful experience such as falling or receiving a scare will generally not damage mother or fetus (Stott & Latchford, 1976). It is only when mothers experience *prolonged and severe* emotional stress and anxiety during their pregnancies (for example, due to an abusive relationship or a series of crises in the family) that damage may be done. The most likely effect is stunted prenatal growth, which can result in low birth weight, premature birth, and birth complications (Lobel, 1994; Paarlberg et al., 1995). Babies of highly stressed mothers tend to be small, hyperactive, irritable, and quite irregular in their feeding, sleeping, and bowel habits (Sameroff & Chandler, 1975; Vaughn et al., 1987). Studies of monkeys and other animals show even more clearly that maternal stress during pregnancy can cause offspring to be socially inhibited, anxious, and reluctant to explore, even as adolescents (Clarke, Soto, Bergholz, & Schneider, 1996).

How might maternal stress stunt fetal growth and contribute to the offspring's irritability and anxiety? The mechanisms are not yet clear. The link between stressful experiences and small, premature babies might be the product of stress hormones, or changes in the immune system, or even a poor diet and unhealthy lifestyle (Paarlberg et al., 1995). Whatever the mechanism, it is clear that not all stressed mothers have babies who are small and arrive early. In one revealing study (McCubbin et al., 1996), pregnant mothers were brought to the laboratory and asked to take a somewhat stressful arithmetic test. Those whose blood pressures rose the most dramatically during this mild stress test were more likely than other women to deliver premature babies with low birth weights. Thus, the *presence* of stress in a woman's life may not be as important as her *responsiveness* to stress in determining outcomes.

The link between maternal stress and active, irritable infants is harder to explain. Hypotheses include the idea that stress directly causes behavioral problems, that the baby of an emotional mother may simply be genetically predisposed to have a "difficult" temperament, and that a mother's emotional tensions may affect her care of her baby *after* birth. Since experimentation is impossible, establishing causal links is difficult. Still, mothers who experience severe stress during pregnancy should probably seek therapeutic help. In one study, the babies of stressed mothers who received counseling weighed more at birth than the babies of stressed mothers who did not get help (Rothberg & Lits, 1991).

Nutritional Condition

Forty years ago, doctors often advised mothers to gain no more than two pounds a month while pregnant, believing that a total gain of 15 to 18 pounds was quite sufficient. Today, doctors are more likely to recommend a healthy, high-protein, high-calorie diet with a weight gain of two to five pounds during the first three months of pregnancy and about a pound a week thereafter—a total increase of 25 to 35 pounds (Ratcliffe, Byrd, & Sakornbut, 1996). We now know that inadequate prenatal nutrition can be harmful. Severe maternal malnutrition, which occurs during famine, stunts prenatal growth and produces small, underweight babies (Stein et al., 1975; Susser & Stein, 1994). The effects of malnutrition depend on when it occurs. During the first trimester, malnutrition can disrupt the formation of the spinal cord, result in fewer brain cells, and even cause stillbirth (Susser & Stein, 1994). During the third trimester, it is most likely to result in smaller neurons, a smaller brain, and a smaller child overall.

The offspring of malnourished mothers sometimes show cognitive deficits as infants and children. Poor prenatal nutrition also puts some children at risk for certain diseases in adulthood, especially hypertension, coronary heart disease, and diabetes (Barker, 1994; Goldberg & Prentice, 1994). In many cases, though, prenatal malnutrition does not have serious long-term effects on development (Golub et al., 1996). Much depends on whether a child receives an adequate diet and good care *post*natally. Dietary supplements, especially when combined with stimulating day care, can go a long way toward heading off the potentially damaging effects of prenatal malnutrition (Super, Herrera, & Mora, 1990; Zeskind & Ramey, 1981). Best, of course, is good nourishment before *and* after birth.

Teratogens

A **teratogen** is any disease, drug, or other environmental agent that can harm a developing fetus (for example, by causing deformities, blindness, brain damage, or even death). The list of teratogens has grown frighteningly long over the years, and there are many more potential teratogens in the environment whose effects on development have not yet been assessed. Before considering the effects of some major teratogens, let's emphasize that over 90% of babies born in the United States are normal and that many of those born with defects have mild, temporary, or reversible problems (Baird, Anderson, Newcombe, & Lowry, 1988; Heinonen, Slone, & Shapiro, 1977).

Let me begin with a few generalizations about the effects of teratogens, which I will then illustrate with examples (Abel, 1989; Friedman & Polifka, 1996; Spreen et al., 1984):

1. The effects of a teratogenic agent are worst during the critical period when an organ system grows most rapidly.
2. Not all embryos and fetuses are affected, or affected equally, by a teratogen.
3. Susceptibility to harm is determined by the unborn child's genetic makeup as well as by the mother's, and by the quality of the prenatal environment.
4. The higher the exposure to a teratogen, the more likely it is that serious damage will occur.
5. The effects of a teratogen often depend on the quality of the postnatal environment.

Let's look more closely at the first generalization, for it is particularly important. A period of rapid growth is a **critical period** for that organ system: a time during which the developing organism is especially sensitive to environmental influences, positive or negative. As you'll recall, organogenesis takes place during the period of the embryo (weeks 3 to 8 of prenatal development). As Figure 4.4 shows, it is during this time—before a woman is even likely to know she is pregnant—that most organ systems are most vulnerable to damage. Moreover, each organ has a critical period that corresponds to its own time of most rapid development (for example, weeks 3 to 6 for the heart, 4 to 7 for the arms). Once an organ or body part is fully formed, it is usually less susceptible to damage. However, because some organ systems—most importantly, the nervous system—can be damaged throughout pregnancy, sensitive periods might be a better term than "critical periods."

Diseases

The principles of teratology can be illustrated by surveying just a few of the many diseases that can disrupt prenatal development.

Rubella. A woman affected by **rubella** (German measles) during pregnancy may bear a child with one or more of a variety of defects, including blindness, deafness, heart defects, and mental retardation. Rubella is most dangerous during the first trimester, a critical period in which the eyes, ears, heart, and brain are rapidly forming. Yet not all babies whose mothers had

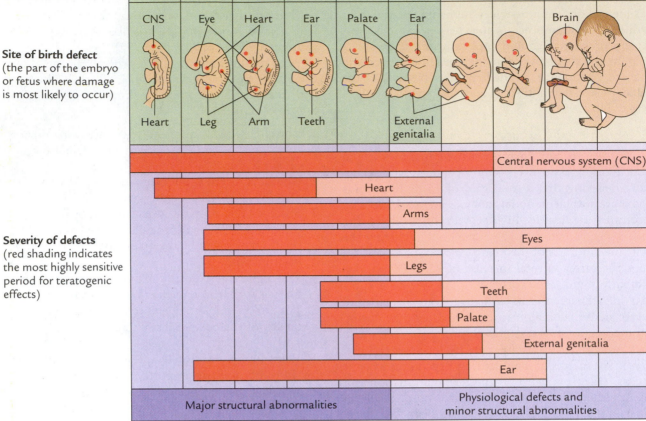

Site of birth defect
(the part of the embryo
or fetus where damage
is most likely to occur)

Severity of defects
(red shading indicates
the most highly sensitive
period for teratogenic
effects)

FIGURE 4.4 *The critical periods of prenatal development. Teratogens are more likely to produce major structural abnormalities during the third through the eighth prenatal week. Note, however, that many organs and body parts remain sensitive to teratogenic agents throughout the nine-month prenatal period.* (Adapted from Moore, 1977)

rubella, even during the most critical period of prenatal development, will have problems. Birth defects occur in 60% to 85% of babies whose mothers had the disease in the first eight weeks of pregnancy, in about 50% of those infected in the third month, and in only 16% of those infected in weeks 13 to 20 (Kelley-Buchanan, 1988). Consistent with the critical-period principle, damage to the nervous system, eyes, and heart is most likely during that part of the first eight weeks of pregnancy when each of these organs is forming, whereas deafness is more likely when the mother contracts rubella in weeks 6 to 13 of the pregnancy. Today, doctors stress that a woman should not try to become pregnant unless she has been immunized against rubella or has already had it.

Syphilis. Now consider another teratogen, the sexually transmitted disease **syphilis.** Like the babies of mothers who have rubella, the babies of mothers who have syphilis often suffer from blindness, deafness, heart problems, or brain damage, assuming that they live long enough to be born (Miller, 1976). This illus-

trates the principle that different teratogens, here syphilis and rubella, can be responsible for the same problem. However, whereas rubella is most damaging early in pregnancy, syphilis is most damaging in the middle and later stages of pregnancy. This is because syphilitic organisms cannot cross the placental barrier until the 18th prenatal week. A mother-to-be who finds out she has the disease can thus be treated with antibiotics long before the disease can harm her fetus. A number of maternal conditions that may affect prenatal development are listed in Table 4.1.

AIDS. The sexually transmitted disease of greatest concern today is **acquired immune deficiency syndrome (AIDS),** the disease caused by the human immunodeficiency virus (HIV). AIDS destroys the immune system and makes victims susceptible to "opportunistic" infections that may eventually kill them. HIV-infected mothers can transmit the virus to their babies (1) prenatally, if the virus passes through the placenta; (2) during birth, when blood may be exchanged between mother and child as the umbilical cord separates

TABLE 4.1

Maternal diseases and conditions that may affect an embryo, fetus, or newborn

Disease or Condition	Effects
SEXUALLY TRANSMITTED DISEASES	
Acquired immune deficiency syndrome (AIDS)	If transmitted from mother to child, destroys defenses against disease and may lead to death. Mothers can acquire it through sexual contact or contact with contaminated blood (see text).
Gonorrhea	Attacks the eyes of the child during birth; blindness is prevented by administering silver nitrate eyedrops to newborns.
Herpes simplex (genital herpes)	May cause eye and brain damage or death in the first trimester. Mothers with active herpes are advised to undergo cesarean deliveries to avoid infecting their babies during delivery, but the odds of such infection are actually low (Ratcliffe, Byrd, & Sakornbut, 1996).
Syphilis	Untreated, can cause miscarriage or serious birth defects such as blindness and mental retardation (see text).
OTHER MATERNAL CONDITIONS OR DISEASES	
Chicken pox	Can cause spontaneous abortion or premature delivery and slow growth, though not malformations.
Influenza (flu)	The more powerful strains can cause spontaneous abortions or neural abnormalities early in pregnancy.
Rubella	May cause blindness, deafness, mental retardation, and heart defects (see text).
Toxemia	Affecting about 5% of mothers in the third trimester, its mildest form, *preeclampsia*, causes high blood pressure and rapid weight gain in the mother. Untreated, preeclampsia may become *eclampsia* and cause maternal convulsions and coma and death of mother and/or unborn child. Surviving infants may be brain damaged (Simpson, 1997).
Toxoplasmosis	This mild and common disease, caused by a parasite present in raw meat and cat feces, can produce serious eye or brain damage or even death in the unborn child.

SOURCES: Based in part on information from Edelman and Mandle (1990); Kelley-Buchanan (1988); Ratcliffe, Byrd, & Sakornbut (1996); and Simpson & Creehan (1996)

from the placenta, or (3) after birth, if the virus is transmitted during breast feeding (Eldred & Chaisson, 1996). Despite all these possibilities for infection, it appears that only around 25% of babies born to HIV-infected mothers are infected (Gabiano et al., 1992); the rate is much lower if the mother is taking AZT to treat the HIV (Cowley, 1994; Friedman & Polifka, 1996). Infected infants live longer today than they did at the outset of the AIDS epidemic, thanks to the development of appropriate treatments; over half are now living beyond age 6 and many are surviving into adolescence (Hutton, 1996). Mother-to-child transmission of HIV in the United States is especially common among inner-city minority women who take drugs intravenously or have sexual partners who do (Eldred & Chaisson, 1996).

Drugs

Up to 60% of pregnant women take at least one prescription or over-the-counter drug during pregnancy (Schnoll, 1986). Under a doctor's close supervision, medications used to treat ailments and medical conditions are usually safe for mother and fetus (McMahon & Katz, 1996). However, certain individuals exposed to certain drugs in certain doses at certain times during the prenatal period are damaged for life.

Thalidomide. In 1960, a West German drug company began to market **thalidomide,** an over-the-counter tranquilizer that was said to relieve morning sickness (the periodic nausea many women experience during the first trimester of pregnancy). Presumably, the drug was perfectly safe, for it had no ill effects in tests on pregnant rats. More than any other drug, thalidomide alerted the world to the dangers of taking drugs during pregnancy.

Thousands of women who used thalidomide during the first two months of pregnancy gave birth to babies with tragic defects—most notably, with all or

FIGURE 4.5 *This boy has the flipper-like arms and deformed hands produced by the drug thalidomide.*

parts of their limbs missing, with the feet or hands attached directly to the torso like flippers. (See Figure 4.5.) Eyes, ears, noses, and hearts were also often badly deformed. It soon became clear that there are critical periods for different deformities. If the mother had taken thalidomide on or around the 35th day after her last menstrual period, her baby was likely to be born without ears. If she had taken it on the 39th through 41st day after her last menstruation, the baby often had grossly deformed arms or no arms at all; if thalidomide was taken between the 40th and 46th day, the child was likely to have deformed legs or no legs. And if the mother waited until the 52nd day after menstruating before using thalidomide, her baby was usually not affected (Apgar & Beck, 1974).

Tobacco. Pregnant women today do not take thalidomide, of course, but many do smoke. Although the rate has fallen in recent years, about 14% of pregnant women smoke during pregnancy, despite warnings on cigarette packages that smoking may be damaging to fetuses (Guyer et al., 1996). The babies of mothers who smoke tend to grow more slowly in the womb and are likely to be born prematurely and small (Fried et al., 1992; Nordentoft et al., 1996). In some, the growth of the limbs is stunted because smoking restricts blood flow to the fetus (Källén, 1997). The more the mother smokes, the stronger the growth retardation. "Passive smoking" is risky as well; babies have lower birth weights if their *fathers* smoke than if they do not (Rubin et al., 1986). Often the small babies of smokers experience catch-up growth after they are born and reach normal size by late infancy, but the more their mothers smoke, the less likely it is that their growth will catch up completely (Streissguth et al., 1994).

The babies of smokers are also more susceptible than other babies to respiratory infections and breathing difficulties (Diaz, 1997). In fact, even smoking half a pack a day, especially if a mother is also anemic, can increase the odds of sudden infant death syndrome (SIDS), in which a sleeping baby suddenly stops breathing and dies (Bulterys, Greenland, & Kraus, 1990). Finally, some studies link maternal smoking to at least mild cognitive difficulties and to behavior problems such as impulsivity (Diaz, 1997). However, there is disagreement about whether these psychological effects endure beyond childhood.

In sum, maternal smoking during pregnancy is unwise, as it slows fetal growth and contributes to respiratory and, possibly, cognitive difficulties. These effects may be due to nicotine and other chemicals in cigarettes as well as to the fact that smoking reduces the flow of blood and oxygen to the fetus.

Alcohol. A cluster of symptoms dubbed **fetal alcohol syndrome (FAS)** was identified in 1973 (Jones, Smith, Ulleland, & Streissguth, 1973). The most noticeable physical symptoms are a small head and distinctive facial abnormalities (see Figure 4.6). Children with FAS are smaller and lighter than normal, and their physical growth lags behind that of their age mates.

Affected children show signs of brain damage. As newborns, they are likely to display excessive irritability, hyperactivity, seizures, or tremors. The majority of children with fetal alcohol syndrome score well below average on intelligence tests throughout childhood and adolescence, and many are mentally retarded (Abel, 1981; Streissguth, Randels, & Smith, 1991). Hyperactive behavior and attention deficits are also common among these children. Longitudinal research by Ann Streissguth and her colleagues indicates that over 90% of them have mental health problems later in life; they are likely to get into trouble at school, break the law, and lose jobs (Colburn, 1996). About 20% of pregnant women drink during pregnancy, and up to 4% abuse alcohol (Stratton, Howe, & Battaglia, 1996). As a result, 3 in 1000 babies nationally are born with FAS and suffer its symptoms all their lives.

How much drinking does it take to harm an unborn baby? In keeping with the dosage principle of teratology, the symptoms of fetal alcohol syndrome are most severe when the level of alcohol is highest—that is, when the mother is clearly an alcoholic. Heavy drinkers (who consume five or more drinks a day) run a 30% or higher risk of having a child with fetal alcohol syndrome (Vorhees & Mollnow, 1987). However, even moderate alcohol consumption or "social drinking" (1–3 ounces a day) can lead to less serious problems called "fetal alcohol effects" in some babies. Such effects include retarded physical growth and minor physical abnormalities, as well as such problems as

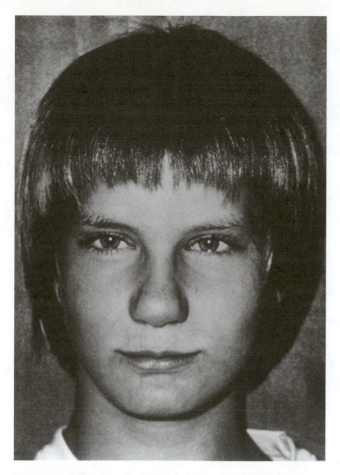

FIGURE 4.6 *This girl's widely spaced eyes, flattened nose, and underdeveloped lip are characteristics common of fetal alcohol syndrome.*

condition influence its ability to resist and recover from damage. So, for example, one fraternal twin may show all the physical abnormalities associated with FAS whereas the other twin, though exposed to the same prenatal environment, may show almost none; by contrast, identical twins respond very similarly when they are exposed to alcohol prenatally (Streissguth & Dehaene, 1993). As our third principle of teratology states, both the child's and the mother's characteristics influence the extent to which a given teratogen proves damaging.

Cocaine. Recently, much concern has centered on the risks associated with cocaine use and the characteristics of so-called "crack" babies. Although there is no "cocaine syndrome" with characteristic physical abnormalities like those associated with fetal alcohol syndrome, cocaine use can indeed damage the fetus (Lester, Freier, & LaGasse, 1995). It can cause spontaneous abortion in the first trimester of pregnancy and premature detachment of the placenta or fetal strokes later in pregnancy (Diaz, 1997). Because cocaine constricts the blood vessels, reducing the flow of oxygen to the fetus, and because it suppresses appetite, it contributes to fetal malnourishment, retarded growth, and low birth weight (Hawley & Disney, 1992). At birth, a small proportion of babies born to cocaine users experience withdrawal-like symptoms such as tremors and extreme irritability, as well as respiratory difficulties (Diaz, 1997; Singer, Farkas, & Kliegman, 1992). Their cries are either frequent and high-pitched or infrequent and more subdued (Lester et al., 1991). This suggests that exposure to cocaine has caused them to be either extremely irritable or extremely sluggish (Lester et al., 1991).

Cocaine-exposed infants seem to take less interest in learning than other infants (Alessandri et al., 1993), and they may be at risk for later deficits in their cognitive and language development, as well as in their play and social skills (Lester et al., 1995). However, we still know too little about the longer-term development of the babies of cocaine and crack cocaine users. And we often cannot be sure whether any problems they do display are due to prenatal exposure to cocaine or to other prenatal or postnatal risk factors they may experience as the children of substance-abusing parents (Hawley & Disney, 1992).

Table 4.2 catalogs a number of other substances and their known or suspected effects on the child. What should we make of these findings? We now understand that drugs do not damage all fetuses exposed to them in a simple, direct way. Instead, complex transactions between an individual with a certain genetic makeup and his or her prenatal, perinatal, and postnatal environments influence whether or not prenatal drug exposure does lasting damage (Jacobson &

poor fine and gross motor skills, attention deficits, and low IQ and mental performance scores. No amount of drinking seems to be entirely safe. Even a mother who drinks less than an ounce a day is likely to have a sluggish or placid newborn (Jacobson, Fein, et al., 1984) whose mental development is slightly below average (Jacobson et al., 1993). What's more, there is no well-defined critical period before or after which fetal alcohol effects cannot occur; drinking late in pregnancy can be as risky as drinking soon after conception (Jacobson et al., 1993).

Why do some babies of drinking mothers suffer ill effects while others do not? The chances of damage depend in part on the mother's physiology—for example, on how efficiently she metabolizes alcohol and, therefore, how much is passed on to the fetus (Abel, 1989). Complicating the situation is the fact that problem drinkers often have other problems that can aggravate the effects of alcohol on the fetus or cause damage in their own right—among them malnutrition, use of drugs other than alcohol, cigarette smoking, and lack of prenatal care (Stratton et al., 1996). In addition, the embryo's genetic makeup and physical

TABLE 4.2

Some drugs taken by the mother that affect the fetus or newborn

Drug	Effects
Alcohol	Small head, facial abnormalities, heart defects, low birth weight, and intellectual retardation (fetal alcohol syndrome; see text).
Aspirin	Occasional low dose okay, but used in large quantities, may cause neonatal bleeding and gastrointestinal discomfort. Aspirin *may* be associated with low birth weight and lower intelligence test scores, and mild motor skill deficits (Barr, Streissguth, Darby, & Sampson, 1990; Vorhees & Mollnow, 1987).
Marijuana	Heavy use of marijuana has been linked to premature birth, low birth weight, and mild behavioral abnormalities, such as irritability at birth, but does not cause physical abnormalities or have long-lasting effects on most children (Fried, O'Connell, & Watkinson, 1992).
Narcotics	Addiction to heroin, codeine, methadone, or morphine increases the risk of premature delivery and low birth weight. The newborn is often addicted and experiences potentially fatal withdrawal symptoms; e.g., vomiting and convulsions. Longer-term cognitive deficits are sometimes evident.
Sex hormones	Birth control pills containing female hormones have been known to produce heart defects and cardiovascular problems (Heinonen et al., 1977; Schardein, 1985), but today's pill formulas are safer. Progesterone in drugs used to prevent miscarriage may masculinize the fetus. Diethylstilbestrol (DES), once also prescribed to prevent miscarriage, caused reproductive problems and cervical cancer in exposed daughters (Hamm, 1981).
Stimulants	Caffeine use has been linked to abnormal reflexes and irritability at birth (Jacobson, Fein, et al., 1984) but does not seem to have longer-lasting effects on development (Barr & Streissguth, 1991). Cocaine use can cause spontaneous abortion, slows fetal growth, and may result in later learning and behavior problems (see text). Amphetamine use has been linked to aggressive behavior and low school achievement (Billing et al., 1994).
Tobacco	Babies of smokers tend to be small and premature, have respiratory problems, and sometimes show intellectual deficits or behavior problems later in development. "Passive smoking" is risky as well (see text).

SOURCES: Based in part on information from Abel (1989); Diaz (1997); Friedman & Polifka (1996); and Kelley-Buchanan (1988)

Jacobson, 1996b). Still, women who are planning to become pregnant or who are pregnant should avoid all drugs unless they are prescribed by a physician and essential to health.

Environmental Hazards

Radiation. A mother can control what she ingests, but sometimes she cannot avoid a hazardous external environment. After atomic bombs were dropped on Hiroshima and Nagasaki in 1945, not one pregnant woman who was within one-half mile of the blasts gave birth to a live child, and 75% of those who were within a mile and a quarter of the blasts had stillborn infants or seriously handicapped children who died soon after birth (Apgar & Beck, 1974); surviving children of these mothers had a higher than normal rate of mental retardation (Vorhees & Mollnow, 1987). Even clinical doses of radiation, like those used in X rays and cancer treatment, are capable of causing mutations, spontaneous abortions, and a variety of birth defects, especially if the mother is exposed during the first trimester of pregnancy. For this reason, expectant mothers are routinely advised to avoid X rays unless they are essential to their own survival, and women who work with X-ray equipment must take proper precautions. (Despite some concern about it, by the way, a woman who works in front of a computer screen all day does not appear to place her fetus at risk (Parazzini et al., 1993).)

Pollutants. Pollutants in the air we breathe and the water we drink include "heavy metals," such as lead, which are discharged by smelting operations and other industries and may be present in paint, dust, or water pipes in old houses. Children who were exposed to lead prenatally show impaired intellectual functioning as infants in proportion to the amount of lead in their umbilical cords (Bellinger et al., 1987; and see Figure 4.7). This is true even when other differences among children, such as socioeconomic status, are controlled for. However, the same high levels of lead in the blood *after* birth are not related to poorer mental performance, which further indicates that the prenatal period is an especially vulnerable time (Bellinger et al., 1987).

Although the polluting chemicals called **polychlorinated biphenyls (PCBs)**, formerly used in electrical insulation, were outlawed in 1977, they are still

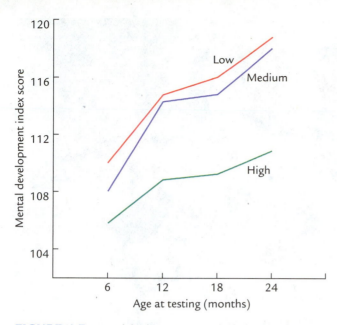

FIGURE 4.7 *Mental development scores of infants with low, medium, or high levels of lead in their umbilical cords before birth* (From Bellinger et al., 1987)

present in the environment, and are another hazard. Joseph Jacobson and his colleagues found that newborns who were exposed to low levels of PCBs because their mothers ate fish from Lake Michigan during pregnancy were neurologically immature, and that some were also born small or prematurely (Jacobson, Jacobson, et al., 1984). At age 4 these children showed deficiencies in short-term memory, to an extent that corresponded to the dose of PCBs they received prenatally (Jacobson, Jacobson, & Humphrey, 1990). Even at age 11 they scored an average of six points lower on IQ tests than control children (Jacobson & Jacobson, 1996a). The principle of critical periods was also borne out: Although larger quantities of PCBs are passed through breast feeding than through the placenta, exposure after birth through nursing had no relationship to cognitive performance.

It is critical to note that a *father's* exposure to environmental toxins can affect a couple's children. How? It seems that a father's prolonged exposure to radiation, anesthetic gases used in operating rooms, pesticides, or other environmental toxins can damage the chromosomes in his sperm and cause genetic defects in his children (Stone, 1992; Strigini et al., 1990). Clearly, there is a critical need for more research aimed at identifying a huge number of chemicals, wastes, and other environmental hazards that may affect unborn children.

Summing Up

The message is clear: The chemistry of the prenatal environment often determines whether an embryo

or fetus survives and how it looks and functions after birth. By becoming familiar with the information touched on here, and by keeping up with new knowledge, parents-to-be can do much to increase the already high odds that their unborn child will be normal as it approaches its next challenge: the birth process.

THE PERINATAL ENVIRONMENT

The **perinatal environment** is the environment surrounding birth; it includes influences such as drugs given to the mother during delivery, delivery practices, and the social environment shortly after birth. Like the prenatal environment, the perinatal environment can greatly affect human development.

Childbirth is a three-stage process. The first stage of labor begins as the mother experiences *contractions* of the uterus spaced at 10-minute to 15-minute intervals and ends when her cervix has fully dilated (widened) so that the fetus's head can pass through. This stage of labor lasts an average of 8 to 14 hours for firstborn children, compared to only 3 to 8 hours for later-borns. The second stage of labor is *delivery,* which begins as the fetus's head passes through the cervix into the vagina and ends when the baby emerges from the mother's body. This is the time when the mother is often told to "bear down" (push) with each contraction to assist her baby through the birth canal. A quick delivery may take a half hour, whereas a long one may take more than an hour and a half. Finally, the third stage of the birth process is the *afterbirth,* or the expulsion of the placenta, which lasts only a few minutes.

When the birth process is completed, the mother (and often the father too, if he is present) is typically physically exhausted, relieved to be through the ordeal of giving birth, and exhilarated all at once. Meanwhile, the fetus has been thrust from its quite carefree, but cramped, existence into a strange new world.

Possible Hazards

In the large majority of births, the entire process goes smoothly, and parents and newborn quickly begin their relationship. Occasionally problems arise.

Anoxia

One clear hazard during the birth process is **anoxia,** or oxygen shortage (also called asphyxia). Anoxia can occur for any number of reasons—for example, because the umbilical cord becomes pinched or tangled during birth, because sedatives given to the mother reach the fetus and interfere with the baby's

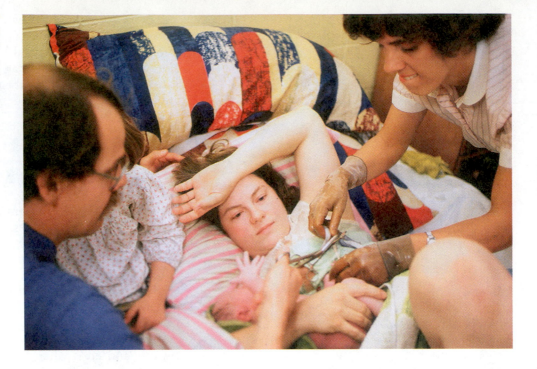

breathing, or because mucus lodged in the baby's throat prevents normal breathing. Why is anoxia dangerous? Largely because brain cells die if they are starved of oxygen for more than a few minutes. Severe anoxia can result in *cerebral palsy,* a motor disability in which the affected individual has difficulties controlling muscles of the arms, legs, or head (Vaughn, McKay, & Behrman, 1984). Severe anoxia can also cause mental retardation.

Milder cases of anoxia make some infants irritable at birth or delay their motor and cognitive development. However, many victims, especially those whose environments after birth are optimal, function perfectly normally later in childhood (Sameroff & Chandler, 1975). In one study, for example, children who suffered from relatively brief anoxia scored below normal as a group on measures of intellectual development at age 3 but had average intelligence test scores by age 7 (Corah et al., 1965). Only a minority of these children showed persisting problems. Thus prolonged anoxia can cause permanent disabilities, but the effects of milder anoxia are typically overcome as a child gets older.

Another bit of good news is that the chances of anoxia have been greatly reduced by the use of fetal monitoring procedures during labor and delivery. Doctors are now alert to the risk of anoxia if the fetus is not positioned in the usual head-down position, for then the birth process takes longer. If the baby is born feet or buttocks first (a **breech presentation**) delivery becomes more complex, although the vast majority of breech babies are normal. A vaginal delivery is nearly impossible for the one fetus in a hundred lying side-

ways in the uterus. The fetus must be turned to assume a head-first position or be delivered by **cesarean section,** a surgical procedure in which an incision is made in the mother's abdomen and uterus so that the baby can be removed. And that leads us to the potential hazards associated with delivery procedures and technologies themselves.

Complicated Delivery

During the 19th century, many doctors believed that the routine use of *forceps* (an instrument resembling an oversized pair of salad tongs) was the best way to deliver babies (Edwards & Waldorf, 1984). Unfortunately, the use of forceps on the soft skull of the newborn sometimes caused serious problems, including cranial bleeding and brain damage. Now forceps are used with great care only when a baby may die if it is not removed.

As for the cesarean section, it too has been controversial. Use of this alternative to normal vaginal delivery has prevented the death of many babies—for example, when the baby is too large or the mother is too small to permit normal delivery, when a fetus out of position cannot be repositioned, or when fetal monitoring reveals that a birth complication is likely. Medical advances have made cesarean sections about as safe as vaginal deliveries, and few ill effects on mothers and infants have been observed (Kochanevich-Wallace et al., 1988). However, mothers who have "C-sections" do take longer to recover from the birth process (Gottlieb & Barrett, 1986), and they are less satisfied with the birth process and less positive toward and involved with their babies, at least during the first month after birth (DiMatteo et al., 1996). Nonetheless, the development of babies born by cesarean appears to be perfectly normal (Mutryn, 1993).

Many observers began to question why cesarean deliveries became so much more common over the past two or three decades, until they accounted for "almost 25% of births in the United States in 1988 (Clarke & Taffel, 1996). The U.S. government has made it a national goal to decrease the rate, and it has indeed dropped down closer to 20%. It is also understood now that mothers who have one cesarean birth need not have all their subsequent babies by cesarean, as was believed only a decade ago (Simpson & Creehan, 1996). Nonetheless, some obstetricians continue to rely heavily on this procedure because it protects them from the costly malpractice suits that might arise from complications in vaginal deliveries (Localio et al., 1993). Overall, birth by cesarean delivery can be lifesaving in some cases and is unlikely to disrupt normal development but is more common than it needs to be in our society.

Medications

Concerns have also been raised about medications given to mothers during the birth process—analgesics and anesthetics to reduce their pain, sedatives to relax them, and stimulants to induce or intensify uterine contractions (Simpson & Creehan, 1996). Yvonne Brackbill and her associates (1985) found that babies whose mothers receive large doses of obstetrical medication smile infrequently, are generally sluggish and irritable, and are difficult to feed or cuddle during the first few weeks of life. In short, they act as though they are drugged. Think about it: Doses of medication large enough to affect mothers can have much greater impacts on newborns who weigh only 7 pounds and have immature circulatory and excretory systems that cannot get rid of drugs for days or even weeks.

So should mothers avoid obstetric medications at all costs? That advice is perhaps too strong. For example, some women are at risk of experiencing birth complications because of their size or body shape or because their babies are large. For such women, sedatives in appropriate doses can actually *reduce* the chances of complications such as anoxia (Myers & Myers, 1979).

It is also important to recognize that there are many drugs, some safer than others. For example, sedatives such as Demerol disrupt the newborn's functioning and responsiveness to stimuli more than local anesthetics that deaden the pelvic area only (Emory, Schlackman, & Fiano, 1996). How much of a drug is taken, when it is taken, and by which mother it is taken are also important. More alert to the potentially negative effects of medications given during labor and delivery, doctors today are more likely than doctors of the past to use drugs only when clearly necessary and to use the least toxic drugs in the lowest effective doses at the safest times (Simpson & Creehan, 1996). Thus, taking obstetric medications is not as risky a business today as it once was, but it is still a decision that requires weighing the pros and cons carefully.

Identifying High-Risk Newborns

In the end, a small minority of infants are in great jeopardy at birth because of genetic defects, prenatal hazards, or perinatal damage. It is essential to these infants' survival and well-being that they are identified as early as possible. Although much more sophisticated methods of assessing the health and functioning of newborns exist (Molfese, 1989), the **Apgar test** is routinely used to provide a quick assessment of the newborn's heart rate, respiration, color, muscle tone, and reflexes (Apgar & James, 1962; and see Table 4.3). It is given immediately after birth and then 5 minutes later.

The simple test yields scores of 0, 1, or 2 for each of the five factors. The five scores are then added to yield a total score that can range from 0 to 10. Infants who score 7 or higher are in good shape. However, infants scoring 4 or lower are at risk—their heartbeats are sluggish or nonexistent, their muscles are limp,

TABLE 4.3

The Apgar test			
	Score		
Characteristic	*0*	*1*	*2*
Heart rate	Absent	Slow (under 100 beats per minute)	Over 100 beats per minute
Respiratory effort	Absent	Slow or irregular	Good; baby is crying
Muscle tone	Flaccid; limp	Weak; some flexion	Strong; active motion
Color	Blue or pale	Body pink, extremities blue	Completely pink
Reflex irritability	No response	Frown, grimace, or weak cry	Vigorous cry

and their breathing, if they are breathing, is shallow and irregular. These babies will immediately experience a different postnatal environment from the normal baby's, for they require medical intervention in intensive care units to survive, as we will see at the end of the chapter.

The birth of a baby is a dramatic experience for the whole family. However, it was not that long ago that most hospitals barred fathers from the delivery room and snatched babies away from their mothers soon after delivery to place them in nurseries. Let us briefly look at the birth experience from a family perspective.

The Mother's Experience

What is it really like to give birth to a child? In a study of Swedish mothers (Waldenström et al., 1996), most mothers admitted they experienced severe pain and a good deal of anxiety, including feelings of outright panic. Yet most also emerged from the delivery room feeling very good about their achievement and their ability to cope ("I did it!"). Overall, 77% felt the experience was positive, and 10% said it was negative. Despite longer labors and more medication, first-time mothers did not perceive labor and delivery much differently than experienced mothers did.

What factors influence a mother's experience? Psychological factors such as the mother's attitude toward her pregnancy, her knowledge and expectations about the birth process, her sense of control over childbirth, and the social support she receives from her partner or someone else are important determinants of her experience of delivery and of her new baby (Waldenström et al., 1996; Wilcock, Kobayashi, & Murray, 1997). Social support can be especially important. When the father, or another supportive person whose main role is to comfort the mother, is present during labor and delivery, women experience less pain, use less medication, are less likely to have cesarean sections, and are likely to feel better about the whole birth process (Hodnett & Osborn, 1989; Kennell et al., 1991).

Cultural Factors

The experience of childbearing is shaped by the cultural context in which it occurs. For example, different cultures have different views of the desirability of having children. In some, a large family is a status symbol, whereas in the People's Republic of China, a "one-child policy" discourages multiple childbearing in hopes of slowing population growth and raising the standard of living. As a result of this policy, the average number of children a Chinese woman bears has dropped from 4.8 in 1970 to 1.8 in 1994 (Post, 1994). The ratio of boys to girls has also changed; many parents want their one child to be a boy and therefore abort female fetuses who have been identified through ultrasound tests or abandon their female babies after they are born (Post, 1994).

Practices surrounding birth also differ widely (Chalmers, 1996; S. Steinberg, 1996). Among the Pokot people of Kenya, for example, cultural beliefs and rituals help to ensure strong social support of the mother and a successful birth (O'Dempsey, 1988). The whole community celebrates the coming birth, and the father-to-be must stop hunting lest he be killed by animals. As a result, he is available to support his wife. A midwife, aided by female relatives, delivers the baby. The placenta is buried in the goat enclosure, and the baby is washed in cold water and given a mixture of hot ash and boiled herbs so that it will vomit the amniotic fluid that it has swallowed. Mothers are given plenty of time to recover. They go into seclusion for a month and devote themselves entirely to their babies for three months.

In Uttar Predesh in northern India, by contrast, the blood associated with childbirth is viewed as polluting, and the whole event as shameful (Jeffery & Jeffery, 1993). The baby is delivered by a *dai*, a poorly paid attendant hired by the woman's mother-in-law who hates her menial, disgusting job, provides no pain relievers, discourages the mother from crying out in pain, and offers little emotional support. The mother is kept in the house for several days and in the family compound for weeks so that she will not pollute others. Because the baby is also believed to be polluted, its hair is shaved off.

Many observers charge that childbirth in highly industrialized Western societies has become too "medicalized" and that we should go back to the traditional ways observed in less developed countries. Yet as the Indian example illustrates, not all "traditional" practices are in the best interests of parents and babies (Jeffery & Jeffery, 1993). Also, Western societies do a far better job of preventing mother and infant mortality than developing countries. In some areas of sub-Saharan Africa, for example, about 15% of babies die during childbirth or in the first year of life (Caldwell, 1996). In Western, industrial societies, infant mortality rates have dropped from almost 20% in the late 18th century to only 1% recently (Caldwell, 1996). The secret to a more optimal birth experience may be to blend beneficial traditional practices such as offering emotional support to new mothers with modern medical know-how (Chalmers, 1996).

Early Bonding

How important are the first few hours after birth to the relationship between parent and child? Marshall Klaus and John Kennell hypothesized that the first 6 to 12 hours after birth are a sensitive period for the emotional *bonding* of a mother to her infant. The mother is likely to be exhilarated and often shows an

engrossment with her baby—an intense fascination and a desire to touch, hold, and caress this new family member (Greenberg & Morris, 1974; Peterson, Mehl, & Liederman, 1979). She is especially ready to develop a strong affection for her baby, and her baby is especially alert and responsive as well (Kennell, Voos, & Klaus, 1979). In a study testing their hypothesis, Klaus and Kennell (1976) compared new mothers who received traditional hospital care to mothers in an "extended contact" experimental group who were allowed 5 "extra" hours a day to cuddle their babies, including an hour of skin-to-skin contact within 3 hours of birth. A month later, mothers who had extended contact with their infants were more involved with them and held them closer during feeding sessions. A year later, these mothers were still more nurturing, and their 1-year-olds outperformed control infants on tests of physical and mental development.

Subsequent research has shown that "early contact" effects are not as large or as lasting as Klaus and Kennell initially found them to be (Goldberg, 1983). Such contact can be a pleasant experience for both mother and baby, and it can help a mother *begin* to form an emotional bond to her child. However, secure attachments between infants and caregivers are not formed in a matter of minutes or hours. They develop slowly, through social interactions taking place over many weeks and months, and can develop even when there is no early contact at all between parent and infant.

Postpartum Depression

The mother–child relationship can get off to a rocky start if the new mother suffers from postpartum depression. For these new mothers, the experience of giving birth is anything but joyful; it is a time of profound sadness and hopelessness. Valerie Whiffen (1992) points out that there are actually three distinct depressive states that sometimes affect new mothers. A mother experiencing the *maternity blues* is tearful, irritable, moody, anxious, and depressed within the first 10 days after birth. This condition is relatively mild, passes quickly, and is probably linked to the steep drops in levels of female hormones that normally occur after delivery, as well as to the stresses associated with delivering a child and taking on the responsibilities of parenthood. As many as half of new mothers may experience the maternity blues (Kraus & Redman, 1986).

A second, and far more serious, condition is *postpartum psychosis;* a very small minority of new mothers who have had previous histories of psychological disorder experience hallucinations and other symptoms of severe psychopathology after giving birth and require hospitalization. In between these extremes is the condition of primary interest to us here, **postpartum depression,** or an episode of clinical depression that

The minutes after birth can be a wonderful time to start a relationship, but close attachments can grow even without this early bonding experience.

lasts for a matter of months rather than days in a woman who has just given birth.

Postpartum depression affects about 13% of new mothers (Whiffen, 1992). Only very rarely does a woman who has never had significant emotional problems become clinically depressed for the first time after giving birth (Whiffen, 1992). Instead, most of the affected women have histories of depression, and many were depressed during pregnancy as well. Also, women who are vulnerable to depression are more likely to actually become depressed if they are experiencing other life stresses on top of the stresses of becoming a mother (O'Hara et al., 1991). Lack of social support—especially a poor relationship with one's partner—also increases the odds (Gotlib et al., 1991). Researchers have not been able to detect any simple or straightforward connection between hormonal changes in the postpartum period and postpartum depression (O'Hara et al., 1991). At this point, environmental factors such as marital conflict seem more important than hormonal changes.

Is postpartum depression a unique form of depression? Although some would argue that the hormonal changes accompanying it make it unique, Valerie Whiffen (1992) concludes that it is basically no different from other cases of clinical depression. She suggests that we may not really need to speak of "postpartum depression" any more than we need to speak of "postbreakup depression" or "postretirement depression." Postpartum or not, depression tends to occur when a vulnerable individual experiences overwhelming stress (see Chapter 16). In this case, the stresses simply center on the transition to new parenthood.

Whether it is a unique syndrome or not, postpartum depression has significant implications for the mother–infant relationship. One study compared 70 mothers experiencing postpartum depression and nondepressed mothers over a 24-month period (Campbell et al., 1992). Depressed women often did not want their babies in the first place and perceived them as difficult babies. They also interacted less positively with their infants and in some cases seemed hostile toward them. Other studies suggest that depressed mothers have trouble responding to their babies' signals and establishing reciprocal, give-and-take relationships with them (Leadbeater, Bishop, & Raver, 1996). When mothers are depressed, withdrawn, and unresponsive like this, the mother–infant attachment is likely to become an insecure one, and infants sometimes develop depressive symptoms and behavior problems of their own (Field et al., 1985; Murray, 1992; Radke-Yarrow et al., 1985). For their own sake and for the sake of their infants, then, mothers experiencing more than a mild case of the "maternity blues" should seek professional help in overcoming their depression.

The Father's Experience

Fathers, like mothers, experience the birth process as a significant event in their lives that involves a mix of positive and negative emotions. Like mothers, fathers tend to be anxious during pregnancy and birth. The new fathers interviewed in one study admitted that they experienced mounting fear during labor, but said that they tried hard to look calm nonetheless (Chandler & Field, 1997). They found labor to be more work than they had expected and sometimes felt excluded as the nurses took over. For Tim, whose wife Angie dilated only 2 centimeters in 12 hours, then received drugs to induce labor, and eventually had to have a cesarean delivery, the process was even more agonizing. Despite the stresses, though, negative emotions usually give way to relief, pride, and joy when the baby finally arrives (Chandler & Field, 1997).

Most fathers find early contact with their babies special. Like a new mother, a new father may find himself engrossed with the baby:

When I come up to see [my] wife . . . I go look at the kid and then I pick her up and then I put her down. . . . I keep going back to the kid. It's like a magnet. That's what I can't get over, the fact that I feel like that. [Greenberg & Morris, 1974, p. 524]

Some studies find that fathers who handle and help care for their babies in the hospital later spend more time with them at home than fathers who have not had these early interactions (Greenberg & Morris, 1974). Other studies fail to find these long-term effects on the father–infant relationship but suggest that early contact with the newborn makes a father feel closer to his partner and more a part of a family (Palkovitz, 1985). Like mothers, however, fathers who miss out on early contact can simply learn to love their children later on.

THE EARLY POSTNATAL ENVIRONMENT

After the prenatal environment and the perinatal environment, we experience the postnatal environment— for a lifetime. In chapters to come, I will have much to say about a wide range of environmental influences on life-span development: influences of parents, peers, schools, workplaces, and so on. Here I simply want to make the point that human development is influenced by the broader social context in which it occurs—by cultural factors (or what Urie Bronfenbrenner, as discussed in Chapter 2, calls the *macrosystem*).

Culture and Early Socialization

Parents are products of their broader culture, and they in turn transmit that culture to their offspring. **Socialization** is the process by which individuals acquire the beliefs, values, and behaviors judged important in their society. By socializing the young, society controls their undesirable behavior, prepares them to adapt to the environment in which they must function, and ensures that cultural traditions will be carried on by future generations. The socialization process begins at birth. Robert LeVine (1974, p. 230, and see LeVine, 1988) maintains that parents everywhere share three very broad goals for their children:

1. *Survival:* to promote the physical survival and health of the child, ensuring that the child lives long enough to have children of his or her own.
2. *Economic self-sufficiency:* to foster the skills and traits that the child will need for economic self-maintenance as an adult.
3. *Self-actualization:* to foster capacities for maximizing other cultural values (for example, morality,

religion, achievement, wealth, prestige, and a sense of personal satisfaction).

LeVine also maintains that these universal goals of parenting form a hierarchy. Until parents are confident that their children will survive, higher-order goals such as teaching them to talk, count, or follow moral rules can wait. And only when parents and other caregivers believe that their children have acquired many of the basic attributes that will eventually contribute to their economic self-sufficiency will they encourage such goals as self-actualization or self-fulfillment.

Because different peoples must adapt to different environments, they sometimes emphasize different parenting goals, and their child-care and child-rearing practices differ accordingly. In societies where infant mortality is high, the survival goal of parenting is top priority. Babies may not even be named or viewed as persons until they seem likely to survive (Nsamenang, 1992). Parents keep infants close 24 hours a day to protect them. Among the !Kung, a hunting and gathering society of the Kalahari Desert in southern Africa, for example, babies are carried upright in slings during the day, and they sleep in the same bed with their mothers at night (Konner, 1981). They are breast-fed, suckling several times an hour as desired, and may not be weaned until the ripe old age of 4. In general, infants in hunter-gatherer societies are indulged considerably, at least until their survival is assured.

Infant-care practices are considerably different in modern, industrialized societies where infant mortality is lower. Babies typically sleep apart from their parents; they breast feed, if at all, for only a few months before being switched to the bottle and then to solid food; and they generally must learn to accommodate their needs to their parents' schedules (Konner, 1981). Not surprisingly, Mayan mothers in Guatemala, who sleep in the same bed with their babies until they are toddlers, express shock at the American practice of leaving infants alone in their own bedrooms (Morelli, Rogoff, Oppenheim, & Goldsmith, 1992).

Parenting practices in the early postnatal period are influenced not only by the extent to which infant survival is in doubt but by specific cultural belief systems. Amy Richman and her associates (1988) have observed mothers interacting with their babies in five societies, two agrarian and three industrial. Figure 4.8 shows some striking differences between how Gusii mothers in Kenya and white middle-class mothers in Boston interact with their 9- to 10-month-old infants (see also Richman, Miller, & LeVine, 1992). Gusii mothers hold their infants and make physical contact to soothe them far more than American mothers but look at and talk to their babies less.

Why the differences? Like so many parents in non-Western societies with high infant mortality rates,

In many cultures, parents attempt to achieve the survival goal of parenting by keeping their babies close at all times.

Gusii mothers emphasize the survival goal of parenting, keeping their offspring comfortable and safe by holding them close. In addition, the Gusii believe that babies cannot understand speech until about age 2. No wonder, then, that they rarely converse with their young charges. And because cultural norms in their society demand that they avert their gaze during conversations, they rarely make eye contact with their babies either, even during lengthy breast-feeding sessions. In Boston, by contrast, playpens and infant seats are available as substitutes for mothers' arms, and their use probably reflects the value American parents place on teaching their children to be autonomous. Moreover, American mothers believe that babies *can* understand speech and that they should get an early start on developing language skills in order to succeed in school; as a result, these mothers chat away while they interact with their babies.

Although we do not know what long-term effects cultural differences in parenting practices may have, it is clear that infants respond to the parenting they receive. Thus, for example, Sara Harkness and Charles Super report that Kipsigis babies in Kenya wake every 3 to 4 hours to feed, whereas by 6 months of age,

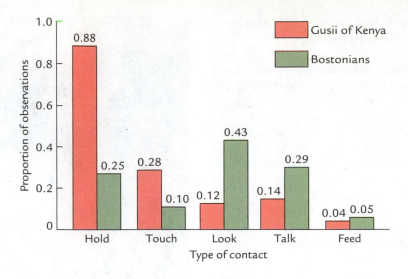

FIGURE 4.8 *Compared to parents in Boston, Gusii parents in Kenya hold and touch their infants more but look at and talk to them less.* (From Richman et al. in LeVine et al., 1988)

American babies sleep 8 or 9 hours straight at night and Dutch babies sleep about 10 (Russell, 1995). In Boston, where mothers established regular schedules for their infants and wanted their babies to be alert and responsive to their stimulation during the day but quiet at night, a baby who could not learn to sleep through the night was quickly labeled a "problem baby" (Super & Harkness, 1981). Dutch parents are even more insistent that babies follow regular schedules, which helps explain why Dutch babies sleep even longer at night than U.S. babies (Russell, 1995). In Kenya, a baby who wakes at night is not viewed as difficult at all. Because mothers and infants sleep together, it is perfectly acceptable for babies to rouse their mothers now and then during the night to feed. Of special significance for development, then, may be the *goodness of fit* between an infant's behavior and the culture's demands. The baby whose temperament is well matched to its cultural "niche" is likely to have an easier experience of infancy than the baby whose temperament is not. More generally, development can and does proceed normally in a wide range of cultures, but it is also colored by the specific cultural context in which it occurs.

RISK AND RESILIENCE

To what extent is harm done in the prenatal or perinatal period long-lasting, and to what extent can postnatal experiences make up for it? We have encountered many examples in this chapter of what can go wrong before or during birth. Certainly some damaging effects are irreversible: The thalidomide baby will never grow nor-

mal arms or legs, and the child who is mentally retarded owing to fetal alcohol syndrome will always be mentally retarded. And yet many of us turned out fine despite the fact that our mothers, unaware of many risk factors that concern us today, smoked and drank during their pregnancies or received heavy doses of medication during delivery. As we have already emphasized, not all embryos, fetuses, or newborns exposed to hazards are affected by them. Is it also possible that some babies who are exposed and who are clearly affected recover from their deficiencies later in life?

Indeed it is, and we now have longitudinal follow-up studies to tell us so (Kopp & Kahler, 1989). Consider these findings:

- Nine to 11 years after they were born, the children of mothers who smoked during pregnancy were no smaller, no less intelligent, no less achievement-oriented, and no less socially adjusted than the children of nonsmokers (Lefkowitz, 1981).

- As young adults entering the military, Dutch males whose mothers experienced famine during their pregnancies scored no lower on a test of intelligence than males who received adequate prenatal nutrition (Stein & Susser, 1976; Stein et al., 1975).

And then we have the results of major longitudinal studies of babies who were "at risk" at birth—for example, who had low birth weights, had been exposed to prenatal hazards, or suffered poor health (Baker & Mednick, 1984; Werner, 1989; Werner & Smith, 1982, 1992). These studies indicate that babies at risk—particularly those whose problems at birth are severe—have more intellectual and social problems as children and as adolescents than normal babies do. And yet many of these at-risk babies outgrow their problems with time. Emmy Werner and Ruth Smith (1982), in reporting on their longitudinal study of all babies born in 1955 on the island of Kauai in Hawaii, went so far as to title their book *Vulnerable but Invincible*, so impressed were they by the **resilience** of young human beings, the "self-righting" tendencies that allow many of them—about a third—to recover from early disadvantages, such as prenatal and perinatal difficulties, poverty, and disorganized families, and to get on a very healthy course of development (Garmezy, 1991). The Kauai babies have now been followed into their early 30s, and it is clear that their outcomes in life have had more to do with their experiences since birth—including their experiences as adults—than with whether or not they experienced problems at birth (Werner & Smith, 1992).

The interesting question, then, is this: *Why do some children recover from early deficiencies while others continue to have problems later in life?* Developmentalists have begun to search for possible **protective factors,** factors that work to prevent individuals who are at risk for developing problems from doing so. Two sets of protective factors have proven important (Garmezy, 1991; Werner, 1989):

◆ *Personal resources.* Possibly because of their genetic makeup, some children have qualities such as intelligence, sociability, and communication skills that help them to choose or create more nurturing and stimulating environments and to cope with challenges.
◆ *A supportive postnatal environment* (Baker & Mednick, 1984; Werner & Smith, 1992). Some children at risk receive the social support they need, within or outside the family. Most importantly, they are able to find at least one person who loves them unconditionally (Werner & Smith, 1992).

Both personal resources and supportive postnatal environments can help prevent developmental problems and allow resilient children to thrive despite early disadvantages. With this as background, let's look more closely at one particular group of at-risk babies: those with low birth weight.

Low-Birth-Weight Babies

Some low-birth-weight babies are small but have experienced a normal rate of prenatal growth. More often, low birth weight is a sign of problems such as inadequate nutrition. When the environment in the womb is not supportive, it may be adaptive for the fetal growth rate to slow, for this helps ensure survival (Hay, Catz, Grave, & Yaffe, 1997). Still, low-birth-weight babies are at risk. The 8% to 9% of infants who weigh less than 2500 grams (5½ pounds) at birth are especially likely to have difficulty if they (1) arrive prematurely (more than 3 weeks before their due dates) and (2) are smaller than they should be considering the time they have been in the womb (Kopp & Parmelee, 1979).

As we have seen, a mother's smoking or drinking, fetal malnutrition, and a number of other factors can contribute to prematurity and low birth weight. Premature, low-birth-weight babies must first be helped to survive. They are likely to develop infections because their immune systems have not matured enough, and they are prone to respiratory difficulties and even death because they have not yet produced enough **surfactant,** a substance that aids breathing by preventing the air sacs of the lungs from sticking together. As Table 4.4 illustrates, the smaller these babies are, the lower their odds of survival (Lin, 1993). Assuming they do survive, they may be difficult for some parents to accept because they are often tiny and wrinkled, as well as both unresponsive and irritable. What's more, they may be stereotyped as intellectually and socially limited (Stern & Hildebrandt, 1986).

It doesn't sound good. And yet, researchers are learning that the fates of premature and low-birth-weight babies depend considerably on two factors. The first is their biological condition—their health and neurological status in particular (Koller et al., 1997). The second is the quality of the postnatal environment they experience. Consider what Ronald Wilson (1985) found in his study of twins who were especially small at birth (weighing under 1750 grams, or less than about 3¾ pounds) and who were also small for their (short) gestation ages. These babies were indeed deficient in mental development as infants, but they caught up over time. Indeed, those whose families had high socioeconomic status caught up *completely* to the average child by age 6. Problems were more lasting among at-risk twins who grew up in lower-income homes, but they too showed self-righting tendencies. It seems that premature, low-birth-weight babies can achieve normal levels of intellectual functioning during childhood when they live in middle-class homes, when their mothers are relatively educated, and most importantly, *when their mothers, rich or poor, are attentive and responsive when interacting with them* (Beckwith & Parmelee, 1986; Brooks-Gunn et al., 1993).

Studies like these raise a larger issue about the importance of early experience. Some developmentalists take seriously the concept of critical (or sensitive) periods in early development. Others stress the resilience of human beings, their ability to rebound from early disadvantages and to respond to environmental influences throughout their lives rather than only during so-called critical periods. Which is it?

TABLE 4.4

Infant mortality as a function of birth weight			
	Birth Weight		**Percentage of Babies Who Die**
	In Grams	*In Pounds*	
Very low birth weight	500–749	1 lb, 9 oz or less	67
	750–999	1 lb, 10 oz–2 lb, 3 oz	33
	1000–1249	2 lb, 4 oz–2 lb, 12 oz	16
Low birth weight	1249–1499	2 lb, 13 oz–3 lb, 4 oz	9
	1500–2500	3 lb, 5 oz–5 lb, 8 oz	6
Average birth weight	2500–3000	5 lb, 9 oz–6 lb, 9 oz	2
	3001–4500	6 lb, 10 oz–9 lb, 14 oz	1

SOURCE: Lin (1993)

We have encountered evidence in favor of both positions. Hazards during the important prenatal and perinatal periods *can* leave lasting scars, and yet many children show remarkable resilience. Isn't this the lesson we learn from the case of Genie described at the beginning of the chapter? Yes, she was permanently affected by extreme deprivation during sensitive periods of development early in life. Yet even she showed considerable resilience when her environment improved. There *do* seem to be some points in the life span, especially early on, in which both positive and negative environmental forces have especially strong impacts. Yet at the same time, *environment matters throughout life*. Certainly, it would be a mistake to assume that all children who have problems at birth are doomed. In short, early experience by itself can, but rarely does, make or break development; later experience counts too, sometimes enough to turn a negative course of development completely around.

APPLICATIONS: GETTING LIFE OFF TO A GOOD START

The more we learn about important environmental influences on human development, the better able we are to optimize the environment and therefore to optimize development. Although the nature and quality of an individual's environment matters throughout the life span, it seems sensible to do as much as possible to get a baby's life off to a good start.

Before Birth

For starters, it would be good for babies if more of them were planned and wanted. Moreover, a woman should begin making positive changes in her lifestyle, such as giving up smoking, before she even thinks about becoming pregnant. Once a woman is preg-

nant, she should seek good prenatal care as quickly as possible so that she will learn how to optimize the well-being of both herself and her unborn child and so that any problems during the pregnancy can be managed appropriately. As we have seen, the guidelines for pregnant women are not that complicated, though they are often violated. They boil down to such practices as eating an adequate diet, protecting oneself against diseases, and avoiding drugs. Research suggests that special intervention programs, such as home visits to mothers who smoke, to encourage healthy habits and provide social support can prevent damage to the children (Olds, Henderson, & Tatelbaum, 1994).

Today many couples also enroll in classes that prepare them for childbirth. The "natural childbirth" movement arose from the work of Grantly Dick-Read, in England, and Fernand Lamaze, in France. These two obstetricians discovered that many women could give birth with minimal pain, without medication, through what has come to be called the **Lamaze method** of prepared childbirth. This approach teaches women to associate childbirth with pleasant feelings and to ready themselves for the process by learning exercises, breathing and pushing methods, and relaxation techniques that make childbirth easier (Dick-Read, 1933/1972; Lamaze, 1958). Parents typically attend Lamaze classes for six to eight weeks before the delivery. The father or another supportive person becomes a coach who helps the mother train her muscles and perfect her breathing for the event that lies ahead. He will usually be there to help his partner during delivery.

Women who regularly attend Lamaze or similar childbirth classes are indeed more relaxed during labor, experience less pain, less often need medication, have an easier time delivering, and have more positive attitudes toward themselves, their families, and the childbirth process (Wideman & Singer, 1984). Childbirth education can be made even more effective if it is supplemented with effective pain-management techniques such as hypnosis (Harmon, Hynan, & Tyre, 1990).

During Birth

Today's women have more choices about how and where they want to give birth than women 20 years ago did. Gone are the days when almost all women gave birth in a hospital, on their backs with their legs in stirrups, and under the influence of medication. For some years there has been a movement to return to the days when birth was a natural family event that occurred at home rather than a medical problem to be solved with high technology (Ackermann-Liebrich et al., 1996; Edwards & Waldorf, 1984).

Today, more and more couples are opting for home deliveries, often with the aid of one of the growing number of certified nurse-midwives who are trained in nonsurgical obstetrics. Those who favor home delivery argue that the relaxed atmosphere of the home setting calms the mother, making her delivery quicker and easier. Although the mothers who choose home delivery are usually those who can expect an easy time of it, home deliveries are no riskier for mothers or babies than hospital deliveries when mothers are at low risk for birth complications (Ackermann-Liebrich et al., 1996).

Similarly, many couples today are choosing to have their babies in **alternative birth centers** that provide a homelike atmosphere but still make medical technology available (Klee, 1986). Some are in hospitals, others are independent centers that place the task of delivery in the hands of nurse-midwives. In either case, mates or other close companions, and often even the couple's children, can be present during labor, and healthy infants can remain in the same room with their mothers (rooming-in) rather than spending their first days in the hospital nursery. So far, the evidence suggests that delivery by nurse-midwives in alternative birth centers is no more risky to mothers and their babies than delivery in hospitals by physicians and is less likely to involve interventions such as anesthesia and cesarean sections (Fullerton & Severino, 1992; Harvey et al., 1996). Today, the woman whose pregnancy is going smoothly has considerable freedom to give birth as she chooses.

After Birth

So now that you have a baby, what do you do? New parents are often uncertain about how to relate to their babies and may find the period after birth stressful. T. Berry Brazelton (1979) has devised a way to help parents appreciate their baby's competencies and feel competent themselves as parents. He has developed a newborn assessment technique, the *Brazelton Neonatal Behavioral Assessment Scale*, that assesses the strength of infant reflexes as well as the infant's responses to 26 situations (for example, reactions to cuddling, general irritability, and orienting to the examiner's face and voice). Brazelton uses this test to teach parents to understand their babies as individuals and to appreciate many of the pleasing competencies that they possess. During "Brazelton training," parents observe the test being administered and also learn how to administer it themselves to elicit smiles and other heart-warming responses from their babies.

In some studies, mothers of high-risk (and sometimes difficult) infants who receive Brazelton training become more responsive in their face-to-face interactions with their babies than mothers who do not, and their infants score higher on developmental tests (Britt & Myers, 1994; Widmayer & Field, 1980). Compared to untrained parents, trained parents may also become more knowledgeable about infant behavior, more confident of their caretaking abilities, and more satisfied with their infants (Myers, 1982). Although this brief intervention appears to be a good way to help parents and babies get off to a good start, it cannot accomplish miracles and sometimes has little impact (Britt & Myers, 1994).

Giving the seriously premature and low-birthweight infant a good start requires more effort. Neonatal intensive care units, with their high-tech life-sustaining machines and computerized monitoring systems, have greatly improved the odds that babies who are at high risk will survive the perinatal period. Consider Baby Brittany, born after 27 weeks in the womb weighing just over a pound (Colburn, 1995). She had only about 8 teaspoons of blood, had to be fed a high-nutrient fluid through a thin wire into her leg, and received, every 6 hours through a tube running from her nose to her stomach, a bit of formula intended to prepare her digestive tract to process food. Although she spent 2 days on a small respirator, her lungs worked well compared to those of many premature babies in neonatal intensive care. Brittany was lucky, for she was older and more mature than most 1 pounders. Yet only 20 years ago, without the "high-tech" neonatal care she received, she probably would not have lived.

Much is still being learned about how to optimize the rather abnormal environment in which infants like Brittany spend the first several weeks of life. Since "preemies" are not still fetuses and yet not quite normal newborns, it is not clear whether they should be handled like babies or given womblike accommodations befitting fetuses (Smotherman & Robinson, 1996). Not long ago, these babies simply lay in their isolettes receiving little stimulation and contact at all. They were, in effect, deprived of the sensory stimulation that they would have received either in the womb or in a normal home environment. Today, their perinatal sensory environment is much improved,

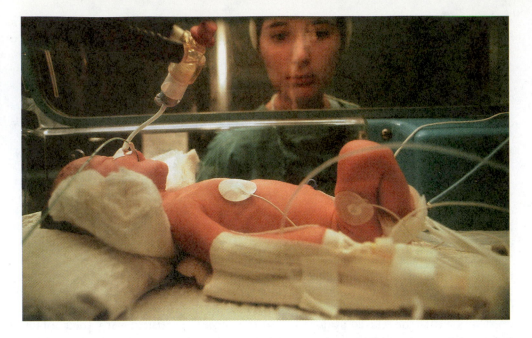

thanks to research on the effects of sensory stimulation programs.

Many sensory stimulation programs have centered on the "body senses" because much bodily stimulation is provided in the womb. Preterm infants have been stroked, held upright, rocked, and even put on waterbeds (Schaefer, Hatcher, & Barglow, 1980). For example, Frank Scafidi and his colleagues (1986, 1990) provided preterm infants with just three 15-minute stimulation sessions a day over 10 days. These babies' bodies were massaged and their limbs were flexed and extended. Stimulated babies gained 21% more weight per day, showed more mature behaviors on the Brazelton scale, and were able to leave the hospital 5 days earlier than control infants (Scafidi et al., 1990). It appears that fairly simple and inexpensive environmental changes and special stimulation programs can help the high-risk infant develop normally.

Finally, high-risk infants can benefit from programs that teach their parents how to provide responsive care and appropriate intellectual stimulation to them once they are home. Home visits to advise parents, combined with a stimulating day-care program for low-birth-weight toddlers, can teach mothers how to be better teachers of their young children and stimulate these children's cognitive development. In an ambitious project called the Infant Health and Development Program, premature and low-birth-weight infants at eight sites have benefited from such early intervention (Bradley et al., 1994; Brooks-Gunn et al., 1993; McCarton et al., 1997). The program involved weekly home visits during the first year of life and then biweekly home visits and attendance by the infant at a special day-care center for half a day every day from age 1 to age 3. Mothers were given child-care education and support as well. The program appears to help parents provide a more growth-enhancing home environment—for example, to give their babies appropriate toys and learning materials and to interact with them in stimulating ways.

The intervention helped these high-risk babies, especially the heavier ones, achieve more cognitive growth by age 3 than they would otherwise achieve. However, an impressive 14-point boost in IQ scores at age 3 for heavier low-birth-weight children who received the intervention had dropped to a 4-point advantage at age 8 (McCarton et al., 1997). Children who weighed 2000 g (5 lb, 4 oz) or less at birth did not get much benefit. We have more to learn, then, about what it takes to keep the development of at-risk children on a positive track after the perinatal period comes to a close. However, everything we do know about life-span environmental forces suggests that supportive parents and programs can do a great deal to optimize every child's development.

As Chapter 3 and this chapter have testified, both nature and nurture contribute to life-span human development. Certain genes and early environments can have profound negative impacts on development. Yet the vast majority of us come into existence with an amazingly effective genetic program to guide our development. Most of us, whether we grow up in Kenya or Japan or the United States, also receive the benefits of a normal human environment, an environment that joins forces with this genetic program to promote normal development (Gottlieb, 1996). Sometimes early insults cannot be undone, but other times only very adverse conditions over a long period of time—conditions like those experienced by Genie—can keep us from developing normally. Even then, we often show a good deal of resilience if given half a chance.

We will encounter numerous examples in the remainder of this text of the positive and negative impacts that environmental forces can have on development throughout the life span. We will also want to bear in mind throughout that each person's genetic endowment affects what experiences he or she has and how he or she is affected by them.

SUMMARY POINTS

1. The environment of human development includes all events or conditions outside the person that affect or are affected by the person's development, including both the physical and the social environment.

2. Environmental influences on development start at conception as the zygote begins its passage through three stages of prenatal development: (1) the germinal period, (2) the period of the embryo, and (3) the period of the fetus.

3. The prenatal physical environment is most supportive when a mother is between 16 and 35, is not stressed, and is well-nourished. A variety of teratogens such as diseases and drugs can significantly affect development, especially during critical or sensitive periods when the embryo's organs are rapidly forming. Effects depend on the dose of a teratogen, the mother's and child's makeup, and the postnatal environment.

4. The perinatal environment (the environment surrounding birth) is also important. Childbirth is a three-step process consisting of the contractions of labor, delivery, and the afterbirth (expulsion of the placenta). Despite recent concerns about overuse, cesarean sections are still common; perinatal risks to the baby include anoxia and the effects of medications given to the mother.

5. Most new parents are anxious during labor and delivery but find the experience a positive one. Support for new mothers varies across cultures. Emotional bonding in the hours immediately following birth, though pleasant, does not seem necessary for loving attachments to form.

6. Part of the postnatal environment is the cultural context. Survival, economic self-sufficiency, and self-actualization goals of parenting are universal, but parents in cultures with high infant mortality must concentrate on infant survival and therefore keep their infants with them around the clock. Some babies are temperamentally more suited to their cultural niche than others and respond better to socialization efforts.

7. Some problems created by prenatal and perinatal hazards are long-lasting, but many babies at risk show remarkable resilience and outgrow their problems, especially if they have personal resources such as sociability and intelligence and grow up in stimulating and supportive postnatal environments where someone loves them.

8. Ways of getting human lives off to a good start today include prenatal care, Lamaze classes, alternative birth centers, neonatal intensive care units, and training for parents of high-risk infants.

FOOD FOR THOUGHT

1. Thinking about the material in Chapter 3 and this chapter, develop a plan for preventing mental retardation that involves consideration of both genetic and environmental contributors to significantly limited intellectual development.

2. Some people argue that women who abuse alcohol or other drugs during pregnancy should be charged with attempted murder—or actual murder if they have a miscarriage. What is your view and why?

3. Thinking about the material on birth and the perinatal environment, arrange the perfect birth experience for you and your baby and justify its features. Where would you be, who would be there, what would be done?

4. Pretend you are a newborn reflecting on the difference between your prenatal home and the postnatal environment into which you have just been thrust. What are some key differences between these environments in terms of the kinds of stimulation and support they provide? What do you miss most about the womb, and what is most interesting to you about this new world? Why do you think you're ready for a change of environment, and how well does this new postnatal environment meet your needs?

W ON THE WEB

1. *Pregnancy and Birth*   Web sites aimed at parents are cropping up all over, among them "Baby Web," which offers information aimed at parents-to-be and parents about pregnancy and prenatal care, birth, and infant care.
http://www.netaxs.com:80/~iris/infoweb/baby.html

2. *Best Bet on Pregnancy and Birth*   "ParentsPlace" features practical advice, in Question and Answer format, from a midwife about everything from conceiving a child to handling morning sickness, having prenatal screening tests such as amniocentesis, handling last trimester weight gain, and giving birth. A number of teratogens are also discussed.
http://www.parentsplace.com/genobject.cgi/readroom/pregnant.html

KEY TERMS

prenatal environment	period of the fetus	perinatal environment
germinal period	age of viability	anoxia
blastula	infant states	breech presentation
period of the embryo	teratogen	cesarean section
organogenesis	critical period	Apgar test
amnion	rubella	engrossment
chorion	syphilis	postpartum depression
placenta	acquired immune deficiency syndrome (AIDS)	socialization
umbilical cord		resilience
artificial insemination	thalidomide	protective factors
in vitro fertilization (IVF)	fetal alcohol syndrome (FAS)	surfactant
cloning	polychlorinated biphenyls (PCBs)	Lamaze method
testosterone		alternative birth centers

CHAPTER 5

The Physical Self

THE ENDOCRINE SYSTEM

THE NERVOUS SYSTEM
Early Brain Development
Later Brain Development
The Aging Brain

THE INFANT
The Newborn
Physical Growth
Physical Behavior

THE CHILD
Steady Growth
Physical Behavior

THE ADOLESCENT
Physical and Sexual Maturation
Physical Behavior

THE ADULT
Physical Appearance and Structure
Functioning and Health
The Reproductive System
Physical Behavior
Disease, Disuse, and Abuse

APPLICATIONS: OPTIMIZING HEALTHY DEVELOPMENT
Nutrition
Exercise
Avoiding Known Health Risks

SUMMARY POINTS

FOOD FOR THOUGHT

ON THE WEB

KEY TERMS

When you are very young, each of your cells, based on its individual personality and aptitude, selects an area of specialization, such as the thigh, in which to pursue its career. As you grow, the cell multiplies, and it teaches its offspring to be thigh cells also. Thus the proud thigh-cell tradition is handed down from generation to generation, so that by the time you're a teenager, you have an extremely competent, efficient, and hard-working colony down there, providing you with thighs so sleek and taut that they look great even when encased in Spandex garments that would be a snug fit on a Bic pen. But as your body approaches middle age, this cellular discipline starts to break down. The newer cells become listless and bored, and many of them, looking for "kicks," turn to cellulite. Your bodily tissue begins to deteriorate, gradually becoming saggier and lumpier, until one day you glance in the mirror and realize, to your horror, that you look as though for some reason you are attempting to smuggle out of the country an entire driveway's worth of gravel concealed inside your upper legs. [Barry, 1990, pp. 19–20]

You don't get old all at once. You notice the first wrinkle, the first gray hair . . . but you are too busy living to really think of "when you'll be old." Then, one day, you are "over 75!" Out of habit, you continue doing all the things you did all you life. [Rose Rudin at age 77, cited in Saul, 1983, p. 152]

Humorist Dave Barry's view of physical development and aging is more dismal than the one expressed by Rose Rudin and the one I am about to present. We live in a society that pictures physical aging as nothing but inevitable decline. The realities of the aging experience may surprise you.

In this chapter we trace the body's developing size and proportions, and the functioning of selected body systems, emphasizing the nervous and endocrine systems because we could not function without them. We will look at the development and aging of the brain. We will also examine the reproductive system as it matures during adolescence and changes during adulthood. And we will watch the physical self in action, as motor skills develop during childhood and physical fitness and motor behavior change during adulthood. We will identify influences on physical development and aging, so that we can better understand why some children develop—and some older adults age—more rapidly than others.

The human body is marvelously complex, with many parts working together to make the full range of behavior possible. As we saw in Chapter 4, all the major organs take shape during the first eight weeks of the prenatal period. Each bodily system has an orderly course of development (Tanner, 1990). For example, the nervous system develops very rapidly, completing most of its important growth by the end of infancy. The reproductive system, by contrast, is slower to develop than most of the organs and systems. To understand physical growth and sexual maturation, we must understand the endocrine (hormonal) system. And if we want to know why adults are physically and mentally more competent than infants, we must understand the nervous system.

THE ENDOCRINE SYSTEM

How *does* the human body grow? All humans have a distinctly human genetic makeup that makes them develop physically in similar directions and at similar rates. Individual heredity also influences the individual's rate of physical development and final size—in interaction, of course, with environmental factors such as whether his or her diet includes milk and other nutritious foods.

But how are genetic messages translated into action? It is here that the endocrine system plays its role. **Endocrine glands** secrete chemicals called *hormones* directly into the bloodstream. Perhaps the most critical of the endocrine glands is the **pituitary gland,** the so-called master gland located at the base of the brain. Directly controlled by the *hypothalamus* of the brain, it triggers the release of hormones from all other endocrine glands by sending hormonal messages to those glands. Moreover, the pituitary produces **growth hormone,** which stimulates the rapid growth and development of body cells. Children who lack this hormone are unlikely to exceed 4 feet (130 cm) in height as adults (Tanner, 1990), but can now be treated successfully with synthetic growth hormones. By contrast, administering human growth hormone to children who are just plain short and do not have an endocrine problem is likely to do no good and can even backfire. Hormone treatment tends to induce an early and short puberty and these children are either early to attain the height they would have attained anyway or actually end up smaller than they would have been (Rosenfeld, 1997).

The *thyroid gland* also plays a key role in growth and development, as well as in the development of the nervous system. Babies born with a thyroid deficiency become mentally retarded and grow slowly if their condition goes unnoticed and untreated (Robertson, 1993; Tanner, 1990). Children who develop a thyroid deficiency later in life will not suffer brain damage, since most of their brain growth has already occurred, but their physical growth will slow drastically.

In Chapter 4 we encountered still another critical role of the endocrine system. A male fetus will not develop male reproductive organs unless (1) a gene on

TABLE 5.1

Hormonal influences on growth and development

Endocrine Gland	Hormones Produced	Effects on Growth and Development
Pituitary	Growth hormone	Regulates growth from birth through adolescence; triggers adolescent growth spurt.
	Activating hormones	Signal other endocrine glands (such as the ovaries and testes) to secrete their hormones.
Thyroid	Thyroxine	Affects growth and development of the brain and helps to regulate growth of the body during childhood.
Testes	Testosterone	Is responsible for development of the male reproductive system during the prenatal period; directs male sexual development during adolescence.
Ovaries	Estrogen Progesterone	Responsible for regulation of menstrual cycle; estrogen directs female sexual development during adolescence.
Adrenal glands	Adrenal androgens	Play a supportive role in the development of muscle and bones; contribute to sexual motivation.

his Y chromosome triggers the development of the testes (which are endocrine glands), and (2) the testes secrete the most important of the male hormones, *testosterone.* Male sex hormones become highly important again during adolescence. When people speak of adolescence as a time of "raging hormones," they are quite right. The testes of a male secrete large quantities of testosterone and other male hormones (called **androgens**). These hormones stimulate the production of growth hormone, which in turn triggers the adolescent growth spurt. Androgens are also responsible for the development of the male sex organs and contribute to sexual motivation during adulthood (Tanner, 1990).

Meanwhile, in adolescent girls, the ovaries (also endocrine glands) produce larger quantities of the primary female hormone, **estrogen,** and of progesterone. Estrogen increases dramatically at puberty, stimulating the production of growth hormone and the adolescent growth spurt, much as testosterone does in males. It is also responsible for the development of the breasts, pubic hair, and female sex organs, as well as for the control of menstrual cycles throughout a woman's reproductive years. Finally, the *adrenal glands* secrete androgenlike hormones that contribute to the maturation of the bones and muscles in both sexes (Tanner, 1990). There is now evidence that the maturation of the adrenal glands during middle childhood results in sexual attraction well before puberty in both boys and girls (McClintock & Herdt, 1996). The roles of different endocrine glands in physical growth and development are summarized in Table 5.1.

In adulthood, endocrine glands continue to secrete hormones, under the direction of the hypothalamus and the pituitary, to regulate bodily processes (Andres & Tobin, 1977). For example, thyroid hormones help the body's cells metabolize (break down) foods into usable nutrients, and the adrenal glands help the body cope with stress. Throughout the life span, then, the endocrine system works together with the nervous system to keep the body on an even keel. Yet changes occur; for example, there are declines in levels of sexual hormones associated with menopause. And, as we will see in Chapter 17, some theorists believe that changes in the functioning of the endocrine glands late in life bring about aging and death.

In short, the endocrine system, in collaboration with the nervous system, is centrally involved in growth during childhood, physical and sexual and maturation during adolescence, functioning over the entire life span, and aging later in life.

THE NERVOUS SYSTEM

None of the physical or mental achievements that we regard as human would be possible without a functioning nervous system. Briefly, the nervous system consists of the brain and spinal cord (central nervous system) and neural tissue that extends into all parts of the body (peripheral nervous system). Its basic unit is a **neuron** (see Figure 5.1). Although neurons come in many shapes and sizes, they have some common features. Branching, bushy *dendrites* receive signals from other neurons, and the long *axon* of a neuron transmits signals—to another neuron or, in some cases, directly to a muscle cell. The axon of one neuron makes a connection with another neuron at a tiny gap called a **synapse.** By releasing *neurotransmitters* stored at the ends of its axons, one neuron can either stimulate or

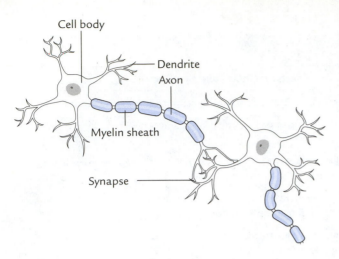

FIGURE 5.1 *Two neurons forming a synapse. A synapse between neurons links the axon of one to the dendrites of the other. When the first neuron is activated, it releases neurotransmitters that stimulate (or inhibit) electrical activity in the second neuron.* (From Janowsky & Carper, 1996)

inhibit the action of another neuron. During development, axons become covered by a waxy material called **myelin,** which acts like insulation to speed the transmission of neural impulses.

Now imagine a brain with as many as 100 billion neurons, each communicating through synapses to thousands of others (Cowan, 1979). How does this brain develop to make adults more physically and mentally capable than young infants? Is it that adults have more neurons than infants do? More synapses connecting neurons or a more organized pattern of connections? And what actually happens to the brain in later life?

Early Brain Development

The evolution of the brain's structure during the prenatal period is shown in Figure 5.2. The main parts of the brain begin as swellings or lumps on the "neural tube," a tubelike structure that forms very early and resembles the brain of a worm (Thompson, 1993). By 50 days, the brain resembles that of a fish. The areas of the brain that develop earliest are the "primitive" or "lower" portions such as the spinal cord, brain stem, and midbrain. These portions of the brain control the infant's states of waking and sleeping, permit simple motor reactions, and regulate such biological functions as digestion, respiration, and elimination, making life possible. However, we would be little different from snakes if the higher centers of the brain did not develop.

By 5 months after conception, the fetus's brain resembles that of other primates. Steadily, the hemispheres of the **cerebral cortex,** the outer covering of the brain involved in higher mental processes, become larger and more convoluted, making for a characteristically human brain. The cortex continues to develop well after birth and becomes organized into areas that control voluntary body movements, perception, and higher intellectual functions such as learning, thinking, and speaking.

Most important developments in the brain take place during the prenatal period and early infancy. Key processes involved in early brain development include the proliferation of brain cells, their migration to particular regions of the brain, their differentiation as specialized neurons, and the formation of synapses that link neurons in functioning networks (Janowsky & Carper, 1996; Johnson, 1997; Spreen, Risser, & Edgell, 1995; Thompson, 1993).

Proliferation

Neurons multiply at a staggering rate during the prenatal period; by one estimate, the number of neurons increases by 250,000 every minute from conception to birth (Thompson, 1993). After birth, though, neurons no longer divide to form new neurons. Since we have all the neurons we will ever have as infants, the number of neurons cannot explain why adults are cognitively more adept than babies.

Migration

Through a process not fully understood but influenced by both genetic instructions and the biochemical environment in which brain cells find themselves, neurons migrate to particular locations within the brain where they will become part of particular functioning units of neurons. They then grow axons that extend out to connect with other neurons. Like the proliferation of neurons, the migration of neurons is complete by birth and therefore cannot explain cognitive development thereafter (Janowsky & Carper, 1996).

Differentiation

Influenced by the locations in which they end up, neurons take on specialized functions—for example, as cells of the visual cortex or cells of the hippocampus (a brain structure concerned with memory and emotion). If a neuron that would normally migrate to the visual cortex of an animal's brain is transplanted into the area of the cortex that controls hearing, it will differentiate as an auditory neuron instead of a visual neuron (Johnson, 1997). Every neuron starts out with the potential to become any specific type of neuron; what it actually becomes depends on where it migrates.

Synaptogenesis

Perhaps the most important process in early brain development is **synaptogenesis,** the formation of con-

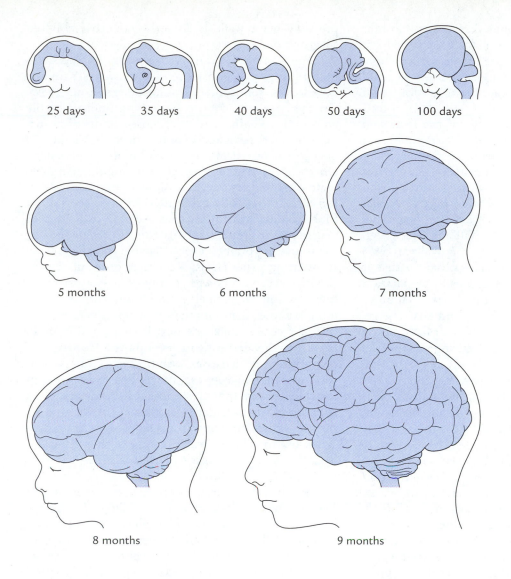

FIGURE 5.2 *The brain from 25 days after conception to birth. The brains from 25 days to 100 days are much enlarged; the diagrams for the brains from 5 to 9 months are about a third of their actual sizes.* (From Thompson, 1993)

25 days   35 days   40 days   50 days   100 days

5 months   6 months   7 months

8 months   9 months

nections among neurons. The genetic code does not fully specify which neurons will form synapses with which and therefore what the specific architecture of the brain will be. Instead, genes provide a general sketch of how the brain should be wired, and early experience then plays a critical role in determining which neurons and connections between them will survive.

To understand how the brain becomes "wired," we must look more closely at brain development during the last three months of prenatal life and the first two years after birth. This prenatal and postnatal stretch has been termed the period of the **brain growth spurt,** for several reasons:

◆ Neurons are proliferating rapidly during the prenatal period, as we have seen.
◆ Neural cells are increasing in size and weight both before and after birth. At birth a baby's brain is only 25% of its eventual adult weight; by age 2, it has already reached 75% of its adult weight.

◆ Neurons are rapidly being covered with the waxy myelin that increases their ability to transmit signals effectively.
◆ Levels of neurotransmitters are increasing.
◆ Neurons are forming synapses with one another and organizing themselves into intricately interconnected groups that take on specialized functions, such as the control of motor behavior or visual perception.

But neurons are also dying in massive numbers during this same early period of rapid brain development! Researchers estimate that almost *half* of the neurons produced in early life die soon afterward (Janowsky & Finlay, 1986). Similarly, large numbers of the many synapses formed during the brain growth spurt later disappear, so that we actually have more synapses during infancy than before or after (Huttenlocher, 1994). As Richard Thompson (1993) notes, "If you are worried about reports that people lose a few neurons and synapses as they grow old, remember that you lost far more by the time you were born" (p. 308). If we liken the developing brain to a house under construction, we must imagine that the builder decides to build many rooms and many hallways between rooms and later goes back and knocks about half of them out!

What is happening? The brain of the fetus and young infant has a great deal of *plasticity*, meaning that its cells are highly responsive to the effects of experience, both normal and abnormal, both growth-producing and damaging. During the sensitive period of the brain growth spurt, the brain needs stimulation in order to develop normally and can be permanently damaged without it. As William Greenough and his colleagues (Greenough, Black, & Wallace, 1987) explain, the immature brain has evolved so that it produces an excess of neural synapses in preparation for receiving early sensory and motor stimulation of the sort available to all developing humans. The genetic code supplies only a rough sketch of the wiring of the brain; it is up to experience, during sensitive periods for brain development early in life, to finalize and fine tune the neural circuitry. As neurons extend their axons to other neurons and form synapses, these synapses enter into a kind of competition. The neural connections most often activated by the infant's early experiences will survive; the synapses that are faulty and are used infrequently will disappear.

Assuming that the infant does indeed have normal opportunities to explore and experience the world, the result will be a normal brain and normal development. To return to our house-building analogy, it is like waiting to see which rooms and hallways get the most traffic before deciding which to retain in the final house. In sum, the development of the brain early in life is not due entirely to the unfolding of a maturational program; it is the handiwork of both a genetic program and early experience.

An important implication is that a lack of normal experiences can interfere with normal brain development. Classic studies conducted by noted researchers David Hubel and Torsten Wiesel showed that sewing one eye of a kitten shut so that it was deprived of the normal experience of seeing light during the cat's critical period for brain development resulted in a lack of normal connections between that eye and the visual cortex—and blindness even after the eye had been reopened (Wiesel & Hubel, 1965; and see Thompson, 1993). By contrast, depriving an adult cat's eye of light did no permanent damage. In humans, the critical period for the visual cortex appears to extend for six years; children who have cataracts or for some other reason are unable to see during this period also suffer permanent damage to their vision (Thompson, 1993). Similarly, movement contributes to the development of the motor cortex; a child who must be in a body cast until age 4 will learn to walk with time but will probably never walk as smoothly as other children (Begley, 1996).

The immature brain is also plastic in the sense that it is highly responsive to each individual's unique experiences (Johnson, 1997; Greenough et al., 1987). On the negative side, the developing brain is highly vulnerable to damage if it is exposed to drugs or diseases (recall the discussion of teratogens in Chapter 3) or if it is deprived of sensory and motor experiences. On the positive side, though, this highly adaptable brain can often recover successfully from injuries. Neurons are not yet fully committed to their specialized functions and can often take over the functions of neurons that are damaged (Rakic, 1991). Moreover, the immature brain is especially able to benefit from stimulating experiences. Rats that grow up in enriched environments with plenty of sensory stimulation develop larger, better-functioning brains with more synapses than rats that grow up in barren cages (Bennett et al., 1964; Greenough et al., 1987). Brain plasticity is greatest early in development. However, the organization of synapses within the nervous system continues to change in response to experience throughout the life span. Indeed, synapses can come and go in a matter of hours or days (Thompson, 1993). Animals put through their paces in mazes grow bushier dendrites, but their brains will lose some of their complexity if the animals are moved to less stimulating quarters (Thompson, 1993).

In short, the critical period for brain development, the time when it occurs most rapidly, is during the late prenatal period and early infancy. The processes of proliferation, migration, differentiation, and synaptogenesis all contribute to the final product. The developing brain is characterized by a good deal of plasticity; normal genes may provide rough guidelines as to how the brain should be configured, but early experience determines the specific architecture of the brain.

Later Brain Development

Although new neurons are no longer forming during childhood, the brain is still developing. By a child's fifth birthday the brain has achieved fully 90% of its adult weight. The myelination of neurons continues throughout childhood, and the different areas of the brain become more specialized.

One important example of the developing organization of the brain is the **lateralization,** or specialization, of the two hemispheres of the cerebral cortex. In most people the left cerebral hemisphere controls the right side of the body and is specially equipped to process language, whereas the right hemisphere controls the left side of the body and specializes in processing music and in carrying out such spatial activities as mentally visualizing designs. Because of lateralization, we come to rely more on one hand or side of the body than on the other. About 90% of us rely on our right hands (or left hemispheres) to write and perform other motor activities.

When exactly does the brain become lateralized? Signs of brain lateralization are clearly evident at birth. From the first day of life, speech sounds stimulate slightly more electrical activity in the left side of the cerebral cortex than in the right (Molfese, 1977). In addition, most newborns turn to the right rather than to the left when they lie on their backs, and these same babies later tend to reach for objects with their right hands (Michel, 1981). This evidence suggests that young brains are already organized in a lateralized fashion (Kinsbourne, 1989).

Nonetheless, hand preferences usually do not stabilize until after infancy. As children develop, they come to rely more and more consistently on one hemisphere or the other to carry out various tasks. This developmental trend involves a change in how the two sides of the brain are *used,* however, rather than a fundamental change in the brain's structure (Kinsbourne, 1989).

Stanley Coren, Clare Porac, and Pam Duncan (1981) showed that preferences for using one side of the body or the other become stronger between the preschool years and the high school years. They asked 3- to 5-year-olds and high school students to do such things as pick up a crayon, kick a ball, look into an opaque bottle to identify what was inside, or put an ear close to a box to hear sounds coming from it. In this way they could see which hand, foot, eye, or ear each child favored. Although most preschoolers already preferred their right hands and feet, right eyes and ears were preferred more clearly by high school students than by the young children. Moreover, only about 32% of the preschoolers consistently demonstrated preference for the right side of the body on all tasks, whereas about 52% of the adolescents did.

Overall, then, the brain appears to be structured very early so that the two hemispheres of the cortex will be capable of specialized functioning. As we develop, the large majority of us come to rely more on the left hemisphere to carry out language activities and more on the right hemisphere to do such things as perceive shapes and listen to music. We also come to rely more consistently on one hemisphere, usually the left, to control many of our physical activities.

When does the brain complete its development? Through the ages, adults have noticed that teenagers are more likely than children to ask hypothetical "what if" questions and to reason about weighty abstractions such as truth and justice. Are these shifts in thinking tied to late developments within the brain? Some researchers believe that growth spurts in the brain occur at just the times in infancy, childhood, and adolescence at which Jean Piaget and others believe major cognitive breakthroughs occur (Case, 1992; Somsen et al., 1997). They believe that a reorganization of the brain is responsible for breakthroughs in adolescent thinking.

Indeed, the brain enters a final phase of development between ages 12 and 20. By about age 16 the brain reaches its full adult weight (Tanner, 1990). Myelination of certain pathways, including those that allow us to concentrate for lengthy periods of time, continues during adolescence (Benes, 1989; Tanner, 1990). This may help explain why infants, toddlers, school-age children, and even young adolescents have shorter attention spans than do older adolescents and adults (Tanner, 1990). The speed at which the nervous system processes information also continues to increase during adolescence (Kail, 1991).

Finally, organization of the neural circuitry of the prefrontal cortex, which is involved in higher-level cognitive activities such as strategic planning, impulse control, and self-monitoring of thought continues until the age of 20 or so (Spreen et al., 1995; Stuss, 1992). Twelve-year-olds, even those who are intellectually gifted, are often "clever" but are rarely what one would call "wise." They can solve many problems correctly, but they are not as skilled as adults at showing foresight or adopting broad perspectives on problems (Segalowitz, Unsal, & Dywan, 1992). Although changes in the brain during adolescence are less dramatic than those earlier in life, it is quite likely that some of the cognitive growth we observe during the teenage years becomes possible only after adolescents' brains undergo a process of reorganization and fine-tuning.

The Aging Brain

Many people fear that aging means losing one's brain cells and ultimately becoming "senile." As we'll see in Chapter 16, *Alzheimer's disease* (and other conditions that cause serious brain damage and dementia) are *not* part of normal aging; they do not affect the majority of older people. Normal aging *is* associated with gradual and relatively mild *degeneration* within the nervous system—a loss of neurons, diminished functioning of many remaining neurons, and potentially harmful changes in the tissues surrounding and supporting neurons (Selkoe, 1992). As people age, more and more of their neurons atrophy or shrivel, transmit signals less effectively, and ultimately die (Bondareff, 1985). Just as brain weight and volume increase over the childhood years, they decrease over the adult years, especially after age 50 (Yamaura, Ito, Kubota, & Matsuzawa, 1980). Elderly adults may end up with 5 to 30% fewer neurons, depending on the brain site studied, than they had in young adulthood (Selkoe, 1992). Neuron loss is greater in the areas of the brain that control sensory and motor activities than in either the association areas of the cortex (involved in thought) or the brain stem and lower brain (involved in basic physiological functions such as breathing; Whitbourne, 1985).

Other signs of brain degeneration besides neuron loss include (1) declines in the levels of important neurotransmitters; (2) the formation of "senile plaques," hard areas in the tissue surrounding neurons that may interfere with neuronal functioning and are seen in abundance in people with Alzheimer's disease; and (3) reduced blood flow to the brain, which may starve neurons of the oxygen and nutrients they need in order to function (Bondareff, 1985). One of the main implications of such degeneration, as we will see later, is that older brains typically process information more slowly than younger brains do.

However, recent research suggests that the aging brain is characterized not only by degeneration but also by *plasticity*. The brain can change in response to experience and develop new capabilities *throughout the life span* (Black, Isaacs, & Greenough, 1991; Johnson, 1997). For example, one team of researchers compared brain tissue collected from autopsies of middle-aged adults, normal elderly adults, and elderly adults who had Alzheimer's disease (Buell & Coleman, 1979; Flood et al., 1987; Flood & Coleman, 1990). Like other researchers, they found evidence of neural loss with age. But they also discovered that neurons often had longer, bushier dendrites—and presumably were able to make more new synapses with other neurons—in early old age than in middle age (Coleman & Flood, 1987). Dendrites were sparser among very old people and among Alzheimer's patients.

In part, brain plasticity in later life may be a compensation for brain degeneration; surviving neurons seem to step in to carry out the functions of dead or dying neurons (Bondareff, 1985; Flood & Coleman, 1990). This may allow the aging person to maintain abilities quite well despite some normal neural loss. But brain growth in old age is also a direct response to stimulation or experience. For example, placing adult rats in living environments that are more complex and stimulating than their usual laboratory cages results in measurable neural growth (Black et al., 1989; Connor, Diamond, & Johnson, 1980). The aging brain is clearly less plastic, less influenced by environmental enrichment or deprivation, than the infant brain (Black et al., 1991). However, the brain clearly retains some of its plasticity *throughout* the life span.

What does it mean for older adults that both degeneration and plasticity—both losses and gains—characterize the aging brain? In some people, degeneration may win out, and intellectual performance will decline. In other people, plasticity may prevail; their brains may form new and adaptive neural connections faster than they are lost so that performance on some tasks may actually *improve* with age (at least until very old age). As we'll see in chapters 7, 8, and 9, older adults differ widely in how effectively they learn, re-

Mental "exercise" in later life is likely to contribute to neural growth in the aging brain and compensate for neural degeneration.

member, and think, as well as in how well their intellectual abilities hold up as they age (Morse, 1993). On average, though, plasticity and growth may make up for degeneration until people are in their 70s and 80s. One key to maintaining or even improving performance in old age is to avoid the many diseases that can interfere with nervous-system functioning. Another key is to remain intellectually active—to create an "enriched environment" for one's brain. Certainly we can reject the view that aging involves nothing but a slow death of neural tissue. Old brains *can* learn new tricks!

Having looked at the development of the endocrine system and the nervous system, we are in a position to examine the development and aging of the physical self. We concentrate on the body (its size, composition, and functioning) and the use of body and brain in physical activities such as locomotion and finely controlled movements.

THE INFANT

Tremendous amounts of growth and physical development occur during the two years of infancy. Understanding the newborn's capacities and limitations brings a fuller appreciation of the dramatic changes that take place between birth and adulthood.

The Newborn

Newborns used to be viewed as helpless little organisms unprepared to cope with the world outside the

TABLE 5.2

Reflexes	Developmental Course	Significance
SURVIVAL REFLEXES		
Breathing reflex	Permanent	Provides oxygen and expels carbon dioxide
Eye-blink reflex	Permanent	Protects eyes from bright light or foreign objects
Pupillary reflex: Constriction of pupils to bright light; dilation to dark or dimly lit surroundings	Permanent	Protects against bright lights; adapts visual system to low illumination
Rooting reflex: Turning of cheek in direction of a tactile (touch) stimulus	Gradually weakens over the first 6 months of life	Orients child to breast or bottle
Sucking reflex: Sucking on objects placed (or taken) into mouth	Is gradually modified by experience over the first few months of life	Allows child to take in nutrients
Swallowing reflex	Is permanent but modified by experience	Allows child to take in nutrients and protects against choking
PRIMITIVE REFLEXES		
Babinski reflex: Fanning and then curling toes when bottom of foot is stroked	Usually disappears within the first 8 months to 1 year of life	Presence at birth and disappearance in first year indicate normal neurological development
Grasping reflex: Curling of fingers around objects (such as a finger) that touch baby's palm	Disappears in first 3–4 months; is replaced by a voluntary grasp	Presence at birth and later disappearance indicate normal neurological development
Moro reflex: Loud noise or sudden change in position of baby's head will cause baby to throw arms outward, arch back, and then bring arms toward each other as if to hold onto something	Disappears over the first 6–7 months; however, child continues to react to unexpected noises or a loss of bodily support by showing a startle reflex (which does not disappear)	Presence at birth and later disappearance (or evolution into the startle reflex) indicate normal neurological development
Swimming reflex: Infant immersed in water will display active movements of arms and legs and involuntarily hold breath (thus staying afloat for some time)	Disappears in first 4–6 months	Presence at birth and later disappearance indicate normal neurological development
Stepping reflex: Infants held upright so that their feet touch a flat surface will step as if to walk	Disappears in first 8 weeks unless infant has regular opportunities to practice it	Presence at birth and later disappearance indicate normal neurological development

NOTE: Preterm infants may show little or no evidence of primitive reflexes at birth, and their survival reflexes are likely to be irregular or immature. However, the missing reflexes will typically appear soon after birth and will disappear a little later than they do among full-term infants.

womb. We now know that they are far better equipped for life than that. What *are* the capabilities of the newborn? Reflexes, functioning senses, a capacity to learn, and organized, individualized patterns of waking and sleeping are among them.

One of the newborn's greatest strengths is a full set of useful **reflexes.** A reflex is an unlearned and automatic response to a stimulus, as when the eye automatically blinks in response to a puff of air. Reflexes can be contrasted with the newborn's spontaneous arm waving, leg kicking, and thrashing—movements that have no obvious stimulus. Table 5.2 lists some reflexes that can be readily observed in all normal newborns. These seemingly simple reactions are actually quite graceful, varied, and complex patterns of behavior (Prechtl, 1981).

Some reflexes are called *survival reflexes* because they have clear adaptive value. Examples include the breathing reflex (useful for obvious reasons), the eye-blink reflex (which protects against bright lights or

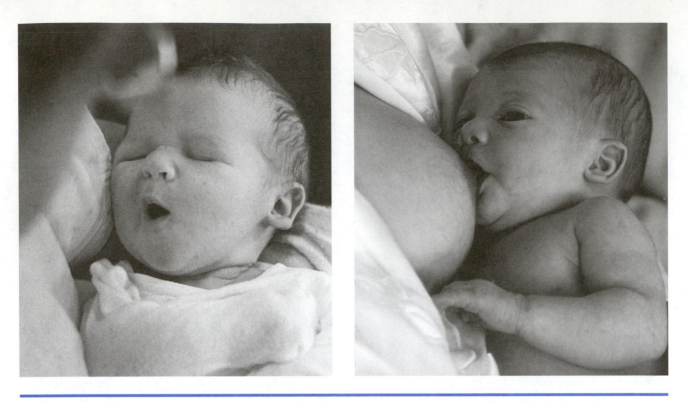

The rooting reflex (left) and the sucking reflex (right) are two of the newborn's adaptive reflexes. The infant will turn in the direction of a touch on the cheek, searching for something to suck, and then will suck an object placed in its mouth.

foreign particles), and the sucking reflex (needed to obtain food). The so-called *primitive reflexes* are not nearly as useful; in fact, many are believed to be remnants of our evolutionary history that have outlived their purpose. The *Babinski reflex* is a good example. Why would it be adaptive for infants to fan their toes when the bottoms of their feet are stroked? We don't know. Other primitive reflexes may have adaptive value, at least in some cultures. For example, the grasping reflex may help infants who are carried in slings or on their mothers' hips to hang on. Finally, other primitive reflexes—for example, the grasping reflex and the stepping reflex—may be forerunners of useful voluntary behaviors that develop later in infancy (Fentress & McLeod, 1986).

Primitive reflexes typically disappear during the early months of infancy. For instance, the grasping reflex becomes very weak by 4 months. These primitive reflexes are controlled by the lower, "subcortical" areas of the brain and are lost as the higher centers of the cerebral cortex develop and make voluntary motor behaviors possible. Even though many primitive reflexes are not very useful to infants, they have proven to be extremely useful in diagnosing infants' neurological problems. If such reflexes are *not* present at birth—or if they last too long in infancy—we know that something is wrong with a baby's nervous system. The existence of reflexes at birth tells us that infants come to

life ready to respond to stimulation in adaptive ways. The disappearance of certain reflexes tells us that the nervous system is developing normally and that experience is having an impact on both brain and behavior.

A second strength of newborns is their *senses*. As we saw in Chapter 4, the sensory systems are developing before birth, and (as we shall see in Chapter 6) all of the senses are functioning reasonably well at birth. Newborns do indeed see and hear, and they respond to tastes, smells, and touches in predictable ways too. For instance, newborns scan the borders between white and black squares, as though they follow this rule of seeing: "Look for edges in the visual world" (Haith, 1980). They turn away from loud noises, but turn in the direction of softer sounds (Field et al., 1980).

A third strength of newborns is their *ability to learn* from their experiences. They can, for example, learn to suck faster if sucking produces a pleasant-tasting sugary liquid rather than plain water (Kron, 1966; Lipsitt, 1990). In other words, they can change their behavior according to its consequences (see Chapter 8 on learning capacities).

Finally, the fact that newborns have *organized and individualized patterns of daily activity* is another sign that they are well equipped for life. As we saw in Chapter 4, *infant states* are the different levels of consciousness that newborns experience in a typical day.

They include quiet sleep; active sleep that involves a good deal of body movement and irregular breathing; drowsiness; nonalert waking, in which the infant is active but not attentive; alert waking, in which the infant has bright eyes and is very attentive; and fussing or crying (Thoman & Whitney, 1990; Wolff, 1966). These states help regulate the infant's interactions with its environment and tell us that the infant's physiological processes are well organized from birth (Thoman & Whitney, 1990). Infants rarely have problems establishing regular sleep cycles, for example, unless their nervous systems are abnormal in some way, so assessment of infant states can help identify babies with neurological abnormalities (Halpern, MacLean, & Baumeister, 1995).

Newborns average about 70% of their time (16–18 hours a day) sleeping and only two to three hours in a state of alert inactivity actively taking in what is going on around them (Berg, Adkinson, & Strock, 1973; Hutt, Lenard, & Prechtl, 1969). Moreover, newborns spend fully half of their sleeping hours in active sleep, also called **REM sleep** (for the rapid eye movements that occur during it). By comparison, infants older than 6 months spend only 25 to 30% of their total sleep in REM sleep, children and adults about 20%. During REM sleep, brain activity is more typical of wakefulness than of regular (non-REM) sleep; adults awakened from REM sleep usually report that they were dreaming. Why, then, do young infants spend so much time in REM sleep? It has been suggested that REM sleep provides young infants with plenty of internal stimulation that allows their nervous systems to mature (Boismier, 1977; Roffwarg, Muzio, & Dement, 1966).

Research on infant states also makes it clear that newborns have a good deal of individuality (Thoman & Whitney, 1990). In a study by Brown (1964), one newborn was observed to be in an alert waking state only 4% of the time, whereas another was alert 37% of the time. Similarly, one newborn cried only 17% of the time, but another spent fully 39% of its time crying. Such variations among infants have obvious implications for parents. It is likely to be far more pleasant to be with a baby who is often alert and rarely cries than it is to interact with a baby who is rarely attentive and frequently fussy. As we saw in Chapter 3, both genetic endowment and environment contribute to these kinds of differences in infant temperament.

Newborn infants are indeed competent and ready for life. They have a wide range of reflexes, functioning senses, a capacity to learn, and an organized and unique pattern of waking and sleeping. But think for a moment about newborns in comparison to adults: Let's also bear in mind that newborns are quite limited beings. Their brains are not nearly as developed as they will be by the end of infancy. Their capacity to move *voluntarily and intentionally* is limited, and al-though their senses are working, they are not as able to interpret stimuli as an older individual is. They can learn, but they are slow learners compared to older children, often requiring many learning trials before they form an association between stimulus and response. And they clearly lack important social and communication skills. In short, newborns have *both* strengths and limitations—strengths that can serve as building blocks for later development, limitations that tell us much remains to be accomplished.

Physical Growth

Newborns are typically about 20 inches long and weigh 7 to 7½ pounds. Boys are longer than girls at birth and during the first two years of life, although not during the preschool years (Hauspie et al., 1996). Weight and length at birth can mislead us about eventual weight and height, though, because the growth of some fetuses is stunted by a poor prenatal environment (Hauspie et al., 1996). In the first few months of life, infants grow rapidly, gaining nearly an ounce of weight a day and an inch in length each month. By age 2, they have already attained about half of their eventual adult height and weigh 27 to 30 pounds. If they continued growing at this rapid pace until age 18, they would stand about 12 feet 3 inches high and weigh several tons!

We usually think of growth as a slow and steady process, but daily measurements of infant length show that babies grow in fits and starts (Lampl, Veldhuis, & Johnson, 1992). They may grow a couple of centimeters one day and then not grow at all for a few days before experiencing another little growth spurt. In the end, 90 to 95 percent of an infant's days are growth free, and yet their occasional bursts of physical growth add up to substantial increases in size.

Bones and muscles also develop quickly during infancy. At birth most of the infant's bones are soft, pliable, and difficult to break. They are too small and flexible to allow newborns to sit up or balance themselves when pulled to a standing position. The soft cartilage-like tissues of the young infant gradually ossify (harden) into bony material as calcium and other minerals are deposited into them. In addition, more bones develop, and they become more closely interconnected. As for muscles, young infants are relative weaklings. They have all the muscle cells they will ever have, but their strength will increase as their muscles grow larger.

Principles of Growth

You have probably noticed that young infants seem to be all head compared to older children and adults. That is because growth follows the **cephalo-caudal principle**: it occurs in a head-to-tail direction. This pattern is clear in Figure 5.3: The head is far

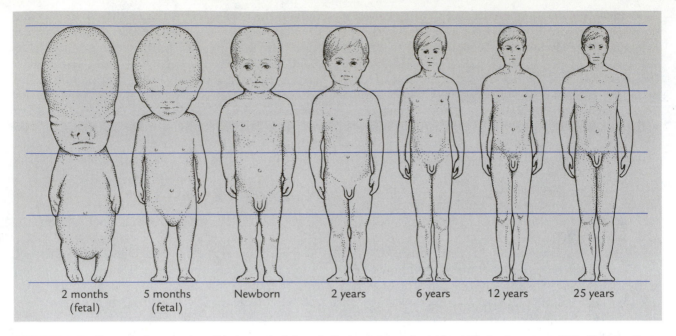

FIGURE 5.3 *Changes in the proportions of the human body from the fetal period through adulthood. The head represents 50% of body length at two months after conception but only 12–13% of adult height. By contrast, the legs constitute only about 12–13% of the length of a 2-month-old fetus but 50% of an adult's height.*

ahead of the rest of the body during the prenatal period and accounts for about 25% of the newborn's length. But the head accounts for only 12% of an adult's height. During the first year after birth, the trunk grows the fastest; in the second year, the legs are the fastest growing part of the body. Muscles develop and neurons become myelinated in the same head-to-tail order.

While infants are growing from the head downward, they are also growing and developing muscles from the center outward to the extremities. This **proximodistal principle** of growth can be seen during the prenatal period, when the chest and internal organs form before the arms, hands, and fingers. During the first year of life, the trunk is rapidly filling out while the arms remain short and stubby until they undergo their own period of rapid development.

A third important principle of growth and development is the **orthogenetic principle** set forth by pioneering developmental theorist, Heinz Werner (1957): "Wherever development occurs it proceeds from a state of relative globality and lack of differentiation to a state of increasing differentiation, articulation, and hierarchical integration" (p. 126). A human starts out as a single, undifferentiated cell at conception; this is the global state of which Werner wrote. But then, as growth proceeds, that single cell becomes billions of highly specialized cells (neurons, blood cells, liver cells, and so on). Moreover, these differentiated cells become organized, or integrated, into functioning systems such as the brain or the digestive system. Overall,

then, physical growth is orderly, obeying the cephalocaudal, proximodistal, and orthogenetic principles. As we will see shortly, motor development follows these very same principles.

The rapid physical and muscular growth that occurs during infancy, combined with the development of the nervous system, helps make possible the tremendous advances in motor development that we see during these two years.

Physical Behavior

The motor behaviors of newborns are far more organized and sophisticated than they appear to be at first glance (Prechtl, 1981). Yet newborns are not ready to dance or thread needles. By age 2, however, immobile infants have become toddlers, walking up and down stairs by themselves and using their hands to accomplish simple self-care tasks and to operate toys. How do the motor skills involved in walking and manipulating objects develop?

Locomotor Development

Examine the motor milestones listed in Table 5.3. Column 2 shows the age at which 50% of U.S. infants master each skill. This average age of mastery is called the **developmental norm** for a skill. Column 3 indicates when almost all infants (90%) have mastered each milestone. Developmental norms like these must be interpreted carefully. They depend on the group studied (children walk earlier today than they used to and walk earlier in some cultures than in others), and they hide a good deal of variation among children, even in the sequence in which skills are mastered (von Hofsten, 1993). Finally, most children who master a skill earlier or later than the developmental norm are still within the normal range of development. Parents should not be alarmed if their child is a month or two "behind" the norm; only significantly delayed achievement of new skills is cause for concern.

Can you recognize the workings of the cephalocaudal and proximodistal principles of development in the milestones in Table 5.3? Early motor development does obey the *cephalocaudal principle,* because the neurons between the brain and the muscles myelinate in a head-to-tail manner. Thus, infants can lift their heads before they can control their trunks enough to sit, and they can sit before they can control their legs to walk. The *proximodistal principle* of development is less obvious in Table 5.3 but is also evident in early motor development. Activities involving the trunk are mastered before activities involving the arms and legs, and activities involving the arms and legs are mastered before activities involving the hands and fingers or feet and toes. Therefore, infants can roll over before they can walk or bring their arms together to grasp a bottle, and children generally master **gross motor skills** (skills such as kicking the legs or drawing large circles that involve large muscles and whole body or limb movements) before mastering **fine motor skills** (skills such as picking Cheerios off the breakfast table or writing letters of the alphabet that involve precise movements of the hands and fingers or feet and toes). As the nerves and muscles mature in a downward and outward direction, infants gradually gain control over the lower and the peripheral parts of their bodies.

The *orthogenetic principle* is also evident in early motor development. A very young infant is likely to hurl his whole body as a unit at a bottle of milk held close by (global response). An older infant gains the ability to move specific parts of her body separately (differentiation); she may be able to extend one arm toward the bottle without extending the other arm, move the hand but not the arm to grasp it, and so on, making distinct, differentiated movements. Finally, the still older infant is able to coordinate separate movements in a functional sequence—reaching for, grasping, and pulling in the bottle while opening the mouth to receive it and closing the mouth when the prize is captured (integration). The orthogenetic principle applies to the learning of motor skills in adulthood, too. For example, a novice tennis player may have to practice the elements of a good serve separately before integrating them into a smooth serving motion. Indeed, in many areas of development humans increasingly master a range of more and more specific responses (differentiation) and combine these responses into more organized and coherent patterns (integration).

TABLE 5.3

Age norms (in months) for important motor milestones (based on Anglo-American, Hispanic, and African-American children in the United States)

Skill	Month When 50% of Infants Have Mastered the Skill	Month When 90% of Infants Have Mastered the Skill
Lifts head 90° while lying on stomach	2.2	3.2
Rolls over	2.8	4.7
Sits without support	5.5	7.8
Stands holding on	5.8	10.0
Walks holding on	9.2	12.7
Walks well	12.1	14.3
Walks up steps	17.0	22.0
Kicks ball forward	20.0	24.0

SOURCE: Adapted from Frankenburg & Dodds, 1967

Crawling. Life changes dramatically for infants and their parents when the infants first begin to crawl or creep, normally at around 7 months of age. Different infants find different ways to navigate at first; one may slither on her belly in a kind of combat crawl, another may use only his forearms to pull ahead, another may chug along backward. However, infants end up crawling on their hands and knees at about 10 months of age, and they all seem to figure out that the best way to keep their balance is to move the arm and leg that are diagonal to one another at the same time (Freedland & Bertenthal, 1994).

With their new mobility, infants are better able to explore the objects around them and to interact with other people. Experience moving through the spatial world contributes to cognitive, social, and emotional development (see Bertenthal, Campos, & Kermoian, 1994). For example, crawlers, as well as noncrawlers who are made mobile with the aid of special walkers, are more able to search for and find hidden objects than are infants of the same age who are not mobile. Crawling also contributes to more frequent social interactions with parents and to the emergence of a healthy fear of heights.

Walking. Although parents must be on their toes when their infants first begin walking, at about one year of age, they take great delight in witnessing this new milestone in motor development, as do infants themselves. According to Esther Thelen (1984, 1995), the basic motor patterns required for walking are present at birth. They are evident in the newborn's stepping reflex and in the spontaneous kicking that infants do when they are lying down. Indeed, Thelen noticed that the stepping reflex and early kicking motions were actually identical, and she then began to question the idea that early reflexes, controlled by subcortical areas of the brain, are inhibited once the cortex takes control of movements. Thelen showed that it simply required more strength to make the walking motion standing up (as in the stepping reflex) than to make it lying down (as in kicking); she also showed that babies who no longer showed the stepping motion when placed on a table *did* show it when their legs were in water and less muscle power was needed to move their chunky legs.

The upshot? Infants need more than a more mature nervous system in order to walk; they must also develop more muscle and become less top-heavy. Even when they do begin to walk, they lack good balance, partly because of their big heads and short legs. Steps are short; legs are wide apart; and hips, knees, and ankles are flexed. There is much teetering and falling, and a smooth gait and good balance will not be achieved for some time. Thelen's point is that we would walk funny too if we, like infants, were "fat, weak, and unstable" (Thelen, 1984, p. 246).

Manipulating Objects

When we look at what infants can do with their hands, we also see a progression from reflexive activity to more voluntary, coordinated behavior. As we saw, newborns come equipped with a grasping reflex. It weakens at 2 to 4 months of age, and for a time infants cannot aim their grasps very well. They take swipes at objects, and even make contact more than you'd expect by chance, but they often miss. And rather than opening their hands in order to grasp what they are reaching for, they make a fist (Bower, 1982; von Hofsten, 1993).

By the middle of the first year, infants can once again grasp objects well, although they use a rather clumsy, clamplike grasp in which they press the palm and outer fingers together. Their eyes and hands are better coordinated than the younger infant's; they reach for an object along a straighter path and can correct their reach, if necessary, to obtain the target (von Hofsten, 1993; Mathew & Cook, 1990). The workings of the proximodistal principle of development can be seen when infants who could control their arms and then their hands finally become able to control the individual fingers enough to use a **pincer grasp.** Involving only the thumb and the forefinger (or another finger), the pincer grasp appears at about 9 to 12 months (Halverson, 1931).

By 16 months of age infants can scribble with a crayon, and by the end of the second year they can copy a simple horizontal or vertical line and even build towers of five or more blocks. They are rapidly

Young toddlers have difficulty maintaining their balance because of their large, heavy heads and torsos and their weak muscles.

gaining control of specific, *differentiated* movements and then *integrating* those movements into whole, coordinated actions. They use their new locomotor and manipulation skills to get to know and adapt to the world around them. By cornering bugs and stacking Cheerios, they develop their minds.

Nature, Nurture, and Motor Development

Infants do not need to be taught basic motor skills. Motor development depends in part on the maturation of body and brain, and infants all over the world progress through the same motor milestones in just about the same order and at just about the same times.

Yet experience plays a critical role in motor development as well. For one thing, it affects the rate at which infants progress through the sequence of motor milestones. For example, infants who are given opportunities to practice their stepping reflex early in life walk at an earlier age than infants who do not receive this early training (Zelazo, Zelazo, & Kolb, 1972). Moreover, cross-cultural studies tell us that the ages at which infants attain milestones in motor development are influenced by their parents' beliefs about motor development and by the opportunities available to practice motor skills. For example, Brian

Hopkins (1991) compared the motor development of white infants in England to that of black infants whose families immigrated to England from Jamaica. The black infants developed motor skills at earlier ages but did so primarily when their mothers adhered to traditional Jamaican practices for handling infants and nurturing motor development. These handling routines involve massaging infants, stretching and rotating their limbs, eliciting their stepping responses, holding them by the arms and shaking them gently up and down, throwing them into the air, and even holding them by the ankles upside down. Jamaican mothers expect early motor development, work to achieve it, and get it.

Yet infants who do not receive nearly so much opportunity to practice their motor skills still develop normal motor skills. It seems that infants do not need special motor training, but they *do* need normal opportunities to move around. For example, Wayne Dennis (1960) studied infants in institutional settings who spent most of their time lying on their backs, often on hollowed-out mattresses that made it impossible for them even to roll over onto their stomachs. Only 8% of the 2- and 3-year-olds and 15% of the 3- and 4-year-olds could walk alone!

Early in the study of human development, it was believed that motor development was due entirely to maturational processes—that motor skills naturally emerge as the brain and body mature. Now a new perspective on motor development (and on other aspects of development as well), the **dynamic systems approach,** has emerged. It proposes that more and more sophisticated patterns of motor behavior emerge over time through a "self-organizing" process in which children use the sensory feedback they receive when they try different movements to modify their motor behavior in adaptive ways (Smith & Thelen, 1993). In this view, motor milestones such as crawling and walking are the learned outcomes of a process of interaction with the environment in which infants do the best they can with what they have in order to achieve their goals (Thelen, 1995). Neural maturation, physical growth, muscle strength, balance, and other characteristics of the child interact with gravity, floor surfaces, and characteristics of the specific task to influence what children can and cannot learn to do with their bodies.

Consider what happens when 6-month-old babies are placed in a contraption called a Jolly Jumper, a harness hanging from a spring attached to a door frame from which infants dangle with their feet barely touching the floor (see Figure 5.4). As Eugene Goldfield, Bruce Kay, and William Warren (1993) observed, infants placed in a Jolly Jumper for the first time must discover on their own how to make it do interesting things. At first, infants in the study tried out a variety of actions, engaging in a form of experimentation,

FIGURE 5.4 *The Jolly Jumper*

or motor "babbling" (Sveistrup & Woollacott, 1996), that allowed them to discover the possibilities. Infants pushed off against the floor now and then and found that they could bounce up and down. Over a period of weeks, using the sensory feedback they received, they then fine-tuned this bouncing motion, figuring out how to use the correct leg thrusts at just the right times to get the best rhythmic bouncing action possible. It would be wrong to say that these infants entered a "bouncing stage" of motor development or to say that their bouncing skills "matured" (Thelen, 1995). Instead, they learned and remembered a coordinated pattern of movement well adapted to the situation they were in—being strapped into the Jolly Jumper.

Similarly, infants who want to get across the room to an interesting person or toy, but who are too pudgy and weak-legged to walk there, learn to navigate on their bellies or on their hands and knees. It is the infant's active exploration of the possibilities for movement that drives them on to more advanced solutions. As infants get older and gain more muscle and more control of their limbs and posture, their solutions to the problem of navigating become more sophisticated. According to the dynamic systems perspective, we walk not because our genetic code programs us to do so but because we *learn* that walking works pretty well, given our biomechanical properties as humans and the characteristics of the environments we must navigate (Thelen, 1995). In the dynamic systems approach, nature (maturation) and nurture (sensory and motor experience) are both essential and largely inseparable.

THE CHILD

Development of the body and motor behavior during childhood is slower than it was during infancy, but it is steady. One need only compare the bodies and the physical feats of the 2-year-old and the 10-year-old to be impressed by how much change occurs over childhood.

Steady Growth

From age 2 until puberty, children gain about 2 to 3 inches in height and 6 to 7 pounds in weight every year. During middle childhood (ages 6–11), children may *seem* to grow very little, probably because the gains are small in proportion to the child's size (4–4½' tall and 60–80 pounds) and therefore harder to detect (Eichorn, 1979). The cephalocaudal and proximodistal principles of growth continue to operate. As the lower parts of the body and the extremities fill out, the child takes on more adultlike body proportions. The bones are continuing to grow and harden, and the muscles are becoming stronger.

Physical Behavior

Infants and toddlers are quite capable of controlling their movements in relation to a stationary world. What they will master during childhood is the ability to move capably in a *changing* environment—when a ball is thrown at them and they must bring their hands together at just the right time to catch it, when they must navigate on a crowded sidewalk, or when the surface they are standing on unexpectedly moves (Keough & Sugden, 1985; Sveistrup & Woollacott, 1996). They will also refine many motor skills. For example, young children throw a ball only with the arm, but older children learn to step forward as they throw. Thus, older children can throw farther than younger ones can, not just because they are bigger and stronger but also because they use more refined and efficient techniques of movement (Haywood, 1986).

The toddler in motion appears awkward compared to the older child, who takes steps in more fluid and rhythmic strides and is better able to avoid obstacles. And children quickly become able to do more than just walk. By age 3, they can walk or run in a straight line, though they cannot easily turn or stop while running. Four-year-olds can skip and hop on one foot (Corbin, 1973). By age 5, children are becom-

Children are not as coordinated in preschool as they will be a few years later.

ing rather graceful. With each passing year, school-age children can run a little faster, jump a little higher, and throw a ball a little farther (Herkowitz, 1978; Keough & Sugden, 1985).

From age 3 to 5, eye/hand coordination and control of the small muscles are improving rapidly, giving children more and more sophisticated use of their hands. Three-year-olds find it difficult to button their shirts, tie their shoes, or copy simple designs. By age 5, children can accomplish all of these feats and can even cut a straight line with scissors or copy letters and numbers with a crayon. By age 8 or 9, they can use household tools such as screwdrivers and have become skilled performers at games that require eye/hand coordination. Handwriting quality and speed also improve steadily from age 6 to age 15 (Van Galen, 1993).

Finally, older children have quicker reactions than young children do. When dogs suddenly run in front of their bikes, they can do something about it. In studies of **reaction time,** a stimulus, such as a light, suddenly appears, and the subject's task is to respond to it as quickly as possible—for example, by pushing a button. These studies reveal that reaction time improves steadily throughout childhood (Thomas, Gallagher, & Purvis, 1981; Wilkinson & Allison, 1989). Indeed, as children get older, they can carry out any number of cognitive processes more quickly (Kail, 1991; Van Galen, 1993). This speeding of neural responses with age contributes in important ways to steady improvements in memory and other cognitive skills from infancy to adolescence (see Chapter 8).

In short, no matter what aspect of physical growth and motor behavior we consider, we see steady and impressive improvement over the childhood years. But these changes are not nearly so dramatic as those that will occur during the adolescent years, as the child becomes an adult.

THE ADOLESCENT

Physical and Sexual Maturation

Think back to the dramatic physical changes of adolescence and your reactions to them. You rapidly grew taller during the **adolescent growth spurt** and took on the body size and proportions of an adult. Moreover, you experienced **puberty,** the processes of biological change that result in an individual's attaining sexual maturity and becoming capable of producing a child. The term *puberty,* by the way, is derived from a Latin word meaning "to grow hairy." Sprouting hair here and there is at least part of what it means to be an adolescent.

The Growth Spurt

Typically, a girl's rapid growth begins at age 10½ and reaches a peak at age 12 (Tanner, 1981). Boys lag behind girls by about two years, so that their growth spurt typically begins at age 13 and peaks at age 14. As a result, there is a period in middle school when many boys appear "shrimpy" compared to many girls. Both sexes return to a slower rate of growth after the peak of their growth spurts. Like infants, adolescents may grow in fits and starts rather than continuously (Lampl et al., 1992).

Different parts of the body grow at different rates. One of the most disturbing aspects of growth for many adolescents is that the extremities of the body enlarge before the trunk and central areas do. Thus, adolescents may be embarrassed by having monstrous feet or protruding noses before the rest of their bodies have caught up. This direction of growth is the opposite of the proximodistal (center to extremities) direction that characterizes early physical development.

Muscles also develop rapidly in both sexes, with boys normally gaining a higher proportion of muscle mass than girls do. Girls gain extra fat, primarily in the breasts, hips, and buttocks. Total body weight increases in both sexes, but it is distributed differently: The hips broaden in young women, the shoulders in young men.

Sexual Maturation

For most girls the first visible sign of sexual maturation is the accumulation of fatty tissue around their nipples, forming small "breast buds" at about age 9 or 10 (Herman-Giddens et al., 1997). Straight, soft pubic hair usually begins to appear a little later, although as many as one-third of all girls develop some pubic hair before their breasts begin to develop (Tanner, 1990). As a girl enters her growth spurt, the breasts grow rapidly and the internal sex organs begin to mature. The most dramatic event in the sexual maturation process is the achievement of **menarche**—the first menstruation—normally between the ages of 11 and 15, with an average of 12½ in the United States (Tanner, 1990). Menstruation freshens the lining of the uterus so that it is ready to support a fertilized egg. However, young girls often begin to menstruate before they have begun to ovulate, so they *may* not actually be capable of reproducing for 12 to 18 months after menarche (Tanner, 1990). In the year after menarche, the breasts and kinky pubic hair also complete their development, and axillary (underarm) hair grows, only to be shaven off by most females in our society (see Figure 5.5).

Physical and sexual maturation among girls in the United States appears to occur a good deal earlier than norms based on older studies indicate, and it proceeds at different rates in different ethnic groups. A recent study by Marcia Herman-Giddens and her colleagues (1997) of physicians' records shows that African-American girls begin to experience pubertal changes a year or more earlier than white girls. At the age of 8, for example, 48% of African-American girls, compared to only 15% of white girls, had begun to develop breasts, pubic hair, or both. African-American girls reached menarche at an average age of 12.1, white girls at 12.9. Wide variation was evident in both racial groups, however; a few girls (1% of whites, 3% of blacks) showed signs of breast or pubic hair development at age 3, while a few had not begun to mature even at age 12!

For the average boy the sexual maturation process begins at about age 11 to 11½ with an initial enlargement of the testes and scrotum (the saclike structure that encloses the testes). Unpigmented, straight pubic hair appears soon thereafter, and about six months later the penis grows rapidly at about the same time that the adolescent growth spurt begins (Tanner, 1990; and see Figure 5.5). The marker of sexual maturation that is most like menarche in girls is a boy's first ejaculation—the emission of seminal fluid in a "wet dream" or while masturbating. It typically occurs at about age 13 to 14. Just as girls often do not ovulate until some time after menarche, boys often do not produce viable sperm until some time after their first ejaculation.

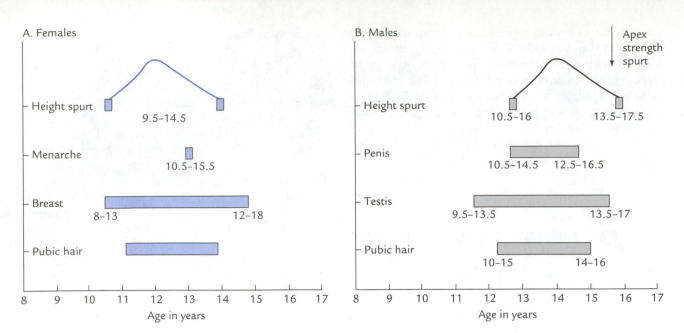

FIGURE 5.5 *Sequence of events in the sexual maturation of females (A) and males (B). The numbers represent the variation among individuals in the ages at which each aspect of sexual maturation begins or ends. For example, we see that the growth of the penis may begin as early as age 10½ or as late as age 14½.* (Adapted from Marshall & Tanner, 1970)

Somewhat later, boys begin to sprout facial hair, first at the corners of the upper lip and finally on the chin and jawline. As the voice lowers, many boys have the embarrassing experience of hearing their voices "crack" uncontrollably up and down between a squeaky soprano and a deep baritone, sometimes within a single sentence. Boys may not see the first signs of a hairy chest until their late teens or early twenties, if at all.

Variations in Timing

As noted above, there are large individual differences in the timing of physical and sexual maturation. An early-maturing girl may develop breast buds at age 8 and reach menarche at age 10, while a late-developing boy may not begin to experience a growth of his penis until age 14½ or a height spurt until age 16. Within a junior high school, then, one will find a wide assortment of bodies, ranging from those that are entirely childlike to those that are fully adultlike. No wonder adolescents are self-conscious about their appearance.

What determines an adolescent's rate of development? Genes are part of the answer: Identical twins typically experience changes at similar times, and early or late maturation tends to run in families (Tanner, 1990). In both sexes the changes involved in physical and sexual maturation are triggered when the hypothalamus of the brain stimulates activity in the endocrine system (see discussion at start of chapter). Boys and girls have similar levels of both male and female sex hormones during childhood. However, by the time sexual maturation is complete, males have larger quantities of male hormones (androgens, including testosterone) circulating in their blood than females do, while females have larger quantities of female hormones (estrogen, progesterone, and others).

Physical and sexual maturation, then, are processes set in motion by the genes and executed by hormones. But environment also plays its part in the timing of maturation. This is dramatically illustrated by the **secular trend,** a historical trend in industrialized societies toward earlier maturation and greater body size. In 1880, for example, the average girl reached menarche at about age 16. In 1900 the average was down to about 14 to 15, and by the 1980s it was down to 12½ (Tanner, 1981). In addition, people have been growing taller and heavier over the past century: Many adolescents are taller than their grandparents, although the secular trend now appears to be leveling off in our society (Tanner, 1981). One can still find cultures where sexual maturity is reached much later than it is in industrialized nations. For example, in one part of New Guinea it was observed that the average girl did not reach menarche until age 18 (Tanner, 1990). Many Third World countries are now experiencing their own secular trends, however.

What explains the secular trend? Better nutrition and advances in medical care seem to be most responsible (Tanner, 1990). Today's children are more likely than their parents or grandparents to reach their genetic potentials for maturation and growth because they are better fed and less likely to experience growth-retarding illnesses. Even within our own relatively affluent society, poorly nourished adolescents mature later than well-nourished ones do. Girls who are tall and overweight as children tend to mature earlier than other girls (St. George, Williams, & Silva, 1994). By contrast, girls who engage regularly in strenuous physical activity and girls who suffer from *anorexia nervosa* (the life-threatening eating disorder that involves dieting to the point of starvation) may begin menstruating very late or stop menstruating after they have begun (Frisch, Wyshak, & Vincent, 1980; Hopwood et al., 1990). Similarly, undernourished boys grow more slowly and are likely to produce fewer viable sperm than their well-fed peers do (Frisch, 1983). Truly, then, physical and sexual maturation are the products of an *interaction* between heredity and environment.

Psychological Implications

What psychological effects do the many changes associated with puberty really have on adolescents? In our culture, girls typically become quite concerned about appearance and worry about how others will respond to them (Greif & Ulman, 1982). One adolescent girl may think she is too tall, another that she is too short. One may try to pad her breasts, whereas another may hunch her shoulders to hide hers. Yet most girls do start to feel better about their bodies, their relationships with peers, and their abilities when they develop breasts (Brooks-Gunn & Warren, 1988). Their emotional reactions to menarche are mixed (Greif & Ulman, 1982). Girls are often a bit excited, but they are often scared and confused as well, especially if they mature early or, like many girls, do not fully understand menstruation or have internalized negative cultural myths about what to expect (Koff & Rierdan, 1995; Moore, 1995). Some develop poor body images because they are bothered by the weight gains that typically accompany menarche (Duncan et al., 1985).

What about boys? Their body images are more positive than those of girls, and they are more likely to welcome their weight gain (Richards et al., 1990). But they hope to be tall, hairy, and handsome, and they may become preoccupied with their physical and athletic prowess (Berscheid, Walster, & Bohrnstedt, 1973). Whereas menarche is a memorable event for girls, boys are often unaware of some of the physical changes they are experiencing (Zani, 1991). Although they notice their first ejaculation, they rarely tell anyone about it, often were not prepared for it, and, like females, express a mix of positive and negative reactions to becoming sexually mature (Gaddis & Brooks-Gunn, 1985; Stein & Reiser, 1994).

Adolescents who are maturing physically and sexually not only come to feel differently about themselves but come to be viewed and treated differently by other people. In many nonindustrial societies of the world, rituals called **rites of passage** communicate to the whole community that a child has become an adult (van Gennep, 1908/1960; Schlegel & Barry, 1991). Among the Kaguru of eastern Africa, for example, boys as young as age 10 to 12 are led into the bush, stripped of their clothes, and shaved of all hair, symbolically losing their status as children (Beidelman, 1971). They then undergo the painful experience of being circumcised without benefit of anesthesia. They learn about sexual practices and are taught ritual songs and riddles that instruct them in the ways of adulthood. Finally, they are "anointed" with red earth to mark their new status as adults and led back to the village for celebrations and feasts. The Kaguru girl is initiated by herself whenever she experiences her first menstruation. Her genital area is cut as a mark of her new status; she is instructed in the ways of adulthood, often by her grandmother; and she too is welcomed back into society as an adult rather than a child.

Pubertal changes may also prompt changes in family relations. Laurence Steinberg (1981, 1988) has found that, around age 11 to 13, when pubertal changes are peaking, the white adolescents he studied in the United States tended to become more independent, less close to their parents, and more likely to experience conflicts with their parents, especially with their mothers. Conflict with parents more often involved minor squabbles about unmade beds, late hours, and loud music than arguments about core values, but it was common. Hormonal changes in early adolescence may contribute to this increased conflict with parents, as well as to moodiness, bouts of depression, lower or more variable energy levels, and restlessness during this period (Buchanan, Eccles, & Becker, 1992). However, cultural beliefs about family relations or about the significance of becoming an adult also influence parent/child interactions during adolescence. For example, many Mexican-American boys and their parents appear to become *closer* rather than more distant during the peak of pubertal changes (Molina & Chassin, 1996).

Even when parent/child relationships are disrupted during early adolescence, they become warmer again once the pubertal transition is completed. Parents—mothers and fathers alike—can help adolescents adjust successfully to puberty by maintaining close relationships and helping adolescents accept themselves (Swarr & Richards, 1996). Overall, we should not imagine that the physical and hormonal changes of puberty cause psychological changes in the individual in a direct and straightforward way. Instead, biological changes interact with psychological characteristics of the person and changes in the social environment to influence how adolescence is experienced (Magnusson, 1995; Paikoff & Brooks-Gunn, 1991).

BOX 5.1

Struggling through puberty

Late-maturing boys and early-maturing girls have the most difficulty adjusting to puberty and its accompanying physical and social changes, perhaps because they stand out as different from their peers for a time. Here, two college students reflect on their experiences.

Late-Maturing Boy:

I didn't grow until I was almost 16 years old. Even after that growth spurt of six inches in six months, I was only 5'6" tall. I still had baby fat around my waist, barely had hair under my arms, and was years away from even thinking about shaving. The fact that everyone around me was developing and I wasn't made me stay home, become less autonomous. I would come home from school, plop myself on the couch, and watch TV for the rest of the day.

Things really started to change in college. I grew to about 5'11" and lost my baby fat. With my maturity, my self-confidence grew.

Early-Maturing Girl:

Suddenly my entire world was drastically and permanently altered by my first outward sign of sexual maturation, the budding of my breasts at age 8. Other girls in my class would make fun

of me or isolate me and make me feel different from them. They would tease me by telling the boys that I wore a bra. Although this does not seem like a big deal now, in the fourth grade it was a very emotionally painful experience.

By the end of fifth grade, I had begun menstruating. It was at this point that older boys became interested in

me. Naturally, I was at first flattered by all of their attention, but I quickly realized what it was that they were after and once again felt very alone. From the day of my first menstruation on, though, I honestly feel that my mom began to give me more responsibility and listen to me.

Early versus Late Development

If "timely" maturation has psychological implications, what is it like to be "off time," to be an especially early or late developer? The answer depends on whether we are talking about males or females and also on whether we examine their adjustment during adolescence or later on (see Box 5.1).

Consider the short-term impacts of being an early-developing or late-developing boy. Other things being equal, the early-developing boy should be at an advantage during the years when he is developed and other boys are not. He is likely to star on the athletic field, impress the girls, and have his way in fights, if nothing else. Indeed, early maturers tend to be poised and confident in social settings, are judged to be attractive, and often win athletic honors and student elections (Jones & Bayley, 1950). The only negative aspect of being an early-maturing boy is earlier involvement in substance use and other problem behaviors (Tschann

et al., 1994). By comparison, late maturation in boys has several disadvantages. Late-maturing boys tend to be more anxious and attention seeking; they tend to feel unsure of themselves and inferior (Jones & Bayley, 1950; Livson & Peskin, 1980). As a group they even score lower than other students do, at least in early adolescence, on school achievement tests (Dubas, Graber, & Petersen, 1991).

Now consider early- and late-maturing girls. Traditionally, physical prowess has not been as important in girls' peer groups as in boys', so an early-developing girl may not gain much status from being larger and more muscled. In addition, since girls develop about two years earlier than boys do, she may be subject to ridicule for a time—the only one in her grade who is developed and thus the target of some teasing. Perhaps for some of these reasons, early maturation appears to be more of a disadvantage than an advantage for girls. Especially when most girls are not yet developed, the early-maturing girl tends to be *less* popular than her prepubertal classmates (Faust, 1960; Jones & Mussen, 1958). She is more likely to report symptoms of depression and anxiety, especially if she had psychological problems as a child (Hayward et al., 1997). And, like the early-maturing boy she is more likely to become involved in the "teen scene" of dating, drinking, having sex, and engaging in minor troublemaking (Simmons & Blyth, 1987; Stattin & Magnusson, 1990; Tschann et al., 1994). But this is a case where the interaction of biological and environmental factors is critical to the outcome: It is when early-maturing girls hang out with older adolescents, especially older boys, that they become involved in early sexuality and other rebellious behaviors and jeopardize their school achievement (Stattin & Magnusson).

Late-maturing girls (like late-maturing boys) may experience some anxiety as they wait to mature, but they are not nearly as disadvantaged as late-maturing boys. Indeed, whereas later-developing boys tend to perform poorly on school achievement tests, later-developing girls outperform other students (Dubas et al., 1991).

Do differences between early and late developers persist into later adolescence and adulthood? Typically they fade with time. By late high school, for example, differences in academic performance between early and late maturers have already disappeared (Dubas et al., 1991), and early-maturing girls are no longer less popular or more prone to depression than other girls (Faust, 1960; Hayward et al., 1997). Some of the advantages of being an early-maturing boy may carry over into adulthood, but early maturers also seem to be more rigid and conforming than late maturers, who may learn some lessons about coping in creative ways from their struggles as adolescents (Jones, 1965). Similarly, struggle may stimulate psy-

chological growth and effective coping skills in early-maturing girls (Livson & Peskin, 1980; Peskin, 1973). In short, those individuals who have a relatively difficult time coping with physical and sexual maturation—late-developing boys and early-developing girls—may learn through their struggles to cope with adversity and respond flexibly to change.

Overall, then, both the advantages of maturing early and the disadvantages of maturing late are greater for males than for females. Late-maturing boys and early-maturing girls are especially likely to find the adolescent period disruptive. However, psychological differences between early- and late-maturing adolescents become smaller and more mixed in quality by adulthood. Finally, let's note that differences between early and late maturers are relatively small and that many other factors besides the timing of maturation influence whether this period of life goes smoothly or not.

Physical Behavior

The dramatic physical growth that occurs during adolescence makes teenagers stronger and more physically competent than children. Rapid muscle development over the adolescent years makes both boys and girls noticeably stronger than they were as children (Faust, 1977). Performance of large-muscle activities continues to improve: An adolescent can throw a ball farther, cover more ground in the standing long jump, and run much faster than a child can (Keough & Sugden, 1985). However, as the adolescent years progress, the physical performance of boys continues to improve, while that of girls often levels off or even declines (Thomas & French, 1985; see also Figure 5.6).

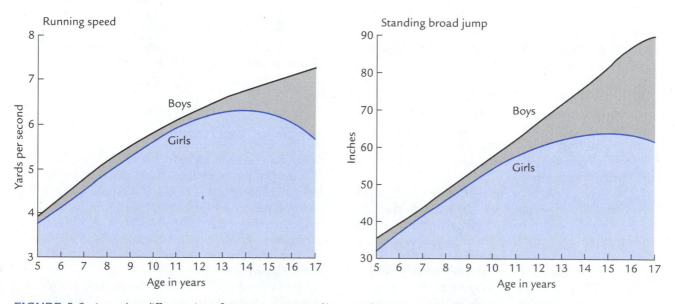

FIGURE 5.6 *Age and sex differences in performance on two tests of large-muscle activity* (From Johnson & Buskirk, 1974)

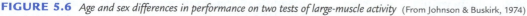

It is easy to see that larger muscles enable boys to outperform girls in activities that require strength. But biological differences cannot entirely explain sex differences in physical performance (Smoll & Schutz, 1990). Gender-role socialization may be partly responsible (Herkowitz, 1978). As girls mature sexually and physically, they are often encouraged to be less "tomboyish" and to become more interested in traditionally "feminine" (and, often, more sedentary) activities. However, studies of world records in track, swimming, and cycling suggest that, as gender roles have changed in the past few decades, women have been improving their performances, and the male/female gap in physical performance has narrowed dramatically (Dyer, 1977; Whipp & Ward, 1992). As today's girls participate more often in sports and other strenuous physical activities, their performance on tests of large-muscle activity is likely to improve during adolescence rather than decline. Then both young women and young men will be likely to enter adulthood in peak physical condition.

THE ADULT

The body of the mature adolescent or young adult is at its prime in many ways. It is strong and fit; its organs are functioning efficiently. But it is aging, as it has been all along. Physical aging occurs slowly and steadily over the entire life span. It begins to have noticeable effects on physical appearance and functioning in middle age and has had an even more significant impact by the time old age is reached, though more in some people than in others. We'll now examine the physical aging process.

Physical Appearance and Structure

Only minor changes in physical appearance occur in the 20s and 30s, but many people do notice signs that they are aging as they reach their 40s. The skin wrinkles, and the hair thins and turns gray (and may drop out by the handfuls in balding men). Middle-age spread may strike as people put on extra weight (and have the "love handles" and potbellies to prove it). Some people find these changes difficult to accept, for they are influenced by societal stereotypes to equate "old" with "unattractive."

The body shows additional effects of aging in old age. After gaining weight from their 20s to their 50s, people typically begin to lose it starting in their 60s (Haber, 1994). Loss of weight in old age is usually coupled with a loss of muscle over the entire span of adulthood (Montoye & Lamphiear, 1977; Murray et al., 1985). The result may be sagging flesh. "Age spots" also appear on the skin, which wrinkles and thins.

The bones lose tissue so that the vertebrae collapse a bit. As a result, people tend to get shorter as they age—by half an inch from about age 60 to 70 if they are men, by an inch if they are women (Adams, Davies, & Sweetnam, 1970). It may seem that elderly adults have shrunk even more than that, but recall the secular trend: Recent cohorts are growing taller than cohorts of the past, and today's older adults are therefore relatively short, even without the bone loss that most experience.

Extreme bone loss in later life results from the disease **osteoporosis,** a disease in which a serious loss of minerals leaves the bones fragile and easily fractured. It involves pain and can actually result in death if the victim falls down and fractures a hip. It is a special problem for older women, who never had as much bone mass as men to start with and whose bones tend to thin rapidly after menopause (Johnston et al., 1985). White and Asian women with light frames who smoke and have a family history of osteoporosis are especially at risk (Haber, 1994). Women with osteoporosis often have the so-called dowager's hump, a noticeably rounded upper back (see Figure 5.7). One long-term victim lost almost six inches in height by age 70 (far more than the average loss of one inch) and ended up with her rib cage sitting on her hip bones (Franklin, 1995).

What can be done to prevent osteoporosis? Increased calcium intake (many adults do not get nearly enough to maintain strong bones), exercise (it must be weight-bearing exercise such as walking or jogging), and female hormones taken to treat menopause (see later section) have all been shown to help prevent or slow osteoporosis (Soules & Bremner, 1982).

The joints are also aging over the adult years. The cushioning between bones wears out, and the joints become stiffer. In its extreme this normal aging process takes the form of *osteoarthritis,* one of the most common disabilities of old age. The older person who can no longer fasten buttons, stoop to pick up dropped items, or even get into and out of the bathtub may easily feel incompetent and dependent (Whitbourne, 1985).

Functioning and Health

Aging also involves a gradual decline in the efficiency of most bodily systems from the 20s on (Christofalo, 1988; Whitbourne, 1985). No matter what physical function we look at—strength, the capacity of the heart or lungs to meet the demands of exercise, the ability of the body to control its temperature, or the ability of the immune system to fight disease—the gradual effects of aging are evident.

Each system of the body seems to have its own timetable of development and aging. However, most

FIGURE 5.7 *The "dowager's hump" associated with osteoporosis*

systems increase to a peak sometime between childhood and early adulthood and decline slowly thereafter (Bafitis & Sargent, 1977; Whitbourne, 1985). During the peak years of physiological functioning, death rates are lower than they are in either infancy or later adulthood. Neither the infant nor the old person is well equipped to cope with such stresses to the body as pneumonia, extreme temperature changes, or exhausting activity.

Yet, it is important to note that individual differences in physiological functioning grow larger with age (Harris et al., 1992). One finds more differences in aerobic capacity and other physiological measures among 70-year-olds than among 20-year-olds. In other words, *not all older people have poor physiological functioning, even though the average old person is less physiologically fit than the average young person.*

Another fact of physical aging is a decline in the **reserve capacity** of many organ systems—that is, their ability to respond to demands for extraordinary output, as in emergencies (Goldberg & Hagberg, 1990). For example, old and young do not differ much in resting heart rates, but older adults, unless they are completely disease-free, will have lower *maximal* heart rates (Lakatta, 1990). This means that older adults

who do not feel very old at all as they go about their normal routines may feel very old indeed if they try to run up mountains.

By the time people are 65 or older, it is hard to find many of them who do not have something or other wrong with their bodies. Acute illnesses such as colds and infections actually become less frequent with age from childhood on, but chronic diseases and disorders become more common (U.S. Bureau of the Census, 1996). National health surveys indicate that over 85% of the 65-and-older age group have at least one chronic impairment, whether it is a sensory loss, a physical disability, or a degenerative disease (Harris, 1978). Arthritis alone affects 48%; in addition, about 37% have hypertension (high blood pressure), and about 30% a heart condition (Jette, 1996). Among older adults who live in poverty, many of whom are minority group members, health problems and difficulties in day-to-day functioning are even more common and also more severe (Clark & Maddox, 1992; Hobbs, 1996).

Yet, despite their chronic diseases and impairments, about 70% of people 65 and older say they are in excellent, very good, or good health (Hobbs, 1996). Moreover, relatively few say they need assistance with daily activities, though the figure climbs with age from 9% of those age 65 to 69 to 50% of those 85 and older (Hobbs, 1996). Also, while having a chronic disease or disability does tend to lower an older person's sense of well-being, many people with arthritis, diabetes, and other difficulties are no less content with their lives than anyone else (Kempen et al., 1997). Clearly the majority of older people are able to retain their sense of well-being and ability to function independently despite an increased likelihood of impairments.

The Reproductive System

During most of adulthood, the sex hormones that start to be secreted during adolescence help to ensure interest in sexual behavior and the ability to have children, but they also have psychological implications and affect the experience of aging. Hormone levels in men fluctuate somewhat from day to day (Harman & Talbert, 1985), and men with high levels of testosterone tend to be more sexually active and aggressive than other men (Schiavi et al., 1991; Archer, 1991). Otherwise, it is not clear that changes in men's hormone levels are tied to changes in their moods and behavior.

By contrast, hormone levels shift drastically each month as women progress through their menstrual cycles, and the shifts have psychological implications for some women. Estrogen and progesterone levels rise to a peak at midcycle, when a woman is ovulating, and decline as she approaches her menstrual period. A minority of women—probably fewer than 10%—experience significant **premenstrual syndrome (PMS)**—irritability, moodiness, and physical symptoms such as breast tenderness and headaches during the days just before the menstrual flow (Woods, Most, & Dery, 1982). However, when women are simply asked to complete mood surveys every day and don't know that their menstrual cycles are being studied, most report little premenstrual mood change at all, suggesting that hormonal fluctuations have little effect on them (Englander-Golden et al., 1986). We can quickly dispense with the sexist notion that a woman could not be president because she might fall apart if an international crisis occurred at the wrong time of the month.

We now know that genetic endowment influences the extent to which a woman experiences both premenstrual and menstrual distress (Condon, 1993; Kendler et al., 1992). Social factors also enter in. Learned societal stereotypes of what women "should" experience at different phases of the menstrual cycle appear to influence what women do experience and report (Ainscough, 1990; Englander-Golden et al., 1986). Most likely, then, biological, psychological, social, and cultural factors all contribute to a woman's experience of the menstrual cycle during her adult life (McFarlane & Williams, 1990).

Menopause

Like other systems of the body, the reproductive system ages. The ending of a woman's menstrual periods in midlife is called **menopause.** Humorist Dave Barry (1990) calls it the stage of life when a woman's body senses that "her furniture is much too nice for her to have a baby barfing on it" (p. 89). Consider the basic facts of this "change of life" (see Matthews, 1992; Voda, 1993). The average woman experiences menopause at age 51, and the usual age range is from 42 to 58. The process actually takes place over about four years on average, as periods become either more or less frequent and less regular (McKinlay, Brambilla, & Posner, 1992). Levels of estrogen and other female hormones decline, so that the woman who has been through menopause has a hormone mix that is less "feminine" and more "masculine" than that of the premenopausal woman. When menopause is completed, a woman is no longer ovulating, no longer menstruating, and no longer capable of conceiving a child.

The age at which a woman reaches menopause is unrelated to the age at which she reached menarche (Treloar, 1982). Although the age of menarche has declined over history as part of the secular trend, the age of menopause does not appear to have changed much and is similar from culture to culture (Greene, 1984). What *has* changed is that women are now living long enough to experience a considerable period of postmenopausal life.

What is your image of a "menopausal woman"? The stereotyped image is this: She is irritable and will scream at you or burst into tears without provocation; she is depressed and emotionally unstable. How much truth is there to this stereotype? Not much at all. About two-thirds of women in our society do experience **hot flashes,** sudden experiences of warmth and sweating, usually centered around the face and upper body, that occur at unpredictable times, last for a few seconds or minutes, and are often followed by a cold shiver (Robinson, 1996). Many also experience *vaginal dryness* and irritation or pain during intercourse as a result. Still other women experience no symptoms at all, however.

What about the psychological symptoms—the irritability and depression? Once again we discover that there is wide variation among menopausal women—and not much truth at all to the negative stereotypes. In a particularly well-designed study, Karen Matthews and her associates (Matthews, 1992; Matthews et al., 1990) studied 541 initially premenopausal women over a three-year period, comparing those who subsequently experienced menopause with women of similar ages who did not become menopausal. The typical woman entering menopause initially experienced some physical symptoms such as hot flashes. Some women also reported mild depression and temporary emotional distress, probably in reaction to their physical symptoms, but only about 10% could be said to have become seriously depressed in response to menopause. Typically, menopause had no effect whatsoever on women's levels of anxiety, anger, perceived stress, or job dissatisfaction. When women *do* experience severe psychological problems during the menopausal transition, they often had those problems well before the age of menopause (Greene, 1984).

Women who have been through menopause generally claim that it had little effect on them or that it even improved their lives; they're usually more positive about it than women who have not been through it yet (Neugarten et al., 1963; Wilbur, Miller, & Montgomery, 1995). For most women, menopause brings no changes one way or the other in sexual interest and activity, although sexual activity does gradually decline in both women and men over the adult years (Greene, 1984). In short, despite all the negative stereotypes, menopause seems to be "no big deal" for most women.

Why do some women experience more severe menopausal symptoms than others do? Partly because some women undergo greater biological changes, but also due to psychological and social factors of the sort that influence women's reactions to sexual maturation and to their menstrual cycles. For example, women who expect menopause to be a negative experience are likely to get what they expect (Matthews, 1992). There is also a good deal of variation across cultures in how menopause is experienced (see Box

BOX 5.2

Cultural differences in the experience of menopause

Menopause is universal, but the experience of it is not. In one study, for example, 69% of a sample of Canadian women reported experiencing at least one hot flash during the menopausal period, but only 20% of Japanese women recalled having had any (Lock, 1993). Indeed, the Japanese have no word for hot flashes and have little use for hormone replacement therapy (Lock, 1993).

Psychological symptoms of menopause vary even more widely from culture to culture (Robinson, 1996). For instance, Marcha Flint (1982) surveyed women of a high and socially advantaged caste in India and found that few of these women experienced any symptoms at all. Women who had not reached menopause looked forward to it, and women who had reached it were pleased that they had. Why? According to Flint, menopause brought social

rewards to these Indian women. They were freed from the taboos associated with menstruation that had kept them veiled and segregated from male society as younger women. They could now mingle with men other than their husbands and fathers and even drink the local brew with the fellows. Moreover, they still had meaningful work roles and were seen as wise by virtue of their years. In our society, by comparison, aging often means a loss of status to older women, and menopause is regarded as a medical condition of aging to be treated with hormones.

Cultural attitudes can clearly influence adjustment to biological change. Within any cultural or socioeconomic group, of course, individual women will also differ tremendously in their responses to this universal transition. Biological, psychological, and social factors all play a part.

5.2). It appears that the impact of menopause is colored by the meaning it has to a woman, as influenced by her society's prevailing views of menopause and by her own personal characteristics.

In our society, **hormone replacement therapy (HRT)** (taking estrogen and progestin to compensate for hormone loss due to menopause) is increasingly recommended to women who are beginning to experience menopausal changes. This hormone treatment relieves physical symptoms of menopause such as hot flashes and vaginal dryness, prevents or slows osteoporosis, and protects against the increased risk of coronary heart disease associated with the loss of estrogen (Grodstein et al., 1996; Matthews, 1992). It may relieve depression (Zweifel & O'Brien, 1997), and it may even lower the odds of Alzheimer's disease (Henderson, 1997; Paganini-Hill & Henderson, 1996). Not everyone agrees with the philosophy of treating a natural change associated with aging as though it were a medical condition, however, and concern remains about a small increase in the risk of breast cancer associated with hormone replacement therapy (Col et al., 1997; Voda, 1993).

The Male Climacteric

Despite popular references to the "male menopause," men cannot experience menopause, since they do not menstruate. What they can experience is captured by the term **climacteric**—meaning "critical time" or, more specifically, the loss of reproductive capacity in either sex in later life. Women experience their climacteric within a relatively narrow age range around age 50. Men, however, may lose the ability to father children around then, much later, or even never: Men in their 90s have been known to father children. The sperm produced by older men may not be as active as those produced by younger men. Levels of testosterone also decrease very gradually over the adult years in most men (Schiavi et al., 1991), although not in extremely healthy men (Harman & Tsitouras, 1980). In sum, the changes associated with the climacteric in men are more gradual, more variable, and less complete than those in women (Soules & Bremner, 1982). As a result, they have few psychological impacts. Frequency of sexual activity does decline as men age. However, this trend cannot be blamed entirely on decreased hormone levels, because sexual activity often declines even when testosterone levels remain high (Tsitouras, Martin, & Harman, 1982; see also Chapter 11 on sexuality).

For both sexes, then, changes in the reproductive system are a normal part of aging. Yet neither women nor men seem to suffer much as their ability to have children wanes or disappears. Sexual activity becomes less frequent, but it remains an important part of life for most older adults.

Physical Behavior

How well can older adults carry out physical activities in daily life? Obviously those who have severe arthritis may have difficulty merely walking or dressing themselves without pain, but here we focus on two more typical changes in physical behavior over the adult years: a slowing of behavior and a decreased ability to engage in strenuous activities.

Slowing Down

You may have noticed, as you breeze by them on the sidewalk, that older adults often walk more slowly than young people do. Indeed, a recent study suggests that the amount of time stoplights provide for pedestrians to cross the street is just not enough for the 99% of people age 72 or older who walk at a pace slower than four feet per second (Langlois et al., 1997). Some older adults also walk as if they were treading on a slippery surface—with short, shuffling steps and not much arm movement (Murray, Kory, & Clarkson, 1969; see also Figure 5.8). Why is this?

For one thing, the sensory systems involved in balance do not function as well in old age as they did in earlier years (Ochs, Newberry, Lenhardt, & Harkins, 1985). Elderly people, like young children, have difficulty performing tests in which they must maintain their balance when they are placed on a moving platform or are given misleading sensory feedback (Stelmach et al., 1989; Woollacott, Shumway-Cook, & Nashner, 1986). Thus, many older people may walk slowly to compensate for poor balance. More generally, older adults who fear they will fall make many adaptive changes in their walk to protect themselves (Maki, 1997).

An older person's slow pace of walking may also be due to reduced cardiovascular functioning. The pace at which adults of any age choose to walk and the fastest pace at which they can walk are associated with their cardiovascular capacity (Cunningham et al., 1982). Older people with strong hearts may walk very briskly, but those who have cardiovascular limitations may slow down.

On average, older adults perform many motor actions more slowly and with less coordination than younger adults do (Morgan et al., 1994; Stelmach & Nahom, 1992). The underlying reason is a slowing of the brain. Gerontologist James Birren has argued that *the* central change that comes about as we age is a slowing of the nervous system (Birren & Fisher, 1995). It affects not only motor behavior but mental functioning as well, and it affects a majority of elderly people to at least some degree. We have already seen that young children have slow reaction times. Speed on a variety of perceptual-motor tasks improves until the 20s and then gradually decreases over the adult years (Earles & Salthouse, 1995; Wilkinson & Allison,

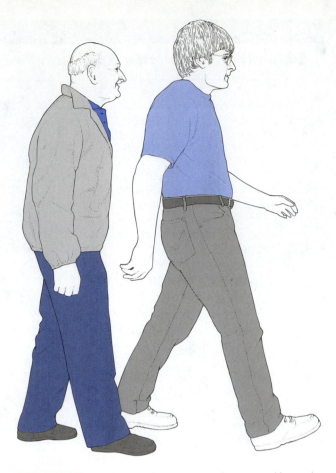

FIGURE 5.8 *Compared to the young man, the average older man takes shorter strides, does not achieve as large an angle between heel and floor, and swings his arms less widely. He appears to be treading cautiously.* (Based on Murray, Kory, & Clarkson, 1969)

1989). Elderly adults are especially slow to react when tasks are novel and when they are complex—for example, when any one of several stimuli might appear on a screen and each requires a different response (Sliwinski et al., 1994; Spirduso & MacRae, 1990). On average, older adults take one and a half to two times longer to respond than young adults do when they perform a wide range of cognitive tasks that require speedy answers (Lima, Hale, & Myerson, 1991).

We should not expect all old people to be slow in all situations, however. Physically fit older people and those who are free from cardiovascular diseases have quicker reactions than their peers who lead sedentary lives or have diseases, although they are likely to be slower than they were when they were younger (Earles & Salthouse, 1995; Spirduso & MacRae, 1990). Aerobic exercise or experience playing video games can also speed the reactions of older adults (Dustman et al., 1989, 1992). In addition, experience can help elderly people compensate for a slower nervous system so that they can continue to perform well on familiar motor tasks.

To illustrate, Timothy Salthouse (1984) tested the psychomotor performance of female typists ranging in age from 19 to 72. On average, and in keeping with the results of countless studies, the older women performed more slowly than the younger ones on a reaction-time task in which they had to quickly press one typewriter key when the letter *R* appeared and another when the letter *L* appeared on a screen. Yet older women typed written material just as fast as the younger women did. Apparently these experienced typists were better than younger typists at processing information about the next letters to be typed, giving themselves more time to get ready (see also Bosman, 1993). Thus, practice at a skill may allow older people who perform quite slowly on reaction time tasks in the laboratory to perform familiar motor tasks very quickly and effectively in everyday life. This is an excellent example of a common process in aging: **compensation for decline,** or finding a way, often unconsciously, to make up for or get around age-related losses of function in order to function well (Baltes, Smith, & Staudinger, 1992). Turning up the volume on the TV set if one is hearing impaired, driving more slowly if one's reactions are slower, and writing reminder notes to oneself if one's memory is failing are all common examples of how adults deal actively and adaptively with some of the losses associated with aging and disease in later life.

The slowing of the nervous system and of motor performance is one important fact of aging. Another is that many people become out of shape. Typically, adults decrease their involvement in vigorous physical activity as they get older—females earlier than males (Shephard & Montelpare, 1988). By late adulthood they may find that they get tired just climbing stairs or carrying groceries; running a marathon is out of the question. Because of declines in reserve capacity, aging bodies are at a greater disadvantage when they must perform tasks requiring maximal strength, speed, or endurance than when they are asked to perform normal daily activities (Goldberg & Hagberg, 1990). The average older person tires more quickly and needs more time to recover after vigorous activity than the average younger person.

Yet once again there is more diversity among older adults than among younger ones. *Some* older people can perform vigorous physical activities with distinction. Michael Stones and Albert Kozma (1985) cite the examples of the 70-year-old woman who competed in the 1972 Olympic equestrian events and the 98-year-old man who could run a marathon (26 miles) in 7½ hours!

Disease, Disuse, and Abuse

As we've seen, many aspects of physical functioning decline over the adult years in many individuals. But

Some older adults have a good deal of reserve capacity and can perform strenuous activities even in their 80s or 90s.

an important question arises: *When we look at the performance of older people, are we seeing the effects of aging alone or the effects of something else?* The "something else" could be disease, disuse of the body, abuse of the body—or all three.

As we have seen, most older people have at least some chronic *disease* or impairment such as arthritis or heart disease (Jette, 1996). How would an elderly person function if he or she could manage to stay completely disease-free? James Birren and his colleagues (1963) addressed just this question in a classic study of men aged 65 to 91. Extensive medical examinations were conducted to identify two groups of elderly men: (1) those who were almost perfectly healthy and had *no* signs of disease at all and (2) those who had slight traces of disease-in-the-making but no clinically diagnosable diseases. Several aspects of physical and intellectual functioning were assessed in these men, and the participants were compared to young men.

The most remarkable finding was that the healthier group of older men hardly differed at all from the younger men! They were equal even in their capacity for physical exercise, and they actually beat the younger men on measures of intelligence requiring general information or knowledge of vocabulary words. Their main limitations were the slower brain activity and reaction times that seem to be so basic to the aging process. Overall, *aging itself in the absence of disease had little effect on physical and psychological functioning.* However, the men with slight traces of impending disease *were* deficient on several measures. Diseases that have progressed to the point of symptoms have even more serious consequences for performance.

So it is possible that disease, rather than aging itself, accounts for many declines in functioning in later life (see also Houx, Vreeling, & Jolles, 1991). We must note, however, that Birren and his colleagues had a tough time finding the perfectly healthy older people they studied. Most older people experience *both* aging and disease, and it is difficult to separate the effects of the two. Although aging and disease are distinct, increased vulnerability to disease is one part—and an important part—of normal aging.

Disuse of the body also contributes to steeper declines in physical functioning in some adults than in others (Wagner et al., 1992). Masters and Johnson (1966) proposed a "use it or lose it" maxim to describe the fact that sexual functioning deteriorates if a person engages in little or no sexual activity. The same maxim can be applied to other systems of the body. Muscles atrophy if they are not used, and the heart functions less well if a person leads a sedentary life. Changes like these in some aging adults are much like the changes observed in people of any age who are confined to bed for a long time (Goldberg & Hagberg, 1990). The brain also needs "mental exercise" in order to display plasticity and to continue to function effectively in old age (Black et al., 1991). In short, most systems of the body seem to thrive on *use,* but too many people become inactive as they age (Wagner et al., 1992).

Finally, *abuse* of the body contributes to declines in functioning in some people. Excessive alcohol consumption, a high-fat diet, and smoking are all clear examples (Haber, 1994). Additionally, although elderly adults are not often recreational drug abusers, many do take several prescribed medications. Drugs typically affect older adults more powerfully than they do younger adults; they can also interact with one another and with the aging body's chemistry to impair functioning (Cherry & Morton, 1989; Lamy, 1986).

Overall, then, poor functioning in old age may represent any combination of the effects of aging, disease, disuse, and abuse. We may not be able to do much to change basic aging processes, but we quite certainly can change our lifestyles to optimize the odds of a long and healthy old age.

APPLICATIONS: OPTIMIZING HEALTHY DEVELOPMENT

Throughout the ages, human beings have searched for the secret to a longer and healthier life. The Spanish explorer Ponce de León searched for a fountain of youth in Florida. Other seekers of immortality, guided by the mistaken theory that decreases in levels of sex hormones were responsible for aging, transplanted ape testicles into old men in an effort to prolong their lives (Walford, 1983). If biologists identify the genes at the root of basic aging processes and figure out how to alter them, we might all live to be 500. In the meantime, the best we can do is try to avoid the diseases and disabilities that can make us function poorly and die young. A nutritious diet, regular exercise, and avoidance of known health risks can have very positive effects on health and longevity, especially if healthy lifestyles are adopted in childhood and continued throughout the life span (Haber, 1994; Margolis, Sparrow, & Swanson, 1989).

Nutrition

As we saw in Chapter 4, adequate nutrition is essential for getting development off to a good start. The baby whose mother is severely malnourished during her pregnancy is likely to be small, to have fewer than the normal number of brain cells, and to be at risk for developmental difficulties and even death. Prenatally malnourished babies can achieve normal intellectual growth if they receive appropriate cognitive and social stimulation after birth (Sigman, 1995).

Infants and young children who are malnourished after birth seem able to cope with a *temporary* shortage of food. Although their growth is likely to slow while they are malnourished, they grow much faster than normal when their diets become adequate again (Tanner, 1990). This **catch-up growth** after a period of malnutrition or illness reflects the body's struggle to get back on the growth course that it is genetically programmed to follow. To prevent malnutrition in the United States, the government established the WIC program, which provides nutrition education and nutritious foods to low-income women, infants, and children. Supplemental nutrition programs of this sort have been shown to have positive effects on both motor development and cognitive development (Sigman, 1995).

Good nutrition contributes to healthy development after childhood as well. Perhaps because they grow so rapidly but often subsist on a diet of junk food, many adolescents take in too much fat and too little fiber (Clavien et al., 1996). Inadequate nutrition is also a problem for some elderly adults (Pos-

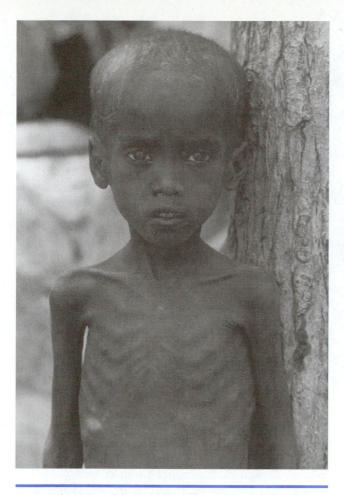

Severe malnutrition, of the kind epidemic in African nations like Somalia, can seriously impair both physical and intellectual development.

kidney disease, high blood pressure, diabetes, liver problems, and even arthritis. Obesity is usually the product of both nature and nurture: Heredity is perhaps the most important factor (Grilo & Pogue-Geile, 1991), but overeating and inactivity also contribute.

Up to 30% of American children are estimated to be overweight (Wolfe et al., 1994), and being an overweight child or adolescent usually means becoming an overweight adult (Boodman, 1995). Children who watch more than five hours of television a day are about five times more likely to be overweight than children who watch zero to two hours a day, perhaps because they get little exercise and eat the junk foods they see advertised on TV (Gortmaker et al., 1996). Weight loss programs are likely to be more successful with child "couch potatoes" than with adult ones, though; self-control may not be as necessary if parents can control their children's eating habits for them (Wilson, 1994).

Teenagers face increased risks of obesity because their metabolism rates slow down as they mature physically. Individuals who are overweight as adolescents—even those who slim down as adults—run a greater-than-average risk of coronary heart disease and a host of other health problems some 55 years later (Must et al., 1992). Middle-aged adults also run a special risk of gaining weight, especially if they become less physically active but keep eating as much as they did as younger adults (Haber, 1994).

Overall, people who manage to keep their weight in the normal range tend to live longer than individuals who are either seriously overweight or seriously underweight (Guralnik & Kaplan, 1989). Most importantly, humans of all ages benefit when they eat a nutritious diet that provides an adequate number of calories overall and that contains adequate amounts of protein, vitamins, and fiber—as well as less fat, cholesterol, and salt than most Americans consume (Haber, 1994).

Exercise

Many children in the United States do not get as much exercise as they should (Simons-Morton et al., 1997), and those teenagers who exercise very little tend to be the same teenagers who eat poorly, smoke cigarettes, and otherwise take poor care of themselves (Pate et al., 1996). What if more people exercised vigorously throughout their lives? If disuse of the body contributes to poor physical functioning, can exercise prevent health problems and slow the aging process?

Regular exercise—for example, the widely recommended 30 minutes or more of moderate activity most days of the week—has many beneficial effects on the body at any age and can make an old body function more like a younger one (Haber, 1994). In older adults,

ner et al., 1994). People typically reduce their total caloric intake in old age, in part because they become less physically active. Some then eat so little that they do not get enough nutrients, especially if they are uneducated and poor (Davis, Murphy, & Neuhaus, 1988; Posner et al., 1994). Older adults who are malnourished may feel unwell, become more susceptible to illnesses, and even begin to show the cognitive impairments associated with dementia (Weg, 1983). Programs such as Meals on Wheels that deliver nourishing food to the homes of disabled or ill senior citizens can play an important role in preventing such problems.

There are also health risks associated with being overweight. The term *obesity* is commonly used to describe individuals who are at least 20% above the "ideal" weight for their height, age, and sex. Obesity is clearly a threat to health, and rates of it have been increasing recently in our society at all ages, even among children (Galuska et al., 1996). Obese people do not live as long as their normal-weight peers, and they are at greater risk for such problems as heart and

exercise can improve cardiovascular and respiratory functioning, slow bone loss, strengthen muscles, and enhance mental functioning. For example, Robert Dustman and his colleagues (1989) involved elderly adults in four months of aerobic training—three 1-hour sessions a week of fast walking and occasional jogging. The result was improvement in oxygen uptake capacity, reaction time, memory, and several other aspects of cognitive functioning. In another study, elderly adults who did low-intensity exercise and weight lifting for a year became stronger and more flexible and experienced less pain as a result (Sharpe et al., 1997). Participating in exercise programs can also make aging adults feel less stressed and happier (Haber, 1994; King et al., 1993).

Overall, it is estimated that regular fitness training at retirement age can delay becoming physically dependent by as many as eight years (Shephard, 1978, 1990). What exercise cannot do is halt the inevitable aging process. Even the hearts of long-time athletes lose some of their capacity over time (Heath et al., 1981). And even frequent joggers gain weight and add inches to their waists as they enter middle age (Williams, 1997). True, people who exercise generally weigh less and have slimmer waists than those who do not, but a 30-year-old man who runs 20 to 30 miles a week until he is 50 would add almost two inches to his waist anyway and would have to run farther and farther each year to avoid it. To try to beat aging, then, it is not enough to remain active; one must become *more* active over the years (Williams, 1997).

Avoiding Known Health Risks

Finally, we can maintain our health and extend our lives by avoiding known health risks and adopting habits that promote health (Margolis et al., 1989; Walford, 1983). Adults who have good health practices in middle age are more likely than adults who do not to be in excellent physical shape in old age (Guralnik & Kaplan, 1989). It is well-known that smoking increases one's risks of coronary heart disease, cancer, emphysema, and a host of other ailments. Because most people begin smoking before they are 20, early prevention efforts can save lives (Margolis et al., 1989). Moderate alcohol consumption—for example, a glass of wine or a beer with dinner at night—appears to protect the heart and reduce the risk of death from cardiovascular disease, whereas heavy drinking is a health hazard (Scherr et al., 1992). Eating breakfast every day, getting seven to eight hours of sleep, and avoiding between-meal snacks are also linked to better physical health and functioning in later life (Guralnik & Kaplan, 1989).

One team of researchers estimated that we could prevent 19% of deaths in the United States each year by eliminating tobacco use, and another 14% by improving people's diets and activity patterns (McGinnis & Foege, 1993). Through better nutrition, hygiene, health habits, and health care, recent cohorts of Americans have experienced longer and healthier lives than previous cohorts (Manton, Stallard, & Corder, 1997). If today's young people are really getting the message about the effects of lifestyle on health, their old age experience should last even longer and be more enjoyable.

As this chapter shows, physical and psychological development are intimately intertwined throughout the life span. Changes in the body require psychological adjustments and bring psychological change. Newly mobile infants benefit cognitively and emotionally from access to a larger physical and social world; adolescents alter their body images in response to physical and sexual maturation; and aging adults change in response to disease and disability. At the same time, psychological and social factors influence reactions to these physical changes. It is fitting, then, that we keep our focus on the *whole person*, body and mind, as we now turn toward the more "psychological" aspects of human development.

◆ SUMMARY POINTS

1. Each of the many systems of the human body develops and ages at its own rate, guided by a genetic program set into action by the brain and hormones released by the endocrine system.

2. The nervous system, billions of neurons communicating by means of neurotransmitter chemicals, is central to all human functioning. Neurons proliferate, differentiate, and organize themselves into interconnected groups. The plasticity of the infant brain allows it to select certain neural connections over others in response to normal early experiences, as well as to benefit from enriching stimulation.

3. During childhood, neural transmission speeds up, and lateralization of various brain functions, though present at birth, becomes more evident in behavior. During adolescence, the brain, especially the prefrontal cortex, continues to develop, permitting sustained attention and strategic planning.

4. There is both degeneration and plasticity in the aging brain; neurons atrophy and die, levels of neurotransmitters decrease, and blood flow to the brain decreases, but the aging brain forms new synapses to compensate for neural loss and reorganizes itself in response to learning experiences.

5. Newborns have a wide range of reflexes (both survival and primitive reflexes), working senses, a capacity to learn, and organized sleeping and waking states; they are competent but also limited creatures.

6. Infants grow physically according to the cephalocaudal, proximodistal, and orthogenetic principles. Bones harden, muscles strengthen.

7. As the motor areas of the brain's cortex mature, motor milestones are achieved in a predictable cephalocaudal and proximodistal order, and differentiated responses are integrated into meaningful sequences of movement. Maturation is a factor in early motor development, but normal opportunities to interact with the environment and learn motor behaviors are also necessary, according to the dynamic systems approach.

8. During childhood the body steadily grows, and both large muscle and small muscle control and reaction time improve.

9. The adolescent growth spurt and pubertal changes make adolescence a time of dramatic physical change: Girls reach menarche at an average age of 12½; boys experience their first ejaculation a bit later. Rates of maturation vary widely, in part because of genetic makeup and in part because of nutrition and health status.

10. Most adolescent girls and boys react to the maturation process with mixed feelings, worry about their physical appearance or capabilities, and experience heightened conflict with parents in early adolescence. Advantages of early maturation are greater for boys than for girls, but differences between early and later maturers fade over time.

11. Physical capabilities of boys improve whereas those of many girls level off or even decline during adolescence, perhaps because of gender stereotypes.

12. Most systems of the body reach a peak of functioning between childhood and early adulthood and decline gradually thereafter; decreases in reserve capacity are especially noticeable. However, individual differences in physiological functioning become greater with age.

13. During the reproductive years of adulthood, some women experience mood swings during the menstrual cycle, but few women are incapacitated by premenstrual syndrome. Men's hormone levels also fluctuate, though not in monthly cycles.

14. Women reach menopause and lose their reproductive capacity at about age 50; most experience hot flashes and vaginal dryness, but few experience severe psychological symptoms. The reproductive systems of men age more gradually and less completely during the male climacteric.

15. As people age, they experience a slowing of their nervous systems, reaction times, and motor behavior; their capacity for vigorous activity is also reduced.

16. Aging, disease, disuse, and abuse of the body all affect performance in later life. Perfectly healthy older people function much like younger people except for their slower reactions, but the development of chronic diseases is a fact of aging for most people.

17. A healthy lifestyle at any age includes proper nutrition, exercise, and avoidance of known health risks. Such a lifestyle can slow, though not completely halt, the aging process.

FOOD FOR THOUGHT

1. We now know that the architecture of the brain is created in response to early experience rather than laid down by the genes. In what ways might a brain "fine-tuned" by experience be superior to a brain whose structure is entirely determined at birth?

2. Recall a time when you learned a new motor skill—for example, how to roller skate or hit a golf ball. Can you apply the dynamic systems approach to understand how your skill developed over time and what influenced its development?

3. Dave Barry, who was quoted at the start of the chapter, has an overly grim view of the physical aging process. What in this chapter gives you reason to be more optimistic about aging, and why? Cite specific concepts and research findings.

4. Suppose you set as your goal reaching the age of 100 in superb physical condition. Describe and justify a plan for achieving your goal and then indicate why you might not make it despite your best efforts.

(W) ON THE WEB

1. *Puberty*   The Health Department of Western Australia has created useful Web sites on a number of health-related topics, including two on pubertal changes directed at adolescents and filled with solid information about physical and sexual changes. The first site concerns girls, the second boys:
http://www.public.health.wa.gov.au/hp2107.htm
http://www.public.health.wa.gov.au/hp2106.htm

2. *Physical Aging*   The National Institute on Aging serves up lots of information about aging, especially under a heading called "Age Pages—Brochures and Fact Sheets for the Public." There you will find brief and excellent descriptions of such health problems as osteoporosis, high blood pressure, and arthritis; a discussion of sexuality in later life; and information about exercise and other health-promoting practices.
http://www.nih.gov/nia/

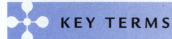
endocrine gland
pituitary gland
growth hormone
androgens
estrogen
neuron
synapse
myelin
cerebral cortex
synaptogenesis
brain growth spurt
lateralization
reflex

REM sleep
cephalocaudal principle
proximodistal principle
orthogenetic principle
developmental norm
gross motor skills
fine motor skills
pincer grasp
dynamic systems approach
reaction time
adolescent growth spurt
puberty
menarche

secular trend
rites of passage
osteoporosis
reserve capacity
premenstrual syndrome
 (PMS)
menopause
hot flash
hormone replacement
 therapy (HRT)
climacteric
compensation for decline
catch-up growth

CHAPTER 6

Perception

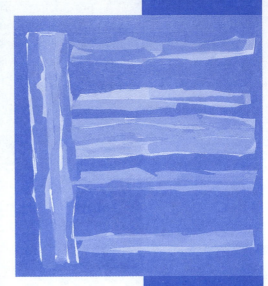

ISSUES OF NATURE AND NURTURE

THE INFANT
Assessing Perceptual Abilities
Vision
Hearing
Taste and Smell
Touch, Temperature, and Pain
Integrating Sensory Information
Influences on Early Perceptual Development

THE CHILD
The Development of Attention
Learning to Read

THE ADOLESCENT

THE ADULT
Vision
Hearing
Taste and Smell
Touch, Temperature, and Pain
The Adult in Perspective

**APPLICATIONS: AIDING PEOPLE WITH
HEARING IMPAIRMENTS**

SUMMARY POINTS

FOOD FOR THOUGHT

ON THE WEB

KEY TERMS

It's your first day in the world, and the room is bright and noisy, nurses bustling here and there. You are sponged, swaddled, and handed to your mother, who says, "Oh, hello," and gently strokes your head and shoulders before passing you on to your father. Having spent nine months in a dark, watery womb, what do you make of all this sensory input?

In what ways are the perceptual experiences of infants and adults similar, and in what ways are they different because of the adult's greater experience with the world?

Psychologists have long distinguished between sensation and perception. **Sensation** is the process by which sensory receptor neurons detect information and transmit it to the brain. From birth, infants sense the environment. They detect light, sound, odor-bearing molecules in the air, and other stimuli. But do they make "sense" of it? **Perception** is the interpretation of sensory input: recognizing what you see, understanding what is said to you, knowing that the odor you have detected is a sizzling steak, and so on. It is affected by one's history of learning experiences. Does the newborn really perceive the world, then, or merely sense it? And what happens to sensory and perceptual capacities as we age? Perhaps we should start with a more basic question: Why

should you care about the development of sensation and perception?

Because sensation and perception are at the very heart of human functioning. Just try to think of one thing you do that does not depend on your perceiving the world around you. You certainly would have a tough time as a student if you could neither read the printed word nor understand speech. Indeed, you would not be able to walk to class without the aid of the body senses that control movement. Possibly one of the reasons that sensation and perception may not seem important is that they occur so effortlessly. We simply take them for granted—unless perhaps we are made to imagine what it might be like to be blind or deaf. Then most of us are terrified.

There is another reason to be interested in sensation and perception. They have been at the center of a debate among philosophers and more recently developmental scientists about how we gain knowledge of reality.

ISSUES OF NATURE AND NURTURE

Must humans learn how to perceive a meaningful world, or are we equipped to do so from the start? Philosophers were raising the nature/nurture issue about perception long before anyone had conducted research on the perceptual capabilities of young infants. **Empiricists** such as the 17th-century British philosopher John Locke (1690/1939) took the nurture side of the nature/nurture issue; they believed that the infant enters the world as a *tabula rasa* (blank slate) who knows nothing except what he or she learns through the senses. Empiricists think infants perceive the world very differently than adults do; only by accumulating perceptual experience do they learn how to interpret sensory stimuli in meaningful ways.

Nativists take the nature side of the nature/nurture issue and argue that we come to the world equipped with knowledge that allows us to perceive a meaningful world from the start. For example, Rene Descartes (1638/1965) and Immanuel Kant (1781/1958) believed that we are born with an understanding of the spatial world. Presumably infants don't need to learn that receding objects will appear smaller or that approaching objects will seem larger; perceptual understandings like these are innate or at least mature very rapidly. According to nativists, these abilities have been built into the human nervous system through the course of evolution, making the infant perceiver quite similar to the adult perceiver.

Many of today's developmental theorists take less extreme stands on the nature/nurture issue. They understand that human beings' innate biological endowment, maturational processes, and experience all contribute to perceptual development. Yet they still grapple with nature/nurture issues, and some still take a strong stand on either the nature or the nurture side of the debate. Some researchers have concluded that the infant is equipped to interpret sensory experience much as adults do almost from birth (Spelke, 1994), whereas others argue that the perceptual areas of the brain and perceptual skills evolve gradually as the infant responds to sights, sounds, and other stimuli (Smith & Katz, 1996). Researchers who study perceptual development attempt to determine which perceptual capacities are evident so early in life as to seem innate and which take longer to emerge and appear to be learned. They also attempt to identify the kinds of experiences that are required for normal perceptual development, sometimes by studying children who have been deprived of certain experiences. Their work is some of the most exciting in all of developmental psychology.

Nature/nurture issues also arise in the study of declines in sensory and perceptual abilities in later life. Are these declines universal, suggesting that they are the product of fundamental aging processes? Or do they differ a good deal from person to person and result from factors other than aging, such as disease, exposure to ultraviolet rays, loud noise, and other environmental influences known to damage the senses? Just as we must pin down the contributions of nature and nurture to early perceptual development, we must clarify their roles in perceptual aging.

So let us get into it. We will look very closely at sensation and perception in infancy, for this is when most fundamental perceptual capacities emerge. We will also see how much more "intelligent" the senses become during childhood and adolescence and question the image of old age as a time of little more than sensory decline. Finally, we will look more closely at how nature and nurture contribute to perceptual development across the life span.

THE INFANT

The pioneering American psychologist William James (1890) claimed that sights, sounds, and other sensory inputs formed a "blooming, buzzing confusion" to the young infant. James was actually noting that impressions from the several senses are fused rather than separable, but his statement has since been quoted to represent the view that the world of the young infant is hopelessly confusing.

Today the accepted view is that young infants have far greater perceptual abilities than anyone ever suspected. Their senses are functioning even before birth, and in the early months of life they show many signs that they are perceiving a coherent rather than a chaotic world. Why the change in views? It is not that babies have gotten any smarter. It is that researchers have gotten smarter. They have developed more sophisticated methods of studying exactly what infants can and cannot do. Infants, after all, cannot tell us directly what they perceive, so the trick has been to develop ways to let their behavior speak for them.

Assessing Perceptual Abilities

As researchers have devised more and more ingenious ways of testing the perceptual capacities of young infants, they have uncovered more and more sophisticated capacities at younger and younger ages. The main methods used to study infant perception are the habituation, preferential looking, and operant-conditioning techniques (see Rosser, 1994).

Habituation

Infants, and humans of all ages for that matter, lose interest in a stimulus that is presented over and over again. This process of learning to be bored is called **habituation.** If an infant who has habituated to one stimulus then regains interest when a somewhat different stimulus is substituted, we know that the two stimuli—for example, different visual designs, tones, or touches—have been discriminated from each other (Rosser, 1994).

Preferential Looking

Alternatively, we can present an infant with two stimuli at the same time and measure the length of time the infant spends looking at each. A preference for one over the other, like responding to a novel stimulus in the habituation paradigm, indicates that the infant discriminates the two stimuli. And if the infant looks equally long at the two stimuli? Then it's unclear what we can conclude; the infant may well discriminate the stimuli but simply not like one better than the other.

Operant Conditioning

As B. F. Skinner established, humans will repeat a response that has a pleasant consequence; that is, they are capable of learning through *operant conditioning* (see Chapter 8). Young infants are not easily conditioned, but they can learn to suck faster or slower or to turn their head to the side when a certain stimulus is presented if they are reinforced for that response. Suppose that we want to determine whether infants can distinguish two speech sounds. First, the infants might be conditioned over several trials to turn their heads every time they hear Sound 1—perhaps by being shown an interesting toy or being given a taste of milk. Then, Sound 2 would be presented; if the infant turns his head, that suggests that the two sounds are perceived as equivalent; if not, we can conclude that the two sounds have been discriminated.

The habituation, preferential looking, and operant-conditioning techniques for studying infant perception have their limitations. Most importantly, infants can fail to respond to some difference between stimuli for reasons that have nothing to do with an inability to discriminate between them (Rosser, 1994). Still, these techniques, along with others, have revealed a good deal about what infants perceive and what they do not, as we will now see.

Vision

Most of us tend to think of vision as our most indispensable sense. Because vision is indeed important, we'll examine its early development in some detail before turning to the other major senses.

Basic Capacities

The eye functions by taking in stimulation in the form of light and converting it to electrochemical signals to the brain. How well does the newborn's visual system work? Quite well, in fact. From the first, the infant can detect changes in brightness, though not as sensitively as adults (Banks & Shannon, 1993). The ability to discriminate degrees of brightness develops rapidly. By only 2 months of age, infants can distinguish a white bar that differs only 5% in luminance from a solid white background (Peeples & Teller, 1975).

Very young infants also see the world in color, not in black and white, as some early observers had thought. How do we know this? Suppose we accustom an infant to a blue disk using the habituation technique. What will happen if we now present either a blue disk of a different shade or a green disk? As Marc Bornstein and his colleagues established, 4-month-old infants will show little interest in a disk of a different blue but will be very attentive to a green disk—even when the light reflected from these two stimuli differs in wavelength from the original blue stimulus by exactly the same amount (Bornstein, Kessen, & Weiskopf, 1976). Four-month-olds appear to discriminate colors and categorize portions of the continuum of wavelengths of light into the same basic color categories (red, blue, green, and yellow) that adults do. Color vision is present at birth, but newborns cannot discriminate some color differences because their receptors are not yet mature. By 2 to 3 months of age, though, color vision is mature (Matlin & Foley, 1997; Teller & Lindsey, 1993).

Are objects clear or blurry to young infants? This is a matter of **visual acuity,** or the ability to perceive detail. By adult standards the newborn's visual acuity is poor. You have undoubtedly heard of 20/20 vision, as measured by the familiar Snellen eye chart with the big E at the top. Infants cannot be asked to read eye charts. However, they do prefer to look at a patterned stimulus rather than a blank one—unless it is so fine-grained that it looks no different from a blank. So, by using the preferential looking technique and presenting increasingly fine-grained striped disks paired with blank disks to infants, we can find the point at which their perception of the stripes is lost and translate this into an estimate of visual acuity.

Although estimates differ, the newborn's vision may be as poor as 20/600, which means that an adult with normal vision can see at 600 feet what the infant sees clearly only at 20 feet (Banks & Salapatek, 1983). Objects are blurry to the young infant unless they are about 8 inches from the face or are bold patterns with sharp light/dark contrasts—the faces of parents, for example (Aslin, 1988; Matlin & Foley, 1997). The young infant's world is also blurred because of limitations in **visual accommodation,** the ability of the lens of the eye to change shape in order to bring objects at different distances into focus. It is likely to take six months to a year before the infant will see as well as an adult (Banks & Shannon, 1993). In short, the eyes of the young infant are not working at peak levels, but they are certainly working. Newborns can perceive light and dark, focus on nearby objects, distinguish colors, and see patterns that are not too finely detailed (Hainline & Abramov, 1992). But does all this visual stimulation make any sense?

Pattern Perception

It is one thing to say that young infants (those under 2 months of age) can see, but it is another to say that they can discriminate different patterns of visual stimulation. In the early 1960s, Robert Fantz (1961, 1963) conducted a number of pioneering studies to determine whether infants can discriminate various forms or patterns. He found that babies less than 2 days old could indeed discriminate visual forms. They preferred to look at patterned stimuli such as faces or concentric circles rather than at unpatterned

Young infants are attracted to visual stimuli with well-defined contours (or areas of light-dark contrast), to movement, and to bold patterns that are neither too simple nor too complex.

disks. They also seemed to have a special interest in the human face, for they looked at faces longer than at other patterned stimuli such as a bull's-eye or newsprint. However, young infants looked only a little bit longer at a face drawing than at a stimulus with facial features in a scrambled array (Fantz, 1961). Here, then, was evidence that human faces are of interest to very young infants not because they are perceived as meaningful faces, but because they have certain physical properties that create interest, whether those properties show up in a real face or a scrambled face.

So the search began for the properties of patterns that "turn infants on." For one thing, young infants are attracted to patterns that have a large amount of light/dark transition, or **contour;** they respond to sharp boundaries between light and dark areas (Banks & Shannon, 1993). Since faces and scrambled faces have an equal amount of contour, they are equally interesting.

Second, young infants are attracted to movement. Newborns can and do track a moving target with their eyes, although their tracking at first is imprecise and likely to falter unless the target is moving slowly (Kremenitzer et al., 1979). They also look longer at moving objects and perceive their forms better than those of stationary ones (Johnson & Aslin, 1995; Slater et al., 1990).

Finally, young infants seem to be attracted to *moderately complex* patterns. They prefer a clear pattern of some kind (for example, a bold checkerboard pattern) to either a blank stimulus or a very elaborate one like a page from the *New York Times* (Fantz & Fagan, 1975). As infants mature, they come to prefer more and more complex stimuli.

In sum, we know that infants under 2 months of age have visual preferences, and we also know something about the physical properties of stimuli that attract their attention. They seek out contour, movement, and moderate complexity. As it happens, human faces have all of these physical properties. Martin Banks and his colleagues have offered a very simple explanation for these early visual preferences: *Young infants prefer to look at whatever they can see well* (Banks & Ginsburg, 1985). Using a complex mathematical model, Banks has been able to predict what different patterns might look like to the eye of a young infant. Figure 6.1 gives an example. Because the young infant's eye is small and its neural receptors immature, it has poor visual acuity and sees a highly complex checkerboard as a big dark blob. The pattern in a moderately complex checkerboard can be seen. Less-than-perfect vision would therefore explain why young infants prefer moderate complexity to high complexity. Indeed, limited vision can account for a number of the infant's visual preferences. Young infants seem to actively seek out exactly the visual input that they can see well, input that will stimulate the development of

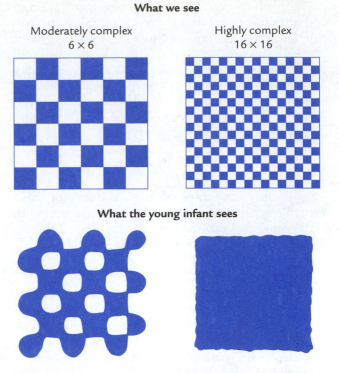

What we see

Moderately complex
6 × 6

Highly complex
16 × 16

What the young infant sees

FIGURE 6.1 *What the young eye sees. By the time these two checkerboards are processed by eyes with undeveloped vision, only the checkerboard on the left may have any pattern remaining. Blurry vision in early infancy helps to explain a preference for moderately complex rather than highly complex stimuli.* (From Banks & Salapatek in Mussen, 1983)

the visual centers of their brains (Banks & Shannon, 1993; Hainline & Abramov, 1992).

To this point we have established that, from birth, infants discriminate patterns and prefer some over others. But do they really perceive forms or patterns? For example, do they just see an angle or two when they view a triangle, or do they see a whole triangular form that stands out from its background as a distinct shape? Some research suggests that even newborns and 1-month-olds are sensitive to information about whole shapes or forms (Slater et al., 1991; Treiber & Wilcox, 1980). But most studies point to an important breakthrough in the perception of forms starting at about 2 or 3 months of age.

Part of the story is told in Figure 6.2. One-month-olds focus on the outer contours of forms such as faces (Johnson, 1997; Salapatek, 1975). Interestingly, even babies a few days old can recognize their mothers' faces, but only when they can see the shape of the mother's head, not when they have only her facial features to work with (Pascalis et al., 1995)! Starting at about 2 months of age, infants no longer focus on some external boundary or contour; instead, they explore the interiors of figures thoroughly (for example, looking at a person's facial features rather than just at the chin, hairline, and top of the head). It is as though

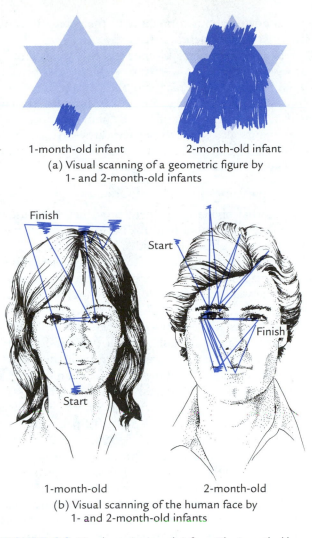

1-month-old infant   2-month-old infant
(a) Visual scanning of a geometric figure by
1- and 2-month-old infants

Finish   Start

Finish

Start

1-month-old   2-month-old
(b) Visual scanning of the human face by
1- and 2-month-old infants

FIGURE 6.2 *Visual scanning in early infancy. The 1-month-old seems to be trying to locate where an object begins and ends, whereas the 2-month-old seems to be on the way to figuring out what an object is by exploring it inside and out.* (Adapted from Salapatek, 1975)

they are no longer content to locate where an object starts and where it ends, as 1-month-olds tend to do; they seem to want to know what it is.

Some researchers find that even newborns prefer well-formed human faces to scrambled face forms that have the same features in some random array (Valenza et al., 1996). Most studies, however, reveal that a clear preference for a normal face over a scrambled face emerges only at 2 or 3 months of age (Dannemiller & Stephens, 1988; Johnson & Gilmore, 1996). James Dannemiller and Benjamin Stephens (1988) demonstrated that at 3 months of age, but not at 6 weeks, infants even prefer a normal face drawing to an otherwise identical pattern in which areas that are normally dark on a face (facial features, hair) were made light and areas that are normally light (the cheeks, for example) were made dark. Some researchers think that the preference for well-formed faces sometimes ob-

served in newborns is an innate response controlled by a subcortical area of the brain; they note that it disappears in a matter of weeks (Johnson, 1997). By contrast, the preference for face forms evident at 2 to 3 months of age most likely reflects the maturing of the cortex of the brain and the infant's growing familiarity with faces (Hainline & Abramov, 1992; Johnson, 1997). Infants now smile when they see faces, as though they recognize them as familiar and appreciate their significance.

Mainly, there is much left to learn about early perception of faces. An intense nature/nurture debate still rages about whether infants have an innate ability to perceive face forms or can do so only after they have had some experience looking at faces. Still, we can conclude that infants truly perceive a meaningful face form, not merely an appealing pattern of light and dark, by 2 to 3 months of age. So it goes with pattern perception more generally: As infants gain experience with different objects, their attention is drawn to certain objects not only because they have certain physical properties but because their forms are recognized as familiar (Kagan, 1971).

Depth Perception

Another important aspect of visual perception involves perceiving depth and knowing when objects are near or far away. Although it can take years to learn to judge the size of objects off in the distance, very young infants have some intriguing abilities to interpret spatial cues involving nearby objects. For example, they react defensively when objects move toward their faces; blinking in response to looming objects first appears at about 1 month of age and becomes much more consistent over the next few months (Nanez & Yonas, 1994). Moreover, even newborns seem to operate by the principle of **size constancy:** They recognize that an object is the same size despite changes in its distance from the eyes. In one study (Slater, Mattock, & Brown, 1990), newborns who were habituated to a particular cube presented at different distances preferred to look at a different-sized cube when given a choice. This was the case even when the new cube took up the same amount of the visual field as the original cube.

Does this evidence of early spatial perception mean that infants who have begun to crawl know enough about space to avoid crawling off the edges of beds or staircases? The first attempt to examine depth perception in infants was carried out by Eleanor Gibson and Richard Walk (1960), using an apparatus called the **visual cliff.** This cliff (see Figure 6.3) consists of an elevated glass platform divided into two sections by a center board. On the "shallow" side a checkerboard pattern is placed directly under the glass. On the "deep" side the pattern is several feet below the glass, creating the illusion of a drop-off or "cliff." Infants

FIGURE 6.3 *An infant on the edge of a visual cliff, being lured to cross the "deep" side*

are placed on the center board and coaxed by their mothers to cross both the "shallow" and the "deep" sides. Testing infants 6 ½ months of age and older, Gibson and Walk found that 27 of 36 infants would cross the shallow side to reach Mom, but only 3 of 36 would cross the deep side. Most infants of crawling age (typically 7 months or older) clearly perceive depth and are afraid of drop-offs.

But the testing procedure used by Gibson and Walk depended on the ability of infants to crawl. Would younger infants who cannot yet crawl be able to perceive a drop-off? Joseph Campos and his colleagues (Campos, Langer, & Krowitz, 1970) figured that the heart rates of young infants might tell them. So they lowered babies over the shallow and deep sides of the visual cliff. Babies as young as 2 months of age had a slower heart rate on the deep side than on the shallow side. Why slower? When we are afraid, our hearts beat faster, not slower. A slow heart rate is a sign of interest. So 2-month-old infants *perceive a difference* between the deep and shallow sides of the visual cliff, but they have not yet learned to *fear* drop-offs.

Fear of drop-offs appears to be learned through experience crawling about—and perhaps falling now and then, or at least coming close to it (Campos, Bertenthal, & Kermoian, 1992). Some beginning crawlers will shuffle right off the ends of beds or the tops of stairwells if they are not watched carefully. However, fear of drop-offs is stronger in infants who have logged a few weeks of experience crawling than in infants of the same age who do not yet crawl; also, providing infants who do not crawl with walkers that allow them to move about hastens the development of a healthy fear of heights (Campos, Bertenthal, & Kermoian, 1992). Both maturation and normal experi-

ences moving about contribute to the perception and interpretation of depth, it seems.

In summary, perception of space develops rapidly in early infancy. The ability to see that an object is looming toward the face and the perception of size constancy despite variations in distance are evident within the first month of life. By about 2 months of age, infants also seem to perceive drop-offs, but it is only in the second half of the first year that maturation and experience result in a fear of drop-offs.

Organizing a World of Objects

Another challenge in perceptual development is to separate the visual field into distinct objects, even when parts of objects are hidden behind other objects. From an early age, infants show remarkable abilities to organize and impose order on visual scenes in much the same way that adults do. For example, Katherine Van Giffen and Marshall Haith (1984) reported that 3-month-olds, though not 1-month-olds, will focus their attention on a small irregularity in an otherwise well-formed circle or square pattern, as if they appreciated that it is indeed a deviation from an otherwise well-formed and symmetrical pattern.

Infants must also determine where one object ends and another begins. Elizabeth Spelke and her colleagues (Kellman & Spelke, 1983; Spelke, 1990) have concluded that young infants are sensitive to a number of cues about the wholeness of objects, especially cues available when an object moves. For example, 4-month-olds seem to expect all the parts of an object to move in the same direction at the same time, and they therefore use *common motion* as an important cue in determining what is or what is not part of the same object (Kellman & Spelke, 1983). It takes infants longer, until about 6 months of age, to determine the boundaries of objects that are stationary (Kellman, 1993). Thus babies appear to have an unlearned ability to organize a visual scene into distinct objects, and they are better able to make sense of a world in motion—a world like the one they live in—than of a stationary world.

The Infant as Intuitive Theorist

That's not all. Recently, researchers have been exploring infants' understandings of the physical laws that govern objects. For example, Elizabeth Spelke and her colleagues have been testing infants to determine what they know of Newtonian physics and the basic laws of object motion (Spelke & Hermer, 1996). Do babies know that a falling object will move downward along a continuous path until it encounters an obstruction? Spelke's studies suggest that infants only 4 months of age seem surprised when a ball that is dropped behind a screen is later revealed to have ended up below a shelf rather than resting upon it. They look longer at this "impossible" event than at the comparison event in which the ball's motion stops when it reaches a barrier. By 6 months of age, infants also seem surprised when a ball drops behind a screen and then, when the screen is lifted, appears to be suspended in midair rather than lying at the bottom of the display unit (Kim & Spelke, 1992; Spelke et al., 1992). This hints that they know something about the laws of gravity.

Findings like these have led some developmentalists to conclude that young infants do much more than just sense the world—that instead, they come equipped with organized systems of knowledge called **intuitive theories** that allow them to make sense of the world (Wellman & Gelman, 1992; Gelman, 1996). From an early age, children distinguish among the domains we know as physics, biology, and psychology. They organize their knowledge in each domain around causal principles and seem to understand that different causal forces operate in different domains (for example, that desires influence the behavior of humans but not of rocks). According to this intuitive theories perspective, young infants have innate knowledge of the world, and they perceive and even reason about it in much the same ways adults do. Coming to know the physical world is then a matter of fleshing out understandings that we have had all along rather than constructing entirely new ones as we get older (Spelke, 1994).

As you'll see in Box 6.1, some researchers also believe that babies understand number concepts long before they ever step into a math class. All in all, it's becoming clearer than ever that young infants know a good deal more about the world around them than anyone imagined, though they still learn more and more as they get older.

In sum, the development of visual perception proceeds with remarkable speed during the first few months of life. Infants either come equipped with the perceptual skills we take for granted or soon acquire them. Perhaps because their nervous systems are immature and their vision poor, newborns prefer sights with light-dark contour, movement, and moderately complex patterning. Within a couple of months, infants more clearly perceive whole forms such as faces; in a few more months, they fear drop-offs and show evidence of having intuitive theories of the physical world that allow them to recognize violations of laws of motion and perceive number, among other things. Perceptual development and cognitive development are intertwined as infants become better and better at interpreting what their senses detect.

Hearing

Hearing is at least as important to us as vision, especially since we depend on it to communicate with others through spoken language. Sound striking the ear

From birth, infants will look in the direction of an interesting sound. This ability to localize sound improves and becomes more voluntary by 4 months of age.

creates vibrations of the eardrum, which are transmitted to the cochlea in the inner ear and converted to signals to the brain.

Basic Capacities

Newborns can hear quite well—better than they can see (Matlin & Foley, 1997). They can also localize sounds: They are startled by loud noises and will turn away from them, but they will turn in the direction of softer sounds (Field et al., 1980; Morrongiello et al., 1994). By 4 months of age, what was a reflexive reaction has become a voluntary one, and infants can shift their eyes and heads in the appropriate direction quickly and accurately (Morrongiello, Fenwick, & Chance, 1990; Muir, 1985).

Newborns appear to be a little less sensitive to very soft sounds than adults are (Aslin, Pisoni, & Jusczyk, 1983). As a result, a soft whisper may not be heard. However, newborns can discriminate among sounds within their range of hearing that differ in loudness, duration, direction, and frequency or pitch, and these basic capacities improve rapidly during the first months of life (Bower, 1982; Trehub et al., 1991).

Perceiving Speech

Young infants seem to be well equipped to respond to human speech, for they can discriminate basic speech sounds—called **phonemes**—very early in life. Peter Eimas (1975b, 1985) pioneered research in this area by demonstrating that infants 2 to 3 months

BOX 6.1

Can babies count?

Although you may think it ridiculous to ask whether babies can count, developmentalists have discovered that very young infants have some impressive understandings of the abstract quality we call number. Karen Wynn (1992) sought to determine whether 5-month-old infants could add and subtract numbers by seeing how long infants looked at different addition and subtraction "problems." Her test procedure, summarized in the figure here, involved showing the infants a display area with a single Mickey Mouse doll in it, raising a screen in order to hide the doll, and having the infant watch as a hand placed a second doll in the display area and came out empty. Infants then were observed to see how long they looked at each of two outcomes when the screen was dropped again: a correct outcome in which two dolls were in the display area when the screen was removed (1+1=2), or an incorrect outcome in which only one doll was present (1+1=1).

Which of these two events attracted more attention? Infants looked longer at the incorrect outcome, as though surprised by the mathematical error it represented. They also looked longer at a 1+1=3 scenario than at the correct 1+1=2 outcome. In other words, they did not merely expect there to be some greater number of dolls present after the addition of one doll; they expected precisely one more doll. These 5-month-olds also seemed to excel at

subtraction: They were surprised when two dolls minus one doll resulted in two dolls rather than one.

Why do babies look longer at the incorrect math outcomes? Is it because these outcomes are mathematically impossible, or is it because they are physically impossible, in that objects cannot just cease to exist or magically appear out of nowhere as they do in the "impossible" scenarios? Tony Simon, Susan Hespos, and Philippe Rochat (1995) replicated Wynn's experiment but attempted to determine whether infants are sensitive to mathematical impossibility or physical impossibility. For example, infants were shown an Elmo puppet alone on a stage like Wynn's and then saw another Elmo puppet added to make two. They were also shown scenarios in which one Elmo plus one Elmo added to only one Elmo (mathematically incorrect) or one Elmo plus one Elmo made an Elmo and an Ernie (mathematically correct but physically impossible) or two Elmos yielded one Ernie (mathematically and physically impossible). The 5-month-olds tested did not seem bothered at all when the identity of the puppets changed—when an Elmo became an Ernie. Instead the findings of Wynn's study were supported: babies looked long and hard at and seemed surprised by incorrect math.

Researchers are still unsure whether infants can coordinate visual and au-

ditory information about number—for example, by expecting to see two items when two drumbeats are sounded but three items when three drumbeats are sounded (Mix, Levine, & Huttenlocher, 1997; Starkey, Spelke, & Gelman, 1990). And it is clear that they cannot handle numbers greater than three or at most four (Wynn, 1995). Still, research to date suggests that infants have what may be an innate sensitivity to number, whether the items involved are objects, sounds, or events (Wynn, 1995).

This research illustrates larger issues in the study of infant perception and cognition. The fact that infants look more at incorrect mathematical outcomes than at correct ones is difficult to interpret (Canfield & Smith, 1996): What competencies are babies actually showing? We do not yet know exactly. It may be that researchers are so intent on pinpointing exactly when infants have particular competencies that they are missing the real story of development. Infant "mathematicians" are showing only one rudimentary skill (noticing a mathematically incorrect result) in one situation, when mathematical competence actually consists of many skills displayed in many situations and acquired over many years (Fischer & Bidell, 1991; Haith, 1997). Babies may well have an innate sensitivity to number, but they still have a lot left to learn before they will be ready to take calculus!

---

old could distinguish consonant sounds that are very similar (for example, *ba* and *pa*). Indeed, infants seem to be able to tell the difference between the vowels *a* and *i* from the second day of life (Clarkson & Berg, 1983). Moreover, just as babies divide the spectrum of light into basic color categories, they seem to divide the continuum of speech sounds into categories corresponding to the basic sound units of language, as early as 3 months of age (Kuhl, 1991; Miller & Eimas, 1996). Among other things, this sound category system allows them to recognize a phoneme as the same phoneme even when it is spoken by different people (Marean, Werner, & Kuhl, 1992). These are impressive accomplishments.

Indeed, there are actually some speech sound discriminations that an infant can make better than an adult (Werker & Desjardins, 1995). We begin life biologically prepared to learn any language humans anywhere speak. As we mature, we normally become especially sensitive to the sound differences that are significant in our own language and less sensitive to sound differences that are irrelevant to our own language. For example, young infants can easily discriminate the consonants *r* and *l* (Eimas, 1975a). So can adults who speak English, French, Spanish, or German. However, Chinese and Japanese make no distinction between *r* and *l,* and adult native speakers of those languages cannot make this particular au-

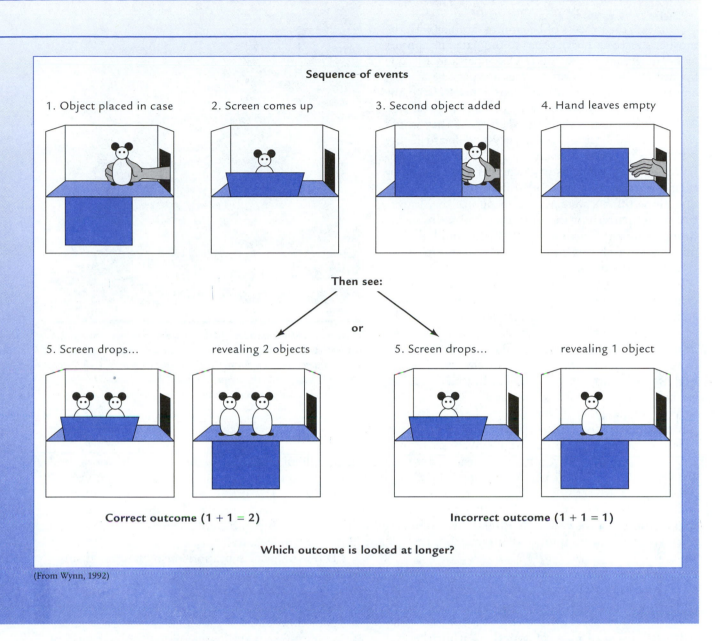

Sequence of events

1. Object placed in case 2. Screen comes up 3. Second object added 4. Hand leaves empty

Then see:

or

5. Screen drops... revealing 2 objects 5. Screen drops... revealing 1 object

Correct outcome (1 + 1 = 2) **Incorrect outcome (1 + 1 = 1)**

Which outcome is looked at longer?

(From Wynn, 1992)

ditory discrimination as well as young infants can (Miyawaki et al., 1975). Similarly, infants raised in English-speaking homes can make discriminations that are important in Hindi but nonexistent in English, but English-speaking adults have trouble doing so (Werker et al., 1981).

By a year of age, when infants are just beginning to utter their first words, they have already become insensitive to sound contrasts that are not made in their native language (Werker & Desjardins, 1995). What has happened is that their early auditory experiences have shaped the formation of neural connections, or synapses, in the auditory areas of their brains so that they are optimally sensitive to the sound contrasts

that they have been listening to and that are important in the language they will learn.

Newborns are especially attentive to female voices (Ecklund-Flores & Turkewitz, 1996), but can they recognize their mothers' voices? Using the operant-conditioning technique of studying perception, Anthony DeCasper and William Fifer (1980) found that babies can indeed recognize their mothers' voices, and during the first 3 days of life. For half of the newborns they studied, sucking faster than usual on a pacifier would activate a recording of the mother's voice, whereas sucking more slowly than usual would elicit a recording of a female stranger. Just the opposite was true for the remaining infants. These 1- to 3-day-old babies learned to suck either rapidly or slowly—whichever it took—to hear their mothers rather than strange women.

Indeed, the process of becoming familiar with the mother's voice and with other sound patterns appears to begin prenatally. Anthony DeCasper and Melanie Spence (1986) had mothers recite a passage (for example, portions of Dr. Seuss's *The Cat in the Hat*) many times during the last six weeks of their pregnancies. At birth the infants were tested to see if they would suck more to hear the story they had heard before birth or to hear a different story. Remarkably, they preferred the familiar story, whether it was read by their own mother or by another baby's mother. Somehow these infants were able to recognize the distinctive sound pattern of the story they had heard in the womb. Auditory learning before birth could also explain why newborns prefer to hear their mothers' voices to those of unfamiliar women.

Before we get carried away with the notion of educating youngsters before they are even born, however, we should bear in mind that the acoustics of the womb are poor and the nervous systems of fetuses are immature. Although some parents today seem willing to try almost anything to get their children's education off to an early start, it is doubtful that factual information can be instilled prenatally. The real message of this research is that infants seem to have an innate readiness to perceive speech. They are similarly sensitive to musical sounds (Schellenberg & Trehub, 1996). For example, newborns like music better than arrhythmic noise (Butterfield & Siperstein, 1972), and older infants are sensitive enough to the pattern or structure in a piece of music that they prefer music that is stopped at the ends of natural phrases to music that is stopped in midphrase (Krumhansl & Jusczyk, 1990).

In sum, hearing is more developed than vision at birth. Infants can distinguish between speech sounds and recognize familiar sound patterns such as their mothers' voices soon after birth, and they are similarly responsive to musical sounds. Within the first year, they lose sensitivity to sound contrasts that are not significant in the language they are starting to learn, and they further refine their auditory perception skills.

Taste and Smell

Can newborns detect different tastes and smells? The sensory receptors for taste—taste buds—are located mainly on the tongue. In ways not fully understood, taste buds respond to chemical molecules and give rise to perceptions of sweet, salty, bitter, or sour tastes. We are apparently born with a sweet tooth, for shortly after birth babies will suck faster and longer for sweet

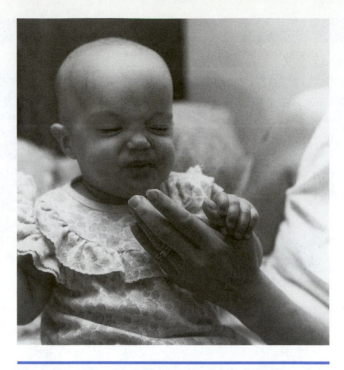

From birth, infants respond to tastes. In response to a sugar solution, newborns part their lips, lick their upper lips, make sucking movements, and sometimes smile. In response to bitter tastes, they purse their lips or open their mouths with the corners down and drool. This older baby is trying to rid herself of unwanted food.

(sugary) liquids than for bitter, sour, salty, or neutral (water) solutions (Crook, 1978). Indeed, sugar water—though not plain water—seems to have a marvelous ability to calm even premature babies and can help them cope with painful events such as needle pricks (Smith & Blass, 1996).

Different taste sensations also produce distinct facial expressions in the newborn. Jacob Steiner and his colleagues (Ganchrow, Steiner, & Daher, 1983; Steiner, 1979) have found that newborns lick their lips and sometimes smile when they are tasting a sugar solution but purse their lips and even drool to get rid of the foul taste when they are given bitter quinine. Their facial expressions become increasingly pronounced as a solution becomes sweeter or more bitter, suggesting that newborns can discriminate different concentrations of a substance.

The sense of smell, or **olfaction,** depends on sensory receptors in the nasal passage that react to chemical molecules in the air. It, too, is working well at birth. Newborns react vigorously to unpleasant smells such as vinegar or ammonia and turn their heads away (Rieser, Yonas, & Wilkner, 1976). Even more remarkable is evidence that babies who are breast-fed can recognize their mothers solely by the smell of their breasts or underarms within a week or two of birth

(Cernoch & Porter, 1985; Porter et al., 1992). Babies who are bottle-fed cannot, probably because they have less contact with their mothers' skin. Thus the sense of smell we often take for granted may help babies and their parents get to know each other right from the start.

In sum, both the sense of taste and the sense of smell are working very well at birth. Later development is mainly a matter of learning to recognize what it is that is being tasted or smelled. As wine tasters illustrate, these senses can become highly educated indeed.

Touch, Temperature, and Pain

Receptors in the skin detect touch or pressure, heat or cold, and painful stimuli. The sense of touch seems to be operating quite nicely well before birth and may, along with the body senses that detect motion, be one of the first senses to develop (Field, 1990). We saw in Chapter 5 that newborns respond with reflexes if they are touched in appropriate areas. Even in their sleep, newborns will habituate to strokes of the same spot on the skin but respond again if the tactile stimulation is shifted to a new spot—from the ear to the lips, for example (Kisilevsky & Muir, 1984).

Newborns are also sensitive to warmth and cold (Pratt, 1954). Finally, young babies clearly respond to painful stimuli such as pin pricks (Stevens, 1996). For obvious ethical reasons, researchers have not exposed infants to severely painful stimuli. However, analyses of boys' cries as they undergo circumcisions leave no doubt that these surgical procedures are painful (Porter, Miller, & Marshall, 1986). Such research challenges the medical wisdom of giving babies who must undergo major surgery little or no anesthesia. It turns out that infants are more likely to survive heart surgery if they receive deep anesthesia that keeps them unconscious during the operation and for a day afterward than if they receive light anesthesia that does not entirely protect them from the stressful experience of pain (Anand & Hickey, 1992).

We have now seen that each of the major senses is operating in some form at birth and that perceptual abilities increase dramatically during infancy. Let's ask one final question about infant perception: Can infants meaningfully integrate information from the different senses?

Integrating Sensory Information

It would obviously be useful for the infant who is attempting to understand the world to be able to put together information gained from viewing, fingering, sniffing, and otherwise exploring objects. It now seems clear that the senses do indeed function in an inte-

grated way at birth. For instance, the fact that newborns will look in the direction of a sound they hear suggests that vision and hearing are linked. Moreover, infants 8 to 31 days old expect to feel objects that they can see and are frustrated by a visual illusion that looks like a graspable object but proves to be nothing but air when they reach for it (Bower, Broughton, & Moore, 1970). Thus vision and touch, as well as vision and hearing, seem to be interrelated early in life. This integration of the senses helps babies perceive and respond appropriately to the objects and people they encounter (Hainline & Abramov, 1992; Walker-Andrews, 1997).

A somewhat more difficult task is to recognize through one sense an object that is familiar through another; this is called **cross-modal perception.** This capacity is required by children's games that involve feeling objects hidden in a bag and identifying what they are by touch alone. A vivid demonstration of cross-modal perception in early life involved familiarizing infants with an object through touch and then determining if they could recognize the object by sight (Meltzoff & Borton, 1979). One-month-old infants were given one of two pacifiers to suck without being allowed to see what they were sucking. One pacifier was round and smooth, and the other had hard nubs on it. Infants then saw two styrofoam forms, one shaped like the smooth pacifier and the other like the nubbed pacifier. They tended to look more at the pacifier they had sucked than at the unfamiliar one, suggesting that they recognized by sight a stimulus that was familiar only through touch.

Although this oral-to-visual cross-modal transfer may be evident very early, other forms of cross-modal perception are not consistently or reliably displayed until about 4 to 7 months of age (Streri & Pecheux, 1986; Walker-Andrews, 1997). Then, for example, infants integrate vision and hearing to judge distance; they actually prefer to look at an approaching train that gets louder and a departing one that gets quieter rather than at videos in which sound and sight are mismatched (Pickens, 1994). Performance on more complex cross-modal perception tasks that require matching patterns of sounds with patterns of visual stimuli continues to improve all the way through childhood and adolescence, however (Botuck & Turkewitz, 1990).

In sum, impressions from the different senses are "fused" early in life, much as William James believed, but not so as to create the "blooming, buzzing confusion" he described. Rather, this early sensory integration may make it easier for babies to perceive and use information that comes to them through multiple channels simultaneously (Walker-Andrews, 1997). Then, as the separate senses continue to develop and each becomes a more effective means of exploring

Intersensory perception. The ability to recognize through one sense (here, touch) what has been learned through another (vision) increases with age during infancy and childhood. Here, the birthday girl must identify prizes in the bag by touch alone.

objects, babies become more skilled at cross-modal perception and are able to coordinate information gained through one sense with information gained through another.

Influences on Early Perceptual Development

What remarkable perceptual competencies even the very young infant has, and what remarkable progress is made within the first few months of life. All of the major senses begin working before birth and are clearly functioning at birth; parents would be making a huge mistake to assume that their newborn is not taking in the sensory world. Many perceptual abilities—for example, the ability to perceive depth or to distinguish melodies—then emerge within just a few months after birth. Gradually, basic perceptual capacities are fine-tuned, and, importantly, infants become more and more able to interpret their sensory experiences—to recognize a pattern of light as a face, for example. By the time infancy ends, the most important aspects of perceptual development are complete (Bornstein, 1992). The senses and the mind are working to create a meaningful world of recognized objects, sounds, tastes, smells, and bodily sensations.

The fact that perceptual development takes place so quickly can be viewed as support for the "nature" side of the nature/nurture debate. Many basic perceptual capacities appear to be innate or to develop rapidly in all normal infants. What, then, is the role of early sensory experience in perceptual development?

Early Experience and the Brain

As we saw in Chapter 5, sensory experience is critically important in determining the organization of the developing brain (Johnson, 1997; Newberger, 1997). To expand a bit on this theme, imagine what visual perception would be like in an infant who was blind at birth but later had surgery to permit vision. In sensory-deprivation research involving animals, young animals are temporarily deprived of sensory stimulation. If they later show a perceptual deficit, the experiences that they did *not* have are judged to have been necessary for normal development.

Nearly half a century ago, Austin Riesen and his associates discovered that chimpanzees raised in the dark experience a degeneration of the optic nerve that seriously restricts their vision (Riesen et al., 1951). If the chimps spent no more than seven months in the dark, the damage could be reversed; otherwise it was permanent. In chimps exposed to diffuse, unpatterned light for brief periods every day, damage to the optic nerves did not occur. Yet animals deprived of patterned stimulation later had difficulty discriminating forms such as circles and squares—a task that normal chimps easily master (Riesen, 1965).

In short, the visual system requires stimulation early in life, including patterned stimulation, to develop normally—in humans as well as in chimpanzees. Some babies are born with cataracts that make them nearly blind. Once surgery restores their sight, they (like Riesen's chimps) have difficulty, at least initially, discriminating common forms such as spheres and cubes (Walk, 1981). Because the wiring of connections between the optic nerve and the brain is disrupted by sensory deprivation, full and lasting recovery of perceptual abilities after a period of early visual deprivation is sometimes very difficult to achieve (Thompson, 1993).

It is also now clear that young animals not only need visual stimulation but require specific forms of it if neurons in the visual areas of the brain are to develop properly (Greenough, Black, & Wallace, 1987; Johnson, 1997). Pioneering neuropsychologists David Hubel and Torsten Wiesel paved the way in studying how early experience affects the architecture of the visual areas of the cat's brain (Hubel & Wiesel, 1963; Wiesel & Hubel, 1965; and see Chapter 5). In mature cats, for example, specific neural cells respond to either horizontal, vertical, or oblique (slanted) lines. When Blakemore and Price (1987) compared the responses of kittens' and cats' brains to lines at different orientations, they found that the brain cells of 7-day-old kittens were not yet specialized; they either did not respond at all or did not respond selectively (only to lines of a particular orientation). After about 4 weeks of visual experience, though, particular cells responded only to horizontal, vertical, or oblique lines, indicating that an adultlike brain organization was rapidly taking shape. What happens if a kitten is fitted with goggles that allow it to view only vertical stripes? Then it develops an abundance of "vertical" cells but loses some of the cells that would enable it to detect horizontal and oblique lines (Stryker et al., 1978). Similarly, humans who have severe *astigmatism—* misshapened lenses that distort images—often have lasting difficulty seeing lines equally well in all orientations even after their vision is corrected (Mitchell et al., 1973).

The same message about the importance of early experience applies to the sense of hearing: Exposure to auditory stimulation early in life affects the architecture of the developing brain, which in turn influences auditory perception skills (Finitzo, Gunnarson, & Clark, 1990). The conclusion is clear: *Maturation alone is not enough; normal perceptual development also requires normal perceptual experience.* The practical implication is also clear: Visual and hearing problems in children should be detected and corrected as early in life as possible.

The Infant's Active Role

Parents need not worry about arranging just the right sensory environment for their children because young humans actively seek just the stimulation they need in order to develop properly. Infants are active explorers and stimulus seekers from the start; they orchestrate their own perceptual, motor, and cognitive development through their exploratory behavior (Gibson, 1988; Ruff & Rothbart, 1996).

According to Eleanor Gibson (1988), infants proceed through three phases of exploratory behavior:

1. From birth to 4 months they explore their immediate surroundings, especially their caregivers, by looking and listening, and they learn a bit about objects by mouthing them and watching them move;
2. From 5 to 7 months, once the ability to voluntarily grasp objects has developed, babies pay far closer attention to objects, exploring objects with their eyes as well as with their hands;
3. By 8 or 9 months of age, after they have begun to crawl, infants extend their explorations out into the larger environment and carefully examine the objects they encounter on their journeys, learning all about their properties. Whereas a young infant may merely mouth a new toy and look at it now and then, a 12-month-old will give

it a thorough examination—turning it, fingering it, poking it, and watching it intently all the while (Ruff et al., 1992).

By combining perception and action in their exploratory behavior, infants actively create sensory environments that meet their needs and contribute to their own development (Eppler, 1995). As children become more able to attend selectively to the world around them, they become even more able to choose the forms and levels of stimulation that suit them best.

Cultural Variation

Do infants who grow up in different cultural environments encounter different sensory stimulation and ultimately perceive the world in different ways? Perceptual preferences obviously differ from culture to culture. In some cultures, people think hefty women are more beautiful than slim ones or relish eating sheep's eyeballs or chicken heads. Are more basic perceptual competencies also affected by socialization?

People from different cultures differ very little in basic sensory capacities such as the ability to discriminate degrees of brightness or loudness (Berry et al., 1992). However, their perceptions and interpretations of sensory input can vary considerably. For example, we have already seen that children, starting at the end of the first year of life, become insensitive to speech sound contrasts that they do not hear because they are not important in their primary language. Michael Lynch and his associates (1990) have shown that the same is true with respect to perceptions of music. Infants from the United States, they found, noticed equally well notes that violated either Western musical scales or the Javanese pelog scale. This suggests that humans are born with the potential to perceive music from a variety of cultures. However, American adults were less sensitive to bad notes in the unfamiliar Javanese musical system than to mistuned notes in their native Western scale, suggesting that their years of experience with Western music had shaped their perceptual skills.

Another example of cultural influence concerns the ability to translate one's perceptions of the human form into a drawing. In Papua New Guinea, where there is no cultural tradition of drawing and painting, children ages 10 to 15 who have had no schooling do not have much luck drawing the human body; they draw scribbles or tadpole-like forms far more often than children in the same society who have attended school and have been exposed many times to drawings of people (Martlew & Connolly, 1996; and see Figure 6.4). We all have the capacity to create two-dimensional representations, but we apparently develop that capacity more rapidly if our culture provides us with relevant experiences. Many other

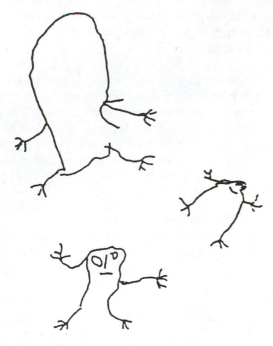

FIGURE 6.4 *Children ages 10 to 15 in Papua New Guinea, unless they have attended school, lack experience with drawings of the human form and produce drawings much like those done by far younger children in our society. Cultural experience influences the ability to translate visual perceptions into representations on the page.* (From Martlew & Connolly, 1996)

examples of the effects of cultural learning experiences on visual and auditory perception can be cited (Berry et al., 1992).

In sum, a common biological heritage and common sensory experiences combine to ensure that all normal humans develop the same basic perceptual abilities. However, perceptual development is also shaped by specific sensory experiences that only some children have, as influenced by their own explorations of the world and by the cultural context in which they develop.

THE CHILD

If most sensory and perceptual development is complete by the end of infancy, what is left to accomplish during childhood? Mostly it is a matter of learning to use the senses more intelligently. As a result, it becomes even harder to separate perceptual development from cognitive development. For example, children rapidly build knowledge of the world so that they can recognize and label what they sense, giving it greater meaning. In addition, much of perceptual development in childhood is really a matter of the development of **attention,** the focusing of perception and cognition on something in particular. Youngsters be-

come better able to use their senses deliberately and strategically to gather the information most relevant to a task at hand. They also become more skilled at making the kinds of perceptual discriminations that are so important in complex cognitive tasks such as learning to read.

The Development of Attention

From the start, infants actively use their senses to explore their environment, and they prefer some sensory stimuli to others. Still, there is some truth to the idea that the attention of the infant or very young child is "captured by" something and that of the older child is "directed toward" something. Selective as they are, 1-month-old infants do not really deliberately choose to attend to faces and other engaging stimuli. Instead, a novel stimulus attracts their attention and, once their attention is "caught," they sometimes seem unable to turn away (Ruff & Rothbart, 1996). As children get older, three things change: (1) their attention spans become longer, (2) they become more selective in what they attend to, and (3) they are better able to plan and carry out systematic strategies for using their senses to achieve goals.

Longer Attention Span

Young children do have short attention spans. Researchers know that they should limit their experimental sessions with young children to a few minutes, and nursery school teachers often switch classroom activities every 15 to 20 minutes. Even when they are doing things they like, such as watching a television program or playing with a toy, 2- and 3-year-olds spend far less time actually concentrating on the program or the toy than older children do (Anderson et al., 1986; Ruff & Lawson, 1990). In one study of sustained attention, children were asked to put strips of colored paper in appropriately colored boxes (Yendovitskaya, 1971). Children aged 2½ to 3½ worked for an average of 18 minutes and were easily distracted; children aged 5½ to 6 often persisted for an hour or more. Further improvements in attention span occur later in childhood.

More Selective Attention

Although young infants clearly deploy their senses in a selective manner, they are not very good at controlling their attention—deliberately concentrating on one thing while ignoring something else. With age, infant attention becomes more selective. As infants approach two years of age, they also become able to form plans of action, which then guide what they focus upon and what they ignore (Ruff & Rothbart, 1996). As school-age children get older, they become more and more able to selectively focus their attention

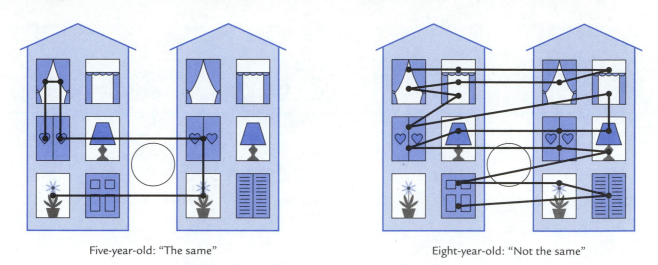

Five-year-old: "The same"   Eight-year-old: "Not the same"

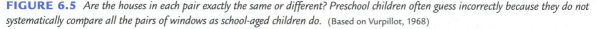

FIGURE 6.5 *Are the houses in each pair exactly the same or different? Preschool children often guess incorrectly because they do not systematically compare all the pairs of windows as school-aged children do.* (Based on Vurpillot, 1968)

so that they can find a target visual stimulus while disregarding distractor stimuli (Strutt et al., 1975). Similarly, children become more able to tune in one speaker while ignoring another who is talking at the same time—or to monitor two conversations at the same time and recall what was said (Maccoby, 1967). These findings should suggest to teachers of young children that performance will be better if distractions in task materials and in the room are kept to a minimum.

More Systematic Attention

Finally, as they get older, children become more able to plan and carry out systematic perceptual searches. We have already seen that older infants are more likely than younger ones to thoroughly explore a pattern. Research with children in the former Soviet Union reveals that visual scanning becomes considerably more detailed or exhaustive over the first six years of life (Zaporozhets, 1965). But the most revealing findings come from studies of how children go about a *visual search*. Elaine Vurpillot (1968) recorded the eye movements of 4- to 10-year-olds who were trying to decide whether two houses, each with several windows containing various objects, were identical or different. As Figure 6.5 illustrates, children aged 4 and 5 were not at all systematic. They often looked at only a few windows and as a result came to wrong conclusions. In contrast, most children older than 6½ were very systematic, they typically checked each window in one house with the corresponding window in the other house, pair by pair.

In summary, learning to control attention is an important part of perceptual development during childhood. Infants and young children are without question selectively attentive to the world around

them, but they haven't fully taken charge of their attentional processes. With age, children become more able to concentrate on a task for a long period, to focus on relevant information and ignore distractions, and to use their senses in purposeful and systematic ways to achieve goals. As you might expect, children who have difficulty controlling their attention have difficulty learning and performing well in school (Ruff & Rothbart, 1996).

Learning to Read

One of the most challenging perceptual tasks that children face in our culture is learning to read. How do they learn to translate printed language into spoken language? Eleanor Gibson and Harry Levin (1975) identified three phases in learning to read. First, children equate reading with storytelling: They may pick up a storybook and "read" very sensible sentences—most of which have no relation to the words on the page.

Next, children recognize that the squiggles on the printed page represent words. They may try to match the spoken words of a familiar story to the symbols on the page, but their matches are not correct. This kind of activity sets the stage for learning that each letter is related to a particular sound and that combinations of letters (and sounds) make up printed words.

In the third and final phase of learning to read, children have become quite skilled at decoding letters; they can sound out unknown words by breaking them into individual sounds or syllables. Children gain solid mastery of the rules for translating letters into sounds by the third or fourth grade (Morrison, 1984). However, the complexities of letter/sound correspondences in English can give even older readers problems. For

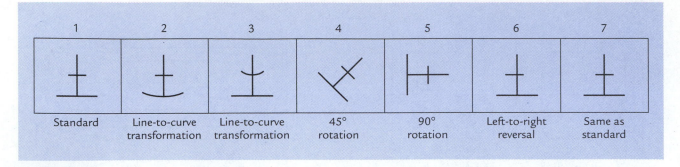

FIGURE 6.6 *Examples of figures used to test children's ability to detect the distinctive features of letterlike forms* (Adapted from Gibson, Gibson, Pick, & Osser, 1962)

example, the *c* in *circle* is pronounced very differently from the *c* in *cannery,* and the *gh* in *ghetto* does not sound a bit like the *gh* in *rough.*

In part, reading is an exercise in visual form perception. As Eleanor Gibson (1969) puts it, readers must learn to recognize the **distinctive features** of letters—the specific elements (such as straight and curved lines) that distinguish one letter from another. Gibson and her colleagues tested for this skill by showing children aged 4 to 8 a standard letterlike form and asking them to select those identical to the standard from among a set of similar forms (Gibson, Gibson, Pick, & Osser, 1962; see also Figure 6.6). The 4- and 5-year-olds often mistakenly selected stimuli that were not identical to the standard. The 6- to 8-year-olds in Gibson's study were far more able than younger children to detect the distinctive features that differentiated the variations from the standard form. Perhaps it is because young children have difficulty discriminating letters that serious reading instruction normally begins around age 5 to 7 in many countries.

To make sense of all those squiggles on the page, of course, children must not only differentiate among them but also must learn how they correspond to sounds in spoken language. To do so, they first must acquire an auditory skill called **phonological awareness;** that is, they must realize that spoken words can be decomposed into basic sound units, or *phonemes.* Children who have phonological awareness can recognize that *cat* and *trouble* both have the phoneme /t/ in them, can tell you how many distinct sounds there are in the word *bunch,* and can tell you what will be left if you take the "f" sound out of *fat.* Once they have the auditory skills to isolate the phonemes in spoken language, children are in a position to detect correspondences between these sounds and printed letters (an intersensory perception task).

Children who have serious difficulties learning to read, even though they have normal intellectual ability and no sensory impairments or emotional difficul-

ties that could account for their problems, are said to have **dyslexia,** or a reading disability. Dyslexic children have varied disabilities. A minority have the kind of visual perception problem that used to be seen as the heart of dyslexia; they cannot distinguish between letters with similar appearances, or they read words backward (*top* might become *pot*). However, it is now clear that the difficulties of the large majority of dyslexic children concern auditory perception more than visual perception.

Specifically, children who become dyslexic readers often show deficiencies in phonological awareness well before they enter school (Bruck, 1992; Vellutino et al., 1996). They also have trouble recognizing spoken words if given their initial sounds (Metsala, 1997). Because these youngsters have difficulty analyzing the sounds in speech, they also have trouble detecting sound/letter correspondences, which in turn impairs their ability to recognize printed words automatically and effortlessly (Bruck, 1990; Vellutino, 1991). They must then devote so much effort to decoding the words on the page that they have little attention to spare for interpreting and remembering what they have read. Dyslexic children continue to perform very poorly on tests of phonological awareness and tests of word recognition as adolescents and adults, even if they have managed to become decent readers (Bruck, 1990, 1992). It is now clear that dyslexia is a lifelong disability, not just a developmental delay that is eventually overcome (Bruck, 1992; Francis et al., 1996).

What does all this suggest about teaching children to read? For years there has been debate over the merits of two broad approaches to reading instruction: the phonics approach and the whole-language approach. The phonics or code-oriented approach teaches children to analyze words into their component sounds—that is, it systematically teaches them letter/sound correspondence rules (Vellutino, 1991). By contrast, the whole-language (or look-say) approach emphasizes reading for meaning and teaches children

to recognize specific words by sight or to figure out what they mean using clues in the surrounding context. It assumes that the parts of printed words (the letters) are not as meaningful as the whole words and that children can learn to read as effortlessly and naturally as they learn to understand speech.

Research most strongly supports the phonics approach. To read well, children must somehow learn that spoken words are made up of sounds and that the letters of the alphabet correspond to these sounds (Foorman, 1995). Teaching phonological awareness skills can pay off in better reading skills (Castle, Riach, & Nicholson, 1994). One research team, knowing that dyslexic children have special difficulty discriminating speech sounds that are made rapidly such as *b, d,* and *t,* developed an entertaining computer game that allows children to practice discriminating pairs of these hard-to-distinguish sounds when they are altered so that they are stretched out in time and thereby made easier to perceive (Merzenich et al., 1996; Tallal et al., 1996). After only a month of such game playing, the ability to recognize fast sequences of speech sounds and understand language improves dramatically. These gains are likely to pay off in improved reading performance as children become more able to sound out the words on the page. Despite the importance of phonological awareness, though, there is no reason why reading programs cannot attempt to make good use of both the phonics and whole-language forms of instruction, teaching letter/sound correspondences but also helping children find meaning and enjoyment in what they read (Adams, 1990).

THE ADOLESCENT

There is little to report about perception during adolescence, except that some of the developments of childhood are not quite completed until then. For example, portions of the brain that help regulate attention are not fully myelinated until adolescence (Tanner, 1990). Perhaps this helps explain why adolescents and young adults have incredibly long attention spans on occasion, as when they spend hours cramming for tests or typing term papers into the wee hours of the morning. The ability to sustain attention improves considerably between childhood and adulthood (McKay et al., 1994).

In addition, adolescents become still more efficient at ignoring irrelevant information so that they can concentrate on the task at hand. Not only do they learn more than children do about material they are supposed to master, but they learn *less* about distracting information that could potentially interfere with their performance (Miller & Weiss, 1981). Similarly, adolescents can divide their attention more systematically between two tasks. For instance, Andrew Schiff and Irwin Knopf (1985) watched the eye movements of 9-year-olds and 13-year-olds during a two-part visual search task. Children were to push a response key when particular symbols appeared at the center of a screen and also remember letters flashed at the corners of the screen. The adolescents developed an efficient strategy for switching their eyes back and forth from the center to the corners at the right times. The

9-year-olds had an unfortunate tendency to look at blank areas of the screen or to focus too much attention on the letters in the corners of the screen, thereby failing to detect the symbols in the center.

In short, adolescence appears to be a time when basic perceptual and attentional skills are perfected. Adolescents are better than children at sustaining their attention and using it selectively and strategically to solve the problem at hand.

THE ADULT

What becomes of sensory and perceptual capacities during adulthood? There is good news and bad news, and we might as well dispense with the bad news first: Sensory and perceptual capacities decline gradually with age in the normal person. Whispers become harder to hear, seeing in the dark becomes difficult, food may not taste as good, and so on. Often these declines begin in early adulthood and become noticeable in one's 40s, sometimes giving middle-aged people a feeling that they are getting old. Further declines take place in later life, to the point that one would have a hard time finding a person aged 65 or older who does not have at least a mild sensory or perceptual impairment. The good news is that these changes are gradual and usually minor. As a result we can usually compensate for them, making small adjustments such as turning up the volume on the TV set or adding a little extra seasoning to food. Because losses are not severe, and because of the process of compensation, only a minority of old people develop serious problems such as blindness and deafness.

The losses we are talking about take two general forms. First, sensation is affected, as indicated by raised **sensory thresholds.** The threshold for a sense is the point at which low levels of stimulation can be detected—a dim light can be seen, a faint tone can be heard, a slight odor can be detected, and so on. Stimulation that is below the threshold cannot be detected, so a raising of the threshold with age means that sensitivity to very low levels of stimulation is lost. (We saw that the very young infant is also insensitive to some very low levels of stimulation.)

Second, perceptual abilities also decline in some aging adults. Even when stimulation is intense enough to be well above the detection threshold, older people sometimes have difficulty processing or interpreting sensory information. As we'll see, they may have trouble searching a visual scene, understanding rapid speech in a noisy room, or recognizing the foods that they are tasting.

So, sensory and perceptual declines are typical during adulthood, although they are far steeper in some individuals than in others and can often be compensated for. These declines involve both a raising of thresholds for detecting stimulation and a loss of some perceptual abilities.

Vision

Several changes in the eye and in the parts of the nervous system related to vision take place over the adult years, leading to vision problems in later life (Kline & Scialfa, 1996; Fozard, 1990). You may have noticed that the eyes of old people are often slightly discolored and dull. However, the more significant changes take place *within* the eye. The pupil of an old person normally is smaller than that of a young adult and does not change in size as much when lighting conditions change. The lens that focuses light to cast a sharp image on the retina has been gaining new cells from childhood on, making it denser and less flexible later in life: It cannot change shape, or accommodate, as well to bring objects at different distances into focus. The lens is also yellowing, and both it and the gelatinous liquid behind it are becoming less transparent. Finally, the sensory receptor cells in the retina, especially those that allow us to see things off to the side, die or function less efficiently than they once did, as do the complex nerves leading from the retina to the visual areas of the brain. What impacts do these physical and neural changes have on visual sensation and perception?

Basic Capacities

Gradual changes in the eye are often not noticeable until middle age. In their 40s many people notice a loss of near vision. This very common change is the main sign of **presbyopia** (a term meaning "aging sight") and is related to a decreased ability of the lens to accommodate to objects that are close to the eye. Over the years an adult may, without even being aware of it, gradually move newspapers and books farther from the eye to make them clearer—a form of compensation for decline. Eventually, however, the arms may simply be too short to do the trick any longer. So middle-aged adults cope by getting reading glasses (or, if they also have problems with distance vision, bifocals); reading the fine print may still be a problem, however (Kosnik et al., 1988).

As for distance vision, visual acuity as measured by standard eye charts increases in childhood, peaks in the 20s, remains quite steady through middle age, and steadily declines in old age (Pitts, 1982). The implications for the average adult are fairly minor. For example, in one major study, 69% of 75- to 85-year-olds had corrected vision between 20/10 and 20/25 (Kahn et al., 1977). At worst, then, most of them could see at 20 feet what a person with standard acuity can see at 25 feet. Only 3.3% of them had corrected vision of 20/200 or worse—a cutoff commonly used to define legal blindness. Most of us needn't fear becoming blind in old age, then, though most of us will indeed wear corrective lenses (see Figure 6.7).

The minority of elderly people who experience serious declines in visual acuity typically suffer from pathological conditions of the eye. These conditions become more prevalent in old age but are not part of aging itself (Pitts, 1982). For example, **cataracts**— opaque areas of the lens—are the leading cause of blindness in old age. Over half of elderly adults have cataracts but they can be removed through surgery to prevent blindness (Suro, 1997). A contributing factor is lifelong heavy exposure to sunlight and its damaging ultraviolet rays (Kline & Schieber, 1985).

Over age 50, **glaucoma** also becomes more common. In this condition, increased fluid pressure in the eye can damage the optic nerve and cause a progressive loss of peripheral vision and ultimately blindness. The key is to prevent the damage before it occurs through eye drops or surgery to lower eye fluid pressure. In many cases the damage is done before people experience any visual problems, though; only regular eye tests can reveal the buildup of eye pressure that spells trouble (Suro, 1997).

Because older people also have higher visual detection thresholds than younger adults do, they are less sensitive to dim lights and may have trouble making things out in the dark. This can make night driving and navigating in a dark house difficult. In addition, **dark adaptation**—the process in which the eyes adapt to darkness and become more sensitive to the low levels of light available—occurs more slowly in older individuals than in younger ones. As a result, the older person driving at night may have special problems when turning onto a dark road from a lighted highway.

Many older adults also have difficulty with glare from bright lights (Kline & Scialfa, 1996). The glare from headlights or from the lights in a very brightly lit room may interfere with clear vision, and old people may take some time to recover from sudden glares (for example, popping flashbulbs). In short, some older people are in a bind: They cannot make things out well in the dark, but they are also bothered by the glare of bright lights.

Finally, perceiving moving objects is a problem for older adults, even those who have good visual acuity (Sivak, Olson, & Pastalan, 1981). Older adults have difficulty reading street signs while they are driving (Kosnik et al., 1988), and they are less able than younger adults to judge the speed of other vehicles (Scialfa et al., 1991). They also have a smaller field of vision, so objects off to the side (cars coming from intersecting streets, for example) may not be detected until there is little time to react (Owsley et al., 1991).

In case you have formed the impression that old people should not be allowed to drive, let's quickly

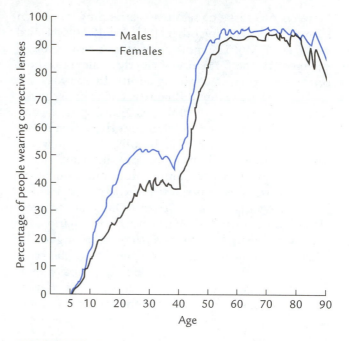

FIGURE 6.7 *The percentage of people wearing glasses or contact lenses rises from less than 1% among 3-year-olds to 92% of those aged 75 or older! Notice the steep rise during the 40s, when many people find they need reading glasses because the lenses of their eyes become less able to change shapes.* (From National Center for Health Statistics, 1983)

note that the drivers who cause the most accidents are those under 25. When we take into account the fact that young people do more driving than elderly people do, it turns out that both elderly drivers and young drivers have more accidents *per mile driven* than middle-aged drivers do (Williams & Carsten, 1989). Yet, the driving records of older adults are not as bad as might be expected, because many of them compensate for visual and other perceptual difficulties and slower reactions by driving less frequently, especially at night and during rush hour—or by being more cautious when they do drive (Kline et al., 1992). So, young drivers might try to be patient the next time they find themselves behind a slow-moving elderly driver: He or she is doing everyone a favor by compensating for declines rather than denying them and driving like a young maniac!

Attention and Visual Search

As we saw when we examined perceptual development during infancy and childhood, perception is more than just seeing: It is using the senses intelligently and allocating attention efficiently. Young children have more difficulty performing complex visual search tasks and ignoring irrelevant information than older children do. Do older adults also have more difficulty than younger adults?

Older adults do worse than younger ones on a number of tests that require dividing one's attention between two tasks or selectively attending to certain stimuli while ignoring others (Hartley, 1992; McDowd & Birren, 1990). The more distractors a task involves, the more the performance of elderly adults falls short of the performance of young adults. In everyday life, this may translate into difficulty carrying on a conversation while driving or problems locating the asparagus amid all the frozen vegetables at the supermarket.

In one test of visual search skills, Dana Plude and William Hoyer (1981) asked young adults and elderly adults to sort cards containing from one to nine letters into two bins, depending on whether or not they contained specific target letters. Older adults were clearly more distracted by irrelevant information, for they were especially slow compared to young adults when the number of distractor letters on the cards was high. In some situations, elderly people appear to have difficulty inhibiting responses to irrelevant stimuli so that they can focus their attention more squarely on relevant stimuli (Dywan & Murphy, 1996; Hasher et al., 1991).

Yet this difficulty inhibiting responses is not always seen (Kieley & Hartley, 1997). For example, the older adults in Plude and Hoyer's study had difficulty only when the letters to be hunted for changed from session to session. When sorters got to practice over all six sessions with the same target letters, older adults were no longer especially bothered by having to search through many distractors. Similarly, older adults search more effectively when they know in advance where to look for a target in a larger display than when the location of a target is unpredictable (Farkas & Hoyer, 1980).

In short, older adults have their greatest difficulties in processing visual information: (1) when the situation is *novel,* when they're not sure exactly what to look for or where to look, and (2) when it is *complex,* when there's a great deal of distracting information to search through, or two tasks must be performed at once (Plude & Hoyer, 1985). By contrast, they have fewer problems when they have clear expectations about what they are to do and when the task is not overly complex. Thus, an older factory worker who has inspected radios for years may be just as speedy and accurate as a younger worker at this well-practiced, familiar task, but he or she might perform relatively poorly if suddenly asked to inspect pocket calculators and look for a much larger number of possible defects—a novel and complex task.

In summary, it is normal for adults to experience a gradual loss of near vision as they age and to encounter special problems when they are in either darkness or bright light and when they are viewing moving objects. Performance on novel and complex visual perception tasks may also suffer in old age, partly because older adults are less able than younger people to filter out distracting information.

An older adult is likely to find the ice cream as efficiently as a younger adult in a familiar supermarket but may have difficulty with this visual search task if the supermarket is unfamiliar.

Hearing

There is some truth to the stereotype of the hard-of-hearing older person. The older the age group, the greater the percentage of people who have at least a mild hearing loss: about 20% in the 45 to 54 age group and as many as 75% in the 75 to 79 age group (Butler & Lewis, 1977). Most older people experience only mild hearing impairments, though; few are deaf.

Basic Capacities

Sources of hearing problems range from excess wax buildup in the ears to a sluggish nervous system. Most age-related hearing problems seem to originate in the inner ear, however (Kline & Scialfa, 1996). The cochlear hair cells that serve as auditory receptors, their surrounding structures, and the neurons leading from them to the brain degenerate gradually over the adult years. The most noticeable result is a loss of sensitivity to high-frequency or high-pitched sounds, the most common form of **presbycusis,** or problems of the aging ear (Northern, 1996). Thus the older person may have difficulty hearing a child's high voice, the flutes in an orchestra, and high-frequency consonant sounds such as *s, z,* and *ch* (Whitbourne, 1985) but may have less trouble with deep voices, tubas, and sounds like *b.* After age 50, lower-frequency sounds also become increasingly difficult to hear (Kline & Scialfa, 1996). By one estimate, adults under 55 suffer a 3-decibel hearing loss each decade; people over 55 lose 9 decibels of hearing each decade (Davis, Ostri, & Parving, 1991). The implication is clear: To be heard by the average older adult a sound—especially a high-pitched sound but, ultimately, any sound—must be louder than it needs to be to exceed the hearing threshold of a younger adult.

Is this loss of hearing with age the inevitable result of basic aging processes or is it caused by other factors? We know that the loss is more noticeable among men than among women, that men are more likely to work in noisy industrial jobs, and that those who do hold such jobs experience more hearing loss than other men (Bergman, 1980; Martin, 1994). And yet, even when adults who have held relatively quiet jobs are studied, men show detectable hearing losses earlier in life (in their 30s) and lose hearing sensitivity at a faster rate than women (Pearson et al., 1995). It seems, then, that most people, men more than women, will experience some loss of sensitivity to high-frequency sounds as part of the basic aging process but that certain people will experience more severe losses owing to their experiences. Fans of loud music, beware: The noise at rock concerts and discos is often in the 120 to 130 decibel range and is loud enough to cause a temporary raising of hearing thresholds (Hetu & Fortin, 1995) and possibly even permanent hearing loss in individuals who are regularly exposed to it (Hartman, 1982).

Speech Perception

Perhaps the most important thing we do with our ears in everyday life is listen to other people during conversations. The ability to hear is one requisite for understanding speech, but this complex auditory perception task also depends on cognitive processes such as attention and memory. How well do aging adults do?

Under ideal listening conditions, older adults typically have somewhat more difficulty discriminating words that are read to them than younger adults do, perhaps because of degeneration within the ear. However, these problems are minor compared to those that some older adults, especially those with hearing losses, experience under *poor listening conditions* (Fozard, 1990; Kline & Scialfa, 1996). Here cognitive skills become more critical (Sommers, 1997). For example, when you are trying to understand what someone is saying in the presence of loud background noise, you must keep your attention focused and "hear between the lines," inferring what a word is from context when you cannot make it out completely.

Older adults are especially likely to have problems understanding speech if there is a great deal of background noise. The performance gap between them and younger adults is also greater when the speech signal is "degraded" in other respects—for example, when it is fast, when it reverberates in a room, or when some of its frequencies are filtered out or distorted, as is the case when listening to a voice on the telephone or on a videocassette (Bergman et al., 1976; Fozard, 1990).

In addition, auditory perception tasks, like visual perception tasks, are more difficult for older people when they are novel and complex. In familiar, everyday situations, older adults are able to make good use of contextual cues to interpret what they hear (Fozard, 1990). In one study, for example, elderly adults were about as able as young adults to recall meaningful sentences they had just heard (Wingfield et al., 1985). However, they had serious difficulties in repeating back grammatical sentences that made no sense or random strings of words, especially when these meaningless stimuli were spoken rapidly. So an older person may be able to follow an ordinary conversation but not a technical presentation on an unfamiliar topic—especially if the speaker makes the task even harder by talking too fast.

Overall, then, most older adults have only mild hearing losses, especially for high-frequency sounds, and only minor problems understanding everyday speech, and they can compensate for their difficulties quite successfully—for example, by reading lips and relying on contextual cues. Novel and complex speech heard under poor listening conditions is likely to cause more trouble. For those rarer older people who develop a significant hearing loss, the psychological effects can be far more serious, as we'll see at the end of this chapter.

Taste and Smell

Does the aging of sensory systems also mean that older people become less able to appreciate tastes and aromas? Studies designed to measure taste thresholds suggest that with increasing age, many of us have more difficulty detecting weak taste stimulation—for example, a little bit of salt or citric acid in water (Bartoshuk & Beauchamp, 1994; Stevens et al., 1995). In addition, both middle-aged and older adults sometimes have difficulty discriminating among tastes that differ in intensity. In one study, for example, adults over 70 were less able than young adults to reliably judge one solution to be saltier, or more bitter, or more acidic, than another (Weiffenbach, Cowart, & Baum, 1986). Interestingly, older adults did not have difficulty distinguishing degrees of sweetness; we don't seem to ever lose the sweet tooth that we are born with.

The ability to perceive odors also typically declines with age. Sensitivity to odors increases from childhood to early adulthood and then declines during adulthood, more so with increasing age (Doty et al., 1984; Ship et al., 1996). All things considered, age takes a greater toll on the sense of smell than on the sense of taste (Bartoshuk & Beauchamp, 1994). However, differences between age groups are usually small, and many older people retain their sensitivity to odors quite well. Women are more likely than men to maintain their ability to label odors in scratch-and-sniff tests (Ship & Weiffenbach, 1993), partly because they are less likely than men to have worked in factories and been exposed to chemicals (Corwin, Loury, & Gilbert, 1995). Also, healthy adults of both sexes retain their sense of smell somewhat better than those who have diseases and take medications (Ship & Weiffenbach, 1993). Once again, then, we see that perceptual losses in later life are part of the basic aging process but vary from person to person depending on environmental factors.

How do declines in the senses of taste and smell affect the older person's enjoyment of food? Susan Schiffman (1977) blindfolded young adults and elderly adults and asked them to identify blended foods by taste and smell alone. As Table 6.1 reveals, the older people were less often correct than the college students. But was this due to a loss of taste sensitivity or to a loss of smell sensitivity? Or was it instead a cognitive problem—difficulty coming up with the name of a food that was in fact sensed?

Claire Murphy (1985) attempted to shed light on these questions by presenting young and elderly adults with 12 of the blended foods used by Schiffman. She observed that older people often came up with the wrong specific label but the right idea (identifying sugar as fruit or salt as peanuts, for example). Thus at least some of their difficulty might have been cognitive in nature. Murphy also tested women whose nostrils were blocked and found that both young and elderly women did very poorly when they could not smell and had to rely on taste alone. This finding suggests that reduced ability to identify foods in old age is due less to losses in the sense of taste than to losses in the sense of smell and declines in the cognitive skills required to remember and name what one has tasted.

If foods do not have much taste, the older person may lose interest in eating and not get proper nourishment (Whitbourne, 1985). Or the older person may overuse seasonings such as salt or eat spoiled food, which would threaten health in still another way. Yet these problems can be remedied. For example, when flavor enhancers were added to the food in one nursing home, elders ate more, gained muscle strength, and had healthier immune system functioning than they did when they ate the usual institutional fare (Schiffman & Warwick, 1993).

Touch, Temperature, and Pain

By now, we've seen numerous indications that older adults are often less able than younger adults to detect weak sensory stimulation. This holds true regarding the sense of touch as well. The detection threshold for touch increases and sensitivity is gradually lost from middle childhood on (Kenshalo, 1977; Verrillo & Verrillo, 1985). It is not clear that minor losses

TABLE 6.1

Age differences in recognition of foods

	Percentage Recognizing Food	
Pureed Food Substance	College Students (ages 18–22)	Elderly People (ages 67–93)
Apple	93	79
Banana	93	59
Pear	93	86
Pineapple	93	86
Strawberry	100	79
Walnut	33	28
Broccoli	81	62
Cabbage	74	69
Carrot	79	55
Celery	89	55
Corn	96	76
Cucumber	44	28
Green bean	85	62
Green pepper	78	59
Potato	52	59
Tomato	93	93
Beef	100	79
Fish	89	90
Pork	93	72
Rice	81	55

Elderly adults have more difficulty than young college students identifying most blended foods by taste and smell alone. Percentages of those recognizing food include reasonable guesses such as "orange" in response to "apple." Notice that some foods (for example, cucumber) are very difficult for people of any age to identify by taste and smell alone. Appearance and texture are important to our recognition of such foods.
SOURCE: From Schiffman, 1977

in touch sensitivity have many implications for daily life, however.

Similarly, older people may be less sensitive to changes in temperature than younger adults are (Verrillo & Verrillo, 1985). Some keep their homes too cool because they are unaware of being cold; others may fail to notice that it is too hot. Since older bodies are also less able than younger ones to maintain an even temperature, elderly people face an increased risk of death in heat waves or cold snaps (Rango, 1985).

It seems only fair that older people should also be less sensitive to painful stimulation, but are they? They are indeed less likely than younger adults to report weak levels of stimulation as painful, although the age differences in pain thresholds are not large or totally consistent (Verrillo & Verrillo, 1985). Yet older people seem to be no less sensitive to stronger pain stimuli. Older adults with arthritis, osteoporosis, cancer, and other diseases may not complain much about their chronic pain, but they feel it and it clearly has the potential to interfere with their daily functioning and decrease their psychological well-being (Moss, Lawton, & Glicksman, 1991).

The Adult in Perspective

Of all the changes in sensation and perception during adulthood that we have considered, those involving vision and hearing appear to be the most important and the most nearly universal. Not only are these senses less keen, but they are used less effectively in such complex perceptual tasks as searching a cluttered room for a missing book or following rapid conversation in a noisy room. Declines in the other senses are less serious and do not affect as many people.

Still, the vision and hearing of most elderly adults remain reasonably good. It is the minority of older adults with severe or multiple losses that we must worry about. In our complex society, difficulties in driving, watching television, reading newspapers, and getting around can limit satisfaction and social interaction in old age. People who have sensory impairments usually have intellectual impairments as well, most likely due to general declines in neural functioning that affect both perception and cognition (Baltes & Lindenberger, 1997; Salthouse et al., 1996). Finally, sensory impairments may even increase the risk of death, especially when deficits in vision and balance conspire to cause life-threatening falls. So what can be done to help optimize the development of individuals with significant sensory impairments? Let's consider hearing impairments across the life span.

APPLICATIONS: AIDING PEOPLE WITH HEARING IMPAIRMENTS

Although sensory impairments can change the course of normal life-span development, much can be done to help even individuals who are born totally deaf or blind to develop in positive directions and function effectively in everyday life. We close this chapter by briefly examining interventions for children and adults who have hearing impairments.

If they are to master spoken language, babies born with impaired hearing need to be identified as early as possible. A committee of the National Institutes of Health noted, however, that the average hearing-impaired child is not identified until the age of 2½, usually when it becomes clear that his or her language skills have not developed normally (National Institutes of Health, 1993). Because children who receive no special intervention before the age of 3 usually have lasting difficulties with speech and language skills, the committee recommended that all newborns

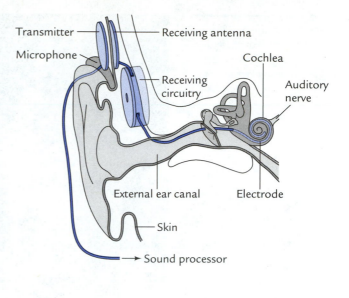

FIGURE 6.8 *A cochlear implant*

in the United States be given hearing tests soon after birth. How do you test the hearing of newborns? The recommended testing procedure involves making clicking sounds in the infant's ear and then determining with sensors attached to the head whether the brain is responding appropriately (National Institutes of Health, 1993).

Once hearing-impaired infants are identified, interventions can be planned. Many programs attempt to capitalize on whatever residual hearing these children have by equipping them with hearing aids. Today, even profoundly deaf children can be helped to hear through an advanced amplification device called the **cochlear implant.** It is implanted in the inner ear through surgery and connected to a microphone worn outside the ear. It works by bypassing damaged hair cells and directly stimulating the auditory nerve with electrical impulses (see Figure 6.8).

Deaf children who are provided with cochlear implants before the age of 5 recognize more spoken words and speak more intelligibly than do children who receive them later in childhood, though even children given implants later in life can benefit (Tye-Murray et al., 1995; Fryauf-Bertschy et al., 1997). Why aren't all hearing-impaired children provided with cochlear implants, then? First, they require surgery and are expensive. Also, despite their benefits, cochlear implants do not have the full support of the deaf community. Deaf children who use them, some claim, will be given the message that one should be ashamed of being deaf. They will be deprived of participation in the unique culture that has developed in communities of

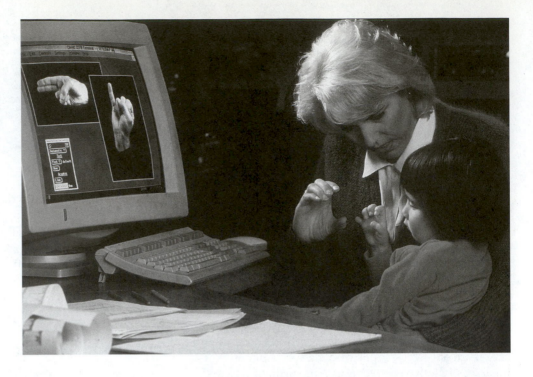

deaf people who share a common language and identity. And, because their hearing will still be far from normal, they may end up feeling that they do not belong to either the deaf or the hearing world (Arana-Ward, 1997; Fryauf-Bertschy et al., 1997).

Another important element in early intervention programs for hearing-impaired children is parent involvement (Maxon & Brackett, 1992). In one program for hearing-impaired children, infants are fitted with hearing aids and teachers then go into the home to show parents how to make their children more aware of the world of sound (Bess & McConnell, 1981). For instance, on hearing the screech of a car's brakes outside, parents might put their hands to their ears, rush their child to the window, and talk about the noise. Similarly, parents are urged to slam doors, deliberately rattle pots and pans, and create other such opportunities for the child to become alert to sounds. All the while, parents are using words to describe everyday objects, people, and events.

This combination of the right amplification device and auditory training in the home has proven quite effective in improving the ability of hearing-impaired infants and preschoolers to hear speech and learn to speak. Yet for other deaf and severely hearing-impaired children, the most important thing may be early exposure to sign language. Early intervention programs for parents of deaf infants can teach them strategies for getting their infants' attention and involving them in conversations using sign (Chen, 1996). The earlier in life deaf children acquire some language system, whether spoken or signed, the better their command of language is likely to be later in life (May-

berry & Eichen, 1991). Deaf children whose parents are deaf and use sign language with them, as well as deaf children of hearing parents who participate in early intervention programs, generally show normal patterns of development, whereas children who are not exposed to any language system early in life suffer for it (Marschark, 1993).

What about the other end of the life span? Most hearing-impaired adults were born with normal hearing. Many are reluctant at first to admit that they have a hearing problem and to seek help because they interpret their problem negatively as a sign of aging (Goffinet, 1992). Yet those who do not have their hearing corrected may end up suffering from depression, decreased independence, and strained relationships (Appollonio et al., 1996). Imagine how hard social interaction can become when one cannot understand what is being said, misinterprets what is said, or has to keep asking people to repeat what they said. One 89-year-old woman became extremely depressed and isolated: "There is an *awfulness* about silence . . . I am days without speaking a word. It is affecting my voice. I fear for my mind. I can't hear the alarm clock, telephone ring, door bell, radio, television—or the human voice" (Meadows-Orlans & Orlans, 1990, pp. 424–425). We tend to think of vision as our most important sense, but hearing impairments may be more disruptive than visual impairments to cognitive and social functioning. Still, many individuals cope very well with their hearing impairments and maintain active, satisfying lifestyles.

Hearing aids, though beneficial, cannot really restore normal hearing; they tend to distort sounds and to magnify background noise as well as what one is trying to hear. In addition, many older people are ill-served by hearing aids that are of poor quality or that are poorly matched to their specific hearing problems (Corso, 1981). Because cochlear implants work best for individuals who were exposed to spoken language before they lost their hearing, elderly people are ideal candidates for them. They tolerate the surgical procedure required for implantation well, and their hearing test scores increase significantly (Kelsall et al., 1995). In addition, over 80% of them report that their quality of life improved significantly.

Finally, the physical and social environment can be modified to help people of all ages with hearing losses (see National Institute on Aging and National Institute on Deafness and Other Communication Disorders, 1996). For example, furniture can be arranged to permit face-to-face contact; lights can be turned on to permit use of visual cues such as gestures and lip movements. Then there are the simple guidelines we can follow to make ourselves understood by hearing-impaired persons. One of the most important is to avoid shouting. Shouting not only distorts speech but raises the pitch of the voice (therefore making it more difficult for elderly people to hear) and makes it harder for the individual to lip read. It is best to speak at a normal rate, clearly but without overarticulating, with one's face fully visible, at a distance of about 3 to 6 feet.

With modern technology, appropriate education, effective coping strategies, and help from those of us who hear, hearing-impaired and deaf individuals of all ages can thrive. The stakes are high, for perception is indeed our primary means of knowing the world. How would infants gain knowledge of teddy bears, spoons, or videocassettes without being able to see them, hear them, finger them, or pop them into their mouths? How would we know anything at all without the input that our senses provide? Perception is truly at the heart of human cognitive development, the topic to which we turn next.

SUMMARY POINTS

1. *Sensation* is the detection of sensory stimulation; *perception* is the interpretation of what is sensed. Developmentalists and philosophers differ about whether basic knowledge of the world is innate (the nativist position) or must be acquired through the senses (the empiricist position).

2. Methods of studying infant perception include the preferential looking, habituation, and operant-conditioning techniques.

3. From birth the visual system is working reasonably well. Infants under 2 months of age discriminate brightness and colors and are attracted to contour, moderate complexity, and movement. Starting at 2 or 3 months of age, they more clearly perceive whole patterns such as faces and seem to understand a good deal about objects and their properties, possibly because they already have intuitive theories of the physical world. Spatial perception also develops rapidly, and by about 7 months infants not only perceive drop-offs but also fear them.

4. Young infants can recognize their mothers' voices, distinguish speech sounds that adults cannot discriminate, and analyze features of musical sounds.

5. The senses of taste and smell are also well developed at birth. Newborns avoid unpleasant tastes and enjoy sweet tastes, and they soon recognize their mothers by odor alone. Newborns are also sensitive to touch, temperature, and pain.

6. The senses are interrelated at birth but, as they develop, performance on cross-modal perception tasks improves.

7. Although many basic perceptual abilities unfold early in life and may be innate, early perceptual development also requires normal sensory stimulation and can take somewhat different forms depending on the sensory experiences available in one's culture.

8. During childhood we learn to sustain attention for longer periods of time, to direct it more selectively (filtering out distracting information), and to plan and carry out more systematic perceptual searches. Children must develop phonological awareness, detect distinguishing features of letters, and grasp letter/sound correspondence rules in order to read.

9. During adolescence, the ability to sustain and control attention improves still more, and sensation and perception are at their peaks.

10. During adulthood, sensory and perceptual capacities gradually decline in most individuals, though many changes are minor and can be compensated for. Visual difficulties include a loss of near vision in middle age, problems perceiving motion, and difficulty performing novel and complex visual searches.

11. Hearing difficulty associated with aging most commonly involves loss of sensitivity to high-frequency (high-pitched) sounds. Even elderly people without significant hearing losses may experience difficulty understanding novel and complex speech spoken rapidly under poor listening conditions.

12. Many older people have difficulty recognizing or enjoying foods, largely because of declines in the sense of smell; touch, temperature, and pain sensitivity also decrease slightly but intense pain stimuli still hurt.

13. Hearing-impaired individuals can benefit from early detection, early exposure to sign language and oral language (with the help of cochlear implants), and the help of hearing people who follow simple communication guidelines.

☼ FOOD FOR THOUGHT

1. Drawing on your knowledge of the sensory and perceptual capacities of newborns, put yourself in the place of a newborn in the delivery room just emerging from the womb and describe your perceptual experiences.

2. The Fosters have decided that their precious 3-year-old, Fenwick, should attend Harvard and deserves a head start. They have brought in a tutor to give him reading lessons for two hours each day. In view of what you know about the development of attention and of other skills relevant to reading, why might this experiment be doomed to failure?

3. You have been hired to teach a cooking course to elderly adults. First, analyze the perceptual strengths and weaknesses of your students: What perceptual tasks might be easy for them and what tasks might be difficult? Second, considering at least three senses, think of ten strategies you can use to help your students compensate for the declines in perceptual capacities that some of them may be experiencing.

Ⓦ ON THE WEB

1. *Hearing Impairment*   This site provides information about deafness and hearing loss, sign language, and related topics. Those of you who listen to loud music might be interested in a fact sheet on noise-induced hearing loss. This and other fact sheets are available through the National Institute on Deafness and Other Communication Disorder.
http://curry.edschool.virginia.edu/go/cise/ose/categories/hi.html

2. *Dyslexia*   For the latest information and research on dyslexia and its causes, try the Web site of the International Dyslexia Association. The Research page is especially interesting and includes interpretations of recent studies of dyslexia.
http://www.interdys.org/

3. *Aging and the Senses*   In the Web site of the National Institute on Aging, under the heading, "Age Pages—Brochures and Fact Sheets for the Public" (click the "Health Information" button), you will find brief and excellent descriptions of presbyopia and presbycusis and other problems in vision and hearing affecting older adults.
http://www.nih.gov/nia/

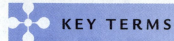

sensation

perception

empiricist

nativist

habituation

visual acuity

visual accommodation

contour

size constancy

visual cliff

intuitive theories

phoneme

olfaction

cross-modal perception

attention

distinctive feature

phonological awareness

dyslexia

sensory threshold

presbyopia

cataracts

glaucoma

dark adaptation

presbycusis

cochlear implant

CHAPTER 7

Cognition and Language

PIAGET'S APPROACH TO COGNITIVE DEVELOPMENT
What Is Intelligence?
How Does Intelligence Develop?

THE INFANT
Substages of the Sensorimotor Stage
The Development of Object Permanence

THE CHILD
The Preoperational Stage
The Concrete Operations Stage

THE ADOLESCENT
The Formal Operations Stage
Implications of Formal Thought

THE ADULT
Limitations in Cognitive Performance
Growth beyond Formal Operations?
Aging and Cognitive Skills

PIAGET IN PERSPECTIVE
Piaget's Contributions
Challenges to Piaget

VYGOTSKY'S SOCIOCULTURAL PERSPECTIVE
Culture and Thought
Social Interaction and Thought
Language and Thought

MASTERING LANGUAGE
What Must Be Mastered
The Course of Language Development
How Language Develops

APPLICATIONS: IMPROVING COGNITIVE FUNCTIONING

SUMMARY POINTS

FOOD FOR THOUGHT

ON THE WEB

KEY TERMS

A very bright 18-month-old was approached by a woman in the supermarket who smiled and said, "Coochie, coochie, coo." The little girl, puzzled, turned to her mother and asked, "Is she trying to talk to me?" (Rowe, 1994, p. 97)

From an early age, humans are beings who think and who communicate their thoughts to others. In this chapter, we begin to examine the development of cognition—the activity of knowing and the processes through which knowledge is acquired and problems are solved. Human beings are cognitive beings throughout the life span, but their minds change in important ways. In this chapter I concentrate on the very influential theory of cognitive development proposed by Jean Piaget, who traced growth in cognitive capacities during infancy, childhood, and adolescence and then asked what becomes of these capacities during adulthood. I also consider an alternative view: Vygotsky's sociocultural perspective on cognitive development and the contributions of language to it. Finally, I trace the development of language and explore relationships between language and thought.

PIAGET'S APPROACH TO COGNITIVE DEVELOPMENT

Piaget at one time worked in Alfred Binet's laboratories on the development of standardized intelligence tests (see Chapter 2) but quickly became disenchanted with an approach that seemed to be concerned only with determining the ages at which children could correctly answer certain questions. Piaget became intrigued by children's *mistakes*, for he noticed that children of the same age often made similar kinds of mistakes—errors that were typically quite different from those made by younger or older children. Could these age-related differences in error patterns reflect developmental steps, or stages, in intellectual growth? Piaget thought so, and he devoted his life to studying how children think, not just what they know (Flavell, 1963).

Interested in basic questions of philosophy, Piaget defined his field of interest as **genetic epistemology,** the study of how we come to know reality and basic dimensions of it such as space, time, and causality. Epistemology is the branch of philosophy that studies knowledge of reality, and "genetic" can be translated as "developmental." In other words, Piaget sought to shed new light on the nature of human knowledge by studying how children come to know the world. His studies began with close observation of his own three

children as infants: how they explored new toys, solved simple problems that he arranged for them, and generally came to understand themselves and their world. Later Piaget studied larger samples of children through what has become known as his **clinical method,** a flexible question-and-answer technique used to discover how children think about problems. Many contemporary researchers consider the method imprecise because it does not involve asking standardized questions to all children tested, but Piaget (1929) believed that the investigator should have the flexibility to pursue an individual child's line of reasoning so as to fully understand the particular child's mind. From his naturalistic observations of his own children and by using the clinical method to explore how children understand everything from the rules of games to the concepts of space and time, Piaget formulated his view of the development of intelligence.

What Is Intelligence?

Piaget defined intelligence as a basic life function that helps the organism adapt to its environment. We observe adaptation as we watch the toddler figuring out how to work a jack-in-the-box, the school-age child figuring out how to divide candies among friends, or the adult figuring out how to program a video recorder. The newborn enters an unfamiliar world with few means of adapting to it other than working senses and reflexes. But Piaget viewed infants as active agents in their own development, learning about the world of people and things by observing, investigating, and experimenting.

Knowledge gained through active exploration takes the form of one or another **scheme** (sometimes called a *schema* in the singular, *schemata* in the plural). Schemes are cognitive structures: organized patterns of action or thought that we construct to organize or interpret our experience (Piaget, 1952, 1977). For example, the infant's grasping actions and sucking responses are early behavioral schemes, patterns of action used to adapt to different objects. During their second year, children develop symbolic schemes, or concepts. They use internal mental symbols such as images and words to represent or stand for aspects of experience, as when a young child sees a funny dance and carries away a mental model of how it was done. Older children become able to manipulate symbols in their heads to help them solve problems.

As children develop more sophisticated schemes, or cognitive structures, they become increasingly able to adapt to their environments. Because they gain new schemes as they develop, children of different ages will respond to the same stimuli differently. The infant may get to know a shoe mainly as a "thing-to-chew," the preschooler may decide to let the shoe

The grasping scheme. Infants have a range of behavioral schemes that allow them to explore new objects. Each scheme is a general pattern of behavior that can be adjusted to fit specific objects.

symbolize or represent a telephone and put it to her ear, and the school-age child may mentally count its shoelace eyelets.

How Does Intelligence Develop?

Piaget believed that all schemes—all forms of understanding—are created through the operation of two inborn intellectual functions, which he called organization and adaptation. Through **organization,** children combine existing schemes into new and more complex ones. For example, the young infant who gazes, reaches, and grasps will organize these simple schemes into a complex structure, *visually directed reaching.* Complex cognitive structures in older children grow out of reorganizations of more primitive structures.

Adaptation is the process of adjusting to the demands of the environment. It occurs through two complementary processes, assimilation and accommodation. Imagine that you are a 2-year-old, that the world is still new, and that you see your first horse. What will you make of it? In all likelihood you will try to relate it to something familiar. **Assimilation** is the process by which we interpret new experiences in terms of existing schemes or cognitive structures. Thus, if you already have a scheme that mentally represents your knowledge of dogs, you may label this new beast "doggie." Through assimilation we deal with the environment in our own terms, sometimes bending the world to squeeze it into our existing categories. Throughout the life span we rely on our existing cognitive structures to understand new events.

But if you notice that this "doggie" is bigger than most dogs and has a mane and an awfully odd "bark,"

you may then be prompted to change your understanding of the world of four-legged animals. **Accommodation** is the process of modifying existing schemes to better fit new experiences. Perhaps you will need to invent a new name for this horse or ask what it is and revise your concept of four-legged animals accordingly.

If we always assimilated new experiences, our understandings would never advance. Piaget believed that all new experiences are greeted with a mix of assimilation and accommodation. Once we have schemes, we apply them to make sense of the world, but we also encounter puzzles that force us to modify our understandings through accommodation. According to Piaget, when new events seriously challenge old schemes, or prove our existing understandings to be inadequate, we experience cognitive conflict. This *cognitive disequilibrium* then stimulates cognitive growth and the formation of more adequate understandings (Piaget, 1985).

Intelligence, then, develops through the *interaction of the individual with the environment.* Piaget took an interactionist position on the nature/nurture issue, maintaining that children "construct reality," or actively create knowledge of the world, from their experiences. They are neither born with innate ideas nor programmed with knowledge by adults. Piaget also viewed human beings as active creators of their own intellectual development. Their knowledge of the world, which takes the form of cognitive structures or schemes, changes as they organize and reorganize their existing knowledge and adapt to new experiences through the complementary processes of assimilation and accommodation. As a result of the interaction of biological maturation and experience, humans progress through four distinct stages of cognitive development:

1. the *sensorimotor* stage (birth to 2 years)
2. the *preoperational* stage (2 to 7 years)
3. the stage of *concrete operations* (7 to 11 years)
4. the stage of *formal operations* (11 years or later and beyond)

These stages represent qualitatively different ways of thinking and occur in an *invariant sequence*—that is, in the same order in all children. However, depending on their experiences, children may progress through the stages rapidly or slowly; the age ranges associated with the stages are only averages.

THE INFANT

Piaget's **sensorimotor stage,** spanning the two years of infancy, involves coming to know the world through one's senses and actions. The dominant cog-

TABLE 7.1

Summary of the substages and intellectual accomplishments of the sensorimotor period	
Substage	*Description*
1. Reflex activity (Birth to 1 month)	Active exercise and refinement of inborn reflexes (e.g., accommodate sucking to fit the shapes of different objects)
2. Primary circular reactions (1–4 months)	Repetition of interesting acts centered on one's own body (e.g., repeatedly suck thumb, kick legs, or blow bubbles)
3. Secondary circular reactions (4–8 months)	Repetition of interesting acts on objects (e.g., repeatedly shake a rattle to make an interesting noise, or bat a mobile to make it wiggle)
4. Coordination of secondary schemes (8–12 months)	Combining of actions to solve simple problems (e.g., bat aside a barrier in order to grasp an object, using the scheme as a means to an end); first evidence of intentionality
5. Tertiary circular reactions (12–18 months)	Experimentation to find *new* ways to solve problems or produce interesting outcomes (e.g., explore bath water by gently patting it, then hitting it vigorously and watching the results; stroking, pinching, squeezing, and patting a cat to see how it responds to varied actions)
6. Beginning of thought (18–24 months)	First evidence of insight; can solve problems mentally now using symbols to stand for objects and actions (e.g., visualize how a stick could be used to move an out-of-reach toy closer); is no longer limited to thinking by doing

nitive structures are *behavioral schemes*—patterns of action that evolve as infants begin to coordinate sensory input (seeing and tasting an object) and motor responses (grasping it). Because infants solve problems through their actions rather than with their minds, their mode of thought is qualitatively different from that of older children.

Substages of the Sensorimotor Stage

The six substages of the sensorimotor stage are outlined in Table 7.1. At the start of the sensorimotor period, infants may not seem highly intelligent, but they are already active explorers of the world around them. We see increasing signs of intelligent behavior as infants pass through the substages, for they are gradually learning about the world and about cause and effect by observing the effects of their actions. They are transformed from *reflexive* creatures who adapt to their environment using their innate reflexes, to *reflective* ones who can solve simple problems in their heads and carry them out.

The crowning achievement of the sensorimotor stage is internalizing behavioral schemes to construct mental symbols that can then guide future behavior. Now the infant can experiment *mentally* and can therefore show a kind of insight into how to solve a problem. This new **symbolic capacity**—the ability to use images, words, or gestures to represent or stand for objects and experiences—will show itself not only in more sophisticated problem solving but also in the

language explosion and pretend play that are so evident in the preschool years.

The advances in problem-solving ability reflected in the six substages of the sensorimotor period bring with them other important changes. Consider changes in the quality of infants' play activities. They are more interested in their own bodies than in manipulating toys until the substage of *secondary circular reactions* (4 to 8 months), when they repeat an action, like sucking or banging a toy over and over. When they reach the substage of *tertiary circular reactions* (12 to 18 months), they experiment in varied ways with toys, exploring them thoroughly and learning all about their properties. With the final substage, the *beginning of thought*, at about 18 months, comes the possibility of letting one object represent another, so that a cooking pot becomes a hat, or a shoe becomes a telephone—a simple form of pretend play made possible by the capacity for symbolic thought. It is also in this stage, according to Piaget, that infants can imitate models who are no longer present, because they can now create and later recall mental representations of what they have seen.

The Development of Object Permanence

Another important change during the sensorimotor period concerns the infant's understanding of the existence of objects. According to Piaget, newborns lack the concept of **object permanence**. This is the very fundamental understanding that objects continue to

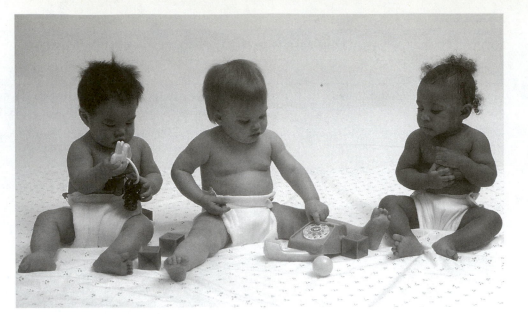

One-year-olds who have entered the stage of tertiary circular reactions experiment with objects and delight in making their toys respond in new and interesting ways.

exist when they are no longer visible or otherwise detectable to the senses. It probably doesn't occur to you to wonder whether your coat is still in the closet after you shut the closet door (unless perhaps you have taken a philosophy course). But very young infants, because they rely so heavily on their senses, seem to operate as though objects exist only when they are perceived or acted on. According to Piaget, the infant must construct the notion that reality exists apart from one's experience of it.

Piaget believed that the concept of object permanence develops gradually over the entire sensorimotor period. Up through roughly 4 to 8 months, it's "out of sight, out of mind." Infants will not search for a toy if you quickly cover it with a cloth or screen. By Substage 4 (8 to 12 months), they master that trick but still rely very much on their perceptions and actions to "know" an object (Piaget, 1954). After his 10-month-old daughter, Jacqueline, had repeatedly retrieved a toy parrot from one hiding place, Piaget put it in a new spot while she watched him. Amazingly, she looked in the original hiding place. She seemed to assume that her behavior determined where the object would appear; she did not treat the object as if it existed apart from her own actions. The surprising tendency of 8- to 12-month-olds to search for an object in the place where they last found it (A) rather than in its new hiding place (B) is called the **A, not B, error.**

In Substage 5, the 1-year-old overcomes this error but continues to have trouble with invisible displacements—as when you hide a toy in your hand, move your hand under a pillow, and remove the hand. The infant will search where the object was last seen, seeming confused when it is not in your hand and failing to look under the pillow, where it was deposited. Finally, by 18 months or so, the infant is capable of *mentally representing* such invisible moves and conceiving of the object in its final location. According to Piaget, the concept of object permanence is fully mastered at this point.

Does research support Piaget? Recent studies suggest that infants may develop at least some understanding of object permanence far earlier than Piaget claimed (Fischer & Hencke, 1996). For example, Renee Baillargeon and Marcia Graber (1988) devised a test of the A, not B, error that did not require reaching for a hidden object, only looking toward where it should be. The 8-month-old infants they studied seemed surprised when a toy that had disappeared behind one screen was snatched from behind a second screen 15 seconds later; the infants seemed to remember very well where the toy had been hidden. Evidence like this suggests that infants who make the A, not B, error and search in the site of their previous success can remember, at least for several seconds, where the object was actually hidden. However, they may not yet be able to act appropriately on this knowledge by searching in location B, possibly because they cannot inhibit a tendency to reach toward A, the spot they last searched (Baillargeon & Graber, 1988; Diamond, 1985).

More generally, it seems that babies sometimes know a good deal more about object permanence than they reveal through their actions when they are given the kinds of search tasks Piaget devised (Baillargeon & DeVos, 1991). Gradually they become more skilled at acting on their knowledge by searching in the right spot. By the end of the sensorimotor period, they are masters of even very complex hide-and-seek games.

All in all, children's intellectual achievements during the six substages of the sensorimotor period are truly remarkable. By its end, they have become deliberate thinkers with a symbolic capacity that allows them to solve some problems in their heads, and with a grasp of object permanence and of many other concepts as well.

THE CHILD

No one has done more to make us aware of the surprising turns that children's minds can take than Jean Piaget, who described how children enter the preoperational stage of cognitive development in their preschool years and progress to the concrete-operational stage as they enter their elementary school years.

The Preoperational Stage

The **preoperational stage** of cognitive development extends from roughly 2 to 7 years of age. The symbolic capacity that emerged at the end of the sensorimotor stage runs wild in the preschool years and is the greatest cognitive strength of the preschooler. Imagine the possibilities: The child can now use words to refer to things, people, and events that are not physically present. Instead of being trapped in the immediate present, the child can refer to both past and future. Pretend or fantasy play flourishes at this age: blocks can stand for telephones, cardboard boxes for trains. Some children even invent imaginary friends and elaborate make-believe worlds. Although parents may worry about such flights of fancy, they are perfectly normal. In fact, imaginative uses of the symbolic capacity are associated with advanced cognitive and social development (Singer & Singer, 1990; Taylor, Cartwright, & Carlson, 1993).

Yet the young child's mind is limited compared to that of an older child, and it was the limitations of preoperational thinking that Piaget explored most thoroughly. Although less so than infants, preschoolers are still highly influenced by their immediate perceptions, focus on the most perceptually salient aspects of a situation, and therefore can be fooled by appearances. They have difficulty with tasks that require them to use logic to arrive at the right answer. We can best illustrate this reliance on perceptions and lack of logical thought by considering Piaget's classic tests of conservation.

Lack of Conservation

One of the many lessons about the physical world that children must master is the concept of **conservation,** the idea that certain properties of an object or substance do not change when its appearance is altered in some superficial way. So, find yourself a 4- or 5-year-old and try Piaget's conservation-of-liquid-quantity task. Pour equal amounts of water into two identical glasses, and get the child to agree that they have the same amount of water to drink. Then, *as the child watches,* pour the water from one glass into a shorter, wider glass. Now ask whether the two containers—the tall, narrow glass and the shorter, broader one—have the same amount of water to drink or whether one has more water. Children younger than 6 or 7 will usually say that the taller glass has more water than the shorter one (see Figure 7.1). Thus they lack the understanding that the volume of liquid is *conserved* despite the change in the shape it takes in different containers.

How can young children be so easily fooled by their perceptions? According to Piaget, the preschooler is unable to engage in **decentration,** the ability to focus on two or more dimensions of a problem at one time. Consider the conservation task: The child must focus on height and width simultaneously and recognize that the increased width of the short, broad container compensates for its lesser height. Preoperational thinkers engage in **centration**—the tendency to center attention on a single aspect of the problem. They focus on height alone and conclude that the taller glass has more liquid; or, alternatively, they focus on width and conclude that the short, wide glass has more. In other ways as well, preschoolers seem to have one-track minds.

A second contributor to success on conservation tasks is **reversibility,** the process of mentally undoing or reversing an action. Older children often display mastery of reversibility by suggesting that the water be poured back into its original container to prove that it is still the same amount. The young child shows *irreversibility* of thinking and may insist that the water would overflow the glass if it were poured back. Indeed, one young child tested by a student of mine shrieked, "Do it again!" as though pouring the water back without causing the glass to overflow were some unparalleled feat of magic.

Finally, preoperational thinkers fail to demonstrate conservation because of limitations in **transformational thought,** the ability to conceptualize *transformations,* or processes of change from one state to another, as when water is poured from one glass to another (see Figure 7.2). Preoperational thinking is *static,* or fixed.

Preoperational children do not understand the concept of conservation, then, because they engage in centration, irreversible thought, and static thought. The older child, in the stage of concrete operations, has mastered decentration, reversibility, and transformational thought. The correct answer to the conservation task is now a matter of logic; there is no longer a need to rely on perception as a guide. Indeed, a 9-year-old tested by another of my students grasped the logic so well and thought the question of which

  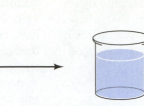 

Liquids: Two identical beakers are filled to the same level, and the child agrees that they have the same amount to drink.

Contents of one beaker are poured into a different-shaped beaker so that the two columns of water are of unequal height.

Conserving child recognizes that each beaker has the same amount to drink (on the average, conservation of liquids is attained at age 6–7 years).

Mass (continuous substance): Two identical balls of playdough are presented. The child agrees that they have equal amounts of dough.

One ball is rolled into the shape of a sausage.

Conserving child recognizes that each object contains the same amount of dough (average age, 6–7).

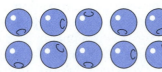

Number: Child sees two rows of beads and agrees that each row has the same number.

One row of beads is increased in length.

Conserving child recognizes that each row still contains the same number of beads (average age, 6–7).

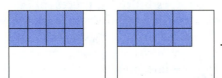

Area: The child sees two identical sheets, each covered by the same number of blocks. The child agrees that each sheet has the same amount of uncovered area.

The blocks on one sheet are scattered.

Conserving child recognizes that the amount of uncovered area remains the same for each sheet (average age, 9–10).

 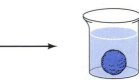 

Volume (water displacement): Two identical balls of clay are placed in two identical beakers that had been judged to have the same amount to drink. The child sees the water level rise to the same point in each beaker.

One ball of clay is taken from the water, molded into a different shape, and placed above the beaker. Child is asked whether the water level will be higher than, lower than, or the same as in the other beaker when the clay is reinserted into the water.

Conserving child recognizes that the water levels will be the same because nothing except the shape of the clay has changed — that is, the pieces of clay displace the same amount of water (average age, 9–12).

FIGURE 7.1 *Some common tests of the child's ability to conserve*

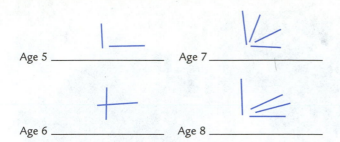

Age 5 _____   Age 7 _____

Age 6 _____   Age 8 _____

FIGURE 7.2 *Preoperational thought is static. Slowly and repeatedly drop a pencil in front of a preschooler, and then ask the child to draw the falling of the pencil (or give the child a number of strips of paper to be arranged to show the falling of the pencil). Preoperational thinkers (the 5- and 6-year-olds) generally show you the before and after but nothing in between. Older children are better able to conceptualize transformations like the falling of the pencil.*

glass had more water so stupid that she asked, "Is *this* what you do in college?!"

Egocentrism

Piaget believed that preoperational thought also involves **egocentrism**—a tendency to view the world solely from one's own perspective and to have difficulty recognizing other points of view. For example, he asked children to choose the drawing that shows what a display of three mountains would look like from a particular vantage point. Young children often chose the view that corresponded to their own position (Piaget & Inhelder, 1956). Similarly, young children often assume that, if they know something, other people do too (Ruffman & Olson, 1989). The same holds for desires: The 4-year-old who wants to go to McDonald's for dinner may say that Mom and Dad want to go to McDonald's too, despite the fact that Mom's on a diet and Dad prefers Pizza Hut.

Difficulty with Classification

The limitations of relying on perceptions and intuitions are also apparent when preoperational children are asked to classify objects and think about classification systems. When 2- or 3-year-old children are asked to sort objects on the basis of similarities, they make interesting designs or change their sorting criteria from moment to moment. Older preoperational children can group objects systematically on the basis of shape, color, function, or some other dimension of similarity (Inhelder & Piaget, 1964). However, even children aged 4 to 7 have trouble thinking about relations between classes and subclasses, or wholes and parts. Given a set of wooden beads, most of which are brown but a few of which are white, preoperational children do fine when they are asked if all the beads are wooden and if there are more brown beads than white beads. That is, they can conceive of the whole class (wooden beads) or of the two subclasses (brown and white beads). However, when the question is "Which would make the longer necklace, the brown beads or the wooden beads?" they usually say "The brown beads." They cannot *simultaneously* relate the whole class to its parts; they lack what Piaget termed the concept of **class inclusion,** or the logical understanding that the parts are included within the whole. Notice that the child centers on the most striking perceptual feature of the problem—the fact that brown beads are more numerous than white ones—again being fooled by appearances.

Did Piaget Underestimate the Preschool Child?

Are preschool children really as perception-bound and egocentric as Piaget believed? Many developmentalists believe that Piaget seriously underestimated the competencies of preschool children by giving them very complex tasks to perform (Bjorklund, 1995). Consider a few examples of the strengths uncovered by researchers using simpler tasks.

Rochel Gelman (1972) simplified Piaget's conservation-of-number task (shown in Figure 7.1) and discovered that children as young as 3 have some grasp of the concept that number remains the same even when items are rearranged spatially. She first got children to focus their attention on number by playing a game in which two plates, one holding two toy mice and one with three toy mice, were presented, and the plate with the larger number was always declared the winner. Then Gelman started introducing changes, sometimes adding or subtracting mice but sometimes just bunching up or spreading out the mice. Young children were not fooled by spatial rearrangements; they seemed to understand that number remained the same. However, they showed their limitations when they were given larger sets of numbers that they could not count.

Similarly, by reducing tasks to the bare essentials, several researchers have demonstrated that preschool children are not as egocentric as Piaget claimed. In one study, 3-year-olds were shown a card with a dog on one side and a cat on the other (Flavell, Everett, Croft, & Flavell, 1981). The card was held vertically between the child (who could see the dog) and the experimenter (who could see the cat). When children were asked what the experimenter could see, these 3-year-olds performed flawlessly.

Finally, preschool children seem to have a good deal more understanding of classification systems than Piaget believed (Markman, 1989; Taylor & Gelman, 1989; Waxman & Hatch, 1992). Sandra Waxman and Thomas Hatch (1992) asked 3- and 4-year-olds to teach a puppet all the different names they could think of for certain animals, plants, articles of clothing, and

pieces of furniture. The goal was to see if children knew terms associated with familiar classification hierarchies—for example, if they knew that a rose is a type of flower and is also a member of the larger category of plants. Children performed quite well, largely because a clever method of prompting responses was used. Depending on which term(s) the child forgot to mention (rose, flower, or plant), he or she was asked about the rose: "Is this a dandelion?" "Is this a tree?" "Is this an animal?" Very often children came up with the proper terms in response (for example, "No, silly, [it's not an animal] it's a plant!)." Even though young children typically fail the tests of class inclusion that Piaget devised, then, they appear to have a fairly good grasp of familiar classification hierarchies.

Studies like these have raised important questions about the adequacy of Piaget's theory and have led to a more careful consideration of the demands placed on children by cognitive assessment tasks. Simplified tasks that focus youngsters' attention on relevant aspects of the task and do not place heavy demands on their memories or verbal skills tend to reveal that young children develop sound understandings of the physical world earlier than Piaget thought. Yet Piaget was right in arguing that preschool children, although they have a number of sound intuitions about the world, are more perception-bound and egocentric thinkers than elementary school children are. Preschool children still depend on their perceptions to guide their thinking and fail to grasp the logic behind concepts such as conservation. They also have difficulty applying their emerging understanding to complex tasks that involve coordinating two or more dimensions.

The Concrete Operations Stage

About the time children start elementary school, their minds undergo another transformation. Piaget's third stage of cognitive development extends from roughly 7 to 11 or more years of age. The **concrete operations stage** involves mastering the logical operations that were missing in the preoperational stage—becoming able to perform *mental* actions on objects, such as adding and subtracting Halloween candies, classifying dinosaurs, or arranging objects from largest to smallest. This allows school-age children to think very effectively about the objects and events they experience in everyday life. For every limitation of the preoperational child, we can see a corresponding strength of the concrete-operational child.

Conservation

Given the conservation-of-liquid task (Figure 7.1), the preoperational child centers on either the height or the width of the glasses, ignoring the other dimension. The concrete-operational child can *decenter* and juggle two dimensions at once. *Reversibility* now allows the child to mentally reverse the pouring process and imagine the water in its original container. *Transformational thought* allows the child to better understand the process of change involved in pouring the water. Overall, armed with logical operations, the child now knows that there must be the same amount of water after it is poured into a different container; he or she has logic, not just appearance, as a guide.

Looking back at the conservation tasks in Figure 7.1, you will notice that some forms of conservation (for example, mass and number) are understood years earlier than others (area or volume). Piaget maintained that operational abilities evolve in a predictable order as simple skills that appear early are reorganized into increasingly complex skills. He used the term **horizontal décalage** to characterize the fact that different cognitive skills related to the same stage of cognitive development emerge at different times.

Seriation and Transitivity

To appreciate the nature and power of logical operations, consider the child's ability to think about relative size. A preoperational child given a set of sticks of different lengths and asked to arrange them in order from biggest to smallest is likely to struggle along, awkwardly comparing one pair of sticks at a time. Concrete-operational children are capable of the logical operation of **seriation,** which enables them to arrange items mentally along a quantifiable dimension such as length or weight. Thus they perform this seriating task quickly and correctly.

Concrete-operational thinkers also master the related concept of **transitivity,** which describes the necessary relations among elements in a series. If, for example, John is taller than Mark, and Mark is taller than Sam, who is taller—John or Sam? It follows *logically* that John must be taller than Sam, and the concrete operator grasps the transitivity of these size relationships. Lacking the concept of transitivity, the preoperational child will need to rely on perceptions to answer the question; he or she may insist that John and Sam stand next to each other in order to determine who is taller. Preoperational children probably have a better understanding of such transitive relations than Piaget gave them credit for (Gelman, 1978; Trabasso, 1975), but they still have difficulty grasping the logical necessity of transitivity (Chapman & Lindenberger, 1988).

Other Advances

The school-age child overcomes much of the egocentrism of the preoperational period, becoming better and better at recognizing other people's perspectives. Classification abilities improve as the child comes to grasp the concept of *class inclusion* and can bear in mind that subclasses (brown beads + white beads) are included in a whole class (wooden beads). Mastery of mathematical operations improves the child's ability to solve arithmetic problems and results in an interest in measuring and counting things precisely (and sometimes fury if companions don't keep accurate score in games). Overall, school-age children appear more logical than preschoolers because they now possess a powerful arsenal of "actions in the head."

But surely, if Piaget proposed a fourth stage of cognitive development, there must be some limitations to concrete operations. Indeed there are. This mode of thought is applied to objects, situations, and events that are real or readily imaginable (thus the term *concrete* operations). As we'll see, concrete operators have difficulty thinking about abstract ideas and hypothetical propositions that have no basis in reality.

THE ADOLESCENT

Although tremendous advances in cognition occur from infancy to the end of childhood, still other transformations of the mind are in store for the adolescent. If teenagers become introspective, question their parents' authority, dream of perfect worlds, and contemplate their futures, cognitive development may help explain why.

The Formal Operations Stage

Piaget set the beginning of the **formal operations stage** of cognitive development at age 11 or 12, or possibly later. If concrete operations are mental actions on *objects* (tangible things and events), formal operations are mental actions on *ideas*. Thus the adolescent who acquires formal operations can mentally juggle and think logically about ideas, which cannot be seen, heard, tasted, smelled, or touched. In other words, formal-operational thought is more hypothetical and abstract than concrete-operational thought; it also involves adopting a more systematic and scientific approach to problem solving (Keating, 1980).

Hypothetical and Abstract Thinking

If you could have a third eye and put it anywhere on your body, where would you put it, and why? That question was posed to 9-year-old fourth-graders (i.e., concrete operators) and to 11- to 12-year-old sixth-graders (the age when the first signs of formal operations often appear). In their drawings, all the 9-year-olds placed the third eye on their foreheads between their existing eyes; many thought the exercise was stupid. The 11- and 12-year-olds were not as bound by the realities of eye location. They could invent ideas that were contrary to fact (for example, the idea of an eye in one's palm) and think logically about the implications of such ideas (see Figure 7.3). Thus, concrete operators deal with realities, whereas formal operators can deal with possibilities, including those that contradict known reality. This may be one reason why adolescents come to appreciate absurd humor, as we see in Box 7.1.

Formal-operational thought is also more abstract than concrete-operational thought. The school-age child might define the justice system in terms of police and judges; the adolescent might define it more abstractly as a branch of government concerned with balancing the rights of different interests in society.

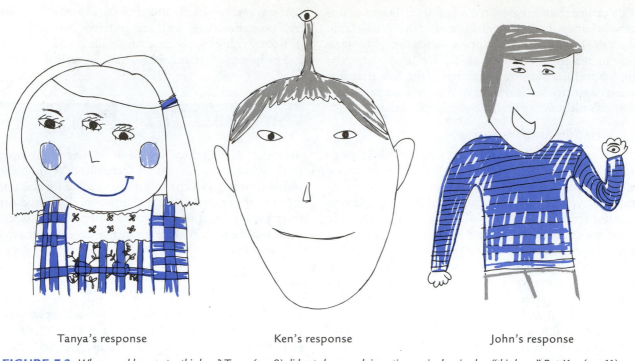

Tanya's response   Ken's response   John's response

FIGURE 7.3 *Where would you put a third eye? Tanya (age 9) did not show much inventiveness in drawing her "third eye." But Ken (age 11) said of his eye on top of a tuft of hair: "I could revolve the eye to look in all directions." John (also 11) wanted a third eye in his palm: "I could see around corners and see what kind of cookie I'll get out of the cookie jar." Ken and John show early signs of formal-operational thought.*

Also, the school-age child might be able to think logically about concrete and factually true statements, as in this syllogism: If you drink poison, you will die. Fred drank poison. Therefore, Fred will die. The adolescent can engage in such if-then thinking about either contrary-to-fact statements ("If you drink milk, you will die") or symbols (If *P*, then *Q. P*, therefore, *Q*).

Problem Solving

Formal operations also permit systematic and scientific thinking about problems. One of Piaget's famous tests for formal-operational thinking is the pendulum task. The child is given a number of weights that can be tied to a string to make a pendulum and is told that he or she may vary the length of the string,

the weight attached to it, and the height from and force with which the weight is released in order to find out which of these factors alone or in combination determines how quickly the pendulum makes its arc (Figure 7.4). How would you go about solving this problem?

The concrete operator is likely to jump right in without much advanced planning, using a *trial-and-error* approach. That is, the child may try a variety of things but fail to test out different hypotheses systematically—for example, the hypothesis that the shorter the string is, the faster the pendulum swings, all other factors remaining constant. Concrete operators are therefore unlikely to solve the problem. What they can do is draw proper conclusions from their observations—for example, from watching as someone else

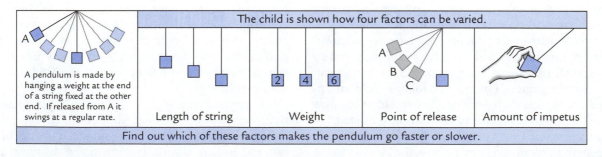

FIGURE 7.4 *The pendulum problem* (From Labinowicz, 1980)

BOX 7.1

Children's humor and cognitive development

Where does the fish keep its money? Answer: In the riverbank.

Do you remember going through a phase in early elementary school of telling terrible jokes like this one? A preschooler hearing this joke may laugh at the silly idea of a fish having money but if asked to rephrase the joke, the child is likely to say the answer was "In the bank." A child of this age misses the whole idea that the humor of the joke depends on the double meaning of "bank." Anything that looks or sounds silly may amuse preschoolers—calling a "shoe" a "floo" or a "poo," for example. Once children realize that everything has a correct name, playing with language by mislabeling things and using taboo words such as "poo-poo" becomes wonderfully amusing (Ely, 1997; McGhee, 1979).

With the onset of concrete-operational thought and advances in awareness of the nature of language, children come to appreciate jokes and riddles that involve linguistic ambiguities. The riverbank joke boils down to a classification task: There is a large category of banks, with at least two subclasses, financial institutions and the banks of streams. School-age children who have mastered the concept of class inclusion can keep the class and subclasses in mind at once and move back and forth mentally between the two meanings of "bank." Appreciation of such puns is high among second-graders (7- to 8-year-olds) and continues to grow until fourth or fifth grade (McGhee & Chapman, 1980; Yalisove, 1978). And the better children are at solving riddles, the better they tend to

be at reading and other language tasks (Ely, 1997).

As their command of language strengthens, children also become more able to understand sarcasm, irony, and other discrepancies between what is said and what is meant, as when a teacher says to a noisy 8-year-old, "My, but you're quiet today" (Capelli, Nakagawa, & Madden, 1990). The more they understand ironic statements, the more they appreciate the humor in them (Dews et al., 1996).

Children's tastes in humor change again when they enter the stage of formal operations at about age 11 or 12 (Yalisove, 1978). Simple riddles and puns are no longer cognitively challenging enough, it seems, and are likely to elicit loud groans (McGhee, 1979). Adolescents do, however, appreciate jokes that involve an absurd or contrary-to-

fact premise and a punchline that is quite logical if the absurd premise is accepted. The humor in "How do you fit six elephants into a Volkswagen?" depends on appreciating that "Three in the front and three in the back" is a perfectly logical answer only if one accepts the hypothetical premise that multiple elephants could fit into a small car (Yalisove, 1978). Reality-oriented school-age children might simply judge this joke stupid; after all, elephants *can't* fit into cars. Clearly, then, children cannot appreciate certain forms of humor until they have the required cognitive abilities. Research on children's humor suggests that children and adolescents are most attracted to jokes that challenge them intellectually by requiring them to use the cognitive skills they are just beginning to master (McGhee, 1979).

demonstrates what happens if a pendulum with a short string is compared to a pendulum with a long string.

What will the formal-operational individual do? In all likelihood, he or she will first sit and think, planning an overall strategy for solving the problem. To begin with, *all* the possible hypotheses should be generated; after all, the one that is overlooked may be the right one. Then it must be determined how each hypothesis can be tested. This is a matter of **hypothetical-**

deductive reasoning, or reasoning from general ideas to their specific implications. In the pendulum problem it means starting with a hypothesis and tracing the specific implications of this idea in an if-then fashion: "If the length of the string matters, then I should see a difference when I compare a long string to a short string while holding other factors constant." The trick in hypothesis testing is to vary each factor (for example, the length of the string) while holding all the others constant (the weight, the height from which the weight is dropped, and so on). (It is, by the way, the length of the string that matters; the shorter the string, the faster the swing.)

In summary, formal-operational thought involves being able to think systematically about hypothetical ideas and abstract concepts. It also involves mastering the hypothetical-deductive approach that scientists use—forming many hypotheses and systematically testing them through an experimental method.

Progress toward Mastery

Are 11- and 12-year-olds really capable of all these sophisticated mental activities? In most cases, no. Piaget (1970) himself described the transition from concrete operations to formal operations as taking place gradually over several years. Many researchers have found it useful to distinguish between early and late formal operations. For example, 11- to 13-year-olds just entering the formal operations stage are able to consider simple hypothetical propositions such as the three-eye problem. But most are not yet able to devise an overall game plan for solving a problem or to systematically generate and test hypotheses. These achievements are more likely later in adolescence.

Consider the findings of Suzanne Martorano (1977), who gave 80 girls in grades 6, 8, 10, and 12 a battery of ten Piagetian tasks. Among them were the pendulum problem, a task requiring students to identify all the possible combinations of chemicals that could produce a particular chemical reaction, and analyzing how the behavior of a balance beam is affected by the heaviness of weights on the beam and their distances from the fulcrum, or center. The sixth- and eighth-graders (ages 11–12 and 13–14) passed only two or three of the ten tasks on the average, and the tenth- and twelfth- graders (ages 15–16 and 17–18) passed an average of five or six. Thus even the twelfth-graders did not consistently show formal operations across tasks.

Progress toward mastery of formal operations is obviously slow, at least as measured by Piaget's scientific tasks. These findings have major implications for secondary-school teachers, who are often trying to teach very abstract material to students with a wide range of thinking patterns. Teachers may need to give concrete thinkers extra aid by using specific examples and demonstrations to help clarify general principles.

Implications of Formal Thought

Formal-operational thought contributes to other changes in adolescence—some good, some not so good. First the good news: As we'll see in upcoming chapters, formal-operational thought may prepare the individual to gain a sense of identity, think in more complex ways about moral issues, and understand other people. Advances in cognitive development help to lay the groundwork for advances in many other areas of development.

Now the bad news: Formal operations may also be related to some of the more painful aspects of the adolescent experience. Children tend to accept the world as it is and to heed the words of authority figures. The adolescent armed with formal operations can think more independently, imagine alternatives to present realities, and raise questions about everything from why parents set down the rules they do to why there is injustice in the world. Questioning can lead to confusion and sometimes to rebellion against ideas that do not seem logical enough. Some adolescents become idealists, inventing perfect worlds and envisioning logical solutions to problems they detect in the imperfect world around them, sometimes losing sight of practical considerations and real barriers to social change. Just as infants flaunt the new schemes they develop, adolescents may go overboard with their new cognitive skills, irritate their parents, and become frustrated when the world does not respond to their flawless logic.

Some years ago, David Elkind (1967) proposed that formal-operational thought also leads to **adolescent egocentrism,** difficulty differentiating one's own thoughts and feelings from those of other people. The young child's egocentrism is rooted in ignorance that different people have different perspectives, but the adolescent's reflects an enhanced ability to reflect about one's own and others' thoughts. Elkind identified two types of adolescent egocentrism: the imaginary audience and the personal fable. The **imaginary audience** phenomenon involves confusing your own thoughts with those of a hypothesized audience for your behavior. Thus the teenage girl who spills soda on her dress at a party may feel extremely self-conscious: "They're all thinking what a slob I am! I wish I could crawl into a hole." She assumes that everyone else in the room is as preoccupied with the blunder as she is. Or a teenage boy may spend hours in front of the mirror getting ready for a date and then be so concerned with how he imagines his date is reacting to him that he hardly notices her: "Why did I say that? She looks bored. Did she notice my pimple?" (She, of course, is equally preoccupied with how she is playing to her audience. No wonder teenagers are often awkward and painfully aware of their every slip on first dates!)

The second form of adolescent egocentrism is the **personal fable,** a tendency to think that you and your thoughts and feelings are unique (Elkind, 1967). If the imaginary audience is a product of the inability to differentiate between self and other, the personal fable is a product of differentiating too much. Thus the adolescent who is in love for the first time imagines that no one in the history of the human race has ever felt such heights of emotion. When the relationship

breaks up, of course, no one—least of all a parent—could possibly understand the crushing agony. The personal fable may also lead adolescents to feel that rules that apply to others do not apply to them. Thus *they* won't be hurt if they speed down the highway without wearing a seat belt or drive under the influence of alcohol. And *they* won't become pregnant if they engage in sex without contraception, so they don't need to bother with contraception! As it turns out, high scores on measures of adolescent egocentrism are associated with behaving in risky ways (Greene et al., 1996; Holmbeck et al., 1994).

Elkind hypothesized that the imaginary audience and the personal fable phenomena should increase when formal operations are first being acquired and then decrease as adolescents get older, gain fuller control of formal operations, and assume adult roles that require fuller consideration of others' perspectives. Indeed, both the self-consciousness associated with the imaginary audience and the sense of specialness associated with the personal fable are most evident in early adolescence and decline by late high school (Elkind & Bowen, 1979; Enright, Lapsley, & Shukla, 1979). Adolescent egocentrism may persist, though, when adolescents have insecure relationships with their parents that may make them self-conscious and lacking in self-confidence even as older adolescents (Ryan & Kuczkowski, 1994).

Contrary to what Piaget and Elkind hypothesized, however, researchers have been unable to link the onset of formal operations to the rise of adolescent egocentrism (Gray & Hudson, 1984; O'Connor & Nikolic, 1990). It now seems that adolescent egocentrism may arise when adolescents acquire advanced social perspective-taking abilities and contemplate how other people might perceive them and react to their behavior (Lapsley et al., 1986; Vartanian & Powlishta, 1996). The truth is that researchers have not yet figured out precisely why young adolescents often feel that the whole world is watching them or that not one person in the world can truly understand them. We can conclude, though, that the acquisition of formal operations brings with it both new competencies and new challenges.

THE ADULT

Do adults think differently from adolescents? Does cognition change over the adult years? Until recently, developmentalists have not asked such questions. After all, Piaget indicated that the highest stage of cognitive development, formal operations, was fully mastered by most people by age 15 to 18. Why bother studying cognitive development in adulthood? As it turns out, it has been well worth the effort. Research has revealed limitations in adult performance that must be explained, and it also suggests that at least some adults progress beyond formal operations to more advanced forms of thought.

Limitations in Cognitive Performance

If many high school students are shaky in their command of formal operations, do most of us gain fuller

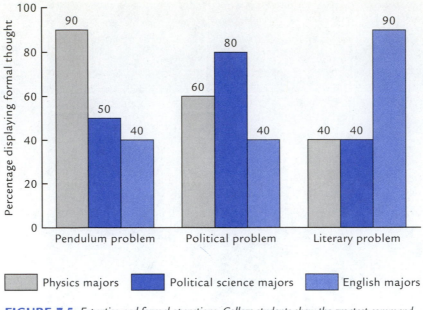

FIGURE 7.5 *Expertise and formal operations. College students show the greatest command of formal-operational thought in the subject area most related to their major.*
(Data from De Lisi & Staudt, 1980)

mastery after the high school years? Gains are indeed made between adolescence and adulthood (Blackburn & Papalia, 1992), but, still, only about half of all college students show firm and consistent mastery of formal operations on Piaget's scientific reasoning tasks (Neimark, 1975). Similarly, sizable percentages of American adults do not solve scientific problems at the formal level, and there are some societies in which *no* adults solve formal-operational problems (Neimark, 1975).

Why don't more adults do well on Piagetian tasks? An average level of performance on standardized intelligence tests seems to be necessary for a person to achieve formal-operational thought (Inhelder, 1966). What seems more important than basic intelligence, though, is formal education (Neimark, 1979). In cultures in which virtually no one solves Piaget's problems, people do not receive advanced schooling. If achieving formal-operational thought requires education, Piaget's theory may be culturally biased and his stages may not be universal as he believed.

But neither lack of intelligence nor lack of formal education is a problem for most college students. Instead, they have difficulty with tests of formal operations when they lack *expertise in a domain of knowledge.* Piaget (1972) himself suggested that adults are likely to use formal operations in a field of expertise but to use concrete operations in less familiar areas. This is precisely what seems to happen. For example, Richard De Lisi and Joanne Staudt (1980) gave three kinds of formal-operational tasks—the pendulum problem, a

political problem, and a literary criticism problem—to college students majoring in physics, political science, and English. As Figure 7.5 illustrates, each group of majors did very well on the problem relevant to their field of expertise. On problems outside their fields, however, about half the students failed. Very possibly, then, many adolescents and adults fail to use formal reasoning on Piaget's scientific problems simply because these problems are unfamiliar to them and they lack expertise.

As Kurt Fischer (1980; Fischer, Kenny, & Pipp, 1990) maintains, each person may have an optimal level of cognitive performance that will show itself in familiar and well-trained content domains. However, performance is likely to be highly inconsistent across content areas unless the person has had a chance to build knowledge and skills in all these domains. More often, adults may use and strengthen formal modes of thinking *only in their areas of expertise.* By adopting a contextual perspective on cognitive development, we can appreciate that the individual's experience and the nature of the tasks he or she is asked to perform influence cognitive performance across the life span (Salthouse, 1990).

Growth beyond Formal Operations?

While some researchers have been asking why adults sometimes perform so poorly on cognitive tasks, others have been asking why they sometimes perform so well. Take Piaget himself. Was his ability to generate a complex theory of development no more than the application of formal-operational thought? Or are there advances in cognitive development during adulthood that would better explain the remarkable cognitive achievements of some adults?

At this point there are several intriguing ideas about stages of cognitive development that may lie beyond formal operations—that is, about **postformal thought** (see Commons, Richards, & Armon, 1984; Labouvie-Vief, 1992; Sinnott, 1996; Yan & Arlin, 1995). As noted earlier, adolescents who have attained formal operations sometimes get carried away with their new powers of logical thinking. They insist that there is a logically correct answer for every question—that, if you simply apply logic, you'll arrive at the right answer—at some absolute truth. Perhaps formal-operational adolescents need a more complex way of thinking in order to adapt to the kinds of problems adults face everyday—problems in which there are many ways to look at an issue, no one right answer, and yet a need to make a decision (Sinnott, 1996).

How might thought be qualitatively different in adulthood from what it is in adolescence? What might a truly adult stage of cognitive development be like? Several researchers have suggested that adults are more likely than adolescents to see knowledge as relative rather than absolute (Kitchener et al., 1989; Labouvie-Vief, 1992). **Relativistic thinking** in this sense means understanding that knowledge depends on the subjective perspective of the knower. An *absolutist* assumes that truth lies in the nature of reality and that there is only one truth; a *relativist* assumes that one's own starting assumptions influence the "truth" that is discovered and that there are multiple ways of viewing a problem.

Consider this logic problem: " 'A' grows 1 cm per month. 'B' grows 2 cm per month. Who is taller?" (Yan & Arlin, 1995, p. 230). From the information given, an absolutist might say "B," but a relativist would be more likely to say, "It depends." It *does* depend, on how tall A and B were to begin with and on how much time passes before their heights are measured. A relativistic thinker will recognize that the problem is ill-defined and that further information is needed, and he or she will be able to think flexibly about what the answer would be if we made certain assumptions rather than others.

Or consider this problem, given to preadolescents, adolescents, and adults by Gisela Labouvie-Vief and her colleagues (Labouvie-Vief et al., 1983):

> John is known to be a heavy drinker, especially when he goes to parties. Mary, John's wife, warns him that if he gets drunk one more time she will leave him and take the children. Tonight John is out late at an office party. John comes home drunk. (p. 5)

Does Mary leave John? Most preadolescents and many adolescents quickly and confidently said "yes." They did not question the assumption that Mary would stand by her word; they simply applied logic to the information they were given. Adults were more likely to realize that different starting assumptions were possible and that the answer depended on which assumptions were chosen. One woman, for example, noted that, if Mary had stayed with John for years, she would be unlikely to leave him now. This same woman said "There was no right or wrong answer. You could get logically to both answers" (p. 12). Postformal thinkers seem able to devise more than one logical solution to a problem (Sinnott, 1996).

In a fascinating study of cognitive growth over the college years, William Perry (1970) found that beginning college students often assumed that there were absolute, objective truths to be found if only they applied their minds or sought answers from their textbooks or their professors. As their college careers progressed, they often became frustrated in their search for absolute truths. They saw that many questions seemed to have a number of alternative answers, depending on the perspective of the answerer. Taking the extremely relativistic view that any opinion was as good as any other, several of these students said they weren't sure how they could ever decide what to believe. Eventually, many of them understood that some opinions can be better supported than others; they were then able to commit themselves to specific positions while being fully aware that they were choosing among relative perspectives. Between adolescence and adulthood, then, many people start out as absolutists, then become relativists, and finally are able to make commitments to

Relativism in the college years. As one student said, "I am the type of person who would never tell anyone that their idea is wrong—if they searched, well, even if they hadn't searched, even if they just believed it—that's cool for them" (Kitchener & King, 1981, p. 96). Many of these students later decide that there are sound reasons for preferring some beliefs to others.

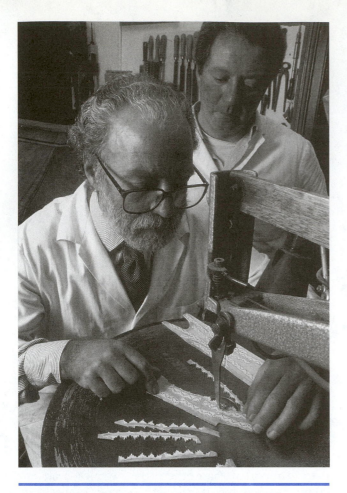

Adults think very efficiently once they gain expertise on the job.

positions despite their more sophisticated awareness of the nature and limits of knowledge (Sinnott, 1996).

It has also been suggested that advanced thinkers thrive on detecting paradoxes and inconsistencies among ideas and trying to reconcile them—only to repeat the process of challenging and changing their understandings again and again (Basseches, 1984; Riegel, 1973). Advanced thinkers also seem to be able to think systematically and logically about abstract systems of knowledge (Fischer et al., 1990; Richards & Commons, 1990). If the concrete-operational thinker performs mental actions such as addition on concrete *objects,* and the formal-operational thinker performs mental actions on *ideas,* the postformal thinker seems able to manipulate whole *systems* of ideas—for example, by comparing and contrasting psychological theories or analyzing abstract similarities and differences between mathematical operations such as addition and division.

It is not yet entirely clear whether relativistic thinking or other forms of advanced thinking might really qualify as a new, postformal stage of cognitive development. It is clear, though, that these types of thinking are shown by only a minority of adults, par-

ticularly those who have received advanced education, who are open to rethinking issues, and who live in a culture that nourishes their efforts to entertain new ideas (Irwin, 1991; Sinnott, 1996). It is also clear that cognitive growth does not end in adolescence. Yet, age itself does not tell us much about how an adult thinks; life circumstances and the demands placed on people to think at work, in the home, and in the community often tell us more.

Aging and Cognitive Skills

What becomes of cognitive capacities in later adulthood? Some mental abilities decline as the average person ages, and it appears that older adults often have trouble solving Piagetian tests of formal-operational thinking (Blackburn & Papalia, 1992). Indeed, elderly adults sometimes perform more poorly than young and middle-aged adults even on *concrete*-operational tasks assessing conservation and classification skills (Blackburn & Papalia, 1992; Denney, 1982).

This does not mean that elderly adults regress to immature modes of thought, however (Blackburn & Papalia, 1992). For one thing, these studies have involved cross-sectional comparisons of different age groups. The poorer performance of older groups does not necessarily mean that cognitive abilities are lost as one ages. It could be due to a cohort effect, for the average older adult today has had less formal schooling than the average younger adult has had. In fact, older adults who are attending college tend to perform just as well as younger college students on tests of formal operations (Blackburn, 1984; Hooper, Hooper, & Colbert, 1985). Moreover, very brief training can quickly improve the performance of older adults long out of school, which suggests that the necessary cognitive abilities are there but merely need to be reactivated (Blackburn & Papalia, 1992).

Questions have also been raised about the relevance of the skills assessed in Piagetian tasks to the lives of older adults (Labouvie-Vief, 1985). Not only are these problems unfamiliar to many older adults, but they resemble the intellectual challenges that children confront in school, not those that most adults encounter in everyday contexts. Thus, older people may not be very motivated to solve them. Also, older adults may rely on modes of cognition that have proved useful to them in daily life but that make them look cognitively deficient in the laboratory (Salthouse, 1990).

Consider this example. Kathy Pearce and Nancy Denney (1984) found that elderly adults, like young children but unlike other age groups, often group two objects on the basis of some functional relationship between them (for example, putting a pipe and matches together because matches are used to light pipes) rather than on the basis of similarity (for example, putting a pipe and a cigar together because they both contain tobacco products). In school and in some job situations, Pearce and Denney suggest, people are asked to group objects on the basis of similarity, but in everyday life it may make more sense to associate objects that are commonly used together.

Such findings suggest that what appear to be deficits in older people may merely be differences in style. Similar stylistic differences in classification skills have been observed cross-culturally and can, if researchers are not careful, lead to the incorrect conclusion that uneducated adults from non-Western cultures lack basic cognitive skills. A case in point: Kpelle adults in Africa, when asked to sort foods, clothing, tools, and cooking utensils into groups, sorted them into pairs based on functional relationships. "When an exasperated experimenter asked finally, 'How would a fool do it?' he was given back sorts of the type that were initially expected—four neat piles with foods in one, tools in another, and so on" (Glick, 1975, p. 636)!

In sum, today's older adults appear not to perform concrete- and formal-operational tasks as well as their younger contemporaries do. Planners of adult education for senior citizens might bear in mind that some of their students (though by no means all) may benefit from more concrete forms of instruction. However, these differences may be related to factors other than age, such as education and motivation; an actual age-related decline in operational abilities has not been firmly established. Most important, older adults who perform poorly on unfamiliar problems in laboratory situations often perform far more capably on the sorts of problems that they encounter in everyday contexts (Cornelius & Caspi, 1987; Salthouse, 1990).

PIAGET IN PERSPECTIVE

Now that we have examined Jean Piaget's theory of cognitive development, it is time to evaluate it. Let's start by giving credit where credit is due. Then we'll consider challenges to Piaget's version of things.

Piaget's Contributions

Piaget is a giant in the field of human development. As one scholar quoted by Harry Beilin (1992) put it, "assessing the impact of Piaget on developmental psychology is like assessing the impact of Shakespeare on English literature or Aristotle on philosophy—impossible" (p. 191). It is hard to imagine that we would know even a fraction of what we know about intellectual development without his groundbreaking work. One sign of a good theory is that it stimulates research. Piaget asked fundamentally important questions about how humans come to know the world and

showed that we can answer them "by paying attention to the small details of the daily lives of our children" (Gopnik, 1996, p. 225). His cognitive-developmental perspective has now been applied to almost every aspect of human development, and the important questions he raised continue to guide the study of cognitive development.

We can credit Piaget with some lasting insights (Flavell, 1996). He showed us that infants are active in their own development—that from the start they seek to master problems and to understand the incomprehensible. He taught us that young humans do indeed think differently than older humans—and often in ways we never would have suspected.

Finally, and quite importantly, Piaget was largely right in his basic description of cognitive development. The *sequences* he proposed seem to describe quite well the course and content of intellectual development for children and adolescents from the hundreds of cultures and subcultures that have now been studied (Flavell, Miller, & Miller, 1993). Although cultural factors do influence the *rate* of cognitive growth, the direction of development is always from sensorimotor thinking to preoperational thinking to concrete operations and, for many, to formal operations.

Challenges to Piaget

Partly because Piaget's theory has been so enormously influential, it has had more than its share of criticism (see Lourenco & Machado, 1996). We will focus on five major criticisms here:

1. *Underestimating young minds:* Piaget seems to have underestimated the cognitive abilities of infants and young children, though he emphasized that he was more interested in understanding sequences of changes than in the specific ages at which they occur (Lourenco & Machado, 1996). When researchers use more familiar problems than Piaget's and reduce tasks to their essentials, hidden competencies of young children—and of adolescents and adults too—are sometimes revealed.

2. *Failing to distinguish between competence and performance:* Piaget was concerned with identifying underlying cognitive competencies that guide performance on cognitive tasks. But there is an important difference between understanding a concept and successfully completing a task designed to measure it. The age ranges Piaget proposed for some stages may have been off target in part because he tended to ignore the many factors besides competence that can influence task performance: everything from the individual's motivation, verbal abilities, and memory capacity to the nature, complexity, and familiarity of the specific task used to assess mastery. Piaget may have been too quick to assume that children who failed at one of his

tasks lacked competence; they may only have failed to demonstrate their competence in a particular situation.

3. *Claiming that broad stages of development exist:* According to Piaget, each new stage of cognitive development is a coherent mode of thinking that is applied across a wide range of specific problems. Yet there is often little consistency in the individual's performance on different tasks that presumably measure the abilities defining a given stage. More and more researchers are arguing that cognitive development is *domain specific*—that is, it is a matter of building skills in particular content areas, and growth in one domain may proceed much faster than growth in another (Fischer et al., 1990).

4. *Failing to adequately explain development:* Several critics suggest that Piaget did a better job of describing development than of explaining how it comes about (Bruner, 1997). To be sure, Piaget wrote extensively about his interactionist position on the nature/nurture issue and did as much as any developmental theorist to tackle the question of how development comes about. Presumably humans are always assimilating new experiences in ways that their level of maturation allows, accommodating their thinking to those experiences, and reorganizing their cognitive structures into increasingly complex modes of thought. Yet this explanation is rather vague. We need to know far more about how specific maturational changes in the brain and specific kinds of experiences contribute to important cognitive advances.

5. *Giving limited attention to social influences on cognitive development:* Piaget may have paid too little attention to how children's minds develop through their social interactions with more competent individuals and develop differently in different cultures. Piaget's child often resembles an isolated scientist exploring the world alone, when in fact children develop their minds through interactions with parents, teachers, and more competent peers and siblings. True, Piaget had interesting ideas about the role of peers in helping children overcome their egocentrism and take other perspectives (see Chapter 12 on moral development). However, as we will see shortly, the significance of social interaction and culture for cognitive development is the basis of the perspective on cognitive development offered by one of Piaget's early critics, Lev Vygotsky.

So, Piaget's theory of cognitive development might have been stronger if he had designed tasks that could better reveal the competencies of infants and young children; if he had explored the many factors besides underlying competence that influence actual performance; if he had been able to provide more convincing evidence that his stages are indeed coherent; if he had been more specific about *why* development proceeds as it does; and if he had more fully considered social and cultural influences on the development of thought. It may be unfair, however, to expect an innovator who accomplished so much to have achieved everything.

VYGOTSKY'S SOCIOCULTURAL PERSPECTIVE

To view Piaget's work from a new vantage point and lay the groundwork for a discussion of language development, let's consider the sociocultural perspective of Lev Vygotsky (1934/1962, 1930-1935/1978; see Bodrova & Leong, 1996; Glassman, 1994; Wertsch & Tulviste, 1992). This Russian psychologist was born in 1896, the same year as Piaget, and was an active scholar in the 1920s and 1930s when Piaget was formulating his theory. Vygotsky died of tuberculosis at the age of 38, before his own theory was fully developed. However, his main theme is clear: *Cognitive growth occurs in a sociocultural context and evolves out of the child's social interactions.*

Culture and Thought

Vygotsky very much believed that both what people know and how they think are shaped by the cultural and historical context in which they develop. Each culture has certain "tools of the mind" that it passes on to its members—tools such as language, problem-solving tactics, and memory strategies (Bodrova & Leong, 1996; Vygotsky, 1978). Vygotsky would not be surprised to learn that formal-operational thought is rarely used in some cultures, for he expected cognitive development to vary from society to society depending on what mental tools the culture valued and made available. How do children acquire their society's mental tools? By interacting with parents and other more experienced members of the culture and by adopting their language.

Social Interaction and Thought

Consider this scenario: Annie, a 4-year-old, receives a jigsaw puzzle, her first, for her birthday. She attempts to work the puzzle but gets nowhere until her father comes along, sits down beside her, and gives her some tips. He suggests that it would be a good idea to put the corners together first. He points to the pink area at the edge of one corner piece and says "Let's look for another pink piece." When Annie seems frustrated, he places two interlocking pieces near each other so that she will notice them. And when she succeeds, he offers words of encouragement. As Annie gets the hang of it, he steps back and lets her work more and more independently. This kind of social interaction, claimed Vygotsky, fosters cognitive growth.

How? First, Annie and her father are operating in what Vygotsky called the **zone of proximal development**—the gap between what a learner can accomplish independently and what he or she can accomplish with the guidance and encouragement of a more skilled partner. Skills within the zone are ripe for development and are the skills at which instruction should be aimed. Skills outside the zone are either well-mastered already or still too difficult. In our example, Annie obviously becomes a more competent puzzle-solver with her father's help than without it. More important, she will internalize the problem-solving techniques that she discovered in collaboration with her father, working together in her zone of proximal development, and she will ultimately use them on her own, rising to a new level of independent mastery. What began as a social process involving two people becomes a cognitive process within one.

In many cultures, children do not go to school with other children to learn; nor do their parents explicitly teach them tasks such as weaving and hunting. Instead, they learn through **guided participation**—by actively participating in culturally relevant activities with the aid and support of their parents and other knowledgeable guides (Rogoff, 1997; Rogoff et al., 1993). Jerome Bruner (1983) had a similar concept in mind when he wrote of the many ways in which parents provide "scaffolding" for their children's development, structuring learning situations so that learning becomes easier. In short, Vygotsky rejects Piaget's view of children as independent explorers in favor of the view that they learn more sophisticated cognitive strategies through their interactions with more mature thinkers. To Piaget, the child's level of cognitive development determines what he or she can learn; to Vygotsky, learning in collaboration with more knowledgeable companions drives development.

Language and Thought

In Vygotsky's view, language is the primary vehicle through which adults pass culturally valued modes of thinking and problem solving on to their children. It also comes to serve as our most important tool of thinking. Whereas Piaget maintained that cognitive development influences language development, Vygotsky argued that language shapes thought in important ways and that thought changes fundamentally once we begin to think in words (Bodrova & Leong, 1996).

Piaget and Vygotsky both noticed that preschool children often talk to themselves as they go about their daily activities, almost as if they were play-by-play sports announcers. ("I'm putting the big piece in the corner. I need a pink one. Not that one—this one.") Two preschool children playing next to each other sometimes carry on their own separate mono-

According to Vygotsky's theory, cognitive development is shaped by the culture in which children live and by the kinds of problem-solving strategies that adults and other knowledgeable guides pass on to them.

logues rather than truly conversing. Piaget (1926) regarded such speech as egocentric, as further evidence that preoperational thinkers cannot yet take the perspectives of other people (in this case, their conversation partners) and therefore have not mastered the art of social speech. He did not believe that egocentric speech played any useful role in cognitive development. Vygotsky, however, called it **private speech**—speech to oneself that guides one's thought and behavior. Rather than viewing it as a sign of cognitive immaturity, he saw it as a critical step in the development of mature thought and as the forerunner of the silent thinking-in-words that we adults engage in every day.

Studies conducted by Vygotsky and other researchers support his claim (see Berk, 1992). *Social speech* (for example, the conversation between Annie and her father as they jointly worked a puzzle) gives rise to *private speech* (Annie's talking aloud, much as her father talked to her, as she then tries to work the puzzle on her own), which in turn goes "underground" to become first mutterings and lip movements and then *inner speech* (Annie's silent verbal thought). Use

TABLE 7.2

A comparison of Vygotsky and Piaget

Vygotsky's Sociocultural View	*Piaget's Cognitive-Developmental View*
1. Cognitive development is different in different social and historical contexts	Cognitive development is mostly the same universally
2. Cognitive growth results from social interactions (guided participation in the zone of proximal development)	Cognitive growth results from the child's independent explorations of the world
3. Children and their partners "co-construct" knowledge	Each child constructs knowledge on his/her own
4. Social processes become individual psychological ones (e.g., social speech becomes inner speech)	Individual, egocentric processes become more social (e.g., egocentric speech becomes social speech)
5. Adults are especially important (because they know the culture's tools of thinking)	Peers are especially important (because children must learn to take peers' perspectives into account)
6. Learning precedes development (tools learned with adult help become internalized)	Development precedes learning (children cannot master certain things until they have the requisite cognitive structures)

of private speech increases during the early preschool years and then decreases during the early elementary school years.

Intellectually capable children rely more heavily on private speech in the preschool years and make the transition to inner speech earlier in the elementary school years than their less academically capable peers do (Berk & Landau, 1993; Kohlberg, Yaeger, & Hjertholm, 1968). This suggests that the preschool child's self-talk is indeed a sign of cognitive maturity, as Vygotsky claimed, rather than a sign of immature egocentrism, as Piaget claimed. In further support of Vygotsky's views, it has been found that young children rely most heavily on private speech when they are struggling to solve difficult problems (Berk, 1992). Even adults sometimes revert to thinking aloud when they are stumped by a problem (John-Steiner, 1992).

In addition, heavy use of private speech contributes to effective problem-solving performance—if not immediately then later, when children encounter similar problems in the future (Behrend, Rosengren, & Perlmutter, 1989; Bivens & Berk, 1990). Thus, private speech not only helps children think their way through challenging problems but also allows them to incorporate into their own thinking the problem-solving strategies that they learned initially during their collaborations with adults. Notice that, as in guided participation, what is at first a social process becomes an individual psychological process.

In sum, Vygotsky's sociocultural perspective stresses social influences on cognitive development that Piaget largely ignored. Children's minds develop (1) in response to cultural influences, (2) in collaborative in-

teractions with skilled partners on tasks that are within their zone of proximal development, and (3) as they incorporate what skilled partners say to them into what they say to themselves. As social speech is transformed into private speech and then inner speech, the culture's preferred tools of problem solving work their way from the language of competent guides into the thinking of the individual. Table 7.2 summarizes some of the differences between Vygotsky's sociocultural perspective and Piaget's cognitive-developmental view.

As Vygotsky maintained, language does shape the nature of thought, and yet Piaget was also right to point out that children's cognitive skills influence their progress in mastering language. Hold on to the idea that language and thought influence one another as we turn to language development and further consider its relationship to cognitive development.

MASTERING LANGUAGE

Although language is one of the most intricate forms of knowledge we will ever acquire, all normal children master a language very early in life. Indeed, many infants are talking before they can walk. Can language be all that complex, then? It certainly can be. Linguists (scholars who study language) have yet to fully describe the rules of English (or of any other language), and so far computers cannot understand speech as well as most 5-year-olds can. What exactly is the task facing young language learners?

What Must Be Mastered

Linguists define **language** as a communication system in which a limited number of signals—sounds or letters (or gestures, in the case of the sign language used by deaf people)—can be combined according to agreed-upon rules to produce an infinite number of messages. As Vygotsky appreciated, any human language is both a marvelously versatile means of social communication and an essential tool of thought. To master a spoken language such as English, a child must know basic sounds, how sounds are combined to form words, how words are combined to form meaningful statements, what words and sentences mean, and how to use language effectively in their social interactions. That is, the child must master five aspects of language: phonology, morphology, syntax, semantics, and pragmatics.

Phonology is the sound system of a language, and the basic units of sound in any given language are its phonemes. The child in an English-speaking country must come to know the 45 phonemes used in English (which correspond roughly to the familiar vowel and consonant sounds) and must also learn which ones can be combined in English and which ones cannot (for example, *st-*, but not *sb-*). Other languages have other basic sounds (or, in a sign language, basic hand shapes and motions). Children must learn to hear and to pronounce the phonemes of their language in order to make sense of the speech they hear and to be understood when they speak.

Rules of **morphology** are rules for the formation of words from sounds. Rules of morphology in English include the rule for forming past tenses of verbs by adding *-ed* and the rule for forming plurals by adding *-s*, as well as rules for using other prefixes and suffixes and rules that say that you cannot combine sounds to say *vlow* but can say *flow*. Exceptions to these rules must be learned as well.

Rules of **syntax** are rules for forming sentences from words. Consider these three sentences: (1) Fang Fred bit, (2) Fang bit Fred, and (3) Fred bit Fang. The first, as even very young children recognize, violates the rules of English sentence structure or syntax, although this word order would be perfectly acceptable in French. The second two sentences are grammatical English sentences that have very different meanings conveyed by their different word orders. Children must master rules of syntax to understand or use language, from simple declarative sentences like these to complex sentences with many phrases.

Semantics is the aspect of language that concerns meanings. Words stand for things, and the child must map the relationships between words and things. Knowledge of semantics is also required to interpret whole sentences or speeches or paragraphs. Grasping semantics obviously depends on understanding the world and thus on cognitive development.

Finally, language learners must also master **pragmatics**—rules specifying how language is used appropriately in different social contexts. That is, children have to learn when to say what to whom. They must learn to communicate effectively by taking into account who the listener is, what the listener already knows, and what the listener needs or wants to hear. "Give me that cookie" may be grammatical English, but the child is far more likely to win Grandma's heart (not to mention a cookie) with a polite "May I please try one of your yummy cookies, Grandma?"

In short, mastering language is an incredible challenge, for it requires learning phonology, semantics, morphology, syntax, and pragmatics. What's more, human communication involves not only language but also forms of *nonverbal communication* (facial expressions, tone of voice, gestures, and so on). For example, **intonation,** the variations in pitch, loudness, and timing used when saying words or sentences, is very important. Using intonation, speakers put emphasis on grammatically important words, signal that they are asking questions rather than making statements, and so on. Children must also learn these nonverbal signals, which often clarify the meaning of a verbal message and are important means of communicating in their own right. Let's look at the course of language development and then ask how nature and nurture contribute to the child's remarkable accomplishment.

The Course of Language Development

For the first 10 to 13 months of life, infants are not yet capable of speaking meaningful words, but they are building up to that achievement.

Before the First Words

As we learned in Chapter 6, newborns seem to tune in to human speech immediately. Very young infants can distinguish between phonemes such as *b* and *p* or *d* and *t* (Eimas, 1975). Indeed, as we saw in Chapter 6, infants from homes where English is spoken are better than English-speaking adults at differentiating certain phonemes that are *not* used in English (Werker & Desjardins, 1995). Before they ever speak a word, infants are also becoming sensitive to the fact that pauses in speech fall *between* clauses, phrases, and words rather than in the middle of these important language units (Fisher & Tokura, 1996; Myers et al., 1996). This sensitivity may help them learn the rules of grammar.

What about producing sounds? Prelinguistic vocalizations develop in stages related to the maturation of motor control over the muscles involved in articulating sound (Hoff-Ginsberg, 1997). At birth, infants produce a "hunger" cry, a "mad" cry, and a "pain" cry (Wolff, 1969). By the third week of life, they also produce a "fake" cry, which may be what Piaget would call a primary circular reaction—the repeating of an interesting noise for the sheer pleasure of making it (Wolff, 1969).

The next milestone in vocalization, at about 3 to 5 weeks of age, is **cooing:** repeating vowel-like sounds such as "ooooooh" and "aaaaah." Babies coo when they are contented. At about 3 to 4 months of age, infants expand their range considerably as they begin to produce consonant sounds. They enter a period of **babbling** between about 4 and 6 months of age, repeating consonant/vowel combinations such as "baba" or "dadadada" over and over (again, a primary circular reaction in Piaget's terminology).

Up to about 6 months of age, infants all over the world, even deaf ones, sound pretty much alike, but the effects of experience soon become apparent. At roughly this age, deaf infants fall behind hearing infants in their ability to produce well-formed syllables (Oller & Eilers, 1988). By the time infants are about 8 months old, they babble with something of an accent; adults can often tell from their babbling whether babies have been listening to French, Chinese, or Arabic (de Boysson-Bardies, Sagart, & Durand, 1984). These advanced babblers increasingly restrict their sounds to those that are phonemes in the language they are hearing, and they pick up the intonation patterns of that language as well (Hoff-Ginsberg, 1997). Apparently, then, babies are "learning the tune before the words" (Bates, O'Connell, & Shore, 1987, p. 157).

As they attempt to master the semantics of language, infants come to understand many words before they can produce them. That is, *comprehension is ahead of production, or expression, in language development.* Before they really understand the specific words in a command, they will obey commands (for example; "Get the ball") in familiar contexts, probably by interpreting tone of voice and context cues (Benedict, 1979). Shortly before speaking their first true words, however, as they approach a year of age, they really seem to understand familiar words. If their mothers name a familiar toy, they will look at it rather than at other nearby objects (Thomas et al., 1981). From infancy on, we generally understand more words than we are able to control in our own speech or writing.

In their first year, infants are also learning basic lessons about the pragmatics of language. For example, during the first six months they are most likely to coo or babble *while* a partner is speaking (Freedle & Lewis, 1977). After that point, however, they seem to have mastered the rule of conversational turn-taking, for they vocalize when a partner has stopped talking. This marks a basic, highly important step in learning to use language appropriately in social interactions.

Indeed, infants learn a great deal about how to communicate before they ever utter a meaningful word.

The First Words

An infant's first meaningful word, spoken at about a year of age, is a special event for parents. First words have been called **holophrases** because a single word sometimes conveys an entire sentence's worth of meaning. These single-word "sentences" can serve different communication functions depending on the way they are said and the context in which they are said (Greenfield & Smith, 1976). For example, 17-month-old Shelley used the word *ghetti* (spaghetti) in three different ways over a five-minute period. First she pointed to the pan on the stove and seemed to be asking, "Is that spaghetti?" Later the function of her holophrase was to name the spaghetti when shown the contents of the pan, as in "It's spaghetti." Finally, there was little question that she was requesting spaghetti when she tugged at her companion's sleeve as he was eating and used the word in a whining tone.

Although there are limits to the meaning that can be packed into a single word and its accompanying tone of voice and gestures, 1-year-olds in the holophrastic stage of language development do seem to have mastered such basic language functions as naming, questioning, requesting, and demanding. And at the same time they begin to use words as symbols, they also begin to use nonverbal symbols—gestures such as pointing, raising their arms to signal "up," or panting heavily to say "dog" (Acredolo & Goodwyn, 1988; Bates et al., 1987).

What do 1-year-olds talk about? They talk mainly about objects and actions on objects (Pan & Gleason, 1997; and see Table 7.3). Katherine Nelson (1973) studied 18 infants as they learned their first 50 words and found that nearly two-thirds of early words referred to objects, including familiar people. These objects were nearly all either manipulatable by the child (bottles, shoes) or capable of moving themselves (animals, trucks).

Toddlers' first words also include many references to familiar actions (Nelson, Hampson, & Shaw, 1993); in other words, they talk a lot about the "sensorimotor schemes" that Piaget believed were so important to their cognitive development. Yet there are individual differences in speaking style right from the start. Some children use a referential style loaded with nouns referring to objects. Others seem to treat language as a social tool; they use an expressive style of speaking with more personal pronouns and memorized social routines such as "Byebye" and "I want it" (Bates et al., 1994; Nelson, 1973).

Initial language acquisition proceeds literally one word at a time. Three or four months may pass before the child has a vocabulary of 10 words (Nelson, 1973). Then, in what is called the **vocabulary spurt,** at

TABLE 7.3

Examples of words used by children younger than 20 months

SOUND EFFECTS
baa baa, meow, moo, ouch, uh-oh, wolf, yum-yum

FOOD AND DRINK
apple, banana, cookie, cheese, cracker, juice, milk, water

ANIMALS
bear, bird, bunny, dog, cat, cow, duck, fish, kitty, horse, pig, puppy

BODY PARTS AND CLOTHING
diaper, ear, eye, foot, hair, hand, hat, mouth, nose, toe, tooth, shoe

HOUSE AND OUTDOORS
blanket, chair, cup, door, flower, keys, outside, spoon, tree, tv

PEOPLE
baby, daddy, gramma, grampa, mommy, [child's own name]

TOYS AND VEHICLES
ball, balloon, bike, boat, book, bubbles, plane, truck, toy

ACTIONS
down, eat, go, sit, up

GAMES AND ROUTINES
bath, bye, hi, night-night, no, peekaboo, please, shhh, thank you, yes

ADJECTIVES AND DESCRIPTIVES
allgone, cold, dirty, hot

SOURCE: From Pan & Gleason in Gleason (1997)

around 18 months of age when the child has mastered about 30 to 50 words, the pace of word learning quickens dramatically (Goldfield & Reznick, 1996; Nelson, 1973). By 24 months of age, children are producing an average of 186 words (Nelson, 1973). What changes? During the vocabulary spurt, toddlers seem to arrive at the critical realization that everything has a name; they then want to learn all the names they possibly can (Reznick & Goldfield, 1992).

Getting the Meaning

How do toddlers figure out what words mean? It's a huge challenge. Think about it: the word "cat," used to refer to Gooseberry the family pet, could mean Gooseberry only, felines in general, fur, orange-colored, liable to tear your flesh, or a number of other things. Children accomplish the feat of determining what words mean by using several strategies that help them narrow down the possible meanings that a new word could have (de Villiers & de Villiers, 1992; Markman, 1989). For example, they tend to assume that a new word refers to a whole object rather than to some part of the object and to a class of similar objects (eye-

glasses in general) rather than to one specific object (Mommy's reading glasses). They also assume that each word has a unique meaning. As a result, when they hear the new word *macaroon*, they are likely to conclude that it does not mean exactly the same thing as the more familiar word *cookie* and most likely refers to a particular kind of cookie (Taylor & Gelman, 1989). Finally, young language learners infer word meanings by paying close attention to the contexts in which unfamiliar words are used (Nelson et al., 1993). This includes noticing how a word is used in sentences. The child who hears a new word, *zav*, used as a noun to refer to a toy ("This is a zav") concludes that this new word refers to a kind of toy. However, the child who hears *zav* used as an adjective ("This is a zav one") will infer that *zav* is some attribute of a toy, such as its color (Taylor & Gelman, 1988).

Despite the soundness of their strategies for inferring word meanings, children do not always succeed at first. They only rarely get the meaning entirely wrong, but they fairly often use a word too broadly or too narrowly (Pan & Gleason, 1997). One error is **overextension,** or using a word to refer to too wide a range of objects or events, as when a 2-year-old calls all furry, four-legged animals *doggie*. The second, and opposite, error is **underextension,** as when a child initially uses the word "doggie" to refer only to basset hounds like the family pet. Notice that both overextension and underextension are examples of Piaget's concept of assimilation, using existing concepts to interpret new experiences. Getting semantics right seems to be mainly a matter of discriminating similarities and differences—for example, categorizing animals on the basis of size, shape, the sounds they make, and other perceptual features (Clark & Clark, 1977).

But might children know more about the world than their semantic errors suggest? Yes. Two-year-olds who say "doggie" when they see a cow will point to the cow rather than the dog when asked to find the cow (Thompson & Chapman, 1977). In fact, children who overextend the word "doggie" in their speech are no less able than children who do not to look toward the cow rather than the dog when asked, "Where's the cow?" (Naigles & Gelman, 1995). Children may overextend the meaning of certain words like "doggie" not because they misunderstand word meanings but because they want to communicate, have only a small vocabulary with which to do so, and haven't yet learned to call something a "whatchamacallit" when they cannot come up with the word for it (Naigles & Gelman, 1995).

Telegraphic Speech

The next step in language development, normally taken at about 18 to 24 months of age, is combining two words into a simple sentence. Toddlers all over the world use two-word sentences to express the same

TABLE 7.4

Two-word sentences serve similar functions in different languages.

Function of Sentence	Language	
	English	German
To locate or name	There book	Buch da (book there)
To demand	More milk Give candy	Mehr milch (more milk)
To negate	No wet Not hungry	Nicht blasen (not blow)
To indicate possession	My shoe Mama dress	Mein ball (my ball) Mamas hut (Mama's hat)
To modify or qualify	Pretty dress Big boat	Armer wauwau (poor dog)
To question	Where ball	Wo ball (where ball)

SOURCE: Adapted from Slobin (1979)

basic ideas (see Table 7.4). Early combinations of two, three, or more words are sometimes called **telegraphic speech** because, like telegrams, many of these sentences contain critical content words and omit frills such as articles, prepositions, and auxiliary verbs.

Now, it is ungrammatical in adult English to say "No wet" or "Where ball." However, these two-word sentences are not just random word combinations or mistakes; they reflect children's *own* systematic rules for forming sentences. Psycholinguists have approached early child language as though it were a foreign language and have tried to describe the rules that young children seem to be using to form sentences. At first, psycholinguists such as Martin Braine (1963) focused on the order of the two words in two-word sentences, believing that children followed predictable rules of word order. Toddlers do indeed use some predictable formulas in their early speech, before they really grasp the rules of grammar (Lieven, Pine, & Baldwin, 1997). For example, they often use a certain word in combination with a variety of other words to create sentences ("want ball," "want book," "want more"). Still, to understand child grammar, developmentalists found it necessary to consider not only word order but the *meanings* that children are attempting to convey, the functions their sentences are serving.

Two-word sentences, like holophrases, serve several communication functions: naming, demanding, negating, and so on. Lois Bloom (1970) and others feel that it is therefore appropriate to describe early language in terms of a **functional grammar**—one that emphasizes the semantic relations between words, or the meanings being expressed. For example, young children often use the same word order to convey different meanings. "Mommy nose" might mean "That's Mommy's nose" in one context, but for one 22-month-old girl it meant "Mommy, I've just wiped my runny nose the length of the living room couch." Word order sometimes does matter: "Billy hit" and "Hit Billy" may mean different things. Body language and tone of voice also communicate meanings, as when a child points and whines to request ice cream, not merely note its existence.

Overall, children learn to make combinations of words, accompanied by body language, perform basic communication functions as they interact with others. By the age of 2, they are typically understanding quite a bit, are using many words appropriately either alone or in two-word telegraphic sentences, and are positioning themselves for the language explosion that will occur during the preschool years.

Mastering Grammatical Rules

In the short period from age 2 to 5, children come to speak sentences that are remarkably complex and adultlike. Table 7.5 gives an inkling of how fast things move in the particularly important period from age 2 to age 3. From the two-word stage of language acquisition, children progress to three-word telegraphic sentences and then to still longer sentences, beginning to add the little function words like articles and prepositions that were often missing in their early telegraphic sentences (Hoff-Ginsberg, 1997). They infer more and more of the rules of adult language.

How do we know when children are mastering new rules? Oddly enough, their progress sometimes reveals itself in new "mistakes." Consider the task of learning rules of morphology for forming plurals and past tenses (Brown, 1973; Mervis & Johnson, 1991). Typically this happens sometime during the third year. A child who has been saying "feet" and "went" may suddenly start to say "foots" and "goed." Does this represent a step backward? Not at all. The child was probably using the correct irregular forms at first by imitating adult speech, without really understanding the meaning of plurality or verb tense. The use of "foots" and "goed" is a breakthrough: He or she has now inferred the morphological rules of adding *-s* to pluralize nouns and adding *-ed* to signal past tense. At first, however, the youngster engages in **overregularization,** overapplying the rules to cases in which the proper form is irregular. When the child masters exceptions to the rules, he or she will say "feet" and "went" once more.

Children must also master rules for creating variations of the basic declarative sentence; that is, they must learn the rules for converting a basic idea such

TABLE 7.5

Samples of Kyle's speech at 24 months and 11 months later. At 24 months, Kyle speaks in telegraphic sentences no more than three words long; by 35 months, his sentences are much longer and grammatically complex, though not error-free, and he is far more able to participate in the give-and-take of conversation (if not to heed his mother and respect the dignity of potato bugs).

Age 24 Months (His second birthday party)	Age 35 Months (Playing with a potato bug)
Want cake now.	Mother: Kyle, why don't you take the bug back to his friends?
Boons! Boons! [pointing to balloons]	Kyle: After I hold him, then I'll take the bug back to his friends. Mommy, where did the bug go? Mommy, I didn't know where the bug go. Find it. Maybe Winston's on it [the family dog]. Winston, get off the bug! [Kyle spots the bug and picks it up.]
They mine! [referring to colors]	
I wan' see.	Mother: Kyle, *please* let the bug go back to his friends.
See sky now.	Kyle: He does not want to go to his friends. [He drops the bug and squashes it, much to his mother's horror.] I stepped on it and it will not go to his friends.
Ow-ee [pointing to knee]	

as "I am eating pizza" into such forms as questions ("Am I eating pizza?"), negative sentences ("I am not eating pizza"), and imperatives ("Eat the pizza!"). The prominent linguist Noam Chomsky (1968, 1975) drew attention to the child's learning of these rules by proposing that language be described in terms of a **transformational grammar,** or rules of syntax for transforming basic underlying thoughts into a variety of sentence forms.

How do young children learn to phrase the questions that they so frequently ask to fuel their cognitive growth? The earliest questions often consist of nothing more than two- or three-word sentences with rising intonation ("See kitty?"). Sometimes "wh" words like *what* or *where* appear ("Where kitty?"). During the second stage of question asking, children begin to use auxiliary, or helping, verbs, but their questions are of this form: "What Daddy is eating?" "Where the kitty is going?" Their understanding of transformation rules is still incomplete (Dale, 1976). Finally, they learn the transformation rule that calls for moving the auxiliary verb ahead of the subject (as in the adult-like sentence "What is Daddy eating?").

By the end of the preschool period (ages 5 to 6), children's sentences are very much like those of adults, even though they have never had a formal lesson in grammar. It's an amazing accomplishment. Yet there is still more to accomplish.

Later Language Development

Not only do school-age children improve their pronunciation skills, produce longer and more complex sentences, and continue to expand their vocabularies, but they also begin to think about and manipulate language in ways that were previously impossible (Ely, 1997).

Listening to preschool children talk, we notice that many of them have difficulty articulating certain

phonemes; *spaghetti* may come out as *pasketti, scissors* as *thithors.* Most such articulation problems disappear during the early elementary school years (Klein, 1996). School-age children also master many complex syntactical rules such as those for forming and interpreting passive sentences like "Goofy was liked by Donald" and conditional sentences like "If Goofy had come, Donald would have been delighted" (Boloh & Champaud, 1993; Sudhalter & Braine, 1985). Command of grammar actually continues to improve through adolescence; teenagers' spoken and written sentences are increasingly long and complex (Clark & Clark, 1977; Hunt, 1970).

School-age children and adolescents are also expanding their knowledge of semantics. Thanks to the remarkable vocabulary spurt of the preschool period, 6-year-olds already understand some 8000 to 14,000 words and will continue to expand their vocabularies at a rate of about 15 words a day for many years to come (Carey, 1977). During adolescence, with the help of formal-operational thought, children become better able to understand and define abstract terms (McGhee-Bidlack, 1991). They also become better able with age to infer meanings that are not explicitly stated and must be inferred (Beal, 1990).

Finally, children are mastering the pragmatics of language and are becoming increasingly able to communicate effectively in different situations (Oliver, 1995). As they become less cognitively egocentric, they are more able to take the perspective of their listeners (Hoff-Ginsberg, 1997). Throughout childhood and adolescence, then, advances in cognitive development are accompanied by advances in language and communication skills.

Language in Adulthood

Clearly, language skills improve steadily throughout childhood and adolescence, but what happens during adulthood? Adults simply hold on to the knowledge of the phonology they gained as children, though elders can have difficulty distinguishing speech sounds if they have hearing impairments or deficits in the cognitive abilities required to make out what they hear (Sommers, 1997). They also retain their knowledge of grammar very well. Older adults do tend to use less complex sentences than younger adults do, however. Also, those with memory difficulties may have trouble understanding sentences that are highly complex syntactically (for example, "The children warned about road hazards refused to fix the bicycle of the boy who crashed"); they may not be able to remember the beginning of the sentence by the time they get to the end (Kemtes & Kemper, 1997; Stine, Soederberg, & Morrow, 1996).

Meanwhile, knowledge of the semantics of language, of word meanings, often *expands* during adulthood, at least until people are in their 70s or 80s (Obler & Albert, 1985; Schaie, 1996). After all, adults gain experience with the world from year to year, so it is not surprising that their vocabularies continue to grow and they enrich their understandings of the meanings of words. However, older adults do more often have the "tip-of-the-tongue" experience of not being able to come up with the name of an object (or especially a person's name) when they need it (Au et al., 1995; MacKay & Abrams, 1996). This problem is a matter of not being able to retrieve information stored in memory rather than a matter of no longer knowing words, though. Overall, command of language holds up very well in later life unless the individual experiences major declines in cognitive functioning (Light, 1990; Stine et al., 1996).

In sum, we cannot help but be awed by the pace at which children master the fundamentals of language during their first five years of life, but we must also appreciate the continued growth that occurs in childhood and adolescence and the maintenance of language skills throughout the life span. It is time to ask how these remarkable skills are acquired.

How Language Develops

What abilities must young children bring to the language-learning task, and what help must their companions provide? Theorists attempting to explain language acquisition have differed considerably in their positions on the nature/nurture issue, as illustrated by the learning, nativist, and interactionist perspectives on language development (see Bohannon & Bonvillian, 1997).

The Learning Perspective

How do children learn language? Most adults would say that children imitate what they hear, receiving praise when they get it right and being corrected

Language competencies are typically well maintained in old age.

when they get it wrong. Different learning theorists emphasize different aspects of this broad process. Social-learning theorist Albert Bandura (1971) and others emphasize observational learning—learning by listening to and then imitating older companions. Behaviorist B. F. Skinner (1957) and others emphasize the role of reinforcement. As children achieve better and better approximations of adult language, parents and other adults praise meaningful speech and correct errors. Children are also reinforced by getting what they want when they speak correctly. In general, learning theorists consider the child's social environment to be critical to what and how much he or she learns.

How well does the learning perspective account for language development? Certainly it is no accident that children end up speaking the same language that their parents speak, down to the regional accent. Children do learn the words that they hear spoken by others—even on television programs (Rice & Woodsmall, 1988). In addition, young children are more likely to start using new words if they are reinforced for doing so than if they are not (Whitehurst & Valdez-Menchaca, 1988). And, finally, children whose caregivers frequently encourage them to converse by asking questions, making requests, and the like are more advanced in early language development than those whose parents are less conversational (Bohannon & Bonvillian, 1997; Pine, 1994).

However, learning theorists have had an easier time explaining the development of phonology and semantics than accounting for how syntactical rules are acquired. For example, after analyzing conversations between mothers and young children, Roger Brown, Courtney Cazden, and Ursula Bellugi (1969) discovered that a mother's approval or disapproval depended on the truth value or semantics of what was said, *not* on the grammatical correctness of the statement. Thus, when a child looking at a cow says "Her cow" (accurate but grammatically incorrect), Mom is likely to provide reinforcement ("That's right, darling"), whereas if the child were to say "There's a dog, Mommy" (grammatically correct but untruthful), Mom would probably correct the child ("No, silly—that's a cow"). Similarly, parents seem just as likely to reward a grammatically primitive request ("Want milk") as a well-formed version of the same idea (Brown & Hanlon, 1970). Such evidence casts doubt on the idea that the major mechanism behind syntactic development is reinforcement.

Could imitation of adults account for the acquisition of syntax? We have already seen that young children produce many sentences that they are unlikely to have heard adults using ("Allgone cookie," overregularizations such as "It swimmed," and so on). These kinds of sentences are not imitations. Also, an adult is likely to get nowhere in teaching syntax by saying "Repeat after me" unless the child already has at least some knowledge of the grammatical form to be learned (Baron, 1992; McNeill, 1970). Young children *do* frequently imitate other people's speech, and this may help them get to the point of producing new structures themselves. But it is hard to see how imitation and reinforcement alone can account for the learning of grammatical rules.

The Nativist Perspective

Nativists have made little of the role of the language environment and much of the role of the child's biologically programmed capacities in explaining language development. Noted linguist Noam Chomsky (1968, 1975) proposed that humans have an inborn mechanism for mastering language called the **language acquisition device (LAD).** The LAD was conceived as an area in the brain equipped to identify certain universal features of language and to figure out the specific rules of any particular language. To learn to speak, children need only hear other humans speak; using the LAD, they quickly grasp the rules of whatever language they hear (see Figure 7.6).

What evidence supports a nativist perspective on language development? First, there are indeed areas of the brain that specialize in language functions;

Broca's area in the frontal lobe controls speaking, for example, whereas Wernicke's area controls speech recognition (Thompson, 1993). Second, children do acquire an incredibly complex communication system very rapidly. Third, they all progress through the same sequences at roughly similar ages, and they even make the same kinds of errors, which suggests that language development is guided by a specieswide maturational plan. Fourth, these universal aspects of early language development occur despite cultural differences in the styles of speech that adults use in talking to young children. In some cultures, for example, parents believe that babies are incapable of understanding speech and do not even talk directly to them (Richman, Miller, & LeVine, 1992; Schieffelin & Ochs, 1983).

Last but not least, we have evidence that the capacity for acquiring language has a genetic basis. The fact that some of our linguistic competencies, including the ability to combine symbols to form short sentences, are shared with chimpanzees and other primates suggests that they arose during the course of evolution and are part of our genetic endowment as humans (Greenfield & Savage-Rumbaugh, 1993). Identical twins score more similarly than fraternal twins on measures of verbal skills, and certain speech, language, and reading disorders run in families, indicating that individual heredity also influences the course of language development (Lewis & Thompson, 1992; Plomin, 1990).

Although nativists are correct to emphasize the importance of biologically based capacities in language acquisition, there are two major limitations of the nativist perspective. First, attributing language development to a built-in language acquisition device does not really explain it. Explanations would require knowing *how* such an inborn language processor sifts through language input and infers the rules of language (Moerk, 1989). Second, nativists, in focusing on the defects of learning theories of language development, tend to underestimate the contributions of the child's language environment. The nativists base much of their argument on three assumptions: (1) that the only thing children need to develop language is exposure to speech, (2) that the speech children hear is so

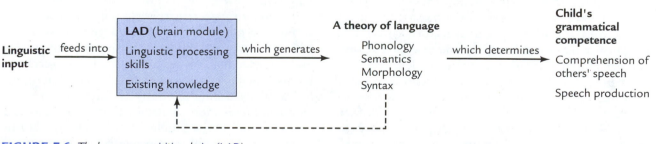

FIGURE 7.6 *The language acquisition device (LAD)*

incredibly complex that only a highly powerful brain could possibly detect regularities in it, and (3) that adults give children little useful feedback about whether their sentences are grammatically correct. These assumptions now seem to be inaccurate, and most researchers currently believe that language development depends on both nature and nurture.

The Interactionist Perspective

Interactionists believe that *both* learning theorists and nativists are correct: Children's biologically based competencies *and* their language environment interact to shape the course of language development (Bohannon & Bonvillian, 1997). They emphasize that acquisition of language skills depends on and is related to the acquisition of many other capacities: perceptual, cognitive, motor, social, and emotional. They point out that the capacity for acquiring language is not unique (as nativists who speak of the LAD claim); milestones in language development often occur at the same time as milestones in other aspects of cognitive development and involve the same underlying mental processes (Bates et al., 1987). For example, young children first begin to use words as meaningful symbols at the time they begin to display nonlinguistic symbolic capacities, such as the ability to use gestures (waving bye-bye), and to engage in pretend play (treating a bowl as if it were a hat).

The interactionists' position is not unlike that taken by Piaget (1970). He too believed that milestones in cognitive development pave the way for progress in language development and that maturation and environment interact to guide both cognitive development and language development. Like Piaget (but unlike learning theorists), many interactionists argue that language development depends on the maturation of cognitive abilities such as the capacity for symbolic thought. However, the interactionist position also emphasizes—as Vygotsky did but Piaget did not—ways in which social interactions with adults contribute to cognitive and linguistic development. Language is primarily a means of communicating—one that develops in the context of social interactions as children and their companions strive to get their messages across, one way or another.

Long before infants use words, Jerome Bruner (1983) claims, their caregivers show them how to take turns in conversations—even if the most these young infants can contribute when their turn comes is a laugh or a bit of babbling. As adults converse with young children, they create a supportive learning environment—a "scaffold" in Bruner's terms, a zone of proximal development in Vygotsky's—that helps the children grasp the regularities of language (Bruner, 1983; Harris, 1992). For example, parents may go through their children's favorite picture books at bedtime asking "What's this?" and "What's that?" This

gives their children repeated opportunities to learn that conversing involves taking turns, that things have names, and that there are proper ways to pose questions and give answers. Soon the children are asking "What's this?" and "What's that?" themselves. As children gain new language skills, adults adjust their styles of communication accordingly.

Language researchers use the term **child-directed speech** (also called "motherese," though it is used by fathers too) to describe the speech adults use with young children (Gelman & Shatz, 1977; Pine, 1994): short, simple sentences, spoken slowly and in a high-pitched voice, often with much repetition, and with exaggerated emphasis on key words (usually words for objects and activities). For example, the mother trying to get her son to eat his peas might say "Eat your peas now. Not the cracker. See those *peas*? Yeah, eat the *peas*." Child-directed speech seems to be used by adults speaking to young children in the large majority of language communities that have been studied (Fernald et al., 1989). And infants, from the earliest days of life, seem to pay more attention to the high-pitched sounds and varied intonational patterns of child-directed speech than to the "flatter" speech adults use when communicating with one another (Cooper & Aslin, 1990; Pegg, Werker, & McLeod, 1992).

Would children learn language just as well if adults talked to them in an adultlike style? Perhaps not. The nativists seem to have underestimated the contributions of environment to language development. Mere exposure to speech is simply not enough; children must be actively involved in using language (Locke, 1997). Catherine Snow and her associates, for example, found that a group of Dutch-speaking children, despite the fact that they watched a great deal of German television, did not acquire any German words or grammar (Snow et al., 1976). True, there are cultural groups (the Kaluli of New Guinea, the natives of American Samoa, and the Trackton people of the Piedmont Carolinas) in which motherese does not seem to be used. Children in these societies still seem to acquire language without noticeable delays (Gordon, 1990; Ochs, 1982; Schieffelin, 1986). Yet even these children overhear speech and participate in social interactions in which language is used, and that is what seems to be required in order to master a human language (Lieven, 1994). Those parents who do use child-directed speech further simplify the child's task of figuring out the rules of language (Harris, 1992). They converse with children daily in attention-getting and understandable ways about the very objects and events that have captured the youngsters' attention.

Adults speaking to young children also use specific communication strategies that foster language development. For example, if a child says "Kittie goed," an adult may respond with an **expansion**—a more grammatically complete expression of the same

"Motherese" is used by fathers, too. Both mothers and fathers—and siblings, too, for that matter—adapt their speech to young language learners. (Barton & Tomasello, 1994)

thought ("Yes, the cat went in the car"). Adults use conversational techniques like expansions mainly to improve communication, not to teach grammar (Penner, 1987). However, these techniques also serve as a subtle form of correction after children produce grammatically incorrect sentences and show them more grammatical ways to express the same ideas (Bohannon & Stanwicz, 1988; Saxton, 1997). It's not quite true, then, that adults provide no corrective feedback concerning children's grammatical errors, as nativists claim. True, they rarely say, "No, that's wrong; say it this way." They do, however, provide a good deal of subtle corrective feedback through their responses to children, and this feedback helps children grow linguistically (Bohannon & Bonvillian, 1997).

How can adults best facilitate young children's language learning? What cognitive capacities enable children to learn how language works? Much remains to be learned about language development, but it does seem to require the interaction of a biologically prepared child with at least one conversational partner, ideally one who tailors his or her own speech to the child's level of understanding.

A Critical Period for Language?

Young children are so adept at learning languages that some scholars have wondered whether a critical

(or at least sensitive) period for language acquisition may exist. Some years ago, Eric Lenneberg (1967) claimed that there is such a critical period and that it lasts until puberty, when the development of lateralization of language functions in the left hemisphere of the brain is completed. Although we now know that lateralization of the brain occurs more rapidly than Lenneberg thought (Locke, 1997; and see Chapter 5), researchers continue to be very interested in determining whether young children are uniquely capable of language learning.

What evidence supports the critical period hypothesis of language acquisition? Some comes from studies of deaf children, some of whom (especially those with hearing parents) do not have an opportunity to learn *any* language, oral or signed, in their early years. Rachel Mayberry (1994) has studied language mastery in deaf college students who were exposed to American Sign Language at different ages and has found that the rule "the earlier, the better" applies. Mastery of the morphology, syntax, and semantics of sign language was greatest among students exposed to it in infancy or early childhood. Those who learned sign later in their development (ages 9–16) mastered it better if they had had some exposure to English early in life than if they had not been exposed to any language system at all before they encountered sign language (see Box 7.2 for more on how the language development of deaf children compares to that of hearing children).

Meanwhile, Elissa Newport and her colleagues (Newport, 1991) have uncovered similar evidence of a critical period for second-language learning. In one study (Johnson & Newport, 1989), native speakers of Korean or Chinese who had come to the United States between the ages of 3 and 39 were tested for mastery of English grammar. Among those who began learning English before puberty, those who learned it earliest learned it best. Among those who arrived in the United States after puberty, performance was generally poor, regardless of age of arrival or number of years using English. But, you may argue, adults may structure the language environment in more helpful ways for young learners than for older ones, making the child's task easier than the adult's. How can adults have more difficulty than children acquiring languages when they are more adept cognitively? Although it is true that adults learn faster than children in the short run if they are given the same language input, adults are less likely than children to ever attain nativelike proficiency in a second language (Mayberry, 1994). Quite possibly, then, the language processing areas of the brain are shaped for a lifetime by early experience with language in ways that limit later learning of other languages.

We would want a good deal more evidence before accepting the critical-period hypothesis, however, and

BOX 7.2

Language acquisition among deaf children

Many deaf children gain their first exposure to language by learning American Sign Language (ASL). This language system is a true language. For example, signs are arbitrary symbols, not attempts to mimic objects and events, and they are used according to a system of grammatical rules that determines their ordering. We ought to be able to learn something about language acquisition in general, then, by studying language acquisition among deaf children.

On average, deaf children acquire sign language in much the same sequence and at much the same rate as hearing children acquire spoken language, and they make many of the same kinds of errors on their way (Bellugi, 1988; Meier, 1991; Locke, 1997). Interestingly, deaf infants whose parents are deaf and communicate to them in sign "babble" in sign language. They experiment with gestures in much the same way that hearing infants experiment with sounds in preparation for their first meaningful communications (Petitto & Marentette, 1991). They then sign their first meaningful single words at about 12 months of age, use their first syntax (combinations of two signs) at 18 to 24 months, and master many rules of morphology such as past tense formation between 2 and 3 years of age (Meier, 1991). Just as hearing children have difficulty with the pronunciation of certain words and overgeneralize certain rules, deaf children make predictable errors in their signing (Meier, 1991). Moreover, for both deaf and hearing children, advances in language development are linked closely to advances in cognitive development; for example, children start putting signs or words together in sentences at about the same age that they put sequences of actions together in their play (Spencer, 1996).

The language environment experienced by deaf infants is also far more similar to that of hearing infants than you would imagine. For example, deaf mothers sign in motherese; they present signs at a slower pace, repeat signs more, and exaggerate their signing motions more when they talk to their infants than when they talk to their deaf friends (Masataka, 1996). Moreover, just as hearing babies prefer the exaggerated intonations of motherese, deaf infants pay more attention and show more emotional response when they are shown tapes of infant-directed signing than tapes of adult-directed signing.

Finally, it turns out that language areas of the brain develop much the same in deaf children exposed to sign as in hearing children exposed to speech. For example, Helen Neville and her colleagues (1997) examined brain activity during the processing of sentences by deaf and hearing ASL users, hearing individuals (interpreters) who acquired sign late in life, and hearing individuals who did not know ASL. For the most part, reliance on areas of the left hemisphere of the cortex to process sentences was just as evident among those who acquired ASL early in life as among hearing individuals who acquired English early in life. Early learners of ASL did use their right hemispheres more in responding to sentences, perhaps because spatial skills based in the right hemisphere come into play in interpreting the gestures of someone who is signing. Reliance on the left hemisphere to process syntax was not as clear among individuals who acquired a language later in life.

As we have seen, language development is sometimes delayed among deaf children of hearing parents if they cannot hear well enough to understand spoken language but are not exposed to sign language either (Mayberry, 1994). Overall, then, studies of language acquisition among deaf children suggest that young humans are biologically prepared to master language and will do so, if they are given the opportunity, whether that language is signed or spoken, whether it involves visual-spatial skills or auditory ones (Meier, 1991).

might be better off calling it a "sensitive" period in any case. Also, it is not yet clear whether this sensitive period for language acquisition ends at around age 5 or extends to puberty (Hoff-Ginsberg, 1997). Perhaps the main message is that young children are supremely capable of learning languages and advancing their cognitive development in the process. Meanwhile, college students learning a foreign language for the first time may have to appreciate that they will never speak it as well as someone who learned it as a young child.

APPLICATIONS: IMPROVING COGNITIVE FUNCTIONING

Having examined both Piaget's and Vygotsky's theories of cognitive development, we might ask what each has to contribute to the goal of optimizing mental functioning. As Piaget's views first became popular in the United States and Canada, psychologists and educators designed studies to determine whether they could speed cognitive development and help children and adults solve problems more effectively. Some researchers had a different motive: to challenge Piaget's view that concepts like conservation cannot be mastered until the child is intellectually ready.

What has been learned from these training studies? Generally, they suggest that many Piagetian concepts can be taught to children who are slightly younger than the age at which the concepts would naturally emerge. Training is sometimes difficult, and it does not always generalize well to new problems, but progress can be achieved. Dorothy Field (1981), for example, demonstrated that 4-year-olds could be trained to recognize the identity of a substance like a ball of clay before and after its appearance is altered—that is, to understand that, although the clay looks different, it is still the *same* clay and has to be the same amount of clay. Field found that nearly 75% of the children given this identity training could solve at least three out of five conservation problems 2.5 to 5 months after training.

Similar training studies have demonstrated that children who function at the late concrete operations stage can be taught formal operations (Adey & Shayer, 1992). Researchers have had even more luck improving the cognitive performance of older adults, sometimes with very simple interventions (Blackburn & Papalia, 1992). Such studies suggest that many elderly individuals who perform poorly on Piagetian problem-solving tasks simply need a quick refresher course to show their underlying competence. Make no mistake: *No one* has demonstrated that 2-year-olds can be taught formal operations. But at least these studies establish that specific training experiences can somewhat speed a child's progress through Piaget's stages or bring out more advanced capacities in an adult who is performing at a less advanced level.

Piaget himself disapproved of attempts by Americans to speed children's progress through his stages (Piaget, 1970). He believed that parents should simply provide young children with opportunities to explore their world and that teachers should use a discovery approach in the classroom that allows children to learn by doing. Given their natural curiosity and normal opportunities to try their hand at solving problems, children would construct ever more complex understandings on their own. Many educators began building Piaget's ideas about discovery-based education into school curricula, especially in science classes (see Gallagher & Easley, 1978). Teachers have also taken seriously Piaget's notion that children best understand material that they can assimilate into their existing understandings. So, for example, they have designed curricula to guide severely mentally retarded adults through the substages of the sensorimotor period (Williams, 1996). Finding out what the learner already knows or can do and providing instruction matched to the child's level of development are in the spirit of Piaget.

And what would Lev Vygotsky recommend to teachers who want to stimulate cognitive growth? As you might guess, Vygotsky's theoretical orientation leads to a very different approach to education from Piaget's—a more social one. Whereas students in Piaget's classroom would most likely be engaged in independent exploration, students in Vygotsky's classroom would be involved in guided participation, "co-constructing" knowledge during interactions with teachers and more knowledgeable peers. The roles of teachers and other more skillful collaborators would be to organize the learning activity, break it into steps, provide hints and suggestions carefully tailored to the child's current abilities, and gradually turn over more and more of the mental work to the student. According to Vygotsky's sociocultural perspective, the guidance provided by a skilled partner will then be internalized by the learner, first as private speech and eventually as silent inner speech. Education ends up being a matter of providing children with tools of the mind important in their culture, whether hunting strategies or computer skills (Bodrova & Leong, 1996; Berk & Winsler, 1995).

Is there any evidence that Vygotsky's guided participation approach might be superior to Piaget's discovery approach? Consider what Lisa Freund (1990) found when she had 3- to 5-year-old children help a puppet with a sorting task: deciding which furnishings (sofas, beds, bathtubs, stoves, and so on) should be placed in each of six rooms of a dollhouse that the puppet was moving into. First the children were tested to determine what they already knew about proper furniture placement. Then each child worked at a similar task, either alone (as might be the case in Piaget's discovery-based education, though here children were provided with corrective feedback by the experimenter) or with his or her mother (Vygotsky's guided learning). Finally, to assess what they had learned, Freund asked the children to perform a final, rather complex, furniture-sorting task. The results were clear: Children who had sorted furniture with help from their mothers showed dramatic improvements in sorting ability, whereas those who had practiced on their own showed little improvement. Moreover, the children who gained the most from guided participation with their mothers were those whose mothers talked the most about how to tackle the task. Collaborating with a competent peer can also produce cognitive gains that a child might not achieve working alone (Azmitia, 1992; Gauvain & Rogoff, 1989).

So children do not always learn the most when they function as solitary scientists, seeking discoveries on their own; often, conceptual growth springs more readily from children's interactions with other people—particularly with competent people who provide an optimal amount of guidance. Yet it would seem that many children might benefit most from the best of both worlds: opportunities to explore on their own *and* supportive companions to offer help when needed.

Pause for a moment and consider the truly remarkable accomplishments that we have described in this chapter. The capacities of the human mind for thought and language are truly awesome. Because the human mind is so complex, we should not be surprised that it is not yet understood. Piaget attacked only part of the puzzle, and he only partially succeeded. Vygotsky alerted us to sociocultural influences on cognitive development but died before he could formalize his theory. As we see in Chapters 8 and 9, other ways to think about mental development are needed.

◆ SUMMARY POINTS

1. Jean Piaget, through his clinical method, formulated four stages of cognitive development, in which children construct increasingly complex schemes through an interaction of maturation and experience. Children adapt to the world through the processes of organization and adaptation (assimilating new experience to existing understandings and accommodating existing understandings to new experience).

2. According to Piaget, infants progress through six substages of the sensorimotor stage by perceiving and acting on the world; they progress from using their reflexes to adapt to the environment to using symbolic or representational thought to solve problems in their heads. Their symbolic capacity permits full mastery of object permanence.

3. In Piaget's preoperational stage (ages 2–7), children make many uses of their symbolic capacity but are limited by their dependence on appearances, lack of logical mental operations, and egocentrism. They fail to grasp the concept of conservation because they engage in centration, irreversible thinking, and static thought, though recent research suggests that preschool children's capacities are greater than Piaget supposed.

4. School-age children enter the stage of concrete operations (ages 7–11) and begin to master conservation tasks through decentration, reversibility, and transformational thought. They can think about relations, grasping seriation and transitivity, and they understand the concept of class inclusion.

5. Adolescents often show the first signs of formal operations at 11 or 12 and later master the hypothetical-deductive reasoning skills required to solve scientific problems. Cognitive changes result in other developmental advances and may also contribute to confusion, rebellion, idealism, and adolescent egocentrism (the imaginary audience and the personal fable).

6. Adults are most likely to display formal-operational skills in their areas of expertise. Some adults, especially well-educated ones, may advance to postformal modes of thought such as relativistic thinking. Although aging adults often perform less well than younger adults on Piagetian tasks, factors other than biological aging may explain this difference.

7. Piaget has made huge contributions to the field of human development but has been criticized for underestimating the capacities of infants and young children, not considering factors besides competence that influence performance, failing to demonstrate that his stages have coherence, offering vague explanations of development, and underestimating the role of language and social interaction in cognitive development.

8. Vygotsky's sociocultural perspective emphasizes cultural and social influences on cognitive development more than Piaget's theory does. Through guided participation

in culturally important activities, children learn problem-solving techniques from knowledgeable partners sensitive to their zone of proximal development; language also shapes their thought as social speech becomes private speech and later inner speech.

9. To acquire language, children must master phonology (sound), semantics (meaning), morphology (word structure), and syntax (sentence structure), as well as learn how to use language appropriately (pragmatics) and to understand nonverbal communication.

10. Infants begin to discriminate speech sounds and progress from crying, cooing, and babbling to one-word holophrases (at 1 year of age) and then to telegraphic speech (at 18 months), guided by a functional grammar that allows them to name things, make requests, and achieve other communication goals.

11. Language abilities improve dramatically in the preschool years, as illustrated by overregularizations and new transformation rules. School-age children and adolescents refine their language skills and become less egocentric communicators. Knowledge of semantics continues to expand during adulthood, and language abilities hold up well in old age, despite some difficulties with speech sound perception, the tip-of-the-tongue phenomenon, and the processing of complex syntax.

12. Theories of language development include learning theories, nativist theories, and interactionist theories that emphasize both the child's biologically based capacities and experience conversing with adults who use child-directed speech and strategies such as expansion that simplify the language-learning task. A critical or at least sensitive period for language acquisition appears to exist in early childhood.

13. Attempts to teach cognitive skills suggest that development can be speeded up, though with some difficulty and with limits, and that older adults can be helped to use their cognitive competencies more effectively. Piaget advocated a discovery approach to learning, whereas Vygotsky's followers emphasize guided participation involving collaboration between the learner and a more capable adult or peer.

FOOD FOR THOUGHT

1. Thinking about the differences between preoperational thought, concrete-operational thought, and formal-operational thought, what should parents keep in mind as they attempt to communicate with 4-year-old, 8-year-old, and 17-year-old children?

2. Create descriptions of a Piagetian preschool and a Vygotskian preschool. What are the main differences in terms of how children will be assessed, what they will be taught, and how they will be taught? How do teachers in each school view the role of language in education?

3. Imagine that you are a computer scientist and are given the task of writing a computer program that can comprehend spoken English as well as the average 3-year-old does. What information should your computer program contain, and what does it have to do with incoming speech samples? Why do you think writing such a computer program is a hugely complex task?

ON THE WEB

1. *Piaget*   The material at this site can be tough reading, but if you are interested in what researchers inspired by Piaget's work are doing, try the site of the Jean Piaget Society. You will find abstracts of scholarly papers (sometimes whole papers) on topics related to Piaget's theory and a short biography of Piaget as well. Many developmentalists who study cognitive development but are not necessarily

Piagetians participate in the annual meetings of the Jean Piaget Society and contribute to its Web site.
http://www.sunnyhill.bc.ca/Lalonde/JPS/

2. *Vygotsky* To find explanations of some of Vygotsky's concepts, such as inner speech and the zone of proximal development, and to read his biography, try this site. Though not fancy, it links you to some useful information. One piece compares Piaget and Vygotsky.
http://www.infoline.ru/g23/3533/proc/vygee/links.htm

KEY TERMS

genetic epistemology
clinical method
scheme (schema)
organization
adaptation
assimilation
accommodation
sensorimotor stage
symbolic capacity
object permanence
A, not B, error
preoperational stage
conservation
decentration
centration
reversibility
transformational thought
egocentrism
class inclusion

concrete operations stage
horizontal décalage
seriation
transitivity
formal operations stage
hypothetical-deductive reasoning
adolescent egocentrism
imaginary audience
personal fable
postformal thought
relativistic thinking
zone of proximal development
guided participation
private speech
language
phonology
morphology

syntax
semantics
pragmatics
intonation
cooing
babbling
holophrase
vocabulary spurt
overextension
underextension
telegraphic speech
functional grammar
overregularization
transformational grammar
language acquisition device (LAD)
child-directed speech
expansion

CHAPTER 8

Learning and Information Processing

BASIC LEARNING PROCESSES
Classical Conditioning
Operant Conditioning
Observational Learning
Stability and Change in Learning

THE INFORMATION-PROCESSING APPROACH

THE INFANT
Early Memory
Infantile Amnesia

THE CHILD
Learning and Memory
Problem Solving

THE ADOLESCENT

THE ADULT
Developing Expertise
Learning, Memory, and Aging
Problem Solving and Aging

APPLICATIONS: IMPROVING MEMORY

SUMMARY POINTS

FOOD FOR THOUGHT

ON THE WEB

KEY TERMS

"W here did you learn *that*?"
"I can't believe I remembered that."
"Larry . . . Larry . . . Larry Murphy?"
"It's on the tip of my tongue."
"Sorry, I completely forgot."

Lines like these appear often in our conversations; learning and remembering, failing to learn and forgetting—these are all important parts of our daily lives. Moreover, individuals develop as they do partly because of what they have learned and remembered from their experiences. Both Piaget and Vygotsky were centrally interested in the question of how children come to know the world around them. In this chapter our examination of cognitive development continues, but we consider other approaches to answering this key question. The chapter begins with the messages of traditional learning theories about basic learning mechanisms important at all ages. But learning theories could not explain complex forms of cognitive activity, and so cognitive psychologists, influenced by the rise of computer technology, began to think of the brain as a computer that processes input and converts it to output (correct answers on tests, for example). This information-processing perspective on the mind has revealed much about how the capacities to acquire, remember, and use information change over the life span.

BASIC LEARNING PROCESSES

The capacity to learn, to change in response to one's experience, is in place even before birth and strongly affects development and adaptation throughout the life span. Here we briefly review three fundamental types of learning featured in major learning theories of human development: classical conditioning, operant conditioning, and observational learning (see also Chapter 2 on learning theories).

Classical Conditioning

In **classical conditioning,** a stimulus that initially had no effect comes to elicit a response through its association with a stimulus that already elicits the response. That is, a new association between stimulus and response is learned. The Russian physiologist Ivan Pavlov discovered classical conditioning and demonstrated that dogs who automatically salivated at the sight of food could learn to salivate at the sound of a bell alone if, during a training period, the bell was regularly sounded just before they ate.

What role does classical conditioning play in human development? It is highly involved in the learning of emotional responses and attitudes. In a classic study, John Watson, founder of behavioral psychology, and Rosalie Raynor (1920) set out to demonstrate that fears can be learned—that they are not necessarily inborn, as was commonly thought at the time. These researchers presented a gentle white rat to a now-famous infant named Albert, who showed no fear of it whatsoever. However, every time the rat was brought forth, Watson would slip behind Albert and bang a steel rod with a hammer.

In this situation, the loud noise served as an **unconditioned stimulus (UCS)**—that is, a built-in and unlearned stimulus—for fear, which in turn is an unlearned or **unconditioned response (UCR)** to loud noises (as babies are naturally upset by them). During conditioning, the stimuli of the white rat and the loud noise were presented together several times. Afterward, Watson presented the white rat to Albert without banging the steel rod, and Albert now whimpered and cried in response to the white rat alone. His behavior had changed as a result of his experience. Specifically, an initially neutral stimulus, the white rat, had become a **conditioned stimulus (CS)** for a **conditioned response (CR),** fear, as Figure 8.1 shows. This learned response generalized to other furry things such as a rabbit and a Santa Claus mask. By today's standards Watson's experiment would be viewed as unethical, but he had made his point: Emotional responses can be learned.

Perhaps you can identify a fear or phobia you learned when an object or event that is not fearsome in itself became associated with a frightening experience. To this day, I shiver at the sight (or even the thought) of antiseptic cotton, undoubtedly because cotton just happened to be there when the iodine swabbed on a skinned knee caused painful shivers. Fortunately, responses that are learned through classical conditioning can be unlearned through the same process, in this case called **counterconditioning.** Mary Cover Jones (1924) demonstrated that a 2-year-old named Peter overcame his fear of furry animals after being exposed to a rabbit (for him, a CS for fearful responses) while he ate a favorite food (a UCS for pleasant feelings). Peter gradually came to associate the rabbit with pleasurable rather than fearful feelings.

Classical conditioning is undoubtedly involved when infants learn to love their parents, who at first may be neutral stimuli but who become associated with the positive sensations of receiving milk, being rocked, and being comforted. And classical conditioning helps explain why adults find that certain songs on the radio, scents, or articles of clothing "turn them on." You can see how a wide range of emotional associations and attitudes could be acquired through classical conditioning.

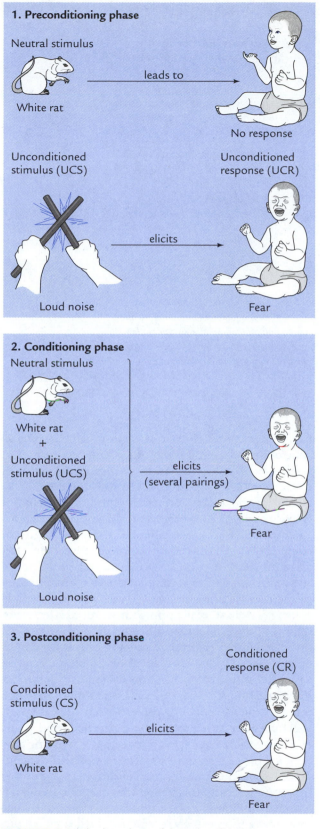

1. Preconditioning phase

Neutral stimulus

White rat → leads to → No response

Unconditioned stimulus (UCS)

Loud noise → elicits → Unconditioned response (UCR)

Fear

2. Conditioning phase

Neutral stimulus

White rat
+
Unconditioned stimulus (UCS)

Loud noise → elicits (several pairings) → Fear

3. Postconditioning phase

Conditioned stimulus (CS)

White rat → elicits → Conditioned response (CR)

Fear

FIGURE 8.1 *The three phases of classical conditioning*

Operant Conditioning

Another highly important form of basic learning is **operant conditioning** (sometimes called instrumental conditioning). In classical conditioning, responses are elicited or provoked by a stimulus. In operant conditioning, a learner first *emits* a response, or behaves in some way, and then comes to associate this action with the positive or negative consequences that follow it. B. F. Skinner (1953) made this form of conditioning famous. The basic principle makes a good deal of sense: We tend to repeat behaviors that have pleasant consequences and cut down on behaviors that have unpleasant consequences. Through operant conditioning, we learn new skills and a range of habits, both good and bad.

In the language of operant conditioning, *reinforcement* occurs when a consequence *strengthens* a response, or makes it more likely to occur in the future. If a child cleans his room and then receives a hug, the hug will probably provide **positive reinforcement** for room cleaning and make the behavior more likely in the future. *Positive* here means that something has been *added* to the situation, and *reinforcement* means that the behavior is strengthened. Thus a positive reinforcer is an event that, when introduced following a behavior, makes that behavior more probable in the future. **Negative reinforcement** also involves the strengthening of some behavioral tendency, but the behavior is strengthened because something negative or unpleasant is *removed* from the situation, or is escaped or avoided, after the behavior occurs. Have you been in a car in which an obnoxious buzzer sounds until you fasten your seat belt? The idea is that your "buckling up" behavior will become a habit through *negative reinforcement*, because buckling up allows you to escape the unpleasant buzzer. No candy or hugs follow the buckling up, so it is not positive reinforcement that makes you likely to perform this behavior. It is negative reinforcement.

We are likely to keep doing things that allow us to escape or avoid unpleasantness, so we learn many habits through negative reinforcement. If a teenager finds that lying to Mom is the secret to avoiding long lectures, she will keep right on lying. If a man finds that a few beers allow him to escape his feelings of anxiety, he'll keep right on drinking. In each case a behavior is strengthened through negative reinforcement—through the removal or elimination of something unpleasant.

I have labored the point about negative reinforcement because there is a common—and absolutely incorrect—tendency to think that the term *negative reinforcement* is a fancy name for punishment. Contrast reinforcement, whether it is positive or negative, with punishment: Whereas reinforcement increases the strength of the behavior that preceded it, punishment

	Positive stimulus (pleasant)	Negative stimulus (unpleasant)
Administered	**Positive reinforcement, adding a positive stimulus** (strengthens the behavior) Dad gives in to the whining and lets Moosie play Nintendo, making whining more likely in the future.	**Positive punishment, adding a negative stimulus** (weakens the behavior) Dad calls Moosie a "baby." Moosie does not like this at all and is less likely to whine in the future.
Withdrawn	**Negative punishment, withdrawing a positive stimulus** (weakens the behavior) Dad confiscates Moosie's favorite Nintendo game to discourage whining in the future.	**Negative reinforcement, withdrawing a negative stimulus** (strengthens the behavior) Dad stops joking with Lulu. Moosie gets very jealous when Dad pays attention to Lulu, so his whining enables him to bring this unpleasant state of affairs to an end.

FIGURE 8.2 *Possible consequences of behavior. Moosie comes into the TV room and sees his father talking and joking with his sister, Lulu, as the two watch a football game. Soon Moosie begins to whine, louder and louder, that he wants them to turn off the television so he can play Nintendo games. Here are four possible consequences of his behavior. Consider both the type of consequence—whether it is a positive or negative stimulus—and whether it is administered ("added to" the situation) or withdrawn.*

decreases the strength of that behavior. There are two forms of punishment paralleling the two forms of reinforcement. **Positive punishment** occurs when an unpleasant event is added to the situation following a behavior (for example, a cashier is criticized for coming up short of cash at the end of the day); **negative punishment** occurs when something pleasant is removed from the situation following the behavior (the amount she was short is deducted from her pay). Both positive and negative punishment decrease the likelihood that a behavior will be repeated.

The four possible consequences of a behavior are summarized in Figure 8.2. In addition, some behavior is simply ignored; that is, it has no particular consequence. Behavior that is ignored, or no longer reinforced, tends to weaken, in a process called **extinction.** Indeed, a good alternative to punishment, at least for behavior that is not dangerous, is to ignore it while reinforcing desirable behavior that is incompatible with it. All too often the well-behaved child is ignored and the misbehaving child gets the attention—which serves as positive reinforcement for the misbehavior.

Skinner and other behavioral theorists emphasize the power of positive reinforcement in raising children. When a child is first being taught a new habit, such as making the bed or saying "Thank you," it is best to provide **continuous reinforcement,** reinforcing the new behavior every time it occurs (perhaps with warm praise). Then, to maintain the desirable behavior over long periods, it is best to switch to **partial reinforcement,** reinforcing only some occurrences of the behavior, ideally on an unpredictable schedule of reinforcement. If continuous reinforcement comes to an abrupt end, extinction (fading) of the new behavior is likely to occur. However, if a child never quite knows when another dose of parental approval might be coming, the behavior is likely to continue even after all reinforcement ceases. Many parents feel that positive reinforcement of desirable behavior must be supplemented by punishment of bad behavior in child rearing. They can make punishment more effective by following the guidelines in Box 8.1.

Behaviorists claim that learning processes may explain aspects of development that are often assumed to be the result of maturation (Tarabulsy, Tessier, & Kappas, 1996). For example, at about 9 months of age, infants typically begin to protest when the caregivers to whom they have now become attached leave them. However, the frequency of an infant's whining and crying upon separation from a parent also depends on how parent and infant condition one another over time during their interactions. The frequency with which infants protest separations increases when mothers reinforce it (by interacting with their infants visually and verbally) but decreases when mothers reinforce other infant behavior instead (Gewirtz & Pelaez-Nogueras, 1992). Indeed, reinforcing protest behavior can cause 6-month-olds, who rarely squawk

BOX 8.1

Using punishment effectively

Although B. F. Skinner emphasized the value of positive reinforcement of good behavior, most parents use punishment at least occasionally. Indeed, 80% of American adults agree that a "good, hard spanking" is sometimes necessary in disciplining a child (Flynn, 1994). In one study of mothers with children under age 4, 63% of inner-city mothers and 20% of suburban mothers had spanked their child in the past week (Socolar & Stein, 1995). Many developmentalists believe that parents should never use physical punishment—that verbal punishment is to be preferred when punishment is necessary. They would also advise parents who do use punishment to follow these guidelines, derived from the research literature (Domjan, 1993; Parke, 1977):

◆ **Punish as soon as possible.** It is best to punish as the child prepares to misbehave or at least during the act. Postponing punishment ("Wait 'til Daddy comes home!") is bad practice. Young children may conclude that Daddy is punishing them for whatever they are doing at the moment—for example, putting toys back in the toy box. Delayed punishment can be effective with older children if the punisher explains why the child is being punished (Verna, 1977).

◆ **Punish with intensity (but not too much intensity).** Laboratory research with young children suggests that intense punishment, in the form of loud buzzers or noises, is more effective than mild punishment. That is, a loud "No" is likely to be more effective than a soft "No." But we should not be misled into thinking that severe physical punishment is a good idea. Severe spankings have several disad-

vantages (Straus, 1994). They create high anxiety, which can interfere with "learning one's lesson" and result in longer-term psychological distress and depression (Turner & Finkelhor, 1996). They can also teach the child to fear (through classical conditioning) and avoid (through operant conditioning) the parent who doles out the punishment. Harsh physical punishment also teaches the child, through observational learning of their parents' use of physical force, to rely on aggression as a way of dealing with problems (Weiss, Dodge, Bates, & Pettit, 1992). So, intense punishment can be effective as long as it is not so intense that it has these sorts of negative side effects.

◆ **Punish consistently.** Acts that are punished only now and then persist. After all, the child is being reinforced part of the time for the (usually fun) misbehavior.

◆ **Be otherwise warm.** Children respond better to punishment from a person who is otherwise affectionate than from someone who is usually cold.

◆ **Explain yourself.** Explaining why the behavior was wrong and is being punished helps children learn to control their own behavior in the future (for example, to recall why the behavior would be unwise). Older children and, in particular, adolescents want and benefit from explanations that point out the social consequences of misbehavior.

◆ **Reinforce alternative behavior.** Since punishment alone tells a child only what *not* to do, it makes sense to strengthen acceptable alternatives to the misbehavior. The parent who does not want a toddler to play with an expensive vase might punish that behav-

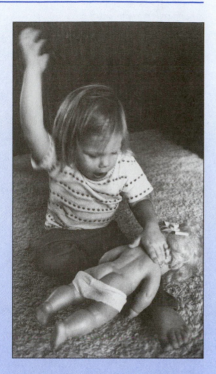

ior but also reinforce play with an unbreakable plastic pot.

◆ **Consider alternative responses to the misbehavior.** Although spanking seems to be the first thing many parents think of when a child misbehaves, punishment can also involve taking away desirable stimuli (for example, TV privileges). And a highly effective alternative to punishment is a procedure called **time out,** which involves removing children from the situation in which their misbehavior is positively reinforced. The boy who is throwing toys around the room might be sent for a few minutes to a quiet room where he is cut off from the pleasure of creating havoc. When misbehavior is no longer reinforced, it weakens through extinction.

at separations from their parents, to protest as often as 12-month-olds do. Such research does not demonstrate that maturational influences on development are unimportant, but it does indicate that parents' decisions about what behaviors to reinforce or punish at what ages can also influence the course of development.

Observational Learning

Finally, consider **observational learning,** learning from observing the behavior of other people. Almost anything can be learned by watching (or listening to) other people. In imitation of parents the child may learn how to speak a language and tackle math problems, as

well as how to swear, snack between meals, and smoke. As we saw in Chapter 2, this form of learning takes center stage in Albert Bandura's social learning theory (1977, 1986, 1989). It is regarded as a more cognitive form of learning than conditioning, as learners construct mental representations (images, verbal summaries) of what they see that can be retrieved from memory at a later time and used to guide behavior.

Bandura set out to demonstrate that people could learn a response that was neither elicited by a conditioned stimulus (classical conditioning) nor performed and then strengthened by a reinforcer (operant conditioning). His classic experiment involved the learning of aggressive behavior by nursery school children (Bandura, 1965). Children watched a short film in which an adult *model* attacked an inflatable "Bobo" doll, hitting the doll with a mallet while shouting "Sockeroo," throwing rubber balls at the doll while shouting "Bang, bang, bang," and so on. There were three experimental conditions: (1) a *model-rewarded* condition in which children saw a second adult give the aggressive model some candy and a soft drink for a "championship performance"; (2) a *model-punished* condition in which the second adult scolded and spanked the model for beating up on Bobo, and (3) a *no-consequences* condition in which children simply saw the model behave aggressively. After the film ended, it was the children's turn to be in a playroom with the Bobo doll and many of the props the model had used to work Bobo over.

What did children in the three conditions learn from this adventure in observational learning? Children who saw the model rewarded and children in the no-consequences condition imitated more of the model's aggressive acts than children who had seen the model punished for aggression. But Bandura also devised a learning test that asked children to reproduce all of the model's behavior they could remember. As it turned out, children learned about the same amount from observing the model regardless of the experimental condition they were in. Apparently the children who had seen the model punished imitated fewer of the model's behaviors on the initial "performance" test because they had learned from the film that they too might be punished for striking Bobo. Nonetheless, these children learned a great deal about how to behave aggressively—knowledge that could be acted upon in the future if their expectation and fear of punishment were not so great.

This study demonstrates that children can indeed learn new behavior simply through observing a model—even though they have not tried out the aggressive behaviors before and have not been reinforced for performing them. Moreover, the study points out an important distinction between *learning* and *performance*: Children can learn from observation without imitating (performing) the learned responses. Whether they will perform what they learn depends in part on whether the model was reinforced (or punished) for his or her actions—a process called **vicarious reinforcement.** In addition, although children can learn by observing even without being reinforced, reinforcing them directly for imitating will increase the chances that they will continue to perform what they have learned.

You can see why social learning theorists such as Albert Bandura are considered far more cognitively oriented than behavioral theorists such as John Watson and B. F. Skinner. Observational learning, unlike classical and operant conditioning, requires a mind that attends to, remembers, and interprets information about other people's behavior. Finally, learners also process information about the vicarious consequences of behavior, form expectations about the likelihood of reinforcement or punishment in the future, and even *mentally* reinforce or punish their own actions—all very cognitive activities.

Stability and Change in Learning

The same basic learning processes can explain changes in behavior in both young and old. Humans of all ages learn positive and negative emotional associations to a wide range of stimuli (classical conditioning). They form habits, good and bad, by being influenced by the reinforcing or punishing consequences of what they do (operant conditioning). And they change their own understandings and behaviors after watching other people behave (observational learning). Yet the capacity to learn changes as we develop.

Can Young Infants Learn?

Infants *can* learn, and they can do so even before birth (Lipsitt, 1990; Rovee-Collier, 1987). For example, newborns can be classically conditioned, although not always easily. Lewis Lipsitt and Herbert Kaye (1964) paired a musical tone with the presentation of a nipple (an unconditioned stimulus for sucking). After several of these conditioning trials, 2- to 3-day-old infants began to suck at the sound of the tone, which had become a conditioned stimulus (CS) for the sucking response. Operant conditioning is also possible at birth. At the tender age of 1 day, infants will learn to suck faster on a nipple if their sucking is positively reinforced by sugary rather than plain water (Kron, 1966).

Whether true observational learning exists at birth is controversial. In some studies, newborns have proven able to imitate certain facial expressions, such as surprise and sadness, and certain actions, such as sticking out the tongue or opening the mouth (Field et al., 1982; Meltzoff & Moore, 1983, 1989; see also Figure 8.3). These findings were exciting because they challenged Piaget's claim that infants cannot imitate actions until about a year of age, when they have some ability to represent mentally what they have seen. However, a careful review of the research suggests that very young babies stick out their tongues in response to a model's doing so far more reliably than they display other imitative responses such as mouth opening (Anisfeld, 1996). Moreover, even the ability to imitate

tongue protrusions fades with age after the first month or two of life (Abravanel & Sigafoos, 1984). Imitation in the newborn, then, is largely restricted to tongue thrusting and is a temporary phenomenon.

Does imitative tongue protrusion really qualify as observational learning, then? Some researchers now doubt it (Bjorklund, 1995; Vinter, 1986). They maintain that early "imitation" is actually a reflexlike, automatic response to a specific stimulus that disappears with age (just as many of the newborn's reflexes do). Another possibility, suggested by Susan Jones (1996), is that tongue protrusion is not imitation at all but just a young infant's way of trying to explore interesting sights with their mouths before they have mastered the art of reaching. Jones demonstrated that young infants (1) stick out their tongues in reaction to many interesting sights, (2) find an adult who sticks out her tongue more interesting than one who merely opens and closes her mouth, and (3) more often stick out their tongues to snag interesting toys before they are capable of reaching for objects than afterwards. So, newborns who match the behavior of adults who stick out their tongues may be showing an automatic, biologically programmed response or engaging in an attempt to explore interesting sights rather than engaging in imitation (Jones, 1996). True observational learning that involves storing representations of what a model did and repeating it emerges later in infancy after the cortex of the brain is further developed.

Developmental Changes

The basic learning processes that emerge before or not long after birth continue to operate throughout the life span in much the same way. However, learning capacities also improve considerably with age.

Although newborns can learn, they are not always very competent learners. They are most adept at learning responses that produce food or are otherwise significant biologically (Rovee-Collier, 1987). However, they are often slow to learn. They may need nearly 200 conditioning trials to learn to turn their heads at the sound of a bell in order to be reinforced with milk (Papousek, 1967). By 3 months of age, infants need only about 40 trials to learn the same response, and by 5 months they need fewer than 30. Second, the range of responses that a newborn can learn and perform is quite limited. Only a few reflexes can be classically conditioned, and only behaviors already within the newborn's repertoire can be learned through operant conditioning or observation. Entirely novel behaviors cannot be learned. As infants develop, they rapidly become able to learn more kinds of responses, and to learn them faster.

Changes in the ability to learn through observation are particularly striking. **Deferred imitation,** the ability to imitate a novel act after a delay, is not evident

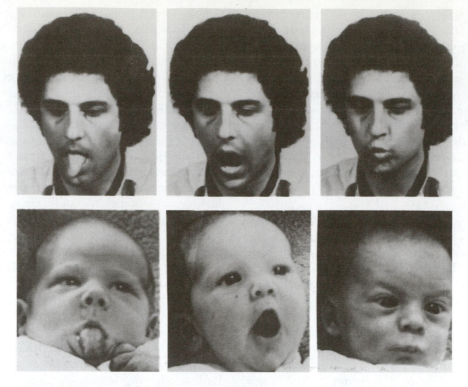

FIGURE 8.3 *Andrew Meltzoff is one of the researchers who has demonstrated imitation of facial expressions in newborns. These sample photographs are from videotaped recordings of 2- to 3-week-old infants imitating tongue protrusion, mouth opening, and lip protrusion. Of the three responses shown here, tongue protrusion is the most reliably observed.*
From A. N. Meltzoff & M. K. Moore (1977). "Imitation of facial and manual gestures by human neonates." *Science, 198,* 75–78.

at birth. As early as 9 months of age, though, and possibly earlier if they have had repeated exposure to what a model did, infants can imitate novel actions (for example, pushing a button on a box to produce a beep) after a 24-hour delay (Barr, Dowden, & Hayne, 1996; Meltzoff, 1988). With age, their ability to imitate *sequences* of novel actions improves (Bauer, 1996). Observational learning skills improve still further during childhood as children become able to use words to describe what they have seen so that they can remember more about it (Coates & Hartup, 1969).

Learning processes are as important in later life as they are in early life, and older adults continue to learn every day. However, they tend to be slower learners than younger adults. For example, it takes adults over age 50 more trials than younger adults to learn classically conditioned responses (Kausler, 1994; Woodruff-Pak, 1990); in one study, people in their 80s required twice as many trials as people in their 40s to learn to blink their eyes at the sound of a tone (Solomon et al., 1989). The fact that other animals show similar changes in basic learning processes suggests that these changes are part of the basic aging process and are caused by neural loss in relevant areas of the brain

(Kausler, 1994). For the most part, however, basic forms of learning are both evident and important at *all* ages. An adult might develop a classically conditioned fear of flying after a very rough flight, might cease to work hard on the job after receiving the punishment of a pay cut, or might learn World Wide Web search skills by watching a colleague. Changes in all of us are partly the result of learning experiences.

Important as basic classical conditioning, operant conditioning, and observational learning are, many psychologists have concluded that learning theories do not adequately explain how humans learn complex material, remember it, and use it to solve problems. Let's look now at an approach that addresses these issues.

THE INFORMATION-PROCESSING APPROACH

As the behavioral perspective on learning gained a firm hold among psychologists, it became unfashionable to study mental events that could not be directly observed. According to Howard Gardner (1985), the "cognitive revolution" in psychology could not have occurred without (1) a demonstration of the inadequacies of the behaviorist approach and (2) the rise of computer technology.

Showing deficiencies in the behaviorist approach was easiest in relation to complex learning and memory tasks. Consider learning from this textbook. Obviously some very complex processes occur between your registering of the pattern of print on this page and your writing of an essay about it. To account for these processes, behaviorists like Watson and Skinner would have to talk about chains of mental stimuli and responses between an external stimulus (for instance, the printed page) and an overt response. This approach proved cumbersome at best, as more cognitively oriented learning theorists such as Albert Bandura recognized.

Then came computers with their capacity for systematically converting input to output. The computer seemed to provide a good analogy to the human mind, and efforts to program computers to play chess and solve other problems as well as human experts do has revealed a great deal about the strengths and limitations of human cognition (Newell & Simon, 1961; Simon, 1995). Any computer has a limited capacity, associated with its hardware and software, for processing information. The computer's *hardware* is the machine itself—its keyboard (or input system), its storage capacity, and so on. The mind's "hardware" is the nervous system, including the brain, the sensory receptors, and their neural connections. The computer's *software* consists of the programs used to manipulate received and stored information: word-processing and statistics programs and the like. The mind, too, has its software—rules, strategies, and other mental "programs" that specify how information is to be registered, interpreted, stored, retrieved, and analyzed.

The computer, then, was the model for the **information-processing approach** to human cognition, which emphasizes the basic mental processes involved in attention, perception, memory, and decision making. When the information-processing approach began to guide studies of development, the challenge became one of determining how the hardware and software of the mind change over the life span. Just as today's more highly developed computers have greater capacity than those of the past, maturation of the nervous system plus experience presumably enable adults to remember more than young children can and to perform more complex cognitive feats with greater accuracy (Kail & Bisanz, 1992).

Figure 8.4 presents an early and very influential conception of the human information-processing system offered by Richard Atkinson and Richard Shiffrin (1968) over 30 years ago. If your history professor says

that the U.S. Constitution was ratified in 1789, this statement is an environmental stimulus. Assuming that you are not lost in a daydream, your **sensory register** will log it, holding it for a fraction of a second as a kind of afterimage (or, in this example, a kind of echo). Much that strikes the sensory register quickly disappears without further processing. Attentional processes (see Chapter 6) have a good deal to do with which sensory stimuli enter the sensory register in the first place and which are processed even further. If you think you may need to remember 1789, it will be moved into **short-term memory,** which can hold a limited amount of information (perhaps only about seven items or chunks of information) for several seconds. For example, short-term memory can hold on to a telephone number while you dial it. Today, cognitive researchers distinguish between passive and active forms of short-term memory and use the term **working memory** to refer to a mental "scratch pad" that temporarily stores information while actively operating on it. It is what is "on one's mind," or in one's consciousness, at any moment. As you know, people can juggle only so much information at once without having some of it slipping away.

To illustrate working memory, look at the following seven numbers. Then look away, and then add the numbers in your head while trying to remember them (Byrnes, 1996, p. 55):

$$7 \quad 2 \quad 5 \quad 6 \quad 1 \quad 4 \quad 7$$

Most likely, having to actively manipulate the numbers in working memory in order to add them disrupted your ability to rehearse them in order to remember them. People who are fast adders would have better luck than most people, because they would have more working memory space left for remembering the items (Byrnes, 1996).

To be remembered for any length of time, information must be moved from short-term memory into **long-term memory,** a relatively permanent store of information that represents what most people mean by memory. More than likely, you will hold the professor's statement in short-term memory just long enough to record it in your notes. Later, as you study your notes, you will rehearse the information in working memory to move it into long-term memory so that you can retrieve it the next day when you are taking the test.

This simplified model shows what you must do to learn and remember something. The first step is **encoding** the information: getting it into the system, learning it, moving it from the sensory register to short-term memory and then to long-term memory while organizing it in a form suitable for storage. If it never gets in, it cannot be remembered. Then there is **storage,** or the holding of information in the long-term memory store. Memories fade over time unless

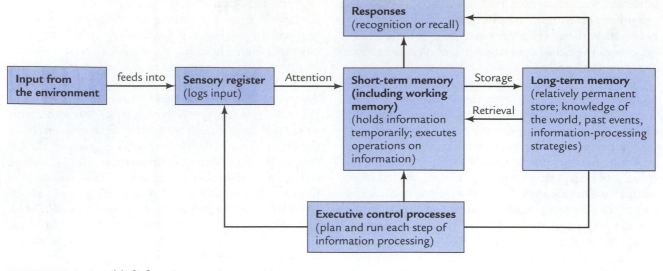

FIGURE 8.4 *A model of information processing* (Adapted from Atkinson & Shiffrin in Spence & Spence, 1968)

they are appropriately stored in long-term memory. And finally, there is **retrieval,** or the process of getting information out again when it is needed.

If you are asked a multiple-choice question about when the Constitution was ratified, you need not actively retrieve the correct date; you merely need to recognize it among the options. This is an example of **recognition memory.** But assume you were asked "When was the Constitution ratified?" This would be a test of **recall memory,** which requires active retrieval without the aid of cues. In between recognition and recall memory is **cued recall memory,** in which one is given a hint or cue to facilitate retrieval (for example, "When was the Constitution ratified? It's the year the French Revolution began and rhymes with *wine.*"). Most people find questions requiring recognition memory easier to answer than those requiring cued recall, and those requiring cued recall are easier than those requiring pure recall. This is true across the life span, which suggests that many things that we have apparently encoded or learned are "in there someplace," although we have trouble retrieving them without cues. Failures to remember can involve difficulties in initial encoding, storage, or retrieval.

Now imagine that you are asked how many years passed between the signing of the Declaration of Independence (1776, remember?) and the ratification of the Constitution. Here we have a simple example of **problem solving,** or use of the information-processing system to achieve a goal or arrive at a decision (in this case, to answer the question). Here, too, the information-processing model describes what happens between stimulus and response. The question will move through the memory system. You will need to draw on your long-term memory to understand the question, and then you will have to search long-term memory for

the two relevant dates. Moreover, you will need to locate your stored knowledge of the mathematical operation of subtraction. You will then transfer this stored information to working memory so that you can use your subtraction "program" (1789 minus 1776) to derive the correct answer.

Notice that processing information successfully requires both knowing what you are doing and making decisions. This is why the information-processing model includes **executive control processes** involved in planning and monitoring what is done. These control processes run the show, guiding the selection, organization, manipulation, and interpretation of information all the way along. Stored knowledge about the world and about information processing guides what is done with new information.

Cognitive psychologists now recognize that information processing is more complex than this model or similar models suggest (Bjorklund, 1997). For example, they now appreciate that people, like computers, engage in "parallel processing," carrying out many cognitive activities simultaneously rather than performing operations one step at a time in a sequence. They also appreciate that different processing approaches are used in different domains of knowledge. Still, the information-processing approach to cognition has the advantage of focusing attention on *how* people remember things or solve problems, not just on what they recall or what answer they give. A young child's performance on a problem could break down in any number of ways: The child might not be paying attention to the relevant aspects of the problem, might be unable to hold all the relevant pieces of information in working memory long enough to do anything with them, might lack the strategies for transferring new information into long-term memory or retrieving information from long-term memory as needed, might simply not have enough stored knowledge to understand the problem, or might not have the executive control processes needed to manage the steps in problem solving. If we can identify how information processes in the younger individual differ from those in the older person, we will have gained much insight into cognitive development.

Many processes involved in learning, memory, and problem solving improve between infancy and adulthood and then decline somewhat in old age, although this pattern is not uniform for all processes or all people. Our task in this chapter is to describe these age trends and, more interestingly, to try to determine why they occur.

THE INFANT

We have already seen that infants explore the world thoroughly through their senses and are capable of learning. But are they remembering anything of their experiences? Both the traditional learning theory and information-processing perspectives have helped us find out.

Early Memory

Assessing infant memory has required ingenuity, since infants cannot just tell us what they recall. Chapter 6 introduced a very simple and often overlooked form of learning called *habituation,* or learning *not* to respond to a stimulus that is repeated over and over. Habituation might be thought of as learning to be bored by the familiar (for example, the continual ticking of a clock) and is evidence that a stimulus is recognized as familiar. From birth, humans habituate to repeatedly presented lights, sounds, and smells; such stimuli are recognized as "old hat" (Friedman, 1972; Willemsen, 1979). In other words, newborns are capable of recognition memory. They prefer a new sight to something they have seen many times (Fagan, 1984), and they show reduced interest in a word they heard spoken repeatedly 24 hours earlier (Swain, Zelazo, & Clifton, 1993). As they get older, infants need less "study time" before a stimulus becomes old hat, and they can *retain* what they have learned for days or even weeks (Fagan, 1984; Richards, 1997).

Another method of establishing the existence of memory in early infancy, one that relies on operant-conditioning techniques, has been used extensively by Carolyn Rovee-Collier and her colleagues (Rovee-Collier, 1997; Rovee-Collier & Boller, 1995) to explore infant memory capacities. If a ribbon is run between a baby's ankle and an attractive mobile, as shown in Figure 8.5, the infant will shake a leg now and then and learn in a matter of minutes that leg kicking brings

FIGURE 8.5 *When ribbons are tied to their ankles, young infants soon learn to make a mobile move by kicking their legs. Carolyn Rovee-Collier has made use of this operant conditioning paradigm to find out how long infants will remember the trick for making the mobile move.*

about a positively reinforcing consequence: the jiggling of the mobile.

In order to test infant memory, the mobile is presented at a later time to see whether the infant will kick again. To succeed at this task, the infant must not only recognize the mobile but *recall* that the thing to do is to kick. Infants 2 months old remember how to make the mobile move for up to two days, 3-month-olds for about a week, and 6-month-olds for over two weeks (Rovee-Collier & Boller, 1995). What if stronger cues to aid recall were provided? Two to four weeks after their original learning experience, infants who are "reminded" of their previous learning by seeing the mobile move kick up a storm as soon as the ribbon is attached to their ankles, whereas infants who are not reminded show no sign of remembering to kick (Rovee-Collier & Boller, 1995). It seems, then, that *cued recall* (in this case, memory cued by the mere presence of the mobile or, better yet, its rotation by the experimenter) emerges during the first couple of months of life and that infants remember best when they are reminded of what they learned.

However, this research also suggests that young infants have difficulty recalling what they have learned if cues are insufficient. They have trouble remembering if the mobile (for example, the specific animals hanging from it) or the context in which they encountered it (for example, the design on the playpen liner) is even slightly different from the original mobile or context in which they learned. In short, early memories are very *cue-dependent* and *context-specific*.

When are infants capable of pure recall—of actively retrieving information from memory when no cues are available? A big breakthrough is made at about 8 to 12 months of age (Nelson, 1995). At about 8 to 9 months of age, infants will search for and find a hidden toy in tasks like those used to test for Piaget's concept of object permanence (Sophian, 1980). This is evidence of recall. So is deferred imitation, evident as we saw in 9-month-old infants (Meltzoff, 1988). Patricia Bauer (1996) and her colleagues have shown infants of different ages sequences of actions and then asked them to imitate what they saw—for example, putting a teddy bear in bed, covering him with a blanket, and reading him a story. Infants as young as 13 months of age appear to be capable of reconstructing a sequence of actions eight months afterward. Much like children and adults, they remember best when they have repeated exposures to what they are to remember, when they are given plenty of cues to help them remember, and when the events they must remember occur in a meaningful or logical order.

By age 2, infants have become verbal and can use words to reconstruct events that happened months earlier (Howe & Courage, 1993). Katherine Nelson (1984), for example, relates how Emily, at only 24 months of age, reconstructed a trip to the library with her grandmother that took place four months earlier: "Go library. I sat in Mormor's lap. I went to the library. Probably that's what we did. Probably we did in the *bus!*" (p. 122).

In sum, developmentalists have gone from believing that infants have no memory at all beyond a few seconds to appreciating that even 1-year-olds can recall experiences for weeks and even months under certain conditions. Infants clearly show recognition memory for familiar stimuli at birth and cued recall memory by about 2 months of age. As they get older, they can retain information longer and longer. Recall memory, which requires actively retrieving an image of an object or event that is no longer present, appears to emerge toward the end of the first year. And by age 2 it is even clearer that infants can consciously and deliberately recall events that happened long ago, for they, like us, use language to represent and describe what happened. And yet, although infants clearly store memories, the infant years are a blank for most of us. Why is this?

Infantile Amnesia

Lack of memory for the early years of life has been termed **infantile amnesia.** To determine how old we have to be at the time of significant life events in order to remember them, JoNell Usher and Ulric Neisser (1993) asked college students who had experienced (1) the birth of a younger sibling, (2) hospitalization, (3) the death of a family member, or (4) a family move early in life to answer questions about those experiences (for example, who told them their mothers were going to the hospital to give birth, what they were doing when she left, and where they were when they first saw the new baby). As Figure 8.6 shows, the proportion of memory questions students were able to answer increased dramatically as age at the time of the experience increased. Overall, children had to be at least 2 to recall the birth of a sibling or hospitalization and age 3 to recall the death of a family member or a move.

So why can't we remember our infant years? As we have seen, the problem is *not* that the infant brain is so primitive that it cannot form lasting memories (Howe & Courage, 1993; Rovee-Collier & Boller, 1995). Also, young preschool children seem to be able to

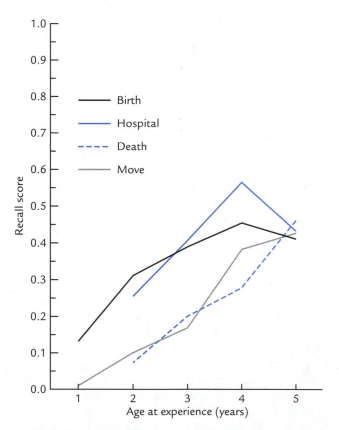

FIGURE 8.6 *College students' recall of early life events increases as a function of how old they were at the time of the event.* (From Usher & Neisser, 1993)

remember a good deal about events that occurred when they were infants, even though older children and adults cannot (Bauer, 1996; Fivush, Gray, & Fromhoff, 1987). Sigmund Freud thought infantile amnesia was a matter of blocking out or repressing from consciousness highly emotional events, but contemporary researchers favor more cognitive explanations. One suggestion is that infants may not have enough space in working memory to hold the multiple pieces of information about actor, action, and setting that are needed to encode a coherent memory of an event (White & Pillemer, 1979). Also, infants do not use language and adults do. Perhaps early memories are stored in some cryptic nonverbal code that we cannot retrieve once we are verbal adults (Bauer, 1996).

Possibly memories that are no longer useful once we reach new developmental levels and face new developmental tasks are no longer retrieved and therefore are lost (Rovee-Collier & Boller, 1995). Or maybe what is lacking is not cognitive or language abilities but a sense of self around which memories of personally experienced events can be organized, as "events that happened to *me*" (Howe & Courage, 1993). As you can see, there are plenty of ideas about the cause of infantile amnesia but still no firm explanation of why a period of life that is highly important to later development is a blank for most of us (Perlmutter, 1986).

THE CHILD

The 2-year-old is already a highly capable information processor, as evidenced by the rapid language learning that takes place at this age. But dramatic improvements in learning, memory, and problem solving occur throughout the childhood years, as children learn everything from how to flush toilets to how to work advanced math problems.

Learning and Memory

In countless learning situations, older children learn faster and remember more than younger children do (Kail, 1990). For example, 2-year-olds can repeat back about two digits immediately after hearing them, 10-year-olds about six digits. But *why?* Here are four major hypotheses about why learning and memory improve, patterned after those formulated by John Flavell and Henry Wellman (1977):

1. *Changes in basic capacities.* Older children have higher-powered "hardware" than young children do; their brains have more working memory space for manipulating information and can process information faster.

2. *Changes in memory strategies.* Older children have better "software"; they have learned and consistently use effective methods for getting information into long-term memory and retrieving it when they need it.

3. *Increased knowledge about memory.* Older children know more about memory (for example, how long they must study to learn things thoroughly, which kinds of memory tasks take more effort, which strategies best fit each task, and so on).

4. *Increased knowledge about the world.* Older children know more about the world in general than young children. This knowledge, or expertise, makes material to be learned more familiar, and familiar material is easier to learn and remember than unfamiliar material.

Do Basic Capacities Change?

Since the nervous system continues to develop in the early years of life, it seems plausible that older children remember more than younger children do because they have a better "computer"—a larger or more efficient information-processing system. However, we can quickly rule out the idea that the storage capacity of long-term memory enlarges. There is no consistent evidence that it changes after the first month of life (Perlmutter, 1986). In fact, both young and old alike have more room for storage than they could ever possibly use. Nor does the capacity of the sensory register to take in stimuli seem to change much (Bjorklund, 1995; House, 1982). It does seem, however, that the speed of mental processes improves with age and that this allows older children and adults to perform more mental operations at once in working memory than young children can (Kail & Salthouse, 1994).

This idea has been featured in revisions of Piaget's theory of cognitive development proposed by neo-Piagetian theorists such as Robbie Case (1985, Marini & Case, 1994). He seeks to build on Piaget's insights into cognitive development but has also been strongly influenced by the information-processing approach. He proposes that more advanced stages of cognitive development are made possible by increases in the capacity of working memory. For example, Piaget stressed the preschooler's tendency to *center* on one aspect of a problem and lose sight of another (for example, to attend to the height of a glass but ignore its width, or vice versa). Perhaps, say the neo-Piagetians, this is not a matter of lacking certain cognitive structures; perhaps young children simply do not have enough working memory capacity to keep both pieces of information in mind at once and coordinate them. Similarly, young children may do poorly on memory tasks because they cannot keep the first items on a list in mind while processing newer ones. And they may fail to solve mathematical problems correctly because they cannot keep the facts of the problem in mind while they are performing calculations.

The *total* capacity of short-term memory for passively storing information does not seem to change with age (Dempster, 1985), but older children *are* able to manipulate more information at once in working memory (Case, 1985; Kail, 1990). Partly, this is because they have become faster and more efficient at executing basic mental processes, such as identifying numbers or words to be learned (Kail, 1991); these processes become *automatized* so that they can be done with little mental effort. This, in turn, frees space in working memory for other purposes, such as storing the information needed to solve a problem.

Improvements with age in operating speed and working memory efficiency could be due to maturational changes in the brain or could reflect the older child's greater familiarity with numbers, letters, and other stimuli (Bjorklund, 1995). There is general agreement, though, that older children can process more information in working memory and process it faster than younger children can, and this is one reason why memory improves over childhood.

Do Memory Strategies Change?

A good sign of the memory limitations of young children is the fact that their recognition memory is way ahead of their recall memory. If 4-year-olds were shown the 12 items in Figure 8.7, they would *recognize* nearly all of them if asked to select the objects they had seen from a larger set of pictures (Brown, 1975). But if asked to *recall* the objects, they might remember only 2 to 4 of them—a far cry from the 7 to 9 items that an 8-year-old would recall or the 10 to 11 an adult would recall several minutes later. What specific strategies evolve during childhood to permit this dramatic improvement in performance?

Children as young as 2 can deliberately remember to do "important" things, such as reminding Mom to buy candy at the grocery store (Somerville, Wellman, & Cultice, 1983). They are more likely to use external memory aids (for example, pointing at or holding a toy pig when asked to remember where it is hidden) if they are instructed to remember than if they are not (Fletcher & Bray, 1996). Yet preschoolers have not mastered many effective strategies for moving information into long-term memory. For example, when instructed to remember toys they have been shown, 3- and 4-year-olds will look very carefully at the objects and will often label them once, but only rarely do they use the memory strategy called **rehearsal,** the repeating of items one is trying to learn and remember (Baker-Ward, Ornstein, & Holden, 1984). To rehearse the objects in Figure 8.7, you might simply say over and over "Apple, truck, grapes, ..." John Flavell and

FIGURE 8.7 *A memory task. Imagine that you have 120 seconds to learn the 12 objects pictured here. What tricks or strategies might you devise to make your task easier?*

his associates (Flavell, Beach, & Chinsky, 1966) found that, whereas only 10% of 5-year-olds repeated the names of pictures they were asked to recall, more than half of 7-year-olds and 85% of 10-year-olds used this strategy.

Another important memory strategy is **organization,** or classifying items into meaningful groups. You might lump the apple, the grapes, and the hamburger in Figure 8.7 into a category of "foods" and form other categories for "animals," "vehicles," and "baseball equipment." You would then rehearse each category and recall it as a cluster. Another organizational strategy, *chunking,* is used when we break a long number (6065551843) into manageable subunits (606-555-1843, a phone number). Organization is mastered a bit later in childhood than rehearsal. Until about age 9 or 10, children are not much better at recalling lists of items that lend themselves readily to grouping than they are at recalling lists of unrelated words (Flavell & Wellman, 1977).

Finally, the strategy of **elaboration** involves actively creating meaningful links between items to be remembered. Elaboration is achieved by adding something to the items, in the form of either words or images. Creating and utilizing a sentence like "The apple fell on the horse's nose" would help you remember two of the items in Figure 8.7. Elaboration is especially helpful in learning foreign languages. For example, one might link the Spanish word *pato* (pronounced pot-o) to the English word *duck* by imagining a duck in a pot of boiling water. This is the most mentally taxing of the three memory strategies; perhaps for that reason, it is rarely used spontaneously before adolescence (Pressley, 1982).

Using effective memory strategies to learn material is only half the battle. *Retrieval strategies* can also influence how much is ultimately recalled, even when effective memory strategies were used to learn the material initially. Indeed, retrieving something from memory can often be a complex adventure in problem solving, as when you try to remember when you went on a trip by searching for cues that might trigger your memory ("Well, I still had long hair then, but it was after Muffy's wedding, and . . ."). Strange as it may seem, even when young schoolchildren are shown how to use the memory strategy of elaboration, they still may do less well than older children on memory tests because it does not occur to them to *use* the images they worked so hard to create to help them retrieve what they learned (Pressley & Levin, 1980).

Does Knowledge about Memory Change?

The term **metamemory** refers to knowledge of memory and memory processes. It is knowing, for example, what one's memory limits are, which memory strategies are more or less effective, and which memory tasks are more or less difficult (Flavell, Miller, & Miller, 1993). Metamemory is one aspect of **metacognition,** or knowledge of the human mind and of the whole range of cognitive processes. Your store of metacognitive knowledge might include an understanding that you are better at language learning than at algebra, that it is harder to pay attention to a task when there is distracting noise in the background than when it is quiet, and that it is wise to check out a proposed solution to a problem before concluding that it is correct.

When do children first show evidence of metamemory? If instructed to remember where the *Sesame Street* character Big Bird has been hidden so that they can later wake him up, even 2- and 3-year-olds will go stand near the hiding spot, or at least look or point at that spot; they do not do these things as often if Big Bird is visible and they don't need to remember where he is (DeLoache, Cassidy, & Brown, 1985). By age 2, then, children have acquired at least one simple bit of knowledge about memory: To remember something, you have to work at it!

Children learn a good deal more about memory during their preschool years, but they also have much left to learn (O'Sullivan, 1997; Wellman, 1977). In one study (Yussen & Levy, 1975), preschoolers, third-graders, and adults were asked to estimate whether they would be able to recall sets of pictures of varying sizes. Preschoolers' estimates were highly unrealistic—as if they believed they could perform any memory feat imaginable—and they were unfazed by information about how another child had done on the task. Only by age 7 or so do most children realize that related items or those that can be organized into categories are easier to recall than unrelated items (Kreutzer, Leonard, & Flavell, 1975). And, although 7- and 9-year-olds realize that rehearsing and catego-

rizing are more effective strategies than merely looking at items or naming them, only 11-year-olds know that organization is more effective than rehearsal (Justice, 1985).

Are increases in metamemory a major contributor to improved memory performance over the childhood years? The evidence is mixed. Metamemory and memory performance are positively correlated, but often quite weakly (Bjorklund, 1995). Good metamemory apparently is not required for good recall (Bjorklund & Zeman, 1982). Moreover, children who know what to do may not always do it, so good metamemory is no guarantee of good recall (Salatas & Flavell, 1976). It seems that children must not only know that a strategy is useful but *why* it is useful in order to be motivated to use it and to actually benefit from its use (Justice et al., 1997). Overall, there are at least some links between metamemory and memory performance—enough to suggest the merits of teaching children more about how memory works and how they can make it work more effectively for them.

Does Knowledge of the World Change?

Ten-year-olds obviously know considerably more about the world in general than 2-year-olds do. The individual's knowledge of a content area to be learned, or **knowledge base,** as it has come to be called, clearly affects learning and memory performance. Think about the difference between reading about a topic that you already know well and reading about a new topic. In the first case, you can read quite quickly because you are able to link the information to the knowledge you have already stored. All you really need to do is check for any new information or information that contradicts what you already know. Learning about a highly unfamiliar topic is more difficult ("It's Greek to me").

Perhaps the most dramatic illustration of the powerful influence of knowledge base on memory was provided by Michelene Chi (1978). She demonstrated that even though adults typically outperform children on tests of memory, this age difference could be reversed if children have more expertise than adults. Chi recruited children who were expert chess players and compared their memory skills to those of adults who were familiar with the game but lacked expertise. On a test of memory for sequences of digits, the children recalled fewer than the adults did, demonstrating their usual "deficiencies." But on a test of memory for the locations of *chess pieces,* the children clearly beat the adults (Figure 8.8). Because they were experts, these children were able to form more and larger meaningful mental "chunks" or groups of chess pieces, and that was what allowed them to remember more.

Pause to consider the implications: On most tasks, young children are the novices and older children or adults are the experts. Perhaps older children

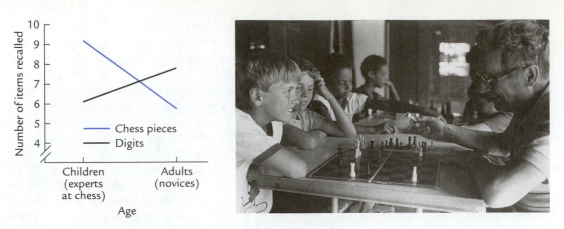

FIGURE 8.8 *Effects of expertise on memory. Michelene Chi found that child chess experts outperformed adult chess novices on a test of recall for the location of chess pieces (though, in keeping with the usual developmental trend, these children could not recall strings of numbers as well as adults could).* (Adapted from Chi in Siegler, 1978)

and adults recall longer strings of digits because they are more familiar with numbers than young children are, not because they have better basic learning capacities. Perhaps they recall more words in word lists simply because they have more familiarity with language. Perhaps memory improves over childhood simply because older children know more about all kinds of things than younger children do (Bjorklund, 1995).

In their areas of expertise, whether the topic is math or dinosaurs or soccer, children appear to develop highly specialized and effective strategies of information processing, just as the young chess players studied by Chi apparently had (Chi, Hutchinson, & Robin, 1989). Indeed, children with low general intellectual ability but high expertise sometimes understand and remember more about stories in their area of expertise than children with higher intellectual ability but less expertise (Schneider, Bjorklund, & Maier-Bruckner, 1996). It seems that the more one knows, the more one *can* know. It also seems that how well a child does on a memory task depends not only on age but also on familiarity with the specific task at hand.

A Summing Up

We can now draw four conclusions about the development of learning and memory:

1. Older children have a greater information-processing *capacity* than younger children do, particularly in the sense that they are faster information processors and can juggle more information in working memory.
2. Older children use more effective *memory strategies* in encoding and retrieving information.
3. Older children know more about memory, and, although evidence of the importance of *meta-memory* is mixed, good metamemory may help children to choose more appropriate strategies

and to control and monitor their learning more effectively.
4. Older children know more in general, and their larger *knowledge base* improves their ability to learn and remember.

Can we choose a best hypothesis? Probably not at this point. All these phenomena may contribute something to the dramatic improvements in learning and memory that occur over the childhood years. They may also interact. For example, the automatization of certain information processes may leave the child with enough working memory space to use effective memory strategies that were just too mentally demanding earlier in childhood (Bjorklund, 1995). Or, increased knowledge may permit faster information processing. We will return to these same four hypotheses when we consider changes in learning and memory in adulthood.

Problem Solving

To solve any problem, one must process information about the task, as well as use stored information, to achieve a goal. How do problem-solving capacities change during childhood? Piaget provided one answer to this question by proposing that children progress through broad stages of cognitive growth, but information-processing theorists were not satisfied with this explanation. They sought to pinpoint more specific reasons why problem-solving prowess improves so dramatically as children get older.

Consider the problem of predicting what will happen to the balance beam in Figure 8.9 when weights are put on each side of the fulcrum, or balancing point. The goal is to decide which way the balance beam will tip when it is released. To judge correctly, one must take into account both the number of

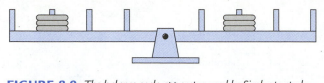

FIGURE 8.9 *The balance-scale apparatus used by Siegler to study children's problem-solving abilities*

weights and their distances from the fulcrum. Piaget believed that concrete-operational thinkers can appreciate the significance of either the amount of weight or its distance from the center but will not grasp the inverse relationship between the two factors until they reach the stage of formal operations. Then new cognitive structures allow them to understand that balance can be maintained by decreasing a weight but moving it farther away from the fulcrum or by increasing a weight but moving it closer to the fulcrum (Piaget & Inhelder, 1966/1969).

Robert Siegler (1981) proposed that the information-processing perspective could provide a fuller analysis. His **"rule assessment" approach,** determines what information about a problem children take in and what rules they then formulate to account for this information. This approach assumes that children's problem-solving attempts are rule governed rather than hit-or-miss, and that children fail to solve problems because they fail to encode all the critical aspects of the problem and are guided by faulty rules.

Siegler (1981) administered balance beam problems to individuals aged 3 to 20. He detected clear age differences in the extent to which both weight and distance from the fulcrum were taken into account in the rules that guided decisions about which end of the balance beam would drop. Few 3-year-olds used any kind of rule; they guessed. By contrast, 4- and 5-year-olds were rule governed; more than 80% of them used a rule that said that the side of the balance beam with more weight would drop; they totally ignored distance from the fulcrum. By age 8, most children had begun to consider distance from the fulcrum as well as weight; at least when the weights were equal, they appreciated that the side of the balance beam with the weights farthest from the fulcrum would drop. By age 12, the vast majority of children considered both weight and distance on a range of problems, although they still became confused on complex problems in which one side had more weights but the other had its weights farther from the fulcrum. Finally, 30% of 20-year-olds had discovered the correct rule: the pull on each arm is a function of weight times distance. For example, if there are three weights on the second peg to the left and two weights on the fourth peg to the right, the left torque is $3 \times 2 = 6$ and the right torque is $2 \times 4 = 8$, so the right arm will go down.

In most important areas of problem solving, Siegler (1996) has now concluded, children do not progress from just one way of thinking to another way of thinking as they get older, as his balance beam research suggested. Instead, in working problems in arithmetic, spelling, science, and other school subjects, most children in any age group use *multiple* rules or problem-solving strategies rather than just one. In working subtraction problems like $12 - 3 = 9$, for example, children sometimes count down from 12 until they have counted off 3 and arrive at 9, but other times count up from 3 until they reach 12. In one study of second and fourth graders (Siegler, 1989), over 90% of the children used three or more different strategies in working subtraction problems.

Siegler now believes that cognitive development works much as evolution does, through a process of *natural selection* in which many ways of thinking are available and the most adaptive survive. Rather than picturing development as a series of stages resembling stairsteps, he argues, we should picture it as overlapping waves, as shown in Figure 8.10. At each age, children have multiple problem-solving strategies available to them; it's not "one child, one rule." As children get older, they use less adaptive strategies less, and more adaptive strategies more, and now and then, whole new strategies may appear. Cognitive change goes on all the time, not just during transitions between stages, as Piaget believed.

Imagine how effective teachers might be if they, like Siegler, could accurately diagnose the information-processing strategies of their learners to know exactly what each child is noticing (or failing to notice) about a problem and exactly what rules or strategies each child is using when. Like a good car mechanic, the teacher would be able to pinpoint the problem and replace faulty strategies and rules with more adaptive

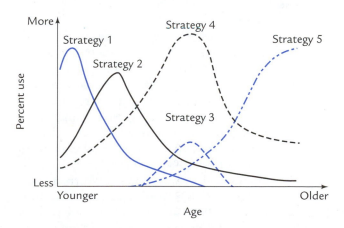

FIGURE 8.10 *Cognitive development may resemble overlapping waves more than a staircase leading from one stage to another. Children of a particular age typically use multiple thinking strategies rather than just one.* (From Siegler, 1996)

ones. Much remains to be learned about how and why problem-solving strategies evolve as children get older. However, the rule assessment approach gives us a fairly specific idea of what children are doing (or doing wrong) as they attack problems and illustrates how the information-processing approach to cognitive development provides a different view of development than Piaget's account does.

THE ADOLESCENT

Although parents who are in the midst of reminding their adolescent sons and daughters to do household chores may wonder whether teenagers process any information at all, learning, memory, and problem solving continue to improve considerably during the adolescent years. How exactly?

First, new learning and memory strategies emerge. It is during adolescence that the memory strategy of elaboration is mastered (Pressley, 1982). Adolescents also develop and refine advanced learning and memory strategies that are highly relevant to school learning—for example, note taking and underlining skills. Ann Brown and Sandra Smiley (1978) asked students from the fifth-grade (age 11) to twelfth-grade to read and recall a story. Some learners were asked to recall the story immediately; others were given an additional five minutes to study it before they were tested. Amazingly, fifth-graders gained almost nothing from the extra study period, except for those few who used the time to underline or take notes. Junior high school students benefited to an extent, but only in senior high school did most students use underlining and note taking effectively to improve their recall. When some groups of students were told that they could underline or take notes if they wished, fifth-graders still did not improve, largely because they tended to underline everything rather than highlighting the most important points.

Second, adolescents make more deliberate use of strategies that younger children use more or less unconsciously (Bjorklund, 1985). For example, they may deliberately organize a list of words instead of simply using any natural organization or grouping that happens to be there already. And they use existing strategies more selectively. For example, they are adept at using their strategies to memorize the material on which they know they will be tested and at deliberately forgetting anything else (Bray, Hersh, & Turner, 1985; Lorsbach & Reimer, 1997). To illustrate, Patricia Miller and Michael Weiss (1981) asked children to remember the locations of animals that had been hidden behind small doors, ignoring the household objects hidden behind other doors. As Figure 8.11 shows, 13-year-olds recalled more than 7- and 10-year-olds about where the animals had been hidden, but they remembered *less*

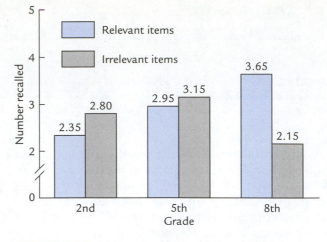

FIGURE 8.11 *Adolescents are better able than children to concentrate on learning relevant material and to ignore irrelevant material.* (From Miller & Weiss, 1981)

about task-irrelevant information (the locations of the household objects). Apparently, they are better able to push irrelevant information out of working memory so that it does not interfere with task performance (Lorsbach & Reimer, 1997). So, during elementary school, children get better at distinguishing between what is relevant and what is irrelevant, but during adolescence they advance even farther by selectively using their memory strategies only on the relevant material. If it's not going to be on the test, forget it!

Other strides are made in adolescence besides these changes in *memory strategies. Basic capacities* continue to increase; for example, adolescents perform any number of cognitive operations more speedily than children do (Kail, 1991). Of course, adolescents also continue to expand their *knowledge base,* so they may do better than children on some tasks simply because they know more about the topic. *Metamemory* and *metacognition* also improve. For example, adolescents become better able to tailor their reading strategies to different purposes (studying versus skimming) and better able to realize when they don't understand something (Baker & Brown, 1984). Growth in strategies, basic capacities, knowledge base, and metacognition probably also helps explain the growth in everyday problem-solving ability that occurs during the adolescent years (Berg, 1989). Teenagers perfect a number of information-processing skills and become able to apply them *deliberately and spontaneously* across a wide variety of tasks (Brown et al., 1983).

THE ADULT

If you are about age 20, you will be pleased to know that the young adult college student has served as the standard of effective information processing against which all other age groups are compared. Although information processes are thought to be most efficient in young adults, improvements in cognitive performance do occur during the adult years before aging begins to take its toll on some memory and problem-solving capacities.

Developing Expertise

Comparisons of people who are new to their chosen fields of study with those who are more experienced tell us that experience pays off in more effective memory and problem solving. In Chapter 7, we saw that people in Piaget's highest stage of cognitive development, formal operations, often perform better in their areas of specialization than in unfamiliar areas. Similarly, information-processing research tells us that adults often function best cognitively in domains in which they have achieved expertise (Byrnes, 1996; Ericsson, 1996; Glaser & Chi, 1988). It seems to take about ten years of training and experience to become a true expert in a field and to build a rich and well-organized knowledge base (Ericsson, 1996). But once this is achieved, one not only knows and remembers more but thinks more effectively than individuals who lack expertise.

Consider first the effects of knowledge base on memory. How might adults who are baseball experts and adults who care little for baseball perceive and remember the same game? George Spilich and his associates (1979) had baseball experts and novices listen to a tape of a half inning of play. Experts recalled more of the information that was central to the game—the important plays and the fate of each batter, in proper order—whereas novices were caught up by less central facts such as the threatening weather conditions and the number of people attending the game. Experts also recalled more details—for example, noting that a double was a line drive down the left-field line rather than just a double. At any age, experts in a field are likely to remember new information in that content domain more fully than novices do (Morrow et al., 1994).

In addition, experts are able to use their elaborately organized and rich knowledge bases to solve problems effectively and efficiently. They are able to size up a situation quickly, see what the problem really is, and recognize how the new problem is similar to and different from problems encountered in the past (Glaser & Chi, 1988). They can quickly, surely, and almost automatically call up just the right information from their extensive knowledge base to devise effective solutions to problems and carry them out efficiently.

Are the benefits of expertise content-specific, or does gaining expertise in one domain carry over into other domains and make one a more generally effec-

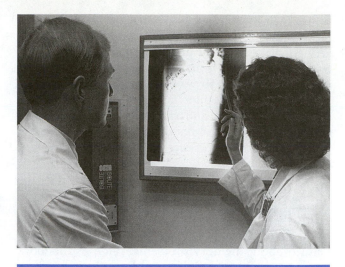

Adults who have gained proficiency in their chosen fields can draw from their well-organized knowledge bases to find just the right information to fit the problem at hand. Solving problems is automatic and effortless for experts.

tive learner or problem solver? This is an interesting and important question. One research team (Ericsson, Chase, & Faloon, 1980) put an average college student to work at improving the number of digits he could recall. He practiced for about an hour a day, three to five days a week, for more than a year and a half—over 200 hours in all. His improvement? He went from a memory span of 7 digits to one of 79 digits! His method involved forming meaningful associations between strings of digits and running times—for example, seeing 3492 as "3 minutes and 49 point 2 seconds, near world-record mile time" (p. 1181). It also involved chunking numbers into groups of three or four and then organizing the chunks into large units.

Did all this work pay off in a better memory for information other than numbers? Not really. When he was given letters of the alphabet to recall, this young man's memory span was unexceptional (about six letters). Clearly the memory ability he developed was based on strategies of use only in the subject matter he was trying to remember. Similarly, Rajan Mahadevan, a man with an exceptional memory for arrays of numbers, turns out to possess no special ability at all for remembering the positions and orientations of objects (Biederman et al., 1992), and Shakuntala Devi, a woman who can solve complex mathematical problems in her head at amazing speeds, is apparently no faster than average at performing other cognitive operations (Jensen, 1990). Each of these experts apparently relies on *domain-specific* knowledge and *domain-specific* information-processing strategies to achieve their cognitive feats (Ericsson & Kintsch, 1995).

In sum, experts know more than novices do, their knowledge base is more organized, and they are able to use their knowledge and specialized strategies they have devised to learn, remember, and solve problems very efficiently in their areas of expertise—but not in other domains. In effect, experts do not need to think much; they are like experienced drivers who can put themselves on "autopilot" and carry out well-learned routines very quickly and accurately. By gaining expertise over the years, adults can often compensate for losses in information-processing capacities, which is our next topic.

Learning, Memory, and Aging

No less an expert on learning than B. F. Skinner complained about memory problems: "One of the more disheartening experiences of old age is discovering that a point you have just made—so significant, so beautifully expressed—was made by you in something you published a long time ago" (Skinner, 1983, p. 242). In fact, most elderly adults report that they have at least minor difficulties remembering things (Smith et al., 1996). They are especially likely to have trouble remembering names, routines like filling the car with gas, and items they will need later, and they are also more upset than young adults by memory lapses, perhaps because they view them as signs of aging (Cavanaugh, Grady, & Perlmutter, 1983).

Areas of Strength and Weakness

Much research indicates that, on average, older adults learn new material more slowly and sometimes learn it less well than young and middle-aged adults do and that they remember what they have learned less well. However, the following qualifications are important:

◆ Most of the research is based on cross-sectional studies comparing age groups, which suggests that the age differences detected could be related to factors other than age.
◆ Declines, when observed, typically do not become noticeable until the late 60s and the 70s.
◆ Difficulties in remembering affect elderly people more noticeably as they continue to age and are most severe among the oldest-old.
◆ Not all older people experience these difficulties.
◆ Not all kinds of memory tasks cause older people difficulty.

Studies of memory skills in adulthood suggest that the aspects of learning and memory in which older adults look most deficient in comparison with young and middle-aged adults are some of the same areas in which young children compare unfavorably to older children (for reviews, see Guttentag, 1985; Smith & Earles, 1996). Here are some of the major

weaknesses—and, by implication, strengths—of the older adult:

Timed Tasks. On the average, older adults are slower than younger adults to learn and retrieve information; they may need to go through the material more times to learn it equally well and may need more time to respond when their memory is tested. Thus they are hurt by time limits (Botwinick, 1984).

Unfamiliar Tasks. Older adults fare especially poorly compared to younger adults when the material to be learned is unfamiliar or meaningless—when they cannot tie it to their existing knowledge. In a convincing demonstration of how familiarity influences memory, Barrett and Wright (1981) had young and elderly adults examine modern words likely to be more familiar to young adults (for example, *dude, disco,* and *bummer*) and words from the past likely to be more familiar to older adults (for example, *pompadour, gramophone,* and *vamp*). Sure enough, young adults outperformed older adults on the "new" words, but older adults outperformed young adults on the "old" words. Many laboratory tasks involve learning material that is unfamiliar and thus do not allow older adults to make use of their knowledge base.

Unexercised Skills. Older adults are also likely to be at a disadvantage when they are required to use learning and memory skills that they rarely use in daily life. They hold their own when they can rely on well-practiced skills that have become effortless and automatic with practice. For example, Lynne Reder, Cynthia Wible, and John Martin (1986) found that elderly adults were just as good as young adults at judging whether sentences presented to them were plausible based on a story they had read. Judging whether something makes sense in the context of what one has read is a well-exercised ability. However, older adults were deficient when it came to judging whether specific sentences had or had not appeared in the story—a skill that is seldom used outside school. It seems that older adults read to get the gist or significance of a story and do not bother with the details, a strategy that may be very adaptive if they have no need to memorize details and if their ability to do so has fallen off with age (Adams, 1991; Stine-Morrow, Loveless, & Soederberg, 1996). In other ways as well, age differences are smaller when well-practiced skills are assessed than when less-practiced skills are assessed (Denney, 1982).

Recall versus Recognition. Older adults are likely to be more deficient on tasks requiring recall memory than on tasks requiring only recognition of what was learned. In one study of memory for high school classmates (Bahrick, Bahrick, & Wittlinger, 1975), even adults who were almost 35 years past graduation could still recognize which of five names matched a picture in their yearbook about 90% of the time. However, the ability to actively recall names of classmates when given only their photos as cues dropped considerably as the age of the remember increased. A large gap between recognition and recall tells us that older people have encoded and stored the information but cannot retrieve it without the help of cues. Sometimes older adults fail to retrieve information because they never thoroughly encoded or learned it in the first place, but at other times they simply cannot retrieve information that is "in there."

Deliberate, Effortful Memory Tasks. Finally, older adults seem to have more trouble with tasks that require mental effort than with tasks that involve more automatic mental processes. Memory researchers have concluded that humans have distinct memory systems that operate by different rules. They now distinguish between **implicit memory,** which occurs unintentionally, automatically, and without awareness, and **explicit memory,** which involves deliberate, more effortful recollection of events (Howard, 1996; Roediger, 1990; Schacter, 1996). Explicit memory is tested through traditional recognition and recall tests. When implicit memory is tested, learners do not even know that their memory is being assessed. For example, individuals might be exposed to a list of words (orange, tablet, forest, and so on) to be rated for likability, not memorized. In a second task, they are given word stems such as TAB____ and asked to complete them with the first word that comes to mind. People who are exposed to the word *tablet* in the initial task are more likely than people who are not to come up with the word *tablet* rather than *table* or *tabby* to complete the word stem, demonstrating that they learned something from their earlier exposure to the words, even though they were not trying to learn. Adults with amnesia do poorly on tests of explicit memory in which they study words and then are asked to finish word stems like TAB____ with a word they studied earlier. Amazingly, though, if they are merely exposed to a list of words and then given an implicit memory test that asks them to write the first word that comes to mind, they do fine (Graf, Squire, & Mandler, 1984)! Many forms of amnesia destroy explicit memory but leave implicit memory intact (Schacter, 1996).

Some scholars believe that implicit memory develops earlier in infancy than explicit memory (Nelson, 1995; Schacter, 1996). Others believe that both forms of memory are evident very early in infancy (Rovee-Collier, 1997). All agree, though, that the two types of memory follow very different developmental paths. As we have seen, explicit memory increases from infancy to adulthood and then declines in later adulthood. By contrast, implicit memory capacity does not change much at all; young children often do no worse than older children, and elderly adults often do no worse than younger adults on tests of implicit memory (Graf, 1990; Howard, 1996; Russo et al., 1995). Research on implicit memory tells us that young and old alike learn and retain a tremendous amount of information from their everyday experiences without any effort at all.

Overall, these findings suggest that older adults, like young children, have difficulty with tasks that are *cognitively demanding*—that require speed, the learning of unfamiliar material, the use of unexercised abilities, recall rather than recognition, or explicit and effortful rather than implicit or automatic memory. Yet older adults and young children have difficulty for different reasons, as we will now see.

Explaining Declines in Old Age

In asking *why* some older adults struggle with some learning and memory tasks, we can first return to the same hypotheses we used to explain childhood improvements in performance and consider basic processing capacities, strategy use, metamemory, and knowledge base. Then we will consider some additional possibilities.

Knowledge Base. Let's start with the hypothesis that differences in *knowledge base* explain differences between older and younger adults. We immediately encounter a problem: Young children may be ignorant, but elderly adults are not. Older adults are generally at least as knowledgeable as young adults (Camp, 1989; Hess & Pullen, 1996). They often equal or surpass younger adults on measures of vocabulary and knowledge of word meanings (Light, 1991; West, Crook, & Barron, 1992). Moreover, they know a lot about the world. For example, they are as adept as younger adults at answering questions about major events of past decades (Hess & Pullen, 1996; Poon et al., 1979). They also still know a surprising amount of information they learned in high school Spanish, algebra, and geometry courses taken as many as 50 years earlier (Bahrick, 1984; Bahrick & Hall, 1991). So, deficiencies in knowledge base are probably not the source of most of the memory problems that older adults display. On the contrary, gains in knowledge probably help older adults compensate for losses in information-processing efficiency (Salthouse, 1993). Thus, older pilots are as adept as younger pilots and better than nonpilots at repeating back flight commands, but they show the usual effects of aging if they are given tasks less relevant to their work (Morrow et al., 1994). As Paul Baltes has put it, "Knowledge is power!" (Baltes, Smith, & Staudinger, 1992, p. 143).

Many adults continue to expand their knowledge bases well into old age.

Metamemory. Could elderly adults, like young children, be deficient in the specific knowledge called metamemory? Is their knowledge of some of the strategies that prove useful in school learning—and in laboratory memory tasks—a bit rusty? This theory sounds plausible, but research shows that older adults seem to know as much as younger adults about such things as which memory strategies are best and which memory tasks are hardest (Light, 1991).

Yet there's a difference between knowing about memory and believing that you can remember things. Older adults *do* express more negative beliefs about their memory skills than younger adults do (Cavanaugh, 1996). Although actual memory loss may contribute to a drop in confidence in one's memory skills, negative beliefs about one's memory skills also appear to hurt memory performance (Cavanaugh, 1996; McDonald-Miszczak, Hertzog, & Hultsch, 1995).

Becca Levy and Ellen Langer (1994) suggest that part of the problem lies in our society's negative stereotypes of aging—specifically the stereotype of old people as forgetful. These researchers tested the memory of young and elderly adults (ages 59–91) in three groups: hearing Americans, deaf Americans, and hearing Chinese. In both the American deaf and Chinese cultures, elders are respected and negative stereotypes of intellectual aging are not as prevalent as they are among hearing Americans. As Figure 8.12 shows, young adults in the three groups performed equally well on a set of recall tasks, but Chinese elders outperformed deaf American elders (who were second best) and hearing American elders. In fact, elderly Chinese adults actually scored only a little lower than young Chinese adults, despite having less education. In addi-

tion, those older people in the study who believed that aging brings about memory loss performed more poorly than those who did not. Levy (1996) has also shown that activating negative stereotypes in the minds of elderly adults (through rapid, subliminal presentation of words like "Alzheimer's" and "senile" on a computer screen) causes them to perform worse on memory tests and express less confidence in their memory skills than when positive stereotypes of old age are planted in their minds (through words like "wise" and "sage"). Findings like these clearly call into question the idea of a universal decline in memory skills in later life and point to the influence of culture and its views of aging on performance.

Memory Strategies. What about the hypothesis that failure to use effective *memory strategies* accounts for deficits in old age? Many older adults do not spontaneously use strategies such as organization and elaboration, even though they know them and are capable of using them (Light, 1991; Smith & Earles, 1996). This may indeed be an important part of the problem when older adults are asked to deliberately memorize something. But *why* do many older adults fail to use effective strategies?

Basic Processing Capacities. The answer may lie in our fourth hypothesis—the notion that *basic processing capacities* change with age. Which capacities? Much attention has focused on declines in the capacity to use working memory to actively operate on a lot of information simultaneously. Working-memory capacity declines during adulthood, after having increased during childhood and adolescence. Moreover, an adult's

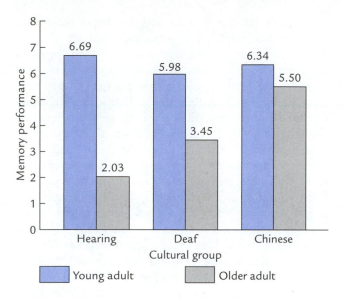

FIGURE 8.12 *Declines in memory skills in old age are not universal. In deaf culture and in Chinese culture, elderly people are not stereotyped as forgetful and senile. Perhaps as a result, Chinese elders perform almost as well as young Chinese adults on memory tasks, whereas in the United States, elders, especially in the hearing population, perform poorly.* (Adapted from Levy & Langer, 1994)

working-memory capacity predicts how well she or he will perform on a wide range of cognitive tasks (Salthouse, 1992).

Both young children and older adults, it seems, need to devote more space in working memory than older children or young adults do to carrying out basic mental operations such as recognizing stimuli (Guttentag, 1985; Kail & Salthouse, 1994). This leaves less space for other purposes, such as thinking about or rehearsing material. We have seen that both younger children and older adults do relatively well when learning and remembering can take place automatically—when mental effort is *not* required—but struggle when they must exert a great deal of mental effort or carry out several mental operations at once.

Limitations in working-memory capacity are most likely rooted in slow functioning of the nervous system both early and late in life (Kail & Salthouse, 1994; and see Chapter 5). Much research tells us that speed of processing increases during childhood and adolescence, peaks in early adulthood, and then declines slowly over the adult years (Kail & Salthouse, 1994). Much research also tells us that age differences in performance on cognitive tasks often shrink in size when age differences in speed of information processing are taken into account and controlled. Experience in a domain of learning can certainly enhance performance, but if children and older adults generally have a sluggish "computer," they simply may not be able to keep up with the processing demands of complex learning

and memory tasks (Kail & Salthouse, 1994). Slow neural transmission, then, may be behind limitations in working memory in childhood and old age, and limitations in working memory may in turn contribute not only to limitations in long-term memory but also to difficulties performing a wide range of cognitive tasks, including problem-solving tasks and tests of intelligence, even those that have no time limits (Fry & Hale, 1996; Kail & Salthouse, 1994).

To this point, then, we might conclude that many older adults, although they have a vast knowledge base and a good deal of knowledge about learning and memory, experience declines in basic processing capacities (and concerns about them) that make it difficult for them to carry out memory strategies that will drain their limited working-memory capacity. But the basic-processing-capacity hypothesis cannot explain everything about age differences in memory (Light, 1991). We must consider some additional hypotheses—ones suggesting that age differences in learning and memory are not so much the result of biological decline as of a variety of contextual factors.

Contextual Contributors. Impressed by the influence of such factors as cohort differences, motivation, and task characteristics on the performance of elderly adults, many researchers are adopting a *contextual perspective* on learning and memory (Dixon, 1992). They emphasize that performance on learning and memory tasks is the product of an interaction among (1) characteristics of the learner, such as goals, motivations, and abilities; (2) characteristics of the particular task at hand; and (3) characteristics of the broader context, including the cultural context, in which a task is performed. They are not convinced that there is a universal biological decline in basic learning and memory capacities, for older individuals often perform very capably in certain contexts.

First, *cohort differences in education, health, and lifestyle* can explain some of the deficits in some learning and memory skills in old age. Elderly people today are less educated, on average, than younger adults are, and they are further removed from their school days. In some cultures, *only* those individuals who have had formal schooling use memory strategies such as verbal rehearsal (Kuhn, 1992; Wagner, 1978). Moreover, education can compensate for aging. Older adults who are highly educated or who have strong verbal skills sometimes perform just as well as younger adults do (Cavanaugh, 1983; West et al., 1992).

Similarly, older adults are more likely than younger adults to have chronic or degenerative diseases, and even mild diseases can impair memory performance (Houx, Vreeling, & Jolles, 1991; Hultsch et al., 1993). Older adults also lead less active lifestyles and perform fewer cognitively demanding activities than younger adults do on average. These age-group differences in lifestyle also contribute to age differences in cognitive performance (Luszcz, Bryan, & Kent, 1997). Older college professors, perhaps because they remain mentally active, outperform other older adults and equal young professors on some tests of recall (Shimamura et al., 1995).

The implications of such research are clear: Declines in information-processing skills are not inevitable or universal. Older adults may be able to maintain their memory skills quite well if they are relatively well educated, manage to stay healthy, and exercise their minds. At the same time, factors such as education and health cannot account completely for age differences in cognitive performance (Smith & Earles, 1996).

Second, older adults may perform poorly on some cognitive tasks not because of deficient abilities but because of *motivational factors*. Motivation is important at all ages, but older adults seem to be especially likely to ask whether information is potentially useful to them before they invest energy in learning it (Schaie, 1977/1978). In one study in which adults were to learn nonsense syllables, fully 80% of the elderly subjects simply dropped out of the study; they saw no point in learning such nonsense (Hulicka, 1967)! Research suggests that older adults sometimes do poorly on cognitive tasks because of underarousal (insufficient motivation), overarousal (anxiety, especially when faced with challenging tasks), and adoption of a cautious style of responding that results in their giving answers only when they are sure of them (Schaie & Willis, 1996).

Finally, we must consider the hypothesis that older adults display learning and memory deficits mainly because the *kinds of tasks* that have typically been presented to them are so far removed from the everyday contexts in which they normally learn and remember (Hess & Pullen, 1996). Think about the difference between remembering a list of food terms in the laboratory and remembering what to buy at the grocery store. In learning a list, the person may have no choice but to use mental memory strategies such as organization and elaboration. But in everyday life both young and old adults rely far less on such internal strategies than on *external memory aids*—notes, lists, and the like (Cavanaugh et al., 1983). After all, why conjure up images to help you remember what to buy at the supermarket when you can simply write out a shopping list? You can even use other people as an aid to memory (Dixon, 1992); for example, you can ask your spouse to remind you to get soy sauce and have a grocery clerk help you find it!

In the everyday task of grocery shopping, the job of remembering where to find the brown sugar or the cream cheese is simplified immensely because we can draw on our previous experience in the store (our knowledge base). Moreover, items are embedded in a meaningful context (such as the baking section or the dairy section), so cues are available in the store to help us remember. In one demonstration of the importance of such contextual cues, Kathryn Waddell and Barbara Rogoff (1981) showed that elderly adults did just as well as middle-aged adults at remembering the locations of objects (toy cars, pieces of furniture,

FIGURE 8.13 *Older adults are even more likely than younger adults to remember the locations of items better when they are placed in the context of a meaningful landscape than when they are placed in cubicles. The contextual perspective on information processing reminds us that older adults can perform well or poorly depending on the nature of the task they confront.* (From Waddell & Rogoff, 1981)

and so on) that had been placed in a meaningful landscape consisting of a parking lot, houses, a church, and other landmarks. They had difficulty only when these items were stripped of a meaningful context and were placed in cubicles (see Figure 8.13). In everyday situations, then, elderly adults can place new information in the context of what they already know and can make use of situational cues to help them remember. While older adults do have difficulty sometimes with everyday tasks like remembering people's names and remembering whether they locked the door or turned off the oven, they are generally able to perform much better in real life than in the lab (Hess & Pullen, 1996).

Summing Up.   Perhaps the truth lies somewhere between (1) *the basic-processing-capacity* view, which points to a universal decline in cognitive resources, such as speed and working memory, that affects performance on many cognitive tasks, and (2) *the contextual view,* which stresses variability from person to person and situation to situation based on cohort differences, motivational factors, and task demands. Most adults, at least if they live to an advanced old age, may well experience some loss of basic processing resources. However, they may also have developed specialized knowledge and strategies that allow them to compensate for these losses as they carry out the everyday cognitive activities most important to them (Baltes et al., 1992).

Problem Solving and Aging

We know that problem-solving skills improve steadily from early childhood through adolescence, but what becomes of them in adulthood? On the one hand, we might expect to see a decline in problem-solving prowess paralleling declines in learning and memory performance. But if adults also increase their knowledge bases and develop expertise as they get older, might not older adults outwit younger novices on many problem-solving tasks?

When they are given traditional problem-solving tasks to perform in the laboratory, young adults typically perform better than middle-aged adults, who in turn outperform older adults (Denney, 1989). However, consider research using the Twenty Questions task. Subjects are given an array of items and asked to find out, in as few yes/no questions as possible, which item the experimenter has in mind (see Figure 8.14). The soundest problem-solving strategy is to ask **constraint-seeking questions**—ones that rule out more than one item (for example, "Is it an animal?"). Young children and older adults tend to pursue specific hypotheses instead ("Is it a pig?" "Is it a pencil?"). Consequently, they must ask more questions to identify the right object. However, older adults do far better if the task is altered to make it more familiar;

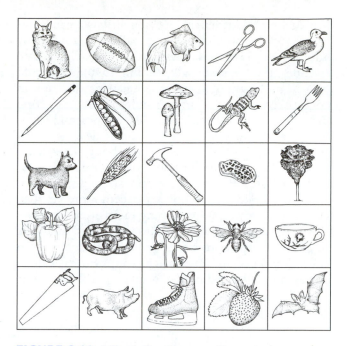

FIGURE 8.14 *A Twenty Questions game. You can try it on a young child or a friend by thinking of one item in the group and asking your testee to find out which it is by asking you yes/no questions. Look for constraint-seeking questions (for example, "Is it animate?"), and note the total number of questions required to identify the correct item.*

they then draw on their knowledge base to solve the problem. For example, when Denney (1980) used an array of playing cards, older adults asked plenty of constraint-seeking questions ("Is it a heart?" "Is it a face card?"). Thus older adults are capable of using effective problem-solving strategies but do not use them in some contexts, especially when given unfamiliar tasks in a laboratory.

What if adults are asked to deal with real-life problems like grease fires in the kitchen, warm refrigerators, or family squabbles? Nancy Denney and Kathy Pearce (1989) asked elderly adults to help them devise everyday problems that would be meaningful and familiar to older individuals. One problem was to generate ideas about how a 65-year-old recently widowed woman could improve her social life; another was to advise an elderly couple living on Social Security what to do when they were unable to pay their heating bill one winter. On these everyday problems, performance increased from early adulthood to middle age and declined in old age.

Other findings echo this one: When given everyday problems to which they can apply the expertise they have gained through experience, middle-aged adults often outperform young adults. Elderly adults sometimes equal and sometimes do worse than young and middle-aged adults; either way, they show smaller deficits than they do on unfamiliar problems in the laboratory (Berg & Klaczynski, 1996; Marsiske &

Willis, 1995). Ultimately, declines in basic capacities may limit the problem-solving skills of many elderly adults not only in the laboratory but in real life as well (Denney, 1989; Kasworm & Medina, 1990). We should bear in mind, though, that there is wide variation in cognitive competence among older adults, reflecting differences in health, education, experience, and so on.

In sum, we get much the same message about problem-solving skills that we got about memory capacities. Although performance on unfamiliar, meaningless laboratory tasks often appears to decline after early adulthood, the ability to perform more familiar, everyday information-processing tasks often improves through middle age and is maintained until quite late in life. Once again, this supports a contextual view of cognition: The gap between age groups can be wide or nonexistent, depending on what a problem-solving task demands and whether it allows the problem solver to make use of his or her expertise.

Some cognitive researchers feel that what appear to be cognitive deficits in old age may actually be signs of cognitive adaptation and growth (Dixon, 1992; Perlmutter, 1986). Older adults may let little-needed cognitive skills grow rusty in order to maintain and strengthen those skills that are most useful to them in everyday life. They may use their expertise in important domains to compensate for losses in basic processing capacities (Baltes et al., 1992). Children improve their ability to do all kinds of things; older adults may improve their ability to perform critical learning, memory, and problem-solving tasks and forget the rest!

APPLICATIONS: IMPROVING MEMORY

Have you noticed that the material in this chapter has great potential value to teachers? Skinner's operant-conditioning principles have long been widely applied in behavior modification programs to improve classroom learning and motivation, and Bandura's social learning theory is the basis for programs that rely on modeling of the behaviors to be learned. The information-processing perspective has yielded better methods for diagnosing learning problems and improving instruction. Here we'll focus on interventions aimed at boosting the memory skills of young children and older adults. Just how much can be achieved through training?

Garrett Lange and Sarah Pierce (1992) took on the challenge of teaching the memory strategy of organization (grouping) to 4- and 5-year-olds. Using pictures of objects and animals as the stimuli, they taught these preschoolers a "group-and-name trick" that in-

volved sorting items to be learned into groups based on similarity, naming the group, naming the items within the group, and, at recall, naming the group before calling out the items within that group. Because such memory-training programs have not always been successful, these researchers also attempted to increase motivation through encouragement and praise. They even included training in metamemory: They made sure children understood the rationale for the sorting strategy, knew when it could be used, and could see firsthand that it could improve their performance.

How successful was the training? These children did virtually no sorting of items to be learned before they were trained, but they did a good deal of it after training, even seven days later. They clearly learned to use the organization strategy they were taught. They also outperformed untrained control children on measures of recall. However, the gains in recall were fairly small compared to the much larger gains in strategy use that occurred. These young children apparently could not derive full benefit from the memory strategy they were taught, possibly because they did not have the working-memory capacity to carry out the strategy. Programs that teach memory strategies and metacognitive skills to elementary school children often work much better, especially with children who are underachievers and who may be capable of executing strategies but fail to do so on their own (Hattie, Biggs, & Purdie, 1996). Still, the benefits of training are often domain specific; they do not generalize to learning tasks different from those that were the focus of training. Perhaps this makes sense if we realize that the strategies that may work best in learning math skills may be quite different from the strategies that work best in learning historical facts or basketball skills.

How well do older adults respond to attempts to teach them more effective memory strategies? Although a number of studies have shown that such training can be very effective (Verhaeghen, Marcoen, & Goossens, 1992), there are limits. Consider the interesting work of Paul Baltes and his colleagues (Baltes et al., 1992). In one study (Kliegl et al., 1989) these researchers trained young adults (ages 19–29) and elderly adults (ages 65–83) in a mnemonic technique called the **method of loci.** It involves devising a mental map of a route through a familiar place (such as one's home) and then creating images linking items to be learned to landmarks along the route. For example, the German adults in the study were taught to associate words on word lists with 40 well-known landmarks in West Berlin, and they continued to practice for many sessions so that their maximal level of performance could be assessed.

The accomplishments of these adults were quite remarkable, as Figure 8.15 shows. Older adults im-

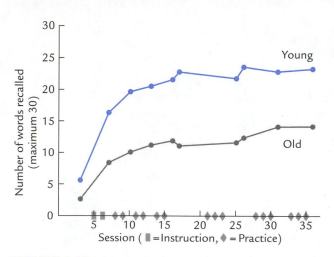

FIGURE 8.15 *Trained to use the method of loci and then given many practice sessions, young adults improved their ability to recall word lists more than older adults did, suggesting that aging places limits on maximal performance. Still, elderly adults benefited considerably from training in this memory strategy.* (From Baltes & Kliegl, 1992)

proved from recalling fewer than 3 words in correct order after hearing a 30-word list only once to recalling 10 words, and young adults upped their performance even more, from 6 to 20 words. These findings tell us that there is a great deal of cognitive plasticity and potential throughout the life span. As Baltes and his colleagues put it, older adults have considerable "reserve capacity" that can be tapped through intensive training. Indeed, despite limitations in basic processing capacity, older adults can master powerful memory techniques that enable them to outperform young adults who have not learned and practiced these techniques. Memory training programs can also improve aspects of metamemory, particularly elders' negative beliefs about their memory capacities (Floyd & Scogin, 1997).

At the same time, this study and others show that older adults, especially those who have experienced steep cognitive declines, profit less from memory training than young adults do (Verhaeghen & Marcoen, 1996). Both children and elderly adults coached to use memory strategies often fail to use them in new learning situations, perhaps because these strategies simply require too much mental effort (Pressley et al., 1985; Storandt, 1992).

What, then, is the solution? If some memory strategies are too mentally taxing for many young children and elderly adults, it may make more sense to capitalize on their memory strengths. Knowing that implicit memory holds up better than explicit memory, for example, Cameron Camp and his colleagues (Camp et al., 1996; Camp & McKitrick, 1992) have tried to help patients with dementia caused by Alz-

heimer's disease make use of the implicit memory capacities that they, like people with amnesia, retain even though they have serious deficits in explicit memory. For example, they have taught patients with Alzheimer's disease to remember the names of staff members by having the patients name photos of staff members repeatedly and at ever-longer intervals between trials. People who could not retain names for more than a minute were able to recall them weeks later after training. The technique appears to work because it makes use of implicit memory processes; adults learn quite effortlessly when they repeatedly encounter the material to be learned.

Finally, it sometimes makes more sense to change the learning environment than to change the learner (Pressley, 1983). If, for example, young children and some older adults do not spontaneously organize the material they are learning to make it more meaningful, one can organize it for them. Indeed, giving children practice at learning highly organized material can help them master the grouping strategy on their own (Best, 1993). Similarly, if the material to be learned is unfamiliar, one can use examples or analogies that will help learners relate it to something that *is* familiar (for example, teaching a senior citizens' group about the federal budget by likening it to their personal budgets). If young children and older adults need more time, let them set their own pace.

To use a real-world example, it turns out that older adults have more trouble understanding and remembering information about their drug prescriptions than young adults do (Morrell, Park, & Poon, 1989). Yet by writing clear, organized instructions and spending time explaining to older patients what they are to do, health-care professionals can simplify the learning task (Morrell et al., 1989). Alternatively, older adults can be given external memory aids. Denise Park and her colleagues (1992) explored the benefits of two such aids—an organization chart (a poster or pocket-sized table giving an hour-by-hour account of when drugs should be taken) and a medication organizer (a dispenser with columns for different days of the week and pill compartments for times of the day). Adults over 70 more often took their pills correctly when they were given both the chart and the organizer than when they were given one or the other or neither. Because we know that poor health is one contributor to poor memory functioning, it makes awfully good sense to reduce the cognitive demands on old and ailing patients by letting external memory aids do the mental work for them. Surely the best of all possible worlds for the learner would be one in which materials and teaching techniques are tailored to the learner's information-processing capacities, *and* training is offered in how to stretch those capacities.

1. Basic learning processes such as classical conditioning, operant conditioning, and observational learning change with age and contribute in important ways to human development.

2. In classical conditioning, an initially neutral stimulus is repeatedly paired with an unconditioned stimulus that always elicits an unconditioned response; consequently, the neutral stimulus becomes a conditioned stimulus for the response. Many emotional responses are acquired this way.

3. In operant conditioning, what is learned is an association between a response or behavior and the consequences that it produces. In reinforcement (positive or negative), consequences strengthen behavior. Punishment (positive or negative) decreases the strength of behavior, and extinction occurs when no consequences follow the behavior.

4. In observational learning, the individual learns from observing another person (a model). Learning may occur in the absence of reinforcement even if performance (imitation) does not, but the vicarious consequences of the action for the model or the learner can affect the likelihood of performance. Observational learning is highly cognitive learning, involving selective attention and symbolic representation of what was seen. All forms of learning except observational learning are clearly evident at birth and all, especially observational learning, become more efficient with age until late in adulthood.

5. The behaviorist perspective has given way to the more cognitive information-processing approach. The human "computer" takes in information into a sensory register, short-term and working memory, and long-term memory during encoding; stores it; retrieves it (demonstrating recognition, cued recall, or recall memory); and uses it to solve problems.

6. Infants are capable of learning from the start. They show recognition memory at birth, simple recall in the presence of cues at 2 or 3 months, recall in the absence of cues toward the end of the first year, and deliberate, conscious attempts to retrieve memories by age 2.

7. Learning and memory continue to improve during childhood: (a) Basic information-processing capacity increases as the brain matures and fundamental processes are automatized to free working-memory space; (b) memory strategies such as rehearsal, organization, and elaboration improve; (c) metamemory improves; and (d) the general knowledge base grows, improving the processing of new information in areas of expertise.

8. Even young children use systematic rules to solve problems, but their problem-solving skills improve as they replace faulty rules with ones that incorporate all the relevant aspects of the problem. Multiple strategies are used at any age, so that development resembles overlapping waves more than a set of stairsteps leading from one way of thinking to the next.

9. Adolescents master advanced learning strategies such as elaboration, note taking, and underlining; use their strategies more deliberately and selectively; and use their increased metacognitive abilities to guide learning and remembering.

10. As adults gain expertise in a domain, they develop large and organized knowledge bases as well as highly effective, specialized, and automatized ways of retrieving and using their knowledge.

11. Many older adults, though not all, perform less well than young adults on learning and memory tasks that require speed, the learning of unfamiliar or meaningless material, the use of unexercised abilities, recall rather than recognition memory, and explicit rather than implicit memory.

12. Older adults retain their knowledge base well and have only limited deficiencies in metamemory, though their performance can be hurt by negative beliefs about memory and aging. Late-life decreases in processing speed and working-memory capacity may limit the use of memory strategies and hurt performance. According

to the contextual perspective, factors such as cohort differences, low motivation, and the irrelevance of many laboratory tasks to everyday life also contribute to age differences in learning and memory.

13. On average, older adults also perform less well than younger adults on laboratory problem-solving tasks, but everyday problem-solving skills are likely to improve from early adulthood to middle adulthood and to be maintained fairly well in old age.

14. Basic learning theories and the information-processing approach can be applied to improve education. Memory-skills training can benefit both young children and elderly adults. However, since transfer to new situations does not always occur, altering instruction to better match the capacities of the learner is also appropriate.

☀ FOOD FOR THOUGHT

1. Benjamin is spanked hard by his father after he hit his sister on the head with his toy fire engine. Explain exactly how classical conditioning, operant conditioning, and observational learning could each result in Benjamin's learning a "lesson" from this experience.

2. You are a first-grade teacher, and one of the first things you notice is that some of your students remember a good deal more than others about the stories you read to them. From what you have read in this chapter, what are your main hypotheses about why some children have better memories than other children the same age?

3. As a teacher in an ElderHostel program, you want to base your teaching methods on knowledge of the information-processing capacities of elderly adults. What practical recommendations would you derive from (1) the view that there is a universal decline with age in basic processing capacities, and (2) the contextual perspective on cognitive aging?

Ⓦ ON THE WEB

1. *Learning* For great examples of classical conditioning, operant conditioning, and observational learning, give this site a look. You might even come away with the expertise required to train your dog. (Learning principles do not work with cats, of course!).
   http://www.rrcc.mb.ca/~psych/learning
   . . . and then select learning-resources from the list.

2. *Memory Tips* Useful guidance on improving your memory can be found on "The Memory Page," developed by a college student who walks you through memory tasks and teaches you strategies that can be applied to them. He also offers tips on studying and retaining what you study. As you read the material, ask yourself which concepts and generalizations discussed in this chapter are illustrated in the Memory Page.
   http://www.geocities.com/HotSprings/3602/

❖ KEY TERMS

classical conditioning	conditioned stimulus (CS)	negative reinforcement
unconditioned stimulus (UCS)	conditioned response (CR)	positive punishment
unconditioned response (UCR)	counterconditioning	negative punishment
	operant conditioning	extinction
	positive reinforcement	continuous reinforcement

partial reinforcement

time out

observational learning

vicarious reinforcement

deferred imitation

information-processing approach

sensory register

short-term memory

working memory

long-term memory

encoding

storage

retrieval

recognition memory

recall memory

cued recall memory

problem solving

executive control processes

infantile amnesia

rehearsal

organization (as memory strategy)

elaboration

metamemory

metacognition

knowledge base

rule assessment approach

implicit memory

explicit memory

constraint-seeking questions

method of loci

CHAPTER 9

Intelligence and Creativity

WHAT IS INTELLIGENCE?
The Psychometric Approach
Gardner's Theory of Multiple Intelligences
Sternberg's Triarchic Theory

HOW IS INTELLIGENCE MEASURED?
The Stanford-Binet Test
The Wechsler Scales
The Distribution of IQ Scores
Intelligence Testing Today

THE INFANT
Developmental Quotients
Infant Intelligence and Later Intelligence

THE CHILD
How Stable Are IQ Scores during Childhood?
Causes of Gain and Loss

THE ADOLESCENT
Continuity between Childhood and Adulthood
IQ and School Achievement

THE ADULT
IQ and Occupational Success
Change in IQ with Age
Predictors of Decline
Potential for Wisdom

FACTORS THAT INFLUENCE IQ SCORES
Genes
Home Environment
Social-Class Differences
Racial and Ethnic Differences

THE EXTREMES OF INTELLIGENCE
Mental Retardation
Giftedness

CREATIVITY AND SPECIAL TALENTS
What Is Creativity?
Creativity in Childhood and Adolescence
Creative Achievement in Adulthood

APPLICATIONS: BOOSTING INTELLECTUAL PERFORMANCE ACROSS THE LIFE SPAN
Early Intervention for Preschool Children
Enrichment for Low-IQ Adolescents
IQ Training for Aging Adults

SUMMARY POINTS

FOOD FOR THOUGHT

ON THE WEB

KEY TERMS

When he was 3 years old, the 19th-century English philosopher John Stuart Mill began to study Greek under his father's direction. At age 6½, he wrote a history of Rome. He tackled Latin at age 8, and before age 9 he was reading original Latin works. At 8 he also began his study of geometry and algebra. Mill's IQ score has been estimated at 190, on a scale on which 100 is average (Cox, 1926).

At the age of 35, Michael lives in an institution for the mentally retarded. He has been labeled profoundly retarded and has an IQ score of 17, as nearly as it can be estimated. Michael responds to people with grins and is able to walk haltingly, but he cannot feed or dress himself and does not use language.

Some gifted children thrive as college students. Some minds develop faster and farther than others.

As these examples indicate, the range of human cognitive abilities is immense. So far, our exploration of cognitive development has focused mainly on what human minds have in common, not on how they differ. Piaget, after all, was interested in identifying *universal* stages of cognitive development. And the information-processing approach has been used mainly to understand the basic cognitive processes *all* people rely on to learn, remember, and solve problems.

This chapter continues our exploration of how the human mind normally changes over the life span. Still another approach to the study of the mind is introduced: the *psychometric*, or testing, approach to intelligence, which led to the creation of intelligence tests. You, like many students I have taught, may find it hard to say anything nice about IQ tests. They do indeed have their limitations, and they have been misused. Yet they have also told us a good deal about intellectual development and about variations in intellectual performance. The chapter examines how performance on intelligence tests typically changes and

stays the same over the life span, what IQ tests tell us about a person, and why people's IQ scores differ. It also looks at both gifted and mentally retarded individuals from a life-span perspective. Finally, it considers creativity, a type of intellectual ability not measured by intelligence tests. Before going further, take the quiz in Box 9.1 to see if you may have some misconceptions about intelligence and intelligence tests; the chapter will clarify why the correct answers are correct.

WHAT IS INTELLIGENCE?

There is no clear consensus about what intelligence is. Piaget defined intelligence as "adaptive thinking or action" (Piaget, 1950). Other experts have offered different definitions, many of them centering in some way on the ability to think abstractly or to solve problems effectively (Sternberg, 1991; Sternberg & Berg, 1986). Early definitions of intelligence tended to reflect the assumption that intelligence is innate intellectual ability, genetically determined and thus fixed at conception. But it has now become clear that intelligence is *not* fixed, that it is changeable and subject to environmental influence (Perkins, 1996). As a result, an individual's intelligence test scores sometimes vary considerably over a lifetime. Bear in mind that understandings of this complex human quality have changed since the first intelligence tests were created at the turn of the century—and that there is still no single, universally accepted definition of intelligence.

The Psychometric Approach

The research tradition that spawned the development of standardized tests of intelligence is the **psychometric approach** (Thorndike, 1997). According to psychometric theorists, intelligence is a trait or a set of traits that characterizes some people to a greater extent than others. The goals, then, are to identify these traits precisely and to measure them so that differences among individuals can be described. But, from the start, experts could not agree on whether intelligence is one general cognitive ability or many specific abilities.

A Single Attribute or Many Attributes?

One way of trying to determine whether intelligence is a single ability or many abilities is to ask people to perform a large number of mental tasks and then to analyze their performance using a statistical procedure called **factor analysis.** This technique identifies clusters of tasks or test items (called *factors*) that are highly correlated with one another but unrelated to other clusters of items. Suppose, for example, that the items given to a group of people include many that require verbal skills (for example, defining words) and many that require mathematical skills (solving arith-

BOX 9.1

What do you know about intelligence and creativity?

Answer each question true or false.

1. On the leading tests of intelligence, a score of 100 is average.
2. Most scholars now conclude that there is no such thing as general intelligence; there are only separate mental abilities.
3. Individuals who are intellectually gifted are typically gifted in all mental abilities.
4. Intellectually gifted children do well in school but are more likely than most children to have social and emotional problems.

5. IQ predicts both a person's occupational status and his or her success compared to others in the same occupation.
6. On average, performance on IQ tests declines in people's 70s and 80s.
7. Qualities we associate with "wisdom" are as common among young and middle-aged adults as among elderly adults.
8. It has been established that children's IQs are far more influenced by their environments than by their genes.

9. How well a child does on a test of creativity cannot be predicted very well from his or her IQ score.
10. Creative achievers (great musicians, mathematicians, writers, and so on) typically do all their great works before about age 40 or 45 and produce only lesser works from then on.

Answers: 1-T, 2-F, 3-F, 4-F, 5-T, 6-T, 7-T, 8-F, 9-T, 10-F

---

metic puzzles). Now suppose that people who do well on any verbal item also do well on other verbal items, and those who do well on any math problem also do well on other math problems. Further suppose that people who do well on verbal problems may or may not perform well on math problems, and vice versa. In this case, math performance does not correlate highly with verbal performance, and factor analysis would reveal a "verbal ability factor" that is distinct from a "math ability factor." If, by contrast, correlations among the items revealed that those people who do well on any item in the test tend to do well on others as well, it would seem that one general ability factor underlies performance on both verbal and math problems.

Charles Spearman (1927) was among the first to use factor analysis to try to determine whether intelligence is one or many abilities. He concluded that a general mental ability (called *g*) contributes to performance on many kinds of tasks. However, he also noticed that a student who excelled at most tasks might also score very low on a particular measure (for example, memory for words). So he proposed that intelligence has two aspects: *g*, or general ability, and *s*, or special abilities, each of which is specific to a particular kind of task.

When Louis Thurstone (1938; Thurstone & Thurstone, 1941) factor-analyzed test scores obtained by eighth-graders and college students, he identified seven fairly distinct factors that he called *primary mental abilities:* spatial ability, perceptual speed (the quick noting of visual detail), numerical reasoning (arithmetic skills), verbal meaning (defining of words), word fluency (speed in recognizing words), memory, and inductive reasoning (formation of a rule to describe a set of observations). Thus Thurstone concluded that

Spearman's general ability factor should be broken into several distinct mental abilities.

The controversy was not over. J. P. Guilford (1967, 1988) proposed that there are as many as 180 distinct mental abilities! According to his **structure-of-intellect model,** there are five kinds of intellectual *contents* (things that people can think about, such as sights, ideas, or the behaviors of other people); six types of mental *operations* or actions that can be performed on these contents (such as recognizing, remembering, or evaluating); and six kinds of intellectual *products* or outcomes of thinking (such as a concept or an inference). Simple multiplication tells us that there are $5 \times 6 \times 6 = 180$ possible combinations of the contents, operations, and products (see Figure 9.1).

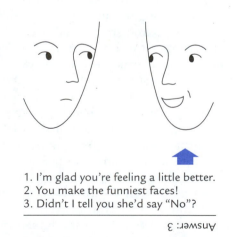

1. I'm glad you're feeling a little better.
2. You make the funniest faces!
3. Didn't I tell you she'd say "No"?

Answer: 3

FIGURE 9.1 *An item from one of Guilford's tests of social intelligence. The task is to read the characters' expressions and decide what the person marked by the arrow is probably saying to the other person.*
(Adapted from Guilford, 1967)

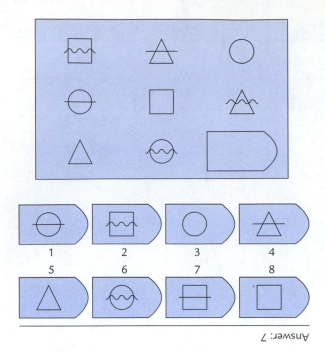

Answer: 7

FIGURE 9.2 *An item assessing fluid intelligence (similar to those in a test called the Raven Progressive Matrices Test). Which of the numbered pieces completes the design?*

Fluid versus Crystallized Intelligence

More recently, Raymond Cattell and John Horn have greatly influenced current thinking concerning intelligence by focusing attention on two broad dimensions of intellect: fluid intelligence and crystallized intelligence (Cattell, 1963; Horn & Cattell, 1967; Horn & Noll, 1997). **Fluid intelligence** is the ability to use one's mind actively to solve novel problems—for example, to solve verbal analogies, remember unrelated pairs of words, or recognize relationships among geometric figures. The skills involved—reasoning, seeing relationships among stimuli, drawing inferences—are usually not taught and are believed to be relatively free of cultural influences (see Figure 9.2). **Crystallized intelligence,** in contrast, is use of knowledge acquired through schooling and other life experiences. Tests of general information ("At what temperature does water boil?"), word comprehension ("What is the meaning of *duplicate*?"), and numerical abilities are all measures of crystallized intelligence. Thus, fluid intelligence involves using one's mind in new and flexible ways, whereas crystallized intelligence involves using what one has already learned through experience.

Obviously the use of factor analysis has not exactly settled the question of what intelligence is. Much depends on what tasks are given to test takers and how the resulting patterns of correlations are interpreted. Nonetheless, some consensus is emerging today. Intelligence is most often viewed as a hierarchy that includes (1) a general ability factor at the top that influences how well people do on a wide range of cognitive tasks, (2) a few broad dimensions of ability that are distinguishable from one another in factor analyses (for example, fluid intelligence, crystallized intelligence, memory capacity, perceptual skills, and processing speed), and (3) at the bottom, a large number of specific abilities such as numerical reasoning, spatial discrimination, and word comprehension that also influence just how well a person performs specific cognitive tasks that tap these specific abilities (Carroll, 1993; Horn & Noll, 1997).

The concepts of general ability, fluid and crystallized intelligence, and a hierarchy of abilities have proved useful, but in the end, the intelligence tests guided by psychometric theories of intelligence have emphasized general intellectual ability by summarizing performance in a single IQ score, and they have assessed only some of the specialized abilities that humans possess. Critics believe these tests have not fully described what it means to be an intelligent person. Let's examine two ways of thinking about intelligence that represent challenges to the traditional view that guided the development of intelligence tests. Doing so will help us capture the nature of intelligence and help us appreciate the limitations of the tests used to measure it.

Gardner's Theory of Multiple Intelligences

Howard Gardner (1983; Chen & Gardner, 1997) rejects the idea that a single IQ score is a meaningful measure of human intelligence. He argues that there are many intelligences, most of which have been ignored by the developers of standardized intelligence tests. Instead of asking, "How smart are you?" Gardner claims, we should be asking, "How are you smart?" and identifying people's strengths and weaknesses across the full range of human mental faculties (Chen & Gardner, 1997). In his book *Frames of Mind,* Gardner (1983) argues that there are at least seven distinct intellectual abilities:

1. *linguistic intelligence* (language skills, as seen in the poet's facility with words)
2. *logical-mathematical intelligence* (the abstract thinking and problem solving shown by mathematicians and scientists and emphasized by Piaget)
3. *musical intelligence* (based on an acute sensitivity to sound patterns)
4. *spatial intelligence* (most obvious in great artists who can perceive things accurately and transform what they see)
5. *bodily-kinesthetic intelligence* (the "intelligent" movement shown by dancers, athletes, and surgeons)
6. *interpersonal intelligence* (social intelligence, social skill, exceptional sensitivity to other people's motivations and moods)

7. *intrapersonal intelligence* (understanding of one's own feelings and inner life)

Traditional IQ tests emphasize linguistic and logical-mathematical intelligence, perhaps because those are the forms of intelligence Western societies value most highly and work the hardest to nurture in school. But IQ tests can be faulted for ignoring most of the other forms of intelligence. Although Gardner does not claim that his is *the* definitive list of intelligences, he does present evidence suggesting that each of these seven abilities is distinct. For example, it is clear that a person can be exceptional in one ability but poor in others—witness the **savant syndrome,** the phenomenon in which extraordinary talent in a particular area is displayed by a person who is otherwise mentally retarded (Nettelbeck & Young, 1996). Leslie Lemke, one such individual, is blind, has cerebral palsy, is mentally retarded, and could not talk until he was an adult (Monty, 1981). Yet he can hear a musical piece once and play it flawlessly on the piano or imitate songs in perfect German or Italian even though his own speech is still primitive. Other savants, despite IQs below 70, can draw well enough to gain admittance to art school or calculate on the spot what day of the week it was January 16, 1909 (O'Connor & Hermelin, 1991). Some scholars think that the skills shown by savants are so specific and depend so much on memory that they do not really qualify as separate "intelligences" (Nettelbeck & Young, 1996). However, Gardner insists that savant syndrome simply cannot be explained by theories that emphasize a general intelligence factor, g.

Gardner also marshals evidence to show that each intelligence has its own distinctive developmental course. Many of the great musical composers and athletes, for example, revealed their genius in childhood, whereas exceptional logical-mathematical intelligence typically shows up later, after the individual has gained the capacity for abstract thought and has mastered an area of science. Finally, Gardner links his distinct intelligences to distinct structures in the brain, arguing that the seven intelligences are neurologically distinct as well.

Sternberg's Triarchic Theory

Agreeing with Gardner that traditional IQ tests do not capture all that it means to be an intelligent person, Robert Sternberg (1985, 1988) has proposed a **triarchic theory of intelligence** that emphasizes three aspects of intelligent behavior: context, experience, and information-processing skills.

Contextual Component

First, Sternberg argues that what is defined as intelligent behavior depends on the sociocultural *context* in which it is displayed. Intelligent people adapt to the

How would you define an intelligent child? Mexican-American parents, like Cambodian, Filipino, and Vietnamese parents, say that the intelligent child is motivated, socially skilled, and able to manage his or her own behavior. Euro-American parents place less emphasis on these noncognitive aspects of intelligence (Okagaki & Sternberg, 1993). Each cultural group defines intelligence in its own way.

environment they are in (for example, a job setting), shape that environment to make it suit them better, or find a better environment. Such people have "street smarts." Psychologists, according to Sternberg, must begin to understand intelligence as behavior in the real world, not as behavior in taking tests (Sternberg et al., 1995).

This perspective views intelligent behavior as varying from one culture or subculture to another, from one period in history to another, and from one period of the life span to another. For example, Sternberg describes attending a conference in Venezuela and showing up at 8:00 A.M. sharp, only to find that he and four other North Americans were the only ones there. A behavior that is "intelligent" in North America proved to be rather "dumb" in a culture where expectations about punctuality are different. Each culture or subculture defines the ingredients of intelligent behavior in its own way (Miller, 1997). As a result, it is challenging to devise ways of measuring intelligence that are appropriate across cultures.

Sternberg also notes that what is intelligent can change over time. Numerical abilities may not play as important a role in intelligent behavior now that calculators and computers are widely used, for example, whereas analytical skills may be more important than ever in a complex, urban world. And certainly the infant learning how to master new toys shows a different kind of intelligence from that of the adult mastering a college curriculum. Thus, our definition of the intelligent infant must differ from our definition of the intelligent adult.

Experiential Component

The second aspect of the triarchic theory focuses on the role of *experience* in intelligence. What is intelligent when one first encounters a new task is not the same as what is intelligent after extensive experience with that task. The first kind of intelligence, *response to novelty,* requires active and conscious information processing. Sternberg believes that relatively novel tasks provide the best measures of intelligence because they tap the individual's ability to come up with good ideas or fresh insights.

In daily life, however, people also perform more or less intelligently on tasks they have done over and over (reading the newspaper, for example). This second kind of intelligence reflects **automatization,** or an increased efficiency of information processing with practice. It is intelligent to develop little "programs in the mind" for performing common everyday activities efficiently and unthinkingly. Most important, says Sternberg, it is crucial to know how familiar a task is to a person in order to assess that person's behavior fairly. For example, giving people of two different cultural groups an intelligence test whose items are familiar to one group and novel to the other introduces **culture bias** into the testing process, making it difficult to obtain a fair assessment of the groups' relative abilities.

Information-Processing Component

The third aspect of the triarchic theory focuses on *information-processing components.* As an information-processing theorist, Sternberg believes that the theories of intelligence underlying the development of IQ tests ignore *how* people produce intelligent answers. He argues that the components of intelligent behavior range from identifying the problem to carrying out strategies to solve it; a full picture of intelligence includes not only the number of answers people get right but also the processes they use to arrive at their answers and the efficiency with which they use those processes.

So, fully assessing how intelligent Harry and Huang are requires consideration of the *context* in which they perform (their age, culture, and historical period); their previous *experience* with a task (whether their behavior reflects response to novelty or automatized processes); and their *information-processing* strategies. Individuals who are intelligent according to this triarchic model are able to carry out logical thought processes efficiently and effectively in order to solve both novel and familiar problems and adapt to their environment. Unfortunately, today's widely used tests of intelligence do not reflect this sophisticated view of intelligence.

HOW IS INTELLIGENCE MEASURED?

When psychologists first began to devise intelligence tests at the turn of the century, their concern was not with defining the nature of intelligence but with the more practical task of determining which schoolchildren were likely to be slow learners—and doing so in a way that would be less biased than letting teachers judge the matter (Thorndike, 1997). Consequently, many tests had no precisely defined theory of intelligence behind them and were originally intended to assess intelligence in children, not in adults.

The Stanford-Binet Test

Alfred Binet and a colleague, Theodore Simon, produced the forerunner of our modern intelligence tests. In 1904 they were commissioned by the French government to devise a test that would identify "dull" children who might need special instruction. Binet and Simon devised a large battery of tasks measuring the skills believed to be necessary for classroom learning: attention, perception, memory, reasoning, verbal comprehension, and so on. Items that discriminated between normal children and those described by their teachers as slow were kept in the final test.

The test was soon revised to make the items *age graded.* For example, a set of "6-year-old" items could be passed by most 6-year-olds but few 5-year-olds; "12-year-old" items could be handled by most 12-year-olds but not by younger children. This approach permitted the testers to describe a child's **mental age (MA),** the level of age-graded problems that the child is able to solve. Thus, a child who passes all items at the 5-year-old level but does poorly on more advanced items—regardless of her actual age—is said to have an MA of 5.

Binet's influence is still with us in the form of the modern *Stanford-Binet Scale.* In 1916 Lewis Terman of Stanford University translated and published a revised version of Binet's test for use with American children. It contained age-graded items for ages 3 to 13. Moreover, Terman made use of a procedure that had been developed for comparing mental age to chronological age. It is one thing to have a mental age of 10 when one is chronologically only 8, but another thing entirely to have that same mental age when one is 15. The **intelligence quotient,** or **IQ,** was originally calculated by dividing mental age by chronological age and then multiplying by 100: IQ = MA/CA × 100. An IQ score of 100 indicates average intelligence, regardless of a child's age: The normal child passes just the items that agemates typically pass; mental age increases each year but so does chronological age. The child of 8 with a mental age of 10 has experienced rapid intellectual growth and has a high IQ (specifically, 125); the child of 15 with a mental age of 10 has an IQ of only 67 and is clearly below average compared to children of the same age.

A revised version of the Stanford-Binet is still in use (Thorndike, Hagen, & Sattler, 1986). Its **test norms**— standards of normal performance expressed as average scores and the range of scores around the average—are based on the performance of a large and representative sample of people (2-year-olds through adults) from many socioeconomic and racial backgrounds. The concept of mental age is no longer used to calculate IQ; instead, individuals receive scores that reflect how well or how poorly they do as compared with others of the same age. An IQ of 100 is still average, and the higher the IQ score an individual attains, the better the performance is in comparison to agemates.

The Wechsler Scales

David Wechsler constructed a set of intelligence tests that is also in wide use. The Wechsler Preschool and Primary Scale of Intelligence (WPPSI) is for children between the ages of 3 and 8 (Wechsler, 1989). The Wechsler Intelligence Scale for Children (WISC-III) is appropriate for schoolchildren aged 6 to 16 (Wechsler, 1991), and the Wechsler Adult Intelligence Scale-Revised (WAIS-R) is used with adults (Wechsler, 1981). The Wechsler tests yield a *verbal IQ* score based on items measuring vocabulary, general knowledge, arithmetic reasoning, and the like, as well as a *performance IQ* based on such nonverbal skills as the ability to assemble puzzles, solve mazes, reproduce geometric designs with colored blocks, and rearrange pictures to tell a meaningful story (see Figure 9.3). As with the Stanford-Binet, a score of 100 is defined as average performance for one's age. A person's *full-scale IQ* is a combination of the verbal and performance scores.

The Distribution of IQ Scores

To more fully interpret an IQ score of 130 or 85, it helps to know how IQ scores are distributed in the population at large. Scores for large groups of people form a **normal distribution,** or a symmetrical, bell-shaped spread around the average score of 100 (see Figure 9.4). Scores around the average are common; very high and very low scores are rare. Over two-thirds of us have IQs between 85 and 115. Fewer than 3% have scores of 130 or above, a score that has often been used as one criterion of giftedness. John Stuart Mill, with his estimated IQ of 190, was very rare indeed! Similarly, fewer than 3% have IQs below 70, a cutoff that is commonly used today to define mental retardation.

Intelligence Testing Today

Traditional IQ tests continue to be used, and new ones are continually being developed. However, some scholars, disenchanted with the way in which intelligence has traditionally been defined and measured, have sought to develop entirely new approaches to intellectual assessment.

One promising approach, called **dynamic assessment,** attempts to evaluate how well children actually learn new material when an examiner provides them with competent instruction (Campione et al., 1984; Lidz, 1997). Reuven Feuerstein and his colleagues, for example, have argued that, even though intelligence is often defined as a *potential* to learn from experience, IQ tests typically assess only *what has been learned,* not what can be learned (Feuerstein, Feuerstein, & Gross, 1997). This approach may be biased against children from culturally different or disadvantaged backgrounds who lack opportunities to learn what the tests measure. Feuerstein's *Learning Potential Assessment Device* asks children to learn new things with the guidance of an adult who provides increasingly helpful cues. This test interprets intelligence as the ability to learn quickly with minimal guidance. Robert Sternberg (1985, 1991) uses a similar approach in a test he has constructed based on his triarchic theory of intelligence. It turns out that dynamic assessment of learning capacity provides information over and above what traditional IQ tests provide about a child's intellectual competence and likely achievement (Day et al., 1997; Lidz, 1997).

Despite their vast influence, IQ tests have been roundly criticized. A single IQ score derived from a test that assesses only some of the many intelligences that humans can display certainly does not do justice to the complexity of human mental functioning. Moreover, it is a measure of the individual's *performance* at one point in time—an estimate that is not always a good indicator of the person's underlying intellectual *competence.* And, as Sternberg (1992) notes, it is high time to bring modern information-processing theory to bear on the testing of intelligence in order to understand *how* highly intelligent individuals succeed

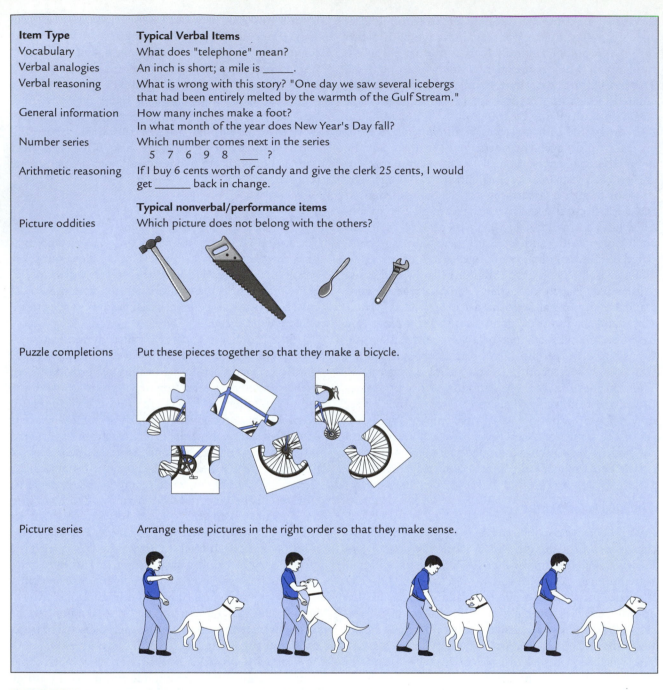

Item Type	Typical Verbal Items
Vocabulary	What does "telephone" mean?
Verbal analogies	An inch is short; a mile is _____.
Verbal reasoning	What is wrong with this story? "One day we saw several icebergs that had been entirely melted by the warmth of the Gulf Stream."
General information	How many inches make a foot? In what month of the year does New Year's Day fall?
Number series	Which number comes next in the series 5 7 6 9 8 ___ ?
Arithmetic reasoning	If I buy 6 cents worth of candy and give the clerk 25 cents, I would get _____ back in change.

Typical nonverbal/performance items

Picture oddities — Which picture does not belong with the others?

Puzzle completions — Put these pieces together so that they make a bicycle.

Picture series — Arrange these pictures in the right order so that they make sense.

FIGURE 9.3 *Items similar to those appearing on the Wechsler intelligence test for children* (From Shaffer, 1996)

where others fail. In sum, the nature of intelligence is still poorly understood. We do, however, have a vast store of information about how IQ scores change over the life span and about the implications for development and achievement of having a low or high IQ.

THE INFANT

As we saw in Chapters 7 and 8, the mind develops very rapidly in infancy. But how can an infant's intellectual growth be measured? Is it possible to identify infants who are more or less intelligent than their agemates? And how well does high (or low) intelligence in infancy predict high (or low) intelligence in childhood and adulthood?

Developmental Quotients

None of the standard intelligence tests can be used with children much younger than 3, because the test items require verbal skills and attention spans that in-

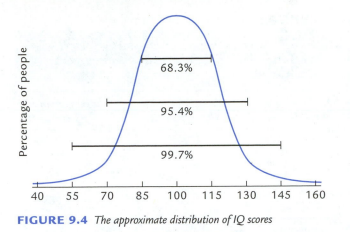

FIGURE 9.4 *The approximate distribution of IQ scores*

fants do not have. Some developmentalists have tried to measure infant intelligence by assessing the rate at which infants achieve important developmental milestones. Perhaps the best known and most widely used of the infant tests is the *Bayley Scales of Infant Development* (Bayley, 1969, 1993). This test, designed for infants aged 2 to 30 months, has three parts:

1. The *motor scale,* which measures the infant's ability to do such things as grasp a cube and throw a ball.
2. The *mental scale,* which includes adaptive behaviors such as reaching for a desirable object, searching for a hidden toy, and following directions.
3. The *infant behavioral record,* a rating of the child's behavior on dimensions such as goal-directedness, fearfulness, and social responsivity.

On the basis of the first two scores, the infant is given a **DQ,** or **developmental quotient,** rather than an IQ. The DQ summarizes how well or how poorly the infant performs in comparison to a large norm group of infants of the same age.

Infant Intelligence and Later Intelligence

As they grow older, infants do progress through many developmental milestones of the kind assessed by the Bayley Scales, so such scales are useful in charting infants' developmental progress. They are also useful in diagnosing neurological problems and mental retardation—even when these conditions are fairly mild and difficult to detect through standard pediatric or neurological examinations (Escalona, 1968; Honzik, 1983). But developmentalists have also been interested in the larger issue of continuity versus discontinuity in intellectual development: Can we predict which infants are likely to be gifted, average, or mentally retarded during the school years?

Apparently not from their DQs. Correlations between infant DQ and child IQ are very low, sometimes

close to zero. The infant who does well on the Bayley Scales or other infant tests may or may not obtain a high IQ score later in life (Honzik, 1983; Rose et al., 1989). True, the infant who scores very low on an infant test often turns out to be mentally retarded, but otherwise there seems to be a good deal of discontinuity between early and later scores—at least until a child is 4 or older.

Why don't infant development scales do a better job of predicting children's later IQs? Perhaps the main reason is that infant tests and IQ tests tap qualitatively different kinds of abilities (McCall, Eichorn, & Hogarty, 1977). Piaget would undoubtedly approve of this argument. Infant scales focus heavily on the sensory and motor skills that Piaget believed are so important in infancy; IQ tests such as the Stanford-Binet and WISC emphasize more abstract abilities, such as verbal reasoning, concept formation, and problem solving.

Robert McCall (1981, 1983) offers a second explanation, arguing that the growth of intelligence during infancy is highly influenced by powerful and universal maturational processes. Maturational forces pull infants back on course if environmental influences cause them to stray. For this reason, higher or lower infant test scores are likely to be nothing more than temporary deviations from a universal developmental path. As the child nears age 2, McCall argues, maturational forces become less strong, so individual differences become larger and more stable over time. Consistent differences related to both individual genetic makeup and environment now begin to emerge (see Yeates et al., 1983, for relevant evidence).

Should we give up on trying to predict later IQ on the basis of development in infancy? Perhaps not yet. The information-processing approach has given new life to the idea that there is continuity in intelligence from infancy to childhood. Several researchers have found that certain measures of infant attention predict later IQ better than infant intelligence tests do. For example, *speed of habituation* (the speed with which an infant loses interest in a repeatedly presented stimulus) and *preference for novelty* (the infant's tendency to prefer a novel stimulus to a familiar one), assessed in the first year of life, have an average correlation of about +.45 with IQ in childhood, particularly with verbal IQ and memory skills (Bornstein & Sigman, 1986; McCall & Carriger, 1993; and see Rose & Feldman, 1995). Fast reaction time in infancy (time taken to look in the direction of a visual stimulus as soon as it appears) predicts later IQ about as well (Dougherty & Haith, 1997).

Perhaps, then, we can characterize the "smart" infant as the speedy information processor—the infant who quickly gets bored by the same old thing, seeks out novel experiences, and soaks up information rapidly. There seems to be some continuity between infant intelligence and childhood intelligence after all. Such Bayley Scale accomplishments as throwing a ball are unlikely to carry over into vocabulary learning or problem-solving skills in childhood. However, the extent to which the young infant processes information quickly can predict the extent to which he or she will learn quickly and solve problems efficiently later in childhood.

TABLE 9.1

Correlations of IQs measured during the preschool years and middle childhood with IQs measured at ages 10 and 18

Age of Child	Correlation with IQ at Age 10	Correlation with IQ at Age 18
4	.66	.42
6	.76	.61
8	.88	.70
10	—	.76
12	.87	.76

SOURCE: From Honzik, Macfarlane, & Allen (1948)

THE CHILD

Over the childhood years, children generally become able to answer more questions, and more difficult questions, on IQ tests. That is, their mental ages increase. But what happens to the IQ scores of individual children, which reflect how they compare with peers?

How Stable Are IQ Scores during Childhood?

It was once assumed that a person's IQ reflected his or her genetically determined intellectual capacity and therefore would remain quite stable over time. In other words, a child with an IQ of 120 at age 5 was expected to obtain a similar IQ at age 10, 15, or 20. Is this idea supported by research? As we have seen, infant DQs do not predict later IQs well at all. However, starting at about age 4 there is a fairly strong relationship between early and later IQ, and the relationship grows even stronger by middle childhood. Table 9.1 summarizes the results of a longitudinal study of more than 250 children (Honzik, Macfarlane, & Allen, 1948; also see Sameroff et al., 1993): The shorter the interval between two testings, the higher the correlation between children's IQ scores. Even when a number of years have passed, IQ seems to be a very stable attribute: The scores that children obtain at age 6 are clearly related to those they obtain 12 years later, at age 18.

There is something these correlations are not telling us, however. They are based on a large *group* of children, and they do not necessarily mean that the IQs of *individual children* will remain stable over the years. As it turns out, many children show sizable ups and downs in their IQ scores over the course of childhood. Patterns of change over time differ considerably from child to child, as though each were on his or her own developmental trajectory (Gottfried et al., 1994). One team of researchers looked at the IQ scores of 140 children who had taken intelligence tests at regular intervals from age 2½ to age 17 (McCall, Applebaum, & Hogarty, 1973). The average difference between a child's highest and lowest scores was a whopping 28.5 points. About one-third showed changes of more than 30 points, and one child changed by 74 IQ points!

How do we reconcile the conclusion that IQ is relatively stable with this clear evidence of instability? We can still conclude that, within a group, children's standings (high or low) in comparison with peers stay quite stable from one point to another during the childhood years. But, at the same time, many individual children experience drops or gains in IQ scores over the years. Remember, though, that we are talking about performance on IQ tests rather than underlying intellectual competence. IQ scores are influenced not only by a person's intelligence but by his or her motivation, testing procedures and conditions, and many other factors. As a result, IQ may be more changeable over the years than intellectual ability.

Causes of Gain and Loss

Some wandering of IQ scores upward or downward over time is just random fluctuation—a good day at one testing, a bad day at the next. Yet there are patterns, too. Children whose scores fluctuate the most tend to live in unstable home environments; their life experiences had fluctuated between periods of happiness and turmoil (Honzik et al., 1948).

In addition, some children gain IQ points over childhood and others lose them. Who are the gainers, and who are the losers? Gainers seem to have parents who foster achievement and who are neither too strict nor too lax in child rearing (McCall et al., 1973). On the other hand, noticeable drops in IQ with age often occur among children who live in poverty. Otto Klineberg (1963) proposed a **cumulative-deficit hypothesis** to explain this: Impoverished environments inhibit intellectual growth, and these negative effects accumulate over time. There is some support for the cumulative-deficit hypothesis, especially when a child's parents are not only poor but low in intellectual functioning themselves (Jensen, 1977; Ramey & Ramey, 1992). Overall, then, although mental age rises during childhood, IQ scores show both continuity and change and can rise and fall.

THE ADOLESCENT

Intellectual growth is very rapid during infancy and childhood. What happens during adolescence, and how well does IQ predict school performance?

Continuity between Childhood and Adulthood

Intellectual growth continues its rapid pace in early adolescence and then slows down and levels off in later adolescence (Thorndike, 1997). A spurt in brain development, some studies suggest, occurs at roughly the age of 11 or 12, when children are believed to enter Piaget's formal-operational stage (Case, 1992; Andrich & Styles, 1994). Brain development may give children the information-processing speed and working-memory capacity they need to perform at adultlike levels on IQ tests as well (Kail & Salthouse, 1994). Thus, basic changes in the brain in early adolescence may underlie a variety of cognitive advances—the achievement of formal operations, improved memory and information-processing skills, and better performance on tests of intelligence.

Although adolescence is a time of impressive mental growth, it is also a time of increased stability of individual differences in intellectual performance. During the teen years, IQ scores become even more stable than they were in childhood and predict IQ in middle age very well (Eichorn, Hunt, & Honzik, 1981). Even while adolescents as a group are experiencing cognitive growth, then, each adolescent is establishing a characteristic level of intellectual performance that will most likely be carried into adult life unless the individual's environment changes dramatically.

IQ and School Achievement

If the original purpose of IQ tests was to estimate how well children would do in school, have these tests achieved their purpose? Yes, fairly well. The correlation between children's and adolescents' IQ scores and their grades is about +.50, making general intellectual ability one of the best predictors of school achievement available (Neisser et al., 1996). Adolescents with high IQs are also less likely to drop out of high school and more likely to go on to college than their peers with lower IQs; the correlation between IQ and years of education obtained averages +.55 (Neisser et al., 1996). However, IQ scores do not predict college grades as well as they predict high school grades (Brody & Brody, 1976). This is probably because most college students have at least the average intellectual ability needed to succeed in college. Actual success is therefore more influenced by personal qualities such as motivation. Overall, an IQ score is a good predictor of academic achievement, but it does not tell us everything about a

student. Factors such as work habits, interests, and motivation to succeed also affect academic achievement.

THE ADULT

Do IQ scores predict achievement after people have left school? Does performance on IQ tests change during the adult years? And do IQ scores decline in old age, as performance on Piagetian cognitive tasks and some memory tasks do?

IQ and Occupational Success

There is indeed a relationship between IQ and occupational status. White collar workers consistently score higher than blue collar, or manual, workers (Weakliem, McQuillan, & Schaer, 1995). The gap is smaller for recent cohorts than for earlier ones, but it still exists. As shown in Table 9.2, the average IQ score for an occupation increases as the prestige of the occupation increases (Gottfredson, 1986). The reason for this relationship is clear: It undoubtedly takes more intellectual ability to complete law school and become a lawyer than it does to be a farmhand. Yet notice too that IQs vary considerably in every occupational group, so many people in low-status jobs have high IQs.

Now a second question: Are bright lawyers, electricians, or farmhands more successful or productive than their less intelligent colleagues? The answer here is also "yes." The correlation between scores on tests of intellectual ability and such measures of job performance as supervisor ratings average +.30 to +.50 (Neisser et al., 1996). General intellectual ability seems to predict job performance in a wide range of occupations better than any other indicator yet devised, and it predicts likelihood of success as accurately for members of racial and ethnic minority groups as for whites (Hunter & Hunter, 1984). More intellectually capable adults are better able to learn what they need to know about their occupations and to solve the problems that arise day by day.

In sum, IQ does have some bearing on occupational success, predicting both what kind of occupation an individual chooses and how well he or she performs in it. At the same time, an IQ score does not tell the whole story; personal qualities such as motivation and environmental factors such as social support for one's aspirations also affect vocational outcomes (see Chapter 15).

Change in IQ with Age

Perhaps no question about adult development has been studied as thoroughly as that of how intellectual abilities change with age. Early cross-sectional studies comparing different age groups of adults yielded

TABLE 9.2

Average IQs and range of IQs for enlisted military personnel who had worked in different civilian occupations. Average IQs increase with the prestige of the occupation, and some occupations are rarely entered by individuals with below-average IQs. At the same time, each field has its more and less intelligent workers.

Occupation	Average IQ	Range of IQs
Accountant	128.1	94–157
Lawyer	127.6	96–157
Engineer	126.6	100–151
Chemist	124.8	102–153
Reporter	124.5	100–157
Teacher	122.8	76–155
Pharmacist	120.5	76–149
Bookkeeper	120.0	70–157
Sales manager	119.0	90–137
Purchasing agent	118.7	82–153
Radio repairman	115.3	56–151
Salesman	115.1	60–153
Artist	114.9	82–139
Stock clerk	111.8	54–151
Machinist	110.1	38–153
Electrician	109.0	64–149
Riveter	104.1	50–141
Butcher	102.9	42–147
Bartender	102.2	56–137
Carpenter	102.1	42–147
Chauffeur	100.8	46–143
Cook and baker	97.2	20–147
Truck driver	96.2	16–149
Barber	95.3	42–141
Farmhand	91.4	24–141
Miner	90.6	42–139

SOURCE: From Harrell & Harrell (1945)

disturbing findings—disturbing, at least, to anyone over 20. For example, extensive testing during World War I using the *Army Alpha Test* showed that scores on this IQ-type test steadily decreased from the young groups of 20 years of age or less to the older groups of up to 50 and 60 years of age (Yerkes, 1921). Does this finding mean that we're brightest at 20 and it's downhill from there? Not really. In longitudinal follow-up studies, the scores a group of middle-aged people obtained on the Army Alpha Test were compared to the scores these same adults had obtained when they were college freshmen. The middle-age scores turned out to be *higher* on every subtest except the one dealing with arithmetic (Owens, 1953). This finding, along with longitudinal evidence that IQs decline only modestly in old age, startled psychologists who had long assumed that intellectual performance peaked at age 20 (Cunningham & Owens, 1983).

Why the big discrepancy? As noted in Chapter 1, both cross-sectional and longitudinal studies have their problems. Cross-sectional studies compare people of different cohorts who have had different levels of education and life experiences because they were born at different times. Yet longitudinal studies are also flawed. People die or drop out of such studies. Those who are left—those whose scores can be charted across the years—tend to be individuals with better health and higher intellectual functioning, the very people who may be most likely to improve their abilities in earlier adulthood and maintain them in old age (Schaie, 1983).

So neither kind of study is entirely adequate in determining how IQ test performance changes with age. The best information about changes in intellectual abilities has come from a sophisticated *sequential study* directed by K. Warner Schaie that combines the cross-sectional and the longitudinal approaches (see Schaie, 1983, 1996). Schaie's study began in 1956 with a sample of members of a health maintenance organization ranging in age from 22 to 70. They were given a revised test of primary mental abilities that yielded scores for five separate mental abilities (see Box 9.2). Seven years later, as many of them as could be found were retested. In addition, a new sample of adults ranging in age from their 20s to their 70s was tested. This design made it possible to determine how the performance of the same individuals changed over a period of seven years *and* to compare the performance of people who were 20 years old in 1956 with that of a different cohort of people who were 20 in 1963. This same strategy was repeated in 1970, 1977, and 1984, giving the researchers a wealth of information about different cohorts, including longitudinal data on some of the same people over a 28-year period.

What has this important study revealed? First, it seems that when a person is born has at least as much influence on intellectual functioning as age does. In other words, cohort or generational effects on performance exist. This evidence confirms the suspicion that cross-sectional comparisons of different age groups yield too grim a picture of declines in intellectual abilities during adulthood. Specifically, recently born cohorts (the youngest people in the study were born in 1959) have tended to outperform earlier generations (the oldest were born in 1889) on most tests. Yet on the test of numerical ability, people born between 1903 and 1924 actually performed better than both earlier and later generations. So different generations may have a special edge in different areas of intellectual performance, showing that when one is born *does* affect one's intellectual abilities. Judging from Schaie's findings, young and middle-aged adults today can look forward to better intellectual functioning in old age than their grandparents have experienced.

The primary mental abilities measured in Schaie's Seattle study

- **Verbal meaning:** One must recognize the meaning of a word by identifying the best synonym for it from a list of four words. This ability comes in handy in reading and understanding speech.
- **Space:** This is the ability to imagine how an object would look if it were rotated in space. Given one figure (an *F*, for example), one must quickly determine whether six other figures are or are not the *F* at another angle (for example, upside down). Spatial ability would aid in reading maps or assembling pieces of equipment.
- **Reasoning:** The test of reasoning involves foreseeing the pattern in a

series of letters. Given the pattern "*b c r c d r d e r*," one would have to figure out that the next letter should be *e*. Reasoning enters into solving problems in real life, as when one analyzes a situation on the basis of past experience and plans an appropriate future course.
- **Number:** This is the ability to deal with basic arithmetic problems quickly. Given an addition problem that has been worked to yield a sum, one must decide whether it has been worked correctly. Although mathematics abilities may be less useful today now that we have calculators, they still play a role in daily life.

- **Word fluency:** Finally, the word-fluency test measures the quick recall of words. During a five-minute period one must write down as many words as possible that begin with the letter *s*. Presumably this ability enters into talking and reading easily.

SOURCE: These descriptions are based on those provided by Schaie (1983, pp. 73–74) of the following test: Thurstone, L. L., & Thurstone, T. G. (1948). *SRA Primary Mental Abilities, Ages 11–17, Form AM.* Chicago: Science Research Associates.

What happens to the mental abilities of adults as they age? Figure 9.5 charts longitudinal data on changes in five intellectual abilities over a period of 28 years. For the most part, modest gains in abilities occur in the 30s, 40s, and even 50s; scores level off in the late 50s and early 60s. Declines begin to occur in the late 60s and 70s and become steep in the 80s—far later than was previously thought. By 80 or so, significant declines in several abilities are evident. Before that age, however, the average older person functions within the normal range of ability for young adults.

But another important message of Schaie's study, and of other research as well, is that patterns of aging differ for different abilities. For one thing, *fluid intelligence* (those abilities requiring active thinking and reasoning applied to novel problems, as measured by tests like the primary mental abilities tests of reasoning and space) usually declines earlier and more steeply than *crystallized intelligence* (those abilities involving the use of knowledge acquired through experience, as in answering the verbal meaning test used by Schaie). Consistently, adults lose some of their ability to grapple with new problems starting in middle age, but their "crystallized" general knowledge and vocabulary stay steady or even improve through the 60s and then decline somewhat (Horn & Noll, 1997; Kaufman & Kaufman, 1997). An overall IQ score obscures this important fact of cognitive aging.

Similarly, scores on the performance subtests of the Wechsler adult IQ test (which include many nonverbal items posing novel problems) decline earlier

than verbal IQ scores do (Busse & Maddox, 1985). Why is this? Both tests of fluid intelligence and tests of performance IQ are often timed, and performance on timed, or speeded, tests declines more in old age than performance on unspeeded tests does (Jarvik & Bank, 1983). Fluid, performance, and speeded IQ test items may be less familiar to older adults who have been out of school for years than to younger adults; in this sense, the tests may be subtly biased against older adults (Cornelius, 1984; Labouvie-Vief, 1985). However, declines in these fluid aspects of intelligence have also been linked to the slowing of central nervous system functioning that most people experience as they age (Schaie, 1996).

A clear message here is that speed of information processing is related to intellectual functioning across the life span. Not only is rapid information processing in infancy associated with high IQ scores in childhood, but young adults with quick reaction times outperform their more sluggish agemates on IQ tests, and adults who lose information-processing speed in later life lose some of their ability to think through complex and novel problems as well (Jensen, 1993). And it is not just that older adults can't finish tests that have time limits, for declines in fluid intelligence in later life occur even on untimed tests (Kaufman & Kaufman, 1997). The problem is that the slower information processor cannot keep in mind and process simultaneously all relevant aspects of a complex problem.

We now have an overall picture of intellectual functioning in adulthood. Age-group differences in performance suggest that older adults today are at a

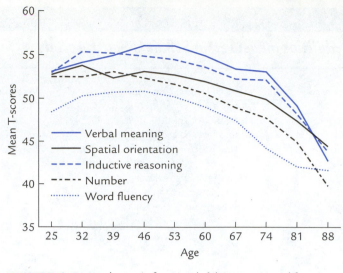

FIGURE 9.5 *Age changes in five mental abilities as estimated from longitudinal data for different cohorts of adults studied over a 28-year period* (From Schaie, 1996)

disadvantage on many tests compared to younger adults, partly because of deficiencies in the quality of education they received early in life. But actual declines in intellectual abilities associated with aging are generally minor until people reach their late 60s or 70s. Even in old age, declines in fluid intelligence, performance intelligence, and performance on speeded tests are more apparent than declines in crystallized intelligence, verbal intelligence, and performance on untimed tests.

One last message of this research is worth special emphasis: *Declines in intellectual abilities are not universal.* Even among the 81-year-olds in Schaie's study, only about 30 to 40% had experienced a significant decline in intellectual ability in the previous seven years (Schaie, 1990). Moreover, although few 81-year-olds maintained all five mental abilities, almost all retained at least one ability from testing to testing, and about half retained four out of five (Schaie, 1989). The range of differences in intellectual functioning in a group of older adults is extremely large (Morse, 1993), and anyone who stereotypes all elderly adults as intellectually limited is likely to be wrong most of the time.

Predictors of Decline

What is most likely to determine whether or not a person experiences declines in intellectual performance in old age? *Poor health,* not surprisingly, is one risk factor. People who have cardiovascular diseases or other chronic illnesses show steeper declines in mental abilities than their healthier peers (Schaie, 1996). Diseases (and most likely the drugs used to treat them as well) also contribute to a rapid decline in intellectual abilities within a few years of death (Johansson, Zarit, &

Berg, 1992; Kleemeier, 1962). This phenomenon has been given the depressing label **terminal drop.** Perhaps there really is something, then, to the saying "Sound body, sound mind."

A second factor in decline is an *unstimulating lifestyle.* Schaie and his colleagues found that the biggest intellectual declines were shown by elderly widows who had low social status, engaged in few activities, and were dissatisfied with their lives (Schaie, 1996). These women lived alone and seemed disengaged from life. Individuals who maintain their performance or even show gains tend to have above-average socioeconomic status, advanced education, intact marriages, intellectually capable spouses, and physically and mentally active lifestyles. Interestingly, married adults are affected by the intellectual environment they provide for each other. Their IQ test scores become more similar over the years, largely because the lower functioning partner's scores rise closer to those of the higher functioning partner (Gruber-Baldini, Schaie, & Willis, 1995).

The moral is "Use it or lose it!" This rule, applicable to muscular strength and sexual functioning, also pertains to intellectual functioning in later life (Schaie, 1983). The plasticity of the nervous system throughout the life span enables elderly individuals to benefit from intellectual stimulation and training, to maintain the intellectual skills most relevant to their activities, and to compensate for the loss of less-exercised abilities (Dixon et al., 1985). There is still much to learn about how health, lifestyle, and other factors shape the individual's intellectual growth and decline. What is certain is that most of us can look forward to many years of optimal intellectual functioning before *some* of us experience losses of *some* mental abilities in later life.

Potential for Wisdom

Many people believe, incorrectly as we have seen, that intellectual decline is an inevitably part of aging—and yet many people also believe that old people are wise. Indeed, this belief has been expressed in many cultures throughout history (Clayton & Birren, 1980; Holliday & Chandler, 1986). It is also featured in Erik Erikson's influential theory of life-span development. Erikson claims that older adults often gain wisdom as they face the prospect of death and attempt to find meaning in their lives (Erikson, 1982; see also Chapter 10). Notice, too, that the word *wise* is never used to describe children, adolescents, or even young adults (unless perhaps it is to call one of them a "wise guy"). Is the association between wisdom and old age just a stereotype or is there some truth to it?

But first we must ask, what is wisdom, and how can one assess it? There is no consensus as yet among developmental psychologists, and very little research (see Sternberg, 1990). Paul Baltes and his colleagues offer this definition of **wisdom:** "good judgment and advice about important but uncertain matters of life" (Staudinger, Smith, & Baltes, 1992, p. 272). In this view, the wise person has exceptional insight into what life is all about. Others add that the wise person takes the time to reflect about life, is able to accept the human condition as it is, and genuinely cares for other people (Ardelt, 1997).

Does wisdom typically increase with age, or are one's life experiences more important than one's age in determining whether or not one is wise? Ursula Staudinger, Jacqui Smith, and Paul Baltes (1992) attempted to find out by interviewing young (ages 25–35) and elderly (ages 65–82) women who were either clinical psychologists or similarly well-educated professionals in other fields. The goal was to assess the relative contributions of age and specialized experience to wisdom, based on the assumption that clinical psychologists stand to gain special sensitivity to human problems from their professional training and practice.

These women were interviewed about a person named Martha, who had chosen to have a family but no career and who met up with an old friend who had chosen to have a career but no family. The women were asked to talk about how Martha might review and evaluate her life after this encounter. Answers were scored for five qualities judged to be indicators of wisdom: (1) knowledge of the human condition (for example, of the concerns of mothers and professional women); (2) sound strategies for analyzing life problems and weighing the pros and cons of different decisions; (3) awareness of the relevance of contextual factors, such as norms regarding women's roles, in shaping the developmental paths people take; (4) awareness that life goals are relative and depend on

We tend to believe that age brings wisdom. It can—but does not do so often.

the culture and the individual; and (5) insight into the unpredictability of life.

What was found? First, wisdom proved to be rare; it seems that only about 5% of the answers given by adults to problems like these qualify as "wise" (Smith & Baltes, 1990). Second, expertise proved to be more relevant than age to the development of wisdom. That is, clinical psychologists, whether they were young or old, displayed more signs of wisdom than other women did. Older women were generally no wiser—or less wise—than younger women.

So far, then, research does not support the common belief that wisdom is acquired *only* in old age. Yet the knowledge base that contributes to wisdom holds up very well later in life, like other crystallized intellectual abilities (Baltes et al., 1995). Older adults, like younger adults, are more likely to display wisdom if they have life experiences (such as work as a clinical psychologist) that sharpen their insights into the human condition. The immediate social context also influences the degree to which wisdom is expressed; wiser problem solutions are generated when adults have an opportunity to discuss problems with someone whose judgment they value and when they are encouraged to reflect after such discussions (Staudinger & Baltes, 1996). Thus, consulting with your fellow students and work colleagues and thinking about their advice may well be the beginning of wisdom.

At this early stage in the study of wisdom, there is much disagreement about what it is, how it develops, and how it is related to other mental abilities. However, research on wisdom provides still more evidence that different mental faculties develop and age differently over the adult years. Paul Baltes has offered a life-span perspective on intellectual development that highlights this fact (see Baltes & Graf, 1996). Performance on the sorts of problem-solving tests that measure fluid intelligence, especially those that require speedy information processing, does indeed decline in later life as biological aging takes its toll. However, older adults are often able to compensate for this decline by making good use of their crystallized abilities—the knowledge they have accumulated over a lifetime, and, for a few people, the wisdom that comes only with experience.

FACTORS THAT INFLUENCE IQ SCORES

Now that we have surveyed changes in intellectual functioning over the life span, let's address a different question: Why do children or adults who are *the same age* differ in IQ? Part of the answer is that they differ in the kinds of motivational and situational factors that can affect performance on a given day. Yet there are real differences in underlying intellectual ability to be explained, too, and, as usual, our best explanation is that genetic and environmental factors interact to make us what we are.

Genes

The pioneers of the IQ testing movement believed that individual differences in IQ exist simply because some people inherit better genes at conception than others do. Even though IQ scores are now known *not* to be determined entirely by genes, heredity does help explain individual differences in intellectual performance. As we saw in Chapter 3, identical twins obtain more similar IQ scores than fraternal twins do, even when they have been raised apart all their lives. Moreover, the IQs of adoptive children, once they reach adolescence anyway, are more strongly correlated with those of their biological parents than with those of their adoptive parents. Overall, about half of the variation in IQ scores within a group of individuals is associated with genetic differences among them (Neisser et al., 1996). This leaves about half of the variation attributable to differences in the environments in which people develop. Here we find that children growing up in the same home show family resemblance in IQ scores (an effect of shared environment) while they are children but

not by the time they reach adolescence and adulthood (Loehlin, Horn, & Willerman, 1997; McGue et al., 1993). Most effects of environment on IQ are unique to the individual, then, and are not shared by siblings.

The fact that differences in IQ are linked to differences in genetic makeup says nothing about the extent to which IQ can be increased. Height is even more strongly associated with genetic endowment than IQ. Yet it can clearly be decreased by poor nutrition or increased by good nutrition and has, in fact, increased over several generations as nutrition has improved (Sternberg, 1997). So let's look further at aspects of the environment in infancy and early childhood that can stimulate or inhibit intellectual growth. Then we will see how far this information can take us in explaining differences in IQ scores associated with socioeconomic status and race or ethnicity.

Home Environment

A recent study by Arnold Sameroff and his colleagues (1993) provides a broad overview of some of the environmental factors that put children at risk for having low IQ scores—and, by implication, some of the factors associated with higher IQs. These researchers assessed the ten risk factors shown in Table 9.3 at age 4 and again at age 13. Every one of these factors was related to IQ at age 4, and most also predicted IQ at age 13. In addition, the greater the number of these risk factors affecting a child, the lower his or her IQ. Which particular risk factors a child experienced was less important than how many he or she experienced. Clearly it is not good for intellectual development to grow up in a disadvantaged home with an adult who is unable to provide much intellectual nurturance.

In what specific ways do parents influence their children's intellectual development? Bettye Caldwell and Robert Bradley have developed a widely used instrument for determining how intellectually stimulating or impoverished a home environment is (Caldwell & Bradley, 1984; Bradley & Caldwell, 1984). Sample items from the preschool version of their **HOME inventory** (*Home Observation for Measurement of the Environment*) are shown in Table 9.4 (Caldwell & Bradley, 1984). Bradley and his colleagues (1989) have found that scores on the HOME predict African-American and Euro-American children's IQs at age 3 quite well; the correlations are about .50. Moreover, gains in IQ from age 1 to age 3 are likely to occur among children from stimulating homes, whereas children from families with low HOME scores often experience drops in IQ over the same period. The early IQ scores of Mexican-American children are not very closely related to their families' HOME scores, however, so we know less about how the home environments that Hispanic parents provide influence their children's intellectual development.

TABLE 9.3

Ten environmental risk factors associated with low IQ and mean IQs at age 4 of children who did or did not experience each risk factor

Risk Factor	Mean IQ at Age 4 if:	
	Child Experienced Risk Factor	Child Did Not Experience Risk Factor
Child is member of minority group	90	110
Head of household is unemployed or low-skilled worker	90	108
Mother did not complete high school	92	109
Family has four or more children	94	105
Father is absent from family	95	106
Family experienced many stressful life events	97	105
Parents have rigid child-rearing values	92	107
Mother is highly anxious/distressed	97	105
Mother has poor mental health/diagnosed disorder	99	107
Mother shows little positive affect toward child	88	107

SOURCE: Data and descriptions compiled from Sameroff et al. (1993)

TABLE 9.4

Subscales and sample items from the HOME inventory

SUBSCALE 1: EMOTIONAL AND VERBAL RESPONSIVITY OF PARENT (11 ITEMS)
Sample items: Parent responds verbally to child's vocalizations or verbalizations
                           Parent's speech is distinct, clear, and audible
                           Parent caresses or kisses child at least once

SUBSCALE 2: AVOIDANCE OF RESTRICTION AND PUNISHMENT (8 ITEMS)
Sample items: Parent neither slaps nor spanks child during visit
                           Parent does not scold or criticize child during visit
                           Parent does not interfere with or restrict child more than three times during visit

SUBSCALE 3: ORGANIZATION OF PHYSICAL AND TEMPORAL ENVIRONMENT (6 ITEMS)
Sample items: Child gets out of house at least four times a week
                           Child's play environment is safe

SUBSCALE 4: PROVISION OF APPROPRIATE PLAY MATERIALS (9 ITEMS)
Sample items: Child has a push or pull toy
                           Parent provides learning facilitators appropriate to age—mobile, table and
                               chairs, highchair, playpen, and so on
                           Parent provides toys for child to play with during visit

SUBSCALE 5: PARENTAL INVOLVEMENT WITH CHILD (6 ITEMS)
Sample items: Parent talks to child while doing household work
                           Parent structures child's play periods

SUBSCALE 6: OPPORTUNITIES FOR VARIETY IN DAILY STIMULATION (5 ITEMS)
Sample items: Father provides some care daily
                           Child has three or more books of his or her own

SOURCE: Adapted from Caldwell & Bradley (1984)

What particular aspects of the home environment best predict high IQs? Studies using the HOME inventory indicate that the most important factors are parental involvement with the child and opportunities for stimulation (Gottfried et al., 1994). Other researchers (e.g., Crockenberg, 1983) would add that the sheer amount of stimulation parents provide to their young children may not be as important as whether that stimulation is responsive to the child's behavior (a smile in return for a smile) and matched to the child's competencies so that it is neither too simple nor too challenging (Hunt & Paraskevopoulos, 1980; Miller, 1986). In short, an intellectually stimulating home is one in which parents are eager to be involved with their children and are responsive to their developmental needs and behavior (MacPhee, Ramey, & Yeates, 1984).

Do differences in stimulation in the home really *create* individual differences in IQ? We know that more intelligent parents are more likely than less intelligent parents to provide intellectually stimulating home environments for their children *and* to pass on to their children genes that contribute to high intelligence; that is, we have evidence of the *gene/environment correlations* discussed in Chapter 3. Could it be, then, that bright children are bright because of the genes they inherited rather than the home environment their bright parents provided? Keith Yeates and his colleagues (Yeates, MacPhee, Campbell, & Ramey, 1983) evaluated this hypothesis in a longitudinal study of 112 mothers and their children aged 2 to 4. They measured the mothers' IQs, the children's IQs from age 2 to age 4, and the families' HOME environments. The best predictor of a child's IQ at age 2 was the mother's IQ, just as a genetic hypothesis would suggest; home environment had little effect. But the picture changed by the time children were 4 years old, when mother's IQ and the quality of the home environment were about equally important predictors of the child's IQ. Moreover, the researchers established statistically that differences in the quality of the home environment influenced children's IQs over and above the effects of their mothers' IQs, and that much of the effects of mothers' IQs could be attributed to the fact that high-IQ mothers provided more stimulating home environments than low-IQ mothers (see also Luster & Dubow, 1992). We also know that adopted children's IQ scores rise considerably when they are moved from less stimulating to more stimulating homes (Turkheimer, 1991), and we know that the quality of day care children receive predicts their verbal IQ scores (Broberg et al., 1997).

In sum, the argument that genetic influences can fully explain the apparent effects of home environment on IQ does not hold up. Yet we cannot ignore genetic influences either, for gifted children are more likely than their less gifted peers to seek intellectual stimulation (Gottfried et al., 1994). Overall, intellectual development seems to go best when a motivated, intellectually capable child begging for intellectual nourishment is fortunate enough to get it from involved and responsive parents.

Social-Class Differences

Children from lower-class homes average some 10 to 20 points below their middle-class agemates on IQ

tests. This is true in all racial and ethnic groups (Helms, 1997). What if socioeconomic conditions were to improve?

Over the 20th century, average IQ scores have increased in all countries studied, a phenomenon called the **Flynn effect** after its discoverer, James Flynn (1987, 1996). In the United States, the increase has amounted to 3 to 4 IQ points per decade, perhaps 20 or more IQ points overall. Increases of this size cannot be due to genetic evolution and therefore must have environmental causes (Flynn, 1996). Interestingly, the Flynn effect is clearer for measures of fluid intelligence than for measures of crystallized intelligence, even though one might expect crystallized intelligence to benefit more from improved educational opportunities. Flynn believes that a good portion of the trend reflects increases in performance on IQ tests but not in true intellectual capacity; for example, today's test takers are probably more test-wise than test takers of the past. Yet he also concludes that improved nutrition, education, and living conditions over this century have contributed to real improvements in intellectual functioning.

Similarly, improving the economic conditions of children's homes can improve their IQs. For example, Sandra Scarr and Richard Weinberg have charted the intellectual growth of black and white children adopted before their first birthdays (Scarr & Weinberg, 1983; Weinberg, Scarr, & Waldman, 1992). Many of these children came from disadvantaged family backgrounds and had biological parents who were poorly educated and somewhat below average in IQ. The children were placed in middle-class homes with adoptive parents who were highly educated and above average in intelligence. Throughout childhood and adolescence, these adoptees have posted average or above average scores on standardized IQ tests—higher scores than they would have obtained if they had stayed in the disadvantaged environments offered by their natural parents.

Could social-class differences in IQ be due to differences in the quality of the home environment that parents of different socioeconomic levels provide? Yes, at least partially. Scores on the HOME inventory are higher in middle-class homes than in lower-class homes, indicating that middle-class homes are more intellectually stimulating on average (Bradley et al., 1989; Gottfried, 1984). Poor nutrition, drug abuse, disruptive family experiences, and other factors associated with poverty may also contribute to the social-class gap in IQ (Gottfried & Gottfried, 1984).

Racial and Ethnic Differences

Controversy regarding racial and ethnic differences in IQ has raged for many years, but the publication of

Differences in intellectual functioning within any racial or ethnic group are far greater than differences among groups.

The Bell Curve in 1994 by Richard Herrnstein and Charles Murray caused a major stir. The main theme of the book was that IQ scores have become more and more important in determining people's occupational success and socioeconomic standing and that we are becoming a society with a high-IQ, educated, and wealthy elite and a lower-IQ, less educated class of poor people. They also argued that racial differences in average IQ scores exist, that they cannot be explained entirely by socioeconomic differences between racial groups, and that these IQ differences are probably rooted, at least in part, in genetic differences between the races.

What do we know about this controversial topic? Racial and ethnic differences in IQ scores do exist; everyone acknowledges that. In the United States, for example, Asian-American and Euro-American children tend to score higher on IQ tests than African-American, Native-American, and Hispanic-American children, on average (Neisser et al., 1996). Different subcultural groups sometimes also show distinctive profiles of mental abilities; for example, black children often do particularly well on verbal tasks, whereas Hispanic children, perhaps because of language differences, tend to excel on nonverbal items (Neisser et al., 1996; Taylor & Richards, 1991). Of course, it is essential to keep in mind that we are talking about *group averages*. Like the IQ scores of white children, those of minority children run the whole range, from the mentally retarded to the gifted. We certainly cannot predict an individual's IQ merely on the basis of racial or ethnic identity.

Having said that, we must ask why these average group differences exist. Let's consider the following hypotheses: (1) bias in the tests, (2) motivational factors, (3) genetic differences between groups, and (4) environmental differences between groups.

Culture Bias

There may be *culture bias* in testing; that is, IQ tests may be more appropriate for children from white middle-class backgrounds than for those from other subcultural groups (Helms, 1992; Lopez, 1997). Low-income African-American children who speak a different dialect of English from that spoken by middle-class Anglo children, as well as Hispanic children who hear Spanish rather than English at home, may not understand some test instructions or items. What's more, their experiences may not allow them to become familiar with some of the information that is called for on the tests (for example, "What is a 747?" "Who wrote Hamlet?").

It is true that minority-group children often do not have as much exposure to the culture reflected in the tests as nonminority children do. If IQ tests assess "proficiency in white culture," minority children are bound to look deficient (Helms, 1992). Using IQ tests designed to be fair to all ethnic groups and introducing procedures to help minority children feel more comfortable and motivated can cut the usual IQ gap between African-American and white children in half (Kaufman, Kamphaus, & Kaufman, 1985). But, even though standardized IQ test items sometimes have a white middle-class flavor, group differences in IQ probably cannot be traced solely to test bias. *Culture-fair IQ tests* include items that should be equally unfamiliar (or familiar) to people from all ethnic groups and social classes—for example, items that require completing a geometric design with a piece that matches the rest of the design. Still, racial and ethnic differences emerge on such tests (Jensen, 1980). In addition, IQ tests predict future school achievement as well for blacks and other minorities as they do for whites (Neisser et al., 1996).

Motivational Factors

Another possibility is that minority individuals are not motivated to do their best in testing situations because they are anxious or resist being judged by whites (Moore, 1986; Ogbu, 1994; Steele, 1997). They may be wary of strange examiners, may see little point in trying to do well, and may shake their heads as if to say they don't know the answer before the question is ever completed. Disadvantaged children do indeed score some 7 to 10 points better when they are given time to warm up to a friendly examiner or are given a mix of easy and hard items so that they do not become discouraged by a long string of difficult items (Zigler et al., 1982). Even though almost all children do better with a friendly examiner (Sacks, 1952), it still seems that black children, even those from middle-class homes, are often less comfortable in testing situations than white middle-class children are (Moore, 1986).

Claude Steele and his colleagues have argued that the performance of African Americans is likely to suffer whenever negative stereotypes of their group come into play (Steele, 1997; Steele & Aronson, 1995). In one study, female students at Stanford University were given very difficult test items; some were told that they were taking a test of verbal abilities and would get feedback about their strengths and weaknesses; others were told that they were going to do some verbal problems but that their ability would not be evaluated. As Figure 9.6 shows, African-American students performed poorly when they were led to believe that the test would reveal their level of intellectual ability, but performed more like white students when they did not think their ability would be judged. Even being asked to identify their race in a personal information section at the start of a test of intellectual ability can undermine the performance of African-American college students (Steele & Aronson, 1995).

Why? Steele concluded that African Americans perform poorly on IQ tests partly because of "stereotype threat," fear that they will be judged to have the qualities associated with negative stereotypes of African Americans. It is not that African Americans have internalized stereotypes and believe that they are intellectually inferior, according to Steele. Instead, they become anxious and unable to perform well in testing situations that arouse concerns about being negatively stereotyped.

Genetic Influences

Perhaps no idea in psychology has sparked more heated debate than the suggestion that racial and eth-

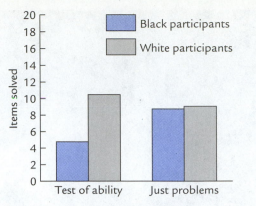

FIGURE 9.6 *African-American students perform poorly on tests of mental abilities when they think they are taking a test that may result in their being stereotyped as unintelligent.* (Adapted from Steele & Aronson, 1995)

nic differences in IQ scores could be due to group differences in genetic makeup. We know that differences in genetic makeup contribute, along with differences in environment, to IQ differences *within* either the white or the black population. Scholars such as Arthur Jensen (1969) and Herrnstein and Murray (1994) have gone a step further to suggest that IQ differences *between* whites and blacks may be due to genetic differences between the races.

However, most psychologists do not think that evidence that heredity contributes to within-group differences says much at all about the reasons for between-group differences. Richard Lewontin (1976) makes this point with an analogy. Suppose that corn seeds with different genetic makeups are randomly drawn from a bag and planted in two fields—one that is barren and one that has fertile soil. Since all the plants within each field were grown in the same soil, their differences in height would have to be due to differences in genetic makeup. A genetic explanation would fit. But, if the plants in the fertile field are generally taller than those in the barren field, this *between-field* variation must be entirely due to environment. Similarly, even though genes partially explain individual differences in IQ *within* black groups and white groups, the average difference *between* the racial groups may still reflect nothing more than differences in the environments they typically experience. There is currently no direct evidence that differences in genetic makeup between the races account for average group differences in IQ (Neisser et al., 1996).

Environmental Influences

It is time to return to an environmental hypothesis about racial and ethnic differences in IQ. Many of the intellectual and academic differences that have been attributed to race or ethnicity probably reflect racial and ethnic differences in socioeconomic status instead (Patterson, Kupersmidt, & Vaden, 1990). Research on adopted children is very relevant here. Placement in more advantaged homes has allowed lower-income black children to equal or exceed the average IQ in the general population and to exceed the IQs of comparable black children raised in more disadvantaged environments by 20 points (Moore, 1986; Scarr & Weinberg, 1983; Weinberg et al., 1992). This could not have happened if black children were genetically deficient.

The major message of this research is that children, whether they are black or white, perform better on IQ tests when they grow up in intellectually stimulating environments with involved, responsive parents and are exposed to the "culture of the tests and the schools" (Scarr & Weinberg, 1983, p. 261). How much of the racial gap in IQ can be explained by racial differences in neighborhood and family socioeconomic conditions, mother's education, and qualities of the home environment? Jeanne Brooks-Gunn, Pamela Klebanov, and Greg Duncan (1996) used statistical procedures to correct for these environmental differences between African-American and white children so that they could estimate what the IQ difference would be if the two racial groups had been raised in similar environments. Without any controls for environmental differences, there was an IQ gap of 18 points. The gap narrowed to only 8 points when family and neighborhood income levels were controlled and was reduced to only 3 points, a trivial difference, when racial differences in the provision of a stimulating home environment (HOME scores) were controlled. In short, the fact that more African-American than white children live in poverty and have limited learning opportunities at home has a lot to do with the racial difference in average IQ scores.

There are signs that the IQ gap between black and white children has been decreasing in recent years as educational and economic opportunities for African Americans have improved (Vincent, 1991). Perhaps the issue of racial and ethnic differences in IQ will largely disappear as life conditions for minority-group families improve further. Culture bias, motivational factors such as stereotype threat, and socioeconomic differences between groups may all contribute to the differences we see today.

THE EXTREMES OF INTELLIGENCE

Although we have identified some of the factors that contribute to individual differences in intellectual performance, we cannot fully appreciate the magnitude of these differences without considering people at the extremes of the IQ continuum. Just how different are mentally retarded and gifted individuals? And how different are their lives?

Mental Retardation

Mental retardation is currently defined by the American Association on Mental Retardation (Luckasson et al., 1992) as significantly below-average intellectual functioning associated with limitations in areas of adaptive behavior such as self-care and social skills and originating before age 18. To be diagnosed as mentally retarded, an individual must obtain an IQ score of 70 to 75 or lower *and* have difficulties meeting age-appropriate expectations in important areas of everyday functioning. According to this definition, mental retardation is not merely a deficiency within the person; rather, it is the product of the interaction between person and environment, strongly influenced by the type and level of supportive help the individual receives (Reiss, 1994).

Individuals with mental retardation differ greatly in their levels of functioning. A mildly retarded adult with an IQ in the range of about 55 to 70 is likely to have a mental age comparable to that of an 8- to 12-year-old child. Mildly retarded persons can learn both academic and practical skills in school, and they can potentially work and live independently or with occasional help as adults. At the other end of the continuum, so-called profoundly retarded persons, with IQs below 20 to 25 and mental ages below 3 years, show major delays in all areas of development and require basic care, sometimes in institutional settings. They, too, can benefit considerably from training, though.

Mental retardation has many causes. Severely retarded persons are often affected by **organic retardation,** meaning that their retardation is due to some identifiable biological cause associated with hereditary factors, diseases, or injuries. *Down syndrome*, the condition associated with an extra 21st chromosome, and *phenylketonuria (PKU)* are familiar examples of organic retardation associated with genetic factors (Simonoff, Bolton, & Rutter, 1996; and see Chapter 3). Other forms of organic retardation are associated with prenatal risk factors—an alcoholic mother, exposure to rubella, and so on (see Chapter 4). Organically retarded children, because many of them are significantly behind other children developmentally, can often be identified at birth or during infancy. However, the most common form of mental retardation, **cultural-familial retardation,** is typically milder and appears to be due to a combination of low genetic potential and a poor, unstimulating environment (Simonoff et al., 1996). Whereas children with organic retardation come from all socioeconomic levels, children with cultural-familial retardation often come from poverty areas and have a parent or sibling who is also retarded (Zigler, 1995). From one-half to three-quarters of mental retardation is of the cultural-familial type: exact cause unknown (Zigler & Hodapp, 1991).

Overall, as many as 3% of school-age children are classified as mentally retarded (Luckasson et al., 1992;

Roeleveld, Zielhuis, & Gabreels, 1997). What becomes of these children as they grow up? As a general rule, they proceed along the same paths and through the same sequences of developmental milestones as other children do (Zigler & Hodapp, 1991). Because they are developing at a slower-than-normal pace, their mental ages continue to increase well into adulthood, whereas normally mental growth levels off in adolescence (Fisher & Zeaman, 1970). Their IQs remain low, of course, because they do not achieve the same level of growth that others do. They, like nonretarded people, show signs of intellectual aging in later life, especially on tests that require speed (Devenny et al., 1996). Individuals with Down syndrome may experience even greater intellectual deterioration, as they are at risk for premature Alzheimer's disease (Day & Jancar, 1994).

As for their outcomes in life, consider a follow-up study of individuals with mild and borderline mental retardation who had been placed in segregated special education classes during the 1920s and 1930s (Ross et al., 1985). The individuals studied had a mean IQ of 67. They were compared with their siblings and with nonretarded peers about 35 years later. Generally, these mentally retarded adults had poor life outcomes in middle age in comparison with nonretarded groups (see also Schalock et al., 1992). About 80% of the retarded men were employed, but they usually held semiskilled or unskilled jobs that required little education or intellectual ability. Women often married and became homemakers. Compared with nonretarded peers, retarded men and women fared worse on other counts as well. For example, they had lower incomes, less adequate housing, poorer adjustment in social relationships, and a greater dependency on others.

Yet the authors of the study still found grounds for optimism. These individuals had done much better during adulthood than stereotyped expectations of mentally retarded persons would predict. After all, most of them worked and had married, and about 80% reported having had no need for public assistance in the 10 years before they were interviewed. This study, like others before it, suggests that many children who are labeled mentally retarded by the schools—and who do indeed have difficulty with the tasks demanded of them in school—"vanish" into the general population after they leave school. Apparently they can adapt to the demands of adult life. As the authors put it, "It does not take as many IQ points as most people believe to be productive, to get along with others, and to be self-fulfilled" (Ross et al., 1985, p. 149).

Giftedness

The gifted child used to be identified solely by an IQ score—one that was at least 130 or 140. Programs for gifted children still focus mainly on those with very high IQs, but there is increased recognition that some

Gifted children have either high IQ scores or special abilities. This four-year-old Chinese girl is already entering musical competitions in Beijing.

children are gifted because they have special abilities rather than because they have high general intelligence. Even high-IQ children are usually not equally talented in all areas; contrary to myth, they cannot just become anything they choose (Winner, 1996). More often, high-IQ children have exceptional talent in an area or two and otherwise are good, but not exceptional, performers (Achter, Benbow, & Lubinski, 1997). So today's definitions emphasize that **giftedness** involves having a high IQ *or* showing special abilities in areas valued in our society, such as mathematics, the performing and visual arts, or even leadership (Coleman, 1985). Here we focus on individuals with exceptional IQs.

How early can intellectually gifted children be identified? By toddlerhood, according to a longitudinal study by Allen Gottfried and his colleagues (1994). They tracked a large sample of children from age 1 to age 8, determined which children had IQs of 130 or above at age 8, and then looked for differences between these gifted children and other children earlier in life. The gifted children turned out to be identifiable as early as 18 months of age, primarily by their advanced language skills. They were also highly curious and motivated to learn; they even enjoyed the challenge of taking IQ tests more than most children.

The rest of the story of the development of high-IQ children is told by a major longitudinal study launched in 1921 by none other than Lewis Terman, developer of the Stanford-Binet test (Fincher, 1973; Terman, 1954; Oden, 1968). The participants were more than 1500 California schoolchildren who were nominated by their teachers as gifted and who had IQs of 140 or higher. It soon became apparent that these high-IQ children (who came to be called Termites) were exceptional in many other ways as well. For example, they had weighed more at birth and had learned to walk and talk sooner than most toddlers. They reached puberty somewhat earlier than average and had better-than-average health. Their teachers rated them as better adjusted and more morally mature than their less-intelligent peers. And, although they were no more popular than their classmates, they were quick to take on leadership responsibilities. Taken together, these findings destroy the stereotype that most gifted children are frail, sickly youngsters who are socially inadequate and emotionally immature.

Another demonstration of the personal and social maturity of most gifted children comes from a study of high-IQ children who skipped high school entirely and entered the University of Washington as part of a special program to accelerate their education (Robinson & Janos, 1986). Contrary to the common wisdom that gifted children will suffer socially and emotionally if they skip grades and are forced to fit in with much older students, these youngsters showed no signs at all of maladjustment. Indeed, on several measures of psychological and social maturity and adjustment, they equaled their much older college classmates, as well as similarly gifted students who attended high school. Many of them thrived in college, for the first time finding friends like themselves—friends who "got their jokes" (Noble, Robinson, & Gunderson, 1993, p. 125).

Yet it is inaccurate to conclude that intellectually gifted children are models of good adjustment, perfect in every way. Their main social advantage lies in their ability to think maturely about social dilemmas; they are not any more or less prone to behavioral and emotional problems than other children (Gottfried et al., 1994). Some research also suggests that children with IQs closer to 180 than 130 are quite often unhappy and socially isolated, perhaps because they are so out of step with their peers, and sometimes even have serious problems (Winner, 1996).

What becomes of gifted children as adults? Failure can come even to the most gifted of prodigies. In *Terman's Kids*, Joel Shurkin (1992) describes several less-than-happy life stories of some of Terman's Termites. A woman who graduated from Stanford at age 17 and was headed for success as a writer became a landlady instead; an emotionally disturbed boy took cyanide at age 18 after being rejected in love. Box 9.3 describes a particularly tragic case of failed genius.

BOX 9.3

William Sidis: A case of unrealized potential

No failed genius is more notorious than William Sidis. According to Amy Wallace's (1986) biography *The Prodigy,* Sidis was the son of a brilliant Harvard psychologist and the godson of the pioneering psychologist William James. From infancy, "Billy" was the subject of an experiment designed by his father to prove that magnificent talents can be developed in any child. Given the most enriched of early environments (and probably some good genes as well), Billy could read the newspaper at 18 months of age and had learned eight languages by the time he reached school age. His school years were brief, however, for he entered Harvard at age 11 and was teaching mathematics at Rice University by age 17.

Unfortunately, his parents invested so much energy in developing his mind that they apparently neglected his social and emotional development. His

social incompetence and odd habits were as widely publicized as his intellectual feats, and finally William Sidis had apparently had enough of it all. He

quit the academic life, took a series of menial jobs, and lived as a hermit, writing about obscure topics and jumping at every opportunity to show children his prodigious collection of streetcar and subway tickets. Sidis seemed content with his life of obscurity, but he certainly did not achieve the greatness that might have been predicted. He died of a stroke at age 46.

William Sidis was clearly the exception to all we know about gifted children and their outcomes. Nonetheless, his story reminds us that early blooming is no guarantee of later flowering. And it works the other way, too: Late blooming does not rule out eminence in adulthood. We need only cite the case of Albert Einstein, whose name is synonymous with genius. Einstein didn't speak until age 4, could not read until age 7, and was judged by his teachers to have little future at all (Feldman, 1982)!

These are the exceptions, however; most of Terman's gifted children remained as remarkable in adulthood as they had been in childhood. Fewer than 5% were rated as seriously maladjusted. Their rates of such problems as ill health, mental illness, alcoholism, and delinquent behavior were but a fraction of those observed in the general population (Terman, 1954), although they were no less likely to divorce (Holahan & Sears, 1995).

The occupational achievements of the men in the sample were impressive. In middle age, 88% were employed in professional or high-level business jobs, compared to 20% of men in the general population (Oden, 1968). As a group they had taken out more than 200 patents and written some 2000 scientific reports, 100 books, 375 plays or short stories, and more than 300 essays, sketches, magazine articles, and critiques. And gifted women? Because of the influence of gender-role expectations during the period covered by the study, gifted women achieved less than gifted men vocationally, often interrupting their careers or sacrificing their career goals entirely to raise families. Yet they were more likely to have careers and to have accomplished ones than most women of their generation.

Finally, the Termites aged well. In their 60s and 70s, most of the men and women in the Terman study were highly active, involved, healthy, and happy people (Holahan & Sears, 1995). The men kept working longer than most men do and stayed involved in work even after they retired. The women too led exceptionally active lives. Contrary to the stereotype that gifted individuals burn out early, then, the Termites continued to burn bright throughout their lives.

Overall, most of Terman's gifted children moved through adulthood as healthy, happy, and highly productive individuals. Yet some fared better than others. Even within this elite group, for example, the quality of the individual's home environment was important. The most well-adjusted and successful adults had highly educated parents who offered them both love and intellectual stimulation (Tomlinson-Keasey & Little, 1990).

CREATIVITY AND SPECIAL TALENTS

Despite their many positive outcomes in life, not one of Terman's high-IQ gifted children became truly eminent. Recall that Terman had teachers nominate bright children for inclusion in the study. Is it possible that teachers overlooked some children who would be considered gifted by today's criteria, but because of their special talents rather than their high IQs? Might they have missed children capable of outstanding work in a particular area such as music, art, or writing? The word *creativity* comes to mind. Perhaps creativity is more important than IQ in allowing a Michelangelo or a Mozart to break new ground. But what is creativity, and what do we know about its development?

What Is Creativity?

Creativity is most often defined as the ability to produce *novel* responses that are appropriate in context and valued by others—products that are both original and meaningful (Richards, 1996). In his structure-of-intellect model, J. P. Guilford (1967, 1988) captured the idea of creativity by proposing that it involves divergent rather than convergent thinking. **Divergent thinking** requires coming up with a variety of ideas or solutions to a problem when there is no one right answer. **Convergent thinking** involves "converging" on the one best answer to a problem and is precisely what IQ tests measure. The most common measure of creativity, at least in children, is what is called **ideational fluency** or the sheer number of different (including novel) ideas that one can generate. Quick—list all the uses you can think of for a pencil. An uncreative person might say you could write letters, notes, postcards, and so forth; by contrast, one creative person envisioned a pencil as "a backscratcher, a potting stake, kindling for a fire, a rolling pin for baking, a toy for a woodpecker, or a small boat for a cricket" (Richards, 1996, p. 73).

Creativity and divergent thinking truly are distinct from general intelligence and convergent thinking. For example, Getzels and Jackson (1962) gave more than 500 students in grades 6 to 12 intelligence tests and five creativity tests:

1. A word-association test in which students were asked to give as many definitions as possible for fairly common words.
2. A test of alternative uses, in which students were asked to think of as many uses as they could for familiar objects.
3. A hidden-shapes test that required them to find geometric figures hidden in more complex figures.
4. A fables test in which they furnished the last line for an unfinished fable.
5. A make-up-problems test in which they were to make up a variety of mathematical problems from a large amount of numerical information.

Scores on these creativity measures and scores on IQ tests were not highly correlated; typically such correlations are only about .20 (Torrance, 1969). Creativity and general intelligence are related in the sense that highly creative people rarely have below-average IQs. Thus, a *minimum* of intelligence is probably required for creativity (Runco, 1992; Wallach, 1971). However, among people who have average or above-average IQs,

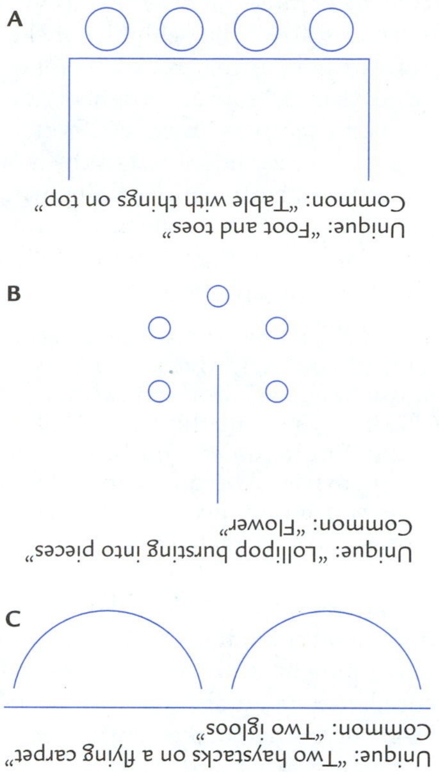
A
Common: „Table with things on top"
Unique: „Foot and toes"
B
Common: „Flower"
Unique: „Lollipop bursting into pieces"
C
Common: „Two igloos"
Unique: „Two haystacks on a flying carpet"

FIGURE 9.7 *Are you creative? Indicate what you see in each of the three drawings. Below each drawing you will find examples of unique and common responses, drawn from a study of creativity in children.* (From Wallach & Kogan, 1965)

an individual's IQ score is essentially unrelated to his or her level of creativity. In all likelihood, then, the IQs of you and your classmates will not necessarily predict which of you will give the most creative answers to the problems in Figure 9.7.

Creativity in Childhood and Adolescence

What is the child who scores high on tests of creativity like? Getzels and Jackson (1962) compared children who had high creativity scores but normal-range IQ scores with children who scored high in IQ but not in creativity. Personality measures suggested that the creative children showed more freedom, originality, humor, violence, and playfulness than the high-IQ children. Perhaps as a result, the high-IQ children were more success oriented and received more approval from teachers. Compared with their less creative peers, creative children also engaged in more fantasy or pretend play (Kogan, 1983). Such play often involves inventing new uses for familiar objects and new roles for oneself.

Although average IQ scores differ across racial and socioeconomic groups, scores on creativity tests often do not (Kogan, 1983). Moreover, genetic influences (a source of individual differences in IQ), have little to do with performance on tests of creativity; twins are similar in the degree of creativity they display, but identical twins are no more similar than fraternal twins (Plomin, 1990; Reznikoff et al., 1973). This suggests that certain qualities of the home environment tend to make brothers and sisters alike in their degree of creativity. What qualities? Although we have little research to go on, parents of creative children and adolescents tend to value nonconformity and independence, accept their children as they are, encourage their curiosity and playfulness, and grant them a good deal of freedom to explore new possibilities on their own (Getzels & Jackson, 1962; Harrington, Block, & Block, 1987; Runco, 1992). In some cases the parent/child relationship is even distant; a surprising number of eminent creators seem to have experienced rather lonely, insecure, and unhappy childhoods (Ochse, 1990). Out of their adversity may have come a strong desire to excel. Overall, then, creative abilities are influenced by factors quite distinct from those that influence the cognitive abilities measured on IQ tests.

How does the capacity to be creative change with age? We really are not sure. Performance on tests of creativity generally increases over the childhood and adolescent years, but there appear to be certain ages along the way when it drops off (Kogan, 1983). Howard Gardner (Gardner, Phelps, & Wolf, 1990) suggests that preschool children are highly original, playful, and uninhibited but that school-age children become restricted in their creative expression as they attempt to master their culture's rules for art, music, dance, and other creative endeavors so that they can do things the "right" way. During adolescence, Gardner believes, some individuals give up the desire to express themselves creatively, but others regain the innovativeness and freedom of expression they had as preschoolers and put it to use, along with the technical skills they gained as children, to produce highly creative works. The ages at which creativity flourishes or is stifled seem to vary from culture to culture, depending on when children are pressured to conform (Torrance, 1975). Overall, the developmental course of creativity is not so predictable or steady as the increase in mental age seen on measures of IQ. Instead, creativity seems to wax and wane with age in response to developmental needs and cultural demands.

How well does performance on tests of creativity predict actual creative accomplishments such as original artwork or outstanding science projects? Some researchers have found that scores on creativity tests administered in either elementary or secondary school predict actual creative achievements, such as inventions and novels, in adulthood (Howieson,

FIGURE 9.8 *When most children are drawing scribbles, a gifted child artist named Eytan was drawing sophisticated vehicles like this cement truck, drawn at the age of 2 years and 7 months. Eytan's parents enjoyed his drawings but did nothing to teach him how to draw; nor did he merely copy drawings. Instead, he figured out on his own how to represent three dimensions on a two-dimensional piece of paper.* (From Golumb, 1992)

1981; Runco, 1992; Torrance, 1988). However, just as it is a mistake to expect IQ to predict creative accomplishments, it may also be a mistake to expect tests of creativity to do so with any great accuracy (Albert, 1996). Why? First, creativity is expressed in different ways at different points in the life span; engaging in imaginative play as a child is correlated with high scores on tests of creativity (Russ, 1996), but all of this may have little to do with being a creative scientist or musician as an adult. Also, creativity tests, like IQ tests, attempt to measure *general* cognitive abilities when, in fact, many *specific talents* exist, and each of them (artistic, mathematical, musical, and so on) requires distinct skills and experiences, as suggested by Gardner's theory of multiple intelligences.

So researchers are now looking at individuals who do indeed show exceptional talent in a particular field and are trying to identify the factors that contribute to their accomplishments (Sternberg & Lubart, 1996; and see Figure 9.8). David Feldman (1982, 1986), for example, has studied children who are "prodigies" in such areas as chess, music, and mathematics. These individuals were generally similar to other children in areas outside their fields of expertise. What contributed to their special achievements? They had *talent*, of course, but they also seemed to have a powerful *motivation* to develop their special talents—a real passion for what they were doing. The Olympic gymnast Olga Korbutt put it well: "If gymnastics did not exist, I would have invented it" (Feldman, 1982, p. 35). Moreover, these achievers were blessed with an *environment* that recognized, valued, and nurtured their talent and motivation (see also Winner, 1996). They were strongly encouraged and supported by their families and intensively tutored or coached by experts. According to Feldman, the child with creative potential

in a specific field must become intimately familiar with the current state of the field if he or she is to advance or transform it, as the groundbreaking artist or musician does. But parents and trainers must not be too pushy. For example, David Helfgott, the Australian pianist who was the subject of the movie *Shine*, was nearly destroyed by an abusive father who pushed him unmercifully to master difficult pieces (Page, 1996). Cellist Yo-Yo Ma, a prodigy himself, says this about nurturing young musicians:

> If you lead them toward music, teach them that it is beautiful, and help them learn—say, "Oh, you love music, well, let's work on this piece together, and I'll show you something" . . . That's a *creative* nurturing. But if you just push them to be stars, and tell them they'll become rich and famous—or, worse, if you try to live through them—that is damaging. (Page, 1996, p. G10)

K. Anders Ericsson and Neil Charness (1994) go even further than Feldman in emphasizing the importance of environment in the development of creative talent. Indeed, they maintain that it is practice rather than innate talent that makes great creators great, that nature is overrated and nurture is underrated when it comes to creative achievement. Their research shows that prolonged training in a set of skills can alter cognitive and physiological processes and permit levels of performance that would have been unimaginable without training. Motivation also enters in, however, because only some individuals are willing to do what Ericsson and Charness believe is necessary to become outstanding in a field—work hard every day over a period of more than ten years.

In summary, there are many forms of giftedness, many "intelligences." Studies of creativity have revealed that performance on creativity tests is distinct from performance on IQ tests. Yet neither tests of general intelligence nor tests of general creativity are very good at predicting which children will show exceptional talent in a *specific* field. Instead, that kind of creative achievement seems to be related to characteristics of the individual, including exceptional talent and motivation, *and* characteristics of the environment, especially support and the extensive training required to master a field.

Creative Achievement in Adulthood

Studies of creativity during the adult years have focused on a very small number of so-called eminent creators in such fields as art, music, science, and philosophy. The big question has been this: *When* in adulthood are such individuals most productive and most likely to create their best works? Is it early in adulthood, when they can benefit from youth's enthusiasm and freshness of approach? Or is it later in adulthood, when they have fully mastered their field and have the experience and knowledge necessary to make a breakthrough in it? And what becomes of the careers of eminent creators in old age?

Early studies by Harvey Lehman (1953) and Wayne Dennis (1966) provided a fairly clear picture of how creative careers unfold (see also Simonton, 1990). In most fields, creative production increases steeply from the 20s to the late 30s and early 40s and then gradually declines thereafter, though not to the same low levels that characterized very early adulthood. Peak times of creative achievement also vary from field to field. As Figure 9.9 shows, the productivity of scholars in the humanities (for example, historians and philosophers) continues well into old age and actually peaks in the 60s, possibly because creative work in these fields often involves integrating knowledge that has "crystallized" over many years. By contrast, productivity in the arts (for example, music or drama) peaks in the 30s and 40s and declines quite steeply thereafter, perhaps because artistic creativity depends on a more "fluid" or innovative kind of thinking. Scientists seem to be intermediate, peaking in their 40s and declining only in their 70s. Even within the same general field, differences in peak times have been noted. For example, poets reach their peak before novelists do, and mathematicians peak before other scientists do (Dennis, 1966; Lehman, 1953).

Still, in many fields (including psychology, by the way), creative production rises to a peak in the late 30s or early 40s, and there are some declines in both total number of works and number of high-quality works thereafter (Simonton, 1990). This same pattern can be detected across different cultures and historical periods. Even so, the percentage of a creator's works that are major, significant ones does not change much at all over the years (Simonton, 1990). This means that many creators are still producing outstanding works in old age—sometimes their greatest works—not just rehashes of earlier triumphs. Michelangelo, for instance, was in his 70s and 80s when he worked on St. Peter's Cathedral, and Goethe was polishing *Faust* at 83. Indeed, the most eminent among the eminent seem to start early and finish late (Simonton, 1990).

How can we account for changes in creative production over the adult years? One explanation, proposed long ago (Beard, 1874, cited by Simonton, 1984), is that creative achievement requires both enthusiasm and experience. In early adulthood the enthusiasm is there, but the experience is not; in later adulthood the experience is there, but the enthusiasm or vigor has fallen off. People in their 30s and 40s have it all.

Dean Simonton (1984, 1990, 1991) has offered another theory: Each creator may have a certain potential to create that is realized over the adult years; as the potential is realized, less is left to express. According

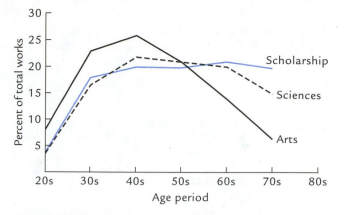

FIGURE 9.9 *Percentage of total works produced in each decade of the lives of eminent creators. The "scholarship" group includes historians and philosophers; the "sciences" category includes natural and physical scientists, inventors, and mathematicians; and the "arts" creators include architects, musicians, dramatists, poets, and so on.* (Data from Dennis, 1966)

to Simonton, creative activity involves two processes: *ideation* (generating creative ideas) and *elaboration* (executing ideas to produce actual poems, paintings, or scientific publications). After a career is launched, some time elapses before any ideas are generated or any works actually completed. This would explain the rise in creative achievement between the 20s and 30s. Also, some kinds of work take longer to formulate or complete than others, which helps explain why a poet (who can generate and carry out ideas quickly) might reach a creative peak earlier in life than, say, a historian (who may need to devote years to the research and writing necessary to complete a book once the idea for it is hatched).

Why does creative production eventually begin to taper off? Simonton (1990, 1991) suggests that older creators may simply have used up much of their total stock of potential ideas. They never totally exhaust their creative potential, but they have less of it left to realize. Simonton argues, then, that changes in creative production over the adult years have more to do with the nature of the creative process than with a loss of mental ability in later life. Creators who start their careers late are likely to experience the very same rise and fall of creative output that others do, only later in life. And those lucky creators with immense creative potential to realize will not burn out; they will keep right on producing great works until they die.

What about mere mortals like us? Here, researchers have fallen back on tests designed to measure creativity. In one study, scores on a test of divergent thinking abilities decreased at least modestly after about age 40 and decreased even more steeply starting at about 70 (McCrae, Arenberg, & Costa, 1987). It seems that elderly adults do not differ much from younger adults in the originality of their ideas; the main difference is that they generate fewer of them (Jaquish & Ripple, 1981). Generally, then, these studies agree with the studies of eminent achievers: Creative behavior becomes less frequent in later life, but it remains possible throughout the adult years.

APPLICATIONS: BOOSTING INTELLECTUAL PERFORMANCE ACROSS THE LIFE SPAN

How much can special training improve performance on tests of intelligence? Is such training effective only early in life, when intellectual growth is most rapid, or can it also work later in life? Intervention studies have explored how plastic, or moldable, intelligence is in early childhood, adolescence, and old age. Most of these interventions have been offered to those most in need of them—disadvantaged infants and preschoolers, mentally retarded individuals, and adults whose intellectual abilities are declining in old age.

Early Intervention for Preschool Children

During the 1960s a number of programs were launched to enrich the early learning experiences of disadvantaged preschoolers. *Project Head Start* is perhaps the best known of these interventions. The idea was to provide a variety of social and intellectual experiences that might better prepare these children for school. At first, Head Start and similar programs seemed to be a smashing success; children in the programs were posting average gains of about 10 points on IQ tests. But then discouragement set in: By the time children reached the middle years of grade school, their IQs were no higher than those of control-group children (Gray, Ramsey, & Klaus, 1982). Such findings led Arthur Jensen (1969, p. 2) to conclude that "compensatory education has been tried and it apparently has failed."

But that was not the end of it. Children in some of these programs have now been followed into their teens and even 20s. Irving Lazar and Richard Darlington (1982) reported on the long-term effects of 11 early intervention programs in several areas of the United States. Other follow-up studies of Head Start and similar early education programs for disadvantaged children have been conducted since then (see Campbell & Ramey, 1995; Zigler & Styfco, 1994). These long-term studies indicate the following:

1. Children who participate in early intervention programs show immediate gains on IQ and school achievement tests, whereas nonparticipants do not. However, the gains rarely last for more than three or four years after the program has ended. Impacts on measures other than IQ are more encouraging.

2. Compensatory education improves both children's and mothers' attitudes about achievement. When asked to describe something that has made them feel proud of themselves, program participants are more likely than nonparticipants to mention scholastic achievements or (in the case of 15- to 18-year-olds) job-related successes. Mothers of program participants tend to be more satisfied with their children's school performance and to hold higher occupational aspirations for their children.

3. Program participants are more likely to meet their school's basic requirements than nonparticipants are. They are less likely to be assigned to special education classes, to be retained in a grade, or to drop out of high school.

4. There is even some evidence (though not in all studies) that teenagers who have participated in early compensatory education are less likely than nonparticipants to become pregnant, to require welfare assistance, and to be involved in delinquent behavior.

In sum, longitudinal evaluations suggest that compensatory education has been tried and works. Programs seem most effective if they start early, last long, and involve several components. For example, Craig Ramey and his colleagues (see Campbell & Ramey, 1995; Ramey & Ramey, 1992) have reported outstanding success with the Abecedarian Project, an early intervention for extremely disadvantaged, primarily African-American, children that involved an intellectually stimulating day-care program, home visits and efforts to involve parents in their children's development, and medical and nutritional care from early infancy to kindergarten entry. Program participants outperformed nonparticipants throughout childhood and into adolescence. By age 15, the impressive IQ advantage they had shown as young children had narrowed to less than 5 points, but they continued to perform better on math and reading achievement tests, were less likely to have been held back a grade, and were less in need of special education services. Some children in the study were randomly assigned to a group whose intervention did not begin until school age, when a teacher worked with their regular teachers and their parents over a three-year period. These children did not show as many gains as those who received the preschool intervention, suggesting that it is best to intervene early in children's lives (Campbell & Ramey, 1995).

These findings are indeed encouraging, but is it really too late to intervene after the years of infancy

High-quality Head Start programs provide the nutrition, health care, parent training, and intellectual stimulation that can get disadvantaged children off to a good start.

and early childhood have passed? Not according to Israeli psychologist Reuven Feuerstein.

Enrichment for Low-IQ Adolescents

Early in this chapter we described Feuerstein's dynamic assessment approach, which involves testing intelligence by directly testing the potential to learn with guidance. He has also developed cognitive training programs for culturally different, learning disabled, and mentally retarded adolescents and young adults (Feuerstein et al., 1981). According to Feuerstein, such individuals are not absorbing as much from their experiences as more advantaged learners are, mainly because they have not had many opportunities to learn thinking skills from more competent thinkers. What they need, then, is a "mediator," a guide who structures and interprets the environment for them at first. They will then come to learn more from their experiences on their own. (This approach should remind you of Lev Vygotsky's theory, described in Chapter 7, that children acquire new ways of thinking through their social interactions with more experienced problem solvers; it is based in part on Vygotsky's work.)

In Feuerstein's "Instrumental Enrichment" program, a mediator leads students through several cognitive tasks, teaching them the cognitive strategies they need to perform well. For example, the mediator might direct students' attention to key aspects of the task, ask them what they think should be done, prompt them to think about strategies they could use, and encourage them to evaluate the correctness of their solutions. Participants in one intervention study were 12- to 15-year-old mentally retarded and nearly mentally retarded adolescents who were three to four years behind their peers academically (Feuerstein et al., 1981). Compared to a control group that received a general enrichment program, participants in Feuerstein's special program showed immediate gains on intellectual and cognitive measures. Moreover, participants were still ahead of nonparticipants two years later, when they took both a military intelligence test and the Primary Mental Abilities test. Even more impressively, benefits of the training appeared to *increase* over this two-year period, rather than fading away as the gains of intervention programs often do. This kind of cumulative effect is precisely what Feuerstein expected, for the whole idea of his approach is to help students learn more in the future from their own experiences. Not all attempts to implement Feuerstein's curriculum have worked this well (Blagg, 1991; Frisby & Braden, 1992). However, it is clear that cognitive interventions need not occur in infancy to be successful.

IQ Training for Aging Adults

But can you teach old dogs new tricks? And can you reteach old dogs who have suffered declines in mental abilities the old tricks they have lost? K. Warner Schaie and Sherry Willis (1986) sought to find out by training elderly adults in spatial ability and reasoning, two of the fluid mental abilities that are most likely to decline in old age. Within a group of older people ranging in age from 64 to 95 who participated in Schaie's longitudinal study of intelligence, they first identified individuals whose scores on one of the two abilities had declined over a 14-year period, as well as individuals who had remained stable over the same period. The goal with the decliners would be to restore lost ability; the goal with those who had maintained their ability would be to improve it. Participants took pretests measuring both abilities, received five hours of training in either spatial ability or reasoning, and then were given posttests on both abilities. The spatial training involved learning how to rotate objects in space, at first physically and then mentally. Training in reasoning involved learning how to detect a recurring pattern in a series of stimuli (for example, musical notes) and to identify what the next stimulus in the sequence should be.

The training worked. And both those who had suffered ability declines and those who had maintained their abilities prior to the study improved, though decliners showed significantly more improvement in spatial ability than nondecliners did. Schaie and Willis estimated that 40% of the decliners gained enough through training to bring them back up to the level of performance they had achieved 14 years earlier, before decline set in. What's more, effects of the training among those who had experienced declines in performance were still evident seven years later (Schaie, 1996).

The larger messages? You *can* teach old dogs new tricks—and reteach them old tricks—in very little time. This research does not mean that cognitive abilities can be restored in elderly people who have Alzheimer's disease or other brain disorders and have experienced significant neural loss. Instead, it suggests that many intellectual skills decline in later life because they are not used—and that these skills can be revived with a little coaching and practice. This research, combined with research on children, provides convincing evidence of the plasticity of cognitive abilities over the entire life span.

Now that our account of cognitive development over the life span is now complete, you should appreciate that each of the three major approaches to the mind that we have considered—the Piagetian cognitive-developmental approach discussed in Chapter 7, the information-processing approach discussed in Chapter 8, and the psychometric or testing approach discussed here—offers something of value. Perhaps we can summarize it this way: Piaget has shown us that comparing the thought of a preschooler to the thought of an adult is like comparing a tadpole to a frog. Modes of thought change qualitatively with age. The information-processing approach has helped us understand thinking processes and explain why the young child cannot remember as much information or solve problems as effectively as the adult can. Finally, the psychometric approach has told us that, if we look at the wide range of tasks to which the mind can be applied, we can recognize distinct mental abilities that each person consistently displays in greater or lesser amounts. We need not choose one approach and reject the others. Our understanding of the mind is likely to be richer if all three approaches continue to thrive. There are truly many "intelligences," and it is foolish to think that a single IQ score can possibly describe the complexities of human cognitive development.

◆ SUMMARY POINTS

1. The psychometric or testing approach to cognition defines intelligence as a set of traits that allows some people to think and solve problems more effectively than others. It can be viewed as a hierarchy consisting of a general factor *g*, broad abilities such as fluid and crystallized intelligence, and many specific abilities. Gardner's theory of multiple intelligences, with its focus on seven distinct forms of intelligence, offers an alternative view. Sternberg's triarchic theory of intelligence, with its contextual, experiential, and information-processing components, offers another.

2. Intelligence tests such as the Stanford-Binet and the Wechsler scales compare an individual's performance on a variety of cognitive tasks with the average performance of agemates. Scores on these tests in a large population form a normal or bell-shaped distribution, with an average score of 100. Some testers are experimenting with dynamic assessment methods that determine how well individuals learn new material with guidance.

3. In infancy, mental growth is rapid and is measured by developmental quotients derived from tests such as the Bayley Scales. However, infant scores do not predict later IQ as well as measures of speed of information processing such as rapid habituation and preference for novelty do.

4. During childhood, mental growth continues, and IQs at one age predict IQs at later ages quite well. However, many individuals show wide variations in their IQ scores over time. Those who gain IQ points often have favorable home environments, whereas disadvantaged children often show a cumulative deficit.

5. In adolescence, further mental growth occurs; IQs continue to be relatively stable over time and predict school achievement and years of education obtained.

6. IQ is related to the status or prestige of an adult's occupation, as well as to his or her success within that occupation. Both cross-sectional studies and longitudinal studies tend to distort the picture of age-related change. Schaie's sequential study suggests that (a) date of birth (cohort) influences test performance, (b) no major declines in mental abilities occur until the late 60s or 70s, (c) some abilities (especially fluid ones) decline more than others (especially crystallized ones), and (d) not all people's abilities decline. Decline is most likely in those who have poor health and unstimulating lifestyles.

7. Meanwhile, wisdom, or exceptional insight into the human condition, is no more common, but also no less common, in later adulthood than in earlier adulthood and depends less on age than on life experiences.

8. Individual differences in IQ at a given age are linked to genetic factors and to intellectually stimulating qualities of the home environment. The low average scores of some minority groups on IQ tests may be explained better by culture bias in testing, low motivation (including anxiety caused by negative group stereotypes), and low socioeconomic status than by genetic differences. Minority children perform much better when they grow up in intellectually stimulating homes.

9. Mentally retarded individuals show varied levels of functioning, depending on their IQs and the causes (organic or cultural-familial) of their retardation. Mildly retarded individuals appear to meet the demands of adult life better than the demands of school. Children identified as gifted on the basis of high IQ scores have been found to be above average in virtually all ways.

10. Creativity, the ability to produce novel and socially valued works, is a distinct mental ability that demands divergent rather than convergent thinking; it is largely independent of IQ once a minimum IQ is exceeded, increases with age during childhood, and is fostered in homes where independence is valued. Eminent creators are typically more productive during their 30s and 40s than before or after, but continue to produce great works in later life. Performance on creativity tests declines in later life, but creative capacities clearly survive into old age.

11. Attempts to boost performance on IQ tests suggest that Head Start programs can have long-lasting benefits and that mental abilities are plastic throughout the life span.

FOOD FOR THOUGHT

1. All things considered, do you think it was a good idea or a bad idea for psychologists such as Binet and Terman to devise IQ tests? What value do these tests have? What problems do they create?

2. Imagine that you are chosen to head a presidential commission on intelligence testing whose task it is to devise a better IQ test for use in the schools than any that currently exists. Drawing on material in this chapter, sketch out the features of your model IQ test. What would be included and excluded from your definition of intelligence? How would you go about measuring intelligence as you define it? In what ways would your test improve upon the Stanford-Binet or WISC?

3. Putting together material from chapters 7, 8, and 9, how would you describe the cognitive functioning of a typical 70-year-old person? What are the greatest cognitive strengths of older adults, what are their greatest limitations, and how much can an individual do to optimize his or her functioning?

4. The Maori are a socioeconomically disadvantaged group in New Zealand, a country colonized by the British long ago. Maori children typically score lower on IQ tests than children of British background. Knowing what you know about minorities in the United States, what are your top two hypotheses about why Maori children perform relatively poorly, and how might you test these hypotheses?

W ON THE WEB

1. *Testing in an Educational Context* The Web site of Harcourt Brace Educational Measurement contains excellent information about testing ability and achievement in educational settings. It includes a glossary of measurement terms (for example, reliability, percentile, norm) and a set of frequently asked questions and their answers.
   http://www.hbem.com/

2. *Intelligence Test* If you enjoy mental challenges, try the IQ test items and puzzles at this site. Don't take your scores too seriously, however, as the intelligence tests are not standardized. Rather than seek a definitive IQ score, you might see if you can determine which of the seven Primary Mental Abilities used in Schaie's major study of IQ and aging are represented in the items offered up here. Are they measures of crystallized or fluid intelligence?
   http://webusers.anet-stl.com/~chimera/puzzles.html

3. *Mental Retardation* The Web site of the Association for Retarded Citizens provides news items on the latest developments in the field of mental retardation and allows you to search its database to retrieve information on every imaginable related topic.
   http://thearc.org/welcome.html

KEY TERMS

psychometric approach
factor analysis
structure-of-intellect model
fluid intelligence
crystallized intelligence
savant syndrome
triarchic theory of intelligence
automatization
culture bias
mental age (MA)

intelligence quotient (IQ)
test norms
normal distribution
dynamic assessment
developmental quotient (DQ)
cumulative-deficit hypothesis
terminal drop
wisdom
HOME inventory

Flynn effect
mental retardation
organic retardation
cultural-familial retardation
giftedness
creativity
divergent thinking
convergent thinking
ideational fluency

CHAPTER 10

Self-Conceptions and Personality

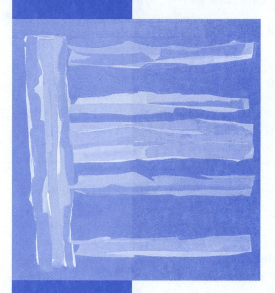

CONCEPTUALIZING THE SELF
Theories of Personality Development

THE INFANT
The Emerging Self
Temperament

THE CHILD
Elaborating on a Sense of Self
Self-Esteem
Influences on Self-Esteem
The Personality Stabilizes

THE ADOLESCENT
Self-Conceptions
Self-Esteem
Forming a Sense of Identity

THE ADULT
Self-Perceptions
Continuity and Discontinuity in Personality
Psychosocial Growth

APPLICATIONS: BOOSTING SELF-ESTEEM

SUMMARY POINTS

FOOD FOR THOUGHT

ON THE WEB

KEY TERMS

In the late 1960s, a conventional-looking assistant professor of psychology at Harvard University, Richard Alpert, began experimenting with drugs, went to India, and reemerged as Baba Ram Dass, a mystic in a white robe preaching the value of living for the moment. A remarkable transformation? Perhaps not, according to his former colleague, David McClelland:

> When I first saw Ram Dass again in the early 1970s he seemed like a completely transformed person. . . . He was wearing long Indian style clothes with beads around his neck; he was nearly bald but had grown a long bushy beard. He had given away all his possessions, refused his father's inheritance, carried no money on his person, and for a time lived as a nomad in a van which was all he had in the world. He had given up drugs, abandoned his career as a psychologist. . . . Yet after spending some time with him, I found myself saying over and over again, "it's the same old Dick.". . . He was still very intelligent . . . he was still verbally fluent. . . . And he was still charming. . . . At a somewhat less obvious level, Alpert was very much involved in high drama, just as he had always been. . . . (McClelland, 1981, pp. 89–91)

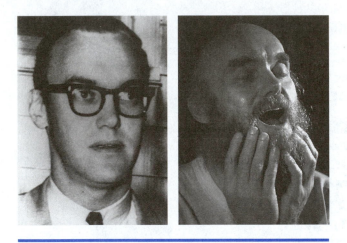

Harvard professor Richard Alpert (left) changed dramatically in appearance after he became Ram Dass (right), but there were signs of continuity in his personality nonetheless.

Do humans remain "the same people" in most significant respects, or do they undergo dramatic transformations in personality over the years from infancy to old age? The issue of continuity (stability) and discontinuity (change) in development is an important and fascinating one that was introduced in Chapter 2. This chapter is about the ways in which our personalities, and our perceptions of those personalities, change—and remain the same—over the life span. Let me begin by clarifying some terms and laying out some theoretical perspectives on personal-

ity. Then we will see how self-perceptions and aspects of temperament and personality change from infancy to old age.

CONCEPTUALIZING THE SELF

Personality is often defined as the organized combination of attributes, motives, values, and behaviors that is unique to each individual. Most people describe personalities in terms of *personality traits*—dispositions such as sociability, independence, dominance, anxiety, and so on. Traits are assumed to be relatively consistent across different situations and over time; if you peg a classmate as insecure, you expect this person to behave insecurely at school and at work, now and next year.

When you describe yourself, you may not be describing your actual personality so much as you are revealing your **self-concept**—your *perceptions,* positive or negative, of your unique attributes and traits. We all know people who seem to have unrealistic self-conceptions—the fellow who thinks he is "God's gift to women" (who don't agree) or the woman who believes she is a dull plodder (but is actually quite brilliant). A closely related aspect of self-perception is **self-esteem**—your overall evaluation of your worth as a person, high or low, based on all the positive and negative self-perceptions that make up your self-concept. This chapter examines how self-concept and self-esteem change and remain the same over the life span. It also takes up the question of how adolescents pull together their various self-perceptions to form an **identity,** an overall sense of who they are, where they are heading, and where they fit in society.

Theories of Personality Development

How does the personality develop? Is it formed in childhood and stable from then on, or does it continue to evolve and change throughout our lives? To get some feel for current debates about the nature of personality development, let's look at some striking differences between three major theoretical perspectives on the nature of personality and personality development: psychoanalytic theory, psychometric (trait) theory, and social learning theory.

Psychoanalytic Theory

As you recall from Chapter 2, Sigmund Freud was concerned with the development and inner dynamics of three parts of the personality: the selfish id, the rational ego, and the moralistic superego. He strongly believed that biological urges residing within the id push all children through universal stages of psycho-

TABLE 10.1

The eight stages of Erikson's psychosocial theory

Stage	Age Range (years)	Central Issue
1. Trust versus mistrust	Birth to 1	Can I trust others?
2. Autonomy versus shame and doubt	1–3	Can I act on my own?
3. Initiative versus guilt	3–6	Can I carry out my plans successfully?
4. Industry versus inferiority	6–12	Am I competent compared to others?
5. Identity versus role confusion	12–20	Who am I, really?
6. Intimacy versus isolation	20–40	Am I ready for a relationship?
7. Generativity versus stagnation	40–65	Have I left my mark?
8. Integrity versus despair	65 and older	In the end, has my life been meaningful?

sexual development, starting with the oral stage of infancy and ending with the genital stage of adolescence when sexual maturity is attained. Freud did not imagine psychosexual growth continuing during adulthood. Rather, he believed that the personality was formed in infancy and early childhood—during the first five years of life, essentially—and showed considerable continuity thereafter. Anxieties arising from harsh parenting or other unfavorable early experiences, he claimed, would leave a permanent mark on the personality and reveal themselves in adult personality traits.

The psychosocial theory of Erik Erikson, a neo-Freudian theorist whose contributions to the understanding of personality we highlight later in this chapter, was also introduced in Chapter 2. Like Freud, Erikson concerned himself with the inner dynamics of personality and proposed that the personality evolves through systematic stages that confront people with different challenges (Erikson 1963, 1968, 1982). Compared to Freud, however, Erikson came to place more emphasis on social influences on development such as peers, teachers, schools, and churches; the rational ego and its adaptive powers; possibilities for overcoming the effects of harmful early experiences; and the potential for growth throughout the life span.

Erikson's eight stages of psychosocial development are listed in Table 10.1 and will be discussed in relation to research findings later in this chapter. Both maturational forces and social demands, Erikson believed, push human beings everywhere through these eight psychosocial crises. Later conflicts may prove difficult to resolve if early conflicts were not resolved successfully. For development to proceed optimally, a healthy balance between the terms of the conflict must be struck: In infancy, for example, trust of caregivers should outweigh mistrust, but an element of skepticism is needed as well.

Erikson clearly did not agree with Freud that the personality is largely formed by the end of early childhood; discontinuity was possible, he thought. Erikson also appreciated that development continues throughout the life span. Yet, like Freud, he believed that people everywhere progress through stages of personality development, undergoing similar personality changes at similar ages.

Psychometric Theory

The approach to personality that has most strongly influenced efforts to study it is the *psychometric approach*—the same testing approach that guided the development of intelligence tests. According to this approach—which embodies psychometric, or trait, theory—personality is a set of trait dimensions along which people can differ (for example, sociable–unsociable, responsible–irresponsible). Personality scales are administered to people, and statistical procedures such as *factor analysis* are used to identify groupings of personality test items that appear to be distinct trait dimensions. Trait theorists assume that personality traits are relatively enduring, so, like psychoanalytic theorists, they expect to see carryover in personality over the years. Unlike psychoanalytic theorists, they do not believe that the personality unfolds in a series of stages.

How many personality trait dimensions are there? Just as scholars have disagreed about how many distinct mental abilities exist, they have disagreed about how many personality dimensions exist. However, a consensus is now forming around the idea that human personalities can be described in terms of five major dimensions, now called the **big five,** believed by many theorists to capture the essential ways in which personalities differ (Digman, 1990; Halverson et al., 1994; Costa & McCrae, 1994). These five personality dimensions—neuroticism, extraversion, openness to experience, agreeableness, and conscientiousness—are shown in Table 10.2. We have evidence that all five are genetically influenced and that they begin to show themselves during childhood, some of them in infancy (Rowe, 1994; Vikem et al., 1994). The "big five"

TABLE 10.2

The "big five" personality dimensions		
Dimension	Basic Definition	Key Characteristics
Neuroticism	Emotional instability vs. stability	Anxiety, hostility, depression, self-consciousness, impulsiveness, vulnerability
Extraversion	Sociability and outgoingness vs. introversion	Warmth, gregariousness, assertiveness, activity, excitement seeking, positive emotions
Openness to experience	Curiosity and interest in variety vs. preference for sameness	Openness to fantasy, esthetics, feelings, actions, ideas, values
Agreeableness	Compliance and cooperativeness vs. suspiciousness	Trust, straightforwardness, altruism, compliance, modesty, tender-mindedness
Conscientiousness	Discipline and organization vs. lack of seriousness	Competence, order, dutifulness, achievement striving, self-discipline, deliberation

SOURCE: Adapted from Costa & McCrae (1992)

also seem to be universal; they capture personality differences in cultures with very different parenting styles, value systems, and languages, such as Portuguese, Hebrew, and Chinese (McCrae & Costa, 1997). We will soon see what happens to them as we get older.

Social Learning Theory

Finally, social learning theorists such as Albert Bandura (1986) and Walter Mischel (1973; Mischel & Shoda, 1995) not only reject the notion of universal stages of personality development but question the very existence of enduring personality traits that show themselves in a wide variety of situations and long stretches of the life span. Instead, they emphasize that people change if their environments change. An aggressive boy can become a warm and caring man if his aggression is no longer reinforced; a woman who has been socially withdrawn can become more outgoing if she begins to interact closely with friends who serve as models of outgoing, sociable behavior. From this perspective, personality is a set of behavior tendencies shaped by our interactions with other people in specific social situations.

Social learning theorists believe strongly in situational influences on behavior. If there is consistency in personality, they claim, it is most likely to be a matter of our consistently behaving one way in one situation and another way in another situation. Luis may hate being the center of attention, whereas Robert may relish it; Luis may love quiet time, Robert may get easily bored if nothing is going on. Each person can be characterized as reacting in particular ways in particular situations (Mischel & Shoda, 1995). Consistency in personality would be even more likely if the social environment remained the same. If Rick the rancher continues to do the same ranching on the same ranch in the same small town for a lifetime, he might well stay the "same old Rick."

However, most of us experience major changes in our social environments as we become older. Just as we behave differently when we are in a library than when we are at a party, we become "different people" as we take on new roles in life, develop new relationships, or move to new locations. To the social learning theorist, then, personality development is a very individual process whose direction depends on each person's social experiences. Theorists who adopt a contextual perspective on development (see Chapter 2) make similar assumptions. Indeed, contextual theorists are likely to say that personality traits, considered apart from the social contexts that shape and give meaning to a person's actions, are meaningless abstractions.

Obviously, stage theorists (represented by Freud, Erikson, and other psychoanalytic theorists) and nonstage theorists (trait theorists, social learning theorists) do not see eye to eye about how the personality develops. Stage theorists propose universal, age-related personality changes, whereas nonstage theorists propose that change may occur at any time in life and can proceed in many directions. Moreover, some theorists (including trait theorists) agree with Freud that personality emerges early in life and remains largely stable thereafter, whereas other theorists (Erikson, social learning theorists) emphasize the discontinuity side of the continuity/discontinuity issue and suspect that we never stop changing as individuals. Whether or not our personality traits do in fact remain highly consistent across the life span is a central question in the study of personality development.

This chapter is concerned with continuity and discontinuity in both personality traits and self-conceptions and evaluations. When do infants become aware of themselves as unique individuals, and when do they begin to display their unique personalities? What influences how children perceive and evaluate themselves, and to what extent are the personalities they will have as adults already evident? How do adolescents go about finding their identities as individuals? Finally, do people's personalities and self-perceptions systematically change over the adult years, or do they remain essentially the same, and why?

THE INFANT

Do infants have any awareness that they exist or any sense of themselves as distinct individuals? Let's explore this issue and then see if it makes any sense to say that infants have unique "personalities."

The Emerging Self

Many developmental theorists believe that infants are born without a sense of self. Margaret Mahler (Mahler, Pine, & Bergman, 1975) likens the newborn to a "chick in an egg" whose needs are met and who has no reason to differentiate itself from the surrounding environment. It is not easy to determine when infants first gain a sense of themselves as beings separate from the world around them, but the first glimmers of this capacity can be detected in the first two or three months of life (Samuels, 1986; Stern, 1983). For example, 2-month-old infants whose arms are connected by strings to audiovisual equipment delight in producing the sight of a smiling infant's face and the theme from *Sesame Street* by pulling the strings (Lewis, Alessandri, & Sullivan, 1990). When the strings are disconnected and they can no longer produce such effects, they pull all the harder and become frustrated and angry. By 3 months of age, babies also seem to be able to put together information from their eyes and their sense of bodily movement to recognize videotapes of their leg kicking as their own (Rochat & Morgan, 1995). These studies suggests that young infants discover properties of their physical selves, distinguish between the self and the rest of the world, and appreciate that they can act upon other people and objects.

When do infants recognize themselves as distinct individuals and become able to tell themselves apart from other infants? To find out, Michael Lewis and Jeanne Brooks-Gunn (1979) used an ingenious technique first used with chimpanzees to study **self-recognition,** the ability to recognize oneself in a mirror or photograph. Mother daubs a spot of rouge on the infant's nose and then places the infant in front of

Does this boy really know that the fascinating tot in the mirror is him? Probably not if he is younger than 18 months of age, for that is about when self-recognition is mastered by most toddlers.

a mirror. If infants have some mental image of their own faces and recognize their mirror images as themselves, they should soon notice the red spot and reach for or wipe their own noses rather than the nose of the mirror image. When infants 9 to 24 months old were given this rouge test, the youngest infants showed no self-recognition: They seemed to treat the image in the mirror as if it were "some other kid." Some 15-month-olds recognized themselves, but only among 18- to 24-month-olds did a large majority of infants show clear evidence of self-recognition (see also Asendorpf, Warkentin, & Baudonnière, 1996). They touched their noses rather than the mirror, apparently realizing that they had a strange mark on their faces that warranted investigation. They knew exactly who that kid in the mirror was!

Good performance on the rouge test depends on skills such as being able to point and appreciate mirror reversals. Hence, other approaches to studying self-recognition have been used. According to Lewis and Brooks-Gunn, babies form a **categorical self,** classifying themselves into social categories based on age, sex, and other visible characteristics, figuring out what is "like me" and what is "not like me." By the end of the first year, infants are already able to distinguish between strange babies and strange adults or between strange women and strange men (Brooks-Gunn & Lewis, 1981; Lewis & Brooks-Gunn, 1979). Before they are 18 months old, toddlers can tell themselves apart from toddlers of the other sex or from older individuals but are less able to distinguish between photos of themselves and photos of other infants of the same sex. As they approach age 2, they also master this task. By 18 to 24 months of age, then, most infants definitely have an awareness of who they are—at least as a physical self with a unique appearance and as a categorical self belonging to specific age and gender categories.

To what can we attribute this emerging self-awareness? First, the ability to recognize the self depends on *cognitive development* (Bertenthal & Fischer, 1978). Children who are mentally retarded are slow to recognize themselves in a mirror but can do so once they have attained a mental age of at least 18 to 20 months (Hill & Tomlin, 1981). Second, self-awareness depends on social experiences. Chimpanzees who have been raised in complete isolation, unlike those who have had contact with other chimps, fail to recognize themselves in a mirror (Gallup, 1979). As it turns out, human toddlers who have formed secure attachments to their parents are better able to recognize themselves in a mirror and know more about their names and genders than do toddlers whose relationships are less secure (Pipp, Easterbrooks, & Harmon, 1992).

The critical role of *social interaction* in the development of the self was appreciated long ago by Charles Cooley (1902) and George Herbert Mead (1934). Cooley used the term **looking-glass self** to emphasize that our understanding of self is a reflection of how other people respond to us; that is, our self-concepts are the images cast by a social mirror. Through their actions and words, parents and other companions communicate to infants that they are babies and are also either girls or boys. Later, social feedback helps children determine what they are like and what they can and cannot do well. Throughout life we forge new self-concepts through our social interactions. Thus the development of the self is closely related to both cognitive development and social interaction, beginning in infancy.

Awareness of the self paves the way for many important emotional and social developments (Pipp-Siegel & Foltz, 1997). Toddlers who recognize themselves in the mirror are more able than those who do not to experience self-conscious emotions such as embarrassment—for example, if asked to show off by dancing in front of strangers (Lewis et al., 1989). Also, toddlers who have gained awareness of self are more aware of other people. They are more able than other toddlers to communicate with their playmates by imitating their actions (Asendorpf et al., 1996) and they can even cooperate in simple ways with peers to achieve common goals such as retrieving toys from containers (Brownell & Carriger, 1990). Once infants are aware of themselves, then, they become able to coordinate their own perspective with that of another individual.

Temperament

Even though it takes infants some time to become aware of themselves as individuals, they *are* individuals with their own distinctive personalities from the very first weeks of life. The study of infant personality has centered on dimensions of **temperament,** early genetically based tendencies to respond in predictable ways to events that serve as the building blocks of personality by influencing the kinds of interactions the individual has with his or her environment. Learning theorists have tended to view babies as "blank slates" who can be shaped in any number of directions by their experiences. However, it is now clear that babies differ from the start in such characteristics as how they react to stimuli (for example, whether they smile or fuss, and how strongly) and how they regulate these reactions (for example, whether they attend to arousing stimuli or avoid them; Rothbart, Derryberry, & Posner, 1994).

Temperament influences later personality. For example, a baby who is uncomfortable interacting with people may miss out on opportunities to learn social interaction skills as a child, become more and more socially awkward as a result, and end up an introverted adult. Although there is much agreement that babies differ in their temperaments from an early age, temperament has been defined and measured in a number of ways, as we will now see.

Emotionality, Activity, and Sociability

Arnold Buss and Robert Plomin (1984) have called attention to three dimensions of temperament: **emotionality, activity,** and **sociability.** Some babies are more emotionally reactive (or easily and intensely irritated by events) than others are; some are highly active while others are quite sluggish; and some are very sociable, or interested in and responsive to people, while others are standoffish. Behavioral genetics research using twins and adopted children tells us that these aspects of temperament are partly influenced by genetic endowment and partly influenced by the individual's unique experience (Braungart et al., 1992; Schmitz et al., 1996). Identical twins have quite similar temperaments, whereas fraternal twins hardly resemble each other at all (Buss & Plomin, 1984; Rowe, 1994). Growing up in the same home does nothing to make adoptive brothers and sisters alike in these aspects of temperament (Schmitz et al., 1996).

Behavioral Inhibition

Jerome Kagan and his colleagues have been investigating another aspect of early temperament that they believe is highly significant—**behavioral inhibition,** or the tendency to be extremely shy, restrained, and distressed in response to unfamiliar people and situations (Kagan, 1994; Reznick et al., 1986). Inhibited children could be considered extremely high in emotionality and low in sociability. Kagan (1989) estimates that about 15% of toddlers have this inhibited temperament, whereas 10% are extremely uninhibited, eager to jump into new situations.

At 4 months of age, infants who will later be recognized as inhibited children are highly reactive to novel stimuli; they wriggle and fret more than most infants in response to new sights and sounds, such as a cotton swab dipped in alcohol or a moving mobile. At 21 months, they take a long time to warm up to a strange examiner, retreat from unfamiliar objects such as a large robot, and fret and cling to their mothers. By contrast, uninhibited toddlers readily and enthusiastically interact with strangers, robots, and all manner of new experiences.

In follow-up tests at 5½ and 7½ years of age, most children who were either highly inhibited or highly uninhibited at 21 months of age still displayed the same temperament they showed as toddlers. Those who had been inhibited as toddlers were more likely than children who had been uninhibited to be shy in a group of strange peers and to be afraid of trying out a balance beam. Even at age 13, differences between inhibited and uninhibited children were still evident (Kagan, 1994). The inhibited adolescents talked and smiled less than the uninhibited ones. After failing a difficult task, the inhibited adolescents just looked glum, whereas the uninhibited children smiled, as though laughing at themselves. Overall, of the children who had maintained the same temperament from age 2 to age 7, about half still had the same temperament by adolescence, suggesting a fair amount of continuity.

Kagan and his colleagues have also found that inhibited youngsters show distinctive physiological reactions to novel events; they become highly aroused (as indicated by high heart rates) in situations that barely faze other children. And their behavioral inhibition is genetically influenced; anxiety and phobias run in their families (Kagan, 1994). In one study (DiLalla, Kagan, & Reznick, 1994), the correlation between the inhibition scores of identical twins was +.82, that for fraternal twins .47. Very possibly, then, genes affect temperament by influencing the development of the nervous system and the way it responds to stimuli.

Easy versus Difficult Temperament

Still another useful way of describing infant temperament comes from the pioneering work of Alexander Thomas, Stella Chess, and their colleagues (Chess & Thomas, 1984; Thomas & Chess, 1977, 1986; Thomas, Chess, & Birch, 1970). These researchers gathered information about several dimensions of infant behavior such as typical mood, regularity or predictability of biological functions such as feeding and sleeping habits, tendency to approach or withdraw from new stimuli, intensity of emotional reactions, and adaptability to new experiences and changes in routine. Most infants could be placed into one of three categories on the basis of the overall patterning of these temperamental qualities:

1. *Easy temperament:* Infants with an **easy temperament** are even tempered, typically content or happy, and quite open and adaptable to new experiences such as the approach of a stranger or their first taste of strained plums. They have regular feeding and sleeping habits, and they tolerate frustrations and discomforts well.

2. *Difficult temperament:* Infants with a **difficult temperament** are active, irritable, and irregular in their habits. They often react very negatively (and vigorously) to changes in routine and are slow to adapt to new people or situations. They cry frequently and loudly and often have tantrums when they are frustrated by such events as being restrained or having to live with a dirty diaper.

3. *Slow-to-warm-up temperament:* Infants with a **slow-to-warm-up temperament** are quite inactive, somewhat moody, and only moderately regular in their daily schedules. Like difficult infants, they are slow to adapt to new people and situations, but they typically respond in mildly, rather than intensely, negative ways. For example, they may resist cuddling by looking away from the cuddler rather than by kicking or screaming. They do eventually adjust, showing a quiet interest in new foods, people, or places.

Of the infants in Thomas and Chess's New York longitudinal study, 40% were easy infants, 10% were difficult infants, 15% were slow-to-warm-up infants, and the remaining third could not be clearly placed in one category or another because they shared qualities of two or more categories. Thomas and Chess went on to study the extent of continuity and discontinuity in temperament over the years from infancy to early adulthood (Chess & Thomas, 1984; Thomas & Chess, 1986). Difficult infants who had fussed when they could not have more milk often became children who fell apart if they could not work math problems correctly, but they did not necessarily become maladjusted adults. By the age of 3 or 4, being difficult (or easy) in temperament *did* predict being difficult (or easy) in temperament and being poorly or well adjusted as a young adult, but the relationships were far from perfect. For example, 39% of the individuals tested fell in the same temperamental category as young adults that they had been in as 4-year-olds, but the rest changed (Korn, 1984): Although some

BOX 10.1

The case of Carl: Goodness of fit

The case of Carl illustrates the importance to later personality development of the match between a child's temperament and his or her social environment. Early in life, Carl was one of the most difficult children Stella Chess and Alexander Thomas had ever encountered: "Whether it was the first bath or the first solid foods in infancy, the beginning of nursery and elementary school, or the first birthday parties or shopping trips, each experience evoked stormy responses, with loud crying and struggling to get away" (1984, p. 188). Carl's mother became convinced that she was a bad parent, but his father accepted and even de-

lighted in Carl's "lusty" behavior and patiently and supportively waited for him to adapt to new situations. As a result, Carl did not develop serious behavior problems as a child.

Carl's difficult temperament did come out in force when he entered college and had to adapt to a whole new environment. He became extremely frustrated and thought about dropping out but eventually reduced his course load and got through this difficult period successfully. By age 23 he was no longer considered by the researchers to have a difficult temperament. How different his later personality and adjustment might have been

had the fit between his difficult temperament and his parents' demands and expectations been poor! When children have difficult temperaments and grow up with parents who cannot control their behavior effectively, they are likely to have serious behavior problems as adolescents (Maziade et al., 1990). Clearly, then, healthy personality development depends on the goodness of fit between child and home environment. The moral for parents is clear: Get to know your baby as an individual, and allow for his or her personality quirks.

---

individuals maintained the same temperament, then, some easy children turned into maladjusted adults, and some difficult children outgrew their behavior problems. Both continuity and discontinuity in temperament were evident.

Goodness of Fit

What determines whether or not temperamental qualities persist, then? Much may depend on what Thomas and Chess call the **goodness of fit** between child and environment—the extent to which the child's temperament is compatible with the demands and expectations of the social world to which he or she must adapt (see also Lerner et al., 1989). A good example comes from observations of the Masai of East Africa (DeVries, 1984). In most settings an easy temperament is likely to be more adaptive than a difficult one, but among the Masai during famine babies with *difficult* temperaments outlived easy babies. Why? Perhaps because Masai parents believe that difficult babies are future warriors or perhaps because babies who cry loud and long get noticed and fed. As this example suggests, a particular temperament may be a good fit to the demands of one environment but maladaptive under other circumstances. The goodness-of-fit concept is another example of how individual predispositions and the environment interact to influence developmental outcomes.

In their longitudinal study, Chess and Thomas (1984) found that difficult children often continued to display difficult temperaments later in life if the person/environment fit was bad—if their parents were impatient, inconsistent, and demanding with them. However, difficult infants whose parents adapted to

their temperaments and gave them more time to adjust to new experiences enjoyed a good fit to the environment and became able to master new situations effectively and energetically (see Box 10.1). Similarly, Jerome Kagan (1994) and his colleagues find that parents of inhibited children make a mistake if they overprotect their sensitive children from stress, for then their children do not learn to control their inhibition; parents also err if they become angry and impatient. Instead, it is best for parents to prepare inhibited youngsters for potentially upsetting experiences and then make reasonable demands that they cope.

In sum, by the end of the first two years of life, infants have become aware of themselves as individuals. Toddlers recognize themselves in a mirror, refer to themselves by name, and understand that they are physically distinct from other human beings. Cognitive development and experiences with the social looking glass make this new self-awareness possible. Moreover, each toddler has his or her own distinct temperamental qualities that are sketched in the genetic code and expressed from the first days of life. However, the personality is by no means set in infancy; there is both continuity and discontinuity. Early temperamental qualities *may or may not* carry over into childhood and adulthood, depending on the goodness of fit between the individual's predispositions and his or her social environment.

THE CHILD

Children's personalities continue to take form, and children acquire much richer understandings of themselves as individuals, as they continue to experience cognitive growth and interact with other people. Ask children of different ages to tell you about themselves. You'll find their responses amusing, and you'll learn something about how children come to know themselves as individuals.

Elaborating on a Sense of Self

Once toddlers begin to talk, they can and do tell us about their emerging self-concepts. By age 2 some toddlers are already using the personal pronouns *I, me, my,* and *mine* (or their names) when referring to the self and *you* when addressing a companion (Lewis & Brooks-Gunn, 1979; Stipek, Gralinski, & Kopp, 1990). This linguistic distinction suggests that 2-year-olds have formed a concept of "self" and can distinguish self from other. Toddlers also show us that they are developing a categorical self when they describe themselves in terms of age and sex ("Katie big girl").

The preschool child's self-concept is very concrete and physical (Damon & Hart, 1982, 1988). When asked to describe themselves, preschoolers dwell on their physical characteristics ("I look like a kid. I have skin. I have clothes"), their possessions ("I have a bike"), and the physical actions they can perform ("I can jump"). In one study (Keller, Ford, & Meachum, 1978), 3- to 5-year-olds were asked to say ten things about themselves and to complete the sentences "I am a _____" and "I am a boy/girl who _____." Fully half of the children's responses were *action* statements such as "I play baseball" or "I walk to school." Very few of these young children made any mention of their psychological traits or inner qualities. At most, young children use global terms such as "nice" or "mean," "good" or "bad," to describe themselves and others (Livesley & Bromley, 1973). However, their descriptions of characteristic behavior patterns and preferences ("I like to play by myself at school") may provide the foundation for later personality trait descriptions ("I'm shy") (Eder, 1989, 1990).

By the age of 8 or so, children are more capable of describing their enduring inner qualities (Livesley & Bromley, 1973), and their self-descriptions are filled with personality-trait terms ("I'm friendly," "I'm funny," "I'm curious," and so on). Moreover, they now describe not just what they typically do or what they can do but how their abilities compare with those of their companions (Secord & Peevers, 1974). The preschooler who claimed to be able to hit a baseball now becomes the elementary school child who claims to be a better batter than any of her classmates. What has changed? For one thing, children have gained the cognitive skills needed to infer from regularities in their behavior that they have certain consistent traits. For another, they are more capable of evaluating themselves through **social comparison**—of using informa-

Preschool children emphasize the "active self" in their self-descriptions, noting things they can do but saying little at all about their psychological traits.

tion about how they stack up compared to other individuals to judge themselves (Pomerantz et al., 1995). They then define and evaluate themselves in terms of whether they are more or less competent than other children.

Young children often seem to be rather oblivious to information about how they compare to others and have difficulty interpreting such information when they receive it (Butler, 1990; Ruble, 1983). They tend to believe that they are the greatest, even in the face of direct evidence that they have been outclassed by their peers. By age 5 or so, children do watch their classmates and make social comparisons (Frey & Ruble, 1985). However, they usually do this to be sociable ("Same lunchbox—we're twinsies!") or to find out how to do their work ("Where did you write your name?") rather than to evaluate themselves. By contrast, first-grade children begin to seek information that will tell them whether they are more or less competent than their peers; they glance at each other's papers, ask "How many did you miss?" and say things like "I got more than you did." Older elementary school children are more politically astute and avoid making potentially embarrassing social comparisons

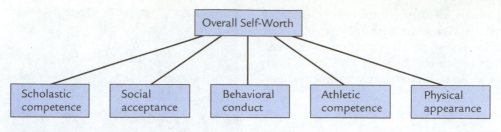

FIGURE 10.1 *The multidimensional and hierarchical nature of self-esteem* (From Harter, 1996)

out loud. Yet they most certainly sneak looks at other children's papers and pay close attention to information about where they stand in the classroom pecking order (Frey & Ruble, 1985; Pomerantz et al., 1995).

So, social comparison increases and becomes more subtle with age. Yet the extent to which children engage in social comparison is very much influenced by the social context. It is common in the United States because parents, teachers, and others emphasize individual achievement. However, Israeli children living in communal kibbutzim do less of it than children raised in Israeli cities, perhaps because cooperation and teamwork are so strongly emphasized in the kibbutzim (Butler & Ruzany, 1993).

Social comparisons help school-age children understand both how they are like others and how they are different from others. On the one hand, elementary school children are more likely than preschoolers to define themselves as part of social units ("I'm a Kimball, a second-grader at Brookside School, a Brownie Scout"). They are forming a social identity that ties them to similar others (Damon & Hart, 1988). On the other hand, school-age children also take special notice of how they differ from others. An African-American girl in a largely white school, for example, is more likely to mention her race when she is asked to tell about herself than is a black girl in an all-black school (McGuire et al., 1978). Why? Simply because children do attempt to understand what makes them unique as individuals.

Self-Esteem

As children amass a wide range of perceptions of themselves and engage in social comparisons, they begin to evaluate their worth. Susan Harter (1982, 1986, 1996) has developed a self-perception scale that assesses children's self-worth by asking them to evaluate their *scholastic competence* (for example, feeling smart, doing well in school), *social acceptance* (being popular, feeling liked), *behavioral conduct* (not getting in trouble), *athletic competence* (being good at sports), and *physical appearance* (feeling good-looking). When the scale was given to third- through ninth-graders, even third-graders showed that they had well-defined positive or negative feelings about themselves. Moreover, chil-

dren made important distinctions between their competency in one area and their competency in another; they did not just have generally high or generally low self-esteem. This suggests that self-esteem is *multidimensional* rather than unidimensional. But it is also *hierarchical,* for during the elementary school years children also come to integrate their self-perceptions in different domains to form an overall, abstract sense of self-worth (Harter, 1996; Marsh & Hattie, 1996). As Figure 10.1 shows, the self-esteem hierarchy that results has global self-worth at the top and specific dimensions of self-concept below it.

The accuracy of self-evaluations increases steadily over the elementary school years (Butler, 1990; Harter, 1982). Young children (4- to 7-year-olds) can be accused of having inflated egos; their self-esteem scores sometimes reflect their *desires* to be liked or to be "good" at various activities as much as their actual competencies (Eccles et al., 1993; Harter & Pike, 1984). However, starting at about age 8, children's self-evaluations become more realistic and accurate. For example, those with high scholastic self-esteem are rated as intellectually competent by their teachers, and those with high athletic self-esteem are frequently chosen by peers in sporting events. At the same time, children are increasingly realizing what they "should" be like and are forming an ever-grander "ideal self." As a result, the gap between the real self and the ideal self increases with age, and older children run a greater risk than younger children do of thinking that they fall short of what they could or should be (Glick & Zigler, 1985; Oosterwegel & Oppenheimer, 1993).

Influences on Self-Esteem

Why do some children have higher self-esteem than others? Basically because some children (1) are more competent than others, and (2) receive more positive social feedback (Shirk & Harter, 1996). Some children are in fact more competent and socially attractive than others; they experience more success in areas important to them and come out better in social comparisons (Luster & McAdoo, 1995). Apart from competence, though, social feedback from parents, teachers, peers, and other important people can play a critical role. Most notably, children with high self-esteem tend to have parents who are both warm and democratic (Coopersmith, 1967; Lamborn et al., 1991).

Parents who are loving, form secure attachments with their children, and frequently communicate approval and acceptance are likely to help their children think positively about themselves (Felson, 1990; Verschueren, Marcoen, & Schoefs, 1996). Saying, whether through words, looks, or actions, "You're not important" or "Why can't you be more like your older brother?" is likely to have the opposite effect on self-esteem. This is the concept of the looking-glass self in action: Children will form self-concepts that reflect the evaluations of significant people in their lives.

Parents whose children have high self-esteem also enforce clearly stated rules of behavior while allowing their children to express their opinions and participate in decision making. This democratic parenting style may contribute to self-esteem by giving children a firm basis for evaluating whether their behavior is good or bad and by sending them the message that their opinions are respected. The relationship between high self-esteem and this nurturing parenting style has been observed in most ethnic groups in the United States as well as in other countries such as Australia, Germany, and China (Scott, Scott, & McCabe, 1991; Steinberg et al., 1992).

Teachers, peers, and other significant individuals contribute to self-esteem in much the same way that parents do. As children get older, peer influences on self-esteem become more and more evident (Thorne & Michaelieu, 1996). The judgments of other people, along with all the information that children gain by observing their own behavior and comparing it with that of their peers, shape their overall self-evaluations. Once self-esteem has been established, it tends to remain quite stable over the elementary school years, and it is positively correlated with a variety of measures of good adjustment (Coopersmith, 1967; Harter, 1996).

In sum, a major change in self-conception occurs at about age 8 as children shift from describing their physical and active selves to talking of their psychological and social qualities. Other changes include increased social comparison, formation of an overall sense of self-worth, more accurate self-evaluation, and widening of the ideal self/real self gap. Competence and positive social feedback from warm, democratic parents contribute to high self-esteem.

The Personality Stabilizes

When can you tell what a child's personality will be like by the time he or she reaches adulthood? The biologically based response tendencies that we call temperament will be shaped by the individual's social experiences into a full-blown personality during childhood. Certain aspects of early temperament clearly carry over into later personality. For example, inhibited 3-year-olds are less impulsive, less willing to take risks, and less aggressive than uninhibited children, even as adolescents (Caspi & Silva, 1995). Yet we cannot always be confident that the sociable or inhibited infant or young child will remain that way. Many important dimensions of personality do not really begin to "gel" and become fairly stable until the elementary school years (Hartup & van Lieshout, 1995; Moss & Susman, 1980; Guerin & Gottfried, 1994).

As the years go by, some behavior patterns are reinforced and strengthened because they set in motion certain kinds of interactions with the social environment and evoke certain reactions from other people (Caspi, Elder, & Bem, 1987, 1988). For example, a child who has an explosive personality, who is irritable and prone to temper tantrums, may lose friends and alienate teachers as a child, lose jobs or experience marital problems as an adult, and so experience a snowballing of the negative consequences of her early personality. She may also evoke hostile reactions from other people that further reinforce her tendency to be ill-tempered.

The goodness of fit between person and environment also helps determine which traits carry over into later life and which do not. Consider Figure 10.2, which reports the results of a classic longitudinal study of development from birth to early adulthood conducted by Jerome Kagan and Howard Moss (1962). Achievement orientation, sex-typed (or sex-appropriate) activity, and spontaneity were reasonably stable over time in both males and females, as indicated by high correlations between behavior in childhood and behavior in adulthood. By contrast, tendencies toward anger or aggression and initiation of activities with the other sex were stable for males but not for females, whereas tendencies to react passively in stressful situations and to be dependent on other people were much more stable for females.

How can we explain this pattern of results? Kagan and Moss (1962) suggest that the stability of a personality trait over time depends on its being valued by society and consistent with society's prescribed gender roles (that is, on its goodness of fit to social expectations). Only then will it be reinforced. Parents, peers, teachers, and other agents of socialization value achievement in both sexes, so early socialization experiences encourage both boys and girls to remain achievement oriented. Society also encourages sex-typed activities for both boys and girls. But aggressive tendencies may persist less in girls, and passivity and dependence may be less stable in boys, because our society has traditionally not tolerated either aggressive girls or passive, dependent boys (see also Asendorpf & Van Aken, 1991; Kerr et al., 1994). Thus traits that conflict with cultural norms may be discouraged and may fail to endure. Other people's reactions to a

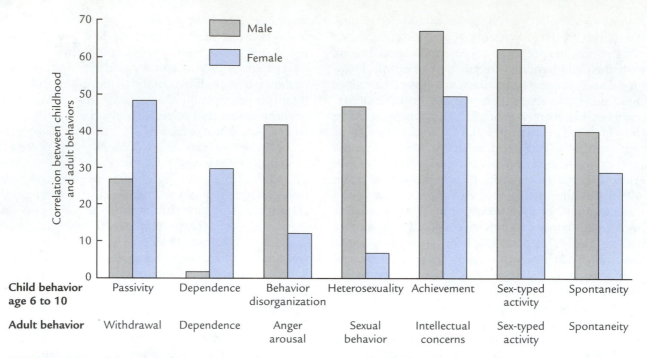

FIGURE 10.2 *Stability and change in seven classes of behavior between childhood and early adulthood. Note: Each bar shows the correlation between child behavior and adult behavior. The higher the correlation, the more the individual's standing within that group on the trait remains consistent over time.* (Adapted from Kagan & Moss, 1962)

child's behavior, including those based on cultural beliefs, help determine which of their distinctive personality traits children are most likely to carry with them into later life.

THE ADOLESCENT

Perhaps no period of the life span is more important to the development of the self than adolescence. Adolescence is truly a time for "finding oneself," as we see from considering adolescent self-conceptions, self-esteem, and identity formation.

Self-Conceptions

Raymond Montemayor and Marvin Eisen (1977) learned a great deal about the self-concepts of children and adolescents from grades 4 to 12 by asking students to write 20 answers to the question "Who am I?" What age differences can you detect in these answers given by a 9-year-old, an 11-year-old, and a 17-year-old (pp. 317–318)?

9-year-old: My name is Bruce C. I have brown eyes. I have brown hair. I love! sports. I have seven people in my family. I have great! eye sight. I have lots! of friends. I live at. . . . I have an uncle who is almost 7 feet tall. My teacher is Mrs. V. I play

hockey! I'm almost the smartest boy in the class. I love! food. . . . I love! school.

11½-year-old: My name is A. I'm a human being . . . a girl . . . a truthful person. I'm not pretty. I do so-so in my studies. I'm a very good cellist. I'm a little tall for my age. I like several boys. . . . I'm old fashioned. I am a very good swimmer. . . . I try to be helpful. . . . Mostly I'm good, but I lose my temper. I'm not well liked by some girls and boys. I don't know if boys like me. . . .

17-year-old: I am a human being . . . a girl . . . an individual. . . . I am a Pisces. I am a moody person . . . an indecisive person . . . an ambitious person. I am a big curious person. . . . I am lonely. I am an American (God help me). I am a Democrat. I am a liberal person. I am a radical. I am conservative. I am a pseudoliberal. I am an Atheist. I am not a classifiable person (i.e., I don't want to be).

There are several notable differences between the self-descriptions of children and adolescents (see also Damon & Hart, 1988; Harter, 1990; Livesley & Bromley, 1973). First, self-descriptions become *less physical and more psychological* as children get older. Second, these self-portraits become *less concrete and more abstract*. Recall Piaget's theory that children begin to shift from concrete-operational to formal-operational thinking at about age 11 or 12. Although 9- to 10-year-olds are capable of describing their psychological traits, they often do so in fairly concrete terms ("I love! food"). Children entering adolescence (11- to 12-year-olds) more often generalize about their broader personality traits ("I am a truthful person"). High school students' self-descriptions are even more abstract, focusing not only on personality traits but also on important values and ideologies or beliefs ("I am a pseudoliberal").

Third, adolescents reflect more about what they are like; they are *more self-aware* than children are (Selman, 1980). Their new ability to think about their own and other people's thoughts and feelings can make them painfully self-conscious. Fourth, adolescents have a *more differentiated* self-concept than children (Harter, 1996). For example, the child's "social self," which reflects perceived acceptance by peers, splits into distinct aspects such as acceptance by the larger peer group, acceptance by close friends, and acceptance in romantic relationships (Connolly & Konarski, 1995). Finally, older adolescents seem able to combine their differentiated self-perceptions into a *more integrated, coherent self-portrait.* Instead of merely listing traits, they organize their self-perceptions, including those that seem contradictory, into a coherent picture—a theory of what makes them tick.

As an illustration, consider an interesting study by Susan Harter and Ann Monsour (1992) in which 13-, 15-, and 17-year-olds were asked to describe themselves when they are with parents, with friends, in romantic relationships, and in the classroom. These adolescents were then asked to sort through their self-descriptions, identify any opposites or inconsistencies, and indicate which opposites confused or upset them. The 13-year-olds were quite unaware of inconsistencies within themselves. If they did detect any, they were not especially bothered by them. By age 15, students identified many more inconsistencies and were clearly confused by them. One ninth-grade girl, for example, noted that she was both attentive and lazy in school, talkative and nervous in romantic relationships, smart at school and fun-loving with friends, and so on. In discussing her tendency to be happy with friends but depressed at home, she said, "I really think of myself as a happy person, and I want to be that way with everyone because I think that's my true self, but I get depressed with my family and it bugs me because that's not what I want to be like" (Harter & Monsour, 1992, p. 253). These 15-year-olds, especially the girls, seemed to feel that there were several different selves inside them and were concerned about finding the "real me." Harter has also found that adolescents this age are often afraid to express the "real me" even when they find it, as we see in Box 10.2.

Only the 17-year-olds Harter and Monsour studied were able to integrate their conflicting self-perceptions into a more coherent view of themselves. Thus a 17- or 18-year-old boy might conclude that it is perfectly understandable to be relaxed and confident in most situations but nervous on dates if one has not yet had much dating experience or that "moodiness" can explain being cheerful with friends on some occasions but irritable on others. Harter and Monsour believe that cognitive development—specifically the ability to compare abstract trait concepts and ultimately integrate them through higher-order concepts like "moodiness"—is behind this change in self-perceptions.

In sum, self-understandings become more psychological, abstract, differentiated, and integrated, and self-awareness increases, from childhood to adolescence and over the course of adolescence. Truly, the adolescent becomes a sophisticated personality theorist who reflects upon and understands the workings of his or her personality (and who also has a richer understanding of other people).

Self-Esteem

The founder of developmental psychology, G. Stanley Hall, characterized adolescence as a time of emotional turmoil and psychological *storm and stress*. By this account, adolescents might be expected to experience low, or at least very unstable, levels of self-esteem. Does research support this view?

For about 20% of teenagers, adolescence is indeed a time of storm and stress characterized by significant mental health problems, including drops in self-esteem (Offer & Schonert-Reichl, 1992). Roberta Simmons and her colleagues (Simmons, Rosenberg, & Rosenberg, 1973) compared the self-perceptions of children aged 8 to 11, 12 to 14, and 15 or older. Self-image problems were greatest among the 12- to 14-year-olds. These early adolescents had relatively low self-esteem, were highly self-conscious, and reported that their self-perceptions were highly changeable. Leaving elementary school as the oldest and most revered of students and entering the larger world of junior high school as the youngest and least competent sometimes damages self-esteem temporarily (Seidman et al., 1994; Simmons et al., 1987; Wigfield et al., 1991). However, this dip in self-esteem does not affect everyone. It is likely to be greatest among females facing multiple stressors—for example, making the transition to junior high school and also coping with pubertal changes, beginning to date, and perhaps dealing with a family move all at the same time (Simmons et al., 1987). Some of us do indeed remember seventh grade as a year we would like to forget!

Overall, though, adolescence is not hazardous to the self, and most adolescents do not experience significant drops in self-esteem. Instead, most emerge from this developmental period with essentially the same level of self-esteem they had at the outset (Block

BOX 10.2

False self behavior during adolescence

Once adolescents begin to notice that they behave differently in different social contexts (with parents, peers, and romantic partners), they often become concerned about which "me" is the "real me." They also become aware that they are playing parts that are not the "real me" in some contexts. According to Susan Harter and her colleagues, they engage in **false self behavior,** putting on false fronts or acting out of character, usually in an attempt to win the approval of parents or peers (Harter et al., 1996).

Harter and her colleagues (1996) gave adolescents in grades 6 to 12 scales measuring perceived support received from parents and peers and a measure of true/false self behavior asking whether or not the adolescent is able to express his or her true self (for example, "Some kids feel that they can be their 'true self' around their mothers but other kids feel that they *can't* be their 'true self' around their mothers," p. 365). The adolescents who engaged in the most false self behavior around their parents felt that (1) they got little support from their parents, (2) the support they did get was conditional

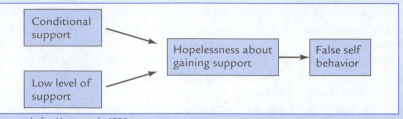

Patterned after Harter et al., 1996

on whether they conformed to their parents' standards, and (3) there was little hope that they would be accepted and supported in the future. As one adolescent put it:

> My mom is really on my case because I'm not living up to what she wants me to be. If I get A's in school she acts like she is proud of me. But if I don't, she doesn't approve of me, you could say how she treats me is conditional on how I do. There is no way I can ever please her, it's pretty hopeless. (Harter, 1996, p. 361)

Similarly, Harter found that some adolescents engaged in more false self behavior with their peers than others did and that those who did felt that their friends were "fair weather"

friends who accepted them only if they behaved like everyone else. Some adolescents engaged in false self behavior as a way of experimenting with different images in order to find their true identity or in order to impress people. Those reasons proved to be healthy. However, when adolescents engaged in false self behavior because they did not like themselves and did not believe that anyone would accept them, they were likely to score high on measures of depression and to lack a sense of self-worth. Once again, then, we see signs of the looking-glass self in action: Adolescents are most likely to accept themselves if important people in their lives accept them as they are and provide what noted psychotherapist Carl Rogers (1951) called "unconditional positive regard."

& Robins, 1993; Crain, 1996). Apparently they revise their self-concepts in fairly minor ways as they experience the physical, cognitive, and social changes of adolescence. Overall, then, Hall's characterization of adolescence as a stormy time for the self is inaccurate for most adolescents.

Forming a Sense of Identity

Like G. Stanley Hall, Erik Erikson believed that adolescence is a time of dramatic changes in the self. It was Erikson (1968) who characterized adolescence as a critical period in the lifelong process of forming one's identity as a person and who proposed that adolescents experience the psychosocial conflict of **identity versus role confusion.** The concept of identity, introduced at the start of the chapter, is slippery. It refers to a firm and coherent definition of who you are, where you are going, and where you fit into society. To achieve a sense of identity, the adolescent must somehow integrate the many separate perceptions that are part of the self-concept into a coherent sense of self and must

feel that he or she is, deep down, the same person yesterday, today, and tomorrow—at home, at school, or at work (Blasi & Glodis, 1995). The search for identity involves grappling with many important questions: What kind of career do I want? What religious, moral, and political values can I really call my own? Who am I as a man or woman and as a sexual being? Where do I fit in the world? What do I really want out of my life?

Can you recall struggling with identity issues yourself? Are you currently struggling with some of them? If so, you can appreciate the uncomfortable feelings that adolescents may experience when they can't seem to work out a clear sense of who they are. Erikson believed that many young people in complex societies like the United States experience a full-blown and painful "identity crisis"; indeed, he coined the term. There are many reasons why they might do so. First, their bodies change, and they must therefore revise their body images (a part of their self-concepts) and become accustomed to being sexual beings. Second, cognitive growth allows adolescents to think systematically about hypothetical possibilities, including possible future selves. Third, social demands are placed on them to "grow up"—to decide what they want to do in life and to get on with it. According to Erikson (1968), our society supports youth by allowing them a period of time in high school and college when they are relatively free of responsibilities and can experiment with different roles in order to find themselves—a so-called **moratorium period.** But it also makes establishing an identity harder than it may be in many other cultures by giving youth a huge number of options and encouraging them to believe that they can be anything they want to be.

Developmental Trends

James Marcia (1966) expanded on Erikson's theory and stimulated much research on identity formation by developing an interview that allows investigators to assess where an adolescent is in the process of identity formation. Adolescents are classified into one of four *identity statuses* based on their progress toward an identity in each of several domains (for example, occupational, religious, and political/ideological). The key questions are whether or not an individual has experienced a *crisis* (or has seriously grappled with identity issues and explored alternatives) and whether or not he or she has achieved a *commitment* (that is, a resolution of the questions raised). On the basis of crisis and commitment, the individual is classified into one of the four identity statuses shown in Table 10.3.

How long does it take to achieve a sense of identity? Philip Meilman's (1979) study of college-bound boys between 12 and 18, 21-year-old college males, and 24-year-old young men provides an answer (see Figure 10.3). Most of the 12- and 15-year-olds were in either the identity diffusion or the foreclosure status. At these ages many adolescents simply have not yet thought about who they are—either they have no idea or they know that any ideas they do have are very likely to change (the **diffusion status,** with no crisis and no commitment). Other adolescents may say things like "I'm going to be a doctor like my dad" and appear to have their acts together. However, it becomes apparent that they have never really thought through *on their own* what suits them best and have simply accepted identities suggested to them by their parents or other people (the **foreclosure status,** involving a commitment without a crisis).

As Figure 10.3 indicates, progress toward identity achievement becomes more evident starting at age 18. Notice that more individuals now begin to fall into the **moratorium status,** in which the individual is currently experiencing a crisis or is actively exploring identity issues. Presumably, entering the moratorium status is a good sign; if the individual can find answers to the questions raised, he or she will move on to the identity achievement status. Yet notice that only 20% of the 18-year-olds, 40% of the college students, and slightly over half of the 24-year-olds in Meilman's study had achieved a firm identity based on a careful weighing of alternatives (the **identity achievement status**).

Is the identity formation process different for females from what it is for males? In most respects, no (Archer, 1992; Kroger, 1997). Females progress toward

TABLE 10.3

The four identity statuses, as shown by current religious beliefs		
	No Crisis Experienced	*Crisis Experienced*
NO COMMITMENT MADE	**DIFFUSION STATUS** The person has not yet thought about or resolved identity issues and has failed to chart directions in life. *Example:* "I haven't really thought much about religion, and I guess I don't know what I believe exactly."	**MORATORIUM STATUS** The individual is currently experiencing an identity crisis and is actively raising questions and seeking answers. *Example:* "I'm in the middle of evaluating my beliefs and hope that I'll be able to figure out what's right for me. I like many of the answers provided by my Catholic upbringing, but I've also become skeptical about some teachings and have been looking into Unitarianism to see if it might help me answer my questions."
COMMITMENT MADE	**FORECLOSURE STATUS** The individual seems to know who he or she is but has latched on to an identity prematurely, without much thought (e.g., by uncritically becoming what parents or other authority figures suggest he or she should). *Example:* "My parents are Baptists and I'm a Baptist; it's just the way I grew up."	**IDENTITY ACHIEVEMENT STATUS** The individual has resolved his or her identity crisis and made commitments to particular goals, beliefs, and values. *Example:* "I really did some soul-searching about my religion and other religions too and finally know what I believe and what I don't."

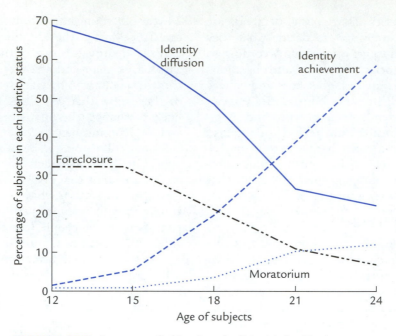

FIGURE 10.3 *Percentages of subjects in each of Marcia's four identity statuses as a function of age. Note that only 4% of the 15-year-olds and 20% of the 18-year-olds had achieved a stable identity.* (Based on Meilman, 1979)

achieving a clear sense of identity at about the same rate that males do. However, one intriguing sex difference has been observed: Although today's college women are just as concerned about establishing a career identity as men are, they attach greater importance to and think more about the aspects of identity that center on sexuality and how to balance career and family goals (Archer, 1992; Kroger, 1997; Patterson, Sochting, & Marcia, 1992). Perhaps it is the continuing influence of traditional gender roles we see here.

Judging from such research, identity formation *takes quite a bit of time.* Not until the late teens and early 20s do many young men and women move from the diffusion or foreclosure status into the moratorium status and then achieve a sense of identity (Waterman, 1982). But this is by no means the end of the identity formation process. Some adults continue in a moratorium status for years; others reopen the question of who they are after thinking they had all the answers earlier in life (Kroger, 1996). A divorce, for example, may cause a woman to rethink what it means to be a woman and reraise questions about other aspects of her identity as well. The result may be new psychosocial growth.

Not only does identity formation take a long time but it *occurs at different rates in different domains of identity* (Kroger, 1996). For example, Sally Archer (1982) assessed the identity statuses of 6th- to 12th-graders in four domains: occupational choice, gender-role attitudes, religious beliefs, and political ideologies. Only

5% of the adolescents were in the same identity status in all four areas, and more than 90% were in two or three categories across the four areas. Apparently, then, some aspects of identity take shape earlier than others. The process may be even more complex for members of racial and ethnic minority groups. As Box 10.3 shows, they are typically more concerned than white adolescents with forming a positive ethnic identity.

Influences on Identity Formation

The adolescent's progress toward achieving identity is a product of at least four factors: (1) cognitive growth, (2) relationships with parents, (3) experiences outside the home, and (4) the broader cultural context. *Cognitive development* seems to enable adolescents to imagine and contemplate possible future identities. Adolescents who have achieved solid mastery of formal-operational thought and who think in complex and abstract ways are more likely to raise and resolve identity issues than adolescents who are less cognitively mature (Waterman, 1992). In addition, adolescents in the moratorium and achievement statuses adopt an information-processing style that involves actively seeking out relevant information rather than relying on others for guidance, as foreclosed adolescents tend to do, or putting off decisions and making impulsive choices at the last minute, as diffused adolescents tend to do (Berzonsky & Neimeyer, 1994).

Second, adolescents' *relationships with parents* affect their progress in forging an identity (Markstrom-Adams,

BOX 10.3

Forging a positive ethnic identity

The process of forming an identity includes forming an **ethnic identity,** a sense of personal identification with an ethnic group and its values and cultural traditions (Phinney, 1996). Everyone has an ethnic and racial background, but members of minority groups tend to think more than white adolescents do about who they are ethnically and racially.

The process begins during the preschool years, when children learn that different racial and ethnic categories exist and gradually become able to classify themselves correctly into one group or another (Spencer & Markstrom-Adams, 1990). For example, Mexican-American preschool children may learn behaviors associated with their culture such as how to give a Chicano handshake, but they often do not know until about the age of 8 what ethnic labels apply to them, what they mean, or that they will last a lifetime (Bernal & Knight, 1997).

Forming a positive ethnic identity during adolescence seems to proceed through the same steps as forming a vocational or religious identity, even though we don't choose our racial or ethnic heritage in the way we choose our occupations (Phinney, 1993). School-age children and young adolescents either say that they identify with their racial or ethnic group because their parents and other members of the group influenced them to do so (foreclosure status) or have not given the issue much thought (diffusion status).

Between the ages of 16 and 19, many minority youths move into the moratorium and achievement statuses with respect to ethnic identity. One Mexican-American female described her moratorium period this way: "I want to know what we do and how our culture is different from others. Going to festivals and cultural events helps me to learn more about my own culture and about myself" (Phinney, 1993, p. 70). When ethnic identity is achieved, youths feel comfortable being what they are.

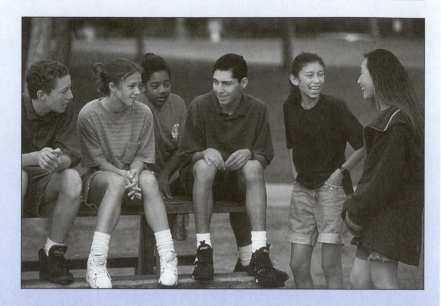

Questioning regarding ethnic identity is sometimes triggered by being discriminated against or by having one's group loyalty questioned. According to Signithia Fordham and John Ogbu (1986), for example, many low-income African-American adolescents who perform well in the classroom experience a good deal of ambivalence about their accomplishments because they run the risk of being accused of "acting white" by their black peers if they try to succeed by white standards. Virtually all North American minorities have a term for community members who identify too closely with the mainstream white culture, be it the "apple" (red on the outside, white on the inside) for Native Americans, the "coconut" for Hispanics, the "banana" for Asians, or the "Oreo" for African Americans. Minority adolescents must decide what *they* are inside.

Biracial adolescents sometimes face even greater dilemmas. For example, adolescents who are both African American and white may feel that they do not quite fit in either racial group, or they may be pressured by friends to choose an identity as black *or* white but not *both* (DeBerry, Scarr, & Weinberg, 1996; Kerwin et al., 1993). Those who are able to identify clearly as either an African American or a white are likely to be more well-adjusted than those who cannot decide what they are (DeBerry et al., 1996). Erik Erikson, by the way, had firsthand experience with these sorts of ethnic identity struggles; he was the blond, blue-eyed son of a Danish mother and a Jewish stepfather and was nicknamed "the goy" (non-Jew) by the Jewish boys in his neighborhood (Coles, 1970).

Somehow, minority adolescents must work out a resolution to these sorts of conflicts between their own culture and the majority culture. They are likely to do so more successfully if their parents teach them about their group's cultural traditions, try to prepare them to live in a culturally diverse society and deal with prejudice, and provide the warm and democratic parenting that seems to foster self-esteem and healthy identity development (Bernal & Knight, 1997; Marshall, 1995). Most minority adolescents cope well with the special challenges in identity formation they face. They settle questions of ethnic identity and resolve other identity issues at about the same ages as Euro-American youths (Markstrom-Adams & Adams, 1995), and they end up with about the same levels of self-esteem (Crain, 1996).

1992; Waterman, 1982). Youth in the diffusion status of identity formation are more likely than those in the other categories to be neglected or rejected by their parents and to be distant from them. Perhaps it is difficult to forge one's own identity without first having the opportunity to identify with respected parental figures and to take on some of their desirable qualities. At the other extreme, adolescents categorized as being in the foreclosure status appear to be extremely close—possibly too close—to parents who are loving but overly protective and controlling. Because they love their parents and have little opportunity to make decisions on their own, foreclosed adolescents may never question parental authority or feel any need to forge a separate identity.

By comparison, students who are classified in the moratorium and identity achievement statuses appear to have a solid base of affection at home combined with considerable freedom to be individuals in their own right (Campbell, Adams, & Dobson, 1984; Grotevant & Cooper, 1986). In family discussions, for example, these adolescents experience a sense of closeness and mutual respect while feeling free to disagree with their parents (Grotevant & Cooper, 1986). Notice that this is the same warm and democratic parenting style that seems to help younger children gain a strong sense of self-esteem.

Experiences outside the home are a third influence on identity formation. For example, adolescents who go to college are exposed to diverse ideas and encouraged to think issues through independently. Although college students may be more confused for a time about their identities than peers who begin working after high school (Munro & Adams, 1977), going to college provides the kind of "moratorium period" that Erikson felt was essential to identity formation.

Finally, identity formation is influenced by *the broader cultural context* in which it occurs—a point that Erikson himself strongly emphasized. The whole notion that adolescents should choose a personal identity after carefully exploring many options may well be peculiar to industrialized Western societies in the 20th century (Cote & Levine, 1988). As was true of adolescents in earlier eras, adolescents in many traditional societies today simply adopt the adult roles they are expected to adopt, without any soul searching or experimentation. For many of these adolescents, what Marcia calls identity foreclosure is probably the most adaptive route to adulthood (Cote & Levine, 1988). Even in our society, many disadvantaged young women foreclose identity by becoming mothers; early child bearing is common in their environment, and they may see few other options (Cohler & Musick, 1996).

In Western society at least, the adolescent who is able to raise serious questions about the self and an-

Adolescents sometimes experiment with a variety of looks in their search for a sense of identity.

swer them—that is, the individual who achieves identity—is likely to be better off for it. Identity achievement is associated with psychological well-being and high self-esteem, complex thinking about moral issues and other matters, a willingness to accept and cooperate with other people, and a variety of other psychological strengths (Waterman, 1992). By contrast, those individuals who fail to achieve a sense of identity may find themselves lacking self-esteem and drifting aimlessly, trapped in the identity diffusion status. Erikson recognized that identity issues can and do crop up later in life even for those people who form a positive sense of identity during adolescence. Nonetheless, he quite rightly marked the adolescent period as a key time in life for defining who we are.

THE ADULT

As we enter adulthood, having gained a great deal of understanding of what we are like as individuals, we clearly have our own unique personalities. What happens during the adult years? Are self-conceptions and personality traits highly changeable, or do they remain much the same?

Self-Perceptions

Let's first ask whether self-concepts and levels of self-esteem change over the adult years. On the one hand, we might expect that many people would gain self-esteem as they cope successfully with the challenges of adult life. On the other hand, we might guess that aging, disease, and losses of roles and relationships in later life could undermine self-esteem. As it turns out, neither view is accurate. Most researchers find no evidence at all that young, middle-aged, and elderly adults differ in self-esteem or in the ways they describe themselves (McGue, Hirsch, & Lykken, 1993; Ruth & Coleman, 1996). For instance, there is little truth at all to the stereotyped view that older adults suffer from a poor self-image. The interesting question has become this: *How do elderly people manage to maintain positive self-images even as they experience some of the losses that come with aging?*

First, *the gap between the real self and the ideal self closes in later life.* Adults of different ages do not differ much in how they evaluate their present selves, but they *do* differ in their views of what they could or should be in the future. Carol Ryff (1991) asked young, middle-aged, and elderly adults to assess their (1) ideal, (2) likely future, (3) present, and (4) past selves. As Figure 10.4 shows, ratings of the present self did not change much from age group to age group—further evidence that older adults do not suffer from low self-esteem. However, older adults scaled down their visions of what they could ideally be and what they will be in the future (and judged more positively what they had been in the past). Thus the gap between the ideal self and real self that grows larger during childhood and adolescence and gives us a sense of falling short apparently closes again in later life (see also Fleeson & Heckhausen, 1997).

Second, Laura Carstensen and Alexandra Freund (1994) suggest that many "losses" experienced in later life are not interpreted as losses at all because *the individual's goals and standards change with age.* The 45-year-old may be devastated at being passed over for a promotion, whereas the 60-year-old nearing retirement may not be any more bothered by this than 45-year-olds are by "not being able to jump on their beds, and draw pictures with crayons" (Carstensen & Freund, 1994, p. 87). Perhaps, then, as our goals change over the life span, we apply different measuring sticks in evaluating ourselves and do not mind failing to achieve goals that are no longer important to us.

Third, *the people with whom we compare ourselves change* (Brandtstädter & Greve, 1994). Older adults do not compare themselves to young adults but to people

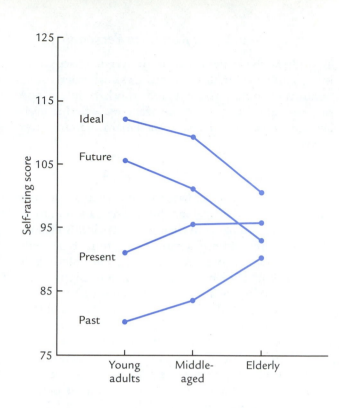

FIGURE 10.4 *Favorability of ratings of their ideal, likely future, present (real), and past selves by young, middle-aged, and elderly adults. The gap between ideal and real self that widens during childhood and adolescence shrinks during adulthood, as indicated by the converging lines in the graph. As they age, adults become more comfortable with the idea of remaining as they are and as they have been in the past.* (Adapted from Ryff, 1991)

who may have the same kinds of chronic diseases and impairments they have. Indeed, societal stereotypes of aging are so bleak that older adults can feel good about their own aging simply by conjuring up images of how bad aging normally is (Brandtstädter & Greve, 1994).

In sum, adults of different ages appear to feel equally good about themselves and to describe themselves in similar ways. This may be true in part because older adults perceive a smaller gap between their real and ideal selves, set different goals and evaluate their self-worth by different standards, and engage in different social comparisons. Each adult also maintains much the same level of self-esteem over time, although positive and negative life events can certainly bring about temporary changes in self-perception (Mortimer, Finch, & Kumka, 1982; Tran, Wright, & Chatters, 1991). Do we distort our self-perceptions so that we can have the comforting sense of feeling that we are basically the same people we always were? Or are unchanging self-perceptions a reflection of continuity in personality traits? Let's see.

Continuity and Discontinuity in Personality

To address the issue of continuity versus discontinuity in adult personality, we must ask whether adults retain their rankings compared to others in a group on trait dimensions over the years *and* whether average scores increase, decrease, or remain the same over the years.

Do People Retain Their Rankings?

Paul Costa, Robert McCrae, and their colleagues have closely studied personality change and continuity by giving adults from their 20s to their 90s personality tests and administering these tests repeatedly over the years (Costa & McCrae, 1994; McCrae & Costa, 1990). They have focused on the "big five" dimensions of personality listed in Table 10.2 and have found a good deal of stability of individual differences, as indicated by high correlations between scores on the same trait dimensions at different ages. In other words, the person who tends to be extraverted as a young adult is likely to be extraverted as an elderly adult, and the introvert is likely to remain introverted over the years. Similarly, the adult who shows high or low levels of neuroticism, conscientiousness, agreeableness, or openness to new experiences is likely to retain that ranking compared to peers years from now. Correlations between personality trait scores on two occasions 20 to 30 years apart average about .60 across the five personality dimensions. This means that 36% of the variation among individuals at a later testing can be predicted from differences in their earlier scores. It suggests consistency in personality over time but also room for change (Costa & McCrae, 1994). Personalities are still forming in the teens and 20s but then become more firmly established by the time adults are in their 30s (Carmichael & McGue, 1994; Costa & McCrae, 1992). And despite stereotypes suggesting that elderly adults are "rigid" in their ways, personality is no more stable at 70 or 80 than at 30 or 40.

We should note, though, that Costa and McCrae have found greater stability of personality traits than some other researchers have found (for example, Connolly, 1991; Finn, 1986). When correlation coefficients between early and later traits are in the neighborhood of .50 or less, as they often are after many years have passed, they can be interpreted to suggest either continuity or discontinuity in personality—and probably both. Overall, major personality traits such as extraversion and neuroticism show less stability over the years than intelligence but more stability than such aspects of personality as self-esteem, attitudes, values, goals, and interests (Bengtson et al., 1985; Ruth & Coleman, 1996). Moreover, this consistency is not due simply to a desire on the part of adults to *think* they remain the same, for it also shows up when their spouses are asked to rate them over the years (Connolly, 1991; Costa & McCrae, 1988).

In sum, research has confirmed the argument of trait theorists that relatively enduring personality traits exist, and yet it also tells us that people change over the years. Evidence of continuity may explain why we often perceive ourselves as being the same basic people we used to be and why people we have not seen for years often seem not to have changed much at all. If this is bad news for people who are dissatisfied with their current personalities, it is good news for those who want to predict what they and other people will be like in the future or how they will respond to life events. For example, individuals who consistently score high on measures of neuroticism and low on measures of extraversion are likely to experience more negative and fewer positive life events than other people (Magnus et al., 1993) and to have more difficulty coping with stressful life events than do other individuals (Hoffman, Levy-Shiff, & Malinski, 1996; McCrae & Costa, 1990).

Even though individuals' rankings on many personality dimensions remain fairly stable during adulthood, many individuals must be changing, or the correlations between scores on repeated personality tests would be higher. Even if people's rankings were identical from time to time, it is still possible that most people systematically change in certain common directions. You may be consistently more extraverted than I over the years, and yet both of us, along with our peers, could become less extraverted at age 70 than we were at age 20. So let's examine the second major meaning of continuity in personality: stability in the average level of a trait displayed over the years.

Do Personalities Change Systematically?

Early cross-sectional studies suggested that younger and older adults have quite different personalities on average. For example, Bernice Neugarten and her colleagues found that elderly men and women were more introverted, introspective, and in touch with their inner feelings than middle-aged adults were (Neugarten, 1977). They seemed less concerned with demands placed on them by other people and more attuned to voices within themselves. However, some of these age-group differences turned out to be generational, or cohort, differences rather than true maturational changes. It turns out that people's personalities are considerably affected by when they were born and by what sorts of experiences they had in their formative years (Schaie & Parham, 1976). For example, today's older men are more restrained about expressing their feelings and less assertive than today's young men. Yet, when men are assessed repeatedly over the years, there is no sign that they *become* more emotionally restrained or less assertive as they get older (Douglas & Arenberg, 1978). Possibly, then, today's elderly people grew up in a time when self-expression was less strongly encouraged than it has been in more recent times.

Only longitudinal studies can tell us whether people's personalities actually become different *as they age*. Some longitudinal studies point to personality growth from adolescence to middle age. People seem to become more intellectual and achievement oriented, more self-aware and introspective, more self-confident and assertive, more independent, and more nurturant toward others (Haan, 1981; Helson & Wink, 1992; Stevens & Truss, 1985). Adults apparently have opportunities to gain personality strengths as they get their lives off the ground and settle into specific work and family roles.

What about the period from middle age to old age? There are only a few signs that most people change in similar ways during this period. Adults' activity levels (their tendencies to be energetic, fast working, and action oriented) begin to decline in the 50s and continue declining through the 80s and 90s (Costa & McCrae, 1994). Some longitudinal studies also reinforce the idea that people tend to become less extraverted and more introspective in old age (Field & Millsap, 1991; Leon et al., 1979). Still, most of us will not undergo similar personality changes as part of the aging experience. Either we will remain much the same, as the work of Costa and McCrae suggests, or we will change in response to life experiences, but in our own individual ways, depending on our personalities (Wink, 1996).

Where do we stand, then? Most evidence suggests this:

1. There is a good deal of cross-age consistency in people's rankings within a group on "big five" personality trait dimensions such as extraversion and neuroticism, but change in them occurs too, and other aspects of personality may be even more changeable.
2. Different generations of people often have somewhat distinctive personality profiles as groups, indicating that the historical context in which people grow up affects their personality development.
3. There is some personality growth from adolescence to middle adulthood—a strengthening of qualities such as achievement orientation, self-confidence, autonomy, and nurture; evidently we do not stop developing as individuals once we turn 20.
4. There are very few ways in which the personality traits of adults systematically change in similar directions as they progress from middle adulthood to later adulthood, although some decreases in

activity level and increases in introspectiveness may be observed.

Overall, then, whether we look at individuals' relative positions on trait dimensions, as indicated by correlations, or at the average levels of different traits expressed by younger and older adults, there seem to be both continuity and discontinuity in personality during adulthood—considerable stability as well as room for change, especially in very early adulthood but later on as well.

Why Do People Change or Remain the Same?

Having figured out that there are both stability and change in personality traits over the life span, developmentalists are beginning to ask why people stay the same and why they change. What makes a personality stable? First, the influence of *heredity* is at work (see Chapter 3). Just as we have evidence of the heritability of infant temperament, we know that genes contribute to individual differences in adult personality. To cite an example, one large-scale study of adult twins in Sweden ranging in age from their 20s to their 80s yielded correlations between the extraversion and neuroticism scores of identical twin pairs of about .50 (Floderus-Myrhed, Pedersen, & Rasmuson, 1980). Obviously, identical genes do not make for identical personalities; the unique experiences of identical twins must have contributed to differences in their levels of extraversion and neuroticism. However, the correlations for fraternal twins were considerably lower (about .20), suggesting that adult personality is genetically influenced. Genetic influence is still apparent in old age, for elderly identical twins, even those who have been separated all their lives, continue to be more alike than elderly fraternal twins in personality (Plomin et al., 1988).

Second, *lasting effects of childhood experiences* may contribute to stability of personality. We have seen, for example, that parents can either help a child overcome a difficult temperament or contribute to its becoming an enduring pattern of response.

Third and finally, traits remain stable because our *environments remain stable*. Here the argument is not just that early experiences have lasting effects—it is that both early and later experiences promote personality stability because we consistently seek out and have experiences that suit and reinforce our personalities (Caspi, 1993). The mechanism here may be *gene-environment correlations*: Genetic endowment influences the kinds of experiences we have, and those experiences, in turn, strengthen genetically based predispositions (see Chapter 3). Suppose that Thelma, because of some mix of genes and early experience, shows an early tendency to be extraverted, whereas Louise is a shy introvert from the start. Thelma's friendliness is likely to elicit friendliness from other people throughout her life. Moreover, as an extravert, she will seek out and create environments to her liking—placing herself in crowds, at parties, and in jobs where she can socialize. In these environments, Thelma is likely to maintain or even strengthen her initial tendency to be extraverted. Louise, meanwhile, might go out of her way to avoid parties, keep to herself, and therefore remain an introverted individual, comfortable with herself and her lifestyle. Each will be exposed to and will actively seek experiences that are likely to sustain and strengthen their early personality predispositions. In a kind of snowball effect, the consequences of having one early temperament rather than another will cumulate over the years (Caspi, 1993).

What, then, might cause the significant changes in personality that some adults experience? *Biological factors* such as disease could contribute. The nervous system deterioration associated with *Huntington's disease,* for example, causes victims to become moody and irritable. A more likely possibility is that adults change in response to *changes in the social environment,* including major life events (Caspi, 1993). For example, young adults who leave school and start working experience more personality changes than those who stay in school (van der Velde, Feij, & Taris, 1995), and those who land good jobs with high incomes and much freedom to make decisions tend to gain confidence after college, whereas those who face job insecurity and unemployment in their early careers lose it (Mortimer et al., 1982). In this way, life events help determine whether traits evident in early adulthood will persist or change, much as social learning theorists claim. If their lives change dramatically enough, adults can become very different people from what they were earlier in life.

Finally, change may be more likely when *the fit between person and environment is poor.* Consider some fascinating research conducted by Florine Livson (1976). She identified two groups of women, both of whom were mentally healthy at age 50. "Traditional" women were conventional and well suited for the stereotypically feminine role. They had been outgoing and popular as teenagers and continued to show these same traits in adulthood, changing little at all. By contrast, "independents" did not fit traditional feminine roles as well. As teenagers they had tended to be unconventional, introspective, and motivated to achieve. During adulthood these nontraditional women, like most women of their era, abandoned careers to pursue the lives of housewives and mothers. They then found themselves confronting a midlife crisis in their 40s: They were depressed and up in the air about what to do with their lives as their children prepared to leave the nest. Yet by age 50 these independent women were able to redirect their lives and rebound toward a level of psychological health equal to that of the traditional women.

Similarly, Livson (1981) found that men who fitted the traditional male role well changed less over the years than "nontraditional" men, who felt cramped by the traditional male role and only after a crisis in their 40s began to express their more feminine, emotional sides. Livson's studies tell us that people are most likely to change when the fit between their personalities and their environments (or lifestyles) is poor. This message about the importance of goodness of fit is the very one that has emerged from research on children with easy, difficult, and slow-to-warm-up temperaments. And it supports an important theme of contextual theorists: Personalities unfold through the ongoing transactions between person and environment.

In conclusion, the personality is both stable and changeable during adulthood. Genes, early childhood experiences, and the tendency to seek out or end up in environments that match and reinforce earlier predispositions all contribute to stability. Change in personality becomes more likely if people's environments change considerably or if there is a poor fit between their personalities and their lifestyles. Finally, even if personalities remain basically the same for long stretches of the life span, this does not mean that they cannot change—as, for example, with the help of a skilled psychotherapist (Costa & McCrae, 1992). Powerful experiences have the capacity to alter us at any stage of life.

Psychosocial Growth

Researchers who conclude that adults hardly change at all over the years typically study personality by administering standardized personality scales. These tests were designed to assess enduring traits and may well tell us about the most stable aspects of personality. However, researchers who interview people in depth about their lives often detect considerably more change and growth (Wrightsman, 1994). This is quite clear in research on Erikson's theory of psychosocial development through the life span. Let's review what this chapter has told us about psychosocial changes through adolescence and then ask whether Erikson was right to call attention to the potential for further psychological growth during adulthood.

Before Adulthood

During Erikson's first psychosocial conflict, **trust versus mistrust,** infants supposedly learn to trust other people to be responsive to their needs. If caregivers respond inconsistently, the balance of trust versus mistrust will tip in the direction of mistrust. Erikson believed that infants, in resolving the psychosocial conflict of basic *trust versus mistrust,* begin to recognize that they are separate from the caregivers

The "fit" between the personalities of independent, unconventional women and the traditional wife/mother role can be poor. This may result in dissatisfaction and stimulate changes in lifestyle or personality.

who respond to their needs. Indeed, as this chapter revealed, infants begin to distinguish self from other (typically the mother) during the first two or three months of life.

Toddlers acquire an even clearer sense of themselves as individuals as they struggle with the psychosocial conflict of **autonomy versus shame and doubt.** According to Erikson, they develop a sense of themselves and assert that they have wills of their own. Consistent with this view, toddlers recognize themselves in the mirror and lace their speech with the words "me" and "no" at about 18 months of age. Four- and 5-year-olds who have achieved a sense of autonomy then enter Erikson's stage of **initiative versus guilt.** They develop a sense of purpose by devising bold plans and taking great pride in accomplishing the goals they set. As we have seen, preschoolers define themselves primarily in terms of their physical activities and accomplishments.

A sense of initiative, Erikson believed, paves the way for success when elementary school children face the conflict of **industry versus inferiority** and focus on mastering important cognitive and social skills. As we have seen, elementary school children seem intent on evaluating their competencies; they engage in more social comparison than younger children and are likely to acquire a sense of industry rather than inferiority only if those comparisons turn out favorably.

According to Erikson, children who successfully master each of these childhood psychosocial conflicts gain new ego strengths. Moreover, they learn a good deal about themselves and position themselves to resolve the adolescent crisis of *identity versus role confusion.* As we have seen in some detail, adolescence is indeed a time for raising and answering identity questions. But what happens to adolescents with newfound identities during the adult years? Erikson was one of the first developmentalists to claim that stagelike changes in personality continue during adulthood.

Early Adult Intimacy

As Erikson saw it, young adulthood is a time for dealing with the psychosocial conflict of **intimacy versus isolation.** He theorized that one must achieve a sense of individual identity before becoming able to commit oneself to a *shared identity* with another person—that is, you must know yourself before you can love someone else. The young adult who has no clear sense of self may be threatened by the idea of entering a committed, long-term relationship and being "tied down," or he or she may become overdependent on a romantic partner (or possibly a close friend) as a source of identity. We will consider other perspectives on adult romantic relationships in Chapter 13 but here ask only whether identity does indeed pave the way for genuine intimacy.

To find out, Susan Whitbourne and Stephanie Tesch (1985) measured both identity status and intimacy status among college seniors and 24- to 27-year-old alumni from the same university. The researchers interviewed people about their closest relationships and placed each person in one of six intimacy statuses. These included being a social isolate with no close relationships, being in a shallow relationship with little communication or involvement, being in a deep relationship but not yet being ready to make a long-term commitment to one's partner, and being in a genuinely intimate relationship that has it all—involvement, open communication, and a long-term commitment.

More alumni than college students fell into either the moratorium (active questioning) or the achievement status of identity formation. Thus, progress toward achieving identity continues to be made *after* college graduation. College graduates had also progressed farther than college seniors in resolving intimacy issues; more of them were involved in long-term, committed relationships. Finally, and most important, the college graduates who had well-formed identities

Early adulthood is the time, according to Erik Erikson, for deciding whether to commit to a shared identity with another person.

were more likely than those who did not to be capable of genuine and lasting intimacy—precisely what Erikson had theorized. Other research too suggests that the ability to enter into a committed relationship is associated with successful resolution of Erikson's earlier stages (Orlofsky, 1993).

So far, so good, then. As Erikson claimed, we apparently must know ourselves before we can truly love another person. Yet there are interesting differences between women and men in this process (Adams & Archer, 1994; Hodgson & Fischer, 1979). Erikson believed that women cannot fully resolve identity questions until they choose a mate and fashion an identity around their roles as wife and mother-to-be. Is this rather sexist view correct? Not quite; it goes more like this. Most men follow the identity-then-intimacy route, becoming psychologically ready for a serious relationship only after they have settled on a career and perhaps even launched it. Women with masculine gender-role orientations and many masculine-stereotyped traits such as assertiveness tend to follow this same identity-then-intimacy route (Dyk & Adams, 1990). But other women follow quite different developmental pathways. In past generations, some women resolved intimacy issues before identity issues: They married, raised children, and only after the children were more self-sufficient asked who they really were as individuals (Hodgson & Fischer, 1979; Schiedel & Marcia, 1985). Today, women with feminine gender-role orientations tend to tackle identity and intimacy issues simultaneously, perhaps forging a personal identity that centers on caring for other people or defining themselves in the context of a love relationship (Dyk & Adams, 1990). For feminine women only, then, Erikson may have been right in saying that women

must fuse the tasks of achieving identity and intimacy. Overall, though, Erikson's theory seems to fit men better than it fits women because fewer women follow the identity-then-intimacy scenario. Sex differences in the paths to identity and intimacy are likely to diminish as more women postpone marriage to pursue their careers.

Middle-Age Generativity

Is there continuing psychosocial growth in middle age? George Vaillant (1977), a psychoanalytic theorist, conducted an in-depth longitudinal study of mentally healthy Harvard men from college to middle age, as well as a longitudinal study of blue-collar workers (Vaillant, 1983; Vaillant & Milofsky, 1980). Vaillant found support for Erikson's view that the 20s are a time to raise intimacy issues. He found that, in their 30s, men shifted their energies to advancing their careers and were not very reflective or concerned about others. Finally, in their 40s, many men became concerned with Erikson's issue of **generativity versus stagnation,** which involves gaining the capacity to produce something that outlives you and to genuinely care about the welfare of future generations. These men expressed more interest than ever before in passing on something of value, either to their own children or to younger people at work. They reflected on their lives and experienced the kind of intellectual vitality that adolescents sometimes experience as they struggle with identity issues. Few of these men experienced a full-blown and turbulent midlife crisis, just as few had experienced a severe identity crisis as college students. Nonetheless they were growing as individuals, often becoming more caring and self-aware as they entered their 50s. One of these men expressed the developmental progression Vaillant detected perfectly: "At 20 to 30, I think I learned how to get along with my wife. From 30 to 40, I learned how to be a success in my job. And at 40 to 50, I worried less about myself and more about the children" (1977, p. 195).

More recently, Dan McAdams (1993) and his associates have found that middle-aged men and women (and elderly ones as well) are more likely than young adults to have achieved a sense of generativity. Generative adults are caring people, committed parents, productive workers and mentors, and community leaders (see also Peterson & Klohnen, 1995). Erikson believed that nurturing one's children as they prepare to leave the nest is central to gaining a sense of generativity. Indeed, among men, although not among women, the experience of parenthood helps adults attain a sense of generativity (McAdams, 1993). Women may achieve generativity earlier in adulthood, even if they do not become parents, through the nurturing and mentoring roles they often adopt.

Gisela Labouvie-Vief and her colleagues (1995) find that middle-aged adults also come to know themselves in deeper ways than younger adults do. At least some of them are able to integrate contradictory aspects of their personalities, confront and make sense of their successes and failures in life, and emerge with a deeper understanding of who they are. Overall, then, we find support for Erikson's view that women and men are capable of impressive psychosocial growth during early and middle adulthood.

Old-Age Integrity

Elderly adults, according to Erikson, confront the psychosocial issue of **integrity versus despair.** They try to find a sense of meaning in their lives that will help them face the inevitability of death. Most older adults, when asked what they would do differently if they had their lives to live over again, say there is little, if anything, they would change (Erikson, Erikson, & Kivnick, 1986; Field & Millsap, 1991). This suggests that most older adults do attain a sense of integrity. But how?

Gerontologist Robert Butler (1963, 1975) has proposed that elderly adults engage in a process called **life review,** in which they reflect on unresolved conflicts of the past in order to come to terms with themselves, find new meaning and coherence in their lives, and prepare for death. Do older adults in fact engage in life review, and does it help them achieve a healthy sense of integrity? Contrary to the stereotype, elderly people do not really spend more time thinking about the old days or dwelling in the past than younger people do (Gambria, 1979–1980; Webster & Cappeliez, 1993). However, older adults *are* more likely than younger adults to use their reminiscences to evaluate and integrate the pieces of their lives, and

What is generativity? It is singer Cissy Houston saying this about her highly successful singing daughter, Whitney: "To be singing with someone you brought into the world, who you cradled in your arms—it's nice. It's wonderful to see something you do that comes out halfway right." (*Newsweek,* January 5, 1987, p. 61)

that's what life review is all about (Molinari & Reichlin, 1984–1985).

More important, those elders who use the life-review process to confront and come to terms with their failures display a stronger sense of ego integrity and better overall adjustment than those who do not reminisce or those who obsess about how poorly life has treated them (Taft & Nehrke, 1990; Wong & Watt, 1991). Believing that life review can be beneficial in later life, Butler and others have used it as a form of therapy, asking elderly adults to reconstruct and reflect on their lives with the help of photo albums and other memorabilia. Participation in life-review therapy can indeed help elderly adults feel less anxious and more content with themselves and their lives (Haight, 1988, 1992).

A Summing Up

On balance, Erikson's theory of psychosocial development seems to be partially, though not fully, supported. Although some of Erikson's themes are reflected in research on the development of the personality and the self during infancy and childhood, very few studies have directly tested Erikson's theory of early psychosocial development, perhaps because it is rather general and therefore difficult to test. Erikson's theorizing about the adolescent stage of identity versus role confusion has been tested extensively, however, and is quite well supported.

The evidence is also quite convincing that achieving a sense of identity in adolescence paves the way for forming a truly intimate relationship with another person as a young adult. Moreover, generativity does seem to be an issue for many middle-aged adults, and many older adults seek a sense of integrity through the process of life review. As Erikson proposed, then, humans experience personal growth and change throughout the life span. Personality traits such as extraversion and neuroticism may remain quite consistent over the years, but people do confront new psychological conflicts as they age.

APPLICATIONS: BOOSTING SELF-ESTEEM

We all know that individuals who have low self-esteem suffer for it, so how can self-esteem be increased? Earlier in this chapter we noted that parents can do a lot to foster high self-esteem in their children by blending love with democratic and consistent discipline. Such parents are able to express their disapproval of a child's misbehavior while conveying the message that the child is a valuable and lovable person. They set clear guidelines for behavior and yet allow their children to express their own views and become individuals in their own right. These same parental practices are also associated with the achievement of a solid sense of identity in adolescence.

But sometimes, despite the efforts of parents, children still have low self-esteem. Stephen Shirk and Susan Harter (1996) argue that psychotherapists would do well to put more emphasis on treating low self-esteem in children and adolescents than they do. Many children with psychological disorders such as learning disabilities, substance abuse disorders, and eating disorders have low self-esteem. Moreover, low self-esteem can contribute to problems such as depression and poor academic performance, whereas high self-esteem can help protect youngsters against the harmful effects of stress (Shirk & Harter, 1996). As Susan Harter's own research has shown, children may have low self-esteem either because they think they fall short in domains they consider important or because they look in the social looking glass and feel unaccepted by significant people in their lives. When low self-esteem is rooted in negative self-evaluations, children can either be helped to gain the skills they wish they had (for example, through social skills training) or to establish more realistic standards of judging themselves. When low self-esteem is rooted in parental neglect or rejection, the therapist may help by providing the unconditional acceptance that the child lacks or by using family therapy to help parents communicate love to their children. When children feel rejected by their peers, the solution may be to teach them more effective social skills or to convince them that their peers are not as rejecting as they may seem.

Consider the case of Chris, a 16-year-old high school junior who wanted to kill himself, despite the fact that he was an A student, a starter on the basketball team, a popular student, and a model son (Shirk & Harter, 1996). A perfectionist, he was highly self-critical when he fell short of his demanding standards (for example when he did not get the highest grade on a physics exam). He had supportive parents and caring friends, so negative social feedback was not the source of his low self-esteem. Instead, he had come to link lack of perfection in schoolwork with social rejection, figuring that no one would accept him if he were a "loser." An adopted child, he had concluded that his birth mother gave him away because he was imperfect: "If I had been flawless (perfect), she would have kept me" (p. 192). Therapy then focused on helping Chris understand the distortions in his thinking about himself, revise his standards of self-evaluation, and see that there was nothing wrong with him.

What about elderly adults who have low opinions of themselves? Although older adults typically score no lower than young adults on self-esteem measures, some older people may have taken to heart society's negative views of old age. **Ageism** is the term used to describe prejudice against elderly people (Butler, 1975). Ageists believe the stereotypes that old people are sickly, cranky, dependent, forgetful, or otherwise incompetent or unpleasant. Although the majority of older adults see themselves as better off than most other older people (Heckhausen & Krueger, 1993), they are aware of and tend to share society's negative images of old age (Bodily, 1991).

With this in mind, Judith Rodin and Ellen Langer (1980) set out to boost the self-esteem of a particularly vulnerable group: new nursing-home residents. These researchers discovered that 80% of the residents, a week after entering the nursing home, blamed aging for many of the difficulties in functioning that they were experiencing. It did not occur to them that the nursing-home environment could be a source of these problems. In an experiment designed to change their attributions, Rodin and Langer taught one group of residents a new "theory": The fact that they found walking difficult was not because they were old and feeble; it was because the nursing-home floors were tiled and therefore very slippery for people of all ages. The fact that they grew tired in the evening was not due to the weariness of old age; *anyone* would be tired after being awakened at 5:30 in the morning.

Compared to both an untreated control group and a group that was merely given medical information to the effect that physical aging was not the major source of their difficulties, the group that learned to attribute their difficulties to the environment rather than to old age fared well. They became more active and sociable, and even more healthy, than the other groups. The moral? Elderly people who can avoid taking negative stereotypes of old people to heart and who can avoid blaming all their difficulties on the ravages of old age—that is, older adults who can avoid thinking like ageists—appear to have a good chance of feeling good about themselves in later life. Perhaps the worst thing about old age is thinking the worst about old age.

Clearly, self-esteem can be increased through systematic interventions (Hattie, 1992). But should we as a society put so much emphasis on boosting self-esteem? Developmental psychologist William Damon (1994) believes that we err by trying to make all children feel good about themselves, regardless of their behavior. Self-esteem, he maintains, means nothing unless it grows out of one's accomplishments. Besides, children need opportunities to learn not only about their successes and strengths but about their failures and limitations. And, he argues, by emphasizing the importance of loving oneself, we underemphasize the importance of caring about others. Perhaps there is merit in being more selective about if and when we intervene to make young and older individuals feel better about who they are.

◆ SUMMARY POINTS

1. Personality is an organized combination of attributes unique to the individual; self-concept (perceptions of one's attributes) and self-esteem (overall evaluations of one's worth) do not always coincide with objective personality traits.

2. Psychoanalytic theorists maintain that we experience similar, stagelike personality changes at similar ages. Erik Erikson saw more potential for personality growth during adulthood than Freud did, but believed, like Freud, that there is carryover from early stages to later stages. Psychometric (trait) theorists, such as those who conceptualize personality in terms of the "big five" trait dimensions, also believe that aspects of personality are enduring but do not propose stages of personality development. Social learning theorists and contextual theorists maintain that people can change in any number of directions at any time in life if their social environments change.

3. Early in their first year, infants acquire some sense that they exist separately from the world around them; by 18 to 24 months of age, they display self-recognition and form a categorical self based on age and sex.

4. Even young infants display distinctive personalities. They differ in emotionality, activity, and sociability; behavioral inhibition; and easy, difficult, and slow-to-warm-up temperaments. Temperament is partially influenced by genetic endowment but also shaped by the goodness of fit between child and environment and is only moderately related to later personality.

5. The self-concepts of preschool children are very concrete and physical. By about age 8, children begin to describe their inner psychological traits and evaluate their competencies through social comparison processes. Children are most likely to develop high self-esteem if they are competent, fare well in social comparisons, and have parents who are warm and democratic.

6. During middle childhood, the personality "gels"; traits become more consistent and enduring than they were earlier in life, especially if they are culturally valued and therefore represent a good fit to the environment.

7. During adolescence, self-concepts become more psychological, abstract, and integrated, and self-awareness increases. Most adolescents experience no more than temporary disturbances in self-esteem at the onset of adolescence.

8. The most difficult challenge of adolescence is resolving Erikson's conflict of identity versus role confusion. From the diffusion and foreclosure identity statuses, many college-age youths progress to the moratorium status and ultimately to the identity achievement status. Identity formation is uneven across domains of identity, often continues into adulthood, and is influenced by cognitive development and by social experiences such as interactions with loving parents who encourage individuality.

9. During adulthood, self-conceptions and self-esteem change relatively little. Older adults maintain self-esteem by bringing their ideal selves closer to their real selves, changing their goals and standards of self-evaluation, and comparing themselves to other older adults.

10. Individuals' rankings on "big five" dimensions of personality such as neuroticism and agreeableness remain quite stable after very early adulthood, but there is both continuity and discontinuity in personality. From adolescence to middle adulthood, many people appear to gain confidence, autonomy, nurturance, and other personal strengths; from middle age to old age, only a few systematic changes occur, notably decreased activity and increased introspectiveness.

11. Stability of personality may be due to genetic makeup, lasting effects of early experience, and the fact that people seek out and encounter experiences that reinforce their earlier personalities. Personality change may be associated with changes in the social environment and a poor fit between person and environment.

12. Erikson's theory of psychosocial development is supported by evidence that resolution of conflicts centering on trust, autonomy, initiative, and industry paves the way for achieving a positive sense of identity in adolescence. Identity then lays a foundation for achieving intimacy in early adulthood, middle-aged adults become concerned with achieving generativity, and life review helps elderly people resolve Erikson's final crisis of integrity versus despair.

13. Children's self-esteem can be strengthened through warm and democratic parenting as well as through psychotherapy and special interventions, and the self-esteem of older adults can be increased by reducing their tendency to be ageists and attribute difficulties in functioning to old age.

☀ FOOD FOR THOUGHT

1. Write four brief descriptions of yourself to show how you might have answered the question "Who am I?" at age 4, age 9, age 14, and age 21. What developmental changes in self-conceptions do your self-descriptions illustrate?

2. Teddie the Toddler tends to get very stressed when his routines are changed, or a stranger comes to the door, or he is asked to try something he has never tried before. Help his parents understand his temperament and what it may mean for his personality as a 70-year-old.

3. What might parents and society do to make the process of achieving a positive identity during adolescence particularly difficult, and what might they do to help adolescents find themselves? Also, do you agree with Erikson that a period of serious questioning and experimentation in adolescence is necessary in order for adult development to proceed well? Why or why not?

4. Interview ten adults and ask them how well-adjusted, on a scale of 1 to 10, they felt they were in early childhood, adolescence, and now adulthood. You might also ask respondents to explain the basis for their ratings. The answers for early childhood will probably be based on what their parents told them. Does your survey suggest continuity or discontinuity of adjustment?

Ⓦ ON THE WEB

1. *Temperament*   Browse through the free downloads page if you'd like to learn more about how Thomas and Chess measured infants' temperaments with the New York Longitudinal Scales, see sample items from the Carey Temperament Scales, or learn more about the measurement of temperament.
http://www.temperament.com/downloads.html

2. *The Big Five Personality Dimensions*   This site will acquaint you with the "big five" and the specific traits that belong under each of the five major dimensions. You'll find background information, a comparison of this model of personality to others, and information about tests available for assessing the "big five."
http://www.centacs.com/

✦ KEY TERMS

personality	easy temperament	identity achievement status
self-concept	difficult temperament	ethnic identity
self-esteem	slow-to-warm-up temperament	trust versus mistrust
identity	goodness of fit	autonomy versus shame and doubt
"big five"	social comparison	initiative versus guilt
self-recognition	false self behavior	industry versus inferiority
categorical self	identity versus role confusion	intimacy versus isolation
looking-glass self	moratorium period	generativity versus stagnation
temperament	diffusion status	integrity versus despair
emotionality	foreclosure status	life review
activity	moratorium status	ageism
sociability		
behavioral inhibition		

CHAPTER 11

Gender Roles and Sexuality

MALE AND FEMALE
Gender Norms and Stereotypes
Actual Gender Differences

THE INFANT
Differential Treatment
Early Learning

THE CHILD
Acquiring Gender Stereotypes
Gender-Typed Behavior

THE ADOLESCENT
Adhering to Gender Roles
Theories of Gender-Role Development

THE ADULT
Gender Roles
Masculinity, Femininity, and Androgyny

SEXUALITY OVER THE LIFE SPAN
Are Infants Sexual Beings?
Childhood Sexuality
Adolescent Sexuality
Adult Sexuality

APPLICATIONS: CHANGING GENDER-ROLE ATTITUDES AND BEHAVIOR

SUMMARY POINTS

FOOD FOR THOUGHT

ON THE WEB

KEY TERMS

Developmental psychologist Carole Beal (1994) learned an interesting lesson about the significance of being a girl or a boy when she was interviewing 9-year-olds:

I had just finished one interview and was making some quick notes when the next child came into the office. I looked up, and an odd thing happened: I could not tell whether the child was a boy or a girl. The usual cues were not there: The child's hair was trimmed in a sort of pudding-bowl style, not really long but not definitively short either. The child was dressed in a gender-neutral outfit of jeans, sneakers, and a loose t-shirt, like most of the children at the school. The name on the interview permission slip was "Cory," which did not clarify matters much as it could be either a boy's or a girl's name. Still puzzled, I began the interview and found myself becoming increasingly frustrated at not knowing Cory's sex. I quickly realized how many unconscious assumptions I usually made about boys and girls; for example, that a girl would probably like a particular story about a horse and be willing to answer a few extra questions about it, or that a boy would probably start to get restless after a certain point and I would have to work a bit harder to keep his attention. (p. 3)

Gender-role socialization begins very early as parents provide their infants with "gender-appropriate" clothing, toys, and hairstyles.

Unlike Cory, most children are readily identified as girls or boys and treated accordingly. How much does it really matter, in terms of development, whether a child is perceived and treated as a girl or perceived and treated as a boy? How much does it matter whether a child actually *is* a girl or a boy biologically? These are the kinds of questions we tackle in this chapter.

In our society, gender clearly matters. When proud new parents telephone to announce a birth, the first question friends and family tend to ask is "Is it a boy or a girl?" (Intons-Peterson & Reddel, 1984). Before long, girls discover that they are girls and many acquire a taste for frilly dresses and dollhouses, while boys discover that they are boys and often wrestle each other on the lawn. As adults, we never lose our awareness of being either men or women. We define ourselves partly in terms of our "feminine" or "masculine" qualities, and we play roles that conform to society's view of what a woman or a man should be. In short, being female or male is a highly important aspect of the self throughout the life span.

In this chapter we'll be looking at how the characteristics and life experiences of male and female humans are similar and different—and why. We'll see how girls and boys learn to play their parts as girls or boys and how they are groomed for their roles as women or men. We'll also consider some of the ways in which adult men and women are steered along different developmental paths. In addition, we'll examine the development of sexuality and its implications for relationships between the sexes. Before going any further, try the quiz in Box 11.1 to see if you know which of our many ideas about male/female differences have some truth to them.

MALE AND FEMALE

What difference does it make whether one is a male or a female? It matters in terms of physical differences, psychological differences, and differences in roles played in society. The physical differences are undeniable. A zygote that receives an X chromosome from each parent is a genetic (XX) female, whereas a zygote that receives a Y chromosome from the father is a genetic (XY) male. In rare cases of gender chromosome abnormalities (see Chapter 3), this is not the case; a girl may have only one X chromosome or a boy may have three chromosomes (XYY or XXY). Chromosomal differences result in different prenatal hormone balances in males and females, and hormone balances before and after birth are responsible for the facts that the genitals of males and females differ and that only females can bear children. Moreover, males typically grow to be taller, heavier, and more muscular than females, although females may be the hardier sex in that

BOX 11.1

Which of these sex differences is real?

Which of the following sex differences do you think is a consistent difference demonstrated to exist in studies comparing males and females? Mark each true or false. Answers are printed upside-down and will become clear in the discussion that follows.

1. Males are more aggressive than females.
2. Males are more active than females.
3. Females are more social than males.
4. Females have stronger verbal abilities than males.
5. Males have greater achievement motivation than females.
6. Males are more analytical than females.
7. Females are more suggestible and prone to conform than males.
8. Females are more emotionally unstable than males.
9. Males are more rational and logical than females.
10. Males have greater spatial and mathematical abilities than females.

Answers: 1-T, 2-T, 3-F, 4-T, 5-F, 6-F, 7-F, 8-F, 9-F, 10-T

---

they live longer and are less susceptible to many physical disorders. As we'll see later in the chapter, some theorists argue that biological differences between males and females are ultimately responsible for psychological and social differences as well.

However, there is much more to being male or female than biology. Virtually all societies expect the two sexes to adopt different **gender roles,** the parts or patterns of behavior that females and males should play in a particular society (for example, the parts of wife, mother, and woman or of husband, father, and man).[1] Characteristics and behaviors viewed as desirable for males or females are specified in **gender-role norms**—that is, society's expectations or standards concerning what males and females *should* be like (Pleck, 1981). Each society's norms generate **gender-role stereotypes,** which are overgeneralized and largely inaccurate beliefs about what males and females *are* like (Pleck, 1981).

Through the process of **gender typing,** children not only become aware that they are biological males or females but also acquire the motives, values, and patterns of behavior that their culture considers appropriate for members of their biological sex. Through the gender-typing process, for example, Susie might learn a gender-role norm stating that women should strive to be good mothers and gender-role stereotypes indicating that women are more skilled at nurturing children than men are. As an adult, Susan might then

adopt the traditional feminine role by switching from full- to part-time work when her first child is born and devoting herself to the task of mothering.

We would be very mistaken, then, to credit any differences that we observe between girls and boys (or women and men) to biological causes. They could just as easily be due to differences in the ways males and females are perceived and raised. But, before we try to explain sex differences, perhaps we should find out what these differences are believed to be and what they actually are.

Gender Norms and Stereotypes

Which sex is more likely to express emotions? To be tidy? To be competitive? To use harsh language? If you are like most people, you undoubtedly have ideas about how men and women differ psychologically and can offer some ready answers to these questions.

The female's role as childbearer has shaped the gender-role norms that prevail in many societies, including our own. Girls have typically been encouraged to assume an **expressive role** that involves being kind, nurturant, cooperative, and sensitive to the needs of others (Parsons, 1955). These psychological traits, it is assumed, will prepare girls to play the roles of wife and mother—to keep the family functioning and to raise children successfully. By contrast, boys have been encouraged to adopt an **instrumental role,** for as a traditionally defined husband and father the male faces the tasks of providing for the family and protecting it from harm. Thus boys are expected to become dominant, independent, assertive, and competitive. Similar norms for males and females apply in many, though certainly not all, societies (Whiting & Edwards, 1988; Williams & Best, 1990).

Because cultural norms demand that females play an expressive role and males play an instrumental

---

[1] I use the term *sex* when I am referring to the distinction between biological males and biological females and the term *gender* when I am discussing masculine and feminine traits and behavior patterns that develop as social influences interact with biology. Although many developmentalists speak of *sex roles* or *sex-role stereotypes* where I speak of *gender roles* or *gender-role stereotypes,* I believe that it is useful to emphasize through our use of terms that most differences between the sexes are not purely biological but are related as well to socialization experiences.

role, we tend to form stereotypes saying that females possess expressive traits and males possess instrumental traits (Broverman et al., 1972; Williams & Best, 1990). If you're thinking that these stereotypes have disappeared as attention to women's rights has increased and as more women have entered the labor force, think again. Although some change has occurred, adolescents and young adults still endorse many traditional stereotypes about men and women (Bergen & Williams, 1991). Moreover, they describe themselves differently. When Jean Twenge (1997) analyzed studies conducted from the 1970s to the 1990s in which standard scales assessing gender-relevant traits were administered, she found that men and women today describe themselves more similarly than men and women 20 years ago did, largely because women now see themselves as having more masculine traits. However, male and female personality profiles continue to differ in ways consistent with gender stereotypes. Might beliefs about sex differences have a basis in fact, then? Let's see.

Actual Gender Differences

In a classic review of more than 1500 studies comparing males and females, Eleanor Maccoby and Carol Jacklin (1974) concluded that only four common gender stereotypes are reasonably accurate (that is, consistently supported by research). Here are their conclusions, with some updates and amendments:

1. Females have greater *verbal abilities* than males. According to Maccoby and Jacklin's review, girls tend to develop verbal skills at an earlier age than boys and show a small but consistent advantage on tests of vocabulary, reading comprehension, and speech fluency. However, sex differences in verbal ability have all but disappeared in more recent studies (Cahan & Ganor, 1995; Feingold, 1988; Hyde & Linn, 1988).

2. Males outperform females on tests of *spatial ability* (for example, arranging blocks in patterns, identifying the same figure from different angles; see Figure 11.1). Although Maccoby and Jacklin concluded that these differences emerge only in adolescence, differences on some tests can be detected in childhood and then persist across the life span (Kerns & Berenbaum, 1991; Linn & Petersen, 1985; Voyer, Voyer, & Bryden, 1995).

3. Similarly, males outperform females, on the average, on tests of *mathematical ability*, starting in adolescence. A more recent review of the evidence by Janet Hyde and her associates (1990) suggests that girls actually have a slight edge in computational skills, that the sexes do not differ in their understanding of math concepts, and that starting in adolescence, males outperform females primarily on mathematical word problems. The male advantage in mathematical problem-

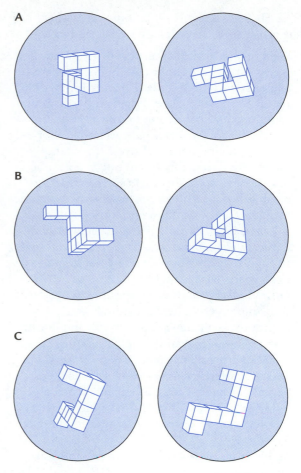

Answer: *The two figures in items A and B are the same, but the two in item C are different.*

FIGURE 11.1 *A spatial-ability task. Are the two figures in each pair alike or different? This task assesses the ability to mentally rotate visual information and is a task on which average differences between females and males are quite large.* (From Shepard & Metzler, 1971)

solving skills is especially clear in samples of high math performers; that is, more males than females are mathematically talented (Stumpf & Stanley, 1996). As it turns out, more males than females are also *low* math achievers; on a number of cognitive ability tests, more males than females show up at both the top and the bottom of the scale (Feingold, 1992).

4. Finally, males engage in more physical and verbal *aggression* than females, starting as early as age 2. Males clearly commit more serious crimes (Knight, Fabes, & Higgins, 1996), but sex differences are clearer for physical aggression than for other forms of aggression. For example, females tend to specialize in subtle, indirect, and relational forms of aggression such as gossiping about and excluding others (Bjorkqvist, 1994; Crick, 1996).

Since the publication of Maccoby and Jacklin's monumental review, researchers have continued to argue over how many true sex differences exist (Eagly,

1995; Hyde & Plant, 1995). Some researchers believe that other sex differences are well-established:

1. Even before birth (DiPietro et al., 1996) and continuing throughout childhood, boys are *more physically active* than girls (Eaton & Enns, 1986; Eaton & Yu, 1989); they fidget and squirm more as infants and run around more as children.

2. Boys are *more developmentally vulnerable,* not only to prenatal and perinatal stress (for example, they die more often before birth) but to a number of diseases and to disorders such as reading disabilities, speech defects, hyperactivity, emotional problems, and mental retardation (Henker & Whalen, 1989; Jacklin, 1989; Raz et al., 1994).

3. Girls are *more compliant with the requests of adults,* though they are no more likely than boys to give in to peers (Maccoby, 1990).

4. Girls are *more tactful and cooperative* as opposed to using forceful and demanding tactics when attempting to persuade others to comply with them (Cowan & Avants, 1988; Maccoby, 1990).

5. Females are *more nurturant and empathic;* though this sex difference is clearer in self-ratings than in actual behavior (Fabes, Eisenberg, & Miller, 1990; Feingold, 1994a). They also take more interest in and are more responsive to infants (Reid & Trotter, 1993).

6. Females are *more anxious,* cautious, and fearful, though not in social situations (Feingold, 1994a). They are also more prone to develop anxiety disorders and phobias (Myers et al., 1984).

Other researchers take the contrasting view that even the largest of the "real" psychological differences between the sexes are trivial. For example, if you imagine all the differences in aggressiveness among individuals, from the most aggressive to the least aggressive person in a group, it turns out that only 5% of that variation can be traced to whether a person is a male or a female (Hyde, 1984). Apparently the remaining 95% of the variation is due to other differences among people. In other words, *average* levels of aggression for males and females may be noticeably different, but within each sex there are both extremely aggressive and extremely nonaggressive individuals: *It is impossible to predict accurately how aggressive a person is simply by knowing his or her gender.* Sex differences in most other abilities and personality traits are similarly small (see Figure 11.2). Moreover, some sex differences are smaller today than they used to be (Hyde et al., 1990; Stumpf & Stanley, 1996).

Where is all the evidence that males possess instrumental traits and females possess expressive traits? Where is the evidence that females are more suggestible or that they have lower self-esteem, lack achievement motivation, or are less capable of logical thought? Most of our stereotypes of males and females are just

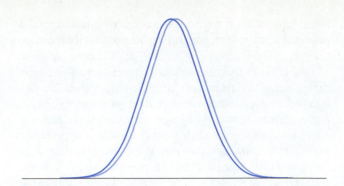

FIGURE 11.2 *These two distributions of scores—one for males, one for females—indicate the size of the gap between the sexes in mathematical abilities. Despite a small difference in average performance, the scores of males and females overlap considerably. Some sex differences are larger than this, but most detectable differences are small.* (Adapted from Hyde et al., 1990)

that—overgeneralizations unsupported by fact (Maccoby & Jacklin, 1974). Females and males are far more psychologically similar than different.

Why do unfounded stereotypes persist? Partly because we, as the holders of male/female stereotypes, are biased in our perceptions. We are more likely to notice and remember behaviors that confirm our beliefs than to notice exceptions such as independent behavior in a woman or emotional sensitivity in a man (Martin & Halverson, 1981). Alice Eagly's (1987) **social-role hypothesis** suggests that differences in the roles that women and men play in society also do a lot to create and maintain gender-role stereotypes. For example, men have traditionally occupied powerful roles in business and industry that require them to be dominant and forceful. Women have more often filled the role of homemaker and therefore have been called upon to be nurturant and sensitive to their children's needs. As a result, we begin to see men as by nature "dominant" and women as by nature "nurturant." We lose sight of the fact that it is differences in the social roles they play that cause men and women to behave differently. It could be that sex differences in behavior might actually be reversed if women ran companies and men raised children.

As Eagly's social-role hypothesis suggests, we must adopt a contextual perspective on psychological differences between males and females. Sex differences that are evident in one culture or social context often are not evident in another (Deaux & Major, 1990; Feingold, 1994b). For example, women do better on tests of mathematical ability—and sometimes even outperform men—in countries like Israel, where women have excellent occupational opportunities in technical fields (Baker & Jones, 1992). This suggests that sex differences in abilities are not biologically inevitable. From a contextual perspective, it is really quite silly to speak about the "nature of women" or the "nature of men."

Differences between males and females can be large or small, depending on the social contexts in which they find themselves.

Although psychological sex differences are often small, it still makes a very real difference in our society whether one is a male or a female. First, gender norms and stereotypes, even when they are unfounded, affect how we perceive ourselves and other people. As long as people expect females to be less competent in math than males, for example, females may well lack confidence in their abilities and perform less competently (Eccles, Jacobs, & Harold, 1990). The fact that many stereotypes are unfounded does not make them any less potent.

In addition, even though males and females are not very different psychologically, they are still steered toward different *roles in society*. In childhood, girls and boys conform to their gender roles by segregating themselves by sex and developing different interests and play activities (Huston, 1985). As adolescents and adults, males and females pursue different vocations and lifestyles. Although more women are entering male-dominated fields today than in the past, they are underrepresented in many traditionally male-dominated fields, and men are not often entering female-dominated fields (U.S. Bureau of the Census, 1997). If you go to a college graduation ceremony today, you will still see relatively few women among the engineers and few men among the nursing graduates. More men are sharing child-rearing and household responsibilities with their partners today, but most couples still divide the labor along traditional lines, so that she is primarily responsible for child care and housework while he is primarily responsible for income and money management (Zick & McCullough, 1991). When we think about who asks whom out on a date, who stays home from work when a child has the chicken pox, or who sews the buttons back on shirts, we must conclude that, despite significant social change, traditional gender roles are alive and well!

In short, we continue to live in a society where, for better or for worse, being male or female *matters*. The psychological differences between the sexes may be few and small, but the physical differences are always visible, and the roles that most men and women play in society continue to differ. So now let's trace how girls and boys master their "gender-role curriculum" and how they apply what they learn throughout their lives.

THE INFANT

At birth there are very few differences, other than the obvious anatomical ones, between males and females (Maccoby & Jacklin, 1974), and even these few differ-

ences tend to be small and inconsistent. Nonetheless, it does not take long at all after newborns are labeled as girls or boys for gender stereotypes to affect how they are perceived and treated—and for infants themselves to notice that males and females are different.

Differential Treatment

While the baby is still in the hospital delivery room or nursery, parents tend to call an infant son "big guy" or "tiger" and to comment on the vigor of his cries, kicks, and grasps. Girl infants are more likely to be labeled "sugar" or "sweetie" and to be described as soft, cuddly, and adorable (Maccoby, 1980; MacFarlane, 1977). Even when objective examinations reveal no such differences between boys and girls at birth, parents perceive boys as strong, large featured, and coordinated while viewing girls as weaker, finer featured, and more awkward (Rubin, Provenzano, & Luria, 1974; see also Burnham & Harris, 1992; Stern & Karraker, 1989). Soon boys and girls are decked out in either blue or pink and provided with "sex-appropriate" hairstyles, toys, and room furnishings (Pomerleau et al., 1990; Rheingold & Cook, 1975).

In one study (Condry & Condry, 1976), college students watched a videotape of a 9-month-old infant who was introduced as either a girl ("Dana") or a boy ("David"). Students who saw "David" interpreted his strong reaction to a jack-in-the-box as "anger," whereas students who watched "Dana" concluded that the very same behavior was "fear." Although stereotyping of boys and girls from birth could be partly the effect of actual differences between the sexes (Burnham & Harris, 1992), it is also likely to be a *cause* of such differences.

Early Learning

Yet infants are not merely the passive targets of other people's reactions to them; they are actively trying to get to know the social world around them, as well as themselves. By the end of the first year, babies can already distinguish women from men in photographs (women are the long-haired ones) and look longer when male or female voices match up properly with male or female faces (Fagot & Leinbach, 1993; Poulin-Dubois et al., 1994). As they begin to categorize other people as males and females, they also figure out which of these two significant social categories they themselves belong to. By 18 months of age, most toddlers seem to have an emerging understanding that they are either like other males or like other females, even if they cannot verbalize it (Lewis & Weinraub, 1979). Almost all children give verbal proof that they have acquired a basic sense of **gender identity,** or an awareness that they are either a boy or a girl, by the age of 2½ to 3 (Thompson, 1975).

As they acquire their gender identities, boys and girls are also beginning to behave differently. Boys aged 14 to 22 months usually prefer trucks and cars to other playthings, whereas girls of this age would rather play with dolls and soft toys (Smith & Daglish, 1977). Many 18- to 24-month-old toddlers will actually refuse to play with toys regarded as appropriate for the other sex—even when there are no other toys to play with (Caldera, Huston, & O'Brien, 1989). As they approach the age of 2, then, infants are already beginning to behave in ways that are considered gender appropriate in our society.

In sum, the two years of infancy lay the groundwork for later gender-role development. Because their sex is important to those around them, and because they see for themselves that males and females differ, infants begin to form categories of "male" and "female," establish a basic gender identity, and pursue "gender-appropriate" pastimes (Lewis & Weinraub, 1979).

THE CHILD

Much of the "action" in gender-role development takes place during the toddler and preschool years. Having already come to understand their basic gender identity, young children rapidly acquire (1) gender stereotypes, or ideas about what males and females are supposedly like; and (2) gender-typed behavior patterns, or tendencies to favor "gender-appropriate" activities and behaviors over those typically associated with the other sex.

Acquiring Gender Stereotypes

Remarkable as it may seem, toddlers begin to learn society's gender stereotypes at about the same time they become aware of their basic gender identities. Deanna Kuhn and her associates (Kuhn, Nash, & Brucken, 1978) showed a male doll ("Michael") and a female doll ("Lisa") to children aged 2½ to 3½ and asked each child which of the two dolls would engage in various sex-stereotyped activities. Even among the 2½-year-olds, many boys and girls agreed that girls talk a lot, never hit, often need help, like to play with dolls, and like to help their mothers with chores such as cooking and cleaning. Boys, of course, like to play with cars, help their fathers, build things, and utter comments like "I can hit you." Apparently 2- and 3-year-olds know a lot already about gender stereotypes.

Over the next several years, children's heads become filled with considerably more "knowledge" about the toys and activities considered appropriate for girls or boys (Serbin, Powlishta, & Gulko, 1993; Welch-Ross & Schmidt, 1996). As we saw in Chapter 10, during the elementary school years children begin to describe themselves in terms of their underlying psychological traits, rather than just their observable physical characteristics and activities. They also begin to understand gender stereotypes that describe the supposed psychological traits of males and females. For example, Deborah Best and her colleagues (1977) found that fourth- and fifth-graders in England, Ireland, and the United States typically believed that women are weak, emotional, softhearted, sophisticated, and affectionate, whereas men are ambitious, assertive, aggressive, dominating, and cruel.

How seriously do children take the gender-role norms and stereotypes that they are rapidly learning? It depends on how old they are. William Damon (1977) told children aged 4 to 9 a story about a little boy named George who insists on playing with dolls, even though his parents have told him that dolls are for girls and that boys should play with other toys. When questioned, 4-year-olds said that doll play and other cross-sex behaviors are okay if that is what George really wants to do. As 4-year-old Jack put it, "It's up to him" (Damon, 1977, p. 249). By age 6,

Calvin and Hobbes

by **Bill Watterson**

though, about the time they understand that their sex will remain constant, children become extremely rigid in their thinking and intolerant of anyone who violates traditional gender-role standards. These norms now have the force of absolute moral laws and must be obeyed. Consider the reaction of 6-year-old Michael to George's doll play:

> (*Why do you think people tell George not to play with dolls?*) Well, he should only play with things that boys play with. The things that he is playing with now is girls' stuff.... (*Can George play with Barbie dolls if he wants to?*) No sir! ... (*What should George do?*) He should stop playing with girls' dolls and start playing with G.I. Joe. (Damon, 1977, p. 255; italics added)

The oldest children in Damon's sample were more flexible in their thinking and less chauvinistic. Nine-year-old James, for example, felt that George could legitimately be punished for breaking windows but not for playing with dolls, something he felt boys can do even though they usually don't. He distinguished between moral rules, which we are obligated to obey, and gender-role standards, which are more like customs.

Why do 6- or 7-year-olds interpret gender stereotypes as though they were absolute moral rules rather than social conventions? Perhaps it is because they view any rule or custom as a natural law, like the law of gravity, that must always be correct (Carter & Patterson, 1982). Or perhaps young children must exaggerate gender roles in order to "get them cognitively clear" (Maccoby, 1980). Once their gender identities are more firmly established, children can afford to be more flexible in their thinking about what is "for boys" and what is "for girls." They still know the stereotypes, but they no longer believe as many of them (Signorella, Bigler, & Liben, 1993).

Gender-Typed Behavior

Finally, children rapidly come to behave in "gender-appropriate" ways. As we have seen, preferences for gender-appropriate toys are already detectable in infancy. Apparently, babies establish preferences for "boy" toys or "girl" toys even before they have established clear identities as males or females or can correctly label toys as "boy things" or "girl things" (Blakemore, LaRue, & Olejnik, 1979; Fagot, Leinbach, & Hagan, 1986). Moreover, children quickly come to favor same-sex playmates. In one study (Jacklin & Maccoby, 1978), pairs of 33-month-old toddlers (two boys, two girls, or a boy and a girl) were placed in a laboratory playroom and observed to see how often they engaged in solitary activities and how often they engaged in social play. As we see in Figure 11.3, both boys and girls were more sociable with same-sex peers than with other-sex peers.

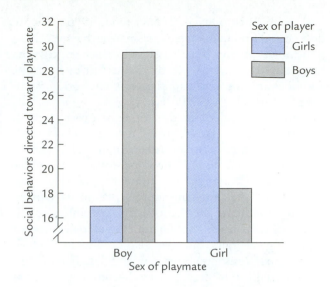

FIGURE 11.3 *Do toddlers prefer playmates of their own sex? Apparently so, for boys are much more sociable with boys than with girls, whereas girls are more outgoing with girls than with boys.* (Based on Jacklin & Maccoby, 1978)

During the elementary school years, boys and girls develop even stronger preferences for peers of their own sex and show increased **gender segregation,** separating themselves into boys' and girls' peer groups and interacting far more often with their own sex than with the other sex (Thorne, 1993). Gender segregation occurs in a variety of cultures, from Kenya to India to the Philippines, and increases with age (Leaper, 1994; Whiting & Edwards, 1988). At age 4½, children in the United States spend three times more time with same-sex peers than with peers of the other sex; by age 6½, they spend 11 times more time (Maccoby & Jacklin, 1987). This is due in part to incompatibilities between boys' and girls' play styles. Basically, boys are too rowdy, domineering, and unresponsive to suit the tastes of many girls, so girls gravitate toward other girls and develop a style of interacting among themselves that is quite different from the rather timid style they adopt in the company of boys (Maccoby, 1990; Moller & Serbin, 1996).

As it turns out, children who insist most strongly on clear boundaries between the sexes and avoid consorting with "the enemy" tend to be socially competent and popular, whereas children who violate gender segregation rules tend to be less well adjusted and run the risk of being rejected by their peers (Kovacs, Parker, & Hoffman, 1996; Sroufe et al., 1993). Boys face stronger pressures to adhere to gender-role expectations than girls do. This may be why they develop stronger gender-typed preferences at earlier ages (Blakemore et al., 1979; Bussey & Bandura, 1992). Just ask your female classmates if they were "tomboys" when they were young, and you're likely to find that about half were (Burn, O'Neil, & Nederend, 1996). But we defy you to find many male classmates who are willing to admit that they were "sissies" in their youth! The masculine role is very clearly defined in our society, and boys are ridiculed and rejected if they do not conform to it (Martin, 1990).

In sum, gender-role development proceeds with remarkable speed. By the time they enter school, children have long been aware of their basic gender identities, have acquired many stereotypes about how the sexes differ, and have come to prefer gender-appropriate activities and same-sex playmates. During middle childhood their knowledge continues to expand as they learn more about gender-stereotyped psychological traits, but they also become more flexible in their thinking about gender roles. Their *behavior*, especially if they are boys, becomes even more gender-typed, and they segregate themselves even more from the other sex.

THE ADOLESCENT

After going their separate ways in childhood, boys and girls come together in the most intimate ways during adolescence. How do they prepare for the masculine or feminine gender roles that they will be asked to play in adulthood?

Adhering to Gender Roles

As we have just seen, young elementary school children are highly rigid in their thinking about gender roles, whereas older children think more flexibly, recognizing that gender norms are not absolute, inviolable laws. Curiously, children once again seem to become highly intolerant of certain role violations and stereotyped in their thinking about the proper roles of males and females in adolescence. They are more likely than somewhat younger children to make negative judgments about peers who violate expectations by engaging in cross-sex behavior or expressing cross-sex interests (Alfieri, Ruble, & Higgins, 1996; Sigelman, Carr, & Begley, 1986).

Consider what Trish Stoddart and Elliot Turiel (1985) found when they asked children aged 5 to 13 questions about boys who wear a barrette or put on nail polish and about girls who sport a crewcut or wear a boy's suit. As Figure 11.4 reveals, both the kindergartners and the adolescents judged these behaviors to be very wrong, whereas third- and fifth-graders viewed them far more tolerantly. Like the elementary school children, eighth-graders clearly understood that gender-role expectations are just social conventions that can easily be changed and do not necessarily apply in all societies. However, these adolescents

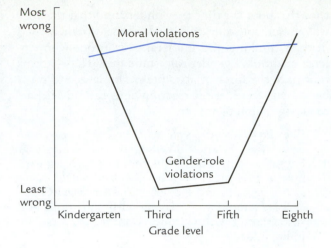

FIGURE 11.4 *Children's rankings of the wrongness of gender-role transgressions (such as a boy's wearing nail polish) and violations of moral rules (such as pushing another child from a swing). Notice that children of all ages deplore immoral acts, but that only kindergartners and adolescents view gender-role violation as wrong. Elementary school children come to think about gender-role standards more flexibly than they did earlier, but adolescents become concerned about the psychological implications of deviating from one's "proper" role.* (Adapted from Stoddart & Turiel, 1985)

had also begun to conceptualize gender-role violations as a sign of psychological abnormality and could not tolerate them.

Increased intolerance of deviance from gender-role expectations is tied to a larger process of **gender intensification,** in which sex differences may be magnified by hormonal changes associated with puberty and increased pressure to conform to gender roles (Boldizar, 1991; Galambos, Almeida, & Petersen, 1990; Hill & Lynch, 1983). Boys begin to see themselves as more masculine; girls emphasize their feminine side. Girls often become more involved with their mothers, boys with their fathers (Crouter, Manke, & McHale, 1995). Why might this gender intensification occur? Hormonal influences may be at work, or adolescents may emphasize gender more once they begin to look like either a man or a woman. Parents may also contribute: As children enter adolescence, mothers do more with their daughters and fathers do more with their sons (Crouter, Manke, & McHale, 1995).

Peers may be even more important. Adolescents increasingly find that they must conform to traditional gender norms in order to appeal to the other sex. A girl who was a tomboy and thought nothing of it may find, around age 12 to 13, that she must dress and behave in more "feminine" ways to attract boys and must give up her tomboyish ways (Burn et al., 1996). A boy may find that he is more popular if he projects a more sharply "masculine" image. Social pressures on adolescents to conform to traditional roles may even help explain why sex differences in cognitive abilities sometimes become more noticeable as children enter adolescence (Hill & Lynch, 1983; Roberts et al., 1990). Later in adolescence, teenagers become more comfortable with their identities as men and women and more flexible in their thinking once again (Urberg, 1979).

We have now surveyed some major milestones in gender-role development from infancy to adolescence—the development of basic gender identity in toddlerhood, gender segregation in childhood, and a return to quite rigid thinking about gender as part of gender intensification during adolescence. Now the most intriguing question about gender-role development in childhood and adolescence: How can it be explained?

Theories of Gender-Role Development

"Once there was a baby named Chris . . . [who] went to live on a beautiful island . . . [where] there were only boys and men; Chris was the only girl. Chris lived a very happy life on this island, but she never saw another girl or woman" (Taylor, 1996, p. 1559). Do you think Chris developed traditionally masculine or traditionally feminine characteristics? When Marianne Taylor (1996) asked children about Chris's toy preferences, occupational aspirations, and personality traits, she found that 4- to 8-year-olds took the nature side of the nature-nurture controversy: They expected Chris's biological status as a girl to determine her development. The 9- and 10-year-olds in the study emphasized the role of nurture in Chris's development, expecting her to be influenced by the masculinizing environment in which she was raised. *Where do you come down in this debate, and why?*

Several theories of the development of gender roles have been proposed. Some theories emphasize the role of biological differences between the sexes, whereas others emphasize social influences on children. Some emphasize what society does to children, others what children do to themselves as they try to understand gender and all its implications. Let's briefly examine a biologically oriented theory and then consider the more "social" approaches offered by psychoanalytic theory, social learning theory, cognitive-developmental theory, and gender schema theory.

Biosocial Theory

The biosocial theory of gender-role development proposed by John Money and Anke Ehrhardt (1972) calls attention to the ways in which biological events influence the development of boys and girls. But it also focuses on ways in which early biological developments influence how people *react* to a child and suggests that these social reactions then have much to do with children's assuming gender roles.

Chromosomes, Hormones, and Social Labeling.

Money and Ehrhardt stress that the male (XY) or female (XX) chromosomes most of us receive at conception are merely a starting point in biological differentiation of the sexes. A number of critical events affect a person's eventual preference for the masculine or feminine role (see also Breedlove, 1994).

1. If certain genes on the Y chromosome are present, a previously undifferentiated tissue develops into testes as the embryo develops; otherwise it develops into ovaries.
2. At a second critical point, the testes of a male embryo normally secrete more of the male hormone *testosterone,* which stimulates the development of a male internal reproductive system, and another hormone that inhibits the development of female organs. Without these hormones the internal reproductive system of a female will develop from the same tissues.
3. At a third critical point, three to four months after conception, secretion of additional testosterone by the testes normally leads to the growth of a penis and scrotum. If testosterone is absent (as in normal females) or if a male fetus's cells are insensitive to the male sex hormones he produces, female external genitalia (labia and clitoris) will form.
4. Finally, the relative amount of testosterone alters the development of the brain and nervous system. For example, it signals the male brain to stop secreting hormones in a cyclical pattern so that males do not experience menstrual cycles at puberty.

Clearly, then, fertilized eggs have the potential to acquire the anatomical and physiological features of either sex. Events at each critical step in the sexual differentiation process determine the outcome.

Once a biological male or female is born, social labeling and differential treatment of girls and boys interact with biological factors to steer development. Parents and other people label and begin to react to the child on the basis of the appearance of his or her genitalia. If a child's genitals are abnormal and he or she is mislabeled as a member of the other sex, this incorrect label will have an impact of its own on the child's future development. For example, if a biological male were consistently labeled and treated as a girl, he would, by about age 3, acquire the gender identity of a girl. Finally, biological factors enter the scene again at puberty when large quantities of hormones are released, stimulating the growth of the reproductive system and the appearance of secondary sex characteristics. These events, in combination with one's earlier self-concept as a male or female, provide the basis for adult gender identity and role

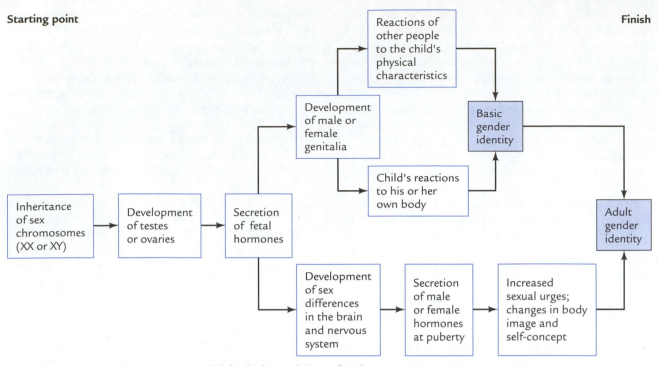

FIGURE 11.5 *Critical events in Money and Ehrhardt's biosocial theory of gender typing* (From Money & Ehrhardt, 1972)

behavior. The complex series of critical points that Money and Ehrhardt (1972) propose is diagrammed in Figure 11.5. But how much is nature and how much is nurture?

Evidence of Biological Influences. A good deal of evidence suggests that biological factors influence the development of males and females in many species of animals (Breedlove, 1994). Evolutionary psychologists notice that most societies socialize males to have instrumental traits and females to have expressive ones and conclude that traditional gender roles may be a reflection of our species heredity (Archer, 1996; Buss, 1995). In addition, individual differences in masculinity and femininity may be partly genetic. Twin studies suggest that individual heredity accounts for 20 to 50% of the variation in the extent to which people describe themselves as having masculine and feminine psychological traits (Loehlin, 1992; Mitchell, Baker, & Jacklin, 1989). In other words, experience does not explain everything.

Biological influences on development are also evident in studies of children who are exposed to the "wrong" hormones prenatally (Ehrhardt & Baker, 1974; Money & Ehrhardt, 1972; see also Gandelman, 1992). Before the consequences were known, some mothers who previously had problems carrying pregnancies to term were given drugs containing progestins, which are converted by the body into the male hormone testosterone. These drugs had the effect of masculinizing female fetuses so that, despite their XX

genetic endowment and female internal organs, they were born with external organs that resembled those of a boy (for example, a large clitoris that looked like a penis and fused labia that resembled a scrotum). Several of these **androgenized females** (girls exposed to excess androgens) were recognized as genetic females, underwent surgery to alter their genitals, and were then raised as girls. When Money and Ehrhardt compared them with their sisters and other girls, it became apparent that many more androgenized girls were tomboys and preferred boys' toys and vigorous activities to traditionally feminine pursuits (see also Berenbaum & Hines, 1992). As adolescents they began dating somewhat later than other girls and felt that marriage should be delayed until they had established their careers. A high proportion (37%) described themselves as homosexual or bisexual (Money, 1985; see also Dittman, Kappes, & Kappes, 1992). Androgenized females also perform better than most other females on tests of spatial ability, further evidence that early exposure to male hormones has "masculinizing" effects on a female fetus (Kimura, 1992; Resnick et al., 1986).

In addition, male exposure to testosterone and other male hormones may be part of the reason why males are more likely than females to commit violent acts (Rubinow & Schmidt, 1996). Evidence from experiments conducted with animals is quite convincing. For example, female rhesus monkeys exposed prenatally to the male hormone testosterone often threaten other monkeys, engage in rough-and-tumble play, and try to "mount" a partner as males do at the beginning of a sexual encounter (Young, Goy, & Phoenix, 1964; Wallen, 1996). Men with high testosterone levels tend to have high rates of delinquency, drug abuse, abusiveness, and violence, although nature interacts with nurture so that these links between testosterone and antisocial behavior are not nearly as evident among men high in socioeconomic status as among men in low socioeconomic status (Dabbs & Morris, 1990).

However, because testosterone levels rise as a result of aggressive and competitive activities, it has been difficult to establish unambiguously that high concentrations of male hormones *cause* aggressive behavior in humans (Archer, 1991). Indeed, animal studies tell us that early experiences can alter the developing nervous systems of males and females and, in turn, their behavior (Breedlove, 1994). Much evidence now suggests that prenatal exposure to male or female hormones has lasting effects on the organization of the brain and, in turn, on sexual behavior, aggression, cognitive abilities, and other aspects of development (Rubinow & Schmidt, 1996). Yet biology does not dictate gender-role development. Instead, *gender-role development evolves from the complex interaction of biology, social experience, and the individual's behavior.*

Evidence of Social-Labeling Influences.

We must also take seriously the *social* aspect of Money and Ehrhardt's biosocial theory. How a child is labeled and treated can also have a considerable impact on gender development. For instance, some androgenized females have been labeled as boys at birth and raised as such until their abnormalities were detected. Money and Ehrhardt (1972) report that the discovery and correction of this condition (by surgery and relabeling as a girl) caused few if any adjustment problems if the sex change took place *before the age of 18 months.* After age 3, sexual reassignment was exceedingly difficult because these genetic females had experienced prolonged masculine gender typing and had already labeled themselves as boys. These findings led Money and Ehrhardt to conclude that there is a *critical period* (between 18 months and 3 years) for the establishment of gender identity when the label society attaches to the child is likely to "stick." Yet studies in which the same infants are presented to some people as boys and to others as girls often indicate that labeling itself has little impact on how people perceive and treat these infants (Stern & Karraker, 1989). And, as Box 11.2 shows, biological males who are labeled as girls during the so-called critical period sometimes adopt a male gender identity later in life, suggesting that we should speak of a *sensitive* rather than a critical period.

In sum, Money and Ehrhardt's biosocial theory stresses the importance of early biological developments that influence how parents and other social agents label a child at birth and that possibly also affect behavior more directly. However, the theory also holds that whether children are socialized as boys or girls strongly influences their gender-role development. In short, biological and social factors interact.

Psychoanalytic Theory

As is true of thinking about most areas of development, thinking about gender-role development was shaped early on by Freud's psychosexual theory. The 3- to 6-year-old child in Freud's phallic stage is said to harbor a strong, biologically based love for the parent of the other sex, experience internal conflict and anxiety as a result of this incestuous desire, and resolve the conflict through a process of **identification** with the same-sex parent. According to Freud, a boy experiencing his **Oedipus complex** loves his mother, fears that his father will retaliate by castrating him, and ultimately is forced to identify with his father, thereby emulating his father and adopting his father's attitudes and behaviors. Freud believed that a boy would show weak masculinity later in life if his father was inadequate as a masculine model, was often absent from the home, or was not dominant or threatening enough to foster a strong identification based on fear.

Meanwhile, a preschool-age girl is said to experience an **Electra complex** involving a desire for her father (and envy of him for the penis she lacks) and a rivalry with her mother. To resolve her unconscious conflict, she identifies with her mother. Her father also contributes to gender-role development by reinforcing her for "feminine" behavior resembling that of her mother. Thus Freud emphasized the role of emotions (love, fear, and so on) in motivating gender-role development and argued that children adopt their roles by patterning themselves after their same-sex parents.

We can applaud Freud for identifying the preschool years as a critical time for gender-role development. In addition, his view that boys, because of fear of castration, have a more powerful motivation than girls to adopt their gender role is consistent with the finding that boys seem to learn gender stereotypes and gender-typed behaviors faster and more completely than girls do. It is also true that boys whose fathers are absent from the home tend to be less traditionally sex-typed than other boys (Stevenson & Black, 1988). Finally, Freud's notion that fathers play an important role in the gender typing of their daughters as well as their sons has been confirmed (Parke, 1996).

However, on other counts psychoanalytic theory has not fared well at all. Many preschool children are so ignorant of male and female anatomy that it is hard to see how most boys could fear castration or most girls could experience penis envy (Bem, 1989; Katcher, 1955). Moreover, Freud assumed that a boy's identification with his father is based on fear, but

BOX 11.2

Is the social label everything, or is biology destiny?

When biological sex and social labeling conflict, which wins out? Consider the fascinating case of a male identical twin whose penis was damaged beyond repair during a botched circumcision (Money & Tucker, 1975). On the advice of John Money, the parents agreed to a surgical procedure that made their 21-month-old boy anatomically a girl. Then they treated him like a girl. By age 5 this boy-turned-girl was quite different from her genetically identical brother. According to John Money and the team in charge of her treatment, she most certainly knew that she was a girl; had developed strong preferences for feminine toys, activities, and apparel; and was far neater and daintier than her brother. This, then, is a vivid demonstration that the most decisive influence on gender-role development is how a child is labeled and treated during the critical period for such development. Or is it?

Milton Diamond and Keith Sigmundson (1997) followed up on this "John" turned "Joan" and found that the story had a twist ending (see also Colapinto, 1997). Joan was never really comfortable with doll play and other traditionally feminine pursuits; she preferred to dress up in men's clothing, play with her twin brother's toys, and take things apart to see how they worked. She used the jumping rope she was given to whip people and tie them up; she was miserable when she was forced to become a Girl Scout rather than a Boy Scout and make daisy chains (Colapinto, 1997). Somewhere around the age of 10, she had the distinct feeling that she was not a girl: "I began to see how different I felt and was. . . . I thought I was a freak or something . . . but I didn't

want to admit it. I figured I didn't want to wind up opening a can of worms" (pp. 299–300). Being rejected by other children because of her masculine looks and feminine dress and being called "cavewoman" and "gorilla" also took their toll, as did continued pressure from psychiatrists to behave in a more feminine manner. Finally, at age 14 and after years of inner turmoil and suicidal thinking, Joan had had it and simply refused to take the female hormones prescribed for her and pretend to be a girl any longer. When finally told that she was a chromosomal male, she/he was relieved: "Suddenly it all made sense why I felt the way I did. I *wasn't* some sort of weirdo" (Colapinto, 1997, p. 92). She then received male hormone shots, a mastectomy, and surgery to construct a penis and emerged as a quite handsome and popular young man who eventually dated girls, married at age 25, and appears to be comfortable with his hard-won identity as John. He now speaks out against the sex reassignment treatment that has long been applied to infants with injured or ambiguous genitals (Colapinto, 1997). Perhaps, then, we should back off from the conclusion that social learning is all that matters. Apparently biology matters too.

A second source of evidence that biology matters is a study of 18 biological males in the Dominican Republic who had a genetic condition that makes their cells insensitive to the effects of male hormones (Imperato-McGinley, Peterson, Gautier, & Sturla, 1979; see also Herdt & Davidson, 1988). They had begun life with ambiguous genitals, were mistaken for girls, and so were labeled and raised as girls. However, under the influence of

male hormones produced at puberty, they sprouted beards and became entirely masculine in appearance. How, in light of Money and Ehrhardt's critical-period hypothesis, could a person possibly adjust to becoming a man after leading an entire childhood as a girl?

Amazingly, 16 of these 18 individuals seemed able to accept their late conversion from female to male and to adopt masculine lifestyles, including the establishment of heterosexual relationships. One retained a female identity and gender role, and the remaining individual switched to a male gender identity but still dressed as a female. This study also casts doubt on the notion that socialization during the first three years is critical to later gender-role development. Instead, it suggests that hormonal influences may be more important than social influences. It is possible, though, that Dominican adults, knowing that this genetic disorder was common in their society, treated these girls-turned-boys differently from other girls when they were young or that these youngsters recognized on their own that their genitals were not normal (Ehrhardt, 1985). As a result, these "girls" may never have fully committed themselves to being girls.

What studies like these of individuals with genital abnormalities appear to teach us is this: We are predisposed by our biology to develop as males or females; the first three years of life are a *sensitive period* perhaps, but not a critical period, for gender-role development; and *both* biology and social labeling contribute to gender-role development.

most researchers find that boys identify most strongly with fathers who are warm and nurturant rather than overly punitive and threatening (Hetherington & Frankie, 1967; Mussen & Rutherford, 1963). Finally, children are not especially similar psychologically to their same-sex parents (Maccoby & Jacklin, 1974). Apparently other individuals besides parents influence a child's gender-related characteristics. And apparently

we must look elsewhere for more complete explanations of gender-role development.

Social Learning Theory

According to social learning theorists such as Albert Bandura (1986) and Walter Mischel (1970), children learn masculine or feminine identities, preferences, and behaviors in two ways. First, through *differential reinforcement*, children are encouraged and rewarded for sex-appropriate behaviors and punished for behaviors considered more appropriate for members of the other sex. Second, through *observational learning*, children adopt the attitudes and behaviors of same-sex models. In this view, a child's gender-role development depends on which of his or her behaviors people reinforce or punish and on what sorts of social models are available. Change the social environment and you change the course of gender-role development.

Differential Reinforcement.   Parents clearly use differential reinforcement to teach boys how to be boys and girls how to be girls (Lytton & Romney, 1991). Beverly Fagot and Mary Leinbach (1989), for example, have found that parents are already encouraging sex-appropriate play and discouraging cross-sex play during the second year of life, before children have acquired their basic gender identities or display clear preferences for male or female activities. By the tender age of 20 to 24 months, daughters are reinforced for dancing, dressing up (as women), following their parents around, asking for help, and playing with dolls; they are discouraged from manipulating objects, running, jumping, and climbing. By contrast, sons are often reprimanded for such "feminine" behavior as playing with dolls or seeking help and are often actively encouraged to play with "masculine" toys such as blocks, trucks, and push-and-pull toys (Fagot, 1978).

Does this "gender curriculum" in the home influence children? It certainly does. Parents who show the clearest patterns of differential reinforcement have children who are relatively quick to label themselves as girls or boys and to develop strongly sex-typed toy and activity preferences (Fagot & Leinbach, 1989; Fagot, Leinbach, & O'Boyle, 1992). It turns out that fathers play a central role in gender socialization; they are more likely than mothers to reward children's gender-appropriate behavior and to discourage behavior considered more appropriate for the other sex (Leve & Fagot, 1997; Lytton & Romney, 1991). Women who choose nontraditional professions are more likely than women in traditionally female fields to have had fathers who encouraged them to be assertive and competitive (Coats & Overman, 1992). Fathers, then, seem to be an especially important influence on the gender-role development of both sons and daughters.

Could differential treatment of boys and girls by parents also contribute to sex differences in ability? Possibly so. Jacquelynne Eccles and her colleagues (1990) have conducted a number of studies to determine why girls tend to shy away from math and science courses and are underrepresented in occupations that involve math and science (see also Benbow & Arjmand, 1990). They suggest that parental expectations about sex differences in mathematical ability become self-fulfilling prophecies. The plot goes something like this:

1. Parents, influenced by societal stereotypes about sex differences in ability, expect their sons to outperform their daughters in math.
2. Parents attribute their sons' successes in math to ability but credit their daughters' successes to hard work (Parsons, Adler, & Kaczala, 1982). These attributions for performance further reinforce the belief that girls lack mathematical talent and turn in respectable performances only through plodding effort.
3. Children begin to internalize their parents' views, so that girls come to believe that they are "no good" in math (Jacobs & Eccles, 1992).
4. Thinking that they lack ability, girls become less interested in math, less likely to take math courses, and less likely than boys to pursue career possibilities that involve math after high school.

In short, parents who expect their daughters to have trouble with numbers get what they expect. The negative effects of low parental expectancies on girls' self-perceptions are evident even when boys and girls perform equally well on tests of math aptitude and attain similar grades in math (Eccles et al., 1990). Girls whose parents are nontraditional in their gender-role attitudes and behaviors do not show the declines in math and science achievement in early adolescence that girls from more traditional families display, so apparently the chain of events Eccles describes can be broken (Updegraff, McHale, & Crouter, 1996).

Peers, like parents, reinforce boys and girls differentially (Beal, 1994). As Beverly Fagot (1985) discovered, boys only 21 to 25 months of age belittle and disrupt each other for playing with "feminine" toys or with girls, and girls express their disapproval of other girls who choose to play with boys. Some scholars believe peers contribute at least as much to gender typing as parents do (Beal, 1994). And as we see in Box 11.3, teachers may contribute too by paying more attention to boys than to girls.

Observational Learning.   Not only do social learning theorists call attention to differential treatment of girls and boys by parents, peers, and teachers, but they emphasize that observational learning also contributes in important ways to gender typing. Children see which toys and activities are "for girls" and which are "for boys" and imitate individuals of their own sex. At about the age of 6 or 7 children begin to pay much closer attention to same-sex models than to other-sex models; for example, they will choose toys that members of their own sex prefer even if it means passing up more attractive toys (Frey & Ruble, 1992). Children who see their mothers perform so-called masculine

BOX 11.3

Are single-sex schools good for girls?

To what extent do teachers treat girls and boys differently in the classroom? We can probably all think of instances in which teachers subtly communicate that boys and girls are different—for example, when teachers ask the boys in the room to help move furniture for the class party but the girls to pour punch. Some scholars feel that sexist treatment in the classroom undermines the confidence and achievement of girls (Beal, 1994). What does research tell us?

A number of studies suggest that teachers pay more attention to boys than to girls (Beal, 1994; Jussim & Eccles, 1992; Sadker & Sadker, 1994). Teachers call on boys more often and give them more feedback. It's not that boys are praised more than girls; instead, they tend to receive both more positive and more negative feedback (Brody, 1985; Hamilton et al., 1991). A good part of the attention they receive is occasioned by their trouble-making, but attention, positive or negative, may signal to girls that boys matter more than they do.

Concerned that girls are being held back academically by this differential treatment, some scholars and educators argue forcefully that girls would be better off in all-girl schools or classrooms than in co-ed ones, and some school systems are experimenting with same-sex education (Sadker & Sad-

ker, 1994). What does the evidence tell us here? Some early studies suggested that all-girl schooling was indeed advantageous to girls (Lee & Bryk, 1986). However, these studies often did not control properly for differences between the students and educational programs in same-sex and co-ed schools. More recent and more carefully designed studies of students attending Catholic schools find few differences at all in school-related attitudes and levels of achievement (LePore & Warren, 1997; Marsh, 1989; Signorella, Frieze, & Hershey, 1996). In

a 1997 study of all-girl, all-boy, and co-ed Catholic high schools, for example, students in single-sex schools generally did no better than students in co-ed schools. The few differences that were observed suggested that boys benefit more academically from same-sex schooling than girls do (LePore & Warren, 1997). It seems, then, that all-girl schooling is not as beneficial as some educators believe, and perhaps the reason is that sexist treatment of girls (and boys too) can occur in any type of school (Lee, Marks, & Byrd, 1994).

tasks and their fathers perform household and child-care tasks tend to be less aware of gender stereotypes and less gender-typed than children who are exposed to traditional gender-role models at home (Turner & Gervai, 1995). Similarly, boys with sisters and girls with brothers have less gender-typed activity preferences than children who grow up with same-sex siblings (Colley et al., 1996).

Not only do children learn by watching the children and adults with whom they interact, but they also learn from the media—radio, television, movies, magazines—and even from their picture books and elementary school readers. Although sexism in children's picture books has decreased over the past 50 years, it is still the case that male characters are more

likely than female characters to engage in active, instrumental activities such as climbing, riding bikes, and making things, whereas female characters are depicted as passive, dependent, and often helpless, spending their time picking flowers, playing quietly indoors, and "creating problems that require masculine solutions" (Kortenhaus & Demarest, 1993; and see Turner-Bowker, 1996).

It is similar in the world of television: Typically, male characters are dominant individuals who work at a profession, whereas many females are passive, emotional creatures who manage a home or work at "feminine" occupations such as nursing (Liebert & Sprafkin, 1988). Children who watch a large amount of television are more likely to choose gender-appropriate

toys and to hold stereotyped views of males and females than their classmates who watch little television (McGhee & Frueh, 1980; Signorielli & Lears, 1992). As more women play detectives and more men raise families on television, children's notions of female and male roles are likely to change. Indeed, watching *The Cosby Show* and other nonsexist programs is associated with holding *less*-stereotyped views of the sexes (Rosenwasser, Lingenfelter, & Harrington, 1989).

In sum, there is much evidence that both differential reinforcement and observational learning contribute to gender-role development. However, social learning theorists have often portrayed children as the passive recipients of external influences: Parents, peers, television characters, and others show them what to do and reinforce them for doing it. Perhaps this perspective does not put enough emphasis on what children *themselves* contribute to their own gender socialization. Youngsters do not receive gender-stereotyped Christmas presents simply because their parents foist those toys upon them. Instead, parents tend to select gender-neutral and often educational toys for their children, but their boys beg for trucks and their girls for tea sets (Robinson & Morris, 1986)!

Cognitive Theory

Some theorists have emphasized cognitive aspects of gender-role development, claiming that, as children acquire understanding of gender, they actively teach themselves to be girls or boys. Lawrence Kohlberg based his cognitive theory on Piaget's cognitive-

developmental theory, whereas Martin and Halverson based their theory on an information-processing approach to cognitive development.

Cognitive-Developmental Theory. Lawrence Kohlberg (1966) proposed a cognitive theory of gender typing that is quite different from the other theories we have considered and helps explain why boys and girls adopt traditional gender roles even when their parents do not want them to do so. Among Kohlberg's major themes are these:

1. Gender-role development depends on stagelike changes in cognitive development; children must acquire certain understandings about gender before they will be influenced by their social experiences.
2. Children engage in self-socialization; instead of being the passive targets of social influence, they actively socialize themselves.

According to both psychoanalytic theory and social learning theory, children are influenced by their companions to adopt "male" or "female" roles and *then* come to view themselves as girls or boys and to identify with (or habitually imitate) same-sex models. Kohlberg suggests that children *first* come to understand that they are girls or boys and then actively seek out same-sex models and a wide range of information about how to act like a girl or a boy. To Kohlberg, it's not "I'm treated like a boy; therefore I must be a boy."

It's more like "I'm a boy, and so now I'll do everything I can to find out how to behave like one."

What understandings are necessary before children will teach themselves to behave like boys or girls? Kohlberg believes that children everywhere progress through the following three stages as they acquire an understanding of what it means to be a female or male:

1. Basic gender identity is established by age 3, when the child recognizes that he or she is a male or a female.
2. Somewhat later the child also acquires **gender stability**—that is, comes to understand that this gender identity is stable *over time*. Boys invariably become men, and girls grow up to be women.
3. The gender concept is complete, somewhere between the ages of 5 and 7, when the child achieves **gender consistency** and realizes that one's sex is also stable *across situations*. Now children know that one's sex cannot be altered by superficial changes such as dressing up as a member of the other sex or engaging in cross-sex activities.

Children 3 to 5 years of age often do lack the concepts of gender stability and gender consistency; they often claim that a boy could become a mommy if he really wanted to or that a girl could become a boy if she cut her hair and wore a hockey uniform. As children enter Piaget's concrete-operational stage of cognitive development and come to grasp concepts like conservation of liquids, they also realize that gender is conserved despite changes in appearance (Marcus & Overton, 1978; Slaby & Frey, 1975). Children have been shown to progress through Kohlberg's three stages in a variety of cultures, which suggests that cognitive maturation is an important influence on the child's emerging understanding of gender (Munroe, Shimmin, & Munroe, 1984).

Criticisms? Sandra Bem (1989) has shown that children need not reach the concrete operations stage to understand gender stability and consistency if they have sufficient knowledge of male and female anatomy to realize that it is one's genitals that make one a male or a female. The most controversial aspect of Kohlberg's cognitive-developmental theory, though, has been his claim that only when children fully grasp that their biological sex is unchangeable, at the age of 5 to 7, do they actively seek out same-sex models and attempt to acquire values, interests, and behaviors that are consistent with their cognitive judgments about themselves. Some evidence supports him (Luecke-Aleksa et al., 1995; Frey & Ruble, 1992). And yet, as this chapter shows, children learn many gender-role stereotypes and develop clear preferences for same-sex activities and playmates long before they master the concepts of gender stability and gender consis-

tency and then attend more selectively to same-sex models. It seems that only a rudimentary understanding of gender is required before children will learn gender stereotypes and preferences.

Gender Schema Theory. Carol Martin and Charles Halverson (1981, 1987) proposed a somewhat different cognitive theory, an information-processing one, that overcomes the key weakness of Kohlberg's theory. Like Kohlberg, they believe that children are intrinsically motivated to acquire values, interests, and behaviors that are consistent with their cognitive judgments about the self. However, Martin and Halverson argue that self-socialization begins as soon as children acquire a *basic* gender identity, at the age of 2 or 3. According to their *schematic-processing model*, children acquire **gender schemata**—organized sets of beliefs and expectations about males and females that influence the kinds of information they will attend to and remember.

First, children acquire a simple *in-group/out-group schema* that allows them to classify some objects, behaviors, and roles as appropriate for males and others as appropriate for females (for example, cars are for boys, girls can cry but boys should not, and so on). Then they seek out more elaborate information about the role of their own sex, constructing an *own-sex schema*. Thus a young girl who knows her basic gender identity might first learn that sewing is for girls and building model airplanes is for boys. Then, because she is a girl and wants to act consistently with her own self-concept, she gathers a great deal of information about sewing to add to her own-sex schema, largely ignoring any information that comes her way about how to build model airplanes (see Figure 11.6).

Consistent with this schematic-processing theory, children do appear to be especially interested in learning about objects or activities that fit their own-sex schemata. In one study, 4- to 9-year-olds were given boxes of gender-neutral objects (hole punches, burglar alarms, and so on) and were told that the objects were either "girl" items or "boy" items (Bradbard et al., 1986). Boys explored "boy" items more than girls did, and girls explored "girl" items more than boys did. A week later the children easily recalled which items were for boys and which were for girls; they had apparently sorted the objects according to their "in-group/out-group" schemata. In addition, boys recalled more in-depth information about "boy" items than did girls, whereas girls recalled more than boys about these very same objects if they had been labeled "girl" items. If children's information-gathering efforts are indeed guided by their own-sex schemata in this way, we can easily see how boys and girls might acquire very different stores of knowledge as they develop.

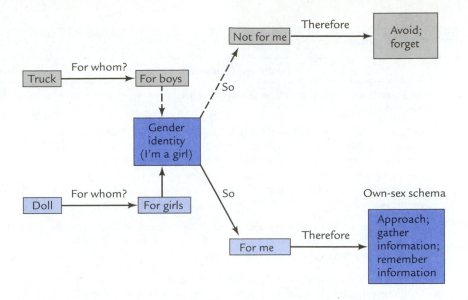

FIGURE 11.6 *Gender schema theory in action. A young girl classifies new information according to an "in-group/out-group schema" as either "for boys" or "for girls." Information about boys' toys and activities is ignored, but information about toys and activities for girls is relevant to the self and so is added to an ever-larger "own-sex schema."* (Adapted from Martin & Halverson in Carter, 1987)

Once gender schemata are in place, children will actually distort new information in memory so that it is consistent with their schemata (Liben & Signorella, 1993; Martin & Halverson, 1983). For example, Martin and Halverson (1983) showed 5- and 6-year-olds pictures of children performing gender-consistent activities (for example, a boy playing with a truck) and pictures of children performing gender-inconsistent activities (for example, a girl sawing wood). A week later the children easily recalled the sex of the actor when activities were gender-consistent; when an actor's behavior was gender-inconsistent, though, children often distorted the scene to make it gender-consistent (for example, by saying that it was a boy, not a girl, who had sawed wood). Thus this research gives us some insight into why inaccurate gender stereotypes persist. The child who believes that women cannot be doctors may be introduced to a female doctor but is likely to remember meeting a nurse and still insist that women cannot be doctors!

An Attempt at Integration

The biosocial, social learning, and cognitive perspectives all contribute to our understanding of sex differences and gender-role development. The biosocial model offered by Money and Ehrhardt notes the importance of biological developments that influence how people label and treat a child. And yet socialization agents—parents, as noted by Freud, and siblings, peers, and teachers as well, as noted by social-learning theorists—are teaching children how to be girls or boys well before they even understand that they *are* girls or boys. Differences in social learning experiences

may also help explain why, even though virtually *all* children form gender concepts and schemata, *some* children are far more gender-typed than others in their preferences and activities (Serbin et al., 1993).

Kohlberg's cognitive-developmental theory and Martin and Halverson's gender schema approach convince us that cognitive growth and self-socialization processes also contribute to gender-role development. Once children acquire a basic gender identity as a boy or a girl and form gender schemata, they become highly motivated to learn their appropriate roles. When they finally grasp, at age 5 to 7, that their sex will never change, they become even more determined to learn their gender roles and pay special attention to same-sex models. Parents who want to avoid socializing their children into traditional gender roles are often amazed to see their children turn into traditional girls and boys all on their own.

In short, children have a male or female biological endowment that helps guide their development, are influenced by other people from birth on how to become "real boys" or "real girls," and actively socialize themselves to behave in ways that seem consistent with their understandings that they are either boys or girls (see Table 11.1). Most developmentalists today would agree that what children learn regarding how to be males or females depends on an interaction between biological factors and social influences. Thus we must respect the role of genes and hormones in gender-role development but also view this process from a contextual perspective and appreciate that the patterns of male and female development that we observe in our society today may not be inevitable. In

TABLE 11.1

An integrative overview of the gender-typing process

Developmental Period	Events and Outcomes	Pertinent Theory(ies)
Prenatal period	The fetus develops male or female genitalia, which others will react to once the child is born.	Biosocial
Birth to 3 years	Parents and other companions label the child as a boy or a girl and begin to encourage gender-consistent behavior while discouraging cross-sex activities. As a result of these social experiences and the development of very basic classification skills, the young child acquires some gender-typed behavioral preferences and the knowledge that he or she is a boy or a girl (basic gender identity).	Social learning
3 to 6 years	Once children acquire a basic gender identity, they begin to seek information about sex differences, form gender schemas, and actively try to behave in ways viewed as "appropriate" for their own sex.	Gender schema
6 to puberty	Children finally acquire the concepts of gender stability and consistency, recognizing that they will be males or females for all their lives and in all situations. At this point, they begin to look closely at the behavior of same-sex models in order to acquire attributes consistent with their firm categorization of themselves as male or female.	Cognitive-developmental
Puberty and beyond	The biological changes of adolescence, along with social pressures, cause an intensification of gender differences and stimulate formation of an adult gender identity.	Biosocial Social learning Gender schema Cognitive-developmental

another era, in another culture, the process of gender-role socialization could produce quite different kinds of boys and girls.

THE ADULT

You might think that, once children and adolescents have learned their gender roles, they simply play them out during adulthood. Instead, as people face the challenges of adult life and enter new social contexts, their gender roles and their concepts of themselves as men and women change. So do their sex lives.

Gender Roles

Although males and females fill their masculine or feminine roles throughout their lives, the specific content of those roles changes considerably over the life span. The young boy may act out his masculine role by playing with trucks or wrestling with his buddies; the grown man may play his role by holding down a job. Moreover, the degree of difference between male and female roles also changes. Children and adolescents do adopt behaviors consistent with their "boy" or "girl" roles, but the two sexes otherwise adopt quite similar roles in society—namely, those of children and

students. Even as they enter adulthood, males' and females' roles do not differ much, because members of both sexes are often single and in school or working.

However, the roles of men and women become more distinct when they marry and, especially, when they have children. Even among newlyweds, for example, the wife typically does the lion's share of the housework, whether or not she is employed, and specific tasks tend to be parceled out along traditional lines: she doing the cooking, he taking out the garbage (Atkinson & Huston, 1984). The birth of a child tends to make even quite egalitarian couples divide their labors in more traditional ways than they did before the birth (Cowan, Cowan, Heming, & Miller, 1991). It is she who becomes primarily responsible for child care and household tasks; he tends to emphasize his role as "breadwinner" and center his energies on providing for the family. Even as men today increase their participation in child care and housework, they still tend to play a "helper" role (Baruch & Barnett, 1986). At least two-thirds of what gets done at home is still done by women (Pleck, 1985; Zick & McCullough, 1991).

What happens after the children are grown? The roles played by men and women become more similar again starting in middle age, when the nest empties and child-care responsibilities end. The similarity between gender roles continues to increase as adults enter old age; as retirees and grandparents, men and women lead similar lives. It would seem, then, that the roles of men and women are fairly similar before marriage, maximally different during the child-rearing years, and more similar again later on (Gutmann, 1997).

Do these sorts of shifts in the roles played by men and women during adulthood affect them psychologically? Let's see.

Masculinity, Femininity, and Androgyny

For many years, psychologists assumed that masculinity and femininity were at opposite ends of a continuum. If one possessed highly masculine traits, one must be very unfeminine; being highly feminine implied being unmasculine. Sandra Bem (1974) challenged this assumption by arguing that individuals of either sex can be characterized by psychological **androgyny**—that is, by a balancing or blending of *both* desirable masculine-stereotyped traits (being assertive, analytical, forceful, independent) and desirable feminine-stereotyped traits (being affectionate, compassionate, gentle, understanding). In Bem's model, then, masculinity and femininity are *two separate dimensions* of personality. A male or female who has many desirable masculine-stereotyped traits and few feminine ones is defined as a *masculine sex-typed* person. One who has many feminine- and few masculine-stereotyped traits is said to be *feminine sex-typed*. The androgynous person possesses both masculine and feminine traits, whereas the *undifferentiated* individual lacks both of these kinds of attributes (see Figure 11.7).

How many of us are androgynous? Bem (1974, 1979) and other investigators (Spence & Helmreich, 1978) have developed self-perception inventories that contain both a masculinity (or instrumentality) scale and a femininity (or expressivity) scale. In one large sample of college students (Spence & Helmreich, 1978), roughly 33% of the test takers were "masculine" men or "feminine" women; about 30% were androgynous, and the remaining individuals were either undifferentiated (low on both scales) or "sex-reversed" (masculine sex-typed females or feminine sex-typed males). Around 30% of children can also be classified as androgynous (Boldizar, 1991; Hall & Halberstadt, 1980). So androgynous individuals do indeed exist, and in sizable numbers. But do perceived masculinity, femininity, and androgyny change over the adult years?

Changes with Age

David Gutmann (1987, 1997) has offered the intriguing hypothesis that gender roles and gender-related traits in adulthood are shaped by what he calls the **parental imperative,** the requirement that

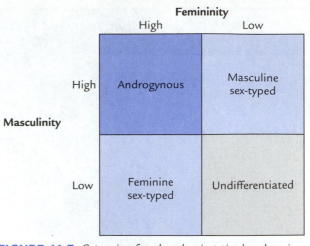

FIGURE 11.7 *Categories of gender-role orientation based on viewing masculinity and femininity as separate dimensions of personality.*

mothers and fathers adopt different roles in order to raise children successfully. Drawing on his own cross-cultural research and that of others, he suggests that in many cultures young and middle-aged men must emphasize their "masculine" qualities in order to feed and protect their families, whereas young and middle-aged women must express their "feminine" qualities in order to nurture the young and meet the emotional needs of their families.

According to Gutmann, all this changes dramatically starting in midlife, when men and women are freed from the demands of the parental imperative. Men become less active and more passive, take less interest in community affairs, and focus more on religious contemplation and family relationships. They also become more sensitive and emotionally expressive. Women, meanwhile, are changing in precisely the opposite direction. After being quite passive, submissive, and nurturing in their younger years, they become more active, domineering, and assertive in later life. In many cultures they take charge of the household after being the underlings of their mothers-in-law and become stronger forces in their communities. In short, Gutmann's parental imperative hypothesis states that, over the course of adulthood, psychologically "masculine" men become "feminine" men, while "feminine" women become "masculine" women—that the psychological traits of the two sexes flipflop.

A similar but somewhat different hypothesis is that adults experience a midlife **androgyny shift.** Instead of giving up traits they had as young adults, men and women retain their gender-typed qualities but add to them qualities traditionally associated with the other sex; that is, they become more androgynous. Ideas along this line were proposed some time ago by the psychoanalytic theorist Carl Jung (1933),

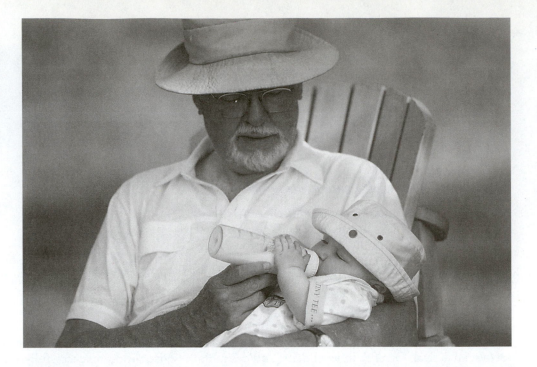

who believed that we have masculine and feminine sides all along but learn to integrate them and express both facets of our human nature only in middle age. Let's see how these ideas have fared.

What age differences do researchers find when they administer masculinity and femininity scales to men and women of different ages? In one study, Shirley Feldman and her associates (1981) gave Bem's androgyny inventory to individuals at eight different stages of the family life cycle. Consistent with Gutmann's notion of a parental imperative, taking on the role of parent seemed to lead men to perceive themselves as more masculine in personality and women to perceive themselves as having predominantly feminine strengths (see also Abrahams, Feldman, & Nash, 1978). Moreover, among adults who were beyond their parenting years, especially among grandparents, sex differences in self-perceptions decreased. Contrary to Gutmann's hypothesis, however, grandfathers did not replace their masculine traits with feminine traits and grandmothers did not become less feminine and more masculine. Instead, both sexes experienced an androgyny shift: Grandfathers retained their masculine traits while gaining feminine attributes, and grandmothers retained their feminine traits while taking on masculine attributes as well (see also Wink & Helson, 1993). This finding is particularly interesting in view of the fact that today's older people should, if anything, be *more* traditionally gender-typed than younger adults who have grown up in an era of more flexible gender norms.

In sum, young adults who are not parents are relatively androgynous, the parenting role brings out traditionally sex-typed traits in both men and women,

and androgyny once again emerges when the parenting years are over. These changes in gender-role orientations during adulthood appear to be related more to the roles men and women play than to how old they are, as Alice Eagly's social-role hypothesis would predict. For example, young mothers are more psychologically feminine than nonmothers of the same age (Feldman et al., 1981), and working women are more assertive and independent than nonworking women (Wink & Helson, 1993). Again, we must adopt a contextual perspective on gender-role development and appreciate that males and females can develop in any number of directions depending on their social, cultural, and historical context and on the social roles they play.

Is Androgyny Advantageous?

If a person can be both assertive and sensitive, both independent and understanding, being androgynous sounds psychologically healthy. Is it? Bem (1975, 1978) demonstrated that androgynous men and women behave more flexibly than more sex-typed individuals. For example, androgynous people, like masculine sex-typed people, can display the "masculine," instrumental trait of independence by resisting social pressure to judge very unamusing cartoons as funny just because their companions do. Yet they are as likely as feminine sex-typed individuals to display the "feminine," expressive quality of nurturance by interacting positively with a baby. Androgynous people seem to be highly adaptable, able to adjust their behavior to the demands of the situation at hand (Shaffer, Pegalis, & Cornell, 1992). In addition, androgynous individuals appear to enjoy higher self-esteem and are perceived as better adjusted than their traditionally sex-typed peers, though this is largely because of the masculine qualities they possess (Boldizar, 1991; Spence & Hall, 1996).

But, before we jump to the conclusion that androgyny is a thoroughly desirable attribute, can you imagine any disadvantages of androgyny? During *childhood,* expressing too many of the traits considered more appropriate in the other sex can result in rejection by peers and low self-esteem (Lobel, Slone, & Winch, 1997). It may be premature, then, to conclude that it is better in all respects to be androgynous rather than either masculine or feminine in orientation—at least while traditional gender thinking prevails. Still, we can at least conclude that it is unlikely to be damaging for men to become a little more "feminine" or for women to become a little more "masculine" than they have been traditionally.

SEXUALITY OVER THE LIFE SPAN

An important part of becoming a woman or a man is becoming a sexual being. Sexual development is a lifelong process that starts in infancy.

Are Infants Sexual Beings?

It was Sigmund Freud who made the seemingly outrageous claim that humans are sexual beings from birth onward. We are born, he said, with a reserve of sexual energy that is redirected toward different parts of the body as we develop. Freud may have been wrong about some things, but he was quite right about the fact that infants are sexual beings.

Babies are, of course, biologically equipped at birth with male or female chromosomes, hormones, and genitals. Moreover, young infants in Freud's oral stage of development *do* appear to derive pleasure from sucking, mouthing, biting, and other oral activities. But the clincher is this: Both male babies and female babies have been observed to touch and manipulate their genital areas, to experience physical arousal, and to undergo what appear to be orgasms (Leung & Robson, 1993). Parents in some cultures, well aware of the pleasure infants derive from their genitals, occasionally use genital stimulation as a means of soothing fussy babies (Ford & Beach, 1951).

What should we make of this infant sexuality? Infants feel bodily sensations, but they are hardly aware that their behavior is "sexual." How unfortunate, then, that the mother of one infant girl studied by Bakwin (1973) was apparently shocked by this "immoral" behavior and slapped and scolded her innocent child (to no avail). Infants are sexual beings primarily in the sense that their genitals are sensitive and their nervous systems allow sexual responses. They are also as curious about their bodies as they are about the rest of the world. It will not be too long, however, before they begin to learn what human sexuality is about and how the members of their society regard it.

Childhood Sexuality

Although boys and girls spend much of their time in gender-segregated groups, they are nonetheless preparing for the day when they will participate in sexual relationships with the other sex. They learn a great deal about sexuality and reproduction, continue to be curious about their bodies, and begin to interact with the other sex in ways that will prepare them for dating in adolescence.

Knowledge of Sex and Reproduction

As children get older, they learn that sexual anatomy is the key differentiator between males and females and acquire a more correct and explicit vocabulary for discussing sexual organs (Goldman & Goldman, 1982; Gordon, Schroeder, & Abrams, 1990). As Anne Bernstein and Philip Cowan (1975) have shown, their understandings of "where babies come from" also change as they develop cognitively. Young children often seem to assume either that babies are just there all along or that they are somehow manufactured, much as toys might be. According to Jane, aged 3½, "You find [the baby] at a store that makes it. . . . Well, they get it and then they put it in the tummy and then it goes quickly out" (p. 81). Another preschooler, making what he could of a book about reproduction in the animal world, created this scenario:

> (*How would the lady get a baby to grow in her tummy?*) Um, get a rabbit . . . they just get a duck or a goose and they get a little more growned . . . and then they turn into a baby. (*A rabbit will turn into a baby?*) They give them some food, people food, and they grow like a baby. (*If I asked you to tell me just one way that people get babies, what would you say?*) I would say, a store, buy a duck. . . . (Bernstein & Cowan, 1975, p. 87; italics supplied)

As these examples illustrate, young children construct their own understandings of reproduction well before they are told the "facts of life." Between the ages of 9 and 11, most children come to understand that sexual intercourse plays a role in the making of babies (Goldman & Goldman, 1982). By 11 or 12 most children have integrated information about sexual intercourse with information about the biological union of egg and sperm (Bernstein & Cowan, 1975). Thus, as children mature cognitively and as they gain access to information, they are able to construct

ever more accurate understandings of sexuality and reproduction.

Sexual Behavior

According to Freudian theory, preschoolers in the *phallic stage* of psychosexual development are actively interested in their genitals and seek bodily pleasure through masturbation, but school-age children enter a *latency period* during which they repress their sexuality and turn their attention instead to schoolwork and friendships with same-sex peers. It turns out that Freud was half right and half wrong.

Freud was correct that preschoolers are highly curious about their bodies, masturbate, and engage in both same-sex and cross-sex sexual play. He was wrong to believe that such activities occur infrequently among school-age children. In analyzing interviews with children aged 4 to 14, James Elias and Paul Gebhard (1969) found that about 50% of the boys and 30% of the girls reported that they had masturbated before reaching puberty and had engaged in some form of sexual play with same-sex peers (exhibition of genitals, manipulation of each other's genitals, and so on), and over a third of both sexes reported similar forms of heterosexual play. Latency-period children may be more discreet about their sexual experimentation than preschoolers, but they have by no means lost their sexual curiosity.

Indeed, Martha McClintock and Gilbert Herdt (1996) have gathered evidence that age 10 is an important landmark in sexual development, a time when many boys as well as girls experience their first sexual attraction (for a member of the other sex if they later become heterosexual, for a member of their own sex if

they later become gay or lesbian). This milestone in development appears to be influenced by the maturation of the adrenal glands (which produce male androgens). It comes well before the maturation of the sex organs during puberty and therefore challenges the view of Freud (and many of the rest of us) that puberty is the critical milestone in sexual development. As McClintock and Herdt note, our society does little to encourage fourth graders to have sexual thoughts, especially about members of their own sex, so perhaps a hormonal explanation of early sexual attraction makes more sense than an environmental one.

Yet sexual development is also shaped by the cultural context in which children develop. Judging from the anthropological research of Clellan Ford and Frank Beach (1951), the diversity in sexual attitudes and behaviors among cultures of the world is staggering. In *restrictive* societies, children are not allowed to express any sexuality until they reach puberty or sometimes until they marry. In New Guinea, for example, Kwoma boys are not allowed to touch themselves, and a boy caught having an erection is likely to have his penis beaten with a stick! In *semirestrictive* societies like the United States and most industrialized Western nations, rules prohibiting childhood masturbation and sex play exist; but they are frequently violated, and adults rarely punish children unless the violations are flagrant. In *permissive* societies, children are free to express their sexuality and are encouraged to prepare for their roles as mature sexual beings. On the island of Ponape, for example, 4- and 5-year-olds receive a thorough sex education from adults and are free to try out what they have learned on one another. In other societies, such as among certain groups in

New Guinea, men engage in sexual behavior with boys in order to initiate them, a practice we would label sexual abuse (Konker, 1992).

In our semirestrictive society, children learn from their peers how to relate to the other sex. As Barrie Thorne's (1993) observations in elementary schools demonstrate, boys and girls may be segregated by gender, but they are hardly oblivious to each other. They talk constantly about who "likes" whom and who is "cute"; they play kiss-and-chase games in which girls attempt to catch boys and infect them with "cooties"; and they have steady boyfriends and girlfriends (if only for a few days). At times boys and girls seem like mortal enemies. But by loving and hating each other, kissing and running away, they are grooming themselves for more explicitly sexual—but still often ambivalent—heterosexual relationships later in life (Thorne, 1993).

Child Sexual Abuse

Every day in this country, children, adolescents, and even infants are sexually abused by the adults closest to them. A typical scenario would be this: A girl aged 7 or 8—though it happens to boys too—is abused repeatedly by her father, stepfather, or another male relative or family friend (Trickett & Putnam, 1993). Estimates of the percentages of girls and boys who are sexually abused vary wildly, perhaps because so many cases go unreported. In one representative sample of U.S. adults, though, 27% of the women and 16% of the men reported having experienced some form of childhood sexual abuse ranging from being touched in ways they considered abusive to being raped (Finkelhor et al., 1989). This study suggests it is a serious and widespread social problem.

What are the impacts of sexual abuse on the victims? A useful account is offered by Kathleen Kendall-Tackett, Linda Williams, and David Finkelhor (1993) based on their review of 45 studies. There is no one distinctive "syndrome" of psychological problems that characterizes abuse victims. Instead, these individuals may experience any number of problems commonly seen in emotionally disturbed individuals, including anxiety, depression, low self-esteem, aggression, acting out, withdrawal, and school learning problems. Roughly 20 to 30% experience each of these problems, and boys seem to experience much the same types and degrees of disturbance as girls do.

Many of these aftereffects boil down to a lack of self-worth and a difficulty trusting others (Cole & Putnam, 1992). A college student of my acquaintance who had been abused repeatedly by her father and by other relatives as well had this to say about her experience:

It was very painful, emotionally, physically, and psychologically. I wanted to die to escape it. I wanted to escape from my body. . . . I developed a "good" self and a "bad" self. This was the only way I could cope with the experiences. . . . I discovered people I trusted caused me harm. . . . It is difficult for me to accept the fact that people can care for me and expect nothing in return. . . . I dislike closeness and despise people touching me.

Two problems seem to be uniquely associated with being sexually abused. First, about a third of victims engage in "sexualized behavior," acting out sexually by putting objects in vaginas, masturbating in public, behaving seductively, or, if they are older, behaving promiscuously (Kendall-Tackett et al., 1993). One theory is that this sexualized behavior helps victims master or control the traumatic events they experienced (Tharinger, 1990). Second, about a third of victims display the symptoms of **posttraumatic stress disorder.** This clinical disorder, involving nightmares, flashbacks to the traumatizing events, and feelings of helplessness and anxiety in the face of danger, affects some soldiers in combat and other victims of extreme trauma (Kendall-Tackett et al., 1993).

In a minority of children, sexual abuse may contribute to severe psychological disorders, including multiple-personality disorder, the splitting of the psyche into distinct personalities (Cole & Putnam, 1992; Ross et al., 1991). Yet about a third of children seem to experience no psychological symptoms at all (Kendall-Tackett et al., 1993). Some of these symptomless children may experience problems in later years. But it is also true that some children are less severely damaged and more able to cope than others are.

Which children have the most difficulty? We know that the effects of abuse are likely to be most severe when the abuse involved penetration and force and occurred frequently over a long period of time; when the perpetrator was a close relative such as the father; and when the child's mother did not serve as a reliable source of emotional support (Beitchman et al., 1991; Kendall-Tackett et al., 1993; Trickett & Putnam, 1993). Children are likely to recover much better if their mothers believe their stories and can offer them a stable and loving home environment (Kendall-Tackett et al., 1993). Psychotherapy aimed at treating the anxiety and depression many victims experience and teaching them coping and problem-solving skills so that they will not be revictimized can also contribute to the healing process (Finkelhor & Berliner, 1995). Recovery takes time, but it does take place.

Adolescent Sexuality

Although infants and children are sexual beings, sexuality assumes far greater importance once sexual maturity is achieved. Adolescents must now incorporate into their identities as males or females concepts of themselves as *sexual* males or females. Moreover, they must figure out how to express their sexuality in the context of interpersonal relationships. As part of their search for identity, teenagers raise questions about their sexual attractiveness, their sexual values, and their goals in close relationships. They also experiment with sexual behavior—sometimes with good outcomes, sometimes with bad ones. The psychological aspects of dating relationships are explored further in Chapter 13; here we'll focus on the sexual aspects.

Sexual Orientation

Part of establishing a sexual identity, part of the larger task of resolving Erikson's conflict of identity versus role confusion, is becoming aware of one's **sexual orientation**—that is, one's preference for sexual partners of the same or other sex. Sexual orientation exists on a continuum; not all cultures categorize sexual preferences as ours does (Paul, 1993), but we commonly describe people as having primarily heterosexual, homosexual, or bisexual orientations. Most adolescents establish a heterosexual sexual orientation without much soul searching. For youths who are attracted to members of their own sex, however, the process of accepting that they have a homosexual orientation and establishing a positive identity in the face of negative societal attitudes can be a long and torturous one. Many have an initial awareness of their sexual preference before reaching puberty but do not accept being gay or lesbian, or gather the courage to "come out," until their mid-20s (Garnets & Kimmel, 1991; Savin-Williams, 1995).

Experimentation with homosexual activity is fairly common during adolescence, but few adolescents become part of the estimated 5 to 6% of adults who establish an enduring homosexual or bisexual sexual orientation (Smith, 1991). Contrary to societal stereotypes of gay men as effeminate and lesbian women as masculine, gay and lesbian individuals have the same wide range of psychological and social attributes that heterosexual adults do. Knowing that someone prefers same-sex romantic partners tells us no more about his or her personality than knowing that someone is heterosexual.

What influences the development of one's sexual orientation? Part of the answer lies in the genetic code. Dean Hamer and his colleagues (1993) have reported evidence that some gay men are gay in part because they have a particular gene on the X chromosome they inherited from their mothers. Moreover, twin studies have established that identical twins are more alike in sexual orientation than fraternal twins (Bailey & Pillard, 1991; Bailey et al., 1993). As Table 11.2 reveals, though, in about half the identical twin pairs, one twin is homosexual or bisexual but the other is heterosexual. This means that environment contributes at least as much as genes to the development of sexual orientation.

TABLE 11.2

If one twin is gay (or lesbian), in what percentage of twin pairs does the other twin also have a homosexual or bisexual sexual orientation? Higher rates of concordance (similarity) for identical twin pairs than for fraternal twin pairs provide evidence of genetic influence on homosexuality. Less-than-perfect concordance points to the operation of environmental influences as well.

	Identical Twins	Fraternal Twins
Both male twins are gay/bisexual if one is:	52%	22%
Both female twins are lesbian/bisexual if one is:	48%	16%

SOURCE: Male figures from Bailey & Pillard (1991); female figures from Bailey et al. (1993)

Other research tells us that many gay men and lesbian women expressed strong cross-sex interests when they were young, despite being subjected to the usual pressures to adopt a traditional gender role (Bailey & Zucker, 1995; LeVay, 1996). Richard Green (1987), for example, studied a group of highly feminine boys who didn't just engage in cross-sex play now and then but who strongly and consistently preferred female roles, toys, and friends. He found that 75% of these boys (compared with 2% of a control group of gender-typical boys) were exclusively homosexual or bisexual 15 years later. Yet the genetic research by Bailey and Pillard suggests that sexual orientation is every bit as heritable among gay men who were typically masculine boys and lesbian women who were typically feminine girls as among those who showed early cross-sex interests (Bailey & Pillard, 1991; Bailey et al., 1993). All that is clear, then, is that many gay and lesbian adults know from an early age that traditional gender-role expectations do not suit them.

What environmental factors may help to determine whether or not a genetic predisposition toward homosexuality is actualized? We really do not know as yet. The old psychoanalytic view that male homosexuality stems from having a domineering mother and a weak father has received little support at all (LeVay, 1996). Growing up with a gay or lesbian parent also seems to have little impact on later sexual orientation (Golombok & Tasker, 1996; Patterson, 1992). Nor is there support for the idea that homosexuals were seduced into a homosexual lifestyle by older individuals.

A more promising hypothesis is that hormonal influences during the prenatal period influence sexual orientation (Ellis et al., 1988; Meyer-Bahlburg et al., 1995). For example, the fact that androgenized females are more likely than most other women to adopt a lesbian or bisexual orientation suggests that high prenatal doses of male hormones may predispose at least some females to homosexuality (Dittman et al., 1992; Money, 1988). Another possibility is that nature and nurture interact. Biological factors may predispose an individual to have certain psychological traits, which in turn influence the kinds of social experiences the person has, which in turn shape his or her ultimate sexual orientation (Byne, 1994). However, the fact is that no one yet knows exactly which factors in the prenatal or postnatal environment contribute, along with genes, to a homosexual orientation (Byne, 1994; LeVay, 1996).

Sexual Morality

Whatever their sexual orientations, adolescents establish attitudes regarding what is and is not appropriate sexual behavior. The sexual attitudes of adolescents have changed dramatically during this century, especially during the 1960s and 1970s, and yet many of the "old" values have endured. Philip Dreyer (1982) noted three important historical changes.

First, most adolescents have come to believe that *sex with affection is acceptable*. They no longer buy the traditional view that premarital intercourse is always morally wrong. They also don't go so far as to view casual sex as acceptable, though males have more permissive attitudes about this than females (Oliver & Hyde, 1993). Most adolescents insist that the partners be "in love" or feel a close emotional involvement with each other.

A second important change is the *decline of the* **double standard.** According to the double standard, sexual behavior that is viewed as appropriate for males is considered inappropriate for females; there is one standard for males, another for females. Thus in the "old days" a young man was expected to "sow some wild oats," whereas a young woman was expected to remain a virgin until she married. The double standard has not entirely disappeared. For example, fathers still look more favorably on the sexual exploits of their sons than on those of their daughters (Brooks-Gunn & Furstenberg, 1989), and college students still tend to believe that a woman who has many sexual partners is more immoral than an equally promiscuous man (Robinson et al., 1991). However, Western societies have been moving for some time toward a single standard of sexual behavior used to judge both males and females.

The third change might be described as *increased confusion about sexual norms*. Adolescents continually receive mixed messages about sexuality (Darling & Hicks, 1982). They are encouraged to be popular and attractive to the other sex, and they watch countless television programs and movies that glamorize sexual behavior. Yet they are also told to value virginity and to fear and avoid pregnancy, bad reputations, and

AIDS and other sexually transmitted diseases. The standards for males and females are now more similar, and adolescents tend to agree that sexual intercourse in the context of emotional involvement is acceptable; but teenagers still must forge their own codes of behavior, and they differ widely in what they decide.

Sexual Behavior

If attitudes about sexual behavior have changed over the years, has sexual behavior itself changed? Yes, it has. Today's teenagers are involved in more intimate forms of sexual behavior at earlier ages than adolescents of the past were. Figure 11.8 shows the percentages of high school students who had premarital intercourse in each of five historical periods. This figure illustrates three themes:

1. Rates of sexual activity climbed in the 1960s and continued to climb through the 1980s (Dreyer, 1982; Forrest & Singh, 1990). This upward trend showed its first signs of dropping off in the early 1990s (Vobejda & Havemann, 1997).
2. These changes in rates of sexual activity are evident among both males and females.
3. Perhaps because of the decline of the double standard, the sexual behavior of females has changed much more than that of males, to the point that sex differences in sexual activity have all but disappeared (Leigh et al., 1994).

The percentage of adolescents with sexual experience increases steadily with age over the adolescent years. One-fourth of 14-year-olds and about half of 16-year-olds have had sexual intercourse (Leigh et al., 1994). Among college students, the rate is around 70 to 80% (Baier, Rosenzweig, & Whipple, 1991; Reinisch et al., 1992). Early sexual involvement is most likely among adolescents whose mothers were teenage parents; indeed, twin studies indicate that age of first intercourse is genetically influenced (Dunne et al., 1997). In addition, adolescents who become sexually active early are not very invested in school; instead they are involved in problem behaviors such as substance abuse and delinquency (Crockett et al., 1996).

Males and females feel differently about their sexual encounters. For example, females are more insistent than males that sex and love—physical intimacy and emotional intimacy—go together. In one survey, 61% of college women, but only 29% of college men, agreed with the idea "No intercourse without love" (Darling, Davidson, & Passarello, 1992). Females are also more likely than males to have been in a steady relationship with their first sexual partner (Darling et al., 1992). This continuing gap between the sexes can sometimes create misunderstandings and hurt feelings, and it may partly explain why females are

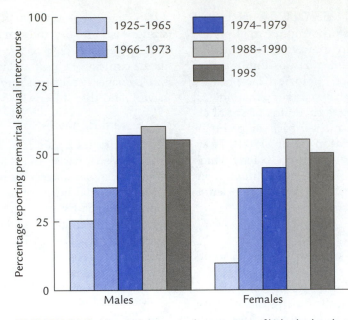

FIGURE 11.8 *Historical changes in the percentages of high school students reporting premarital sexual intercourse* (Data for the first three time periods adapted from Dreyer, 1982; data for the most recent two periods from Centers for Disease Control, 1992; Vobejda & Havemann, 1997)

more likely than males to wish they had waited to have sex (de Gaston, Jensen, & Weed, 1995).

In sum, both the sexual attitudes and the sexual behaviors of adolescents have changed considerably in this century. Sexual involvement is now part of the average adolescent's experience. This is true of all major ethnic groups, and of rich and poor. In fact, the differences in sexual activity among social groups have been shrinking (Forrest & Singh, 1990). Although most adolescents seem to adjust successfully to becoming sexually active, there have also been some casualties among those who are psychologically unready for sex or who end up with an unintended pregnancy or a sexually transmitted disease.

Sexually active adolescent couples often fail to use contraception, partly because they are cognitively immature and do not take seriously the possibility that their behavior could have unfortunate long-term consequences (Loewenstein & Furstenberg, 1991; Morrison, 1985). In one survey, only about one-third of sexually active teenagers said they always used a condom during intercourse in the past year (Leigh et al., 1994). For the adolescent who gives birth, the consequences of teenage sexuality are likely to include an interrupted education, low income, and a difficult start for both her and her child (Furstenberg, Lincoln, & Menken, 1981). This young mother's life situation and her child's developmental status are likely to improve later on, especially if she goes back to school and limits her family size, but she is likely to remain economically disadvantaged compared with her peers

who postpone parenthood until their 20s (Furstenberg, Brooks-Gunn, & Morgan, 1987).

What effect has the threat of AIDS had on adolescent sexual behavior? Most studies find change but perhaps not enough. Teens are more likely to use condoms than they used to be, and rates of teenage pregnancy have actually begun to decline recently as a result (Vobejda & Havemann, 1997). However, few adolescents are doing what they would need to do to protect themselves from HIV infection: abstaining from sex or using a condom (latex, with a spermicide) *every* time. Even college students have failed to change enough: only 30% of students in the United States who had had sexual intercourse in the past three months used a condom in their last sexual encounter (Centers for Disease Control, 1997). No wonder many educators are now calling for stronger programs of sex education and distribution of free condoms at school. There is little chance of preventing the unwanted consequences of teenage sexuality unless more adolescents either postpone sex or practice safer sex.

Adult Sexuality

Just as adults' sexual orientations are varied, so are their sexual lifestyles. Some adults remain single—some of them actively seeking a wide range of partners, others having one partner at a time, and still others leading celibate lives. Over 9 of 10 Americans marry at some point, and most adults are married at any given time. Men have more sexual partners than

Many of today's adolescents become involved in sexual activity very early and give little thought to the long-term consequences of their behavior.

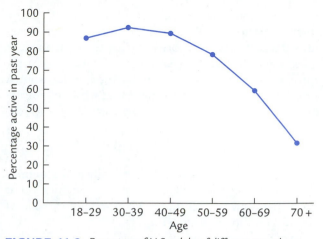

FIGURE 11.9 *Percentage of U.S. adults of different ages who reported having at least one sexual partner in the past year. Cross-sectional data like these can be misleading about the degree to which sexual activity declines with age, but longitudinal studies also point to decreased involvement.* (Adapted from Smith, 1991)

women during their adult lives, but most members of both sexes have just one sexual partner at a time (Laumann et al., 1994).

What becomes of people's sex lives as they get older? Many young people can barely conceive of their parents or—heaven forbid—their grandparents as sexual beings. We tend to stereotype elderly people as sexless or asexual. But we are wrong: People continue to be sexual beings throughout the life span. Perhaps the most amazing discoveries about sex in late adulthood are those of Bernard Starr and Marcella Weiner (1981), who surveyed 800 elderly volunteers aged 60 to 91. In this group, over 90% claimed to like sex, almost 80% were still sexually active, and 75% said that their sex lives were the same as or better than when they were younger. One 70-year-old widow, asked how often she would like to have sex, was not bashful at all about replying "Morning, noon, and night" (p. 47).

Obviously people can remain highly interested in sex and sexually active in old age. Yet Starr and Weiner's findings are likely to be exaggerated, since only the most sexually active people may have agreed to complete such a survey. More reliable findings are reported by Tom Smith (1991) based on a survey of a representative sample of American adults that asked about many things, including sexual behavior. As Figure 11.9 shows, the percentage of adults who reported at least some sexual contact in the past year declined quite steadily from age group to age group, although almost a third of adults in their 70s and older were

still sexually active. Men were more likely to be sexually active than women, and, as you might expect, adults were more likely to be sexually active if they were married (91%) than if they were separated or divorced (74-80%) or widowed (only 14%).

In sum, sexual activity declines with age, especially among older women. Yet most people do not end their sex lives when they turn 65. Many older adults continue having sexual intercourse, and many of those who cease having it or have it less frequently continue to be sexually motivated (Clements, 1996).

Explanations for Declining Activity

How can we explain declines with age in sexual interest and activity? Consider first the physiological changes in sexual capacity that occur with age, as revealed by the pioneering research of William Masters and Virginia Johnson (1966, 1970). Males are at their peak of sexual responsiveness in their late teens and early 20s and gradually become less responsive thereafter. A young man is easily and quickly aroused; his orgasm is intense; and he may have a refractory, or recovery, period of only minutes before he is capable of sexual activity again. The older man is likely to be slower—slower to arouse, slower to ejaculate after being aroused, and slower to recover afterward. In addition, levels of male sex hormones decline gradually with age in many men. This may contribute to diminished sexual functioning among older men (Schiavi et al., 1991), although most researchers do not believe that hormonal factors fully explain the changes in sexual behavior that most men experience (Kaye, 1993).

Physiological changes in women are far less dramatic. Females reach their peak of sexual responsiveness later than men do, often not until their late 30s. Women are capable of more orgasms in a given time span than men are because they have little or no refractory period after orgasm, and this capacity is retained into old age. As noted in Chapter 5, menopause does not seem to reduce sexual activity or interest for most women. However, like older men, older women typically are slower to become sexually excited. Moreover, some experience discomfort associated with decreased lubrication.

All things considered, the physiological changes that men and women experience don't really explain why many of them become less sexually active in middle and old age. Masters and Johnson concluded that both men and women are physiologically capable of sexual behavior well into old age. Women retain this physiological capacity even longer than men, yet they are the ones who are less sexually active in old age.

Apparently we must turn to factors other than biological aging to explain changes in sexual behavior. In summarizing these factors, Pauline Robinson (1983) quotes Alex Comfort (1974): "In our experience, old folks stop having sex for the same reason they stop riding a bicycle—general infirmity, thinking it looks ridiculous, and no bicycle" (p. 440).

Under the category of infirmity, diseases and disabilities, as well as the drugs prescribed for them, can limit sexual functioning (Clements, 1996; Marsiglio & Donnelly, 1991). This is a particular problem for men, who may become impotent if they have high blood pressure, coronary disease, diabetes, or other health problems. *Mental* health problems are also very important: Many cases of impotence among middle-aged and elderly men are attributable to psychological causes such as stress at work and depression rather than to physiological causes (Felstein, 1983; Persson & Svanborg, 1992).

The second source of problems is social attitudes that view sexual activity in old age as "ridiculous," or at least inappropriate. Old people are stereotyped as sexually unappealing and sexless (or as "dirty old men") and are discouraged from expressing sexual interests. These negative attitudes may be internalized by elderly people, causing them to suppress their sexual desires (Kaye, 1993; Purifoy, Grodsky, & Giambra, 1992). Older females may be even further inhibited by the "double standard of aging," which regards aging in women more negatively than aging in men (Arber & Ginn, 1991).

Third, there is the "no bicycle" part of Comfort's analogy—namely, the lack of a partner, or at least of a willing and desirable partner (Clements, 1996). Most older women are widowed, divorced, or single and face the reality that, for every 100 women, there are only 69 men. Moreover, most of these men are married, and those who are single are very often looking for a younger partner (Robinson, 1983). Lack of a partner, then, is *the* major problem for elderly women, many of

Most older adults continue to be sexual beings who seek love and affection.

whom continue to be interested in sex, physiologically capable of sexual behavior, and desirous of love and affection.

Perhaps we should add one more element to Comfort's bicycle analogy: lack of cycling experience. Masters and Johnson (1966, 1970) proposed a "use it or lose it" principle of sexual behavior to reflect two findings. First, an individual's level of sexual activity early in adulthood predicts his or her level of sexual activity in later life. The relationship is not necessarily causal, by the way; it could simply be that some people are more sexually motivated than others throughout adulthood. A second aspect of the "use it or lose it" rule may well be causal, however: Middle-aged and elderly adults who experience a long period of sexual abstinence often have difficulty regaining their sexual capacity afterward.

In summary, elderly people can continue to enjoy an active sex life if they retain their physical and mental health, do not allow negative attitudes surrounding sexuality in later life to stand in their way, have a willing and able partner, and can avoid long periods of abstinence. It seems likely that elderly people of the future, influenced by trends toward increased sexual permissiveness during this century, will be freer than the elderly people of today to express their sexual selves.

APPLICATIONS: CHANGING GENDER-ROLE ATTITUDES AND BEHAVIOR

Some people believe that the world would be a better place if boys and girls were no longer socialized to adopt traditional masculine or feminine roles, interests, and behaviors. Children of both sexes would then have the freedom to be androgynous; women would no longer suffer from a lack of assertiveness in the world of work, and men would no longer be forced to suppress their emotions. Just how successful are efforts to encourage more flexible gender roles?

In a number of projects designed to change gender-role behavior, children have been exposed to nonsexist films, encouraged to imitate models of cross-sex behavior, reinforced by teachers for trying out cross-sex activities, and provided with nonsexist educational materials (Katz, 1986; Katz & Walsh, 1991). For example, Rebecca Bigler and Lynn Liben (1990) reasoned that, if they could alter children's gender stereotypes, they could head off the biased information processing that stereotypes promote. They exposed 6- to 11-year-olds to a series of problem-solving discussions emphasizing that (1) the most important considerations in deciding who could perform well in such traditionally masculine or feminine occupations as construction worker and beautician are the person's interests and willingness to learn and (2) the person's gender is irrelevant. Compared to children who received no such training, program participants showed a clear decline in occupational stereotyping, especially if they had entered the study with firm ideas about which jobs are for women and which are for men. Moreover, this reduction in stereotyping brought about the predicted decrease in biased information processing: Participants were more likely than nonparticipants to remember counterstereotypic information presented to them in stories (for example, recalling that the "garbage man" in a story was actually a woman).

Yet many efforts at change work in the short run but fail to have lasting effects. Children encouraged to interact in mixed-sex groups revert to their preference for same-sex friends as soon as the program ends (Lockheed, 1986; Serbin, Tonick, & Sternglanz, 1977). Why is it so difficult to change children's thinking? Perhaps because children are groomed for their traditional gender roles from birth and are bombarded with traditional gender-role messages every day. A short-term intervention project may have little chance of succeeding in this larger context. If, on the other hand, the broad social changes of this century continue, children may all react as one 13-year-old did when asked whether a new mother of her acquaintance had delivered a boy or a girl: "Why do you want to know?" (Lorber, 1986, p. 567).

◆◆ SUMMARY POINTS

1. Differences between males and females can be detected in the physical, psychological, and social realms; gender differences arise from an interaction of biological influences and socialization into gender roles (including the learning of gender-role norms and stereotypes).

2. Research comparing males and females indicates that the two sexes are far more similar than different psychologically. The average male is better at spatial and mathematical problem-solving tasks and more aggressive but less adept at verbal tasks than the average female. Males also tend to be more active, assertive, and developmentally vulnerable than females, who tend to be more compliant with adults' requests, tactful, nurturant, and anxious. Most sex differences are small, however, and some are becoming even smaller.

3. During infancy, boys and girls are very similar, but adults treat them differently. By age 2, infants have often gained knowledge of their basic gender identity and display "gender-appropriate" play preferences.

4. Gender typing progresses most rapidly during the toddler and preschool years, with 2- and 3-year-olds already learning gender stereotypes; school-age children are at

first quite rigid and then more flexible in their thinking about gender norms and segregate themselves by sex.

5. Adolescents become intolerant in their thinking about gender-role deviations and, through gender intensification, show increased concern with conforming to gender norms.

6. Theories of gender-role development include the biosocial theory proposed by Money and Ehrhardt, which emphasizes prenatal biological developments but also stresses the importance of how a child is labeled and treated during a critical period for gender identity information. From Freud's psychoanalytic perspective, gender-role development results from the child's identification with the same-sex parent. Social learning theorists focus on differential reinforcement and observational learning. Cognitive perspectives emphasize understanding of gender and active self-socialization: Kohlberg's cognitive-developmental theory emphasizes that children master gender roles once they master the concepts of gender identity, gender stability, and gender consistency; gender schema theory holds that children socialize themselves as soon as they have a basic gender identity and can construct gender schemata. Each theory has some support but none is completely right.

7. Adults are influenced by the changing demands of gender roles. Marriage and parenthood appear to cause men and women to adopt more traditionally sex-typed roles. Freed from the parental imperative, middle-aged and elderly adults tend to experience a shift toward androgyny, blending desirable masculine-stereotyped and feminine-stereotyped qualities (though not switching personalities). Androgyny tends to be associated with good adjustment and adaptability.

8. We are sexual beings from infancy onward. Contrary to Freud's theory, sexual curiosity continues into the latency period; school-age children engage in sex play and appear to experience their first sexual attractions at about age 10.

9. In adolescence, forming a positive sexual identity is an important task, one that can be difficult for those with a gay or lesbian sexual orientation. During this century, we have witnessed increased endorsement of the view that sex with affection is acceptable, a weakening of the double standard, and increased confusion about sexual norms. Although the trend reversed in the 1990s, more adolescents have been engaging in sexual behavior at earlier ages than in the past.

10. Most adults marry and become less sexually active as they get older. Declines in the physiological capacity for sex cannot fully explain declines in sexual activity; poor physical or mental health, lack of a partner, negative societal attitudes, and periods of sexual abstinence also contribute.

11. Attempts to change the gender-role attitudes and behaviors of children have been partially successful but often fail to have lasting effects, perhaps because socialization into traditional roles is so pervasive. Yet societal pressure to adopt narrowly defined gender roles appears to be lessening.

FOOD FOR THOUGHT

1. Jen and Ben are fraternal twins whose parents are determined that they should grow up to be androgynous. Nonetheless, when the twins are only 4, Jen wants frilly dresses and loves to play with her Barbie doll and Ben wants a machine gun and loves to pretend he's a football player and tackle people. Each seems headed for a traditional gender role. Which of the theories in this chapter do you think is most able to explain this, and which has the most difficulty explaining it, and why?

2. Not as many women as men become architects. Drawing on the material in this chapter, discuss the extent to which nature and nurture may be responsible for this, citing evidence.

3. The extent to which males and females differ changes from infancy to old age. When are gender differences in psychological characteristics and roles played in society greatest and when are they least evident—and how would you account for this pattern?

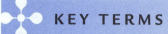
1. *Gender Equity*   This site is focused on the Women's Educational Equity Act and issues surrounding gender equity in education, including the issue of whether single-sex education is a good idea. It links to over 200 other organizations that have some stake in the issues and will give you a sense of what is being done at a national level to ensure equal opportunity for girls and women.
    http://www.edc.org/womensequity/
2. *Sexuality*   The site of Planned Parenthood Federation of America has a wealth of information about sexual and reproductive health, birth control, sexually transmitted diseases, and sex education.
    http://www.plannedparenthood.org

KEY TERMS

gender role
gender-role norm
gender-role stereotype
gender typing
expressive role
instrumental role
social-role hypothesis
gender identity
gender segregation

gender intensification
androgenized females
identification
Oedipus complex
Electra complex
gender stability
gender consistency
gender schema (plural: schemata)

androgyny
parental imperative
androgyny shift
posttraumatic stress disorder
sexual orientation
double standard

CHAPTER 12

Social Cognition and Moral Development

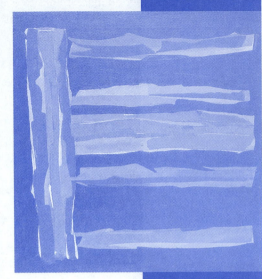

SOCIAL COGNITION
Developing a Theory of Mind
Person Perception
Role-Taking Skills
Social-Cognitive Development in Adulthood

PERSPECTIVES ON MORAL DEVELOPMENT
Moral Affect: Psychoanalytic Theory
Moral Reasoning: Cognitive-Developmental Theory
Moral Behavior: Social Learning Theory

THE INFANT
Early Moral Training
Prosocial Behavior

THE CHILD
Research on Kohlberg's View
Research on Piaget's View
Moral Behavior

THE ADOLESCENT
Changes in Moral Reasoning
Antisocial Behavior

THE ADULT
Moral Development
Religion and Adult Life

KOHLBERG'S THEORY IN PERSPECTIVE
Support for Kohlberg
Factors That Promote Moral Growth
Is the Theory Biased?
Is the Theory Incomplete?

APPLICATIONS: COMBATING YOUTH VIOLENCE
Improving Moral Reasoning
Building Social Information-Processing Skills
Breaking Coercive Cycles

SUMMARY POINTS

FOOD FOR THOUGHT

ON THE WEB

KEY TERMS

Jennifer Ertman and Elizabeth Pena called their parents to say they were on their way home from the pool party they had attended and took a shortcut through a heavily wooded area. They were spotted by six gang members, ages 14 to 18, who had been drinking beer and fistfighting as part of an initiation ritual for two new recruits. The bodies of the girls were found four days later; they had been raped repeatedly and strangled. One gang member, appearing on a television program about gangs just the day before the murders, had said it all: "Human life means nothing." (Ingrassia, 1993)

Roger Lindsay was fishing when he spotted a man in the middle of the lake starting to go under. Without thinking, Roger jumped in and swam out after him, dragged him back to shore, and resuscitated him. What makes his act particularly heroic is that he was wearing a heavy artificial limb, having lost his leg in a motorcycle accident years earlier. (Kreutz, 1991)

Roger Lindsay and the teenagers who killed Jennifer Ertman and Elizabeth Pena all made moral choices—choices that reflected the ways in which they were raised and the kinds of people they had become. How, we wonder, can human beings be capable of such good and yet such bad? In this chapter we continue our examination of the development of the self by exploring how we come to understand the world of people and think through social problems, including issues of right and wrong. When and how do children acquire a set of moral standards, and how do they go about deciding what is right and what is wrong? How do our ways of dealing with moral choices change over the life span? We will begin by setting the development of a sense of morality in the broader context of the development of **social cognition**—thinking about the perceptions, thoughts, emotions, motives, and behaviors of the self and other people (Flavell, 1985).

SOCIAL COGNITION

Infants come to know parents, siblings, and other companions by appearance and form expectations about how their familiar companions will behave. However, infants cannot analyze the personalities of other people or recognize that their companions have their own distinct needs, feelings, and thoughts. These skills are examples of social cognition, which includes thinking not only about individuals—self and others—but about groups and whole social systems. We have already touched on some important aspects of social-cognitive development in this book, seeing, for ex-

ample, that older children think differently than younger children about what they are like as individuals and about how males and females differ. Here we'll focus on developmental changes in the ability to understand human psychology, describe other people, and adopt other people's perspectives.

Developing a Theory of Mind

Imagine that you are a young child and are brought to the laboratory and led through the research scenario portrayed in Figure 12.1. A doll named Sally puts her marble in her basket and leaves the room. While she is gone, Anne moves the marble to her box. Sally returns to the room. Now you are asked the critical question: Where will Sally look for her marble?

This task is called a **false belief task** because it assesses the understanding that people can hold incorrect beliefs and be influenced by these beliefs, wrong though they may be. The task was used in a pioneering study by Simon Baron-Cohen, Alan Leslie, and Uta Frith (1985) to determine whether young children, children with Down syndrome, and children with autism (see Chapter 16) have a **theory of mind.** A theory of mind is the understanding that people have mental states such as desires, beliefs, and intentions and that their behavior is guided ("caused" if you like) by these mental states. Children pass the false belief task in Figure 12.1 and show evidence of having a theory of mind when they say that Sally will look for her marble in the basket (where she *believes* it to be) rather than in the box (where it actually is). Children who have a theory of mind believe that Sally's behavior will be guided by her false belief about the marble's location; they are able to set aside their own knowledge of where the marble ended up after Anne moved it. They have formulated what Chapter 6 described as an *intuitive theory,* here a theory of human psychology that helps them, and most of the rest of us too, explain why people do what they do.

In Baron-Cohen's study, about 85% of both 4-year-olds of normal intelligence and children with Down syndrome passed the false belief task. Yet despite mental ages greater than those of the children with Down syndrome, 80% of the autistic children *failed.* They incorrectly claimed that Sally would look where they knew the marble to be (in the box) rather than where Sally had every reason to believe it was (in the basket).

This study served as the basis for hypothesizing that autistic children experience the severe problems in social interaction that they display because they lack a theory of mind and suffer from a kind of "mind blindness" (Baron-Cohen, 1995). Imagine trying to understand and interact with people if you are unable to appreciate such fundamentals of human psychology as the fact that people look for things where they

1 Sally places her marble in basket

2 Exit Sally

3 Anne transfers Sally's marble to box

4 Re-enter Sally

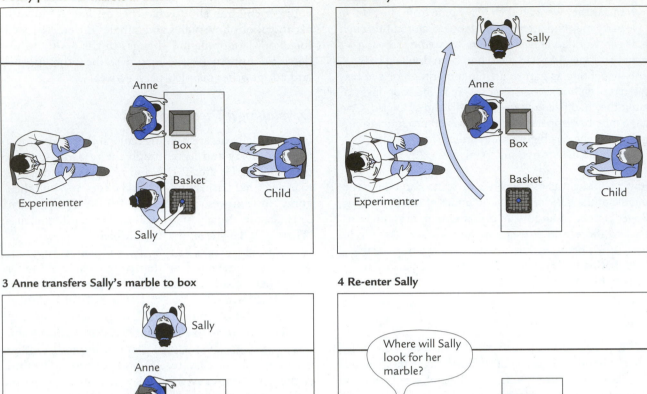

Where will Sally look for her marble?

FIGURE 12.1 *The experimental arrangement in the false belief task involving Sally and Anne. Since Sally does not know that Anne transferred Sally's marble from Sally's basket to Anne's box, she believes it is in her basket and should be predicted to look for it there.* (Adapted from Baron-Cohen et al., 1985)

believe they are, choose things that they want and reject things that they hate, sometimes attempt to plant false beliefs in others, and so on. Temple Grandin, a woman with autism who is intelligent enough to be a professor of animal sciences, describes having to compensate for lack of a theory of mind by creating a memory bank of how people behave and what emotions they express in various situations and then having to "compute" how people might be expected to behave in similar situations (Sacks, 1993). Although she could grasp simple emotions such as happiness, she had trouble understanding more complex ones, and never could quite get what *Romeo and Juliet* was all about. Just as we cannot understand falling objects without employing the concept of gravity, we cannot understand human beings without invoking the

concept of mental states. In all likelihood, the ability to read people's minds proved adaptive to our ancestors and became part of our biological endowment (Mitchell, 1997).

Not only has research on theory of mind stimulated a great deal of thinking about the nature and causes of autism, but it has led many researchers to begin asking when and how normal children develop a theory of mind. Although children normally do not pass false belief tasks until the age of 4 or at the earliest 3, researchers have detected forerunners of a theory of mind as early as the end of the first year of life (Leekam, 1993; Mitchell, 1997). For example, starting at about 9 months of age, infants and their caregivers engage in a good deal of **joint attention,** both looking at the same object at the same time. At this age, in-

Even 1-year-olds show a primitive awareness that other people may have mental states (perceptions) different from their own when they point at objects so that their companions and they can jointly attend to the same object.

fants sometimes point to toys and then look toward their companions, encouraging others to look at what they are looking at. By doing so, infants show an awareness that other people have perceptual experiences and can share perceptions with one another.

And when infants engage in their first simple pretend play between 1 and 2 years of age, pretending to eat from a bowl or to talk on the phone, they show at least a primitive understanding of the difference between pretense (a kind of false belief) and reality. They know the difference between a pretend tea party and a real one, for example. Yet if you pretend to spill pretend tea on the table and hand a 2-year-old a paper towel, he or she will quickly wipe it up, no questions asked (Harris, 1989)!

Children also begin to refer to mental states in their speech starting at around age 2 (Bretherton & Beeghly, 1982). Ross (at 2 years and 7 months) was asked why he keeps asking why, and replied, "I want to say 'why,'" explaining his behavior in terms of his desire; Adam (at 3 years, 3 months of age), said about a bus, "I thought it was a taxi," seemingly aware that he had a false belief (Wellman & Bartsch, 1994, p. 345).

Finally, some research suggests that children as young as 2½ years old will attempt to deceive an adult about which of several containers holds a bag of gold coins and jewels (Chandler, Fritz, & Hala, 1989). They seem capable of trying to plant a false belief in another person once they are given the skills they need to erase telltale footprints leading toward the hiding place and to lay new footprints heading in the wrong direction. They are especially adept at deception if they help to plan it themselves (Chandler & Hala, 1994). Other studies suggest that 3-year-olds are too young to deceive other people deliberately and will lay false tracks even when they are supposed to help

someone find rather than keep someone from finding a prize (Sodian, 1994). The notion that deceit is not possible until age 4 jibes with parents' observations: 77% of the mothers polled in one study claimed that 4-year-olds are capable of deliberately lying, but only 29% thought 3-year-olds have this capacity (Stouthamer-Loeber, 1991).

Children clearly understand perceptions, desires, and pretense before they understand beliefs (Gopnik, Slaughter, & Meltzoff, 1994; Custer, 1996). Henry Wellman (1990) theorizes that children first develop a **desire psychology** at about age 2; they talk about what they want and even explain their own behavior and that of others in terms of wants or desires. They appreciate, for example, that an experimenter who expresses a strong distaste for crackers would rather eat raw vegetables than the crackers the child prefers (Repacholi & Gopnik, 1997).

By age 4, and possibly as early as age 3, children normally progress to a **belief-desire psychology.** Not only do they understand that people's desires guide their behavior, but they begin to pass false belief tasks like the one about Sally and her marble and demonstrate an understanding that beliefs are not always an accurate reflection of reality. They appreciate that people do what they do because they desire certain things and believe that certain actions will help them fulfill their desires. By age 3, children even understand in a rudimentary way how desires and beliefs are linked to emotions (Wellman & Banerjee, 1991). They know that if people want things and get them, they are happy, but if they want things and do not get them, they are sad or disappointed. They appreciate that when people believe that one thing will happen and something else happens instead, they are surprised. Age 3 or 4—researchers disagree—is often cited as the time when children "have" a theory of mind. However, it is better to think of theory of mind as a set of understandings that children begin to develop well before age 3 or 4 and continue to refine long afterwards (Mitchell, 1997).

Developing a theory of mind is partly just a matter of getting older and maturing neurologically and cognitively. Abnormal brain development in children with autism may be the reason for their great difficulty with tasks assessing theory of mind (Bailey, Phillips, & Rutter, 1996). However, acquiring a theory of mind also requires experience interacting with other humans. Children with siblings seem to grasp the elements of a theory of mind earlier than children without siblings (Jenkins & Astington, 1996; Lewis et al., 1996; Perner, Ruffman, & Leekam, 1994). Engaging in pretend play with siblings may help, since this provides practice understanding that belief and reality are not necessarily the same (Taylor & Carlson, 1997; Youngblade & Dunn, 1995). In multichild families, there may also be more talk about mental states ("She thought you finished your ice cream," "He didn't mean to step on your head"), and such discussion may contribute to early mastery of a theory of mind (Dunn et al., 1991). Preschoolers who interact with many adults also do well on theory of mind tasks, though (Lewis et al., 1996). By contrast, even 8-year-old children growing up among the Junin Quechua people of Peru have trouble understanding that beliefs can be false, most likely because the Junin Quechua rarely talk about mental states (Vinden, 1996). Clearly, then, acquiring a theory of mind—the groundwork necessary for all later social-cognitive development—requires both normal neurological and cognitive development and social experiences that require understanding other people's mental states.

Person Perception

Although research on theory of mind tells us that even preschool children are budding psychologists, they still have a way to go to understand other people in terms of their enduring personality traits and to use their knowledge of other people's personalities to predict how they will react and what they will do. In studies of *person perception,* children are asked to describe people they know (parents, friends, disliked classmates, and so on) or to infer people's traits from their behavior. The ways in which young children and older children perceive people differ considerably.

As we discovered in Chapter 10, children younger than 7 or 8 describe themselves primarily in physical rather than psychological terms. Not surprisingly, they describe other people that way too (Livesley & Bromley, 1973; Ruble & Dweck, 1995; Yuill, 1993). Four-year-old Evan says of his father, "He has one nose, one Mom, two eyes, brown hair." Five-year-old Jenny says, "My daddy is big. He has hairy legs and eats mustard. Yuck! My daddy likes dogs—do you?" Not much of a personality profile there!

Young children perceive others in terms of their physical appearance, possessions, and activities. When they use psychological terms at all, the terms are often global, evaluative ones such as "nice" or "mean," "good" or "bad," rather than specific personality trait labels (Livesley & Bromley, 1973; Ruble & Dweck, 1995). Moreover, traits are not yet viewed as enduring qualities that can predict how a person will behave in the future or explain why a person behaves as he or she does (Rholes et al., 1990; Yuill, 1993). The 5-year-old who describes a friend as "dumb" is often using this trait label only to describe that friend's recent "dumb" behavior; he or she may well expect "smart" behavior tomorrow (Rholes & Ruble, 1984; Yuill, 1993). Some researchers do find that young children are able to use information about classmates' previous behavior to predict their future behavior if the task is made simple enough. For example, kindergartners choose peers

they judge to be "smart" as teammates for an upcoming academic contest, but peers they judge to be "nice" when asked to select future playmates (Droege & Stipek, 1993). Still, young children use trait terms more to describe or evaluate behavior than to explain it (Ruble & Dweck, 1995).

Around age 7 or 8, children become more able to "get below the surface" of human beings and infer their enduring psychological traits. Ten-year-old Kim describes her friend Tonya: "She's funny and friendly to everyone, and she's in the gifted program because she's smart, but sometimes she's too bossy." As children reach the age of 11 or 12, they become more likely to make *social comparisons* on important psychological dimensions, noting that one classmate is smarter or shyer than another (Barenboim, 1981). They also make more use of psychological traits to explain why people behave as they do, claiming, for instance, that Mike pulled the dog's tail *because* he's cruel (Gnepp & Chilamkurti, 1988). Clearly, then, children become more psychologically minded as their emerging social-cognitive abilities permit them to make inferences about enduring inner qualities from the concrete behavior they observe in the people around them.

When asked to describe people they know, adolescents offer personality profiles that are even richer in psychological terminology than those provided by children (Livesley & Bromley, 1973; O'Mahony, 1986). They see people as unique individuals with distinctive personality traits, interests, values, and feelings. Moreover, they are able to create more integrated, or organized, person descriptions, analyzing how an individual's diverse and often inconsistent traits fit together and make sense as a whole personality. Dan, for example, may notice that Noriko brags about her abilities at times but seems very unsure of herself at other times, and he may integrate these seemingly discrepant impressions by concluding that Noriko is basically insecure and boasts only to hide that insecurity. Some adolescents spend hours "psychoanalyzing" their friends and acquaintances, trying to figure out what really makes them tick.

Just as was the case with children's descriptions of themselves, then, we can detect a progression in person perception from physical descriptions and global evaluations of other people as good or bad during the preschool years, to more differentiated descriptions that refer to specific personality traits starting at age 7 or 8; and finally to more integrated personality profiles that show how even seemingly inconsistent traits fit together during adolescence.

Role-Taking Skills

Another important aspect of social-cognitive development involves outgrowing the *egocentrism* that Piaget believed characterizes young children (see Chapter 7) and developing **role-taking skills:** the ability to assume another person's perspective and understand his or her thoughts and feelings in relation to one's own. Role-taking skills are essential in thinking about moral issues and appreciating the consequences of one's actions for others; indeed, it is hard to interact with other people without adopting their perspectives now and then. Robert Selman (1976, 1980; Yeates & Selman, 1989) studied role-taking abilities by asking children questions about interpersonal dilemmas:

Holly is an 8-year-old girl who likes to climb trees. She is the best tree climber in the neighborhood. One day while climbing down from a tall tree, she falls . . . but does not hurt herself. Her father sees her fall. He is upset and asks her to promise not to climb trees anymore. Holly promises.

Later that day, Holly and her friends meet Shawn. Shawn's kitten is caught in a tree and can't get down. Something has to be done right away or the kitten may fall. Holly is the only one who climbs trees well enough to reach the kitten and get it down but she remembers her promise to her father. (Selman, 1976, p. 302)

To assess how well a child understands the perspectives of Holly, her father, and Shawn, Selman asks: "Does Holly know how Shawn feels about the kitten? How will Holly's father feel if he finds out she climbed the tree? What does Holly think her father will do if he finds out she climbed the tree? What would you do in this situation?" Children's responses to these questions led Selman (1976) to conclude that role-taking abilities develop in a stagelike manner.

According to Selman, children aged 3 to 6 years are largely egocentric. Unaware of perspectives other than their own, they assume that they and other people see eye to eye. If young children like kittens, for example, they assume that Holly's father does too and therefore will be delighted if Holly saves the kitten.

However, as concrete-operational cognitive abilities emerge, children become better able to consider another person's point of view. By age 8 to 10, for example, they appreciate that two people can have different points of view even if they have access to the same information, they are able to think about their own thoughts and the thoughts of another person, and they realize that their companions can do the same. Thus they can appreciate that Holly may think about her father's concern for her safety but conclude that he will understand her reasons for climbing the tree.

Finally, adolescents who have reached the formal-operational stage of cognitive development roughly at age 12, become capable of mentally juggling multiple perspectives, including the perspective of the "generalized other," or the broader social group. The adoles-

cent thus might consider how fathers *in general* react when children disobey them, while also considering whether Holly's father is similar to or different from the typical father (Selman, 1980; Yeates & Selman, 1989). Adolescents become mental jugglers, then, keeping in the air their own perspective, that of another person, *and* that of an abstract "generalized other" representing a larger social group.

Role-taking skills often come into play when conflicts arise and must be settled. Suppose that 14-year-old Beth is arguing with her parents about whether she should be allowed to go on single dates. If Beth has advanced role-taking skills, she may realize that her parents are motivated by a concern for her welfare and may imagine how "parents in general" and "teenagers in general" would view the issue. Instead of merely pushing her own perspective, she may be able to integrate her perspective and her parents' into a solution that is best for *the relationship*. Thus she may decide that going on double dates until she demonstrates that she is responsible is the best way to balance her interest in freedom with her parents' concerns for her welfare. Not all 14-year-olds are this mature, of course, but Selman has observed considerable growth in the ability to understand and resolve interpersonal conflicts during the adolescent years (Selman et al., 1986).

Adolescents who have advanced role-taking skills are capable of resolving their conflicts with their parents because they can accept the perspectives of their parents and try to seek a mutually beneficial agreement.

What implications do these advances in social cognition have for children's and adolescents' relationships? Important ones. Experience interacting with peers seems to sharpen role-taking skills, and, in turn, sophisticated role-taking skills help make a child a more sensitive and desirable companion. As it turns out, children whose role-taking skills are advanced are more likely than agemates who perform poorly on tests of role taking to be sociable and popular and to have established close friendships with peers (Gnepp, 1989; Kurdek & Krile, 1982; LeMare & Rubin, 1987; McGuire & Weisz, 1982). Good role takers are in a position to infer the needs of others so that they can respond appropriately to those needs (Hudson, Forman, & Brion-Meisels, 1982). Moreover, they are skilled at figuring out how to resolve the disagreements that inevitably arise in peer interactions (Yeates & Selman, 1989).

Social-Cognitive Development in Adulthood

As adults go about the business of life, they too rely on their social-cognitive skills to make sense of other people. As we have seen in earlier chapters, *non*social cognitive abilities, such as those used in testing scientific hypotheses, often improve during early and middle adulthood. Compared with adolescents, who seem to want to force facts into one neat and logical system, some adults become better able to accept contradictions in the real world and are more aware that problems can be viewed from a number of different perspectives (see Chapter 7). However, some elderly people experience declines in performance on tasks that assess nonsocial cognition. Do important social-cognitive skills like the ability to adopt other people's perspectives also increase early in adulthood but decline in later life?

Social cognitive development during adulthood does seem to involve both gains and losses (Blanchard-Fields, 1996; Hess, 1994). Fredda Blanchard-Fields (1986) presented adolescents, young adults, and middle-aged adults with three dilemmas requiring them to engage in role taking and integrate discrepant perspectives: (1) two conflicting historical accounts, (2) a conflict between a teenage boy and his parents over whether he must visit his grandparents with the family, and (3) a disagreement between a man and a woman about an unintended pregnancy. As Figure 12.2 shows, adults—especially middle-aged adults—were better able than adolescents to see both sides of the issues and to integrate the perspectives of *both* parties into a workable solution. Here, then, is evidence that the social-cognitive skills of adults may continue to expand after adolescence. Indeed, through a combination of social experience and cognitive growth, middle-aged adults have the potential to become quite sophisticated students of human psychology. As we

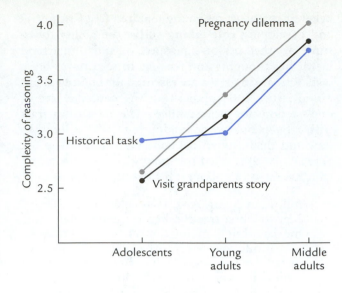

FIGURE 12.2 *Social-cognitive skills increase from adolescence to adulthood. In this study, adolescents had special difficulty applying their social-cognitive skills to the two most emotionally involving vignettes (those about the grandparents and pregnancy).* (Adapted from Blanchard-Fields, 1986)

saw in Chapter 9, a few even gain a kind of wisdom that gives them exceptional insight into the complexity of human problems.

Do elderly people continue to display the sophisticated social-cognitive skills that middle-aged adults display? For the most part, yes. They perform as well as young and middle-aged adults on many social-cognitive tasks (Hess, 1994; Pratt et al., 1991). Yet other studies suggest that, on average, older adults are not always as adept as middle-aged adults at taking others' point of view, integrating different perspectives, and thinking in complex ways about the causes of people's behavior (Blanchard-Fields, 1996; Pratt et al., 1996).

Because longitudinal studies have not been done, we do not know whether age differences reflect real declines with age or generational differences. Besides, these age differences are small. The social-cognitive abilities of adults depend far more on the extent and nature of their social experiences than on their age. Those elderly adults who have the sharpest social-cognitive skills tend to be socially active; they are deeply involved in meaningful social roles such as those of spouse, grandparent, church member, and worker (Dolen & Bearison, 1982). They have opportunities to talk to other people about problems they are experiencing (Pratt et al., 1996). And they are often well-educated and have better than average health (Pratt et al., 1996).

So, individuals may actually gain social-cognitive abilities during adulthood that they did not possess as adolescents, and elderly people may continue to display sophisticated social-cognitive skills as long as they continue to use those skills every day in their social interactions. It is mainly when elderly people become socially isolated or inactive that they seem to experience difficulties in reasoning complexly about personal and interpersonal issues.

Having now examined some important and dramatic changes in social cognition over the life span, let's look more closely at an important area of development in which social-cognitive skills play a critical role—moral development.

PERSPECTIVES ON MORAL DEVELOPMENT

Although we could debate endlessly about what **morality** really is, most of us might agree that the term implies an ability (1) to distinguish right from wrong, (2) to act on this distinction, and (3) to experience pride when one does the right thing and guilt or shame when one does not. Accordingly, three basic components of morality have been identified:

1. An *affective,* or emotional, component, consisting of the feelings (guilt, concern for others' feelings, and so on) that surround right or wrong actions and that motivate moral thoughts and actions.
2. A *cognitive* component, centering on how we think about right and wrong and go about deciding how to behave; this component involves social-cognitive skills like role taking.
3. A *behavioral* component, reflecting how we actually behave when, for example, we experience the temptation to cheat or are called upon to help a needy person.

As it turns out, each of the three major theoretical perspectives on moral development has focused on a different component of morality. So let's briefly see what psychoanalytic theory has to say about moral affect, what cognitive-developmental theory has to say about moral cognition or reasoning, and what social learning theory can tell us about moral behavior.

Moral Affect: Psychoanalytic Theory

What kinds of **moral affects,** or emotions, do you feel if you contemplate cheating or lying? Chances are you experience such negative feelings as shame, guilt, anxiety, and fear of being detected—feelings that keep you from doing things you know are wrong. **Empathy,** the vicarious experiencing of another person's feelings (for example, smiling at the good fortune of another or experiencing another person's distress), is another important moral affect. Empathizing with individuals

Learning to resist the temptation to break moral rules (here, one against biting!) is an important part of moral development.

who are suffering ("feeling their pain") can motivate **prosocial behavior,** positive social acts such as helping or sharing that reflect a concern for their welfare. Positive emotions like pride and self-satisfaction when one has done the right thing are also an important part of morality. We will generally be motivated to avoid negative moral emotions and experience positive ones by acting in moral ways.

Assuming that young infants are unlikely to feel these sorts of moral emotions, when do they arise? Freud's (1935/1960) psychoanalytic theory offered an answer (see Chapter 2). Freud believed that the mature personality has three components: the selfish and irrational id, the rational ego, and the moralistic superego. The *superego,* or conscience, has the important task of ensuring that any plans formed by the ego to gratify the id's urges are morally acceptable. Infants and toddlers, Freud claimed, lack a superego and are essentially "all id." They will therefore act on their selfish motives unless their parents control them.

During the phallic stage (ages 3–6), when children are presumed to experience an emotional conflict over their love for the other-sex parent, the superego is formed. To resolve his *Oedipus complex,* Freud claimed, a boy identifies with and patterns himself after his father, particularly if the father is a threatening figure who arouses fear. Not only does he learn his masculine role in this manner, but he takes on as his own, through the process called **internalization,** his father's moral standards. Similarly, a girl resolves her *Electra complex* by identifying with her mother and internalizing her mother's moral standards. However, Freud believed that girls, because they do not experience the intense fear of castration that boys experience, are not as motivated to resolve their psychic conflict and develop weaker superegos than males do.

Having a superego, then, is like having a parent inside your head—always there, even when someone else isn't, to tell you what is right or wrong and to arouse emotions such as shame and guilt if you so much as think about doing wrong. We can applaud Freud for pointing out that emotion is a very important part of morality, that parents contribute in important ways to moral development, and that children must somehow internalize moral standards if they are to behave morally even when no authority figure is present to detect and punish them.

However, the specifics of Freud's theory are largely unsupported:

1. Cold, threatening, and punitive parents do *not* raise morally mature youngsters; instead, as modern psychoanalytic thinkers appreciate, children form strong consciences when they are securely attached to warm and responsive parents (Emde et al., 1991; Kochanska, 1997b).
2. Males do *not* appear to have stronger superegos than females.
3. Moral development begins well before the phallic stage, as we will see shortly.
4. Children who are 6 or 7 years old, and who have presumably achieved moral maturity by resolving their Oedipal conflicts, have *not* completed their moral growth.

Although Freud's broad themes have merit, it may be time to lay the particulars of his theory of moral development to rest.

Moral Reasoning: Cognitive-Developmental Theory

Cognitive developmentalists study morality by looking at the development of **moral reasoning**—the thinking process that occurs when we decide whether an act is right or wrong. Jean Piaget and theorists influenced by him assume that moral development depends on social-cognitive development and unfolds through a series of stages. To cognitive-developmental theorists, what is really of interest is *how we decide* what to do, not what we decide or what we actually do. A young child and an adult might both decide not to steal a pen that is there for the taking, but the reasons they give for their decision might be entirely different.

Piaget's Theory

Piaget (1932/1965) studied children's concepts of the nature of rules by asking Swiss children about their games of marbles, and he explored children's concepts of justice by presenting them with moral dilemmas to ponder. For example, he told children about two boys, John, who accidentally knocked over a tray of 15 cups while coming to dinner as requested, and Henry, who broke only one cup while sneaking jam from the cupboard. The key question he posed was which child was naughtier and why.

From children's responses to such questions, Piaget formulated a theory of moral development that generated a good deal of research (see Lapsley, 1996). Basically, Piaget claimed the following:

1. Preschool children are "premoral" and have little awareness or understanding of rules.
2. Children between the ages of about 6 and 10 take rules dead seriously, believing that rules are handed down by parents and other authority figures and are sacred and unalterable. They also believe that rule violations are wrong to the extent that they have damaging consequences, even if the violator had good intentions (as the boy who broke 15 cups did).
3. At the age of 10 or 11, most children enter a final stage of moral development in which they begin to appreciate that rules are agreements between individuals—agreements that can be changed through a consensus of those individuals. In judging actions, they pay more attention to whether an actor's intentions were good or bad, seeing Henry, the misbehaving boy who broke one cup, as naughtier than John, the well-intentioned boy who broke 15.

According to Piaget, progress through these stages depends on both cognitive maturation and social experience, especially with peers. He actually believed that peers contribute more to moral development than parents do because peers are equals and must learn to take one another's perspectives and resolve disagreements among themselves fairly.

Kohlberg's Theory

Inspired by Piaget's pioneering work on moral development, Lawrence Kohlberg (1963, 1981, 1984; Colby & Kohlberg, 1987) formulated the cognitive-developmental theory that has come to dominate the study of moral development (Lapsley, 1996).[1] He began

[1] Lawrence Kohlberg was born in 1927 and died in 1987. He put his own moral principles into action as a youth by helping to transport Jewish refugees from Europe to Israel after World War II. He devised his theory of moral development as a doctoral student at the University of Chicago and then spent most of his career at Harvard studying moral development and promoting moral education (Green, 1989).

his work by asking 10-, 13-, and 16-year-old boys questions about various moral dilemmas to assess how they were thinking about these issues. Careful analysis of the responses led Kohlberg to conclude that moral growth progresses through a universal and invariant sequence of three broad moral levels, each of which is composed of two distinct stages. Each stage grows out of the preceding stage and represents a more complex way of thinking about moral issues. Kohlberg insists that people cannot skip stages and will not regress to earlier stages once they have reached higher stages in the sequence.

Think about how you would respond to the following moral dilemma posed by Kohlberg and his colleagues:

> There was a woman who had very bad cancer, and there was no treatment known to medicine that would save her. Her doctor, Dr. Jefferson, knew that she had only about 6 months to live. She was in terrible pain, but she was so weak that a good dose of a pain killer like ether or morphine would make her die sooner. She was delirious and almost crazy with pain, and in her calm periods she would ask Dr. Jefferson to give her enough ether to kill her. She said she couldn't stand the pain and she was going to die in a few months anyway. Although he knows that mercy killing is against the law, the doctor thinks about granting her request. (Colby, Kohlberg, Gibbs, & Lieberman, 1983, p. 79)

What do you think? Should Dr. Jefferson give her the drug that would make her die? Why or why not? Should the woman have the right to make the final decision? Why or why not? These are among the questions that people are asked after hearing the dilemma. Remember, Kohlberg's goal is to understand *how* an individual thinks, not whether he or she is for or against providing the woman with the drug. Individuals at each stage of moral reasoning might well endorse *either* of the alternative courses of action, but for different reasons. Kohlberg's three levels of moral reasoning, and the two stages within each level, are as follows:

Level 1: Preconventional morality.
At the level of **preconventional morality,** rules are really external to the self rather than internalized. The child conforms to rules imposed by authority figures in order to avoid punishment or to obtain personal rewards. The perspective of the self dominates: What is right is what one can get away with or what is personally satisfying.

Stage 1: Punishment-and-obedience orientation. The goodness or badness of an act depends on its consequences. The child will obey authorities to avoid punishment but may not consider an act wrong if it will not be punished. The greater the harm done or the more severe the punishment, the more "bad" the act is.

Stage 2: Instrumental hedonism. A person at the second stage of moral development conforms to rules in order to gain rewards or satisfy personal needs. There is some concern for the perspectives of others, but it is ultimately motivated by the hope of benefit in return. "You scratch my back and I'll scratch yours" is the guiding philosophy.

Level 2: Conventional morality.
At the level of **conventional morality,** the individual *has* internalized many moral values. He or she strives to obey the rules set forth by others (parents, peers, the government) in order to win their approval and recognition for good behavior or to maintain social order. The perspectives of other people are clearly recognized and given serious consideration.

Stage 3: "Good boy" or "good girl" morality. What is right is now that which pleases, helps, or is approved by others. People are often judged by their intentions, "meaning well" is valued, and being "nice" is important.

Stage 4: Authority and social-order-maintaining morality. Now what is right is what conforms to the rules of legitimate authorities. The reason for conforming is not so much a fear of punishment as a belief that rules and laws maintain a social order that is worth preserving. Doing one's duty and respecting law and order are valued.

Level 3: Postconventional morality.
At the third and final level of moral reasoning, **postconventional morality,** the individual defines what is right in terms of broad principles of justice that have validity apart from the views of particular authority figures. The individual may distinguish between what is morally right and what is legal, recognizing that some laws—for example, the racial segregation laws that Dr. Martin Luther King, Jr., challenged—violate basic moral principle. Thus the person transcends the perspectives of particular social groups or authorities and begins to take the perspective of *all* individuals.

Stage 5: Morality of contract, individual rights, and democratically accepted law. At this "social contract" stage, there is an increased understanding of the underlying purposes served by laws and a concern that rules be arrived at through a democratic consensus so that they express the will of the majority or maximize social welfare. Whereas the person at Stage 4 is unlikely to challenge an established law, the Stage-5 moral reasoner might call for democratic change in a law that compromises basic rights. The principles embodied in the U.S. Constitution illustrate Stage-5 morality.

BOX 12.1

Sample responses to the mercy-killing dilemma at Kohlberg's three levels of moral reasoning

Preconventional Morality

Give the drug:

Stage 1: Dr. Jefferson should give the terminally ill woman a drug that will kill her because there is little chance that he will be found out and punished and he would not have to live with her agony anymore.

Stage 2: Dr. Jefferson should give her the drug because he might benefit from the gratitude of her family in the long run if he does what she wants. He should think of it as the right thing to do if it serves his purposes.

Do not give the drug:

Stage 1: The doctor runs a big risk of losing his license and being thrown in prison if he gives her the drug.

Stage 2: Besides, he really has little to gain personally by taking such a big chance. If the woman wants to kill herself, that's her business, but why should he help her if he stands to gain little in return?

Conventional Morality

Give the drug:

Stage 3: Most people would understand that the doctor was motivated by concern for the woman rather than by self-interest. They would be able to forgive him for what was essentially an act of kindness. (*Note:* Many Stage 3 thinkers would be likely to disapprove of mercy killing, however.)

Stage 4: The doctor should give the woman the drug because of the Hippocratic oath, which spells out a doctor's duty to relieve suffering. This oath should be taken seriously by all doctors.

Do not give the drug:

Stage 3: Most people are likely to disapprove of mercy killing. Dr. Jefferson would clearly lose the respect of his colleagues and friends if he administered the drug. A good person simply would not do this.

Stage 4: Mercy killing is against the laws that we as citizens are obligated to uphold. The Bible is another compelling authority, and it too says, "Thou shalt not kill." Dr. Jefferson simply can't take the law into his own hands; instead, he has a duty to uphold the law.

Postconventional Morality

Give the drug:

Stage 5: Although most of our laws have a sound basis in moral principle, laws against mercy killing do not. The doctor's act is morally justified in that it relieves the suffering of an agonized human being. Yet, if Dr. Jefferson breaks the law in the service of a greater good, he should still be willing to be held legally accountable because society would be damaged if everyone simply ignored laws they do not like.

Stage 6: One must consider the effects of this act on everyone concerned— the doctor, the dying woman, other terminally ill people, all people everywhere. Basic moral principle dictates that all people have a right to dignity and self-determination, as long as others are not harmed by their decisions. Assuming that no one else will be hurt, then, the dying woman has a right to live and die as she chooses. The doctor is doing right by respecting her integrity as a person and saving her, her family, and all of society from needless suffering.

Do not give the drug:

Stage 5: The laws against mercy killing protect citizens from harm at the hands of unscrupulous doctors and should be upheld. If the laws were to be changed through the democratic process, that might be another thing. But right now the doctor can best serve society by adhering to them.

Stage 6: If we truly adhere to the principle that human life should be valued above all else and all lives should be valued equally, it is morally wrong to "play God" and decide that some lives are worth living and others are not. Before long we would have a world in which no life has value.

Stage 6: Morality of individual principles of conscience. At this "highest" stage of moral reasoning, the individual defines right and wrong on the basis of self-formulated principles that are broad and universal in application. The Stage-6 thinker does *not* just make up whatever principles he or she happens to favor but instead arrives at abstract principles of respect for all individuals and their rights that *all* religions or moral authorities might view as compelling and fair. Kohlberg (1981) described Stage-6 thinking as a kind of "moral musical chairs" in which the person facing a moral dilemma is able to take the perspective or "chair" of each and every person or group that could potentially be affected by a decision and arrive at a solution that would be regarded as just from every "chair." Stage 6 is Kohlberg's vision of ideal moral reasoning, but it is so rarely observed that Kohlberg stopped attempting to measure its existence.

In Box 12.1 we present examples of how people at the preconventional, conventional, and postconventional levels might reason about the mercy-killing dilemma. Progress through Kohlberg's stages of moral reasoning depends in part on the development of perspective-taking abilities (Selman, 1980). Specifically, as individuals become more able to consider perspectives other than their own, moral reasoning progresses from a rather egocentric focus on personal welfare at the preconventional level, to a concern with the perspectives of other people (parents, friends, and even members of the society in which one lives) at the conventional level, and, ultimately, to a concern with what is right from the perspective of *all* people at the postconventional level.

Moral Behavior: Social Learning Theory

Social learning theorists such as Albert Bandura (1986, 1991) and Walter Mischel (1974) have been primarily interested in the behavioral component of morality—in what we actually *do* when faced with temptation. These theorists claim that moral behavior is learned in the same way that other social behaviors are learned: through reinforcement and punishment and through observational learning. They also consider moral behavior to be strongly influenced by the nature of the specific situations in which people find themselves. That is, a person may behave morally in one situation but transgress in another or proclaim that nothing is more important than honesty but then lie.

To highlight the difference between social learning theory and other perspectives, let's see how different theorists might attempt to predict whether a teenager (Waldo, we'll call him) will cheat on his upcoming math test. Freud would certainly want to know whether Waldo feared and identified strongly with his father in early childhood. If he did, presumably he has developed a strong superego as part of his personality and therefore will be less likely to cheat, lie, or steal than a child with a weak superego (unless, of course, his father had a weak superego).

Piaget and Kohlberg, meanwhile, would be interested in Waldo's cognitive development and, specifically, in the stage at which he reasons about moral dilemmas. Although Kohlberg insists that one's level of moral reasoning does not necessarily predict which decision one will make, Kohlberg would at least expect Waldo's mode of decision making to be consistent across many moral situations. Moreover, since Kohlberg believes that each higher stage permits a more adequate way of making moral decisions, he might expect the child whose moral reasoning is advanced to be less likely to cheat than the child who still thinks at the preconventional level. Notice, then, that both the psychoanalytic perspective and the cognitive-developmental perspective view morality as a kind of personality trait—a quality that each of us possesses and that consistently influences our judgments and actions.

What might social learning theorists say about Waldo? They would be curious about the moral habits he has learned and the expectations he has formed about the probable consequences of his actions. If Waldo's parents, for example, have consistently reinforced him when he has behaved morally and punished him when he has misbehaved, he will be more likely to behave in morally acceptable ways than a child who has not had adequate moral training. Waldo will also be better off if he has been exposed to many models of morally acceptable behavior rather than brought up in the company of liars, cheaters, and thieves. Like Freudians, social learning theorists view parents as important socialization agents. Rather than focusing on the emotional relationship between parent and child and the identification process, though, they are more concerned about the opportunities for observational learning and reinforcement and punishment that parents provide.

And yet social learning theorists are skeptical of the notion that morality is a single, highly consistent trait or mode of thinking that will show itself in all situations. Even if Waldo's parents have taught him to be honest, for example, that learning may not generalize well to the math class when Waldo faces an opportunity to cheat. Moreover, *situational* influences in the math class might have more influence on Waldo's behavior than his prior learning. What if it is obvious to him that he stands no chance of being caught and punished? What if his friend Willard promises to get him a date on Friday night (a powerful reinforcer) if he joins a cheating conspiracy? What if he observes his classmates cheating on the test and sees that they are getting away with it?

In sum, the social learning perspective on moral development holds that morality is *situation-specific behavior* rather than a generalized trait such as a strong superego or a postconventional mode of moral reasoning. Influenced by specific learning experiences, we do acquire moral (or immoral) habits that express themselves in situations in which it is possible to cheat, lie, steal, help a person in need, and so on. And yet each specific moral situation we encounter also affects our behavior.

We are now ready to trace the development of morality from infancy to old age. Our coverage charts the development of the self as a moral being, examining moral affect, cognition, and behavior as they have been conceptualized by psychoanalytic, cognitive-developmental, and social learning theorists.

THE INFANT

Do infants have any sense of right or wrong? If a baby takes a toy that belongs to another child, would you label the act stealing? If an infant hits another child in

the head with a toy, would you insist that the infant be put on trial for assault? Of course not. Adults in our society, including psychologists, view infants as **amoral**—that is, lacking any sense of morality. Since we do not believe that infants are capable of evaluating their behavior in the light of moral standards, we do not hold them morally responsible for any wrongs they commit (although we certainly attempt to prevent them from harming others). Nor do we expect them to be "good" when we are not around to watch them. Yet it is now clear that these initially amoral creatures begin to learn fundamental moral lessons during their first two years of life (Emde et al., 1991; Gralinski & Kopp, 1993; Kochanska, 1993).

Early Moral Training

Moral socialization begins early. Roger Burton (1984) relates how his daughter Ursula, age 1½, was so taken by the candy that she and her sisters had gathered on Halloween that she snatched some from her sisters' bags. The sisters immediately said, "No, that's mine," and conveyed their outrage in the strongest terms. A week later the sisters again found some of their candy in Ursula's bag and raised a fuss, and it was their mother's turn to explain the rules to Ursula. The problem continued until finally Burton himself came upon Ursula in a bedroom looking at some forbidden candy. Ursula looked up and said, "No, this is Maria's, not Ursula's" (p. 199).

It is through such social learning experiences, accumulated over the years, that children come to understand moral rules and standards. Children must learn two lessons, really: (1) to experience negative emotions

when they violate rules, and (2) to control their impulses to engage in prohibited behaviors (Kochanska, 1993). Ursula and other young children learn from being reprimanded to associate the act of stealing with negative emotional responses. As they near the age of 2, children are already beginning to show visible signs of distress when they break things or otherwise violate standards of behavior (Cole, Barrett, & Zahn-Waxler, 1992; Kagan, 1981; Kochanska, 1993). Made to think that they have caused a doll's head to fall off, some toddlers even show signs of guilt, as opposed to mere distress, and try to make amends (Kochanska, Casey, & Fukumoto, 1995). This means 18- to 24-month-old children are beginning to internalize rules and to anticipate disapproval when they fail to comply with them. They are also able, at least to a limited degree, to exert the self-control it takes to resist the temptation to engage in forbidden behaviors (Kochanska, Murray, & Coy, 1997).

Parents contribute to moral socialization by establishing rules, reacting to children's rule-breaking behavior, and working toward mutual understandings of what is acceptable and what is not (Emde et al., 1991; Gralinski & Kopp, 1993). If parents are firm but not harsh as they attempt to get toddlers to comply with their demands, these young children are likely to become cooperative rather than defiant and will become able to control their own behavior even when parents are not around (Crockenberg & Litman, 1990).

The approach to socialization adopted by parents is not the only important influence on early moral development, however. The child's temperament may interact with the parents' approach to influence outcomes. Grazyna Kochanska (1995, 1997a) has discovered that the children who are easiest to socialize are temperamentally *fearful,* or inhibited (see Chapter 10); they are hesitant to try things like jumping on a trampoline or trying on an ape mask, and they become highly anxious when they are reprimanded. As a result, they can be socialized effectively to refuse to touch toys they are not to touch and to comply cheerfully with requests through a gentle approach to discipline—one that capitalizes on their anxiety but does not terrorize them so much that they cannot pay attention to the lesson they are to learn (Kochanska, 1995).

Other toddlers, though, are *fearless,* or uninhibited; they are not very emotionally reactive to mild reprimands (but will not internalize their parents' rules if they are treated harshly, either). Fearless children are most likely to learn to comply with rules and requests when their parents are warm and responsive and create a secure attachment bond that makes children want to cooperate with and please their parents (Kochanska, 1997a). Most children are more eager to comply with adults with whom they have secure, give-and-take relationships than with adults who are insensitive to their needs (Kochanska, 1997b). However, a secure attachment seems to be especially critical in motivating fearless children, as fear tactics do not work on them.

Here, then, is another example of the importance of the *goodness of fit* between a child's temperament and his or her social environment. Children with a fearful temperament respond best to gentle persuasion and mild discipline that makes them anxious (but not too anxious), whereas fearless children, not bothered much by reprimands, respond to warm, responsive parenting that makes them want to cooperate. Given appropriate socialization, most toddlers will internalize many rules of conduct and acquire the beginnings of a moral sense.

Prosocial Behavior

Not only are infants capable of internalizing rules of behavior, but they are not quite so selfish, egocentric, and unconcerned about other people as Freud, Piaget, Kohlberg, and many other theorists have assumed. Perhaps the strongest evidence of this comes from studies of empathy and prosocial behavior. Even newborns display a very primitive form of empathy: they become distressed by the cries of other newborns (Hoffman, 1988; Martin & Clark, 1982). It is unlikely that they really distinguish between another infant's distress and their own, though. Moreover, they are not yet capable of acting on their primitive empathy by behaving altruistically to relieve another's distress (Hoffman, 1981).

Instead, the capacity to act prosocially emerges in the second year of life. Carolyn Zahn-Waxler and her colleagues (1992) report that over half of the 13- to 15-month-old infants they studied were observed to engage in at least one act of prosocial behavior—helping, sharing, expressing concern, comforting, and so on. These behaviors became increasingly common from age 1 to age 2, when all but one child in the study acted prosocially. Consider the reaction of 21-month-old John to his distressed playmate, Jerry:

> Today Jerry was kind of cranky; he just started . . . bawling and he wouldn't stop. John kept coming over and handing Jerry toys, trying to cheer him up. . . . He'd say things like "Here, Jerry," and I said to John "Jerry's sad; he doesn't feel good; he had a shot today." John would look at me with his eyebrows wrinkled together like he really understood that Jerry was crying because he was unhappy. (Zahn-Waxler, Radke-Yarrow, & King, 1979, pp. 321–322)

Overall, then, infants are amoral in some senses, particularly when it comes to making judgments of right and wrong. Yet, at the same time, their "moral socialization" has begun, they internalize rules of conduct and become distressed when they violate the rules, and they already show the rudiments of empathy, an important motivator of moral behavior that may well be part of our species heredity as human beings (Hoffman, 1993).

THE CHILD

During the years from age 2 to age 12, children's standards of morality and their motivation to live up to these standards grow out of their social experiences in the family, peer group, and wider society. Research on moral development during childhood has explored how children of different ages think about moral issues and has tested some of the ideas of Piaget and Kohlberg. It has also told us a good deal about how children actually behave when their moral values are tested.

Research on Kohlberg's View

The hypothetical moral dilemmas that Lawrence Kohlberg devised to assess stages of moral reasoning (for example, the mercy-killing dilemma presented earlier) are too complex for preschool children to understand, but they have been given to school-age children. These children generally reason at the preconventional level, taking an egocentric perspective on morality and defining as right those acts that are rewarded and as wrong those acts that are punished (Colby et al., 1983). At best, they are beginning to make the transition to conventional moral reasoning by displaying a Stage-3 concern with being a "good boy" or a "good girl" who gains the approval of others.

FIGURE 12.3 *Examples of drawings used by Nelson to convey an actor's intentions to preschool children. Here we see negative intent and a negative consequence.* (From Nelson, 1980)

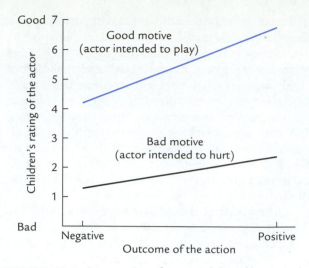

FIGURE 12.4 *Average ratings of an actor's behavior for actors who had either good or bad intentions and produced either positive or negative outcomes* (From Nelson, 1980)

In short, from Kohlberg's perspective most children, and especially young children, are not really moral beings yet, for they have not yet adopted conventional societal values as their own. Kohlberg's stages seem to be more useful in describing the moral reasoning of adolescents and adults than in describing that of young children. However, other researchers have looked more closely at some of Piaget's claims about the moral reasoning of young children and find that both Kohlberg and Piaget may have underestimated the child's ability to think about right and wrong.

Research on Piaget's View

Consistent with Piaget's theory of moral development, children gain a deeper understanding of rules as they get older, and their levels of moral reasoning depend on their levels of cognitive development (Lapsley, 1996). At the same time, however, it has become clear that Piaget, like Kohlberg, failed to appreciate the ability of preschool and young grade school children to consider the intentions behind people's actions and to appreciate the distinction between moral rules and more arbitrary rules.

Ignoring Intentions?

Consider Piaget's claim that young children judge acts as right or wrong on the basis of their consequences rather than the intentions that guided them. As it turns out, his moral-decision story about John and Henry and the cups was flawed. It asked whether a child who causes a small amount of damage in the service of bad intentions (the boy who broke one cup while misbehaving) is naughtier than a child who causes a large amount of damage despite good intentions (the boy who broke 15 cups while obeying his mother). It therefore did not allow a clear separation of the effects of consequences and intentions on the child's thinking.

Sharon Nelson (1980) overcame this flaw in an interesting experiment. Three-year-olds listened to stories in which a character threw a ball to a playmate.

The actor's motive was described as *good* (his friend had nothing to play with) or *bad* (the actor was mad at his friend), and the consequences of his act were either *positive* (the friend caught the ball and was happy to play with it) or *negative* (the ball hit the friend in the head and made him cry). To make the task even simpler, Nelson showed children drawings of what happened (see Figure 12.3 for an example).

Not surprisingly, the 3-year-olds in the study judged acts that had positive consequences more favorably than acts that caused harm. However, as Figure 12.4 illustrates, they also judged the well-intentioned child who had wanted to play more favorably than the child who intended to hurt his friend, *regardless of the consequences of his actions*. Apparently, then, even very young children can base their moral judgments on *both* an actor's intentions and the consequences of his or her act (see also Bussey, 1992). Indeed, as we saw earlier, preschool children have formulated a theory of mind and know enough about intentions to cry, "I didn't mean it! I didn't mean it!" when they stand to be punished. Overall, Piaget was correct to conclude that young children assign more weight to consequences and less weight to intentions than older children do, but he was wrong to conclude that young children are incapable of weighing both factors at once when they evaluate others' conduct (Lapsley, 1996; Zelazo, Helwig, & Lau, 1996).

Viewing Rules as Sacred?

Piaget also claimed that 6- to 10-year-old children view rules as sacred prescriptions laid down by respected authority figures. These moral absolutes cannot be questioned or changed. However, Elliot Turiel (1978, 1983) has observed that children actually distinguish between two kinds of rules in daily life:

(1) **moral rules,** or standards that focus on the welfare and basic rights of individuals, and (2) **social-conventional rules,** standards determined by social consensus that tell us what is appropriate in a particular social setting. Moral rules include rules against hitting, stealing, lying, and otherwise harming others or violating their rights. Social-conventional rules are more like rules of social etiquette and include the rules of games as well as school rules that forbid eating snacks in class or using the restroom without permission.

Even preschool children understand that moral and social-conventional rules are different and that moral rules are more compelling and unalterable (Nucci & Nucci, 1982; Smetana, Schlagman, & Adams, 1993). Judith Smetana (1981), for example, discovered that children as young as age 2 ½ regard moral transgressions such as hitting, stealing, or refusing to share as much more serious and deserving of punishment than social-conventional violations such as not staying in one's seat in nursery school or not saying grace before eating. Even more remarkable is what these youngsters said when asked if a violation would be okay if there were no rule against it: They claimed that it was *always* wrong to hit people or commit other moral transgressions, rule or no rule, but they felt that it would be perfectly okay for children to get out of their seats at nursery school or violate other social conventions in the absence of any explicit rules.

Moreover, 6- to 10-year-old children, who should be even more likely than preschool children to regard the laws laid down by adults as "sacred," are very capable of questioning adult authority (Tisak & Tisak, 1990). These children claim that it is perfectly fine for parents to enforce rules against stealing and other moral violations, but they believe that it can be inappropriate and unjustifiable for parents to arbitrarily restrict their children's friendships. And they maintain that not even God can proclaim that stealing is morally right and make it so (Nucci & Turiel, 1993). It turns out that school-age children will not blindly accept any dictate offered by an authority figure as legitimate.

Overall, then, it seems that both Piaget and Kohlberg failed to appreciate how much moral growth takes place in early childhood. Both regarded young children as selfish and amoral creatures who have not yet internalized rules of moral conduct and cannot be expected to behave morally. Yet we now know that even toddlers learn rules of conduct, experience moral emotions such as guilt and empathy, and behave in prosocial ways. And we know that even preschool children are quite capable of judging acts as right or wrong according to whether the actor's intentions were good or bad, even though they do often put more weight on an act's consequences than on the motives behind it. In addition, they do not view *all* rules as absolute, sa-

cred, and unchangeable, for they realize that social-conventional rules are more arbitrary and less binding than moral rules, and they challenge adult authority when they believe it is illegitimate. Young children have by no means completed their moral growth, but they are well on their way to becoming moral beings long before late childhood and early adolescence, the periods that Piaget and Kohlberg mark as the time of substantial moral growth.

Moral Behavior

To many people, the ultimate goal of moral socialization is to produce a child who not only has internalized moral rules but will abide by them. Can children be trusted to abide by rules? Will they cheat if they think they can get away with it? What factors influence whether or not a child will behave morally? These are just the sorts of questions that social learning theorists have asked, and their findings add greatly to our understanding of moral development and how it can be fostered.

Consider a classic study of moral behavior reported by Hugh Hartshorne and Mark May (1928–1930). Their purpose was to investigate the moral character of 10,000 children (ages 8–16) by tempting them to lie, cheat, or steal in a variety of situations. It readily became apparent that almost all children espoused "sound" moral values, claiming that honesty was good, that cheating and stealing were wrong, and so on. Yet children who cheated or violated other moral rules in a particular situation were just as likely as those who did not to state that cheating is wrong. Moreover, most children *did* violate their own moral rules in at least one situation. In other words, Hartshorne and May had a tough time finding children who not only espoused the right values but consistently acted according to those values. Most children's moral behavior was quite inconsistent from situation to situation; correlations between the tests of stealing, lying, and other forms of misconduct were low, ranging from .00 to no more than about .40.

Reanalyses of these data and new investigations suggest that children are somewhat more consistent in their behavior than Hartshorne and May had concluded (Burton, 1963; Nelson, Grinder, & Mutterer, 1969; Rushton, 1980). Across a set of situations, some children tend to be more honest, more likely to resist temptation, or more helpful than other children. Still, moral thought, affect, and behavior are not as closely interrelated in childhood as they will be by adolescence or adulthood (Blasi, 1980).

Why are children relatively inconsistent in their moral behavior? One explanation may be that they are reasoning at Kohlberg's preconventional level. When punishment and reward are the primary considerations in defining acts as right or wrong, perhaps it is

Although it is often difficult to tell whether children are working together or using each other's work, most youngsters can be tempted to cheat if the situational factors are right. Children's moral conduct is fairly inconsistent from situation to situation.

not surprising that the child may see nothing much wrong with cheating when the chances of detection and punishment are slim. In addition, as social learning theorists would emphasize, moral inconsistency results from *situational* influences on behavior such as the importance of the goal that can be achieved by transgressing, the probability of being detected, and the amount of encouragement provided by peers (Burton, 1976). How, then, can parents best raise a child who can be counted on to behave morally in most situations?

How Does One Raise Moral Children?

Social learning theorists would advise parents who want to foster moral maturity in their children to *reinforce moral behavior, punish immoral behavior, and serve as models of moral behavior.* Reinforcement can be used to strengthen prosocial behaviors such as sharing or to teach children acceptable alternatives to acts one wants to discourage (Fischer, 1963; Perry & Parke, 1975). Punishment of misdeeds, including a loud "No" or a critical comment, can also contribute to moral growth if it is not overly harsh, if it teaches children to associate negative emotions with their wrongdoing, if it is accompanied by an explanation of why the forbidden act is wrong and should be avoided, and if it is supplemented by efforts to encourage and reinforce more acceptable behavior (Perry & Parke, 1975; see also Chapter 8). The problem with punishment, especially severe physical punishment, is that it may have undesirable side effects (such as making children resentful or overly anxious or teaching them that aggression is an appropriate means of solving problems).

Finally, social learning theorists emphasize that parents should serve as models of moral behavior. Children usually will follow the example of an adult who resists temptation (Toner, Parke, & Yussen, 1978). They are especially likely to do so if the model states the rule he or she is following and a rationale for not committing the prohibited act (Grusec, Kuczynski, Rushton, & Simutis, 1979) and if the model is someone with whom they have a close relationship (Grusec & Goodnow, 1994).

The important work of Martin Hoffman (1970, 1983, 1988) has provided additional insights into how to foster not only moral behavior but moral thought and affect as well. Several years ago, Hoffman (1970) reviewed the child-rearing literature to determine which parental approaches were associated with high levels of moral development. Three major approaches were compared:

1. **Love withdrawal:** withholding attention, affection, or approval after a child misbehaves—or, in other words, creating anxiety by threatening a loss of reinforcement from parents.
2. **Power assertion:** using power to administer spankings, take away privileges, and so on—in other words, using punishment.
3. **Induction:** explaining to a child why the behavior is wrong and should be changed by emphasizing how it affects other people.

Suppose that little Ronnie has just put the beloved family cat through a cycle in the clothes dryer. Using love withdrawal, a parent might say, "How could you do something like that? I can't even bear to look at you!" Using power assertion, a parent might say "Get to your room this minute; you're going to catch it." Using induction, a parent might say "Ronnie, look how scared Fluffy is. You could have killed her, and you know how sad we'd all be if she died." Induction, then, is a matter of providing rationales or explanations that focus special attention on the consequences of wrongdoing for other people (or cats, as the case may be).

Which approach best fosters moral development? As you can see in Table 12.1, induction is more often positively associated with children's moral maturity than either love withdrawal or power assertion (Brody & Shaffer, 1982). The use of power assertion is actually more often associated with moral *immaturity* than with moral maturity, although one recent study suggests that the negative effects of punishment are more evident among white children than among African-American children (Deater-Deckard et al., 1996). Love withdrawal has been found to have positive effects in some studies but negative effects in others.

Why is induction particularly effective? By explaining *why* an act is wrong, parents can (1) communicate

TABLE 12.1

Relationships between parents' use of three disciplinary strategies and children's moral development

	Type of Discipline		
Direction of Relationship between Parents' Use of a Disciplinary Strategy and Children's Moral Maturity	*Love Withdrawal*	*Power Assertion*	*Induction*
Positive correlation	8	7	38
Negative correlation	11	32	6

NOTE: Table entries represent the number of occasions on which a particular disciplinary technique was found to be associated (either positively or negatively) with a measure of children's moral affect, reasoning, or behavior.
SOURCE: Adapted from Brody & Shaffer (1982)

standards and provide children with cognitive rationales that they can use to evaluate their own behavior, (2) help children empathize with the individuals they may have hurt and associate moral emotions such as guilt and shame with their wrongdoing, and (3) point out what the child should have done instead. In short, induction calls attention to the cognitive, affective, and behavioral aspects of morality and may help children to integrate them.

Hoffman's work provides a fairly clear picture of how parents can best contribute to the moral growth of their children. Yet we must also appreciate that a particular moral socialization technique can have different effects, depending on the particular misdeed, child, and parent involved (Grusec & Goodnow, 1994). For example, a child's temperament helps to determine how morally trainable he or she is and even what approach to moral training parents use. As we saw earlier, Grazyna Kochanska (1993) has found that some children are, by temperament, more fearful than others and therefore are more likely to become appropriately anxious and distressed when they are disciplined. In addition, some children are less impulsive than others and therefore are more able to inhibit their urges to engage in wrongdoing (Kochanska et al., 1997).

Children who are high in emotionality but low in impulsivity are relatively easy to socialize using positive disciplinary techniques such as induction. They get nervous if they think they might be punished, and they are able to stop themselves from misbehaving. As a result, their parents are likely to use induction frequently and may not have much need to resort to power assertion (Keller & Bell, 1979). Children who are not easily led to associate guilt and other negative emotions with their wrongdoings or who have difficulty controlling their impulses appear to drive parents to use more power-assertive (and ineffective) dis-

cipline (Anderson, Lytton, & Romney, 1986; Lytton, 1990). Such children are difficult to socialize by any means. Clearly, then, parents affect children, but children also affect parents as moral socialization proceeds.

THE ADOLESCENT

As adolescents gain the capacity to think about abstract and hypothetical ideas and as they begin to chart their future identities, many of them reflect a great deal on their values and moral standards. Others do not reflect enough, it seems, and end up behaving in antisocial ways.

Changes in Moral Reasoning

Although most teenagers break the law now and then, adolescence is actually a period of considerable growth in moral reasoning and a time when many individuals become increasingly motivated to behave morally. Consider first the results of a 20-year longitudinal study that involved repeatedly asking the 10-, 13-, and 16-year-old boys originally studied by Kohlberg to respond to moral dilemmas (Colby et al., 1983). Figure 12.5 shows the percentage of judgments offered at each age that reflected each of Kohlberg's six stages.

A number of interesting developmental trends can be seen here. Notice that the preconventional reasoning (Stage 1 and 2 thinking) that dominates among 10-year-olds decreases considerably during the teen years, when conventional reasoning (Stages 3 and 4) is becoming the dominant mode of moral thinking. So, among 13- to 14-year-olds, most moral judgments reflect either a Stage-2 (instrumental hedonism) approach—"You scratch my back and I'll scratch

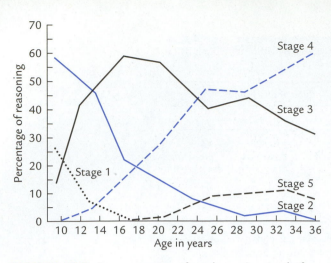

FIGURE 12.5 *Average percentage of moral reasoning at each of Kohlberg's stages for males from age 10 to age 36* (From Colby et al., 1983)

yours"—or a Stage-3 ("good boy"/"good girl") concern with being nice and earning approval. Over half of the judgments offered by 16- to 18-year-olds embodied Stage-3 reasoning, but about a fifth were scored as Stage-4 (authority and social-order-maintaining morality) arguments. These older adolescents were beginning to take a broad societal perspective on justice and were concerned about acting in ways that would help maintain the social system.

Where are all the postconventional moral reasoners? Kohlberg's work suggests that postconventional reasoning does not appear until early adulthood in our society. In short, the main developmental trend in moral reasoning during adolescence is a shift from preconventional thinking to more conventional reasoning. It is during adolescence that most individuals seem to rise above a concern with external rewards and punishments and begin to express a genuine concern with living up to the moral standards that parents and other authorities have taught them and ensuring that laws designed to make human relations orderly and fair are taken seriously and maintained.

William Damon and Daniel Hart (1992) have observed another important breakthrough in moral development during adolescence: Many teens begin to view morality as an important part of their identity. Because adolescents are more sensitive than children to the expectations of those around them, they are more motivated to portray and view themselves as honest, fair, and caring individuals. Many come to feel that they would lose self-respect if they selfishly ignored others' needs (Eisenberg et al., 1991). A few even become moral leaders who devote their lives to achieving social justice (Colby & Damon, 1992).

In short, most adolescents have clearly internalized conventional moral values, and many are highly motivated to be the kinds of moral beings that people around them want them to be. But what about those adolescents who seem to have no moral values at all?

Antisocial Behavior

Although most adolescents are law abiding most of the time, a small minority of youth, like the gang members mentioned at the beginning of this chapter, are involved in serious antisocial conduct—muggings, rapes, armed robberies, knifings, drive-by shootings. Might adolescents who engage repeatedly in aggressive, antisocial acts be cases of arrested moral development who have not internalized the conventional values of society? Studies do suggest that juvenile offenders are more likely than nondelinquents to engage in preconventional, egocentric, moral reasoning (Gregg, Gibbs, & Basinger, 1994; Trevethan & Walker, 1989). Some offenders clearly lack a sense of right and wrong and feel little remorse about their criminal acts. Yet the relationship between moral reasoning and antisocial behavior is weak; a sizable number of delinquents are capable of conventional moral reasoning but commit illegal acts anyway (Blasi, 1980). This suggests that we must consider a wider range of factors to understand the origins of antisocial conduct.

Dodge's Social-Information Processing Model

Kenneth Dodge has advanced our understanding by offering a social information-processing model of social behavior that has been used most often to analyze contributors to aggressive behavior (Crick & Dodge, 1994; Dodge, 1986, 1993). Imagine that you are walking down the aisle in a classroom and trip over a classmate's leg. As you fall to the floor, you are not quite sure what happened. Dodge and other social information-processing theorists believe that the individual's reactions to frustration, anger, or provocation depend not so much on the social cues present in the situation as on the ways in which the person processes and interprets this information.

An individual who is provoked (as by being tripped) progresses through six steps in information processing, according to Dodge:

1. *encoding* (taking in information),
2. *interpretation* (making sense of this information and deciding what caused the other person's behavior),
3. *clarification of goals* (deciding what one wants to achieve in the situation),
4. *response search* (thinking of possible actions to achieve the goal),
5. *response evaluation* (weighing the pros and cons of these alternative actions), and
6. *behavioral enactment* (doing something).

TABLE 12.2

The six steps in Dodge's social information-processing model and likely responses to provocation by a highly aggressive youth

Step	Behaviors	Likely Response of Aggressive Youth
1. Encoding of cues	Search for, attend to, and register cues in the situation	Focus on cues suggesting hostile intent; ignore other relevant information
2. Interpretation of cues	Interpret situation; infer other's motive	Infer that provoker had hostile intent
3. Clarification of goals	Formulate goal in situation	Make goal to retaliate
4. Response search	Generate possible responses	Generate few options, most of them aggressive
5. Response evaluation	Assess likely consequences of responses generated; choose the best	See advantages in responding aggressively rather than nonaggressively (or fail to evaluate consequences at all, act impulsively)
6. Behavioral enactment	Produce chosen response; act	Behave aggressively

NOTE: Social information processors make use of a database of information about past social experiences, social rules, and social behavior at each step of the process and skip around from step to step. See Crick & Dodge (1994) for further details and relevant research.

We do not necessarily go through these steps in precise order; we can cycle back and forth among them or work on two or more simultaneously (Crick & Dodge, 1994). And at any step, we may draw not only on information available in the immediate situation but on a stored database that includes memories of previous social experiences and information about the social world.

As you might imagine, the skills involved in carrying out these six steps in social information processing improve with age (Dodge & Price, 1994). Older children are more able than younger ones to do such things as encode all the relevant cues in a situation, accurately interpret cues to determine what caused another person to behave as he or she did, generate a range of responses, and carry off intended behaviors skillfully. Why, then, are some children of a given age more aggressive than others?

Highly aggressive youth, including adolescents incarcerated for violent crimes (Slaby & Guerra, 1988), show deficient or biased information processing at every step in Dodge's model (Dodge, 1993; Slaby & Guerra, 1988). For example, a highly aggressive adolescent who is tripped by a classmate is likely to (1) process relatively few of the available cues in the situation and show a bias toward information suggesting that the tripping was deliberate rather than accidental (for example, noticing a fleeting smirk on the classmate's face); (2) make an *attribution of hostile intent*, inferring from the information gathered that the classmate meant to cause harm; (3) set a goal of getting even (rather than, for example, a goal of smoothing relations); (4) think of only a few possible ways to react, mostly aggressive ones; (5) conclude, after evaluating alternative actions, that an aggressive response will have favorable outcomes (or perhaps not

think enough about the negative consequences of aggression); and (6) carry out the particular aggressive response selected (see Table 12.2).

Many aggressive youths also skip steps of the model and act impulsively, "without thinking"; they respond automatically on the basis of their data bank of past experiences. These youth tend to see the world as a hostile place and are easily angered. If a situation is ambiguous (as a tripping or bumping incident is likely to be), they are more likely than nonaggressive youth to attribute hostile intent to whoever harms them (Crick & Dodge, 1994; Slaby & Guerra, 1988). Indeed, some respond so automatically that they are ready to fight even when no harm was intended *and* they correctly perceive that no harm was intended (Waldman, 1996)!

In addition, aggressive youth tend to evaluate the consequences of aggression far more positively than other adolescents do. They expect their aggressive acts to achieve the desired results, view being "tough" and controlling others as important to their self-esteem, and feel morally justified in acting because they believe they are only retaliating against individuals who are "out to get them" (Coie et al., 1991; Quiggle et al., 1992).

Dodge's social information-processing model is helpful in understanding why children and adolescents might be provoked to behave aggressively in particular situations. However, it leaves somewhat unclear the extent to which the underlying problem is how one thinks (how skilled one is at processing social information), whether one thinks (how impulsive one is, how much one's emotions rule), or what one thinks (for example, whether one believes that other people are hostile and that aggression pays). Finally, only recently have Dodge and his colleagues begun to

BOX 12.2

Reactive and proactive aggressors

In studying the social information processing of aggressive children, Kenneth Dodge and his colleagues began to notice two distinct types of aggression (Crick & Dodge, 1996; Dodge et al., 1997). **Reactive aggression** is a "hot" form of aggression that occurs when a person is frustrated and highly aroused and lashes out in anger. Reactive aggressors blow up when they are provoked and are known for their hot tempers. They overattribute hostile intent to others, even in ambiguous situations, and then they retaliate quickly, without enough consideration of the consequences of their actions (Crick & Dodge, 1996). **Proactive aggression** is a more cold-blooded, deliberate kind of aggression designed to achieve instrumental goals such as getting valued resources and dominating others. Proactive aggressors consciously decide to bully or harm others because they expect their displays of force to work and get them what they want.

In a recent study, Dodge and a number of colleagues (1997) tested some of their thinking about the developmental experiences that might underlie reactive and proactive aggression. They studied boys and girls classified on the basis of teachers' reports as reactive aggressors, proactive aggressors, pervasive aggressors who showed both types of aggression, and nonaggressors. The children were studied from kindergarten to third grade.

Reactive aggressors tended to have problems paying attention and controlling their impulses, and they had often been exposed to harsh discipline or even physical abuse at home. Dodge and his collaborators were able to show that abuse early in childhood was linked to reactive aggression later in childhood, perhaps because these children learned early to expect others to be hostile toward them. In a second study involving chronically violent boys, the researchers found that reactive aggressors became aggressive earlier in life than proactive aggressors and had more emotional problems.

By contrast, proactive aggressors could not easily be distinguished from the nonaggressive children. They did not seem to have as many problems with impulse control or poor social information processing as reactive aggressors did, and their family situations were not unusual. What was missing from the study, though, was an attempt to collect information about these children's reinforcement histories in hopes of explaining how they came to expect aggression to have positive consequences. If they were frequently reinforced by parents or peers for fighting back or being "tough," or if they simply learned through experience that they could dominate others through brute force, simple social learning principles might explain their behavior.

Much remains to be learned about the developmental histories of chronically aggressive children. The unfortunate truth is that many aggressive children go on to engage in delinquency as adolescents and in crime and explosive behavior as adults (Huesmann et al., 1984; Newman et al., 1997). Dodge's work suggests that reactive aggressors need to be protected from abusive parents and taught to control their anger and to react less impulsively and more thoughtfully in social situations. Proactive aggressors may be easier to treat, in that they mainly need to learn that aggression does not pay in the long run and that there are better ways to achieve their goals.

explain how aggressive and nonaggressive individuals come to have such different information-processing styles in the first place. The interesting research in Box 12.2 gives us some hints, as does the research described below.

Contributors to Aggression

Severe antisocial behavior is most likely the product of an interplay between genetic predisposition and social learning experiences. Twin studies suggest that some individuals are genetically predisposed to have hostile, irritable temperaments and to engage in aggressive, delinquent, and criminal behavior. Genetic differences between people account for as much as half of the variation among them in aggression (Miles & Carey, 1997). This does *not* mean that certain people are doomed to become antisocial individuals, however, for the social environments in which they are raised also play a crucial role in determining their conduct.

What social influences are important? Some cultural contexts are more likely to breed aggression than others. In Japan, children are taught very early to value social harmony; even during the preschool years, Japanese children are less angered by interpersonal conflicts and less likely to react to them aggressively than American children are (Zahn-Waxler et al., 1996). By contrast, children in the United States see violence glorified on television every day and live in a country that leads all industrialized countries in rapes and murders (Wolff, Rutten, & Bayer, 1992). In addition, rates of violent crime are over three times higher in lower socioeconomic neighborhoods and communities than in middle-class ones (Elliott & Ageton, 1980). In these neighborhoods, norms support the use of violence to resolve conflicts, and the stresses of daily life make it difficult for parents to monitor and manage their children (Jagers, Bingham, & Hans, 1996; McLoyd, 1990). A poor African-American child living in a single-parent family is much less likely

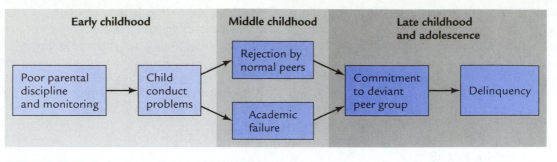

FIGURE 12.6 *Patterson's model of the development of antisocial behavior starts with poor discipline and coercive cycles of family influence.* (Adapted from Patterson et al., 1989)

to become an aggressive, delinquent teenager in a middle-class neighborhood than in a lower-class one (Kupersmidt et al., 1995).

Then there are family influences on aggression. Gerald Patterson and his colleagues have found that highly antisocial children and adolescents often experience **coercive family environments** in which family members are locked in power struggles, each trying to control the others through coercive tactics such as threatening, yelling, and hitting (Dishion et al., 1991; Patterson, DeBaryshe, & Ramsey, 1989). Parents find that they can stop their children's misbehavior, temporarily at least, by threatening, yelling, and hitting, while children learn that they can get their parents to lay off by throwing a temper tantrum and fighting back. But as both parents and children come to rely more and more on coercive tactics, parents increasingly lose control over their children's behavior until even the loudest lectures and hardest spankings have little effect.

The next steps in the making of an antisocial adolescent are predictable (see Figure 12.6): The child, already aggressive and unpleasant to be around, ends up performing poorly in school and being rejected by other children. By default, he or she becomes involved in a peer group made up of other low-achieving, antisocial, and unpopular youths and then is steered even further in the direction of a delinquent career by these colleagues in crime (Dishion et al., 1991, 1995). There are signs that the effects of unaffectionate and coercive parenting are stronger for boys than for girls (McFadyen-Ketchum et al., 1996), but there is a good deal of support for the basic view that ineffective parenting is a major contributor to the development of aggression (Kazdin, 1995).

In sum, the severe antisocial behavior that some adolescents display is more than a matter of immature moral reasoning, although many delinquent youth do reason at Kohlberg's preconventional level. Antisocial behavior can also be traced to deficiencies in social information-processing skills that make youngsters quick to attribute hostile intentions to other people and

convinced of the value of aggression. This information-processing style, in turn, may be rooted both in genetically influenced temperamental traits and in social learning experiences in the family (coercive family environments), peer group, and wider society. All these factors help to determine whether youth enter adulthood as model citizens or menaces to society.

THE ADULT

Adults assume responsibilities as parents, work supervisors, and community leaders, so their moral decisions affect not only their own lives but those of people around them. How does moral thinking change during adulthood, and what role do religious beliefs play in the moral thinking of adults?

Moral Development

As we have discovered already (see Figure 12.5, p. 346), Kohlberg's postconventional moral reasoning appears to emerge *only* during the adult years (if it emerges at all). In Kohlberg's 20-year longitudinal study (Colby et al., 1983), the large majority of adults in their 30s still reasoned at the conventional level, although many of them had shifted from Stage 3 to Stage 4. A minority of individuals—one-sixth to one-eighth of the sample—had begun to use Stage-5 postconventional reasoning, showing a deeper understanding of the basis for laws and distinguishing between just and unjust laws. Clearly there is moral growth in early adulthood (Rest, Thoma, & Edwards, 1997; Walker, 1989). Do these trends continue into later adulthood, or do older adults instead revert to less mature forms of moral reasoning?

Most studies suggest that there are no real age differences in stage of moral reasoning, at least when relatively educated adults are studied and when the age groups compared have similar levels of education (Chap, 1985–1986; Pratt et al., 1991, 1996). Older adults seem to reason as complexly as younger adults do, whether they are given Kohlberg's hypothetical dilemmas to ponder or are asked to discuss real-life situations in which they were "unsure about the right thing to do" (Pratt et al., 1991). Even when their skills are tracked longitudinally over a four-year period, they show no declines in moral thinking and perform just as well as young adults (Pratt et al., 1996). Here, then, is an aspect of social-cognitive development that holds up very well in later life.

Religion and Adult Life

James Fowler (1981, 1991) has argued that religious development closely parallels moral development as described by Kohlberg. His interviews with individuals ranging in age from 3 to 84 indicate that children think very concretely about the religious images to which they are exposed; that adolescents and adults formulate more abstract belief systems of their own; and that a few middle-aged and elderly adults progress to a kind of universalizing faith in which they transcend specific belief systems and achieve a sense of oneness with all beings.

Many of us believe that religion plays an increasingly central role in people's lives and moral thinking as they get older. Although many older individuals are indeed highly religious, there is actually little change from middle age to late old age in the tendency to view religion as important and as greatly comforting (Blazer & Palmore, 1976; McFadden, 1996; Palmore, 1981). In other words, research offers no support for the idea that people "get religion" or cling to it more strongly as they approach death. In fact, poor health forces some elderly people to cut back on their participation in organized religious activities, although many of them compensate with increased involvement in private religious activities such as prayer and Bible study (Ainlay & Smith, 1984; Young & Dowling, 1987).

As it turns out, those older adults who *do* remain highly involved in religion appear to be happier and better adjusted than those who do not (Blazer & Palmore, 1976; Coke, 1992). Religion seems to be especially important to the well-being of elderly African Americans and other minority elders (Hatch, 1991); for many of them, religion serves as a key means of coping with life's problems (McFadden, 1996). Although we cannot be sure that the relationship between religious involvement and well-being is causal, old and young alike seem to have a greater sense of well-being if they believe that life has purpose and meaning than if they do not (Reker, Peacock, & Wong, 1987).

In short, adults have the potential for both moral and religious growth during early and middle adulthood and are then likely to maintain the levels of moral reasoning and religious commitment in old age that they established earlier. Kohlberg (1973) himself argued that experience confronting moral issues and taking responsibility for one's decisions during a lifetime may help adults form more coherent philosophies of life and continue their growth as moral beings.

KOHLBERG'S THEORY IN PERSPECTIVE

Kohlberg's theory of moral development has dominated research in this area for many years. We have now seen that children think about hypothetical moral dilemmas primarily in a preconventional manner, that adolescents adopt a conventional mode of moral reasoning, and that a minority of adults progress to the postconventional level. Kohlberg appears to have discovered an important developmental progression in moral thought. But let's now complete our discussion of moral development by evaluating Kohlberg's influential theory, examining both its supporting evidence and its criticisms.

Support for Kohlberg

As you'll recall, Kohlberg claims that his stages form an invariant and universal sequence of moral growth. Do all people progress through the stages in precisely the order Kohlberg specified? It appears that they do, to a point. Longitudinal studies of moral growth in Turkey, Israel, and the United States demonstrate this (see Colby & Kohlberg, 1987; Rest et al., 1997). Regardless of their culture, individuals do not skip stages. Moreover, only about 5% of them regress from a higher stage to a lower stage from one testing to the next, and these instances of regression are so few that they probably reflect scoring errors.

However, the idea that everyone progresses through Stages 1 to 4 in order is better supported than the idea that people continue to progress from Stage 4 to Stages 5 and 6. Stage 3 or 4 is the end of the developmental journey for most individuals worldwide (Snarey, 1985). And, contrary to Kohlberg's view that each person is guided by one coherent way of viewing moral issues, most people continue to draw on the thinking of lower stages of moral reasoning even after they have advanced to higher stages. In one study (Wark & Krebs, 1996), 85% of the adults studied reasoned at more than one stage across three different moral dilemmas. How people reason turns out to be highly influenced by contextual factors, especially the nature of the particular moral dilemmas they face.

Factors That Promote Moral Growth

How much support is there for Kohlberg's thinking about the factors that contribute to moral growth? Basically, he has argued, as Piaget did, that two influences are most important: cognitive growth and relevant social experiences.

Cognitive Growth

What kind of cognitive growth is necessary? The preconventional reasoner adopts an egocentric, very concrete perspective on moral issues. To reach the conventional stage of moral reasoning and become concerned about living up to the moral standards that significant others transmit, an individual must be capable of taking other people's perspectives (Walker, 1980). Gaining the capacity for postconventional or "principled" moral reasoning requires still more cognitive growth—namely, a solid command of formal-operational thinking (Tomlinson-Keasey & Keasey, 1974; Walker, 1980). The person who bases moral judgments on abstract principles must be able to reason abstractly and take all possible perspectives on a moral issue. Both perspective-taking abilities and more general cognitive abilities appear to be *necessary but not sufficient* for moral growth, however. In other words, not all proficient role takers have reached the conventional level of moral reasoning, and not all formal operators progress to the postconventional level. It is just that these milestones in moral development cannot be achieved without the requisite cognitive skills.

Relevant Social Experience

The second major influence on moral development proposed by Kohlberg is relevant social experience. What social experiences matter? Kohlberg stressed the need for experiences that require people to take the perspectives of others so that they can appreciate that they are part of a larger social order and that moral rules reflect a consensus of individuals in society. Interacting with people who hold views different from one's own also creates *cognitive disequilibrium,* or a conflict between existing cognitive structures and new ideas, which in turn stimulates new ways of thinking.

Like Piaget, Kohlberg felt that interactions with peers or equals, in which children experience differences between their own and others' perspectives, probably contribute more to moral growth than one-sided interactions with adult authority figures in which children are expected to defer to the adults. Parents might make some contribution to moral development, Kohlberg believed, if they provide their children with role-taking opportunities, but they have no special role to play.

Contrary to Piaget's and Kohlberg's claim, parents play a very significant role in moral development, and not just by using inductive discipline and being warm, supportive parents. For example, adolescents who display advanced levels of moral reasoning, especially if they are girls, tend to have parents whose own moral reasoning is advanced (Speicher, 1994). And Lawrence Walker and John Taylor (1991) found that the children who show the most moral growth have parents who, during discussions of moral dilemmas, encourage them to clearly state their positions, paraphrase those positions in a warm and supportive way, and offer more advanced moral arguments that the children can compare to their own arguments. As Piaget and Kohlberg believed, however, parents may slow moral development when they are authoritarian in their approach, challenging the child's judgments and presenting their own ideas in a lecturelike way as lessons to be learned (Walker & Taylor, 1991).

Although parents are more important than Piaget and Kohlberg believed, they were right to call attention to the role of peers in moral development. Children do seem to think more actively and deeply about their own and their partners' moral ideas in discussions with peers than in talks with their mothers or other adults; moreover, discussions with peers are more likely to stimulate moral growth (Kruger, 1992; Kruger & Tomasello, 1986). There seems to be something special about hashing out disagreements with one's equals and having to take their perspectives. Presumably college students' "bull sessions" with their friends, in which they debate the pros and cons of the burning issues of the day, contribute to their moral growth.

Another important kind of social experience is advanced schooling. Consistently, adults who go on to college and receive many years of education think more complexly about moral issues than those who are less educated (Pratt et al., 1991; Speicher, 1994). Advanced educational experiences not only contribute to cognitive growth but also provide exposure to the diverse ideas and perspectives that produce cognitive conflict and soul searching.

Finally, simply participating in a complex, diverse, and democratic society can stimulate moral development. Just as we learn the give-and-take of mutual perspective taking by discussing issues with our friends, we learn in a diverse democracy that the opinions of many groups must be weighed and that laws reflect a consensus of the citizens rather than the arbitrary rulings of a dictator. Indeed, cross-cultural studies suggest that postconventional moral reasoning emerges primarily in Western democracies; people in rural villages in underdeveloped countries show no signs of it (Snarey, 1985). Individuals in these homogeneous communities may have less experience

with the kinds of political conflicts and compromises that take place in a more complex society and so may never have any need to question conventional moral standards.

In sum, Kohlberg not only devised a stage sequence that appears to have universal applicability but he also correctly identified some of the major factors that determine how far an individual progresses in the sequence. Advanced moral reasoning is most likely if the individual has acquired the necessary cognitive skills (particularly perspective-taking skills and, later, the ability to reason abstractly). Moreover, an individual's moral development is highly influenced by social learning experiences, including interactions with parents, discussions with peers, exposure to higher education, and participation in democracy.

Is Kohlberg's theory of moral development sound, then? Not entirely, say the critics. Whenever a theory arouses the enormous interest that Kohlberg's has aroused, you can bet that it will also provoke an enormous amount of criticism (see Lapsley, 1996). Many of the criticisms have centered on the possibility that Kohlberg's theory is biased against certain groups of people and on the fact that it says much about moral reasoning but little about moral affect and behavior.

Is the Theory Biased?

Some critics have charged that Kohlberg's theory reflects a cultural bias, a liberal bias, and/or a sexist bias. That is, it has been said that the stage theory unfairly makes people from non-Western cultures, people with conservative values, or the half of the human race that is female appear to be less than morally mature.

Culture Bias?

Although research indicates that children and adolescents in all cultures proceed through the first three or four of Kohlberg's stages in order, we have seen that postconventional reasoning as Kohlberg defines it simply does not exist in some societies. Critics charge that Kohlberg's highest stages reflect a Western ideal of justice, making the stage theory biased against people who live in non-Western societies or who do not value individualism and individual rights highly enough to want to challenge society's rules (Gibbs & Schnell, 1985; Shweder, Mahapatra, & Miller, 1990). People in societies that emphasize social harmony and place the good of the group ahead of the good of the individual may be viewed as conventional moral thinkers in Kohlberg's system but may actually have very sophisticated concepts of justice (Snarey, 1985; Tietjen & Walker, 1985). The theme that moral development can vary considerably from society to society is explored further in Box 12.3.

Liberal Bias?

Similarly, critics charge that a person must hold liberal values—for example, opposing capital punishment or supporting civil disobedience in the name of human rights—in order to be classified as a postconventional moral reasoner. In one study (de Vries & Walker, 1986), 100% of the college students who showed signs of postconventional thought opposed capital punishment, whereas none of the men and only a third of the women who were transitional between Stage 2 and Stage 3 moral reasoning opposed capital punishment. As de Vries and Walker (1986)

BOX 12.3

Cultural differences in moral thinking

Is each of the following acts wrong? If so, how serious a violation is it?

1. A young married woman is beaten black and blue by her husband after going to a movie without his permission despite having been warned not to do so again.
2. A brother and sister decide to get married and have children.
3. The day after his father dies, the oldest son in a family gets a hair-cut and eats chicken.

These are three of 39 acts presented by Richard Shweder, Manamohan Mahapatra, and Joan Miller (1990, pp. 165–166) to children aged 5 to 13 and adults in India and the United States. You may be surprised to learn that Hindu children and adults rated the son's having a haircut and eating chicken after his father's death as among the most morally offensive of the 39 acts they rated, and the husband's beating of his disobedient wife was not considered wrong at all. American children and adults, of course, viewed beating one's wife as far more serious than breaking seemingly arbitrary rules about appropriate mourning behavior. Although Indians and Americans could agree that a few acts, like brother/sister incest, were serious moral violations, they did not agree on much else.

Moreover, Indian children and adults viewed the Hindu ban against behavior disrespectful of one's dead father as a universal moral rule; they thought it would be best if everyone in the world followed it, and they strongly disagreed that it would be acceptable to change the rule if most people in their society wanted to change it. For similar reasons, they believed that it is a serious moral offense for a widow to eat fish or wear brightly colored clothes or for a woman to cook food for her family or touch her children during her menstrual period. To orthodox Hindus, rules against such behavior are re-

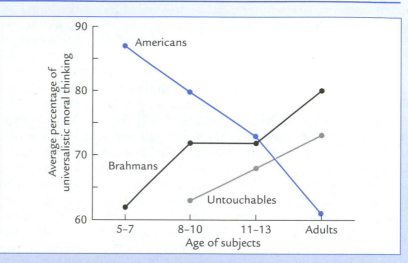

Universalistic moral thinking—the tendency to view rules of behavior as universally valid and unalterable—increases with age among Hindu children in India but decreases with age in the United States. The course of moral development is likely to be different in different societies. (From Shweder in Stigler et al., 1990)

quired by natural law; they are not just arbitrary social conventions created by members of society. Hindus also regard it as morally necessary for a man to beat his disobedient wife in order to uphold his obligations as head of the family.

What effects do cultural beliefs of this sort have on moral development? The developmental trend in moral thinking detected in India was very different from that observed in the United States, as the figure above shows. With age, Indian children saw more and more issues as matters of universal moral principle, whereas American children saw fewer and fewer issues as matters of universal principle (and more and more as matters of arbitrary social convention that can legitimately differ from society to society). Moreover, even the youngest children in both societies expressed moral outlooks very similar to those expressed by adults in their own society and very different from those expressed by either children or adults in the other society.

From these cross-cultural findings, Shweder calls into question Kohlberg's claims that all children everywhere con-

struct similar moral codes at similar ages and that certain universal moral principles exist. In addition, Shweder questions Turiel's claim that children everywhere distinguish from an early age between moral rules and social-conventional rules, for Shweder found that the concept of social-conventional rules was simply not very meaningful to Indians of any age.

Overall, then, these findings challenge the cognitive-developmental position that important aspects of moral development are universal. They tend instead to support a social learning or contextual perspective on moral development, suggesting that children's moral judgments are shaped by the social context in which they develop (see also Haidt, Koller, & Dias, 1993). Perhaps children all over the world think in more and more complex ways about moral issues as they get older, as Kohlberg claimed, but at the same time adopt quite varied notions about what is right and what is wrong, as Shweder claims.

note, it could be that opposition to capital punishment is a more valid moral position than support of capital punishment in that it involves valuing life highly. However, it could also be that the theory is unfair to conservatives who emphasize law-and-order principles (Lapsley et al., 1984).

Gender Bias?

Criticisms of culture bias and liberal bias may have some merit, but no criticism of Kohlberg has stirred more heat than the charge that his theory is biased against women. Carol Gilligan (1977, 1982, 1993) has been disturbed by the fact that Kohlberg's stages were based on interviews with males and that, in some studies, women seemed to be the moral inferiors of men, reasoning at Stage 3 when men usually reasoned at Stage 4. She hypothesizes that females develop a distinctly *feminine* orientation to moral issues, one that is no less mature than the orientation adopted by most men and incorporated into Kohlberg's theory. Gilligan suggests that boys, who are traditionally raised to be independent, assertive, and achievement oriented, come to view moral dilemmas as conflicts between the rights of two or more parties and to view laws and other social conventions as necessary for resolving these inevitable conflicts (a perspective reflected in Kohlberg's Stage-4 reasoning). Girls, Gilligan argues, are brought up to be nurturant, empathic, and concerned with the needs of others and to define their sense of "goodness" in terms of their concern for other people (a perspective that approximates Stage 3 in Kohlberg's scheme). Differences in socialization result in two separate but equal ways of thinking about moral problems: a "masculine" **morality of justice** (in which laws defining individual rights prevail) and a "feminine" **morality of care** (in which one's responsibility for the welfare of other people is most central).

At this point there is little support for Gilligan's claim that Kohlberg's theory is systematically biased against females. Most studies indicate that women reason just as complexly about moral issues as men do when their answers are scored by Kohlberg's criteria (Walker, 1995; Wark & Krebs, 1996). If anything, females are quicker to progress to the conventional level of moral reasoning during early adolescence (Garmon et al., 1996). Moreover, although Gilligan's interviews with women about abortion suggested that they applied a morality of care (Gilligan, 1982), most studies do not support her view that males and females think differently about morality (Lapsley, 1996; Walker, 1989). Several studies do indicate that, when asked to cite moral dilemmas they have actually faced, women are more likely than men to mention problems in interpersonal relationships and then sometimes show more care-based reasoning than men (Pratt et al., 1991; Skoe et al., 1996; Wark & Krebs, 1996). As it

turns out, though, *both* men and women use a lot of care-based reasoning when they face dilemmas involving relationships, and both lean toward justice-based reasoning when issues of rights arise. The nature of the moral dilemma is far more important than the gender of the moral reasoner (Wark & Krebs, 1996).

Finally, there is little support for Gilligan's view that boys and girls are socialized to think differently about morality. Susan Lollis and her colleagues (1996) recorded what parents said to their 2- and 4-year-old children when squabbles broke out between them. Mothers used more care-based reasoning than fathers, so they may have served as models of this approach to moral thinking. However, parents did not use more care-based arguments on girls and more justice-based arguments on boys (Lollis, Ross, & Leroux, 1996). It is not yet clear, then, how sex differences in moral outlook might arise (Walker, 1997).

Although her hypothesis about sex differences in moral reasoning and their origin has not received much support, Gilligan's work *has* increased our awareness that both men and women often think about moral issues—especially real-life as opposed to hypothetical moral issues—in terms of their responsibilities for the welfare of other people. Kohlberg emphasized only one way—a very legalistic way—of thinking about right and wrong. There seems to be merit in tracing the development of *both* a morality of justice and a morality of care in *both* males and females (Brabeck, 1983; Gilligan, 1993).

Is the Theory Incomplete?

Another major criticism of Kohlberg's theory is that it focuses so much on moral reasoning that it almost entirely ignores moral affect and moral behavior (Gibbs & Schnell, 1985; Haan, Aerts, & Cooper, 1985). As Norma Haan and her colleagues (1985) point out, moral dilemmas in everyday life arouse powerful emotions. We care about moral issues and about the people who will be affected by our decisions; we agonize about what to do; we very much want to feel that we are moral beings, and our egos are threatened when we act immorally. Such emotions play a central role in morality by motivating our actions, and any theory that overlooks the role of emotions and motivations in morality is therefore incomplete (see also Haidt et al., 1993; Hart & Chmiel, 1992). Moreover, Haan argues, what we should ultimately be interested in when studying morality is how people actually behave in specific situations.

There is no question that Kohlberg was concerned primarily with moral reasoning rather than with moral affect or behavior. Also, as already noted, a person might decide to uphold or to break a law or a moral rule at any of the stages of moral reasoning.

What distinguishes one stage from the next is the complexity or structure of a person's reasoning, not the specific decisions he or she reaches. Nonetheless, Kohlberg has argued that more advanced moral reasoners are more likely to behave in accordance with widely accepted moral standards than less advanced moral reasoners are. He would predict, for example, that the preconventional thinker might readily decide to cheat on a test if the chances of being detected were small and the potential rewards high. The postconventional thinker would be more likely to appreciate that cheating is wrong in principle, regardless of the chances of detection, because it infringes on the rights of others and undermines social order.

How well *does* a person's stage of moral reasoning predict his or her behavior? Many researchers have found that the moral judgments of young children do *not* predict what they will do when they are given a chance to cheat or violate other moral norms (Nelson, Grinder, & Biaggio, 1969; Toner & Potts, 1981). Studies of older grade school children, adolescents, and adults often do find some consistency between moral reasoning and conduct. Individuals at higher stages of moral reasoning, especially when their empathy is aroused, are more likely than individuals at lower stages to behave prosocially (Miller et al., 1996). And they are less likely to cheat or engage in delinquent and criminal activity (Colby & Kohlberg, 1987; Rest et al., 1997). Kohlberg (1975), for example, found that only 15% of students who reasoned at the postconventional level cheated when given an opportunity to do so, compared with 55% of the students at the conventional level and 70% of those at the preconventional level. Yet the relationship between stage of moral reasoning and moral behavior is typically weak (Bruggeman & Hart, 1996). This suggests that many personal qualities besides level of moral reasoning, and many situational or contextual factors as well, also influence whether a person will behave morally or immorally in daily life (Kurtines, 1986; Thoma, Rest, & Davison, 1991).

In sum, Kohlberg's theory of moral development has become prominent for good reason. It does indeed describe a universal sequence of changes in moral reasoning extending from childhood through adulthood. Moreover, the evidence supports Kohlberg's view that both cognitive growth and social experiences contribute to moral growth. However, there is also some merit to critics' positions. The theory may not be entirely fair to people who live in non-Western societies, who hold values other than liberal, democratic ones, or who emphasize a morality of care rather than a morality of justice. Furthermore, because Kohlberg's theory focuses entirely on moral reasoning, we must rely on other perspectives (such as social learning theory) to understand how moral af-

Gang warfare in inner-city areas is only part of the larger problem of youth violence.

fect and moral behavior develop and how thought, emotion, and behavior interact to make us the moral beings we ultimately become.

APPLICATIONS: COMBATING YOUTH VIOLENCE

In recent years, our society has been struggling with the problem of how to prevent serious aggression and violence on the part of adolescents and, increasingly, children. Three perspectives described in this chapter—Kohlberg's theory of moral development, Dodge's social information-processing model, and Patterson's coercive family environment model—have been applied to the challenge of preventing or reducing aggression. Let's see what the outcomes have been.

Improving Moral Reasoning

How might we best foster basic moral values and encourage prosocial behavior such as sharing, cooperation, and helping among children and adolescents? If, as both Piaget and Kohlberg claim, peers are at least as important as parents in stimulating moral growth, perhaps the most sensible approach is to harness "peer power." This is precisely what many psychologists and educators have attempted to do. They have put children or adolescents together in pairs or small groups to discuss hypothetical moral dilemmas. The rationale is quite simple: Exposure to forms of moral reasoning more mature than their own will create cognitive disequilibrium, which will motivate children to devise more mature modes of thinking.

Does participation in group discussions of moral issues produce more mature moral reasoning? It appears so (Rest et al., 1997). Average changes that are the equivalent of about 4 to 5 years of natural development can be achieved in programs lasting only 3 to 12 weeks. Moreover, researchers have learned what kinds of discussion are most helpful. For example, it is indeed important that students be exposed to reasoning that is slightly more mature than their own (Lapsley, 1996). And moral growth is most likely to occur when students actively transform, analyze, or otherwise act upon what their conversation partners have said—when they say things like "You're missing an important difference here" or "Here's something I think we can agree on" (Berkowitz & Gibbs, 1983).

Does participation in Kohlbergian moral discussion groups raise the level of moral thinking among violent youth? William Niles (1986) tested the effectiveness of moral discussion groups involving institutionalized delinquents and predelinquents (see also Gibbs et al., 1984). Some students were asked to discuss moral dilemmas and attempt to reach a consensus on them; others were asked to clarify their own values as they discussed the dilemmas but not to reach agreement; and still others were not asked to do anything.

A majority of the adolescents involved in discussing moral dilemmas gained at least a third of a stage after two discussion sessions a week for 16 weeks, more growth than youth in the control groups experienced. However, there was no relationship between gains in moral reasoning and improvements in self-control in the classroom, making one wonder whether the training would do anything to decrease delinquent behavior. Kohlberg himself ultimately abandoned the moral discussion group approach, deciding that more significant and lasting changes in moral behavior might be achieved by altering the entire moral atmosphere of a school to create a democratically governed and caring community (Kohlberg, 1985; Power, Higgins, & Kohlberg, 1989).

Building Social Information-Processing Skills

As we saw earlier, Kenneth Dodge's social information-processing model identifies six steps at which a highly aggressive youth might display deficient or biased information processing. Nancy Guerra and Ronald Slaby (1990) coached small groups of incarcerated and violent juveniles of both sexes (1) to look for situational cues other than those suggesting hostile intentions, (2) to control their impulses so that they do not lash out without considering the consequences,

and (3) to generate more nonaggressive solutions to conflicts. As a result of the 12-week intervention, these adolescents showed dramatic improvements in social information-processing skills, believed less strongly in the value of aggression, and behaved less aggressively in their interactions with authority figures and other inmates.

Trained offenders were only somewhat less likely than untrained offenders to violate their paroles after release (34% versus 46% of control youth who received no training), however, suggesting that they may have reverted to their antisocial ways when they returned to the environments in which their aggressive tendencies originated. Indeed, for many young African-American and Hispanic males in gang-dominated inner-city neighborhoods, being quick to detect others' hostile intentions and defend oneself against assault may well be an important survival skill worth preserving (Hudley & Graham, 1993).

Breaking Coercive Cycles

Gerald Patterson and his colleagues, as well as other researchers (see Kazdin, 1995), have maintained that the secret to working with violent youth is to change the dynamics of interactions in their families so that aggressive tactics of controlling other family members are no longer reinforced and the cycle of coercive behavior is broken. Patterson and his team (Bank et al., 1991) randomly assigned adolescent boys who were repeat offenders to either a special parent training intervention or the service usually provided by juvenile court. In the parent training program, therapy sessions held with each family (and usually including the boys) taught parents how to observe both prosocial and antisocial behaviors in their sons; to communicate closely with their son's school and gather teachers' reports on his performance and behavior at school; and, using methods derived from social learning theory, to establish behavior contracts that spell out the reinforcers for prosocial behavior and the penalties for antisocial behavior. The main goal was to break coercive cycles in the family and establish healthier patterns of child management.

Like a similar intervention with younger children (Patterson, 1974), this intervention proved highly effective. More important, rates of serious crime were measured, and they dropped and remained lower even three years after the intervention ended. The standard juvenile court program was equally effective in reducing crime rates but took longer to work its effects. Overall, the parent training intervention was judged only a partial success; it did not fully resolve the problems these dysfunctional families had. The research team concluded that a program involving a six-month placement with foster parents trained in behavioral techniques, combined with parenting skills training for the youth's natural parents, may be more effective (Bank et al., 1991).

In sum, efforts to find effective ways to work with aggressive youth have included attempts to apply the work of Kohlberg (by using discussion of moral issues to raise levels of moral reasoning), Dodge (by teaching effective social information-processing skills), and Patterson (by replacing coercive cycles in the family environment with positive behavior management techniques). Many interventions have achieved short-term gains in skills but have failed to reduce rates of antisocial behavior in the long run. The most promising approaches to preventing and treating aggressive youth appear to recognize that changing patterns of antisocial behavior requires changing not only the individual but patterns of family interaction and the broader social environments in which these youths are developing (Tolan, Guerra, & Kendall, 1995).

We have now completed our series of chapters on the development of the self, or the person as an individual, looking at the development of self-conceptions and distinctive personality traits (Chapter 10), identities as males or females (Chapter 11), and now social-cognitive skills and morality. But individual development does not occur in a vacuum. Repeatedly, we have seen that the individual's development may take different paths, depending on the social context in which it occurs. Our task in upcoming chapters will be to put the individual even more squarely into a social context. It should become clear that throughout our lives we are both independent and interdependent—separate from and connected to other developing persons.

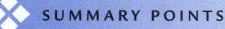

SUMMARY POINTS

1. Social cognition (thinking about self and others) is involved in all social behavior, including moral behavior. By age 3 or 4, children pass false belief tasks and demonstrate that they have acquired a theory of mind, an understanding that mental states exist and guide behavior. Such an understanding requires both normal neurological development and social experience (for example, with siblings).

2. Preschool children describe people in terms of their physical features and activities, whereas children aged 8 or so and older describe people in terms of their inner psychological traits. With age, children also overcome their egocentrism and become more adept at adopting others' perspectives. Both person-perception and role-taking abilities become more abstract during adolescence, and social-cognitive growth continues during adulthood but may decline late in life if a person is socially isolated.

3. Morality has cognitive, affective, and behavioral components; it is the ability to distinguish between right and wrong, to act on that distinction, and to experience appropriate moral emotions.

4. Freud's psychoanalytic theory describes moral development in terms of the formation of the superego and a sense of guilt. Cognitive-developmental theorist Jean Piaget described stages that lead to a better understanding of rules and the intentions behind acts, and Lawrence Kohlberg built on his work to propose three levels of moral reasoning—preconventional, conventional, and postconventional—each with two stages. Social learning theorists have focused on how moral behavior is influenced by past learning and situational pressures.

5. Although infants are amoral in some respects, they begin learning about right and wrong through their early disciplinary encounters, internalize rules, and already display primitive forms of empathy and prosocial behavior. Their moral growth depends on the goodness of fit between their temperament and the approach to moral training their parents adopt.

6. According to Kohlberg, most children operate at the preconventional level of moral reasoning. Both Kohlberg and Piaget underestimated the moral sophistication of young children (for example, their ability to consider both intentions and

consequences in judging acts and to distinguish between moral and social-conventional rules). Situational influences contribute to moral inconsistency. Reinforcement, modeling, and the disciplinary approach of induction can foster moral growth, but the child's temperament also influences moral development.

7. During adolescence, a shift from preconventional to conventional moral reasoning is evident, and many adolescents incorporate moral values into their sense of identity as an individual.

8. Some adults progress from the conventional to the postconventional level of moral reasoning and advance in their religious thinking as well; elderly adults typically do not "regress" in their moral thought and usually maintain the level of commitment to religion they had earlier in adulthood.

9. Kohlberg's stages of moral reasoning form an invariant sequence, with progress through them influenced by cognitive growth and social experiences that involve taking others' perspectives. It has been charged that Kohlberg's theory is biased against people from non-Western cultures, people who do not share his liberal values, and women who express a morality of care rather than a morality of justice. Critics also claim that the theory says too little about moral affect and behavior and cannot predict behavior well.

10. Attempts to prevent and reduce youth violence have applied the work of Kohlberg (through moral discussion groups designed to raise levels of moral reasoning), Dodge (by teaching effective social information-processing skills), and Patterson (teaching parents positive child management strategies and changing coercive family environments). However, the problem is serious, and many interventions have failed to reduce rates of antisocial behavior in the long run.

✴ FOOD FOR THOUGHT

1. Listen closely to a conversation in which your friends talk about people and write down any statements in which they refer to people's beliefs, desires, intentions, and the like in attempting to explain their behavior. Do you see evidence that your friends have a theory of mind? How would humans begin to explain each other's behavior without one?

2. A preconventional thinker, a conventional thinker, and a postconventional thinker all face a moral dilemma on final exam day: There's a very smart student in the row ahead of them whose exam answers are in plain sight. Should they cheat or not? Provide examples of the reasoning you might expect at each level of moral development—one argument in favor of cheating and one against it at each of the three levels. (Are any of these arguments especially difficult to make?)

3. Individuals said to have antisocial personality disorder do not appear to have a sense of right or wrong and have no qualms about harming other people. Drawing on material in this chapter, profile such individuals in terms of (a) their likely temperament, (b) their stage of moral reasoning, (c) their social information-processing style, and (d) the discipline approaches their parents used.

Ⓦ ON THE WEB

1. *Kohlberg*   This site offers biographical information, descriptions of Kohlberg's stages of moral development and examples of thinking at each stage, and links to other Kohlberg sites. It's a good stop if you want to solidify your understanding of the theory.
   http://moon.pepperdine.edu/gsep/class/ethics/kohlberg/

2. *Gilligan* A short but informative outline of Carol Gilligan's ideas on sex differences in moral thinking.
   http://moon.pepperdine.edu/gsep/class/ethics/gilligan/gilligan.html
3. *Youth Violence* This site, created by the National Center for Injury Prevention and Control, Division of Violence Prevention, provides statistics on youth violence and brief descriptions of interventions in 11 cities. You might see whether you can detect the influence of Lawrence Kohlberg, Gerald Patterson, or Kenneth Dodge on these programs. The site is
   http://www.cdc.gov/ncipc.dvp/yvfacts.htm
   but you will be sent to the Centers for Disease Control and Prevention site. From there, go to the link to "Centers, Institutes, and Offices," to find the National Center for Injury Prevention and Control and then Violence Prevention.

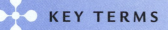

KEY TERMS

social cognition	empathy	social-conventional rules
false belief task	prosocial behavior	love withdrawal
theory of mind	internalization	power assertion
joint attention	moral reasoning	induction
desire psychology	preconventional morality	reactive aggression
belief-desire psychology	conventional morality	proactive aggression
role-taking skills	postconventional morality	coercive family environment
morality	amoral	morality of justice
moral affect	moral rules	morality of care

CHAPTER 13

Attachment and Social Relationships

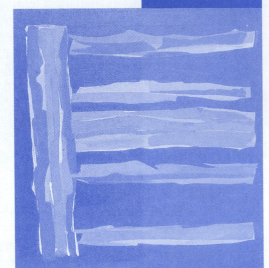

PERSPECTIVES ON RELATIONSHIPS
What Do We Gain from Relationships?
Which Relationships Are Most Critical?

THE INFANT
Early Emotional Development
The First Relationship
Types of Attachment
Early Attachment and Later Development
First Peer Relations

THE CHILD
Parent/Child Attachments
Peer Networks
Play
Peer Acceptance and Popularity
Friendships
Contributions of Peers to Development

THE ADOLESCENT
Attachments to Parents
Friendships
Changing Social Networks
Parent and Peer Influence

THE ADULT
Social Networks
Romantic Relationships
Adult Friendships
Adult Relationships and Adult Development

APPLICATIONS: BUILDING GOOD RELATIONSHIPS

SUMMARY POINTS

FOOD FOR THOUGHT

ON THE WEB

KEY TERMS

o you recognize the little girl in this photo? She is Baby Jessica, it is August 1993, and she is about to be whisked away from the only parents she has ever known (Ingrassia & Springen, 1994). A nation watched in horror as this 2½-year-old was taken from the DeBoers (the parents who thought they had adopted her, though the adoption was contested from the start and never finalized) and awarded by the court to the Schmidts (her biological parents).

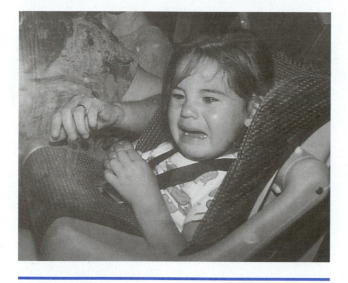

Baby Jessica leaves the only parents she knows.

ow do you think this experience will affect Jessica's later development? Will she be able to form close attachments to her biological parents? Will she be ever fearful of abandonment, whether by parents, friends, or lovers? Think about Jessica as you read this chapter. It concerns our closest relationships across the life span and their implications for our development (and ends with a "Food for Thought" item that will update you on Baby Jessica). Whatever you predict about Baby Jessica's future, you would probably agree that close interpersonal relationships play a critical role in our lives and in development. The poet John Donne wrote, "No man is an island, entire of itself"; it seems equally true that no human being can *become* entire without the help of other human beings.

This chapter addresses questions such as these: What sorts of social relationships are especially important during different phases of the life span, and what is the character of these relationships? When and how do we develop the social competence it takes to interact smoothly with other people and to enter into intimate relationships with them? What are some of the developmental implications of being deprived of close relationships? We begin with some broad perspectives concerning the significance of social relationships for human development.

What is it, really, that social relationships contribute to our development? And what relationships are especially significant? Let's briefly see what developmental theorists have had to say.

What Do We Gain from Relationships?

No doubt you have your own ideas about why you value your relationships with family and friends, but here I'll emphasize how close relationships contribute to development by providing (1) learning opportunities and (2) social support.

The *learning experiences* provided by social interactions affect virtually all aspects of development and have been emphasized by social learning theorists. We acquire language as young children, for example, because people converse with us, serving as models of how to communicate and reinforcing our communication attempts. And, of course, it is other people who teach us social skills and patterns of social behavior. The infant learns from face-to-face interactions with a parent how to take turns with a social partner, the child learns from other children that expressing interest in someone is a better way to make friends than snatching their toys, and the adult continues to look to other people for guidance about how to behave as a lover, parent, worker, or group leader.

A second major function of close relationships is to provide **social support,** or emotional and practical help that bolsters us as individuals and protects us from stress. As Robert Kahn and Toni Antonucci (1980) see it, having reliable sources of social support benefits us both by increasing our sense of well-being and by protecting us from the potentially negative effects of stressful life events. Many researchers use the term *social network* to describe the array of significant individuals who serve as sources of social support. However, Kahn and Antonucci prefer to describe these significant people as a **social convoy** to emphasize the idea of a social support system that changes in size and composition over the life span.

An infant's convoy may consist only of parents. The social convoy enlarges over the years as others (relatives, friends, supportive teachers, romantic partners, colleagues) join it, and then shrinks in old age (Levitt, Guacci-Franco, & Levitt, 1993; Levitt, Weber, & Guacci, 1993). As new members are added, some members drift away. Others, especially family members, remain in the convoy, but we learn to interact with them in new ways, as when the infant son who is thoroughly dependent on his mother becomes the adolescent son clamoring for his independence—and later the middle-aged son who helps his mother manage her money and care for her house.

In sum, other people are important to us for an endless range of reasons, but their most critical roles in the developmental process are as teachers and as sources of social support. We could not learn our culture's patterns of social behavior without them, and we could not meet life's challenges nearly so well without the social support provided by our social convoys.

Which Relationships Are Most Critical?

Many noted developmental theorists have concluded that no social relationship is more important to human development than the very first: the bond between parent and infant. Sigmund Freud (1905/1930) deserves credit for being the first to sound this theme and left no doubt about his opinion: A stable mother/child relationship is essential for normal personality development. Erik Erikson was one of many neo-Freudians who agreed. So was John Bowlby, developer of attachment theory.

Attachment Theory

The most influential theory of parent/child attachment and other relationships today is the theory developed by John Bowlby (1969, 1973, 1980, 1988), a British psychiatrist who died in 1990, and elaborated on by his colleague Mary Ainsworth, an American developmental psychologist (1989; Ainsworth et al., 1978). It has come to be known as **attachment theory** and was based on ethological theory (with its focus on the adaptive value of specieswide behavior), combined with a bit of psychoanalytic theory (Bowlby was a therapist trained in psychoanalytic thought) and modern cognitive psychology (Bowlby believed that the child's expectations about self and other are important, as we'll see).

According to Bowlby (1969), an **attachment** is a strong affectional tie that binds a person to an intimate companion. Most of us form our first attachment at about 6 or 7 months of age, typically to a parent. How do we know when baby Michael becomes attached to his mother? He will try to maintain proximity to her—crying, clinging, approaching, following, doing whatever it takes to maintain closeness. He will prefer her to other individuals, reserving his biggest smiles for her and seeking her out when he is upset, uncomfortable, or afraid; she is irreplaceable in his eyes. He will also be confident about exploring the environment so long as he knows that Mom is there to provide the security he needs.

Notice that an infant attached to a parent is rather like an adult "in love." True, close emotional ties are expressed in different ways, and serve different functions, at different points in the life span. Adults,

for example, do not usually feel compelled to follow their mates around the house, and they look to their loved ones for more than comforting hugs and smiles. Nonetheless, there are basic similarities among the infant attached to a caregiver, the child attached to a best friend, and the adult attached to a mate or lover. *Throughout the life span, the objects of our attachments are special, irreplaceable people with whom we are motivated to maintain proximity and from whom we derive a sense of security* (Ainsworth, 1989).

Nature, Nurture, and Attachment. One of Bowlby's messages to his fellow psychiatrists was that it is normal rather than pathological to need other people throughout the life span. Making use of ethological theory and research, Bowlby argued that infants (and parents too) are biologically predisposed to form attachments. As we saw in Chapter 3, ethologists assume that all species, including human beings, are born with a number of innate behavioral tendencies that have in some way contributed to the survival of the species over the course of evolution. It makes sense to think, for example, that young birds have tended to survive if they have stayed close to their mothers so that they could be fed and protected from predators—but have starved and been gobbled up, and therefore have failed to pass on their genes to future generations, if they have strayed away. Thus chicks, ducks, and goslings may have gradually evolved so that they engage in **imprinting**, an innate form of learning in which the young will follow and become attached to a moving object (usually the mother) during a critical period early in life.

Groundbreaking ethologist Konrad Lorenz (1937) observed imprinting in young goslings and noted that it (1) is automatic—young fowl do not have to be taught to follow; (2) occurs only within a *critical period* shortly after the bird has hatched; and (3) is irreversible—once the gosling begins to follow a particular object, whether that object is its mother or Konrad Lorenz, it will remain attached to it. The imprinting response Lorenz observed is a prime example of a species-specific and largely innate behavior that has evolved over time because it has survival value.

What about human infants? Babies may not become imprinted to their mothers in the same way that young fowl do, but they most certainly follow their love objects around. Bowlby argued that they come equipped with a number of other behaviors besides following that help ensure that adults will love them, stay with them, and meet their needs. Among these behaviors are sucking, clinging, smiling, and vocalizing (crying, cooing, and babbling). Moreover, Bowlby argued that adults are biologically programmed to respond to an infant's signals, just as infants are programmed to respond to the sight, sound, and touch of their caregivers. It is difficult indeed for an adult to

Ethologist Konrad Lorenz demonstrated that goslings would become imprinted to him rather than to their mother if he was the first moving object they encountered during their critical period for imprinting. Human attachment is a bit more complex.

ignore a baby's cry or fail to warm up to a baby's big grin. In short, both human infants and human caregivers have evolved in ways that predispose them to form close attachments, and this ensures that infants will receive the care, protection, and stimulation they need to survive and thrive.

Just as the imprinting of goslings occurs during a critical period, human attachments form during what Bowlby viewed as a sensitive period for attachment, the first three years of life. But attachments do not just form automatically. According to Bowlby, whether an attachment forms and how secure it is will be influenced by the ongoing interaction between infant and caregiver and by the ability of each partner to respond to the other's signals. The infant's preprogrammed signals to other people may eventually wane if they fail to produce favorable reactions because a caregiver is unresponsive to them. And infants themselves must learn to react sensitively to their caregiver's signals so that they can adjust their own behavior to mesh well with that of their love object. So, although Bowlby believes that humans are biologically prepared to form attachments, he also stresses that mutual learning processes contribute to the unfolding of a secure relationship.

Implications of Attachment. Bowlby maintained that the quality of the early parent/infant attachment has important effects on later development, including the kinds of relationships people have with friends, romantic partners, and their own children. He proposed that, from their interactions with caregivers, infants construct **internal working models**—cognitive representations of themselves and other people that shape their expectations about relationships and their processing of social information (Bowlby, 1973; see also Bretherton, 1996). Securely attached infants who have

received responsive care will form internal working models suggesting that they are lovable individuals and that other people can be trusted to care for them. By contrast, insecurely attached infants subjected to insensitive, neglectful, or abusive care may conclude that they are difficult to love and that other people are unreliable. These insecure infants would be expected to have difficulties in later interpersonal relationships; they may, for example, be wary of forming close relationships or be jealous and overly dependent if they do form one.

In sum, attachment theory, as developed by Bowlby and elaborated by Ainsworth, claims that (1) the capacity to form attachments is part of our evolutionary heritage; (2) attachments unfold through an interaction of biological and environmental forces during a sensitive period early in life; (3) the first attachment relationship, that between infant and caregiver, shapes later development and the quality of later relationships; and (4) internal working models of self and others serve as the mechanism through which early experience affects later development.

Peers and the Two Worlds of Childhood

Although the parent/infant relationship is indeed important, some theorists, among them Jean Piaget, argue that relationships with peers are at least as significant. In effect, they argue, there are "two social worlds of childhood," one involving adult/child relationships and the other involving peer relationships and a whole peer culture, and these two worlds contribute differently to development (Harris, 1995; Youniss, 1980; Youniss, McLellan, & Strouse, 1994).

Who is a **peer?** Someone who is one's social equal; someone who functions at a similar level of behavioral complexity—often, though not always, someone of similar age (Lewis & Rosenblum, 1975). As Piaget

(1932/1965) observed, relationships with peers are quite different from relationships with parents. Parent/child relationships are lopsided: Because parents have more power than children do, the children are in a subordinate position and must defer to adult authority. By contrast, peers typically have equal power and influence and must learn to appreciate each other's perspectives, to negotiate and compromise, and to cooperate with each other if they hope to get along. Thus Piaget believed that peers can make a unique contribution to social development that adult authority figures cannot make.

Another theorist who believed that peer relationships contribute significantly to development was neo-Freudian theorist Harry Stack Sullivan (1953; see also Buhrmester & Furman, 1986; Youniss, 1980). He believed that interpersonal needs are important throughout life, but that these needs change as we get older and are gratified through different kinds of social relationships at different ages. According to Sullivan, the parent/child relationship is indeed central up to about age 6; infants need tender care and nurturance from their parents, and preschool children need their parents to serve as playmates and companions. From about age 6 on, however, peers become increasingly important in children's lives. At first children need peers as companions or playmates. Then, in grade school, they need acceptance by the peer group so that they will have opportunities to learn social skills within the group.

Around age 9 to 12, they begin to need intimacy in the form of a close friendship. Sullivan placed special emphasis on the developmental significance of **chumships,** or close friendships with peers of the same sex that emerge at about this age. It is with their close chums, he believed, that children become capable of truly caring about another person and learn the importance of trust, loyalty, and honesty in relationships. In fact, Sullivan believed that a close chumship could do much to make up for any insecurities caused by a poor parent/child relationship or by rejection by the peer group. Moreover, the lessons about intimacy learned in the context of same-sex chumships would then carry over into the intimate romantic relationships formed during adolescence and adulthood. Sullivan believed that a child who never had a chum would be poorly adjusted later in life. We will see later whether he was right.

Developmentalists continue to debate the relative significance of parents and peers for later development, with some agreeing with Freud and Bowlby that the quality of an infant's attachment to an adult is the most significant influence on later personality and social development and others sharing the belief of Piaget and Sullivan that relationships with peers are at least as significant. I think this chapter will convince you that close relationships with *both* caregivers and peers are essential to healthy development across the life span.

THE INFANT

Human infants are social beings from the start, but their social relationships change dramatically once they form close attachments to parents or other companions and develop the social skills that allow them to coordinate their own activities with those of other infants. Since attachments are emotional ties, let us begin by setting the development of parent/infant attachment in the context of early emotional development.

Early Emotional Development

Until fairly recently, most researchers believed that infants did not really have emotional lives—or at least that their emotional expressions were only globally positive or negative in nature. Parents, by contrast, have long felt that their babies' faces reveal a wide range of specific emotions (Johnson et al., 1982). Parents are right.

Development of Specific Emotions

Carroll Izard (1982, 1993) and his colleagues have videotaped infants' responses to such events as grasping an ice cube, having a toy taken away, or seeing their mothers return after a separation. By analyzing specific facial movements (such as the raising of the brows and the wrinkling of the nose) and by asking raters to judge what emotion a baby's face reveals, Izard has established that infants do indeed express distinct emotions in response to different experiences and that adults can readily interpret which emotions they are expressing (see Figure 13.1).

Izard concludes that a number of facial expressions of emotion appear in a predictable order over the first two years. At birth, babies show interest (by staring intently at objects), distress in response to pain, disgust (to foul tastes and odors), and expressions of contentment. Angry expressions appear at 3 to 4 months—about the same time that infants acquire enough control of their limbs to push unpleasant stimuli away. Sadness also emerges at about this same time, with fear making its appearance at age 5 to 7 months. These "primary" emotions seem to be biologically programmed. They emerge in all normal infants at roughly the same ages and are displayed and interpreted similarly in all cultures (Izard, 1982, 1993; Malatesta et al., 1989).

Socialization of Emotions

Although the earliest emotional expressions seem to be biologically programmed, the sociocultural environment soon begins to exert its influence. One of the

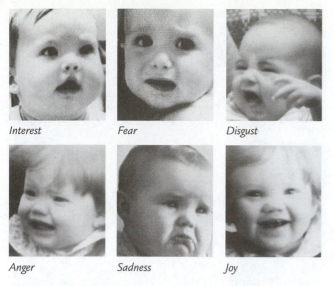

Interest | Fear | Disgust

Anger | Sadness | Joy

FIGURE 13.1 *Infants express a wide range of emotions.*

first lessons babies in our culture learn is that positive emotions such as joy and interest are more welcomed than negative emotions. Observational studies of face-to-face interactions between mothers and infants suggest that young infants display a wide range of positive and negative emotions, changing their expressions with lightning speed (once every 7 seconds) while their mothers do the same (Malatesta et al., 1986, 1989). Mothers, however, restrict themselves mainly to displays of interest, surprise, and joy, thus serving as models of positive emotions. What's more, mothers respond selectively to their babies' expressions; over the early months they become increasingly responsive to their babies' expressions of interest and surprise and less responsive to negative emotions (Malatesta et al., 1986, 1989). Through basic learning processes, then, infants are trained to show a pleasant face more frequently and an unpleasant face less frequently—and they do just this over time. They are beginning to learn which emotional expressions are socially acceptable in their culture.

Precisely what infants learn about emotions can be quite different in one culture than in another. For example, American parents love to stimulate their babies until they reach peaks of delight, whereas Gusii mothers in Kenya hardly ever engage in face-to-face play of this sort and seek instead to keep their infants as calm and content as possible (Dixon et al., 1981). Thus American babies learn that intense emotion is okay as long as it is positive, but Gusii babies learn to restrain both positive and negative emotions.

Babies also learn from parents and other companions which emotions are appropriate in which situations (Denham, 1989; Halberstadt, 1991). One important way in which this may happen is through **social referencing,** the process by which infants monitor others' emotional reactions in ambiguous situations and use this information to regulate their own feelings and behavior (Feinman, 1992; Klinnert et al., 1986). The ability to engage in social referencing emerges in the second half of the first year. For example, Tedra Walden and Tamra Ogan (1988) coached mothers to react either positively or fearfully when their infants were introduced to a toy robot. Mothers donned appropriate facial expressions and said either, "Oh, look at that! What a nice toy! Oh boy! Oh boy! Nice toy!" or "Oh, look at that scary toy! Ooo, what a scary toy! Ooo, scary toy!" (p. 1232). Compared to younger infants, 10 to 13-month-olds not only looked more frequently at their mothers' faces for cues but heeded those cues more, reaching for and touching the "scary" toy less often than the "nice" toy. In many everyday situations, then, infants may learn how they should interpret and respond to people, things, and events by studying the emotional responses of their close companions.

Emotion Regulation

In order to conform to their culture's rules about when and how different emotions should be expressed and in order to keep themselves from being overwhelmed by their emotions, infants must develop strategies for **emotion regulation,** the processes involved in initiating, maintaining, and altering emotional responses (Bridges & Grolnick, 1995). Young infants must make do with only primitive emotion regulation strategies. For example, they are able to reduce their negative arousal by turning away from unpleasant stimuli or sucking vigorously on a pacifier or some other object (Mangelsdorf, Shapiro, & Marzolf, 1995). More often, they rely on their caregivers to help them regulate their emotions—for example, by soothing them when they are distressed (Cole, Michel, & Teti, 1994; Kopp, 1989).

By the end of the first year, infants acquire other strategies such as rocking themselves and moving away from upsetting events. They also actively seek out attachment figures when they are distressed, for the very presence of caregivers has a calming effect. By 18 to 24 months of age, toddlers will try to control the actions of people and objects such as mechanical toys that upset them (Mangelsdorf et al., 1995); they are able to cope with the frustration of waiting for snacks and gifts by playing with toys and otherwise distracting themselves (Grolnick, Bridges, & Connell, 1996); and they will even knit their brows or compress their lips in an attempt to suppress their anger or sadness (Malatesta et al., 1989). As children gain the capacity for symbolic thought and language, they also become able to regulate their distress symbolically—for example, by saying, "Mommy coming soon, Mommy coming soon" after mother goes out the door (Thompson, 1994).

The development of emotions and of strategies for regulating emotions is closely intertwined with the development of attachment relationships. Attachment figures play critical roles in helping infants to regulate their emotions and in teaching them how to do so on their own. Attachment figures also arouse powerful emotions, positive and negative, that need to be controlled; infants can become uncomfortably overstimulated during joyful bouts of play with parents, and they can become highly distressed when their parents leave them. Finally, infants develop styles of emotional expression designed to keep attachment figures close (Bridges & Grolnick, 1995). One infant may learn to suppress negative emotions such as fear and anger so as not to anger an irritable caregiver, whereas another may learn to scream loud and long in order to keep an unreliable caregiver close. It will become clear, as we now trace the development of parent/infant attachments, that emotions and emotion regulation are central in attachment relationships.

In sum, biologically based primary emotions appear in the first year of life and become socialized through modeling, reinforcement, and social referencing. As infants get older, they rely less on caregivers and more on their own emotion regulation strategies to manage their emotions in interactions with attachment objects and other people.

The First Relationship

Like any relationship, the parent/infant attachment is reciprocal. Parents become attached to their infants, and infants become attached to their parents as the relationship unfolds.

Caregiver's Attachment to Infant

Parents have an edge on infants: They often begin to form emotional attachments to their babies even before birth. As we saw in Chapter 4, mothers who have an opportunity for skin-to-skin contact with their babies during the first few hours after birth may form a special bond to them (Klaus & Kennell, 1976). As it turns out, though, such early contact is neither crucial nor sufficient for the development of strong parent-to-infant attachments. Instead, these attachments build during parent/child interactions that take place over many weeks and months.

Parents are drawn to babies because they are "cute"; their chubby cheeks and rounded profiles are appealing (Alley, 1981). Moreover, babies behave in ways that are endearing. Early reflexive behaviors such as sucking, rooting, and grasping help convince parents that their infants enjoy their company (Bowlby, 1969). Smiling may be an especially important signal. It is initially a reflexive response to almost any stimulus but can be triggered by voices at 3 weeks of age and by faces at 5 or 6 weeks of age (Bowlby, 1969;

Smiling is one of the behaviors that helps to ensure that adults will fall in love with babies.

Wolff, 1963). Finally, when infants begin to coo and babble, their parents can enjoy back-and-forth "conversations" with them (Keller & Scholmerich, 1987; Stevenson et al., 1986).

Over the weeks and months, caregivers and infants develop **synchronized routines,** much like dances, in which the partners take turns responding to each other's leads (Stern, 1977; Tronick, 1989). These smooth interactions are most likely to develop if the caregiver limits her social stimulation to those periods when the baby is alert and receptive and avoids pushing things when the infant's message is "Cool it—I need a break from all this stimulation." Edward Tronick (1989, p. 112) described one very synchronous "dance" as a mother played peek-a-boo with her infant:

The infant abruptly turns away from his mother as the game reaches its "peak" of intensity and begins to suck on his thumb and stare into space with a dull facial expression. The mother stops playing and sits back watching. . . . After a few seconds the infant turns back to her with an inviting expression. The mother moves closer, smiles, and says in a high-pitched, exaggerated voice, "Oh, now you're back!" He smiles in response and vocalizes. As they finish crowing together, the infant reinserts his thumb and looks away. The mother again waits. [Soon] the infant turns . . . to her and they greet each other with big smiles.

In sum, infants play an active role in persuading adults to love them. Babies are physically appealing, come equipped with a number of reflexes that promote the formation of an attachment, and are highly responsive to people and capable of synchronizing their behavior with that of their "dance partners." As caregiver and infant perfect their interaction routines, the parent/infant relationship normally blossoms into a strong reciprocal attachment (Isabella & Belsky, 1991).

Yet not all parents become closely attached to their infants. In the first place, some babies are hard to love. Parents may have a difficult time establishing stable and synchronized routines with irritable or unresponsive infants (Field, 1987). Second, some adults have difficulty responding to infants. Parents who were themselves unloved, neglected, or abused as children often start out with the best intentions, but then, when their babies are irritable or inattentive (as all infants are at times), these parents may back off from the relationship, sometimes to the point of neglecting or abusing their babies (Biringen, 1990; Crowell & Feldman, 1991). Mothers who are depressed may also have difficulty responding sensitively to their babies' signals and forming close attachments (Lyons-Ruth et al., 1990).

In addition, the broader social context surrounding caregiver and infant can affect how they react to each other. For example, the stresses associated with poverty or marital difficulties may make it difficult for parents to interact responsively with their babies (Howes & Markman, 1989; Murray et al., 1996). And the cultural context in which caregiver and baby interact can also color their relationship. For instance, German parents strongly encourage independence and discourage clingy behavior in their children, which may explain why German infants are more likely than infants in many other societies to ignore or avoid their parents when they are reunited with them after a separation (Grossmann et al., 1985). By contrast, Japanese babies, who are rarely separated from their mothers early in life, become very distressed by separations (Takahashi, 1990; van IJzendoorn & Kroonenberg, 1988). In short, although most new parents quickly fall in love with their infants, characteristics of the baby, the caregiver, and the surrounding social environment can clearly affect the emerging attachment.

Infant's Attachment to Caregiver

Infants require some time before they are developmentally ready to form attachments. They progress through the following phases (Ainsworth, 1973; Bowlby, 1969):

1. *Undiscriminating social responsiveness* (birth to 2 or 3 months). Very young infants are responsive to voices, faces, and other social stimuli, but any human is of interest to them. They do not yet show a clear preference for one person over another.

2. *Discriminating social responsiveness* (2 or 3 months to 6 or 7 months). Now infants are beginning to express preferences for familiar companions. They are likely to direct their biggest grins and most enthusiastic babbles toward those companions, though they are still quite friendly toward strangers.

3. *Active proximity seeking/true attachment* (6 or 7 months to about 3 years). At about 6 or 7 months of age, infants form their first clear attachments, most often to their mothers. Now able to crawl, an infant will follow along behind her mother to stay close, protest when her mother leaves, and greet her mother warmly when she returns. Within weeks after forming their first attachments, most infants become attached to other people as well—fathers, siblings, grandparents, regular babysitters (Schaffer & Emerson, 1964). By 18 months of age, very few infants are attached to only one person, and some are attached to several.

4. *Goal-corrected partnership* (3 years and older). By about the age of 3, partly because they have more advanced social-cognitive abilities, children can take a parent's goals and plans into consideration and adjust their behavior accordingly to achieve the goal of maintaining optimal proximity to the attachment figure. Thus a 1-year-old cries and tries to follow when Dad leaves the house to talk to a neighbor, whereas the 4-year-old child probably understands where Dad is going and can control her need for his attention until he returns. This final, more partnerlike, phase of attachment lasts a lifetime.

Attachment-Related Fears

Infants no sooner experience the pleasures of love than they discover the agonies of fear. One form of fear, **separation anxiety,** is actually an important sign that an attachment has formed. Once attached to a parent, babies often become wary or fretful when separated from that parent and will follow behind the parent to try to avoid separation. Separation anxiety normally appears at the time infants are forming their first genuine attachments, peaks at 14 to 18 months, and gradually becomes less frequent and less intense throughout infancy and the preschool period (Kagan, 1976; Weinraub & Lewis, 1977). Yet even children and adolescents may become homesick and quite distressed when separated from their parents for a long time (Thurber, 1995).

A second fearful response that often emerges once an attachment is formed is **stranger anxiety,** a wary or fretful reaction to the approach of an unfamiliar person. Most infants react positively to strangers until they form their first attachment and then become

BOX 13.1

Combating stranger anxiety: Tips for babysitters

It is not unusual for 1- or 2-year-olds meeting a new babysitter or being approached by a nurse or doctor at the doctor's office to break into tears and cling to their parents. Stranger-wary infants often stare at the stranger for a moment and then turn away, whimper, and seek the comfort of their parents. Occasionally, infants become terrified and highly upset. Obviously it is in the interests of babysitters and other "strangers" as well to be able to prevent such negative reactions. What might we suggest?

1. *Keep familiar companions available.* Stranger anxiety is less likely to occur if an attachment figure is nearby to serve as a "secure base." In one study, fewer than one-third of 6- to 12-month-olds were wary of an approaching stranger when they were seated on their mothers' laps (Morgan & Ricciuti, 1969). Yet about two-thirds of these infants frowned, turned away, whimpered, or cried if they were seated only 4 feet from their mothers (see also Bohlin & Hagekull, 1993). Babysitters would do well to insist that parents be present when they first meet the children they will tend. If parents must leave, a security blanket or beloved stuffed animal can have much the same calming effect as a parent's presence for some infants (Passman, 1977).

2. *Arrange for the infant's companions to respond positively to you.* As we have seen, infants 6 months of age and older engage in *social referencing* and use other people's emotional reactions to guide their own responses to a situation. The implication is that infants are likely to respond much more favorably to a stranger's approach if their mothers or fathers greet the stranger warmly than if the parents react neutrally or negatively toward this person. It might help, then, for babysitters to initiate a pleasant exchange with Mom or Dad before directing their attention to the infant.

3. *Make the setting more "familiar."* Stranger anxiety is less likely to occur in familiar settings than in unfamiliar ones (Sroufe, Waters, & Matas, 1974). Stranger anxiety should be less severe if the babysitter comes to the child's home than if the child is taken to the babysitter's home or some other unfamiliar place. Yet an unfamiliar environment can become a familiar one if infants are given the time to get used to it. Alan Sroufe and his colleagues (1974) found that over 90% of 10-month-olds became upset if a stranger approached within a minute after they had been placed in an unfamiliar room; only 50% did so when they were given 10 minutes to become accustomed to the room.

4. *Be a sensitive, unobtrusive stranger.* Not surprisingly, an infant's response to a stranger depends on the stranger's behavior (Sroufe, 1977). The meeting is likely to go best if the stranger initially keeps his or her distance and then approaches slowly while smiling, talking,

and offering a familiar toy or suggesting a familiar activity (Bretherton, Stolberg, & Kreye, 1981; Sroufe, 1977). It also helps if the stranger, like any sensitive caregiver, takes his or her cues from the infant (Mangelsdorf, 1992). Babies prefer strangers they can control! Intrusive strangers who approach quickly and force themselves on infants (for example, by trying to pick them up before they have time to adjust) probably get what they deserve.

5. *Try not to look any stranger than you must.* Finally, infants are most likely to be afraid of people who violate their schemas or expectations (Kagan, 1972). Babysitters who have unusual physical features such as beards or Mohawks *or* who dress in unusual outfits elicit more wariness than those who resemble the people infants encounter every day. Babysitters who favor a "punk" or "grunge" look might try to make themselves more readily recognizable as members of the human race!

---

wary of strangers shortly thereafter (Schaffer & Emerson, 1964). Anxious reactions to strangers—often mixed with signs of interest—become common at 8 to 10 months of age, continue through the first year, and gradually decline in intensity over the second year (Sroufe, 1977). Box 13.1 describes the circumstances under which stranger anxiety is most and least likely to occur and suggests how babysitters and health-

TABLE 13.1

The episodes of the Strange Situation test		
Episode	*Event*	*Attachment Behavior Observed*
1.	Experimenter leaves parent and baby to play	
2.	Parent sits while baby plays	Use of parent as secure base
3.	Stranger enters and talks to parent	Stranger anxiety
4.	Parent leaves; stranger lets baby play, offers comfort if needed	Separation anxiety
5.	Parent returns, greets baby, offers comfort if needed; stranger leaves	Reactions to reunion
6.	Parent leaves	Separation anxiety
7.	Stranger enters and offers comfort	Stranger anxiety; ability to be soothed by stranger
8.	Parent returns, greets baby, offers comfort, lets baby return to play	Reactions to reunion

SOURCE: Adapted from Ainsworth et al. (1978)

care professionals can head off outbreaks of fear and trembling.

Exploratory Behavior

Finally, the formation of a strong attachment to a caregiver has another important consequence: It facilitates exploratory behavior. Mary Ainsworth (Ainsworth et al., 1978) emphasizes that an attachment figure serves as a **secure base** for exploration, a point of safety from which an infant can feel free to venture away. Thus Wendy, a securely attached infant visiting a neighbor's home with Mom, may be comfortable exploring the living room as long as she can check back occasionally to see that Mom is still there but may be reluctant to explore if Mom disappears into the bathroom. Paradoxical as it may seem, infants apparently need to rely on another person in order to feel confident about acting independently.

The timetable for the formation of attachments is now clear, and we have seen that the emergence of a specific attachment often brings with it both fearful emotions (separation and stranger anxiety) and confidence (willingness to use the attachment figure as a secure base for exploration). But not all parent/infant attachments are equal.

Types of Attachment

Mary Ainsworth made her most notable contribution to attachment theory by devising a way to assess differences in the quality of parent/infant attachments. She and her associates created the **Strange Situation test,** a technique for measuring the quality of an attachment (Ainsworth et al., 1978). It consists of a series of eight episodes that gradually escalate the amount of stress infants experience as they react to the approaches of an adult stranger and the departures and returns of their caregivers (see Table 13.1). On the basis of an infant's pattern of behavior across the episodes, the quality of his or her attachment to a parent can be characterized as one of four types: secure, resistant, avoidant, or disorganized/disoriented.

1. **Secure attachment.** About 65 to 70% of 1-year-olds in our society are securely attached to their mothers (Ainsworth et al., 1978). The securely attached infant actively explores the room when alone with the mother because she serves as a secure base. The infant may be upset by separation but greets the mother when she returns and welcomes physical contact with her. The child is outgoing with a stranger while the mother is present.

2. **Resistant attachment.** About 10% of 1-year-olds show a resistant attachment, or an insecure attachment characterized by ambivalent reactions. The resistant infant is quite anxious and often does not venture off to play even though the mother is present, which suggests that she does not serve as a secure base for exploration. Yet this infant becomes very distressed when the mother departs, often showing much stronger separation anxiety than the securely attached infant, perhaps because it's not quite clear if mother will ever return. Then, when the mother returns, the infant is ambivalent: He or she may try to remain near the mother but seems to resent her for having left, may resist if she tries to make physical contact, and may even hit and kick her in anger (Ainsworth et al., 1978). Resistant infants are also quite wary of strangers, even when their mothers are present. It seems, then, that the resistant or ambivalent infant works very hard to get love but never quite feels loved.

3. **Avoidant attachment.** Avoidant infants (about 15% of 1-year-olds) seem uninterested in exploring, show little distress when separated from their mothers, and avoid contact when their mothers return. These insecurely attached infants are not particularly wary of strangers but sometimes avoid or ignore them in much the same way that they avoid or ignore their mothers. Avoidant infants, then, seem to have distanced themselves from their parents, almost as if they were denying their need for affection.

TABLE 13.2

Behaviors associated with the secure, resistant, and avoidant attachment styles in the Strange Situation test

Behavior	Type of Attachment			
	Secure	*Resistant*	*Avoidant*	*Disorganized/Disoriented*
Exploration when caregiver is present to provide a "secure base" for exploration?	Yes, actively	No—clings	Yes, but play is not as constructive as that of secure infant	No
Positive response to stranger?	Yes, comfortable if caregiver is present	No, fearful even with caregiver present	No, often indifferent, as they are to caregiver	No, confused responses
Protest when separated from caregiver?	Yes, at least mildly distressed	Yes! *Extremely* upset	No—seemingly unfazed	Sometimes; unpredictable
Positive response to caregiver at reunion?	Yes, happy to be reunited	Yes *and* no. Seeks contact but resents being left; ambivalent	No, ignores or avoids caregiver	Confused; may approach or avoid caregiver or do both

4. **Disorganized/disoriented attachment.** Around 5 to 10% of infants display what is now recognized as a fourth pattern of attachment, one that may reflect even more insecurity than the resistant and avoidant styles (Hertsgaard et al., 1995). Disorganized/disoriented attachment combines features of the resistant and avoidant styles and reflects confusion about whether to approach or avoid the parent (Main & Solomon, 1990). Reunited with their mothers after a separation, these infants may act dazed and freeze; or they may seek contact but then abruptly move away as their mothers approach them; or they may show both patterns in different reunion episodes. Unlike secure, resistant, or avoidant infants, infants with a disorganized/disoriented attachment have not been able to devise any coherent strategy for regulating negative emotions such as separation anxiety.

Table 13.2 summarizes the features of these four patterns of attachment, which have been the subject of considerable research. As we will see later, styles of relating to other people much like these infant attachment styles can be detected when adults are interviewed about their romantic relationships. Indeed, the concepts of attachment theory have now been applied successfully across the life span.

Influences on the Quality of Early Attachments

What determines which of these attachment patterns will characterize a parent/infant relationship? Early studies of the quality of attachments focused almost entirely on the qualities of caregivers that make infants form secure attachments to them, but we now know that infants make their own contributions to the attachment bond as well.

The Caregiver's Contributions. According to Freud, infants in the oral stage of psychosexual development become attached to the individual who provides them with oral pleasure. The attachment will be most secure if a mother is relaxed and generous in her feeding practices. Is there evidence to support Freud's claim? In a classic study conducted by Harry Harlow and Robert Zimmerman (1959), monkeys were separated from their mothers at birth and then reared with two surrogate mothers: a wire "mother" and a cloth "mother" wrapped in foam rubber and covered with terrycloth (see Figure 13.2). Half the infants were always fed by the cloth mother, the other half by the wire mother. To which mother did these infants become attached? There was no contest, really: Infants strongly preferred the cuddly cloth mother, *regardless of which mother had fed them.* Even if their food came from the wire mother, they spent far more time clinging to the cloth mother, ran to "her" when they were upset or afraid, and showed every sign of being attached to her. Harlow's research demonstrated that what he called **contact comfort,** or the pleasurable tactile sensations provided by a soft and cuddly "parent," is a more powerful contributor to attachment in monkeys than feeding or the reduction of hunger.

It may work similarly for humans: One team of researchers (Anisfeld et al., 1990) gave some families with newborns a soft cloth baby carrier that allowed a good deal of physical contact between parent and child and other families a plastic infant seat. Mothers of the babies in the "contact comfort" group were more responsive to them at 3 months of age, and 83% of these infants were securely attached at 13 months of age, compared to only 38% of those in the comparison group. And when Rudolph Schaffer and Peggy

FIGURE 13.2 *The wire and cloth surrogate "mothers" used in Harlow's research. This infant has formed an attachment to the cloth mother that provides "contact comfort," even though it must stretch to the wire mother in order to feed.*

Emerson (1964) asked mothers how they scheduled their feedings and when they weaned their infants, it turned out that the generosity of a mother's feeding practices simply did not predict the strength of her infant's attachment to her. In fact, for 39% of these infants, the person who usually fed, bathed, and changed the child (typically the mother) was not even the child's primary attachment figure! In short, we must reject Freud's view that oral gratification is the basis for attachment.

What *does* matter, then? A great deal of research tells us that *infants develop secure attachments to mothers and fathers who are sensitive and responsive to their needs and emotional signals* (Ainsworth et al., 1978; De Wolff & van IJzendoorn, 1997). This research supports Erikson's version of psychoanalytic theory, for he claimed that a mother's *general responsiveness* to the infant, not just her tendency to gratify oral needs, affects the strength of the attachment formed during his stage of *trust versus mistrust*. It is also consistent with learning theory, in that a highly responsive adult who provides food, fresh diapers, tender touches, and other pleasant experiences should, through association, become reinforcing in his or her own right. Finally, it confirms Bowlby's and Ainsworth's emphasis on sensitive, responsive parenting as the key to secure attachment. Qualities of parenting other than sensitivity and responsiveness count too, though; for example, positive attitudes toward parenting, synchrony in parent/infant

interactions, and provision of emotional support are also associated with secure attachment (De Wolff & van IJzendoorn, 1997).

What parenting styles contribute to insecure attachments? Babies who show a resistant pattern of attachment often have parents who are inconsistent in their caregiving; they react enthusiastically or indifferently, depending on their moods, and are unresponsive a good deal of the time (Isabella, 1993; Isabella & Belsky, 1991). The infant copes with inconsistent caregiving by trying desperately—through clinging, crying, and other attachment behaviors—to obtain emotional support and comfort and then becomes both saddened and resentful when these efforts fail.

The parents of infants with an avoidant attachment tend to provide either too little or too much stimulation. Some tend to be rejecting; they are impatient, unresponsive to the infant's signals, and resentful when the infant interferes with their own plans (Ainsworth, 1979; Isabella, 1993). Interestingly, other parents of infants with avoidant attachments are overzealous, chattering endlessly and providing high levels of stimulation even when their babies become uncomfortably aroused and need a break so that they can regulate their emotions (Belsky, Rovine & Taylor, 1984; Isabella & Belsky, 1991). Infants with an avoidant attachment style may be responding quite adaptively by learning to avoid adults who seem to dislike their company or who bombard them with stimulation they do not want and cannot handle. Whereas resistant infants make vigorous attempts to gain emotional support, avoidant infants seem to have learned not to express their emotional needs (Bridges & Grolnick, 1995). Finally, a disorganized/disoriented style of attachment is evident in as many as 80% of infants who have been physically abused or maltreated (Carlson et al., 1989) and in many infants whose mothers are severely depressed and may tend to mistreat and neglect them (Murray et al., 1996). Infants might naturally be thoroughly confused about whether to approach or avoid a parent who is loving one minute but brutal the next.

The Infant's Contributions. Clearly the ways in which parents interact with their babies relate in predictable ways to the quality of the attachments that form, but the infant's characteristics also have a bearing. Cognitive-developmental theorists emphasize that the ability to form attachments depends in part on the infant's level of cognitive development and knowledge of the surrounding world. For example, in order to experience separation anxiety when a caregiver leaves the room, the infant must recognize that close companions continue to exist even when they are absent (Kohlberg, 1969; Lester et al., 1974). In other words, infants will not form attachments until they have acquired some concept of *person permanence* (a form of the object permanence concept studied by Jean Piaget and discussed in Chapter 7).

The infant's temperament (see Chapter 10) is an even more important influence: An attachment is less likely to be secure if the infant is by temperament fearful and easily distressed (Colin, 1996; Goldsmith & Alansky, 1987). Which has a stronger bearing on the quality of the attachment, then—the caregiver's style of parenting or the infant's temperament? Both are significant, but longitudinal studies suggest that the caregiver's behavior has more to do with whether or not a secure attachment ultimately forms than do characteristics of the infant (Goldberg et al., 1986; Vaughn et al., 1989). Also, if the infant's temperament were the main influence on security of attachment, it would be difficult to explain why almost 4 out of 10 infants are securely attached to one parent but insecurely attached to the other (van IJzendoorn & De Wolff, 1997). Finally, even temperamentally difficult babies are likely to establish secure relationships with caregivers who are patient and adjust their caregiving to the baby's temperamental quirks (Mangelsdorf et al., 1990; van IJzendoorn et al., 1992). These findings are consistent with the *goodness of fit* model introduced in Chapter 10: Secure bonds evolve when parents can respond sensitively to whatever temperamental characteristics their babies display, whereas insecure bonds are more likely when there is a mismatch between caregiving style and infant's temperament (Sroufe, 1985).

Early Attachment and Later Development

From Freud on, almost everyone has assumed that the parent/child relationship is critical in shaping human development. Just how important *is* it? Two lines of research offer us an answer: (1) studies of socially deprived infants, and (2) studies of the later development of securely and insecurely attached infants.

Effects of Social Deprivation

What becomes of babies (like Baby Jessica, mentioned at the start of the chapter) who are separated from their caregivers through illness or death? Worse yet, what happens to infants who never have an opportunity to form *any* attachment bond?

John Bowlby (1960, 1980) was very concerned about the psychological damage that could result from separation from an attachment figure early in life. Drawing on research with families in which an infant or parent was hospitalized or a parent died, he described three phases of grief that infants who are old enough to have formed attachments could be expected to display (see also Colin, 1996):

1. *Protest:* During the first hours or days of a long separation, infants cry, search desperately for their lost caregivers, and cannot be comforted by substitute caregivers;

2. *Despair:* As hope of reunion fades, infants become withdrawn, sad, and listless, much like adults who are mourning a death;

3. *Detachment:* Infants begin to take renewed interest in toys, companions, and other features of the environment; if the caregiver returns, she or he may be ignored or avoided, as if the infant were defending against being hurt again.

If their caregivers return, infants who have displayed these reactions (or some of them, as not all infants display all) then become very needy of the lost caregiver's affection and may not let him or her out of sight. Their grief—and it is truly grief—has run its course. However, infants who experience a series of separations from caregivers or are moved around from foster home to foster home may be permanently marred by their experiences of loving and losing; they may enter a fourth phase of grieving in which they withdraw entirely from human relationships (Bowlby, 1980; Colin, 1996). The strength and duration of protest, despair, and detachment and whether the separation does lasting damage depend on many factors, including the characteristics of the child, the security of the parent/infant attachment, and the quality of care the infant receives after the separation (Rutter, 1981).

So much for having loved and lost. What about never having loved at all? Studies of infants who grow up in deprived institutional settings and never form attachments suggest that this may be worse (Goldfarb, 1943, 1945, 1947; Provence & Lipton, 1962). In the kinds of institutions studied, adults rarely saw the infants except to bathe and change them or to prop a bottle against their pillows at feeding times. Often the infants had few or no crib toys and few opportunities to get out and practice motor skills. Thus they were often deprived of sensory as well as social stimulation.

What are such infants like? They seldom cry, coo, or babble; become rigid when they are picked up; and have few language skills. As for their social development, they tend to form either shallow or anxious relationships; some appear forlorn, withdrawn, and uninterested in their caretakers, while others seem emotionally starved and insatiable in their need for affection. Do these negative effects persist? Apparently so. William Goldfarb (1943, 1947) discovered serious deficits in intellectual functioning, language skills, and social competence among children who spent their first three years in an understaffed orphanage. By adolescence many of these children were loners who had a difficult time relating to peers or family members.

More recently, concerns have been expressed about serious maladjustment observed in some children from deprived institutions in Romania who were adopted into homes in the United States and Canada after the fall of the Romanian government in 1990 (Holden,

Infants do not develop normally if they lack continuing relationships with responsive caregivers—whether one or several.

sive caregivers turn out quite normal in all respects (Kessen, 1975; Oppenheim, Sagi, & Lamb, 1988). Similarly, Efe (Pygmy) infants in Zaire seem to thrive despite being cared for and even nursed by a variety of caregivers besides their mothers (Tronick, Morelli, & Ivey, 1992). Finally, as Box 13.2 illustrates, attending day care all day usually does not disrupt the parent/infant attachment, though it can have negative effects under some circumstances. Apparently, then, normal development requires *sustained interactions with responsive caregivers—whether one or several.*

Later Development of Securely and Insecurely Attached Infants

Now consider infants raised at home. How much difference does having secure or insecure attachment make later in life? According to Bowlby and Ainsworth's attachment theory, a secure attachment should allow "exploration from a secure base," which implies that the securely attached children should be more cognitively competent (because they will be curious, explore the environment freely, and not shy away from challenges) and more socially competent (because they will also explore the world of people freely, will expect positive reactions from others because of the internal working models they form, and will have learned in the parent/child relationship how to interact smoothly with others). Does research support these predictions?

Indeed it does. Everett Waters and his associates (Waters, Wippman, & Sroufe, 1979) measured the quality of infants' attachments to their mothers at 15 months of age and then observed these children in nursery school at age 3½. Children who had been securely attached as infants were social leaders in the nursery school setting: They often initiated play activities, were sensitive to the needs and feelings of other children, and were popular with their peers. Moreover, securely attached infants became children whose teachers described them as curious, self-directed, and eager to learn. By contrast, children who had been insecurely attached at age 15 months, displaying either resistant or avoidant attachment patterns, became 3½-year-olds who were socially and emotionally withdrawn and were hesitant to engage other children in play activities. These children were also less curious, less interested in learning, and less forceful in pursuing their goals than securely attached children, as if they lacked a secure base for exploration. In late childhood and adolescence, children who have enjoyed secure relationships with their parents are still more likely than those who have not to be well-adjusted both intellectually and socially. They are self-confident and do well in school (Jacobsen & Hofmann, 1997), and they are accepted by the peer group and have close friends (Elicker, Englund, & Sroufe, 1992; Kerns, Klepac, & Cole, 1996). As we will see later,

1996). Let it be noted, first, that infants adopted from other countries are usually no more or less likely than other infants to form secure attachments (Juffer & Rosenboom, 1997). However, the Romanian adoptees reportedly spent their infancies in orphanages with 20 to 30 children in a room and only one caregiver for every 10 to 20 children. They spent most of the time rocking back and forth in their cribs with little human contact, much less hugs, bouts of play, and synchronous routines (Fisher et al., 1997). Infants who spent 8 months or more in such orphanages displayed eating problems as well as medical problems; many were withdrawn and seemingly overwhelmed in interactions with siblings and peers (Fisher et al., 1997). These children have also proved to be more likely than most infants to display insecure patterns of attachment; although rarely avoidantly attached, they often display resistant or disorganized patterns of attachment and tend to be indiscriminately friendly, much like some of the children studied decades ago by Goldfarb (Marcovitch et al., 1997).

Why does institutional deprivation have such damaging effects on development? It is probably not just lack of sensory and intellectual stimulation, for institutionalized children who are provided with such stimulation but lack a stable team of caregivers are still developmentally delayed and have emotional difficulties even as adolescents (Hodges & Tizard, 1989). Nor is it the lack of a single "mother figure." In *adequately staffed* institutions in the People's Republic of China and in Israel, infants cared for by a few respon-

BOX 13.2

Is day care good for your infant's attachment?

With about 60% of mothers in the United States now working outside the home at least part time, more and more infants and young children are receiving alternative forms of care. According to U.S. Department of Labor statistics, only 25% of all infants and toddlers are cared for by their parents, whereas 27% are with other relatives, 7% are at home with a sitter, 26% are in day-care homes (typically run by a woman who takes a few children into her own home for payment), and 16% are in large day-care centers (Clarke-Stewart, 1993).

Do infants who attend day-care homes or centers suffer in any way compared to infants who stay at home with a parent? Research to date suggests that they are not necessarily damaged by the experience (Clarke-Stewart, 1993; Scarr & Eisenberg, 1993). Jerome Kagan and his associates (Kagan, Kearsley, & Zelazo, 1978), for example, found that infants who attended a high-quality, university-affiliated day-care center were no less securely attached to their mothers than infants who were raised at home. Moreover, day-care infants were generally indistinguishable from home-reared infants on measures of cognitive, linguistic, and social development.

And now we also have the results of a major study conducted in ten cities in the United States (NICHD Early Child Care Research Network, 1997); it involved assessing infants at 1, 6, and 15 months of age. Overall, infants in alternative forms of care were no less securely attached to their mothers than infants tended by parents; a mother's sensitivity to her infant had a lot more to do with attachment security than whether or not an infant was in alternative care. Other research bolsters the conclusion that high-quality day care can be as good for infants and young children as care at home (Broberg et al., 1997; Clarke-Stewart, 1993; Scarr & Eisenberg, 1993).

However, this broad generalization does not tell the full story. As the horror stories we read now and then in the newspaper suggest, day care can be harmful to some children under some conditions. Consider a few factors that influence how well infants adjust to day care:

1. *Quality of the day care.* The effects of day care depend very much on the quality of care provided in the particular day-care setting (Clarke-Stewart, 1993; Scarr & Eisenberg, 1993). Just as some parents are highly nurturant while others are neglecting or abusive, some day-care experiences are actually more beneficial than at-home care and other experiences are dreadful. An infant's development clearly will suffer if he or she ends up with an alcoholic babysitter or must compete for adult attention as one of many infants in a large, understaffed center. Better developmental outcomes are likely in high-quality day care that has (1) a reasonable child-to-caregiver ratio (up to three infants, four toddlers, or eight preschoolers per adult); (2) caregivers who are warm, emotionally expressive, and responsive to children; (3) little staff turnover, so that children can feel comfortable with and become attached to their caregivers; and (4) planned activities that are age appropriate (Howes, Phillips, & Whitebook, 1992; Zaslow, 1991; and see Clarke-Stewart, 1993, for guidelines for evaluating day-care settings).

2. *Characteristics of the child.* In addition, some infants fare better in alternative care than others do. First, infants from disadvantaged homes who are at risk of delayed development actually experience *faster* intellectual growth if they attend a high-quality day-care program specially designed to meet their needs than if they stay at home and receive little intellectual stimulation (Campbell & Ramey, 1994). Second, girls tend to adapt better to day care than boys (Baydar & Brooks-Gunn, 1991; Belsky & Rovine, 1988). Third, infants and toddlers with easy temperaments are likely to adjust better than children who have "difficult" or "slow to warm up" temperaments (Belsky & Rovine, 1988).

Fourth, age is a consideration. Infants who have already formed attachments to their parents sometimes fare better than younger infants. Several studies suggest that babies who spend many hours in alternative care before the age of 1 are somewhat less likely to be securely attached to their mothers and fathers than are infants tended primarily by their parents during their first year, though most do form secure attachments (Belsky & Rovine, 1988; Lamb, Sternberg, & Prodromidis, 1992). As a result, some researchers continue to be concerned

lasting effects of early attachments can be detected even in adulthood.

Recently, Jay Belsky, Becky Spritz, and Keith Crnic (1996) demonstrated for the first time that children who had secure and insecure attachments as infants have different styles of processing information, consistent with the idea that they have formed very different internal working models of self and other. In the study, 3-year-olds were treated to a series of puppet shows dramatizing positive events such as getting a birthday present and negative ones such as spilling juice. The researchers expected children who had been securely attached as infants to have learned from their pleasant experiences early in life to expect positive experiences and to attend to and remember them especially well; they predicted that children with histories of insecure attachment would expect and find life to be unpleasant. The securely and insecurely attached children in the study did not differ in their attentiveness to positive and negative events, but as Figure 13.3 shows, securely attached children excelled at remembering positive events, whereas insecurely attached children excelled at remembering negative events. This was true even when group differences in temperament about possible negative effects of too much day care too early in life (Belsky, Woodworth, & Crnic, 1996; Clarke-Stewart, 1993).

3. *Parents' attitudes and behaviors.* The outcomes of day-care placement are likely to be better if a mother has positive attitudes about working and about being a mother and if she has the personal qualities it takes to provide warm and sensitive care (Belsky & Rovine, 1988; Crockenberg & Litman, 1991). Ultimately, the quality of parenting that infants receive at home seems to have more to do with their development than with the kind of alternative care they receive when they are not at home (Broberg et al., 1997; Fuller et al., 1996).

Most important of all may be interactions between some of these factors that suggest that day care is fine for some but not for others. In the NICHD (1997) study, for example, infants fared poorly if their mothers were not very responsive to them *and* they were subjected to poor-quality day care; under these circumstances, about half of the infants were insecurely attached to their mothers. By contrast, infants who received high-quality care somewhere, either at home or at day care, were usually securely attached.

In sum, we cannot draw simple conclusions about the effects of alternative care on infant development, for these effects range from beneficial to damaging. It does seem, however, that alternative care is least likely to disrupt development if infants are old enough to have already formed attachments

to their parents and if they interact with *both* responsive substitute caregivers and responsive parents. Infants under age 1, especially boys with difficult temperaments, sometimes do not thrive, especially if they receive low-quality day care and do not have warm, responsive parents.

Meanwhile, many parents who work struggle to find and keep competent sitters or high-quality day-care placements. The infants who receive the poorest, most unstable day care are often those whose parents lack the money to pay for child care, live stressful lives, and are unable to provide responsive care themselves (Fuller, Holloway, & Liang, 1996; Howes, 1990). So far, the U.S. government has been far less willing than the governments of many European countries to finance day care (Clarke-Stewart, 1993). Al-

though a parental-leave policy was finally adopted in 1993, it covers only workers in companies with 50 or more employees and offers only *unpaid* leave, doing little to help most low-income parents, whereas many Western European countries provide paid leave. Day care in the United States is often provided by underpaid and undertrained staff whose turnover rate is high, whereas day care in Western Europe is often government subsidized, staffed by trained and well-paid professionals, and available at affordable prices (Scarr et al., 1993). Until something changes, working parents in the United States will continue to face a serious challenge finding high-quality child care they can afford.

were controlled. The implication? Bowlby was on the right track in theorizing that differences in the internal working models that securely and insecurely attached individuals form are significant for later development. Those children who have positive internal working models of their caregivers are likely to form positive mental representations of other individuals they meet such as peers (Cassidy et al., 1996).

In sum, children are unlikely to develop normally if their first relationships in life are disrupted by separation or if they never have the opportunity to form an attachment. Meanwhile, a secure attachment during infancy has positive implications for both social and intellectual development in childhood and does so by contributing to positive working models of self and other. However, we must avoid concluding that infants who are insecurely attached to their mothers are doomed. First, affectionate ties to *fathers* (or perhaps siblings or grandparents) can compensate for insecure mother/infant relationships. Although most infants have the same kind of attachment with their mothers that they have with their fathers, many infants who are insecurely attached to one parent are securely attached to the other (Fox, Kimmerly, & Schafer,

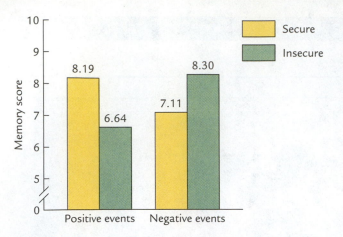

FIGURE 13.3 *Because of differences in their internal working models, securely attached children are biased to remember positive experiences and insecurely attached children to remember negative experiences.* (Based on data from Belsky, Spritz, & Crnic, 1996)

1991; van IJzendoorn & De Wolff, 1997). Infants who have a secure relationship with one parent, whether it is the father or the mother, are more socially competent than infants who are not securely attached to either parent, but those who are securely attached to *both* parents are best off of all (Biller, 1993; Main & Weston, 1981).

In addition, an initially insecure attachment may have no negative long-term consequences if it becomes a secure attachment later on. Unlike diamonds, attachments are not forever. Although most children do experience the same kind of attachment to their parents during childhood that they experienced during infancy (Main & Cassidy, 1988), changing family circumstances often convert insecure attachments into secure ones—or secure attachments into insecure ones. In one recent study, around *half* of the infant-parent pairs studied had different attachment classifications at two assessments 6 or 7 months apart (Belsky, Campbell, Cohn, & Moore, 1996). A secure attachment may become insecure if a mother withdraws from caregiving activities because of such stresses as marital problems, financial woes, or a lack of social support from friends and family members. Meanwhile, initially insecure infants may become securely attached if the lives of their close companions become less stressful (Vaughn et al., 1979). Clearly, the quality of attachment in infancy is unlikely to have long-range effects on development unless the *same* quality is maintained consistently over a reasonably long period (Lamb, 1987).

Finally, we must appreciate that an individual's social relationships *after* infancy affect his or her ultimate social adjustment (Lamb, 1987). Consider what Arlene Skolnick (1986) discovered when she attempted to determine whether an infant who is securely attached to his or her mother at 21 to 30 months of age becomes a child who is well liked, warm, socially per-

ceptive, and otherwise socially competent; an adolescent who is popular and a leader among peers; and a middle-aged adult who is sociable, psychologically healthy, and happily married. Using longitudinal data from the Berkeley Guidance Study, Skolnick found that only about a fourth of the participants in the study had either consistently favorable or consistently poor interpersonal relationships across all four periods of life. The significance of this finding is clear: "Secure attachment to the mother does not make one invulnerable to later problems and socioemotional difficulties, and poor early relations with the mother do not doom a person to a life of loneliness, poor relationships, or psychopathology" (Skolnick, 1986, p. 193).

All things considered, the Bowlby-Ainsworth attachment theory is quite well supported by research evidence, perhaps because it is a broad theory that draws not only on ethological research with animals but also on the psychoanalytic and cognitive perspectives. Although it is difficult to prove that behaviors such as smiling or grasping contribute to the survival of the species, it is likely that many infant behaviors that are innate or maturational in nature do contribute to the formation of attachments. Moreover, Bowlby acknowledges that biological preparedness is not enough to guarantee a firm attachment. The experiences of caregivers and infants as they interact strongly influence whether a secure, resistant, avoidant, or disorganized/disoriented attachment will form.

Moreover, studies of the later consequences of early bonds challenge Freud's strong claim that the quality of an infant's relationship with his or her mother establishes a pattern of personality and social behavior that decisively determines the quality of all future relationships. Instead, they support Bowlby's less extreme position by suggesting that "internal working models" of self and others formed early in life shape later relationships but also can be modified by later relationships. Despite the significance of the infant/parent bond for later development, we apparently have plenty of time to learn new social skills and different attitudes toward relationships in our later interactions with peers, close friends, lovers, and spouses. It is time, then, to supplement our discussion of parent/child relations with a look at the "second world of childhood"—the world of peer relations.

First Peer Relations

Developmentalists have devoted so much effort to studying parent/infant relationships that they have neglected infants' relationships with agemates until fairly recently. When are babies able to interact meaningfully with other infants? Do they become attached to familiar playmates?

Babies show an interest in other babies from the first months of life. By about the middle of the first year, infants will often smile or babble at their tiny companions, vocalize, offer toys, and gesture to one another (Hay, Nash, & Pedersen, 1983; Vandell, Wilson, & Buchanan, 1980). At first many of these friendly gestures go unnoticed and unreciprocated; interactions between infants and adults are a good deal smoother than interactions between infants because adults structure the exchanges (Hay, 1985; Vandell & Wilson, 1987). Still, infants are curious about peers and ready to interact with them from an early age.

Infants then become even more socially adept as they pass through three stages of early sociability from age 1 to age 2 (Mueller & Lucas, 1975; Mueller & Vandell, 1979). At first, in the *object-centered* stage, two infants may jointly focus on a toy but will pay more attention to the toy than to each other. During the second, or *simple interactive,* stage, infants more obviously influence one another and respond appropriately to one another's behavior. They seem to treat peers as if they were interesting "toys" that are responsive and can be controlled (Brownell, 1986). Consider this example:

> Larry sits on the floor and Bernie turns and looks toward him. Bernie waves his hand and says "da," still looking at Larry. He repeats the vocalization three more times before Larry laughs. Bernie vocalizes again and Larry laughs again. This same sequence . . . is repeated twelve more times before Bernie . . . walks off. (Mueller & Lucas, 1975, p. 241)

By about 18 to 24 months of age, infants progress to the third, or *complementary interactive,* stage, in which their interactions are even more clearly social and reciprocal. They now delight in imitating each other and turn these rounds of imitation into social games (Eckerman & Stein, 1990; Howes & Matheson, 1992). Such imitation is the main way in which toddlers coordinate their actions and create a common understanding of what they are doing; only later can they use speech to do this (Eckerman & Didow, 1996). Toddlers also adopt roles in their play and can reverse roles. Thus the toddler who receives a toy may immediately offer a toy in return, or the one who has been the "chaser" will become the "chasee." Toward the end of the second year, infants have become quite proficient at this kind of turn taking and reciprocal exchange. This is especially true if they are securely attached infants, for they are more likely than insecurely attached ones to get positive responses when they reach out in a friendly manner to peers (Fagot, 1997).

Surprising as it may seem, some infants also form special relationships with preferred playmates—friendships (Howes, 1996). On Israeli kibbutzim, where children are cared for in groups, Martha Zaslow (1980) discovered that many pairs of infants as young as 1 year of age became truly attached to each other.

With age, infants' interactions with one another become increasingly skilled and reciprocal.

Hadara and Rivka, for instance, consistently sought each other out as playmates, mourned each other's absence, and disturbed everyone with their loud babbling "conversations" when they were confined to their cribs.

In sum, the caregiver/infant relationship is not the only important social relationship that develops during infancy, although it is the one that comes first and that has the potential to steer social development in either adaptive or maladaptive directions. Through their interactions with significant adults *and* their interactions with peers, infants begin to acquire the social competencies that will permit them to become even more sociable beings during childhood.

THE CHILD

Social relationships change tremendously from infancy to later childhood. How does the parent/child attachment change? Who are the important members of children's social networks, with whom do they spend time, and what is the character of their play? Why are some children more popular than others, and what draws children together as friends? And finally, just how important are children's social relationships to their overall development?

Parent/Child Attachments

The parent/child attachment changes qualitatively during childhood. As John Bowlby (1969) noted, it becomes a "goal-corrected partnership" in which parent and child accommodate to each other's needs and the child becomes more independent of the parent. Older

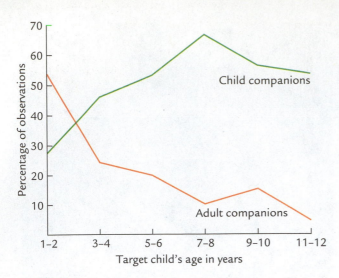

FIGURE 13.4 *Developmental changes in the percentage of their time children spend with adults and other children* (From Ellis, Rogoff, & Cromer, 1981)

preschoolers still seek attention and approval from their parents, and they most certainly rush to their parents for comfort when they are frightened or hurt. But they also become increasingly dependent on *peers* for social and emotional support (Furman & Buhrmester, 1992).

Peer Networks

Over the years from age 2 to age 12, children spend more and more time with peers and considerably less time with adults. This trend is shown vividly in Figure 13.4, which summarizes what Sharri Ellis and her colleagues (1981) found when they observed 436 children playing in their homes and around the neighborhood. Interestingly, this study revealed that youngsters of all ages spent *less* time with agemates (defined as children whose ages were within a year of their own) than with children who were more than a year older or younger than they were. Apparently we must take seriously the idea that peers are not merely agemates but "social equals."

Another finding of this study is a familiar one: Even 1- to 2-year-olds played more often with same-sex companions than with other-sex companions, and this *gender segregation* became increasingly strong with age (see Chapter 11). Once in their sex-segregated worlds, boys and girls experience different kinds of social relationships. You may have heard, for example, that boys travel in "packs," whereas girls travel in "pairs." It's true: by age 6, boys spend about three-fourths of their time in group activities, whereas girls spend only 16% of their time in groups, preferring to play with one other girl at a time (Benenson, Apostoleris, & Parnass, 1997).

Overall, then, children spend an increasing amount of time with peers rather than parents, and these peers are typically *same-sex* children who are only *roughly similar* in age and enjoy the same sex-typed activities.

Play

It is in the context of play that children develop social relationships with their peers and acquire social skills. So important is play in the life of the child from age 2 to age 5 that these years are sometimes called "the play years." This is when children hop about the room shrieking with delight, don capes and go off on dragon hunts, and whip up cakes and cookies made of clay, sand, or thin air. We can detect two major changes in play between infancy and age 5: It becomes more social, and it becomes more imaginative. After age 5 or so, the exuberant and fanciful play of the preschool years gives way to somewhat more serious play.

Play Becomes More Social

Many years ago, Mildred Parten (1932) devised a useful method for classifying the types of play engaged in by nursery school children of different ages. Her six categories of activity, arranged from least to most social, are as follows:

1. *Unoccupied play:* Children stand idly, look around, or engage in apparently aimless activities such as pacing.
2. *Solitary play:* Children play alone, typically with objects, and appear to be highly involved in what they are doing.
3. *Onlooker play:* Children watch others play, taking an active interest and perhaps even talking to the players, but not directly participating.
4. *Parallel play:* Children play next to one another, doing much the same thing, but they interact very little (for example, two girls might sit near each other, both drawing pictures, without talking to each other to any extent).
5. *Associative play:* Children interact by swapping materials, conversing, or following each other's lead, but they are not really united by the same goal (for example, our two girls may swap crayons and comment on each other's drawings as they draw).
6. *Cooperative play:* Children truly join forces to achieve a common goal; they act as a pair or group, dividing their labor and coordinating their activities in a meaningful way (for example, our two girls collaborate to draw a mural for their teacher).

The major message of Parten's study (and of others like it) is that play becomes increasingly social and socially skilled from age 2 to age 5 (Barnes, 1971;

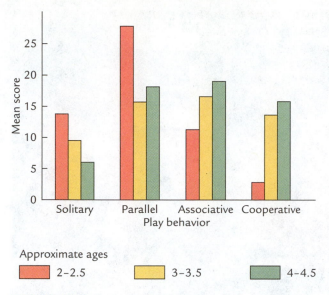

FIGURE 13.5 *Frequency of activities engaged in by preschool children of different ages. With age, solitary and parallel play occur less frequently, whereas associative and cooperative play occur more frequently.* (Adapted from Barnes, 1971)

Smith, 1978; see also Howes & Matheson, 1992). Unoccupied and onlooker activities are quite rare at all ages, solitary and parallel play become less frequent with age (though solitary play has its place throughout childhood), and associative and cooperative play (the most social and complex of the types of play) become more frequent with age (see Figure 13.5).

Play Becomes More Imaginative

The first **pretend play**—play in which one actor, object, or action symbolizes or stands for another—occurs about the age of 1, when an infant may raise an empty cup to her lips, smile, give a parent a knowing glance, and make loud lip-smacking sounds (Nicolich, 1977). The earliest pretend play is just like this: The infant performs actions that symbolize familiar activities such as eating, sleeping, and washing.

By age 2, toddlers readily join in pretense if you hand them a towel and suggest that they wipe up the imaginary tea you just spilled (Harris & Kavanaugh, 1993). Since there is no "tea" in sight, this willingness to clean it up is really quite remarkable. It means that toddlers are capable of using their new symbolic capacity to construct a mental representation of a pretend event and of acting according to this representation (Harris & Kavanaugh, 1993). Pretend play fully blossoms from age 2 to age 5, increasing dramatically in frequency and sophistication (Howes & Matheson, 1992; Rubin et al., 1983). Children can depict heroes and heroines very different from themselves and can enact elaborate dramas using very few props. Most importantly, they combine their capacity for increas-

ingly social play and their capacity for pretense into **social pretend play** (Howes & Matheson, 1992). Starting at age 2½ or 3, children less often enact scenes on their own using dolls and other toys and more often cooperate with playmates to enact their dramas.

The quality of preschoolers' play is shaped by the culture in which they live. In a comparison of the social pretend play of Korean and Euro-American preschoolers, Jo Ann Farver and Yoolim Shin (1997) found that U.S. children liked to play superheroes and act out themes of danger and fantasy (the adventures of superheroes), whereas Korean children took on family roles and enacted everyday activities. American children also talked a lot about their own actions, rejected other children's ideas, and bossed others around, whereas Korean children were more focused on their partners' activities and were more prone to make polite requests and agree with one another. Through their play, then, American children were learning to assert their identities as individuals, whereas Korean children were learning how to keep their egos and emotions under control to achieve group harmony.

Play Becomes More Rule-Governed

After they enter school, children engage less frequently in symbolic play. Now they spend more of their time playing organized games with rules—board games, games of tag or hide-and-seek, organized sports, and so on (Athey, 1984). They also develop individual hobbies, such as building model cars or making scrapbooks, that allow them to develop skills and gain knowledge.

According to Jean Piaget (1932/1965), it is not until children enter the stage of concrete-operational thought, at about age 6 or 7, that they become capable of joining with other children to follow the rules of games. Older children—11- and 12-year-olds who are entering the stage of formal-operational thought—gain a more flexible concept of rules, recognizing that they are arbitrary agreements that can be changed as long as the players agree. Their ability to engage in hypothetical thinking allows them to invent new rules and even new games and to think through strategies in games like chess. Partly because of cognitive gains, then, the play of the school-age child is more organized and rule governed—and less fanciful—than that of the preschool child.

What Good Is Play?

In 19th-century America child's play was discouraged because it was viewed as a frivolous waste of time (Athey, 1984). Now we know better. Play contributes to virtually all areas of children's development. The fact that playful activity occurs among the young of so many species suggests that play is an evolved behavior that serves the adaptive function of preparing

the young for adult life by equipping them with useful skills (Gandelman, 1992).

To illustrate, children who engage in a great deal of pretend play (or are trained to do so) perform better on tests of Piagetian cognitive development, language skills, and creativity than children who rarely pretend (Fisher, 1992; Johnson, 1991). And perhaps because of the social experience they gain, preschoolers who engage in a great deal of social pretend play tend to be more popular and socially mature than children who do not (Connolly & Doyle, 1984; Howes & Matheson, 1992).

In addition, play contributes to healthy emotional development, for children have opportunities to express bothersome feelings, resolve emotional conflicts, and master challenges that they may not be able to master in real life (Curry & Arnaud, 1984; Fein, 1986). If Danny, for example, has recently been scolded by his mother for drawing on the wall, he may gain control of the situation by scolding his "child" for doing the same thing. Children who are suffering from emotional disturbances not only reveal their concerns through their play but have difficulty playing in mature and creative ways (Gordon, 1993). For example, Mavis Hetherington and her colleagues (Hetherington, Cox, & Cox, 1979) found that, compared to children from intact families, children from divorcing families acted out fewer themes in their play, had difficulty using props in multiple ways or getting by without realistic props, and adopted fewer roles. Moreover, the many aggressive themes in their play reflected their angers and anxieties about divorce.

Let it never be said, then, that play is useless. Although children play because it is fun, not because it sharpens their skills, they indirectly contribute to their own development—physical, intellectual, social, and emotional—by doing so. In this sense, play truly is the child's work.

Peer Acceptance and Popularity

As children play and interact, they typically discover that they like some peers more than others. Researchers study peer-group acceptance through **sociometric techniques**—methods for determining who is liked and disliked in a group. In a sociometric survey, children in a classroom may be asked to nominate several classmates whom they like and several whom they dislike, or they may be asked to rate all of their classmates in terms of their desirability as companions (see Terry & Coie, 1991). By finding out who is liked *and* who is disliked in a group, we can classify children into four quite distinct categories of social status (Coie, Dodge, & Coppotelli, 1982): the *popular* (well liked by most and rarely disliked), the *rejected* (rarely liked and often disliked), the *neglected* (isolated children who are neither liked nor disliked but seem instead to be invisible to their classmates), and the *controversial* (children who are liked by many but also disliked by many—for example, the fun-loving child with leadership skills who also has a nasty habit of starting fights).

Why are some children more popular than others, and why are some children rejected by their peers?

Popularity is affected by some personal characteristics that a child can do little about. For instance, physically attractive children are usually more popular than physically unattractive children (Langlois, 1986). As early as the preschool years, children have learned a "beauty is good" stereotype holding that physically attractive peers are friendlier, nicer, smarter, and better in almost every way than their less attractive counterparts.

A child's *competencies* also influence popularity. For example, children who are relatively intelligent and achieve well in school tend to be more socially accepted than those who are less academically competent (Bukowski et al., 1993; Pettit et al., 1996). The most important kind of competence, though, may be *social competence*—the ability to apply social-cognitive skills successfully in initiating social interactions, responding positively to peers, resolving interpersonal conflicts, and so on. Popular children are socially skilled children—cooperative and responsive rather than argumentative and disruptive (Coie, Dodge, & Kupersmidt, 1990; Ladd, Price, & Hart, 1990). "Rejected" children are usually highly aggressive, although some are socially isolated, submissive children who are overly sensitive to teasing and are seen by others as "easy to push around" (Parkhurst & Asher, 1992; Rabiner, Keane, & MacKinnon-Lewis, 1993). Children who fall into the "neglected" category of sociometric status are usually nonaggressive; many of them have reasonably good social skills but tend to be shy, withdrawn, and unassertive (Coie et al., 1990; Harrist et al., 1997). As a result, no one really notices them.

To appreciate how social skills contribute to popularity, consider what happens when children try to enter and gain acceptance in play groups (Dodge et al., 1990; Putallaz & Wasserman, 1989). When children who ultimately become popular want to join a group's activity, they first hold back and assess what is going on and then smoothly blend into the group, commenting pleasantly about whatever the other children are discussing. By contrast, children who are eventually rejected by their peers tend to be pushy and disruptive. Jimmy, for example, may sit beside two boys who are playing a computer game and distract them by talking about a TV program he saw the night before. Even worse, he may criticize the way the boys are playing or even threaten to turn off the computer if he is not allowed to play. By contrast, children who end up being neglected by their peers often hover around a group without taking any positive steps to initiate contact and shy away from peers who attempt to make contact with them.

As we've seen, children who experienced secure attachments to their parents as infants tend to be popular with their peers; they seem to have learned social skills and styles of interacting in the parent-child rela-

Children in the neglected category of sociometric status are shy and tend to hover on the fringes of a group without daring to enter it.

tionship that shape the quality of their relationships with peers (Black & Logan, 1995; Kerns, 1996). Parents of popular children also make explicit attempts to teach their children how to relate to peers, and these attempts pay off (Mize & Pettit, 1997). By contrast, harsh discipline at home tends to breed the aggressive behavior that prompts peers to reject a child (Pettit et al., 1996), and parents who are not very sensitive to their children during conversations tend to produce children who are not very responsive conversation partners and end up being rejected because of it (Black & Logan, 1995).

In sum, popularity is affected by many factors. It helps to have an attractive face and academic skills, but it is probably more important to behave in socially competent ways. Definitions of desirable social behavior, of course, vary from culture to culture. Thus, for example, children who are shy are likely to be unpopular in Canada but popular in China, where being quiet and reserved is more socially desirable (Chen, Rubin, & Sun, 1992). The ingredients of popularity also change with age: Establishing close relationships with members of the other sex enhances popularity during adolescence, but consorting with "the enemy," and thereby violating norms of gender segregation, can *detract* from popularity during childhood (Sroufe et al., 1993). Many such contextual factors influence who is popular and who is not.

Do the outcomes of these popularity polls really matter? Yes—especially for the 10 to 15% of children who are rejected by their peers (Malik & Furman, 1993). Children who are neglected by peers often gain greater acceptance later, but those who are rejected, especially because of aggressive behavior, are likely to maintain their rejected status from grade to grade (Cillessen et al., 1992; Coie et al., 1990). More significantly, children who experience being rejected may consequently end up with worse behavior problems than they had initially (Coie et al., 1992; DeRosier, Kupersmidt, & Patterson, 1994; Morison & Masten, 1991).

Friendships

Close friends are the most important peers a child has. Popular children are more likely than unpopular children to have friends, but even most unpopular children manage to enter into at least one reciprocated friendship (George & Hartmann, 1996), and they are better off if they do have one than if they do not. Not only are they likely to be less lonely (Parker & Asher, 1993), but they are likely to be happier and more competent, especially if their friendships are supportive relationships with peers who are well-adjusted (Hartup & Stevens, 1997). Moreover, just as Harry Stack Sullivan theorized, a true chum can sometimes compensate for a poor relationship with parents and provide children with a sense of self-worth they might otherwise lack (Gauze et al., 1996).

What qualifies someone as a friend? The answer seems to depend on a child's age and level of social-cognitive development, at least when children are asked to explain why their friends are their friends (Selman, 1980). To the preschool child a friend may be "Miguel, who lives next door and plays with me." Before age 8 or so, the principal basis for friendship is *common activity*. Young children form friendships with peers who are similar to themselves in observable characteristics such as age, sex, and racial or ethnic group—and who participate in and enjoy similar activities (Dickens & Perlman, 1981; Hartup & Stevens, 1997). Their descriptions of their friends tend to be egocentric, emphasizing the nice things their friends do for them and the terrific toys they have. Interestingly, their actual friendships are far more sophisticated than their verbal descriptions of their friendships would suggest: Even preschool friends engage in a good deal of give-and-take and genuinely care about one another (Gottman, 1983; Howes, 1996).

Equipped with more sophisticated role-taking skills, 8- to 10-year-old children begin to describe friendships as relationships based on *mutual loyalty*, in which two people exchange respect, kindness, and affection (Aboud & Mendelson, 1996; Furman & Bierman, 1983): "Miguel and I like each other and stick by each other no matter what." No longer are physical and behavioral similarities sufficient; children now insist that their friends be *psychologically* similar to themselves. Moreover, they emphasize that each partner in a friendship must be sensitive to the other's perspective. Perhaps because they rest on a firmer cognitive basis, the friendships (or chumships, as Sullivan would call them) of older children are more long last-

ing than those of younger children (Berndt & Hoyle, 1985; Cairns et al., 1995).

Contributions of Peers to Development

Developmentalists now know that peers, especially friends, may be every bit as important as parents to child development. Parents typically provide a sense of emotional security that enables infants to explore their environment and to appreciate that other people can be interesting companions (Kerns, 1996). However, acceptance by and interactions with peers may be critical in the learning of social skills and normal patterns of social behavior (Newcomb & Bagwell, 1995). Judith Harris (1995) even goes so far as to suggest that children are socialized into the ways of their culture primarily by the peer group and would end up learning much the same things even if they lived in another home, with different parents, in the same neighborhood. She cites the example of immigrant children, who readily learn the local culture from peers, even though it is very different from the culture of their parents.

The influences of peers extend far beyond the realm of social development (Newcomb & Bagwell, 1995; Hartup, 1996). Peers, especially close friends, contribute to emotional development by teaching children how to participate in emotionally intimate relationships and by offering emotional support and comfort that can help children feel better about themselves, weather stressful events such as a divorce, and feel bolder when faced with new challenges such as the first day of kindergarten (Hartup, 1996; Ladd, 1990). Moreover, social interactions with peers stimulate new cognitive growth; children acquire new knowledge and problem-solving skills from other children (Gauvain & Rogoff, 1989; Tudge, 1992).

Acceptance by the larger peer group clearly helps children learn social skills, but friends are important too for what they do to bolster children's self-esteem and provide them with emotional support and opportunities for intimacy (Hartup & Stevens, 1997; Newcomb & Bagwell, 1995). In short, normal child development seems to require both attachments to adults and close relationships with peers and especially friends.

THE ADOLESCENT

Although children are already highly involved in peer activities, adolescents spend even more time with peers and less time with parents (Buhrmester & Furman, 1986; Fallon & Bowles, 1997). The quality of the individual's attachment to parents continues to be highly important throughout adolescence, but peers, including romantic partners, begin to rival or surpass parents in importance as sources of intimacy and sup-

Going to college is a "Strange Situation" that activates attachment behaviors such as hugging and e-mailing designed to maintain contact with attachment figures.

port (Furman & Buhrmester, 1992; Lempers & Clark-Lempers, 1992). Moreover, the *quality* of peer relations changes. Not only do adolescents begin to form boy/girl friendships and go on dates, but they become more capable of participating in truly deep and intimate attachments.

Attachments to Parents

Attachments to parents remain highly important during adolescence. Just as infants must have a secure base if they are to explore, adolescents seem to need the security provided by supportive parents in order to become more independent and autonomous individuals (Kobak et al., 1993; Kenny & Rice, 1995). For many youths in our society, for example, going off to college qualifies as a "naturally occurring strange situation" (Kenny, 1987)—a potentially stressful test of one's ability to cope with the unfamiliar. Students who go home on weekends or call or e-mail home frequently during their first semester are engaging in "attachment behavior" just as surely as the infant who whimpers for his mommy. From an attachment theory perspective, experiencing separation anxiety in this situation is perfectly normal and adaptive. Preoccupa-

tion with parents typically decreases over the first semester and predicts adjustment problems only when it is extreme (Berman & Sperling, 1991).

Students who are securely attached to their parents, as indicated by attachment surveys or interviews, display better psychological and social adjustment during the potentially difficult transition to college than students who are insecurely attached (Kenny & Donaldson, 1991; Lapsley, Rice, & FitzGerald, 1990). Ofra Mayseless and her colleagues (1996) found that securely attached students cope very well with the task of separating from parents; they form close romantic relationships while maintaining close communication with their parents. Resistantly attached students have more difficulty forming romantic relationships and find even minor separations from parents very upsetting. Avoidant youth, although more likely to live with their parents than the other groups, claim not to be bothered much by separation, as if denying that they could need their parents for anything.

More generally, adolescents who enjoy secure attachments with their parents seem to have a stronger sense of identity, higher self-esteem, greater social competence, and better emotional adjustment than their less securely attached peers (Kenny & Rice, 1995). Moreover, the bond to parents remains just as important and just as strong in late adolescence as it is in early adolescence (Kenny & Rice, 1995). When parents provide emotional support and a secure base for exploration but also encourage autonomy, their adolescents seem to thrive.

Friendships

Whereas friendships in early childhood center on common activities, and friendships in late childhood center on mutual loyalty, adolescent friendships increasingly hinge on *intimacy and self-disclosure* (Berndt & Perry, 1990; Buhrmester, 1996). Teenagers continue to form friendships with peers who are similar to themselves and to express feelings of loyalty toward their friends. However, they increasingly choose friends whose *psychological qualities*—interests, attitudes, values, and personalities—seem to match their own. Now they view friends as like-minded individuals who can confide in each other.

The transition to intimate friendships based on a sharing of thoughts and feelings occurs earlier among girls than among boys (Berndt & Perry, 1990; Reis et al., 1993). Teenage girls who are best friends are almost like lovers, intensely attached to each other and inseparable—sometimes even possessive, jealous, and outraged by any betrayal of their trust (Douvan & Adelson, 1966). As girls become more autonomous, gain social-cognitive skills, and become more involved in dating in high school, they become less emotionally dependent on their best friends (Douvan & Adelson,

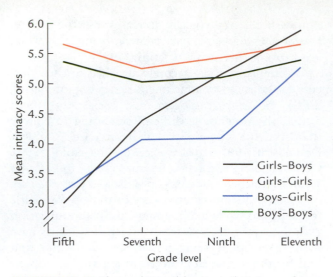

FIGURE 13.6 *Changes during adolescence in the intimacy of same-sex and cross-sex friendships. The "Girls-Boys" scores reflect how girls rated the intimacy of their relationships with boys; "Boys-Girls" scores reflect how boys rated their relationships with girls. Cross-sex friendships clearly become more and more intimate during the adolescent years, ultimately achieving the levels of intimacy that characterize same-sex friendships throughout this developmental period.* (From Sharabany, Gershoni, & Hofman, 1981)

1966). Teenage boys do get to know their buddies well by doing things with them, but their friendships are less emotionally intense and they talk less about their feelings than girls who are best friends do (Berndt, 1982; Buhrmester, 1996).

Although same-sex friendships remain important throughout adolescence, teenagers increasingly enter into close cross-sex friendships. How do these other-sex friendships compare with same-sex friendships? Ruth Sharabany and her colleagues (1981) asked 5th to 11th graders to assess their same- and cross-sex friendships in terms of such aspects of emotional intimacy as spontaneity, trust and loyalty, sensitivity to the other's feelings, attachment, and so on. As you can see in Figure 13.6, same-sex friendships were highly intimate in most respects throughout this age range, but cross-sex friendships did not attain a high level of intimacy until 11th grade. These findings offer some support for Harry Stack Sullivan's view that children learn lessons about intimate attachments in their same-sex chumships that they later apply in their heterosexual relationships (see also Fullerton & Ursano, 1994).

We can also see that girls tended to report higher degrees of intimacy in their friendships than boys did; moreover, girls experienced intimacy in their friendships with boys sooner than boys experienced intimacy in their relationships with girls. These findings confirm that boys are somewhat slower than girls to achieve emotional intimacy in their close relationships.

Changing Social Networks

Elementary school children take interest in members of the other sex and are grooming themselves for heterosexual relationships (Thorne, 1993). Still, one has to wonder how boys and girls who live in their own, gender-segregated worlds arrive at the point of dating "the enemy." Some time ago, Dexter Dunphy (1963) offered a plausible account of how peer-group structures change during adolescence to pave the way for dating relationships. His five stages, outlined in Figure 13.7, are still relevant today.

Cliques and Crowds

The process of change in the organization of the peer group begins in late childhood, when boys and girls become members of same-sex **cliques,** or small friendship groups, and have little to do with the other sex. Next, members of boy cliques and girl cliques begin to interact with each other more frequently. Same-sex cliques provide what amounts to a secure base for exploring ways to behave with members of the other sex: Talking to a girl when your buddies are there is far less threatening than doing so on your own. In the third stage, the most popular boys and girls form a *heterosexual* clique. Popular children are quicker than unpopular children to form cross-sex friendships, so they lead the way (George & Hartmann, 1996).

As less popular peers also enter into heterosexual cliques, a new peer group structure, the **crowd,** completes its evolution. The crowd, a collection of up to about four heterosexual cliques, is involved in arranging organized social activities on the weekend—parties, outings to the lake or mall, and so on. Those adolescents who become members of a mixed-sex clique and a crowd (not all do) have many opportunities to get to know members of the other sex. Eventually, however, interacting with the other sex in group settings is not enough. Couples form and the crowd disintegrates in late high school after having served its purpose of bringing boys and girls together.

Not all high school crowds are the same. The names may vary, but every school has its crowds of "populars," "jocks," "druggies," and "losers," each consisting of adolescents who are similar to one another in some way and different from the adolescents in other crowds (Brown, Mory, & Kinney, 1994; Brown & Lohr, 1987). Everyone in high school seems to recognize these differences: the brains "all wear glasses and 'kiss up' to teachers and after school they all tromp uptown to the library" (Brown et al., 1994, p. 128); "The partyers goof off a lot more than the jocks do, but they don't come to school stoned like the burnouts do" (p. 133). Which crowd an adolescent belongs to has important implications for his or her social iden-

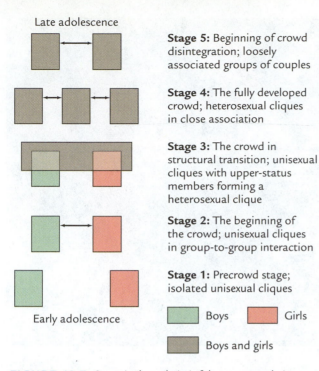

Late adolescence

Stage 5: Beginning of crowd disintegration; loosely associated groups of couples

Stage 4: The fully developed crowd; heterosexual cliques in close association

Stage 3: The crowd in structural transition; unisexual cliques with upper-status members forming a heterosexual clique

Stage 2: The beginning of the crowd; unisexual cliques in group-to-group interaction

Stage 1: Precrowd stage; isolated unisexual cliques

Early adolescence

Boys

Girls

Boys and girls

FIGURE 13.7 *Stages in the evolution of the peer group during adolescence: from same-sex cliques* (bottom) *to dating couples* (top). (Adapted from Dunphy, 1963)

tity and self-esteem; it's easier to feel good about one-self if one is a "popular" or a "jock" rather than a "dweeb," or a "druggie," or a social isolate who does not belong to any crowd (Brown & Lohr, 1987). Crowd membership also has a good deal to do with whether peer pressures pull in the direction of deviant behavior or conventional behavior; "druggies" encourage drug use, whereas "brains" discourage it. So, adolescence is a time of transition from same-sex to cross-sex peer relationships, and peer influences can be healthy or destructive, depending on which cliques and crowds an adolescent belongs to (Hartup & Stevens, 1997).

Dating

Candice Feiring (1996) has recently provided an interesting picture of the dating experiences of a sample of 15-year-olds. Almost 90% of these adolescents had dated by the age of 15, although only 21% were currently dating. Most couples did not go out alone on dates as much as they dated within the context of the peer group or crowd. While dating, couples saw each other or talked on the phone (for an average of 60 minutes per call!) every day. These dating relationships were usually casual and lasted an average of only 4 months. Dating relationships differed from same-sex friendships mainly in that partners were romantically fascinated with one another. In other respects, though, dating relationships were more like same-sex friendships than like adult romantic attachments;

they were mainly sources of companionship rather than of love and security (Feiring, 1996). As we saw in Chapter 11, these relationships of course also involve sexual experimentation.

All things considered, early dating relationships often lack depth and tend to be short-lived. Adolescents face a major developmental challenge in dating, for they must take lessons they have learned in both parent/child and friendship relationships and apply them in a new kind of relationship. In the end, the challenge is to integrate needs for security (satisfied during childhood by parents), intimacy (obtained from same-sex friends, or chums), and sexual gratification (a new need) in a love relationship (Furman & Wehner, 1994). Some adolescent couples form true attachments to one another (Levesque, 1993). More typically, though, romantic attachments that are built on love and provide emotional support do not become common until late adolescence or early adulthood (Furman & Buhrmester, 1992; Laursen, 1996).

Parent and Peer Influence

Should parents worry about the fact that adolescents become more and more involved in both same-sex and cross-sex relationships with peers as they get older? Will they lose influence over their children? One approach to answering these questions has been to study **conformity,** the tendency to yield to the opinions and wishes of others. Conformity to parents' wishes tends to decrease gradually and steadily with age during adolescence, whereas conformity to peers, including peers who advocate lawbreaking, increases until about age 14 or 15 and then declines (Berndt, 1979; Bixenstine, DeCorte, & Bixenstine, 1976; Steinberg & Silverberg, 1986). Thus parents do have some grounds for worrying that their adolescents may get into trouble by "going along with the crowd," especially at around age 14 or 15.

Why does conformity to peers' misconduct *decrease* by the end of high school? As adolescents progress in their quest for autonomy, they become less dependent on *both* parents and peers for guidance and more able to make their own choices. Increased dependence on peers may even be a necessary step in the development of autonomy (Steinberg & Silverberg, 1986). Although parents whose teenagers end up at the police station may not be totally comforted by this thought, teenagers may need the "secure base" that peer acceptance provides before they are ready to become truly autonomous in later adolescence.

Parents retain a good deal more influence over their adolescents than is commonly believed, though. Peers do influence adolescents' social activities and tastes, but parents continue to be the major shapers of their educational and vocational plans and important

values (Sebald, 1986; Wilks, 1986). More important, teenagers who have close attachments to warm and authoritative parents who establish and enforce clear standards of behavior are likely to be academically and socially competent and to internalize their parents' values. What's more, they are likely to associate with conventional rather than antisocial peer groups, are therefore less likely to be exposed to negative peer pressures, and will be less susceptible to such pressures when they do encounter them than are adolescents whose family relationships are poor (Brook et al., 1990; Brown et al., 1993; Fuligni & Eccles, 1993; Mounts & Steinberg, 1995).

Meanwhile, problems for youth who "get in with the wrong crowd" and engage in antisocial behavior usually begin at home. One way parents can go wrong is by being too strict, failing to adjust to adolescents' needs for greater autonomy. This may cause teenagers to become alienated from their parents and overly susceptible to negative peer influences (Fuligni & Eccles, 1993). Parents can also go wrong by failing to provide enough discipline and by not monitoring their children's activities sufficiently (Brown et al., 1993; Dishion et al., 1991). When parents are warm and accepting, are neither too controlling nor too lax, and are consistent in their discipline, adolescents have little need to rebel or to seek acceptance in the peer group that they cannot obtain at home. They are also likely to have the academic and social competencies required for acceptance into crowds that will reinforce their parents' values rather than undermine them (Brown et al., 1993; Dishion et al., 1991).

In summary, adolescent socialization is not a continual war of parents *versus* peers; instead, these two important sources of influence *combine* to affect development. As their teenage children become more involved in activities with peers and more susceptible to peer pressures, parents continue to be important forces in their children's lives. Parent/peer warfare is kept to a minimum because parents and peers often influence different aspects of behavior and decision making and because parents have a hand in ensuring that their children's friends share their views on many important issues. As a result, most adolescents develop healthy peer relationships and acquire social competencies that allow them to form and maintain good relationships as adults.

THE ADULT

Relationships with family and friends are no less important during adulthood than they are earlier in life, but they take on different qualities over the adult years. Let's examine how people's social networks change during adulthood and then look more closely at their romantic relationships and friendships.

Social Networks

With whom do adults of different ages interact, and how socially active are they? Young adults are busily forming romantic relationships and friendships, typically choosing to associate with people who are similar to themselves in important ways, just as children and adolescents do. Harry Reis and his colleagues (1993), in a 10-year study of college students, found that young adults do more socializing with members of the other sex and less with members of the same sex after college graduation than they did while in college; this was true of both sexes and of unmarried as well as married people. In other words, trends toward greater intimacy with the other sex that begin in adolescence continue during early adulthood.

Young adults, especially single ones, seem to have more friends than middle-aged and older adults do (Fischer & Phillips, 1982; Fischer, Sollie, Sorell, & Green, 1989). As adults marry, have children, and take on increasing responsibilities in their jobs, and as they age, their social networks shrink somewhat. Laura Carstensen (1992) has offered a **socioemotional selectivity hypothesis** to account for changes in adults' social networks. As we get older, Carstensen argues, our needs change and we actively choose to narrow our range of social partners to those who can best meet our needs. In middle and late adulthood, we increasingly prefer to interact with people who can meet our emotional needs (usually family members and close friends whose company we enjoy) and have less need for the social stimulation and new information that contacts with strangers and acquaintances often provide. This is an adaptive change that involves sacrificing the quantity of our relationships in order to strengthen their *quality*.

What evidence is there to support the socioemotional selectivity hypothesis? Although middle-aged adults interact less frequently with acquaintances and friends than young adults do, they interact often with their spouses and siblings and actually feel closer emotionally to the significant people in their lives than younger adults do (Carstensen, 1992; see also Fischer & Phillips, 1982). And, although elderly adults have even fewer friends and smaller social networks (Connidis & Davies, 1992), they have about as many close relationships with kin as young and middle-aged adults do (Levitt, 1991). If they do not have living spouses or children, they strengthen relationships with siblings, other relatives, or friends to compensate and maintain an inner circle of intimates (Lang & Carstensen, 1994). So, consistent with the selectivity hypothesis, older adults apparently choose to restrict their interactions to the people who really count and can meet their emotional needs. They end up just as satisfied, if not more satisfied, with their relationships as younger adults, and, at least if they maintain ties to siblings or other kin, they are usually just as able to count on social support (Antonucci, 1985; Bossé et al., 1993; Depner & Ingersoll-Dayton, 1988). They even end up *less* likely than young adults to report feelings of loneliness (Parlee, 1979). So, adults' social networks do shrink in total size from early adulthood to very old age, but most elderly adults enjoy emotionally rich and supportive relationships with a small circle of intimates.

Romantic Relationships

For many adults, the most important member of the social convoy and a key attachment figure is a spouse or romantic partner. As Erik Erikson has emphasized, early adulthood is typically the time for establishing truly intimate and committed relationships—marriages or other enduring emotional attachments.

Partner Selection

Why do we choose the romantic partners we choose? Because we fall in love, you may say. True enough. Yet we do not fall in love with just anyone. As Richard Udry (1971) has emphasized, mate selection is a process of sifting through all potential partners to find one chosen partner. We are most likely to become romantically involved with someone who lives in proximity to us; who is attractive to us; and who matches us in such characteristics as socioeconomic background, education, racial or ethnic group, and religious affiliation.

Assuming that a potential partner passes these tests, similarity with respect to values, attitudes, and interests may help determine whether the relationship endures or crumbles. If potential mates are psychologically similar, they may then favor a relationship in which there is also *complementarity,* or a meshing of strengths and weaknesses that somehow makes each person more complete. Finally, all the compatibility in the world is unlikely to lead to marriage unless both partners have reached a point in their development at which they possess a *readiness for marriage* or for a lasting commitment of some kind. Udry's most important theme is that we gravitate toward those who are similar to ourselves in a wide range of important ways, just as children do when they select friends. Opposites may attract on occasion, but more often birds of a feather flock together.

Attachment Styles

Several researchers, intrigued by the parallels between an infant's attachment to a parent figure and a young adult's love for a romantic partner, have begun to study romantic relationships from the perspective of attachment theory (Ainsworth, 1989; Colin, 1996; Feeney & Noller, 1996). Obviously, parent/infant attachments and adult romantic attachments are not identical. Yet the adult who is in love, like the infant who is attached to a parent, experiences strong affection for his or her partner, wants to be close, takes comfort from the bond, and is upset by separations. Indeed, married adults who are separated from their spouses by war or the demands of work experience the same kinds of distress and despair that infants experience when separated from their mothers and fathers (Vormbrock, 1993). Like parent/child attachment, attachment between romantic partners is biologically

TABLE 13.3

Four types of internal working models associated with having positive or negative views of self and other people based on one's experiences in relationships

	Model of Self	
	Positive	**Negative**
Model of Others **Positive**	**Secure** *Secure attachment history* Have healthy balance of attachment and autonomy (freedom to explore)	**Preoccupied** *Resistant attachment history* Are desperate for love to feel worthy as a person; worry about abandonment; express anxiety and anger openly
Model of Others **Negative**	**Dismissing** *Avoidant attachment history* Shut out emotions; defend against hurt by avoiding intimacy, dismissing the importance of relationships, being "compulsively self-reliant"	**Fearful** *Disorganized/disoriented attachment history* Need relationships but doubt own worth and fear intimacy; lack a coherent strategy for meeting attachment needs

SOURCE: Adapted from Bartholomew & Horowitz (1991)

adaptive; it increases the odds of children, as well as the odds that these children will have two parents to nurture them (Colin, 1996). Perhaps it is not surprising, then, that the concept of romantic love is not just a Western phenomenon, as many people believe. Instead, the phenomenon of romantic love has been documented in at least 88% of the world's cultures, including many in which marriages are arranged by family elders (Jankowiak & Fischer, 1992).

Table 13.3 shows one scheme for thinking about how the internal working models that all of us have constructed from our experiences in early relationships affect romantic relationships (Bartholomew & Horowitz, 1991; see also Shaver & Clark, 1996). Asked questions about their memories of attachment experiences during childhood and their current feelings about relationships, adults with a *secure* working model feel good about both themselves and others; they are not afraid of entering into intimate relationships and do not worry about being abandoned once they do. People with a *preoccupied* working model have a positive view of other people but feel unlovable. Like resistantly attached infants, they crave closeness to others (as a means of validating their self-worth), are highly fearful of abandonment, and tend to become overly dependent on their partners. Adults with a *dismissing* style of attachment have a positive view of self but do not trust other people. Like avoidantly attached infants, they defend themselves against hurt by not expressing their need for love or fear of abandon-

ment; indeed, recent research suggests that they may not be as distressed by thoughts of abandonment as most people (Fraley & Shaver, 1997). They deny that they need people or that relationships really matter to them, find it hard to trust partners, and feel that others want them to be more intimate than they wish to be. Bowlby (1973) described dismissing or avoidant individuals as "compulsively self-reliant." Finally, adults with a *fearful* working model resemble infants with a disorganized/disoriented attachment; they take a dim view of both themselves and other people and display a confusing mix of neediness and fear of closeness.

In an initial study conceptualizing romantic love as attachment, Cindy Hazan and Phillip Shaver (1987) classified 56% of the adults they studied as having a secure attachment style, 19% as resistant, and 25% as avoidant (they did not attempt to measure the fearful or disorganized/disoriented attachment style). Adults' styles of attachments were related to the quality of their romantic relationships (see also Brennan & Shaver, 1995; Colin, 1996). For example, adults with a *secure* attachment style experience a good deal of trust and many positive emotions in their current love relationships. Their relationships also tend to last longer than those of adults with insecure attachment styles. Avoidant lovers fear intimacy, whereas resistant individuals tend to be obsessed with their partners. Both *avoidant* and *resistant* adults report a lot of jealousy and emotional extremes of love and pain in love relationships and are dubious that lasting love can be found. Adults with different attachment styles even express their jealousy differently, it seems: Secure individuals express their anger directly to their partners, resistant individuals hold it in, and avoidant individuals turn their anger on the person who threatened the relationship (Sharpsteen & Kirkpatrick, 1997).

Hazan and Shaver also discovered that adults' characterizations of their early relationships with their parents and their current attachment styles were correlated. Adults with a secure attachment style recalled warm relationships with their parents during childhood, but adults with insecure attachment styles tended to remember their parents as unfair, critical, or cold. Here, then, is more support for Bowlby's (1973) hypothesis that the internal working models of self and others we form on the basis of our earliest attachments affect the quality of later relationships (see also Feeney & Noller, 1996).

As Bowlby theorized, internal working models also predict the extent to which adults have the confidence to take on and master challenges. Hazan and Shaver (1990) find that close relationships with spouses or romantic partners provide the "secure base" that allows adults to explore the environment, work productively, and enjoy life. Securely attached adults enjoy work and are good at it; preoccupied or resistantly attached adults want approval and grumble about not being valued enough by their bosses and coworkers; and dismissing, or avoidantly attached, adults bury themselves in their work and do little socializing.

Finally, the internal working models of self and others that grow out of early experiences in the family also appear to affect an adult's capacity to be a loving parent: Mothers and fathers who had secure relations with their parents tend to interact in more sensitive ways with their children and to form more secure attachments with them than parents whose early attachments were resistant, avoidant, or disorganized (Steele, Steele, & Fonagy, 1996; van IJzendoorn, 1995); indeed, in up to 75% of the cases, mother and infant have the same attachment style. What's more, grandmothers, mothers, and children all tend to fall in the same attachment category (Benoit & Parker, 1994). This research is quite significant, for it suggests that internal working models of relationships may be passed on from one generation to the next. Yet working models are termed "working" models because they are subject to revision if later experiences in relationships suggest that change is warranted (Noam & Fischer, 1996). Although research on secure, preoccupied, dismissing, and fearful styles of attachment in adulthood is intriguing, we must remember that early attachment experiences may predict the future but do not determine it.

Adult Friendships

Even though young adults typically have more friends than older adults do, friends remain an important part of the social convoy throughout the adult years (Blieszner & Adams, 1992; Hartup & Stevens, 1997; Johnson & Troll, 1994). So important are friends to elderly adults that the quality of their relationships with friends has more impact on their well-being than the quality of their relationships with children (O'Connor, 1995). Elderly adults especially value friendships that have lasted a lifetime (Adams, 1985–1986; Matthews, 1986; Shea, Thompson, & Blieszner, 1988). Almost three-fourths of the women Rebecca Adams interviewed claimed that "old friends are the best friends," although they continued to make new friends late in life.

What happens to friendships as older adults begin to develop significant health problems and disabilities? When one friend needs more aid than the other and is able to give less aid in return, this imbalance can cause difficulties (Silverstein & Waite, 1993). Social psychologists have long emphasized the importance of **equity,** or a balance of contributions and gains, in relationships between spouses, friends, and other intimates (Walster, Walster, & Berscheid, 1978).

Close friendships that have lasted for years are particularly important to adults.

Generally, relationships are perceived as more satisfying when they are equitable than when they are inequitable. A person who receives too much from a relationship is likely to feel guilty; a person who gives a great deal and receives little in return may feel angry or resentful (Walster et al., 1978). We are more satisfied with our lives when our close relationships are equitable than when they are lopsided (Antonucci, Fuhrer, & Jackson, 1990).

Consistent with equity theory, Karen Roberto and Jean Scott (1986) report that elderly adults experience less distress in friendships they perceive as equitable than in those they perceive as inequitable. Interestingly, *overbenefited,* or dependent, friends experience more distress than underbenefited, or support-giving, friends. Elderly adults who are unable to contribute equally to a friendship may feel uncomfortable being dependent, whereas friends who find themselves in the helper role may take comfort from knowing they are capable of giving. Perhaps because inequity threatens friendships, older adults usually call on family rather than friends when they need substantial help or emotional support, unless they have no kin nearby (Felton & Berry, 1992; Kendig et al., 1988). By not overburdening their friends, they stand to keep them longer.

In sum, adults of all ages seem to enjoy close friendships, new and old, and often are able to carry with them through life—as part of their social convoy—old friends with whom they share a lifetime of experiences, especially if they can maintain equity in their relationships. Just how much do friendships and other close relationships contribute to well-being, especially in later life?

Adult Relationships and Adult Development

We have emphasized throughout this chapter that close attachments to other people are essential to normal cognitive, social, and emotional development. It should not surprise you to learn, then, that adults are better off in many ways if they enjoy meaningful social relationships. Much attention has been centered on the significance of social networks and social support to elderly people—possibly because researchers, like members of the general public, have incorrectly assumed that most elderly adults are socially isolated. The major generalization that has emerged from this research is this: *It is the quality rather than the quantity of an individual's social relationships that is most closely related to that person's sense of well-being or life satisfaction* (Antonucci & Akiyama, 1991; O'Connor, 1995). Just as people can feel lonely despite being surrounded by others, adults apparently can feel deprived of social support even though they receive a lot of it—or they can have quite restricted social networks and yet feel satisfied with their relationships.

The size of an adult's social network is not nearly so important as whether it includes at least one **confidant**—a spouse, relative, or friend to whom the individual feels an especially close attachment and with whom thoughts and feelings can be shared (de Jong-Gierveld, 1986; Levitt, 1991). For most married adults, spouses are the most important confidants; for older adults whose spouses have died, children or friends often step in to fill these needs; for single adults, siblings sometimes become especially important (Connidis & Davies, 1992). Whoever an older adult's key sources of support are, it is less important how much assistance they provide than that interactions with them are rewarding rather than stressful (Krause, 1995). For example, interactions with adult children may undermine rather than increase well-being if the parent/child attachment is insecure (Barnas, Pollina, & Cummings, 1991).

In sum, a small number of close and harmonious relationships can do much to make negative life events more bearable and improve the overall quality of an adult's life. It's more than that, though: social support, especially from family members, actually has positive effects on the cardiovascular, endocrine, and immune systems; keeps blood pressure in the normal range; improves the body's ability to cope with stress; and can contribute to a longer and, especially in old age, healthier life (Uchino et al., 1995; Uchino, Cacioppo, & Keicholt-Glaser, 1996). Whatever our ages, then, our well-being and development hinge considerably on the quality of our ties to fellow humans—and particularly on our having a close bond with at least one person.

APPLICATIONS: BUILDING GOOD RELATIONSHIPS

Developmentalists naturally have become interested in applying what they have learned about social development to the task of helping individuals to develop richer social relationships. They have been quite successful.

One approach that makes sense if one believes in the importance of the parent/infant attachment for later relationships is to intervene early. Parents who are likely to be insensitive to their infants and whose infants have difficult temperaments are at risk for insecure attachments (see van IJzendoorn, Juffer, & Duyvesteyn, 1995). In one study, low-income mothers in Holland with irritable babies received a series of three 2-hour training sessions designed to make them more sensitive and responsive caregivers (van den Boom, 1995). Home visitors worked with the mothers during everyday interactions to help them respond appropriately to their infants' positive and negative cues. Not only did the mothers who received training become more sensitive caregivers, but their infants were more likely than those of mothers who received no training to be securely attached to their mothers at 12 months of age and to remain more securely attached at $3\frac{1}{2}$. What's more, they apparently transferred positive skills they learned in the parent/infant relationship to their relationships with peers.

Children who are neglected or, worse, rejected by their peers are another group at risk. They can be helped through interventions designed to teach them the social and social-cognitive skills they lack (Malik & Furman, 1993). In social-skills coaching programs, an adult therapist models or displays social skills, explains why they are useful, allows children to practice them, and then offers feedback to help children improve on their performances. Sherrie Oden and Steven Asher (1977) coached third- and fourth-grade social isolates in four important social skills: how to participate in play activities, how to take turns and share, how to communicate effectively, and how to give attention and help to peers. Not only did the children who were coached become more outgoing and positive in their social behavior, but a follow-up assess-

ment a year later revealed that they had achieved gains in sociometric status within the classroom.

Lonely adolescents and young adults are not unlike socially withdrawn children. In many cases they too have social-skills deficits that make it difficult for them to make contact with people, carry on meaningful conversations, and build more intimate relationships (Christopher, Nangle, & Hansen, 1993). For instance, Warren Jones and his associates (1982) discovered that lonely college students needed coaching in how to pay positive attention to their conversation partners by referring to them, pursuing topics they bring up, and asking questions. These researchers designed a coaching program to teach lonely college men to be more attentive to female conversation partners. Compared with students who received no coaching or who simply interacted with a partner without benefit of training, the trained students were more able to offer reinforcing attention to women when they completed the program. Moreover, they left the program reporting that they were less lonely, shy, and self-conscious (see Christopher et al., 1993, for a review of similar successful interventions).

However, not all individuals who are lonely and isolated are socially incompetent. For some individuals the real problem is a restricted social environment—a lack of opportunities for forming close relationships (Rook, 1984, 1991). Such was the case for the socially isolated elderly people described by Marc Pilisuk and Meredith Minkler (1980). Living in inner-city hotels in San Francisco, these individuals were often prisoners of their rooms because of disability, poverty, and fear of crime. To change things, public health nurses began to offer free blood pressure checkups in the lobby of one hotel. As the nurses got to know the residents, they were able to draw them into conversations and to link individuals who had common interests. After about a year, the residents formed their own activities club; organized discussions, film showings, and parties; and were well on their way out of their social isolation. The trick was to change their social environment rather than their social skills.

Because development is influenced by both individual and environmental factors, it makes sense to think that children and adults who lack healthy social relationships can be helped most through efforts to improve their social skills *and* to change their social environments in order to increase their opportunities for meaningful interaction. The ultimate goal might be to ensure that every human being enjoys the many developmental benefits that come from a social convoy that includes a secure bond with at least one caregiver during infancy, a close friendship in childhood or adolescence, and an intimate romantic relationship or friendship in adulthood.

SUMMARY POINTS

1. Social relationships contribute immensely to human development, primarily by providing critical learning opportunities and social support (through our changing social convoys). The developmental significance of early parent/child relationships was emphasized by Freud and continues to be emphasized in the Bowlby-Ainsworth attachment theory, which draws on ethological theory to argue that attachments are built into the human species, develop through an interaction of nature and nurture during a sensitive period early in life, and affect later development by shaping internal working models of self and other. Peer relationships are believed to be especially important by Piaget, who emphasized their reciprocal nature, and Sullivan, who emphasized that childhood chumships can compensate for poor parent/child relationships or peer rejection and prepare children for romantic relationships.

2. Biologically based emotions such as anger and fear appear in the first year of life and quickly become socialized through modeling, reinforcement, and social referencing. As infants get older, they rely less on caregivers and more on their own emotion regulation strategies to manage their emotions in interactions with their attachment objects.

3. Because infants have endearing qualities, parents typically become attached to them before or shortly after birth. Then parent and child normally establish synchronized routines, although some parents have difficulty doing so because of characteristics of the baby, parent, or social context.

4. In forming attachments, infants progress through phases of undiscriminating social responsiveness, discriminating social responsiveness, active proximity seeking, and goal-corrected partnership; the formation of attachments at about 6 or 7 months of age is accompanied by separation anxiety and stranger anxiety.

5. Research using Ainsworth's Strange Situation test indicates that quality of attachment can be classified as secure, resistant, avoidant, or disorganized/disoriented. Although the Freudian view that infants become attached to those who feed them lacks support, Erik Erikson and learning theorists were correct to emphasize the caregiver's responsiveness as the key influence on attachment quality. Secure attachments are associated with sensitive, responsive parenting; resistant attachments with inconsistent, unresponsive care; avoidant attachments with rejection or overstimulation, and disorganized/disoriented attachments with abusive treatment. Infant characteristics (temperament and achievement of cognitive-developmental milestones such as person permanence) also contribute.

6. Severing of attachments can trigger protest, despair, and detachment, but worse is social deprivation that makes it impossible for an infant to attach to anyone. Secure attachments contribute to later competence, but insecurely attached or socially deprived infants are not inevitably doomed to a lifetime of poor relationships.

7. Infants become increasingly able to coordinate their own activity with that of their small companions to participate in complementary interactive exchanges and form friendships.

8. During the years from 2 to 12, children participate in goal-corrected partnerships with their parents and spend increasing amounts of time with peers, especially same-sex ones, engaging in increasingly social and imaginative play, such as social pretend play and then organized games, and forming friendships on the basis of common activity and then mutual loyalty. Physical attractiveness, academic ability, and social competence contribute to popularity. Children who are rejected by their peers are at risk for future problems, for peer interactions affect all aspects of development.

9. During adolescence, same- and cross-sex friendships increasingly involve emotional intimacy and self-disclosure, and heterosexual cliques and crowds facilitate the transition from same-sex peer groups to dating relationships. Although susceptibility to negative peer pressures peaks at about age 14 or 15, adolescence is typically not a continual war of parents versus peers unless poor family relationships result in the adolescent's becoming involved with an antisocial crowd.

10. Most adults of all ages have high-quality relationships, though social networks shrink with age due to increased socioemotional selectivity.

11. In forming romantic attachments, adults favor partners similar to themselves. Adults have secure, preoccupied, dismissing, and fearful attachment styles that appear to be rooted in their early attachment experiences and that influence their romantic relationships and parenting styles.

12. Although adults are highly involved with their spouses or romantic partners, they continue to value friendships, especially long-lasting and equitable ones. Well-being is influenced more by the quality than by the quantity of relationships; it is especially important to have at least one confidant.

13. Individuals who lack close relationships can be helped through interventions to make parents more responsive caregivers, social-skills training, and provision of social-interaction opportunities.

FOOD FOR THOUGHT

1. Remember Baby Jessica, the little girl introduced at the start of the chapter who was snatched at age 2½ from the only parents she had ever known? Now that you have read the chapter, see if you can develop a set of hypotheses, based on attachment theory and research on attachment, about her later development. Do not read further until you do.

    Now it's time to fill you in. By age 3, Jessica had been renamed Anna Jacqueline Schmidt and was reportedly a happy, well-adjusted preschooler (Ingrassia & Springen, 1994). As her mother, Cara Schmidt, reported it, the traumatic effects of loss of attachment figures that theorists like Freud and Bowlby would expect never occurred: "Everyone guaranteed—*guaranteed*—that she would have short-term trauma, that she wouldn't eat, she wouldn't sleep, she'd cry. It didn't happen. She progressed, rapidly" (Ingrassia & Springen, 1994, p. 60). Jessica did remember the day of the van ride ("I got in the van and was crying and crying," p. 66), and she remembered her first parents, the DeBoers, but she did not pine for them. As it turned out, they were far more devastated than Jessica by the severing of the relationship.

    The moral? We should not make too much of one case. Jessica had eight visits with her biological parents before being sent to live with them and therefore had an opportunity to begin to form an attachment to them (Ingrassia & Springen, 1994). We also do not know how she will fare later in life. Yet her story, like the studies of adoptive children discussed earlier, tells us once more that children have a good deal of resilience provided that they are given reasonable opportunities to socialize and to love someone.

2. Ethological theory, psychoanalytic theory, and cognitive psychology all influenced John Bowlby as he formulated attachment theory. Which elements of attachment theory do you think most reflect each of these three theoretical perspectives?

3. Billy Jo, age 10, does not have a best friend and has never really had one. Why do you think this is, and what implications do you think lack of a friend might have for Billy Jo's later development?

ON THE WEB

1. *Attachment Theory*   This site contains one item, a paper in which Mary Ainsworth discusses the concept of security in attachment relationships and provides background on her research on attachment and contributions to attachment theory. http://www.psy.sunysb.edu/ewaters/security.htm

2. *Measuring Adult Attachment*   Ready to diagnose your attachment style or those of your friends? If so, this site allows you to view or download some of the scales that are used in studies of adult attachment (complete with scoring instructions) and to link to the Web pages of such leading researchers as Phillip Shaver. http://www.uwinnipeg.ca/~isspr/att.html

KEY TERMS

social support
social convoy
attachment theory
attachment
imprinting
internal working model
peer
chumship
social referencing

emotion regulation
synchronized routines
separation anxiety
stranger anxiety
secure base
Strange Situation test
secure attachment
resistant attachment
avoidant attachment
disorganized/disoriented
   attachment

contact comfort
pretend play
social pretend play
sociometric techniques
clique
crowd
conformity
socioemotional selectivity
   hypothesis
equity
confidant

CHAPTER 14

The Family

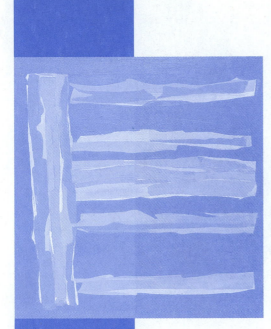

UNDERSTANDING THE FAMILY
The Family as a System
The Family as a System within Other Systems
The Family as a Changing System
A Changing Family System in a Changing World

THE INFANT
The Mother/Infant Relationship
The Father/Infant Relationship
Mothers, Fathers, and Infants: The System at Work

THE CHILD
Dimensions of Child Rearing
Sibling Relationships

THE ADOLESCENT
Parent/Child Closeness
Renegotiating the Relationship

THE ADULT
Establishing the Marriage
New Parenthood
The Child-Rearing Family
The Empty Nest
Grandparenthood
Changing Family Relationships

DIVERSITY IN FAMILY LIFE
Singles
Childless Married Couples
Gay and Lesbian Families
Families Experiencing Divorce
Remarriage and Reconstituted Families

APPLICATIONS: CONFRONTING THE PROBLEM OF FAMILY VIOLENCE
Why Does Family Violence Occur?
What Are the Effects of Abuse?
How Do We Solve the Problem?

SUMMARY POINTS

FOOD FOR THOUGHT

ON THE WEB

KEY TERMS

When Burnam and Addie Ledford hosted the Ledford family reunion, he was 102, she 93. They had married in 1903 and were nearing their 75th wedding anniversary. They had 13 children, 9 of them still surviving, the oldest age 69. They also had 32 grandchildren, the oldest age 42, and 39 great-grandchildren—so many that Burnam marveled, "It's like planting seeds. They keep coming up." (Egerton, 1983)

Not many of us have families as large as the Ledfords', but we are all bound to families. We are born into them, work our way toward adulthood in them, start our own as adults, and remain connected to them in old age. We are part of our families, and they are part of us. James Garbarino (1992) has gone so far as to characterize the family as the "basic unit of human experience" (p. 7).

This chapter examines the family and its diverse and important roles in human development throughout the life span. What is a family, and how has the nature of the family changed in recent years? How do infants, children, and adolescents experience family life, and how are they affected by their relationships with parents and siblings? And what of adults? They are developing individuals, too. How is their development affected by such family transitions as marrying, becoming a parent, watching children leave the nest, and becoming a grandparent? Finally, what are the implications of the diversity that characterizes today's

family lifestyles—and of such decisions as remaining childless or divorcing?

UNDERSTANDING THE FAMILY

The Family as a System

Proponents of **family systems theory** conceptualize the family as a system, meaning that it, like the human body, is truly a whole consisting of interrelated parts, each of which affects and is affected by every other part, and each of which contributes to the functioning of the whole (Klein & White, 1996). In the past, developmentalists did not adopt this family systems perspective. They typically focused almost entirely on the mother/child relationship, assuming that the only process of interest within the family was the mother's influence on the child's development (Ambert, 1992).

The **nuclear family** consists of husband/father, wife/mother, and at least one child. Even a simple man, woman, and infant "system" can be very complex (Belsky, 1981). An infant interacting with her mother is already involved in a process of *reciprocal* influence: The baby's smile is likely to be greeted by a smile from Mom, and Mom's smile is likely to be reciprocated by the infant's grin. However, the presence of *both* parents "transforms the mother-infant dyad into a *family system* [comprising] a husband-wife as well as mother-infant and father-infant relationships" (Belsky, 1981, p. 17). Every individual and every relationship within

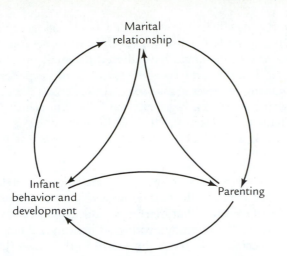

FIGURE 14.1 *A model of the family as a social system. Parents affect infants, who affect each parent and the marital relationship. Of course, the marital relationship may affect the parenting the infant receives, the infant's behavior, and so on. Clearly, families are complex social systems. As an exercise, you may wish to rediagram the patterns of influence within a family after adding a sibling or two.* (From Belsky, 1981)

the family affects every other individual and relationship through reciprocal influence (see Figure 14.1). You can see why it was rather naive to think that the family could be understood by studying only the ways in which mothers mold their children.

Now think about how complex the family system becomes if we add another child (or two or six) to it—and try to understand the unique relationships between each parent and each of these children, as well as relationships between siblings. Or consider the complexity of an **extended family household,** in which parents and their children live with other kin—some combination of grandparents, siblings, aunts, uncles, nieces, and nephews. Extended family households are very common in many cultures of the world, as well as among African Americans in the United States (Pearson et al., 1990; Ruggles, 1994). This family arrangement is likely to be especially adaptive for economically disadvantaged single mothers, who can obtain needed help with child care and social support by living with their mothers (Burton, 1990). Such support helps them parent more effectively, which in turn contributes to good academic performance and psychological adjustment in their children (Taylor, 1996; Taylor & Roberts, 1995; Zimmerman, Salem, & Maton, 1995).

The Family as a System within Other Systems

Whether a family is of the nuclear or the extended type, we cannot think of it as a unit that exists in a vacuum. As we discussed in Chapter 4, it is useful to adopt Bronfenbrenner's *ecological approach* to studying the family (Bronfenbrenner, 1979, 1995; and see Chapter 2), viewing the family as a system embedded in larger social systems such as a neighborhood, a community, a subculture, and a broader culture. For example, parents who are facing financial problems feel less stressed and are better able to maintain effective parenting practices if they have close ties to a larger social support group—a church group, volunteer organization, or set of close friends—than if they do not (Burchinal, Follmer, & Bryant, 1996; Hashima & Amato, 1994). The larger culture is important too; the family experience in our culture is quite different from that in cultures where new brides become underlings in the households of their mothers-in-law, or where men can have several wives. There is an almost infinite variety of family forms and family contexts in the world, and a correspondingly wide range of developmental experiences within the family.

The Family as a Changing System

It would be difficult enough to study the family as a system if it kept the same members and continued to perform the same activities over and over again for as long as it existed. Obviously, this is not the case. Family membership changes as new children are born and as grown children leave the nest. Moreover, the individuals within the family are all developing individuals, and the *relationships* between husband and wife, parent and child, and sibling and sibling also develop in systematic ways over time. Since the family is truly a system, changes in family membership and changes in any individual or relationship within the family are bound to affect the dynamics of the whole.

Thus we have to view the family as a developing organism, and a number of **family development theories** have been proposed to do just that (Klein & White, 1996). The earliest family development theories featured the concept of a **family life cycle,** a sequence of changes in family composition, roles, and relationships from the time people marry until they die (Hill & Rodgers, 1964). Family theorist Evelyn Duvall (1977) outlined eight stages of the family life cycle (see Table 14.1). In each stage, family members play distinctive roles and carry out distinctive developmental tasks—for example, establishing a satisfying relationship as newlyweds, adjusting to the demands of new parenthood in the childbearing phase, and adapting to the departure of children in the "launching" phase.

In this chapter we'll look at the impacts of these family transitions on adults, and we'll examine how the child's experience of the family changes as he or she develops. We'll also see that an increasing number of people do not experience the traditional family life

TABLE 14.1

Stages of the family life cycle

Stage	Available Roles
1. **Married couple** without children	Wife Husband
2. **Childbearing family** oldest child birth to 30 months	Wife/mother Husband/father Infant daughter or son
3. **Family with preschool children** oldest child 30 months to 6 years	Wife/mother Husband/father Daughter/sister Son/brother
4. **Family with school-age children** oldest child up to 12 years	Wife/mother Husband/father Daughter/sister Son/brother
5. **Family with teenagers** oldest child 13 to 20 years	Wife/mother Husband/father Daughter/sister Son/brother
6. **Family launching young adults** first child gone to last child gone	Wife/mother/grandmother Husband/father/grandfather Daughter/sister/aunt Son/brother/uncle
7. **Family without children** empty nest to retirement	Wife/mother/grandmother Husband/father/grandfather
8. **Aging family** retirement to death	Wife/mother/grandmother Husband/father/grandfather Widow or widower

SOURCE: Adapted from Duvall (1977)

cycle, however; they remain single or childless, or they marry multiple times. As a result, many family researchers now reject the simple concept of the family life cycle and its set stages (Dilworth-Anderson & Burton, 1996; Klein & White, 1996). However, they have by no means rejected the idea that families, like the individuals in them, are developing organisms.

In sum, family systems theorists encourage us to view the family as a system in which all members affect all others; Bronfenbrenner and other ecological theorists encourage us to see the family as a system embedded in other systems such as communities and cultures; and family development theorists insist that we understand the family life cycle and the processes of change that each family undergoes.

A Changing Family System in a Changing World

Not only is the family a system embedded within systems, and not only is it a developing system, but the world in which it is embedded is changing rapidly. During the last half of the 20th century, several dramatic social changes have altered the makeup of the typical family and the quality of family experience. Drawing on several analyses of U.S. Census data and other surveys, I'll highlight the following trends (see Chadwick & Heaton, 1992; El-Khorazaty, 1996; Hernandez, 1997; Hobbs, 1996; U.S. Bureau of the Census, 1997):

1. *More single adults:* More adults are living as singles today than in the past. However, don't be deceived into thinking that marriage is out of style, for about 95% of today's young adults can still be expected to marry at some time in their lives (U.S. Bureau of the Census, 1997).

2. *Postponed marriage:* Many adults are not rejecting marriage but are simply delaying it while they pursue educational and career goals. Although the average age of first marriage decreased during the first half of the century, it has now risen again, to about 24 for women and 26 for men (U.S. Bureau of the Census, 1997), despite increased rates of teenage pregnancy among lower-income groups.

3. *Fewer children:* Today's adults are not only waiting longer after they marry to have children, but they are having fewer of them—about 1.8 on average, compared to 3.0 in 1950—and therefore are spending fewer years of their lives raising children (El-Khorazaty, 1996). Increasing numbers of young women are also remaining childless, though few do so by choice (Jacobson & Heaton, 1991).

4. *More women working:* In 1950, 12% of married women with children under age 6 worked outside the home; now the figure is about 63%, a truly dramatic social change (U.S. Bureau of the Census, 1997). Although women still carry the lion's share of child-rearing and housework responsibilities, fewer and fewer children have a mother whose full-time job is that of homemaker.

5. *More divorce:* It is well known that the divorce rate has been increasing over the past several decades. According to one estimate, up to 60% of newly married couples can expect to divorce (Bumpass, 1990).

6. *More single-parent families:* Partly because of a rising rate of out-of-wedlock births, but mostly because of the rise in divorce rates, more children live in single-parent families. In 1960 only 9% of children lived with one parent, usually a widowed one; in 1996, 24% of children under 18 lived with their mothers only, 4% with their fathers only (U.S. Bureau of the Census, 1997).

7. *More children living in poverty:* Unfortunately, the higher numbers of single-parent families have contributed to an increase in the proportion of

children living below the poverty line; 54% of children living in female-headed homes, compared to 10% of children in two-parent families, live in poverty (Eggebeen & Lichter, 1991). As we'll see, economic stresses have many negative effects on the family.

8. *More remarriages:* Simply because more married couples are divorcing, more adults (about 75% of divorced individuals) are remarrying. Often they are forming new, **reconstituted families,** which involve at least a parent, a stepparent, and a child and sometimes blend multiple children from two families into a new family (Glick, 1989). About 25% of American children will spend some time in a reconstituted family (Hetherington & Jodl, 1994).

9. *More years without children:* Because modern couples are compressing their childbearing into a shorter time span, because some divorced individuals do not remarry, and because people are living longer, adults today spend more of their later years as couples—or, especially if they are women, as single adults—without children in their homes (Chadwick & Heaton, 1992; Johnson & Troll, 1996).

10. *More multigeneration families:* As a result of these same trends, more children today know their grandparents and even their great-grandparents. Although three-generation families are still more common than four-generation ones, the family has been evolving into what has come to be called a **beanpole family,** a family with a large number of generations (four or more), each of them small (Bengtson, Rosenthal, & Burton, 1990; Johnson & Troll, 1996). As each generation lives longer, parent/child relationships last longer.

Some of these trends in family life have affected some ethnic and racial groups more dramatically than others. For example, the rise in mother-headed families has been particularly steep among African Americans; partly as a result, almost half of African-American children now live in poverty (Eggebeen & Lichter, 1991). We'll be looking at the impacts of some of these trends on development later in this chapter. Our main point for now is this: *The American family is more diverse than ever before.* Our stereotyped image of the family—the traditional *Leave It to Beaver* nuclear family with breadwinner/father, housewife/mother who does not work, and children—has become just that: a stereotype. By one estimate, about 45% of families in 1960, but only 12% of families in 1995, conformed to this "ideal" (Hernandez, 1997). Although the family is by no means dying, we must broaden our image of it to include the many dual-career, single-parent, reconstituted, and childless families that exist today. Bear that in mind as we begin our excursion into family life at the beginning—with the birth of an infant.

THE INFANT

We begin our look at family development by adopting a child's perspective and following a child's development in the family context from infancy to adolescence. Later we'll adopt the perspective of this child's parents and see how the events of the family life cycle look to them.

The Mother/Infant Relationship

In Chapter 13 we discussed at length the mother/infant attachment and its significance for later development. There is a simple reason why the mother/infant relationship has received far more attention than the father/infant relationship: Mothers have traditionally been the primary caregivers for infants. When mothers are warm, sensitive, and responsive, infants become securely attached to them. By fostering a secure attachment, a parent contributes to other positive outcomes as well—for example, later social competence in interactions with peers, an interest in exploring the world, and rapid intellectual growth.

Yet infants also affect their mothers. Even a sensitive woman may find it difficult to love a baby who cries endlessly. Indeed, babies who have easy temperaments seem to make sensitive and responsive parenting easy, whereas babies who are unresponsive and irritable can sometimes help "produce" rather unaffectionate mothers (van IJzendoorn et al., 1992). The mother/child relationship takes on its distinctive character as a result of the *reciprocal* contributions of mother and infant.

The Father/Infant Relationship

Now that developmentalists have taken seriously the idea that the family is a system, they have discovered that fathers are part of the family too. How much do fathers interact with their children, and what do they really contribute to their children's development?

Gender stereotypes would suggest that fathers are not cut out to care for young children. The evidence suggests that they are (Biller, 1993; Parke, 1996; Phares, 1996). Again and again, researchers find that fathers and mothers are more similar than different in the ways they interact with infants and young children. In one study, for example, mothers and fathers were observed while they fed their babies (Parke & Sawin, 1976). Fathers were no less able than mothers to perform this caregiving task effectively and to ensure that the milk was consumed; nor were they any less sensitive to the infant's cues during the feeding session. Similarly, fathers, just like mothers, become objects of their infants' love and serve as secure bases for their explorations, especially if these fathers have positive attitudes toward parenting and spend a lot of time with their babies (Cox et al., 1992). We really have no basis for thinking that mothers are uniquely qualified to parent or that men are hopelessly inept around babies. However, the fact that fathers are *capable* of sensitive parenting does not necessarily mean they will play the same roles in their children's lives that mothers do. Fathers and mothers do differ in both the quantity and quality of the parenting they provide (Biller, 1993; Parke, 1996; Phares, 1996).

Consider first the matter of quantity. Mothers simply spend more time with children than fathers do, and this seems to be true in most cultures (Phares, 1996; Hewlett, 1992). Fathers in our society are more involved with their children today than they were in the past, especially if their wives work and especially if their wives work on different schedules than they do (Brayfield, 1995). Yet our best estimate is that fathers spend only about a third as much time interacting with their children as mothers do (Phares, 1996).

Now consider the issue of quality. Mothers and fathers differ in their typical styles of interacting with young children. When mothers interact with their babies, a large proportion of their time is devoted to caregiving: offering food, changing diapers, wiping noses, and so on. Although fathers in some societies play an active role in teaching their children, especially their sons, how to perform work activities (Hewlett, 1992), fathers in our society spend much of their time with children in *play*. Specifically, fathers, especially young fathers, are more likely than mothers to provide playful and rowdy physical stimulation and to initiate unusual or unpredictable games (Lamb, 1981; Neville & Parke, 1997). Fathers seem to specialize in tickling, poking, bouncing, and surprising infants, whereas mothers hold, talk to, and play quietly with infants.

Fathers also treat boys and girls more differently than mothers do (see Chapter 11). For one thing, fathers often spend more time with sons than with daughters (Barnett & Baruch, 1987; Phares, 1996). In addition, they are more likely than mothers to encourage boys to play with masculine-stereotyped toys, to encourage girls to play with feminine-stereotyped toys, and to discourage play that is considered more appropriate for the other sex (Snow, Jacklin, & Maccoby, 1983). Thus mothers tend to be "equal opportunity" parents, treating girls and boys much the same, while fathers alter their parenting style according to whether they are interacting with sons or daughters (Lytton & Romney, 1991).

In view of the roles that fathers play in their children's lives, what are their unique contributions to child development? Certainly if a mother is for some

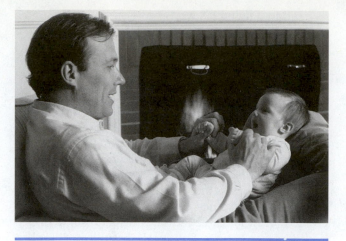

Fathers are just as capable as mothers of sensitive, responsive parenting.

reason unresponsive or rejecting, a father might be crucial to providing the security that infants need so much (Biller, 1993; Main & Weston, 1981). Babies are also likely to be more socially competent if they are securely attached to *both* parents than if they are securely attached to just one (Biller, 1993; Main & Weston, 1981). In addition, children whose fathers are highly involved with them and sensitive to their needs tend to become high achievers in school (Biller, 1993; Cooksey & Fondell, 1996). Because fathers treat boys and girls differently, they also have a lot to do with the masculine gender typing of their sons and, to a lesser extent, the feminine gender typing of their daughters (Stevenson & Black, 1988).

In short, fathers richly deserve the increased respect they have been getting from developmentalists lately. They are not only capable of sensitive and responsive parenting, but they can contribute in many positive ways to their children's development when they use their competencies and take an active part in child rearing.

Mothers, Fathers, and Infants: The System at Work

So far, we have considered mother/child and father/child relationships without viewing the new family as a *three-person* system. The mother/child relationship cannot be understood without adding the father to the picture; nor can father/child interactions be understood without examining how mothers influence that relationship. This is because parents have **indirect effects** on their children through their ability to influence the behavior of their spouses. More generally, indirect effects within the family are instances in which the relationship between two individuals is modified by the behavior or attitudes of a third family member.

Fathers indirectly influence the mother/infant relationship. For example, mothers who have close, supportive relationships with their husbands tend to interact more patiently and sensitively with their babies than mothers who are experiencing marital tension and feel that they are raising their children largely without help (Cox et al., 1992; Howes & Markman, 1989). Meanwhile, mothers indirectly affect the father/infant relationship. For example, fathers tend to be more involved with their infants when their wives believe that a father should play an important role in a child's life (Palkovitz, 1984) and when the two parents talk frequently about their baby (Belsky, Gilstrap, & Rovine, 1984; Levy-Shiff, 1994). In sum, both mothers and fathers can affect their children indirectly through their interactions with their *spouses*. And, overall, children appear to be best off when the marital relationship is solid and couples provide *mutual* support and encouragement that allow *both* to be more sensitive and responsive parents (Biller, 1993; Erel & Burman, 1995).

Now perhaps you can better appreciate the family systems theory view that even the simplest of families is a true social system that is bigger than the sum of its parts. Because mothers, fathers, and children all affect one another, both directly and indirectly, socialization within the family is obviously not a one-way street in which influence flows only from parent to child. Indeed, family socialization is not even just a two-way street—it is more like the busy intersection of many avenues of influence.

THE CHILD

As children reach the age of 2 or 3, parents continue to be caregivers and playmates, but they also become more concerned with teaching their offspring how (and how not) to behave, and they use some approach to child rearing and discipline to achieve this end. Siblings also serve as socialization agents and become an important part of the child's experience of the family.

Dimensions of Child Rearing

How can I be a good parent? Certainly this question is uppermost in most parents' minds. Yet we probably cannot offer any answers that would be good for all times and all social contexts. As John Ogbu (1981, 1994) stresses, a "competent" parent in one cultural or subcultural context could well be an incompetent one in another setting where the skills required for success as an adult are quite different. For example, parents in inner-city ghettos, although extremely affectionate with their infants, tend to use harsh and inconsistent punishment with their older children. From a middle-class perspective, such practices are frowned upon; it

is better, middle-class parents and many researchers would say, to be warm, to reason with children rather than slap them around, and to enforce rules consistently. Yet, to succeed in the street culture of the ghetto, children may need to become fighters and hustlers. Harsh and inconsistent discipline is likely to foster traits such as self-reliance and a mistrust of authority figures in children—just the traits that they may need. So let's bear in mind that "good parenting" is really parenting that prepares children to meet the demands of the specific culture or subculture in which they live.

Having said that, we can nonetheless draw some conclusions about the ingredients of good parenting that will apply in most settings. We can go far in understanding which parenting styles are effective by considering just two dimensions of parenting: *acceptance/responsiveness* and *demandingness/control* (Darling & Steinberg, 1993; Maccoby & Martin, 1983; Schaefer, 1959). Parental **acceptance/responsiveness** refers to the extent to which parents are supportive, sensitive to their children's needs, and willing to provide affection and praise when their children meet their expectations. Accepting, responsive parents are affectionate and often smile at, praise, and encourage their children, though they are also quite critical when a child misbehaves. Less accepting and responsive parents are often quick to criticize, belittle, punish, or ignore their children and rarely communicate to children that they are loved and valued.

Demandingness/control (sometimes it is called permissiveness/restrictiveness) refers to how much control over decisions lies with the parent as opposed to the child. Controlling/demanding parents set rules, expect their children to follow them, and monitor their children closely to ensure that the rules are followed. Less controlling and demanding parents (often called permissive parents) make fewer demands and allow their children a great deal of autonomy in exploring the environment, expressing their opinions and emotions, and making decisions about their own activities.

By crossing these two dimensions, we have four basic patterns of child rearing to consider, as shown in Figure 14.2:

1. **Authoritarian parenting.** This is a restrictive parenting style combining high demandingness-control and low acceptance/responsiveness. Parents impose many rules, expect strict obedience, rarely explain why the child should comply with rules, and often rely on power tactics such as physical punishment to gain compliance.
2. **Authoritative parenting.** Authoritative parents are more flexible; they are demanding and exert control, but they are also accepting and responsive. They set clear rules and consistently enforce them, but they also explain the rationales for their rules and restrictions, are responsive to their children's

Acceptance/Responsiveness

	High	Low
High Demandingness/Control	**Authoritative** Reasonable demands, consistently enforced, with sensitivity to and acceptance of the child	**Authoritarian** Many rules and demands; few explanations and little sensitivity to the child's needs and perspectives
Low	**Permissive** Few rules and demands; children are allowed much freedom by indulgent parents	**Neglectful** Few rules and demands; parents are uninvolved and insensitive to their children's needs

FIGURE 14.2 *The acceptance/responsiveness and demandingness/ control dimensions of parenting. Which combination best describes your parents' approach?* (Based on Maccoby & Martin, 1983)

needs and points of view, and involve their children in family decision making. They are reasonable and democratic in their approach; although it is clear that they are in charge, they communicate respect for their children.

3. **Permissive parenting.** This style is high in acceptance/responsiveness but low in demandingness/control. Permissive parents are indulgent; they make relatively few demands on children to behave maturely, encourage children to express their feelings and impulses, and rarely exert control over their behavior.

4. **Neglectful parenting.** Finally, parents who combine low demandingness/control and low acceptance/responsiveness are relatively uninvolved in their children's upbringing. They seem not to care about their children and may even reject them—or else they are so overwhelmed by their own problems that they cannot devote sufficient energy to setting and enforcing rules (Maccoby & Martin, 1983).

I assume that you have no difficulty deciding that parental acceptance and responsiveness are preferable to parental rejection and insensitivity. As we have seen in this book, warm, responsive, democratic parenting is associated with secure attachments to parents, academic competence, high self-esteem, prosocial tendencies (such as cooperativeness), peer acceptance, a strong sense of morality, and many other virtues. Children want to please loving parents and so are motivated to do what is expected of them and to learn what their parents would like them to learn. By contrast, lack of parental acceptance and affection contributes to depression and other psychological problems (Ge et al., 1996). Because children simply do not

thrive when they are rejected, ethologist Kevin MacDonald (1992) speculates that affection for one's children is an evolved behavior that has allowed parents through the ages to influence their children in any number of adaptive ways.

But degree of demandingness/control is also important. The authoritarian, authoritative, and permissive parenting styles were originally identified and defined by Diana Baumrind (1967, 1977, 1991) in a pioneering longitudinal study. Baumrind found that preschool children raised by authoritative parents were the most well-adjusted: They were cheerful, socially responsible, self-reliant, achievement oriented, and cooperative with adults and peers. Children of authoritarian parents tended to be moody and seemingly unhappy, easily annoyed, relatively aimless, and not very pleasant to be around. Finally, children of permissive parents were often impulsive and aggressive, especially if they were boys. They tended to be bossy and self-centered, rebellious, lacking in self-control, rather aimless, and quite low in independence and achievement.

When Baumrind (1977) reassessed these youngsters at ages 8 to 9, children of authoritative parents still had an edge on their peers. Indeed, the strengths of children raised authoritatively are still evident in adolescence; these teenagers are confident, achievement oriented, and socially competent, and they stay clear of drug abuse and other problem behaviors (Baumrind, 1991).

Subsequent research has shown that the worst developmental outcomes are associated with a neglectful, uninvolved style of parenting. Children of neglectful parents are notable for behavior problems such as aggression and frequent temper tantrums as early as age 3 (Miller et al., 1993). They tend to become hostile and antisocial adolescents who abuse alcohol and drugs and get in a lot of trouble (Lamborn et al., 1991; Weiss & Schwarz, 1996). Parents who communicate that they don't care breed children who are resentful and prone to strike back at their uncaring parents and other authority figures. This may be a problem for at least some so-called **latchkey children,** children who care for themselves after school with little or no adult supervision (see Box 14.1).

In short, children develop best when they have love *and* limits. If they are indulged or neglected and given little guidance, they won't learn self-control and may become quite selfish, unruly, and lacking in direction. And if they receive too much guidance, as the children of authoritarian parents do, they will have few opportunities to learn self-reliance and may lack confidence in their own decision-making abilities.

Social Class, Economic Hardship, and Parenting

Parenting styles are shaped in part by socioeconomic factors. Middle-class and lower-class parents

BOX 14.1

Who's watching the kids?

In the United States, about two to four million elementary school children between the ages of 6 and 13 qualify as latchkey (or self-care) children and are responsible for looking after themselves after school (Zigler & Finn-Stevenson, 1993). Are these children missing out on developmental experiences they should have—or perhaps even getting into trouble—while they are away from the watchful eyes of adults?

Some research suggests that latchkey children have more behavior problems and perform less well in school than other children (Marshall et al., 1997; Pettit et al., 1997; Vandell & Ramanan, 1991). Yet much other research has failed to find differences in academic performance and adjustment between latchkey children and children who are supervised by their mothers or other adults after school (Galambos & Maggs, 1991; Padilla & Landreth, 1989; Posner & Vandell, 1994). This suggests that the experience can be good or bad, depending on the circumstances.

Research by Gregory Pettit and his colleagues (1997) suggests that the age of the child may be one relevant consideration. Children involved in four or more hours of self-care as first-graders were rated less socially competent by their teachers, had lower grades, and scored lower on achievement tests as sixth-graders than children who spent less time in self-care. Latchkey children from low-income families, though not from middle-income ones, also had high levels of antisocial behavior. Similar negative effects were evident among third-graders but not among fifth-graders, suggesting that older children may be better able to cope with looking after themselves.

It also matters how children use their time after school and how well their parents keep tabs on where they are and what they are doing. Laurence Steinberg (1986), studying fifth- through ninth-graders, assessed the extent to which latchkey youth were more than usually susceptible to negative peer influences. He predicted and found that being a latchkey child did no harm to adolescents who spent most of their unsupervised time at home alone, who were raised authoritatively, and who were monitored closely by their parents. By contrast, those latchkey adolescents who were not adequately supervised and who spent their time hanging out with friends were more susceptible to peer pressure than adolescents who spent their time at home alone or were supervised by parents after school. In other words, the more being a latchkey child or adolescent means being rid of adult supervision and doing things that are unlikely to contribute positively to development, the worse its effects.

Although living as a latchkey child is not always harmful, there may be better ways for children to spend their time after school. Especially for younger elementary school children, a structured after-school program that provides supervision, recreation, and academically enriching activities is likely to be a much better option. Jill Posner and Deborah Vandell (1994) compared low-income 9-year-olds who spent their time at the end of the day in formal after-school care programs, with their mothers, being cared for informally by some other adult, or in self-care. Although they did not perform noticeably worse in school or display more behavior problems than other groups, the latchkey children spent more than the usual amount of time watching television. Children who attended formal after-school programs had better academic performance and social adjustment than the other three groups, largely because children in these programs spent more time doing academically relevant activities (see also Rosenthal & Vandell, 1996). So, self-care after school need not be damaging to development, especially among older children whose parents keep tabs on them and ensure that they use their time well. However, it is probably not the best option for young children from lower socioeconomic areas, children who can benefit much more from adult-supervised learning activities.

---

often pursue different goals and emphasize different values in raising their children. Compared to middle- and upper-class parents, lower- and working-class parents tend to (1) stress obedience and respect for authority; (2) be more restrictive and authoritarian, more frequently using power-assertive discipline; (3) reason with their children less frequently, and (4) show less warmth and affection (Maccoby, 1980; McLoyd, 1990). Although we will find a wide range of parenting styles in any social group, these *average* social-class differences in parenting have been observed in many cultures and across racial and ethnic groups in the United States.

Why might they exist? Most explanations center on the stresses associated with low-income living and their effects on parenting (Bolger et al., 1995; McLoyd, 1990). Rand Conger and his associates (1992, 1995), for example, have performed elaborate analyses showing that parents who are experiencing financial problems

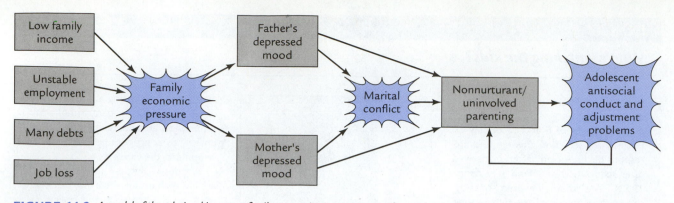

FIGURE 14.3 *A model of the relationship among family economic stress, patterns of parenting, and adolescent adjustment* (Adapted from Conger et al., 1992)

tend to become depressed, which increases conflict between them. Marital conflict, in turn, disrupts each partner's ability to be a supportive, involved, and effective parent, and this breakdown in parenting then contributes to negative child outcomes such as low self-esteem, poor school performance, poor peer relations, and adjustment problems such as depression and aggression (see Figure 14.3).

Another explanation for the link between economic factors and parenting styles focuses on the skills needed by workers in white-collar and blue-collar jobs (Arnett, 1995; Kohn, 1969). Parents from lower socioeconomic groups may quite sensibly emphasize obedience to authority figures if that is what is required in blue-collar jobs like their own. Middle- and upper-class parents may reason with their children and stress individual initiative, curiosity, and creativity more because these are the attributes that count for business executives, professionals, and other white-collar workers. It could be, then, that both middle- and lower-income parents have devised styles of parenting that are well adapted to the distinctive demands of their sociocultural setting.

In sum, the more authoritarian parenting style used by many lower-income parents may reflect *both* (1) the damaging effects of economic stress, particularly of living in poverty or losing one's job, on a parent's ability to parent effectively, and (2) an adaptive attempt to prepare children for jobs in which they will be expected to obey a boss.

Cultural and Ethnic Variation in Parenting

The link between authoritative parenting and positive developmental outcomes is evident in most ethnic groups and socioeconomic groups studied to date in the United States (Glasgow et al., 1997; Steinberg et al., 1995) and in a variety of other cultures as well (Pinto, Folkers, & Sines, 1991; Scott, Scott, & McCabe, 1991). At the same time, even when differences in socioeconomic status are taken into account, par-

ents of different ethnic backgrounds sometimes hold divergent beliefs and values regarding child rearing that shape their parenting practices and affect their children's development (Heath, 1995; MacPhee, Fritz, & Miller-Heyl, 1996).

Consider some examples. Native-American and Hispanic parents, perhaps because their cultures emphasize the goals of the group rather than of the individual, place more emphasis than Euro-American parents on teaching children to be polite and respectful of authority figures (particularly their fathers), as opposed to independent and competitive (MacPhee et al., 1996). These two groups approach their goal in quite different ways, though; Native-American parents are very indulgent and rarely resort to punishment, whereas Hispanic parents are far more likely to use spankings and scoldings to make their points.

In addition, the impacts of a particular parenting style sometimes differ depending on the cultural context in which it is used. For example, use of physical, coercive discipline (short of abuse) is not as strongly linked to aggression and antisocial behavior among African-American youths as among Euro-Americans, possibly because it is commonly used in African-American families and therefore may be viewed by African-American children as a sign of parental caring rather than hostility (Deater-Deckard et al., 1996). Moreover, authoritarian parenting may mean something quite different for Chinese children than for American ones. Ruth Chao (1994), seeking to explain why Chinese children do very well in school despite the fact that their parents often use an authoritarian rather than authoritative style of parenting, notes that Chinese parents are strict because they believe that this is the best way to express their love and train their children properly. A parenting style that may be too controlling to work well in America appears to work very well indeed in China. So, authoritative parenting may stand out as an effective parenting approach in most cultural contexts, but alternative parenting styles also differ in popularity and effectiveness across cultures.

Child Effects on Parents

The study of human development has been guided through most of its history by a simple **parent effects model** in which it is assumed that influences in the family run one way, from parent (particularly mother) to child. We have just reviewed research demonstrating effects of parenting styles on child development. But what if we think a bit differently? Could it be that a child's behavior influences the style of parenting his or her parents use, and that what appear to be parent effects are instead child effects? A **child effects model** of family influence highlights instances in which children influence their parents rather than vice versa (Ambert, 1992; Lerner, 1993).

One clear example of a child effect is the fact that the style of parenting used with a child depends greatly on the age and competence of the child. For example, infants in their first year of life require and elicit sensitive care, whereas older infants who are asserting their wills and toddling here and there force parents to provide more instruction and discipline (Fagot & Kavanaugh, 1993). Normally, parents then become less restrictive as their children mature and gradually, with parental guidance, become capable of making their own decisions (Amato, 1989).

Now consider the possibility that a child's personality influences the parenting he or she receives. Isn't it possible that easygoing, manageable children *cause* their parents to be warm and authoritative? Couldn't difficult, stubborn, and aggressive children help mold parents who are rejecting and who either rule with an iron hand or throw up their hands in defeat and become neglectful? In one demonstration of child effects within the family, Barbara Keller and Richard Bell (1979) challenged the finding (reported in Chapter 12) that a parent's use of the disciplinary technique of *induction* (explanations emphasizing the consequences of a child's behavior for other people) fosters moral maturity in a child. Isn't it possible instead, they reasoned, that children who are already "good" are more likely than less responsive children to elicit inductive explanations from adults?

Keller and Bell asked female college students to convince 9-year-old girls to behave altruistically (for example, to spend more time sewing a pillow for a handicapped child than sewing a pillow for themselves). The trick was that the girls had been taught to act either very attentively (looking at the college student's face, smiling, and answering questions promptly) or very inattentively. As expected, students who were confronted with an attentive child used a great deal of induction; they pointed out how other children might feel if the child behaved selfishly. By contrast, college students who interacted with an inattentive child were more likely to use power-assertion techniques; for example, they promised rewards for altruism and threatened penalties for selfishness.

In another demonstration of child effects in the family, Kathleen Anderson, Hugh Lytton, and David Romney (1986; and see Lytton, 1990) studied mothers of boys who were officially diagnosed as having conduct disorders—boys who were highly aggressive and had histories of arson, truancy, temper outbursts, and other serious problems. The researchers had each of these mothers interact with her own conduct-disordered son, another mother's conduct-disordered son, and a normal boy. Meanwhile, mothers of normal boys also interacted with their own sons and with both another normal boy and a conduct-disordered boy.

The findings were clear: Boys with conduct disorders, quite likely because of their genetic endowment, were so noncompliant and difficult that they brought out a negative, coercive behavior parenting style in every mother with whom they interacted. In this study, at least, there was little evidence that the mothers of conduct-disordered boys were any worse disciplinarians than other mothers or that their parenting was the main cause of their sons' aggressive, destructive behavior.

Other research tells us that severe antisocial behavior probably results when a child who is genetically predisposed to be aggressive behaves in ways that elicit negative parenting and when this negative parenting in turn causes a child to become even more aggressive (Ge et al., 1996; Lytton, 1990; Reiss, 1995). When such a destructive family process develops, and the child elicits coercive and ineffective parenting from parents at the same time that parents elicit antisocial behavior from the child, it becomes hard to say who is more influential. This scenario is best described by a **transactional model** of family influence in which parent and child influence one another reciprocally (Sameroff, 1975). According to this model, child problems can evolve over time if the relationship between parent and child goes bad as the two interact over time, and optimal child development can result when parent/child transactions evolve in a more positive way (see Figure 14.4).

We should not underestimate the role of genes in all this; as Chapter 3 showed, genetic endowment influences not only a child's behavior but the parenting style and home environment he or she experiences (Kendler, 1996; Reiss, 1995; Rowe, 1994). Through the process of gene/environment correlation (Scarr & McCartney, 1983; and see Chapter 3), the genes children inherit (and share with their parents) influence how their parents and other people react to them and what experiences they seek out. The antisocial child will elicit a harsh, controlling style of parenting even from

FIGURE 14.4 *Parent effects, child effects, and transactional models of family influence*

adoptive parents, and then the child's hostile behavior and the parent's ineffective parenting will influence one another and escalate through a transactional process (Ge et al., 1996).

Demonstrations of child effects and transactional effects within the family are tremendously important. We simply cannot take it for granted that parents have sole responsibility for whether their children are "good" or "bad." It is probably still the case that parents influence children more strongly than children influence them (Baumrind, 1991; Simons et al., 1989). Moreover, we have evidence from longitudinal studies that parents who adopt an authoritative parenting style and who firmly demand that their children follow their rules have children who become more compliant and well-behaved over time than other children (Crockenberg & Litman, 1990; Kuczynski & Kochanska, 1995). However, we must remind ourselves again and again that the family is a system in which family members are influenced by their genetic endowments and the environments they create for one another.

Sibling Relationships

A family system consisting of mother, father, and child is perturbed by the arrival of a new baby and becomes a new—and considerably more complex—family system. How do children adapt to a new baby in the house, and how does the sibling relationship change as children get older?

A New Baby Arrives

Judy Dunn and Carol Kendrick (1982; see also Dunn, 1993) have carefully studied young children's reactions to a new sibling. Mothers typically give less attention to their first-borns after the new baby arrives than before. Partly for this reason, first-borns often find being "dethroned" a stressful experience. They become more difficult and demanding or dependent and "clingy," and they often develop problems

with their sleeping, eating, and toileting routines. Most of their battles are with their mothers, but a minority of them are not above hitting, poking, and pinching their younger brothers or sisters. Security of attachment to mother decreases significantly, especially if first-borns are 2 years old or older and can fully appreciate how much they have lost (Teti, Sakin, Kucera, & Corns, 1996). Although positive effects (such as an increased insistence on doing things independently) are also common, it is clear that first-borns are not entirely thrilled to have an attention-grabbing new baby in the house. They resent losing their parents' attention, and their own difficult behavior may alienate their parents even further.

Thus **sibling rivalry**—a spirit of competition, jealousy, or resentment between siblings—often begins as soon as a younger brother or sister arrives. Can it be minimized? Adjustment to a new sibling is easier if the marital relationship is good and if the first-born had secure relationships with both parents before the younger sibling arrived and continues to enjoy close relationships afterward (Dunn & Kendrick, 1982; Teti et al., 1996; Volling & Belsky, 1992). Parents are advised to guard against ignoring their first-born, to continue providing love and attention, and to maintain the child's routines as much as possible. They can also encourage older children to become aware of a new baby's needs and feelings and to assist in their new brother's or sister's care (Dunn & Kendrick, 1982; Howe & Ross, 1990). Ultimately, parents may have to walk a thin line between two traps: becoming so attentive to the new baby that they deprive the older child of attention and love, and becoming so indulgent of the first-born that he or she becomes a "spoiled brat" who resents any competition from the younger sibling (Dunn & Kendrick, 1981).

Ambivalence in Sibling Relationships

Fortunately, most older siblings adjust fairly quickly to having a new brother or sister (Dunn &

Kendrick, 1982). Yet, even in the best of sibling relationships, conflict is normal. Judy Dunn (1993) reports that the number of skirmishes between very young siblings can range as high as 56 per hour! Jealousies, bouts of teasing, shouting matches, and occasional kicks and punches continue to be part of the sibling relationship throughout childhood. These conflicts diminish during adolescence, perhaps because teenage siblings spend more time away from home and from one another (Furman & Buhrmester, 1992; Larson et al., 1996).

Some sibling relationships are consistently closer than others over the years, though (Dunn, Slomkowski, & Beardsall, 1994). The personalities of the siblings are one influence (Stoneman & Brody, 1993), but parents also have a lot to do with just how smooth or stormy the sibling relationship is. Brothers and sisters are likely to get along if their parents get along (Dunn, 1993; MacKinnon, 1989). Sibling relationships are also friendlier and less conflictual if mothers and fathers respond warmly and sensitively to *all* their children and do not consistently favor one child over another (G. Brody, Stoneman, & McCoy, 1994; McHale et al., 1995). Children pay close attention to what goes on between their siblings and their parents, are acutely sensitive to any hints of favoritism, and may resent it if they think they are being treated less warmly or more strictly than other children in the family (Dunn, 1993). But recall the concept of nonshared environmental influences discussed in Chapter 3: Different children in the same family *do* have very different experiences at home and become quite different people as a result, so it is easy to see how sibling rivalries arise.

However, we are dwelling too much on the negative. The most important thing to know about sibling relationships is that they are ambivalent; they involve *both* closeness and conflict, love and hate. Interestingly, school-age siblings who are similar in age report more warmth and closeness than other sibling pairs and yet are also the most likely to experience friction and conflict (Furman & Buhrmester, 1985a, 1985b). Acts of kindness and affection between brothers and sisters typically outnumber hateful or rivalrous acts, but the sibling relationship is by nature both close and conflictual (Abramovitch et al., 1986; Baskett & Johnson, 1982).

Contributions to Development

What positive roles do siblings actually play in one another's development? One of their important functions is to provide *emotional support*. Brothers and sisters confide in one another and protect and comfort one another in rough times. Even preschoolers jump in to comfort their infant siblings when their mothers leave them or when strangers approach (Stewart & Marvin, 1984). For some children, a secure tie to a fa-

In many societies, older siblings are major caregivers for young children.

vorite sibling can help prevent the anxiety and distress that result from being neglected or rejected by peers (East & Rook, 1992; Stormshak et al., 1996).

Second, older siblings often provide *caretaking* services for younger siblings. Indeed, in a study of 186 societies, older children were the *principal* caregivers for infants and toddlers in 57% of the cultures studied (Weisner & Gallimore, 1977; and see Ambert, 1994). In our society as well, older siblings, especially girls, are frequently asked to babysit or tend their younger sibs (McHale & Gamble, 1989).

Finally, older siblings serve as *teachers* of new behavior. One 5-year-old was quite aware of how much her 2-year-old sister learned from her through simple observational learning processes: "See. I said, 'Bye, I'm going on the slide,' and she said, 'Bye.' She says whatever I say." Given a problem to master, young children are likely to learn more when they have an older sibling available to guide them than when they have access to an equally competent older peer (Azmitia & Hesser, 1993). True, older sibs are not always as skilled teachers as parents are; they tend to provide the answers rather than information that can allow their younger sibs to make the right choices on their own

(Perez-Granados & Callanan, 1997). However, older sibs clearly feel a special responsibility to teach, and younger sibs actively seek their guidance. This instruction pays off: When older siblings "play school" with their younger siblings and teach them important lessons such as the ABCs, younger siblings have an easier time learning to read (Norman-Jackson, 1982). What's more, older siblings who tutor their younger sibs may profit as well, for they score higher on tests of academic aptitude and achievement than individuals who have not had these tutoring experiences (Paulhus & Shaffer, 1981; Smith, 1990).

If siblings play so many important roles in development, you may be wondering if children are damaged by not having them. In the People's Republic of China, where government policy limits families to one child, as well as in North America, only children often outperform later-born children in large families on measures of intelligence and academic achievement; moreover, their personalities are not much different from those of other children, suggesting that they are not the "spoiled brats" many believe them to be (Chen, Rubin, & Li, 1994; Falbo & Poston, 1993; Jiao, Ji, & Jing, 1996). Only children, like children with just one sibling, enjoy the advantages of a good deal of attention and stimulation from their parents, and they apparently gain through friendships outside the home whatever social experiences they may miss by not having brothers or sisters. So, although siblings can be very important as emotional supports, caretakers, and teachers, they are not indispensable.

In sum, there is a good deal of reciprocal influence in families that contain preschool or school-age children. Parents, by adopting a particular style of child rearing with each of their children, are influencing their youngsters' development. Children, meanwhile, through child effects, influence the extent to which their parents are accepting/responsive and demanding/controlling. And, once a couple has a second child, the family system changes profoundly. Although rivalry and conflict seem to be a normal part of sibling relationships, brothers and sisters also provide one another with emotional support, caretaking, and teaching.

THE ADOLESCENT

Conjure up an image of a typical relationship between a teenager and his or her parents. Perhaps you envision a teenager who is out all the time with friends, resents every rule and restriction, and talks back at every opportunity. Or perhaps you are imagining parents wringing their hands in despair and wondering if they'll ever survive their children's adolescent years. Many people believe that the period of the family life cycle during which parents have adolescents in the

TABLE 14.2

Percentages of adolescents endorsing different statements about their family relationships

| | Percentage Concurring | | | |
Statement	Males 13–15	Males 16–18	Females 13–15	Females 16–18
My parents are usually patient with me.	84	79	80	76
I can count on my parents most of the time.	78	76	74	77
I feel I have a part in making family decisions.	71	72	70	73
Understanding my parents is beyond me.	18	17	21	18

SOURCE: Adapted from Offer, Ostrov, & Howard (1981)

house is a particularly stressful time, with close parent/child relationships deteriorating into bitter tugs of war. How much truth is there to these characterizations?

Parent/Child Closeness

Although many people believe that adolescents lose respect for their parents and feel less close to them than they did as children, these beliefs simply do not hold up (Galambos, 1992). Most high school students, regardless of age and sex, respect their parents and describe their family relationships in positive ways (Offer, Ostrov, & Howard, 1981; and see Table 14.2). The great majority of teenagers also view their parents as key sources of affection and support (Furman & Buhrmester, 1992; Lempers & Clark-Lempers, 1992).

So far, then, it appears that parent/adolescent relationships are really not very different from parent/child relationships. Yet the parent/child relationship *does* change during adolescence—not so much in its degree of closeness as in the balance of power between parents and adolescents.

Renegotiating the Relationship

A critical developmental task of adolescence is to achieve **autonomy,** the capacity to make decisions independently and manage life tasks without being overly dependent on other people. If adolescents are to "make it" as adults, they can't be rushing home for reassuring hugs after every little setback or depending on parents to get them to work on time or manage their checkbooks. Parents want their adolescents to become autonomous, and adolescents want the freedom to become autonomous.

As children reach puberty and become more physically and cognitively mature and more capable of acting autonomously, conflicts between parents and children become more frequent, at least temporarily, in cultures as diverse as Hong Kong and the United States (Holmbeck & Hill, 1991; Paikoff & Brooks-Gunn, 1991; Yau & Smetana, 1996). These conflicts are usually not severe; most often they are squabbles over such matters as disobedience, homework, or household chores. As adolescents assert themselves more, though, parents turn over more power to them, and the parent/child relationship changes from one in which parents are dominant to one in which parents and their sons and daughters are on a more equal footing (Steinberg, 1996). The process may take longer and be more frustrating for Asian and Asian-American adolescents than for other youths because their parents continue to exert their authority longer and do not place as much value on the development of autonomy (Greenberger & Chen, 1996; Yau & Smetana, 1996).

In the past, many theorists assumed that achieving autonomy required separating from parents—cutting the cords. Now researchers appreciate that it is best for their development if adolescents maintain a close attachment with their families, even as they are gaining autonomy and preparing to leave the nest (Grotevant & Cooper, 1986; Kobak et al., 1993; Lamborn & Steinberg, 1993). Autonomy *and* attachment, or independence *and* interdependence, are the goals.

As it turns out, adolescents are most likely to become autonomous, achievement oriented, and well adjusted if their parents consistently enforce a reasonable set of rules, involve their teenagers in decision making, monitor their comings and goings, *and* continue to be warm and supportive (Brown et al., 1993; Dishion et al., 1991; Lamborn et al., 1991). In other words, the winning approach is an authoritative style of parenting—the same style that appears to foster healthy child development. Although we must, as usual, remind ourselves that children also affect their parents, an authoritative parenting style gives adolescents opportunities to strengthen their independent decision-making skills while still having the benefit of their parents' guidance and advice. It is when parents are rejecting and extremely strict, or rejecting and extremely lax, that teenagers are most likely to be psychologically distressed and get into trouble (Koestner et al., 1991; Lamborn et al., 1991).

The parent/adolescent relationship is truly a partnership, and its quality depends on what both parents and their children do to renegotiate their relationship. Apparently, most parents and their teenagers maintain positive feelings for each other while reworking their relationship so that it allows the adolescent more freedom. As a result, most adolescents are able to achieve autonomy and also shift toward a more mutual relationship with their parents.

THE ADULT

So far we have concentrated on the child's experience of family life. Let's now ask how adults develop and change as they progress through stages of the family life cycle.

Establishing the Marriage

In our society, around 95% of adults choose to marry at some point in their lives (U.S. Bureau of the Census, 1997), and most choose to marry individuals they love. Marriages in many other cultures are not formed on the basis of love but are arranged by leaders of kin groups who are concerned with acquiring property, allies, and the rights to any children produced by a couple (Ingoldsby & Smith, 1995). As Corinne Nydegger (1986) puts it, "These matters are too important to be left to youngsters" (p. 111). So, in reading what follows, remember that our way of establishing families is not the only way.

Marriage is a significant life transition for most adults: It involves taking on a new role (as husband or wife) and adjusting to life as a couple. We rejoice at weddings and view newlyweds as supremely happy beings. Yet individuals who have just been struggling to achieve autonomy and assume adult roles now find that they must compromise with their partners and adapt to each other's personalities and preferences. What happens to couples as they settle into their married lives? Ted Huston and his colleagues find that the honeymoon is short (T. Huston, McHale, & Crouter, 1986; T. Huston & Vangelisti, 1991; see also Johnson, Amoloza, & Booth, 1992; Kurdek, 1991a). In their longitudinal study of over 100 newlywed couples, these researchers discovered that several aspects of the marital relationship deteriorated in the first year after the wedding. For example, couples became less satisfied with their marriages and with their sex lives; they less frequently said "I love you," complimented each other, or disclosed their feelings to each other; and, although they spent only somewhat less time together, more of that time was devoted to getting tasks done and less to having fun or just talking. The couples whose relationships deteriorated the most were those who had engaged in a great deal of mutual criticism and other negative behaviors from the start.

Although most couples are far more satisfied than dissatisfied with their relationships after the "honeymoon" is over, there are clearly strains involved in adapting to marriage. Blissfully happy relationships evolve into still happy but more ambivalent ones.

Pregnancy adds to the challenges faced by newlyweds, who are trying to adjust to life as a couple.

Whether it is because couples begin to see "warts" that they didn't notice before marriage, or stop trying to be on their best behavior, or simply start to take each other for granted, marital relationships no sooner begin than they change in systematic ways.

New Parenthood

Many couples have children within a few years of the marriage ceremony. Children begin to affect their parents even before they arrive; expectant parents often plan ahead by selecting names for the infant, decorating a nursery, moving to larger quarters, and changing or leaving jobs (Grossman et al., 1980). How does the arrival of the new baby affect wife, husband, and the marital relationship? One popular view holds that having children draws a couple closer together; other people believe that children introduce additional strains into a relationship. Which is it?

On average, new parenthood is best described as a stressful life transition that involves both positive and negative changes (Monk et al., 1996). Most parents claim that having a child improves their lives—that their new "bundle of joy" offers them love, companionship, and enjoyment and makes them feel more self-fulfilled or grown up (Emery & Tuer, 1993; Hoffman & Manis, 1979). But let's analyze the situation more closely. Couples have added new roles (as mothers and fathers) to their existing roles (as spouses, workers, and so on). New parents often find juggling work and family responsibilities stressful. They not only have an incredible amount of new work to do as caregivers, but they lose sleep, worry about whether they are doing the right things for their baby, find that they have less time to themselves, do less together just for fun, and often face financial difficulties as well. In addition, even egalitarian couples who previously shared household tasks begin to divide their labors along more traditional lines. She specializes in the "feminine" role by becoming the primary caregiver and housekeeper, while he is likely to become even more involved in his "masculine" role as provider (Cowan et al., 1991; Emery & Tuer, 1993).

What are the effects of increased stress and of the tendency of husband and wife to establish somewhat separate lifestyles? Marital satisfaction typically declines after a baby is born (Belsky, Lang, & Rovine, 1985; Emery & Tuer, 1993). This decline is usually steeper for women than for men, primarily because the burden of child-care responsibilities typically falls more heavily on mothers and they may resent what they regard as an unfair division of labor (Levy-Shiff, 1994; Suitor, 1991).

However, there are wide individual differences in adjustment to new parenthood: Some new parents experience the transition as a bowl of cherries, others as the pits—as a full-blown crisis in their lives. What might make this life event easier or harder to manage? We can answer that question by focusing on the nature of the *event* with which a parent must cope, the *person* who must cope with it, and the *resources* the individual has available.

The *event* is the baby, of course. It is clear that infants who are difficult for some reason (for example, because of an illness that causes endless crying or an irritable temperament) create more stresses and anxieties for parents than infants who are quiet, sociable, responsive, and otherwise easy to love (Levy-Shiff, 1994; Sirignano & Lachman, 1985).

As for the *person,* some adults are better equipped than others to cope with stress, and they find adaptive ways to restructure and organize their lives to accommodate a new baby (Levy-Shiff, 1994; Mylod, Whitman, & Borkowski, 1997). In addition, parents who are older, who conceive after the marriage ceremony, and who wait longer once they are married to have children have an easier time than parents who are young and possibly immature or who must adjust to each other at the same time they are adjusting to a new baby (Belsky, 1981). Similarly, parents who have realistic expectations about how parenthood will change their lives and about children tend to adjust more easily than those who expect the experience to be more positive than it turns out to be (Kalmuss, Davidson, & Cushman, 1992; Mylod et al., 1997). Also, couples who both recall their own parents as warm and accepting are likely to experience a smoother transition to new parenthood and less marital discord than couples in which either spouse was raised in an aloof or rejecting manner—one of many signs that approaches to parenting are passed from one generation to the next (Belsky & Isabella, 1985; van IJzendoorn, 1992).

Finally, *resources* can make a great deal of difference to the new parent. Most important of all is spouse support: Things go considerably better for a new mother when she has a good relationship with her husband and when he shares the burden of childcare and housework responsibilities than when she has no partner or an unsupportive one (Levy-Shiff, 1994; Tietjen & Bradley, 1985). Social support from friends and relatives can also help a new parent cope (Stemp, Turner, & Noh, 1986).

In sum, parents who have an easy baby to contend with, who possess positive personal qualities, and who receive reliable support from their spouses and other intimates are in the best position to cope adaptively with the stresses of new parenthood.

The Child-Rearing Family

What can parents look forward to as they have additional children and as their children grow older? A heavier workload. The stresses and strains of caring for a toddler are greater than those of caring for an infant (Crnic & Booth, 1991), and the arrival of a second child means additional stress on top of that (O'Brien, 1996). Parents must not only devote time to the new baby but deal with their first-born child's normal anxieties about this change in lifestyle. Parents complain of the hassles of cleaning up food and toys, constantly keeping an eye on their children, and dealing with their perfectly normal but irritating demands for at-

Parents can find keeping up with young children draining.

tention, failures to comply with requests, and bouts of whining (O'Brien, 1996). Because the workload is heavier, fathers often become more involved with their children (Phares, 1996). However, the mother who is raising children as a single parent or whose husband is not highly involved in family life may find herself without a moment's rest as she tries to keep up with two active, curious, mobile, and needy youngsters.

Additional challenges sometimes arise for parents when their children enter adolescence. The rewards of parenting may not seem as great as when children were young (Waldron-Hennessey & Sabatelli, 1997). Moreover, as we saw earlier, parent/child conflicts become more frequent as children reach puberty. In addition, there is intriguing evidence that living with adolescents who are becoming physically and sexually mature and beginning to date may cause parents to engage in more than the usual amount of midlife questioning about what they have done with their lives and what they can expect next. Susan Silverberg and Laurence Steinberg (1990) found that parents whose adolescents were highly involved in dating and other mixed-sex activities showed more intense midlife concerns, greater psychological distress, and lower life satisfaction than parents whose children were not as heavily involved in these activities. Other studies suggest that parents of adolescents are especially likely to experience midlife distress if the parent/adolescent relationship is stormy or if their children are attempting to distance themselves emotionally from their parents (Julian, McKenry, & McKelvey, 1991; Silverberg & Steinberg, 1987). Here, then, may be another example of child effects within the family system—Or is it? It is also possible that parents who are psychologically distressed and preoccupied with their own midlife problems cannot provide the emotional support their children need and cause them to seek it elsewhere, in the peer group.

In view of the challenges children create for their parents, perhaps it is not surprising that marital satisfaction continues to decline slightly as additional children join the family (Rollins & Feldman, 1970). Although most parents are more satisfied than dissatisfied with their marriages and take great pleasure in their relationships with their children, children clearly complicate their parents' lives by demanding everything from fresh diapers and close monitoring to college tuition. By claiming time and energy that might otherwise go into nourishing the marital relationship and by adding stresses to their parents' lives, children do seem to have a negative—though typically only slightly negative—effect on the marital relationship.

The Empty Nest

As children reach maturity, the family becomes a launching pad that fires adolescents and young adults off into the world to work and start their own families. The term **empty nest** describes the family after the departure of the last child. Clearly the emptying of the nest involves changes in role and lifestyle for parents, particularly for mothers who have centered their lives on child rearing. How are parents affected by this transition?

Quite positively, it seems! Just as the entry of children into the family causes modest decreases in marital satisfaction, the departure of the last child causes modest *increases* in marital satisfaction (Lee, 1988; White & Edwards, 1990). After the nest empties, women often feel that their marriages are more equitable and that their spouses are more accommodating to their needs (Menaghan, 1983; Suitor, 1991). They, more than their husbands, are likely to feel better about themselves and their lives in general when they no longer have children in the house (Harkins, 1978; McLanahan & Sorensen, 1985). A *minority* of parents do find this transition very disturbing, especially mothers who feel that their departing children are not yet ready to leave and fathers who have poor marriages but very close relationships with their chil-

dren (Harkins, 1978; Lewis, Freneau, & Roberts, 1979). Still, hard as it may be for departing offspring to believe, children appear to cause more stress to their parents when they arrive in the family than when they leave.

Why do parents generally react positively to the empty nest? Possibly it is because they have fewer roles and responsibilities and therefore experience less stress and strain. Empty nest couples also have more time to focus on their marital relationship and to enjoy activities together, as well as more money to spend on themselves. Moreover, parents are likely to view the emptying of the nest as evidence that they have done their job of raising children well and have earned what Erik Erikson called a sense of generativity. One 44-year-old mother put it well: "I have five terrific daughters who didn't just happen. It took lots of time to mold, correct, love, and challenge them. It's nice to see such rewarding results." Of course, most parents continue to enjoy a good deal of contact with their children after the nest empties, so it is not as if they are really losing this important relationship (White & Edwards, 1990).

In recent years an increasing number of adult children have been remaining in the nest or leaving and then "refilling" it, often because of unemployment, limited finances, divorce, or other difficulties in getting their adult lives on track (Ward & Spitze, 1992). Almost 25% of young adults aged 22 to 25 and almost 10% of adults over age 30 live with their parents (Ward, Logan, & Spitze, 1992). Some parents find having adult children in the house distressing (Aquilino, 1991; Umberson, 1992), and adult children who live with their parents feel less close to their parents than adult children who live independently (White & Rogers, 1997). However, most empty nesters adapt well to this arrangement, especially if their children are responsible young adults who are in school or employed rather than irresponsible freeloaders (White & Rogers, 1997).

In the end, parenthood is a source of both stress and satisfaction. We have seen how the demands of parenting can detract from the marital relationship, but there is a positive side too. Although we cannot yet be sure that parenthood itself is the cause, the experience of being a parent may breed personal strengths such as a sense of competence, emotional maturity, and a capacity to care (Palkovitz, 1996). In other words, by nurturing their children parents may well nurture their own development.

Grandparenthood

Although we tend to picture grandparents as white-haired, jovial elders who knit mittens and bake cookies, most adults become grandparents when they are middle-aged, not elderly, and when they are likely to be highly involved in careers and community activities. Grandparenting styles are diverse, as illustrated by the results of a national survey of grandparents of

Most grandparents prefer and adopt a companionate style of grandparenting.

teenagers conducted by Andrew Cherlin and Frank Furstenberg (1986). These researchers determined the prevalence of three major styles of grandparenting:

1. *Remote:* Remote grandparents (29% of the sample) were symbolic figures seen only occasionally by their grandchildren. Primarily because they were geographically distant, they were emotionally distant as well.

2. *Companionate:* This was the most common style of grandparenting (55% of the sample). Companionate grandparents saw their grandchildren frequently and enjoyed sharing activities with them. They only rarely played a parental role, serving as companions rather than caregivers. Like most grandparents, they operated according to a "norm of noninterference," hesitating to meddle in the way their adult children were raising their children. They were quite happy to leave the child-care responsibilities to their children. As one put it, "You can love them and then say, 'Here, take them now, go on home'" (p. 55).

3. *Involved:* Finally, 16% of the grandparents assumed a parentlike role. Like companionate grandparents, they saw their grandchildren frequently and were playful with them, but, unlike companionate grandparents, they also often helped with child care, gave advice, and played other practical roles in their grandchildren's lives. Some involved grandparents were truly substitute parents who lived with and tended their grandchildren because their daughters were unmarried or recently divorced and worked outside the home.

We see, then, that grandparenting can take many forms but that most grandparents frequently see at least some of their grandchildren and prefer a role that is high in enjoyment and affection but low in responsibility. The grandparent/grandchild relationship is likely to be closest when grandparent and grandchild live close to one another and when the grandparent had a close relationship with his or her own grandparents (King & Elder, 1997). The vast majority of grandparents find the role very gratifying (Cherlin & Furstenberg, 1986). Remote grandparents are the least satisfied, largely because they wish they lived closer to their grandchildren and could see them more often.

The grandparent role may have special significance for Native-American and African-American grandmothers, who often are intimately involved in the upbringing of grandchildren and are looked to as teachers of cultural ways and family traditions (Peterson, 1990; Weibel-Orlando, 1990). In our society, relationships between grandchildren and their maternal grandmothers are the closest (Matthews & Sprey, 1985; Roberto & Stroes, 1992). Traditional gender roles may help explain this, for women often serve as "kinkeepers" in the family, keeping up contacts and ensuring that close, affectionate relationships are maintained (Hagestad, 1985; Lye, 1996).

An important feature of the grandparent role is that it is not entirely voluntary. Adults can decide when to become parents, but they become grandparents, ready or not, when their children have babies. Some women become grandparents in their 30s or even late 20s because their teenage daughters have children. These women often become primary caregivers for their grandchildren and tend to be far less enthusiastic about the role than those who become grandmothers "on time" (Burton, 1996).

In addition, grandparents' roles can change dramatically if their children's lives change. As Gunhild Hagestad (1985) puts it, grandparents are "the family national guard" (p. 46); they are on alert and come to the rescue when there is a crisis in the family. When a teenage daughter becomes pregnant, grandmother and grandfather may become key parent figures for the baby (Oyserman, Radin, & Benn, 1993). Grandparents may also be drawn into a more highly involved role when a child divorces (Clingempeel et al., 1992; Cooney & Smith, 1996). Yet if their child does not obtain custody, grandparents' access to their grandchildren may be reduced or even cut off, causing them much anguish.

In short, grandparenthood is an important role in the lives of middle-aged and elderly adults. It can take a remote, companionate, or involved form, depending on such factors as the geographical distance between grandparents and grandchildren and changes in the lives of grandchildren and their parents. And how do grandchildren feel? They typically view their grandparents as important and influential figures in their

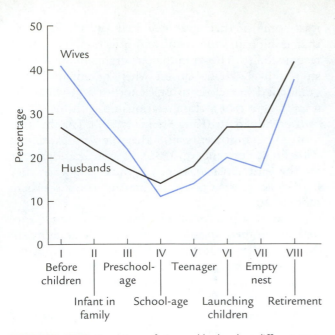

FIGURE 14.5 *Percentages of wives and husbands at different stages of the family life cycle who say their marriage is going well "all the time," as opposed to "most of the time" (the most frequent answer) or less often. Marriages tend to be most blissful before children arrive and after they leave, especially for women.* (From Rollins & Feldman, 1970)

The nature and quality of marital relationships also changes over the years. Women often perceive inequity in their marriages during the parenting years, while they are doing the lion's share of the family's work; their marriages feel fairer, more equal, and less conflictual after the nest empties (Mackey & O'Brien, 1995). And, although frequency of sexual intercourse decreases over the years, psychological intimacy often increases. Elderly couples are more affectionate than middle-aged couples when they interact and are able to resolve conflicts without venting as many negative emotions (Carstensen, Levenson, & Gottman, 1995).

As we've seen, these average changes in marital relationships fit some families much better than others, depending on such factors as the extent to which both parents contribute to child rearing. Moreover, the trends are quite weak: Knowing what stage of the family life cycle an adult is in does not allow us to predict very accurately how satisfied that person is with marriage. To do that, we have to consider many additional factors.

For example, couples who are happy early in their marriage tend to be happy later, and young couples who are miserable early in their marriage tend to remain that way; marital satisfaction, like many personality traits, tends to be quite stable over the years (Dickson, 1995; Johnson et al., 1992). In addition, happily married people are more likely than unhappily married people to have positive personality traits such as self-confidence, social maturity, and an ability to nurture others (Skolnick, 1981). Moreover, their personalities are similar and are likely to remain similar over the years as each partner reinforces in the other the traits that brought them together in the first place (Caspi, Herbener, & Ozer, 1992). In fact, couples become *more* similar in intellectual performance and personality over the years through the intellectual and social stimulation they provide each other (Gruber-Baldini, Schaie, & Willis, 1995). It is when "opposites attract" and find their personalities clashing day after day that marital problems tend to arise (Kurdek, 1991a; Russell & Wells, 1991). Finally, happily married partners genuinely like each other and enjoy each other's company; they do not stay together just because it is convenient, because they believe marriage should be a lifelong commitment, or because they think it is "best for the children" (Lauer & Lauer, 1986; Skolnick, 1981).

The family life cycle ends with widowhood (see Chapter 17 on bereavement and widowhood). By the time they reach age 75 or older, most men are still married and living with their wives, but most women are widowed and living alone (Hobbs, 1996). Even after a spouse dies, the marital relationship often remains centrally important to many adults.

lives (Furman & Buhrmester, 1985a; Roberto & Stroes, 1992), and they benefit when they have frequent contact with these family elders (Falbo, 1991; Wilson, 1986). Indeed, all three generations seem to benefit from maintaining close ties.

Changing Family Relationships

All relationships develop and change with time. What becomes of relationships between spouses, siblings, and parents and their children during the adult years?

The Marital Relationship

As we've seen, marital satisfaction, although generally high for most couples throughout their lives together, dips somewhat after the honeymoon period is over, dips still lower in the new-parenthood phase, continues to drop as new children are added to the family, and recovers only when the children leave the nest. As Figure 14.5 shows, these are precisely the trends discovered by Boyd Rollins and Harold Feldman (1970) when they surveyed adults in the eight phases of the family life cycle about their marital happiness (see also Dickson, 1995; Emery & Tuer, 1993). Moreover, Figure 14.5 reinforces another point we have been making: Women, because they have traditionally been more involved than men in rearing children, tend to be more strongly affected by family life transitions—for good or for bad—than men are.

By permission of Dave Coverly and Creators Syundicate

Sibling Relationships

How do the relationships between brothers and sisters change once siblings no longer live together in the same house and have launched their own separate lives? Starting in adolescence, both closeness and conflict between siblings diminish as brothers and sisters forge their own lives; sibling relationships become less intense and more equal (Buhrmester & Furman, 1990; Cicirelli, 1995). Victor Cicirelli (1982, 1995) finds that adult siblings typically see each other several times a year and communicate through phone calls or letters about how they are getting along. Few of them discuss intimate problems with each other or help each other, though siblings typically know that they can count on each other in a crisis (see also Connidis, 1994).

The same ambivalence that characterizes sibling relationships during childhood seems to carry over into adulthood. A great deal of emotional closeness persists, despite decreased contact; indeed, siblings often grow even closer in old age (Cicirelli, 1995). In Cicirelli's 1982 survey, 68% of middle-aged adults and fully 83% of elderly adults described their relationships with siblings as either "close" or "extremely close." Sisters tend to remain closer than other sibling pairs (Cicirelli, 1995). The potential for sibling rivalry persists too, however. Conflict is far less frequent than during childhood, but old rivalries can and do flare up again during adulthood (Cicirelli, 1995). Siblings who enjoyed a close relationship during childhood are likely to be drawn even closer after significant life events such as a parent's illness or death, whereas sib-

lings who had had poor relationships during childhood are likely to become even more rivalrous in response to the same life events (Lerner et al., 1991; Ross & Milgram, 1982).

The sibling relationship is typically the longest-lasting relationship we have, linking us to individuals who share many of our genes and experiences (Cicirelli, 1991). It is a relationship that can be very close, very tense and conflictual, or, for many people, some of both.

Parent/Child Relationships

Parent and child generations in most families are in close contact and enjoy affectionate give-and-take relationships throughout the adult years. When aging parents eventually need support, children are there to help.

Forming More Mutual Relationships. As young adults leave the nest, they don't sever ties with their parents; instead, they and their parents jointly negotiate a new relationship, often a more intimate one in which they move beyond playing out their roles as "child" and "parent" and become more like friends (Greene & Boxer, 1986; Rossi & Rossi, 1990). The parent/child relationship tends to become closer once children marry, begin their careers, and assume other adult roles (Aquilino, 1997). Young adults often begin to see their parents as individuals in their own right rather than merely as parent figures (White, Speisman, & Costos, 1983). Married daughters are especially likely to establish new and more mutual relationships with their mothers:

> I am understanding her now more than I ever did before. I have started to understand that I had to stop blaming her for everything in my life. I felt she had been a lousy parent. Now, I'm more understanding that my mother is a person and that she has her own problems and her own life. . . . I accepted her as a mother—but she actually is a human being. . . . (White et al., 1983, p. 73)

What happens to the parent/child relationship when children become middle-aged and their parents become elderly? Although tensions in parent/child relationships are normal because parents and children are at different points in their development (Fingerman, 1996), the two generations typically continue to care about, socialize with, and help one another throughout the adult years (Bengtson et al., 1996; Field et al., 1993; Lye, 1996). According to national surveys, 80% of people over 65 have living children, about half either live with a child (18%) or live within 10 minutes of at least one child (34%), and about three-fourths see at least one child at least once a week (Shanas, 1980; see also Taeuber, 1990). Aging mothers enjoy closer relations and more contact with their families than aging fathers do (Field et al., 1993). And African-American, Hispanic-American, and other minority elders often enjoy more supportive relationships with their families than non-Hispanic whites do (Bengtson et al., 1996). So much for the myth that today's families have abandoned the elderly.

What these findings indicate is that the predominant family form in the United States is neither the isolated nuclear family nor the extended family household; instead, it is what has been called the **modified extended family**—an arrangement in which nuclear families live in their own separate households but have close ties and frequent communication and interaction with their other kin (Litwak, 1960). Most elderly people in our society prefer just this pattern. They do not want to have to live with and burden their children when their health fails (E. Brody, Johnsen, & Fulcomer, 1984).

Relationships between the generations are not only close and affectionate, but they are generally quite equitable as well. That is, each generation gives something and each generation receives something in return. In Mexican-American clans, for example, elders receive a great deal of advice and practical help about everything from personal problems to home repairs from their middle-aged children, and their middle-aged children turn to them for advice and help as well (Markides, Boldt, & Ray, 1986). Aging parents can become demoralized when their children help them too much, for then equity is lost and they feel like a burden to the family (Lee, Netzer, & Coward, 1995; Silverstein, Chen, & Heller, 1996).

Similarly, different generations within the family mutually influence each other. Parents transmit their values to their children, and adult children also shape their parents' attitudes and values (Axinn & Thornton, 1993; Rossi & Rossi, 1990). Thus relationships within the family system continue to be reciprocal throughout the life span.

Contrary to myth, then, most aging families do not experience what has been called **role reversal**—a switching of roles late in life such that the parent becomes the needy, dependent one and the child becomes the caregiver (E. Brody, 1990). However, when parents reach advanced ages and begin to develop serious physical or mental problems, middle-aged adults may be called upon to care for them, and then the parent/child relationship may well become less reciprocal.

Caring for Aging Parents.   Elaine Brody (1985, 1990) uses the term **middle generation squeeze** (others call it the "sandwich generation" phenomenon) to describe what middle-aged adults sometimes experience when they are trapped by heavy demands from both the younger and the older generations simultaneously. Put yourself in the shoes of Julia, a 52-year-old African-American working woman:

My girl and grand girl had babies young. Now, they keep on rushin' me, expectin' me to do this

and that, tryin' to make me old 'fore my time. I ain't got no time for myself. I takes care of babies, grown children, and the old peoples. I work too. I get so tired. I don't know if I'll ever get to do somethin' for myself. (Burton, 1996, p. 155)

Julia's situation may not be typical, but it certainly is middle generation squeeze! Middle-aged adults who must foster their children's (and possibly grandchildren's) development while tending to their own development *and* caring for aging parents sometimes find their situation quite overwhelming. They may experience what has come to be called **caregiver burden**, the psychological distress associated with providing care for someone with physical and/or cognitive impairments.

More and more adults with children find themselves caring for their aging parents. Although spouses and siblings also contribute to the care of frail elders, most caregivers are daughters in their 40s and 50s playing out their roles as "kin-keepers." Daughters are about three times more likely than sons to provide assistance to aging parents (Dwyer & Coward, 1991). In many Asian societies, it would be unthinkable for an aging parent not to live with an adult child (usually a son) in later life (Keith, 1992). In our society, aging parents strongly prefer not to burden their children in this way, so much care is provided from a distance (Bengtson et al., 1996).

As you might imagine, adult children playing the role of caregivers for aging parents do experience a burden of emotional, physical, and financial strains (Aneshensel et al., 1995; E. Brody, 1990; Haley et al., 1995). A woman who is almost wholly responsible for a dependent elder often feels angry and resentful because she has no time for herself and little freedom to pursue her own goals. If her parent has Alzheimer's disease or another such cognitive impairment, she may care for the parent for about seven years at home before making the difficult decision to put the parent in a nursing home and then grieving the parent's decline and death (Aneshensel et al., 1995). She may become socially isolated or experience strain in her other relationships because she has little energy left to give to her husband, employer, or children. Some women are forced to quit their jobs or reduce their work hours in order to cope; some become clinically depressed.

Caregiver burden will be especially severe if the elderly parent has cognitive impairments rather than just physical ones (Starrels et al., 1997), especially if he or she also engages in disruptive and socially inappropriate behavior (Aneshensel et al., 1995). The strain is also likely to be worse if the daughter is unmarried and therefore does not have a husband to lean on for practical and emotional support (E. Brody et al., 1992) or if her marriage is an unsupportive one (Stephens &

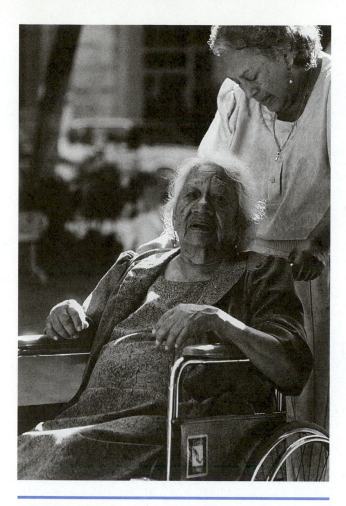

Caring for an ailing parent can result in middle generation squeeze and caregiver burden.

their parents earlier in life and do not have either a strong attachment or a sense of obligation (Whitbeck, Hoyt, & Huck, 1994).

In short, the caregivers most likely to experience psychological distress are those who have highly impaired parents, who are not very close to them, and who help only because they feel they must rather than because they love and cherish their parents. These individuals need support and relief from their burden if they are to continue to provide the estimated 60 to 80% of elder care that they provide (Bengtson et al., 1996).

In sum, generations within a family maintain close relationships throughout adulthood, mutually supporting and influencing each other. Yet the quality of parent/child relationships often changes over the life span. The child who is dependent on parents becomes the adult who can truly be interdependent with them—and in some cases ultimately becomes the person on whom aging parents must depend.

DIVERSITY IN FAMILY LIFE

Useful as it is, the concept of a family life cycle simply does not capture the diversity of adult lifestyles and family experiences (Dilworth-Anderson & Burton, 1996; Klein & White, 1996). Many of today's adults do not progress in a neat and orderly way through the stages of the traditional family life cycle—marrying, having their children, watching them leave the nest, and so on. A small number never marry; a larger number never have children; and a still larger number move in and out of wedded life by marrying, divorcing, and remarrying. So, let's examine some of these variations in family life.

Singles

It is nearly impossible to describe the "typical" single adult, for this category includes not only young adults but middle-aged and elderly people who have experienced divorce or the death of a spouse, as well as adults who have never married. It is typical to start adulthood as a single person, though. Because adults are postponing marriage, the number of young, single adults has been growing; a majority of adults in the 18 to 29 age range are unmarried (Chadwick & Heaton, 1992). Young singles are busy preparing for their careers or getting them off the ground and building social networks. They are likely to have a wider circle of friends than they will have in later years (Carstensen, 1992).

Many young singles today live with a romantic partner without being married—a phenomenon called **cohabitation** (Sweet & Bumpass, 1987). It makes sense to think that couples who live together before marrying would have more opportunity than those

Franks, 1995). In the end, the caregiver/parent relationship and the marital relationship affect one another. A solid marriage can provide social support that lightens the burden of care, a troubled marriage can get in the way; similarly, caregiving can detract from the marital relationship, or it can improve it if it makes a daughter feel better about herself (Stephens & Franks, 1995).

What really motivates adult children to help? In an interesting attempt to understand caregivers' motives, Victor Cicirelli (1993) assessed whether daughters helped their aging mothers out of love or out of duty. Both daughters highly motivated to help based on a strong attachment to their mothers ("I feel lonely when I don't see my mother often") and daughters motivated by a sense of obligation ("I feel that I should do my part in helping") spent more time helping than women whose motivations to help were weaker. However, those who helped out of love experienced helping as far less stressful and burdensome than those who helped mainly out of a sense of duty. Least motivated to help are adult children who felt rejected by who do not to determine whether they are truly compatible. Yet couples who live together and then marry seem to be *more* dissatisfied with their marriages (Thomson & Colella, 1992) and *more* likely to divorce (DeMaris & Rao, 1992) than couples who do not live together before marrying. Why is this? It is unlikely that the experience of cohabitation itself is responsible (Booth & Johnson, 1988). Instead, it seems that the kinds of people who choose to live together may be somewhat more susceptible to marital problems and less committed to marriage than the kinds of people who do not. They tend, for example, to be less religious, less conventional in their family attitudes, less committed to the idea of marriage as a permanent arrangement, and more open to the idea of divorcing (Axinn & Barber, 1997; DeMaris & MacDonald, 1993; Newcomb, 1979). All in all, there is no support for the notion that cohabitation enables people to select their mates more wisely.

What of the 5% or so of single adults who never marry? How do they fare later in adulthood? Not badly at all, it seems, despite stereotypes suggesting that they are miserably lonely and maladjusted. They often manage to make up for their lack of spouse and children by forming close bonds with siblings, friends, or younger adults who become like sons or daughters to them (Rubinstein et al., 1991). They are not a particularly lonely group (Stull & Scarisbrick-Hauser, 1989). As "old-old" people in their 80s and 90s, never-marrieds sometimes do lack relatives who can assist or care for them (Johnson & Troll, 1996). Single adults also tend to have a lower overall sense of well-being or happiness than married adults do during the adult years (Glenn & Weaver, 1988). Yet it is divorced rather than never-married single adults who tend to be the loneliest and least happy of all (Kurdek, 1991b; Peters & Liefbroer, 1997).

Childless Married Couples

Like single adults who never marry, married couples who remain childless do not experience all the stages of the traditional family life cycle. About 12% of women who marry bear no children (U.S. Bureau of the Census, 1997). Most childless couples want children but cannot have them. They are infertile, and some of them try repeatedly to conceive using some of the reproductive technologies discussed in Chapter 4. A growing number of adults, especially highly educated adults with high-status occupations, voluntarily decide to delay having children or to avoid having any at all (Kiernan, 1989).

How are childless couples faring while their peers are having, raising, and launching children? Generally, quite well. Their marital satisfaction is higher than that of couples with children during the child-rearing years (Emery & Tuer, 1993; Somers, 1993). And middle-aged and elderly childless couples seem to be no less satisfied with their lives than parents whose children have left the nest (Glenn & McLanahan, 1981; Rempel, 1985). However, elderly women who are childless *and* widowed may find themselves without anyone to help them if they develop health problems (Johnson & Troll, 1996). It seems, then, that childless couples derive a good deal of satisfaction from their marriages and are happier than single adults but may suffer from a lack of social support very late in life after their marriages end.

Gay and Lesbian Families

The family experiences of gay men and lesbian women are most notable for their diversity (Demo & Allen, 1996; Laird, 1993). In the United States, several million gay men and lesbian women are parents, most through previous heterosexual marriages but others through adoption or artificial insemination (Flaks et al., 1995). Some no longer live with their children, but others raise them as single parents, and still others raise them in families that have two mothers or two fathers. Other gay men and lesbian women remain single and childless or live as couples without children throughout their lives. All in all, the diverse families of gay and lesbian adults are not very well described by traditional family concepts such as the family life cycle, which were developed with heterosexual nuclear families in mind. Moreover, many gay and lesbian families must cope with additional problems because they are not recognized as families by society (Demo & Allen, 1996).

Those gay and lesbian adults who live as couples are likely to have more egalitarian relationships than heterosexual couples do; rather than following traditional gender stereotypes, partners tend to work out a division of labor, through trial and error, based on who is especially talented at what or who hates doing what (Blumstein & Schwartz, 1983; M. Huston & Schwartz, 1995). Otherwise, their relationships evolve through the same stages of development, are satisfying or dissatisfying for the same reasons, and are typically as rewarding as those of married or cohabiting heterosexuals (Kurdek, 1995). Moreover, those gay and lesbian adults who raise children are as likely as heterosexual parents to produce competent and well-adjusted children (Flaks et al., 1995; Patterson, 1995). And, contrary to what many people believe, their children are no more likely than the children of heterosexual parents to develop a homosexual or bisexual sexual orientation; over 90% of the children of gay fathers and lesbian mothers are heterosexual (Bailey et al., 1995; Golombok & Tasker, 1996). There is certainly no evidence that it is in the best interests of children to deny gay and lesbian parents custody of their children or the right to adopt children (Patterson, 1995). Aside from the difficulties they may face because of the stigma attached to homosexuality, families headed by gay or lesbian adults are diverse but more like other families than different from them.

Families Experiencing Divorce

Orderly progress through the family life cycle is disrupted when a couple divorces. Divorce is *not* just one life event; rather, it is a series of stressful experiences for the entire family that begins with marital conflict before the divorce and includes a whole complex of life changes afterward. Families must often cope with "the diminution of financial resources, changes in residence, assumption of new roles and responsibilities, establishment of new patterns of intrafamilial interaction, reorganization of routines and schedules, and eventually the introduction of new relationships into the existing family" (Hetherington & Camara, 1984, p. 398).

Why do people divorce? What effects does divorce typically have on family members? And how can we explain the fact that some adults and children eventually thrive after a divorce whereas others experience persisting problems?

Before the Divorce

We don't know a lot about the processes within the family that ultimately cause couples to divorce rather than stay together despite dissatisfactions. However, Gay Kitson and her colleagues (1985, 1992) have pieced together a portrait of the couples at highest risk for divorce. Generally they are young adults, in their 20s and 30s, who have been married for an average of about seven years and often have young children. They are especially likely to divorce if they married as teenagers, had a short courtship, or conceived a child before marrying—all factors that might suggest an unreadiness for marriage and unusually high financial and psychological stress accompanying new parenthood. Finally, they are more likely to be low in socioeconomic status than high. This profile cannot take us far, however, because all kinds of couples are divorcing today.

Contrary to the notion that today's couples don't really give their marriages a chance to work, research suggests that most divorcing couples experience a few years of marital distress and conflict and often try out separations before they make the final decision to divorce (Gottman & Levenson, 1992; Kitson, 1992). Although the stated reasons for divorcing are varied, they are no longer restricted to severe problems such as nonsupport, alcoholism, or abuse (Gigy & Kelly, 1992). Instead, couples today typically divorce because they feel their marriages are lacking in communication, emotional fulfillment, or compatibility (see Table 14.3). Wives tend to have longer lists of complaints than their husbands do and often have more to do with initiating the breakup (Amato & Rogers, 1997; Kitson et al., 1985; Zeiss, Zeiss, & Johnson, 1980).

After the Divorce: Crisis and Reorganization

Most families going through a divorce experience it as a genuine *crisis*—a period of considerable disruption that often lasts for a year or more (Booth & Amato, 1991; Hetherington, 1989; Kitson, 1992; Lorenz et al., 1997). Typically, both spouses experience emotional as well as practical difficulties. The wife, who usually obtains custody of any children, is likely to be angry, depressed, moody, lonely, and otherwise distressed, although often relieved as well. The husband is also likely to be distressed, particularly if he did not want the divorce and feels shut off from his children. Both individuals must manage the difficult task of revising their identities as single rather than married people. They may both sometimes feel socially isolated from former friends and unsure of themselves as they attempt to establish new romantic relationships. Divorced women with children are likely to face the added problem of getting by with less money—about half of the family income they had before, on average (Smock, 1993). Because of all these stresses, divorced adults are at high risk for depression, physical health problems, and even death (Lorenz et al., 1997; Lillard & Panis, 1996).

As you might suspect, psychologically distressed adults do not make the best of parents. Moreover, children going through a divorce do not make the best of children, for they are suffering too. They are often angry, fearful, depressed, and guilty, especially if they are preschoolers who fear that they are somehow responsible for what happened (Hetherington, 1981). They are also likely to be whiney and dependent, disobedient, and downright disrespectful. A vicious circle of the sort described by the transactional model of family influence results: Children's behavior problems and parents' ineffective parenting styles feed on each other.

Mavis Hetherington and her associates (1982) find that custodial mothers, overburdened by responsibilities and by their own emotional reactions to the divorce, often become edgy, impatient, and insensitive to their children's needs. In terms of the dimensions of child rearing we have discussed, they become less accepting and responsive, less authoritative, and less consistent in their discipline, now and then trying to seize control of their children with a heavy-handed, controlling style of parenting but more often failing to carry through in enforcing rules and making few

TABLE 14.3

Top ten reasons checked by divorcing men and women in California for their divorce. Respondents were given a checklist with 27 items. Notice that incompatibility and lack of emotional fulfillment are strong themes and that more women than men voiced several of these complaints.

Reasons for Divorce Checklist Responses	Percentage of Males (N = 189)	Percentage of Females (N = 212)
1. Gradual growing apart, losing sense of closeness	79	78
2. Not feeling loved and appreciated by spouse	60	73
3. Sexual intimacy problems	65	64
4. Serious differences in lifestyle or values	57	63
5. Spouse not able/willing to meet my major needs	48	64
6. Frequently feel put down or belittled by spouse	37	59
7. Emotional problems of spouse	44	52
8. Conflict regarding spending and handling of money	44	50
9. Severe and intense conflict; frequent fighting	35	44
10. Problems and conflicts with roles (i.e., divisions of responsibility for household jobs or other chores outside the house)	33	47

SOURCE: Adapted from Gigy & Kelly (1992)

demands that their children behave maturely. Noncustodial fathers, meanwhile, are likely to be overpermissive, indulging their children during visits. This is not the formula for producing well-adjusted, competent children. The behavior problems that children display undoubtedly make effective parenting difficult, but a deterioration in parenting style clearly aggravates those behavior problems.

Mother/child relations, particularly between mothers and sons, are likely to be especially poor about a year after the divorce (Hetherington et al., 1982). For children, this breakdown in family functioning is likely to lead not only to behavior problems at home but also to strained relations with peers and academic problems and adjustment difficulties at school (Amato & Keith, 1991; Hetherington et al., 1982). Although older children and adolescents are in a better position to understand the reasons for their parents' divorce, they seem to suffer no less than young children (Amato, 1993; Hetherington, Clingempeel, & Associates, 1992).

How long do these negative consequences last? Hetherington and her colleagues find that families begin to pull themselves back together about two years after the divorce. Girls seem to recover from their difficulties by the end of the second year (Hetherington et al., 1982). Boys improve dramatically during this same period, but many of them continue to show signs of emotional distress and problems in their relationships with parents, siblings, teachers, and peers, even six years after the divorce (Hetherington, 1989).

A word of caution on sex differences, though: Most research concerns mother-headed families and focuses on children's overt behavior problems; some studies suggest that boys fare better in father-headed homes than in mother-headed ones (Zaslow, 1989) and that girls experience more *covert* distress than boys, becoming withdrawn and emotionally upset rather than acting out their frustrations (Chase-Lansdale, Cherlin, & Kiernan, 1995). Overall, then, divorce affects both boys and girls negatively but in somewhat different ways.

Indeed, it has become clear that, even after the crisis phase has passed, divorce can leave a residue of negative effects that lasts for years (Amato & Keith, 1991). Both girls and boys who have experienced divorce are likely to have lower school achievement at age 16 (Jonsson & Gahler, 1997) and more psychological problems at age 23 (Chase-Lansdale, Cherlin, & Kiernan, 1995) than those who have not. Moreover, girls from divorced families tend to leave home early to escape conflict and to become involved in sexual relationships and childbearing earlier than other girls (Cherlin, Kiernan, & Chase-Lansdale, 1995). Even years after the divorce, many adolescents are still negative about what it has done to their lives and harbor fantasies that their parents will reconcile (Wallerstein & Blakeslee, 1989). One girl was quite blunt: "I wish my stepfather would go back to his first wife, I wish my stepmother would go back to her first husband, and I would like my mom and dad to get together again" (Wallerstein, 1984, p. 452). Others fear that they will be unable to find happiness in marriage. There may well be some basis for that fear: Adults whose parents divorced are more likely than adults from intact families to divorce themselves (Amato, 1996).

In sum, divorce is a difficult experience for all involved, and each family member affects others in the family system. Problems reach crisis proportions about a year after the divorce. Although most of them disappear over the next couple of years, some children, negatively affected by their own distress and by a breakdown in parenting, have more persistent problems and may still be struggling with painful feelings many years later.

But now let's offset this gloomy picture of the typical divorce with more encouraging messages. In the first place, a conflict-ridden two-parent family can be more detrimental to a child's development than a stable single-parent family (Hetherington, 1989). Indeed, many of the behavior problems that children display after a divorce are actually evident well before the divorce. They may be caused by long-standing family conflict rather than by the divorce itself (Block, Block, & Gjerde, 1986; Cherlin et al., 1991). In one study, marital problems were linked to both poor parent/child relationships and child behavior problems fully 12 years before parents divorced; divorce further eroded the relationship between fathers and children, but most of the damage to parent/child relationships had already been done by the time couples divorced (Amato & Booth, 1996). There is plenty of evidence that marital conflict contributes to child and adolescent adjustment problems such as anxiety, depression, and conduct disorders; not only does it upset children, but it interferes with a parent's ability to be warm and sensitive (Harold et al., 1997).

Divorce is associated with many factors that can potentially explain its negative effects on child development (Amato, 1993). When Paul Amato (1993) reviewed the literature on these factors, he concluded that marital conflict and deterioration of parenting style were the most important, and that if children could be protected from them divorce need not be damaging (Amato, 1993). Indeed, children may *benefit* if the ending of a stormy marriage ultimately reduces the stress they experience and enables either or both parents to be more sensitive and responsive to their needs (Barber & Eccles, 1992). As we see in Box 14.2, a number of factors can help facilitate a positive adjustment to divorce and keep it from doing lasting damage, among them adequate finances, effective parenting on the part of the custodial parent, involvement of the noncustodial parent, other sources of social support, and a minimum of additional stressors.

Remarriage and Reconstituted Families

Within three to five years of a divorce, about 75% of single-parent families will experience yet another major change when a parent remarries and the children acquire a stepparent—and sometimes new siblings as well (Hetherington, 1989). Imagine the stresses for adults and children who find themselves in a recurring cycle of marriage, marital conflict, divorce, single status, and remarriage. Indeed, the more marital transitions elementary school children have experienced, the poorer their academic performance and adjustment (Kurdek, Fine, & Sinclair, 1995).

How do children fare when their custodial parents remarry? At first there is a period of conflict and disruption as new family roles and relationships are ironed out (Hetherington, 1989; Hetherington et al., 1992). The difficulties are likely to be aggravated if both parents bring children to the family, for parents tend to be warmer toward their biological offspring than toward their stepchildren and children pick up on this and react negatively to it (Mekos, Hetherington, & Reiss, 1996). Interestingly, although boys often suffer more than girls when they live with a single-parent mother in the aftermath of divorce, they benefit more than girls when they gain a stepfather (Hetherington, 1989; Zaslow, 1989). Less is known about the transition from a father-headed single-parent home to a two-parent family with a stepmother, but it appears that this transition is also more difficult for girls, especially if their biological mothers maintain frequent contact with them (Clingempeel & Segal, 1986). Girls, it seems, are often so closely allied with their mothers that they are bothered by either a stepfather competing for their mother's attention or a stepmother attempting to play a substitute-mother role. In sum, the transition from a single-parent family to a reconstituted family requires adjustment and is likely to be more disruptive for girls than for boys.

Even this quick examination of the diverse experiences of single adults, married but childless adults, gay and lesbian adults, and divorced and remarried adults should convince us that it is difficult indeed to generalize about the family. We can gain many insights by tracing the progression of developing human beings through the stages of the traditional family life cycle, but we must also recognize that an increasing number of individuals live and develop in families other than a traditional nuclear one. We must stop talking about *the* family life cycle and start talking about many such cycles (Rowland, 1991). And, recalling the importance of nonshared environmental influences

BOX 14.2

"Good" and "bad" divorces: Factors influencing adjustment

Some adults and children thrive after a divorce, whereas others suffer many negative and long-lasting effects. Of course, an individual's temperament and coping skills are important influences on how well he or she adjusts (Hetherington, 1989). However, other factors can make the individual's task easier:

1. *Adequate financial support.* Families fare better after a divorce if they have adequate finances (Menaghan & Lieberman, 1986; Simons et al., 1993). Unfortunately, only about half of noncustodial fathers pay child support (Sorensen, 1997). Adjustment is likely to be more difficult for mother-headed families that fall into poverty and must struggle to survive, so recent efforts to get more noncustodial parents to pay child support are important.

2. *Involvement of the custodial parent.* The custodial parent obviously plays a critical role in what happens to the family. If she or he can continue to be warm, authoritative, and consistent, children are far less likely to experience problems (Hetherington et al., 1992; Simons et al., 1994). It is difficult to be an effective parent when one is depressed and under stress, but parents who understand the stakes involved may be more able to give their children the love and guidance they need.

3. *Involvement of the noncustodial parent.* If parents continue to squabble after the divorce and are hostile toward each other, both will likely be upset, the custodial parent's parenting is likely to suffer, and children will feel torn in their loyalties and experience behavior problems (Amato, 1993). Children also suffer when they lose contact with their noncustodial parent. Unfortunately, about a third of children living with their mothers lose all contact with their fathers (Seltzer & Bianchi, 1988). By contrast, regular contact with noncustodial fathers who are supportive and who have good parenting skills helps children make a positive adjustment to life in a single-parent home (Amato, 1993; Simons et al., 1994). Ideally, then, children should be able to maintain affectionate ties with both parents and should be protected from any continuing conflict between parents. It may not be as important that parents obtain joint custody as that they both maintain high-quality relationships with their children (Emery & Tuer, 1993; Kline et al., 1989).

4. *Additional social support.* Divorcing adults are less depressed if they have close confidants (Menaghan & Lieberman, 1986). Children also benefit from having close friends to give them social support (Lustig, Wolchik, & Braver, 1992) as well as from participating in peer-support programs in which they and other children of divorce can share their feelings, correct their misconceptions, and learn positive coping skills (Grych & Fincham, 1992). Adolescents in single-parent homes appear to be less likely to engage in delinquent behavior if a second adult (a grandmother, for example) lives in the home than if one parent bears the sole responsibility for child rearing and supervision (Dornbusch et al., 1985). In short, friends, relatives, peers, school personnel, and other sources of social support outside the family can do much to help families adjust to divorce.

5. *A minimum of additional stressors.* Generally, families respond most positively to divorce if additional disruptions are kept to a minimum—for example, if parents do not have to move, go through court hearings, get new jobs, cope with the loss of their children, and so on (Buehler et al., 1985–1986). Obviously it is easier to deal with a couple of changes than a mountain of stressors. Although families cannot always control events, they can strive to keep their lives as simple as possible.

Here, then, we have the first steps in the path toward a positive divorce experience—as well as a better understanding of why divorce is more disruptive for some families than for others. As Paul Amato (1993) concludes, adjustment to divorce will depend on the "total configuration" of stressors the individual faces and resources he or she has available to aid in coping, including both personal strengths (such as good coping skills) and social supports. This research also serves as still another reminder that the family is a system embedded in other systems. Family members influence one another's adjustment to divorce, and the family's experience will also depend on its interactions with the surrounding world.

in the family (see Chapter 3), we must also appreciate that even members of the same family are likely to have very different experiences of family life.

APPLICATIONS: CONFRONTING THE PROBLEM OF FAMILY VIOLENCE

Just as family relationships can be our greatest source of nurturance and support, they can be our greatest source of anguish. Nowhere is this more obvious than in cases of family violence. Child abuse is perhaps the most visible form of family violence. Every day, infants, children, and adolescents are burned, bruised, beaten, starved, suffocated, sexually abused, or otherwise mistreated by their caretakers. In 1994, over 3.1 million reports of maltreatment of children were filed in the United States (American Humane Association, cited in Wiehe, 1996). According to a national survey of U.S. families, 11% of children had reportedly been kicked, bitten, hit, hit with an object, beaten up, burned, or threatened or attacked with a knife or gun by a parent in the past year (Wolfner & Gelles, 1993). Close to half a million are sexually abused each year (see Finkelhor & Dziuba-Leatherman, 1994; and see

In some families, violence is a way of life.

Chapter 11). Others are victims of psychological maltreatment—rejected, verbally abused, or terrorized by their parents (Wiehe, 1996). Still others are neglected and deprived of the basic care and stimulation they need to develop normally.

Abuse of children by their caregivers is only one form of family violence. In all possible relationships within the family the potential for violence exists. Children and adolescents batter, and in rare cases kill, their parents (Agnew & Huguley, 1989); siblings abuse one another in numerous ways (Straus, 1980; Cicirelli, 1995). And spouse abuse, rampant in our society, appears to be the most common form of family violence worldwide. An analysis of family violence in 90 nonindustrial societies by David Levinson (1989) reveals that wife beating occurs in 85% of them; in almost half of these societies it occurs in most or all households, suggesting that it is an accepted part of family life. Although spouse abuse is viewed as intolerable in most segments of our society, Murray Straus and Richard Gelles (1986, 1990) nonetheless estimate, on the basis of their surveys, that 16 of 100 married couples in the United States experience some form of marital violence in a year's time—often "only" a shove or a slap, but violence nonetheless. Almost 6% of the couples surveyed reported at least one instance of severe violence (such as kicking or beating). Where there is spouse abuse, children are likely to be abused as well, especially by their fathers (McCloskey, Figueredo, & Koss, 1995).

As Margaret Hudson (1986) has noted, child abuse and neglect, although they have always existed, were "discovered" as social problems in the 1960s; spouse abuse came to the public's attention in the 1970s; and finally, in the 1980s, it became clear that elderly adults are also the targets of family violence. Frail or impaired older people are physically or psychologically mistreated, neglected, financially exploited, and stripped of their rights—most often by adult children or spouses serving as their caregivers (Lachs et al., 1997; Wolf & Pillemer, 1989). The problem is worldwide (Kosberg & Garcia, 1995). No one really knows how many elderly people are abused, but the onset of cognitive impairments is an important risk factor (Lachs et al., 1997), and 5% of one sample of elderly adults with Alzheimer's disease had been physically abused by their caregivers in the year since they had been diagnosed (Paveza et al., 1992).

This is not a pretty picture. Here we have a social problem of major dimensions that causes untold suffering and inhibits the development of family members of all ages. What can be done to prevent it or to stop it once it occurs? To answer that applied question, we must first try to gain some insight into why family violence occurs in the first place.

Why Does Family Violence Occur?

Child abuse has been studied the longest, and there are many similarities among the various forms of family violence. Therefore, let's see what has been learned about the causes of child abuse.

The Abuser

Anyone examining a badly beaten child might immediately conclude that the abuser must be a psychologically disturbed individual who needs professional help. Strange as it may seem, though, only about 1 child abuser in 10 appears to have a severe mental illness (Kempe & Kempe, 1978). The abusive parent most often is a young mother with many children who lives in poverty, is unemployed, and often has no spouse to share her load (Wiehe, 1996; Wolfner & Gelles, 1993). Yet child abusers come from all races, ethnic groups, and social classes. Many of them appear to be rather typical, loving parents—except for their tendency to become extremely irritated with their children and to do things they will later regret.

There are a few identifiable differences between parents who abuse their children and those who do not. First, although most maltreated children do not abuse their own children when they become parents, roughly 30% do (Kaufman & Zigler, 1989). In other words, abusive parenting, like effective parenting, tends to be passed from generation to generation (Simons et al., 1991; van IJzendoorn, 1992). This "cycle of abuse" is not inevitable, though; it can be broken if abused individuals receive emotional support from parent substitutes, therapists, or spouses and are spared from severe stress as adults (Egeland, Jacobvitz, & Sroufe, 1988; Vondra & Belsky, 1993).

Second, abusive mothers are often battered women, victims of abuse in their romantic relationships (Coohey & Braun, 1997; McCloskey et al., 1995). They may have learned through their experiences as a child and as a wife that violence is the way to solve problems, or they may take out some of their own frustrations on their children.

Third, abusers are often insecure individuals with low self-esteem. Their unhappy experiences in insecure attachment relationships with their parents, reinforced by their experiences in romantic relationships, may lead them to formulate negative internal working models of themselves and others (Pianta, Egeland, & Erickson, 1989; and see Chapter 13). These adults may feel like victims but have also learned to be victimizers (Pianta et al., 1989).

Fourth, abusive parents seem to have unrealistic expectations about what children can be expected to do at different ages and have difficulty tolerating the normal behavior of young children (Haskett, Johnson, & Miller, 1994). For example, Byron Egeland (1979) and his colleagues (Egeland, Sroufe, & Erickson, 1983) found that, when infants cry to communicate needs such as hunger, nonabusive mothers correctly interpret these cries as signs of discomfort; abusive mothers, however, often infer that the baby is somehow criticizing or rejecting them. Indeed, abusive parents seem to find even an infant's smile unpleasantly arousing (Frodi & Lamb, 1980).

In short, abusive parents not only tend to have been exposed to harsh parenting and abusive relationships themselves but also have low self-esteem and find caregiving more stressful, unpleasant, and ego-

threatening than other parents do. Still, it has been difficult to identify a particular kind of person who is highly likely to turn into a child abuser. Could some children bring out the worst in parents?

The Abused

An abusive parent often singles out only one child in the family as a target; this offers us a hint that child characteristics might matter (Gil, 1970). No one is suggesting that children are to *blame* for being abused, but some children do appear to be somewhat more at risk than others. For example, children who are hyperactive or difficult in some way are more likely to be abused than quiet, healthy, and responsive infants who are easier to care for (Ammerman & Patz, 1996; Sherrod et al., 1984). Yet many difficult children are not mistreated, and many seemingly cheerful and easygoing children are.

Just as characteristics of the caregiver cannot fully explain why abuse occurs, then, neither can characteristics of children. It is quite likely that the *combination* of a high-risk parent and a high-risk child spells trouble (Bugental, Blue, & Cruzcosa, 1989), but even the match between child and caregiver may not be enough to explain abuse. We should, as always, consider the ecological context surrounding the family system.

The Context

Quite consistently, abuse is most likely to occur in families under stress. If, for example, a relatively young, poorly educated mother is overburdened with responsibilities and receives little assistance from the father or any other sources of social support, she stands an increased risk of becoming abusive (Egeland et al., 1983; Haskett et al., 1994). Life changes such as the loss of a job or a move to a new residence can also disrupt family functioning and contribute to abuse or neglect (McLoyd et al., 1994; Wolfner & Gelles, 1993). Moreover, some neighborhoods have higher rates of abuse than others with the same demographic and socioeconomic characteristics. These high-risk areas tend to be deteriorating neighborhoods where families are transient, socially isolated, and lacking community services and informal social support (Coulton et al., 1995; Garbarino & Sherman, 1980). Finally, ours is a violent society in which the use of physical punishment is common and the line between physical punishment and child abuse difficult to define (Whipple & Richey, 1997). Cross-cultural studies reveal less child abuse in societies that discourage physical punishment of children and advocate nonviolent ways of resolving interpersonal conflicts (Belsky, 1993; Gilbert, 1997; Levinson, 1989). Child abuse is particularly rare in Scandinavian countries, where steps have been taken to outlaw corporal (physical) punishment of children, not only in the schools but at home (Finkelhor & Dziuba-Leatherman, 1994).

As you can see, child abuse is a complex phenomenon with a multitude of causes and contributing factors. It is not easy to predict who will become a child abuser and who will not, but abuse seems most likely to result when a vulnerable individual faces overwhelming stress with insufficient social support (Wolfner & Gelles, 1993). Much the same is true of spouse abuse, elder abuse, and other forms of family violence.

What Are the Effects of Abuse?

As you might imagine, child abuse is not good for child development. Physically abused and otherwise maltreated children tend to have a number of problems (Trickett & McBride-Chang, 1995). Intellectual deficits and academic difficulties are common (Malinosky-Rummell & Hansen, 1993). John Eckenrode, Molly Laird, and John Doris (1993) have found that children who are neglected are even more likely than those who are physically or sexually abused to obtain low grades and achievement test scores and to have to repeat a grade. Neglected children undoubtedly receive little of the stimulation from nurturing adults that contributes so much to intellectual growth. Meanwhile, behavior problems are more common among physically abused children than among neglected ones. They tend to be explosively aggressive youngsters who are often rejected by their peers for that reason (Haskett & Kistner, 1991; Salzinger et al., 1993; Trickett et al., 1991).

Not surprisingly, abused and neglected children also tend to have emotional problems, rooted in part in insecure attachments to their caregivers (Cicchetti & Barnett, 1991; McCloskey et al., 1995). They are likely to be fearful, anxious, depressed, and low in self-esteem (Bagley, 1995; Emery, 1989). Moreover, these social and emotional difficulties are likely to be long lasting: Adults who were abused as children tend to be violent, both inside and outside the family, and they have higher-than-average rates of substance abuse, depression, and other psychological problems (Bagley, 1995; Malinosky-Rummell & Hansen, 1993).

One of the most disturbing consequences of physical abuse is a lack of normal empathy in response to the distress of peers. When Mary Main and Carol George (1985) observed the responses of abused and nonabused toddlers to the fussing and crying of peers, they found that nonabused children typically attended carefully to the distressed child, showed concern, or even attempted to provide comfort. As shown in Figure 14.6, not one abused child showed appropriate concern; instead, abused toddlers were likely to become angry and attack the crying child (see also Klimes-Dougan & Kistner, 1990). In short, abused children react to the distress of peers much as their abusive parents react to their distress:

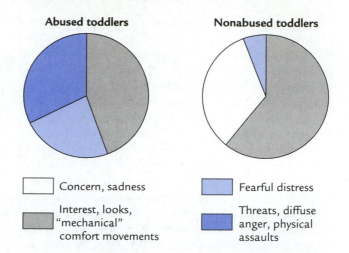

FIGURE 14.6 *Responses to distressed peers observed in abused and nonabused toddlers in day care. Abused children distinguish themselves by a lack of concern and a tendency to become upset, angry, and aggressive when other children cry.* (Adapted from Main & George, 1985)

. . . Martin (an abused boy of 32 months) tried to take the hand of the crying other child, and when she resisted, he slapped her on the arm with his open hand. He then turned away from her to look at the ground and began vocalizing very strongly, "Cut it out! CUT IT OUT!," each time saying it a little faster and louder. He patted her, but when she became disturbed by his patting, he retreated, hissing at her and baring his teeth. He then began patting her on the back again, his patting became beating, and he continued beating her despite her screams. (Main & George, 1985, p. 410)

Surprisingly, many neglected and abused children turn out fine, especially if they have a close relationship with some nonabusive adult (Egeland et al., 1988). Without question, though, child abuse can have negative and often long-lasting effects on cognitive, social, and emotional development. The important question then becomes this: Knowing what we know about the causes and effects of abuse, what can be done to prevent it, stop it, and undo the damage?

How Do We Solve the Problem?

The fact that family violence has many causes is discouraging. Where do we begin to intervene, and just how many problems must we correct before we can prevent or stop the violence? Yet, despite the complexity of the problem, progress has been made.

Consider first the task of preventing violence before it starts. This requires identifying high-risk families—a task that is greatly aided by the kinds of studies we have reviewed. For example, once we know that an infant is at risk for abuse because he or she is particularly irritable or unresponsive, it makes sense to help the child's parents appreciate and evoke the baby's positive qualities. Learning how to elicit smiles, reflexes, and other positive responses from premature infants makes parents more responsive to their babies, which in turn helps these at-risk babies develop more normally (Widmayer & Field, 1980).

Other efforts to prevent abuse have been directed at high-risk parents. Steven Schinke and his associates (1986), for example, decided to teach better coping techniques to one high-risk group of mothers—unwed teenagers who were under a great deal of stress. They conveyed a wide range of stress-management skills: problem-solving strategies, self-praise for handling difficult situations, communication skills (such as refusing unreasonable demands and requesting help), relaxation techniques, and even techniques for building a stronger social-support network. Three months later the mothers who had received the training outperformed the control group on several measures. They had improved their problem-solving skills, had established stronger social-support networks, enjoyed higher self-esteem, and were more confident about their parenting skills. At-risk parents can also benefit from learning effective child-management skills (Wiehe, 1996). The demonstrated success of these and other interventions has led child welfare agencies in several states to develop family support and education programs aimed at preventing child abuse (Zigler & Finn Stevenson, 1993).

What about the parents who are already abusive? Here the problem is more complex. A few visits from a social worker are unlikely to solve the problem. More promising is Parents Anonymous, a self-help approach based on Alcoholics Anonymous that is available to help caregivers understand their problems and to give them the emotional support they often lack (see "On the Web" at the end of the chapter). In extreme cases the abusive parent is prosecuted and the children are taken from the home, although courts have been hesitant to break up families unless the abuse is chronic and severe (Wiehe, 1996). Ultimately, however, a comprehensive approach is likely to be most effective. Abusive parents need emotional support and the opportunity to learn more effective parenting and coping skills, and the victims of abuse need day-care programs and developmental training to help them overcome the cognitive, social, and emotional problems associated with abuse (Culp et al., 1991; Oates & Bross, 1995; Wiehe, 1996). In short, the ultimate goal in attempting to decrease child abuse and other forms of family violence must be to convert a pathological family system into a healthy one.

◆ SUMMARY POINTS

1. The family, whether it is nuclear or extended in form, is best viewed as a changing social system embedded in larger social systems that are also changing. The family systems, family development (family life cycle), and ecological perspectives must all be brought to bear to understand family processes. Social trends affecting family life today include greater numbers of single adults; the postponement of marriage; a decline in childbearing; more female participation in the labor force; more divorces, single-parent families, child poverty, and remarriages; more years with an empty nest; and more multigeneration families.

2. Infants affect and are affected by their parents. Compared to mothers, fathers are less involved in caregiving and more involved in rowdy play. Developmental outcomes are likely to be positive when *both* parents are involved with their children and have positive *indirect* effects on their children by virtue of their influence on each other.

3. Child rearing can be described in terms of the dimensions of acceptance/responsiveness and demandingness/control; generally, children are most socially and cognitively competent when their parents adopt an authoritative style of parenting, combining acceptance and demandingness, and less competent when their parents are authoritarian, permissive, or neglectful.

4. Lower-income parents generally tend to be more punitive and authoritarian than middle-class parents, because of both the demands of blue-collar jobs and the negative effects of economic hardship on parenting. Ethnic differences in parenting also exist, and parenting styles can have different effects in different cultural contexts, but authoritative parenting is generally effective.

5. Research related to the parent effects, child effects, and transactional models of family influence reminds us that children's problem behaviors are not always caused by ineffective parenting—that children's genes influence their behavior, which in turn influences the parenting they receive.

6. When a second child enters the family system, mothers typically become less attentive to their first-borns, and first-borns find the experience stressful. Sibling relationships are characterized by rivalry *and* affection and provide emotional support, caregiving, and teaching.

7. Parent/child relationships typically remain close in adolescence but are renegotiated; adolescents are most likely to gain autonomy when parents remain authoritative, both supportive and appropriately demanding.

8. Marital satisfaction declines somewhat as newlyweds adjust to each other and declines still further as couples face the challenges of new parenthood, which is less stressful if the baby is easy, parents have relevant knowledge and coping skills, and resources such as spouse support are available. Marital satisfaction continues to decline during the child-rearing years and then often increases again after the empty nest transition, which most adults view more positively than negatively. Empty-nest adults take pleasure in becoming grandparents, most often playing a companionate role rather than a remote or involved role.

9. Although marital satisfaction declines during the parenting years, especially among women, it is affected by many additional factors, including previous satisfaction, degree of spousal similarity, and liking for each other.

10. In adulthood, siblings have less contact but normally continue to feel both emotionally close and rivalrous. Young adults sometimes establish more mutual and intimate relationships with their parents. Middle-aged adults continue to experience mutually supportive relationships with their elderly parents rather than role reversal, though some, particularly daughters, do experience the stresses of middle generation squeeze and caregiver burden.

11. Among the adults whose lives are inadequately described by the family life cycle are single adults, some of whom cohabitate; childless married couples, who usually enjoy high marital and life satisfaction; and gay and lesbian adults, whose family patterns are diverse.

12. Divorce significantly disrupts family life for a year or two; some children (especially boys) experience long-lasting social and academic problems, but factors such as financial support, quality of parenting, and social support influence adjustment. Most single-parent families adapt well to becoming part of a reconstituted family, but the transition is often hard for girls.

13. Family violence occurs in all possible relationships within the family. The most recognized form is child abuse; parent characteristics such as a history of abuse and hypersensitivity to child behavior, child characteristics such as a difficult temperament, and contextual factors such as low social support and a deteriorating neighborhood all contribute to the problem and must be considered in formulating solutions.

FOOD FOR THOUGHT

1. Here are four situations a child could experience growing up: being a latchkey child, being physically abused, experiencing a divorce, and living with two parents who fight. Rank these from most to least damaging to child development and justify your decisions.

2. Your 16-year-old daughter's best friend has just called you from the police station to inform you that your daughter, drunk and high on marijuana, just plowed your car into a tree and is being cited for driving under the influence. You need to go to the

police station. How will you respond to this situation, and what parenting style does your planned response seem to reflect?

3. Three months after her divorce, Martha has become depressed and increasingly withdrawn. Her son Matt, age 7, has become a terror around the house and a discipline problem at school. From the perspective of (a) the parent effects model, (b) the child effects model, and (c) the transactional model of family influence, and referring to relevant research, how would you explain what is going on in this single-parent family?

4. Moose is a traditional man, Muffy a traditional woman. Discuss how their experiences of the family life cycle, including new parenthood, the empty nest, and grandparenthood, are likely to be similar and different.

W ON THE WEB

1. *Divorce*   This site contains selected materials from a college course on divorce, on topics such as the effects of divorce on children, coparenting after a divorce, and interventions to help families cope.
   http://www.hec.ohio-state.edu/famlife/divorce/desc.htm#readings

2. *Child Abuse*   For a wealth of information about child abuse, sexual abuse, and other forms of domestic violence, including statistics on the prevalence of abuse, try the site of the National Committee to Prevent Child Abuse.
   http://www.childabuse.org/

3. *Parents Anonymous*   Parents Anonymous has chapters throughout the United States that offer support to parents in an effort to prevent child abuse and neglect. Here at the national Web site is a Network List that will help you find the Web site of the Parents Anonymous organization in your state. Some state sites (for example, that of my home state, Minnesota) have useful resource pages for parents fighting the urge to abuse their children.
   http://www.parentsanonymous-natl.org/

KEY TERMS

family systems theory	demandingness/control	sibling rivalry
nuclear family	authoritarian parenting	autonomy
extended family household	authoritative parenting	empty nest
family development theory	permissive parenting	modified extended family
family life cycle	neglectful parenting	role reversal
reconstituted family	latchkey children	middle generation squeeze
beanpole family	parent effects model	caregiver burden
indirect effects	child effects model	cohabitation
acceptance/responsiveness	transactional model	

CHAPTER 15

Achievement

ACHIEVEMENT MOTIVATION
Need for Achievement
The Value Placed on Achievement
Expectancies of Success
Attributions for Success and Failure

THE INFANT
Early Origins of Achievement Motivation
Mastery through Play

THE CHILD
Mastery-Oriented and Helpless Achievement Styles
Schooling and School Achievement

THE ADOLESCENT
Declining Achievement Motivation
Making Vocational Choices
Working after School
Pathways to Adulthood

THE ADULT
Achievement Motivation
Levinson's Conception of Adult Development
Career Paths during Adulthood
Women, Work, and the Family
Work and Adult Development
Retirement
Successful Aging

APPLICATIONS: IMPROVING THE QUALITY OF EDUCATION

SUMMARY POINTS

FOOD FOR THOUGHT

ON THE WEB

KEY TERMS

At 12 months of age, Robbie shrieks with delight when he finally manages to pry open his mother's purse and make off with her keys. At 3, he concentrates intensely for half an hour on building a tower of blocks, and at 8, he becomes frustrated when he cannot seem to work his new math problems, no matter how hard he tries. At 15, Robert temporarily becomes more motivated to impress the girl who sits behind him in history than to ace the history exam, but he is already thinking that he might like to become an architect when he grows up. And he does become one, after earning his bachelor's degree and then a Master's degree in architecture. After 15 years of working his way up the ladder in an architectural firm, he is restless and decides to start his own firm. He retires at 65, but he certainly does not stop setting new goals for himself. Now he donates his time to Habitat for Humanity and helps build low-income housing.

This life story is not important for its details as much as for what it says about human beings of all ages. Like Robert, most of us have goals and strive to achieve them. We seem to thrive on being stimulated and challenged, for we no sooner achieve one goal than we formulate another. We like to master and control our environment and become distressed when we cannot (Schulz & Heckhausen, 1996). From birth, infants display a powerful urge for mastery that fuels their play and exploratory activities and in turn their intellectual development. Children dis-

play achievement motivation that they channel into schoolwork; yet some achieve more academically than others, and we wonder why.

All of this lays the groundwork for achievement through work as an adult. In many of the world's cultures, children begin their work lives at the tender age of 6 or 7, when they are given responsibilities for tending younger children, gathering food, or watching herds of cattle (Rogoff et al., 1991; Weisner, 1984). By contrast, children in our society are asked to stay in school for a long time in order to acquire the tools they will need to succeed in a highly technological society. Not until late adolescence do most of us settle on career goals and pursue them in earnest. Then, during adulthood, we channel our achievement motivation primarily into work. Just as we experience a family life cycle, we progress through a work life cycle as we begin, maintain, and end our careers. Young adults struggle to balance career and family priorities; middle-aged adults often reflect on their achievements and reevaluate their goals; and elderly adults chart new directions as their working lives come to an end.

As this brief overview suggests, humans are motivated to set and achieve goals throughout the life span. The central questions addressed in this chapter are these: What are the origins of our motivation to master challenges and achieve at a high level? How is this motivation expressed in achievement-related activities such as play, school, and work? And how does participation in these activities in turn affect our development? Let's begin by looking at what achievement motivation really involves.

ACHIEVEMENT MOTIVATION

Researchers exploring the development of achievement motivation initially assumed that behavior in achievement settings could be understood as the product of a single motive: the individual's need for achievement. They soon discovered that influences on achievement behavior are considerably more complex than that.

Need for Achievement

David McClelland and his associates (McClelland, Atkinson, Clark, & Lowell, 1953; see also McClelland, 1985) did much to pioneer the study of achievement motivation. They defined the **need for achievement (n Ach)** as a "learned motive to compete and to strive for success whenever one's behavior can be evaluated against a standard of excellence" (p. 78). In other words, people with strong achievement motivation take pride in their ability to meet high standards and are motivated by this sense of self-fulfillment to work hard, be successful, and outperform others when faced with new challenges.

In their studies of achievement motivation, David McClelland and his colleagues (1953) gave children or adults pictures and asked them to compose stories about the pictures. It was assumed that people would project their own motives onto the pictured situation and that the number of achievement-related themes in the stories would provide a measure of an individual's need for achievement. What story would you tell about the scene portrayed in Figure 15.1? A person with a high need for achievement might say that the men have been working for months on a new scientific breakthrough that will revolutionize medicine, whereas a person with a low need for achievement might say that these fellows are glad the day is over so that they can go home and party. Children who score high on measures of need for achievement do indeed tend to receive better grades in school than those who score low, and *n Ach* predicts adult achievement as well (McClelland et al., 1953).

Yet researchers soon discovered that achievement motivation is influenced by more than a single, global motive. Among the other important factors to be considered are the value placed on achieving a particular goal, the individual's expectancies of success, and the individual's beliefs concerning the causes of success or failure.

The Value Placed on Achievement

John Atkinson (1964) insisted that the *value* of success to the individual (as well as the aversiveness of failing) is an important influence on achievement outcomes

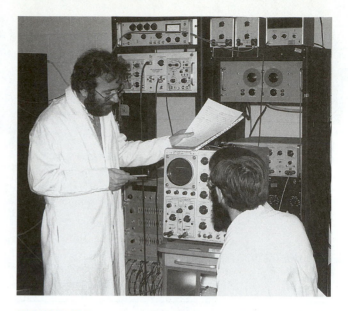

FIGURE 15.1 *Equipment like this was used by David McClelland and his associates to measure need for achievement.*

(see also Wigfield & Eccles, 1992). We are more likely to pursue and strive hard to achieve goals we really care about than goals that are unimportant, and so a strong need for achievement predicts success only when the value placed on achievement is high (Raynor, 1970).

Expectancies of Success

We are also more likely to work hard when we think we are capable and have a reasonable chance of succeeding than when we see no hope of attaining a goal (Atkinson, 1964; Mac Iver, Stipek, & Daniels, 1991). In fact, children with high IQs and low expectancies of academic success often earn poorer grades than their classmates who have lower IQs but higher expectancies (Battle, 1966; Crandall, 1967). Individuals who expect to achieve often do succeed, whereas those who expect to fail may spend little time or effort pursuing goals that they believe are out of reach.

Attributions for Success and Failure

Achievement behavior also depends on how individuals interpret their successes and failures and whether they think they can control these outcomes. Bernard Weiner (1974, 1986) has proposed an **attribution theory** of motivation, in which the explanations (causal attributions) we offer for our outcomes influence our future expectancies of success and our future motivation to succeed. Weiner has emphasized four causes of success or failure: ability (or lack thereof), effort, task difficulty, and luck (either good or bad).

Two of these causes, ability and effort, are internal causes or qualities of the individual, whereas the other

TABLE 15.1

Weiner's classification of the causes of achievement outcomes (and examples of how you might explain a terrible test grade)

Stability		*Locus of Causality*	
		INTERNAL CAUSE	EXTERNAL CAUSE
	STABLE CAUSE	ABILITY "I'm hopeless in math."	TASK DIFFICULTY "That test was incredibly hard and much too long."
	UNSTABLE CAUSE	EFFORT "I should have studied more instead of going out to play."	LUCK "What luck! Every question seemed to be about the one day of class I missed."

two, task difficulty and luck, are external or environmental factors. In other words, Weiner proposes that causal attributions can be grouped along a locus dimension (internal versus external). Here Weiner's thinking corresponds to earlier work on a dimension of personality called **locus of control** (Crandall, 1967, 1969). Individuals with an *internal locus of control* assume that they are personally responsible for what happens to them. For example, they might credit an A grade on a paper to superior writing ability or hard work. Individuals with an *external locus of control* believe that their outcomes depend more on luck, fate, or the actions of others than on their own abilities and efforts. They might say that their A's are due to luck ("The teacher just happened to like my paper topic"), indiscriminate grading, or some other external cause. Children with an internal locus of control earn higher grades and higher scores on academic achievement tests than children with an external locus of control do (Findley & Cooper, 1983), perhaps because they believe their efforts will pay off and therefore work harder.

But Weiner claims that causes also differ along a *stability* dimension. Ability and task difficulty are reasonably stable or unchangeable. If one has low math ability today, one is likely to have the same low ability tomorrow; if algebra problems are difficult today, similar algebra problems are likely to be difficult tomorrow. By contrast, the amount of effort one expends and the workings of luck are highly unstable or variable from situation to situation (see Table 15.1).

Why is it useful to categorize causes of success and failure along both a locus of causality and a stability dimension? Mainly because it is not *always* adaptive to attribute what happens to internal causes, as research on locus of control would lead us to believe. It is indeed healthy to conclude that your successes must be due to high ability; this not only will make you feel proud but will lead you to expect more successes in the future, since ability is relatively stable and should therefore continue to affect future performance. But is it healthy to conclude after a failure that you are hopelessly incompetent, miserably lacking in ability? Hardly! Low ability is an internal cause of poor performance but it is also a stable cause; as a result, attributing failure to low ability is saying that you can do little to improve on your lousy performance. Not only would you have low expectancies of future success and little motivation to strive, but you would also lose self-esteem by admitting that you are "dumb."

Quite clearly, achievement motivation involves far more than just a global need for achievement. Children do differ in their characteristic motives to achieve, but the *value* of success to the individual must also be considered: Why act on any motive to achieve if the goal seems unimportant or irrelevant to your other goals? Moreover, an individual's self-perceived competence and *expectancies* of success also count, for there may be little point in striving if you lack confidence that you can meet the challenge. Finally, drawing on attribution theory, we must recognize that achievement behavior is very much affected by the ways in which an individual interprets successes and failures.

Having laid out some of the key ingredients of achievement motivation, we can look at its origins and evolution and at actual achievements in play, school, and work activities. We will be interested in factors that influence achievement in these activities, as well as in the influences of these activities on subsequent development. Just as children's opportunities for play and classroom learning affect their intellectual and social growth, the daily work experiences and, later, retirement experiences of adults influence their development and well-being. As you will see, this chapter provides many good illustrations of a recurring theme of this book: that the goodness of fit between person and environment matters a great deal in human development.

THE INFANT

Infants spend a good deal of very constructive time exploring the world around them, playing with people and things, and acquiring new competencies in the process. It is during infancy that we can see the roots of achievement motivation.

Early Origins of Achievement Motivation

Some time ago, psychoanalyst Robert White (1959) proposed that human beings are intrinsically motivated from infancy onward to master their environment. He called this **effectance motivation**—a desire to have an effect on or to successfully control the world of objects and people. It has also been called mastery motivation and described as a psychological force that leads infants to attempt to master tasks for the intrinsic joy of doing so (Morgan, MacTurk, & Hrncir, 1995). This effectance, or mastery, motive can be seen clearly when infants struggle to open kitchen cabinets, take their first steps, or figure out how new toys work—and derive great pleasure from their efforts (Busch-Rossnagel, 1997; MacTurk et al., 1987; Mayes & Zigler, 1992). White argued that it is the very nature of human beings to seek out challenges just for the joy of attempting to master them.

Much evidence supports the claim that infants are curious, active explorers who are constantly striving to understand and to exert control over the world around them. This, you'll recall, was one of Jean Piaget's major themes (see Chapter 7). A striving for mastery or competence appears to be inborn and universal, then, and will display itself in the behavior of all normal infants without any prompting from parents. Even so, some infants appear to be more mastery oriented than others. Given a new push toy, one baby may simply look at it, while another may mouth it, bang it, and push it back and forth across the floor (Yarrow et al., 1984). Why might some infants have a stronger effectance motive than others?

Every day, infants and young children display their innate effectance, or mastery, motive.

Influences on Effectance Motivation

Three influences on effectance motivation appear to be important: appropriate stimulation, a responsive environment, and a secure attachment to a caregiver. First, parents whose infants are highly mastery oriented frequently provide *sensory stimulation* designed to arouse and amuse their babies, tickling them, bouncing them, playing games of pat-a-cake, giving them stimulating toys, and so on (Busch-Rossnagel, 1997; Yarrow et al., 1984). Second, mastery motivation will blossom if infants grow up in a *responsive environment* and have plenty of opportunities to see for themselves that they can control their environments (Ford & Thompson, 1985). Parents who return smiles and coos or respond promptly to cries show infants that they can affect people around them. By contrast, the children of parents who are depressed show less interest in and persistence on challenging tasks, perhaps because their parents are not very responsive to them (Redding, Harmon, & Morgan, 1990).

Third and finally, a *secure attachment* to parents seems to promote mastery motivation. As we saw in Chapter 13, sensitive, responsive parenting promotes a secure attachment, which in turn provides a secure base for exploration. Infants who are securely attached to their mothers at 12 to 18 months of age are more likely than those who are insecurely attached

(1) to venture away from their mothers to explore a strange environment (Cassidy, 1986; van den Boom, 1994), (2) to persist until they master new challenges (Frankel & Bates, 1990), and (3) to display a strong sense of curiosity, self-reliance, and eagerness to solve problems as children (see Chapter 13).

An infant's level of effectance motivation affects his or her later achievement behavior. Babies who actively attempt to master challenges at 6 and 12 months of age score higher on tests of mental development at age 2 and 3 than their less mastery-oriented peers (Messer et al., 1986; Yarrow et al., 1975). In short, infants are intrinsically motivated to master challenges; parents may help strengthen this inborn motive by stimulating their infants appropriately, responding to their actions, and developing a secure relationship with them; and the strength of an infant's mastery motivation may influence how much the child learns from experiences and how well he or she functions intellectually late in life.

Mastery through Play

Mastery motivation is very evident in infants' early play (Barrett & Morgan, 1995). Jean Piaget (1951/1962) viewed play as an opportunity for children to practice whatever cognitive competencies they possess and to strengthen them in the process. How does the capacity for play evolve as infants progress through the stages of Piaget's sensorimotor period?

The sequence is much the same in all cultures (Sigman & Sena, 1993). At first infants play with their own bodies—for example, by kicking their legs or sucking their fingers. At only 2 months of age, they display a sense of agency, recognizing that their actions produce certain outcomes. For example, 8-week-old infants delight in pulling their arms in order to tug a string attached to a slide/music device that produces interesting sights and sounds when they do (Alessandri, Sullivan, & Lewis, 1990; Lewis, Alessandri, & Sullivan, 1990). Infants who cannot control the device but who are exposed to the same sights and sounds are not as interested in them. Moreover, infants who have learned to control the device become quite angry and flap their arms furiously if the string is disconnected and they can no longer produce music and slides. Interestingly, a few infants become sad rather than angry and stop tugging on the string, as though they have become helpless (Barrett & Morgan, 1995).

At about 4 months of age infants take a greater interest in toys and will repeatedly suck, pat, bang, and shake rattles and toy animals, often inspecting them closely. During these early months they use the behavioral schemes that they have acquired to explore everything in reach and learn a good deal about the world in the process (Ruff & Saltarelli, 1993). As infants approach their first birthdays, new cognitive capacities allow them to experiment with playthings, performing novel actions rather than merely repeating the same behavior over and over. They also begin to engage in **functional play,** play that involves using objects appropriately to serve the functions they normally serve. Thus 1-year-olds may comb a doll's hair with a comb or turn the dial on a toy phone rather than just sucking or banging it (Belsky & Most, 1981; Sigman & Sena, 1993).

Finally, between age 1 and 2, infants acquire the capacity for *pretend play,* or symbolic play, in which one actor, object, or action represents another (see Chapter 13). Piaget emphasized that the infant's thought changes immensely when he or she acquires the capacity to make one thing stand for another. This *symbolic capacity* is involved in pretend play (where, for example, a clump of mud might symbolize a pie), in language use (where words symbolize or stand for things and events), in delayed imitation (where a mental image symbolizes the behavior that will be imitated), and in problem solving (where solutions can be conjured mentally). As early as 1 year of age, an infant may bring a forbidden cookie to her mouth, pretend to bite it, and smile (Nicolich, 1977). By smiling, this 1-year-old shows awareness that her eating actions stand for or symbolize real eating. The earliest forms of symbolic play are actions just like this: The infant pretends to engage in familiar activities such as eating, sleeping, or washing, using appropriate props.

Pretend play then becomes more sophisticated between the ages of 1 and 2 (Corrigan, 1987; McCune, 1995). Instead of just pretending to be themselves doing the things they normally do, toddlers get outside themselves and pretend to be someone else—mother or father perhaps. They also progress from using objects in familiar ways to using them to stand for things very different from what they are. So, for example, an infant may first pretend to drink from a cup and later pretend to drink from a block. Finally, infants progress from pretending to engage in single acts to pretending to perform multiple acts in meaningful sequences. A young infant may give a doll a drink, whereas an older infant may say "Drink milk," repeatedly raise the cup to the doll's mouth, burp the doll, and wipe its mouth!

Developments in play, language, and imitation go hand in hand; the first simple pretend acts occur around the time that infants utter their first words, and the ability to combine actions in meaningful sequences during pretend play emerges at the same time that 18- to 24-month-olds are starting to combine words into short sentences (McCune, 1995) and to imitate sequences of two or three actions (Brownell, 1988). Advances in cognitive development seem to be behind all these breakthroughs.

In sum, play during infancy is guided by effectance motivation and involves efforts to explore and have an effect upon the environment. From actions centered on the infant's body and then on toys, it progresses to functional play, in which objects are made to perform their usual functions, and culminates in ever-more complex forms of pretend play. Parents can best foster this development by playing alongside their infants and challenging them by playing at a level slightly more complex than the infant's (Damast, Tamis-LeMonda, & Bornstein, 1996).

THE CHILD

When infancy is behind them, children continue to channel their motive to master the environment into play activities but also begin to show true achievement motivation as early as age 2. Now they seem capable of appraising their performances as successes or failures and expecting approval when they succeed and disapproval when they fail (Stipek, Recchia, & McClintic, 1992). By age 3, children have clearly internalized standards of performance and experience true pride or shame, depending on how successfully they meet those standards (Stipek et al., 1992). Some children are clearly more achievement oriented and high achieving than others, and it is these differences we now seek to explain.

Mastery-Oriented and Helpless Achievement Styles

All children experience failure on occasion in their efforts to master challenges and meet achievement standards. Building on the work of Weiner and other attribution theorists, Carol Dweck and her colleagues have attempted to understand differences between children who persist and ultimately triumph in the face of failure and those who give up (Dweck & Elliott, 1983; Dweck & Leggett, 1988). Dweck finds that high achievers tend to attribute their successes to internal and stable causes such as high ability. However, they blame their failures either on external factors beyond their control ("That test was impossibly hard," "That professor's grading is biased") or—and this is even more adaptive—on internal causes that they can overcome (particularly insufficient effort). They do *not* blame the internal but stable factor of low ability ("I'm terrible at this and will never do any better"). Students with this healthy attributional style are said to have a **mastery orientation:** They thrive on challenges and persist in the face of failure, believing that their increased effort will pay off.

By contrast, children who tend to be low achievers often attribute their successes either to the internal cause of hard work or to external causes such as luck or the easiness of the task. Thus they do not experience the pride and self-esteem that come from viewing oneself as highly capable. Yet they often attribute their failures to an internal and stable cause—namely, lack of ability. As a result, they have low expectancies of success and tend to give up. Dweck describes children with this attributional style as having a **learned helplessness orientation,** a tendency to avoid challenges and to cease trying when one experiences failure, based on the belief that one can do little to improve. The learned helplessness phenomenon was first demonstrated by Martin Seligman (1975). His experiments exposed dogs to electric shocks that they could not control. The dogs became incapable of learning responses that would have allowed them to avoid or escape shocks; instead, they just lay down, whined, and bore the pain. So, too, some children may come to feel helpless in the face of failure experiences at school.

Age Differences

Are children really capable of analyzing the causes of success and failure in this way? Perhaps not when they are young. Before the age of 7 or so, children tend to be unrealistic optimists who think they can succeed on almost any task (Stipek & MacIver, 1989). With age, children's perceptions of their academic abilities become more and more accurate (Wigfield et al., 1997). Even after repeated poor performances, young children often continue to think that they have high ability and will do well in the future, whereas older children might become helpless (Miller, 1985; Ruble, Eisenberg, & Higgins, 1994). Young children *can* be made to feel helpless if their failures are very clear-cut and they conclude that they have been bad (Burhans & Dweck, 1995), but they are clearly less susceptible than older children to learned helplessness.

Why is this? Young children are protected from damaging self-perceptions partly because they do not yet fully understand the concept of ability as a stable capacity (Nicholls & Miller, 1984; Pomerantz & Ruble, 1997). They adopt what Carol Dweck calls an **incremental view of ability,** believing that ability is a changeable quality and that they can get smarter if they work hard. This view of ability encourages them to adopt **learning goals** in achievement situations, aiming to learn new things so that they can improve their abilities (Dweck & Leggett, 1988).

As children get older, they tend to acquire an **entity view of ability,** seeing ability as a fixed trait that is not altered much by effort. As a result, more and more of them adopt **performance goals** in school; they aim to *prove* their ability rather than to *improve* it and seek to be judged smart rather than dumb (Dweck & Leggett, 1988; Erdley et al., 1997; and see Table 15.2). These changes in understandings of ability are probably due both to cognitive development—especially an increased ability to analyze the causes of successes and failures and to infer enduring traits from behavior—and to an accumulation of feedback in school (Stipek, 1984).

Those children who manage to hold on to an incremental view of intellectual ability tend to do better in school than those who adopt the entity view (Stipek & Gralinski, 1996). As Table 15.2 illustrates, students who come to believe that ability is a fixed entity that one either has or lacks and conclude that they lack it are the ones who set performance goals for themselves, figure that hard work will not pay off, and run the risk of becoming helpless in the classroom (Dweck & Leggett, 1988). Even gifted students can fall into this trap (Ablard & Mills, 1996). Box 15.1 shows how teachers can use this knowledge to prevent and combat learned helplessness in the classroom; here we look at what parents can do to increase achievement motivation.

Parent Contributions

As we saw earlier, parents can foster mastery motivation in infancy by providing their babies with appropriate sensory stimulation, being responsive, and building a secure attachment relationship. Parents can then strengthen their children's need for achievement

TABLE 15.2

	Mastery orientation versus learned helplessness in the Dweck and Leggett (1988) model	
	Mastery Orientation	*Learned Helplessness*
View of ability	Incremental view (ability can be improved with effort)	Entity view (ability is fixed; cannot be changed)
Goal in classroom	Learning goal (try to become smarter)	Performance goal (try to show the ability you have, avoid looking dumb)
Attributions for success	Due to high ability	Due to luck (or high effort)
Attributions for failure	Due to low effort	Due to low ability
Reactions to failure	Persist; try harder and it will pay off	Give up; perform poorly

and mastery orientation by stressing and reinforcing independence and self-reliance at an early age and by encouraging children to do things on their own (Grolnick & Ryan, 1989; Winterbottom, 1958). They can also emphasize the importance of doing things *well*, or meeting high standards of performance (Rosen & D'Andrade, 1959).

Finally, they can use the same authoritative, or warm and democratic but firm, parenting style that optimizes so many aspects of development (Lamborn et al., 1991; Steinberg, Elmen, & Mounts, 1989). If children are encouraged and supported in a positive manner as they do their schoolwork, they are likely to enjoy new challenges and feel confident about mastering them. They are also unlikely to make the kinds of counterproductive attributions ("I'm dumb") that can cause them to lose interest in schoolwork (Glasgow et al., 1997). By contrast, parents can undermine a child's school performance and intrinsic motivation to learn if they are uninvolved and offer little in the way of guidance *or* if they are highly controlling and do such things as nag continually about homework, offer bribes for good grades, and criticize bad grades (Ginsburg & Bronstein, 1993).

In sum, children approach achievement tasks with either a mastery orientation or a learned helplessness orientation based on the attributions they make for their academic triumphs and disasters. As they get older, children come to understand the concept of ability as a stable trait, and shift from an incremental view of ability and learning goals to an entity view of ability and performance goals. These changes, brought about by both cognitive development and feedback in school, give them a more realistic picture of their own strengths and weaknesses but

also make them more vulnerable to learned helplessness. Yet some children remain far more motivated to succeed in school than others, and authoritative parents who encourage independence and excellence have a lot to do with that.

Let's now look at children's actual achievements in school, particularly at what going to school contributes to child development and why some children get more out of the experience than others.

Schooling and School Achievement

Today the vast majority of children in our society begin their school careers well before age 6—attending kindergarten as 5-year-olds and, in many cases, going to preschool, nursery school, or day care before that (Clarke-Stewart, 1993). David Elkind (1981), author of *The Hurried Child*, fears that the push for earlier and earlier education may be going too far and that young children today are not given enough time simply to be children—to play and socialize as they choose. Elkind even worries that children may lose their self-initiative and intrinsic motivation to learn when their lives are orchestrated by parents who pressure them to achieve at early ages. Is there anything to these concerns?

Benefits of Preschool

Some research seems to confirm Elkind's fears. In one study (Hyson, Hirsch-Pasek, & Rescorla, 1989), 4-year-olds in preschools with a very strong academic thrust gained an initial advantage in basic academic skills, such as knowledge of letters and numbers, but lost it by the end of kindergarten. What's more, they proved to be *less* creative, *more* anxious in testing situations, and *more* negative toward school than chil-

BOX 15.1

Preventing and combating learned helplessness

How can children be encouraged to persist in the face of failure until they master the challenges they face? Elaine Elliott and Carol Dweck (1988) set out to determine whether children might become less susceptible to learned helplessness if they were encouraged to adopt learning goals rather than performance goals in the classroom. In Dweck's view, learned helplessness is rooted in an entity view of ability and the setting of performance goals in the classroom. What if helpless children were encouraged to view difficult tasks as opportunities to *improve* their abilities rather than to display whatever fixed abilities (or inabilities) they currently possess?

In the study, fifth graders were asked to perform a novel task. They were led to believe that they had either low or high ability and were warned that they would soon be performing similar tasks that would prove quite difficult. Half the children worked under a *performance goal* (not unlike the goals emphasized in many classrooms): They were told that their performance would be compared to that of other children and evaluated by an expert. The remaining children were induced to adopt a *learning goal:* Although they would make some mistakes, they were told, working at the tasks would "sharpen the mind" and help them at school.

As expected, the only children who displayed the telltale signs of helplessness (that is, deteriorating performance and attribution of failure to low ability) were those who believed they had low ability and were pursuing a performance goal. For them, continuing to work on the difficult task meant demonstrating again and again that they were stupid! By contrast, even "low ability" students who pursued a learning goal persisted despite their failures and showed remarkably little frustration, probably because they were convinced that they could grow from their experience. Perhaps, then, teachers undermine achievement motivation by distributing gold stars and grades and frequently calling attention to how students stand in comparison to one another. Children might be better off if teachers nurtured their intrinsic motivation to master challenges (see also Boggiano & Katz, 1991; Butler, 1990). Then slow learners could view their mistakes as a sign that they should change strategies to improve their competencies rather than as further proof that they lack ability.

Teachers can also help students who are prone to learned helplessness by coaching them in more adaptive attribution styles. For example, Carol Dweck (1975) exposed children who had become helpless in the face of repeated failures on math problems to a simple "attribution retraining" treatment. Over 25 sessions, these children experienced some successes and were told after each of several prearranged failures that they had not worked fast enough and should have tried harder. Through this retraining, they learned to attribute their failures to lack of effort rather than to low ability (that is, to develop mastery-oriented attributions). They also performed much better on the math problems than they had initially. Interestingly, Dweck used a strategy many educators recommend in another treatment group, giving helpless children nothing but success experiences. These children never learned to cope with failure and retained their helpless ways.

In sum, teachers (and parents too) can do much to foster a mastery-oriented approach to learning by helping children to view learning situations as opportunities to gain competence ("You'll learn a lot by working on this"), to see themselves as having the competence to master challenging work ("You're pretty smart, you know"), and to believe that they can overcome incompetence through effort ("C'mon—you'll get it if you keep trying"). Indeed, mastery-oriented children may be mastery-oriented because their parents already do these things (Hokoda & Fincham, 1995).

dren who attended preschool programs with a social rather than academic emphasis. Similarly, Deborah Stipek and her colleagues (1995) find that highly academic preschool programs raise children's academic achievement test scores but decrease their expectancies of success and pride in accomplishment. So, it may well be possible to undermine achievement motivation by overemphasizing academics in the preschool years.

However, preschool programs that offer a healthy mix of play and academic skill-building activities can be very beneficial to young children, especially disadvantaged ones (Clarke-Stewart, 1993). Although many children who attend preschool programs are no more or less intellectually advanced than those who remain at home, disadvantaged children who attend programs specially designed to prepare them for school *do* experience more cognitive growth and achieve more success in school than disadvantaged children who do not attend such programs (Campbell & Ramey, 1995; Peisner-Feinberg & Burchinal, 1997). Positive effects on later school achievement are especially likely if the preschool experience not only stimulates children's cognitive growth but also gets their parents more involved with the schools (Reynolds et al., 1996). More generally, preschool programs that build school readiness skills but also allow plenty of time for play and social interaction can do a lot to help all children make a smooth transition to elementary school (Zigler & Finn-Stevenson, 1993).

Benefits of School

We should not have to ask why children should attend school, but let's. Attending school contributes substantially to child development. Obviously, children acquire a good deal of basic knowledge and many academic skills at school. They also acquire general strategies for learning new information and thinking about problems that translate into higher scores on IQ tests (Ceci & Williams, 1997). Studies of children in developing countries are especially revealing. They show that children who are exposed to formal education pick up many useful cognitive skills such as effective memory strategies that children who do not attend school lack (see Rogoff, 1990). Even in our society, children who start school early are likely to perform cognitive tasks better than children the same age who start school later (Ceci & Williams, 1997).

Schools also expose children to an **informal curriculum** that teaches them how to fit into their culture. Children learn to obey rules, to cooperate with their classmates, to respect authority, and to become good citizens. Moreover, schools instill basic democratic and social values and help combat such social problems as racism, drug abuse, teenage pregnancy, and AIDS (Comer, 1993; Linney & Seidman, 1989). Like families, then, schools serve as socialization agents, potentially affecting children's social and emotional development as well as providing them with knowledge and cognitive skills that will allow them to lead productive lives. Yet some schools are more effective at all this than others, and it is revealing to see why.

Effective Schools

Some schools are clearly more able than others to accomplish their objectives. You may be surprised by some of the factors that do and do not have a bearing on how effective a school is (Fraser et al., 1987; Mac Iver, Reuman, & Main, 1995; Reynolds, 1992; Rutter, 1983; Wang, Haertel, & Walberg, 1993).

Factors That Often Have Little to Do with a School's Effectiveness. A school's *level of funding* has less to do with the quality of education its students receive than many people believe, once differences in family background characteristics are taken into account. Some analyses conclude that per-pupil expenditure makes a difference (Greenwald, Hedges, & Laine, 1996; Hedges, Laine, & Greenwald, 1994), but others conclude that it does not matter much at all (Hanushek, 1997). States that spend more per pupil do get better results than states that spend little, but this may only be because these states also have more enlightened educational policies (Hanushek, 1997). Most analysts agree that schools need some reasonable level of support in order to function. Moreover, the relationship between funding level and student outcomes is more often positive than negative (Greenwald et al., 1996). However, it may be less important how much money a school has than how effectively it uses the resources it has (Hanushek, 1997).

Another factor that is controversial because it only sometimes seems to be related to school effectiveness is *average class size* (Hanushek, 1997; Rutter, 1983; Toch & Streisand, 1997). Within a range of from 20 to 40 students per class, reducing class sizes (from, say, 36 to 24 students) often has little impact on student achievement and may not be worth the large amount of money it costs. However, class sizes of 50 or more are probably not good, and some studies suggest that large schools are less effective than smaller ones (Fowler & Walberg, 1991). Moreover, class sizes of about 15 in the early grades appear to be beneficial

(Hanushek, 1997), and one-on-one or small-group instruction with beginning students, especially disadvantaged and low-ability ones, can make a big difference in their learning of reading and math (Odden, 1990; Slavin, 1989; Toch & Streisand, 1997).

Finally, it often does not matter much whether or not a school uses **ability tracking,** in which students are grouped according to ability and then taught in classes or work groups with others of similar academic or intellectual standing. Tracking has no clear advantage over mixed-ability grouping for most students (Kulik & Kulik, 1992; Rutter, 1983). It *can* be beneficial, especially to higher-ability students, if it means a curriculum more appropriate to students' learning needs (Kulik & Kulik, 1992). However, low-ability students are unlikely to benefit and may well suffer if they are denied access to the most effective teachers, taught less material than other children, and stigmatized as "dummies" (MacIver et al., 1995; Mehan et al., 1996). Too often, this is just what happens. As Hugh Mehan and his colleagues (1996) put it, "It is not that dumb kids are placed in slow groups or low tracks; it is that kids are made dumb by being placed in slow groups or low tracks" (p. 230).

These, then, are examples of school characteristics that do not so clearly contribute to effective education. No one would recommend putting students in poorly equipped and poorly staffed classes with 50 or more classmates, of course, and the findings discussed here have stirred a lot of controversy. Still, a school that has quite limited financial support (assuming it surpasses a basic minimum), places most students (except perhaps for beginning ones) in fairly large classes, and combines students in mixed-ability learning groups or classes is often just as effective as another school that has ample financial resources, small classes, and ability tracking.

Factors That Matter More.   So what does influence how well children perform? To understand why some schools are more effective than others, we must consider characteristics of the students, characteristics of the learning environment, and the interaction between student and environment.

First, a school's effectiveness is a function of what it has to work with—of the aptitudes of its students (Wang et al., 1993). On average, academic achievement tends to be higher in schools with a preponderance of economically advantaged students; any child is likely to make more academic progress in a school with a high concentration of intellectually capable peers (Brookover et al., 1979; Portes & MacLeod, 1996). However, this does *not* mean that schools are only as good as the students they serve. Many schools that serve disadvantaged populations are highly effective at motivating students and preparing them for jobs or further education (Reynolds, 1992).

In a comfortable and task-oriented classroom, children are motivated to learn.

So what is it about the learning environment of some schools that allows them to accomplish so much? Basically, the effective school environment is a comfortable but businesslike setting in which teachers are involved with students, students are motivated to learn, and serious teaching takes place (Mac Iver et al., 1995; Phillips, 1997; Rutter, 1983). More specifically, in effective schools and classrooms, teachers:

1. Strongly emphasize academics (they demand a lot from their students and expect them to succeed, regularly assign homework, and work hard to achieve their objectives in the classroom).
2. Create a task-oriented but comfortable atmosphere (for example, they waste little time on getting activities started or dealing with distracting discipline problems, provide clear instructions and feedback, and encourage and reward good work).
3. Manage discipline problems effectively (for example, they enforce the rules on the spot rather than sending offenders to the principal's office, and they avoid the use of physical punishment).

Effective schools also have supportive parents and supportive communities behind them (Comer, 1993). Students achieve more when their parents are interested in and value school and school achievement; participate in parent/teacher conferences, PTA meetings, and other school events; and get involved in homework and other school-related activities at home (Bogenschneider, 1997; Sui-Chu & Willms, 1996; Wang et al., 1993). Parents with less education themselves are typically less involved in their children's education than highly educated parents are; yet they can have even more impact on their children's grades if they *do* become involved (Bogenschneider, 1997).

Finally, characteristics of the student and characteristics of the school environment often interact to affect student outcome. Lee Cronbach and Richard Snow (1977) called this phenomenon **aptitude-treatment interaction** (**ATI**), and it is an example of the broader concept of goodness of fit between person and environment that I have emphasized throughout this book. Much educational research has been based on the assumption that *one* teaching method, organizational system, or philosophy of education will prove superior for all students, regardless of their ability levels, learning styles, personalities, and cultural backgrounds. This assumption is often wrong. Instead, many educational practices are highly effective with *some* kinds of students but quite ineffective with other students. The secret is to find an appropriate match between learner and teaching method.

To illustrate the ATI concept, highly achievement-oriented students adapt well to unstructured classrooms in which they have a good deal of choice, whereas less achievement-oriented students often do better with more structure (Peterson, 1977). And sometimes two or more alternative teaching methods work equally well with highly capable students but only one of them suits less capable students. In one study, for example, poor readers learned more from the whole-language approach to reading than from the phonics approach, very likely because it involved more engaging and motivating activities (Sacks & Mergendoller, 1997). In another study, highly distractible students, but not more attentive ones, got more from computer-assisted instruction than from a teacher's presentation of the same material (Orth & Martin, 1994). Evidence of the importance of the fit between student and classroom environment implies that educational programs are likely to be most effective when they are highly individualized—tailored to suit each student's developmental competencies and needs.

In sum, some students (for example, those from advantaged homes) typically outperform others, and some learning environments (especially those in which teachers create a motivating, comfortable, and task-oriented setting and involve parents in their children's schooling) are generally more conducive to learning than others. Still, what works best for one kind of student may not work as well with another kind of student. In aptitude-treatment interactions, we have another nice example of the importance of the fit between individuals and their environments.

Making Integration and Inclusion Work

For many minority students of the past, especially African Americans, additional barriers to school success were created by school segregation. Black children in many states were forced to attend "black schools" that were clearly inferior to "white schools." In its landmark decision in the case of *Brown v. Board of Education of Topeka* in 1954, the Supreme Court ruled that segregated schools were "inherently unequal" and declared that they must be desegregated. What have we learned since this ruling?

Generally, the effects of school integration on children's racial attitudes, self-esteem, and school achievement have been mixed (Gray-Little & Carels, 1997; Stephan, 1978). Some studies do suggest that both African-American and white children tend to have higher self-esteem and higher achievement when they attend racially mixed schools, but the effects are often small (Gray-Little & Carels, 1997). White prejudice toward black students often does not decrease much at all. The self-esteem of black children in integrated schools is only sometimes higher than that of black children in segregated schools (Gray-Little & Carels, 1997). And although minority students sometimes achieve more in integrated schools, especially if they begin to attend them early in their academic careers (St. John, 1975; Entwisle & Alexander, 1992), school integration often does not have much effect on achievement.

Meanwhile, children with developmental disabilities (mental retardation, learning disabilities, physical and sensory handicaps, and other special learning needs) have had a somewhat similar history. They used to be placed in separate schools or classrooms—or, in some cases, rejected as unteachable by the public schools—until the U.S. Congress passed the *Education for All Handicapped Children Act* in 1975 and required schools to provide them with an appropriate education. What has been achieved since? Mixed results have been found in studies of developmentally disabled children integrated into regular classrooms through a practice called **inclusion.** (This practice used to be called mainstreaming; the name change emphasizes the concept that children with special learning needs should spend the entire school day rather than only parts of it in a regular classroom and truly be included in the normal educational process.) Compared with similar students who attend segregated special education classes, these mainstreamed youngsters sometimes fare better in terms of academic performance, self-esteem, and social adjustment but sometimes do not (Buysse & Bailey, 1993; Hunt & Goetz, 1997; Manset & Semmel, 1997).

What we seem to be learning about both racial integration and inclusion is that simply putting diverse students into the same schools and classrooms accomplishes little by itself. Instead, something special must be done to ensure that students of different ethnic backgrounds and ability levels do in fact interact in positive ways and also learn what they are supposed to be learning. Robert Slavin and his colleagues have had much success using **cooperative learning methods,** in which diverse students are assigned to work teams and are reinforced for performing well *as a team* (Slavin, 1986; Stevens & Slavin, 1995).

To illustrate, each member of a math team may be given problems to solve that are appropriate to his or her ability level. Yet members of the team also monitor one another's progress and offer one another aid when needed. To encourage this cooperation, the teams that complete the most math units are rewarded—for example, with special certificates that designate them as "superteams." Here, then, is a formula for ensuring that children of different races and ability levels will interact in a context where the efforts of even the least capable team members are important to the group's success.

Elementary school students come to like school better and learn more when they participate in cooperative learning groups than when they receive traditional instruction (Aronson et al., 1978; Johnson, Johnson, & Maruyama, 1983; O'Donnell & O'Kelly, 1994; Stevens & Slavin, 1995). Moreover, team members gain self-esteem from their successes, and minority students and students with developmental disabilities are more fully accepted by their peers. In short, racial integration and mainstreaming or inclusion *can* succeed if educators deliberately design learning experiences that encourage students from different backgrounds to pool their efforts in order to achieve common goals. Interventions like this are important if children are to be ready for the challenges of secondary school.

THE ADOLESCENT

Adolescents make critical decisions about such matters as how much time to devote to studying, whether to work part time after school, whether to go to college, and what to be when they grow up. They become more capable of making these educational and vocational choices as their cognitive and social skills expand; in turn, the choices they make shape their future development. But many of them lose interest in school as soon as they leave elementary school.

Declining Achievement Motivation

You might think that adolescents would become more dedicated to academic success once they begin to realize that they need a good education in order to succeed in life. But consider what Deborah Stipek (1984) concluded after reviewing studies on the development of achievement motivation from early childhood to adolescence:

> On the average, children value academic achievement more as they progress through school, but their expectations for success and self-perceptions of competence decline, and their affect toward school becomes more negative. Children also become increasingly concerned about achievement outcomes and reinforcement (e.g., high grades) associated with positive outcomes and less concerned about intrinsic satisfaction in achieving greater competence. (p. 153)

Many of the negative trends Stipek describes become especially apparent as young adolescents make the transition from elementary school to a middle school (typically grades 6 to 8) or a junior high school (grades 7 to 9). At this critical juncture, achievement motivation, self-esteem, and grades may all decline (Eccles et al., 1993; Seidman et al., 1994). More and more students become alienated from school; many others continue to work hard at their studies but become extrinsically rather than intrinsically motivated (Harter, 1981): They work to obtain good grades, parent or teacher approval, and other external rewards rather than because they find learning and mastering challenges gratifying in themselves. How can we explain these discouraging trends? We'll consider five contributors: cognitive growth, negative feedback, peer pressures, pubertal changes, and a poor fit between adolescents and the schools they attend.

Cognitive Growth

As we saw earlier, children become increasingly capable with age of analyzing the causes of events, interpreting feedback from teachers, and inferring enduring traits such as high or low ability from their behavior (Stipek & MacIver, 1989). The result is that they come to view their strengths and weaknesses more realistically—and lose some of their high academic self-esteem and high expectancies of success in the process (Stipek & MacIver, 1989; Wigfield et al., 1997).

Negative Feedback

Declines in achievement motivation may also be caused by changes in the kinds of feedback students receive as they get older (Eccles, Lord, & Midgley, 1991; Stipek & MacIver, 1989). Preschool teachers often praise their young charges merely for trying and do not hand out much criticism. As Deborah Stipek (1984) notes, it would be unthinkable for an adult to say to a 5-year-old exhibiting a drawing, "What an ugly picture. You sure can't draw very well" (p. 156). The positive feedback young children receive for their efforts may contribute to their incremental view of ability and their sense that hard work can overcome any barrier (Rosenholtz & Simpson, 1984). By contrast, elementary and secondary school teachers increasingly reserve praise, high grades, and other forms of approval for students who turn in high-quality products. Effort alone is not enough. As they progress through school, then, children receive more and more feedback telling them precisely what capabilities they have and what capabilities they lack.

Peer Pressures

The adolescent's environment also changes in the sense that peers become increasingly important and sometimes can undermine parents' and teachers' efforts to encourage school achievement. Many years ago, when James Coleman (1961) asked high school students how they would like to be remembered, only 31% of the boys and 28% of the girls wanted to be remembered as bright students. They were more concerned with having the athletic and social skills that lead to popularity. Not much has changed (Suitor & Reavis, 1995).

Peer pressures that undermine achievement motivation tend to be especially strong for many lower-income minority students. Laurence Steinberg and his colleagues (Steinberg, Dornbusch, & Brown, 1992) note that the African-American and Hispanic peer cultures in many low-income areas actively discourage academic achievement, whereas Euro- and especially Asian-American peer groups tend to value and encourage it. High-achieving African-American students in some inner-city schools actually run the risk of being rejected by their African-American peers if their academic accomplishments cause them to be perceived as "acting white" (Fordham & Ogbu, 1986). They may feel that they have to abandon their cultural group and racial identity in order to succeed in school, but doing so takes a psychological toll on them (Arroyo & Zigler, 1995; Phelan, Yu, & Davidson, 1994). Although African-American parents are as likely as white parents to value education and to provide the kind of authoritative parenting that encourages school achievement, their positive influences are sometimes canceled out by negative peer influences (Steinberg et al., 1992).

Pubertal Changes

It is also been suggested that the transition to middle school or junior high school is difficult because young adolescents are often experiencing major physical and psychological changes at the same time they are being asked to switch schools. Roberta Simmons and Dale Blyth (1987) found that girls who were reaching puberty at the same time they were moving from sixth grade in an elementary school to seventh grade in a junior high school were more likely to experience drops in self-esteem and other negative changes than girls who remained in a K–8 school during this vulnerable period.

Could it be that more adolescents would remain interested in school if they didn't have to change schools at the very time they are experiencing pubertal changes? This idea became an important part of the rationale for middle schools, which serve grades 6 to 8 and were developed in order to make the transition from elementary school to high school easier for early adolescents (Braddock & McPartland, 1993). Yet Jacquelynne Eccles and her colleagues (Eccles, Lord, & Midgley, 1991; Eccles et al., 1993; Roeser & Eccles, 1998) have shown that students do not necessarily find the transition to middle school any easier than the transition to junior high school. This led them to suspect that it is not as important when adolescents make a school change as what their new school is like.

Poor Person/Environment Fit

Eccles and her colleagues offer a goodness-of-fit explanation for declining achievement motivation in adolescence, arguing that the transition to a new school is likely to be especially difficult when the new school, whether a junior high or a middle school, is ill matched to the developmental needs of early adolescents. These researchers have found that the transition to middle school or junior high school often involves going from a small school with close student/teacher relationships, a good deal of choice regarding learning activities, and reasonable discipline to a larger, more bureaucratized environment in which student/teacher relationships are impersonal, good grades are emphasized but harder to come by, opportunities for choice are limited, assignments are not very intellectually stimulating, and discipline is rigid—all at a time when adolescents are seeking more rather than less autonomy and are becoming more rather than less intellectually capable! Students who had what Carol Dweck calls learning goals in elementary school perceive an increased emphasis on performance goals when they move to middle school (Anderman & Midgley, 1997).

Eccles and her colleagues have demonstrated that the fit between developmental needs and school environment is indeed an important influence on adolescent adjustment to school (Roeser & Eccles, 1998). In one study (MacIver & Reuman, 1988), the transition to junior high school brought about a decline in intrinsic motivation to learn mainly among students who wanted more involvement in classroom decisions but ended up with fewer such opportunities than they had in elementary school. In another study (Midgley, Feldlaufer, & Eccles, 1989), students experienced negative changes in their attitudes toward mathematics only when their move from elementary school to junior high resulted in less personal and supportive relationships with math teachers. For those few stu-

By adolescence, some students have little motivation to achieve in the classroom.

dents whose junior high teachers were more supportive than those they had in elementary school, interest in academics actually *increased*. In still another study, students fared better psychologically and academically when they felt their school encouraged all students to do their best than when competition for grades was emphasized (Roeser & Eccles, 1998).

The message? Declines in academic motivation and performance during early adolescence are not inevitable. Students may indeed form more realistic expectancies of success as their growing cognitive abilities allow them to make use of the increasingly informative feedback they receive from teachers. Experiencing pubertal changes at the same time as other stressful changes and needing to downplay academics in order to gain popularity may also hurt school achievement. However, educators can help to keep adolescents engaged in school by creating school environments that provide a better fit to the developmental needs and interests of adolescents. Whether they are called middle schools or junior high schools, such schools should provide warm, supportive relationships with teachers along with intellectual challenges and increased opportunities for self-direction (Eccles et al., 1993). Specially designed programs can help students adjust to school transitions and reduce the risk that they will drop out (Smith, 1997).

Making Vocational Choices

As they progress through school and learn more about their strengths and weaknesses, adolescents are asked to decide what they want to do with their lives. According to a developmental theory of vocational choice proposed by Eli Ginzberg (1972, 1984), vocational choice unfolds through three stages: (1) the fantasy stage, (2) the tentative stage, and (3) the realis-

tic stage. Children up to about age 10, who are in the *fantasy stage* of vocational development, base their choices primarily on wishes and whims, wanting to be zookeepers, pro basketball players, firefighters, rock stars, or whatever else strikes them as glamorous and exciting. As Linda Gottfredson (1996) emphasizes, however, these youngsters are already beginning to narrow their ideas about future careers to those that are consistent with their emerging self-concepts—as human beings rather than bunnies or ninja turtles, as males or females, and so on. As early as kindergarten, for instance, almost all boys choose traditionally masculine occupations and most girls name traditionally female occupations such as nurse or teacher (Etaugh & Liss, 1992; Phipps, 1995). Many children also develop broad vocational interests that will be reflected in the specific choices they make later (Trice & McClellan, 1993). Still, most are a long way from making realistic choices of a career, and most have little clue what it takes to achieve their dream careers (Phipps, 1995).

According to Ginzberg, it is during the second stage of vocational choice, the *tentative stage,* that adolescents aged 11 to 18 begin to weigh factors other than their wishes and to make preliminary decisions. After considering their *interests* (Would I enjoy counseling people?), they consider their *capacities* (Am I skilled at relating to people, or am I too shy and insecure for this kind of work?) and then also think about their *values* (Is it really important to me to help people, or do I value power, money, or intellectual challenge more?). As they get older, adolescents base their vocational choices more on their values and capacities and less on their fantasies and interests (Kelso, 1977).

As adolescents leave this tentative stage, they also begin to take into account the realities of the job market and the requirements for different occupations (Ginzberg, 1972, 1984). They might now consider the availability of job openings in a field such as psychological counseling, the years of education required, the work conditions, and so on. During this third stage of vocational choice, the *realistic stage,* which spans the ages of about 18 to 22, the individual is likely to narrow things down to a specific choice based on interests, capacities, values, and available opportunities. Now a firm vocational identity is achieved and serious preparation for a chosen occupation begins.

The main developmental trend evident in Ginzberg's stages is increasing realism about what one can be. As adolescents narrow down career choices in terms of both personal factors (their own interests, capacities, and values) and environmental factors (the opportunities available and the realities of the job market), they seek the vocation that best suits them. According to influential vocational theorists such as John Holland and Donald Super, vocational choice is just this: *an effort to find an optimal fit between one's self-concept or personality and an occupation* (Holland, 1985; Spokane, 1996; Super, 1991; Super, Savickas, & Super, 1996).

As they get older, adolescents from lower-income families, especially those from minority backgrounds, often make compromises in their career plans (Gottfredson, 1996). They lower their career aspirations and aim toward the jobs they think they can get rather than the jobs they may most want (Hanson, 1994; Rojewski & Yang, 1997). If they think that discrimination will limit their job prospects, they also tend to stop working hard in school (Taylor et al., 1994).

Similarly, the vocational choices of females have been and continue to be constrained by traditional gender norms. Although young women are increasingly aspiring toward high-status jobs, many do not seriously consider traditionally male-dominated jobs, doubt their ability to attain such jobs, and aim instead toward feminine-stereotyped—and often lower-status—occupations (Lauver & Jones, 1991; Morinaga, Frieze, & Ferligoj, 1993). Those who have adopted traditional gender-role attitudes and expect to marry and start families early in adulthood are especially likely to set their vocational sights low (Aneshensel & Rosen, 1980; Morinaga et al., 1993). They may feel that they cannot achieve important family goals without scaling down their career ambitions.

In short, as adolescents progress through fantasy, tentative, and realistic stages of vocational development, societal influences discourage many low-income youth of both sexes and young women from seriously considering many options that might well fit their interests, capacities, and values. These adolescents are not alone, however. Many other teenagers simply do not do what vocational theorists (and developmental theorist Erik Erikson) would advise them to do: Explore a wide range of possible occupations and then make a choice. Those who *do* consider a wide range of options are more likely than those who do not to choose careers that fit their personalities well (Grotevant, Cooper, & Kramer, 1986). Those who do not at least have opportunities as adults to change their minds and chart new life courses.

Working after School

Would adolescents be able to make more informed and rational vocational choices if they had more experience in the world of work? As things stand, the large majority of adolescents in the United States and Canada do work part time during their high school careers. How do these early work experiences affect their development?

Laurence Steinberg and his associates have compared working and nonworking high school students in terms of such outcomes as their autonomy from parents, self-reliance, self-esteem, sense of investment

Working in fast-food restaurants is not the kind of intellectually challenging work that can contribute positively to adolescent development.

in school, academic performance, delinquency, and drug and alcohol use (Greenberger & Steinberg, 1986; Steinberg, 1984; Steinberg & Dornbusch, 1991; Steinberg, Fegley, & Dornbusch, 1993). Overall, this research offers more bad news than good news. The good news is that working students seem to gain knowledge about the world of work, consumer issues, and financial management and sometimes greater self-reliance from working. However, high school students who worked 20 or more hours a week had grade-point averages about a third of a letter grade lower than those of students who did not work or who worked only 10 or fewer hours per week (Steinberg & Dornbusch, 1991). Working students were also more likely than nonworkers to be disengaged from school—bored and uninvolved in class and prone to cut class and spend little time on homework.

In addition, the more adolescents worked, the more independent they were of parental control, the more likely they were to be experiencing psychological distress (anxiety, depression, and physical symptoms such as headaches), and the more frequently they used alcohol and drugs and engaged in delinquent acts. These negative effects of work generally increased as the number of hours a student worked increased.

In a longitudinal study, Steinberg and his colleagues (1993) established that students who worked long hours were more disenchanted with school and independent of their parents even before they began working. However, working led to *further* alienation from school and *greater* distance from parents and contributed to problems that had not been apparent before. Moreover, students who worked but quit during the course of the study improved their school performance after they stopped working (see also Bachman & Schulenberg, 1993).

Not all research findings are this discouraging. Jeylen Mortimer and his colleagues (1996) also conducted a longitudinal study of high school students in which they controlled carefully for differences between working and nonworking students in factors such as family background and prior academic performance. In their study, working 20 hours or more a week did not hurt academic achievement, self-esteem, or psychological adjustment once other factors were controlled. Students who worked 1 to 20 hours a week actually earned better grades than both nonworkers and students who worked more than 20 hours a week. As in Steinberg's study, though, students who worked more than 20 hours used alcohol more frequently than students who were not employed.

These findings suggest that working while attending high school, although often more damaging than beneficial, is not always bad for adolescents. Much depends on the nature of the work adolescents do. Many teenagers work in food service jobs (pouring soft drinks behind the counter at McDonald's, scooping ice cream, and the like) or perform manual labor (especially cleaning or janitorial work). These routine and repetitive jobs offer few opportunities for self-direction or decision making and only rarely call on academic skills such as reading and math (Steinberg, 1984). They are not the kinds of jobs that "build character" or teach new skills. Adolescents experience increases in mastery motivation and become less depressed over time when the work they do provides opportunities for advancement and teaches useful skills, but lose mastery motivation and become more depressed when they hold menial jobs that interfere with their schooling (Shanahan et al., 1991; Call, Mortimer, & Shanahan, 1995). And working long hours has negative effects on adolescents when their jobs are menial but not when their jobs are of high quality (Barling et al., 1995).

Judging from this research, many adolescents who are flipping hamburgers might be better off postponing work or working only a limited number of hours so that they can concentrate on obtaining a solid education and exploring their career options (Steinberg, 1984). Yet, those adolescents lucky enough to land intellectually challenging jobs, especially jobs that tie in with their emerging vocational interests and teach them useful skills, can benefit from their work experiences.

Pathways to Adulthood

The educational paths and attainments of adolescents are already partially set long before they enter adolescence. Because many individuals' intelligence test scores remain quite stable from childhood on, some children enter adolescence with more aptitude for schoolwork than others do (see Chapter 9). Moreover,

some students have more achievement motivation than others. Quite clearly, a bright and achievement-oriented student is more likely to obtain good grades and go on to college and is less likely to drop out of school than a student with less ability and less need to achieve. By early elementary school, and sometimes even before they enter school, future dropouts are often identifiable by such warning signs as low IQ and achievement test scores, poor grades, aggressive behavior, low socioeconomic status, and troubled homes (Ensminger & Slusarcick, 1992; Lloyd, 1978).

This does *not* mean that adolescents' fates are sealed in childhood, however; experiences during adolescence clearly make a difference. Some teenagers make the most of their intellectual abilities, whereas others who have the ability to do well in school drop out or get poor grades. The quality of an adolescent's school, the extent to which his or her parents are authoritative and encourage school achievement, and the extent to which his or her peers value school can make a big difference (Brown et al., 1993; Rutter et al., 1979; Steinberg et al., 1992).

The stakes are high. Students who achieve good grades are more likely to complete high school; currently, 83% of white students, 74% of African-American students, and an alarmingly low 53% of Hispanic students achieve this milestone (U.S. Bureau of the Census, 1997). They then stand a chance of being among the 24% of whites, 14% of blacks, and 9% of Hispanics who complete four or more years of college (U.S. Bureau of the Census, 1997). These youth, in turn, are likely to have higher career aspirations and end up in higher-status occupations than their peers who do not attend college or do not even finish high school (Featherman, 1980; McCaul et al., 1992). And, if their grades are good, they are likely to perform well in those jobs and advance far in their careers (Roth et al., 1996). In a very real sense, then, individuals are steered along "high success" or "low success" routes starting in childhood. Depending on their own decisions and family, peer, and school influences, adolescents are even more distinctly "sorted out" in ways that will affect their adult lifestyles, income levels, and adjustment. Meanwhile, high school dropouts not only have less successful careers but also miss out on the beneficial effects that every year of schooling has on intellectual functioning (Ceci & Williams, 1997). They also experience more psychological problems than those who stay in school (Kaplan, Damphousse, & Kaplan, 1994).

THE ADULT

The lives of adults are dominated by work—paid or unpaid, outside the home or within the home. What becomes of the need to achieve during the adult years, what does a typical "work life cycle" look like, how do adults blend work and family life, and what are the implications of all this for their development and well-being?

Achievement Motivation

The level of achievement motivation that we acquire in childhood and adolescence carries into adulthood to influence our decisions and life outcomes (Kagan & Moss, 1962; Spence, 1985). For instance, women who have a strong need to achieve are more likely than less achievement-oriented women to work outside the home (Krogh, 1985). Adults with strong achievement needs are also likely to be more competent workers than adults who have little concern with mastering challenges (Helmreich, Sawin, & Carsrud, 1986; Spence, 1985).

What happens to achievement motivation in later life? Is there any support for the common belief that older adults lose some of their drive to excel? Joseph Veroff, David Reuman, and Sheila Feld (1984) explored this question by analyzing motivational themes in stories that American adults told in response to pictures like the one shown in Figure 15.1. Older men displayed only slightly lower levels of achievement motivation than young or middle-aged men did. Here, then, we find no support for the stereotyped idea that older adults are "unmotivated" or have ceased to pursue goals (see also Filipp, 1996; McAdams, St. Aubin, & Logan, 1993).

Veroff and his associates (1984) found that achievement motivation declined fairly steeply from age group to age group among women (see also Mellinger & Erdwins, 1985). However, this age trend pertained mainly to *career-related* motivation and an interest in striving for success in competitive situations. When this study was done, many women set aside career-achievement goals after they had children and made nurturing those children their top priority (Krogh, 1985). However, highly educated women often regained a strong motive to achieve outside the home once the children were older and they could invest more energy in outside work (Baruch, 1967; Malatesta & Culver, 1984). Apparently, then, women are especially likely to be motivated to achieve career success when they have the educational background that would allow them to pursue attractive career goals and when they are not pursuing family-related goals.

Overall, adults' achievement-related motives are far more affected by their changing work and family contexts than by the aging process (Filipp, 1996). Adults of different ages are often more alike than they are different, and different people tend to retain their characteristic levels of achievement motivation over the years, much as they retain many personality traits (Stevens & Truss, 1985). There is certainly little evi-

Most elderly adults continue to be motivated to achieve important goals.

dence that elderly adults inevitably lose their motivation to pursue important goals. Moreover, those elders who do have a strong sense of purpose and direction and feel they are achieving their goals enjoy greater physical and psychological well-being than those who do not (Hooker & Siegler, 1993; Rapkin & Fischer, 1992; Reker et al., 1987). Throughout the life span, then, setting and achieving goals are important. Now let's examine a theory of adult development that has a lot to say about how adults formulate and reformulate their life goals.

Levinson's Conception of Adult Development

Daniel Levinson (1986, 1996; Levinson et al., 1978) proposed an influential stage theory of adult development that can aid us in organizing our examination of adult career paths and achievements. The stages were formulated from interviews with 40 men aged 35 to 45 from four occupational groups (executives, biologists, novelists, and factory workers). Just before his

BOX 15.2

Daniel Levinson's stages of adult development

1. *Early Adult Transition (ages 17 to 22).* Make the transition from adolescence to early adulthood. Try to establish independence from parents and explore possibilities for an adult identity. Form *the dream,* a vision of your life goals.

2. *Entering the Adult World (ages 22 to 28).* Build your first life structure, often by making and testing out a career choice and getting married. Do your best to succeed. Find people who can support your development—a spouse and/or a **mentor** (a guide or advisor, perhaps a trusted faculty member or a supervisor at work). Do not question your life; work hard to get off to a good start as an adult, though always with the idea of keeping doors of opportunity open.

3. *Age-30 Transition (ages 28 to 33).* Ask whether what you are doing is really what you want. Are you becoming locked into a poor career choice or an unsatisfying marriage? If any uncomfortable feelings arise from your questioning, either ignore them and plug away, make small adjustments in your life structure, or plan a more major life change (for example, a job change, a divorce, or a decision to return to school).

4. *Settling Down (ages 33 to 40).* Build a new, and often somewhat different, life structure; "make it," or realize your dream. Outgrow your need for a mentor and become your own person. As in the structure-building period of Entering the Adult World, be ambitious, task oriented, and unreflective.

5. *Midlife Transition (ages 40 to 45).* Begin all over again to question what you have built and where you are heading. If you have been a success, ask whether the dream you formulated as a young adult was really a worthy goal; if you have not achieved your dream, face the fact that you may never achieve it. Confront the facts of aging, and ask what you really want for the future. Consider making major changes in your life structure.

6. *Entering Middle Adulthood (ages 45 to 50).* Create a new life structure appropriate to middle age. If you successfully confronted and resolved midlife issues during the Midlife Transition, you may gain self-understanding, a capacity for mentoring younger adults at work, and a deeper concern for your family—much like the middle-aged adult whom Erik Erikson describes as having acquired a sense of generativity.

Levinson theorizes that this process of building a life structure and then questioning it during a transition period then continues throughout middle and later adulthood.

---

death in 1994, Levinson and his wife, Judy, completed a book reporting that the same stages emerged in interviews with women (Levinson, 1996).

Levinson's stages describe the unfolding of what he calls an individual's **life structure,** an overall pattern of life that reflects the person's priorities and relationships with other people and the larger society. Central to the life structure are family and work roles. Levinson proposes that adults go through a repeated process of first building a life structure and then questioning and altering it. Structure-building periods, during which the person goes about pursuing goals, alternate with transitional periods, when the person questions his or her life decisions. Box 15.2 outlines Levinson's first six stages.

Although Levinson did not interview men or women in their 50s and 60s, he speculates that the same alternating periods of structure building and structure questioning continue into later life. In fact, Levinson is convinced that his stages are both maturational in nature and universal. Environmental factors will influence the specifics of an adult's life, but the basic pattern of building, questioning, and rebuilding will still be evident under the surface. Levinson's perspective has gained much attention as a way of conceptualizing how adults progress in their careers and how they change as individuals. Let's see how well the theory fares when we match it up with research on vocational development during the adult years.

Career Paths during Adulthood

Not all research supports Levinson's theory in all its details, but much research suggests that young, middle-aged, and older adults confront different issues in their roles as workers. After engaging in much experimentation as young adults, people settle down into a chosen occupation. Ultimately, they prepare for the end of their careers and make the transition into retirement.

Exploration and Establishment

According to Levinson, early adulthood is a time for exploring vocational possibilities, launching careers, making tentative commitments, revising them if necessary, seeking advancement, and establishing oneself firmly in what one hopes is a suitable occupation. Most men do formulate what Levinson calls a "dream," centering mainly on occupational goals, in their late teens or early 20s, around the time of Levinson's Early Adult Transition (Drebing & Gooden, 1991). They then test out vocational possibilities and ultimately "settle down" into a career.

Using data from a longitudinal study of males tracked from adolescence to age 36 (see Super et al., 1996), Susan Phillips (1982) examined whether men's decisions about jobs at different ages were tentative and exploratory (for example, "to see if I really liked that kind of work") or more final (for example, "to get started in a field I wanted"). The proportions of decisions that were predominantly exploratory were 80% at age 21, 50% at age 25, and 37% at age 36. In other words, young adults progress from wide-open exploration, to tentative or trial commitments, to a stabilization of their choices. Yet notice that, even in their mid-30s, many men were still trying to figure out what they wanted to be when they grew up! The males in this study held an average of seven full-time jobs or training positions between the ages of 18 and 36, and 30% of them not only changed jobs but changed *fields* between ages 25 and 36 (Phillips, 1982).

Women too are highly likely to change their career goals after they leave school and then to settle on an occupation in their 30s (Jenkins, 1989; Ornstein & Isabella, 1990). Thus, we may make vocational choices as adolescents, but we are obviously very open to making new choices as young adults. It is when the fit between the individual's personality or aptitudes and the demands of the occupation is poor that young adults become dissatisfied and open to exploring other alternatives (Bizot & Goldman, 1993; Bretz & Judge, 1994). Although both men and women change jobs and even careers a good deal during early adulthood, there is little evidence that they do it primarily between the ages of 28 and 33, when Levinson's theory claims that adults experience an Age-30 Transition, in which they question the life structure they have built so far and make changes in both their vocational and personal lives (Dunn & Merriam, 1995).

Midlife Crisis?

According to Levinson, the transition period from ages 40 to 45 is a developmentally significant time of **midlife crisis**—of questioning one's entire life structure, including one's career, and raising unsettling issues about where one has been and where one is heading. True, most of Levinson's middle-aged men did not seek divorces, quit their jobs, buy red sports cars, and behave like lovesick adolescents, as popular images of the midlife crisis might suggest. However, Levinson characterized 80% of the men in his study as having experienced a bona fide crisis—a period of intense inner struggles and disturbing realizations—in their early 40s.

What about women? In his in-depth study of 45 homemakers, women faculty members, and businesswomen between the ages of 35 and 45, Levinson (1996) found that women progressed through the same stages of adult development that men did, faced major issues during his Age-30 Transition (28 to 33), and also experienced significant midlife crises in their early 40s. Indeed, women seemed to have even more to deal with at midlife than men, and almost all found the experience "wrenching," according to Levinson. Homemakers, whose early adult dreams had centered on marriage and motherhood, lived the lives of traditional women during early adulthood but often wanted to express their more independent, nontraditional side at midlife; they were often unhappy with their marriages and ready for a change. The career women had established a dream of career success or of career success combined with happiness in a relatively nontraditional marriage. They also had to deal with inner conflicts between their traditional and nontraditional sides; moreover, they had to cope with the sexism they found in their workplaces and struggle continuously to strike the right balance between career and family—or live with regrets if they could not. Despite the stresses they faced, they were generally happier at midlife than the homemakers.

What have other researchers concluded about the midlife crisis? Almost everyone seems to agree that middle age is a time when many important issues arise and when men and women *can* find themselves engaged in a painful self-evaluation process (Drebing & Gooden, 1991; Farrell & Rosenberg, 1981; Mercer, Nichols, & Doyle, 1989). It is also clear that many middle-aged adults return to a phase of career exploration in which they ask basic questions about what they want to do with their lives and chart new career directions (Smart & Peterson, 1997). Such periods of questioning can be stressful but their rewards in terms of increased job satisfaction can be great.

Still, many researchers seriously doubt that most adults experience a genuine "crisis" at midlife or that this crisis occurs in the narrowly defined age range of 40 to 45, as Levinson claimed. For example, George Vaillant (1977) found that many of the middle-aged men he studied were evaluating their lives but that virtually none could be described as experiencing a painful upheaval, or crisis. In another study, only about 20% of the middle-aged men studied were reevaluating their dreams or raising questions about the meaning of their lives, which suggests that this sort of soul-searching is far from universal (Hedlund & Ebersole, 1983). What's more, men questioned their lives at a variety of ages rather than only in the early 40s, often in response to specific life events such as getting married, changing jobs, or experiencing marital problems.

Studies aimed at determining whether Levinson's stages apply to women suggest that their development is more complex and "messy" than men's. Rather than forming a "dream" that centers on career, many young women formulate "split," or multifaceted, dreams incorporating career, family, and personal goals (Drebing et al., 1995; Roberts & Newton, 1987). Rather than experiencing distinct stages of the sort Levinson describes, many women experience *continuous* struggles with the issue of how to balance career and family goals (Mercer et al., 1989; Roberts & Newton, 1987). Women who had emphasized marriage and family in their 20s sometimes find they want to pursue career goals in their 30s and 40s, whereas career-oriented women sometimes find themselves longing to get married or to have children.

If a stage of midlife crisis in the early 40s were widespread, we might expect men and women to experience significant personality changes at midlife or to show signs of emotional disturbance. This does not seem to be the case (McCrae & Costa, 1990). Finally, if midlife crises were widespread, we might expect middle-aged adults to be dissatisfied with their work. Instead, middle-aged men and women are generally *more* satisfied with their jobs than younger adults are (Warr, 1992). In sum, Levinson may have overestimated the extent to which midlife crisis occurs. It would seem more appropriate to call the phenomenon midlife *questioning* than midlife crisis, to recognize that it can occur in response to life events at a variety of ages and to appreciate that it need not be emotionally wrenching.

How, then, should we evaluate Levinson's theory overall? He has certainly stimulated much thought and research by suggesting that people experience stagelike changes in their life structures during adulthood. He has also captured the flow of vocational development for both men and women in early adulthood quite well. However, because adults are so varied, it is difficult to fit them into a series of universal stages that unfold at predictable ages. The changes that adults undergo seem to be timed more by the life events they experience than by their ages. Thus, some 25-year-olds may be entering the adult world and building preliminary life structures, while others may still be wondering what they want to do in life and still others may be reevaluating their dreams because they dread going to work each morning. The broad themes and developmental trends that Levinson identifies are supported by research, but whether most adult lives change in precisely the ways and at precisely the times that he claims has not been established. And how well Levinson's stages fit adults in other cultures remains to be determined.

Aging Workers

Do we become less able or less motivated to perform well on the job as we enter our 50s and 60s? We can easily think of occupations in which age is a liability. Kareem Abdul Jabbar may have been able to continue the strenuous work of playing pro basketball until age 42, but most pro athletes retire earlier than

that. Aging workers who perform heavy physical labor may also find their work increasingly difficult. But do most adults reach a point at which they are simply over the hill?

As it turns out, the job performance of workers in their 50s and 60s is not very different overall from that of younger workers (Hansson et al., 1997; Rhodes, 1983; Waldman & Avolio, 1986). Age is simply not a very good predictor of how well a person will perform his or her job, and this holds true for both white-collar and blue-collar jobs. Not only are older workers generally as competent as younger workers, but they often have more positive attitudes toward their work (Rhodes, 1983; Warr, 1992). They tend to be *more* satisfied with their jobs, *more* involved in their work, and *less* interested in finding a new job than younger workers are.

Why isn't the performance of older workers hurt by some of the age-related physical and cognitive declines we have discussed in this book? Partly because these declines typically do not become significant until people are in their 70s and 80s, long after they have retired. Older workers have also accumulated a good deal of on-the-job expertise that can help them perform well (Hansson et al., 1997). Finally, the answer may also lie in the strategies aging workers use to cope with aging. Gerontologists Paul and Margaret Baltes (1990) theorize that older people can best cope with aging through a strategy they call **selective optimization with compensation.** Three processes are involved: selection (focus on the skills one most needs and wants to keep sharp), optimization (practice those skills to keep them sharp), and compensation (develop ways to get around the need for other skills). Using selective optimization with compensation, a stressed 60-year-old lawyer might, for example, avoid spreading herself too thin by delegating lower-priority tasks to younger workers (selection), put a lot of time into staying up to date in her main area of specialization (optimization), and do all she can to hide her weaknesses from the head of the law firm (compensation).

In a recent attempt to test this model (Abraham & Hansson, 1995), workers aged 40 to 69 completed scales measuring their reliance on selection, optimization, and compensation strategies. Among older but not younger adults in the sample, especially those with highly stressful jobs, heavy reliance on these strategies did indeed help workers to maintain a high level of performance and attain their goals at work. There are limits, of course, but many older workers seem able to draw on their expertise and on tactics like selective optimization with compensation to maintain a high level of achievement at work, despite age-related declines in their competencies. They are able to maintain a good person/environment fit between any changes in their abilities and the demands of their jobs (Hansson et al., 1997). The federal government

Women today are gradually "breaking through" in traditionally male-dominated fields.

now seems to recognize that older workers are effective workers, for it has raised or eliminated mandatory retirement ages, increased the age of eligibility for Social Security, and, through the Age Discrimination in Employment Act, protected older workers from age discrimination in hiring and retention (Hansson et al., 1997).

Women, Work, and the Family

As we noted in Chapter 14, the employment patterns of women have changed considerably in recent decades. Most women, even mothers of infants and young children, now work outside the home (U.S. Bureau of the Census, 1997). Women are also working for more years (Herring & Wilson-Sadberry, 1993). Finally, women are now entering a wide range of fields that were formerly male dominated or even closed to women: coal mining, truck driving, engineering, and medicine, to name a few.

At the same time, some things have not changed much at all. For example, although the number of female lawyers had risen to about 100,000 by 1984 (about five times as many as there had been a decade earlier) nearly *4 million* women that year were secretaries (Waldman, 1985). And, although the gap between women's and men's earnings has narrowed, it has not closed: Across all jobs, a woman in the 1950s averaged about 60 cents for every dollar a man earned; more recently, the ratio is about 70 cents for every dollar (Bernhardt, Morris, & Handcock, 1995). So why

aren't women achieving more in the workplace? To answer that question, we must focus on two major barriers to women's career achievement: sex discrimination and conflicts between work and family.

Sex Discrimination

It may be difficult for today's young adults to appreciate that, not very long ago, women were simply barred from entering many occupations or were forbidden to work by their husbands, who viewed a wife's "having" to work as a sign that they had failed as breadwinners. Today, women cannot legally be denied entry into prestigious, male-dominated occupations, but they continue to face discrimination in the labor force. For example, traditional "female" jobs often pay less than "male" jobs, even when the intellectual demands are similar (England, Reid, & Kilbourne, 1996). There is still a tendency to view "women's work" as less valuable. Even when women with the same management degrees as men enter the same kinds of management jobs at the same salaries and obtain equal performance ratings from their supervisors, they do not rise as far in the organization or make as much money as men (Cox & Harquail, 1991).

Traditional gender roles also make it difficult for women to obtain the same support for their career ambitions that men receive. For one thing, many women do not receive the mentoring that Daniel Levinson and others have found to be so important to vocational success (Drebing et al., 1995; Roberts & Newton, 1987). In many companies an "old-boy network" helps promising young men make the right connections and rise quickly to the top. However, since few women have made it to the top in business and industry, a comparable "old-girl network" does not yet exist. In addition, working women generally do not receive as much support for their career goals from their husbands as Levinson's men received from their wives (Roberts & Newton, 1987). Clearly, a number of forms of gender-based discrimination make it difficult for women to achieve in the workplace.

Role Conflict and Overload

A second barrier to women's career achievement is **role conflict**—the feeling of being pulled in different directions by the competing demands of different roles (in this instance, family roles and work roles) and the related problem of **role overload**—having too much to do and too little time in which to do it. Role conflict can result when family responsibilities interfere with work performance or when the demands of work interfere with family life, and role overload can occur when both roles are very time demanding (Parasuraman & Greenhaus, 1997; Gutek, Searle, & Klepa, 1991). Many modern women feel they must be "jugglers"—able to feed the children and get them off to school, put in a full day at work, pick up the chil-

dren, swing by the supermarket, fill the gas tank, fix dinner, throw in a couple of loads of laundry, and still find time for meaningful conversations with their husbands. They are perpetual-motion machines, always, it seems, doing two or three things at once.

Because society continues to view women as the primary keepers of home and hearth, many working wives end up coping with role conflict by subordinating career goals to family responsibilities. Steady movement up the career ladder is most likely to occur when an employee works full time and continuously in the same organization (Sorensen, 1991; Van Velsor & O'Rand, 1984). However, women have often interrupted their careers to bear and raise children (Moen, 1992; Sorensen, 1983; Waite, Haggstrom, & Kanouse, 1986). Fewer women today drop out of the labor force while they raise their children, but many women *do* switch from full-time to part-time employment or take less demanding jobs as a means of coping with role conflict, and in the process hurt their chances of rising to high-paid, responsible positions (Moen, 1992; Sorensen, 1991). Meanwhile, the women who *do* make it to the top of the career ladder, especially in male-dominated fields, sometimes cope with role conflict by not marrying, divorcing, or limiting their childbearing (Jenkins, 1989).

Does this mean that it is impossible for women to "have it all"—to combine marriage, family, and a full-time, uninterrupted career? Aren't women who attempt to have it all likely to experience extraordinary role conflict and role overload? Grace Baruch and Rosalind Barnett (1986) have shown that the sheer number of roles a woman plays has little impact on her well-being. Although working outside the home tends to be associated with high self-esteem, women who are wives, mothers, *and* workers are generally neither worse off nor better off than women who play fewer roles and who would be expected to experience less role conflict and overload. Instead, it is the *quality* of a woman's experience in work and family roles that is most closely associated with well-being (see

also Barnett et al., 1995; Vandewater, Ostrove, & Stewart, 1997). Women experience greater happiness and self-esteem, and less depression, when the rewards they gain from *whatever* roles they play outweigh the hassles.

Well-being is also affected by interactions between work lives and family lives. The concept of **spillover** has been used to describe ways in which events at work affect home life, and events at home carry over into the workplace. Much emphasis has been placed on negative spillover effects, in which problems at work adversely affect functioning in the family or family problems undermine effectiveness at work (Barnett et al., 1995; Crouter & McHale, 1993). Too little emphasis has been placed on *positive* spillover effects. A good marriage and rewarding interactions with children can protect a woman from the negative psychological effects of stresses at work (Barnett, 1994), and a rewarding, stimulating job can have positive effects on interactions within the family (Greenberger, O'Neil, & Nagel, 1994).

Barriers to women's career success caused by sex discrimination and role conflict and overload continue to exist, but dual-career couples are coping well with the challenges they face (Shelton, 1992). Women are giving up personal leisure time (not to mention sleep!) and sharing housework tasks with their children to give themselves more time with their children, and their husbands are slowly but steadily increasing their participation in household and child-care activities (Dancer & Gilbert, 1993; Gottfried et al., 1995). If present trends continue, we will see more and more families in which *both* men and women are attempting to balance and integrate their central roles as workers, spouses, and parents—and are finding gratification in each of these roles.

Implications for Children

And what, you might ask, will become of their children? There is no indication that a mother's working—in and of itself—has damaging effects on child development (Beyer, 1995; Hoffman, 1989). Indeed, there are signs that children, especially girls, may benefit from the role model a working mother provides, for they tend to be more independent, to set higher educational and vocational goals, and to adopt less stereotyped views of men's and women's roles than children whose mothers do not work (Hoffman, 1989).

Having a working mother *can* be a negative experience, though, especially for boys (Goldberg, Greenberger, & Nagel, 1996). The key is whether or not a working mother is able to remain a warm and involved parent who shares "quality time" with her children (Beyer, 1995). Martha Moorehouse (1991) found that 6-year-olds whose mothers began working full time were actually more cognitively and socially competent (according to their teachers) than children whose mothers were homemakers *if* these youngsters frequently shared activities such as reading, telling stories, and talking with their mothers. If they lost out on such opportunities, they fared worse than children with stay-at-home mothers. Fortunately, most working mothers manage to spend almost as much time as nonworking mothers with their children (Bryant & Zick, 1996; Nock & Kingston, 1988). As a result, most working mothers, though busy and often stressed, are able to enjoy the personal benefits of working without compromising their children's development.

Work and Adult Development

Play and schooling clearly contribute to a child's development, but what effects does work have on an adult's adjustment and personal growth? For one thing, an adult's occupation is a central part of his or her identity. It means a great deal to people to say that they are psychologists, electricians, or nurses. Work also provides many personal rewards besides money—for example, opportunities to master challenges, gain status and self-esteem, and form enjoyable relationships (Havighurst, 1982).

Perhaps most interesting is evidence that certain kinds of work stretch the capacities of adults, just as certain kinds of play and schooling stretch children's minds. Melvin Kohn and Carmi Schooler (1982, 1983) have explored the implications for adult development of the **substantive complexity** of a job, or the extent to which it provides opportunities for using one's mind and making independent judgments. For example, a secretary with a substantively complex job would do more than merely perform whatever typing assignments are placed on her desk. She might also handle the department budget, decide what office supplies are needed, interact with the public, assign tasks to clerical helpers, and generally take the initiative for making a number of complex decisions every day.

Kohn and Schooler find that substantively complex or intellectually challenging work is associated with greater intellectual flexibility (an ability to handle intellectual problems adeptly and to keep an open mind about issues) and with greater self-direction (a tendency to be self-confident, independent minded, responsible, and tolerant of others). By contrast, people who engage in intellectually unchallenging work tend to be relatively ineffective thinkers, are negative toward themselves and conforming in relation to others, and are often psychologically distressed as well. People who are already intellectually capable and self-directed, of course, are especially likely to land substantively complex jobs. However, Kohn and his colleagues demonstrate that the quality of one's job in turn influences one's subsequent personal qualities (see also Clausen & Gilens, 1990). Moreover, parents whose jobs are substantively complex provide more stimulating home environments for their children and use more effective styles of parenting than parents who hold less intellectually challenging jobs, and these differences in parenting in turn make for differences in children's development (Greenberger et al., 1994; Menaghan & Parcel, 1991; Stewart & Barling, 1996). So, the way we pass our days as adults can have long-term implications for our own and our children's psychological functioning.

Retirement

Although most are still able to work, the large majority of men and women in our society choose to retire sometime in their 60s. Earlier in this century most continued working until they simply could not work any longer. Indeed, as late as 1930, over half of all men aged 65 or older were still working (Palmore et al., 1985). The introduction of Social Security in 1934 and the increased availability of private pension plans changed all that, making it financially possible for more men and women to retire. The result, as Figure 15.2 shows, is that only about 22% of adults aged 65 to 74 and 4% of adults aged 75 and older hold regular jobs (Herzog et al., 1989). The average age of retirement, for white and black men and women alike, is about 63, younger than it used to be (Gendell & Siegel, 1996).

How do people adjust to the final chapter of the work life cycle? Robert Atchley (1976) proposed that adults progress through a series of phases as they make the transition from worker to retiree. The process of adjustment begins with a *preretirement phase,* in which workers nearing retirement gather information and plan for the future (Evans, Ekerdt, & Bossé, 1985). Deciding when to retire is one part of the process. Some workers are forced to retire early because of poor health or because they are pushed out of their

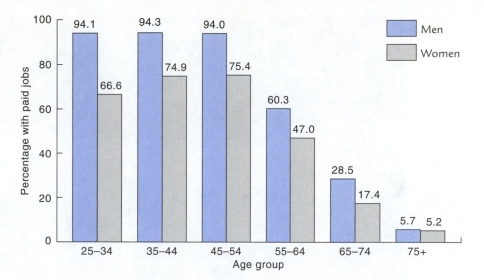

FIGURE 15.2 *Percentages of U.S. adults who have regular paid jobs at various ages (not counted are volunteer work and irregularly paid activities). Women are less involved in paid work than men, especially in early adulthood, but they devote more time to unpaid housework, child care, and helping activities.* (Based on data from Herzog et al., 1989)

jobs, but others choose to retire early because their finances are adequate, they do not feel very attached to their jobs, and they like the prospect of retiring (Hansson et al., 1997). Women often have more positive attitudes toward work and less positive attitudes toward retirement than men (Hanson & Wapner, 1994), but they sometimes retire earlier than they would like because their husbands retire or because other family considerations draw them home (Szinovacz & Ekerdt, 1995).

Just after they retire, workers often experience a *honeymoon phase* when they relish their newfound freedom and perhaps head for the beach, golf course, or camping grounds and do all the projects they never had time to do while they worked. Then, according to Atchley, many enter a *disenchantment phase* as the novelty wears off; they feel aimless and sometimes unhappy. Finally, they move on to a *reorientation phase*, in which they begin to put together a realistic and satisfying lifestyle. Research supports this view. For example, David Ekerdt and his colleagues (1985) found that (1) men who had been retired only a few months were indeed in a honeymoon period in which they were highly satisfied with life and optimistic about the future, (2) men who had been retired 13 to 18 months were rather disenchanted with life, and (3) men who had been retired for longer periods were relatively satisfied once again. In another study, retirees experienced a honeymoon phase (well-being, energy level, and internal locus of control all increased during the first year of retirement); although there were no signs of a disenchantment phase, well-being returned to preretirement levels 6–7 years after

retirement, suggesting reorientation (Gall, Evans, & Howard, 1997).

So, retirement takes getting used to. After retirees have gotten through the initial period of adjustment, though, are they worse off than they were before they retired? Negative images of the retired person abound in our society: He or she supposedly ends up feeling useless, old, bored, sickly, and generally dissatisfied with life. Yet the bulk of research indicates that retirement has few effects at all (Gall et al., 1997; Hansson et al., 1997; Palmore et al., 1985).

Retirement's most consistent effect is a reduction in the individual's income—on average, to about three-fourths of what it was before retirement (Palmore et al., 1985). Retired people generally do *not* experience a decline in their health simply because they retire. Poor health more often causes retirement than vice versa (Hansson et al., 1997). Retirees' activity patterns don't change much either (Palmore et al., 1985; Parnes & Less, 1985). Indeed, retirement has no noticeable effect on the size of people's social networks, the frequency of their social contacts, or their satisfaction with the social support they receive (Bossé et al., 1993; Hansson et al., 1997). Finally, retirement does not seem to disrupt marriages (Ekerdt & Vinick, 1991) or reduce life satisfaction or mental health (Gall et al., 1997; Hansson et al., 1997; Palmore et al., 1985).

Overall, then, retirees are likely to experience an adjustment process involving honeymoon, disenchantment, and reorientation phases and end up adapting quite successfully to retirement and to the drop in income that it typically involves. Yet there are huge individual differences in adjustment. What makes for

Many older adults subscribe to the activity theory of aging, attempting to find substitutes for lost roles and activities. Others find happiness through disengagement and would just as soon sit and watch.

a favorable adjustment? Adults who (1) retire voluntarily rather than involuntarily, (2) enjoy good health, (3) have the financial resources to live comfortably, and (4) are married or otherwise have strong social support typically fare better than those who are forced to retire because of poor health and find themselves with inadequate incomes and few social ties (Gall et al., 1997; Palmore et al., 1985; Szinovacz & Ekerdt, 1995). Unfortunately, many widows and minority-group members, after living on limited incomes during their working years, must spend their "golden years" in poverty (Arber & Ginn, 1991; Clark & Maddox, 1992).

Successful Aging

The fact that adults retire does not mean they cease to be motivated to achieve goals that are important to them. Gerontologists have long been interested in how people's goals shift in later life and what choices make for a happy and fulfilling old age.

One theory of successful aging, **activity theory,** holds that aging adults will find their lives satisfying to the extent that they can maintain their previous lifestyles and activity levels, either by continuing old activities or by finding substitutes—for example, by replacing work with golf, volunteer work, or other stimulating pursuits (Havighurst, Neugarten, & Tobin, 1968; and see Fry, 1992). According to this theory, psychological needs do not really change as people enter old age, and most aging individuals continue to want an active lifestyle.

Other theorists have taken almost precisely the opposite stand on the keys to successful aging. **Disen-**gagement theory claims that successful aging involves a mutual withdrawal of the aging individual and society (Cumming & Henry, 1961; and see Achenbaum & Bengtson, 1994). The aging individual is said to have needs different from those she or he once had and seeks to leave old roles behind and *reduce* activity. Meanwhile, society both encourages and benefits from the older person's disengagement.

Which is it? Throughout this text we have seen evidence that individuals who remain active in old age benefit from their activity. Those who are physically active maintain their health longer than those who lead sedentary lives (see Chapter 5). Those who are intellectually active are likely to maintain their cognitive functions longer (see Chapter 9 and our earlier discussion of the cognitive benefits of substantively complex work). Finally, those who participate in meaningful social relationships are likely to be more satisfied with their lives than those who are socially isolated (Harlow & Cantor, 1996; and see Chapter 13). In other words, there is more support for activity theory than for disengagement theory.

But, before we conclude that activity theory tells us all we need to know about successful aging, let's add three qualifications. First, the relationship between sheer level of activity and life satisfaction or well-being is often quite weak (Fry, 1992). Apparently many individuals who are quite inactive are nonetheless satisfied with their lives, and many who are very busy are nonetheless unhappy. This suggests that the *quality* of one's activity is probably more important than its quantity.

Second, some messages of disengagement theory have merit (Achenbaum & Bengtson, 1994). As we saw in Chapter 10, for example, older adults sometimes adopt a more passive stance toward the world around them and become more introspective than they were earlier in life. This sort of psychological withdrawal could be viewed as a form of disengagement. Moreover, most older people today do withdraw voluntarily from certain roles and activities. Most notably, both older and younger members of society are very supportive of the concept of retirement, suggesting that disengagement from work roles is mutually satisfying to the aging person and to society.

But third, and perhaps most important, neither activity theory *nor* disengagement theory adequately allows for individual differences in personality traits and preferences. Activity theorists assume that most people will benefit from maintaining an active lifestyle; disengagement theorists assume that most people will be best off if they disengage. Instead, it appears that people are most satisfied in old age when they can achieve *a good fit between their lifestyle and their individual needs, preferences, and personality* (Fry, 1992; Seleen, 1982). An energetic and outgoing woman who is denied chances to maintain her active lifestyle in old age may be quite miserable. By contrast, a man who earlier in life found work to be a hassle might like nothing better in his retirement years than to take it easy, do a little fishing, and sit on the porch; he might be extremely unhappy if he were forced to continue working or if he found himself in a nursing home where he was pestered daily to participate in sing-alongs and other planned recreational activities. Still other older adults may find satisfaction from maintaining a few highly important roles, relationships, and activities but selectively withdrawing from others (Carstensen, 1993; Rapkin & Fischer, 1992), possibly a form of selective optimization with compensation.

In short, we cannot assume, as both activity theory and disengagement theory do, that what suits one is likely to suit all. Rather, we should once again adopt an interactional model of development that emphasizes the goodness of fit between person and environment. Box 15.3 explores how the concept of person/environment fit helps to explain why some older adults adjust better to nursing home life than others do.

APPLICATIONS: IMPROVING THE QUALITY OF EDUCATION

Quite obviously, developmental research has much to contribute to the improvement of education, which in turn contributes to the quality of life of adults. Educational practices have been greatly influenced by studies of how children of different ages think and learn, what motivates them, and how their achievement and adjustment to school can be enhanced. Today, many developmental researchers concerned about the quality of education in North American schools are attempting to learn lessons about how best to educate children by studying what appear to be highly effective schools in Japan and other Asian countries.

Cross-cultural research conducted by Harold Stevenson and his colleagues (Chen & Stevenson, 1995; Stevenson & Lee, 1990; Stevenson, Chen, & Lee, 1993) leaves no doubt that schoolchildren in Taiwan, the People's Republic of China, and Japan outperform students in the United States in math, reading, and other school subjects. The gap in math performance is especially striking; in recent testings of 5th graders, for example, only 4% of Chinese children and 10% of Japanese students had scores on a math achievement test as low as those of the average American child (Stevenson et al., 1993). Achievement differences of this sort are evident from the time children enter school and increase as children progress from 1st to 5th to 11th grade (Stevenson et al., 1993). And, contrary to stereotypes, high-achieving Asian students are not more stressed by school than American students; they are less stressed (Crystal et al., 1994). Why do these differences exist, and what insights can they offer about how to improve American education?

The problem is not that American students are "dumber." When they enter school, they perform just about as well on IQ tests as their Asian counterparts (Stevenson et al., 1985), and they score at least as well as Japanese and Chinese students on general-information tests of material *not* typically covered in school (Stevenson et al., 1993). Instead, the achievement gap between American and Asian students seems to be rooted in cultural differences in attitudes concerning education and educational practices:

1. Asian students spend more time being educated. Elementary school teachers in Asian countries devote more class time to academics—for example, two to three times as many hours a week on math instruction (see Figure 15.3). The classroom is also a businesslike place where little time is wasted; Asian students spend about 95% of their time "on task" (in activities such as listening to the teacher and completing assignments), whereas American students spend only about 80% of their time "on task" (Stigler, Lee, & Stevenson, 1987). Asian students also attend school for more hours per day and more days per year (Stevenson et al., 1986).
2. Asian students, especially Taiwanese students, are assigned and complete considerably more homework than American students (Stevenson & Lee, 1990; see also Figure 15.3). While American

BOX 15.3

Personal control and the adjustment of nursing home residents

Some years ago, Ellen Langer and Judith Rodin (1976) began to suspect that declines in physical health and psychological well-being among nursing-home residents might not be entirely due to the ravages of age and illness. Instead, they argued that elderly adults placed in nursing homes lose the feeling that they are in control of their lives and become passive and helpless as a result. Appreciating evidence that a sense of control and mastery is important throughout the life span (Schulz & Heckhausen, 1996), Langer and Rodin tested an intervention designed to increase perceptions of personal control among residents of a Connecticut nursing home.

The administrator of the nursing home gave different talks to the residents of two floors of the facility. The experimental group was told that it was their responsibility to make their wishes known and to make decisions about how to live their lives. He also offered them plants, made it clear that it was their choice whether they wanted to

take one and which one they wanted, and emphasized that the plants were theirs to care for as they would like. Finally, these residents were given a choice about whether and when to see a movie. Residents living on another floor served as the control group and received the message that the *staff* was responsible for their well-being and would do everything possible to see to

their needs. They were given a plant and were told that the nurses would care for it and that a movie would be scheduled on a particular night.

How much difference did it make whether residents were led to believe that control of their lives lay with them or with their caretakers? A great deal! After three weeks, 93% of the experimental group members were rated as

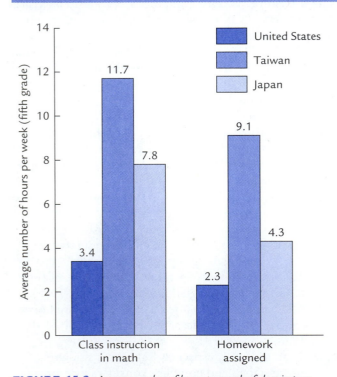

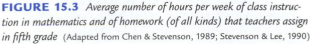

FIGURE 15.3 *Average number of hours per week of class instruction in mathematics and of homework (of all kinds) that teachers assign in fifth grade* (Adapted from Chen & Stevenson, 1989; Stevenson & Lee, 1990)

students are working or socializing with friends, Asian students are hitting the books (Fuligni & Stevenson, 1995).

3. Asian parents are strongly committed to the educational process. They are never quite satisfied with how their children are doing in school or with the quality of education their children are receiving; American parents seem to settle for less (Stevenson et al., 1993). Asian parents also receive frequent communications from their children's teachers in notebooks children carry to and from school each day. They find out how their children are progressing and follow teachers' suggestions for encouraging and assisting their children at home (Stevenson & Lee, 1990).

4. Peers also value school achievement and have high standards; time spent with peers often involves doing homework rather than engaging in activities that interfere with homework (Chen & Stevenson, 1995).

5. Parents, teachers, and students all share a strong belief that hard work or effort will pay off in better learning (they hold an incremental view

improved by nurses unfamiliar with the experimental manipulation. These residents felt happier, were more mentally alert, and were more involved in activities than the comparison group, 71% of whom were judged to have deteriorated during the study period. Even 18 months later, the personal-control residents were rated more sociable, active, interested in their environment, self-initiating, and healthy (Rodin & Langer, 1977). Most significantly, 30% of the comparison-group members had died in the 18-month period following the experiment, compared with only 15% of those encouraged to feel self-determining and in control of their lives.

It seems hard to believe that a brief speech, a plant to care for, and the opportunity to choose to see a movie could have so many beneficial effects on physical health and psychological well-being. Yet studies conducted since agree: Elderly adults fare better when they believe that they have a sense of control over their own lives than when they feel pushed and pulled by external

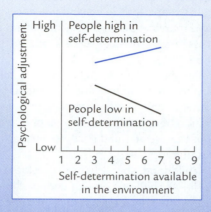

forces (Reich & Zautra, 1989, 1990; Welch & West, 1995).

However, we must, as always, bear in mind that the fit between person and environment is critical in adjustment. Brian O'Connor and Robert Vallerand (1994) administered surveys to nursing-home residents to assess both their tendency to be self-determining (to do things for the intrinsic pleasure of doing them rather than because of external pressures and rewards) and the extent to which their nursing home provided

plenty of opportunity for choice and self-determination. As the graph indicates, residents who had a more self-determining motivational style were better adjusted overall, in terms of satisfaction with their lives and themselves, than those who were less self-determining. More important, motivational style and type of environment interacted. Self-determining, autonomous individuals were better adjusted in environments that allowed them lots of freedom and choice than in environments that limited their ability to be self-determining. However, people who were not very self-determining and therefore had less need for personal control were *less* well adjusted in nursing homes that allowed freedom and choice than in homes in which staff took care of everything for residents. So, opportunities for more freedom and choice can benefit many elderly people (and younger people as well), but we must bear in mind that not everyone wants full control over their lives and not everyone benefits from the opportunity to have it.

of ability), whereas Americans tend to put more emphasis on ability as a cause of good or poor performance. The result may be that Americans give up too quickly on a child who appears to have low intellectual ability.

The formula for more effective education is not so mysterious after all, judging from the success of Japanese and Chinese educational systems. The secret is to get teachers, students, and parents working together to make education the top priority for youth, to set high achievement goals, and to invest the day-by-day effort required to attain those goals. Many states and local school districts have begun to respond to evidence that American schools are being outclassed by schools in other countries by strengthening curricula, tightening standards for teacher certification, raising standards for graduation and promotion from grade to grade, and even lengthen-

ing the school year. Educational reformer James Comer (1993) has been successful at forging closer ties between inner-city schools and the communities they serve and at involving parents as partners with teachers in the educational process. Edward Zigler and his colleagues have worked to convert schools into neighborhood hubs that provide not only education but child care and family support services for children from birth to age 12 (Zigler, Finn-Stevenson, & Stern, 1997). Comer and Zigler have even joined forces to create model schools around the country that combine Comer's community involvement model with Zigler's attempt to expand the services schools provide in order to support child development (Zigler et al., 1997). These educational leaders recognize that improving the school readiness, academic achievement, and vocational preparation of America's youth is a wise investment in the nation's future.

❖ SUMMARY POINTS

1. Achievement motivation, a desire to meet standards of excellence measured as *n Ach,* takes shape early in life and influences our accomplishments in play, school, work, and retirement activities. Achievement is also influenced by the value placed on success, expectancies of success, and attributions for successful and unsuccessful outcomes.

2. Effectance motivation, the forerunner of achievement motivation, is an urge for mastery evident in infancy and is nurtured by sensory stimulation, a responsive environment, and a secure attachment. It is expressed in play, which changes from exploration of objects to functional play and then to pretend play, which emerges at about the age of 1 and becomes increasingly complex with age as cognitive abilities unfold.

3. During childhood, some children develop a stronger need for achievement than others do. As children come to understand the concept of ability, their expectancies of success often decrease and they become more prone to learned helplessness after failure. High academic achievers tend to have mastery-oriented rather than helpless attribution styles; they have an incremental (rather than entity) view of ability and set learning (rather than performance) goals in the classroom. Attempts to combat learned helplessness by emphasizing learning goals and retraining attributions to emphasize the need for greater effort have been successful. Parents can help by being authoritative and encouraging independent mastery and achievement.

4. Within reasonable ranges, a school's effectiveness often is not strongly influenced by financial support, class size, or use of ability tracking. Instead, elementary and secondary school children perform best when (a) they are intellectually capable and motivated; (b) their teachers create a learning environment that is comfortable, task oriented, and motivating, and involves parents; and (c) there is, as aptitude-treatment interaction research suggests, a good "fit" between children's characteristics and the kind of instruction they receive.

5. Neither racial integration nor inclusion (or mainstreaming) for students with developmental disabilities has been very effective overall in increasing students' achievement and social acceptance, but these outcomes can be enhanced through cooperative learning methods.

6. Cognitive development, more negative teacher feedback, peer pressures, puberty, and poor person/environment fit may all contribute to declines in intrinsic achievement motivation as children become adolescents and make the transition to middle school or junior high school. However, adolescents are likely to retain their achievement motivation if they attend schools that provide a good fit to their developmental need for autonomy.

7. According to Eli Ginzberg, adolescents become increasingly realistic as they progress through the fantasy, tentative, and realistic stages of vocational choice. Social factors sometimes constrain the choices made by females and low-income youth of both sexes, and many adolescents do not engage in enough systematic career exploration. Starting in childhood, individuals are channeled along different pathways that determine how much schooling they receive and, in turn, how successful their careers are.

8. Adults of different ages are quite similar in their levels of achievement motivation, although women who turn their attention to child rearing may lose some of their career-oriented achievement motivation.

9. Daniel Levinson's theory that adults go through a recurring process of building life structures and revising them is supported by evidence that young adults engage in much career exploration. Midlife crisis in one's early 40s does not seem to be universal, but many middle-aged adults reevaluate their goals. Older workers are as productive as and often more satisfied than younger workers,

possibly because they use selective optimization with compensation to cope with aging.

10. Despite dramatic changes, most women continue to work in traditionally female and low-paying jobs, owing in part to sex discrimination and role conflict and overload. Yet today's women, like men, typically suffer no damage and can potentially benefit from adding work roles to their other roles, especially if their work is substantively complex. Their children do not suffer if they continue to get quality time with their parents.

11. Retiring workers go through an adjustment process that extends from a preretirement phase to honeymoon, disenchantment, and reorientation phases after retirement; they typically experience a drop in income but little change in health or psychological well-being.

12. Neither activity theory nor disengagement theory places enough emphasis on person/environment fit—on the fact that older adults are likely to be most satisfied when their retirement lifestyles suit their individual personalities and preferences.

13. Educational reform in North America can be guided by research suggesting that the success of Asian schools is rooted in more class time spent on academics, more homework, more parent involvement, more peer support, and a strong belief that hard work pays off.

✦ FOOD FOR THOUGHT

1. Ben, age 12, is doing miserably in math and does not seem to care. Focusing on concepts relevant to achievement motivation, describe how he probably thinks about math, himself as a math student, and his performance in class. And how might he have learned these counterproductive ways of thinking?

2. You have just been installed as the new principal of a racially mixed middle school in which students seem to have given up all interest in learning and discipline in the classroom is a thing of the past. Based on what we know about the transition to middle school and about effective schools, what three new initiatives would you introduce next fall to improve education in your school, and what do you expect them to accomplish?

3. To test Levinson's theory of adult development, one can ask middle-aged adults directly whether they have experienced a midlife crisis, but by doing so, you would be planting ideas in their heads that might not otherwise be there. Instead, develop a short set of questions that you think would allow you to determine whether an adult is currently experiencing a period of midlife questioning or is in one of Levinson's structure-building periods, when such questioning is likely to be minimal. And when you have your questions designed, why not try them out on a parent or professor!

Ⓦ ON THE WEB

1. *Pretend Play*   Produced by the Children's Television Workshop, this site offers a short essay on children's imaginative play, stages in its development, and ways in which parents can help it flourish.
http://www.ctw.org/parents/weekly/0696/069602t1.htm

2. *National Education Association*   The site of the leading professional organization of teachers is a great place to keep up to date on trends in education. The site has a search engine so that you can find information on topics of personal interest, and it offers discussions of hot issues such as the wisdom of giving parents vouchers with

which to purchase their children's education and the controversy over whether schools should offer bilingual education or teach in English only.
http://www/nea.org/neaguide.html

KEY TERMS

need for achievement
  (n Ach)
attribution theory
locus of control
effectance motivation
functional play
mastery orientation
learned helplessness
  orientation
incremental view of ability
learning goal

entity view of ability
performance goal
informal curriculum
ability tracking
aptitude-treatment
  interaction (ATI)
inclusion
cooperative learning
  methods
life structure
mentor

midlife crisis
selective optimization with
  compensation
role conflict
role overload
spillover
substantive complexity
activity theory
disengagement theory

CHAPTER 16

Psychological Disorders Throughout the Life Span

WHAT MAKES DEVELOPMENT ABNORMAL?
Criteria for Diagnosing Psychological Disorders
Developmental Psychopathology

THE INFANT
Infantile Autism
Depression

THE CHILD
Attention-Deficit Hyperactivity Disorder
Depression
Nature, Nurture, and Childhood Disorders
Do Childhood Problems Persist?

THE ADOLESCENT
Is Adolescence Really a Period of Storm and Stress?
Eating Disorders
Drinking and Drug Use
Depression and Suicidal Behavior

THE ADULT
Stress and Coping
Depression
Aging and Dementia

APPLICATIONS: TREATING PSYCHOLOGICAL DISORDERS
Treating Children and Adolescents
Treating Elderly Adults

IS PSYCHOPATHOLOGY ADAPTIVE?

SUMMARY POINTS

FOOD FOR THOUGHT

ON THE WEB

KEY TERMS

*P*eggy, a 17-year-old female, was referred by her pediatrician to a child psychiatry clinic for evaluation of an eating disorder. She had lost 10 pounds in 2 months and her mother was concerned. . . . At the clinic she stated that she was not trying to lose weight, had begun to sleep poorly about 2 months ago unless she had several beers, and that she and friends "got trashed" on weekends. Her relationship with her parents was poor; she had attempted suicide a year previously with aspirin and was briefly hospitalized. The day before this evaluation she had taken a razor to school to try to cut her wrists, but it was taken away by a friend. She admitted being depressed and wanting to commit suicide and finally told of discovering that she was pregnant 4 months earlier. Her boyfriend wanted her to abort, she was ambivalent, and then she miscarried spontaneously about 2 months after her discovery. After that, "It didn't really matter how I felt about anything." (Committee on Adolescence, 1996, pp. 71–72)

*W*e do not all have as many problems as Peggy, but it is the rare human being who makes it through the life span without having at least some difficulty adapting to the challenges of living. Each phase of life has its own unique challenges, and some of us inevitably run into trouble mastering them. This chapter is about some of the ways in which human development can go awry. It looks at how psychopathology, or psychological dysfunction or disorder, can arise from and alter developmental processes. By applying knowledge of human development to the study of psychological disorders, we can understand them better. And by learning more about abnormal patterns of development, we can gain new perspectives on the forces that guide and channel—or block and distort—human development more generally.

WHAT MAKES DEVELOPMENT ABNORMAL?

It is the job of clinical psychologists, psychiatrists, and other mental health professionals to decide who has a psychological disorder and who does not. How do these professionals—indeed, how do we—define the line between normal and abnormal behavior?

Criteria for Diagnosing Psychological Disorders

Three broad criteria are often applied in defining and diagnosing psychological disorders:

1. *Statistical deviance: Does the person's behavior fall outside the normal range of behavior?* By this criterion, a mild case of the "blahs" or "blues" would not be diagnosed as clinical depression because it is so statistically common, but a more enduring, severe, and persistent case might be.

2. *Maladaptiveness: Does the person's behavior interfere with personal and social adaptation or pose a danger to self or others?* Psychological disorders disrupt functioning and create problems for the individual and/or other people.

3. *Personal distress: Does the behavior cause personal anguish or discomfort?* Many psychological disorders involve a good deal of personal suffering and are of concern for that reason alone.

Although these guidelines provide a start at defining abnormal behavior, they are not very specific. We must ask *which* forms of statistical deviation, *which* failures of adaptation, or *which* kinds of personal distress are significant—and *in what contexts*. To define psychological disorder more precisely, we must start by applying more specific standards of behavior—standards that will differ depending on the individual's sociocultural context and age.

Considering Social Norms

Behaviors are normal or abnormal only within some social context. **Social norms** are the expectations about how to behave that prevail in a particular social context, whether it is a culture, subculture, or everyday setting. Thus, hearing the "spirits" speak or seeing visions is defined as abnormal in the mainstream culture of North America, but among the Plains Indians these "symptoms" have been defined as valued skills (Wrightsman, Sigelman, & Sanford, 1979). Similarly, a child's screaming and shouting may be viewed as quite appropriate on the playground but may raise eyebrows if it occurs at a funeral. Definitions of abnormal behavior vary from culture to culture, from subculture to subculture, and from historical period to historical period. In a very real sense, then, abnormality is in the eye of a particular group of beholders.

This becomes clear when we look at how parents in different cultures judge whether child behaviors such as whining or arguing, being fearful or being disobedient, are problems. In one study, John Weisz, Marian Sigman, and their colleagues (1993) compared rates of problem behavior among Embu children in Kenya, Thai children in Thailand, and African-American and white children in the United States, as reported by their parents. Both Embu and Thai parents strongly socialize children to be obedient and self-controlled and are far less tolerant than American parents of rowdy, aggressive behavior. As it turns out, the contrasts between reports of child behavior problems by Embu and American parents were especially sharp (Thai parents fell in between). Embu parents

Childhood as a psychological disorder

What might happen if we failed to take developmental norms into account in defining what is normal and what is not? With tongue in cheek, Jordan Smoller (1986) throws developmental norms out the window and shows us that we might well view *childhood* as a disorder if we judged children entirely by the yardsticks we use to evaluate adult behavior. How do we know when someone is suffering from the disorder called "childhood"? Says Smoller, we look for the following defining features: congenital onset (one is usually born with the condition), dwarfism (unusually short stature), emotional lability and immaturity (a criterion that leads to the misdiagnosis of many adults as children), knowledge deficits (for example, gross ignorance of poli-

tics), and legume anorexia (a refusal to eat vegetables).

The seriousness of "childhood" and the difficulties psychologists face in treating it are illustrated by the case of Billy:

Billy J., age 8, was brought to treatment by his parents. Billy's affliction was painfully obvious. He stood only 4'3" high and weighed a scant 70 pounds, despite the fact that he ate voraciously. Billy presented a variety of troubling symptoms. His voice was noticeably high for a man. He displayed legume anorexia and, according to his parents, often refused to bathe. His intellectual functioning was also below normal—he had little general knowl-

edge and could barely write a structured sentence. Social skills were also deficient. He often spoke inappropriately and exhibited "whining behavior." His sexual experience was non-existent. Indeed, Billy considered women "icky." . . . After years of painstaking treatment, Billy improved gradually. At age 11, his height and weight have increased, his social skills are broader, and he is now functional enough to hold down a paper route. (Smoller, 1986, p. 9)

Enough said: We simply cannot define abnormal behavior at any point in the life span without knowing what is normal at that same age.

were more likely than American parents to claim that their children displayed symptoms of inner distress such as fearful behavior, excessive guilt, and somatic symptoms such as stomachaches. Meanwhile, American parents (white parents more than black) were more likely than Embu parents to claim that their children displayed rowdy symptoms such as arguing, disobeying, and acting cruelly.

By strictly forbidding aggression and disobedience, Embu parents may socialize their children to bottle up negative feelings and to become anxious and distressed rather than to express their frustrations by throwing temper tantrums or slugging their brothers and sisters. Meanwhile, more permissive American parents may end up with unruly children because they tolerate unruly behavior. As Weisz and his colleagues (1993) note, however, there are a number of other possible reasons for cultural differences in rates of child psychopathology. Genetic differences between cultural groups could contribute, or Embu parents may be more sensitive than American parents to the problems of quiet children experiencing inner distress. The living conditions a group experiences may also influence rates of childhood problems. Embu children may have had a large number of somatic symptoms (aches, pains, vomiting, and the like) because they were suffering from malnutrition and disease. It is clear, then, that professionals who assess and treat individuals with problems must understand problem behavior in its cultural context. Abnormal development, like nor-

mal development, is shaped by the broader sociocultural context in which it occurs and must be interpreted in that context.

Considering Age Norms

In addition—and this point is particularly important from a life-span developmental perspective—abnormal behavior must be defined in relation to **age norms,** or societal expectations about what behavior is appropriate or normal at various ages. The 4-year-old boy who frequently cries, acts impulsively, wets his bed, and talks to his imaginary friend may be perceived as—and may be—perfectly normal. The 40-year-old who does the same things needs serious help!

We simply cannot define abnormal behavior and development without having a solid grasp of *normal* behavior and development. Box 16.1 reinforces this point.

Specific Diagnostic Criteria

Psychologists and psychiatrists who diagnose and treat psychological disorders need more specific diagnostic criteria than we have outlined thus far. They find them in the *Diagnostic and Statistical Manual of Mental Disorders,* published by the American Psychiatric Association. The fourth edition of this manual, published in 1994 and known as *DSM-IV,* spells out defining features and symptoms for the whole range of psychological disorders. *DSM-IV* can be faulted for emphasizing observable symptoms of disorder rather than underlying causes and on other grounds as well, but it is the product of a major effort to review research and analyze data on psychological disorders and is the most widely used diagnostic system (see Clark, Watson, & Reynolds, 1995).

Because we will be looking closely at depression in this chapter, we will use it here as an example of how *DSM-IV* defines disorders. Depression is actually a family of several affective or mood disorders, some relatively mild and some severe. One of the most important is **major depressive disorder,** which is defined in *DSM-IV* as at least one episode of feeling profoundly depressed, sad, and hopeless, and/or losing interest in and the ability to derive pleasure from almost all activities, for at least two weeks (American Psychiatric Association, 1994). More specifically, a major depressive episode cannot be diagnosed unless the individual experiences at least five of the following symptoms, including one or the other of the first two, persistently during a two-week period:

1. Depressed mood (or irritable mood in children and adolescents) nearly every day
2. Greatly decreased interest or pleasure in usual activities
3. Significant weight loss or weight gain (or in children, failure to make expected weight gains)
4. Insomnia or too much sleeping
5. Psychomotor agitation or sluggishness/slowing of behavior
6. Fatigue and loss of energy
7. Feelings of worthlessness or extreme guilt
8. Decreased ability to concentrate or indecisiveness
9. Recurring thoughts of death, suicidal ideas, or a suicide attempt

By these criteria, a man suffering from major depression might, for example, feel extremely discouraged; no longer seem to care about his job or even about sexual relations with his wife; lose weight or have difficulty sleeping; speak and move very slowly, as though lacking the energy to perform even the simplest actions; have trouble getting his work done; dwell on how guilty he feels about his many failings; and even begin to think he would be better off dead. Major depressive disorder would *not* be diagnosed if this young man were merely a little "down," if his symptoms were directly due to drug abuse or a medical condition, or if he were going through the normal grieving process after the death of a loved one. Many more people experience depressive *symptoms* than qualify as having a clinically defined depressive *disorder*.

DSM-IV notes cultural and developmental considerations that should be taken into account in making a diagnosis of major depressive disorder. For example, it indicates that Asians who are depressed tend to complain of bodily ailments such as tiredness rather than talking about their psychological symptoms (American Psychiatric Association, 1994). And while *DSM-IV* takes the position that depression in a child is fundamentally similar to depression in an adult, it notes that depressed children often show their depression by being irritable rather than sad.

In sum, diagnosing a psychological disorder such as major depressive disorder involves consideration of the broad criteria of statistical deviance, maladaptiveness, and personal distress and also requires the application of specific diagnostic criteria such as those in *DSM-IV*. What's more, it is important to interpret symptoms in light of relevant social norms and age norms.

As we will see shortly, there are still many unanswered questions about whether the symptoms and significance of major depression—and other psychological disorders as well—change over the life span. Fortunately, there is now keen interest in exploring relationships between psychopathology and development over the life course.

Developmental Psychopathology

In recent years, psychologists have become increasingly aware of the need to adopt a developmental perspective on abnormal behavior (Rutter, 1996; Sroufe, 1997). As a result, a field called **developmental psychopathology,** has emerged. As defined by Alan Sroufe and Michael Rutter (1984), developmental psychopathology is the study of the origins and course of maladaptive behavior. Developmental psychopathologists are well aware of the need to evaluate abnormal behavior in relation to normal development and to attempt to understand how the individual's level of development influences what disorders he or she is likely to display and how those problems are likely to be manifested. They are also interested in finding out how psychological disorders evolve and how they affect later development.

Psychopathology as Development, Not Disease

Some developmental psychopathologists fault *DSM-IV* and similar diagnostic systems for being rooted in a medical or disease model of psychopathology that views psychological problems as diseaselike entities that people either have or do not have. Alan Sroufe (1997) argues that psychopathology is better seen as development than as disease; it is a pattern of adaptation that unfolds over time. And psychological disorders are not defects that lie within the person but the products of complex transactions between person and environment over time.

Figure 16.1 illustrates this model. It shows progressive branchings that lead development on an optimal or less optimal course: Some individuals stay on a route to competence and good adjustment all along; some start out poorly but get back on a more adaptive

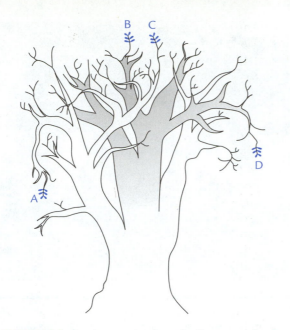

FIGURE 16.1 *Developmental pathways leading to normal and abnormal outcomes. Some individuals start out on a maladaptive course and deviate even further from developmental norms as they get older (route A); others stay on a route to competence and good adjustment all along (B); some start out poorly but get back on a more adaptive course later (C); and still others start off well but deviate later in life (D).*
(Adapted from Sroufe, 1997)

course later; others start off well but deviate later; and still others start on a maladaptive course and deviate further and further from developmental norms as they get older. Different pathways can lead to the same outcome; any particular pathway can lead in multiple directions. Change is possible at many points, and the lines between normal and abnormal development become blurred. A developmental pathways model of this sort may seem complex, but it fits the facts of development.

Developmental Issues

As they attempt to understand developmental pathways associated with adaptive or maladaptive functioning, developmental psychopathologists raise the same developmental issues that have concerned us throughout this book—most notably, the nature/nurture issue and the issue of continuity and discontinuity in development (see Chapter 2). Addressing the nature/nurture issue requires asking important questions such as these:

◆ How do biological, psychological, and social factors interact to give rise to psychological disorders?

◆ Why do some children who grow up in problem-ridden families develop psychological disorders while others in similar circumstances seem to be invulnerable to the stresses they experience?

Questions about the continuity or discontinuity of maladaptive behavior include these:

◆ Are most childhood problems passing disturbances that have no bearing on adult adjustment, or does poor functioning in childhood predict poor functioning later in life?

◆ How do expressions of psychopathology change as the developmental status of the individual changes?

Questions about nature and nurture and continuity and discontinuity are important to answer if we want to gain a more complete understanding of the development of psychological disorders, and we address them in this chapter. Specifically, this chapter introduces a small sampling of developmental problems associated with each phase of the life span (for example, infantile autism to illustrate disorders of infancy, anorexia nervosa to illustrate disorders of adolescence, and Alzheimer's disease to illustrate disorders of old age). In addition, we examine research on depression in *every* developmental period in order to see whether this widespread disorder is indeed the same phenomenon at any age or whether its symptoms and significance change over the life span. Finally, we will see that the successful treatment of psychological disorders requires sensitivity to developmental issues.

THE INFANT

Adults worry about infants who do not eat properly, who cry endlessly, or who seem overly withdrawn and timid. However, because infant development is strongly channeled by biological maturation, very few infants develop severe psychological problems. Yet, psychopathology does exist in infancy, and its effects can be tragic.

Infantile Autism

Infantile autism, or autistic disorder, first identified and described by Leo Kanner in 1943, is a severe disorder that is generally evident starting in infancy and is characterized by impaired social interaction, deviant communication development, and repetitive, stereotyped behavior (American Psychiatric Association, 1994). It is an example of a "pervasive developmental disorder," a condition associated with abnormalities in several areas of development. By definition, autistic children show their abnormal functioning before the age of 3 and therefore can be distinguished from severely disordered children who at first develop normally and only later become disturbed. Fortunately, autism is rare, affecting 2 to 5 of every 10,000 children and about four boys for every girl (American Psychiatric Association, 1994).

To appreciate how very different the autistic child is from the normally developing one, picture the typical infant that we have described in this book: a very social being who responds to others and forms close attachments starting at 6 or 7 months of age, a linguistic being who babbles and later uses one- and two-word sentences to converse, and a curious being who is fascinated by new objects and experiences. Now consider the three defining features of infantile autism highlighted in *DSM-IV* (American Psychiatric Association, 1994; Bristol et al., 1996):

1. *Deviant social development.* Autistic children seem unable to form normal social relationships or to respond appropriately to social cues; they live in a world of their own. They are far less likely than other infants to make eye contact, jointly attend to something with a social partner, seek other people for comfort, snuggle when held, and make friends. In stark contrast to normal children, autistic children seem to find social contact aversive rather than pleasurable. They also have difficulty reading others' emotions or responding with empathy when others are distressed. Although they can form attachments to their parents, they often display what in Chapter 13 was called a disorganized/disoriented pattern of attachment (Capps, Sigman, & Mundy, 1994).

2. *Deviant language and communicative skills.* Many autistic children are mute, whereas others acquire limited language skills but cannot really converse with their companions. Among the unusual features of the autistic child's speech are a very flat, robotlike tone; pronoun reversals (for example, the use of "you" to refer to the self); and **echolalia** (a parroting back of what someone else says). Even those autistic children who have mastered basic sentence structure or grammar have difficulty using language in true give-and-take social exchanges.

3. *Repetitive, stereotyped behavior.* Autistic children have an obsessive need for sameness and can become terribly upset by novelty or change. They engage in stereotyped behaviors such as rocking, flapping their hands in front of their faces, or spinning toys, as though they were seeking sensory stimulation. Yet they also become strongly attached to particular objects and highly distressed when their physical environment is altered (for example, when a chair in the living room is moved a few feet). Very possibly, it is the unpredictability and changeability of human beings that make interacting with them so unpleasant for autistic children.

The autistic child's development is clearly *deviant* or distorted rather than merely delayed (Rutter & Schopler, 1987). Many people believe that autistic

Many individuals with infantile autism continue to function poorly as adolescents and adults, but some improve with age. One "improver," Jerry, described his childhood as a reign of "confusion and terror" in which "nothing seemed constant; everything was unpredictable and strange." (Bemporad, 1979, p. 192)

individuals are exceptionally intelligent. Some do indeed have normal IQs and some show special talents such as the ability to quickly calculate days of the week corresponding to dates on the calendar (see Chapter 9's discussion of *savant syndrome*). However, about three out of four autistic children are mentally retarded (Bailey et al., 1996); they display both the deviant behaviors associated with autism and the developmental delays associated with mental retardation. The condition is indeed "pervasive," for it severely impairs cognitive, social, and emotional development. Yet some researchers now believe that many of the problems autistic children display may be rooted in a cognitive deficit.

Suspected Causes

Most autistic children display a lack of understanding of mental states such as feelings, desires, beliefs, and intentions and of their role in human behavior—a lack of what was characterized in Chapter 12 as a *theory of mind* (see Frith, 1989; Holroyd & Baron-Cohen, 1993; Leslie, 1992). They do not appreciate, for example, that someone who believes she left her running shoes in the hall closet will look there for them and will be surprised if they are not there. Lacking a theory of mind, autistic children simply cannot conceive of someone's having a false belief that contradicts the facts of a situation. Indeed, they do not seem to understand that people have beliefs, false or otherwise.

For a while, many researchers believed that lack of a theory of mind was *the* source of the social, emotional, and communicative problems autistic children display. Now researchers are not so sure: They note that autistic children are not so deficient on theory-of-mind tasks if they have good verbal ability (Yirmiya et al., 1996), and they point to other cognitive deficits that may help explain autism (Charman, 1997; Happé, 1994). Some believe that these children have a broad deficiency in their ability to engage in symbolic, or representational, thought. They note that autistic children are far behind other children in their ability to engage in symbolic or pretend play because they cannot seem to mentally represent pretend events involving pretend objects (Yirmiya & Sigman, 1991) and also have difficulty imitating other people, another skill that requires mental representation (Smith & Bryson, 1994). Other researchers think that the problem is rooted in a deficit in executive functions (planning and organizational functions of the brain), particularly the ability to integrate pieces of information into meaningful wholes (Charman, 1997; Happé, 1994). Whether lack of a theory of mind, a deficiency in symbolic thinking, poor executive or integrative abilities, or some other cognitive impairment will prove to be at the heart of the problems autistic children display is unclear, but this disorder clearly involves a number of severe cognitive impairments.

What causes these impairments? We are not yet sure (Bailey, Phillips, & Rutter, 1996). Early theorists suggested that rigid and cold parenting caused autism, but this harmful myth has long been put to rest (Achenbach, 1982; Donenberg & Baker, 1993). It is now understood that parents and children influence each other and that interacting with an autistic child could easily cause parents to be tense and frustrated. The fact that autism is such a severe disorder present so early in life strongly suggests that it has an organic or physical basis. Indeed, many autistic children, though not all, display neurological abnormalities, though the abnormalities are varied, and up to a third of them develop epilepsy (Bailey et al., 1996; Hooper & Tramontana, 1997). It is not clear which neurological problems are most central to autism or how they arise.

Genes contribute to autism in ways we do not yet understand (LeCouteur et al., 1996). One research team found that, if one identical twin was autistic, the other was autistic in 91% of the twin pairs studied; the concordance rate for fraternal twin pairs was 0% (Steffenburg et al., 1989). Moreover, when one identical twin is autistic but the other is not, the nonautistic twin is highly likely to have deficits in language and social development (Le Couteur et al., 1996). However, the very fact that one identical twin can be autistic when the other is not indicates that early environmental influences must also contribute to at least some cases of the disorder. A few cases have been traced to exposure to rubella or other infections dur-

ing the prenatal period or to extreme environmental deprivation. Complications during pregnancy or delivery were once believed to play a role, but these complications are now believed to reflect rather than cause abnormal development (Bristol et al., 1996). Instead, most cases appear to have one or another of several genetic mechanisms behind them (Bailey et al., 1996). It now seems very unlikely that one, clear-cut biological defect will be found that can explain all cases of autism; instead, this is a complex syndrome associated with many neurological and behavioral problems (Yeung-Courchesne & Courchesne, 1997).

Developmental Outcomes

What becomes of autistic children as they get older? The long-term outcome has usually been poor, undoubtedly because autism is such a pervasive and severe disorder and because it is so often accompanied by mental retardation. Many autistic individuals improve over the years, but most are autistic for life and continue to depend on others for help throughout their lives (Bristol et al., 1996; Piven et al., 1996). Positive outcomes are most likely among those who have normal IQ scores and who can communicate using speech before they are 6 years old (Gillberg & Steffenburg, 1987).

Can treatment help autistic children overcome their problems? Researchers continue to search for drugs that will correct the suspected brain dysfunctions of these children, but they are a long way from discovering a "magic pill." Some autistic children are given drugs to control behavior problems such as hyperactivity or obsessive-compulsive behavior, but these drugs do nothing to cure autism (Campbell et al., 1996).

At present, the main treatment approach is intensive behavioral training, ideally beginning early in life (Campbell et al., 1996). O. Ivar Lovaas and his colleagues pioneered the use of reinforcement principles to shape social and language skills in autistic children and have had startling success (Smith & Lovaas, 1998). In one study, Lovaas (1987) compared two groups of autistic children treated at UCLA. Nineteen children received intensive treatment—more than 40 hours a week of one-on-one treatment for two or more years during their preschool years. Trained student therapists worked with these children using reinforcement principles to reduce their aggressive and self-stimulatory behavior and to teach them developmentally appropriate skills such as how to imitate others, play with toys and with peers, use language, and master academic concepts. Moreover, parents were taught to use the same behavioral techniques at home, and these children were mainstreamed into preschools that served normal children. The children who received this intensive treatment were compared with similarly disturbed children who, because of staff shortages or transportation problems, received a similar treatment program but were exposed to it for only 10 or fewer hours a week.

In the intensively trained group, all but two children scored in the mentally retarded range on tests of intellectual functioning at the start. Yet by age 6 or 7, their IQ scores averaged 83—about 30 points higher than the average in the control group. Moreover, 9 of the 19 not only had average or above-average IQ scores at follow-up but had been mainstreamed into regular first-grade classes and were adapting well. At age 13, 8 of the 19 treated students were still within the normal range of both IQ and school adjustment (Lovaas, Smith, & McEachin, 1989). In contrast, children in the comparison group displayed the usual intellectual deficits of autism, and most attended special classes for autistic and retarded children. Other evidence reinforces the conclusion that some autistic children, especially those who are young and not severely retarded, show a good deal of plasticity and potential if they receive intensive cognitive and behavioral training and comprehensive family services starting early in life (Campbell et al., 1996).

In sum, infantile autism is one of the most vivid examples we have of human development gone awry. The profound problems that autistic children display in their social interactions, language development, and responses to the physical environment make it clear that their development is deviant and not merely delayed. Moreover, most of them remain disordered, at least to some extent, throughout their lives. Yet we can be encouraged by recent reports of the long-term benefits of early behavioral intervention, and we can also hope that researchers will eventually pinpoint the brain dysfunctions and cognitive impairments responsible for this disorder and develop effective treatments to correct them.

Depression

Does it seem possible that an infant could experience major depressive disorder as defined by clinicians? Infants are surely not capable of the negative cognitions that are common among depressed adults—the low self-esteem, guilt, worthlessness, hopelessness, and so on (Garber, 1984). After all, they have not yet acquired the capacity for symbolic thought that would allow them to reflect on their experience. Yet infants *can* exhibit some of the behavioral symptoms (loss of interest in activities, psychomotor slowing) and **somatic symptoms** (bodily symptoms such as loss of appetite and disruption of normal sleep patterns) of depression. Researchers are still debating whether true depressive disorders can occur in infancy, but it is clear that babies can and do experience *depressionlike* states and symptoms (Cytryn & McKnew, 1996).

Depressive symptoms are most likely to be observed in infants who lack a secure attachment relationship or who experience a disruption of their all-important emotional bonds (Cytryn & McKnew, 1996). Infants permanently separated from their mothers between 6 and 12 months of age are likely to become sad, weepy, listless, unresponsive, and withdrawn and to show delays in virtually all aspects of their development (Spitz, 1946). Abused and neglected infants sometimes show similar symptoms (Zeanah, Boris, & Scheeringa, 1997). And infants whose mothers are depressed and therefore emotionally unresponsive to them are also at risk. They begin to adopt an interaction style that resembles that of their depressed caregivers; they vocalize very little and look sad, even when interacting with women other than their mothers, and they begin to show developmental delays by the age of 1 (Field, 1995).

Whether because of genes, learning, or—most likely—both, the children of depressed parents are at increased risk of becoming clinically depressed themselves later in life and developing other psychological disorders as well (Gotlib & Hammen, 1992; Zeanah, Boris, & Scheeringa, 1997). Moreover, these children are likely to interact with their own children in a negative manner, increasing the chances that depression will be passed on to still another generation (Whitbeck et al., 1992). Interventions designed to help depressed mothers appreciate and interact more sensitively with their babies may help to prevent these outcomes, though (Gelfand et al., 1996).

Some infants who are neglected, abused, separated from attachment figures, or otherwise raised in a stressful or unaffectionate manner display a related, and more life-threatening, problem called **failure to thrive.** These youngsters fail to grow normally, lose weight, and become seriously underweight for their age (Bauchner, 1996). They show many of the symptoms of depression, as well as delays in their cognitive and social development and bizarre behaviors such as drinking from toilets (Bauchner, 1996; Green, 1986). In some cases an organic or biological cause, such as an illness or heart defect, can be found, but most cases are said to represent "nonorganic" failure to thrive because the causes seem to be emotional rather than physical.

Lytt Gardner (1972) identified several cases of the failure-to-thrive syndrome, one of which involved twins—a boy and a girl—who grew normally for the first 4 months of life. Soon afterward, their father lost his job, their mother became pregnant with an unwanted baby, and the parents blamed each other for the family's problems. When the father moved out, the mother focused her resentment on her infant son. She fed him and tended to his physical care but became emotionally unresponsive to him. Although his sister continued to grow normally, the boy twin at 13 months of age was about the size of an average 7-month-old.

Like this boy's mother, the mothers of most infants with nonorganic failure to thrive tend to be stressed, depressed, and socially isolated women whose own mothers were emotionally unresponsive or even abusive to them (Gorman, Leifer, & Grossman, 1993). These women tend to neglect their babies, interact in insensitive ways with them, and express tension and anger rather than affection in their interactions (Black et al., 1994; Hutcheson, Black, & Starr, 1993). Almost half of their babies show a disorganized/disoriented pattern of attachment (Ward, Kessler, & Altman, 1993).

These babies gain weight and overcome their depressionlike emotional symptoms almost immediately when they are removed from their homes (Bauchner, 1996). They tend to relapse if they are returned to parents who have not been helped to become more emotionally responsive. Some of these children then remain smaller than normal and display long-term social and intellectual deficits as well (Bauchner, 1996; Heffer & Kelley, 1994).

In sum, even babies can display many of the symptoms of depression, although depression in an infant is not the same as depression in an adult. Most notably, young infants do not have the cognitive capacity to think depressive thoughts but can show many of the behavioral and somatic symptoms of "adult" depression. They can also undergo serious disruptions of their psychological development and fail to thrive if they experience long-term or permanent separation from their attachment figures or are brought up by depressed, unresponsive, or rejecting caregivers.

THE CHILD

Many children experience developmental problems of one sort or another—fears, recurring stomachaches, temper tantrums, and so on. A much smaller proportion are officially diagnosed as having one of the psychological disorders that typically begin in infancy, childhood, or adolescence—or as having a psychological disorder (such as major depressive disorder) that can occur at any age. Table 16.1 lists major childhood disorders as categorized in *DSM-IV*.

Many developmental problems can also be placed in either of two broad categories that reflect whether the child's behavior is out of control or overly inhibited (Achenbach & Edelbrock, 1978). When children have **externalizing problems,** or *undercontrolled disorders,* they "act out" in ways that disturb other people and place them in conflict with social expectations; they may be aggressive, disobedient, difficult to con-

trol, or disruptive. If their problems are severe, they may be diagnosed as having a conduct disorder or as hyperactive. **Internalizing problems,** or *overcontrolled disorders,* involve inner distress; they are more disruptive to the child than to other people and include anxiety disorders (such as persistent worrying about separation from loved ones), phobias, severe shyness and withdrawal, and depression. Externalizing behaviors decrease with age from 6 to 17, whereas internalizing difficulties increase (Crijnen, Achenbach, & Verhulst, 1997). Externalizing problems are more common among boys, whereas internalizing problems are more prevalent among girls, and this is true across cultures (Crijnen et al., 1997). To give you a feel for these two categories of childhood disorder, we will now look at one problem of externalization or undercontrol—hyperactivity—and one problem of internalization or overcontrol—depression.

Attention-Deficit Hyperactivity Disorder

Dusty, a blond 7-year-old, started his day at 5 A.M. with a fit of screaming and kicking; headed for breakfast, grabbed a box of Kix cereal, and began scattering corn puffs around the kitchen; turned to peeling the covering off the TV stand; and noticed the cereal again and began to stomp corn puffs. His mother asked him to get the broom and dustpan and clean up the mess, but the next time she looked he was taking apart the dustpan piece by piece. Soon he was unraveling rolls of toilet paper throughout the house as his exhausted mother looked on (Wallis, 1994). Perhaps you can appreciate why the "undercontrolled" behavior of some hyperactive children is disturbing to other people!

When it was first identified, hyperactivity was defined principally as a problem of excess motor activity, and the term was used to describe children who could not seem to sit still and were continually on the go. Now hyperactivity is viewed as first and foremost a problem of *attention*. According to *DSM-IV* criteria, a child has **attention-deficit/hyperactivity disorder (ADHD)** if some combination of three symptoms are present (and see Dulcan et al., 1997):

1. *Inattention* (for example, the child does not seem to listen, is easily distracted, and does not stick to activities or finish tasks)
2. *Impulsivity* (for example, the child acts before thinking and cannot inhibit an urge to blurt something out in class or have a turn in a group activity)
3. *Hyperactivity* (perpetual fidgeting, finger tapping, chattering, and restlessness)

Around 4% of school-age children are diagnosable as ADHD, and there are at least four ADHD boys for

TABLE 16.1

Some psychological disorders usually first diagnosed in infancy, childhood, or adolescence	

DSM Category	Major Examples
Mental retardation	Subaverage general intellectual functioning
Learning disorders	Reading, math, and writing disorders
Motor skill disorder	Developmental coordination disorder (extreme clumsiness, incoordination)
Communication disorders	Expressive language disorder; stuttering
Pervasive developmental disorders	Autism and similarly severe conditions
Attention-deficit and disruptive behavior disorders	Attention-deficit/hyperactivity disorder; conduct disorders (persistent antisocial behavior); oppositional defiant disorder
Feeding and eating disorders	Pica (eating nonnutritive substances such as paint or sand)
Tic disorders	Tourette's disorder (involuntary grimaces, grunts, foul language)
Elimination disorders	Enuresis (inappropriate urination); encopresis (inappropriate defecation)

SOURCE: Based on *DSM-IV*, American Psychiatric Association, 1994

every ADHD girl (American Psychiatric Association, 1994). Some critics believe that ADHD is overdiagnosed in the United States, and it is indeed more common here than in some countries; but ADHD is reported throughout the world, and rates of it are consistently higher for boys than for girls (Luk, 1996).

Some ADHD children are mainly inattentive rather than hyperactive and impulsive; they are not as disruptive as Dusty, but they, like other ADHD children, often have difficulty in school. Those ADHD children who are hyperactive and impulsive rather than merely inattentive are especially likely to irritate adults and become locked in coercive power struggles with their parents, interactions that only aggravate their problems (Barkley et al., 1991; Buhrmester et al., 1992). Because their behavior is so disruptive, they are also rejected by peers (Whalen et al., 1989). In short, ADHD, like autism, affects cognitive, social, and emotional development in a variety of ways.

Many children with ADHD also have diagnosable learning disabilities; many, because of aggressive, antisocial behavior, also qualify as having conduct disorders; and some suffer from depression or anxiety disorders (Biederman et al., 1996; Silver, 1992). This co-occurrence of two or more conditions in the same individual is called **comorbidity** and is very common; many troubled individuals of all ages, like Peggy at the start of the chapter, have multiple psychiatric diagnoses rather than just one (Clark et al., 1995). Comorbidity complicates the task of understanding the causes and consequences of any particular psychological disorder.

Developmental Course

ADHD expresses itself in somewhat different ways at different ages. The condition often reveals itself first in infancy. Many parents of ADHD children report that their youngsters were very active, had difficult temperaments, or had irregular feeding and sleeping patterns as infants (Crook, 1980; Stewart et al., 1966). In the preschool years, perpetual and seemingly haphazard motor activity is the most noticeable sign of this disorder. Since most young children are energetic and have short attention spans, a child's attention deficits, impulsivity, and hyperactivity must be developmentally inappropriate for a diagnosis of attention-deficit/hyperactivity disorder to be justified (American Psychiatric Association, 1994). Without considering developmental norms, we might well mistake most average 3- and 4-year-olds for hyperactive children! Finally by the grade school years, overactive behavior is less of a problem, but ADHD children are fidgety, restless, and inattentive to schoolwork (American Psychiatric Association, 1994).

What becomes of hyperactive children later in life? It used to be thought that hyperactive children outgrew their problems. Most do outgrow their overactive behavior, and rates of ADHD do decrease with age (Hill & Schoener, 1996). However, many ADHD children continue to have difficulty concentrating and display adjustment difficulties throughout the life span (Fischer et al., 1990; Wender, 1995). About 50% continue to have problems as adolescents (Silver, 1992), and about one-third continue to have problems as adults, sometimes serious ones (Wender, 1995). ADHD adolescents may have difficulty attending to their academic work and may continue to behave impulsively; thus they often perform poorly in school or drop out altogether, and they may commit reckless delinquent acts without thinking about the consequences (Fischer et al., 1990; Wallander & Hubert, 1985). The picture is more positive by early adulthood; most ADHD individuals seem to adjust better to the workplace than they did to school (Wallander & Hubert, 1985). Yet they may find desk jobs hard to tolerate and may continue to get in trouble because they cannot concentrate, make impulsive decisions, and procrastinate (Wender, 1995). Young adults who were diagnosed as hyperactive during childhood are also likely to be involved in more than their share of car accidents and law-breaking, to abuse alcohol and drugs, and to have emotional problems (Mannuzza et al., 1993; Weiss & Hechtman, 1993). Or at least this is true of ADHD children who also have conduct disorders and engage in antisocial behavior as children. Their later adjustment tends to be especially poor compared to that of the relatively invisible ADHD children whose main problem is inattention (Greene et al., 1997; Lynskey & Fergusson, 1995).

Suspected Causes

What causes this disorder? Researchers agree that ADHD has a neurological basis, but they have had difficulty pinpointing it (Hooper & Tramontana, 1997). Initially it was thought that hyperactive children had suffered from "minimal brain damage." The only problem was that researchers could find no evidence of brain damage in most ADHD children, nor could they establish that most children who suffer brain damage become hyperactive (Achenbach, 1982). Researchers are still convinced that the brains of ADHD children process stimulation differently than the brains of other children, but they are now looking for subtle differences in brain chemistry rather than for physical brain damage. Much of their attention is now focused on the possibility that the frontal lobes of individuals with ADHD do not function properly to allow them to plan and control their behavior and inhibit responses when they must (Barkley, 1997; Seidman et al., 1997). Several abnormalities in neurotransmitters may be involved, and very possibly different individuals have different biochemical abnormalities (Wender, 1995).

Similarly, nature and nurture may contribute differently to the origins of these neurological abnormalities in different cases (Cantwell, 1996). We know that some individuals are genetically predisposed to

develop ADHD; one identical twin is highly likely to have it if the other does (Levy et al., 1997; Wender, 1995). Environmental factors also enter in, however. For example, prenatal exposure to the disease rubella, to alcohol, and to nicotine appear to contribute to some cases of ADHD (Deutsch & Kinsbourne, 1990; Milberger et al., 1996; Silver, 1992). An intrusive, highly controlling parenting style may also contribute to, or at least aggravate, the problem in some cases, for when parents are highly intrusive, infants and young children may not learn to regulate their own emotions and behavior (Jacobvitz & Sroufe, 1987; Sroufe, 1997). Family risk factors such as marital conflict and socioeconomic disadvantage may also contribute (Biederman et al., 1995). It has also been proposed that hyperactivity is linked to food allergies and high sugar intake. In Box 16.2, though, we see that these particular theories have not been well supported by research. In sum, ADHD remains a mystery, but it most likely has a number of both genetic and environmental causes and contributors.

Treatment

What can be done to help hyperactive children? Many of them are given stimulant drugs such as methylphenidate (Ritalin); in fact, Dusty's behavior, described earlier, occurred on a day when his doctors asked that he not be given his usual dose! Stimulants help about 70% of the ADHD children for whom they are prescribed (Cantwell, 1996). Although it may seem odd to give overactive children drugs that increase their heart rates and energy levels, stimulants also make ADHD children better able to focus their attention and less distractible and disruptive (Gillberg et al., 1997). These drugs can improve academic performance (Pelham et al., 1993), help bring aggressive behavior under control (Hinshaw, 1991), and positively affect classmates' views of ADHD children (Whalen et al., 1989). Moreover, stimulants seem to work effectively with all age groups; like it or not, they are now given to many preschool children, and they also help ADHD adults who continue to be distractible and impulsive (Musten et al., 1997; Wilens & Biederman, 1992). Some ADHD individuals are prescribed antidepressants as well (Dulcan et al., 1997).

Why, then, does controversy surround the use of stimulants with ADHD children? Some critics feel that these drugs are prescribed to too many children, including some who are not ADHD; have undesirable side effects; and do not really correct the central problems ADHD individuals face. Some children taking stimulants do experience loss of appetite, difficulty sleeping, and stomachaches or headaches, but these side effects are usually mild (Silver, 1992). Long-term stimulant use can also slow physical growth temporarily, but affected individuals ultimately attain normal heights (Spencer et al., 1996).

BOX 16.2

Clearing away the misconceptions about hyperactivity

We do not fully understand what causes attention-deficit/hyperactivity disorder, but researchers are at least weeding out some incorrect ideas about this condition. One early hypothesis was that particular foods, food additives, and preservatives cause or at least aggravate hyperactivity. When Dr. Benjamin Feingold (1975) recommended placing hyperactive children on a diet free of chemical food additives, many parents soon became convinced that the diet achieved miracles. But might these parents have gotten good results only because they expected good results and therefore treated their children more positively? The way to find out is through controlled studies in which children and the adults who are evaluating them do not know whether they are getting the Feingold diet or a diet containing food additives. Such studies clearly indicate that food additives have little apparent effect on the vast majority of ADHD children (Gross et al., 1987; Harley et al., 1978).

What about sugar, though? Many parents believe that their hyperactive children immediately become worse after they eat sweets, and many teachers advise parents to cut their children's sugar intake to help control their hyperactivity (DiBattista & Shepherd, 1993). Again, the research simply fails to support this idea. For example, Richard Milich and William Pelham (1986) had hyperactive boys drink either sugary drinks or ones with the sugar substitute aspartame. Sugar seemed to have no negative effects on these boys' behavior or performance in learning situations. Milich and Pelham suggest an interesting explana-

"He does not have a discipline problem! He's just had a little too much sugar, that's all."

tion for the common observation that sugar makes ADHD children more hyperactive: Perhaps these children simply cannot reorganize their activity after the disruption of stopping to eat a snack—sugary or otherwise.

A very small percentage of ADHD children do seem to have allergic reactions to sugar, food additives, or certain foods, but the various "food theories" that have been offered cannot explain the vast majority of cases of ADHD (Silver, 1992). Many other misconceptions are likely to fall by the wayside before research leads us nearer to the truth—and to better ways of preventing and treating ADHD.

Critics also charge that stimulants do little more than temporarily improve functioning until their effects wear off at the end of the day (Schachar et al., 1997). As it turns out, ADHD individuals who took stimulants as children are often not much better off as adolescents or adults than those who did not (Hart et al., 1995; Wilens & Biederman, 1992). Because of such evidence, and because ADHD is a complex problem affecting all aspects of development, most experts have concluded that drugs should be pre-

scribed with caution and that drugs alone cannot solve all the difficulties faced by ADHD individuals and their families. ADHD children are likely to benefit most from multipronged treatments that involve (1) medication, (2) behavioral programs designed to teach them to stay focused on a task and to control their impulsiveness, and (3) parent training and counseling designed to help parents understand and manage the behavior of these often-difficult youngsters (Cantwell, 1996).

In sum, attention-deficit/hyperactivity disorder interferes with cognitive, social, and emotional development from the early years of life into the adult years. A difficult infant may become an uncontrollable and overactive preschooler, an inattentive grade school student, a low-achieving and delinquent adolescent, and even an impulsive and restless adult. True, many ADHD children do adapt well later in life, but perhaps even more will do so as we learn more about the causes of this disorder and develop treatments that achieve longer-lasting impacts.

Depression

As we saw earlier, the depressionlike symptoms displayed by deprived or traumatized infants probably do not qualify as major depressive disorder. When *can* children experience true clinical depression, then? For years many psychologists and psychiatrists, especially those influenced by psychoanalytic theory, argued that young children simply could not be depressed. Feelings of worthlessness, hopelessness, and self-blame were not believed to be possible until the child formed a strong superego, or internalized moral standards (Garber, 1984).

Finally it was appreciated that even very young children *could* become depressed, but then some researchers argued that childhood depression is qualitatively different from adult depression (Cytryn & McKnew, 1996). Children, it was said, display **masked depression,** or depression in the guise of symptoms such as aggression or anxiety, problems other than those we associate directly with depression (Quay et al., 1987). For example, a depressed child would not talk about being sad; instead, he or she might express depression indirectly by behaving aggressively or being very anxious.

We now know that young children can meet the very same criteria for major depressive disorder that are used in diagnosing adults—and as early as age 3 (Hammen & Compas, 1994; Kovacs, 1996). Depression in children is rarer than depression in adolescents and adults, but an estimated 2% of children have diagnosable depressive disorders (Gotlib & Hammen, 1992). Many youngsters who show the key symptoms of depression *do* have comorbid problems such as conduct disorder and anxiety disorder as well (Harrington, Rutter, & Fombonne, 1996). However, these symptoms of "masked depression" are now understood to be comorbid but distinct problems. They sometimes accompany depression, but they are not veiled symptoms of it and have different implications for development (Harrington et al., 1996).

Although the concept of masked depression in childhood is faulty, there is some truth to the idea that depression expresses itself somewhat differently in a young child than in an adult. Depressed preschool children are more likely to display the behavioral and somatic symptoms of depression (losing interest in activities, eating poorly, and so on) than to display cognitive symptoms (hopelessness, excessive guilt) or to talk about being depressed (American Psychiatric Association, 1994). Some become irritable, but others withdraw quietly to their rooms and cry and may not even be noticed (Cytryn & McKnew, 1996).

Even school-age children do not express their depression in precisely the ways that adults or adolescents do, although there are far more similarities than differences. Like preschoolers, they often show their depression more clearly in how they act than in what they say; some misbehave, have temper tantrums, or get into fights (Borchardt & Meller, 1996; Cytryn & McKnew, 1996). Later in elementary school, depressed children express more cognitive symptoms such as low self-esteem, hopelessness, and self-blame. For example, one 11-year-old said, "The devil is in me"; another claimed, "I'm a burden on the family" (Kosky, 1983, p. 459).

The message is clear, then: Parents and other adults need to become more aware that childhood is not always a happy, carefree time and that children *can* develop serious depressive disorders. If you are still not completely convinced that even very young children can suffer from severely depressed moods, consider evidence that children as young as age $2\frac{1}{2}$ or 3 are capable of attempting suicide (Rosenthal & Rosenthal, 1984). At the tender age of $2\frac{1}{2}$, for example, Elizabeth, reacting to her parents' divorce, a string of many different babysitters, and a depressed mother, ate a bottleful of aspirin the day her mother returned from a brief hospital stay. While pretending to feed her doll aspirin, Elizabeth said, "The baby is going to the hospital because she died today" (p. 522). At age 3, Jeffrey repeatedly hurled himself down a flight of stairs and banged his head on the floor; upset by the arrival of a new brother, he was heard to say, "Jeff is bad, and bad boys have to die" (Cytryn & McKnew, 1996, p. 72).

Other children have jumped from high places, run into traffic, and stabbed themselves, often in response to abuse, rejection, or neglect. One 8-year-old, after writing out her will, approached her father with a large rock and said in all seriousness, "Daddy, would you crush my head, please?" (Cytryn & McKnew, 1996, pp. 69–70). Suicide attempts in childhood are very rare, but the rates are climbing, and they may not tell the whole story because some apparent accidents may actually be suicide attempts (Cytryn & McKnew, 1996). Moreover, children who attempt suicide once often try again (Pfeffer et al., 1994). Again the moral is clear: Children's claims that they want to die should be taken seriously.

Do depressed children tend to have recurring bouts of depression, becoming depressed adolescents and adults? Most children do get through mild episodes of sadness. However, most children diagnosed as having major depression have recurring episodes of serious depression during childhood, adolescence, and even adulthood (Kovacs, 1996; Pataki & Carlson, 1990). In one study, over 60% of children and adolescents with major depression had another episode of it within a one- to five-year follow-up period (Emslie et al., 1997). The depression these children experience disrupts their intellectual development and school achievement as well as their social adjustment (Kovacs & Goldston, 1991). Fortunately, most depressed children respond well to psychotherapy (Birmaher et al., 1996), and over 700,000 children in the United States apparently take Prozac and similar antidepressants (Crowley, 1997). The benefits of antidepressant drugs are not as clear for children as for adolescents and adults, but these drugs do work effectively to relieve symptoms and put severely depressed individuals in a position to respond to psychological treatments (Cytryn & McKnew, 1996; Thase & Kupfer, 1996).

In sum, children, even young ones, can become clinically depressed and even (though rarely) suicidal. Moreover, depression in childhood is very similar to depression in adulthood, although it manifests itself somewhat differently as the developing person gains new cognitive capacities. If adults become more sensitive to signs of depression in children, they will be better able to offer appropriate treatment and perhaps reduce the likelihood of recurrences later in life.

Nature, Nurture, and Childhood Disorders

Most of us have a strong belief in the power of the social environment, particularly the family, to shape child development. This belief often leads us to blame parents—especially mothers (Phares, 1996)—if their children are sad and withdrawn, uncontrollable and "bratty," or otherwise different from most other children. Parents whose children develop problems often draw the very same conclusion, feeling guilty because they assume they are somehow at fault.

It is indeed essential to view developmental disorders from a family systems perspective and to appreciate how emerging problems affect and are affected by family interactions. Yet the power of parents to influence their children's adjustment may not be nearly so great as many of us believe (Sines, 1987). True, youngsters with psychological disorders often come from problem-ridden families and have insecure attachments to their parents (Rutter, 1996; van IJzendoorn & Bakermans-Kranenburg, 1996). For example, both depressed children and hyperactive children are more likely than children without these disorders to have rejecting or hostile parents. In addition, children with psychological disorders are more likely than other children to have mothers or fathers who have histories of psychological disorder themselves (Phares, 1996). For example, children have less than a 10% chance of developing clinical depression over their lifetimes if they have no close relatives with major depressive disorder or another of the major types of depression, a 25 to 30% chance if one close relative suffers from depression, and a 70% chance if both parents were depressed. Surely this means that children develop problems because they live in disturbed family environments with adults whose own psychological problems and marital conflicts make it difficult for them to parent effectively.

Or are there other interpretations? We cannot always be sure that unfavorable home environments *cause* childhood disorders. One alternative explanation is a genetic one. We know, for example, that some individuals are predisposed by their genetic makeup—in interaction, as always, with their experiences—to become clinically depressed (Kendler et al., 1992). The risk is there even if the child is adopted away. Perhaps the son of a depressed mother becomes depressed not so much because his mother was unresponsive or rejecting as because he inherited her genetic predisposition to become depressed.

In addition, "poor parenting" could be partly the *effect* of a child's disorder rather than its cause. As we have seen many times in this book, children contribute to their own development by shaping their social environment. Parental rejection may be a factor in the development of behavior problems, but we cannot ignore the possibility that children's problem behaviors negatively affect their parents' moods, marital relationships, and parenting behaviors (Stice & Barrera, 1995; Wampler, Halverson, & Deal, 1996). Both normal and abnormal development are affected by *reciprocal* influences within the family system.

Consider an example. In a study of the origins of antisocial behavior (Ge et al., 1996), adopted children who either did or did not have a parent with a history of substance abuse or antisocial personality were studied. Children whose biological parents had one of these psychological disorders were more likely to display antisocial behaviors than children whose parents did not, even though they were not raised by their biological parents—clear evidence of a genetic influence on antisocial behavior. More interestingly, the presence of psychiatric problems in biological parents was associated with less warm and involved and more harsh and inconsistent parenting by *adoptive* parents. How could this be? Presumably children whose parents had psychiatric disorders inherited genes that predisposed them to behave in antisocial ways, and their difficult behavior evoked negative responses from their adoptive parents. This is a clear example of the

Because parents and children influence each other, it is not always clear whether a parent's hostility is the cause or the effect of a child's misbehavior.

concept of evocative *gene/environment correlation* discussed in Chapter 3. Finally, this study also uncovered evidence of reciprocal parent/child influence in these families: Antisocial children not only provoked their adoptive parents to treat them in negative ways, but negative parenting aggravated the children's antisocial behavior problems. In view of this evidence, would you want to hold the adoptive parents of these antisocial children solely responsible for their offspring's troublemaking?

Don't mistake us: Family disruption and conflict and ineffective parenting *do* contribute to and aggravate many childhood problems. But many of these problems are also rooted partially in genetic endowment and grow out of a complex transactional process in which children affect and are affected by their parents and their wider social environments (Rutter et al., 1997). It is high time to move beyond the simple view that parents are to blame for all their children's problems. Abnormal development, like normal development, is the product of both nature and nurture and of a history of complex transactions between child and environment (Sroufe, 1997).

Do Childhood Problems Persist?

The parents of children who develop psychological problems very much want to know this: Will my child outgrow these problems, or will they persist? Parents are understandably concerned with the issue of continuity versus discontinuity in development. We have already seen that infantile autism, ADHD, and major depression *do* tend to persist beyond childhood, showing continuity in many individuals. To answer the continuity/discontinuity question

more fully, let's consider the entire spectrum of child-hood problems.

Recall the distinction between externalizing (or undercontrolled) problems and internalizing (or over-controlled) problems. Recently, Avshalom Caspi and his colleagues (1996) used data from a longitudinal study in New Zealand to determine whether children's behavioral styles, or temperamental characteristics, at age 3 predicted their susceptibility to psychological disorders at age 21—a span of 18 years. As part A of Figure 16.2 shows, young children who had undercontrolled, externalizing problems and were described as irritable, impulsive, and rough were more likely than both inhibited, overcontrolled children and well-adjusted children to be diagnosed as having antisocial personality disorder and to have records of criminal behavior as young adults.

Meanwhile, as part B of Figure 16.2 shows, inhibited, overcontrolled children who were shy, anxious, and easily upset were more likely than other children to be diagnosed as depressed later in life; contrary to

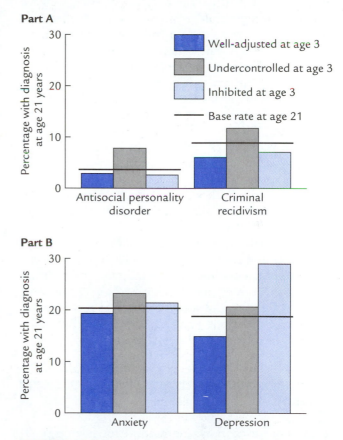

FIGURE 16.2 *Relationships between behavior at age 3 and psychological disorders at age 21. Part A shows that children with undercontrolled, externalizing behavioral styles are more likely than other children to show antisocial behavior at age 21. Part B shows that inhibited, overcontrolled children are at high risk of depression but not anxiety disorders at 21.* (Adapted from Caspi et al., 1996)

prediction, they were not significantly more at risk for anxiety disorders, so here there was not much continuity. Finally, children in both the undercontrolled and inhibited groups were more likely to attempt suicide, and boys in both groups were more likely to become dependent on alcohol. This study and others point to continuity in susceptibility to problems over the years.

Relationships between early behavior problems and later psychopathology in this study and others tend to be weak, though. Notice that most children with temperaments that put them at risk did *not* have diagnosable problems as adults. In a study of Swedish children (von Knorring, Andersson, & Magnusson, 1987), only 11% of children who received psychiatric care before age 10 were still receiving psychiatric care in their early 20s. Certainly having serious psychological problems as a child does not doom most individuals to a life of maladjustment.

Why might we see continuity of problem behavior in some children but discontinuity in others? If children have severe rather than mild psychological problems and continue to live in troubled homes, receiving little help, their difficulties may well persist. We have seen that autistic children remain autistic, that children with major depression often have recurrences, and that severely antisocial children become antisocial adults. However, as Norman Garmezy (1994) and Michael Rutter (1996) emphasize, other children show remarkable resilience, outgrowing early problems. Such children appear to be protected from lasting damage by their own competencies (especially intellectual ability and social skills) and by strong social support (especially by a stable family situation with at least one caring parent figure). Healthy marriages and stable jobs in adulthood can also help turn maladjusted children into well-adjusted adults (Sampson & Laub, 1993).

What we need to understand is that there is *both* continuity and change in children with psychological disorders. Many children, especially those with mild problems, outgrow their difficulties. At the same time, many adolescents and adults with severe problems are continuing to act out a pattern of maladaptive behavior that took form much earlier in life.

THE ADOLESCENT

If any age group has a reputation for having problems and causing trouble, it is adolescents. This is supposedly the time when angelic children are transformed into emotionally unstable, unruly, problem-ridden monsters. The view that adolescence is a time of emotional **storm and stress** was set forth by the founder of developmental psychology, G. Stanley Hall (1904). It has been with us ever since.

Is Adolescence Really a Period of Storm and Stress?

Are adolescents really more likely than either children or adults to experience psychological problems? It seems that adolescents have a far worse reputation than they deserve. In daily life, adolescents are no more likely than children to experience the extreme mood swings that might suggest emotional storm and stress, though adolescents do more often experience mildly negative moods (Larson & Lampman-Petraitis, 1989). And it simply is not the case that *most* adolescents are emotionally disturbed or that *most* develop behavior problems such as drug abuse and chronic delinquency. Instead, significant mental health problems—real signs of storm and stress—characterize about 20% of adolescents (Offer & Schonert-Reichl, 1992). Moreover, many of these adolescents were maladjusted before they reached puberty and continue to be maladjusted during adulthood (Strober, 1986). Overall rates of diagnosed psychological disorder are only slightly higher among adolescents than among children or adults (Offer & Schonert-Reichl, 1992).

Yet adolescence *is* a period of heightened vulnerability to some forms of psychological disorder (Kashani et al., 1989). After all, teenagers must cope with physical maturation, the emergence of new cognitive abilities, dating, changes in family dynamics, moves to new and more complex school settings, societal demands to become more responsible and to assume adult roles, and much more (Hill, 1993). Most adolescents cope with these challenges remarkably well and undergo impressive psychological growth, although it is not unusual for them to feel depressed, anxious, and irritable now and then. For a minority, a buildup of stressors during adolescence can precipitate serious psychopathology.

In sum, it can be a mistake to either overestimate or underestimate levels of psychopathology among adolescents. If we cling too strongly to the storm-and-stress view of adolescence and expect most teens to be half crazy, we may dismiss serious and potentially long-lasting problems as simply a normal "phase kids go through," a phase they will "outgrow." Yet, if we think adolescents are too young to have serious psychological problems, we can also fail to provide emotionally troubled youth with the help they need.

What special mental health risks *do* adolescents face? Among females, eating disorders such as anorexia nervosa and bulimia can make the adolescent period treacherous indeed. In addition, many adolescents of both sexes get themselves into trouble by abusing alcohol and drugs. Finally, rates of depression do increase dramatically from childhood to adolescence, and suicide rates climb accordingly. These problems interfere with normal adolescent development, and yet they become far more understandable when we view them in the context of this development.

Eating Disorders

Perhaps no psychological disorders are more associated with adolescence than the eating disorders that afflict adolescent girls and young women. Both anorexia nervosa and bulimia have become more common in recent years in a number of industrialized countries (Gordon, 1990). And both are serious—indeed, potentially fatal—conditions that are difficult to cure.

Anorexia nervosa, which literally means "nervous loss of appetite," has been defined as a refusal to maintain a weight that is at least 85% of the expected weight for one's height and age (American Psychiatric Association, 1994). Anorexic individuals are also characterized by a strong fear of becoming overweight, a distorted body image (a tendency to view themselves as fat even when they are emaciated), and, if they are females, an absence of regular menstrual cycles. Anorexia and other eating disorders typically emerge in adolescence, although they can emerge for the first time in childhood or even in old age (Beck, Casper, & Andersen, 1996; Smolak & Striegel-Moore, 1996). The typical anorexic may begin dieting soon after reaching puberty and simply continue, insisting, even when she weighs only 60 or 70 pounds and resembles a cadaver, that she is well nourished and could stand to lose a few more pounds (Hsu, 1990). About 1% of adolescent girls suffer from this condition, and 95 out of 100 of its victims are females (American Psychiatric Association, 1994). It is serious; about 6% of affected individuals die (Sullivan, 1995).

Bulimia nervosa, the so-called binge/purge syndrome, involves recurrent episodes of consuming huge quantities of food followed by purging activities such as self-induced vomiting, use of laxatives, or rigid dieting and fasting (American Psychiatric Association, 1994). Like anorexia nervosa, it is rooted in a strong "fear of fat"; its victims believe they are far fatter than they are and want to be far thinner (Williamson et al., 1989). Bulimia is especially prevalent in college populations, affecting few men but as many as 5% of college women (Hsu, 1990). Like anorexia, it is life threatening; laxatives and diuretics used as purging agents can deplete the body of potassium and cause cardiac arrhythmia and heart attacks, and regular vomiting can cause hernias.

A bulimic girl or woman typically binges on the very foods that are taboo to dieters, eating entire half gallons of ice cream, multiple bags of cookies and potato chips, or whole pies and cakes—as much as *55,000 calories* in a single binge session (Johnson et al., 1982). Not surprisingly, bulimic individuals experience a good deal of anxiety and depression in connection with their binge eating. They may learn to engage in purging activities to relieve these negative feelings (Hinz & Williamson, 1987).

Anorexia can be life threatening.

Bulimic individuals can be found in all weight ranges (American Psychiatric Association, 1994). Since anorexic females are, by definition, underweight, they are more "successful," in a perverse way, at avoiding fat than bulimic females are. Some bulimic individuals are also anorexic and, by definition, very thin, but other bulimics are average or overweight. Contrary to myth, these eating disorders are not restricted to white females from upper-middle-class backgrounds. They are evident at all socioeconomic levels; bulimia may even be more prevalent among females from lower-socioeconomic backgrounds (Gard & Freeman, 1996). Eating disorders are also evident in all racial and ethnic groups; Native Americans are especially at risk, Hispanic females are as vulnerable as non-Hispanic whites, and African-American and Asian-American adolescents are the least likely to develop eating disorders (Crago, Shisslak, & Estes, 1996).

Suspected Causes

Eating disorders stem partly from the sociocultural context in which we live—a society obsessed with thinness as the standard of physical attractiveness and femininity. Well before they reach puberty, girls in our society learn to associate being thin with being attractive, to fear becoming fat, and to wish they were thinner (Shapiro, Newcomb, & Loeb, 1997). About 25% of second-grade girls diet (Thelen et al., 1992)! Girls are pressured to work toward impossible standards of beauty: To match the proportions of those Barbie dolls girls love so much, a woman would have to gain 5 inches in the chest and lose 6 inches in the waist (Brownell & Napolitano, 1995)!

As girls experience normal pubertal changes, they naturally gain fat and become, in their minds, less attractive. They have more reason than ever to be obsessed with controlling their weight, especially if they have been socialized to adopt a traditionally feminine role (Murnen & Smolak, 1997; Rodin, Striegel-Moore, & Silberstein, 1990). This may be why adolescence is a prime time for the emergence of eating disorders, especially if a girl matures early, has a lot of body fat, and is highly involved in mixed-sex activities and dating (Cauffman & Steinberg, 1996; Graber et al., 1994).

The weight concerns of both anorexics and bulimics can be best viewed as an extreme version of the body-image concerns that affect most females in our society (Cash & Deagle, 1997; Lowe et al., 1996). Anorexia nervosa can, of course, be viewed as dieting carried to an extreme. Once the path from body dissatisfaction to dieting is taken, dieting itself can contribute to an eating disorder. Attempts to diet, or even periods of involuntary starvation of the sort experienced by prisoners of war, tend to be followed by binge eating and weight gain (Polivy & Herman, 1985; Polivy et al., 1994). Animals and humans are biologically programmed to compensate for a severe restriction of food intake by storing as much fat as possible; once off a crash diet, the body will continue to do this and will therefore gain weight more easily than before the diet was begun. The bulimic individual desperately attempts to fight biology by controlling her eating, but one little lapse from a rigid diet is enough to loosen this control and precipitate serious binge eating.

Still, why do relatively few adolescent females become anorexic or bulimic, even though almost all of them experience social pressure to be thin? Michael Strober and Laura Humphrey (1987) have pieced together an answer. To begin with, genes predispose some individuals to develop an eating disorder (Kendler et al., 1991; Rende, 1996). Genes and unique experiences are about equally important factors, whereas experiences that siblings in the same home share do little to make their odds of developing an eating disorder similar (Kendler et al., 1991). Genes may put certain individuals at risk by contributing to the abnormalities in hormone levels, neurotransmitter levels, and immune function seen in females with anorexia. However, it's not clear; these biological abnormalities could also be effects of the disorder (Study Group on Anorexia Nervosa, 1995). Genes may also put certain individuals at risk by influencing their personalities. Anorexic females tend to be introverted young women who worry a good deal and are perfectionists, whereas bulimic females tend to be extraverted and impulsive (Hsu, 1990). Both groups have low self-esteem, a good deal of self-directed anger, and little sense that they can control their lives (Williams et al., 1993). Often their families have a history of psychopathology (Leung, Geller, & Katzman, 1996). Bulimic women also appear to be vulnerable to other psychological disorders such as depression, anxiety disorders, and alcohol or drug abuse (Kendler et al., 1991).

Yet an eating disorder may not emerge unless a susceptible girl experiences disturbed family relationships and stressful events—that is, unless heredity and environment interact in an unfavorable way. Girls who are overly concerned about their weight tend to be insecurely attached to their parents and to have constructed *internal working models* that lead them to think poorly of themselves and to expect others to as well (Sharpe et al., 1998). Much emphasis has been placed on disturbed mother/daughter relationships, but poor father/daughter relationships also contribute (Swarr & Richards, 1996).

For anorexic girls, though, the problem is not cold, rejecting parents. Salvador Minuchin and his colleagues (Minuchin, Rosman, & Baker, 1978) discovered that anorexic females have difficulty with the adolescent task of forming an identity separate from their parents because their families tend to be "enmeshed," or overly interdependent. Their parents are overprotective and do not allow their daughters to argue or to express negative emotions. The result may be a young woman who has not been able to separate herself from her parents and who desperately wants to establish some sense of control over her life, which she can do by dieting (Smolak & Levine, 1993). Bulimic females, by contrast, often perceive their parents as hostile and distant (Wonderlich, Klein, & Council, 1996).

Finally, a pileup of stressors may serve to push a young woman over the edge. For example, vulnerable adolescents who are experiencing pubertal changes and weight gains, becoming involved in mixed-sex relationships, and changing schools, all at the same time, may have more than they can handle and may then develop an eating disorder (Smolak & Levine, 1996). In eating disorders, then, we have a prime example of how characteristics of the person, family, and wider social environment can interact to produce developmental problems. The young woman who is at risk for eating disorders may be predisposed, partly owing to her genetic makeup, to have difficulty coping with the pressures of adolescence and establishing autonomy. However, she may not actually develop an eating disorder unless she also grows up in a culture

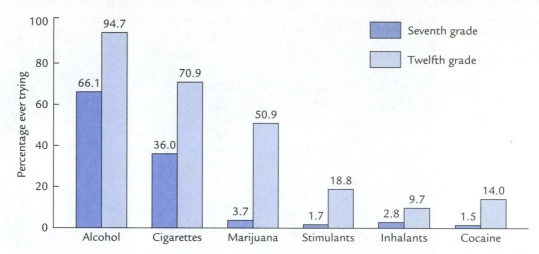

FIGURE 16.3 *Percentages of seventh- and twelfth-graders in New York State who have tried various drugs. These data, like those collected elsewhere in the United States, show that adolescents begin to experiment with drugs early and that more and more of them do so as they get older. Psychedelics, sedatives, tranquilizers, and heroin are not shown here because they were used by fewer than 5% of the students surveyed.* (Based on data from Kandel & Davies, 1991)

that overvalues thinness and in a family that makes it hard for her to form a secure attachment and also express her own identity as an individual—and then faces an accumulation of stressful events.

Treatment

Fortunately, most anorexic and bulimic individuals can be successfully treated, although treatment is challenging. Effective therapies for eating-disordered individuals include behavior modification programs designed to bring their eating behavior under control, individual psychotherapy designed to help them understand and gain control over their problem, family therapy designed to help build healthier parent/child relationships, and, for some, antidepressant medication to treat the depression that often accompanies eating disorders (Bowers, Evans, & Van Cleve, 1996). About half of women with bulimia are fully recovered 5 to 10 years after they are diagnosed; almost 20% continue to meet the full criteria for the disorder, and the remaining 30% still show some of its symptoms (Keel & Mitchell, 1997). Treatment can speed the recovery process, although some individuals improve on their own. Anorexics are more difficult to treat, often relapse, and may require intensive treatment over a long period of time before they recover, but most of them also respond (Eckert et al., 1995; Strober, Freeman, & Morrell, 1997).

Drinking and Drug Use

Just as concern about weight and dieting is quite normal among adolescents, use of alcohol and other drugs is quite common among adolescents—and gets some of them in serious trouble. The data reported in Figure 16.3, which were collected by Denise Kandel

and Mark Davies (1991) in New York State schools, are typical. Alcohol is by far the most widely used drug among adolescents, and its use begins early. By seventh grade, 66% of youth have already tried alcohol; by twelfth grade, about 95% have (Kandel & Davies, 1991). Moreover, almost a third of high school seniors reported being intoxicated at least once in the past month (Johnston, O'Malley, & Bachman, 1995). Marijuana is the most popular illicit drug. It is typical for adolescents to try alcohol before they try marijuana, and to try marijuana before they experiment with other illegal drugs (Yamaguchi & Kandel, 1984). It is also typical for adolescents who use one substance to use others (Bukstein et al., 1997).

In a society in which drug use is widespread, experimenting with tobacco, alcohol, and drugs may well be part of the larger process of experimenting in order to find one's identity and prepare for adult life (Baumrind, 1985). Yet use of these substances is a risk factor not only for substance abuse but for other psychological disorders (Kandel et al., 1997). The earlier that adolescents begin experimenting with substances, the more likely they are to end up with a problem: 47% of adolescents who drink by age 13 develop an alcohol abuse problem, compared with 25% of those who begin to drink at age 17 and only 10% of those who postpone drinking until age 21 (Grant & Dawson, 1997). Why, then, do a minority of adolescents go beyond experimenting and end up abusing drugs?

Most theorists appreciate that adolescent problem behaviors are rooted in interactions among biological, psychological, and sociocultural factors (Bukstein et al., 1997; Igra & Irwin, 1996; Windle, Shope, & Bukstein, 1996). Richard Jessor (1987; Jessor, Donovan, & Costa, 1991) and his colleagues conducted a

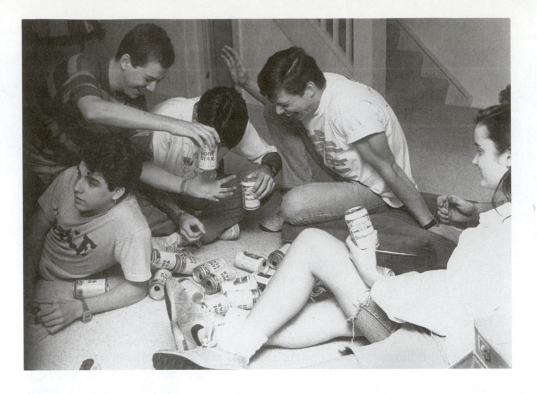

Most adolescents use but do not abuse alcohol. Those who abuse it are often alienated from conventional values, heavily influenced by peers who drink, and prone to other problems.

longitudinal study of problem drinking that started with 13- to 15-year-olds and tracked them until they were age 25 to 27. Problem drinkers were defined as youth who got drunk an average of about 20 times a year and experienced adjustment problems associated with their drinking. Jessor found that three broad factors distinguish problem drinkers from other adolescents: their personal qualities, their perceived social environment, and their other patterns of behavior.

With respect to their *personal qualities,* problem drinkers tend to be alienated from conventional values. They place little value on academic achievement, are not very religious, and generally are not attached to important social institutions such as schools and churches. Other researchers find that problem drinkers have a genetically based susceptibility to alcoholism, are prone to be impulsive and take risks, and have limited problem-solving and coping skills (Igra & Irwin, 1996; Windle et al., 1996).

Second, problem drinkers perceive their *social environment* differently than other adolescents do. Their parents, they say, are unsupportive and have little impact on them, whereas their peers model and reinforce drinking and other problem behaviors. Again and again, researchers find that teenagers who abuse drugs hang out with other teenagers who abuse drugs; meanwhile, their parents are not very warm, do not monitor their behavior well, and are inconsistent or harsh in their parenting style (see also Brook et al., 1990; Frauenglass et al., 1997; Windle et al., 1996). Adolescents are also more likely to drink when their cultural group tolerates and encourages drinking and when alcohol is readily accessible (Windle et al., 1996).

Third, drinking problems occurred within the context of the adolescent's *other behavior problems.* Specifically, problem drinkers are more likely than their peers to engage in other rule violations (smoking, using marijuana, committing delinquent acts, and having sexual intercourse) and are less likely to engage in conventional behaviors (studying and attending worship services).

It seems that any particular adolescent problem is likely to be part of a larger *syndrome* of unconventional and norm-breaking behavior (see also Igra & Irwin, 1996). Consequently, the same personality characteristics and features of the perceived social environment that predict adolescent problem drinking tend to predict other adolescent problem behaviors as well. What's more, these factors predict the continuation of problem behaviors into adulthood (Jessor et al., 1991). In sum, Jessor's model highlights characteristics of the person, his or her perceived social environment, and the context provided by the person's other behavior. It gives us insights into how a wide range of adolescent problems may originate and suggests that preventing and treating such problems may require changing the values of adolescents themselves *and* altering their relationships to parents, peers, schools, and other social institutions.

Depression and Suicidal Behavior

Children become quite a bit more vulnerable to depression as they enter adolescence, especially if they are girls (Cicchetti & Toth, 1998; P. Cohen et al., 1993). Up to 35% of adolescents experience depressed moods at some time, and as many as 7% have diagnosable depressive disorders (Petersen et al., 1993). Why? Pubertal changes in hormone levels can contribute to moodiness during adolescence, but social factors often turn out to be more important than biological factors in explaining the rise in depressive symptoms (Angold & Rutter, 1992). For one thing, adolescents experience more negative life events than children do and may simply have more to be depressed about (Larson & Ham, 1993). Females may be especially at risk because they are more likely than males to experience a cumulation of stressful events such as starting middle school or junior high school, undergoing pubertal changes, and dating in early adolescence (Ge et al., 1994; Nolen-Hoeksema & Girgus, 1994).

We can appreciate that adolescents have one foot in childhood and the other in adulthood when we look at the ways in which depression is manifested during this period. Because they are more intellectually mature than children and have typically become capable of formal-operational thought, depressed adolescents display the same cognitive symptoms of depression that adults display. Hopelessness, feelings of worthlessness, suicidal thinking, and other negative cognitions are common (Garber, Weiss, & Shanley, 1993). Yet depressed adolescents, like depressed children, often show other problems along with their depression—substance abuse, eating disorders, anxiety, antisocial behavior, and more (Petersen et al., 1993). Some depressed teenagers look more like budding juvenile delinquents than like victims of depression. Thus, diagnosing depression during adolescence can still be tricky, for adolescents share some of the qualities of both depressed adults and depressed children.

As depression becomes more common from childhood to adolescence, so do suicidal thoughts, suicide attempts, and actual suicides. Moreover, suicidal behavior among adolescents has been on the rise (Committee on Adolescence, 1996). As a result, suicide is the third leading cause of death for this age group, far behind accidents and just behind homicides; the yearly rate is 13 per 100,000 15- to 24-year-olds (U.S. Bureau of the Census, 1997). For every adolescent suicide there are many unsuccessful attempts—as many as 50 to 200 by some estimates (Garland & Zigler, 1993). Also, suicidal thoughts that may or may not lead to action are shockingly common, to the point of being normal during this period (Committee on Adolescence, 1996). For instance, in one survey of adolescents whose average age was 15, 56% reported at least one instance of suicidal thinking in their lives, and 15% had actually attempted suicide (Windle & Windle, 1997).

Before we conclude that adolescence is the peak time for suicidal behavior, however, let's consider the suicide rates for different age groups (see Figure 16.4). It is clear that *adults* are more likely to commit suicide

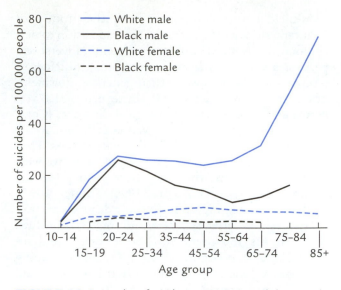

FIGURE 16.4 *Number of suicides per 100,000 people by age and sex among whites and African Americans in the United States. Data from the oldest African Americans are not shown because too few cases were studied.* (Data from U.S. Bureau of the Census, 1996)

than adolescents are. The suicide rate for females peaks in middle age, and the suicide rate for white males climbs throughout adulthood. As a result, elderly white men are the group most likely to commit suicide, possibly because they have high status in society as young men but often experience job failure, retirement, reduced income, and illness as they age (McCall, 1991).

Overall, males are more likely to commit suicide than females, by a ratio of about 3 to 1—a difference that holds up across most cultures studied (Girard, 1993). When we look at suicide *attempts*, this ratio is reversed, with females leading males by a ratio of about 3 to 1. Apparently, then, females attempt suicide more often than males do, but males more often succeed when they try, probably because they use more lethal techniques (especially guns).

If suicide rates are actually higher in adulthood than in adolescence, why do we hear so much about teenage suicide? Maybe it is because adolescents attempt suicide more frequently than adults do, even though they less often succeed. For this reason, the typical adolescent suicide attempt has been characterized as a "cry for help," a desperate effort to get others to notice and help resolve problems that have become unbearable (Berman & Jobes, 1991). The adolescent who attempts suicide often wants a better life; the elderly adult who attempts suicide is more often determined to end his or her life, chooses more lethal methods, and succeeds (Lester, 1994). This by no means suggests that adolescent suicide attempts should be taken lightly, though. Their message is clear: "I've got serious problems; wake up and help me!"

Suicidal behavior is most likely the product of an interaction between genes (a predisposition to psychological disorder) and environment (adverse experiences such as a history of trauma). Suicide attempters, partly because of their genetic endowment, often are severely depressed, abuse drugs, act violently, and have other psychological disorders (Committee on Adolescence, 1996; Vannatta, 1996). Many have histories of troubled family relationships: They have run away from home, or they do not live with both their parents; they may have been physically or sexually abused (Vannatta, 1996; Wagner, 1997). In the period leading up to the suicide attempt, they have often experienced deteriorating relationships with parents and peers, suffered academic and social failures, and begun to feel incapable of coping (Berman & Jobes, 1991). They often have legal and financial problems (Beautrais et al., 1997). Since they often lack effective coping and problem-solving skills, they may see no other way out besides suicide (Yang & Clum, 1996). Many give clear warning by talking about dying or giving away all their possessions; others quietly withdraw or engage in self-destructive behavior such as binge drinking (Committee on Adolescence, 1996). The adolescent who attempts suicide once may try again—and succeed—if he or she receives little help and continues to feel incapable of coping with problems, so professional help is definitely called for after an unsuccessful suicide attempt (Berman & Jobes, 1991).

All in all, adolescence does appear to be a potentially treacherous period of the life span, but only for a minority of individuals. Moreover, problems tend to come in bundles when they come, suggesting that many of the same root causes underlie a wide range of adolescent problem behaviors (Windle & Windle, 1997). However, let's remind ourselves that the large majority of adolescents, even though they may drink too many beers or think a depressive or even suicidal thought now and then, emerge from this period as well-adjusted and competent young adults. They will face new challenges in adapting to the demands of adult life.

THE ADULT

At any age, psychological problems such as depression and anxiety, as well as physical illnesses, may result when an individual faces overwhelming stress. Because the developmental tasks and daily pressures of adult life *are* stress producing, it is time for us to examine the relationship among stress, coping, and psychopathology. We will also continue our exploration of depression across the life span and delve into the special problems of elderly adults who suffer from Alzheimer's disease and other serious brain disorders.

Stress and Coping

According to Richard Lazarus (1993; Lazarus & Folkman, 1984), **stress** is a state that occurs when we perceive events as straining our coping capacities and threatening our well-being. What determines whether or not an experience is stressful, then, is the person's *appraisal* of the event in relation to his or her coping capacities. From this perspective, Faye may find giving birth to be a very stressful experience, whereas Maria may experience little stress in response to this same event because she is confident that she can manage.

What sorts of life experiences create stress and place the person at risk for developing problems? Most of the attention has focused on major life events, which may be either *normative transitions*—events that are typical at certain ages, such as marrying, becoming a parent, or retiring from work—or *nonnormative transitions*—unusual and unforeseen events that can happen at any age, such as being in a car accident, undergoing surgery, or divorcing. Normative life events, because they can be anticipated, are less likely than nonnormative, unscheduled events to be stressful and to cause psychological problems such as anxiety and depression (Pearlin, 1980). For example, retiring typically has little effect on mental health, but being unexpectedly laid off or demoted at work often takes a psychological toll.

Yet even nonnormative major life events do not seem to have as many implications for mental health as ongoing life strains. Lazarus and his colleagues have focused attention on the significance of **daily hassles**—chronic strains or everyday annoyances that may range in magnitude from repeatedly misplacing one's belongings to facing strong pressures to succeed, being trapped in a conflict-ridden relationship, worrying about bills, or living with a chronic illness (Kanner et al., 1981). Morton Lieberman (1983) puts it well: "We are done in more by the drips than by the floods" (p. 133).

In sum, the extent to which people experience stress and its potentially damaging effects depends on both the kinds of events they encounter and the ways in which they appraise them. People generally seem to cope better with major life events that are a normal and expected part of adult development than with life events that they did not expect to occur and are not prepared to manage. Yet the most stress-producing experiences of all may be those "little" daily hassles that, when added up, can make everyday life seem unbearable. The extent to which stress is harmful will then depend in part on the appropriateness and effectiveness of the coping strategies the individual chooses.

With this as background, we can look at stress, coping, and psychopathology across the adult years.

Age and Stressful Experiences

When in their lives do you think adults are most likely to experience stressful events? It seems difficult to decide. After all, young adults face the struggles of building a life—of starting careers, finding mates, marrying, and having children. Yet middle-aged adults are involved in many roles and have heavy burdens of responsibility, and elderly adults often experience hardships associated with declining health and lost roles and relationships.

As it turns out, adults experience the greatest number of life changes and strains in early adulthood (McLanahan & Sorensen, 1985; Pearlin, 1980). Life strains decrease from early adulthood to middle adulthood, perhaps as adults settle into more stable lifestyles. And elderly adults report even fewer hassles than middle-aged adults do, probably because they have fewer roles and responsibilities to juggle or because they appraise events differently, no longer perceiving as many things as stressful (Aldwin, 1994; Folkman et al., 1987).

Age and Coping Skills

If young adults have more to cope with than older adults, do they also have more effective coping strategies at their disposal? We know that coping strategies improve considerably from infancy to adulthood (Aldwin, 1994). Some researchers have proposed that coping capacities then peak in early and middle adulthood and deteriorate with age. According to this "regression" hypothesis, older adults cope with stressful events less actively and effectively than younger adults do (Pfeiffer, 1977). Other researchers, however, propose a "growth" hypothesis of coping, arguing that coping capacities *improve* with age throughout adulthood (Aldwin, 1994; Vaillant, 1977).

As it turns out, neither the regression hypothesis nor the growth hypothesis is very well supported. Instead, individuals at different ages are typically far more similar than different in their coping styles (Aldwin, 1994; Rook, Dooley, & Catalano, 1991). Most likely, we each develop a distinctive coping style that we rely on throughout our adult years (Costa, Zonderman, & McCrae, 1991). However, a few signs of *both* growth and regression have been identified, and they carry an interesting message about adult development.

First, consider some signs of growth. Robert McCrae (1982), for example, asked adults ranging in age from 24 to 91 to describe their responses to a recent stressful life event. Although few age differences in coping styles were detected, young adults were more likely than middle-aged or elderly adults to use immature and usually ineffective coping techniques,

such as expressing anger and hostility or escaping problems through fantasy (see also Diehl, Coyle, & Labouvie-Vief, 1996). Here, then, is some support for the growth hypothesis (see also Felton & Revenson, 1987; Irion & Blanchard-Fields, 1987; Vaillant, 1977).

Now consider some evidence that might be interpreted as regression. Susan Folkman, Richard Lazarus, and their colleagues (1987) compared the coping strategies of middle-aged and elderly adults and found that elderly adults were more passive in some respects (see also Rook et al., 1991). Middle-aged adults were likely to use **problem-focused coping,** attempting to change the stressful situation or eliminate the problem through such tactics as confronting other people, actively planning ways to solve the problem, and seeking social support. Elderly adults relied on more passive, **emotion-focused coping,** changing their appraisal of and emotional response to the problem by trying not to think about it, distancing themselves from it, or making the best of it (see also Blanchard-Fields, Jahnke, & Camp, 1995). An unhappy wife would be using problem-focused coping if she tried to persuade her husband to see a marriage counselor with her but emotion-focused coping if she tried to focus on her husband's endearing qualities and live with his faults.

We might be tempted to conclude, then, that middle-aged and elderly adults are showing growth when they manage to deal with stressful events without venting anger or escaping their problems through fantasy, as younger adults more often do. And we might view elderly adults as having regressed when they do not actively try to change their situations but instead decide to live with them. But it may be more accurate to conclude, as Folkman and her colleagues do, that these few age differences in coping styles mainly reflect age differences in the kinds of problems people face. It may make sense, for example, for a young or middle-aged woman to confront her misbehaving child or her lazy co-worker if she believes that she can change their behavior (a problem-focused strategy). But it may make just as much sense for an elderly man to accept and make the best of a chronic illness that will not go away (an emotion-focused strategy). Elderly adults may rely more heavily on emotion-focused coping strategies only because they are more often faced with problems like chronic disease and disability and the loss of loved ones that simply cannot be solved (Aldwin, 1994). If problem-focused strategies best fit problems that are solvable and emotion-focused strategies best fit problems that are not easily fixed, *both* old and young are probably responding adaptively. Indeed, the key to successful coping at any age may be knowing when to try to change distressing situations and when to learn to live with them (Brandtstädter & Renner, 1990; Folkman et al., 1987).

In sum, both younger and older adults may cope in ways that are appropriate to the kinds of stressful events they are most likely to encounter at their stages of life. Typically, older and younger adults cope in similar ways with similar problems, casting doubt on both the growth and regression hypotheses (Costa et al., 1991). Yet, if young adults experience more major life events and more ongoing hassles than older adults do, but do not differ greatly from older adults in their coping capacities, shouldn't they be more susceptible to psychological disorders than older adults?

When Coping Fails

When in adulthood *are* people most likely to suffer from psychological disorders? The National Institute of Mental Health (NIMH) conducted a major survey of community mental health in New Haven, Baltimore, and St. Louis (Myers et al., 1984; Robins & Regier, 1991). Adults aged 18 or older were interviewed in their homes about the psychological symptoms they were experiencing and estimates were made of the percentages of respondents meeting the criteria for several psychological disorders set out in the forerunner of *DSM-IV*.

Overall, a fairly large proportion of adults—15 to 22% of those surveyed in each city—were judged to have suffered from a diagnosable psychological disorder in the previous six months. Another major study that involved interviews with a national sample of adults (Kessler et al., 1994) suggests that almost half of individuals in the 15-to-54 age range have had a psychological disorder sometime in their life. Moreover, it was more the rule than the exception for people to have two or more disorders if they had one; that is, *comorbidity* was common. A small group, 14% of the population, had multiple and severe problems.

Figure 16.5 shows how prevalent two very common types of disorders proved to be among men and women of different ages in the NIMH study. Notice that both affective disorders (major depression and related mood disorders) and alcohol abuse and dependence affected a larger percentage of young adults than middle-aged or elderly adults. Indeed, the incidence of several other disorders examined in this study, including schizophrenia, anxiety disorders, and antisocial personality, decreased with age. (As you can appreciate, this could be either a true age effect or a cohort effect suggesting that recent generations are more vulnerable than previous generations to psychological disorder.) The only type of impairment that increased with age was cognitive impairment, undoubtedly because some older individuals were falling victim to Alzheimer's disease and other forms of dementia (to be discussed later in this chapter). Otherwise, it appears that young adults, because they experience more stress with no better coping resources

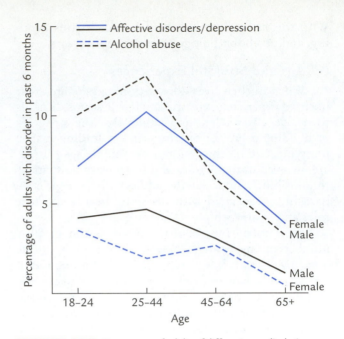

FIGURE 16.5 *Percentages of adults of different ages displaying affective disorders or alcohol abuse/dependence in the past six months* (Created from data reported by Myers et al., 1984)

than older adults possess, are a group at high risk for mental health problems.

Figure 16.5 also reveals that men and women are vulnerable to different sorts of problems. Men are far more likely to abuse alcohol and other drugs than women are, and they are also more likely to display antisocial personality disorder. Women are more likely to report symptoms of depression and other affective disorders, as well as phobias and anxiety disorders (see also Kessler et al., 1994). Overall, the two sexes have very similar rates of psychological disorder.

Finally, psychological disorders are more common in lower socioeconomic groups than in higher socioeconomic groups and vary across racial and ethnic groups. Despite their relatively low income and education, African-American adults have lower rates of affective disorders and substance use disorders than whites, for example, whereas Hispanics have higher rates of affective disorders (Kessler et al., 1994). Let's now look more closely at depression during the adult years.

Depression

Major depression and other affective disorders are among the most common psychological problems experienced by adults. Let's examine more closely who gets depressed and, more interestingly, why.

Age Differences

Contrary to stereotypes, elderly adults overall are *less* vulnerable to major depression and other severe affective disorders than younger adults are (Wolfe, Morrow, & Fredrickson, 1996). This is especially true if they can avoid the diseases and disabilities that can contribute to depression at any age (Roberts et al., 1997). Still, there are good reasons to be concerned about depression in old age, especially when we know that depressed elders are more likely than depressed adolescents to take their own lives.

Depression may be especially difficult to spot in older adults, for example (Blazer & Koenig, 1996). Think about it: Symptoms of depression include fatigue, sleeping difficulties, cognitive deficits, and somatic complaints. What if clinicians noted these symptoms in an elderly person but interpreted them as nothing more than normal aging, or as the result of the chronic illnesses that are so common in old age? Then a case of depression might easily be missed. Elderly adults who are depressed may also "mask" their depression, denying that they are sad and claiming instead that they have medical problems (Lyness et al., 1995; Gallo, Anthony, & Muthen, 1994). This, too, could lead to underdiagnosis of depression in the elderly population. Yet *over*diagnosis of depression in older adults could also occur if bodily complaints attributable to aging and disease are uncritically accepted as signs of depression (Wolfe et al., 1996).

There is currently no reason to conclude that depression in elderly individuals is so different from depression in young and middle-aged adults that entirely different criteria must be developed to detect it (La Rue, Dessonville, & Jarvik, 1985). Still, there seem to be subtle differences across the life span in how depression reveals itself. Clinicians working with elderly adults need to be sensitive to the differences between normal aging processes and psychopathology. Moreover, they should evaluate the health status of elderly individuals, the drugs prescribed for them, and their eating habits to better distinguish between clinical depression and psychological distress stemming from poor health, the side effects of drugs, or poor nutrition (Zarit, Eiler, & Hassinger, 1985). Finally, the fact that relatively few elderly people suffer from severe clinical depression should not blind us to the fact that a much larger number experience depressive symptoms or are demoralized and could benefit from treatment, even though they may not meet *DSM-IV* diagnostic criteria (Blazer & Koenig, 1996). The elderly adults most at risk are those who are very old, physically ill, psychologically disturbed, poor, and socially isolated (Blazer, 1993).

Sex Differences

As we have also seen, women are more likely than men to be diagnosed as depressed—by a margin of two to one (American Psychiatric Association, 1994). This gender gap first emerges during adolescence (Cicchetti

& Toth, 1998). It then reaches its widest point in the 30-to-60 age range and becomes less pronounced or even disappears in old age (Wolfe et al., 1996; Nolen-Hoeksema, 1990). How can we explain this trend?

Female hormones may play a role in depression in early adolescence, postpartum depression, and premenstrual syndrome, but generally biological explanations of the gender gap cannot take us very far (Sprock & Yoder, 1997). Instead, it could be that young and middle-aged women simply have more to cope with and more to be depressed about than men do. Although unmarried adults of both sexes are more likely to be depressed than married ones on average, married women are more depressed than married men. This may be because they carry the burden of responsibility for raising children and holding their families together (Nolen-Hoeksema, 1990; Wu & DeMaris, 1996).

Alternatively, women may be more likely than men to report their symptoms or seek help (Nolen-Hoeksema, 1990). Or it could be that men and women have been socialized to express and deal with their psychological distress in different ways. Men externalize their distress by behaving antisocially or abusing drugs, whereas women may more often internalize theirs (Horwitz & White, 1987; Stapley & Haviland, 1989). And, as Susan Nolen-Hoeksema and her colleagues have suggested, women and men may cope with their bad moods differently. Men tend to respond to depression with *distraction* strategies: They engage in enjoyable activities such as sports to get their minds off their problems. Women more often engage in *rumination*: They think a good deal about their problems and try to analyze why they feel the way they do (Nolen-Hoeksema, 1990; Strauss et al., 1997). Yet ruminating tends to prolong bouts of depression (Nolen-Hoeksema, Morrow, & Frederickson, 1993). By responding as they do, then, men may sidestep or minimize their depression, whereas women may actually aggravate theirs. In sum, biology, heavy burdens of stress, and styles of coping with stress may all contribute to higher rates of depression in females then in males.

Diathesis/Stress

A **diathesis/stress model** of psychopathology has proved very useful in explaining how many psychological problems, including depression, arise, whether in childhood or in adulthood (see Coyne & Whiffen, 1995; Monroe & Simons, 1991). This model proposes that psychopathology results from the interaction over time of a predisposition or vulnerability to psychological disorder (diathesis) and the experience of stressful events. As we have seen, certain people are genetically predisposed to become depressed (Kendler et al., 1992; Weissman et al., 1997). Their genetic risk

Young women who lack coping resources and must deal with the stresses of life in a crime-ridden neighborhood without adequate social support run a high risk of depression.

takes the form of imbalances in a number of key neurotransmitters (Cytryn & McKnew, 1996). According to the diathesis/stress model, though, individuals who are genetically predisposed to become depressed are not likely to do so unless they also experience significant losses or other stressful events. Meanwhile, other individuals may experience high levels of stress but not become depressed because they do not have a vulnerability to depression. In short, depression evolves from the interaction of person and environment. Partly because of their genetic endowment, and partly through socialization, individuals who fail to cope effectively with stress typically lack positive personality traits such as self-confidence and emotional stability. They may even help to bring about more than their share of interpersonal conflicts and other negative life events if they are socially unskilled and emotionally unstable (Gotlib & Hammen, 1992). Rather than taking constructive action to work out their problems, depression-prone individuals often rely on less effective coping strategies such as taking their feelings out on others, denying that they have

problems, or trying to escape their problems by drinking or taking drugs (Holahan & Moos, 1986, 1987).

According to the diathesis/stress model, individuals with limited personal resources for coping must experience stressful life events before they will become depressed. Their odds of becoming depressed increase as the life traumas and stressors they experience mount (Hilsman & Garber, 1995; Kendler et al., 1993). One stressful life event (such as the death of a loved one or a divorce) is usually not enough to trigger major depression, but, when negative events pile up or everyday strains or hassles become overwhelming, a person may succumb (Lieberman, 1983). In sum, depression is an outgrowth of the ongoing interaction between person and environment, just as the diathesis/stress model of psychopathology suggests.

Aging and Dementia

Perhaps nothing scares us more about aging than the thought that we will become "senile." **Dementia,** the technical term for senility, is a progressive deterioration of neural functioning associated with memory impairment, declines in tested intellectual ability, poor judgment, difficulty in thinking abstractly, and, often, personality changes. Becoming "senile" is *not* a normal part of the aging process. Instead, dementia and other moderate and severe cognitive impairments affect about 5% of the 65-and-older population overall (Blazer, 1996; Regier et al., 1988). The rate climbs steadily with age, though, from 3% of those 65 to 74 to about 15 to 20% of those 85 and older (Pollen, 1996; Regier et al., 1988). Although the odds of dementia increase the longer one lives, it is *not* part of normal aging.

Dementia is not a single disorder. Indeed, much damage can be done by labeling any older person with cognitive impairments "senile" and then assuming he or she is a lost cause. Many different conditions can produce the symptoms we associate with senility, and some of them are curable or reversible (Heston & White, 1991). It is also a mistake to assume that any elderly person who becomes somewhat forgetful or absentminded—who occasionally misplaces keys or cannot remember someone's name—is becoming senile. As we saw in Chapter 8, small declines in memory capacities in later life are common and usually do not have much effect on daily functioning. If memory decline were all it took to warrant a diagnosis of dementia, many young and middle-aged adults would qualify too! So let's look at some of the specific forms of dementia.

Alzheimer's Disease

With Alzheimer's disease, you just know you're going to forget things, and it's impossible to put things where you can't forget them because people like me can always find a place to lose things and we have to flurry all over the house to figure where in the heck I left whatever it was. . . . It's usually my glasses. . . . You've got to have a sense of humor in this kind of business, and I think it's interesting how many places I can find to lose things. . . . [People with Alzheimer's] want things like they used to be. And we just hate the fact that we cannot be what we used to be. It hurts like hell. (Cary Henderson, age 64, former history professor diagnosed with Alzheimer's disease at age 55; Rovner, 1994, pp. 12–13)

Alzheimer's disease, or Dementia of the Alzheimer's Type (DAT) as it is termed in *DSM-IV,* is the most common cause of dementia, accounting for about 50% of all cases, including Ronald Reagan's (Williams, 1995). This disease, which can strike in middle age but becomes increasingly likely with advancing age, has two telltale signs: the formation of senile plaques (masses of dying neural material with an abnormal protein called amyloid, a nonsoluble, silklike substance, at their core) and the formation of neurofibrillary tangles (twisted strands of neural fibers within the bodies of neural cells) in the brain (Williams, 1995). Elderly adults without Alzheimer's have senile plaques and neurofibrillary tangles too; it is not only the number but the exact type and location of them that marks the difference between Alzheimer's disease and normal aging (Snowdon, 1997). The result of Alzheimer's disease is a progressive—and irreversible or incurable—deterioration of neurons and increasingly impaired mental functioning, along with personality changes.

The first sign of Alzheimer's disease, detectable 2 to 3 years before dementia can be diagnosed, is difficulty learning and remembering verbal material (Howieson et al., 1997). In the early stages, free recall tasks are difficult but memory is good if cues to recall are provided; over time, individuals cannot recall even with the aid of cues and become increasingly frustrated (Grober & Kawas, 1997; Williams, 1995). As the disorder progresses, Alzheimer's patients have more and more trouble coming up with the words they want during conversations and may forget what they are supposed to do next midway through making a sandwich. If tested, they may be unable to answer simple questions about where they are, what the date is, and who the president of the United States is. Eventually they become incapable of caring for themselves, lose all verbal abilities, and die, some earlier and some later, but on average about 8 to 10 years after onset (Heston & White, 1991). Not only do patients with Alzheimer's disease become increasingly unable to function, but they often test the patience of caregivers by forgetting they have left something cooking on the stove, wandering away and getting lost, accusing people of stealing the items they have misplaced, seeing wild animals in their room, or taking off their clothes in public. Many become highly agitated and uncontrollable, large numbers suffer from depression, and some experience psychotic symptoms such as hallucinations (D. Cohen et al., 1993; Marin et al., 1997; Teri et al., 1995).

What causes Alzheimer's disease? Many cases appear to have a hereditary basis, but there is no single "Alzheimer's gene" (Heston, 1997). Alzheimer's disease does strike repeatedly in some families. In one study of pairs of twins in which one twin had Alzheimer's disease, the other twin did too in 67% of the pairs, compared to 22% of the fraternal twin pairs (Gatz et al., 1997; and see Bergem, Engedal, & Kringlen, 1997). By analyzing blood samples from families with many Alzheimer's victims, genetic researchers were able to locate a gene for the disease on the 21st pair of chromosomes and to conclude that anyone who inherits just one of these apparently dominant genes will eventually develop the disease (Pollen, 1996). Not coincidentally, individuals with *Down syndrome*—the chromosome disorder that is one of the causes of mental retardation—have three rather than the normal two 21st chromosomes and consistently develop the plaques and tangles of Alzheimer's disease, though not always the dementia, in middle age (Haxby & Schapiro, 1992). Yet Alzheimer's disease is more complicated than one gene on one chromosome. Genes associated with Alzheimer's disease have now been identified on chromosomes 1, 14, 19, and 21; all increase the production or accumulation of the amyloid protein associated with Alzheimer's (Selkoe, 1997). The buildup of amyloid inflames and injures neurons; synapses disappear and levels of neurotransmitters drop (Selkoe, 1997).

However, many individuals who fall prey to Alzheimer's disease, especially after age 70, have no apparent history of it in their families (Li et al., 1995). The four genes that have been discovered probably account for only a little over half of the cases of Alzheimer's; even then, environmental factors such as head injury enter in to affect when the disease begins and how quickly it progresses (Plassman & Breitner, 1996). The search for causes, both genetic and environmental, continues. Much attention has centered on the fact that victims have a deficit in the neurotransmitter acetylcholine, which is essential for normal learning and memory (Heston & White, 1991). The hope is that a drug can be developed to correct this problem. No magic pill has been discovered yet, but some drugs that have been tested (tacrine, or Cognex, for example) modestly improve cognitive functioning in some Alzheimer's patients, and more such drugs are likely to follow (Raskind & Peskind, 1997). Recently evidence has also been uncovered suggesting that both the use of anti-inflammatory drugs such as ibuprofen and the taking of estrogen by postmenopausal women may delay the onset and progression of Alzheimer's disease (Breitner, 1997;

Raskind & Peskind, 1997). Chances are that Alzheimer's disease will prove to have several causes and contributors, some genetic and some environmental; it may even turn out to be a group of distinct diseases, each with a different causality (Heston, 1997).

Other Causes of Cognitive Impairment

The second most common type of dementia, affecting 10 to 15% of all cases of dementia by itself and another 10 to 15% in combination with Alzheimer's disease, is **vascular dementia** (Williams, 1995). Also called multi-infarct dementia, it is caused by a series of minor strokes that cut off the blood supply to areas of the brain. Whereas Alzheimer's disease usually progresses slowly and steadily, vascular dementia often progresses in a steplike manner as each small stroke rather quickly brings about a new deterioration in functioning (American Psychiatric Association, 1994). Unlike Alzheimer's disease, which is strongly influenced by genes, vascular dementia is more closely associated with environmental risk factors for cerebrovascular diseases that affect blood flow in the brain, such as smoking and obesity (Bergem et al., 1997; Kaplan & Sadock, 1998). Huntington's disease (a genetic disorder described in Chapter 3), Parkinson's disease, and even AIDS are among the other possible causes of irreversible dementia (Heston & White, 1991). None is as common or as closely linked to old age as Alzheimer's disease (see Figure 16.6).

A minority of cases of dementia—perhaps 10 to 20%—are not related to any of these causes and, more important, are *reversible* or curable (Gurland, 1991). Such problems as alcoholism, toxic reactions to medication, infections, metabolic disorders, and malnutrition can cause symptoms of dementia. If these problems are corrected—for example, if the individual is taken off a recently prescribed medicine or is placed on a proper diet—a once "senile" person can be restored to normal mental functioning. By contrast, if that same person is written off as "senile" or as a victim of Alzheimer's disease, a potentially curable condition may become a progressively worse and irreversible one.

Similarly, elderly adults may be mistakenly diagnosed as suffering from irreversible dementia when they are actually experiencing **delirium.** This reversible condition develops more rapidly than dementia, comes and goes over the course of the day, and is a disturbance of consciousness characterized by periods of disorientation, wandering attention, confusion, and hallucinations (American Psychiatric Association, 1994; Kaplan & Sadock, 1998). Roughly 25% of patients over age 70 who are admitted to hospitals for illness have delirium as one of their symptoms (Williams, 1995). Any number of stresses to the body—illness, surgery, drug overdose, malnutrition, and other factors that can also cause reversible forms of dementia—can result in delirium. Here, too, it is es-

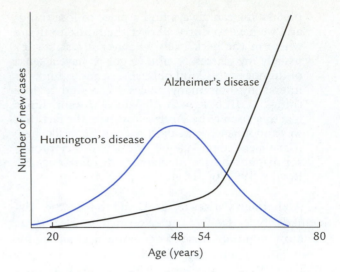

FIGURE 16.6 *Most diseases that cause dementia become more prevalent until middle age and then become less prevalent in later life. The odds of developing Alzheimer's disease, however, continue to rise with each passing year.* (From Heston & White, 1991)

sential to look carefully for such causes and treat them quickly; in most cases, the symptoms will then disappear in a week or two (Kaplan & Sadock, 1998).

Finally, elderly adults who are depressed are all too frequently misdiagnosed as suffering from dementia because they seem forgetful and mentally slow (Kaszniak, 1990). Treatment with antidepressant drugs and psychotherapy can dramatically improve the functioning of such individuals. However, if their depression goes undetected and they are written off as "senile," they are likely to deteriorate further.

The moral is clear: It is absolutely critical to distinguish among irreversible dementias (notably, dementia of the Alzheimer's type and vascular dementia), reversible dementias, delirium, depression, and other conditions that may be mistaken for irreversible dementias—including old age itself (Peskind & Raskind, 1996). Only after all other causes, especially potentially treatable ones, have been ruled out should a diagnosis of Alzheimer's disease be made. But even if such a diagnosis is made, and deterioration leading to death must be expected, a great deal can be done to help family members understand and cope with the Alzheimer's patient and to improve his or her functioning through the use of behavioral management techniques (Miller & Morris, 1993; Mittelman et al., 1993).

APPLICATIONS: TREATING PSYCHOLOGICAL DISORDERS

It can be discouraging to read about the countless ways in which human development can go awry. Ide-

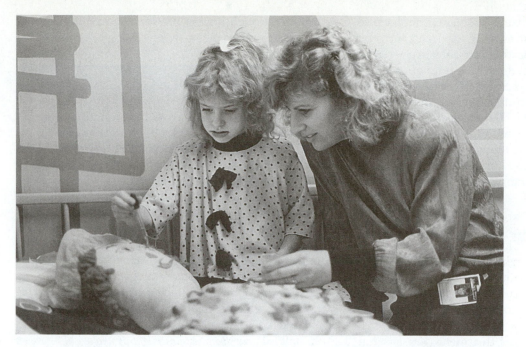

ally, we would seek to prevent developmental problems from arising in the first place through a two-pronged strategy of eliminating risk factors such as defective genes and deviant peer influence and strengthening protective factors such as effective parenting and social support. Yet, if prevention efforts fail, many psychological disorders and developmental problems can be treated successfully, as we have seen in this chapter, either through biological interventions such as medication or through psychological ones such as training and psychotherapy. I would like to close by noting some special challenges that arise in working with either very young or very old clients.

Treating Children and Adolescents

Treating children and adolescents differs in several ways from treating adults. First, children rarely seek treatment on their own (Johnson, Rasbury, & Siegel, 1986). Instead, they are referred for treatment by adults, usually parents, who are disturbed by their behavior. This means that therapists must view the child *and* his or her parents as the "client." Second, children's therapeutic outcomes often depend greatly on the cooperation of their parents. Whether or not a disturbed family environment has contributed to a child's problem, the participation of parents in treatment is critical in resolving the problem (Gelfand & Peterson, 1985). Sometimes all members of the family must be treated in order for any enduring change in the child's behavior to occur—a principle underlying the use of family therapy as a treatment approach.

Third—and this is a point very familiar to students of human development—children function at very different levels of cognitive and emotional devel-

opment than adults, and interventions for them must be designed accordingly (Gardner, 1993; Johnson et al., 1986). Young children cannot easily participate in therapies that require them to verbalize their problems and gain insight into the causes of their behavior (Gardner, 1993). A more appropriate technique might be play therapy, in which disturbed children are encouraged to act out concerns that they cannot easily express in words. All things considered, then, treating children with psychological disorders is particularly challenging. Treatment must involve the family rather than the client alone, and it must be sensitive to the developmental competencies of that client.

John Weisz and Bahr Weiss (1993) pulled together analyses of over 200 studies of the effectiveness of psychotherapy in treating problems of childhood and adolescence. Two major categories of psychotherapy were compared: (1) behavioral therapies (for example, those using reinforcement principles and modeling techniques to alter maladaptive behaviors and teach more adaptive ones) and (2) nonbehavioral therapies (primarily psychoanalytic therapies based on Freudian theory and other "talking cures" in which therapists help clients to express, understand, and solve their problems). These studies examined a wide range of problems (both externalizing and internalizing) and measured a wide range of outcomes (anxiety, cognitive skills and school achievement, personality and self-concept, social adjustment, and so on).

So, does psychotherapy work with children and adolescents? Indeed it does—at least as well as it works with adults, and the benefits appear to be lasting. Moreover, undercontrolled, or externalizing, problems (hyperactivity, aggression) proved to be just as responsive to treatment as internalizing problems (phobias, social withdrawal), suggesting that externalizing problems need not persist if they are effectively treated (Weisz et al., 1987). Behavioral therapies appeared to be more effective with children than nonbehavioral therapies, although these alternative forms of therapy have often proved equally effective in treating adults. Very possibly, this is because children *do*, after all, have limited cognitive skills. Consequently they may have difficulty participating in "talk therapies" but can respond well to direct attempts to alter their behavior or teach them new skills.

Treating Elderly Adults

It can be just as challenging to treat elderly people with psychological problems as it is to treat children. Perhaps the greatest difficulty is that elderly individuals are hesitant to seek treatment. Even young and middle-aged adults with psychological disorders typically receive no professional treatment (Kessler et al., 1994), but the problem is even worse among elderly adults, who turn to their physicians if they turn to anyone but rarely turn to anyone (Gatz & Smyer, 1992; Phillips & Murrell, 1994). Possibly this is because today's elderly generation grew up in a time when a social norm of self-reliance was stronger than it is today and when it was considered shameful to have psychological problems (Gatz et al., 1985). Older adults and members of their families may also believe, wrongly, that problems such as depression and anxiety are just a normal part of getting older or becoming ill (Meador & Davis, 1996). Still another barrier to treatment may be *ageism* in the mental health care system: negative attitudes among mental health professionals that cause them to prefer working with younger people, to perceive elderly individuals as untreatable, and to misdiagnose their problems. Freud may have started it all, for he believed that older adults are not good candidates for psychoanalysis (Meador & Davis, 1996).

What happens when elderly adults do seek treatment? They benefit from psychotherapy every bit as much as younger adults (Wolfe et al., 1996; Scogin & McElreath, 1994). Therapists sometimes need to adapt their techniques to be effective with those elders who are cognitively impaired or who have visual and hearing impairments, but these clients, too, can be helped (Meador & Davis, 1996). Research findings underscore the importance of encouraging elderly people with psychological problems to seek treatment. They also show that working with these individuals can be rewarding for mental health professionals. Just as human beings can fall prey to psychological problems at any point in the life span, they have an impressive capacity throughout the life span to overcome problems and to experience new psychological growth.

IS PSYCHOPATHOLOGY ADAPTIVE?

Psychologists and psychiatrists have long brought major theories of human development to bear in attempting to understand psychological disorders. Freudian psychoanalytic theory once guided thinking about psychopathology and clinical practice; behavioral theorists applied learning principles to the understanding and treatment of problems; cognitive psychologists called attention to how individuals interpret their experiences and perceive themselves. Today, some developmental psychopathologists are applying the perspective of evolutionary psychology (see Chapter 3) to the study of abnormal development and, as a result, are asking a thought-provoking question that rarely gets asked (Fischer et al., 1997; Jensen & Hoagwood, 1997): *What adaptive functions might psychological disorders serve for the individuals who have them?* We traditionally think of psychological disorder in negative ways—as a failure to adapt to or master developmental tasks, as developmental delay or arrested development, as disease. But what we view as maladaptive can also be viewed as an adaptive way of coping with trauma (Fischer et al., 1997). For example, a small number of children who are sexually abused develop multiple personality disorder; by creating elaborate personalities and turning into them, they can often protect themselves from painful realities (Cole & Putnam, 1992).

Evolutionary psychologists would also ask us to consider the possibility that behaviors that appear to be maladaptive in modern society may have played a more useful function for our evolutionary ancestors (Jensen & Hoagwood, 1997). Thus, for example, the darting attention and impulsive behavior we see in hyperactive children may not be very adaptive in a classroom setting where it pays to sit still and be quiet but may have helped some of our ancestors notice predators and act quickly to avoid them, while their more reflective friends were being gobbled up (Jensen et al., 1997). Perhaps hyperactive children would function more effectively in an environment better suited to their characteristics (a soccer field) than in a classroom.

We should not get carried away with the notion that psychological disorders are adaptive. For the most part, they interfere, often seriously, with the individual's ability to meet developmental demands. Nonetheless, it is useful to ask whether symptoms of psychological disorder may serve adaptive functions for the individual and may represent learned ways of coping with stressful environments.

1. To diagnose many psychological disorders, psychologists and psychiatrists consider the broad criteria of statistical deviance, maladaptiveness, and personal distress and judge behavior in light of social norms and age norms. The *Diagnostic and Statistical Manual of Mental Disorders (DSM-IV)* spells out specific diagnostic criteria for a wide range of psychological disorders, including major depressive disorder. Developmental psychopathology is concerned with the origins and course of psychopathology and treats it as a pathway of development rather than as a disease.

2. Infantile autism is characterized by an early onset, deviant social responses, language and communication deficits, and repetitive behavior; it may be rooted partly in cognitive impairments such as lack of a theory of mind or deficiencies in symbolic thought or executive functions. Genetic mechanisms account for most cases and many, but not all, autistic individuals remain impaired in later life, although early, intensive behavioral training can bring about great improvements in their functioning.

3. Some infants who have been emotionally starved or separated from attachment figures, including infants whose parents are depressed and infants suffering from failure to thrive, display depressionlike symptoms, if not true clinical depression.

4. Children with attention-deficit/hyperactivity disorder, an externalizing (under-controlled) disorder, display inattention, impulsivity, and hyperactivity; they can be helped through a combination of stimulant drugs and behavioral training, but many do not entirely outgrow their problems.

5. Diagnosable depression, an internalizing (overcontrolled) disorder, occurs during childhood, manifests itself somewhat differently at different ages, tends to recur, and can be treated with antidepressant drugs and psychotherapy.

6. It is too simple to view "bad" parenting as the cause of all childhood problems; heredity also contributes, and children's problems are partly the cause as well as the effect of disturbed parent/child relationships. Fortunately, despite some continuity, many childhood problems, especially mild ones, are only temporary.

7. Contrary to the "storm and stress" view, adolescents are not much more vulnerable to psychological disorders than children or adults are. Anorexia nervosa and bulimia, both serious eating disorders, seem to arise when a vulnerable adolescent, typically a girl, is raised in a troubled family (in a society that strongly encourages dieting) and experiences stressful events. Experimentation with alcohol and drugs is statistically normal during adolescence, but youth who develop more serious problem behaviors often have unconventional values, perceive their peers as encouraging deviance and their parents as unsupportive, and show a whole syndrome of problems.

8. Risks of depression rise during adolescence, especially among females; adolescents, in a cry for help, are more likely to attempt but less likely to commit suicide than adults (especially older white men).

9. Stressful daily hassles are more likely to cause psychological problems than major life events, even nonnormative ones. Young adults experience more such life strains than older adults do. Young adults may use more problem-focused coping and less emotion-focused coping, but mainly because they face more controllable problems; otherwise age differences are minimal. As a result, most psychological disorders besides cognitive impairment are more common in early adulthood than in later adulthood.

10. Depression tends to be most common in early adulthood and among women, for a number of reasons. It results, according to a diathesis/stress model, when a vulnerable individual who lacks personal resources such as positive personality traits and effective coping strategies experiences multiple stresses.

11. The most common forms of dementia, a progressive loss of cognitive capacities affecting about 5% of the elderly population, are Alzheimer's disease and vascular

dementia. These irreversible dementias must be carefully distinguished from correctable conditions such as reversible dementias, delirium, and depression.

12. Treating children and adolescents with psychological problems is especially challenging but often effective. Elderly adults with psychological disorders also pose special challenges but can benefit just as much as younger adults from psychotherapy.

13. Evolutionary psychologists encourage us to ask whether psychological disorders may serve adaptive functions for the individuals who have them and may reflect sophisticated efforts to cope with difficult environments.

FOOD FOR THOUGHT

1. The major theories of development discussed throughout this book—Freud's or Erikson's psychoanalytic theory, Bandura's social learning theory, Piaget's cognitive-developmental theory, Bronfenbrenner's ecological theory—should have something to say about why a school-age child might become depressed. Try your hand at describing what two of these theorists might say. (You may want to refer back to Chapter 2).

2. A diathesis/stress model of psychopathology is useful in explaining disorders other than depression. Try to sketch out a diathesis/stress model of one of the other psychological disorders discussed in this chapter, using relevant evidence about the disorder.

3. What evidence can you bring to bear in order to evaluate this statement: Psychological problems during adolescence are no more than an attempt to master normal developmental tasks of adolescence such as adjusting to pubertal changes, finding an identity, and gaining peer acceptance.

4. Lucille, though you don't know her, has struggled with major depressive disorder on and off for her entire life. Describe how she may have expressed her depression as an infant, preschool child, school-age child, adolescent, adult, and elderly adult. To what extent is depression depression, regardless of one's age, and to what extent is it manifested differently at different ages?

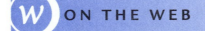 ON THE WEB

There are many, many Web sites devoted to mental health issues, so I'll offer more than the usual number of suggestions for this chapter.

1. *Mental Health Net*   You could spend days at this site alone; it is searchable and links to sites on most of the disorders discussed in this chapter (ADHD, depression, eating disorders, suicide, and so on), as well as to numerous other sites. http://www.cmhc.com/

2. *Internet Mental Health*   Another great encyclopedia of mental disorders, this one links you to sites for the 52 most common disorders, offering information about definition, diagnosis, research, and treatment. You can find material on major depressive disorder and all the other disorders discussed in this chapter. http://www.mentalhealth.com/

3. *Autism*   Autism Resources is an excellent resource if you are interested in infantile autism. Among other things, it links you to "Recovery Zone," a site that centers on the behavioral approach to intervention adopted by Lovaas and his colleagues, as well as to the TEACCH program at the University of North Carolina, another successful intervention. It also links to the site of the Autism Society of America. http://www.autism-info.com/

4. *Hyperactivity*   For the full range of information about attention-deficit/hyperactivity disorder, including a list of famous people with ADHD and a bibliography of readings, try this site.
http://www.cdipage.com/adhd.htm

5. *Eating Disorders*   This site is worth a look if you have a special interest in anorexia, bulimia, and other eating disorders. There are even sections on children and older women to remind us that eating disorders do not strike only in adolescence.
http://www.mirro-mirror.org/eatdis.htm

6. *Depression*   Created by a man who was diagnosed as having major depressive disorder, this site pulls together all kinds of resources on depression, including personal accounts.
http://www.blarg.net/~charlatn/depression/general.html

7. *Alzheimer's Disease*   This site, run by the National Institute on Aging, offers news stories on the latest breakthroughs in research on Alzheimer's disease, as well as publications and resources, many free. It can keep you posted on new developments as researchers continue to seek ways to prevent or cure the leading cause of dementia.
http://www.alzheimers.org

✦ KEY TERMS

social norm
age norm
major depressive disorder
developmental psychopathology
infantile autism
echolalia
somatic symptoms
failure to thrive
externalizing problems

internalizing problems
attention-deficit/hyperactivity disorder (ADHD)
comorbidity
masked depression
storm and stress
anorexia nervosa
bulimia nervosa
stress

daily hassles
problem-focused coping
emotion-focused coping
diathesis/stress model
dementia
Alzheimer's disease
vascular dementia
delirium

CHAPTER 17

The Final Challenge: Death and Dying

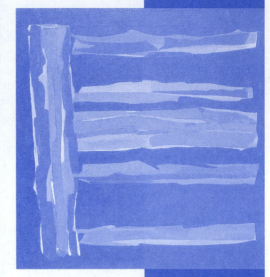

LIFE AND DEATH ISSUES
What Is Death?
What Kills Us and When?
Theories of Aging: But Why Do We Age and Die?

THE EXPERIENCE OF DYING
Kübler-Ross's Stages of Dying
Criticisms and Alternative Views

THE EXPERIENCE OF BEREAVEMENT: AN ATTACHMENT MODEL

THE INFANT

THE CHILD
Grasping the Concept of Death
The Dying Child
The Bereaved Child

THE ADOLESCENT

THE ADULT
Death Anxiety
Death and the Family Life Cycle
Who Copes and Who Succumbs?

APPLICATIONS: LESSENING THE STING OF DEATH
For the Dying
For the Bereaved

SUMMARY POINTS

FOOD FOR THOUGHT

ON THE WEB

KEY TERMS

*J*essica was 5. She showed her mother the picture she had painted. There were black clouds, dark trees, and large red splashes.

"My," said her mother. "Tell me all about this, Jess." Jessica pointed to the red splashes. "That's blood," she said. "And these are clouds." "Oh," said her mother. "See," said Jessica, "the trees are very sad. The clouds are black. They are sad too." "Why are they sad?" asked her mother. "They are sad because their Daddy has died," said Jessica, the tears slowly running down her cheeks. "Sad like us since Daddy died," said her mother and held her closely, and they wept. (Raphael, 1983, p. 138)

*D*eath hurts. Whether we are 5, 35, or 85 when death strikes a loved one, it still hurts. By adulthood, most of us have experienced a significant loss, even if it was "only" the death of a beloved pet. Even when death is not striking so closely, it is there, lurking somewhere in the background—in the newspaper, on television, or in our minds as we go about the tasks of living. And sooner or later we all face the ultimate developmental task: the task of dying.

This chapter explores death and its place in life-span human development. What is death, and why do we die? How have theorists characterized the experiences of dying and bereaved people? What does death mean, and how is it experienced in infancy, childhood, adolescence, and adulthood? Why do some individuals cope far more successfully with death than others do? We will discover that death is part of the human experience throughout the life span but that each person's experience of it depends on his or her level of development, personality, life circumstances, and sociocultural context. Finally, on a practical note, we'll see what can be done to help dying and bereaved individuals through their ordeals.

LIFE AND DEATH ISSUES

What is death, really? When are we most vulnerable to it, and what kills us? And why is it that all of us eventually die of "old age" if we don't die earlier? These "life and death" questions serve to introduce the topic of death and dying.

What Is Death?

As you have probably noticed, there is a good deal of confusion in our society today about when life begins and when it ends. Proponents and opponents of legalized abortion argue vehemently about when life really begins. And we hear similarly heated debates about whether a person in an irreversible coma is truly alive and whether a terminally ill patient who is in agonizing pain should be kept alive with the help of life support machines or allowed to die naturally. Definitions of death as a biological phenomenon are changing; so are the social meanings attached to death.

Biological Definitions of Death

It used to be easy enough to tell that someone was dead: There was no breathing, no heartbeat, no sign of responsiveness. These criteria of biological death are still useful today. However, technological breakthroughs have forced the medical community to rethink what it means to say that someone is dead. The problem is that biological death is not a single event but a *process* (Medina, 1996). Different systems of the body die at different rates, and some individuals who have stopped breathing or who lack a heartbeat or pulse can now be revived before their brains cease to function. Moreover, basic bodily processes such as respiration and blood circulation can be maintained by life support machines in patients who have fallen into a coma and whose brains have ceased to function.

In 1968 an ad hoc committee of the Harvard Medical School offered a definition of death that it hoped would resolve controversies about when a person is dead—a definition that has since gained widespread acceptance and become the basis for modern legal definitions of death (Berger, 1993). The Harvard group defined biological death as **total brain death:** an irreversible loss of functioning in the entire brain, both the higher centers of the cerebral cortex that are involved in thought and the lower centers of the brain that control basic life processes such as breathing. Specifically, to be judged dead a person must meet the following criteria:

1. Be totally unresponsive to stimuli, including painful ones.
2. Fail to move for one hour and fail to breathe for three minutes after being removed from a ventilator.
3. Have no reflexes (for example, no eye blink and no constriction of the eye's pupil in response to light).
4. Register a flat electroencephalogram (EEG), indicating an absence of electrical activity in the cortex of the brain.

As an additional precaution, the testing procedure is repeated 24 hours later. Moreover, since a coma is sometimes reversible if the cause is either a drug overdose or an abnormally low body temperature, these conditions must be ruled out before a coma victim is pronounced dead.

Now consider some of the life and death issues that have revolved around this definition of biological death (Stillion & McDowell, 1996; Urofsky, 1993). In 1975 Karen Ann Quinlan lapsed into a coma at a party, probably because of the combination of alcohol and drugs she had consumed (Urofsky, 1993). Although Quinlan was totally unconscious, her bodily functioning was maintained with the aid of a ventilator and other life support systems. When her parents were finally granted permission to turn off the respirator, Quinlan continued to breathe even without it, much to everyone's surprise. She lived on in a vegetative state, lacking all consciousness and being fed through a tube, until 1985.

Then came the case of Nancy Cruzan (see Berger, 1993; Urofsky, 1993). She was in a car accident one icy night in 1983 and, like Quinlan, fell into a coma and lay for years in a fetal position. She had a heartbeat and breathed on her own but could not survive without being fed through a tube. When her parents sought permission to remove the feeding tube in 1988, the judge agreed, but his decision was appealed by the state of Missouri because Cruzan's own desire to terminate medical care had not been demonstrated. The Supreme Court of the United States agreed, essentially ruling that the Constitution protects an individual's right to refuse unwanted medical treatment but that states can act to preserve life if the individual's wishes are not clear (Urofsky, 1993). In 1990, Ms. Cruzan's parents were allowed to remove the feeding tube because some of her friends recalled her saying that she would not want to be kept alive by artificial means (Urofsky, 1993).

These two famous "right to die" cases highlight the different positions one can take on the issue of when a person is dead. The position laid out in the Harvard definition of total brain death (and in most state laws) is quite conservative. By the Harvard criteria, neither Karen Ann Quinlan nor Nancy Cruzan was dead, even though both were in irreversible comas, because the lower portions of their brains were still functioning enough to support breathing and other "vegetative" functions. Shouldn't we keep such seemingly hopeless patients alive in case we discover ways to revive or cure them? A more liberal position is that a person should be declared dead when the cerebral cortex is irreversibly dead, even if bodily functioning is still maintained by the more primitive portions of the brain. After all, is a person really a person if he or she lacks any awareness and if there is no hope that conscious mental activity will be restored? Should families have to stand by helplessly for years and governments have to pick up the tab for medical care?

Cases like Quinlan's and Cruzan's also raise issues concerning **euthanasia**—a term meaning "happy" or "good" death that usually refers to hastening the death of someone who is suffering from an incurable illness or injury. Box 17.1 explores some of these is-

sues. Clearly life and death decisions such as these are not easy ones (see Kastenbaum, 1998). Our society will continue to grapple with defining life and death and deciding what forms of euthanasia are or are not morally and legally acceptable. And new issues will undoubtedly arise as new life-prolonging medical technologies are introduced.

Social Meanings of Death

Death is not only a biological process but a psychological and social one as well. The social meanings attached to death vary immensely from historical era to historical era, from culture to culture, and from religious group to religious group. Indeed, what we have just discovered is that *society* defines who is dead and who is alive! True, people everywhere die, and people everywhere grieve deaths in some fashion. Moreover, all societies have evolved some manner of reacting to this universal experience—of interpreting its meaning, disposing of corpses, and expressing grief. Beyond these universals, the similarities end.

As Phillippe Ariès (1981) has shown, the social meanings of death have changed over the course of history. In Europe during the Middle Ages, people were expected to recognize that their deaths were approaching so that they could bid their farewells and die with dignity surrounded by loved ones. Since the late 19th century, Ariès argues, Western societies have engaged in a denial of death. We have taken death out of the home and put it in the hospital and funeral parlor; we have shifted responsibility for the care of the dying from family and friends to "experts"—physicians and funeral directors. We have made death a medical failure rather than a natural part of the life cycle. Moreover, we have dispensed with many standard mourning rituals, such as the wearing of armbands or black clothing, and have frowned upon open expressions of grief.

Perhaps this is changing. In the past couple of decades, right-to-die and death-with-dignity advocates have argued forcefully that we should return to some of the old ways, bringing death out into the open rather than avoiding all mention of it, allowing it to occur more naturally, and making it once again an experience to be shared within the family.

If we look at how people in other cultures interpret and manage death, we quickly realize how many alternatives there are to our Western ways (Metcalf & Huntington, 1991; Rosenblatt, 1993; Stroebe et al., 1992). Depending on the society, "funerals are the occasion for avoiding people or holding parties, for fighting or having sexual orgies, for weeping or laughing, in a thousand different combinations" (Metcalf & Huntington, 1991, p. 24). Corpses are treated in a remarkable number of ways too: They "are burned or buried, with or without animal or human sacrifice;

BOX 17.1

Should we hasten death?

Do you believe that euthanasia is appropriate if a person is terminally ill and in constant pain? Before you answer, note that there are actually two very different forms of euthanasia. Active euthanasia, or "mercy killing," is deliberately and directly causing a person's death—for example, by administering a lethal dose of drugs to a pain-racked patient in the late stages of cancer or shooting a spouse who is in the late stages of Alzheimer's disease. Passive euthanasia, by contrast, means allowing a terminally ill person to die of natural causes—for example, by withholding extraordinary lifesaving treatments, as happened when Karen Quinlan was removed from her respirator.

In between active euthanasia and passive euthanasia is **assisted suicide**—not killing someone, as in active euthanasia, but making available to a person who wishes to die the means by which *he* or *she* may do so. Dr. Jack Kevorkian, sometimes known as "Dr. Death," has helped several terminally ill individuals to commit suicide—in some cases by providing them with his "Mercy Machine," a contraption that injects deadly drugs into a patient's veins once he or she pushes a button (Urofsky, 1993). Extreme as the assisted suicide practiced by Dr. Kevorkian may seem, it is not unlike a practice far more common among today's doctors—writing prescriptions for sleeping pills or other drugs at the request of terminally ill patients who have made known their desire to die, in full knowledge that they will probably take an overdose (Quill, 1993).

Where do we stand as a society on the issue of euthanasia, then? There is overwhelming support among medical personnel and members of the general public for passive euthanasia (Stillion & McDowell, 1996). In addition, a surprising 62% of Americans support

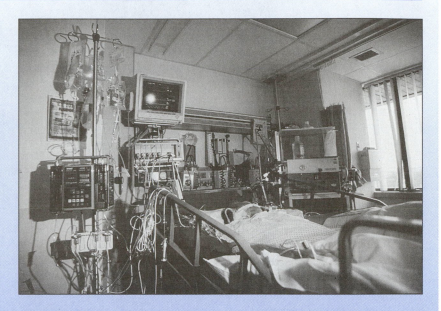

a form of active euthanasia in which a doctor ends a patient's life by some painless means if the patient and his or her family request it (Caddell & Newton, 1995). And, according to a Louis Harris poll, almost as many approve of Dr. Kevorkian's efforts to assist terminally ill people in committing suicide (Colburn, 1994).

In many states, due to the lobbying efforts of the "right to die" movement, it is now legal to withhold lifesaving treatments from terminally ill patients and to "pull the plug" on life support equipment when that is the wish of the dying person or the immediate family (Berger, 1993). In 1994, Oregon became the first state to pass a law allowing physician-assisted suicide in which terminally ill patients who choose can be given drugs with which to take their own lives (Stillion & McDowell, 1996).

Another product of the right-to-die movement is the **Living Will,** a document through which people can state in writing before the fact that they

do no want any extraordinary medical procedures applied if they become hopelessly ill. Most states now honor the wishes expressed in such statements. However, several states do not allow the withdrawal of feeding tubes from patients like Nancy Cruzan, and some groups continue to fight Living Will legislation because they maintain that it promotes more active forms of euthanasia (Berger, 1993). Active euthanasia, meanwhile, is generally viewed under the law as murder.

On many of these life-and-death issues, right-to-die advocates, who maintain that people should have a say in how they die, fight head to head against right-to-life advocates, who claim, often on the basis of strong religious convictions, that everything possible should be done to maintain life and nothing should be done to cut it short. It makes sense to think through these issues now in case you must someday decide whether you or a loved one should live or die.

they are preserved by smoking, embalming, or pickling; they are eaten—raw, cooked, or rotten; they are ritually exposed as carrion or simply abandoned; or they are dismembered and treated in a variety of these ways" (Metcalf & Huntington, 1991, p. 24). In most

societies there is some concept of spiritual immortality. Yet here, too, there is much variety, from concepts of heaven and hell to the idea of reincarnation to a belief in ancestral ghosts who can meddle in the lives of the living (Rosenblatt, 1993).

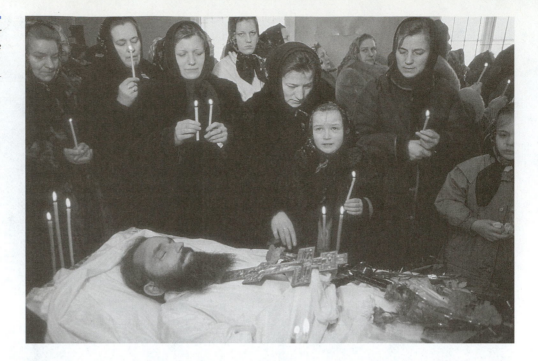

Mourning rituals differ considerably from culture to culture.

We need not look beyond the boundaries of the United States and Canada to find considerable variation in the social meanings of death, for different ethnic and racial groups clearly have different rules for expressing grief (Cook & Dworkin, 1992; Irish, Lundquist, & Nelson, 1993). It is customary among Puerto Ricans, especially women, to display intense, hysterical emotions after a death (Cook & Dworkin, 1992). Japanese Americans, by contrast, are likely to have been taught to restrain their grief—to smile so as not to burden others with their pain and to avoid the shame associated with losing control of oneself (Cook & Dworkin, 1992). Japanese Americans, Euro-Americans, and others socialized to restrain their grief might view Puerto Rican mourners as psychologically disturbed when all they are doing is following the rules for emotional display that prevail in their cultural group.

Different subcultural groups also have different mourning rituals and notions of how long a death should be mourned. Irish Americans are likely to believe that the dead deserve a good send-off—a wake with food, drink, and jokes, the kind of party the deceased might have enjoyed (McGoldrick et al., 1991). Although African Americans share this belief that it is important to go out in style, they are likely to regard the funeral not as a time for rowdy celebration but as a forum for expressing grief, in some congregations by wailing and singing spirituals (McGoldrick et al., 1991; Perry, 1993). Jewish families tend to be even more restrained; they quietly withdraw from normal activities for a week of mourning called *shiva* and then honor the dead again at the one-month and one-year marks (Cytron, 1993). The tradition among the Nava-

jos is to try to forget the loved one as rapidly as possible and resume normal activities after only three or four days of mourning (Cook & Dworkin, 1992). By contrast, Japanese Americans may follow the Japanese tradition of preparing an altar to honor a deceased family member, placing it prominently in their living room, and bowing before it each day so as never to forget (Cook & Dworkin, 1992).

In short, the experiences of dying individuals and of their survivors are very much shaped by the historical and cultural context in which death occurs. Death may be universal, but our experiences of death and dying are not. Death is truly what we humans make of it, which means that we must not presume that there is one "right" way to die or to grieve a death. As Paul Rosenblatt (1993) concludes, "It pays to treat everyone as though he or she were from a different culture" (p. 18).

What Kills Us and When?

How long are we likely to live, and what is likely to kill us? In the United States the **life expectancy** at birth—the *average* number of years a newborn can be expected to live—has risen to almost 76 years (U.S. Bureau of the Census, 1997). This average life expectancy disguises important differences between males and females and among racial and ethnic groups. The life expectancy for white males is 73, whereas the life expectancy for white females is almost 80. Female hormones seem to protect women from high blood pressure and heart problems; avoiding health hazards and performing less dangerous work may also help women live longer. Meanwhile, life expectancies for

African Americans, many of whom experience the many health hazards associated with poverty, are a good deal lower than those for white Americans: 65 for males, 74 for females. As Figure 17.1 shows, several industrialized nations, led by Japan, have higher life expectancies than the United States. Longevity continues to be far more limited in underdeveloped countries plagued by malaria, famine, AIDS, and other such killers.

Infants are relatively vulnerable to death, but by 1993 infant mortality in the United States had fallen to 9 out of 1000 live births—7 out of 1000 among white infants, 16 out of 1000 among African American (U.S. Bureau of the Census, 1997). Assuming that we survive infancy, we have a relatively small chance of dying during childhood, adolescence, or early adulthood. Death rates then climb steadily throughout middle age and old age.

What kills us? The leading causes of death change dramatically over the life span (U.S. Bureau of the Census, 1997). Infant deaths are mainly associated with complications in the period surrounding birth and congenital abnormalities that infants bring with them to life. The leading causes of death among children are accidents (especially car accidents but also poisonings, falls, fires, drownings, and so on) and cancers. Adolescence and early adulthood are generally periods of good health. Accidents (especially car accidents), homicides, and suicides are the leading killers of adolescents. Among young adults ages 25 to 44, the leading killers are accidents and cancers.

Starting in the 45 to 64 age group, chronic diseases—notably cancers and heart diseases—appear at the top of our perverse "hit parade" of leading killers. The incidence of these chronic conditions, climbs steadily with age, raising overall death rates considerably. Among adults 65 and older, heart diseases lead the list by far, followed by cancers and strokes.

In sum, life expectancies are higher than ever. After we make it through the vulnerable period of infancy, we are at low risk of death through early adulthood and if we do die we are most likely to die suddenly because of an accident. As we age, we become more and more vulnerable to death, particularly from chronic diseases. But now a more fundamental question: Why is it that all of us eventually die? Why does no one live to be 200? To understand why death is an inevitable part of human development, we need the help of theories of aging.

Theories of Aging: But Why Do We Age and Die?

There is no simple answer to the question of why we ultimately age and die. However, several theories have been proposed, and each of them says something important about the aging process. These theories can

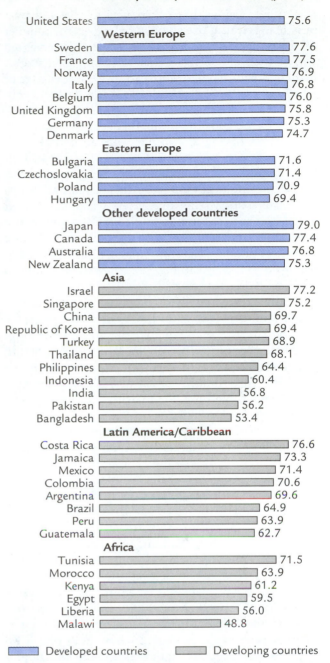

FIGURE 17.1 *Life expectancies for an infant born in 1990 in developed and developing countries. The challenge in countries such as Bangladesh and Malawi is to avoid dying in infancy or childhood.* (From Kinsella & Taeuber, 1993, based on the International Data Base on Aging, U.S. Bureau of the Census, Center for International Research)

be divided into two main categories: **programmed theories of aging** emphasize the systematic genetic control of aging processes, and **damage theories of aging** emphasize the more haphazard processes that cause errors in cells to accumulate and organ systems to deteriorate (Cristofalo, 1996; Medina, 1996; Walford, 1983).

Programmed Theories

Human beings, like other species, have a characteristic **maximum life span**—a ceiling on the number of years that anyone lives. The longest documented and verified life so far is that of Jeanne Louise Calment, a French woman who died in 1997 at the age of 122 (Trueheart, 1997). Nearly blind and deaf and confined to a wheelchair, she maintained her sense of humor to the end, attributing her longevity to everything from having a stomach "like an ostrich's" to being forgotten by God (Trueheart, 1997). Ms. Calment and others who live almost as long are the basis for setting the maximum human life span at 110 to 120. Interestingly, this maximum has not changed much over the centuries, even though the average life expectancy has been increasing dramatically and more and more individuals are managing to avoid dying young so that they can become *centenarians,* living to see their 100th birthdays (Smith, 1997).

Humans are long-lived compared to most species. The maximum life span for the mouse is 3½ years, for the dog 20, for the chimpanzee 50, and for the long-lived Galapagos tortoise 150 (Walford, 1983). The very fact that each species has its own characteristic maximum life span should convince us that specieswide genes have something to do with controlling how long people generally live.

Moreover, we know that the individual's hereditary endowment influences how rapidly he or she ages and how long he or she lives compared to other humans. Many years ago, Franz Kallmann and Gerhard Sander (1949) repeatedly assessed both identical and fraternal twins as they aged and discovered that identical twins show visible signs of aging—graying and thinning of the hair, wrinkling, physical disabilities—at similar times. Identical twins are also more similar than fraternal twins in self-reported health and in the extent to which they suffer from chronic illnesses (Harris et al., 1992). In the end, individual genetic makeup, partly by influencing susceptibility to major diseases, also has a bearing on how long one lives. Twin research suggests that genes account for about a third of the variation in longevity; unique environmental influences not shared with siblings account for most of the rest of the variation (McGue et al., 1993). A fairly good way to estimate how long you will live, then, is to average the longevity of your parents and grandparents (Medvedev, 1991).

In short, we have good reason to believe that aging and death are genetically influenced. But how, exactly, do genes control aging? This is what is not yet known. Probably several genes are involved, some lengthening life, others hastening death (Hodes, McCormick, & Pruzan, 1996). If genes can "turn on" or "turn off" to bring about maturational changes during infancy, or at puberty and menopause, why couldn't they bring about aging and death? Alternatively, a genetic program that

The fact that long life tends to run in families is evidence of a programmed or genetic theory of aging. These identical twins are celebrating their 100th birthday.

has evolved to ensure that we reproduce may run out when the reproductive years are over (Cristofalo, 1996).

Biological researchers have long been investigating the possibility that an aging clock is built into each cell of the body. Their work has built on that of Leonard Hayflick (1976), who grew cells in cultures, allowed them to divide or double, and measured the number of doublings that occurred. He discovered that cells from human embryos could double only a certain number of times—50 times, plus or minus 10, to be exact—an estimate now referred to as the **Hayflick limit.** Hayflick also demonstrated that cells taken from human adults divide even fewer times, presumably because they have already used up some of their capacity for reproducing themselves. Moreover, the maximum life span of a species is related to the number of cell divisions characteristic of that species: The short-lived mouse's cells can go through only 14 to 28 doublings; the very long-lived Galapagos tortoise's cells can manage 90 to 125.

Now researchers believe that the cellular aging clock suggested by Hayflick's limit on cell division is timed through **telomeres,** the stretches of DNA that form the tips of chromosomes. When a cell divides, each of its chromosomes replicates itself, but the chromosome's telomere does not. Instead, half of the telomere goes to one of the new chromosomes that is formed and half goes to the other. The result is shorter and shorter telomeres as we age; eventually, the theory goes, this progressive shortening of telomeres makes cells unable to replicate any more, causes them to malfunction and die, and ultimately causes the organism itself to die (Medina, 1996).

It is not yet certain whether the workings of telomeres and the Hayflick limit are the same for cells in living organisms as for cells grown in petri dishes in the laboratory (Cristofalo, 1996). Many questions also remain about whether the death of cells can ever explain the death of whole organisms (Cristofalo, 1996; Jazwinski, Howard, & Nayak, 1995). Still, the idea that telomeres function as an "aging clock" within cells is a good example of a theory maintaining that aging and death are genetically programmed processes.

Other programmed theories of aging have been offered, some centered on genetically guided and systematic changes in the neuroendocrine and immune systems (Cristofalo, 1996; Medina, 1996). We know that the hypothalamus of the brain, guided by a genetic program, sets in motion the hormonal changes responsible for puberty and menopause (see Chapter 5). Possibly the hypothalamus also serves as an aging clock, systematically altering levels of hormones and brain chemicals in later life so that bodily functioning is no longer regulated properly and we die. Other researchers are investigating genetically governed changes in the immune system that decrease its ability to defend against potentially life-threatening foreign agents such as infections and cause it to mistake normal cells for invaders. All these programmed theories hold that aging and dying are the inevitable products of our biological endowment as human beings.

Damage Theories

In contrast to programmed theories of aging, damage theories generally propose that an accumulation of damage to cells and organs over the years ultimately causes death. Aging and death may not be written in the genetic code from conception on; rather, we are the victims of random destructive processes or errors that accumulate while we live. One early explanation of aging was a "wear-and-tear" theory, proposing that organs simply wear out through use, much as shoes do. We now know that this view is naive. Indeed, using the body (as in regular aerobic exercise) often *improves* rather than diminishes functioning. Nonetheless, more modern versions of the wear-and-tear theory seem to have merit.

According to an **error accumulation theory** of aging, the genetic material DNA is damaged over the years as the cells metabolize nutrients and are increasingly exposed to environmental agents such as pesticides, pollution, and radiation (Medina, 1996). Over time, the genetic code contained in the DNA of more and more cells becomes scrambled, and the body's mechanisms for repairing such damage simply cannot keep up with the chaos. More and more cells then function improperly or cease to function, and the organism eventually dies.

Much attention has focused on errors in the DNA code produced by **free radicals,** molecules that have an extra or "free" electron, that are chemically unstable, and that react with other molecules in the body to produce substances that damage normal cells (Medina, 1996; Kristal & Yu, 1992). "Age spots" on the skin of older people are a visible effect of the damage free radicals can cause, but the damage of most concern is damage to DNA.

Unfortunately, we cannot live and breathe without producing free radicals, for they are a by-product of the metabolism of oxygen. Some studies suggest that "antioxidants" such as vitamin E may increase longevity, though not for very long, by keeping the number of free radicals under control, but the results are not yet conclusive (Cesario & Hollander, 1991; Medina, 1996).

Nature and Nurture Conspiring

The theories just discussed are some of the most promising explanations of why we age and die. Programmed theories of aging generally claim that aging and dying are as much a part of nature's plan as sprouting teeth or uttering one's first words. The telomere explanation of limits on cell replication, changes in endocrine functioning, and declines in the effectiveness of the immune system all suggest that aging and dying are genetically controlled. Damage theories of aging hold that we eventually succumb to haphazard destructive processes such as those caused by free radicals that result in increasingly faulty DNA and abnormal cell functioning.

Neither of these theories of aging has proved to be *the* explanation; instead, many, interacting mechanisms are at work (Cristofalo, 1996; Medina, 1996). For example, genes influence the capacity of cells to keep environmentally caused damage under control, and the random damage caused by free radicals alters genetic material. John Medina (1996) summarizes it this way: "Toxic waste products accumulate because genes shut off. Genes shut off because toxic waste products accumulate" (p. 291). In short, nature and nurture, biological and environmental factors, interact to bring about aging and dying, just as they interact to produce development.

Theories of Aging and Life Extension

What does all this say about our prospects for finding the fountain of youth or extending the life

span? Genetic researchers are making remarkable progress. It is not at all unthinkable that they might discover some of the genetic mechanisms behind aging and dying and devise ways to manipulate genes in order to raise the maximum life span—for example, by intervening to keep telomeres from shortening (Medina, 1996). At present, though, the only technique that has been demonstrated experimentally to extend the life span is **dietary restriction:** a highly nutritious but severely restricted diet representing a 30 to 40% or more cut in normal total caloric intake (Medina, 1996; Masoro, 1988). Laboratory studies involving rats and other animals suggest that dietary restriction extends not only the average longevity but also the maximum life span of a species (Cesario & Hollander, 1991). Dietary restriction brings about many physiological changes, including a reduction in free radicals, but no one is quite sure why half-starved animals live longer than well-fed ones (Medina, 1996). And we certainly do not know whether dietary restriction works as well for humans as it apparently has for rats or what calorie counts and combinations of nutrients are optimal. Experimenting with self-starvation at this point is not a good idea!

While we wait for the breakthroughs that might extend the maximum life span of human beings, we can at least reduce our chances of dying young. As suggested in Chapter 5, for example, we can stop smoking, drink only in moderation, eat nutritious food, exercise regularly, and take other steps to ward off the diseases that make us die prematurely. But none of our efforts to delay death will keep us from dying. So let's turn to the question of how humans cope with death and dying.

THE EXPERIENCE OF DYING

People who die suddenly may be blessed, for those who develop life-threatening illnesses face the challenge of coping with the knowledge that they are seriously ill and are likely to die. Perhaps no one has done more to focus attention on the emotional needs of dying patients than psychiatrist Elisabeth Kübler-Ross (1969, 1974), whose "stages of dying" are widely known.

Kübler-Ross's Stages of Dying

In interviews with over 200 terminally ill patients, Kübler-Ross (1969) detected a common sequence of emotional responses to the knowledge that one had a serious, and probably fatal, illness. She believed that similar reactions might occur in response to any major loss, so bear in mind that the family and friends of the dying person might experience some of these same emotional reactions during the loved one's illness and after the death. Kübler-Ross's five stages of dying are as follows:

1. *Denial and isolation.* A common first response to dreadful news is to say "No! It can't be!" **Denial** is a defense mechanism in which anxiety-provoking thoughts are kept out of, or "isolated" from, conscious awareness. A woman who has just been diagnosed as having lung cancer may insist that the diagnosis is wrong—or accept that she is ill but be convinced that she will beat the odds and recover. Denial can be a marvelous coping device: It can get us through a time of acute crisis until we are ready to cope more con-

structively. Even after dying patients face the facts and become ready to talk about dying, those around them often engage in their own denial, saying such things as "Don't be silly—you'll be well in no time."

2. *Anger.* As the bad news begins to register, the dying person asks "Why me?" Feelings of rage or resentment may be directed at anyone who is handy—doctors, nurses, or family members. Kübler-Ross advises those close to the dying person to be sensitive to this reaction so that they won't try to avoid this irritable person or become angry in return.

3. *Bargaining.* When the dying person bargains, he or she says "Okay, me, but please . . ." The bargainer asks for some concession from God, the medical staff, or someone else. A woman with lung cancer may beg for a cure or perhaps simply for a little more time, a little less pain or a chance to ensure that her children will be taken care of after she dies.

4. *Depression.* When the dying person becomes even more aware of the reality of the situation, depression, despair, and a sense of hopelessness become the predominant emotional responses. Grief focuses on the losses that have already occurred (for example, the loss of the ability to function as one once did) and the losses to come (separation from loved ones, the inability to achieve one's dreams, and so on).

5. *Acceptance.* Assuming that the dying person is able to work through all the complex emotional reactions of the preceding stages, he or she may come to accept the inevitability of death in a calm and peaceful manner. Kübler-Ross (1969) describes the acceptance stage this way: "It is almost void of feelings. It is as if the pain had gone, the struggle is over, and there comes a time for 'the final rest before the long journey,' as one patient phrased it" (p. 100).

In addition to these five "stages of dying," Kübler-Ross emphasizes a sixth response that runs throughout the stages: *hope.* She believes that it is essential for terminally ill patients to retain some sense of hope, even if it is only the hope that they can die with dignity. Now age 71 and weakened by strokes that have left her confined to a wheelchair, Kübler-Ross has reached the point of hoping that her own death will come soon (Cutter, 1998).

Criticisms and Alternative Views

Kübler-Ross deserves immense credit for sensitizing our society to the emotional needs of dying persons and convincing medical professionals to emphasize *caring* rather than curing in working with such persons. At the same time, there are flaws in her account of the dying person's experience (Corr, 1993; Kastenbaum, 1998). Among the most important criticisms are these: (1) Kübler-Ross's use of the term *stage* is inappropriate, (2) she largely ignores the course of the individual's illness, and (3) she makes little of individual differences in emotional responses to dying.

The major problem with Kübler-Ross's "stages" is that they appear not to be stages at all. Research suggests that the dying process is simply not stagelike (Kastenbaum, 1998). Although dying patients usually are depressed as death nears, the other emotional reactions Kübler-Ross describes seem to affect only minorities of individuals (Schulz & Aderman, 1974). Moreover, when these responses do occur, they do not unfold in a set order. Even Kübler-Ross (1974) herself acknowledged that her "stages" do not necessarily follow one another in a lockstep fashion.

As you are by now well aware, developmentalists speak of stages only when most individuals can be shown to proceed through a series of distinct or qualitatively different phases, *in order.* It might have been better if Kübler-Ross had, from the start, described her "stages" simply as common emotional reactions to dying. Unfortunately, some overzealous medical professionals, excited by these "stages," have tried to push dying patients through them in order, believing incorrectly that their patients would never come to accept death unless they experienced the "right" emotions at the "right" times (Kastenbaum, 1998).

Offering an alternative to the idea of stages of dying, Edwin Shneidman (1973, 1980) argues that dying patients alternate between denial and acceptance of death and experience a complex and ever-changing interplay of emotions. One day a patient may seem to accept that death is near; the next day he or she may talk of getting better and going home. Along the way many reactions—disbelief, hope, terror, bewilderment, rage, apathy, calm, anxiety, and others as well—come and go and are even experienced simultaneously. According to Shneidman, then, dying people experience many unpredictable emotional changes rather than distinct stages of dying.

A second major problem in Kübler-Ross's theory is that it pays little attention to how emotional responses are shaped by the course of an illness and the specific events that occur along the way (Glaser & Strauss, 1968). When a patient is slowly and gradually worsening over time, the patient, family members, and staff all have a good deal of time to become accustomed to the fact that death lies ahead, whereas when the path toward death is more erratic, emotional ups or downs are likely each time the patient's condition takes a turn for better or worse. It is generally more difficult to cope with surprises than with a course of dying that is gradual and predictable, but Kübler-Ross expects different patients to experience similar responses even when their diseases and pathways to death are very different.

Finally, by proposing a set of stages to describe most dying people, Kübler-Ross has overlooked the fact that each individual's personality influences how he or she experiences dying. People cope with dying

much as they have coped with the problems of living (Schulz & Schlarb, 1987–1988). For example, John Hinton (1975) found that cancer patients who had faced life's problems directly and effectively, had been satisfied with their lives, and had maintained good interpersonal relationships *before* they became ill displayed less anger and irritability and were less depressed and withdrawn during their illnesses than patients who were less well-adjusted before their illnesses (see also Stein, Linn, & Stein, 1989). Depending on their predominant personality traits, coping styles, and social competencies, some dying persons may deny until the bitter end, some may "rage against the dying of the light," some may quickly be crushed by despair, still others may display incredible strength, and most will display combinations of these responses, each in his or her own unique way.

In sum, the experiences of dying persons are far more complex than Kübler-Ross's five "stages" of dying suggest. As Shneidman emphasizes, there is likely to be a complex interplay of many emotions and thoughts, with swings back and forth between acceptance and denial. Moreover, to understand which emotions will predominate and how these emotions will be patterned over time, we must take into account the nature and course of the individual's condition and the individual's prior personality and coping style.

THE EXPERIENCE OF BEREAVEMENT: AN ATTACHMENT MODEL

Most of us know a good deal more about the process of grieving a death than about the process of dying.

To describe responses to the death of a loved one, we must distinguish among three terms. **Bereavement** is a state of loss, **grief** is the emotional response to loss, and **mourning** consists of culturally prescribed ways of displaying one's reactions. Thus we can speak of a bereaved person who grieves by experiencing such emotions as sadness, anger, and guilt—and who mourns by attending the funeral and laying flowers on the grave each year.

Unless a death is sudden, relatives and friends, like the dying person, have been experiencing many painful emotions *before* the death. They, too, may alternate between acceptance and denial; one day they may express hope that the illness can be halted, and the next day they may despair. Moreover, they often engage in what has been termed **anticipatory grief**, grieving before death occurs for what is happening and for what lies ahead (Rando, 1986).

Yet no amount of preparation and anticipatory grief can eliminate the need to grieve after the death actually occurs. How then, do we grieve? Much important research on the grieving process has been conducted by Colin Murray Parkes and his colleagues in Great Britain (Parkes, 1986, 1991; Parkes & Weiss, 1983). Parkes and John Bowlby (1980), whose influential ethological theory of attachment was outlined in Chapter 13, have conceptualized grieving in the context of attachment theory as a reaction to separation from a loved one that is part of our evolutionary heritage. From this perspective, the grieving adult can be likened to the infant who experiences separation anxiety when his or her mother disappears from view.

The Parkes-Bowlby attachment model of grieving describes four predominant reactions. They overlap considerably and therefore should not be viewed as clear-cut "stages," even though the balances among them do change over time. These reactions are numbness, yearning, disorganization and despair, and reorganization.

1. *Numbness.* In the first few hours or days after the death, the bereaved person is often in a daze—gripped by a sense of unreality and disbelief and almost empty of feelings. He or she may make plane reservations, call relatives, or order flowers—all as if in a dream. Underneath this state of numbness and shock is a sense of being on the verge of bursting, and occasionally painful emotions do break through. The bereaved person is struggling to defend himself or herself against the full weight of the loss. The bad news has not fully registered.

2. *Yearning.* As the numbing sense of shock and disbelief diminishes, the bereaved person experiences more and more agony. Grief comes in pangs or waves that typically are most severe from 5 to 14 days after the death. The grieving person has feelings of panic, bouts of uncontrollable weeping, and physical aches and pains. He or she is likely to be extremely restless, unable to concentrate or to sleep, and preoccupied with thoughts of the loved one and of the events leading to the death.

According to Parkes and Bowlby, the reaction that most clearly makes grieving different from other kinds of emotional distress is *separation anxiety,* the distress of being parted from the object of one's attachment. The bereaved person pines and yearns for the loved one and actually searches for the deceased, as if the finality of the loss has not yet been accepted. A widow may think she heard her husband's voice or saw him in a crowd; she may sense his presence in the house and draw comfort from it; she may be drawn to his favorite chair or wear his bathrobe. Ultimately, of course, the quest to be reunited is doomed to fail.

Both anger and guilt are also common reactions during these early weeks and months of bereavement. Bereaved people often feel irritable and on edge and sometimes experience intense rage—at the loved one for dying, at the doctors for not doing a better job, at almost anyone. To make sense of the death, they seem to need to pin blame somewhere. Unfortunately, they often find reason to blame themselves. It does not take much to trigger guilt feelings in the bereaved. A father may say he should have spent more time teaching his son gun safety; the friend of young man who dies of AIDS may feel that he was not a good enough friend. One of the London widows studied by Parkes actually felt guilty because she never made her husband bread pudding.

3. *Disorganization and despair.* As time passes, pangs of intense grief and yearning become less frequent, though they still occur. As it sinks in that a reunion with the loved one is impossible, depression, despair, and apathy increasingly predominate. During most

Grief is expressed through mourning behaviors such as visiting the cemetery.

of the first year after the death, and longer in many cases, bereaved individuals often feel apathetic or even defeated. They may have difficulty managing their lives or taking any interest in activities.

4. *Reorganization.* Eventually, bereaved persons begin to pull themselves together again as their pangs of grief and periods of apathy become less frequent. They come to invest less emotional energy in their attachment to the deceased and more in their attachments to the living. If married, they begin to make the transition from being a wife or husband to being a widow or widower, slowly shedding their old identities as married persons and forging new identities as individuals. They begin to feel ready for new activities and possibly for new relationships or attachments.

Figure 17.2 visually portrays the first three phases of the grieving process described by Parkes (see also Jacobs et al., 1987–1988; Shuchter & Zisook, 1993). After a death, numbness and disbelief quickly wane, but we may continue to shake our heads in disbelief occasionally even later on. Yearning and pining in response to separation are most intense in the first few months after the death, but these reactions also continue to plague us now and then in later months. Finally, as we gradually accept the finality of death, despair and depression increasingly overwhelm us, until

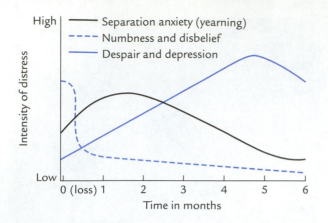

FIGURE 17.2 *The overlapping phases of the grieving process over time* (From Jacobs et al., 1987–1988)

these reactions too give way and we begin to reorganize or recover.

Some researchers would disagree with the specifics of this view of bereavement. However, most would agree on this: *Bereavement is a complex and multidimensional process that varies from person to person and normally takes a long time* (deVries, 1997; Shuchter & Zisook, 1993). Many emotional reactions are involved, and their course and intensity differ from person to person. Most important, recovery after the death of a loved one typically is not evident until a year or two after the death (Cleiren, 1993; W. Stroebe & Stroebe, 1993). Full recovery can take several years, and some people never fully recover from a crushing loss or give up their attachment to the loved one who died (Klass, 1993; Rubin, 1993; Wortman & Silver, 1989).

Yet we expect quick recovery: We are very sympathetic toward the bereaved immediately after a death—eager to help in any way we can—but then we quickly grow weary of someone who is depressed, irritable, or preoccupied. We begin to think, sometimes after only a few weeks, that it is time for the bereaved person to cheer up and get on with life. We are wrong! To be of help to bereaved people, one must understand that their feelings of disbelief, yearning, and despair are likely to linger for a very long time.

We have now presented some of the major theories of how people experience dying and bereavement. However, these theories have been based primarily on the responses of adults. How do infants, children, and adolescents respond to death? What does death even mean to infants and young children? A life-span perspective on death and dying is needed.

THE INFANT

Infants surely do not comprehend death as the cessation of life, but they gain an understanding of concepts that pave the way for an understanding of death. Infants may, for example, come to grasp the concepts of being and nonbeing from such experiences as watching objects and people appear and disappear, playing peek-a-boo, and even going to sleep and "coming alive" again in the morning (Maurer, 1961). As infants begin to acquire the concept of object permanence during Piaget's sensorimotor stage, they search for missing or hidden objects and can become quite frustrated when those objects are "all gone." Very possibly, then, infants first form a global category of things that are "all gone" and later divide it into subcategories, one of which is "dead" (Kastenbaum, 1985).

The experience that is most directly relevant to an emerging concept of death is the disappearance (for whatever reason) of a loved one. It is here that John Bowlby's theory of attachment is helpful. Infants form their first attachments at about the age of 6 or 7 months, when they begin to display signs of separation anxiety or to protest when their beloved caregivers leave them. They have begun to grasp the concept that persons, like objects, have permanent existence, and they expect a loved one who has disappeared to reappear. According to Bowlby, they are biologically programmed to protest separations by crying, searching for their loved one, and attempting to follow, for these behaviors increase the chances that they will be reunited with a caregiver and protected from harm.

Bowlby (1980) goes on to show that infants separated from their attachment figures display many of the same reactions that bereaved adults do. Whether the cause of separation from a parent is death or a vacation trip, infants first engage in vigorous *protest*—yearning and searching for the loved one and expressing outrage when they fail. One 17-month-old girl said only, "Mum, Mum, Mum," for three days after her mother died. She was willing to sit on a nurse's lap but would turn her back, as if she did not want to see that the nurse was not "Mum" (Freud & Burlingham, cited in Bowlby, 1980).

If, after a week or so of protest, an infant has not succeeded in finding the loved one, he or she begins to *despair* and show depressionlike symptoms; the baby loses hope, ends the search, and becomes apathetic and sad. Grief may be reflected in a poor appetite, a change in sleeping patterns, excessive clinginess, or regression to less mature behavior (Furman, 1984; Raphael, 1983; and the discussion in Chapter 16 of infant depression and failure to thrive). Ultimately, such infants begin to seek new relationships and will recover from their loss most completely if they can count on an existing attachment figure (for example, the surviving parent) or can attach themselves to someone new.

Clearly, then, infants who are at least 6 months of age or so and who have formed genuine attachment bonds are old enough to experience intense grief and depressionlike symptoms when a parent or other loved one dies. Moreover, the responses they display—the protest and yearning, the despair and depression—are the same sorts of responses that bereaved adults display. What is the difference? It is mainly that infants lack the concept that death means permanent separation or loss. Without the cognitive capacity to interpret what has happened, an infant whose mother has died may have little idea why she is gone, where she is, or why she does not return.

THE CHILD

As much as parents would like to shelter their children from unpleasant life experiences, children do encounter death in their early years. Of college students reflecting on their first encounters with death, 57% recalled the death of a relative, most often a grandparent, and 28% the death of a pet (Dickinson, 1992). How do children come to understand and cope with these experiences of death?

Grasping the Concept of Death

Contrary to what many adults would like to believe, young children are highly curious about death, think about it with some frequency, and are quite willing to talk about it (Kastenbaum, 1998; Stambrook & Parker, 1987). Yet their beliefs about death are often considerably different from those of adults. In Western societies, a "mature" understanding of death has several components (Essa & Murray, 1994; Hoffman & Strauss, 1985; Speece & Brent, 1984, 1992). We see death as characterized by:

1. *Finality.* It is the cessation of life and of all life processes, such as movement, sensation, and thought.
2. *Irreversibility.* It cannot be undone.
3. *Universality.* It is inevitable and happens to all living things.
4. *Biological causality.* It is the result of natural processes internal to the organism, even if external causes set off these internal changes.

Researchers have studied children's conception of death by asking them the sorts of questions contained in Table 17.1 or having them draw pictures of their images of death. Children between the ages of 3 and 5 have some understanding of death, especially its universality, but they are a long way from having a mature concept of it (Brent et al., 1996). Rather than viewing death as a final cessation of life functions, they tend to think that the dead retain at least some of their capacities. According to preschoolers, the dead may not be as lively and capable as the living, but they may well be able to move around a bit, hear what

TABLE 17.1

Western children's concepts of death and questions pertaining to them

Concept	Questions
Finality	Can a dead person move? Get hungry? Speak? Think? Dream? Do dead people know that they are dead?
Irreversibility	Can a dead person become a live person again? Is there anything that could make a dead animal come back to life?
Universality	Does everyone die at some time? Will your parents die someday? Your friends? Will you die?
Biological causality	What makes a person die? Why do animals die?

SOURCES: Based on Hoffman & Strauss, 1985; Florian & Kravetz, 1985; and other sources

is going on outside their coffins, experience hunger, think, and dream (Hoffman & Strauss, 1985).

Preschool-age children also tend to view death as reversible rather irreversible. They liken it to a sleep (from which one can awaken) or to a trip (from which one can return). With the right medical care, the proper foods, or a bit of magic, a dead person might be brought back to life (Speece & Brent, 1984). As one youngster put it, "Help them, give them hot food, and keep them healthy so it won't happen again" (Koocher, 1974, p. 408). Finally, young children think death is caused by one concrete, external agent or another. One may say that people die because they eat aluminum foil; another may say the cause is eating a dirty bug or a Styrofoam cup (Koocher, 1974; see also Figure 17.3).

Children ages 5 to 7 make considerable progress in acquiring an understanding of death. The majority of children this age do grasp that death is characterized by finality (cessation of life functions), irreversibility, and universality (Grollman, 1995; Speece & Brent, 1992). What most still lack is an understanding of the biological causality of death. In the early elementary school years, children can catalog a number of concrete causes of death (guns, knives, poison, illness, and so on), but they fail to appreciate that all deaths ultimately involve a failure of internal biological processes (Hoffman & Strauss, 1985). Paula, age 12, had mastered this concept: "When the heart stops, blood stops circulating, you stop breathing and that's it. . . . there's lots of ways it can get started, but that's what really happens" (Koocher, 1974, pp. 407–408).

Some children have far more complete understandings of death than their agemates. Why might this be? Children's concepts of death appear to be influenced by (1) their level of cognitive development

FIGURE 17.3 *Young children can talk about and draw pictures of death, but they do not yet understand that it is internally caused. This drawing by a 5-year-old boy focuses on one specific external cause of death—a knife.* (From Wenestam & Wass, 1987)

[annotations in drawing] He got kills too! / and to old he / killed. / That man is killing him / This man is killing people with a knife.

and (2) their life experiences. Young children in Piaget's preoperational stage of cognitive development tend to think magically and very concretely about death and may easily come to wrong conclusions about how or why someone died. Major breakthroughs in the understanding of death occur in about the 5 to 7 age range—precisely when children are making the transition from the preoperational stage of cognitive development to the concrete-operational stage. Children's understandings of death, like their understandings of many other concepts, become more adultlike as they begin to master important logical operations (Essa & Murray, 1994).

But children's concepts of death are also influenced by the cultural context in which they live and the specific cultural and religious beliefs to which they are exposed (Stambrook & Parker, 1987). For example, Jewish and Christian children in Israel, who are taught the Western concept of death we have been discussing, show more understanding of it than Druze children, who are taught to believe in reincarnation (Florian & Kravetz, 1985). Understandably, a child who is taught that people are reincarnated after they die may not view death as an irreversible cessation of all life processes. Indeed, as children in both the United States and China approach adolescence and are increasingly exposed to religious teachings and information about biology and medicine, they lose some of their conviction that death is irreversible and final (Brent et al., 1996). They begin to believe that the dead may well be brought back to life through medical or divine intervention or might live on in an afterlife.

Within any society, children's unique life experiences will also affect their understandings of death. Children who have life-threatening illnesses or who encounter violence and death often grasp death sooner than other children (Essa & Murray, 1994; O'Halloran & Altmaier, 1996). For example, preschool children growing up in conflict-torn areas of Belfast, Northern Ireland, at a time when violent deaths were routine, have been found to have a more complete concept of death than children in more peaceful neighborhoods of the city (McWhirter, Young, & Majury, 1983).

Youngsters' understandings are also influenced by how their parents and others communicate with them about death. How is a young child to overcome the belief that death is temporary, for example, if parents and other adults claim that relatives who have died are "asleep"? Isn't it also understandable that such a child might become afraid of going to bed at night? We must also wonder about statements that liken death to a journey, as in "Grandma has gone away." For all the young child knows, Grandma might be across town or in Chicago and surely could return if she really cared. Experts on death insist that adults only make death more confusing and frightening to young children when they use such euphemisms (Aspinall, 1996). They recommend that parents give children honest but simple answers to the many questions they naturally ask about death and capitalize on events such as the death of a pet to teach children about death and help them understand and express their emotions. Appropriate programs at school can also help familiarize children with the concept of death and accelerate the development of mature understandings of it (Aspinall, 1996; Schonfeld & Kappelman, 1990).

In sum, young children are naturally curious about death and form ideas about it from an early age. During the preschool years, they may understand that death is universal but view it as only a lessening of life processes rather than a cessation of them, as reversible, and as attributable to very concrete external causes. By early elementary school, in Western societies at least, they have mastered the concepts that death is a final, irreversible, and universal cessation of life functions; later, they will come to appreciate that death is ultimately due to a failure of internal biological processes. Each child's grasp of death will depend on his or her level at cognitive development and death-related experience. Is it any different for children who are actually dying?

The Dying Child

Parents and doctors often assume that terminally ill children are unaware that they will die and are better off remaining ignorant. Yet research shows that dying children are far more aware of what is happening to them than adults realize; their tragic experience gives them an understanding of death before their time (Essa & Murray, 1994). Consider what Myra Bluebond-Langner (1977) found when she carefully observed children ranging in age from 2 to 14 who had leukemia. Even preschool children arrived, over time, at an understanding that they were going to die and that death is irreversible. Despite the secretiveness of adults, these children were closely attuned to what was going on around them. They noticed changes in their treatments and subtle changes in the way adults interacted with them, and they noticed what happened to other children who had the same disease and were receiving the same treatments. Over time many of these ill children stopped talking about the long-term future and wanted to celebrate holidays such as Christmas early. A doctor trying to get one boy to cooperate with a procedure said "I thought you would understand, Sandy. You told me once you wanted to be a doctor." Sandy threw an empty syringe at the doctor and screamed "I'm not going to be anything!" (p. 59).

How do terminally ill children cope with the knowledge that they are dying? They are not all the models of bravery that some people suppose them to be. Instead, they experience the same wide range of

Children who are dying need to know that they are loved and to have opportunities to express their concerns and fears.

emotions that dying adults experience—the anger, the depression, and the anxieties over being separated from loved ones, experiencing pain, and wondering what lies ahead (Waechter, 1984). Preschool children may not talk about dying, but they may reveal their fears by having temper tantrums or portraying violent acts in their pretend play (see Figure 17.4). School-age children understand more about their situation and can talk about their feelings if they are given an opportunity to do so. They very much want to participate in normal activities so that they will not feel inadequate compared with their peers, and they want to maintain a sense of control or mastery, even if the best they can do is take charge of deciding which finger should be pricked for a blood sample.

In short, children with terminal illnesses often become painfully aware of the fact that they are dying. They experience a full range of unpleasant emotions and reveal in their behavior, if not in their words, that they are anxious and upset. What, then, can be done to help them cope? Quite obviously, they need the love and support of parents, siblings, and other significant individuals in their lives. Children with cancer who seem to adjust well emotionally to their ordeal have a strong sense that their parents are in control of the situation (Worchel, Copeland, & Barker, 1997). They also have opportunities to talk with adults about their feelings (Faulkner, 1997). In other words, they are not the victims of a well-intentioned but ultimately counterproductive conspiracy of silence on the part of parents and medical care providers.

The Bereaved Child

Children's coping capacities are also tested when a parent, sibling, pet, or other loved one dies. Three major

FIGURE 17.4 *Young children who are dying seem to understand far more about their situation than we give them credit for, and they often express their awareness through their play and drawings. A 5-year-old boy dying of inoperable heart disease drew this self-portrait featuring a big heart with broken lines drawn through it. He then angrily crossed himself out with a black crayon, shouting "Color me gone!"* (From Baker, 1991)

messages have emerged from studies of bereaved children: (1) Children most certainly grieve, (2) they express their grief differently than adults do, and (3) they are vulnerable to long-term negative effects of bereavement (Aspinall, 1996; Osterweis, Solomon, & Green, 1984).

Consider some of the reactions that have been observed in young children whose parents have died (Raphael, 1983; Silverman & Worden, 1993). These children often misbehave or strike out in rage at their surviving parent. They ask endless questions: Where is Daddy? When is he coming back? Will I get a new Daddy? Anxiety about attachment and separation is common; over half of the bereaved children in one study reported being scared that other family members might die (Sanchez et al., 1994). Other children go about their activities as if nothing had happened.

You can readily see how a parent might be disturbed by some of these behaviors—the seemingly inexplicable tantrums, the distressing questions, or, worse, the child's apparent lack of concern about the death. Yet all of these behaviors indicate that the loss is affecting the child greatly. Even an apparent lack of concern may be the child's attempt to deny and avoid emotions that are simply too overwhelming to face (Osterweis et al., 1984). It is important, then, for adults to recognize that children express their grief in ways that reflect their levels of development.

What grief symptoms do children most commonly experience? The preschooler's grief is likely to manifest itself in problems with sleeping, eating, toileting, and other daily routines. Negative moods, dependency, and temper tantrums are also common (Osterweis et al., 1984; Van Eerdewegh, Clayton, & Van Eerdewegh, 1985). Older children express their sadness, anger, and fear more directly (Osterweis et al., 1984), but somatic symptoms such as headaches and other physical ailments are also common (Worden & Silverman, 1996).

Remember, children are highly dependent on their parents. Moreover, they simply do not have the coping capacities that adults do. As a result, children often take years to recover fully from the death of a parent. Even before the death of a terminally ill parent, children show high levels of depression and anxiety symptoms (Siegel, Karus, & Raveis, 1996). Well beyond the first year after the death, some bereaved children continue to display problems such as unhappiness, low self-esteem, social withdrawal, difficulty in school, and problem behavior (Worden & Silverman, 1996; Osterweis et al., 1984). In one longitudinal study of school-age children, one in five children who had lost a parent had serious adjustment problems two years after the death (Worden & Silverman, 1996). Adults who suffer from chronic depression and related forms of psychopathology are more likely than other adults to have experienced the death of a parent in early childhood (Harris & Bifulco, 1991). However, as we will see later, most bereaved children—especially those who have positive coping skills and a good deal of social support—overcome their losses quite successfully.

THE ADOLESCENT

Adolescents typically understand death as the irreversible cessation of biological processes. Moreover, once they have attained Piaget's stage of formal operations, they can think in more abstract ways about death (Corr, 1995; Koocher, 1973; see also Figure 17.5). Although they sometimes ignore the fact that they too will die and take risks that they might not take if they truly believed that death is final, universal, and irreversible (Noppe & Noppe, 1996), adolescents as they get older put their new cognitive capacities to use to ponder and discuss the meaning of death and to think about such hypotheticals as an afterlife (Noppe & Noppe, 1997; Wass, 1991).

Just as children's reactions to death and dying reflect their developmental capacities and needs, adolescents' reactions to becoming terminally ill are likely to reflect the themes of adolescence (Adams & Deveau, 1986; Corr, 1995; Stevens & Dunsmore, 1996). Concerned about their body images as they experience physical and sexual maturation, they may be acutely disturbed if their illness brings with it hair loss, weight gain, amputation, or other such physical changes. Wanting to be accepted by peers, they may feel like "freaks" or become upset when friends who do not know what to say or do abandon them. Eager to become more autonomous, they may be distressed by having to depend on parents and medical personnel and may struggle to assert their wills and maintain a sense of control. Trying to establish their identities and chart future goals, adolescents may be angry and bitter at having their dreams snatched from them.

Similarly, the reactions of an adolescent to the death of a family member or friend are likely to reflect the themes of the adolescent period (Tyson-Rawson, 1996). For example, even though teenagers are becoming increasingly independent of their parents, they still depend quite heavily on them for emotional support and guidance. The adolescent whose parent dies often wants to maintain the attachment and may carry on an internal dialogue with the dead parent for years (Silverman & Worden, 1993). And, given the importance of peers in this developmental period, it is not surprising that adolescents are often devastated when a close friend dies in a car accident, commits suicide, or succumbs to a deadly disease. Unfortunately, the grief of friends often is not taken as seriously as that of family members (Schachter, 1991–1992).

For the most part, adolescents grieve much as adults do. However, they are sometimes reluctant to express their grief for fear of seeming abnormal or losing control and may express their anguish instead

FIGURE 17.5 *Compared to children, adolescents often express very abstract concepts of death that are influenced by their religious training. The 16-year-old girl who drew this picture explained: "The water represents the depth of death. The bubbles represent the releasing of the soul. The tree represents the memories we leave behind. The flame represents Hell and the halo represents Heaven."* (From Wenestam & Wass, 1987)

through delinquent behavior and somatic ailments (Clark, Pynoos, & Goebel, 1994; Osterweis et al., 1984). The adolescent who yearns for a dead parent may feel that he or she is being sucked back into the dependency of childhood and may therefore lock these painful feelings inside:

> "When my mother died I thought my heart would break," recalled Geoffrey, age 14. "Yet I couldn't cry. It was locked inside. It was private and tender and sensitive like the way I loved her. They said to me, 'You're cool man, real cool, the way you've taken it,' but I wasn't cool at all. I was hot—hot and raging. All my anger, all my sadness was building up inside me. But I just didn't know any way to let it out." (Raphael, 1983, p. 176)

In sum, by the time children reach adolescence, they have acquired a mature concept of death, understanding it as a final cessation of life that is irreversible, universal, and biologically caused and thinking more abstractly about it. Whereas young children often express their grief indirectly through their behavior (by wetting their beds, throwing tantrums, and so on), older children and adolescents more directly experience and express painful thoughts and emotions. In each period, children's reactions to bereavement or to the knowledge that they are dying reflect their developmental needs. Thus, when a life-threatening illness strikes, the young child may most want reassurance of parental love and protection, the school-age child may most wish to keep up with peers in school, and the adolescent may most want to maintain a sense of identity and autonomy. They all need their parents and other adults to listen to them and help them cope with their very real emotional reactions.

THE ADULT

How do adults cope with death and dying? We have already introduced models describing adults' experiences of dying and bereavement that partially answer that question. Here we'll elaborate by examining attitudes toward death and dying during the adult years, responses to bereavement in the context of the family life cycle, and factors that determine whether an individual of any age grieves "normally" or pathologically.

Death Anxiety

Adults in our society know full well that death is an irreversible cessation of life processes. However, this by no means suggests that they have mastered their fears of death. **Death anxiety** is a complex set of concerns about death and dying. The person who is highly anxious about death does not want to think about it or be reminded of it, dreads developing a serious illness and facing the pain and stress that dying may entail, and strongly senses that life is too short (see Kastenbaum, 1998; Lonetto & Templer, 1986; Neimeyer, 1994).

Who is most or least anxious about death? On death-anxiety scales, men tend to express less death anxiety than women do, although they may just be less willing to admit their fears (Hickson, Housley, & Boyle, 1988; Lonetto & Templer, 1986). Strongly religious individuals tend to be less anxious about death than other people (Alvarado et al., 1995; Bohannon, 1991), and they manage to cope more successfully with bereavement too, perhaps because they can find meaning in death (McIntosh, Silver, & Wortman, 1993). In addition, personality has a bearing on death anxiety. For example, individuals who have high self-esteem and a sense of mastery are typically less anxious about death and dying than individuals who lack confidence or a sense of control (Lester & Templer, 1992–1993; Rappaport et al., 1993).

Even though elderly adults are nearer to death, they typically express less death anxiety than young or middle-aged adults do, in part because they are more likely to have worked out issues such as those involved in Erikson's stage of integrity versus despair (Rasmussen & Brems, 1996). Older and younger adults also have somewhat different concerns about dying. Richard Kalish and David Reynolds (1977) surveyed

TABLE 17.2

If you were told you had a terminal disease and six months to live, how would you want to spend your time until you died? (*N* = 434)			
Responses	Young (%)	Middle-Aged (%)	Old (%)
Marked change in lifestyle, self-related (travel, sex, drugs, experiences)	24	15	9
Withdrawal (read, contemplate, pray)	14	14	37
Focus concern on others; be with loved ones	29	25	12
Complete projects; tie up loose ends	11	10	3
No change in lifestyle	17	29	31
Other/don't know	5	6	8

SOURCE: From Kalish & Reynolds, 1977

members of four ethnic groups in the Los Angeles area. Table 17.2 shows what these adults said they would want to do if they knew they had only six months to live. Young adults seemed to want to "grab all the gusto" they could by having experiences that would otherwise be forgone and spending time with loved ones. Young adults who are dying often feel angry that life goals will not be realized and important relationships must be left behind (Kalish, 1981). Middle-aged adults were primarily concerned about the welfare of their loved ones. Finally, the elderly adults in this study, having realized many of their goals and raised their children, wanted to contemplate the meaning of their lives.

In sum, death anxiety, though part of the human condition throughout the life span, is likely to be lowest among people who are male, strongly religious, well adjusted, and elderly. Young adults find it especially threatening to be unable to achieve their goals and to enjoy newly formed relationships, middle-aged adults are concerned primarily about the welfare of their families, and elderly adults want to make sense of their lives before they die. Notice the echoes of Erik Erikson here: identity and intimacy concerns in early adulthood, issues of generativity and caring for the younger generation in middle adulthood, and a quest for a sense of personal integrity in old age.

Death and the Family Life Cycle

Given the importance of family attachments throughout the life span, it is not surprising that the deaths of family members are typically harder to bear than other deaths. We really cannot understand bereavement unless we adopt a family systems approach and consider the specific relationships and roles that are altered by a death in the family and the ways in which family members affect one another during the grieving process (Lamberti & Detmer, 1993). So let's examine some of the special challenges associated with three kinds of death in the family: the loss of a spouse, of a child, and of a parent.

The Loss of a Spouse

Most of what we know about bereavement is based on studies of widows and widowers. Experiencing the death of a spouse becomes increasingly likely as we age; it is something most women can expect to endure, for women both outlive men on average and marry men who are older than they are. The marital relationship is a central one for most adults, and the loss of a marriage partner can mean the loss of a great deal indeed. Moreover, the death of a spouse often precipitates other changes—the need to move, enter the labor force or change jobs, assume responsibilities that the spouse formerly performed, parent single-handedly, and so on. Thus widows or widowers must redefine their roles and even their identities in fundamental ways (DeGarmo & Kitson, 1996; Lopata, 1996). Similar challenges confront anyone, married or not, who loses a romantic attachment figure.

As we noted earlier in this chapter, Colin Murray Parkes, in his extensive research on widows and widowers, has concluded that bereaved adults progress through overlapping phases of numbness, yearning, disorganization and despair, and reorganization. What toll does this grieving process take on the individual's physical, emotional, and cognitive functioning? Table 17.3 shows some of the symptoms that widows and widowers commonly report (Parkes, 1986; and see Cleiren, 1993; Shuchter & Zisook, 1993).

Quite clearly, widows and widowers experience many problems. They are at risk for illness and physical symptoms such as loss of appetite, and they tend to overindulge not only in alcohol but in tranquilizers and cigarettes as well. Cognitive functions such as memory and decision making are often impaired. Not surprisingly, their grief creates emotional problems like loneliness and anxiety. Most do not become clinically depressed, but most do display symptoms of depression in the first months after the death (Harlow, Goldberg, & Comstock, 1991). Although losing a spouse is difficult at any age, young and middle-aged adults appear to suffer somewhat more than elderly adults, perhaps because the death of a spouse at these ages is earlier than normal and therefore unexpected (Parkes, 1986; Zisook & Shuchter, 1991).

TABLE 17.3

Percentages of bereaved and nonbereaved adults reporting various symptoms within the past year*

Symptoms	Bereaved	Nonbereaved
Admitted to hospital	18%	6%
Awakening during night	40	12
Changes in appetite	50	29
Increased alcohol consumption	28	3
Sought help for emotional problems	34	7
Wonder if anything is worthwhile	50	26
Worried by loneliness	65	25
Depressed or very unhappy (in past few weeks)	49	29
Restless	49	22
Memory not all right	29	9
Hard to make up mind	53	32
Feel somewhat apart or remote even among friends	34	15

*Responses were gathered in the Harvard Bereavement Study from men and women under the age of 45 who had lost their spouses 14 months before the interviews. Nonbereaved respondents were married adults matched to members of the bereaved sample so that they were similar in age, sex, family size, geographic area, nationality, and socioeconomic status.
SOURCE: Based on Parkes, 1986

Widows and widowers are even at increased risk of death (M. Stroebe & Stroebe, 1993). In an immense study of widowed adults in Finland, risks of death due to accidental and violent causes, alcohol-related causes, heart disease, and lung cancer were all higher than normal, especially in the first six months after a spouse's death (Martikainen & Valkonen, 1996). These extra risks of mortality are higher for men than for women (Lillard & Waite, 1995; M. Stroebe & Stroebe, 1993). Although the stresses of bereavement can undermine the health of both men and women, men often depend particularly heavily on their spouses for social support and must cope with many new responsibilities alone.

We know that the first year after the death is typically the most difficult, that many widows and widowers begin to show signs of recovery in the second year, and that time tends to heal. Yet grieving and symptoms of distress may continue for years after the death (Parkes & Weiss, 1983; Thompson et al., 1991). Darrin Lehman, Camille Wortman, and Allan Williams (1987) compared adults whose spouses had died in car accidents four to seven years previously to similar nonbereaved adults. Even this long after their tragedies, bereaved adults showed more depression, hostility, and anxiety; had more worries; and felt less of a sense of psychological well-being than nonbereaved adults. Perhaps because these deaths had been sudden and violent, 62% still had recurring thoughts that the death was unfair or that they had been cheated, and 68% said that they had been unable to find any meaning in the death.

Mainly, it is difficult to generalize about adults who lose their spouses, as their reactions are diverse. With this diversity in mind, one team of researchers attempted to identify subgroups of widowed men and women based on their patterns of psychological distress over a period of 18 months (Levy, Martinkowski, & Derby, 1994). As Figure 17.6 shows, some adults were quite depressed throughout the 18-month period, others showed little sign of depression at any point, and still others became more and more depressed over time. Only a third showed the pattern most of us would consider typical: high levels of depression early and then a lessening of distress in the months following the death.

In sum, the loss of a spouse is a painful and damaging experience. During the first weeks and months after the death, the psychological pain is typically most acute, and the risks of developing serious physical or mental health problems or even dying are at a peak. However, many widows and widowers experience emotional aftereffects for years afterward. If this picture seems too dismal, let us emphasize that the vast majority of bereaved adults *do not* die and do not develop major physical or psychological disorders, even though their risks are higher than average. Instead, most recover from their grief and get on with their lives—and manage to do so without professional treatment (Parkes, 1986).

The Loss of a Child

My child has died! My heart is torn to shreds. My body is screaming. My mind is crazed. . . . The question is always present on my mind. Why? How could this possibly have happened? The anger is ever so deep, so strong, so frightening. (Bertman, 1991, p. 323, citing a mother's reflections on how she reacted to her 16-year-old daughter's death in a car accident after the initial numbness wore off)

No loss is more difficult for an adult, particularly a mother, than the death of a child (Cleiren, 1993; Lang & Gottlieb, 1993). Even when there is forewarning, the loss of a child is experienced as unexpected, untimely, and unjust: Parents are supposed to protect their children from harm, and children just aren't supposed to die before their parents do (Sprang &

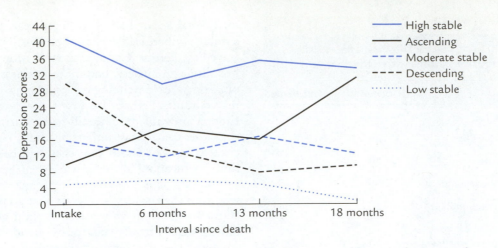

FIGURE 17.6 *Different people show different patterns of bereavement. Here we see five patterns of change in depression scores assessed over 18 months within a sample of widowed men and women. Notice that only a minority show the pattern most of us view as normal: many depression symptoms early, fewer later on.* (Adapted from Levy et al., 1994)

McNeil, 1995). Many children who die do so suddenly in accidents, which only heightens the shock. And let's not forget that the parent role is a central one for most adults, that their attachments to their children run deep, and that their own dreams are tied to the fates of their children.

Compared to adults who have lost a spouse or a parent, parents who have lost a child are exceptionally angry, guilty, and depressed, and they have a greater number of physical complaints (Sanders, 1979–1980; Sprang & McNeil, 1995). Understandably, parents experience a raging anger that something so terrible could happen, and they often feel that they were somehow to blame or failed in their role as parent and protector (Rando, 1991). They often continue to feel attached to an internal representation of the lost child many years after the death (Rubin, 1993).

The age of the child who dies has relatively little impact on the severity of the grief: Parents can experience severe grief reactions even after a miscarriage, stillborn delivery, or abortion (Hutti, 1992; Janssen, Cuisinier, & Hoogduin, 1996). Although most recover in due time, about 10 to 15% of mothers who lose a pregnancy develop a psychological disorder (Janssen et al., 1996). Their difficulties can be aggravated when friends and relatives fail to appreciate that a real loss has occurred and offer no support (Osterweis et al., 1984).

It goes without saying that the death of an infant, child, or adolescent can be devastating. What may be more surprising is the fact that the death of an adult child is usually no less difficult to bear than the death of a younger child (Lesher & Bergey, 1988; Littlefield & Rushton, 1986). The specific issues bereaved parents face may differ depending on the age of the child (de Vries, Lana, & Falck, 1994), but the parent/child attachment bond is strong—even before children are born and even after they leave the nest. Moreover, the death of a child alters the whole family system and affects the well-being of the marital relationship, as well as of siblings and grandparents.

Effects on the Marriage. The odds of divorce sometimes increase after the death of a child, but most couples stay together (Najman et al., 1993). Even so, the marital relationship is likely to be strained because each partner grieves in his or her own way and is not always able to provide social support to the other (Bohannon, 1990–1991). Both sexual and emotional intimacy are likely to decrease (Gottlieb, Lang, & Amsel, 1996; Najman et al., 1993). Strains are likely to be especially severe if the marriage was shaky before the death (Bohannon, 1990–1991; Schwab, 1992).

Effects on Siblings. Grieving parents may also have difficulty giving their surviving children the love and support they need to cope with *their* loss. Children are deeply affected when a brother or sister dies, but their grief is often not fully appreciated (Davies, 1995; Schreder, 1995). Siblings of children battling cancer, for example, may resent it if they are neglected by their parents, may be anxious about their own health, may feel guilty about some of the unsavory feelings of rivalry they have, and may feel pressure after the death to replace the lost child in their parents' eyes (Adams & Deveau, 1987). They have been found to experience stomachaches and headaches and have difficulty sleeping for up to three years after the death (Davies, 1995).

One 12-year-old boy whose brother died described his experience this way: "My Dad can't talk about it, and my mom cries a lot. It's really hard on them. I pre-

The death of a child can threaten the marital relationship and change the entire family system.

tend I'm O.K. I usually just stay in my room" (Wass, 1991, p. 29). If siblings are isolated from their understandably upset parents or if their grief is not taken seriously, they may have an especially hard time recovering. Bereaved children fare better if their parents are not overwhelmed by grief, remain warm and supportive, and encourage open discussion of feelings (Applebaum & Burns, 1991; Graham-Pole et al., 1989).

Effects on Grandparents.
Finally, grandparents also grieve following the death of a child, both for their grandchild *and* for their child, the bereaved parent (Fry, 1997; Ponzetti, 1992). As one grandparent said, "It's like a double whammy!" (DeFrain et al., 1991–1992, p. 178). Grandparents may feel guilty about surviving their grandchildren and helpless to protect their adult children from pain (Fry, 1997). Clearly, then, those who are attempting to help bereaved families need to include the *whole* family in their efforts.

The Loss of a Parent

Even if we escape the death of a child or spouse, the death of a parent is a normative life transition that the vast majority of us will experience. As noted already, children sometimes experience long-lasting problems after the death of a parent. Fortunately, most of us do not have to face this event until we are middle-aged. We are typically less emotionally dependent on our parents by then, and most of us are heavily invested in our own families. Moreover, we expect that our parents will die someday and have prepared ourselves, at least to some degree. Finally, we are likely to share the widespread societal belief that the death of an elderly person is somehow less tragic than that of a young person who has not yet had a chance to live.

Perhaps for all of these reasons, adjusting to the death of a parent is usually not as difficult as adjusting to the death of a spouse or child (Bower, 1997; Cleiren, 1993; Leahy, 1992–1993). This is not to say that a parent's death is easy to bear, however. Adult children may feel vulnerable and alone in the world when their parents no longer stand between them and death (Scharlach & Fredriksen, 1993), and they may experience new pressures as the senior generation in the family (Osterweis et al., 1984). Guilt about not doing enough for the parent who died is also common (Moss et al., 1993). These concerns take a toll: Compared to adults who are not bereaved, adults who have lost a parent in the past three years have higher rates of psychological distress, alcohol use, and health problems (Umberson & Chen, 1994).

Perhaps the soundest conclusion we can reach about deaths in the family is that *all* of them have the potential to cause a great deal of suffering, to put adults at risk for physical and psychological problems and even death, and to perturb the family system. Still, reactions to the loss of a spouse, child, or parent are also influenced by the special qualities of each of those attachments. The death of a child may be particularly difficult because it is so unexpected, whereas the death of a parent may be easier to bear because it is anticipated.

Who Copes and Who Succumbs?

Why do some individuals cope effectively with grief—and even gain strength from their ordeal—whereas others develop serious psychological disorders after a loss? To answer that question, we must first answer another: Where is the boundary line between normal and abnormal grieving?

Defining Pathological Grief

Beverly Raphael (1983) has identified three forms of pathological (or, as psychologists now prefer to say, "complicated") grief (see also Jacobs, 1993). The victim of *chronic grief* grieves for a longer time than is normal. Years after the death, for example, a widow may still burst into tears at any reminder of her husband, set a place at the table for him, and feel highly anxious and unable to function. These reactions are perfectly normal in the year or so after the death, but they may become abnormal if they persist too long. A second form of pathological grief is *distorted grief*, a tendency to show some grief symptoms in exaggerated form and other symptoms hardly at all. Thus a bereaved person may be intensely angry or overwhelmingly guilty, and this one reaction may completely overshadow or interfere with other responses. Finally, pathology may exist if the person grieves too little—if there is an *absence, inhibition, or delay of grief.* A

parent may persist in denying that a child has died long beyond the point at which numbness typically gives way to a fuller awareness of reality, or a widower may find himself unable to cry or to express his painful feelings. In short, either too much or too little of any of the responses that constitute the "normal" bereavement reaction can be a bad sign.

As we discovered in Chapter 16, however, it is not always easy to pin down the dividing line between normal and abnormal behavior. Age norms and social norms must be considered. As we saw earlier, children may express their grief differently than adults do and may be more prone to use denial and acting out as coping mechanisms (Raphael, 1983). In addition, grieving occurs in a cultural context (Lopata, 1996). An Egyptian mother may be conforming to her culture's norms of mourning if she sits alone, withdrawn and mute, for months or even years after a child's death; likewise, a Balinese mother is simply following the rules of her culture if she is calm, composed, and even seemingly cheerful soon after a child's death (Wikan, 1988, 1991). We would certainly be wrong to conclude, on the basis of our own society's norms, that the Egyptian mother is suffering from chronic grief or the Balinese mother from absent or inhibited grief.

Another warning: As Camille Wortman and Roxane Silver (1989) argue, some of our assumptions about what constitutes normal grief are not backed very strongly by research (see also Bonanno et al., 1995; Stroebe et al., 1992). For example, we assume that bereaved persons should confront their loss, experience painful emotions, and "work through" those emotions in order to recover. Yet bereaved individuals who ruminate a lot about what they might have done differently and why they are coping so poorly and who engage in heavy self-analysis after a loss often end up more distressed months later than those who are less reflective (Nolen-Hoeksema, McBride, & Larson, 1997). What's more, bereaved adults who never show much emotional distress often end up better adjusted months later than those who grieve the hardest after their losses (Bonanno et al., 1995; Cleiren, 1993). Particularly in the face of losses as traumatic as those that took place during the Holocaust, repressing painful memories so that one can get on with life may be more adaptive than reviewing them (Kaminer & Lavie, 1993).

Most of us also believe that, once they have grieved sufficiently, bereaved individuals should resolve their grief and detach themselves from their lost attachment figure. As we have seen, though, significant numbers of bereaved individuals continue to grieve many years after a death. Is it then appropriate to insist that grieving lasting more than a year or two is "pathological"? Similarly, we know that many bereaved people maintain their attachments to lost loved ones indefinitely rather than severing those bonds as they resolve their grief (Klass, 1993; Lohnes & Kalter, 1994). Shouldn't we then be more cautious about labeling as abnormal individuals who sense the presence of a lost loved one and consult with him or her about important decisions years after a death?

With those warnings in mind, we can still ask what distinguishes the people who cope well with loss from those who cope poorly. We will consider some of the factors that make it especially difficult for adults—and children as well—to cope with the death of a loved one. As is true of coping following any major life event, coping with bereavement is influenced by the resources possessed by the individual, the nature of the event to be coped with, and the surrounding context of support and stressors.

Personal Resources

Just as some individuals are better able to cope with their own dying than others are, some are more equipped to handle the stresses of bereavement. Bowlby's attachment theory emphasizes that *early experiences in attachment relationships* influence how we later relate to others and handle losses of relationships. If infants and young children receive loving and responsive care, they form internal working models of self and others that tell them that they are lovable and that other people can be trusted (see Chapter 13). They are later able to cope with the deaths of loved ones relatively well. By contrast, infants or young children who receive inconsistent care or who suffer the loss of an important attachment figure by death or abandonment may have more difficulty coping with loss later in life. They may, for example, develop a resistant (or ambivalent) style of attachment that leads them to be overly dependent on others and to display extreme grief and anxiety after a loss (Bowlby, 1980; see also Harris & Bifulco, 1991; Parkes, 1991). Or, they may develop an avoidant attachment style that causes them to be "compulsively self-reliant" and to have difficulty accepting a loss and expressing grief.

Early experiences in the family, as well as genetic endowment, contribute to personality development, and several aspects of *personality and coping style* influence how successfully people cope with death. For example, those individuals who have difficulty coping tend to have low self-esteem (Lund et al., 1985–1986) and lack a sense that they are in control of their lives (Haas-Hawkings et al., 1985). Many were experiencing psychological problems such as depression long before they were bereaved (Norris & Murrell, 1990; Zisook & Shuchter, 1991). So, among the bereaved, as among the dying, the enduring capacity of the individual to cope with life's problems is an important influence on outcomes.

The Nature of the Loss

Bereavement outcomes are also influenced by characteristics of the event with which the person must cope. The closeness of one's *relationship to the deceased* is obviously important (Cleiren, 1993; Jacobs, 1993). We grieve harder for attachment figures such as spouses and children than for people with whom we have not formed true attachment bonds (Cleiren, 1993). Moreover, children grieve especially hard for parents to whom they were closely attached (Umberson & Chen, 1994), and spouses grieve especially hard for partners with whom they shared a common identity and on whom they depended greatly (DeGarmo & Kitson, 1996; Sanders, 1993).

Bereavement reactions are not strongly influenced by the *suddenness or unexpectedness of the death*. Sudden deaths are somewhat—but only somewhat—more difficult than deaths for which there is forewarning (Cleiren, 1993; Sanders, 1993). Possibly this is because the survivors have had no opportunity to engage in anticipatory grief and are thrown into a state of shock. Still, no amount of preparation can eliminate the need to grieve after a death, and the differences in bereavement following sudden death or death after a prolonged illness are surprisingly small. This is probably because having to cope with the threat of separation from a loved one and to care for that individual are stressful experiences in themselves. A long death watch can take as great a toll on mental health as coping with the death that follows (Bodnar & Klecolt-Glaser, 1994; Hays, Kasl, & Jacobs, 1994).

Finally, the *cause of death* influences bereavement outcomes. One of the reasons why the death of a child is so painful is that children's deaths are often the result of "senseless" events such as car accidents, drownings, or homicides. Coping with the suicide of a loved one can also be particularly difficult (Gilewski et al., 1991; Stillion & McDowell, 1996). Suicide survivors may have trouble accepting what happened or figuring out why it happened; they may be plagued by guilt and anger and feel rejected by the deceased. Needless to say, bereavement can also be especially difficult if the bereaved person contributed in some way, even accidentally, to the death (Osterweis et al., 1984).

The Context of Supports and Stressors

Grief reactions are influenced positively by the presence of a strong social support system and negatively by the presence of additional life stressors (de Vries, 1997; Lopata, 1996). Social support is crucial at all ages. It is especially important for the young child whose parent dies to have adequate substitute parenting. Children tend to have more problems if the surviving parent is crippled by grief and insensitive to their needs than if the surviving parent or substitute caregiver helps them express their grief and is able to maintain a loving home environment (Elizur & Kaffman, 1983; Van Eerdewegh et al., 1985). Too often, adults attempt to protect children from the pain of death and inadvertently isolate them from the rest of the family when they are most in need of support.

Bereaved adults also benefit from social support (Norris & Murrell, 1990; Worden & Silverman, 1993). Indeed, family members of all ages recover best when they are close to one another and can share their distress (Kissane et al., 1996). How can family members and friends be most supportive? Bereaved individuals do not appreciate people who try to cheer them up or force them out of their grief. Instead, they are helped most by people who serve as confidants and allow them to express their painful feelings freely (Lehman, Ellard, & Wortman, 1986; Pennebaker & O'Heeron, 1984).

Just as social support helps the bereaved, additional stressors hurt. For example, outcomes tend to be poor for widows who must cope with financial problems after bereavement and for widowers who have difficulty managing household tasks without their wives (Lopata, 1996; Umberson, Wortman, & Kessler, 1992). Widows and widowers may have more than the usual difficulty resolving their grief if they must also take on the challenges of caring single-handedly for young children, finding a new job, or moving (Parkes, 1986; Worden & Silverman, 1993).

By taking into account the person who has experienced a death, the nature of the death, and the context surrounding it, we can put together a profile of the individuals who are most likely to display pathological, or complicated, grief and to develop long-term problems after bereavement. These individuals have had an unfortunate history of interpersonal relationships, perhaps suffering the death of a parent when they were young or insecurity in their early attachments. They have had previous psychological problems and generally have difficulty coping effectively with adversity. The person who died is someone on whom they depended greatly, and the death was sudden, untimely, and seemingly senseless. Finally, these high-risk individuals lack the kinds of social support that can aid them in overcoming their loss, and they experience stresses in addition to the stress of bereavement itself.

Bereavement and Human Development

Guided by common beliefs about bereavement, most researchers have viewed grief as something like an illness. We catch it, it damages our physical and mental health, and we ultimately return to our normal state. Guided by this medical model of grieving, researchers often fail to look for *positive* effects of death on survivors. Yet bereavement is the very kind of life event that has the potential to foster personal growth (de Vries, 1997; Lopata, 1996). Granted, it is a painful way to grow, and we could hardly recommend it as a plan for optimizing human development. Still, the literature on death and dying is filled with testimonials about the lessons that can be learned through suffering.

Many bereaved individuals believe that they have become more confident, family-oriented, open, and religious people who have a greater appreciation of

life (Lehman et al., 1993). Many widows master new skills (including those required to do tasks their husbands performed), become more independent, and emerge with new identities and higher self-esteem (Lopata, 1996; Salahu-Din, 1996). Even while bereavement is undermining their satisfaction with life, it is increasing their sense of self-efficacy (Arbuckle & de Vries, 1995). These testimonials make the point:

> A bereaved sibling: "I won't part with anyone in anger; I want to leave them knowing that I care. I think I have become a more caring person because of my experience." (Rosen, 1986, p. 167)

> A widow, surprised by how successfully she had built a new and satisfying life: "I'm doing things I never thought I could do. I hate being alone but I have good friends and we care about each other. I'm even traveling. I enjoy my work. I never thought I'd hear myself say that I don't mind being single." (Silverman, 1981, p. 55)

> A mother whose infant died: "Now I can survive anything." (DeFrain, Taylor, & Ernst, 1982, p. 57)

So perhaps it is by encountering tragedy that we learn to cope with tragedy, and perhaps it is by struggling to find meaning in death that we come to find meaning in life. Let's now see what can be done to help people cope more effectively with their experiences of death and dying.

APPLICATIONS: LESSENING THE STING OF DEATH

As a society, we are struggling to stop denying and start facing up to the reality of death. A number of efforts are underway to help children and adults who are dying or who are bereaved grapple with death and their feelings about it.

For the Dying

Dramatic changes in the care of dying persons have occurred within the past few decades, thanks in part to the efforts of Elisabeth Kübler-Ross and others. Still, many signs suggest that hospital personnel continue to place too much emphasis on curing terminally ill patients and keeping them alive and too little on controlling their pain and allowing them to "die with dignity" (Colburn, 1995). Out of such concerns has arisen an approach to caring for the dying person intended to be more humane: the hospice.

A **hospice** is a program that supports dying persons and their families through a philosophy of "caring" rather than "curing." The first such facility was St. Christopher's Hospice near London, opened

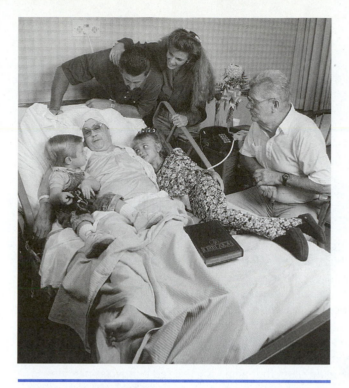

Hospice care helps people live even when they're dying.

off death as long as possible, the setting is sterile and clinical, and family members are too often viewed as a nuisance rather than as the most important of all caregivers. The differences are lessening as more and more hospitals create hospice programs of their own or adopt elements of the hospice philosophy in caring for terminally ill patients (Seale, 1989).

What are the advantages to dying patients and their families of spending their last days together receiving hospice care? In an evaluation of hospice facility care, at-home hospice care, and conventional hospital care in Great Britain, Clive Seale (1991) found that hospice patients spent more of their last days without pain, underwent fewer medical interventions and operations, and received nursing care that was more oriented to their emotional needs. Their families grieved as much as those of hospitalized patients but were more satisfied with the care they received (see also Kastenbaum, 1998). The hospice approach may not work for all, but for some it does mean an opportunity to die with dignity, free of pain and surrounded by loved ones.

in 1967 under the direction of Dr. Cicely Saunders (1977). The concept spread quickly to North America, where hospices have now been established in most communities, serving children with cancer, adults with AIDS, and other dying persons (Kastenbaum, 1998; Siebold, 1992). In many hospice programs today, though, there is no care facility like St. Christopher's; instead, dying patients stay at home and are visited by hospice workers.

What makes hospice care different from hospital care? Whether hospice care is provided in a facility or at home, it entails these key features (Corr & Corr, 1992; Siebold, 1992):

1. The dying person and his or her family—not the "experts"—decide what support they need and want.
2. Attempts to cure the patient or prolong his or her life are deemphasized.
3. Pain control is emphasized.
4. The setting for care is as normal as possible (preferably the patient's own home, or at least a homelike facility that does not have the sterile atmosphere of many hospital wards).
5. Bereavement counseling is provided to the family before and after the death.

The contrasts between hospice care and traditional hospital care are striking. In the hospital, medical experts have control, efforts are directed at staving

For the Bereaved

Part of the mission of hospice programs is to help family members prepare for and cope with their loss. What other help is available for bereaved individuals? Like anyone with psychological problems, bereaved individuals can benefit from individual or group psychotherapy or counseling (Jacobs, 1993; Piper, McCallum, & Azim, 1992). Those whose grief is chronic and disabling may need help in getting beyond it, whereas those whose grief is inhibited may want help expressing their painful emotions (Worden, 1991). Because death takes place in a family context, family therapy often makes a good deal of sense (Gordon, 1995; Sandler et al., 1992). Family therapy can help bereaved parents and children communicate more openly and share their grief, and it can enable parents to maintain the kind of warm and supportive parenting style that will facilitate their children's recovery.

In the United States, still another approach to helping the bereaved has proven popular: the mutual support, or self-help, group. One such mutual support program is Compassionate Friends, serving parents whose children have died. Other groups are aimed at widows and widowers. Parents without Partners, THEOS (They Help Each Other Spiritually), The Widowed Person's Service, and similar support groups bring widows and widowers together to offer one another everything from help and advice in such practical matters as settling finances or finding a job to emotional support and friendship (Lopata, 1996).

Is participation in a mutual support group for widows beneficial? For many individuals, yes (Lieberman,

1993; Lund & Caserta, 1992). Compared to nonparticipants, participants tend to be less depressed and anxious, use less medication, and have a greater sense of well-being and self-esteem (Lieberman & Videka-Sherman, 1986). Perhaps this is because other widows are in the best position to understand what a new widow is going through and to offer effective social support. One widow summed it up this way: "What's helpful? Why, people who are in the 'same boat.' Unless you've been there you just can't understand" (Bankoff, 1983, p. 230).

◆ SUMMARY POINTS

1. In defining death as a biological process, the Harvard definition of total brain death is widely applied, but there are still many controversies surrounding it and the issues of active and passive euthanasia and assisted suicide. The social meanings of death vary across cultures, subcultures, and individuals.

2. The average life expectancy for a newborn in the United States has risen to almost 76 years, higher than that in less developed countries; death rates decline after infancy and rise dramatically after early adulthood; as we age, accidents give way to chronic diseases as primary causes of death.

3. Programmed theories of aging claim that aging is governed by species heredity and individual genetic endowment and include the notion that the shortening of telomeres at the end of chromosomes is responsible for the Hayflick limit on cell reproduction; damage theories of aging focus on an accumulation of random damage to DNA caused by destructive free radicals and other agents. Many genetic and environmental factors interact to bring about aging and death.

4. Elisabeth Kübler-Ross stimulated much concern for dying patients by describing five "stages" of dying (denial/isolation, anger, bargaining, depression, and acceptance). However, dying people do not seem to progress through clear-cut stages, and their experiences depend on their diseases and personalities.

5. Bereavement precipitates grief and mourning, which are expressed, according to Parkes and Bowlby, in overlapping phases of numbness, yearning, disorganization and despair, and, finally, after a year or two, reorganization.

6. Infants do not comprehend death but clearly grieve, protesting and despairing after separations in ways that parallel adults' responses to bereavement.

7. Children are very curious about death. In our society they usually understand by age 5 to 7 that it is a final cessation of life processes that is irreversible and universal and later realize that it is ultimately caused by internal biological changes. Terminally ill children often become very aware of their situations; bereaved children express their grief less directly than adults do and often experience bodily symptoms, academic difficulties, and behavior problems.

8. Adolescents use their advanced cognitive capacities to understand death more abstractly; they cope with dying and bereavement in ways that reflect the developmental themes of adolescence.

9. Death anxiety appears to be lowest among adults who are male, strongly religious, well adjusted, and elderly. Widows and widowers experience many physical, emotional, and cognitive symptoms, are at increased risk of dying, and often show emotional aftereffects for years. The death of a child is often even more difficult for an adult to bear and affects siblings and grandparents as well; the death of an elderly parent, because it is expected, is often easier.

10. Pathological grief (grief that is chronic, distorted, or inhibited) is not easily defined because social and age norms must be considered and some of our common beliefs about "normal" grieving are not well supported. However, intense and prolonged grief is especially likely among individuals who had painful early attachment experiences or lack positive personality traits and coping skills, who had dependent relationships

with individuals who died suddenly and senselessly, and who lack positive social support and face additional stressors.

11. Successful efforts to help people cope with death have included hospice programs for dying patients and their families and mutual support groups for the bereaved.

FOOD FOR THOUGHT

1. Look carefully at the five stages of dying that Kübler-Ross believes terminally ill patients experience and at the four phases of adjustment bereaved persons experience according to Parkes and Bowlby. What common themes do you see? How do they differ?

2. Lucy (age 3), Lilly (age 9), and Lally (age 16) have all been diagnosed with cancer. They have been given chemotherapy and radiation treatments for a number of months but seem to be getting worse rather than better. Write a short monologue for each child expressing (a) whether and how she understands that she is dying, and (b) her major concerns and wishes, based on what you know of normal development at her age.

3. Speaking for all bereaved people everywhere, write a letter to the editor stating what people should understand about normal bereavement and about what they can do to support bereaved people. Your letter should refer to research on normal bereavement.

W ON THE WEB

1. *DeathNET*   This site reflects the views of the right-to-die movement and offers a wealth of material concerning the medical, legal, cultural, and moral aspects of death and dying. You will find information on euthanasia, Dr. Kevorkian, Living Wills, and other topics discussed in this chapter and can search the site for information on topics you choose.
   http://www.islandnet.com/~deathnet/

2. *Euthanasia and Assisted Suicide*   A more balanced look at the debate over euthanasia, starting with an explanation of relevant terms. You can learn how Oregon became the first state to legalize physician-assisted suicide under controlled conditions, and find out how different religions view the issues.
   http://www.religioustolerance.org/euthanas.htm

3. *Death Education*   If you want to explore your own feelings about death and see what's covered in courses on death and dying, Nan P. Chico of California State University at Haywood can help with a variety of material on all aspects of the topic; she also talks very reassuringly about this often painful subject.
   http://isis.csuhayward.edu/ALSS/soc/NAN/dd/dd.htm

KEY TERMS

total brain death	damage theories of aging	denial
euthanasia	maximum life span	bereavement
assisted suicide	Hayflick limit	grief
Living Will	telomere	mourning
life expectancy	error accumulation theory	anticipatory grief
programmed theories of aging	free radicals	death anxiety
	dietary restriction	hospice

Epilogue: Fitting the Pieces Together

MAJOR TRENDS IN HUMAN DEVELOPMENT

1. Infants (Birth to Age 2)
2. Preschool Children (Ages 2 through 5)
3. School-Age Children (Ages 6 through 11)
4. Adolescents (Ages 12 through 19)
5. Young Adults (Ages 20 through 39)
6. Middle-Aged Adults (Ages 40 through 64)
7. Older Adults (Age 65 and Up)

MAJOR THEMES IN HUMAN DEVELOPMENT

1. We Are Whole Persons throughout the Life Span
2. Development Proceeds in Multiple Directions
3. There Is Both Continuity and Discontinuity in Development
4. There Is Much Plasticity in Human Development
5. Nature and Nurture Truly Interact in Development
6. We Are Individuals, Becoming Even More Diverse with Age
7. We Develop in a Cultural and Historical Context
8. We Are Active in Our Own Development
9. Development Is Best Viewed as a Lifelong Process
10. Development Is Best Viewed from Multiple Perspectives

Our survey of human development from conception to death and of the many forces that influence it is now complete. In this epilogue my goal is to help you integrate what you have learned—to see the "big picture." I summarize significant trends in physical, cognitive, personal, and social aspects of development, age period by age period. I then pull together the major themes that have emerged from recent theory and research.

MAJOR TRENDS IN HUMAN DEVELOPMENT

Throughout this book we have seen that each phase of the life span has distinct characteristics. Here, at the risk of oversimplifying, I offer portraits of the developing person in seven periods of life—sketches that show how the strands of development, intertwined, make a *whole person*.

1. Infants (Birth to Age 2)

What is most striking about infant development is the staggering speed with which babies acquire all the basic capacities that make us human. Thanks to orderly and rapid development before birth, the newborn starts life marvelously equipped to adapt to its environment using reflexes, to take in information through all of its senses, and to learn from and remember its experiences. The rapid growth of body and brain during the first two years of life then transforms this neonate into a toddler who is walking, talking, and asserting a newfound sense of self.

As the cortical centers of the brain mature and become organized, many automatic reflexes disappear and are replaced by *voluntary* motor behaviors. In a predictable sequence, infants sit, creep and crawl, and then walk independently, at about 1 year of age; during their first year, they also perfect a pincer grasp and become better able to manipulate objects with their hands. As their perceptual and motor skills improve, so does their capacity to explore the world around them and to actively contribute to their own cognitive development in the process.

As babies progress through the substages of Piaget's *sensorimotor period*, they develop their minds through their own active efforts to perceive and act upon the world around them. They come to understand that objects have permanent existence, even when they are out of sight. They also acquire *symbolic capacity*—the ability to let one thing stand for another—which is central to intellectual activity throughout the remainder of the life span. By the end of the sensorimotor period, they can use symbols such as images to *mentally* devise solutions to problems before trying them out. After cooing and babbling, they will utter their first words at the age of 1 and form two-word sentences such as "Go car" by the age of 2. As Vygotsky would remind us, these cognitive and linguistic breakthroughs grow out of the child's social interactions with parents and other guides.

As their cognitive capacities expand, infants become more aware of themselves as individuals. By age 2 they recognize themselves in the mirror and know that they are girls or boys. In fact, infants are individuals from birth, each with a distinctive and genetically influenced temperament that serves as a foundation for later personality.

Infants' temperaments, coupled with their parents' styles of interacting with them, influence how successfully they resolve Erikson's first psychosocial conflict, that of *trust versus mistrust*, and whether they form secure, resistant, or avoidant attachments to their caregivers starting at about 7 months of age. The parent/child relationship dominates the social world of the infant and serves as a training ground for later social relationships. Cognitive changes and daily exchanges with attachment figures give rise to more sophisticated social skills that infants then apply in encounters with peers. Equipped with the ability to perceive and act upon the environment, with impressive cognitive and linguistic capacities, with an awareness of self, and with trust in their caregivers, infants are ready to venture out into a larger social world.

2. Preschool Children (Ages 2 through 5)

During the preschool years, 2-year-olds who toddle and teeter along and speak in two-word sentences become young children ready for formal schooling. As their brains continue to mature and as they gain motor experience, preschool children acquire the gross motor control they need to hop and catch balls and the fine motor skills they need to trace letters and use scissors.

During Piaget's *preoperational stage* of cognitive development, young children make wonderful use of their symbolic capacity, mastering all the basic rules of language (with the help of adults willing to converse with them) and joining with other children in imaginative sessions of social pretend play. True, young children often have difficulty with problems that require logical thinking. They fail Piaget's tests of *conservation*, thinking that the juice poured from a stocky glass into a tall, narrow glass somehow becomes "more juice." They are egocentric at times, failing to appreciate differences between their own perspectives and those of other individuals and assuming that their listeners know what they know. They are distractible and lack some of the information-processing skills that allow older children to think about two or more aspects of a problem at once and to use strategies such as rehearsal and organization to learn and remember more efficiently.

Preschoolers' personalities continue to take shape as they struggle with Erikson's conflicts of *autonomy versus shame* and *initiative versus guilt*. If all goes well, they develop the confidence to assert themselves and to carry out bold plans, and their self-esteem is high. They learn a good deal about themselves and other people, although their descriptions of people emphasize physical characteristics and activities and say little about inner qualities such as intentions, motives, and enduring personality traits. Although relatively lacking in self-control, they increasingly become socialized by those around them to internalize and follow rules of moral conduct. In no time at all, they also learn what they must know to be a boy or a girl in their society.

Preschool children's attachments to their caregivers continue to be central in their social worlds, but they hone their social skills in interactions with peers, learning to take their playmates' perspectives, engage in truly cooperative play, and enter into friendships. All in all, preschoolers are endlessly fascinating: charming and socially skilled but a bit egocentric at times, immensely curious and intellectually alive but sometimes quite illogical, here one moment but off on some new adventure the next.

3. School-Age Children (Ages 6 though 11)

Compared with preschool children, elementary school children seem considerably more self-controlled, serious, skilled, and logical. Their bodies grow slowly and steadily each year, and they continue to refine their motor skills and use their senses ever more intelligently by directing their attention where it most needs to be directed. As they enter Piaget's *concrete operations stage*, they become able to perform in their heads actions that previously had to be performed with their hands. They can mentally add, subtract, classify, and order objects; grasp conservation problems that fool the preschooler; and draw many logical conclusions about the workings of the physical world. They master the fine points of the rules of language and become better able to take the perspectives of their listeners in conversations. They acquire the memory strategies and other information-processing skills, as well as the knowledge base, it takes to do their schoolwork. And, although their scores on intelligence tests can fluctuate from year to year, their IQs begin to predict fairly well their intellectual standings as adolescents or adults.

The cognitive growth that occurs during the school years, along with social experience, allows children to understand themselves and other people in terms of inner personality traits and underlying motives. School-age children work through Erikson's conflict of *industry versus inferiority* as they attempt to master new skills, compare their accomplishments with those of their classmates, and absorb feedback about where they stand in their reading groups and where they finish in races. The unrealistically high self-esteem of the preschooler drops as children gain a more accurate view of their strengths and weaknesses. Most children also develop fairly consistent personalities, at least parts of which survive into adulthood.

Under the guidance of parents and teachers, and through their interactions with peers, children also learn the values and moral standards of the society around them. Most are at Kohlberg's level of

Arnold Sidney Michlin was born September 2, 1920, in Altoona, Pennsylvania. His parents were Russian immigrants. He was the oldest of three children.

Arnold with his younger brother on a pony during the 1920s. The two boys were very close and worked together for 40 years in the family business.

At 15 with his family in 1935. Arnold (center right) and his brother worked for their father in the business of bottling paint sundries. Times were hard. No pony rides for the family at this stage of their life. The brothers honed their entreprenurial skills and together started a war surplus business after WWII.

Arnold (right) and his wife Florence were high school sweethearts who married in 1941 when she was only 18. He worked for Ford during the war, attended night school at the Detroit Institute of Technology, and graduated as a chemist. Drafted in 1945, he served in the U.S. Army Chemical Warfare Service. Later he founded Michlin Surplus Company in partnership with his brother.

Arnold and Florence raised a family of four in a suburb of Detroit, where he built his dream house in 1950. In 1952, he and his brother purchased a solvent reclamation plant. When their father died in 1954, they took over his paint sundries business. Eventually, the three companies merged, and Arnold's experience as a chemist proved very beneficial at this stage in his life.

Despite the responsibilities of his successful business, Arnold was active in public service. As a young adult he joined the Anti-Defamation League of B'nai B'rith, and was co-founder of Detroit Materials for the People of Palestine. At 50, he founded the Detroit Action Committee for Soviet Jewry; and at 61 he founded the American Arab and Jewish Friends. At 65 he helped organize the Muslim, Jewish, and Christian Trialog, and at 68 he received the United Way "Heart of Gold" award for community service. One of Arnold's fine moments was at the age of 71 when he met Barbara Bush, a guest speaker at the United Way annual banquet. Arnold continues public service, and enjoys spending time with his five grandchildren.

preconventional morality, in which what matters most is whether their acts will be rewarded or punished, but advances in social role-taking skills will help them progress from preconventional to *conventional morality* in early adolescence. School-age children also continue to learn about and conform to prevailing social standards regarding how boys and girls should behave.

The social world of school-age children is more extensive than that of infants and preschool children. Family life is still very important, but more and more time is spent with peers—usually those of the same sex—playing organized games and developing caring friendships or chumships. Youngsters who are rejected by their peers and don't have friends miss out on these important social learning opportunities and tend to become maladjusted adults. Teachers, coaches, TV characters, and sports stars all help to socialize children as well so that they gain the skills and values they will need to do the serious work of adulthood.

4. Adolescents (Ages 12 through 19)

Adolescence, the passage between childhood and adulthood, is a time of dramatic physical, cognitive, and social change. Adolescents who are adjusting to their growth spurt and to the sexual maturation of their bodies at around ages 12 to 14 are naturally preoccupied with their physical appearance and are often more upset by their misshapen noses or gargantuan feet than by any intellectual or character flaws they may possess. Puberty brings with it not only new physical capacities and unfamiliar sexual urges but also new, more adultlike relationships with members of the other sex and with parents.

Meanwhile, the mind is undergoing its own metamorphosis. The child who could reason logically about real-world problems becomes the adolescent who can think systematically about worlds that do not even exist and ideas that contradict reality. When adolescents fully master Piaget's *formal operations stage,* they can formulate and test hypotheses to solve scientific problems and can grasp abstract theories and philosophies. These and other new cognitive capacities result in more effective information processing but sometimes leave adolescents susceptible to *adolescent egocentrism,* thoroughly confused about what to believe, painfully aware of gaps between what is and what should be, and rebellious when their parents or other authority figures are not "logical" enough for their tastes.

Cognitive gains also put adolescents in a position to think about themselves and other people in more sophisticated ways. Teenagers begin to describe themselves in more abstract terms, referring to their core values and philosophies of life. They are more introspective and self-aware than they were as children and can analyze themselves and other people to determine what really makes them tick. By late adolescence many can integrate their self-perceptions into a coherent sense of who they are, resolving Erikson's conflict of *identity versus role confusion* and charting careers and other life goals. Conventional moral reasoning is achieved as adolescents first emphasize the importance of being a "good boy" or "good girl," as defined by parents and society, and later appreciate the need for law and order in the larger social system.

Partly because teenagers become more physically and cognitively mature, and partly because society demands that they take seriously the task of readying themselves for adult roles, social relationships change a good deal during the adolescent years. The balance of power in the family shifts so that adolescents increasingly participate in making decisions about their lives. Adolescents become more and more involved in peer activities, intimate friendships with same- and other-sex peers, and dating relationships. Heightened conformity to peer influence gets many adolescents into a brush or two with the law, but the peer group serves the useful function of helping children who depend heavily on their parents become adults who are less reliant on both parents and peers. Although about 20% of adolescents experience emotional storm and stress during this period of the life span, most teenagers emerge with impressive physical, intellectual, and social competencies and with at least preliminary notions of who they are and what they will be as adults.

5. Young Adults (Ages 20 through 39)

The years of infancy, childhood, and adolescence are all a preparation for entry into adult life. Physiologically, young adults are at their peak; strength, endurance, reaction time, perceptual abilities, and sexual responsiveness are all optimal, even though the aging process is taking slight, and usually not even noticeable, tolls on the body. Early adulthood is also a period of effective cognitive functioning. Some young adults will solidify and possibly expand upon their command of formal-operational thought and devise more efficient information-processing strategies, especially in their areas of expertise. Most adults continue to be conventional moral reasoners, but about one in six begins to think at the level of *postconventional morality,* grasping the moral principles underlying society's rules and regulations. If they continue to use their minds, young adults will often improve some on the IQ test scores they obtained as adolescents.

It is fortunate that young adults are physically and intellectually capable, for they face many challenges. They must often continue to work on the adolescent task of identity formation, exploring different

As a teenager, Alice loved sports. She played on a softball team and started playing tennis with her father at age 10. At 18, she was the first Women's State Tennis Champion in Wisconsin, a title she would earn twice. In college, she worked hard to help support her family through the Depression. Finally, she had to drop out of medical school. She continued taking night courses and met her future husband, whom she followed to California.

Alice at 6 months old. She was born July 9, 1906, in Holly, Michigan, to Gertrude Belle Wright and John Henry Alger.

As a 2-year-old, she was very active. One of her earlist memories is riding in a basket swing suspended from the living room ceiling.

Alice married in 1939 at age 33. She and her husband, George, traveled frequently and visited Catalina during the first year of their marriage. Three years later, they started a family. Alice worked as a manuscript typist for several well-known authors in Santa Barbara, California, and taught tennis to help support the family.

At 45, Alice enjoyed outings with her three young children at Monterey, California. She was involved in her children's activities at home and school. She even hosted an American Field Service exchange student from Germany for a year.

At 80 she poses with her grown children and husband of 47 years in Santa Barbara, California.

Still active at 92, Alice plays tennis 3 days a week, and is seen here flying a sailplane in the Santa Ynez Valley, California. She is also a Literacy Volunteer and knits cotton bandages for lepers through the Direct Relief Foundation. She reads voraciously and loves crossword puzzles. She sadly gave up playing bridge at age 90 because she was tired of being the "designated driver."

options before they settle on a career direction. Meanwhile, they are likely to be working through Erikson's early-adult crisis of *intimacy versus isolation* and, if all goes well, committing themselves to a partner. Young adults are changed by marriage, new parenthood, and other normal events of the family life cycle, just as they are affected by their work experiences. Parenthood tends to lower marital satisfaction and push young husbands and wives into more divergent and traditional gender roles.

In view of the many life changes experienced by young adults, perhaps it is not surprising that this period is characterized by higher divorce rates and more stress-related mental health problems than the later adult years. However, for most young adults this is also an exciting and productive time of life, a time for gaining expertise, independence, and confidence.

6. Middle-Aged Adults (Ages 40 through 64)

Middle adulthood often strikes us as a more settled period than early adulthood, but it is certainly not devoid of change. Gradual declines in the body and its physical capacities that began in the 20s and 30s may now become noticeable. Gray hairs (or no hairs!), a shortness of breath after exercise, and a need for reading glasses proclaim that one is aging. Women experience the changes of menopause around the age of 50; both men and women become more vulnerable to heart diseases and other chronic illnesses. Yet most of the physical changes that middle-aged adults experience occur quite slowly and are not severe, giving people plenty of time to adjust to and compensate for them.

Meanwhile, although intellectual capacities generally remain quite stable, middle-aged adults gradually gain some intellectual capacities and lose others. They amass knowledge and often perform better than young adults on measures of crystallized intelligence (vocabulary or general information). Moreover, they build expertise that allows them to solve everyday problems very effectively and reach peaks of creative achievement in their careers. True, toward the end of middle adulthood some individuals may feel that their memories are slipping a bit or may begin to struggle with the sorts of unfamiliar problems that measure fluid intelligence, but most intellectual skills hold up well in middle age.

Personalities that took form during childhood and that solidified during adolescence and early adulthood tend to persist into later adulthood, although significant change is possible. According to Erikson, middle-aged adults successfully resolve the conflict of *generativity versus stagnation* if they can invest their energies in nurturing the younger generation or in producing something of lasting value, but they may experience a sense of stagnation if they feel they have failed

their children or are preoccupied with their own needs. Midlife crisis is quite rare. Indeed, after the nest empties and middle-aged adults are freed of major parenting responsibilities, they often find their marriages more satisfying, take pride in their grown children and grandchildren, and become more androgynous, expressing both their masculine and feminine sides.

7. Older Adults (Age 65 and Up)

The poet Robert Browning expressed a very positive image of late adulthood when he wrote: "Grow old along with me! The best is yet to be, the last of life for which the first was made." By contrast, William Shakespeare, in *As You Like It* (Act II, Scene 7), characterized the seventh and final age of life as "second childishness and mere oblivion; sans teeth, sans eyes, sans taste, sans everything." The truth lies somewhere in between: Old age *does* bring with it some losses and declines in functioning, but it is also, for most, a period of continued growth and many satisfactions.

By the time adults are in their 60s and 70s, most of them have a physical impairment of some kind—a chronic disease, a disability, failing eyesight or hearing, or, at the least, a slower nervous system and slower reactions. As they enter their 80s and 90s, more and more adults take longer to learn things, experience occasional memory lapses, or have difficulty solving novel problems. Yet only a minority develop Alzheimer's disease, and most retain well the knowledge that they have crystallized over a lifetime and the cognitive and linguistic skills that they practice every day.

Although physical and cognitive declines are part of the experience of aging for most adults, we should be equally impressed by how successfully most adults adapt to these changes. They typically continue to carry out daily activities effectively, and they enjoy just as much self-esteem and life satisfaction as younger adults do. They do not crumble in the face of life changes such as retirement or widowhood. They continue to lead active social lives, use their sophisticated social-cognitive skills to understand other people and engage in complex moral reasoning, and enjoy close ties with both family and friends. And in the end most are able to successfully resolve Erikson's conflict of *integrity versus despair*, finding meaning in their lives and coming to terms with the inevitability of death.

These, then, are the broad themes of later life. Yet what may be most striking of all about elderly adults is their immense diversity. Many people in their 60s to early 70s (the *young old*) are healthy, active, and highly capable, whereas many adults in their 80s, 90s, and 100s (the *old-old* and the *oldest old*) show clear signs of physical and cognitive decline. And, within each of these groups, we find huge differences among individuals, for each adult carries into old age his or her own unique abilities, funds of knowledge, personality traits, and values and will cope with the challenges of aging and dying in his or her own way.

Table E.1 summarizes much of this discussion of physical, cognitive, personal, and social development within each period of the life span. Although this table can serve as a handy description of normal human development, it is important to understand the processes behind these changes.

MAJOR THEMES IN HUMAN DEVELOPMENT

Another way in which to leave you with the "big picture" is by highlighting some major generalizations about human development and the processes behind it. Many of these larger themes are incorporated in the life-span developmental perspective introduced in Chapter 1 (Baltes, 1987); some represent stands on the developmental issues laid out in Chapter 2; and most have been echoed throughout this book. I leave you with the following thoughts:

1. We Are Whole Persons throughout the Life Span

As our review of major developments in each life phase should make clear, it is the intermeshing of physical, cognitive, personal, and social development that gives each period of the life span—and each individual human—a distinctive and coherent quality. Thus the fact that 7-month-old infants become attached to their caregivers is not just a milestone in social development divorced from other aspects of development. The maturation of sensory and motor abilities permits infants to crawl after their parents to maintain the proximity they desire, and their cognitive growth makes them aware that caregivers continue to exist when they leave the room (and therefore can be retrieved). Moreover, the emergence of attachment bonds in turn affects development in other areas—for example, by providing toddlers with the security that allows them to explore the world around them and, in the process, develop their motor skills and cognitive capacities all the more. All the threads of development are interwoven in the whole developing person.

2. Development Proceeds in Multiple Directions

Chapter 5 introduced Heinz Werner's (1957) *orthogenetic principle*, which states that development proceeds from global states to states of increasing differentiation and integration of specific, differentiated states into coherent wholes. The orthogenetic principle is indeed a useful way of summarizing many developmental trends. The single, undifferentiated cell formed at conception becomes billions of highly specialized cells (neurons, blood cells, and so on), all organized into functioning systems (such as the brain). The young infant flails its whole body as a unit (global response); the older child moves specific parts of the body on command (differentiation) and coordinates separate movements to ride a bike (integration). Similarly, young children describe other people's personalities in only the most global terms ("He's nice" "She's mean"); school-age children develop a more differentiated vocabulary of trait labels for characterizing companions; and adolescents become true personality theorists, integrating all they have learned about their companions—contradictions included—into coherent theories about what makes these people tick.

Yet not all developmental change is a matter of acquiring more complex and organized behaviors or progressing toward some "mature" endpoint. As we have seen, human development involves gains *and* losses at every age, as well as systematic changes that make us neither better nor worse than we were before but simply different. Thus children who are gaining many learning skills are also losing some of their intrinsic motivation to learn as they progress through school, and older adults are losing mental speed but at the same time gaining knowledge, and sometimes even wisdom, that helps them compensate for slower information processing. In fact, every gain may have its corresponding loss, and every loss its corresponding gain (Baltes, 1987). Alice James, sister of pioneering psychologist William James and author Henry James, saw this even as her vision failed: "All loss is gain. Since I have become so near-sighted I see no dust or squalor, and therefore conceive of myself as living in splendor" (cited in Baltes, Smith, & Staudinger, 1992, p. 158).

We simply must abandon the old view that human development consists of growth or improvement up to adulthood, stability into middle age, and decline in old age. There are gains, losses, and just plain changes during *all* phases of the life span.

3. There Is Both Continuity and Discontinuity in Development

As we have seen throughout this book, developmentalists have long grappled with the issue of *continuity versus discontinuity* in human development. We now appreciate the wisdom of staking out a middle ground on the continuity/discontinuity issue.

For example, research supports Piaget's claim that children progress through qualitatively different stages of cognitive development, but we now know that these advances in cognitive development are achieved quite

TABLE E.1

Summary of physical, cognitive, personal, and social development across the life span

Period	Physical Development	Cognitive Development
Infant (0 to 2)	Rapid brain and body growth. Reflexes, then more voluntary motor control, walking at 1 year. Functioning senses at birth; early-emerging ability to make sense of sensory information.	Sensorimotor period: Through senses and actions, infants acquire symbolic capacity and object-permanence concept. Cooing, babbling, and then one-word and two-word sentences. Learning capacity and recognition memory from birth.
Preschool child (2 through 5)	Continued rapid brain development. Improved coordination and fine motor skills. Perceptual abilities are good; attention span is short.	Preoperational stage: Thought guided by perceptions rather than logic. Blossoming of symbolic capacity (language acquisition and pretend play). Some limits in information-processing capacity and reasoning; little deliberate use of memory strategies.
School-age child (6 through 11)	Slow physical growth and improved motor skills. Increased ability to control attention and use senses intelligently.	Concrete operations stage: Logical actions in the head; mastery of conservation. Mastery of fine points of language; improved memory strategies and problem solving. IQs begin to stabilize.
Adolescent (12 through 19)	Dramatic growth spurt and attainment of sexual maturity. Improved physical functioning. Concern with body image.	Formal operations stage: Hypothetical and abstract thought. Continued improvement of information-processing skills.
Young adult (20 through 39)	Time of peak functioning, but gradual declines in physical and perceptual capacities begin.	Sophisticated cognitive skills, especially in areas of expertise. Possibility of growth beyond formal thought and gains in knowledge.
Middle-aged adult (40 through 64)	Physical declines become noticeable (e.g., some loss of endurance, need for reading glasses). Increased chronic illness. Menopause and male climacteric.	Mostly stable intellectual functioning and often peak expertise and creative achievement. Fluid intelligence may begin to decline, but crystallized knowledge is maintained well.
Older adult (65+)	Continued physical decline; more chronic disease, disability, and sensory impairment. Slower reaction time.	Declines in cognition are common, but not inevitable. Slower learning, memory problems, declines in IQ and problem solving, especially if skills are rarely exercised.

gradually and occur faster in familiar than in less familiar domains of cognitive functioning (Flavell, Miller, & Miller, 1993). It seems that development often proceeds in a continuous, gradual manner that ultimately leads to stagelike discontinuities—qualitatively different performances that make us appreciate just how much growth has occurred.

Similarly, we have seen that some traits, including general intelligence and "big five" personality traits such as extraversion/introversion, carry over from childhood and become even more stable and consistent during adulthood. However, this continuity or consistency is far from perfect, and there is ample room for change. A bright child may lose intellectual capacity if he or she is abused and neglected at home and attends inferior schools, and an introverted child may gain confidence and blossom into a more outgoing individual with the aid of supportive friends. Such discontinuity means that predicting the character of the adult from knowledge of the child remains a risky business, even in the face of much continuity in development.

4. There Is Much Plasticity in Human Development

Repeatedly we have seen that human beings of all ages are characterized by considerable *plasticity*—by a remarkable capacity to change in response to experience and to get off one developmental pathway and onto

Personal Development	Social Development
Acquisition of sense of self, self-recognition, and awareness of gender identity. Temperament as basis of personality. Conflict of trust versus mistrust.	Social from birth. Attachment to caregiver at 7 months; separation and stranger anxiety follow. Increased social skills with parents and peers; capacity for simple pretend play. Family-centered lifestyle.
Concrete, physical self-concept. Rapid acquisition of gender role. Simple notions of morality. Conflicts of autonomy versus shame and initiative versus guilt.	Parent/child relationship still central in social world. Increased social-cognitive abilities, though egocentric in some ways. More cooperation with peers; social pretend play blossoms. Exposure to schooling.
Self-concept includes psychological traits. Personality "gels." Strong gender typing. Internalization of moral standards, but mainly preconventional morality. Much social comparison and conflict of industry versus inferiority.	Increased involvement with same-sex peers; formation of close chumships. Role-taking skills advance. Play centers on organized games with rules. School and television are important socialization agents.
More abstract and integrated self-concept. Adjustment to sexuality and gender role. Conventional moral reasoning. Conflict of identity versus role confusion.	Peak peer involvement and conformity. More emotionally intimate friendships; dating relationships begin. Parent/child relationship becomes more equal; autonomy increases. Involved in school and career exploration.
Continued work on identity. A minority of individuals shift to postconventional moral reasoning. Increased confidence. Divergence of roles in family according to sex. Personality fairly stable. Conflict of intimacy versus isolation.	Social networks continue to expand, and romantic relationships are formed. Most establish families and take on roles as spouses and parents. Careers are launched; much job switching. Period of much life change; high risk of divorce and psychological problems.
Continued personality stability, but possible midlife questioning and androgyny shift. Conflict of generativity versus stagnation.	Relations center within family. The nest empties and the grandparent role is often added to existing roles. High responsibility for younger and older generations. Career is more stable, and peak success is attained. Family and work roles dominate.
Most maintain characteristic personality traits, self-esteem, and life satisfaction. Growth for many as they resolve conflict of integrity versus despair.	Continued close ties to family and friends; loneliness is rare. Generally smooth adjustment to retirement, and maintenance of social activities. For women especially, adjustment to loss of spouse.

another. Thus, infants whose intellectual development is stunted by early malnutrition can catch up if they are given adequate diets and enriching experiences, and aging adults not only learn new intellectual tricks but sprout new neural synapses in response to intellectual stimulation. Evidence of plasticity and change in later life is especially heartening to those of us who want to foster healthy development. Contrary to what Freud believed, early experiences rarely make or break us. Instead, there are opportunities throughout the life span—within limits, of course—to undo the damage done by early traumas, to teach new skills, and to redirect lives along more fruitful paths. If adverse early experiences are followed by adverse later experiences, we can expect poor outcomes. But,

if potentially damaging early experiences are offset by favorable later experiences, we can expect developing humans to display considerable plasticity and resilience.

5. Nature and Nurture Truly Interact in Development

In a very important sense, the *nature/nurture issue* has been resolved. It is now clear that multiple causal forces, representing *both* nature and nurture and ranging from changes in cell chemistry to changes in the prevailing culture, conspire to determine human development. Biological and environmental influences jointly explain both universal developmental trends and individual differences in development. Consider a universal accomplishment such as acquiring language. Biological maturation, guided by a species-wide genetic blueprint, clearly makes this achievement possible, for no amount of stimulation from adults can make a 1-month-old baby speak sentences. Yet, even though an infant is maturationally ready, language skills will not be acquired without the input from the environment available in all societies—namely, opportunities to converse with speakers of the language. So it goes for many other developmental milestones: Nothing much happens unless the child is maturationally ready to learn *and* has the requisite learning experiences.

And why do individuals differ from one another in, for example, their command of language skills? We could argue that it is because different people inherit different intellectual potentials, but we would also have to acknowledge that a genetic potential for high intelligence would never be realized if a child has no opportunities for intellectual stimulation. We could stress the importance of stimulation, but we would have to acknowledge that children with the genes for high intelligence are more likely to actively seek out, elicit, and profit from such stimulation than children with limited genetic potential. In short, the experiences we have influence whether our genetic potentials are realized or not (*gene/environment interactions*), and the genes we inherit influence what experiences we seek out and have and how we respond to them (*gene/environment correlations*).

As the twin and adoption studies of behavior geneticists reveal, genetic differences among us help explain variation in virtually every human trait, from hair color to verbal ability to depression-proneness. Yet environmental factors count too, particularly the unique experiences that we do not share with siblings. Depending on which aspect of human development we study, we may find that either heredity or environment is more influential, but we cannot escape the conclusion that there would be no development at all without the ongoing contributions of *both*.

Nor can we escape the conclusion that it is often the *goodness of fit* between person and environment that matters in human development (Thomas & Chess, 1986). The child who is genetically predisposed to be irritable and difficult may become the rebellious, angry adolescent if parents are rigid, impatient, and punitive, but the same child may develop in more positive directions if the mesh between his or her temperament and the demands of the social environment is better. The adolescent starving for autonomy may do poorly in a middle school with rigid rules and little room for choice but thrive in a setting that allows more self-direction (Eccles et al., 1993). When there is goodness of fit between genetically influenced tenden-cies and environment, nature and nurture work together in the person's favor.

6. We Are Individuals, Becoming Even More Diverse with Age

In any human development textbook, there is a tendency to emphasize developmental phenomena that are shared by all or most individuals—to highlight the regularities and commonalities. We do indeed share a good deal with our fellow developing humans. But let us not lose sight of the fact that each of us is truly one of kind. Indeed, the diversity of developing humans is so impressive that it often seems impossible to generalize about them.

Individuality is apparent starting at birth if we look closely at each infant's temperament, daily rhythms, and rate of development. As we get older, our individual genetic endowments express themselves more fully, and we increasingly accumulate our own unique histories of life experiences. The result? We can tell a good deal about an individual knowing that he or she is 2 weeks or 2 years old, whereas we know very little indeed about a person simply from learning that he or she is 25 or 65. Indeed, because diversity increases with age, elderly adults are the most diverse group of human beings of all and therefore the most difficult to understand (Harris et al., 1992; Morse, 1993).

7. We Develop in a Cultural and Historical Context

Repeatedly we have seen that humans are embedded in a sociocultural context that affects their development (Bronfenbrenner, 1995). Human development takes different forms in different cultures, social classes, and racial and ethnic groups; human development in the 12th or 17th century was different from human development in the 20th century; and each person's development is influenced by social changes and historical events occurring during his or her lifetime.

We know, for example, that children reach puberty earlier and adults live longer now than they did a century ago. Today's cohorts of adults are also functioning better intellectually and maintaining their intellectual capacities longer than adults who were born early in the 20th century and received less education and poorer health care (Schaie, 1996). Future cohorts of adults are likely to maintain their physical and mental abilities even longer. Changes in the family and in men's and women's roles, technological innovations from the World Wide Web to genetic engineering, and significant social changes yet to take place may all make human development in the 21st century quite different from human development in the 20th century.

We know relatively little about human development in many non-Western societies. Our best guess is that people everywhere develop in some of the same directions but that they are also the products of a particular time and place.

8. We Are Active in Our Own Development

Early developmental theorists tended to view human beings as passively shaped by forces beyond their control. Sigmund Freud saw the developing child as driven by biological urges and molded by early experiences in the family; John Watson and other early learning theorists emphasized that human behavior is controlled by environmental stimuli. Jean Piaget did much to alter this image of developing humans by emphasizing how children *actively* explore the world around them and *actively* invent their own understandings, rather than merely absorbing lessons fed to them by adults. Piaget's insights about the developing child are now firmly embedded in our assumptions about human development at all ages. Certainly we are affected by those around us and are sometimes the passive recipients of environmental influence. But just as certainly we create our own environments, influence those around us, and, by doing so, contribute to our own development. It is this ongoing, dynamic transaction between an active person and a changing environment, each influencing the other in a reciprocal manner, that steers development.

9. Development Is Best Viewed as a Lifelong Process

Developmentalists have never before been as aware of the importance of understanding linkages between earlier and later development as they are today. It is valuable, of course, to study infancy, adolescence, or any other developmental period in its own right. But it is more valuable still to view behavior during any one phase of life from a life-span perspective. It helps

to understand that the teenage girl who bickers with her parents in an effort to forge her own identity might not have the confidence to do so unless she had enjoyed a warm, secure attachment with them as an infant and child. It is important, too, to recognize that this adolescent's quest for a separate identity and increased independence will help her achieve a readiness for intimacy and interdependence with another person. Because development *is* a process, it helps to know where it started and where it is heading.

10. Development Is Best Viewed from Multiple Perspectives

As the content of this book testifies, many disciplines have something to contribute to a comprehensive understanding of human development. Geneticists, developmental neuroscientists, and other representatives of the biological sciences must help us understand the genes, hormones, and neural networks that guide human development and aging. Meanwhile, psychologists must help us understand the individual and his or her relationships, and anthropologists, sociologists, historians, and economists must tell us about the changing sociocultural context in which that individual develops.

Multiple theories must also be brought to bear on the task of understanding human development. As we noted in Chapter 2, many developmentalists are *eclectics*: they embrace several theories rather than feeling that they must select one and reject the rest. As we have seen throughout this book, psychoanalytic, social learning, cognitive-developmental, ethological, and contextual or ecological theories *all* have something important to say about how and why we change and remain the same as we get older.

Some developmentalists believe that it is possible to integrate the best features of theories such as Freud's, Erikson's, and Piaget's, all of which propose universal stages of human development, with a contextual perspective emphasizing variations in development (Lerner & Kauffman, 1985). Such an integrated theory would reflect our understanding that people all over the world develop along certain well-worn pathways but that human development can also take quite different directions depending on the day-by-day transactions between the maturing individual and the particular social world in which he or she is developing.

Often it seems that the more one learns about a topic, the more one realizes how much more there is to learn. This is certainly true of human development. As developmentalists increasingly incorporate contextual assumptions into their thinking, they are asking new questions that might not have occurred to them in the past about how transactions between changing persons and their changing environments actually play themselves out over the years.

For developmentalists, then, there are always more questions than answers. I find this to be both a humbling and an inspiring thought. And I hope that you, too, feel both humbled and inspired as you complete your introduction to life-span human development. For, much as you may have learned, there is much more to be discovered. I hope that you are intrigued enough to observe more closely your own development and that of those around you—or even to take further coursework. And I sincerely hope that you will use what you learn to steer your own and others' development in healthier directions.

Glossary

A, not B, error The tendency of 8- to 12-month-old infants to search for a hidden object in the place where they last found it (A) rather than in its new hiding place (B).

ability tracking The practice in education of grouping students according to ability and then educating them in classes with students of comparable academic or intellectual standing.

acceptance/responsiveness A dimension of parenting capturing the extent to which parents are supportive, sensitive to their children's needs, and willing to provide affection and praise when their children meet their expectations.

accommodation In Piaget's cognitive-developmental theory, the process of modifying existing schemata to incorporate or adapt to new experiences; contrast with *assimilation*. See also *visual accommodation*.

acquired immune deficiency syndrome (AIDS) The disease in which a virus (HIV) destroys the immune system and makes victims susceptible to rare, so-called opportunistic, infections that may eventually kill them. Transmitted through sexual activity and drug needle sharing and from mother to child before or during birth.

activity A dimension of temperament that refers to an individual's vigor or energy level.

activity/passivity issue Issue in developmental theory centering on whether humans are active contributors to their own development or are passively shaped by forces beyond their control.

activity theory A perspective holding that aging adults will find satisfaction to the extent that they maintain an active lifestyle. Contrast with *disengagement theory*.

adaptation In Piaget's cognitive-developmental theory, one's inborn tendency to adjust to the demands of the environment, consisting of the complementary processes of assimilation and accommodation.

adolescent egocentrism A characteristic of adolescent thought that involves difficulty in differentiating between one's own thoughts and feelings and those of other people; evident in the *personal fable* and *imaginary audience* phenomena.

adolescent growth spurt The rapid increase in physical growth that occurs during adolescence.

age effect In developmental research, the effect of getting older or of developing. Contrast with *cohort effect* and *time of measurement effect*.

age grades Socially defined age groups or strata, each with different statuses, roles, privileges, and responsibilities in society.

ageism Prejudice and discrimination directed at older people.

age norm Expectations about what people should be doing or how they should behave at different points in the life span.

age of viability A point (currently at about the 24th prenatal week) when a fetus may survive outside the uterus if excellent medical care is available.

aging To the biologist, deterioration of the organism that leads inevitably to death; to most developmentalists, positive, negative, and neutral changes in the mature organism.

alternative birth center A birthing room or facility that provides a homelike atmosphere but still makes medical technology available.

Alzheimer's disease A pathological condition of the nervous system that results in an irreversible loss of cognitive capacities; the leading cause of dementia.

amniocentesis A method of extracting amniotic fluid from a pregnant woman so that fetal body cells within the fluid can be tested for chromosomal abnormalities and other genetic defects.

amnion A watertight membrane that surrounds the developing embryo, regulating its temperature and cushioning it against injuries.

amoral Lacking any sense of morality; without standards of right and wrong.

androgenized female Genetic female who was exposed to male sex hormones during the prenatal period and therefore developed malelike external genitals and some masculine behaviors.

androgens Male hormones that help trigger the adolescent growth spurt, as well as the development of the male sex organs, secondary sex characteristics, and sexual motivation.

androgyny A gender-role orientation in which the person blends *both* positive masculine-stereotyped and positive feminine-stereotyped personality traits.

androgyny shift A psychological change that begins in midlife, when parenting responsibilities are over, in which both men and women retain their gender-typed qualities but add to them qualities traditionally associated with the other sex, thus becoming more androgynous.

anorexia nervosa A life-threatening eating disorder characterized by failure to maintain a normal weight, a strong fear of weight gain, and a distorted body image; literally, "nervous lack of appetite."

anoxia A lack of sufficient oxygen to the brain; may result in neurological damage or death.

anticipatory grief Grieving before death occurs for what is happening and for what lies ahead.

Apgar test A test that is routinely used to assess a newborn's heart rate, respiration, color, muscle tone, and reflexes immediately after birth and then five minutes later; used to identify high-risk babies.

aptitude-treatment interaction (ATI). A phenomenon in which characteristics of the student and of the school environment interact to affect student outcome, such that any given educational practice may be effective only with a particular kind of student.

artificial insemination A method of conception that involves injecting sperm from a woman's partner or from a donor into the uterus.

assimilation Piaget's term for the process by which children interpret new experiences in terms of their existing schemata. Contrast with *accommodation*.

assisted suicide Making available to an individual who wants to commit suicide the means by which he or she may do so, as when a physician provides a terminally ill patient who wants to die with enough medication to overdose.

attachment A strong affectional tie that binds a person to an intimate companion; characterized by affection and a desire to maintain proximity.

attachment theory Theory of close relationships developed by Bowlby and Ainsworth and grounded in ethological theory (combined with psychoanalytic theory and cognitive theory); it claims that close emotional bonds such as parent/child attachments are biologically based and contribute to species survival.

attention The focusing of perception and cognition on something in particular.

attention-deficit/hyperactivity disorder (ADHD) A disorder characterized by attentional difficulties, impulsiveness, and overactive or fidgety behavior.

attribution theory A theory of motivation emphasizing that explanations or causal attributions for outcomes influence future expectancies of success and motivation to succeed.

authoritarian parenting A restrictive style of parenting, combining high demandingness/control and low acceptance/responsiveness, in which adults impose many rules, expect strict obedience, and often rely on power tactics rather than explanations to elicit compliance.

authoritative parenting A flexible style of parenting, combining high demandingness/control and high acceptance/responsiveness, in which adults lay down clear rules but also grant a fair amount of autonomy to their children and explain the rationale for their restrictions.

autism See *infantile autism*.

automatization The process by which information processing becomes effortless and highly efficient as a result of continued practice or increased expertise.

autonomy The capacity to make decisions independently, serve as one's own source of emotional strength, and otherwise manage life tasks without being overdependent on other people; an important developmental task of adolescence.

autonomy versus shame and doubt Psychosocial conflict in which toddlers attempt to demonstrate their independence from and control over other people; the second of Erikson's stages.

avoidant attachment An insecure infant/caregiver bond or other intimate relationship characterized by little separation anxiety and a tendency to avoid or ignore the attachment object upon reunion.

babbling An early form of vocalization that appears between 4 and 6 months of age and involves repeating consonant-vowel combinations such as "baba" or "dadada."

baby biographies Carefully recorded observations of the growth and development of children by their parents over a period of time; the first scientific investigations of development.

baby boom generation The huge generation of people born between 1945 (the close of World War II) and 1964.

beanpole family A multigenerational family structure characterized by many small generations.

behavioral genetics The scientific study of the extent to which genetic and environmental differences among individuals are responsible for their differences in traits such as intelligence and personality.

behavioral inhibition A temperamental characteristic reflecting one's tendency to withdraw from unfamiliar people and situations.

behaviorism A school of thinking in psychology that holds that conclusions about human development should be based on controlled observations of overt behavior rather than on speculation about unconscious motives or other unobservable phenomena; the philosophical underpinning for early theories of learning.

belief-desire psychology The *theory of mind* reflecting an understanding that both desires and beliefs guide people's behavior and that beliefs are not always an accurate reflection of reality; evident by age 4. Contrast with *desire psychology*.

bereavement A state of loss that provides the occasion for grief and mourning.

"big five" The five major dimensions that best characterize people's personalities: neuroticism, extraversion, openness to experience, agreeableness, and conscientiousness.

blastula A hollow sphere of about 100 to 150 cells that the zygote forms by rapid cell division as it moves through the fallopian tube.

brain growth spurt Period spanning the last three months of prenatal life and the first two years after birth in which the brain undergoes its most rapid development.

breech presentation A delivery in which the fetus emerges feet first or buttocks first rather than head first.

bulimia nervosa A life-threatening eating disorder characterized by recurrent eating binges followed by purging activities such as vomiting.

caregiver burden The psychological distress associated with providing care for someone with physical and/or cognitive impairments.

carrier In genetics, an individual who possesses a recessive gene associated with a disease and who, while he or she does not have the disease, can transmit the gene for it to offspring.

cataracts A pathologic condition of the eye involving opacification (clouding) of the lens that can impair vision or cause blindness.

catch-up growth A phenomenon in which children who have experienced growth deficits will grow very rapidly to "catch up to" the growth trajectory that they are genetically programmed to follow.

categorical self A person's classification of the self along socially significant dimensions such as age and sex.

centenarian An individual who lives to be 100 years of age.

centration In Piaget's theory, the tendency to focus on only one aspect of a problem when two or more aspects are relevant.

cephalocaudal principle The principle that growth proceeds from the head (cephalic region) to the tail (caudal region).

cerebral cortex The convoluted outer covering of the brain that is involved in voluntary body movements, perception, and higher intellectual functions such as learning, thinking, and speaking.

cesarean section A surgical procedure in which an incision is made in the mother's abdomen and uterus so that the baby can be removed through the abdomen.

child-directed speech Speech used by adults speaking with young children; it involves short, simple sentences, spoken slowly and in a high-pitched voice, often with much repetition, and with exaggerated emphasis on key words.

child effects model A model of family influence in which children are believed to influence their parents rather than vice versa.

chorion A membrane that surrounds the amnion and becomes attached to the uterine lining to gather nourishment for the embryo.

chorionic villus biopsy (CVS) An alternative to amniocentesis in which a catheter is inserted through the cervix to withdraw fetal cells from the chorion for prenatal testing to detect genetic defects.

chromosome A threadlike structure made up of genes; in humans, there are 46 chromosomes in the nucleus of each cell.

chromosome abnormalities Conditions in which a child has too few, too many, or incomplete chromosomes because of errors in the formation of sperm or ova.

chumship A close friendship with a peer of the same sex that emerges at about age 9 to 12, according to Sullivan.

classical conditioning A type of learning in which a stimulus that initially had no effect on the individual comes to elicit a response owing to its association with a stimulus that already elicits the response.

class inclusion The logical understanding that parts or subclasses are included in the whole class and that the whole is therefore greater than any of its parts.

climacteric The loss of reproductive capacity in either sex in later life.

clinical method An unstandardized interviewing procedure used by Jean Piaget in which a child's response to each successive question (or problem) determines what the investigator will ask next.

clique A small friendship group that interacts frequently.

cloning The process of converting a single cell from one animal into a new animal that is a genetic duplicate of the original animal.

cochlear implant A surgically implanted amplification device that stimulates the auditory nerve to provide the sensation of hearing to a deaf individual.

codominance In genetics, an instance in which two different but equally powerful genes produce a phenotype in which both genes are equally expressed.

coercive family environment A home in which family members are locked in power struggles, each trying to control the other through aggressive tactics such as threatening, yelling, and hitting.

cognition The activity of knowing and the processes through which knowledge is acquired (e.g., attending, perceiving, remembering, and thinking).

cohabitation The living together of two single adults as an unmarried couple.

cohort A group of people born at the same time; a particular generation of people.

cohort effect In cross-sectional research, the effect on findings of the fact that the different cohorts (age groups) being compared were born at different times and had different formative experiences. Contrast with *age effect* and *time of measurement effect.*

comorbidity The co-occurrence of two or more psychiatric conditions in the same individual.

compensation for decline Finding a way, often unconsciously, to make up for or get around age-related losses of function to perform well.

conception The moment of fertilization, when a sperm penetrates an ovum, forming a zygote.

concordance rate The percentage of cases in which a particular attribute is present for both members of a pair of people (e.g., twins) if it is present for one member.

concrete operations stage Piaget's third stage of cognitive development, lasting from about ages 7 to 11, when children are acquiring logical operations and can reason effectively about real objects and experiences.

conditioned response (CR) A learned response to a stimulus that was not originally capable of producing the response.

conditioned stimulus (CS) An initially neutral stimulus that comes to elicit a particular response after being paired with an unconditioned stimulus that always elicits the response.

confidant A spouse, relative, or friend to whom a person feels emotionally close and with whom he or she can share thoughts and feelings.

conformity The tendency to go along with the opinions or wishes of someone else or to yield to group pressures.

conservation The recognition that certain properties of an object or substance do not change when its appearance is altered in some superficial way.

constraint-seeking questions In the Twenty Questions Task and similar hypothesis-testing tasks, questions that rule out more than one answer to narrow the field of possible choices rather than asking about only one hypothesis at a time.

constructivism Piaget's position that children actively create their own understandings of the world from their experiences, rather than being born with innate ideas or being programmed by the environment.

contact comfort The pleasurable tactile sensations provided by a parent or a soft, terry cloth mother substitute; believed to foster attachments in infant monkeys and possibly humans.

contextual theories Theories of development holding that changes over the life span arise from the ongoing interrelationship between a changing organism and a changing world.

contextual world view A world view underlying certain theories that regards human development as an ongoing historical event or drama and emphasizes the ever-changing relationship between person and environment. Contrast with *mechanistic world view* and *organismic world view*.

continuity/discontinuity issue The debate among theorists about whether human development is best characterized as gradual and continuous or abrupt and stagelike.

continuous reinforcement A schedule of reinforcement in which every occurrence of an act is reinforced.

contour The amount of light/dark transition or boundary area in a visual stimulus.

conventional morality Kohlberg's term for the third and fourth stages of moral reasoning, in which societal values are internalized and judgments are based on a desire to gain approval or uphold law and social order.

convergent thinking Thinking that involves "converging" on the one best answer to a problem; what IQ tests measure. Contrast with *divergent thinking*.

cooing An early form of vocalization that involves repeating vowel-like sounds.

cooperative learning methods Procedures that involve assigning students, usually of different races or ability levels, to work teams that are reinforced for performing well as teams and encourage cooperation among teammates.

correlational method A research technique that involves determining whether two or more variables are related to one another. It cannot indicate that one thing caused another, but it can suggest that a causal relationship exists or allow us to predict one characteristic from our knowledge of another.

correlation coefficient A measure, ranging from +1.00 to −1.00, of the extent to which two variables or attributes are systematically related to each other in either a positive or a negative way.

counterconditioning A treatment based on classical conditioning principles in which the goal is to extinguish an undesirable response to a person, object, or situation and replace it with a new and more adaptive response.

creativity The ability to produce novel responses or works.

critical period A defined period in the development of an organism when it is particularly sensitive to certain environmental influences; outside this period, the same influences will have far less effect.

crossing over A process in which genetic material is exchanged between pairs of chromosomes during meiosis.

cross-modal perception The ability to use one sensory modality to identify a stimulus or pattern of stimuli that is already familiar through another modality.

cross-sectional design A developmental research design in which different age groups (cohorts) are studied at the same point in time and compared.

crowd A network of heterosexual cliques that forms during adolescence and serves to arrange mixed-sex social activities.

crystallized intelligence Those aspects of intellectual functioning that involve making use of knowledge acquired through experience. Contrast with *fluid intelligence*.

cued recall memory Recollecting objects, events, or experiences in response to a hint or cue. Contrast with pure *recall memory* and *recognition memory*.

cultural-familial retardation Mental retardation that appears to be due to some combination of low genetic potential and a poor family environment rather than to a specific biological cause. Contrast with *organic retardation*.

culture A system of meanings shared by a population of people and transmitted from one generation to the next.

culture bias The situation that arises in testing when one cultural or subcultural group is more familiar with test items than another group and therefore has an unfair advantage.

cumulative-deficit hypothesis The notion that impoverished environments inhibit intellectual growth and that these inhibiting effects accumulate over time.

daily hassles Everyday annoyances or chronic life strains that can mount up and cause psychological distress or physical illness.

damage theories of aging Theories that emphasize a number of haphazard processes that cause cells and organ systems to deteriorate; contrast with *programmed theories*.

dark adaptation The process by which the eyes become more sensitive to light over time as they remain in the dark.

death anxiety A complex set of concerns about death and dying.

decentration The ability to focus on two or more dimensions of a problem at one time.

defense mechanisms Mechanisms used by the ego to defend itself against anxiety caused by conflict between the id's impulses and social demands.

deferred imitation The imitation of models who are no longer present.

delirium A clouding of consciousness characterized by alternating periods of disorientation and coherence.

demandingness/control A dimension of parenting reflecting the extent to which parents rather than children exert control over decisions and set and enforce rules; also called permissiveness-restrictiveness.

dementia A progressive loss of cognitive capacities such as memory and judgment that affects some aging individuals and that has a variety of causes.

denial A defense mechanism in which anxiety-provoking thoughts are kept out of, or isolated from, conscious awareness.

dependent variable The aspect of behavior that is measured in an experiment and that is assumed to be under the control of, or "dependent" on, the *independent variable*.

depression See *major depressive disorder*.

desire psychology The earliest *theory of mind*: an understanding that desires guide behavior. Contrast with *belief-desire psychology*.

development Systematic changes in the individual occurring between conception and death; such changes can be positive, negative, or neutral.

developmental norm The age at which half of a large group of infants or children master a skill or display a behavior; the average age for achieving a milestone in development.

developmental psychopathology A field of study concerned with the origins and course of maladaptive or psychopathological behavior.

developmental quotient (DQ) A numerical measure of an infant's performance on a developmental test relative to the performance of other infants the same age.

developmental stage A distinct phase within a larger sequence of development; a period characterized by a particular set of abilities, motives, behaviors, or emotions that occur together and form a coherent pattern.

diathesis/stress model The view that psychopathology results from the interaction of a person's predisposition to psychological problems and the experience of stressful events.

dietary restriction A technique that has been demonstrated to extend the life span of laboratory animals, involving a highly nutritious but severely calorie-restricted diet.

difficult temperament Characteristic mode of response in which the individual is irregular in his or her habits and adapts slowly, often with vigorous protest, to changes in routine or new experiences. Contrast with *easy temperament* and *slow-to-warm-up temperament*.

diffusion status Identity status characterizing individuals who have not questioned who they are and have not committed themselves to an identity.

disengagement theory A perspective holding that successful aging involves a mutually satisfying withdrawal of the aging individual and society from one another. Contrast with *activity theory*.

disorganized/disoriented attachment An insecure infant/caregiver bond, common among abused children, that combines features of the resistant and avoidant attachment styles and is characterized by the infant's dazed response to reunion and confusion about whether to approach or avoid the caregiver.

distinctive feature Any dimension on which two or more objects differ and can be discriminated.

divergent thinking Thinking that requires coming up with a variety of ideas or solutions to a problem when there is no one right answer. Contrast with *convergent thinking*.

dominant gene A relatively powerful gene that is expressed phenotypically and masks the effect of a less powerful, *recessive gene*.

double standard The view that sexual behavior appropriate for members of one gender is inappropriate for members of the other.

Down syndrome A chromosomal abnormality in which the child has inherited an extra 21st chromosome and is, as a result, mentally retarded; also called "trisomy 21."

dynamic assessment An approach to assessing intelligence that evaluates how well individuals learn new material when an examiner provides them with competent instruction.

dynamic systems approach A developmental perspective applied to motor development proposing that increasingly sophisticated patterns of motor behavior emerge over time through a "self-organizing" process in which children adaptively modify their motor behavior on the basis of the sensory feedback they receive when they try different movements.

dyslexia Serious difficulties learning to read in children who have normal intellectual ability and no sensory impairments or emotional difficulties that could account for their learning problems.

easy temperament Characteristic mode of response in which the individual is even-tempered, content, and quite open and adaptable to new experiences. Contrast with *difficult temperament* and *slow-to-warm-up temperament*.

echolalia The repetition of sounds, as when an autistic child parrots what someone says.

eclectic In the context of science, an individual who recognizes that no single theory can explain everything, but that each has something to contribute to our understanding.

ecological approach Bronfenbrenner's view emphasizing that the developing person is embedded in and interacts with a series of environmental systems (*microsystem, mesosystem, exosystem,* and *macrosystem*).

effectance motivation A motive to display competence, master challenges, and affect the world around one.

ego Psychoanalytic term for the rational component of the personality.

egocentrism The tendency to view the world from one's own perspective while failing to recognize that others may have different points of view.

elaboration A strategy for remembering that involves adding something to or creating meaningful links between the bits of information one is trying to retain.

Electra complex Female version of the Oedipus complex, in which a 4- to 6-year-old girl is said to envy her father for possessing a penis and would choose him as a sex object in the hope of sharing this valuable organ that she lacks.

emotionality A dimension of temperament that refers to the tendency to be easily or intensely irritated by events.

emotion-focused coping An approach to dealing with stress that involves changing one's appraisal of a stressful situation rather than changing the situation itself (for example, distancing oneself from a problem, convincing oneself that it is not so bad). Contrast with *problem-focused coping*.

emotion regulation The processes involved in initiating, maintaining, and altering emotional responses.

empathy The vicarious experiencing of another person's feelings.

empiricist An individual whose approach to human development emphasizes the contribution of environmental factors; specifically, one who believes that infants enter the world as blank slates and know nothing except what they learn through their senses. Contrast with *nativist*.

empty nest Term used to describe the family household after the last child departs.

encoding The first step in learning and remembering something; it is the process of getting information into the information-processing system and of learning it and organizing it in a form suitable for storing.

endocrine gland Type of gland that secretes chemicals called hormones directly into the bloodstream. Endocrine glands play critical roles in stimulating growth and regulating bodily functions.

engrossment Parents' fascination with their neonate; a desire to touch, hold, caress, and talk to the newborn baby.

entity view of ability The belief that ability is a fixed trait that cannot be altered by effort. Contrast with *incremental view*.

environment Events or conditions outside the person that are presumed to influence and be influenced by the individual.

equity A balance of contributions and gains in a social relationship that results in neither partner feeling over- or underbenefited.

error accumulation theory The notion that DNA is irreparably damaged over the years, resulting in the death of cells and eventually the organism.

estrogen The female hormone responsible for the development of breasts and the female sex organs and secondary sex characteristics as well as the beginning of menstrual cycles.

ethnic identity A sense of personal identification with one's ethnic group and its values and cultural traditions.

ethology A discipline and theoretical perspective that focuses on the evolved behavior of different species in their natural environments.

eugenics The alteration of the genetic makeup of a population in an attempt to improve the human race.

euthanasia Literally, "good death"; specifically, hastening, either actively or passively, the death of someone who is suffering from an incurable illness or injury.

evolutionary psychology A perspective guided by Darwinian evolutionary theory that asks about the adaptive functions of behavior.

executive control processes Processes that direct and monitor the selection, organization, manipulation, and interpretation of information in the information-processing system.

exosystem In Bronfenbrenner's ecological approach, settings not experienced directly by the individual that still influence his or her development (e.g., effects of events at a parent's workplace on a child's development).

expansion A conversational tactic used by adults in speaking to young children in which they respond to a child's utterance with a more grammatically complete expression of the same thought.

experiment A research strategy in which the investigator manipulates or alters some aspect of a person's environment to measure what effect it has on the individual's behavior or development.

experimental control The holding of all other factors besides the independent variable in an experiment constant, so that any changes in the dependent variable can be said to be caused by the manipulation of the independent variable.

explicit memory Memory that involves consciously recollecting the past. Contrast with *implicit memory*.

expressive role A pattern of behavior, usually instilled in females, that stresses being kind, nurturant, cooperative, and sensitive to the needs of others.

extended family household A family unit composed of parents and children living with other kin such as grandparents, aunts and uncles, and/or cousins. Contrast with *nuclear family*.

externalizing problem Childhood behavior problem that involves "undercontrolled" behavior such as aggression, or acting out difficulties in ways that disturb other people. Contrast with *internalizing problem*.

extinction The gradual weakening and disappearance of a learned response when it is no longer reinforced.

factor analysis A technique that identifies clusters of tasks or test items (called factors) that are highly correlated with one another and unrelated to other items.

failure to thrive A condition observed in infants who are emotionally deprived and characterized by stunted growth, weight loss, and delays in cognitive and socioemotional development.

false belief task A research paradigm used to assess an important aspect of a theory of mind, mainly the understanding that people can hold and be influenced by incorrect beliefs.

false self behavior Behavior that occurs when adolescents put on false fronts or act out of character to win the approval of parents or peers.

family development theory The conceptualization of the family as a developing organism, including concepts such as that of a family life cycle.

family life cycle The sequence of changes in family composition, roles, and relationships that occurs from the time people marry until they die.

family systems theory The conceptualization of the family as a whole consisting of interrelated parts, each of which affects and is affected by every other part, and each of which contributes to the functioning of the whole.

fetal alcohol syndrome (FAS) A group of symptoms commonly observed in the offspring of mothers who use alcohol heavily during pregnancy, including a small head, widely spaced eyes, and mental retardation.

fine motor skills Skills that involve precise movements of the hands and fingers or feet and toes. Contrast with *gross motor skills*.

fixation In psychoanalytic theory, a defense mechanism in which development is arrested and part of the libido remains tied to an early stage of development.

fluid intelligence Those aspects of intelligence that involve actively thinking and reasoning to solve novel problems. Contrast with *crystallized intelligence*.

Flynn effect The rise in average IQ scores over the 20th century.

foreclosure status Identity status characterizing individuals who appear to have committed themselves to a life direction but who have adopted an identity prematurely, without much thought.

formal operations stage Piaget's fourth and final stage of cognitive development (from age 11 or 12 and beyond), when the individual begins to think more rationally and systematically about abstract concepts and hypothetical ideas.

fraternal twins   Twins who are not identical and who result when a mother releases two ova at roughly the same time and each is fertilized by a different sperm.

free radicals   Molecules that have an extra or "free" electron, are chemically unstable, and react with other molecules in the body to produce substances that damage normal cells; highlighted in one damage theory of aging.

functional grammar   An analysis of the semantic relations (meanings such as naming and locating) that children express in their earliest sentences.

functional play   Play that involves using objects appropriately to serve the functions they normally serve.

gender consistency   The stage of gender typing in which children realize that one's sex is stable across situations or despite changes in activities or appearance.

gender identity   One's awareness that one is either a male or a female.

gender intensification   A magnification of differences between males and females during adolescence associated with increased pressure to conform to traditional gender roles.

gender role   A pattern of behaviors and traits that defines how to act the part of a female or a male in a particular society.

gender-role norm   Societal expectation or standard concerning what males or females should be like and how they should behave.

gender-role stereotype   Overgeneralized and largely inaccurate belief about what males or females are like.

gender schema   Organized set of beliefs and expectations about males and/or females that guide information processing.

gender segregation   The formation of separate boys' and girls' peer groups during childhood.

gender stability   The stage of gender typing in which children realize that one's sex remains the same over time.

gender typing   The process by which children become aware of their gender and acquire the motives, values, and behaviors considered appropriate for members of their biological sex.

gene   A functional unit of heredity made up of DNA and transmitted from generation to generation.

gene/environment correlation   A systematic interrelationship between an individual's genes and his or her environment; ways in which genes influence the kind of home environment provided by parents (passive gene-environment correlation), social reactions to the individual (evocative gene-environment correlations), and the types of experiences the individual seeks out (active gene-environment correlation).

gene/environment interaction   The phenomenon in which the effects of one's genes depend on the kind of environment one experiences and in which the effects of the environment depend on one's genetic endowment.

generativity versus stagnation   The psychosocial conflict in which middle-aged adults must gain the sense that they have produced something that will outlive them and genuinely care for younger generations to avoid self-preoccupation; seventh of Erikson's stages.

genetic counseling   A service designed to inform people about genetic conditions they or their unborn children are at risk of inheriting.

genetic engineering   Therapies that involve substituting normal genes for the genes associated with a disease or disorder, or otherwise altering a person's genetic makeup.

genetic epistemology   Piaget's field, the study of how humans come to know reality and basic dimensions of it such as space, time, and causality.

genotype   The genetic endowment that an individual inherits; contrast with *phenotype*.

germinal period   First phase of prenatal development, lasting for about two weeks from conception until the developing organism becomes attached to the wall of the uterus.

gerontology   The study of aging and old age.

giftedness   The possession of unusually high general intellectual potential or of special abilities in such areas as creativity, mathematics, or the arts.

glaucoma   A condition in which increased fluid pressure in the eye damages the optic nerve and causes progressive loss of peripheral vision and ultimately blindness.

goodness of fit   The extent to which the child's temperament and the demands of the child's social environment are compatible or mesh, according to Thomas and Chess; more generally, a good match between person and environment.

grief   The emotional response to loss.

gross motor skills   Skills that involve large muscles and whole body or limb movements (for example, kicking the legs or drawing large circles). Contrast with *fine motor skills*.

growth   The physical changes that occur from conception to maturity.

growth hormone   Hormone produced by the pituitary gland that stimulates childhood physical growth and the adolescent growth spurt.

guided participation   A process in which children learn by actively participating in culturally relevant activities with the aid and support of their parents and other knowledgeable individuals.

habituation   A simple form of learning that involves learning not to respond to a stimulus that is repeated over and over; learning to be bored by the familiar.

Hayflick limit   The estimate that human cells can double only 50 times, plus or minus 10, and then will die.

heritability   The amount of variability in a population on some trait dimension that is attributable to genetic differences among those individuals.

holophrase   A single-word utterance used by an infant that represents an entire sentence's worth of meaning.

HOME inventory   A widely used instrument that allows an observer to determine just how intellectually stimulating or impoverished a home environment is.

horizontal décalage   A term used by Piaget to characterize the fact that different cognitive skills related to the same stage of cognitive development emerge at different times.

hormone replacement therapy   The taking of estrogen and progestin to compensate for hormone loss due to menopause in women.

hospice   A program that supports dying persons and their families through a philosophy of "caring" rather than "curing," either in a facility or at home.

hot flash   A sudden experience of warmth and sweating, often followed by a cold shiver, that occurs in a menopausal woman.

Huntington's disease   A genetic disease caused by a single, dominant gene that strikes in middle age to produce a deterioration of physical and mental abilities and premature death.

hyperactivity   See *attention-deficit/hyperactivity disorder (ADHD)*.

hypothesis   A theoretical prediction about what will hold true if we observe a phenomenon.

hypothetical-deductive reasoning   A form of problem solving in which one starts with general or abstract ideas and deduces or traces their specific implications; "if/then" thinking.

id   Psychoanalytic term for the inborn component of the personality that is driven by the instincts or selfish urges.

ideational fluency   The most common measure of creativity; the sheer number of different, including novel, ideas that one can generate.

identical twins   Monozygotic twins who develop from a single zygote that later divides to form two genetically identical individuals.

identification   Freud's term for the individual's tendency to emulate, or adopt the attitudes and behaviors of, another person, particularly his or her same-sex parent.

identity   One's self-definition or sense of who one is, where one is going, and how one fits into society.

identity achievement status   Identity status characterizing individuals who have carefully thought through identity issues and made commitments or resolved their identity issues.

identity versus role confusion   The psychosocial conflict in which adolescents must form a coherent self-definition or else remain confused about their life directions; the fifth of Erikson's stages.

imaginary audience   A form of adolescent egocentrism that involves confusing your own thoughts with the thoughts of a hypothesized audience for your behavior and concluding that others share your preoccupations.

implicit memory   Memory that occurs unintentionally and without consciousness or awareness. Contrast with *explicit memory*.

imprinting   An innate form of learning in which the young of certain species will follow and become attached to moving objects (usually their mothers) during a critical period early in life.

inclusion   The educational practice of integrating handicapped students into regular classrooms rather than placing them in segregated special education classes; also called "mainstreaming."

incomplete dominance   Condition in which a stronger gene fails to mask all the effects of a weaker partner gene; a phenotype results that is similar but not identical to the effect of the stronger gene.

incremental view of ability   Young children's belief that ability is a changeable quality that can be altered by effort. Contrast with *entity view*.

independent variable   The aspect of the environment that a researcher deliberately changes or manipulates in an experiment to see what effect it has on behavior; a causal variable. Contrast with *dependent variable*.

indirect effects   Instances in which the relationship between two individuals in a family is modified by the behavior or attitudes of a third family member.

induction   A form of discipline that involves explaining why a child's behavior is wrong and should be changed by emphasizing its effects on other people.

industry versus inferiority   Psychosocial conflict in which school-age children must master important cognitive and social skills or else feel incompetent; the fourth of Erikson's stages.

infantile amnesia   A lack of memory for the early years of one's life.

infantile autism   A severe and encompassing developmental disorder that begins in infancy and is characterized by such problems as an aversion to social contact, deviant communication or mutism, and repetitive, stereotyped behavior.

infant states   Coherent patterns of waking and sleeping evident in the fetus and young infant (for example, quiet sleep, active sleep, active waking).

informal curriculum   The nonacademic lessons that children are taught in school about how to fit into their culture (for example, how to obey rules, cooperate, and conform to other important social values).

information-processing approach   An approach to cognition that emphasizes the fundamental mental processes involved in attention, perception, memory, and decision making.

initiative versus guilt   Psychosocial conflict in which preschool children must learn to initiate new activities and pursue bold plans or else become self-critical; the third of Erikson's stages.

instinct   An inborn biological force assumed to motivate a particular response or class of responses.

instrumental role   A pattern of behavior, usually instilled in males, that stresses being dominant, independent, assertive, and competitive.

integrity versus despair   Psychosocial conflict in which elderly adults attempt to find a sense of meaning in their lives and to accept the inevitability of death; the eighth of Erikson's stages.

intelligence quotient (IQ)   A numerical measure of a person's performance on an intelligence test relative to the performance of other examinees of the same age, typically with a score of 100 defined as average.

internalization   The process of adopting as one's own the attributes or standards of other people.

internalizing problem   Childhood behavior problem that represents an "overcontrolled" pattern of coping with difficulties and is expressed in anxiety, depression, and other forms of inner distress. Contrast with *externalizing problem*.

internal working model   In attachment theory, cognitive representations of self and other people that children construct from their interactions with caregivers and that, in turn, shape their expectations about relationships.

intimacy versus isolation   Psychosocial conflict in which young adults must commit themselves to a shared identity with another person or else remain aloof and unconnected to others; the sixth of Erikson's stages.

intonation Variations in pitch, loudness, and timing when saying words or sentences.

intuitive theory Organized system of knowledge, believed to be innate, that allows children to make sense of the world.

in vitro fertilization (IVF) A method of conception in which fertilized eggs are transferred to a woman's uterus in the hopes that one will implant on the wall of the uterus.

joint attention The act of looking at the same object at the same time with someone else; a way in which infants share perceptual experiences with their caregivers.

karyotype A chromosomal portrait created by staining chromosomes, photographing them under a high-power microscope, and arranging them into a predetermined pattern.

Klinefelter syndrome A sex chromosome abnormality in which males inherit two or more X chromosomes (XXY or XXXY); these males fail to develop secondary sex characteristics and often show deficiencies on tests of verbal abilities.

knowledge base One's existing information about a content area, significant for its influence on how well one can learn and remember.

Lamaze method Prepared childbirth in which parents attend classes and learn mental exercises and relaxation techniques to ease delivery.

language A symbolic system in which a limited number of signals can be combined according to rules to produce an infinite number of messages.

language acquisition device (LAD) A set of linguistic processing skills that nativists believe to be innate; presumably the LAD enables a child to infer the rules governing others' speech and then to use these rules to produce language.

latchkey children Children who care for themselves after school with little or no adult supervision.

lateralization The specialization of the two hemispheres of the cerebral cortex of the brain.

learned helplessness orientation A tendency to avoid challenges and to cease trying in the face of failure, resulting primarily from attributing failure to lack of ability and therefore believing that one can do little to improve. Contrast with *mastery orientation.*

learning A relatively permanent change in behavior (or behavior potential) that results from one's experiences or practice.

learning goal A goal adopted by learners in which they seek to learn new things so that they can improve their abilities. Contrast with *performance goal.*

libido Freud's term for the biological energy of the sex instinct.

life expectancy The average number of years a newborn baby today can be expected to live; 75 years at present in the United States.

life review Process in which elderly adults reflect on unresolved conflicts of the past and evaluate their lives; it may contribute to a sense of integrity and readiness for death.

life-span perspective A perspective that views development as a lifelong, multidirectional process that involves gain and loss, is characterized by considerable plasticity, is shaped by its historical/cultural context, has many causes, and is best viewed from a multidisciplinary perspective.

life structure In Levinson's theory of adult development, an overall pattern of life that reflects the person's priorities and relationships.

living will A document in which a person states in advance that he or she does not wish to have extraordinary medical procedures applied if he or she is hopelessly ill.

locus of control A personality dimension differentiating between people who assume they are personally responsible for their life outcomes (internal locus) and people who believe that their outcomes depend on forces outside themselves (external locus).

longitudinal design A developmental research design in which one group of subjects is studied repeatedly over a period of months or years.

long-term memory Memory store in which information that has been examined and interpreted is stored relatively permanently.

looking-glass self The idea that a person's self-concept is largely a reflection of the ways in which other people respond to him or her.

love withdrawal A form of discipline that involves withholding attention, affection, or approval after a child misbehaves.

macrosystem In Bronfenbrenner's ecological approach, the larger cultural or subcultural context of development.

major depressive disorder An affective or mood disorder characterized by at least one episode of feeling profoundly sad and hopeless and/or losing interest in almost all activities.

masked depression Depression, particularly in a child, that seems to manifest itself more in problems such as aggression and anxiety than in overtly depressed behavior and that is therefore "disguised" as problems other than depression.

mastery orientation A tendency to thrive on challenges and persist in the face of failure because of healthy attributions that lead to the belief that increased effort will pay off. Contrast with *learned helplessness orientation.*

maturation Developmental changes that are biologically programmed by genes rather than being caused by learning, injury, illness, or some other life experience.

maximum life span A ceiling on the number of years that any member of a species lives; 110 to 120 for humans.

mechanistic world view A world view underlying certain theories that regards human beings as machines shaped by outside forces and analyzable into their parts. Contrast with *organismic world view* and *contextual world view.*

meiosis The process in which a germ cell divides, producing gametes (sperm or ova), each containing half of the parent cell's original complement of chromosomes; in humans, the products of meiosis normally contain 23 chromosomes.

menarche A female's first menstrual period.

menopause The ending of a woman's menstrual periods and reproductive capacity in midlife.

mental age (MA) A measure of intellectual development that reflects the level of age-graded problems that a child is able to solve; the age at which a child functions intellectually.

mental retardation Significant sub-average general intellectual functioning associated with impairments in adaptive behavior and manifested during the developmental period.

mentor A guide or adviser who provides consultation and practical aid to a younger person.

mesosystem In Bronfenbrenner's ecological approach, interrelationships between microsystems or immediate environments (e.g., ways in which events in the family affect a child's interactions at a day care center).

metacognition Knowledge of the human mind and of the whole range of cognitive processes, including thinking about one's own thought processes.

metamemory One's knowledge about memory and memory processes.

method of loci A mnemonic technique that involves establishing a mental map of a familiar route and then creating images linking each item to be learned to a landmark along the route.

microsystem In Bronfenbrenner's ecological approach, the immediate settings in which the person functions (e.g., the family).

middle generation squeeze Expression describing the phenomenon in which middle-aged adults sometimes experience heavy responsibilities for both the younger and older generations in the family.

midlife crisis A period of major questioning, inner struggle, and reevaluation hypothesized to occur in an adult's early forties.

mitosis The process in which a cell duplicates its chromosomes and then divides into two genetically identical daughter cells.

modified extended family An arrangement in which nuclear families that are related by kinship maintain separate households but frequently interact with one another rather than functioning in isolation.

moral affect The emotional component of morality, including feelings of guilt, shame, and pride regarding one's conduct.

morality The ability to distinguish right from wrong and to act on this distinction. Morality has affec-tive, cognitive, and behavioral components.

morality of care Gilligan's term for what she claims is the dominant moral orientation of females, in which the individual emphasizes concern and responsibility for the welfare of other people rather than abstract rights.

morality of justice Gilligan's term for what she claims is the dominant moral orientation of males, in which moral dilemmas are viewed as inevitable conflicts between the rights of two or more parties that must be settled by law. Contrast with *morality of care*.

moral reasoning The cognitive component of morality; the thinking that occurs when people decide whether various acts are right or wrong.

moral rule Standard of conduct that focuses on the basic rights and privileges of individuals. Contrast with *social-conventional rule*.

moratorium period A period of life in which adolescents are relatively free of responsibility and can experiment to find their identities.

moratorium status Identity status characterizing individuals who are currently experiencing an identity crisis, or actively exploring identity issues, but have not yet achieved an identity.

morpheme One of the smallest meaningful units of language; these include words and grammatical markers such as prefixes, suffixes, and verb tense modifiers (for example, *-ed, -ing*).

morphology Rules governing the formation of words from sounds (for example, rules for forming plurals and past tenses).

mourning Culturally prescribed ways of displaying one's reactions to a loss.

mutation A change in the structure or arrangement of one or more genes that produces a new phenotype.

myelin A waxy substance that insulates neural axons and thereby speeds the transmission of neural impulses.

nativist An individual whose approach to human development emphasizes the contribution of genetic factors; specifically, one who believes that infants enter the world equipped with knowledge that al-lows them to perceive a meaningful world from the start. Contrast with *empiricist*.

naturalistic observation A research method in which the scientist observes people as they engage in common everyday activities in their natural habitats. Contrast with *structured observation*.

natural selection The evolutionary principle that individuals who have characteristics advantageous for survival in a particular environment are the ones who are most likely to survive and reproduce. Over many generations, this process of "survival of the fittest" will lead to changes in a species and the development of new species.

nature/nurture issue The debate within developmental psychology over the relative importance of biological predispositions (nature) and environmental influences (nurture) as determinants of human development.

need for achievement (n Ach) A motive to compete and strive for success whenever one's behavior can be evaluated against a standard of excellence.

negative punishment The process in operant conditioning in which a response is weakened or made less probable when its consequence is the removal of a pleasant stimulus from the situation.

negative reinforcement The process in operant conditioning in which a response is strengthened or made more probable when its consequence is the removal of an unpleasant stimulus from the situation.

neglectful parenting A parenting style that is low in demandingness/control and low in acceptance/responsiveness; uninvolved parenting.

neonate The newborn; the infant from birth to approximately 1 month of age.

neuron The basic unit of the nervous system; a nerve cell.

nonshared environmental influences Experiences unique to the individual that are not shared by other members of the family and that tend to make members of the same family different from one another. Contrast with *shared environmental influences*.

normal distribution A symmetrical (bell-shaped) curve that describes the variability of characteristics within populations; most people fall at or near the average score, with relatively few high or low scores.

nuclear family A family unit consisting of husband/father, wife/mother, and at least one child. Compare with *extended family household*.

object permanence The understanding that objects continue to exist when they are no longer visible or otherwise detectable to the senses; fully mastered by the end of infancy.

observational learning Learning that results from observing the behavior of other people; emphasized in Bandura's social learning theory.

Oedipus complex Freud's term for the conflict that 4- to 6-year-old boys experience when they develop an incestuous desire for their mothers and, at the same time, a jealous and hostile rivalry with their fathers.

oldest-old Older adults, most but not all of whom are 85 and older, who are often extremely frail and dependent. Contrast with *young-old* and *old-old*.

old-old Older adults, most but not all of whom are 75 or older, who often have chronic diseases and impairments, have suffered declines in their abilities, and often depend on others for care. Contrast with *young-old* and *oldest-old*.

olfaction The sense of smell, made possible by sensory receptors in the nasal passage that react to chemical molecules in the air.

operant conditioning A form of learning in which freely emitted acts (or "operants") become either more or less probable depending on the consequences they produce.

organic retardation Mental retardation due to some identifiable biological cause associated with hereditary factors, diseases, or injuries. Contrast with *cultural-familial retardation*.

organismic world view A world view underlying certain theories that regards human beings as whole, living organisms who are active in their own development and change in a stagelike manner. Contrast with *mechanistic world view* and *contextual world view*.

organization In Piaget's cognitive-developmental theory, one's inborn tendency to combine and integrate available schemes into more coherent and complex systems or bodies of knowledge; as a memory strategy, a technique that involves grouping or classifying stimuli into meaningful clusters.

organogenesis The process, occurring during the period of the embryo, in which every major organ takes shape in a primitive form.

orthogenetic principle Werner's principle that development proceeds from global and undifferentiated states toward more differentiated and integrated patterns of response.

osteoporosis A disease in which bone tissue is lost, leaving bones fragile and easily fractured.

overextension The young child's tendency to use a word to refer to a wider set of objects, actions, or events than adults do (e.g., using the word "car" to refer to all motor vehicles).

overregularization The overgeneralization of observed grammatical rules to irregular cases to which the rules do not apply (e.g., saying "mouses" rather than "mice").

parental imperative The notion that the demands of parenthood cause men and women to adopt distinct roles and psychological traits.

parent effects model A model of family influence in which parents (particularly mothers) are believed to influence their children rather than vice versa.

partial reinforcement A schedule of reinforcement in which only some occurrences of a particular act are reinforced, often on an unpredictable schedule.

peer A social equal; one who functions at a level of behavioral complexity similar to that of the self, often someone of similar age.

perception The interpretation of sensory input.

performance goal A goal adopted by learners in which they attempt to prove their ability rather than to improve it. Contrast with *learning goal*.

perinatal environment The environment surrounding birth.

period of the embryo Second phase of prenatal development, lasting from the third through the eighth prenatal week, during which the major organs and anatomical structures begin to develop.

period of the fetus Third phase of prenatal development, lasting from the ninth prenatal week until birth; during this period, the major organ systems begin to function and the fetus grows rapidly.

permissive parenting A lax style of parenting combining low demandingness/control and high acceptance/responsiveness in which adults love their children but make few demands on them and rarely attempt to control their behavior.

personal fable A form of adolescent egocentrism that involves thinking that one's self and one's thoughts and feelings are unique or special.

personality The organized combination of attributes, motives, values, and behaviors that is unique to each individual.

phenotype The way in which a person's *genotype* is actually expressed in observable or measurable characteristics.

phenylketonuria (PKU) A genetic disease in which the child is unable to metabolize phenylalanine; if left untreated, it soon causes hyperactivity and mental retardation.

phoneme One of the basic units of sound used in a particular spoken language.

phonological awareness Understanding that spoken words can be decomposed into some number of basic sound units, or *phonemes;* an important skill in learning to read.

phonology The sound system of a language and the rules for combining these sounds to produce meaningful units of speech.

pincer grasp A grasp in which the thumb is used in opposition to the fingers, enabling an infant to become more dexterous at lifting and manipulating objects.

pituitary gland The "master gland" located at the base of the brain that regulates the other endocrine glands and produces growth hormone.

placenta An organ, formed from the chorion and the lining of the uterus, that provides for the nourishment of the unborn child and the elimination of its metabolic wastes.

plasticity An openness of the brain cells (or of the organism as a whole) to positive and negative environmental influence; a capacity to change in response to experience.

polychlorinated biphenyls (PCBs) Polluting chemicals formerly used in electrical insulation that cause premature birth, neurological immaturity, and lasting cognitive deficits in individuals whose mothers were exposed to them prior to giving birth.

polygenic trait A characteristic that is influenced by the action of many gene pairs rather than a single pair.

population A well-defined group that a researcher who studies a *sample* of individuals is ultimately interested in drawing conclusions about.

positive punishment The process in *operant conditioning* whereby a response is weakened when its consequence is an unpleasant event.

positive reinforcement The process in *operant conditioning* whereby a response is strengthened when its consequence is a pleasant event.

postconventional morality Kohlberg's term for the fifth and sixth stages of moral reasoning, in which moral judgments are based on a more abstract understanding of democratic social contracts or on universal principles of justice that have validity apart from the views of particular authority figures.

postformal thought Proposed stages of cognitive development that lie beyond formal operations.

postpartum depression An episode of severe, clinical depression lasting for months in a woman who has just given birth; to be contrasted with milder cases of the "maternity blues," in which a new mother is tearful and moody in the first days after birth.

posttraumatic stress disorder A psychological disorder involving flashbacks to traumatizing events, nightmares, and feelings of helplessness and anxiety in the face of danger experienced by victims of extreme trauma such as soldiers in combat and sexually abused children.

power assertion A form of discipline that involves the use of superior power to administer spankings, withhold privileges, and so on.

pragmatics Rules specifying how language is to be used appropriately in different social contexts to achieve goals.

preconventional morality Kohlberg's term for the first two stages of moral reasoning, in which society's rules are not yet internalized and judgments are based on the punishing or rewarding consequences of an act.

premenstrual syndrome (PMS) A number of symptoms experienced shortly before each menstrual period that include having tender breasts and a bloated feeling, as well as being irritable and moody.

prenatal environment The environment surrounding an organism between conception and birth.

preoperational stage Piaget's second stage of cognitive development, lasting from about ages 2 to 7, when children think at a symbolic level but have not yet mastered logical operations.

presbycusis Problems of the aging ear, which commonly involve loss of sensitivity to high-frequency or high-pitched sounds.

presbyopia Problems of the aging eye, especially loss of near vision related to a decreased ability of the lens to accommodate to objects that are close to the eye.

pretend play Symbolic play in which one actor, object, or action symbolizes or stands for another.

private speech Nonsocial speech, or speech for the self, commonly used by preschoolers to guide their activities and believed by Vygotsky to be the forerunner of inner speech, or silent thinking-in-words.

proactive aggression A deliberate kind of aggression designed to achieve instrumental goals. Contrast with *reactive aggression.*

problem-focused coping An approach to dealing with stress that involves attempting to change the stress-provoking situation (e.g., confronting other people, actively planning ways to solve a problem, and seeking social support). Contrast with *emotion-focused coping.*

problem solving The use of the information-processing system to achieve a goal or arrive at a decision.

programmed theories of aging Theories that emphasize the systematic genetic control of aging processes; compare with *damage theories of aging.*

prosocial behavior Positive actions toward other people, such as helping and cooperating.

protective factor Factor such as personal resources or a supportive postnatal environment that works to prevent at-risk individuals from developing problems.

proximodistal principle In development, the principle that growth proceeds from the center of the body (or the proximal region) to the extremities (or distal regions).

psychoanalytic theory The theoretical perspective associated with Freud and his followers that emphasizes unconscious motivations for behavior, conflicts within the personality, and stages of psychosexual development.

psychometric approach The research tradition that spawned standardized tests of intelligence and views intelligence as a trait or a set of traits that can be measured and that varies from person to person.

psychosexual stage One of Freud's five stages of development, associated with biological maturation and shifts in the libido: oral, anal, phallic, latency, and genital.

puberty The point at which a person reaches sexual maturity and is physically capable of conceiving a child.

punisher Any consequence of an act that suppresses that act and/or decreases the probability that it will recur.

punishment See *positive punishment* and *negative punishment.*

quasi-experiment An experiment-like study that evaluates the effects of different treatments but does not randomly assign individuals to treatment groups.

random assignment A technique in which research participants are placed in experimental conditions in an unbiased or random way so that the resulting groups are not systematically different from one another.

random sample A sample that is formed by identifying all members of the larger population of interest and then selecting a portion of them in an unbiased or random way to participate in the study; a technique to ensure that the sample studied is representative or typical of the larger population of interest.

reaction time The time interval between the presentation of a stimulus and a response to it.

reactive aggression A form of aggression that occurs when a person is frustrated and highly aroused and

recall memory Recollecting or actively retrieving objects, events, and experiences when examples or cues are not provided. Contrast with *recognition memory* and *cued recall memory*.

recessive gene A less powerful gene that is not expressed phenotypically when paired with a *dominant gene*.

reciprocal determinism The notion in social learning theory that the flow of influence between people and their environments is a two-way street; the environment may affect the person, but the person's characteristics and behavior also influence the environment.

recognition memory Identifying an object or event as one that has been experienced before, as when one must select the correct answer from several options. Contrast with *recall memory* and *cued recall memory*.

reconstituted family A new family that forms after the remarriage of a single parent, sometimes involving the blending of two families into a new one.

reflex An unlearned and automatic response to a stimulus.

regression A defense mechanism that involves retreating to an earlier, less traumatic stage of development.

rehearsal A strategy for remembering that involves repeating the items one is trying to retain.

reinforcer Any consequence of an act that increases the probability that the act will recur.

relativistic thinking A form of postformal thought in which it is understood that there are multiple ways of viewing a problem and that the solutions one arrives at will depend on one's starting assumptions and perspective.

REM sleep A state of active, irregular sleep associated with dreaming; named for the rapid eye movements associated with it.

research ethics Standards of conduct that investigators are ethically bound to honor to protect their research participants from physical or psychological harm.

reserve capacity The ability of many organ systems to respond to demands for extraordinary output, as when the heart and lungs work at maximal capacity.

lashes out in anger. Contrast with *proactive aggression*.

resilience The self-righting or recuperative capacity that allows many children to recover from early disadvantages and get back on a normal course of development.

resistant attachment An insecure infant/caregiver bond or other intimate relationship characterized by strong separation anxiety and a tendency to show ambivalent reactions to the attachment object upon reunion, seeking and yet resisting contact.

retrieval The process of getting information out of long-term memory when it is needed.

reversibility In Piaget's theory, the ability to reverse or negate an action by mentally performing the opposite action.

rite of passage Ritual that signifies the passage from one stage of life to another (e.g., puberty rites).

role conflict The sense of being pulled in different directions by the competing demands of different roles or activities.

role overload The sense of having too much to do in carrying out one's major roles or life activities.

role reversal A switching of child and parent roles late in life such that the parent becomes the dependent one and the child becomes the caregiver.

role-taking skill The ability to assume another person's perspective and understand his or her thoughts, feelings, and behaviors.

rubella A disease that has little effect on a pregnant woman but may cause a number of serious birth defects such as blindness, deafness, and mental retardation in unborn children who are exposed in the first 3 to 4 months of gestation; German measles.

rule assessment approach Robert Siegler's approach to studying the development of problem solving that determines what information about a problem children take in and what rules they then formulate to account for this information.

sample The group of individuals chosen to be the subjects of a study.

savant syndrome The phenomenon in which extraordinary talent in a particular area is displayed by a person who is otherwise mentally retarded.

scheme (or schema; plural, schemes or schemata) A cognitive structure or organized pattern of action or thought that is used to deal with experiences.

schizophrenia A serious form of mental illness characterized by disturbances in logical thinking, emotional expression, and interpersonal behavior.

scientific method An attitude or value about the pursuit of knowledge that dictates that investigators must be objective and must allow their data to decide the merits of their theorizing.

secular trend A trend in industrialized society toward earlier maturation and greater body size now than in the past.

secure attachment An infant/caregiver bond or intimate relationship in which the individual welcomes close contact, uses the attachment object as a source of comfort, and dislikes but can manage separations.

secure base A point of safety, represented by an infant's attachment figure, that permits exploration of the environment.

selective breeding A method of studying genetic influence that involves deliberately determining whether a trait can be bred in animals through selective mating.

selective optimization with compensation The concept that older people cope with aging through a strategy that involves focusing on the skills most needed, practicing those skills, and developing ways to get around the need for other skills.

self-concept One's perceptions of one's unique attributes or traits.

self-esteem One's overall evaluation of one's worth as a person based on an assessment of the qualities that make up the self-concept.

self-recognition The ability to recognize oneself in a mirror or photograph, which occurs in most infants by 18 to 24 months of age.

semantics The aspect of language centering on meanings.

sensation The process by which information is detected by the sensory receptors and transmitted to the brain; starting point in *perception*.

sensorimotor stage Piaget's first stage of cognitive development, spanning the first two years of life, in which infants rely on their senses and motor behaviors in adapting to the world around them.

sensory register The first memory store in information processing, in which stimuli are noticed and are very briefly available for further processing.

sensory threshold The point at which low levels of stimulation can be detected.

separation anxiety A wary or fretful reaction that infants display when they are separated from their attachment objects.

sequential design A developmental research design that combines the cross-sectional approach and the longitudinal approach in a single study to compensate for the weaknesses of each.

seriation A logical operation that allows one to mentally order a set of stimuli along a quantifiable dimension such as height or weight.

sex-linked characteristic An attribute determined by a gene that appears on one of the two types of sex chromosomes, usually the X chromosome.

sexual orientation One's preference for sexual partners of the same or other sex, often characterized as primarily heterosexual, homosexual, or bisexual.

shared environmental influences Experiences that individuals living in the same home environment share and that work to make them similar to one another. Contrast with *nonshared environmental influences*.

short-term memory Memory store in which limited amounts of information are temporarily held; called *working memory* when its active quality is being emphasized.

sibling rivalry A spirit of competition, jealousy, or resentment that may arise between two or more brothers or sisters.

sickle cell disease A genetic blood disease in which red blood cells assume an unusual sickled shape and become inefficient at distributing oxygen throughout the body.

single gene-pair inheritance Genetic mechanism through which a characteristic is influenced by only one pair of genes: one gene from the mother and its partner from the father.

size constancy The tendency to perceive an object as the same size despite changes in its distance from the eyes.

slow-to-warm-up temperament Characteristic mode of response in which the individual is relatively inactive and moody and displays mild resistance to new routines and experiences but gradually adapts. Contrast with *easy temperament* and *difficult temperament*.

sociability A dimension of temperament that refers to the individual's degree of interest in and responsiveness to people.

social clock A personal sense of when things should be done in one's life and when one is ahead of or behind the schedule dictated by age norms.

social cognition Thinking about the thoughts, feelings, motives, and behavior of the self and other people.

social comparison The process of defining and evaluating oneself by comparing oneself to other people.

social-conventional rule Standard of conduct determined by social consensus that indicates what is appropriate within a particular social setting. Contrast with *moral rule*.

social convoy The changing cadre of significant people who serve as sources of social support to the individual during his or her life.

socialization The process by which individuals acquire the beliefs, values, and behaviors judged important in their society.

social learning theory Bandura's theory that children and adults can learn novel responses merely by observing the behavior of a model, making mental notes on what they have seen, and then using these mental representations to reproduce the model's behavior at some future time; more broadly, a learning perspective that emphasizes the cognitive processing of social experiences.

social norm A socially defined expectation about how people should behave.

social pretend play A form of play that involves both cooperation with playmates and the use of pretend or symbolic activity.

social referencing The process, evident starting in infancy, of reading the emotional reactions of other people and using this information to guide one's own behavior in ambiguous situations.

social-role hypothesis Eagly's view that gender-role stereotypes are created and maintained by differences in the roles that men and women play in society rather than being inherent in males and females.

social support The several forms of assistance from other people that bolster individuals and protect them from stress.

socioeconomic status (SES) The position people hold in society based on such factors as income, education, occupational status, and the prestige of their neighborhoods.

socioemotional selectivity hypothesis Carstensen's notion that our needs change as we grow older and that we actively choose to narrow our range of social partners to those who can best meet our needs.

sociometric technique Method for determining who is well liked and popular and who is disliked or neglected in a group.

somatic symptom Physical or bodily sign of distress such as loss of appetite or disruption of normal sleep patterns.

species heredity The genetic endowment that members of a particular species have in common; responsible for universal species traits and patterns of maturation.

spillover The notion that events at work affect home life, and events at home carry over into the workplace.

storage In information processing, the holding of information in the long-term memory store.

storm and stress G. Stanley Hall's term for the emotional ups and downs and rapid changes that he believed characterize adolescence.

stranger anxiety A wary or fretful reaction that infants often display when approached by an unfamiliar person.

Strange Situation test A series of mildly stressful situations to which infants are exposed to determine the quality of their attachments.

stress An aversive state brought about by events that seem to strain the person's coping capacities and threaten his or her well-being.

structured observation A research method in which scientists create special conditions designed to elicit the behavior of interest to achieve greater control over the conditions under which they gather behavioral data. Contrast with *naturalistic observation*.

structure-of-intellect model   Guilford's factor-analytic model of intelligence, which proposes that there are as many as 180 distinct mental abilities.

substantive complexity   The extent to which a job or activity provides opportunities for using one's mind and making independent judgments.

superego   Psychoanalytic term for the component of the personality that consists of one's internalized moral standards.

surfactant   A substance that aids breathing by preventing the air sacs of the lungs from sticking together.

symbolic capacity   The capacity to use symbols such as words, images, or actions to represent or stand for objects and experiences; representational thought.

synapse   The point at which the axon or dendrite of one neuron makes a connection with another neuron.

synaptogenesis   A process in early brain development that involves the formation of connections among neurons.

synchronized routine   Harmonious, dancelike interaction between infant and caregiver in which each adjusts his or her behavior in response to that of the other.

syntax   Rules specifying how words can be combined to form meaningful sentences in a language.

syphilis   A common sexually transmitted disease that may cross the placental barrier in the middle and later stages of pregnancy, causing miscarriage or serious birth defects.

tabula rasa   The idea that the mind of an infant is a "blank slate" and that all knowledge, abilities, behaviors, and motives are acquired through experience.

Tay-Sachs disease   A genetic disease common among Jewish children that is caused by a pair of recessive genes and that results in a degeneration of the nervous system and death.

telegraphic speech   Early sentences that consist primarily of content words and omit the less meaningful parts of speech such as articles, prepositions, pronouns, and auxiliary verbs.

telomere   A stretch of DNA that forms the tip of a chromosome and

that shortens after each cell division, timing the death of cells.

temperament   A genetically based pattern of tendencies to respond in predictable ways; building blocks of personality such as activity level, sociability, and emotionality.

teratogen   Any disease, drug, or other environmental agent that can harm a developing fetus.

terminal drop   A rapid decline in intellectual abilities that people who are within a few years of dying often experience.

test norm   Standard of normal performance on a psychometric instrument that is based on the average scores and range of scores obtained by a large, representative sample of test takers.

testosterone   The most important of the male hormones, or androgens; essential for normal sexual development during the prenatal period and at puberty.

thalidomide   A mild tranquilizer that, taken early in pregnancy, can produce a variety of malformations of the limbs, eyes, ears, and heart.

theory   A set of concepts and propositions designed to organize, describe, and explain a set of observations.

theory of mind   The understanding that people have mental states (feelings, desires, beliefs, intentions) and that these states underlie and help to explain their behavior.

time of measurement effect   In developmental research, the effect on findings of historical events occurring at the time when the data for a study are being collected (e.g., psychological changes brought about by an economic depression rather than as a function of getting older). Contrast with *age effect* and *cohort effect*.

time out   An alternative to punishment that involves removing children from the situation in which their misbehavior is positively reinforced.

total brain death   An irreversible loss of functioning in the entire brain, both the higher centers of the cerebral cortex that are involved in thought and the lower centers of the brain that control basic life processes such as breathing.

transactional model   A model of family influence in which parent and child are believed to influence one another reciprocally.

transformational grammar   Rules of syntax that allow one to transform declarative statements into questions, negatives, imperatives, and other kinds of sentences.

transformational thought   In Piaget's theory, the ability to conceptualize transformations, or processes of change from one state to another, which appears in the stage of concrete operations.

transitivity   The ability to recognize the necessary or logical relations among elements in a serial order (for example, that if A is taller than B, and B is taller than C, then A must be taller than C).

triarchic theory of intelligence   An information-processing theory of intelligence that emphasizes three aspects of intelligent behavior: the context in which people display intelligence, the previous experience they have with cognitive tasks, and the information-processing components they use to go about solving problems.

trust versus mistrust   Psychosocial conflict of infancy, in which infants must learn to trust others to meet their needs in order to trust themselves; the first stage in Erikson's theory.

Turner syndrome   A sex chromosome abnormality in which females inherit only one X chromosome (XO); they remain small in stature, fail to develop secondary sex characteristics, and may show some mental deficiencies.

ultrasound   Method of examining physical organs by scanning them with sound waves—for example, scanning the womb and thereby producing a visual outline of the fetus to detect gross abnormalities.

umbilical cord   A soft tube containing blood vessels that connects the embryo to the placenta and serves as a source of oxygen and nutrients and as a vehicle for the elimination of wastes.

unconditioned response (UCR)   The unlearned response elicited by an unconditioned stimulus.

unconditioned stimulus (UCS)   A stimulus that elicits a particular response without any prior learning.

unconscious motivation   Freud's term for feelings, experiences, and conflicts that influence a person's thinking and behavior, even though they cannot be recalled.

underextension The young child's tendency to use general words to refer to a smaller set of objects, actions, or events than adults do (e.g., using "candy" to refer only to mints).

universality/context-specificity issue The debate over the extent to which developmental changes are common to everyone ("universal," as in most stage theories) or different from person to person ("context-specific").

vascular dementia The deterioration of functioning and cognitive capacities caused by a series of minor strokes that cut off the blood supply to areas of the brain; also called "multi-infarct dementia."

vicarious reinforcement In observational learning, the consequences after a behavior experienced by a model that affect the learner's likelihood of engaging in the behavior.

visual accommodation The ability of the lens of the eye to change shape to bring objects at different distances into focus.

visual acuity The ability to perceive detail in a visual stimulus.

visual cliff An elevated glass platform that creates an illusion of depth, used to test the depth perception of infants.

vocabulary spurt A phenomenon occurring at around 18 months of age when the pace of word learning quickens dramatically.

wisdom Exceptional insight or judgment regarding life's problems.

working memory A memory store, often referred to as a mental "scratch pad," that temporarily holds information while it is being actively operated upon; the active use of the *short-term memory* store.

X chromosome The longer of the two sex chromosomes; normal females have two X chromosomes and normal males have one.

Y chromosome The shorter of the two sex chromosomes; normal males have one Y chromosome and females have none.

young-old Older adults, often but not always between 55 and 75, who are relatively healthy, active, and socially involved. Contrast with *old-old* and *oldest-old*.

zone of proximal development Vygotsky's term for the difference between what a learner can accomplish independently and what he or she can accomplish with the guidance and encouragement of a more skilled partner.

zygote A single cell formed at conception from the union of a sperm and an ovum.

References

CHAPTER 1: Understanding Life-Span Human Development

American Psychological Association. (1982). *Ethical principles in the conduct of research with human participants.* Washington, DC: Author.

Ariès, P. (1962). *Centuries of childhood.* New York: Knopf.

Baltes, P. B. (1987). Theoretical propositions of life-span developmental psychology: On the dynamics between growth and decline. *Developmental Psychology, 23,* 611–626.

Baltes, P. B., Reese, H. W., & Lipsitt, L. P. (1980). Life-span developmental psychology. *Annual Review of Psychology, 31,* 65–110.

Baltes, P. B., Smith, J., & Staudinger, U. M. (1992). Wisdom and successful aging. In T. B. Sonderegger (Ed.), *Nebraska Symposium on Motivation: Vol. 39. Psychology and aging.* Lincoln, NB: University of Nebraska Press.

Belsky, J., Woodworth, S., & Crnic, K. (1996). Trouble in the second year: Three questions about family interactions. *Child Development, 67,* 556–578.

Bengtson, V. L., Cuellar, J. B., & Ragan, P. K. (1977). Stratum contrasts and similarities in attitudes toward death. *Journal of Gerontology, 32,* 76–88.

Biesele, M., & Howell, N. (1981). "The old people give you life": Aging among !Kung hunter-gatherers. In P. T. Amoss & S. Harrell (Eds.), *Other ways of growing old: Anthropological perspectives.* Stanford, CA: Stanford University Press.

Birren, J. E., & Zarit, J. M. (1985). Concepts of health, behavior, and aging.

In J. E. Birren & J. Livington (Eds.), *Cognition, stress, and aging.* Englewood Cliffs, NJ: Prentice-Hall.

Bronfenbrenner, U. (1979). *The ecology of human development: Experiments by nature and design.* Cambridge, MA: Harvard University Press.

Burton, L. M. (1996). Age norms, the timing of family role transitions, and intergenerational caregiving among aging African American women. *Gerontologist, 36,* 199–208.

Charlesworth, W. R. (1992). Darwin and developmental psychology: Past and present. *Developmental Psychology, 28,* 5–16.

Cole, T. R. (1992). *The journey of life: A cultural history of aging in America.* Cambridge, England: Cambridge University Press.

Cunningham, H. (1996). The history of childhood. In C. P. Hwang, M. E. Lamb, & I. E. Sigel (Eds.), *Images of childhood.* Mahwah, NJ: Erlbaum.

Darwin, C. A. (1877). A biographical sketch of an infant. *Mind, 2,* 285–294.

deMause, L. (1974).The evolution of childhood. In L. deMause (Ed.), *The history of childhood.* New York: The Psychohistory Press.

Dublin, L. I., & Lotka, A. J. (1936). *Length of life: A study of the life table.* New York: Ronald Press.

Elder, G. H., Jr., Liker, J. K., & Cross, C. E. (1984). Parent-child behavior in the Great Depression: Life course and intergenerational influences. In P. B. Baltes & O. G. Brim, Jr. (Eds.), *Life-span development and behavior* (Vol. 6). Orlando, FL: Academic.

Elkind, D. (1992, May/June). The future of childhood. Waaah!! Why kids have a lot to cry about. *Psychology Today,* pp. 38–41, 80–81.

Elkind, D. (1994). *Ties that stress: The new family imbalance.* Cambridge, MA: Harvard University Press.

Friedrich, L. K., & Stein, A. H. (1973). Aggressive and prosocial television programs and the natural behavior of preschool children. *Monographs of the Society for Research in Child Development, 38* (4, Serial No. 51).

Fry, C. L. (1985). Culture, behavior, and aging in the comparative perspective. In J. E. Birren & K. W. Schaie (Eds.), *Handbook of the psychology of aging* (2nd ed.). New York: Van Nostrand Reinhold.

Fry, C. L. (1996). Age, aging, and culture. In R. H. Binstock & L. K. George (Eds.), *Handbook of aging and the social sciences* (4th ed.). San Diego: Academic.

Grodin, M., & Glantz, L. H. (Eds.). (1994). *Children as research subjects. Science, ethics, and law.* New York: Oxford University Press.

Haan, N. (1981). Common dimensions of personality development: Early adolescence to middle life. In D. H. Eichorn, J. A. Clausen, N. Haan, M. P. Honzik, & P. H. Mussen (Eds.), *Present and past in middle life.* New York: Academic.

Hall, G. S. (1891). The contents of children's minds on entering school. *Pedagogical Seminary, 1,* 139–173.

Hall, G. S. (1904). *Adolescence* (2 vols.). New York: Appleton.

Hall, G. S. (1922). *Senescence: The last half of life.* New York: Appleton.

Helms, J. E. (1992). Why is there no study of cultural equivalence in standardized cognitive ability testing? *American Psychologist, 47,* 1083–1101.

Kagan, J. (1986). Presuppositions in developmental inquiry. In L. Cirillo & S. Wapner (Eds.), *Value presuppositions in theories of human development.* Hillsdale, NJ: Erlbaum.

Kean, A. W. G. (1937). The history of the criminal liability of children. *Law Quarterly Review, 3,* 364–370.

Keith, J. (1985). Age in anthropological research. In R. H. Binstock & E. Shanas (Eds.), *Handbook of aging and the social sciences* (2nd ed.). New York: Van Nostrand Reinhold.

Keniston, K. (1970). Youth: A "new" stage of life. *American Scholar, 39,* 631–654.

Kett, J. F. (1977). *Rites of passage: Adolescence in America 1790 to the present.* New York: Basic Books.

Koocher, G. P., & Keith-Spiegel, P. (1994). Scientific issues in psychosocial and educational research with children. In M. Grodin & L. H. Glantz (Eds.), *Children as research subjects: Science, ethics, and law.* New York: Oxford University Press.

McCall, R. B. (1977). Challenges to a science of developmental psychology. *Child Development, 48,* 333–344.

McLanahan, S. S., & Sorensen, A. B. (1985). Life events and psychological well-being over the life course. In G. H. Elder, Jr. (Ed.), *Life course dynamics: Trajectories and transitions, 1968–1980.* Ithaca, NY: Cornell University Press.

Minois, G. (1989). *History of old age. From antiquity to the Renaissance* (S. H. Tenison, Trans.). Cambridge, England: Polity Press. (Original work published 1987)

Mize, J., & Ladd, G. W. (1990). A cognitive-social learning approach to social skill training with low-status preschool children. *Developmental Psychology, 26,* 388–397.

Morse, C. K. (1993). Does variability increase with age? An archival study of cognitive measures. *Psychology and Aging, 8,* 156–164.

Neugarten, B. L. (1968). Adult personality: Toward a psychology of the life cycle. In B. L. Neugarten (Ed.), *Middle age and aging: A reader in social psychology.* Chicago: University of Chicago Press.

Neugarten, B. L. (1975). The future and the young-old. *Gerontologist, 15* (Part 2), 4–9.

Neugarten, B. L., Moore, J. W., & Lowe, J. C. (1965). Age norms, age constraints, and adult socialization. *American Journal of Sociology, 70,* 710–717.

Neugarten, B. L., & Neugarten, D. A. (1986). Changing meanings of age in the aging society. In A. Pifer & L. Bronte (Eds.), *Our aging society: Paradox and promise.* New York: Norton.

Ogbu, J. U. (1981). Origins of human competence: A cultural-ethological perspective. *Child Development, 52,* 413–429.

Parke, R. D., Ornstein, P. A., Rieser, J. J., & Zahn-Waxler, C. (1994). The past as prologue: An overview of a century of developmental psychology. In R. D. Parke, P. A. Ornstein, J. J. Rieser, & C. Zahn-Waxler (Eds.), *A century of developmental psychology.* Washington, DC: American Psychological Association.

Pellegrini, A. D. (1996). *Observing children in their natural worlds: A methodological primer.* Mahwah, NJ: Erlbaum.

Reid, T. R. (1993, January 16). 2 million accept duty of being 20. *The Washington Post,* pp. A14, A24.

Remley, A. (1988, October). The great parental value shift: From obedience to independence. *Psychology Today,* pp. 56–59.

Schaie, K. W. (1994). Developmental designs revisited. In S. H. Cohen & H. W. Reese (Eds.), *Life-span developmental psychology: Methodological contributions.* Hillsdale, NJ: Erlbaum.

Singer, J. L., & Singer, D. G. (1981). *Television, imagination, and aggression: A study of preschoolers.* Hillsdale, NJ: Erlbaum.

Society for Research in Child Development, Committee for Ethical Conduct in Child Development Research (1990, Winter). SRCD ethical standards for research with children. *SRCD Newsletter,* pp. 5–7.

Suzman, R. M., Willis, D. P., & Manton, K. G. (Eds.). (1992). *The oldest old.* New York: Oxford University Press.

Tousignant, M. (1995, November 17). The lesson of a lifetime: 2nd-graders thrill to 114-year-old Ella Miller's tales of growing up. *The Washington Post,* p. B01.

Tousignant, M. (1996, November 9). A seasoned voter speaks her mind: At 115 years old, Vienna woman says age of candidate is not an issue. *The Washington Post,* p. B5.

Trafford, A. (1996, March 26). The old gray-haired: They ain't what they used to be. *Washington Post Health,* p. 6.

Tronick, E. Z., Morelli, G. A., & Ivey, P. K. (1992). The Efe forager infant and toddler's pattern of social relationships: Multiple and simultaneous. *Developmental Psychology, 28,* 568–577.

U.S. Bureau of the Census. (1996a). *Statistical abstract of the United States: 1996* (116th ed.). Washington, DC: U.S. Government Printing Office.

U.S. Bureau of the Census. (1996b). 65+ in the United States. *Statistical abstract of the United States: 1996* (116th ed.). Washington, DC: U.S. Government Printing Office.

Vinovskis, M. A. (1996). Changing perceptions and treatment of young children in the United States. In C. P. Hwang, M. E. Lamb, & I. E. Sigel (Eds.), *Images of childhood.* Mahwah, NJ: Erlbaum.

Willems, E. P., & Alexander, J. L. (1982). The naturalistic perspective in research. In B. B. Wolman (Ed.), *Handbook of developmental psychology.* Englewood Cliffs, NJ: Prentice-Hall.

Wilson, M. N. (1989). Child development in the context of the black extended family. *American Psychologist, 44,* 380–385.

CHAPTER 2: Theories of Human Development

Babikian, H. M., & Goldman, A. (1971). A study of teen-age pregnancy. *American Journal of Psychiatry, 128,* 755–760.

Balassone, M. L. (1991). A social learning model of adolescent contraceptive behavior. *Journal of Youth and Adolescence, 20,* 593–616.

Bandura, A. (1977). *Social learning theory.* Englewood Cliffs, NJ: Prentice-Hall.

Bandura, A. (1986). *Social foundations of thought and action: A social cognitive theory.* Englewood Cliffs, NJ: Prentice-Hall.

Bandura, A. (1989). Social cognitive theory. In R. Vasta (Ed.), *Annals of child development: Vol. 6. Theories of child development: Revised formulations and current issues.* Greenwich, CT: JAI Press.

Beilin, H. (1992). Piaget's enduring contribution to developmental psychology. *Developmental Psychology, 28,* 191–204.

Bem, S. L. (1989). Genital knowledge and gender constancy in preschool children. *Child Development, 60,* 649–662.

Benda, B. B., & DiBlasio, F. A. (1994). An integration of theory: Adolescent sexual contacts. *Journal of Youth and Adolescence, 23,* 403–420.

Bijou, S. W., & Baer, D. M. (1961). *Child development: Vol. 1. A systematic and empirical theory.* New York: Appleton-Century-Crofts.

Bronfenbrenner, U. (1979). *The ecology of human development: Experiments by nature and design.* Cambridge, MA: Harvard University Press.

Bronfenbrenner, U. (1989). Ecological systems theory. In R. Vasta (Ed.), *Annals of child development: Vol. 6. Theories of child development: Revised formulations and current issues.* Greenwich, CT: JAI Press.

Bronfenbrenner, U. (1995). Developmental ecology through space and time: A future perspective. In P. Moen, G. H. Elder, Jr., & K. Luscher (Eds.), *Examining lives in context: Perspectives on the ecology of human development.* Washington, DC: American Psychological Association.

Bronfenbrenner, U., & Ceci, S. J. (1994). Nature-nurture reconceptualized in developmental perspective: A bioecological model. *Psychological Review, 101,* 568–586.

Brooks-Gunn, J., & Furstenberg, F. F., Jr. (1989). Long-term implications of fertility-related behavior and family formation on adolescent mothers and their children. In K. Kreppner & R. M. Lerner (Eds.), *Family systems and life-span development.* Hillsdale, NJ: Erlbaum.

Cobliner, W. G. (1974). Pregnancy in the single adolescent girl: The role of cognitive functions. *Journal of Youth and Adolescence, 3,* 17–29.

Cotterell, J. L. (1986). Work and community influences on the quality of child rearing. *Child Development, 57,* 362–374.

Crews, F. (1996). The verdict on Freud [Review of *Freud evaluated: The completed arc*]. *Psychological Science, 7,* 63–68.

Dixon, R. A., & Lerner, R. M. (1992). A history of systems in developmental psychology. In M. H. Bornstein & M. E. Lamb (Eds.), *Developmental psychology: An advanced textbook.* Hillsdale, NJ: Erlbaum.

Emde, R. N. (1992). Individual meaning and increasing complexity: Contributions of Sigmund Freud and Rene Spitz to developmental psychology. *Developmental Psychology, 28,* 347–359.

Erikson, E. H. (1963). *Childhood and society* (2nd ed.). New York: Norton.

Erikson, E. H. (1968). *Identity: Youth and crisis.* New York: Norton.

Erikson, E. H. (1982). *The life cycle completed: A review.* New York: Norton.

Finkel, M. L., & Finkel, D. J. (1978). Male adolescent contraceptive utilization. *Adolescence, 13,* 443–451.

Fisher, S., & Greenberg, R. P. (1977). *The scientific credibility of Freud's theories and therapy.* New York: Basic Books.

Franklin, C., Grant, D., Corcoran, J., Miller, P. O., & Bultman, L. (1997). Effectiveness of prevention programs for adolescent pregnancy: A meta-analysis. *Journal of Marriage and the Family, 59,* 551–567.

Freud, S. (1933). *New introductory lectures in psychoanalysis.* New York: Norton.

Freud, S. (1964). An outline of psychoanalysis. In J. Strachey (Ed.), *The standard edition of the complete psychological works of Sigmund Freud* (Vol. 23). London: Hogarth Press. (Original work published 1940)

Furstenberg, F. F., Jr., Brooks-Gunn, J., & Morgan, S. P. (1987). *Adolescent mothers in later life.* New York: Cambridge University Press.

Furstenberg, F. F., Jr., Lincoln, R., & Menken, J. (Eds.). (1981). *Teenage sexuality, pregnancy, and childbearing.* Philadelphia: University of Pennsylvania Press.

Gewirtz, J. L., & Pelaez-Nogueras, M. (1992). B. F. Skinner: Legacy to human infant behavior and development. *American Psychologist, 47,* 1411–1422.

Gordon, D. E. (1990). Formal operational thinking: The role of cognitive-developmental processes in adolescent decision making about pregnancy and contraception. *American Journal of Orthopsychiatry, 60,* 346–356.

Gruber, H. E., & Voneche, J. J. (Eds.). (1977). *The essential Piaget.* New York: Basic Books.

Grusec, J. E. (1992). Social learning theory and developmental psychology: The legacies of Robert Sears and Albert Bandura. *Developmental Psychology, 28,* 776–786.

Hall, C. S. (1954). *A primer of Freudian psychology.* New York: New American Library.

Hamburg, B. A. (1986). Subsets of adolescent mothers: Developmental, biomedical, and psychosocial issues. In J. B. Lancaster & B. A. Hamburg (Eds.), *School-age pregnancy and parenthood: Biosocial dimensions.* New York: Aldine DeGruyter.

Hart, B., & Hilton, I. (1988). Dimensions of personality organization predictors of teenage pregnancy risk. *Journal of Personality Assessment, 52,* 116–132.

Hatcher, S. L. M. (1973). The adolescent experience of pregnancy and abortion: A developmental analysis. *Journal of Youth and Adolescence, 2,* 53–102.

Henshaw, S. K. (1997). Teenage abortion and pregnancy statistics by state, 1992. *Family Planning Perspectives, 29,* 115–122.

Hingson, R., & Strunin, L. (1992). Monitoring adolescents' response to the AIDS epidemic: Changes in knowledge, attitudes, beliefs, and behaviors. In R. J. DiClemente (Ed.), *Adolescents and AIDS. A generation in jeopardy.* Newbury Park, CA: Sage.

Hopkins, J. R. (1995). Erik Homburger Erikson (1902–1994). *American Psychologist, 50,* 796–797.

Inhelder, B., & Piaget, J. (1958). *The growth of logical thinking from childhood to adolescence: An essay on the construction of formal operational structures* (A. Parsons & S. Milgram, Trans.). New York: Basic Books.

Kaplan, B. (1983). A trio of trials. In R. M. Lerner (Ed.), *Developmental psychology: Historical and philosophical perspectives.* Hillsdale, NJ: Erlbaum.

Katcher, A. (1955). The discrimination of sex differences by young children. *Journal of Genetic Psychology, 87,* 131–143.

Kirby, D. (1985). The effects of selected sexuality education programs: Toward a more realistic view. *Journal of Sex Education and Therapy, 11,* 28–37.

Kirby, D., Short, L., Collins, J., Rugg, D., Kolbe, L., Howard, M., Miller, B., Sonenstein, F., & Zabin, L. S. (1994). School-based programs to reduce sexual risk behaviors: A review of effectiveness. *Public Health Reports, 109,* 339–360.

Kohlberg, L. (1966). Cognitive stages and preschool education. *Human Development, 9,* 5–17.

Kopp, C. B., & Krakow, J. B. (1982). *The child: Development in a social context.* Reading, MA: Addison-Wesley.

Larson, M. S. (1996). Sex roles and soap operas: What adolescents learn about single motherhood. *Sex Roles, 35,* 97–110.

Lerner, R. M., & Kauffman, M. B. (1985). The concept of development in contextualism. *Developmental Review, 5,* 309–333.

Lourenco, O., & Machado, A. (1996). In defense of Piaget's theory: A reply to 10 common criticisms. *Psychological Review, 103,* 143–164.

Macmillan, M. (1991). *Freud evaluated: The completed arc.* New York: Elsevier.

Masson, J. M. (1984). *The assault on truth: Freud's suppression of the seduction theory.* New York: Farrar, Straus, and Giroux.

Morrison, D. M. (1985). Adolescent contraceptive behavior: A review. *Psychological Bulletin, 98,* 538–568.

Muuss, R. E. (1996). *Theories of adolescence* (6th ed.). New York: McGraw-Hill.

Orlofsky, J. L. (1993). Intimacy status: Theory and research. In J. E. Marcia, A. S. Waterman, D. R. Matteson, S. L. Archer, & J. L. Orlofsky (Eds.), *Ego identity: A handbook for psychosocial research.* New York: Springer-Verlag.

Parke, R. D., Ornstein, P. A., Rieser, J. J., & Zahn-Waxler, C. (1994). The past as prologue: An overview of a century of developmental psychology. In R. D. Parke, P. A. Ornstein, J. J. Rieser, & C. Zahn-Waxler (Eds.), *A century of developmental psychology.* Washington, DC: American Psychological Association.

Pepper, S. C. (1942). *World hypotheses: A study in evidence.* Berkeley, CA: University of California Press.

Piaget, J. (1950). *The psychology of intelligence.* New York: Harcourt Brace & World.

Piaget, J. (1952). *The origins of intelligence in children.* New York: International Universities Press.

Reese, H. W., & Overton, W. F. (1970). Models of development and theories of development. In L. R. Goulet & P. B. Baltes (Eds.), *Life-span developmental psychology: Research and theory.* New York: Academic.

Riegel, K. F. (1979). *Foundations of dialectical psychology.* New York: Academic.

Sameroff, A. J. (1983). Developmental systems: Contexts and evolution. In W. Kessen (Vol. Ed.; P. H. Mussen, General Ed.), *Handbook of child psychology: Vol. 1. History, theory, and methods* (4th ed.). New York: Wiley.

Skinner, B. F. (1953). *Science and human behavior.* New York: Macmillan.

Thompson, L., & Spanier, G. B. (1978). Influence of parents, peers, and partners on the contraceptive use of college men and women. *Journal of Marriage and the Family, 40,* 481–492.

Tudge, J. R. H., & Winterhoff, P. A. (1993). Vygotsky, Piaget, and Bandura: Perspectives on the relations between the social world and cognitive development. *Human Development, 36,* 61–81.

Watson, J. B. (1913). Psychology as the behaviorist views it. *Psychological Review, 20,* 158–177.

Watson, J. B. (1925). *Behaviorism.* New York: Norton.

Weisberg, P. (1963). Social and nonsocial conditioning of infant vocalization. *Child Development, 34,* 377–388.

CHAPTER 3: The Genetics of Life-Span Development

Aldridge, S. (1996). *The thread of life: The story of genes and genetic engineering.* Cambridge, Eng.: Cambridge University Press.

Anastasi, A. (1958). Heredity, environment, and the question, "how?" Psychological Review, 65, 197–208.

Archer, J. (1992). *Ethology and human development.* Hertfordshire, Eng.: Harvester Wheatsheaf.

Bailey, J. M., & Pillard, R. C. (1991). A genetic study of the male sexual orientation. *Archives of General Psychiatry, 48,* 1089–1096.

Bailey, J. M., Pillard, R. C., Neale, M. C., & Agyei, Y. (1993). Heritable factors influence sexual orientation in women. *Archives of General Psychiatry, 50,* 217–223.

Baker, L. A., & Daniels, D. (1990). Nonshared environmental influences and personality differences in adult twins. *Journal of Personality and Social Psychology, 58,* 103–110.

Beardsley, T. (1997). Fetal checkup. *Scientific American, 275,* 38.

Begley, S. (with A. Murr & M. Hager) (1995, October 9). Promises, promises. *Newsweek,* pp. 60–62.

Belsky, J., Steinberg, L., & Draper, P. (1991). Childhood experience, interpersonal development, and reproductive strategy: An evolutionary theory of socialization. *Child Development, 62,* 647–670.

Bishop, J. A., & Cooke, L. M. (1975). Moths, melanism, and clean air. *Scientific American, 232,* 90–99.

Bishop, J. E., & Waldholz, M. (1990). *Genome: The story of the most astonishing scientific adventure of our time—The attempt to map all the genes in the human body.* New York: Simon & Schuster.

Bouchard, T. J., Jr. (1984). Twins reared together and apart: What they tell us about human diversity. In S. W. Fox (Ed.), *Individuality and determinism: Chemical and biological bases.* New York: Plenum.

Bouchard, T. J., Jr., Lykken, D. T., McGue, M., Segal, N. L., & Tellegen, A. (1990). Sources of human psychological differences: The Minnesota study of twins reared apart. *Science, 250,* 223–228.

Bouchard, T. J., Jr., & McGue, M. (1981). Family studies of intelligence: A review. *Science, 212,* 1055–1059.

Bronfenbrenner, U., & Ceci, S. J. (1994). Nature-nurture reconceptualized in developmental perspective: A bioecological model. *Psychological Review, 101,* 568–586.

Burns, G. W., & Bottino, P. J. (1989). *The science of genetics* (6th ed.). New York: Macmillan.

Buss, A. H., & Plomin, R. (1984). *Temperament: Early developing personality traits.* Hillsdale, NJ: Erlbaum.

Buss, D. M. (1989). Sex differences in human mate preferences: Evolutionary hypotheses tested in 37 cultures. *Behavioral and Brain Sciences, 12,* 1–49.

Buss, D. M. (1994). *The evolution of desire: Strategies of human mating.* New York: Basic Books.

Cabaniss, M. L. (1996). Amniocentesis. In J. A. Kuller, N. C. Chescheir, & R. C. Cefalo (Eds.), *Prenatal diagnosis and reproductive genetics.* St. Louis, MO: Mosby.

Charlesworth, W. R. (1992). Darwin and developmental psychology: Past and present. *Developmental Psychology, 28,* 5–16.

Daniels, D. (1986). Differential experiences of siblings in the same family as predictors of adolescent sibling personality differences. *Journal of Personality and Social Psychology, 51,* 339–346.

Darwin, C. (1859). *The origin of species.* New York: Modern Library.

Downey, J., Elkin, E. J., Ehrhardt, A. A., Meyer-Bahlburg, H. F., Bell, J. J., & Morishima, A. (1991). Cognitive ability and everyday functioning in women with Turner syndrome. *Journal of Learning Disabilities, 24,* 32–39.

Down syndrome prevalence at birth— United States, 1983–1990 (1994, August 26). *Mortality and Morbidity Weekly Reports, 43,* 617–622.

Dunn, J., & Plomin, R. (1990). *Separate lives. Why siblings are so different.* New York: Basic Books.

Evans, S. (1994, March 22). Study finds risk from prenatal genetic test. *Washington Post Health,* p. 9.

Findlay, I., Atkinson, G., Chambers, M., Quirke, P., Campbell, J., & Rutherford, A. (1996). Rapid genetic diagnosis at 7–9 weeks gestation: Diagnosis of sex, single gene defects, and DNA fingerprint from coelomic samples. *Human Reproduction, 11,* 2548–2553.

Gandelman, R. (1992). *Psychobiology of behavioral development.* New York: Oxford University Press.

Gottesman, I. I. (1991). *Schizophrenia genesis: The origins of madness.* New York: W. H. Freeman.

Gottlieb, G. (1991). Experiential canalization of behavioral development: Theory. *Developmental Psychology, 27,* 4–13.

Gottlieb, G. (1996). Commentary: A systems view of psychobiological development. In D. Magnusson (Ed.), *The lifespan development of individuals: Behavioral, neurobiological, and psychosocial perspectives. A synthesis.* Cambridge: Cambridge University Press.

Grilo, C. M., & Pogue-Geile, M. F. (1991). The nature of environmental influences on weight and obesity: A behavior genetic analysis. *Psychological Bulletin, 110,* 520–537.

Gusella, J. F., Wexler, N. S., Conneally, P. M., Naylor, S. L., Anderson, M. A., Tanzi, R. E., Watkins, P. C., Ottina, K., Wallace, M. R., Sakaguchi, A. Y., Young, A. B., Shoulson, I., Bonilla, E., & Martin, J. B. (1983). A polymorphic DNA marker genetically linked to Huntington disease. *Nature, 306,* 234–238.

Hebb, D. O. (1970). A return to Jensen and his social science critics. *American Psychologist, 25,* 568.

Heston, L. L. (1970). The genetics of schizophrenia and schizoid disease. *Science, 167,* 249–256.

Hinde, R. A. (1983). Ethology and child development. In M. M. Haith & J. J. Campos (Vol. Eds.; P. H. Mussen, General Ed.), *Handbook of child psychology: Vol. 2. Infancy and developmental psychobiology* (4th ed.). New York: Wiley.

Hoffman, L. W. (1991). The influence of the family environment on personality: Accounting for sibling differences. *Psychological Bulletin, 110,* 187–203.

Jarvik, L. F., & Bank, L. (1983). Aging twins: Longitudinal psychometric data. In K. W. Schaie (Ed.), *Longitudinal studies of adult psychological development.* New York: Guilford.

Jockin, V., McGue, M., & Lykken, D. T. (1996). Personality and divorce: A genetic analysis. *Journal of Personality and Social Psychology, 71,* 288–299.

Kendler, K. S. (1996). Parenting: A genetic-epidemiologic perspective. *American Journal of Psychiatry, 153,* 11–20.

Kendler, K. S., Neale, M., Kessler, R., Heath, A., & Eaves, L. (1993). A twin study of recent life events and difficulties. *Archives of General Psychiatry, 50,* 789–796.

Kettlewell, H. B. D. (1959). Darwin's missing evidence. *Scientific American, 200* (3), 48–53.

Khoury, M. J., and the Genetics Working Group. (1996). From genes to public health: The applications of genetic technology in disease prevention. *American Journal of Public Health, 86,* 1717–1722.

Kuller, J. A., Chescheir, N. C., & Cefalo, R. C. (Eds.). (1996). *Prenatal diagnosis and reproductive genetics.* St. Louis, MO: Mosby.

Loehlin, J. C. (1985). Fitting heredity/environment models jointly to twin and adoption data from the California Psychological Inventory. *Behavior Genetics, 15,* 199–221.

Loehlin, J. C. (1992). *Genes and environment in personality development (Individual differences and development series, Vol. 2).* Newbury Park, CA: Sage.

Lykken, D. T., Tellegen, A., & Iacono, W. G. (1982). EEG spectra in twins: Evidence for a neglected mechanism of genetic determination. *Physiological Psychology, 10,* 60–65.

Lytton, H. (1977). Do parents create, or respond to, differences in twins? *Developmental Psychology, 13,* 456–459.

Mandoki, M. W., Sumner, G. S., Hoffman, R. P., & Riconda, D. L. (1991). A review of Klinefelter's syndrome in children and adolescents. *Journal of the American Academy of Child and Adolescent Psychiatry, 30,* 167–172.

Manke, B., McGuire, S., Reiss, D., Howe, G., Hetherington, E., & Plomin, R. (1995). Genetic contributions to adolescents' extrafamilial social interactions: Teachers, best friends, and peers. *Social Development, 4,* 238–256.

Massie, R. K., & Massie, S. (1975). *Journey.* New York: Knopf.

McCall, R. B. (1981). Nature-nurture and the two realms of development: A proposed integration with respect to mental development. *Child Development, 52,* 1–12.

McCartney, K., Harris, M. J., & Bernieri, F. (1990). Growing up and growing apart: A developmental meta-analysis of twin studies. *Psychological Bulletin, 107,* 226–237.

McGue, M., Bouchard, T. J., Jr., Iacono, W. G., & Lykken, D. T. (1993). Behavioral genetics of cognitive ability: A life-span perspective. In R. Plomin & G. E. McClearn (Eds.), *Nature, nurture, and psychology.* Washington, DC: American Psychological Association.

McGue, M., Sharma, A., & Benson, P. (1996). The effect of common rearing on adolescent adjustment: Evidence from a US adoption cohort. *Developmental Psychology, 32,* 604–613.

McKusick, V. A. (1990). *Mendelian inheritance in man* (9th ed.). Baltimore: Johns Hopkins University Press.

Miller, J. A. (1995). Strictest diet avoids subtle detriments of PKU. *Bioscience, 45,* 244–245.

Mitchell, J. J., Capua, A., Clow, C., & Scriver, C. R. (1996). Twenty-year outcome analysis of genetic screening programs for Tay-Sachs and beta-thalassemia disease carriers in high schools. *American Journal of Human Genetics, 59,* 793–798.

Neale, M. C., & Martin, N. G. (1989). The effects of age, sex, and genotype on self-report drunkenness following a challenge dose of alcohol. *Behavior Genetics, 19,* 63–78.

Nightingale, E. O., & Goodman, M. (1990). *Before birth. Prenatal testing for genetic disease.* Cambridge, MA: Harvard University Press.

Pasaro Mendez, E. J., Fernandez, R. M., Goyanes, V., & Mendez, J. (1993). Turner's syndrome: A behavioral and cytogenetic study. *Journal of Genetic Psychology, 154,* 433–447.

Pedersen, N. L., McClearn, G. E., Plomin, R., & Friberg, L. (1985). Separated fraternal twins: Resemblance for cognitive abilities. *Behavior Genetics, 15,* 407–419.

Plomin, R. (1986). *Development, genetics, and psychology.* Hillsdale, NJ: Erlbaum.

Plomin, R. (1990). *Nature and nurture: An introduction to human behavioral genetics.* Pacific Grove, CA: Brooks/Cole.

Plomin, R., & Bergeman, C. S. (1991). The nature of nurture: Genetic influence on environmental measures. *Behavioral and Brain Sciences, 14,* 373–385.

Plomin, R., Corley, R., DeFries, J. C., & Fulker, D. W. (1990). Individual differences in television viewing in early childhood: Nature as well as nurture. *Psychological Science, 1,* 371–377.

Plomin, R., DeFries, J. C., & Loehlin, J. C. (1977). Genotype-environment interaction and correlation in the analysis of human behavior. *Psychological Bulletin, 84,* 309–322.

Plomin, R., DeFries, J. C., McClearn, G. E., & Rutter, M. (1997). *Behavioral genetics* (3rd ed.). New York: W. H. Freeman.

Plomin, R., Pedersen, N. L., Lichtenstein, P., & McClearn, G. E. (1994). Variability and stability in cognitive abilities are largely genetic later in life. *Behavior Genetics, 24,* 207–215.

Plomin, R., Pedersen, N. L., McClearn, G. E., Nesselroade, J. R., & Bergeman, C. S. (1988). EAS temperaments during the last half of the life span: Twins reared apart and twins reared together. *Psychology and Aging, 3,* 43–50.

Plomin, R., Reiss, D., Hetherington, E. M., & Howe, G. W. (1994). Nature and nurture: Genetic contributions to measures of the family environment. *Developmental Psychology, 30,* 32–43.

Reiss, D. (1995). Genetic influence on family systems: Implications for development. *Journal of Marriage and the Family, 57,* 543–560.

Reznikoff, M., Domino, G., Bridges, C., & Honeyman, M. (1973). Creative abilities in identical and fraternal twins. *Behavior Genetics, 3,* 365–377.

Roche, M. I., & Kuller, J. A. (1996). Autosomal disorders: Cystic fibrosis,

Tay-Sachs disease, and Huntington disease. In J. A. Kuller, N. C. Chescheir, & R. C. Cefalo (Eds.), *Prenatal diagnosis and reproductive genetics.* St. Louis, MO: Mosby.

Rose, R. J. (1995). Genes and human behavior. *Annual Review of Psychology, 46,* 625–654.

Rowe, D. C. (1994). *The limits of family influence: Genes, experience, and behavior.* New York: Guilford.

Rowe, D. C., & Plomin, R. (1981). The importance of nonshared (E1) environmental influences in behavioral development. *Developmental Psychology, 17,* 517–531.

Scarr, S., & Kidd, K. K. (1983). Developmental behavior genetics. In M. M. Haith & J. J. Campos (Vol. Eds.; P. H. Mussen, General Ed.), *Handbook of child psychology: Vol. 2. Infancy and developmental psychobiology* (4th ed.). New York: Wiley.

Scarr, S., & McCartney, K. (1983). How people make their own environments: A theory of genotype → environment effects. *Child Development, 54,* 424–435.

Scarr, S., & Weinberg, R. A. (1976). IQ test performance of black children adopted by white families. *American Psychologist, 54,* 260–267.

Scarr, S., & Weinberg, R. A. (1978). The influence of family background on intellectual attainment. *American Sociological Review, 43,* 674–692.

Scarr, S., & Weinberg, R. A. (1983). The Minnesota adoption studies: Genetic differences and malleability. *Child Development, 54,* 260–267.

Shafer, J. H., & Kuller, J. A. (1996). Increased maternal age and prior aneuploid conception. In J. A. Kuller, N. C. Chescheir, & R. C. Cefalo (Eds.), *Prenatal diagnosis and reproductive genetics.* St. Louis, MO: Mosby.

Shiloh, S. (1996). Genetic counseling: A developing area of interest for psychologists. *Professional Psychology: Research and Practice, 27,* 475–486.

Sjogren, B., & Uddenberg, N. (1990). Prenatal diagnosis for psychological reasons: Comparison with other indications, advanced maternal age and known genetic risk. *Prenatal Diagnosis, 10,* 111–120.

Strayer, F. F. (1980). Social ecology of the preschool peer group. In W. A. Collins (Ed.), *Minnesota Symposia on Child Psychology: Vol. 13. Development of cognition, affect, and social relations.* Hillsdale, NJ: Erlbaum.

Strigini, P., Sansone, R., Carobbi, S., & Pierluigi, M. (1990). Radiation and Down's syndrome. *Nature, 347,* 717.

Swavely, S. M., & Falek, A. (1989). Huntington's disease: The prototype for late onset terminal genetic disorders. *Loss, Grief, and Care, 3,* 111–124.

Thompson, R. F. (1975). *Introduction to physiological psychology.* New York: Harper & Row.

Tryon, R. C. (1940). Genetic differences in maze learning in rats. *Yearbook of the National Society for Studies in Education, 39,* 111–119.

Walsh, A. (1995). *Biosociology: An emerging paradigm.* Westport, CT: Praeger.

Weinberg, R. A., Scarr, S., & Waldman, I. D. (1992). The Minnesota Transracial Adoption Study: A follow-up of IQ test performance at adolescence. *Intelligence, 16,* 117–135.

Weiss, R. (1995, October 3). Are we more than the sum of our genes? *Washington Post Health,* pp. 10–12.

Wiggins, S., Whyte, P., Huggins, M., Adam, S., Theilmann, J., Bloch, M., Sheps, S. B., Schechter, M. T., Hayden, M. R. (1992). The psychological consequences of predictive testing for Huntington's disease. *New England Journal of Medicine, 327,* 1401–1405.

Wilson, E. O. (1975). *Sociobiology: The new synthesis.* Cambridge, MA: Belknap Press of Harvard University Press.

Wilson, R. S. (1978). Synchronies in mental development: An epigenetic perspective. *Science, 202,* 939–948.

Wilson, R. S. (1983). The Louisville twin study: Developmental synchronies in behavior. *Child Development, 54,* 298–316.

Wright, L. (1995). Double mystery. *New Yorker, 71,* 44–62.

CHAPTER 4: Early Environmental Influences on Life-Span Development

Abel, E. L. (1981). Behavioral teratology of alcohol. *Psychological Bulletin, 90,* 564–581.

Abel, E. L. (1989). *Behavioral teratogenesis and behavioral mutagenesis. A primer in abnormal development.* New York: Plenum.

Ackermann-Liebrich, U., Voegeli, T., Gunter-Witt, K., Kunz, I., Zullig, M., Schindler, C., & Maurer, M. (1996). Home versus hospital deliveries: Follow-up study of matched pairs for procedures and outcome. *British Medical Journal, 313,* 1313–1318.

Adler, J., & Carey, J. (1982, January 11). But is it a person? *Newsweek,* p. 44.

Aldridge, S. (1996). *The thread of life: The story of genes and genetic engineering.* Cambridge: Cambridge University Press.

Alessandri, S. M., Sullivan, M. W., Imaizumi, S., & Lewis, M. (1993). Learning and emotional responsivity in cocaine-exposed infants. *Developmental Psychology, 29,* 989–997.

Allen, M. C., & Capute, A. J. (1986). Assessment of early auditory and visual abilities of extremely premature infants. *Developmental Medicine and Child Neurology, 28,* 458–466.

Amini, S. B., Catalano, P. M., Dierker, L. J., & Mann, L. I. (1996). Births to teenagers: Trends and obstetric outcomes. *Obstetrics and Gynecology, 87,* 668–674.

Apgar, V., & Beck, J. (1974). *Is my baby all right?* New York: Pocket Books.

Apgar, V., & James, L. S. (1962). Further observations on the newborn scoring system. *American Journal of Diseases of Children, 104,* 419–428.

Baird, P. A., Anderson, T. W., Newcombe, H. B., & Lowry, R. B. (1988). Genetic disorders in children and young adults: A population study. *American Journal of Human Genetics, 42,* 677–693.

Baker, R. L., & Mednick, B. R. (1984). *Influences on human development: A longitudinal perspective.* Boston: Kluwer Nijhoff Publishing.

Barker, D. J. P. (1994). *Mothers, babies, and disease in later life.* London: BMJ Publishing Group.

Barr, H. M., & Streissguth, A. P. (1991). Caffeine use during pregnancy and child outcome: A 7-year prospective study. *Neurotoxicology and Teratology, 13,* 441–448.

Barr, H. M., Streissguth, A. P., Darby, B. L., & Sampson, P. D. (1990). Prenatal exposure to alcohol, caffeine, tobacco, and aspirin: Effects on fine and gross motor performance in 4-year-old children. *Developmental Psychology, 26,* 339–348.

Beck, M. (1994, January 17). How far should we push mother nature? *Newsweek,* pp. 54–57.

Beckwith, L., & Parmelee, A. H., Jr. (1986). EEG patterns of preterm infants, home environment, and later IQ. *Child Development, 57,* 777–789.

Begley, S. (1995, September 4). The baby myth. *Newsweek,* pp. 38–47.

Begley, S. (1997, March 10). Little lamb, who made thee? *Newsweek,* pp. 53–59.

Bellinger, D., Leviton, A., Waternaux, C., Needleman, H., & Rabinowitz, M. (1987). Longitudinal analyses of prenatal and postnatal lead exposure and early cognitive development. *New England Journal of Medicine, 316,* 1037–1043.

Billing, L., Eriksson, M., Jonsson, B., Steneroth, G., & Zetterstrom, R. (1994). The influence of environmental factors on behavioural problems in 8-year-old children exposed to amphetamine during fetal life. *Child Abuse and Neglect, 18,* 3–9.

Brackbill, Y., McManus, K., & Woodward, L. (1985). *Medication in maternity: Infant exposure and maternal information.* Ann Arbor: University of Michigan Press.

Bradley, R. H., Whiteside, L., Mundfrom, D. J., & Casey, P. H. (1994). Impact of the Infant Health and Development Program (IHDP) on the home environments of infants born prematurely and with low birthweight. *Journal of Educational Psychology, 86,* 531–541.

Brazelton, T. B. (1979). Behavioral competence of the newborn infant. *Seminars in Perinatology, 3,* 35–44.

Britt, G. C., & Myers, B. J. (1994). The effects of the Brazelton intervention. *Infant Mental Health Journal, 15,* 278–292.

Bronfenbrenner, U., & Crouter, A. C. (1983). The evolution of environmental models in developmental research. In W. Kessen (Vol. Ed.; P. H. Mussen, General Ed.), *Handbook of child psychology: Vol. 1. History, theory, and methods* (4th ed.). New York: Wiley.

Brooks-Gunn, J., Klebanov, P. K., Liaw, F., & Spiker, D. (1993). Enhancing the development of low birthweight, premature infants: Changes in cognition and behavior over the first three years. *Child Development, 64,* 736–753.

Bulterys, M. G., Greenland, S., & Kraus, J. F. (1990). Chronic fetal hypoxia and sudden infant death syndrome: Interaction between maternal smoking and low hematocrit during pregnancy. *Pediatrics, 86,* 535–540.

Caldwell, P. (1996). Child survival: Physical vulnerability and resilience in adversity in the European past and the contemporary third world. *Social Science and Medicine, 43,* 609–619.

Campell, S. B., Cohn, J. F., Flanagan, C., Popper, S., & Meyers, T. (1992). Course and correlates of postpartum depression during the transition to parenthood. *Development and Psychopathology, 4,* 29–47.

Chalmers, B. (1996). Cross-cultural comparisons of birthing: Psychosocial issues in Western and African birth. *Psychology and Health, 12,* 11–21.

Chandler, S., & Field, P. A. (1997). Becoming a father: First-time fathers' experience of labor and delivery. *Journal of Nurse-Midwifery, 42,* 17–24.

Clarke, A. S., Soto, A., Bergholz, T., & Schneider, M. L. (1996). Maternal gestational stress alters adaptive and social behavior in adolescent rhesus monkey offspring. *Infant Behavior and Development, 19,* 451–461.

Clarke, S. C., & Taffel, S. M. (1996). Rates of cesarean and VBAC delivery, United States, 1994. *Birth, 23,* 166–168.

Colburn, D. (1995, August 22). One pound wonder: The story of Brittany Orange. *Washington Post Health,* p. 7.

Colburn, D. (1996, September 24). Fetal alcohol babies face life of problems. *Washington Post Health,* p. 5.

Corah, N. L., Anthony, E. J., Painter, P., Stern, J. A., & Thurston, D. L. (1965). The effects of perinatal anoxia after seven years. *Psychological Monographs, 79* (Whole No. 596).

Cowley, G. (1994, March 7). Locking HIV out of the womb. *Newsweek,* p. 53.

Curtiss, S. (1977). *Genie: A psycholinguistic study of a modern day "wild child."* New York: Academic.

Diaz, J. (1997). *How drugs influence behavior. A neuro-behavioral approach.* Upper Saddle River, NJ: Prentice-Hall.

Dick-Read, G. (1972). *Childbirth without fear: The original approach to natural childbirth* (Rev. ed.). New York: Harper & Row. (Original work published 1933)

DiMatteo, M. R., Morton, S. C., Lepper, H. S., & Damush, T. M. (1996). Cesarean childbirth and psychosocial outcomes: A meta-analysis. *Health Psychology, 15,* 303–314.

DiMatteo, M. R., Morton, S. C., Lepper, H. S., Damush, T. M., Carney, M. F., Pearson, M., Edelman, C. L., & Mandle, C. L. (1990). *Health promotion throughout the lifespan.* St. Louis, MO: Mosby.

DiPietro, J. A., Hodgson, D. M., Costigan, K. A., Hilton, S. C., & Johnson, T. R. B. (1996b). Fetal neurobehavioral development. *Child Development, 67,* 2553–2567.

DiPietro, J. A., Hodgson, D. M., Costigan, K. A., & Johnson, T. R. B. (1996a). Fetal antecedents of infant temperament. *Child Development, 67,* 2568–2583.

Dollberg, S., Seidman, D. S., Armon, Y., Stevenson, D. K., & Gale, R. (1996). Adverse perinatal outcome in the older primipara. *Journal of Perinatology, 16,* 93–97.

Edelman, C. L., & Mandle, C. L. (1990). *Health promotion throughout the lifespan.* St. Louis, MO: Mosby.

Edwards, M., & Waldorf, M. (1984). *Reclaiming birth: History and heroines of American childbirth reform.* Trumansburg, NY: The Crossing Press.

Eldred, L., & Chaisson, R. (1996). The clinical course of HIV infection in women. In R. R. Faden & N. E. Kass (Eds.), *HIV, AIDS, and childbearing* (pp. 15–30). New York: Oxford University Press.

Emory, E. K., Schlackaman, L. J., & Fiano, K. (1996). Drug-hormone interactions on neurobehavioral responses in human neonates. *Infant Behavior and Development, 19,* 213–220.

Field, T., Sandberg, D., Garcia, R., Vega-Lahr, N., Goldstein, S., & Guy, L. (1985). Pregnancy problems, postpartum depression, and early mother-infant interactions. *Developmental Psychology, 21,* 1152–1156.

Fried, P. A., O'Connell, C. M., & Watkinson, B. (1992). 60- and 72-month follow-up of children prenatally exposed to marijuana, cigarettes, and alcohol: Cognitive and language assessment. *Developmental and Behavioral Pediatrics, 13,* 383–391.

Friedman, J. M., & Polifka, J. E. (1996). *The effects of drugs on the fetus and nursing infant: A handbook for health care professionals.* Baltimore, MD: Johns Hopkins University Press.

Fullerton, J. T., & Severino, R. (1992). In-hospital care for low-risk childbirth. Comparison with results from the National Birth Center Study. *Journal of Nurse Midwifery, 37,* 331–340.

Gabiano, C., Tovo, P. A., de Martino, M., Galli, L., Giaquinto, C., Loy, A., Schoeller, M. C., Giovannini, M., Ferranti, G., Rancilio, L., Caselli, D., Segni, G., Livadiotti, S., Conte, A.,

Rizzi, M., Viggiano, D., Mazza, A., Ferrazzin, A., Tozzi, A. E., & Cappello, N. (1992). Mother-to-child transmission of human immunodeficiency virus type 1: Risk of infection and correlates of transmission. *Pediatrics, 90,* 369–374.

Garmezy, N. (1991). Resiliency and vulnerability to adverse developmental outcomes associated with poverty. *American Behavioral Scientist, 34,* 416–430.

Goldberg, G. R., & Prentice, A. M. (1994). Maternal and fetal determinants of adult diseases. *Nutrition Reviews, 52,* 191–200.

Goldberg, S. (1983). Parent-infant bonding: Another look. *Child Development, 54,* 1355–1382.

Golombok, S., Cook, R., Bish, A., & Murray, C. (1995). Families created by the new reproductive technologies: Quality of parenting and social and emotional development of the children. *Child Development, 66,* 285–298.

Golub, M., Gorman, K., Grantham-McGregor, S., Levitsky, D., Schürch, B., Strupp, B., & Wachs, T. (1996). A re-conceptualization of the effects of undernutrition on children's biological, psychosocial, and behavioral development. *Social Policy Report, Society for Research in Child Development, 10,* 1–21.

Gotlib, I. H., Whiffen, V. E., Wallace, P. M., & Mount, J. (1991). Prospective investigation of postpartum depression: Factors involved in onset and recovery. *Journal of Abnormal Psychology, 100,* 122–132.

Gottlieb, G. (1996). Commentary: A systems view of psychobiological development. In D. Magnusson (Ed.), *The lifespan development of individuals: Behavioral, neurobiological, and psychosocial perspectives. A synthesis.* Cambridge: Cambridge University Press.

Gottlieb, S. E., & Barrett, D. E. (1986). Effects of unanticipated cesarian section on mothers, infants, and their interaction in the first month of life. *Developmental and Behavioral Pediatrics, 7,* 180–185.

Greenberg, M., & Morris, N. (1974). Engrossment: The newborn's impact upon the father. *American Journal of Orthopsychiatry, 44,* 520–531.

Guyer, B., Strobino, D. M., Ventura, S. J., MacDorman, M., & Martin, J. A. (1996). Annual summary of vital statistics—1995. *Pediatrics, 98,* 1007–1019.

Hamm, A. C. (1981). *Questions and answers about DES exposure during pregnancy and birth.* NIH Pub. No. 81-1118. Washington, DC: National Institutes of Health, U.S. Department of Health and Human Services.

Harmon, T. M., Hynan, M. T., & Tyre, T. E. (1990). Improved obstetric outcomes using hypnotic analgesia and skill mastery combined with childbirth education. *Journal of Consulting and Clinical Psychology, 58,* 525–530.

Harvey, S., Jarrell, J., Brant, R., Stainton, C., & Rach, D. (1996). A randomized, controlled trial of nurse-midwifery care. *Birth, 23,* 128–135.

Hawley, T. L., & Disney, E. R. (1992). Crack's children: The consequences of maternal cocaine abuse. *Social Policy Report, Society for Research in Child Development, 6,* 1–23.

Hay, W. W., Jr., Catz, C. S., Grave, G. D., & Yaffe, S. J. (1997). Workshop summary: Fetal growth: Its regulation and disorders. *Pediatrics, 99,* 585–591.

Heinonen, O. P., Slone, D., & Shapiro, S. (1977). *Birth defects and drugs in pregnancy.* Littleton, MA: Publishing Sciences Group.

Hodnett, E. D., & Osborn, R. W. (1989). A randomized trial of the effects of monitrice support during labor: Mothers' views two to four weeks postpartum. *Birth, 16,* 177–183.

Hutton, N. (1996). Health prospects for children born to HIV-infected women. In R. R. Faden & N. E. Kass (Eds.), *HIV, AIDS, and childbearing* (pp. 63–77). New York: Oxford University Press.

Jacobson, J. L., & Jacobson, S. W. (1996a). Intellectual impairment in children exposed to polychlorinated biphenyls in utero. *New England Journal of Medicine, 335,* 783–789.

Jacobson, J. L., & Jacobson, S. W. (1996b). Methodological considerations in behavioral toxicology in infants and children. *Developmental Psychology, 32,* 390–403.

Jacobson, J. L., Jacobson, S. W., Fein, G. G., Schwartz, P. M., & Dowler, J. K. (1984). Prenatal exposure to an environmental toxin. *Developmental Psychology, 20,* 523–532.

Jacobson, J. L., Jacobson, S. W., & Humphrey, H. E. (1990). Effects of in utero exposure to polychlorinated biphenyls and related contaminants on cognitive functioning in young children. *Journal of Pediatrics, 116,* 38–45.

Jacobson, J. L., Jacobson, S. W., Sokol, R. J., Martier, S. S., Ager, J. W., & Kaplan-Estrin, M. G. (1993). Teratogenic effects of alcohol on infant development. *Alcoholism: Clinical and Experimental Research, 17,* 174–183.

Jacobson, S. W., Fein, G. G., Jacobson, J. L., Schwartz, P. M., & Dowler, J. K. (1984). Neonatal correlates of exposure to smoking, caffeine, and alcohol. *Infant Behavior and Development, 7,* 253–265.

Jeffery, R., & Jeffery, P. M. (1993). Traditional birth attendants in rural north India: The social organization of childbearing. In S. Lindenbaum & M. Lock (Eds.), *Knowledge, power, and practice: The anthropology of medicine and everyday life.* Berkeley, CA: University of California Press.

Jones, K. L., Smith, D. W., Ulleland, C. N., & Streissguth, A. P. (1973). Pattern of malformation in offspring of chronic alcoholic mothers. *Lancet, 1,* 1267–1271.

Källén, K. (1997). Maternal smoking during pregnancy and limb reduction malformations in Sweden. *American Journal of Public Health, 87,* 29–32.

Kelley-Buchanan, C. (1988). *Peace of mind during pregnancy: An A-Z guide to the substances that could affect your unborn baby.* New York: Facts on File.

Kennell, J., Klaus, M., McGrath, S., Robertson, S., & Hinkley, C. (1991). Continuous emotional support during labor in a US hospital. A randomized controlled trial. *Journal of the American Medical Association, 265,* 2197–2201.

Kennell, J. H., Voos, D. K., & Klaus, M. H. (1979). Parent-infant bonding. In J. D. Osofsky (Ed.), *Handbook of infant development.* New York: Wiley.

Klaus, M. H., & Kennell, J. H. (1976). *Maternal-infant bonding.* St. Louis, MO: C. V. Mosby.

Klee, L. (1986). Home away from home: The alternative birth center. *Social Science and Medicine, 23,* 9–16.

Kochanevich-Wallace, P. M., McCluskey-Fawcett, K. A., Meck, N. E., & Simons, C. J. (1988). Method of delivery and parent-newborn interaction. *Journal of Pediatric Psychology, 13,* 213–221.

Koller, H., Lawson, K., Rose, S. A., Wallace, I., & McCarton, C. (1997). Patterns of cognitive development in very low birthweight children during the first six years of life. *Pediatrics, 99,* 383–389.

Konner, M. J. (1981). Evolution of human behavior development. In R. H. Munroe, R. L. Munroe, & B. B. Whiting (Eds.), *Handbook of cross-cultural human development.* New York: Garland STPM Press.

Kopp, C. B., & Kahler, S. R. (1989). Risk in infancy. *American Psychologist, 44,* 224–230.

Kopp, C. B., & Parmelee, A. H. (1979). Prenatal and perinatal influences on infant behavior. In J. D. Osofsky (Ed.), *Handbook of infant development.* New York: Wiley.

Kraus, M. A., & Redman, E. S. (1986). Postpartum depression: An interactional view. *Journal of Marital and Family Therapy, 12,* 63–74.

Lamaze, F. (1958). *Painless childbirth: Psychoprophylactic method.* London: Burke.

Leadbeater, B. J., Bishop, S. J., & Raver, C. C. (1996). Quality of mother-toddler interactions, maternal depressive symptoms, and behavior problems in preschoolers of adolescent mothers. *Developmental Psychology, 32,* 280–288.

Lefkowitz, M. M. (1981). Smoking during pregnancy: Long-term effects on offspring. *Developmental Psychology, 17,* 192–194.

Leroy, M. (1988). *Miscarriage.* London: Macdonald & Company.

Lester, B. M., Corwin, M. J., Sepkoski, C., Seifer, R., Peucker, M., McLaughlin, S., & Golub, H. L. (1991). Neurobehavioral syndromes in cocaine-exposed newborn infants. *Child Development, 62,* 694–705.

Lester, B. M., Freier, K., & LaGasse, L. (1995). Prenatal cocaine exposure and child outcome: What do we really know? In M. Lewis & M. Bendersky (Eds.), *Mothers, babies, and cocaine: The role of toxins in development.* Hillsdale, NJ: Erlbaum.

LeVine, R. A. (1974). Parental goals: A cross-cultural view. *Teachers College Record, 76,* 226–239.

LeVine, R. A. (1988). Human parental care: Universal goals, cultural strategies, individual behavior. In R. A. LeVine, P. M. Miller, & M. M. West (Eds.), *Parental behavior in diverse societies: New directions for child development* (No. 40). San Francisco: Jossey-Bass.

Lin, C. (1993). Fetal growth retardation. In C. Lin, M. S. Verp, & R. E. Sabbagha (Eds.), *The high-risk fetus: Pathophysiology, diagnosis, management.* New York: Springer-Verlag.

Lobel, M. (1994). Conceptualizations, measurement, and effects of prenatal maternal stress on birth outcomes. *Journal of Behavioral Medicine, 17,* 225–272.

Localio, A. R., Lawthers, A. G., Bengtson, J. M., Herbert, L. E., Weaver, S. L., Brennan, T. A., & Landis, R. (1993). Relationship between malpractice claims and cesarean delivery. *Journal of the American Medical Association, 269,* 366–373.

MacFarlane, A. (1977). *The psychology of childbirth.* Cambridge, MA: Harvard University Press.

McCarton, C. M., Brooks-Gunn, J., Wallace, I. F., Bauer, C. R., Bennett, F. C., Bernbaum, J. C., Broyles, S., Casey, P. H., McCormick, M. C., Scott, D. T., Tyson, J., Tonascia, J., & Meinert, C. L. (1997). Results at age 8 years of early intervention for low-birth-weight premature infants. *Journal of the American Medical Association, 277,* 126–132.

McCubbin, J. A., Lawson, E. J., Cox, S., Sherman, J. J., Norton, J. A., Read, J. A. (1996). Prenatal maternal blood pressure response to stress predicts birth weight and gestational age: A preliminary study. *American Journal of Obstetrics and Gynecology, 175,* 706–712.

McMahon, M. J., & Katz, V. L. (1996). Clinical teratology. In J. A. Kuller, N. C. Chescheir, & R. C. Cefalo (Eds.), *Prenatal diagnosis and reproductive genetics.* St. Louis, MO: Mosby.

Miller, S. S. (1976). *Symptoms: The complete home medical encyclopedia.* New York: Thomas Y. Crowell.

Molfese, V. J. (1989). *Perinatal risk and infant development. Assessment and prediction.* New York: Guilford Press.

Moore, K. L. (1977). *The developing human.* Philadelphia: W. B. Saunders.

Morelli, G. A., Rogoff, B., Oppenheim, D., & Goldsmith, D. (1992). Cultural variation in infants' sleeping arrangements: Questions of independence. *Developmental Psychology, 28,* 604–613.

Murray, L. (1992). The impact of postnatal depression on infant development. *Journal of Child Psychology and Psychiatry and Allied Disciplines, 33,* 543–561.

Mutryn, C. S. (1993). Psychosocial impact of cesarean section on the family: A literature review. *Social Science and Medicine, 37,* 1271–1281.

Myers, B. J. (1982). Early intervention using Brazelton training with middle-class mothers and fathers of newborns. *Child Development, 53,* 462–471.

Myers, R. E., & Myers, S. E. (1979). Use of sedative, analgesic, and anesthetic drugs during labor and delivery: Bane or boon. *American Journal of Obstetrics and Gynecology, 133,* 83–104.

Nordentoft, M., Lou, H. C., Hansen, D., Nim, J., Pryds, O., Rubin, P., & Hemmingsen, R. (1996). Intrauterine growth retardation and premature delivery: The influence of maternal smoking and psychosocial factors. *American Journal of Public Health, 86,* 347–354.

Nsamenang, A. B. (1992). *Human development in cultural context—A third world perspective.* Newbury Park, CA: Sage.

O'Dempsey, T. J. D. (1988). Traditional belief and practice among the Pokot people of Kenya with particular reference to mother and child health: 2. Mother and child health. *Annals of Tropical Paediatrics, 8,* 125.

O'Hara, M. W., Schlechte, J. A., Lewis, D. A., & Varner, M. W. (1991). Controlled prospective study of postpartum mood disorders: Psychological, environmental, and hormonal variables. *Journal of Abnormal Psychology, 100,* 63–73.

Olds, D. L., Henderson, C. R., Jr., & Tatelbaum, R. (1994). Prevention of intellectual impairment in children of women who smoke cigarettes during pregnancy. *Pediatrics, 93,* 228–233.

Paarlberg, K. M., Vingerhoets, Ad J. J. M., Passchier, J., Dekker, G. A., & van Geijn, H. P. (1995). Psychosocial factors and pregnancy outcome: A review with emphasis on methodological issues. *Journal of Psychosomatic Research, 39,* 563–595.

Palkovitz, R. (1985). Fathers' birth attendance, early contact, and extended contact with their newborns: A critical review. *Child Development, 56,* 392–406.

Parazzini, F., Luchini, L., La Vecchia, C., & Crosignani, P. G. (1993). Video display terminal use during pregnancy and reproductive outcomes—a meta-analysis. *Journal of Epidemiology and Community Health, 47,* 265–268.

Peterson, G. H., Mehl, L. E., & Liederman, P. H. (1979). The role of some birth-related variables in father attachment. *American Journal of Orthopsychiatry, 49,* 330–338.

Post, T. (1994, November 28). Quality not quantity. *Newsweek,* pp. 36–37.

Radke-Yarrow, M., Cummings, E. M., Kuczynski, L., & Chapman, M. (1985). Patterns of attachment in two- and three-year-olds in normal families and families with parental depression. *Child Development, 56,* 884–893.

Ratcliffe, S. D., Byrd, J. E., & Sakornbut, E. L. (1996). *Handbook of pregnancy and perinatal care in family practice: Science and practice.* Philadelphia: Hanley & Belfus.

Richman, A. L., LeVine, R. A., New, R. S., Howrigan, G. A., Welles-Nystrom, B., & LeVine, S. E. (1988). Maternal behavior to infants in five cultures. In R. A. LeVine, P. M. Miller, & M. M. West (Eds.), *Parental behavior in diverse societies: New directions for child development* (No. 40). San Francisco: Jossey-Bass.

Richman, A. L., Miller, P. M., & LeVine, R. A. (1992). Cultural and educational variations in maternal responsiveness. *Developmental Psychology, 28,* 614–621.

Roberts, C. J., & Lowe, C. R. (1975). Where have all the conceptions gone? *Lancet, 1,* 498–499.

Rothberg, A. D., & Lits, B. (1991). Psychosocial support for maternal stress during pregnancy: Effect on birth weight. *American Journal of Obstetrics and Gynecology, 165,* 403–407.

Rubin, D. H., Krasilnikoff, P. A., Leventhal, J. M., Weile, B., & Berget, A. (1986). Effect of passive smoking on birth-weight. *Lancet, 2,* 415–417.

Russell, C. (1995, March 28). Baby study links busy days, fussy nights. *Washington Post Health,* p. 7.

Rymer, R. (1993). *Genie: An abused child's first flight from silence.* New York: HarperCollins.

Sadler, T. W. (1996). Embryology and experimental teratology. In J. A. Kuller, N. C. Chescheir, & R. C. Cefalo (Eds.), *Prenatal diagnosis and reproductive genetics.* St. Louis, MO: Mosby.

Sameroff, A. J., & Chandler, M. J. (1975). Reproductive risk and the continuum of caretaking casualty. In F. D. Horowitz, M. Hetherington, S. Scarr-Salapatek, & G. Siegel (Eds.), *Review of child development research* (Vol. 4). Chicago: University of Chicago Press.

Scafidi, F. A., Field, T. M., Schanberg, S. M., Bauer, C. R., Vega-Lahr, N., Garcia, R., Poirier, J., Nystrom, G., & Kuhn, C. M. (1986). Effects of tactile/kinesthetic stimulation on the clinical course and sleep/wake behavior of preterm neonates. *Infant Behavior and Development, 9,* 91–105.

Scafidi, F. A., Field, T. M., Schanberg, S. M., Bauer, C. R., Vega-Lahr, N., Garcia, R., Poirer, J., Nystrom, G., & Kuhn, C. M. (1990). Massage stimulates growth in preterm infants: A replication. *Infant Behavior and Development, 13,* 167–188.

Schaefer, M., Hatcher, R. P., & Barglow, P. D. (1980). Prematurity and infant stimulation: A review of research. *Child Psychiatry and Human Development, 10,* 199–212.

Schardein, J. L. (1985). *Chemically induced birth defects.* New York: Dekker.

Schnoll, S. H. (1986). Pharmacologic basis of perinatal addiction. In I. J. Chasnoff (Ed.), *Drug use in pregnancy: Mother and child.* Boston: MTP Press Limited.

Simpson, K. R. (1997). Preterm birth in the United States: Current issues and future perspectives. *Journal of Perinatal and Neonatal Nursing, 10,* 11–15.

Simpson, K. R., & Creehan, P. A. (1996). *Perinatal nursing.* Philadelphia, PA: Lippincott-Raven.

Singer, L., Farkas, K., & Kliegman, R. (1992). Childhood medical and behavioral consequences of maternal cocaine use. *Journal of Pediatric Psychology, 17,* 389–406.

Smotherman, W. P., & Robinson, S. R. (1996). The development of behavior before birth. *Developmental Psychology, 32,* 425–434.

Spreen, O., Risser, A. H., & Edgell, D. (1995). *Developmental neuropsychology.* New York: Oxford University Press.

Spreen, O., Tupper, D., Risser, A., Tuokko, H., & Edgell, D. (1984). *Human developmental neuropsychology.* New York: Oxford University Press.

Stein, Z. A., & Susser, M. W. (1976). Prenatal nutrition and mental competence. In J. D. Lloyd-Still (Ed.), *Malnutrition and intellectual development.* Littleton, MA: Publishing Sciences Group.

Stein, Z. A., Susser, M. W., Saenger, G., & Marolla, F. (1975). *Famine and human development: The Dutch hunger winter of 1944–1945.* New York: Oxford University Press.

Steinberg, L. (1996). *Adolescence* (4th ed.). New York: McGraw-Hill.

Steinberg, S. (1996). Childbearing research: A transcultural review. *Social Science and Medicine, 43,* 1765–1784.

Stern, M., & Hildebrandt, K. A. (1986). Prematurity stereotyping: Effects on mother-infant interaction. *Child Development, 57,* 308–315.

Stone, R. (1992). Can a father's exposure lead to illness in his children? *Science, 258,* 31.

Stott, D. H., & Latchford, S. A. (1976). Prenatal antecedents of child health, development, and behavior: An epidemiological report of incidence and association. *Journal of the American Academy of Child Psychiatry, 15,* 161–190.

Stratton, K., Howe, C., & Battaglia, F. (Eds.). (1996). *Fetal alcohol syndrome: Diagnosis, epidemiology, prevention, and treatment.* Washington, DC: National Academy Press.

Streissguth, A. P., & Dehaene, P. (1993). Fetal alcohol syndrome in twins of alcoholic mothers: Concordance of diagnosis and IQ. *American Journal of Medical Genetics, 47,* 857–861.

Streissguth, A. P., Randels, S. P., & Smith, D. F. (1991). A test-retest study of intelligence in patients with fetal alcohol syndrome: Implications for care. *Journal of the American Academy of Child and Adolescent, 30,* 584–587.

Streissguth, A. P., Sampson, P. D., Barr, H. M., Bookstein, F. L., & Olson, H. C. (1994). The effects of prenatal exposure to alcohol and tobacco: Contributions from the Seattle Longitudinal Prospective Study and implications for public policy. In H. L. Needlebaum & D. Bellinger (Eds.), *Prenatal exposure to toxicants.* Baltimore, MD: Johns Hopkins University Press.

Strigini, P., Sansone, R., Carobbi, S., & Pierluigi, M. (1990). Radiation and Down's syndrome. *Nature, 347,* 717.

Super, C. M., & Harkness, S. (1981). Figure, ground, and Gestalt: The cultural context of the active individual. In R. M. Lerner & N. A. Busch-Rossnagel (Eds.), *Individuals as producers of their development: A life-span perspective.* New York: Academic Press.

Super, C. M., Herrera, M. G., & Mora, J. O. (1990). Long-term effects of food supplementation and psychoso-cial intervention on the physical growth of Colombian infants at risk of malnutrition. *Child Development, 61,* 29–49.

Susser, M., & Stein, Z. (1994). Timing in prenatal nutrition: A reprise of the Dutch Famine Study. *Nutrition Reviews, 52,* 84–94.

van Balen, F. (1996). Child-rearing following in vitro fertilization. *Journal of Child Psychology and Psychiatry and Allied Disciplines, 37,* 687–693.

Vaughn, B. E., Bradley, C. F., Joffe, L. S., Seifer, R., & Barglow, P. (1987). Maternal characteristics measured prenatally are predictive of ratings of temperamental "difficulty" on the Carey Infant Temperament Questionnaire. *Developmental Psychology, 23,* 152–161.

Vaughn, V. C., McKay, J. R., & Behrman, R. E. (1984). *Nelson textbook of pediatrics* (12th ed.). Philadelphia: Saunders.

Vorhees, C. V., & Mollnow, E. (1987). Behavioral teratogenesis: Long-term influences on behavior from early exposure to environmental agents. In J. D. Osofsky (Ed.), *Handbook of infant development* (2nd ed.). New York: Wiley.

Waldenström, U., Borg, I., Olsson, B., Sköld, M., & Wall, S. (1996). The childbirth experience: A study of 295 new mothers. *Birth, 23,* 144–153.

Werner, E. E. (1989). High-risk children in young adulthood: A longitudinal study from birth to 32 years. *American Journal of Orthopsychiatry, 59,* 72–81.

Werner, E. E., & Smith, R. S. (1982). *Vulnerable but invincible: A longitudinal study of resilient children and youth.* New York: McGraw-Hill.

Werner, E. E., & Smith, R. S. (1992). *Overcoming the odds: High-risk children from birth to adulthood.* Ithaca, NY: Cornell University Press.

Whiffen, V. E. (1992). Is postpartum depression a distinct diagnosis? *Clinical Psychology Review, 12,* 485–508.

Wideman, M. V., & Singer, J. E. (1984). The role of psychological mechanisms in preparation for childbirth. *American Psychologist, 39,* 1357–1371.

Widmayer, S., & Field, T. (1980). Effects of Brazelton demonstrations on early interactions of preterm infants and their teenage mothers. *Infant Behavior and Development, 3,* 79–89.

Wilcock, A., Kobayashi, L., & Murray, I. (1997). Twenty-five years of obstetric patient satisfaction in North America: A review of the literature. *Journal of Perinatal and Neonatal Nursing, 10,* 36–47.

Wilson, R. S. (1985). Risk and resilience in early mental development. *Developmental Psychology, 21,* 795–805.

Zeskind, P. S., & Ramey, C. T. (1981). Preventing intellectual and interactional sequelae of fetal malnutrition: A longitudinal, transactional, and synergistic approach to development. *Child Development, 52,* 213–218.

CHAPTER 5: The Physical Self

Adams, P., Davies, G. T., & Sweetnam, P. (1970). Osteoporosis and the effects of aging on bone mass in elderly men and women. *Quarterly Journal of Medicine, 39,* 601–615.

Ainscough, C. E. (1990). Premenstrual emotional changes: A prospective study of symptomatology in normal women. *Journal of Psychosomatic Research, 34,* 35–45.

Andres, R., & Tobin, J. D. (1977). Endocrine systems. In C. E. Finch & L. Hayflick (Eds.), *Handbook of the biology of aging.* New York: Van Nostrand Reinhold.

Archer, J. (1991). The influence of testosterone on human aggression. *British Journal of Psychology, 82,* 1–28.

Bafitis, H., & Sargent, F., II. (1977). Human physiological adaptability through the life sequence. *Journal of Gerontology, 32,* 402–410.

Baltes, P. B., Smith, J., & Staudinger, U. M. (1992). Wisdom and successful aging. In T. B. Sonderegger (Ed.), *Nebraska Symposium on Motivation: Vol. 39, Psychology and aging.* Lincoln: University of Nebraska Press.

Barry, D. (1990). *Dave Barry turns 40.* New York: Crown.

Begley, S. (1996, February 19). Your child's brain. *Newsweek,* pp. 55–62.

Beidelman, T. O. (1971). *The Kagura: A matrilineal people of East Africa.* New York: Holt, Rinehart & Winston.

Benes, F. M. (1989). Myelination of cortical-hippocampal relays during late adolescence. *Schizophrenia Bulletin, 15,* 585–593.

Bennett, E. L., Diamond, M. C., Krech, D., & Rosenzweig, M. R. (1964). Chemical and anatomical plasticity of the brain. *Science, 146,* 610–619.

Berg, W. K., Adkinson, C. D., & Strock, B. D. (1973). Duration and frequency of periods of alertness in neonates. *Developmental Psychology, 9,* 434.

Berscheid, E., Walster, E., & Bohrnstedt, G. (1973, June). The happy American body: A survey report. *Psychology Today,* pp. 119–131.

Bertenthal, B. I., Campos, J. J., & Kermoian, R. (1994). An epigenetic perspective on the development of self-produced locomotion and its consequences. *Current Directions in Psychological Science, 3,* 140–145.

Birren, J. E., Butler, R. N., Greenhouse, S. W., Sokoloff, L., & Yarrow, M. R. (Eds.). (1963). *Human aging: A biological and behavioral study.* Washington, DC: U.S. Government Printing Office.

Birren, J. E., & Fisher, L. M. (1995). Aging and speed of behavior: Possible consequences for psychological functioning. *Annual Review of Psychology, 46,* 329–353.

Black, J. E., Isaacs, K. R., & Greenough, W. T. (1991). Usual vs. successful aging: Some notes on experiential factors. *Neurobiology of Aging, 12,* 325–328.

Black, J. E., Sirevaag, A. M., Wallace, C. S., Savin, M. H., & Greenough, W. T. (1989). Effects of complex experience on somatic growth and organ development in rats. *Developmental Psychobiology, 22,* 727–752.

Boismier, J. D. (1977). Visual stimulation and the wake-sleep behavior in human neonates. *Developmental Psychobiology, 10,* 219–227.

Bondareff, W. (1985). The neural basis of aging. In J. E. Birren & K. W. Schaie (Eds.), *Handbook of the psychology of aging* (2nd ed.). New York: Van Nostrand Reinhold.

Boodman, S. G. (1995, June 13). Researchers study obesity in children. *Washington Post Health,* pp. 10–15.

Bosman, E. A. (1993). Age-related differences in the motoric aspects of transcription typing skill. *Psychology and Aging, 8,* 87–102.

Bower, T. G. R. (1982). *Development in infancy* (2nd ed.). San Francisco: W. H. Freeman.

Brooks-Gunn, J., & Warren, M. P. (1988). The psychological significance of secondary sexual characteristics in nine- to eleven-year-old girls. *Child Development, 59,* 1061–1069.

Brown, J. L. (1964). States in newborn infants. *Merrill-Palmer Quarterly, 10,* 313–327.

Buchanan, C. M., Eccles, J. S., & Becker, J. B. (1992). Are adolescents the victims of raging hormones: Evidence for activational effects of hormones on moods and behavior at adolescence. *Psychological Bulletin, 111,* 62–107.

Buell, S. J., & Coleman, P. D. (1979). Dendritic growth in the aged human brain and failure of growth in senile dementia. *Science, 206,* 854–856.

Case, R. (1992). The role of the frontal lobes in the regulation of cognitive development. *Brain and Cognition, 20,* 51–73.

Cherry, K. E., & Morton, M. R. (1989). Drug sensitivity in older adults: The role of physiologic and pharmacokinetic factors. *International Journal of Aging and Human Development, 28,* 159–174.

Christofalo, V. J. (1988). An overview of the theories of biological aging. In J. E. Birren & V. L. Bengtson (Eds.), *Emergent theories of aging.* New York: Springer.

Clark, D. O., & Maddox, G. L. (1992). Racial and social correlates of age-related changes in functioning. *Journal of Gerontology: Social Sciences, 47,* S222–S232.

Clavien, H., Theintz, G., Rizzoli, R., & Bonjour, J. P. (1996). Does puberty alter dietary habits in adolescents living in a Western society? *Journal of Adolescent Health, 19,* 68–75.

Col, N. F., Eckman, M. H., Karas, R. H., Pauker, S. G., Goldberg, R. J., Ross, E. M., Orr, R. K., & Wong, J. B. (1997). Patient-specific decisions about hormone replacement therapy in postmenopausal women. *Journal of the American Medical Association, 277,* 1140–1147.

Coleman, P. D., & Flood, D. G. (1987). Neuron numbers and dendritic extent in normal aging and Alzheimer's disease. *Neurobiology of Aging, 8,* 521–545.

Condon, J. T. (1993). The premenstrual syndrome: A twin study. *British Journal of Psychiatry, 162,* 481–486.

Connor, J. R., Jr., Diamond, M. C., & Johnson, R. E. (1980). Aging and environmental influences on two types of dendritic spines in the rat occipital cortex. *Experimental Neurology, 70,* 371–379.

Corbin, C. (1973). *A textbook of motor development.* Dubuque, IA: William C. Brown.

Coren, S., Porac, C., & Duncan, P. (1981). Lateral preference behaviors in preschool children and young adults. *Child Development, 52,* 443–450.

Cowan, W. M. (1979). The development of the brain. *Scientific American, 241,* 112–133.

Cunningham, D. A., Rechnitzer, P. A., Pearce, M. E., & Donner, A. P. (1982). Determinants of self-selected walking pace across ages 19 to 66. *Journal of Gerontology, 37,* 560–564.

Davis, M. A., Murphy, S. P., & Neuhaus, J. M. (1988). Living arrangements and eating behavior of older adults in the United States. *Journal of Gerontology: Social Sciences, 43,* S96–S98.

Dennis, W. (1960). Causes of retardation among institutional children: Iran. *Journal of Genetic Psychology, 96,* 47–59.

Dubas, J. S., Graber, J. A., & Petersen, A. C. (1991). The effects of pubertal development on achievement during adolescence. *American Journal of Education, 99,* 444–460.

Duncan, P. D., Ritter, P. L., Dornbusch, S. M., Gross, R. T., & Carlsmith, J. M. (1985). The effects of pubertal timing on body image, school behavior, and deviance. *Journal of Youth and Adolescence, 14,* 227–235.

Dustman, R. E., Emmerson, R. Y., Steinhaus, L. A., Shearer, D. E., & Dustman, T. J. (1992). The effects of videogame playing on neuropsychological performance of elderly individuals. *Journal of Gerontology, 47,* 168–171.

Dustman, R. E., Ruhling, R. O., Russell, E. M., Shearer, D. E., Bonekat, H. W., Shigeoka, J. W., Wood, J. S., & Bradford, D. C. (1989). Neurobiology of aging. In A. C. Ostrow (Ed.), *Aging and motor behavior.* Indianapolis, IN: Benchmark Press.

Dyer, K. F. (1977). The trend of the male-female performance differential in athletics, swimming, and cycling, 1948–1976. *Journal of Biosocial Science, 9,* 325–338.

Earles, J. L., & Salthouse, T. A. (1995). Interrelations of age, health, and speed. *Journal of Gerontology: Psychological Sciences and Social Sciences, 50,* P33–P41.

Eichorn, D. H. (1979). Physical development: Current foci of research. In J. D. Osofsky (Ed.), *Handbook of infant development.* New York: Wiley.

Englander-Golden, P., Sonleitner, F. J., Whitmore, M. R., & Corbley, G. J. M. (1986). Social and menstrual cycles: Methodological and substantive findings. In V. L. Olesen & N. F. Woods (Eds.), *Culture, society, and menstruation*. Washington, DC: Hemisphere.

Faust, M. S. (1960). Developmental maturity as a determinant of prestige in adolescent girls. *Child Development, 31,* 173–184.

Faust, M. S. (1977). Somatic development of adolescent girls. *Monographs of the Society for Research in Child Development, 42,* (Whole No. 169).

Fentress, J. C., & McLeod, P. J. (1986). Motor patterns in development. In E. M. Blass (Ed.), *Handbook of behavioral neurobiology: Vol. 8. Developmental psychobiology and developmental neurobiology*. New York: Plenum.

Field, J., Muir, D., Pilon, R., Sinclair, M., & Dodwell, P. (1980). Infants' orientation to lateral sounds from birth to three months. *Child Development, 51,* 295–298.

Flint, M. (1982). Male and female menopause: A cultural put-on. In A. M. Voda, M. Dinnerstein, & S. R. O'Donnell (Eds.), *Changing perspectives on menopause*. Austin, TX: University of Texas Press.

Flood, D. G., Buell, S. J., Horwitz, G. J., & Coleman, P. D. (1987). Dendritic extent in human dentate gyrus granule cells in normal aging and senile dementia. *Brain Research, 402,* 205–216.

Flood, D. G., & Coleman, P. D. (1990). Hippocampal plasticity in normal aging and decreased plasticity in Alzheimer's disease. *Progress in Brain Research, 83,* 435–443.

Frankenburg, W. K., & Dodds, J. B. (1967). The Denver Development Screening Test. *Journal of Pediatrics, 71,* 181–191.

Franklin, M. B. (1995, April 25). New hope for osteoporosis sufferers? *Washington Post Health*, pp. 8–9.

Freedland, R. L., & Bertenthal, B. I. (1994). Developmental changes in interlimb coordination: Transition to hands-and-knees crawling. *Psychological Science, 5,* 26–32.

Frisch, R. E. (1983). Fatness, puberty, and fertility. The effects of nutrition and physical training on menarche and ovulation. In J. Brooks-Gunn & A. C. Petersen (Eds.), *Girls at puberty:*

Biological and psychosocial perspectives. New York: Plenum.

Frisch, R. E., Wyshak, G., & Vincent, L. (1980). Delayed menarche and amenorrhea of ballet dancers. *New England Journal of Medicine, 303,* 17–19.

Gaddis, A., & Brooks-Gunn, J. (1985). The male experience of pubertal change. *Journal of Youth and Adolescence, 14,* 61–69.

Galuska, D. A., Serdula, M., Pamuk, E., Siegel, P. Z., & Byers, T. (1996). Trends in overweight among US adults from 1987 to 1993: A multistate telephone survey. *American Journal of Public Health, 86,* 1729–1735.

Goldberg, A. P., & Hagberg, J. M. (1990). Physical exercise in the elderly. In E. L. Schneider & J. W. Rowe (Eds.), *Handbook of the biology of aging* (3rd ed.). San Diego: Academic.

Goldfield, E. C., Kay, B. A., & Warren, W. H., Jr. (1993). Infant bouncing: The assembly and tuning of action systems. *Child Development, 64,* 1128–1142.

Gortmaker, S. L., Must, A., Sobol, A. M., Peterson, K., Colditz, G. A., & Dietz, W. H. (1996). Television viewing as a cause of increasing obesity among children in the United States. *Archives of Pediatric and Adolescent Medicine, 150,* 356–362.

Greene, J. G. (1984). *The social and psychological origins of the climacteric syndrome.* Hants, England & Brookfield, VT: Gower.

Greenough, W. T., Black, J. E., & Wallace, C. S. (1987). Experience and brain development. *Child Development, 58,* 539–559.

Greif, E. B., & Ulman, K. J. (1982). The psychological impact of menarche on early adolescent females: A review. *Child Development, 53,* 1413–1430.

Grilo, C. M., & Pogue-Geile, M. F. (1991). The nature of environmental influences on weight and obesity: A behavior genetic analysis. *Psychological Bulletin, 110,* 520–537.

Grodstein, F., Stampfer, M. J., Manson, J. E., Colditz, G. A., Willett, W. C., Rosner, B., Speizer, F. E., & Hennekens, C. H. (1996). Postmenopausal estrogen and progestin use and the risk of cardiovascular disease. *New England Journal of Medicine, 335,* 453–461.

Guralnik, J. M., & Kaplan, G. A. (1989). Predictors of healthy aging: Prospec-

tive evidence from the Alameda County Study. *American Journal of Public Health, 79,* 703–708.

Haber, D. (1994). *Health promotion and aging*. New York: Springer.

Haith, M. (1980). *Rules that babies look by.* Hillsdale, NJ: Erlbaum.

Halpern, L. F., MacLean, W. E., & Baumeister, A. A. (1995). Infant sleep-wake characteristics: Relation to neurological status and the prediction of developmental outcome. *Developmental Review, 15,* 255–291.

Halverson, H. M. (1931). An experimental study of prehension in infants by means of systematic cinema records. *Genetic Psychology Monographs, 10,* 107–286.

Harman, S. M., & Talbert, G. B. (1985). Reproductive aging. In C. E. Finch & E. L. Schneider (Eds.), *Handbook of the biology of aging* (2nd ed.). New York: Van Nostrand Reinhold.

Harman, S. M., & Tsitouras, P. D. (1980). Reproductive hormones in aging men. I. Measurement of sex steroids, basal luteinizing hormone, and Leydig cell response to human chorionic gonadotropin. *Journal of Clinical Endocrinology and Metabolism, 51,* 35–40.

Harris, C. S. (1978). *Fact book on aging: A profile of America's older population.* Washington, DC: National Council on Aging.

Harris, J. R., Pedersen, N. L., McClearn, G. E., Plomin, R., & Nesselroade, J. R. (1992). Age differences in genetic and environmental influences for health from the Swedish Adoption/ Twin Study of Aging. *Journal of Gerontology: Psychological Sciences, 47,* P213–P220.

Hauspie, R. C., Chrzastek-Spruch, H., Verleye, G., Kozlowska, M. A., & Susanne, C. (1996). Determinants of growth in body length from birth to 6 years of age: A longitudinal study of Dublin children. *American Journal of Human Biology, 8,* 21–29.

Hayward, C., Killen, J. D., Wilson, D. M., Hammer, L. D., Litt, I. F., Kraemer, H. C., Haydel, F., Varady, A., & Taylor, C. B. (1997). Psychiatric risk associated with puberty in adolescent girls. *Journal of the American Academy of Child and Adolescent Psychiatry, 36,* 255–262.

Haywood, K. M. (1986). *Life span motor development*. Champaign, IL: Human Kinetics Publishers.

Heath, G. W., Hagberg, J. M., Ehsani, A. A., & Holloszy, J. O. (1981). A physiological comparison of young and older endurance athletes. *Journal of Applied Physiology, 51,* 634–640.

Henderson, V. W. (1997). The epidemiology of estrogen replacement therapy and Alzheimer's disease. *Neurology, 48,* S27–S35.

Herkowitz, J. (1978). Sex-role expectations and motor behavior of the young child. In M. V. Ridenour (Ed.), *Motor development: Issues and applications.* Princeton, NJ: Princeton Book Company.

Herman-Giddens, M. E., Slora, E. J., Wasserman, R. C., Bourdony, C. J., Bhapkar, M. V., Koch, G. G., & Hasemeier, C. M. (1997). Secondary sexual characteristics and menses in young girls seen in office practice: A study from the Pediatric Research in Office Settings Network. *Pediatrics, 99,* 505–512.

Hobbs, F. B. (with B. L. Damon). (1996). *65+ in the United States.* Washington, DC: U.S. Bureau of the Census.

Hopkins, B. (1991). Facilitating early motor development: An intracultural study of West Indian mothers and their infants living in Britain. In J. K. Nugent, B. M. Lester, & T. B. Brazelton (Eds.), *The cultural context of infancy: Vol. 2. Multicultural and interdisciplinary approaches to parent-infant relations.* Norwood, NJ: Ablex.

Hopwood, N. J., Kelch, R. P., Hale, P. M., Mendes, T. M., Foster, C. M., & Beitins, I. Z. (1990). The onset of human puberty: Biological and environmental factors. In J. Bancroft & J. M. Reinisch (Eds.), *Adolescence and puberty.* New York: Oxford University Press.

Houx, P. J., Vreeling, F. W., & Jolles, J. (1991). Rigorous health screening reduces age effect on memory scanning task. *Brain and Cognition, 15,* 246–260.

Hutt, S. J., Lenard, H. G., & Prechtl, H. E. R. (1969). Psychophysiology of the newborn. In L. P. Lipsitt & H. W. Reese (Eds.), *Advances in child development and behavior.* New York: Academic.

Huttenlocher, P. R. (1994). Synaptogenesis, synapse elimination, and neural plasticity in human cerebral cortex. In C. A. Nelson (Ed.), *Threats to optimal development: The Minnesota Symposium on Child Psychology* (Vol. 27). Hillsdale, NJ: Erlbaum.

Janowsky, J. S., & Carper, R. (1996). Is there a neural basis for cognitive transitions in school-age children? In A. J. Sameroff & M. M. Haith (Eds.), *The five to seven year shift: The age of reason and responsibility.* Chicago: University of Chicago Press.

Janowsky, J. S., & Finlay, B. L. (1986). The outcome of perinatal brain damage: The role of normal neuron loss and axon retraction. *Developmental Medicine and Child Neurology, 28,* 375–389.

Jette, A. M. (1996). Disability trends and transitions. In R. H. Binstock & L. K. George (Eds.), *Handbook of aging and the social sciences.* San Diego: Academic Press.

Johnson, M. H. (1997). *Developmental cognitive neuroscience: An introduction.* Cambridge, MA: Blackwell.

Johnson, W. R., & Buskirk, E. R. (1974). *Science and medicine of exercise and sport* (2nd ed.). New York: Harper and Row.

Johnston, C. C., Jr., Hui, S. L., Witt, R. M., Appledorn, R., Baker, R. S., & Longcope, C. (1985). Early menopausal changes in bone mass and sex steroids. *Journal of Clinical Endocrinology and Metabolism, 61,* 905–911.

Jones, M. C. (1965). Psychological correlates of somatic development. *Child Development, 36,* 899–911.

Jones, M. C., & Bayley, N. (1950). Physical maturing among boys as related to behavior. *Journal of Educational Psychology, 41,* 129–148.

Jones, M. C., & Mussen, P. H. (1958). Self-conceptions, motivations, and interpersonal attitudes of early- and late-maturing girls. *Child Development, 29,* 491–501.

Kail, R. (1991). Developmental change in speed of processing during childhood and adolescence. *Psychological Bulletin, 109,* 490–501.

Kempen, G. I-J. M., Ormel, J., & Relyveld, J. (1997). Adaptive responses among Dutch elderly: The impact of eight chronic medical conditions on health-related quality of life. *American Journal of Public Health, 87,* 38–44.

Kendler, K. S., Silberg, J. L., Neale, M. C., Kessler, R. C., Heath, A. C., & Eaves, L. J. (1992). Genetic and environmental factors in the aetiology of menstrual, premenstrual, and neurotic symptoms: A population-based twin study. *Psychological Medicine, 22,* 85–100.

Keough, J., & Sugden, D. (1985). *Movement skill development.* New York: Macmillan.

King, A. C., Taylor, C. B., & Haskell, W. L. (1993). Effects of differing intensities and formats of 12 months of exercise training on psychological outcomes in older adults. *Health Psychology, 12,* 292–300.

Kinsbourne, M. (1989). Mechanisms and development of hemisphere specialization in children. In C. R. Reynolds & E. Fletcher-Janzen (Eds.), *Handbook of clinical child neuropsychology.* New York: Plenum.

Koff, E., & Rierdan, J. (1995). Early adolescent girls' understanding of menstruation. *Women and Health, 22,* 1–19.

Kron, R. E. (1966). Instrumental conditioning of nutritive sucking behavior in the newborn. *Recent Advances in Biological Psychiatry, 9,* 295–300.

Lakatta, E. G. (1990). Heart and circulation. In E. L. Schneider & J. W. Rowe (Eds.), *Handbook of the biology of aging* (3rd ed.). San Diego: Academic Press.

Lampl, M., Veldhuis, J. D., & Johnson, M. L. (1992). Saltation and stasis: A model of human growth. *Science, 258,* 801–803.

Lamy, P. P. (1986). The elderly and drug interactions. *Journal of the American Geriatrics Society, 34,* 586–592.

Langlois, J. A., Keyl, P. M., Guralnik, J. M., Foley, D. J., Marottoli, R. A., & Wallace, R. B. (1997). Characteristics of older pedestrians who have difficulty crossing the street. *American Journal of Public Health, 87,* 393–397.

Lima, S. D., Hale, S., & Myerson, J. (1991). How general is general slowing: Evidence from the lexical domain. *Psychology and Aging, 6,* 416–425.

Lipsitt, L. P. (1990). Learning processes in the human newborn. Sensitization, habituation, and classical conditioning. *Annals of the New York Academy of Sciences, 608,* 113–127.

Livson, N., & Peskin, H. (1980). Perspectives on adolescence from longitudinal research. In J. Adelson (Ed.), *Handbook of adolescent psychology.* New York: Wiley.

Lock, M. (1993). *Encounters with aging: Mythologies of menopause in Japan and North America.* Berkeley, CA: University of California Press.

Magnusson, D. (1995). Individual development: A holistic, integrated model. In P. Moen, G. H. Elder, Jr., &

K. Luscher (Eds.), *Examining lives in context: Perspectives on the ecology of human development.* Washington, DC: American Psychological Association.

Maki, B. E. (1997). Gait changes in older adults: Predictors of falls or indicators of fear? *Journal of the American Geriatrics Society, 45,* 313–320.

Manton, K. G., Stallard, E., & Corder, L. (1997). Changes in the age dependence of mortality and disability: Cohort and other determinants. *Demography, 34,* 135–157.

Margolis, L. H., Sparrow, A. W., & Swanson, G. M. (1989). *Growing into healthy adults: Pediatric antecedents of adult disease* (Health Monograph Series No. 3). Lansing, MI: Michigan Department of Public Health.

Marshall, W. A., & Tanner, J. M. (1970). Variations in the pattern of pubertal changes in boys. *Archives of Disease in Childhood, 45,* 13–23.

Masters, W. H., & Johnson, V. E. (1966). *Human sexual response.* Boston: Little, Brown.

Mathew, A., & Cook, M. L. (1990). The control of reaching movements by young infants. *Child Development, 61,* 1238–1257.

Matthews, K. A. (1992). Myths and realities of the menopause. *Psychosomatic Medicine, 54,* 1–9.

Matthews, K. A., Wing, R. R., Kuller, L. H., Meilahn, E. N., Kelsey, S. F., Costello, E. J., & Caggiula, A. W. (1990). Influences of natural menopause on psychological characteristics and symptoms of middle-aged healthy women. *Journal of Consulting and Clinical Psychology, 58,* 345–351.

McClintock, M. K., & Herdt, G. (1996). Rethinking puberty: The development of sexual attraction. *Current Directions in Psychological Science, 5,* 178–183.

McFarlane, J. A., & Williams, T. M. (1990). The enigma of premenstrual syndrome. *Canadian Psychology, 31,* 95–108.

McGinnis, J. M., & Foege, W. H. (1993). Actual causes of death in the United States. *Journal of the American Medical Association, 270,* 2207–2211.

McKinlay, S. M., Brambilla, D. J., & Posner, J. G. (1992). The normal menopause transition. *Maturitas, 14,* 103–115.

Michel, G. F. (1981). Right-handedness: A consequence of infant supine head-orientation preference. *Science, 212,* 685–687.

Molfese, D. L. (1977). Infant cerebral asymmetry. In S. J. Segalowitz & F. A. Gruber (Eds.), *Language development and neurological theory.* Orlando, FL: Academic.

Molina, B. S. G., & Chassin, L. (1996). The parent-adolescent relationship at puberty: Hispanic ethnicity and parent alcoholism as moderators. *Developmental Psychology, 32,* 675–686.

Montoye, H. J., & Lamphiear, D. E. (1977). Grip and arm strength in males and females, age 10 to 69. *Research Quarterly for Exercise and Sport, 48,* 108–120.

Moore, S. M. (1995). Girls' understanding and social constructions of menarche. *Journal of Adolescence, 18,* 87–104.

Morgan, M., Phillips, J. G., Bradshaw, J. L., Mattingley, J. B., Iansek, R., & Bradshaw, J. A. (1994). Age-related motor slowness: Simply strategic? *Journal of Gerontology, 49,* M133–M139.

Morse, C. K. (1993). Does variability increase with age? An archival study of cognitive measures. *Psychology and Aging, 8,* 156–164.

Murray, M. P., Duthie, E. H., Jr., Gambert, S. R., Sepic, S. B., & Mollinger, L. A. (1985). Age-related differences in knee muscle strength in normal women. *Journal of Gerontology, 40,* 275–280.

Murray, M. P., Kory, R. C., & Clarkson, B. H. (1969). Walking patterns in healthy old men. *Journal of Gerontology, 24,* 169–178.

Must, A., Jacques, P. F., Dallal, G. E., Bajema, C. J., & Dietz, W. H. (1992). Long-term morbidity and mortality of overweight adolescents. A follow-up of the Harvard Growth Study of 1922 to 1935. *New England Journal of Medicine, 327,* 1350–1355.

Neugarten, B. L., Wood, V., Kraines, R. J., & Loomis, B. (1963). Women's attitudes toward the menopause. *Vita Humana, 6,* 140–151.

Ochs, A. L., Newberry, J., Lenhardt, M. L., & Harkins, S. W. (1985). Neural and vestibular aging associated with falls. In J. E. Birren & K. W. Schaie (Eds.), *Handbook of the psychology of aging* (2nd ed.). New York: Van Nostrand Reinhold.

Paganini-Hill, A., & Henderson, V. W. (1996). Estrogen replacement therapy and risk of Alzheimer disease. *Archives of Internal Medicine, 156,* 2213–2217.

Paikoff, R. L., & Brooks-Gunn, J. (1991). Do parent-child relationships change during puberty? *Psychological Bulletin, 110,* 47–66.

Pate, R. R., Heath, G. W., Dowda, M., & Trost, S. G. (1996). Associations between physical activity and other health behaviors in a representative sample of US adolescents. *American Journal of Public Health, 86,* 1577–1581.

Peskin, H. (1973). Influence of the developmental schedule of puberty on learning and ego functioning. *Journal of Youth and Adolescence, 2,* 273–290.

Posner, B. M., Jette, A., Smigelski, C., Miller, D., & Mitchell, P. (1994). Nutritional risk in New England elders. *Journal of Gerontology: Medical Sciences, 49,* M123–M132.

Prechtl, H. F. R. (1981). The study of neural development as a perspective of clinical problems. In K. J. Connolly & H. F. R. Prechtl (Eds.), *Maturation and development.* Philadelphia: Lippincott.

Rakic, P. (1991). Plasticity of cortical development. In S. E. Brauth, W. S. Hall, & R. J. Dooling (Eds.), *Plasticity of development.* Cambridge, MA: Bradford/MIT Press.

Richards, M. H., Boxer, A. W., Petersen, A. C., & Albrecht, R. (1990). Relation of weight to body image in pubertal girls and boys from two communities. *Developmental Psychology, 26,* 313–321.

Robertson, N. R. C. (1993). *A manual of neonatal intensive care* (3rd ed.). London: Edward Arnold.

Robinson, G. (1996). Cross-cultural perspectives on menopause. *Journal of Nervous and Mental Disease, 184,* 453–458.

Roffwarg, H. P., Muzio, J. W., & Dement, W. C. (1966). Ontogenetic development of the human sleep-dream cycle. *Science, 152,* 604–619.

Rosenfeld, R. G. (1997). Is growth hormone just a tall story? *Journal of Pediatrics, 130,* 172–174.

Salthouse, T. A. (1984). Effects of age and skill in typing. *Journal of Experimental Psychology: General, 113,* 345–371.

Saul, S. (1983). *Aging: An album of people growing old* (2nd ed.). New York: Wiley.

Scherr, P. A., LaCroix, A. Z., Wallace, R. B., Berkman, L., Curb, J. D., Cornoni-Huntley, J., Evans, D. A., & Hennekens, C. H. (1992). Light to moderate alcohol consumption and mortality in the elderly. *Journal of the American Geriatrics Society, 40,* 651–657.

Schiavi, R. C., Schreiner-Engel, P., White, D., & Mandeli, J. (1991). The relationship between pituitary-gonadal function and sexual behavior in healthy aging men. *Psychosomatic Medicine, 53,* 363–374.

Schlegel, A., Barry, H., III. (1991). *Adolescence: An anthropological inquiry.* New York: Free Press.

Segalowitz, S. J., Unsal, A., & Dywan, J. (1992). Cleverness and wisdom in 12-year-olds: Electrophysiological evidence for late maturation of the frontal lobe. *Developmental Neuropsychology, 8,* 279–298.

Selkoe, D. J. (1992). Aging brain, aging mind. *Scientific American, 267,* 135–142.

Sharpe, P. A., Jackson, K. L., White, C., Vaca, V. L., Hickey, T., Gu, J., & Otterness, C. (1997). Effects of a one-year physical activity intervention for older adults at congregate nutrition sites. *Gerontologist, 37,* 208–215.

Shephard, R. J. (1978). *Physical activity and aging.* Chicago: Year Book Medical Publishers.

Shephard, R. J. (1990). The scientific basis of exercise prescribing for the very old. *Journal of the American Geriatrics Society, 38,* 62–70.

Shephard, R. J., & Montelpare, W. (1988). Geriatric benefits of exercise as an adult. *Journal of Gerontology: Medical Sciences, 43,* M86–M90.

Sigman, M. (1995). Nutrition and child development: More food for thought. *Current Directions in Psychological Science, 4,* 52–55.

Simmons, R. G., & Blyth, D. A. (1987). *Moving into adolescence: The impact of pubertal change and school context.* New York: Hawthorne, Aldine de Gruyter.

Simons-Morton, B. G., McKenzie, T. J., Stone, E., Mitchell, P., Osganian, V., Strikmiller, P. K., Ehlinger, S., Cribb, P., & Nader, P. R. (1997). Physical activity in a multiethnic population of third graders in four states. *American Journal of Public Health, 87,* 45–50.

Sliwinski, M., Buschke, H., Kuslansky, G., Senior, G., & Scarisbrick, D. (1994). Proportional slowing and addition speed in old and young adults. *Psychology and Aging, 9,* 72–80.

Smith, L. B., & Thelen, E. (1993). *A dynamic systems approach to development:*

Applications. Cambridge, MA: MIT Press.

Smoll, F. L., & Schutz, R. W. (1990). Quantifying gender differences in physical performance: A developmental perspective. *Developmental Psychology, 26,* 360–369.

Somsen, R. J. M., van Klooster, B. J., van der Molen, M. W., van Leeuwen, H. M. P., & Licht, R. (1997). Growth spurts in brain maturation during middle childhood as indexed by EEG power spectra. *Biological Psychology, 44,* 187–209.

Soules, M. R., & Bremner, W. J. (1982). The menopause and climacteric: Endocrinologic basis and associated symptomatology. *Journal of the American Geriatrics Society, 30,* 547–561.

Spirduso, W. W., & MacRae, P. G. (1990). Motor performance and aging. In J. E. Birren & K. W. Schaie (Eds.), *Handbook of the psychology of aging* (3rd ed.). San Diego: Academic.

Spreen, O., Risser, A. H., & Edgell, D. (1995). *Developmental neuropsychology.* New York: Oxford University Press.

Stattin, H., & Magnusson, D. (1990). *Paths through life: Vol. 2. Pubertal maturation in female development.* Hillsdale, NJ: Erlbaum.

Stein, J. H., & Reiser, L. W. (1994). A study of white middle-class adolescent boys' responses to "semenarche" (the first ejaculation). *Journal of Youth and Adolescence, 23,* 373–384.

Steinberg, L. (1988). Reciprocal relation between parent-child distance and pubertal maturation. *Developmental Psychology, 24,* 122–128.

Steinberg, L. D. (1981). Transformations in family relations at puberty. *Developmental Psychology, 17,* 833–840.

Stelmach, G. E., & Nahom, A. (1992). Cognitive-motor abilities of the elderly driver. *Human Factors, 34,* 53–65.

Stelmach, G. E., Phillips, J., DiFabio, R. P., & Teasdale, N. (1989). Age, functional postural reflexes, and voluntary sway. *Journal of Gerontology: Biological Sciences, 44,* B100–B106.

St. George, I. M., Williams, S., & Silva, P. A. (1994). Body size and the menarche: The Dunedin study. *Journal of Adolescent Health, 15,* 573–576.

Stones, M. J., & Kozma, A. (1985). Physical performance. In N. Charness (Ed.), *Aging and human performance.* Chichester, England & New York: Wiley.

Stuss, D. T. (1992). Biological and psychological development of executive functions. *Brain and Cognition, 20,* 8–23.

Sveistrup, H., & Woollacott, M. J. (1996). Longitudinal development of the automatic postural response in infants. *Journal of Motor Behavior, 28,* 58–70.

Swarr, A. E., & Richards, M. H. (1996). Longitudinal effects of adolescent girls' pubertal development, perceptions of pubertal timing, and parental relations on eating problems. *Developmental Psychology, 32,* 636–646.

Tanner, J. M. (1981). Growth and maturation during adolescence. *Nutrition Review, 39,* 43–55.

Tanner, J. M. (1990). *Foetus into man: Physical growth from conception to maturity* (rev. & enl. ed.). Cambridge, MA: Harvard University Press.

Thelen, E. (1984). Learning to walk: Ecological demands and phylogenetic constraints. In L. P. Lipsitt & C. Rovee-Collier (Eds.), *Advances in infancy research* (Vol. 3). Norwood, NJ: Ablex.

Thelen, E. (1995). Motor development: A new synthesis. *American Psychologist, 50,* 79–95.

Thoman, E. B., & Whitney, M. P. (1990). Behavioral states in infants: Individual differences and individual analyses. In J. Columbo and J. Fagen (Eds.), *Individual differences in infancy: Reliability, stability, prediction.* Hillsdale, NJ: Erlbaum.

Thomas, J. R., & French, K. E. (1985). Gender differences across age in motor performance: A meta-analysis. *Psychological Bulletin, 98,* 260–282.

Thomas, J. R., Gallagher, J. D., & Purvis, G. J. (1981). Reaction time and anticipation time: Effects of development. *Research Quarterly for Exercise and Sport, 52,* 359–367.

Thompson, R. F. (1993). *The brain: A neuroscience primer* (2nd ed.). New York: W. H. Freeman.

Treloar, A. E. (1982). Predicting the close of menstrual life. In A. M. Voda, M. Dinnerstein, & S. R. O'Donnell (Eds.), *Changing perspectives on menopause.* Austin: University of Texas Press.

Tschann, J. M., Adler, N. E., Irwin, C. E., & Millstein, S. G. (1994). Initiation of substance use in early adolescence: The roles of pubertal timing and emotional distress. *Health Psychology, 13,* 326–333.

Tsitouras, P. D., Martin, C. E., & Harman, S. M. (1982). Relationship of serum testosterone to sexual activity in healthy elderly. *Journal of Gerontology, 37,* 288–293.

U.S. Bureau of the Census. (1996). *Statistical abstract of the United States: 1996* (116th ed.). Washington, DC: U.S. Government Printing Office.

Van Galen, G. P. (1993). Handwriting: A developmental perspective. In A. F. Kalverboer, B. Hopkins, & R. H. Geuze (Eds.), *Motor development in early and later childhood: Longitudinal approaches.* Cambridge: Cambridge University Press.

van Gennep, A. (1960). *The rites of passage* (M. B. Vizedom & G. L. Caffee, Trans.). Chicago: University of Chicago Press. (Original work published 1908)

Voda, A. M. (1993). A journey to the center of the cell: Understanding the physiology and endocrinology of menopause. In J. C. Callahan (Ed.), *Menopause: A midlife passage.* Bloomington, IN: Indiana University Press.

von Hofsten, C. (1993). Studying the development of goal-directed behaviour. In A. F. Kalverboer, B. Hopkins, & R. H. Geuze (Eds.), *Motor development in early and later childhood: Longitudinal approaches.* Cambridge: Cambridge University Press.

Wagner, E. H., LaCroix, A. Z., Buchner, D. M., & Larson, E. B. (1992). Effects of physical activity on health status in older adults. I. Observational studies. *Annual Review of Public Health, 13,* 451–468.

Walford, R. L. (1983). *Maximum life span.* New York: Norton.

Weg, R. B. (1983). Changing physiology of aging. In D. S. Woodruff & J. E. Birren (Eds.), *Aging. Scientific perspectives and social issues.* Pacific Grove, CA: Brooks/Cole.

Werner, H. (1957). The concept of development from a comparative and organismic point of view. In D. B. Harris (Ed.), *The concept of development: An issue in the study of human behavior.* Minneapolis: University of Minnesota Press.

Whipp, B. J., & Ward, S. A. (1992). Will women soon outrun men? *Nature, 355,* 25.

Whitbourne, S. K. (1985). *The aging body. Physiological changes and psycho-*

logical consequences. New York: Springer-Verlag.

Wiesel, T. N., & Hubel, D. H. (1965). Comparison of the effects of unilateral and bilateral eye closure on cortical unit responses in kittens. *Journal of Neurophysiology, 28,* 1029–1040.

Wilbur, J., Miller, A., & Montgomery, A. (1995). The influence of demographic characteristics, menopausal status, and symptoms on women's attitudes toward menopause. *Women and Health, 23,* 19–39.

Wilkinson, R. T., & Allison, S. (1989). Age and simple reaction time: Decade differences for 5,325 subjects. *Journal of Gerontology: Psychological Sciences, 44,* P29–P35.

Williams, P. T. (1997). Evidence for the incompatibility of age-neutral overweight and age-neutral physical activity standards from runners. *American Journal of Clinical Nutrition, 65,* 1391–1396.

Wilson, G. T. (1994). Behavioral treatment of childhood obesity: Theoretical and practical implications. *Health Psychology, 13,* 371–372.

Wolfe, W. S., Campbell, C. C., Frongillo, E. A., Haas, J. D., & Melnik, T. A. (1994). Overweight schoolchildren in New York State: Prevalence and characteristics. *American Journal of Public Health, 84,* 807–813.

Wolff, P. H. (1966). The causes, controls, and organization of behavior in the neonate. *Psychological Issues, 5* (1, Whole No. 17).

Woods, N. F., Most, A., & Dery, G. K. (1982). Prevalence of perimenstrual symptoms. *American Journal of Public Health, 72,* 1257–1264.

Woollacott, M. H., Shumway-Cook, A., & Nashner, L. M. (1986). Aging and posture control: Changes in sensory organization and muscular coordination. *International Journal of Aging and Human Development, 23,* 97–114.

Yamaura, H., Ito, M., Kubota, K., & Matsuzawa, T. (1980). Brain atrophy during aging: A quantitative study with computed tomography. *Journal of Gerontology, 35,* 492–498.

Zani, B. (1991). Male and female patterns in the discovery of sexuality during adolescence. *Journal of Adolescence, 14,* 163–178.

Zelazo, P. R., Zelazo, N. A., & Kolb, S. (1972). "Walking" in the newborn. *Science, 176,* 314–315.

Zweifel, J. E., & O'Brien, W. H. (1997). A meta-analysis of the effect of hormone replacement therapy upon depressed mood. *Psychoneuroendocrinology, 22,* 189–212.

CHAPTER 6: Perception

Adams, M. J. (1990). *Beginning to read: Learning and thinking about print.* Cambridge, MA: MIT Press.

Anand, K. J., & Hickey, P. R. (1992). Halothane-morphine compared with high-dose sufentanil for anesthesia and postoperative analgesia in neonatal cardiac surgery. *New England Journal of Medicine, 326,* 1–9.

Anderson, D. R., Lorch, E. P., Field, D. E., Collins, P. A., & Nathan, J. G. (1986). Television viewing at home: Age trends in visual attention and time with TV. *Child Development, 57,* 1024–1033.

Appollonio, I., Carabellese, C., Frattola, L., & Trabucchi, M. (1996). Effects of sensory aids on the quality of life and mortality of elderly people: A multivariate analysis. *Age and Aging, 25,* 89–96.

Arana-Ward, M. (1997, May 11). As technology advances, a bitter debate divides the deaf. *The Washington Post,* p. A1.

Aslin, R. N. (1988). Perceptual development. *Annual Review of Psychology, 39,* 435–473.

Aslin, R. N., Pisoni, D. B., & Jusczyk, P. W. (1983). Auditory development and speech perception in infancy. In M. M. Haith & J. J. Campos (Eds.), *Handbook of child psychology: Vol. 2. Infancy and developmental psychobiology* (4th ed.). New York: Wiley.

Baltes, P. B., & Lindenberger, U. (1997). Emergence of a powerful connection between sensory and cognitive functions across the adult life span: A new window to the study of cognitive aging? *Psychology and Aging, 12,* 12–21.

Banks, M. S., & Ginsburg, A. P. (1985). Infant visual preferences: A review and new theoretical treatment. In H. W. Reese (Ed.), *Advances in child development and behavior* (Vol. 19). Orlando, FL: Academic.

Banks, M. S., in collaboration with Salapatek, P. (1983). Infant visual perception. In M. M. Haith & J. J. Campos (Eds.; P. H. Mussen, Gen. Ed.), *Handbook of child psychology: Vol. 2. Infancy and developmental psychobiology* (4th ed.). New York: Wiley.

Banks, M. S., & Shannon, E. (1993). Spatial and chromatic visual efficiency in human neonates. In C. E. Granrud (Ed.), *Visual perception and cognition in infancy*. Hillsdale, NJ: Erlbaum.

Bartoshuk, L. M., & Beauchamp, G. K. (1994). Chemical senses. *Annual Review of Psychology, 45,* 419–449.

Bergman, M. (1980). *Aging and the perception of speech*. Baltimore, MD: University Park Press.

Bergman, M., Blumenfeld, V. G., Cascardo, D., Dash, B., Levitt, H., & Margulies, M. K. (1976). Age-related decrement in hearing for speech: Sampling and longitudinal studies. *Journal of Gerontology, 31,* 533–538.

Berry, J. W., Poortinga, Y. H., Segall, M., & Dasen, P. R. (1992). *Cross-cultural psychology: Research and applications.* Cambridge: Cambridge University Press.

Bess, F. H., & McConnell, F. E. (1981). *Audiology, education, and the hearing impaired child*. St Louis, MO: C. V. Mosby.

Blakemore, C., & Price, D. J. (1987). The organization and post-natal development of area 18 of the cat's visual cortex. *Journal of Physiology, 384,* 263–292.

Bornstein, M. H. (1992). Perception across the lifespan. In M. H. Bornstein & M. E. Lamb (Eds.), *Developmental Psychology: An advanced textbook* (3rd ed.). Hillsdale, NJ: Erlbaum.

Bornstein, M. H., Kessen, W., & Weiskopf, S. (1976). Color vision and hue categorization in young human infants. *Journal of Experimental Psychology: Human Perception and Performance, 2,* 115–129.

Botuck, S., & Turkewitz, G. (1990). Intersensory functioning: Auditory-visual pattern equivalence in younger and older children. *Developmental Psychology, 26,* 115–120.

Bower, T. G. R. (1982). *Development in infancy* (2nd ed.). San Francisco: W. H. Freeman.

Bower, T. G. R., Broughton, J. M., & Moore, M. K. (1970). The coordination of vision and tactile input in infancy. *Perception and Psychophysics, 8,* 51–53.

Bruck, M. (1990). Word recognition skills of adults with childhood diagnoses of dyslexia. *Developmental Psychology, 26,* 439–454.

Bruck, M. (1992). Persistence of dyslexics' phonological awareness deficits. *Developmental Psychology, 28,* 874–886.

Butler, R. N., & Lewis, M. I. (1977). *Aging and mental health* (2nd ed.). St Louis, MO: C. V. Mosby.

Butterfield, E. C., & Siperstein, G. N. (1972). Influence of contingent auditory stimulation upon non-nutritional suckle. In J. F. Bosma (Ed.), *Third symposium on oral sensation and perception: The mouth of the infant.* Springfield, IL: Charles C. Thomas.

Campos, J. J., Bertenthal, B. I., & Kermoian, R. (1992). Early experience and emotional development: The emergence of wariness of heights. *Psychological Science, 3,* 61–64.

Campos, J. J., Langer, A., & Krowitz, A. (1970). Cardiac responses on the visual cliff in prelocomotor human infants. *Science, 170,* 196–197.

Canfield, R. L., & Smith, E. G. (1996). Number-based expectations and sequential enumeration by 5-month-old infants. *Developmental Psychology, 32,* 269–279.

Castle, J. M., Riach, J., & Nicholson, T. (1994). Getting off to a better start in reading and spelling: The effect of phonemic awareness instruction within a whole language program. *Journal of Educational Psychology, 86,* 350–359.

Cernoch, J. M., & Porter, R. H. (1985). Recognition of maternal axillary odors by infants. *Child Development, 56,* 1593–1598.

Chen, D. (1996). Parent-infant communication: Early intervention for very young children with visual impairment or hearing loss. *Infants and Young Children, 9,* 1–12.

Clarkson, M. G., & Berg, W. K. (1983). Cardiac orienting and vowel discrimination in newborns: Crucial stimulation parameters. *Child Development, 54,* 162–171.

Corso, J. F. (1981). *Aging sensory systems and perception*. New York: Praeger.

Corwin, J., Loury, M., & Gilbert, A. N. (1995). Workplace, age, and sex as mediators of olfactory function: Data from the national geographic smell survey. *Journal of Gerontology: Psychological Sciences, 50,* P179–P186.

Crook, C. K. (1978). Taste perception in the newborn infant. *Infant Behavior and Development, 1,* 52–69.

Dannemiller, J. L., & Stephens, B. R. (1988). A critical test of infant pattern preference models. *Child Development, 59,* 210–216.

Davis, A. C., Ostri, B., & Parving, A. (1991). Longitudinal study of hearing. *Acta Otolaryngologica, 476,* 12–22.

DeCasper, A. J., & Fifer, W. P. (1980). Of human bonding: Newborns prefer their mothers' voices. *Science, 208,* 1174–1176.

DeCasper, A. J., & Spence, M. J. (1986). Prenatal maternal speech influences newborns' perception of speech sounds. *Infant Behavior and Development, 9,* 133–150.

Descartes, R. (1965). La dioptrique. In R. J. Herrnstein & E. G. Boring (Eds.), *A sourcebook in the history of psychology*. Cambridge, MA: Harvard University Press. (Original work published 1638)

Doty, R. L., Shaman, P., Applebaum, S. L., Giberson, R., Siksorski, L., & Rosenberg, L. (1984). Smell identification ability: Changes with age. *Science, 226,* 1441–1443.

Dywan, J., & Murphy, W. E. (1996). Aging and inhibitory control in text comprehension. *Psychology and Aging, 11,* 199–206.

Ecklund-Flores, L., & Turkewitz, G. (1996). Asymmetric headturning to speech and nonspeech in human newborns. *Developmental Psychobiology, 29,* 205–217.

Eimas, P. D. (1975a). Auditory and phonetic cues for speech: Discrimination of the (r-l) distinction by young infants. *Perception and Psychophysics, 18,* 341–347.

Eimas, P. D. (1975b). Speech perception in early infancy. In L. B. Cohen & P. Salapatek (Eds.), *Infant perception: From sensation to cognition.* New York: Academic Press.

Eimas, P. D. (1985). The perception of speech in early infancy. *Scientific American, 252,* 46–52.

Eppler, M. A. (1995). Development of manipulatory skills and the deployment of attention. *Infant Behavior and Development, 18,* 391–405.

Fantz, R. L. (1961). The origin of form perception. *Scientific American, 204,* 66–72.

Fantz, R. L. (1963). Pattern vision in newborn infants. *Science, 140,* 296–297.

Fantz, R. L., & Fagan, J. F. (1975). Visual attention to size and number of pattern details by term and preterm infants during the first six months. *Child Development, 46,* 3–18.

Farkas, M. S., & Hoyer, W. J. (1980). Processing consequences of perceptual grouping in selective attention. *Journal of Gerontology, 35,* 207–216.

Field, J., Muir, D., Pilon, R., Sinclair, M., & Dodwell, P. (1980). Infants' orientation to lateral sounds from birth to three months. *Child Development, 51,* 295–298.

Field, T. (1990). *Infancy.* Cambridge, MA: Harvard University Press.

Finitzo, T., Gunnarson, A. D., & Clark, J. L. (1990). Auditory deprivation and early conductive hearing loss from otitis media. *Topics in Language Disorders, 11,* 29–42.

Fischer, K. W., & Bidell, T. (1991). Constraining inferences about cognitive capacities. In S. Carey & R. Gelman (Eds.), *The epigenesis of mind: Essays on biology and knowledge* (pp. 199–235). Hillsdale, NJ: Erlbaum.

Foorman, B. R. (1995). Research on "The Great Debate": Code-oriented versus whole language approaches to reading instruction. *School Psychology Review, 24,* 376–392.

Fozard, J. L. (1990). Vision and hearing in aging. In J. E. Birren & K. W. Schaie (Eds.), *Handbook of the psychology of aging* (3rd. ed.). San Diego: Academic Press.

Francis, D. J., Shaywitz, S. E., Stuebing, K. K., Shaywitz, B. A., & Fletcher, J. M. (1996). Developmental lag versus deficit models of reading disability: A longitudinal, individual growth curves analysis. *Journal of Educational Psychology, 88,* 3–17.

Fryauf-Bertschy, H., Tyler, R. S., Kelsay, D. M. R., Gantz, B. J., & Woodworth, G. G. (1997). Cochlear implant use by prelingually deafened children: The influence of age at implant and length of device use. *Journal of Speech, Language, and Hearing Research, 40,* 183–199.

Ganchrow, J. R., Steiner, J. E., & Daher, M. (1983). Neonatal facial expressions to different qualities and intensities of gustatory stimuli. *Infant Behavior and Development, 6,* 189–200.

Gelman, S. A. (1996). Concepts and theories. In R. Gelman & T. K. Au (Eds.), *Perceptual and cognitive development.* San Diego, CA: Academic Press.

Gibson, E. J. (1969). *Principles of perceptual learning and development.* New York: Appleton-Century-Crofts.

Gibson, E. J. (1988). Exploratory behavior in the development of perceiving, acting, and the acquiring of knowledge. *Annual Review of Psychology, 39,* 1–41.

Gibson, E. J., Gibson, J. J., Pick, A. D., & Osser, H. A. (1962). A developmental study of the discrimination of letterlike forms. *Journal of Comparative and Physiological Psychology, 55,* 897–906.

Gibson, E. J., & Levin, H. (1975). *The psychology of reading.* Cambridge, MA: MIT Press.

Gibson, E. J., & Spelke, E. S. (1983). The development of perception. In J. H. Flavell & E. M. Markman (Eds.; P. H. Mussen, Gen. Ed.), *Handbook of child psychology: Vol. 3. Cognitive development* (4th ed.). New York: Wiley.

Gibson, E. J., & Walk, R. D. (1960). The "visual cliff." *Scientific American, 202,* 64–71.

Goffinet, J. M. (1992). Hearing loss and hearing aid use by the elderly: A primer for the geriatric care professional. *Educational Gerontology, 18,* 257–264.

Greenough, W. T., Black, J. E., & Wallace, C. S. (1987). Experience and brain development. *Child Development, 58,* 539–559.

Hainline, L., & Abramov, I. (1992). Assessing visual development: Is infant vision good enough? *Advances in Infancy Research, 7,* 39–102.

Haith, M. M. (1980). Visual competence in early infancy. In R. Held, H. Liebowitz, & H. R. Teuber (Eds.), *Handbook of sensory physiology* (Vol. 8). Berlin: Springer-Verlag.

Haith, M. M. (1997, April). *Who put the cog in infant cognition: Is rich interpretation too costly?* Paper presented at the biennial meeting of the Society for Research on Child Development, Washington, DC.

Hartley, A. A. (1992). Attention. In F. I. M. Craik & T. A. Salthouse (Eds.), *The handbook of aging and cognition.* Hillsdale, NJ: Erlbaum.

Hartman, B. T. (1982). An exploratory study of the effects of disco music on the auditory and vestibular sys-

tems. *Journal of Auditory Research, 22,* 271–274.

Hasher, L., Stoltzfus, E. R., Zacks, R. T., & Rypma, B. (1991). Age and inhibition. *Journal of Experimental Psychology: Learning, Memory, and Cognition, 17,* 163–169.

Hetu, R., & Fortin, M. (1995). Potential risk of hearing damage associated with exposure to highly amplified music. *Journal of the American Academy of Audiology, 6,* 378–386.

Hubel, D. H., & Wiesel, T. N. (1963). Receptive fields of cells in striate cortex of very young, visually inexperienced kittens. *Journal of Neurophysiology, 26,* 994–1002.

James, W. (1890). *Principles of psychology* (2 vols.). New York: Holt.

Johnson, M. H. (1997). *Developmental cognitive neuroscience.* Oxford, England: Blackwell.

Johnson, M. H., & Gilmore, R. O. (1996). Developmental cognitive neuroscience: A biological perspective on cognitive change. In R. Gelman & T. K. Au (Eds.), *Perceptual and cognitive development.* San Diego: Academic Press.

Johnson, S. P., & Aslin, R. N. (1995). Perception of object unity in 2-month-old infants. *Developmental Psychology, 31,* 739–745.

Kagan, J. (1971). *Change and continuity in infancy.* New York: Wiley.

Kahn, H. A., Leibowitz, H. M., Ganley, J. P., Kini, M. M., Colton, T., Nickerson, R. S., & Dawber, T. R. (1977). The Framingham eye study. I. Outline and major prevalence findings. *American Journal of Epidemiology, 106,* 17–32.

Kant, I. (1958). *Critique of pure reason.* New York: Modern Library. (Original work published 1781)

Kellman, P. J. (1993). Kinematic foundations of infant visual perception. In C. Granrud (Ed.), *Visual perception and cognition in infancy.* Hillsdale, NJ: Erlbaum.

Kellman, P. J., & Spelke, E. S. (1983). Perception of partly occluded objects in infancy. *Cognitive Psychology, 15,* 483–524.

Kelsall, D. C., Shallop, J. K., & Burnelli, T. (1995). Cochlear implantation in the elderly. *American Journal of Otology, 16,* 609–615.

Kenshalo, D. R. (1977). Age changes in touch, vibration, temperature, kinesthesis and pain sensitivity. In J. E.

Birren & K. W. Schaie (Eds.), *Handbook of the psychology of aging*. New York: Van Nostrand Reinhold.

Kieley, J. M., & Hartley, A. A. (1997). Age-related equivalence of identity suppression in the stroop color-word task. *Psychology and Aging, 12*, 22–29.

Kim, K., & Spelke, E. J. (1992). Infants' sensitivity to effects of gravity on visible object motion. *Journal of Experimental Psychology: Human Perception and Performance, 18*, 385–393.

Kisilevsky, B. S., & Muir, D. W. (1984). Neonatal habituation and dishabituation to tactile stimulation during sleep. *Developmental Psychology, 20*, 367–373.

Kline, D. W., Kline, T. J. B., Fozard, J. L., Kosnik, W., Schieber, F., & Sekuler, R. (1992). Vision, aging, and driving: The problems of older drivers. *Journal of Gerontology: Psychological Sciences, 47*, P27–P34.

Kline, D. W., & Schieber, F. (1985). Vision and aging. In J. E. Birren & K. W. Schaie (Eds.), *Handbook of the psychology of aging* (2nd ed.). New York: Van Nostrand Reinhold.

Kline, D. W., & Scialfa, C. T. (1996). Visual and auditory aging. In J. E. Birren & K. W. Schaie (Eds.), *Handbook of the psychology of aging* (4th ed.). San Diego, CA: Academic Press.

Kosnik, W., Winslow, L., Kline, D., Rasinski, K., & Sekuler, R. (1988). Visual changes in daily life throughout adulthood. *Journal of Gerontology: Psychological Sciences, 43*, P63–P70.

Kremenitzer, J. P., Vaughn, H. G., Jr., Kurtzberg, D., & Dowling, K. (1979). Smooth-pursuit eye movements in the newborn infant. *Child Development, 50*, 442–448.

Krumhansl, C. L., & Jusczyk, P. W. (1990). Infants' perception of phrase structure in music. *Psychological Science, 1*, 70–73.

Kuhl, P. K. (1991). Perception, cognition, and the ontogenetic and phylogenetic emergence of human speech. In S. E. Brauth, W. S. Hall, & R. J. Dooling (Eds.), *Plasticity of development*. Cambridge, MA: A Bradford Book, MIT Press.

Locke, J. (1939). An essay concerning human understanding. In E. A. Burtt (Ed.), *The English philosophers from Bacon to Mill*. New York: Modern Library. (Original work published 1690)

Lynch, M. P., Eilers, R. E., Oller, D. K., & Urbano, R. C. (1990). Innateness, experience, and music perception. *Psychological Science, 1*, 272–276.

Maccoby, E. E. (1967). Selective auditory attention in children. In L. P. Lipsitt & C. C. Spiker (Eds.), *Advances in child development and behavior*. New York: Academic Press.

Marean, G. C., Werner, L. A., & Kuhl, P. K. (1992). Vowel categorization by very young infants. *Developmental Psychology, 28*, 396–405.

Marschark, M. (1993). *Psychological development of deaf children*. New York: Oxford University Press.

Martin, F. N. (1994). *Introduction to audiology* (5th ed.). Englewood Cliffs, NJ: Prentice Hall.

Martlew, M., & Connolly, K. J. (1996). Human figure drawings by schooled and unschooled children in Papua New Guinea. *Child Development, 67*, 2743–2762.

Matlin, M. W., & Foley, H. J. (1997). *Sensation and perception* (4th ed.). Boston: Allyn and Bacon.

Maxon, A. B., & Brackett, D. (1992). *The hearing-impaired child. Infancy through high school years*. Boston: Andover Medical Publishers.

Mayberry, R. I., & Eichen, E. B. (1991). The long-lasting advantage of learning sign language in childhood: Another look at the critical period for language acquisition. *Journal of Memory and Language, 30*, 486–512.

McDowd, J. M., & Birren, J. E. (1990). Aging and attentional processes. In J. E. Birren & K. W. Schaie (Eds.), *Handbook of the psychology of aging* (3rd. ed.). San Diego: Academic Press.

McKay, K. E., Halperin, J. M., Schwartz, S. T., & Sharma, V. (1994). Developmental analysis of three aspects of information processing: Sustained attention, selective attention, and response organization. *Developmental Neuropsychology, 10*, 121–132.

Meadows-Orlans, K. P., & Orlans, H. (1990). Responses to loss of hearing in later life. In D. F. Moores & K. P. Meadows-Orlans (Eds.), *Educational and developmental aspects of deafness*. Washington, DC: Gallaudet University Press.

Meltzoff, A. N., & Borton, R. W. (1979). Intermodal matching by human neonates. *Nature, 282*, 403–404.

Merzenich, M. M., Jenkins, W. M., Johnston, P., Schreiner, C., Miller, S. L., & Tallal, P. (1996). Temporal processing deficits of language-learning impaired children ameliorated by training. *Science, 271*, 77–81.

Metsala, J. L. (1997). Spoken word recognition in reading disabled children. *Journal of Educational Psychology, 89*, 159–169.

Miller, J. L., & Eimas, P. D. (1996). Internal structure of voicing categories in early infancy. *Perception and Psychophysics, 58*, 1157–1167.

Miller, P. H., & Weiss, M. G. (1981). Children's attention allocation, understanding of attention, and performance on the incidental learning task. *Child Development, 52*, 1183–1190.

Mitchell, D. E. (1988). The recovery from early monocular visual deprivation in kittens. In A. Yonas (Ed.), *Minnesota Symposia on Child Psychology: Vol. 20. Perceptual development in infancy*. Hillsdale, NJ: Erlbaum.

Mitchell, D. E., Freeman, R. D., Millodot, M., & Haegerstrom, G. (1973). Meridional amblyopia: Evidence for modification of the human visual system by early visual experience. *Vision Research, 13*, 535–558.

Mix, K. S., Levine, S. C., & Huttenlocher, J. (1997). Numerical abstraction in infants: Another look. *Developmental Psychology, 33*, 423–428.

Miyawaki, K., Strange, W., Verbrugge, R., Liberman, A. M., Jenkins, J. J., & Fujimura, D. (1975). An effect of linguistic experience: The discrimination of [r] and [l] by native speakers of Japanese and English. *Perception and Psychophysics, 18*, 331–340.

Morrison, F. J. (1984). Reading disability: A problem in rule learning and word decoding. *Developmental Review, 4*, 36–47.

Morrongiello, B. A., Fenwick, K. D., & Chance, G. (1990). Sound localization activity in very young infants: An observer-based testing procedure. *Developmental Psychology, 26*, 1003.

Morrongiello, B. A., Fenwick, K. D., Hillier, L., & Chance, G. (1994). Sound localization in newborn human infants. *Developmental Psychobiology, 27*, 519–538.

Moss, M. S., Lawton, M. P., & Glicksman, A. (1991). The role of pain in the last year of life of older persons. *Journal of Gerontology: Psychological Sciences, 46*, P51–P57.

Muir, D. W. (1985). The development of infants' auditory spatial sensitivity.

In S. E. Trehub & B. Schneider (Eds.), *Advances in the study of communication and affect: Vol. 10. Auditory development in infancy*. New York: Plenum.

Murphy, C. (1985). Cognitive and chemosensory influences on age-related changes in the ability to identify blended foods. *Journal of Gerontology, 40*, 47–52.

Nanez, J. E., & Yonas, A. (1994). Effects of luminance and texture motion on infant defensive reactions to optical collision. *Infant Behavior and Development, 17*, 165–174.

National Center for Health Statistics, G. S. Poc. (1983). Eye care visits and use of eyeglasses or contact lenses: United States, 1979 and 1980. *Vital and Health Statistics*, Series 10 (No. 145).

National Institute on Aging and National Institute on Deafness and Other Communication Disorders. (1996). Hearing and older people. In L. M. Ross (Ed.), *Communication Disorders Sourcebook* (Vol. 11, pp. 183–184). Detroit: Omnigraphics.

National Institutes of Health. (1993, March 1–3). Consensus statement on the early identification of hearing impairment in infants and young children. In L. M. Ross (Ed.), *Communication Disorders Sourcebook* (Vol. 11, pp. 51–53). Detroit: Omnigraphics.

Newberger, J. J. (1997). New brain development research—A wonderful window of opportunity to build public support for early childhood education! *Young Children, 52*, 4–9.

Northern, J. L. (1996). *Hearing disorders* (3rd ed.). Boston: Allyn and Bacon.

Owsley, C., Ball, K., Sloane, M. E., & Bruni, J. R. (1991). Visual/cognitive correlates of vehicle accidents in older drivers. *Psychology and Aging, 6*, 403–415.

Pascalis, O., Deschonen, S., Morton, J., Deruelle, C., & Fabregrenet, M. (1995). Mother's face recognition by neonates: A replication and an extension. *Infant Behavior and Development, 18*, 79–85.

Pearson, J. D., Morell, C. H., Gordon-Salant, S., Brant, L. J., Metter, E. J., Klein, L., & Fozard, J. L. (1995). Gender differences in a longitudinal study of age-associated hearing loss. *Journal of the Acoustical Society of America, 97*, 1196–1205.

Peeples, D. R., & Teller, D. Y. (1975). Color vision and brightness discrimination in two-month-old human infants. *Science, 189*, 1102–1103.

Pickens, J. (1994). Perception of auditory-visual distance relations by 5-month-old infants. *Developmental Psychology, 30*, 537–544.

Pitts, D. G. (1982). The effects of aging on selected visual functions: Dark adaptation, visual acuity, stereopsis, and brightness contrast. In R. Sekuler, D. Kline, & K. Dismukes (Eds.), *Aging and human visual function*. New York: Alan R. Liss.

Plude, D. J., & Hoyer, W. J. (1981). Adult age differences in visual search as a function of stimulus mapping and processing load. *Journal of Gerontology, 36*, 598–604.

Plude, D. J., & Hoyer, W. J. (1985). Attention and performance: Identifying and localizing age deficits. In N. Charness (Ed.), *Aging and human performance*. Chichester, England: Wiley.

Porter, F. L., Miller, R. H., & Marshall, R. E. (1986). Neonatal pain cries: Effects of circumcision on acoustic features and perceived urgency. *Child Development, 57*, 790–802.

Porter, R. H., Makin, J. W., Davis, L. B., & Christensen, K. M. (1992). Breast-fed infants respond to olfactory clues from their own mother and unfamiliar lactating females. *Infant Behavior and Development, 15*, 85–93.

Pratt, K. C. (1954). The neonate. In L. Carmichael (Ed.), *Manual of child psychology* (2nd ed.). New York: Wiley.

Rango, N. (1985). The social epidemiology of accidental hypothermia among the aged. *Gerontologist, 25*, 424–430.

Riesen, A. H. (1965). Effects of visual deprivation on perceptual function and the neural substrate. In J. deAjuriaguerra (Ed.), *Dessaferentation experimental et clinique*. Geneva: Georg.

Riesen, A. H., Chow, K. L., Semmes, J., & Nissen, H. W. (1951). Chimpanzee vision after four conditions of light deprivation. *American Psychologist, 6*, 282.

Rieser, J., Yonas, A., & Wilkner, K. (1976). Radial localization of odors by human newborns. *Child Development, 47*, 856–859.

Rosser, R. (1994). *Cognitive development: Psychological and biological perspectives*. Boston: Allyn and Bacon.

Ruff, H. A., & Lawson, K. R. (1990). Development of sustained, focused attention in young children during free play. *Developmental Psychology, 26*, 85–93.

Ruff, H. A., & Rothbart, M. K. (1996). *Attention in early development—Themes and variations*. New York: Oxford University Press.

Ruff, H. A., Saltarelli, L. M., Coppozzoli, M., & Dubiner, K. (1992). The differentiation of activity in infants' exploration of objects. *Developmental Psychology, 27*, 851–861.

Salapatek, P. (1975). Pattern perception in early infancy. In L. B. Cohen & P. Salapatek (Eds.), *Infant perception: From sensation to cognition* (Vol. 1). New York: Academic.

Salthouse, T. A., Hancock, H. E., Meinz, E. J., & Hambrick, D. Z. (1996). Interrelations of age, visual acuity, and cognitive functioning. *Journal of Gerontology: Psychological Sciences, 51*, 317–330.

Schellenberg, E. G., & Trehub, S. E. (1996). Natural musical intervals: Evidence from infant listeners. *Psychological Science, 7*, 272–277.

Schiff, A. R., & Knopf, I. J. (1985). The effect of task demands on attention allocation in children of different ages. *Child Development, 56*, 621–630.

Schiffman, S. (1977). Food recognition by the elderly. *Journal of Gerontology, 32*, 586–592.

Schiffman, S. S., & Warwick, Z. S. (1993). Effect of flavor enhancement of foods for the elderly on nutritional status: Food intake, biochemical indices, and anthropometric measures. *Physiological Behavior, 53*, 395–402.

Scialfa, C. T., Guzy, L. T., Liebowitz, H. W., & Garvey, P. M. (1991). Age differences in estimating vehicle velocity. *Psychology and Aging, 6*, 60–66.

Ship, J. A., Pearson, J. D., Cruise, L. J., Brant, L. J., & Metter, E. J. (1996). Longitudinal changes in smell identification. *Journal of Gerontology: Medical Sciences, 51*, M86–M91.

Ship, J. A., & Weiffenbach, J. M. (1993). Age, gender, medical treatment, and medication effects on smell identification. *Journal of Gerontology: Medical Sciences, 48*, M26–M32.

Simon, T. J., Hespos, S. J., & Rochat, P. (1995). Do infants understand simple arithmetic? A replication of Wynn (1992). *Cognitive Development, 10*, 253–269.

Sivak, M., Olson, P. L., & Pastalan, L. A. (1981). Effect of driver's age on nighttime legibility of highway signs. *Human Factors, 23,* 59–64.

Slater, A., Mattock, A., & Brown, E. (1990). Size constancy at birth: Newborn infants' response to retinal and real size. *Journal of Experimental Child Psychology, 49,* 314–322.

Slater, A., Mattock, A., Brown, E., & Bremner, J. G. (1991). Form perception at birth: Cohen and Younger (1984) revisited. *Journal of Experimental Child Psychology, 51,* 395–406.

Slater, A., Morison, V., Somers, M., Mattock, A., Brown, E., & Taylor, D. (1990). Newborn and older infants' perception of partly occluded objects. *Infant Behavior and Development, 13,* 33–49.

Smith, B., & Blass, E. M. (1996). Taste-mediated calming in premature, preterm, and full-term human infants. *Developmental Psychology, 32,* 1084–1089.

Smith, L. B., & Katz, D. B. (1996). Activity-dependent processes in perceptual and cognitive development. In R. Gelman & T. K. Au (Eds.), *Perceptual and cognitive development.* San Diego: Academic Press.

Sommers, M. S. (1997). Speech perception in older adults: The importance of speech-specific cognitive abilities. *Journal of the American Geriatrics Society, 45,* 633–637.

Spelke, E. S. (1990). Principles of object perception. *Cognitive Science, 14,* 29–56.

Spelke, E. S. (1994). Initial knowledge: Six suggestions. *Cognition, 50,* 431–445.

Spelke, E. S., Breinlinger, K., Macomber, J., & Jacobson, K. (1992). Origins of knowledge. *Psychological Review, 99,* 605–632.

Spelke, E. S., & Hermer, L. (1996). Early cognitive development: Objects and space. In R. Gelman & T. K. Au (Eds.), *Perceptual and cognitive development.* San Diego: Academic Press.

Starkey, P., Spelke, E. S., & Gelman, R. (1990). Numerical abstraction by human infants. *Cognition, 36,* 97–127.

Steiner, J. E. (1979). Human facial expressions in response to taste and smell stimulation. In H. W. Reese & L. P. Lipsitt (Eds.), *Advances in child development and behavior* (Vol. 13). New York: Academic Press.

Stevens, B. (1996). Pain management in newborns: How far have we progressed in research and practice? *Birth: Issues in Perinatal Care, 23,* 229–235.

Stevens, J. C., Cruz, L. A., Hoffman, J. M., & Patterson, M. Q. (1995). Taste sensitivity and aging: High incidence of decline revealed by repeated threshold measures. *Chemical Senses, 20,* 451–459.

Streri, A., & Pecheux, M. (1986). Vision-to-touch and touch-to-vision transfer of form in 5-month-old infants. *British Journal of Developmental Psychology, 4,* 161–167.

Strutt, G. F., Anderson, D. R., & Well, A. D. (1975). A developmental study of the effects of irrelevant information on speeded classification. *Journal of Experimental Child Psychology, 20,* 127–135.

Stryker, M. P., Sherk, H., Leventhal, A. G., & Hirsch, V. H. B. (1978). Physiological consequences for the cat's visual cortex of effectively restricting early visual experience with oriented contours. *Journal of Neurophysiology, 41,* 896–909.

Suro, M. D. (1997, March 11). Sight for sore eyes: New research aims at preventing vision loss. *Washington Post Health,* pp. 12–14.

Tallal, P., Miller, S. L., Bedi, G., Byma, G., Wang, X., Nagarajan, S. S., Schreiner, C., Jenkins, W. M., & Merzenich, M. M. (1996). Language comprehension in language-learning impaired children improved with acoustically modified speech. *Science, 271,* 81–84.

Tanner, J. M. (1990). *Foetus into man: Physical growth from conception to maturity* (rev. & enl. ed.). Cambridge, MA: Harvard University Press.

Teller, D. Y., & Lindsey, D. T. (1993). Motion nulling techniques and infant color vision. In C. Granrud (Ed.), *Visual perception and cognition in infancy.* Hillsdale, NJ: Erlbaum.

Thompson, R. F. (1993). *The brain: A neuroscience primer* (2nd ed.). New York: W. H. Freeman.

Trehub, S. E., Schneider, B. A., Thorpe, L. A., & Judge, P. (1991). Observational measures of auditory sensitivity in early infancy. *Developmental Psychology, 27,* 40–49.

Treiber, F., & Wilcox, S. (1980). Perception of a "subjective contour" by infants. *Child Development, 51,* 915–917.

Tye-Murray, N., Spencer, L., & Woodworth, G. G. (1995). Acquisition of speech by children who have prolonged cochlear implant experience. *Journal of Speech and Hearing Research, 38,* 327–337.

Valenza, E., Simion, F., Cassia, V. M., & Umilta, C. (1996). Face preference at birth. *Journal of Experimental Psychology: Human Perception and Performance, 22,* 892–903.

Van Giffen, K., & Haith, M. M. (1984). Infant visual response to Gestalt geometric forms. *Infant Behavior and Development, 7,* 335–346.

Vellutino, F. R. (1991). Introduction to three studies on reading acquisition: Convergent findings on theoretical foundations of code-oriented versus whole language approaches to reading instruction. *Journal of Educational Psychology, 83,* 437–443.

Vellutino, F. R., Scanlon, D. M., Sipay, E. R., & Small, S. G. (1996). Cognitive profiles of difficult-to-remediate and readily remediated poor readers: Early intervention as a vehicle for distinguishing between cognitive and experiential deficits as basic causes of specific reading disability. *Journal of Educational Psychology, 88,* 601–638.

Verrillo, R. T., & Verrillo, V. (1985). Sensory and perceptual performance. In N. Charness (Ed.), *Aging and human performance.* Chichester, England: Wiley.

Vurpillot, E. (1968). The development of scanning strategies and their relation to visual differentiation. *Journal of Experimental Child Psychology, 6,* 632–650.

Walk, R. D. (1981). *Perceptual development.* Pacific Grove, CA: Brooks/Cole.

Walker-Andrews, A. S. (1997). Infants' perception of expressive behaviors: Differentiation of multimodal information. *Psychological Bulletin, 121,* 437–456.

Weiffenbach, J. M., Cowart, B. J., & Baum, B. J. (1986). Taste intensity perception in aging. *Journal of Gerontology, 41,* 460–468.

Wellman, H. M., & Gelman, S. A. (1992). Cognitive development: Foundational theories of core domains. *Annual Review of Psychology, 43,* 337–375.

Werker, J. F., & Desjardins, R. N. (1995). Listening to speech in the first year of life: Experiential influences on phoneme perception. *Current Directions in Psychological Science, 4,* 76–81.

Werker, J. F., Gilbert, J. H. V., Humphrey, K., & Tees, R. C. (1981). Developmental aspects of cross-language speech perception. *Child Development, 52,* 349–355.

Whitbourne, S. K. (1985). *The aging body. Physiological changes and psychological consequences.* New York: Springer-Verlag.

Wiesel, T. N., & Hubel, D. H. (1965). Comparison of the effects of unilateral and bilateral eye closure on cortical unit responses in kittens. *Journal of Neurophysiology, 28,* 1029–1040.

Williams, A. F., & Carsten, O. (1989). Driver age and crash involvement. *American Journal of Public Health, 79,* 326–327.

Wingfield, A., Poon, L. W., Lombardi, L., & Lowe, D. (1985). Speed of processing in normal aging: Effects of speech rate, linguistic structure, and processing time. *Journal of Gerontology, 40,* 579–595.

Wynn, K. (1992). Addition and subtraction by human infants. *Nature, 358,* 749–750.

Wynn, K. (1995). Infants possess a system of numerical knowledge. *Current Directions in Psychological Science, 4,* 172–177.

Yendovitskaya, T. V. (1971). Development of attention. In A. V. Zaporozhets & D. B. Elkonin (Eds.), *The psychology of preschool children.* Cambridge, MA: MIT Press.

Zaporozhets, A. V. (1965). The development of perception in the preschool child. *Monographs of the Society for Research in Child Development, 30* (2, Serial No. 100, pp. 82–101).

CHAPTER 7: Cognition and Language

Acredolo, L., & Goodwyn, S. (1988). Symbolic gesturing in normal infants. *Child Development, 59,* 450–466.

Adey, P. S., & Shayer, M. (1992). Accelerating the development of formal thinking in middle and high school students: II. Postproject effects on science achievement. *Journal of Research in Science Teaching, 29,* 81–92.

Au, R., Joung, P., Nicholas, M., Obler, L. K., Kass, R., & Albert, M. L. (1995). Naming ability across the adult life span. *Aging and Cognition, 2,* 300–311.

Azmitia, M. (1992). Expertise, private speech, and the development of self-regulation. In R. M. Diaz & L. E. Berk (Eds.), *Private speech: From social interaction to self-regulation.* Hillsdale, NJ: Erlbaum.

Baillargeon, R., & DeVos, J. (1991). Object permanence in young infants: Further evidence. *Child Development, 62,* 1227–1246.

Baillargeon, R., & Graber, M. (1988). Evidence of location memory in 8-month-old infants in a nonsearch AB task. *Developmental Psychology, 24,* 502–511.

Bandura, A. (1971). An analysis of modeling processes. In A. Bandura (Ed.), *Psychological modeling.* New York: Lieber-Atherton.

Baron, N. S. (1992). *Growing up with language: How children learn to talk.* Reading, MA: Addison-Wesley.

Barton, M. E., & Tomasello, M. (1994). The rest of the family: The role of fathers and siblings in early language development. In C. Gallaway & B. J. Richards (Eds.), *Input and interaction in language acquisition.* Cambridge: Cambridge University Press.

Basseches, M. (1984). *Dialectical thinking and adult development.* Norwood, NJ: Ablex.

Bates, E., Marchman, V., Thal, D., Fenson, L., Dale, P., Reznick, J. S., Reilly, J., & Hartung, J. (1994). Developmental and stylistic variation in the composition of early vocabulary. *Journal of Child Language, 21,* 85–123.

Bates, E., O'Connell, B., & Shore, C. (1987). Language and communication in infancy. In J. D. Osofsky (Ed.), *Handbook of infant development* (2nd ed.). New York: Wiley.

Beal, C. R. (1990). The development of text evaluation and revision skills. *Child Development, 61,* 247–258.

Behrend, D. A., Rosengren, K., & Perlmutter, M. (1989). A new look at children's private speech: The effects of age, task difficulty, and parent presence. *International Journal of Behavioral Development, 12,* 305–320.

Beilin, H. (1992). Piaget's enduring contribution to developmental psychology. *Developmental Psychology, 28,* 191–204.

Bellugi, U. (1988). The acquisition of a spatial language. In F. S. Kessel (Ed.), *The development of language and language researchers: Essays in honor of Roger Brown.* Hillsdale, NJ: Erlbaum.

Benedict, H. (1979). Early lexical development: Comprehension and production. *Journal of Child Language, 6,* 183–200.

Berk, L. E. (1992). Children's private speech: An overview of theory and the status of research. In R. M. Diaz & L. E. Berk (Eds.), *Private speech: From social interaction to self-regulation.* Hillsdale, NJ: Erlbaum.

Berk, L. E., & Landau, S. (1993). Private speech of learning disabled and normally achieving children in classroom academic and laboratory contexts. *Child Development, 64,* 556–571.

Berk, L. E., & Winsler, A. (1995). *Scaffolding children's learning: Vygotsky and early childhood education.* Washington: National Association for the Education of Young Children.

Bivens, J. A., & Berk, L. E. (1990). A longitudinal study of the development of elementary school children's private speech. *Merrill-Palmer Quarterly, 36,* 443–463.

Bjorklund, D. F. (1995). *Children's thinking: Developmental function and individual differences.* Pacific Grove, CA: Brooks/Cole.

Blackburn, J. (1984). The influence of personality, curriculum, and memory correlates on formal reasoning in young adults and elderly persons. *Journal of Gerontology, 39,* 207–209.

Blackburn, J. A., & Papalia, D. E. (1992). The study of adult cognition from a Piagetian perspective. In R. J. Sternberg & C. A. Berg (Eds.), *Intellectual development.* New York: Cambridge University Press.

Bloom, L. (1970). *Language development: Form and function in emerging grammars.* Cambridge, MA: MIT Press.

Bodrova, E., & Leong, D. J. (1996). *Tools of the mind: The Vygotskian approach to early childhood education.* Englewood Cliffs, NJ: Prentice Hall.

Bohannon, J. N., III, & Bonvillian, J. D. (1997). Theoretical approaches to language acquisition. In J. K. Gleason (Ed.), *The development of language* (4th ed.). Boston: Allyn and Bacon.

Bohannon, J. N., III, & Stanowicz, L. (1988). The issue of negative evidence: Adult responses to children's language errors. *Developmental Psychology, 24,* 684–689.

Boloh, Y., & Champaud, C. (1993). The past conditional verb form in French children: The role of semantics in late grammatical development. *Journal of Child Language, 20,* 169–189.

Braine, M. D. S. (1963). The ontogeny of English phrase structure: The first phrase. *Language, 39,* 1–13.

Brown, R. (1973). *A first language: The early stages.* Cambridge, MA: Harvard University Press.

Brown R., Cazden, C., & Bellugi, U. (1969). The child's grammar from I–III. In J. P. Hill (Ed.), *Minnesota Symposia on Child Psychology* (Vol. 2). Minneapolis: University of Minnesota Press.

Brown, R., & Hanlon, C. (1970). Derivational complexity and order of acquisition. In J. R. Hayes (Ed.), *Cognition and the development of language*. New York: Wiley.

Bruner, J. S. (1983). *Child's talk: Learning to use language.* New York: Norton.

Bruner, J. S. (1997). Celebrating divergence: Piaget and Vygotsky. *Human Development, 40,* 63–73.

Capelli, C. A., Nakagawa, N., & Madden, C. M. (1990). How children understand sarcasm: The role of context and intonation. *Child Development, 61,* 1824–1841.

Carey, S. (1977). The child as word learner. In M. Halle, J. Bresnan, & G. A. Miller (Eds.), *Linguistic theory and psychological reality.* Cambridge, MA: MIT Press.

Chapman, M., & Lindenberger, U. (1988). Functions, operations, and decalage in the development of transitivity. *Developmental Psychology, 24,* 542–551.

Chomsky, N. (1968). *Language and mind.* New York: Harcourt, Brace & World.

Chomsky, N. (1975). *Reflections on language.* New York: Pantheon Books.

Clark, H. H., & Clark, E. V. (1977). *Psychology and language: An introduction to psycholinguistics.* New York: Harcourt Brace Jovanovich.

Commons, M. L., Richards, F. A., & Armon, C. (Eds.). (1984). *Beyond formal operations: Late adolescent and adult cognitive development.* New York: Praeger.

Cooper, R. P., & Aslin, R. N. (1990). Preference for infant-directed speech in the first month after birth. *Child Development, 61,* 1584–1595.

Cornelius, S. W., & Caspi, A. (1987). Everyday problem solving in adulthood and old age. *Psychology and Aging, 2,* 144–153.

Dale, P. S. (1976). *Language development: Structure and function.* New York: Holt, Rinehart & Winston.

De Boysson-Bardies, B., Sagart, L., & Durand, C. (1984). Discernible differences in the babbling of infants according to target language. *Journal of Child Language, 11,* 1–16.

De Lisi, R., & Staudt, J. (1980). Individual differences in college students' performance on formal operations tasks. *Journal of Applied Developmental Psychology, 1,* 163–174.

Denney, N. W. (1982). Aging and cognitive changes. In B. B. Wolman (Ed.), *Handbook of developmental psychology.* Englewood Cliffs, NJ: Prentice-Hall.

de Villiers, P. A., & de Villiers, J. G. (1992). Language development. In M. H. Bornstein & M. E. Lamb (Eds.), *Developmental psychology: An advanced textbook.* Hillsdale, NJ: Erlbaum.

Dews, S., Winner, E., Kaplan, J., Rosenblatt, E., Hunt, M., Lim, K., Mcgovern, A., Qualter, A., & Smarsh, B. (1996). Children's understanding of the meaning and functions of verbal irony. *Child Development, 67,* 3071–3085.

Diamond, A. (1985). The development of the ability to use recall to guide action, as indicated by infants' performance on AB. *Child Development, 56,* 868–883.

Eimas, P. D. (1975). Speech perception in early infancy. In L. B. Cohen & P. Salapatek (Eds.), *Infant perception: From sensation to cognition* (Vol. 2). New York: Academic Press.

Elkind, D. (1967). Egocentrism in adolescence. *Child Development, 38,* 1025–1034.

Elkind, D., & Bowen, R. (1979). Imaginary audience behavior in children and adolescents. *Developmental Psychology, 15,* 38–44.

Ely, R. (1997). Language and literacy in the school years. In J. K. Gleason (Ed.), *The development of language* (4th ed.). Boston: Allyn and Bacon.

Enright, R., Lapsley, D., & Shukla, D. (1979). Adolescent egocentrism in early and late adolescence. *Adolescence, 14,* 687–695.

Fernald, A., Taeschner, T., Dunn, J., & Papousek, M., & Fukui, I. (1989). A cross-language study of prosodic modifications in mothers' and fathers' speech to preverbal infants. *Journal of Child Language, 16,* 477–501.

Field, D. (1981). Can preschool children really learn to conserve? *Child Development, 52,* 326–334.

Fischer, K. W. (1980). A theory of cognitive development: The control and construction of hierarchies of skills. *Psychological Review, 87,* 477–531.

Fischer, K. W., & Hencke, R. W. (1996). Infants' construction of actions in context: Piaget's contribution to research on early development. *Psychological Science, 7,* 204–210.

Fischer, K. W., Kenny, S. L., & Pipp, S. L. (1990). How cognitive processes and environmental conditions organize discontinuities in the development of abstractions. In C. N. Alexander & E. J. Langer (Eds.), *Higher stages of human development: Perspectives on adult growth.* New York: Oxford University Press.

Fisher, C., & Tokura, H. (1996). Acoustic cues to grammatical structure in infant-directed speech: Cross-linguistic evidence. *Child Development, 67,* 3192–3218.

Flavell, J. H. (1963). *The developmental psychology of Jean Piaget.* New York: Van Nostrand Reinhold.

Flavell, J. H. (1996). Piaget's legacy. *Psychological Science, 7,* 200–203.

Flavell, J. H., Everett, B. H., Croft, K., & Flavell, E. R. (1981). Young children's knowledge about visual perception: Further evidence for the level 1–level 2 distinction. *Developmental Psychology, 17,* 99–103.

Flavell, J. H., Miller, P. H., & Miller, S. A. (1993). *Cognitive development.* Englewood Cliffs, NJ: Prentice Hall.

Freedle, R., & Lewis, M. (1977). Prelinguistic conversation. In M. Lewis & L. Rosenblum (Eds.), *Interaction, conversation, and the development of language.* New York: Wiley.

Freund, L. S. (1990). Maternal regulation of children's problem-solving behavior and its impact on children's performance. *Child Development, 61,* 113–126.

Gallagher, J. M., & Easley, J. A., Jr. (Eds.). (1978). *Knowledge and development (Vol. 2). Piaget and education.* New York: Plenum.

Gauvain, M., & Rogoff, B. (1989). Collaborative problem-solving and children's planning skills. *Developmental Psychology, 25,* 139–151.

Gelman, R. (1972). The nature and development of early number concepts. In H. W. Reese (Ed.), *Advances in child development and behavior* (Vol. 7). New York: Academic.

Gelman, R. (1978). Cognitive development. *Annual Review of Psychology, 29,* 297–332.

Gelman, R., & Shatz, M. (1977). Appropriate speech adjustments: The operation of conversational constraints on talk to two-year-olds. In M. Lewis & L. Rosenblum (Eds.), *Interaction, conversation, and the development of language.* New York: Wiley.

Glassman, M. (1994). All things being equal: The two roads of Piaget and Vygotsky. *Developmental Psychology, 14,* 186–214.

Glick, J. C. (1975). Cognitive development in cross-cultural perspective. In F. Horowitz (Ed.), *Review of child development research* (Vol. 1). Chicago: University of Chicago Press.

Goldfield, B., & Reznick, J. S. (1996). Measuring the vocabulary spurt: A reply to Mervis and Bertrand. *Journal of Child Language, 23,* 241–246.

Gopnik, A. (1996). The post-Piaget era. *Psychological Science, 7,* 221–225.

Gordon, P. (1990). Learnability and feedback. *Developmental Psychology, 26,* 217–220.

Gray, W. M., & Hudson, L. M. (1984). Formal operations and the imaginary audience. *Developmental Psychology, 20,* 619–627.

Greene, K., Rubin, D. L., Hale, J. L., & Walters, L. H. (1996). The utility of understanding adolescent egocentrism in designing health promotion messages. *Health Communication, 8,* 131–152.

Greenfield, P. M., & Savage-Rumbaugh, E. S. (1993). Comparing communicative competence in child and chimp: The pragmatics of repetition. *Journal of Child Language, 20,* 1–26.

Greenfield, P. M., & Smith, J. H. (1976). *The structure of communication in early language development.* New York: Academic.

Harris, M. (1992). *Language experience and early language development: From input to uptake.* Hove, UK: Erlbaum.

Hoff-Ginsberg, E. (1997). *Language development.* Pacific Grove, CA: Brooks/Cole.

Holmbeck, G. N., Crossman, R. E., Wandrei, M. L., & Gasiewski, E. (1994). Cognitive development, egocentrism, self-esteem, and adolescent contraceptive knowledge, attitudes, and behavior. *Journal of Youth and Adolescence, 23,* 169–193.

Hooper, F. H., Hooper, J. O., & Colbert, K. K. (1985). Personality and memory correlates of intellectual functioning in adulthood: Piagetian and psychometric assessments. *Human Development, 28,* 101–107.

Hunt, K. W. (1970). Syntactic maturity in schoolchildren and adults. *Monographs of the Society for Research in Child Development, 35* (1, Serial No. 134).

Inhelder, B. (1966). Cognitive development and its contribution to the diagnosis of some phenomena of mental deficiency. *Merrill-Palmer Quarterly, 12,* 299–319.

Inhelder, B., & Piaget, J. (1964). *Early growth of logic in the child: Classification and seriation.* New York: Harper & Row.

Irwin, R. R. (1991). Reconceptualizing the nature of dialectical postformal operational thinking: The effects of affectively mediated social experiences. In J. D. Sinnott & J. C. Cavanaugh (Eds.), *Bridging paradigms: Positive development in adulthood and cognitive aging.* New York: Praeger.

Johnson, J., & Newport, E. (1989). Critical period effects in second language learning: The influence of maturational state on the acquisition of English as a second language. *Cognitive Psychology, 21,* 60–99.

John-Steiner, V. (1992). Private speech among adults. In R. M. Diaz & L. E. Berk (Eds.), *Private speech: From social interaction to self-regulation.* Hillsdale, NJ: Erlbaum.

Keating, D. P. (1980). Thinking processes in adolescence. In J. Adelson (Ed.), *Handbook of adolescent psychology.* New York: Wiley.

Kemler Nelson, D. G., Hirsh-Pasek, K., Jusczyk, P. W., & Cassidy, K. W. (1989). How the prosodic cues in motherese might assist in language learning. *Journal of Child Language, 16,* 55–68.

Kemtes, K. A., & Kemper, S. (1997). Younger and older adults' on-line processing of syntactically ambiguous sentences. *Psychology and Aging, 12,* 362–371.

Kitchener, K. S., & King, P. M. (1981). Reflective judgment: Concepts of justification and their relationship to age and education. *Journal of Applied Developmental Psychology, 2,* 89–116.

Kitchener, K. S., King, P. M., Wood, P. K., & Davison, M. L. (1989). Sequentiality and consistency in the development of reflective judgment: A six-year longitudinal study. *Journal of Applied Developmental Psychology, 10,* 73–95.

Klein, W. (1996). Language acquisition at different ages. In D. Magnusson (Ed.), *The lifespan development of individuals: Behavioral, neurobiological, and psychosocial perspectives. A synthesis.* Cambridge: Cambridge University Press.

Kohlberg, L., Yaeger, J., & Hjertholm, E. (1968). Private speech: Four studies and a review of theories. *Child Development, 39,* 691–736.

Labinowicz, E. (1980). *The Piaget primer.* Menlo Park, CA: Addison-Wesley.

Labouvie-Vief, G. (1985). Intelligence and cognition. In J. E. Birren & K. W. Schaie (Eds.), *Handbook of the psychology of aging* (2nd ed.). New York: Van Nostrand Reinhold.

Labouvie-Vief, G. (1992). A neo-Piagetian perspective on adult cognitive development. In R. J. Sternberg & C. A. Berg (Eds.), *Intellectual development.* New York: Cambridge University Press.

Labouvie-Vief, G., Adams, C., Hakim-Larson, J., & Hayden, M. (1983, April). *Contexts of logic: The growth of interpretation from pre-adolescence to mature adulthood.* Paper presented at the biennial meeting of the Society for Research in Child Development, Detroit, Michigan.

Lapsley, D. K., Milstead, M., Quintana, S. M., Flannery, D., & Buss, R. R. (1986). Adolescent egocentrism and formal operations: Tests of a theoretical assumption. *Developmental Psychology, 22,* 800–807.

Lenneberg, E. H. (1967). *Biological foundations of language.* New York: Wiley.

Lewis, B. A., & Thompson, L. A. (1992). A study of developmental speech and language disorders in twins. *Journal of Speech and Hearing Research, 35,* 1086–1094.

Lieven, E. V. M. (1994). Crosslinguistic and crosscultural aspects of language addressed to children. In C. Gallaway & B. J. Richards (Eds.), *Input and interaction in language acquisition.* Cambridge: Cambridge University Press.

Lieven, E. V. M., Pine, J. M., & Baldwin, G. (1997). Lexically based learning and early grammatical development. *Journal of Child Language, 24,* 187–219.

Light, L. L. (1990). Interactions between memory and language in old age. In J. E. Birren & K. W. Schaie (Eds.), *The handbook of the psychology of aging* (3rd ed.). San Diego: Academic Press.

Locke, J. L. (1997). A theory of neurolinguistic development. *Brain and Language, 58,* 265–326.

Lourenco, O., & Machado, A. (1996). In defense of Piaget's theory: A reply to 10 common criticisms. *Psychological Review, 103,* 143–164.

MacKay, D. G., & Abrams, L. (1996). Language, memory, and aging: Distributed deficits and the structure of new-versus-old connections. In J. E. Birren & K. W. Schaie (Eds.), *Handbook of the psychology of aging* (4th ed). San Diego: Academic Press.

Markman, E. M. (1989). *Categorization and naming in children*. Cambridge, MA: MIT Press.

Martorano, S. C. (1977). A developmental analysis of performance on Piaget's formal operations tasks. *Developmental Psychology, 13,* 666–672.

Masataka, N. (1996). Perception of motherese in a signed language by 6-month-old deaf infants. *Developmental Psychology, 32,* 874–879.

Mayberry, R. I. (1994). The importance of childhood to language acquisition: Evidence from American Sign Language. In J. C. Goodman & H. C. Nusbaum (Eds.), *The development of speech perception: The transition from speech sounds to spoken words.* Cambridge, MA: MIT Press.

McGhee, P. E. (1979). *Humor: Its origin and development.* San Francisco: W. H. Freeman.

McGhee, P. E., & Chapman, A. J. (1980). *Children's humour.* London: Wiley.

McGhee-Bidlack, B. (1991). The development of noun definitions: A metalinguistic analysis. *Journal of Child Language, 18,* 417–434.

McNeill, D. (1970). *The acquisition of language.* New York: Harper & Row.

Meier, R. P. (1991). Language acquisition by deaf children. *American Scientist, 79,* 69–70.

Mervis, C. B., & Johnson, K. E. (1991). Acquisition of the plural morpheme: A case study. *Developmental Psychology, 27,* 222–235.

Moerk, E. L. (1989). The LAD was a lady and the tasks were ill-defined. *Developmental Psychology, 9,* 21–57.

Myers, J., Jusczyk, P. W., Nelson, D. G. K., Charles-Luce, J., Woodward, A. L., & Hirsh-Pasek, K. (1996). Infants' sensitivity to word boundaries in fluent speech. *Journal of Child Language, 23,* 1–30.

Naigles, L. G., & Gelman, S. A. (1995). Overextensions in comprehension and production revisited: Preferential-looking in a study of dog, cat, and cow. *Journal of Child Language, 22,* 19–46.

Neimark, E. D. (1975). Longitudinal development of formal operations thought. *Genetic Psychology Monographs, 91,* 171–225.

Neimark, E. D. (1979). Current status of formal operations research. *Human Development, 22,* 60–67.

Nelson, K. (1973). Structure and strategy in learning to talk. *Monographs of the Society for Research in Child Development, 38* (Serial No. 149).

Nelson, K., Hampson, J., & Shaw, L. K. (1993). Nouns in early lexicons: Evidence, explanations, and implications. *Journal of Child Language, 20,* 61–84.

Neville, H. J., Coffey, S. A., Lawson, D. S., Fischer, A., Emmorey, K., & Bellugi, U. (1997). Neural systems mediating American Sign Language: Effects of sensory experience and age of acquisition. *Brain and Language, 57,* 285–308.

Newport, E. L. (1991). Contrasting conceptions of the critical period for language. In S. Carey & R. Gelman (Eds.), *The epigenesis of mind: Essays on biology and cognition.* Hillsdale, NJ: Erlbaum.

Obler, L. K., & Albert, M. L. (1985). Language skills across adulthood. In J. E. Birren & K. W. Schaie (Eds.), *Handbook of the psychology of aging* (2nd ed.). New York: Van Nostrand Reinhold.

Ochs, E. (1982). Talking to children in western Samoa. *Language in Society, 11,* 77–104.

O'Connor, B. P., & Nikolic, J. (1990). Identity development and formal operations as sources of adolescent egocentrism. *Journal of Youth and Adolescence, 19,* 149–158.

Oliver, E. I. (1995). The writing quality of seventh, ninth, and eleventh graders, and college freshmen: Does rhetorical specification in writing prompts make a difference? *Research in the Teaching of English, 29,* 422–450.

Oller, D. K., & Eilers, R. E. (1988). The role of audition in infant babbling. *Child Development, 59,* 441–449.

Pan, B. A., & Gleason, J. K. (1997). Semantic development: Learning the meanings of words. In J. K. Gleason (Ed.), *The development of language* (4th ed.). Boston: Allyn and Bacon.

Pearce, K. A., & Denney, N. W. (1984). A lifespan study of classification preference. *Journal of Gerontology, 39,* 458–464.

Pegg, J. E., Werker, J. F., & McLeod, P. J. (1992). Preference for infant-directed over adult-directed speech: Evidence from 7-week-old infants. *Infant Behavior and Development, 15,* 325–345.

Penner, S. G. (1987). Parental responses to grammatical and ungrammatical child utterances. *Child Development, 58,* 376–384.

Perry, W. G., Jr. (1970). *Forms of intellectual and ethical development in the college years: A scheme.* New York: Holt, Rinehart & Winston.

Petitto, L. A., & Marentette, P. F. (1991). Babbling in the manual mode: Evidence for the ontogeny of language. *Science, 251,* 1493–1496.

Piaget, J. (1926). *Language and thought in the child.* London: Routledge & Kegan Paul.

Piaget, J. (1929). *The child's conception of the world.* New York: Harcourt, Brace & World.

Piaget, J. (1952). *The origins of intelligence in children.* New York: International Universities Press.

Piaget, J. (1954). *The construction of reality in the child.* New York: Basic Books.

Piaget, J. (1970). Piaget's theory. In P. H. Mussen (Ed.), *Carmichael's manual of child psychology* (Vol. 1). New York: Wiley.

Piaget, J. (1972). Intellectual evolution from adolescence to adulthood. *Human Development, 15,* 1–12.

Piaget, J. (1977). The role of action in the development of thinking. In W. F. Overton & J. M. Gallagher (Eds.), *Knowledge and development* (Vol. 1). New York: Plenum.

Piaget, J. (1985). *The equilibration of cognitive structures: The central problem of intellectual development* (Trans. by T. Brown & K. J. Thampy). Chicago: University of Chicago Press.

Piaget, J., & Inhelder, B. (1956). *The child's conception of space.* New York: Norton.

Pine, J. M. (1994). The language of primary caregivers. In C. Gallaway & B. J. Richards (Eds.), *Input and interaction in language acquisition.* Cambridge: Cambridge University Press.

Plomin, R. (1990). *Nature and nurture: An introduction to human behavioral genetics.* Pacific Grove, CA: Brooks/Cole.

Reznick, J. S., & Goldfield, B. A. (1992). Rapid change in lexical development in comprehension and production. *Developmental Psychology, 28,* 406–413.

Rice, M. L., & Woodsmall, L. (1988). Lessons from television: Children's word learning when viewing. *Child Development, 59,* 420–429.

Richards, F. A., & Commons, M. L. (1990). Postformal cognitive-developmental theory and research: A review of its current status. In C. N. Alexander & E. J. Langer (Eds.), *Higher stages of human development: Perspectives on adult growth.* New York: Oxford University Press.

Richman, A. L., Miller, P. M., & LeVine, R. A. (1992). Cultural and educational variations in maternal responsiveness. *Developmental Psychology, 28,* 614–621.

Riegel, K. F. (1973). Dialectic operations: The final period of cognitive development. *Human Development, 16,* 346–370.

Rogoff, B. (1997, April). *Development as transformation of participation in sociocultural activities.* Paper presented at the biennial meeting of the Society for Research in Child Development, Washington, DC.

Rogoff, B., Mistry, J., Goncu, A., & Mosier, C. (1993). Guided participation in cultural activity by toddlers and caregivers. *Monographs of the Society for Research in Child Development, 58* (8, Serial No. 236).

Rowe, D. C. (1994). *The limits of family influence. Genes, experience, and behavior.* New York: Guilford.

Ruffman, T. K., & Olson, D. R. (1989). Children's ascriptions of knowledge to others. *Developmental Psychology, 25,* 601–606.

Ryan, R. M., & Kuczkowski, R. (1994). The imaginary audience, self-consciousness, and public individuation in adolescence. *Journal of Personality, 62,* 219–238.

Salthouse, T. A. (1990). Cognitive competence and expertise in aging. In J. E. Birren & K. W. Schaie (Eds.), *The handbook of the psychology of aging* (3rd ed.). San Diego: Academic Press.

Saxton, M. (1997). The contrast theory of negative input. *Journal of Child Language, 24,* 139–161.

Schaie, K. W. (1996). *Intellectual development in adulthood: The Seattle Longitudinal Study.* Cambridge: Cambridge University Press.

Schieffelin, B. B. (1986). *How Kaluli children learn what to say, what to do, and how to feel.* New York: Cambridge University Press.

Schieffelin, B. B., & Ochs, E. (1983). A cultural perspective on the transi-tion from prelinguistic to linguistic communication. In R. M. Golinkoff (Ed.), *The transition from prelinguistic to linguistic communication.* Hillsdale, NJ: Erlbaum.

Singer, D. G., & Singer, J. L. (1990). *The house of make-believe: Children's play and the developing imagination.* Cambridge, MA: Harvard University Press.

Sinnott, J. (1996). The developmental approach: Postformal thought as adaptive intelligence. In F. Blanchard-Fields & T. M. Hess (Eds.), *Perspectives on cognitive change in adulthood and aging.* New York: McGraw-Hill.

Skinner, B. F. (1957). *Verbal behavior.* New York: Appleton-Century-Crofts.

Snow, C. E., Arlman-Rupp, A., Hassing, Y., Jobse, J., Joosken, J., & Vorster, J. (1976). Mother's speech in three social classes. *Journal of Psycholinguistic Research, 5,* 1–20.

Sommers, M. S. (1997). Speech perception in older adults: The importance of speech-specific cognitive abilities. *Journal of the American Geriatrics Society, 45,* 633–637.

Spencer, P. E. (1996). The association between language and symbolic play at two years: Evidence from deaf toddlers. *Child Development, 67,* 867–876.

Stine, E. A. L., Soederberg, L. M., & Morrow, D. G. (1996). Language and discourse processing through adulthood. In F. Blanchard-Fields & T. M. Hess (Eds.), *Perspectives on cognitive change in adulthood and aging.* New York: McGraw-Hill.

Sudhalter, V., & Braine, M. D. S. (1985). How does comprehension of passives develop? A comparison of actional and experiential verbs. *Journal of Child Language, 12,* 455–470.

Taylor, M., Cartwright, B. S., & Carlson, S. M. (1993). A developmental investigation of children's imaginary companions. *Developmental Psychology, 29,* 276–285.

Taylor, M., & Gelman, S. A. (1988). Adjectives and nouns: Children's strategies for learning new words. *Child Development, 59,* 411–419.

Taylor, M., & Gelman, S. A. (1989). Incorporating new words into the lexicon: Preliminary evidence for language hierarchies in two-year-old children. *Child Development, 60,* 625–636.

Thomas, D., Campos, J. J., Shucard, D. W., Ramsay, D. S., & Shucard, J. (1981). Semantic comprehension in infancy: A signal detection approach. *Child Development, 52,* 798–803.

Thompson, J. R., & Chapman, R. S. (1977). Who is "Daddy" revisited? The status of two-year-olds' overextended words in use and comprehension. *Journal of Child Language, 4,* 359–375.

Thompson, R. F. (1993). *The brain: A neuroscience primer* (2nd ed.). New York: W. H. Freeman.

Tomasello, M., Strosberg, R., & Akhtar, N. (1996). Eighteen-month-old children learn words in non-ostensive contexts. *Journal of Child Language, 23,* 157–176.

Trabasso, T. (1975). Representation, memory, and reasoning: How do we make transitive inferences? In A. D. Pick (Ed.), *Minnesota symposia on child psychology* (Vol. 9). Minneapolis: University of Minnesota Press.

Vartanian, L. R., & Powlishta, K. K. (1996). A longitudinal examination of the social-cognitive foundations of adolescent egocentrism. *Journal of Early Adolescence, 16,* 157–178.

Vygotsky, L. S. (1962). *Thought and language* (E. Hanfmann & G. Vakar, Eds. & Trans.). Cambridge, MA: MIT Press. (Original work published 1934)

Vygotsky, L. S. (1978). *Mind in society: The development of higher mental processes* (M. Cole, V. John-Steiner, S. Scribner, & E. Souberman, Eds.). Cambridge, MA: Harvard University Press. (Original work published 1930, 1933, 1935)

Waxman, S. R., & Hatch, T. (1992). Beyond the basics: Preschool children label objects flexibly at multiple hierarchical levels. *Journal of Child Language, 19,* 153–166.

Werker, J. F., & Desjardins, R. N. (1995). Listening to speech in the first year of life: Experiential influences on phoneme perception. *Current Directions in Psychological Science, 4,* 76–81.

Wertsch, J. V., & Tulviste, P. (1992). L. S. Vygotsky and contemporary developmental psychology. *Developmental Psychology, 28,* 548–557.

Whitehurst, G. J., & Valdez-Menchaca, M. C. (1988). What is the role of reinforcement in early language acquisition? *Child Development, 59,* 430–440.

Williams, K. C. (1996). Piagetian principles: Simple and effective application.

Journal of Intellectual Disability Research, 40, 110–119.

Wolff, P. H. (1969). The natural history of crying and other vocalizations in early infancy. In B. M. Foss (Ed.), *Determinants of infant behavior* (Vol. 4). London: Methuen.

Yalisove, D. (1978). The effect of riddle structure on children's comprehension of riddles. *Developmental Psychology, 14,* 173–180.

Yan, B., & Arlin, P. K. (1995). Nonabsolute/relativistic thinking: A common factor underlying models of postformal reasoning? *Journal of Adult Development, 2,* 223–240.

CHAPTER 8: Learning and Information Processing

Abravanel, E., & Sigafoos, A. D. (1984). Exploring the presence of imitation during early infancy. *Child Development, 55,* 381–392.

Adams, C. (1991). Qualitative age differences in memory for text: A life-span developmental perspective. *Psychology and Aging, 6,* 323–336.

Anisfeld, M. (1996). Only tongue protrusion modeling is matched by neonates. *Developmental Review, 16,* 149–161.

Atkinson, R. C., & Shiffrin, R. M. (1968). Human memory: A proposed system and its control processes. In K. W. Spence & J. T. Spence (Eds.), *The psychology of learning and motivation: Advances in research and theory* (Vol. 2). New York: Academic Press.

Bahrick, H. P. (1984). Semantic memory content in permastore: Fifty years of memory for Spanish learned in high school. *Journal of Experimental Psychology: General, 113,* 1–29.

Bahrick, H. P., Bahrick, P. O., & Wittlinger, R. P. (1975). Fifty years of memory for names and faces: A cross-sectional approach. *Journal of Experimental Psychology: General, 104,* 54–75.

Bahrick, H. P., & Hall, L. K. (1991). Lifetime maintenance of high school mathematics content. *Journal of Experimental Psychology: General, 120,* 20–33.

Baker, L., & Brown, A. L. (1984). Metacognitive skills and reading. In P. D. Pearson (Ed.), *A handbook of reading research.* New York: Longman.

Baker-Ward, L., Ornstein, P. A., & Holden, D. J. (1984). The expression of memorization in early childhood. *Journal of Experimental Child Psychology, 37,* 555–575.

Baltes, P. B., & Kliegl, R. (1992). Further testing of limits of cognitive plasticity: Negative age differences in a mnemonic skill are robust. *Developmental Psychology, 28,* 121–125.

Baltes, P. B., Smith, J., & Staudinger, U. M. (1992). Wisdom and successful aging. In T. B. Sonderegger (Ed.), *Nebraska Symposium on Motivation: Vol. 39. Psychology and aging.* Lincoln, NB: University of Nebraska Press.

Bandura, A. (1965). Influence of models' reinforcement contingencies on the acquisition of imitative responses. *Journal of Personality and Social Psychology, 1,* 589–595.

Bandura, A. (1977). *Social learning theory.* Englewood Cliffs, NJ: Prentice-Hall.

Bandura, A. (1986). *Social foundations of thought and action: A social cognitive theory.* Englewood Cliffs, NJ: Prentice-Hall.

Bandura, A. (1989). Social cognitive theory. In R. Vasta (Ed.), *Annals of child development. Vol. 6: Theories of child development: Revised formulations and current issues.* New York: Appleton-Century-Crofts.

Barr, R., Dowden, A., & Hayne, H. (1996). Developmental changes in deferred imitation by 6- to 24-month-old infants. *Infant Behavior and Development, 19,* 159–170.

Barrett, T. R., & Wright, M. (1981). Age-related facilitation in recall following semantic processing. *Journal of Gerontology, 36,* 194–199.

Bauer, P. J. (1996). What do infants recall of their lives? Memory for specific events by one- to two-year-olds. *American Psychologist, 51,* 29–41.

Berg, C. A. (1989). Knowledge of strategies for dealing with everyday problems from childhood through adolescence. *Developmental Psychology, 25,* 607–618.

Berg, C. A., & Klaczynski, P. A. (1996). Practical intelligence and problem solving: Searching for perspectives. In F. Blanchard-Fields & T. M. Hess (Eds.), *Perspectives on cognitive change in adulthood and aging.* New York: McGraw-Hill.

Best, D. L. (1993). Inducing children to generate mnemonic organizational strategies: An examination of long-term retention and materials. *Developmental Psychology, 29,* 324–336.

Biederman, I., Cooper, E. E., Fox, P. W., & Mahadevan, R. S. (1992). Unexceptional spatial memory in an exceptional memorist. *Journal of Experimental Psychology: Learning Memory and Cognition, 18,* 654–657.

Bjorklund, D. F. (1985). The role of conceptual knowledge in the development of organization in children's memory. In C. J. Brainerd & M. Pressley (Eds.), *Basic processes in memory development: Progress in cognitive development research.* New York: Springer-Verlag.

Bjorklund, D. F. (1995). *Children's thinking: Developmental function and individual differences.* Pacific Grove, CA: Brooks/Cole.

Bjorklund, D. F. (1997). In search of a metatheory for cognitive development (or, Piaget is dead and I don't feel so good myself). *Child Development, 68,* 144–148.

Bjorklund, D. F., & Zeman, B. R. (1982). Children's organization and metamemory awareness in their recall of familiar information. *Child Development, 53,* 799–810.

Botwinick, J. (1984). *Aging and behavior: A comprehensive integration of research findings* (3rd ed.). New York: Springer.

Bray, N. W., Hersh, R. E., & Turner, L. A. (1985). Selective remembering during adolescence. *Developmental Psychology, 21,* 290–294.

Brown, A. L. (1975). The development of memory: Knowing, knowing about knowing, and knowing how to know. In H. W. Reese (Ed.), *Advances in child development and behavior* (Vol. 10). New York: Academic Press.

Brown, A. L., Bransford, J. D., Ferrara, R. A., & Campione, J. C. (1983). Learning, remembering, and understanding. In J. H. Flavell & E. M. Markman (Eds.), *Handbook of child psychology: Vol. 3. Cognitive development* (4th ed.). New York: Wiley.

Brown, A. L., & Smiley, S. S. (1978). The development of strategies for studying text. *Child Development, 49,* 1076–1088.

Byrnes, J. P. (1996). *Cognitive development and learning in instructional contexts.* Boston: Allyn and Bacon.

Camp, C. J. (1989). World-knowledge systems. In L. W. Poon, D. C. Rubin, & B. A. Wilson (Eds.), *Everyday cognition in adulthood and late life.* Cambridge: Cambridge University Press.

Camp, C. J., Foss, J. W., O'Hanlon, A. M., & Stevens, A. B. (1996). Memory interventions for persons with dementia. *Applied Cognitive Psychology, 10,* 193–210.

Camp, C. J., & McKitrick, L. A. (1992). Memory interventions in Alzheimer's-type dementia populations: Methodological and theoretical issues. In R. L. West & J. D. Sinnott (Eds.), *Everyday memory and aging: Current research and methodology* (pp. 155–172). New York: Springer-Verlag.

Case, R. (1985). *Intellectual development: Birth to adulthood.* Orlando, FL: Academic Press.

Cavanaugh, J. C. (1983). Comprehension and retention of television programs by 20- and 60-year-olds. *Journal of Gerontology, 38,* 190–196.

Cavanaugh, J. C. (1996). Memory self-efficacy as a moderation of memory change. In F. Blanchard-Fields & T. M. Hess (Eds.), *Perspectives on cognitive change in adulthood and aging.* New York: McGraw-Hill.

Cavanaugh, J. C., Grady, J. G., & Perlmutter, M. (1983). Forgetting and use of memory aids in 20 to 70 year olds' everyday life. *International Journal of Aging and Human Development, 17,* 113–122.

Chi, M. T. H. (1978). Knowledge structures and memory development. In R. Siegler (Ed.), *Children's thinking: What develops?* Hillsdale, NJ: Erlbaum.

Chi, M. T. H., Hutchinson, J. E., & Robin, A. F. (1989). How inferences about novel domain-related concepts can be constrained by structured knowledge. *Merrill-Palmer Quarterly, 35,* 27–62.

Coates, B., & Hartup, W. W. (1969). Age and verbalization in observational learning. *Developmental Psychology, 1,* 556–562.

DeLoache, J. S., Cassidy, D. J., & Brown, A. L. (1985). Precursors of mnemonic strategies in very young children's memory. *Child Development, 56,* 125–137.

Dempster, F. N. (1985). Short-term memory development in childhood and adolescence. In C. J. Brainerd & M. Pressley (Eds.), *Basic processes in memory development: Progress in cognitive development research.* New York: Springer Verlag.

Denney, N. W. (1980). Task demands and problem-solving strategies in middle-aged and older adults. *Journal of Gerontology, 35,* 559–564.

Denney, N. W. (1982). Aging and cognitive changes. In B. B. Wolman (Ed.), *Handbook of developmental psychology.* Englewood Cliffs, NJ: Prentice-Hall.

Denney, N. W. (1989). Everyday problem solving: Methodological issues, research findings, and a model. In L. W. Poon, D. C. Rubin, & B. A. Wilson (Eds.), *Everyday cognition in adulthood and late life.* Cambridge: Cambridge University Press.

Denney, N. W., & Pearce, K. A. (1989). A developmental study of practical problem solving in adults. *Psychology and Aging, 4,* 438–442.

Dixon, R. A. (1992). Contextual approaches to adult intellectual development. In R. J. Sternberg & C. A. Berg (Eds.), *Intellectual development.* New York: Cambridge University Press.

Domjan, M. J. (1993). *Principles of learning and behavior* (3rd ed.). Pacific Grove, CA: Brooks/Cole.

Ericsson, K. A. (1996). The acquisition of expert performance: An introduction to some of the issues. In K. A. Ericsson (Ed.), *The road to excellence: The acquisition of expert performance in the arts and sciences, sports, and games.* Mahwah, NJ: Erlbaum.

Ericsson, K. A., Chase, W. G., & Faloon, S. (1980). Acquisition of a memory skill. *Science, 208,* 1181–1182.

Ericsson, K. A., & Kintsch, W. (1995). Long-term working memory. *Psychological Review, 102,* 211–245.

Fagan, J. F., Jr. (1984). Infant memory: History, current trends, relations to cognitive psychology. In M. Moscovitch (Ed.), *Infant memory: Its relation to normal and pathological memory in humans and other animals.* New York: Plenum.

Field, T. M., Woodson, R., Greenberg, R., & Cohen, D. (1982). Discrimination and imitation of facial expressions by neonates. *Science, 218,* 179–181.

Fivush, R., Gray, J. T., & Fromhoff, F. A. (1987). Two-year-olds talk about the past. *Cognitive Development, 2,* 393–409.

Flavell, J. H., Beach, D. R., & Chinsky, J. M. (1966). Spontaneous verbal rehearsal in a memory task as a function of age. *Child Development, 37,* 283–299.

Flavell, J. H., Miller, P. H., & Miller, S. A. (1993). *Cognitive development.* Englewood Cliffs, NJ: Prentice Hall.

Flavell, J. H., & Wellman, H. M. (1977). Metamemory. In R. V. Kail & J. W. Hagen (Eds.), *Perspectives on the development of memory and cognition.* Hillsdale, NJ: Erlbaum.

Fletcher, K. L., & Bray, N. W. (1996). External memory strategy use in preschool children. *Merrill-Palmer Quarterly, 42,* 379–396.

Floyd, M., & Scogin, F. (1997). Effects of memory training on the subjective memory functioning and mental health of older adults: A meta-analysis. *Psychology and Aging, 12,* 150–161.

Flynn, C. P. (1994). Regional differences in attitudes toward corporal punishment. *Journal of Marriage and the Family, 56,* 314–324.

Friedman, S. B. (1972). Habituation and recovery of visual response in the alert human newborn. *Journal of Experimental Child Psychology, 13,* 339–349.

Fry, A. F., & Hale, S. (1996). Processing speed, working memory, and fluid intelligence: Evidence for a developmental cascade. *Psychological Science, 7,* 237–241.

Gardner, H. (1985). *The mind's new science: A history of the cognitive revolution.* New York: Basic.

Gewirtz, J. L., & Pelaez-Nogueras, M. (1992). Infants' separation difficulties and distress due to misplaced maternal contingencies. In T. Field, P. McCabe, & N. Schneiderman (Eds.), *Stress and coping in infancy and childhood* (pp. 19–46). Hillsdale, NJ: Erlbaum.

Glaser, R., & Chi, M. T. H. (1988). Overview. In M. T. H. Chi, R. Glaser, & M. Farr (Eds.), *The nature of expertise.* Hillsdale, NJ: Erlbaum.

Graf, P. (1990). Life-span changes in implicit and explicit memory. *Bulletin of the Psychonomic Society, 28,* 353–358.

Graf, P., Squire, L. R., & Mandler, G. (1984). The information that amnesic patients do not forget. *Journal of Experimental Psychology: Learning, Memory, and Cognition, 10,* 164–178.

Guttentag, R. E. (1985). Memory and aging: Implications for theories of memory development during childhood. *Developmental Review, 5,* 56–77.

Hattie, J., Biggs, J., & Purdie, N. (1996). Effects of learning skills interventions on student learning: A meta-analysis. *Review of Educational Research, 66,* 99–136.

Hess, T. M., & Pullen, S. M. (1996). Memory in context. In F. Blanchard-Fields & T. M. Hess (Eds.), *Perspectives on cognitive change in adulthood and aging.* New York: McGraw-Hill.

House, B. J. (1982). Learning processes: Developmental trends. In J. Worell (Ed.), *Psychological development in the elementary years.* New York: Academic Press.

Houx, P. J., Vreeling, F. W., & Jolles, J. (1991). Rigorous health screening reduces age effect on memory scanning task. *Brain and Cognition, 15,* 246–260.

Howard, D. V. (1996). The aging of implicit and explicit memory. In F. Blanchard-Fields & T. M. Hess (Eds.), *Perspectives on cognitive change in adulthood and aging.* New York: McGraw-Hill.

Howe, M. L., & Courage, M. L. (1993). On resolving the enigma of infantile amnesia. *Psychological Bulletin, 113,* 305–326.

Hulicka, I. M. (1967). Age differences in retention as a function of interference. *Journal of Gerontology, 22,* 180–184.

Hultsch, D. F., Hammer, M., & Small, B. J. (1993). Age differences in cognitive performance in later life: Relationships to self-reported health and activity life style. *Journal of Gerontology: Psychological Sciences, 48,* P1–P11.

Jensen, A. R. (1990). Speed of information processing in a calculating prodigy. *Intelligence, 14,* 259–274.

Jones, M. C. (1924). A laboratory study of fear: The case of Peter. *Pedagogical Seminary, 31,* 308–315.

Jones, S. S. (1996). Imitation or exploration? Young infants' matching of adults' oral gestures. *Child Development, 67,* 1952–1969.

Justice, E. M. (1985). Categorization as preferred memory strategy: Developmental changes during elementary school. *Developmental Psychology, 21,* 1105–1110.

Justice, E. M., Bakerward, L., Gupta, S., & Jannings, L. R. (1997). Means to the goal of remembering: Developmental changes in awareness of strategy use performance relations. *Journal of Experimental Child Psychology, 65,* 293–314.

Kail, R. (1990). *The development of memory in children* (3rd ed.). New York: W. H. Freeman.

Kail, R. (1991). Developmental change in speed of processing during childhood and adolescence. *Psychological Bulletin, 109,* 490–501.

Kail, R., & Bisanz, J. (1992). The information-processing perspective on cognitive development in childhood and adolescence. In R. J. Sternberg & C. A. Berg (Eds.), *Intellectual development.* New York: Cambridge University Press.

Kail, R., & Salthouse, T. A. (1994). Processing speed as a mental capacity. *Acta Psychologica, 86,* 199–225.

Kasworm, C. E., & Medina, R. A. (1990). Adult competence in everyday tasks: A cross-sectional secondary analysis. *Educational Gerontology, 16,* 27–48.

Kausler, D. H. (1994). *Learning and memory in normal aging.* San Diego: Academic Press.

Kliegl, R., Smith, J., & Baltes, P. B. (1989). Testing-the-limits and the study of adult age differences in cognitive plasticity of a mnemonic skill. *Developmental Psychology, 25,* 247–256.

Kreutzer, M. A., Leonard, C., & Flavell, J. H. (1975). An interview study of children's knowledge about memory. *Monographs of the Society for Research in Child Development, 40* (1, Serial No. 159).

Kron, R. E. (1966). Instrumental conditioning of nutritive sucking behavior in the newborn. *Recent Advances in Biological Psychiatry, 9,* 295–300.

Kuhn, D. (1992). Cognitive development. In M. H. Bornstein & M. E. Lamb (Eds.), *Developmental psychology: An advanced textbook* (3rd ed.). Hillsdale, NJ: Erlbaum.

Lange, G., & Pierce, S. H. (1992). Memory-strategy learning and maintenance in preschool children. *Developmental Psychology, 28,* 453–462.

Levy, B. (1996). Improving memory in old age through implicit self-stereotyping. *Journal of Personality and Social Psychology, 71,* 1092–1107.

Levy, B., & Langer, E. (1994). Aging free from negative stereotypes: Successful memory in China and among the American deaf. *Journal of Personality and Social Psychology, 66,* 989–997.

Light, L. L. (1991). Memory and aging: Four hypotheses in search of data. *Annual Review of Psychology, 42,* 333–376.

Lipsitt, L. P. (1990). Learning and memory in infants. *Merrill-Palmer Quarterly, 36,* 53–66.

Lipsitt, L. P., & Kaye, H. (1964). Conditioned sucking in the human newborn. *Psychonomic Science, 1,* 29–30.

Lorsbach, T. C., & Reimer, J. F. (1997). Developmental changes in the inhibition of previously relevant information. *Journal of Experimental Child Psychology, 64,* 317–342.

Luszcz, M. A., Bryan, J., & Kent, P. (1997). Predicting episodic memory performance of very old men and women: Contributions from age, depression, activity, cognitive ability, and speed. *Psychology and Aging, 12,* 340–351.

Marini, Z., & Case, R. (1994). The development of abstract reasoning about the physical and social world. *Child Development, 65,* 147–159.

Marsiske, M., & Willis, S. L. (1995). Dimensionality of everyday problem solving in older adults. *Psychology and Aging, 10,* 269–283.

Mcdonald-Miszczak, L., Hultsch, D. F., & Hertzog, C. (1995). Stability and accuracy of metamemory in adulthood and aging: A longitudinal analysis. *Psychology and Aging, 10,* 553–564.

Meltzoff, A. N. (1988). Infant imitation and memory: Nine-month-olds in immediate and deferred tests. *Child Development, 59,* 217–225.

Meltzoff, A. N., & Moore, M. K. (1983). Newborn infants imitate adult facial gestures. *Child Development, 54,* 702–709.

Meltzoff, A. N., & Moore, M. K. (1989). Imitation in newborn infants: Exploring the range of gestures initiated and the underlying mechanisms. *Developmental Psychology, 25,* 954–962.

Miller, P. H., & Weiss, M. G. (1981). Children's attention allocation, understanding of attention, and performance on the incidental learning task. *Child Development, 52,* 1183–1190.

Morrell, R. W., Park, D. C., & Poon, L. W. (1989). Quality of instructions on prescription drug labels: Effects on memory and comprehension in young and old adults. *Gerontologist, 29,* 345–354.

Morrow, D., Leirer, V., Altieri, P., & Fitzsimmons, C. (1994). When expertise reduces age differences in performance. *Psychology and Aging, 9,* 134–148.

Nelson, C. A. (1995). The ontogeny of human memory: A cognitive neuroscience perspective. *Developmental Psychology, 31,* 723–738.

Nelson, K. (1984). The transition from infant to child memory. In M. Moscovitch (Ed.), *Infant memory: Its relation to normal and pathological memory in humans and other animals.* New York: Plenum.

Newell, A., & Simon, H. A. (1961). Computer simulation of human thinking. *Science, 134,* 2011–2017.

O'Sullivan, J. T. (1997). Effort, interest, and recall: Beliefs and behaviors of preschoolers. *Journal of Experimental Child Psychology, 65,* 43–67.

Papousek, H. (1967). Experimental studies of appetitional behavior in human newborns and infants. In H. W. Stevenson, E. H. Hess, & H. L. Rheingold (Eds.), *Early behavior: Comparative and developmental approaches.* New York: Wiley.

Park, D. C., Morrell, R. W., Frieske, D., & Kincaid, D. (1992). Medication adherence behaviors in older adults: Effects of external cognitive supports. *Psychology and Aging, 7,* 252–256.

Parke, R. D. (1977). Some effects of punishment on children's behavior—revisited. In E. M. Hetherington & R. D. Parke (Eds.), *Contemporary readings in child psychology.* New York: McGraw-Hill.

Perlmutter, M. (1986). A life-span view of memory. In P. B. Baltes, D. L. Featherman, & R. M. Lerner (Eds.), *Life-span development and behavior* (Vol. 7). Hillsdale, NJ: Erlbaum.

Piaget, J., & Inhelder, B. (1969). *The psychology of the child* (H. Weaver, Trans.). New York: Basic Books. (Original work published 1966)

Poon, L. W., Fozard, J. L., Paulshock, D. R., & Thomas, J. C. (1979). A questionnaire assessment of age differences in retention of recent and remote events. *Experimental Aging Research, 5,* 401–411.

Pressley, M. (1982). Elaboration and memory development. *Child Development, 53,* 296–309.

Pressley, M. (1983). Making meaningful materials easier to learn: Lessons from cognitive strategy research. In M. Pressley & J. R. Levin (Eds.), *Cognitive strategy research: Educational applications.* New York: Springer-Verlag.

Pressley, M., Forrest-Pressley, D. L., Elliott-Faust, D., & Miller, G. (1985). Children's use of cognitive strategies, how to teach strategies, and what to do if they can't be taught. In M. Pressley & C. J. Brainerd (Eds.), *Cognitive learning and memory in children: Progress in cognitive development research.* New York: Springer-Verlag.

Pressley, M., & Levin, J. R. (1980). The development of mental imagery retrieval. *Child Development, 51,* 558–560.

Reder, L. M., Wible, C., & Martin, J. (1986). Differential memory changes with age: Exact retrieval versus plausible inference. *Journal of Experimental Psychology: Learning, Memory, and Cognition, 12,* 72–81.

Richards, J. E. (1997). Effects of attention on infant's preference for briefly exposed visual stimuli in the paired-comparison recognition-memory paradigm. *Developmental Psychology, 32,* 22–31.

Roediger, H. L. (1990). Implicit memory: Retention without remembering. *American Psychologist, 45,* 1043–1056.

Rovee-Collier, C. (1987). Learning and memory in infancy. In J. D. Osofsky (Ed.), *Handbook of infant development* (2nd ed.). New York: Wiley.

Rovee-Collier, C. (1997). Dissociations in infant memory: Rethinking the development of implicit and explicit memory. *Psychological Review, 104,* 467–498.

Rovee-Collier, C., & Boller, K. (1995). Current theory and research on infant learning and memory: Application to early intervention. *Infants and Young Children, 7,* 1–12.

Russo, R., Nichelli, P., Gibertoni, M., & Cornia, C. (1995). Developmental trends in implicit and explicit memory: A picture completion study. *Journal of Experimental Child Psychology, 59,* 566–578.

Salatas, H., & Flavell, J. H. (1976). Behavioral and metamnemonic indicators of strategic behaviors under remember instructions in first grade. *Child Development, 47,* 81–89.

Salthouse, T. A. (1992). Why do adult age differences increase with task complexity. *Developmental Psychology, 28,* 905–918.

Salthouse, T. A. (1993). Speed and knowledge as determinants of adult age differences in verbal tasks. *Journal of Gerontology: Psychological Sciences, 48,* P29–P36.

Schachter, D. L. (1996). *Searching for memory: The brain, the mind, and the past.* New York: Basic Books.

Schaie, K. W. (1977/1978). Toward a stage theory of adult cognitive development. *International Journal of Aging and Human Development, 8,* 129–138.

Schaie, K. W., & Willis, S. L. (1996). *Adult development and aging* (4th ed.). New York: HarperCollins.

Schneider, W., Bjorklund, D. F., & Maier-Bruckner, W. (1996). The effects of expertise and IQ on children's memory: When knowledge is, and when it is not enough. *International Journal of Behavioral Development, 19,* 773–796.

Shimamura, A. P., Berry, J. M., Mangels, J. A., Rusting, C. L., & Jurica, P. J. (1995). Memory and cognitive abilities in university professors: Evidence for successful aging. *Psychological Science, 6,* 271–277.

Siegler, R. S. (1981). Developmental sequences within and between concepts. *Monographs of the Society for Research in Child Development, 46* (2, Serial No. 189).

Siegler, R. S. (1989). Hazards of mental chronometry: An example from children's subtraction. *Journal of Educational Psychology, 81,* 497–506.

Siegler, R. S. (1996). *Emerging minds: The process of change in children's thinking.* New York: Oxford University Press.

Simon, H. A. (1995). The information-processing theory of mind. *American Psychologist, 50,* 507–508.

Skinner, B. F. (1953). *Science and human behavior.* New York: Macmillan.

Skinner, B. F. (1983). Intellectual self-management in old age. *American Psychologist, 38,* 239–244.

Smith, A. D., & Earles, J. L. K. (1996). Memory changes in normal aging. In F. Blanchard-Fields & T. M. Hess (Eds.), *Perspectives on cognitive change in adulthood and aging.* New York: McGraw-Hill.

Smith, G. E., Petersen, R. C., Ivnik, R. J., Malec, J. F., & Tangalos, E. G. (1996). Subjective memory complaints, psychological distress, and longitudinal change in objective memory performance. *Psychology and Aging, 11,* 272–279.

Socolar, R. R., & Stein, R. E. (1995). Spanking infants and toddlers: Maternal belief and practice. *Pediatrics, 95,* 105–111.

Solomon, P. R., Pomerleau, D., Bennett, L., James, J., & Morse, D. L. (1989). Acquisition of the classically conditioned eyeblink response in humans over the life span. *Psychology and Aging, 4,* 34–41.

Somerville, S. C., Wellman, H. M., & Cultice, J. C. (1983). Young children's deliberate reminding. *Journal of Genetic Psychology, 143,* 87–96.

Sophian, C. (1980). Habituation is not enough: Novelty preferences, search, and memory in infancy. *Merrill-Palmer Quarterly, 26,* 239–257.

Spilich, G. J., Vesonder, G. T., Chiesi, H. L., & Voss, J. F. (1979). Text processing of domain-related information for individuals with high and low domain knowledge. *Journal of Verbal Learning and Verbal Behavior, 18,* 275–290.

Stine-Morrow, E. A. L., Loveless, M. K., & Soederberg, L. M. (1996). Resource allocation in on-line reading by younger and older adults. *Psychology and Aging, 11,* 475–486.

Storandt, M. (1992). Memory-skills training for older adults. In T. B. Sonderegger (Ed.), *Nebraska Symposium on Motivation: Vol. 39. Psychology and aging.* Lincoln: University of Nebraska Press.

Straus, M. A. (1994). *Beating the devil out of them: Corporal punishment in American families.* New York: Lexington Books.

Swain, I. U., Zelazo, P. R., & Clifton, R. K. (1993). Newborn infants' memory for speech sounds retained over 24 hours. *Developmental Psychology, 29,* 312–323.

Tarabulsy, G. M., Tessier, R., & Kappas, A. (1996). Contingency detection and the contingent organization of behavior in interactions: Implications for socioemotional development in infancy. *Psychological Bulletin, 120,* 25–41.

Turner, H. A., & Finkelhor, D. (1996). Corporal punishment as a stressor among youth. *Journal of Marriage and the Family, 58,* 155–166.

Usher, J. A., & Neisser, U. (1993). Childhood amnesia and the beginnings of memory for four early life events. *Journal of Experimental Psychology: General, 122,* 155–165.

Verhaeghen, P., & Marcoen, A. (1996). On the mechanisms of plasticity in young and older adults after instruction in the method of loci: Evidence for an amplification model. *Psychology and Aging, 11,* 164–178.

Verhaeghen, P., Marcoen, A., & Goossens, L. (1992). Improving memory performance in the aged through mnemonic training: A meta-analytic study. *Psychology and Aging, 7,* 242–251.

Verna, G. B. (1977). The effects of a four-hour delay of punishment under two conditions of verbal instruction. *Child Development, 48,* 621–624.

Vinter, A. (1986). The role of movement in eliciting early imitations. *Child Development, 57,* 66–71.

Waddell, K. J., & Rogoff, B. (1981). Effect of contextual organization on spatial memory of middle-aged and older women. *Developmental Psychology, 17,* 878–885.

Wagner, D. A. (1978). Memories of Morocco: The influence of age, schooling, and environment on memory. *Cognitive Psychology, 10,* 1–28.

Watson, J. B., & Raynor, R. (1920). Conditioned emotional reactions. *Journal of Experimental Psychology, 3,* 1–14.

Weiss, B., Dodge, K. A., Bates, J. E., & Pettit, G. S. (1992). Some consequences of early harsh discipline: Child aggression and a maladaptive social information processing style. *Child Development, 63,* 1321–1335.

Wellman, H. M. (1977). Preschoolers' understanding of memory relevant variables. *Child Development, 48,* 1720–1723.

West, R. L., Crook, T. H., & Barron, K. L. (1992). Everyday memory performance across the life span: Effects of age and noncognitive individual differences. *Psychology and Aging, 7,* 72–82.

White, S. H., & Pillemer, D. B. (1979). Childhood amnesia and the development of a socially accessible memory system. In J. F. Kihlstrom & F. J. Evans (Eds.), *Functional disorders of memory.* Hillsdale, NJ: Erlbaum.

Willemsen, E. (1979). *Understanding infancy.* San Francisco: W. H. Freeman.

Woodruff-Pak, D. S. (1990). Mammalian models of learning, memory, and aging. In J. E. Birren & K. W. Schaie (Eds.), *The handbook of the psychology of aging* (3rd ed.). San Diego: Academic Press.

Yussen, S. R., & Levy, V. M. (1975). Developmental changes in predicting one's own memory span of short-term memory. *Journal of Experimental Child Psychology, 19,* 502–508.

CHAPTER 9: Intelligence and Creativity

Achter, J. A., Benbow, C. P., & Lubinski, D. (1997). Rethinking multipotentiality among the intellectually gifted: A critical review and recommendations. *Gifted Child Quarterly, 41,* 5–15.

Albert, R. S. (1996). Some reasons why childhood creativity often fails to make it past puberty into the real world. In M. A. Runco (Ed.), *Creativity from childhood through adulthood: The developmental issues.* San Francisco: Jossey-Bass.

Andrich, D., & Styles, I. (1994). Psychometric evidence of intellectual growth spurts in early adolescence. *Journal of Early Adolescence, 14,* 328–344.

Ardelt, M. (1997). Wisdom and life satisfaction in old age. *Journal of Gerontology: Psychological Sciences and Social Sciences, 52,* P15–P27.

Baltes, P. B., & Graf, P. (1996). Psychological aspects of aging: Factors and frontiers. In D. Magnusson (Ed.), *The lifespan development of individuals: Behavioral, neurobiological, and psychosocial perspectives: A synthesis.* Cambridge: Cambridge University Press.

Baltes, P. B., Staudinger, U. M., Maercker, A., & Smith, J. (1995). People nominated as wise: A comparative study of wisdom-related knowledge. *Psychology and Aging, 10,* 155–166.

Bayley, N. (1969). *Bayley Scales of Infant Development.* New York: Psychological Corporation.

Bayley, N. (1993). *Bayley Scales of Infant Development* (2nd ed.). San Antonio, TX: Psychological Corporation.

Blagg, N. (1991). *Can we teach intelligence? A comprehensive evaluation of Feuerstein's instrumental enrichment program.* Hillsdale, NJ: Erlbaum.

Bornstein, M. H., & Sigman, M. D. (1986). Continuity in mental development from infancy. *Child Development, 57,* 251–274.

Bradley, R. H., & Caldwell, B. M. (1984). 174 children: A study of the relationship between home environment and cognitive development during the first 5 years. In A. W. Gottfried (Ed.), *Home environment and early cognitive development: Longitudinal research.* Orlando, FL: Academic.

Bradley, R. H., Caldwell, B. M., Rock, S. L., Ramey, C. T., Barnard, K. E., Gray, C., Hammond, M. A., Mitchell, S., Gottfried, A. W., Siegel, L., & Johnson, D. L. (1989). Home environment and cognitive development in the first 3 years of life: A collaborative study involving six sites and three ethnic groups in North America. *Developmental Psychology, 25,* 217–235.

Broberg, A. G., Wessels, H., Lamb, M. E., & Hwang, C. P. (1997). Effects of day care on the development of cognitive abilities in 8-year-olds: A longitudinal study. *Developmental Psychology, 33,* 62–69.

Brody, E. B., & Brody, N. (1976). *Intelligence: Nature, determinants, and consequences.* New York: Academic Press.

Brooks-Gunn, J., Klebanov, P. K., & Duncan, G. J. (1996). Ethnic differences in children's intelligence test scores: Role of economic deprivation, home environment, and maternal characteristics. *Child Development, 67,* 396–408.

Busse, E. W., & Maddox, G. L. (1985). *The Duke longitudinal studies of normal aging. 1955–1980: Overview of history, design, and findings.* New York: Springer.

Caldwell, B. M., & Bradley, R. H. (1984). *Manual for the Home Observation for Measurement of the Environment.* Little Rock: University of Arkansas at Little Rock.

Campbell, F. A., & Ramey, C. T. (1995). Cognitive and school outcomes for high-risk African-American students at middle adolescence: Positive effects of early intervention. *American Educational Research Journal, 32,* 743–772.

Campione, J. C., Brown, A. L., Ferrara, R. A., & Bryant, N. R. (1984). The zone of proximal development: Implications for individual differences and learning. In B. Rogoff & J. V. Wertsch (Eds.), *Children's learning in the "zone of proximal development"* (New Directions for Child Development, No. 23). San Francisco: Jossey-Bass.

Carroll, J. B. (1993). *Human cognitive abilities: A survey of factor-analytic studies.* Cambridge: Cambridge University Press.

Case, R. (1992). The role of the frontal lobes in the regulation of cognitive development. *Brain and Cognition, 20,* 51–73.

Cattell, R. B. (1963). Theory of fluid and crystallized intelligence: A critical experiment. *Journal of Educational Psychology, 54,* 1–22.

Chen, J. Q., & Gardner, H. (1997). Alternative assessment from a multiple intelligences theoretical perspective. In D. P. Flanagan, J. Genshaft, &

P. L. Harrison (Eds.), *Contemporary intellectual assessment: Theories, tests, and issues.* New York: Guilford.

Clayton, V. P., & Birren, J. E. (1980). The development of wisdom across the life span: A reexamination of an ancient topic. In P. B. Baltes & O. G. Brim, Jr. (Eds.), *Life-span development and behavior* (Vol. 3). New York: Academic Press.

Coleman, L. J. (1985). *Schooling the gifted.* Menlo Park, CA: Addison-Wesley.

Cornelius, S. W. (1984). Classic pattern of intellectual aging: Test familiarity, difficulty, and performance. *Journal of Gerontology, 39,* 201–206.

Cox, C. M. (1926). *Genetic studies of genius. Vol. 2: The early mental traits of three hundred geniuses.* Stanford, CA: Stanford University Press.

Crockenberg, S. (1983). Early mother and infant antecedents of Bayley Scale performance at 21 months. *Developmental Psychology, 19,* 727–730.

Cunningham, W. R., & Owens, W. A., Jr. (1983). The Iowa State study of the adult development of intellectual abilities. In K. W. Schaie (Ed.), *Longitudinal studies of adult psychological development.* New York: Guilford.

Day, J. D., Engelhardt, J. L., Maxwell, S. E., & Bolig, E. E. (1997). Comparison of static and dynamic assessment procedures and their relation to independent performance. *Journal of Educational Psychology, 89,* 358–368.

Day, K., & Jancar, J. (1994). Mental and physical health and ageing in mental handicap: A review. *Journal of Intellectual Disability Research, 38,* 241–256.

Dennis, W. (1966). Creative productivity between the ages of 20 and 80 years. *Journal of Gerontology, 21,* 1–8.

Devenny, D. A., Silverman, W. P., Hill, A. L., Jenkins, E., Sersen, E. A., & Wisniewski, K. E. (1996). Normal ageing in adults with Down's syndrome: A longitudinal study. *Journal of Intellectual Disability Research, 40,* 208–221.

Dixon, R. A., Kramer, D. A., & Baltes, P. B. (1985). Intelligence: A life-span developmental perspective. In B. B. Wolman (Ed.), *Handbook of intelligence: Theories, measurements, and applications.* New York: Wiley.

Dougherty, T. M., & Haith, M. M. (1997). Infant expectations and reaction time as predictors of childhood speed of processing and IQ. *Developmental Psychology, 33,* 146–155.

Eichorn, D. H., Hunt, J. V., & Honzik, M. P. (1981). Experience, personality, and IQ: Adolescence to middle age. In D. H. Eichorn, J. A. Clausen, N. Haan, M. P. Honzik, & P. H. Mussen (Eds.), *Present and past in middle life.* New York: Academic Press.

Ericsson, K. A., & Charness, N. (1994). Expert performance: Its structure and acquisition. *American Psychologist, 49,* 725–747.

Erikson, E. H. (1982). *The life cycle completed: A review.* New York: Norton.

Escalona, S. (1968). *The roots of individuality: Normal patterns of individuality.* Chicago: Aldine.

Feldman, D. H. (1986). *Nature's gambit: Child prodigies and the development of human potential.* New York: Basic Books.

Feldman, R. D. (1982). *Whatever happened to the Quiz Kids? Perils and profits of growing up gifted.* Chicago: Chicago Review Press.

Feuerstein, R., Feuerstein, R., & Gross, S. (1997). The Learning Potential Assessment Device. In D. P. Flanagan, J. Genshaft, & P. L. Harrison (Eds.), *Contemporary intellectual assessment: Theories, tests, and issues.* New York: Guilford.

Feuerstein, R., Miller, R., Hoffman, M. B., Rand, Y., Mintzker, Y., & Jensen, M. R. (1981). Cognitive modifiability in adolescence: Cognitive structure and the effects of intervention. *Journal of Special Education, 15,* 269–287.

Fincher, J. (1973). The Terman study is 50 years old: Happy anniversary and pass the ammunition. *Human Behavior, 2,* 8–15.

Fisher, M. A., & Zeaman, D. (1970). Growth and decline of retardate intelligence. In N. R. Ellis (Ed.), *International review of research in mental retardation* (Vol. 4). New York: Academic Press.

Flynn, J. R. (1987). Massive IQ gains in 14 nations: What IQ tests really measure. *Psychological Bulletin, 101,* 171–191.

Flynn, J. R. (1996). What environmental factors affect intelligence: The relevance of IQ gains over time. In D. K. Detterman (Ed.), *Current topics in human intelligence: Vol. 5. The environment.* Norwood, NJ: Ablex.

Frisby, C. L., & Braden, J. P. (1992). Feuerstein's dynamic assessment approach: A semantic, logical, and empirical critique. *Journal of Special Education, 26,* 281–301.

Gardner, H. (1983). *Frames of mind: The theory of multiple intelligences.* New York: Basic Books.

Gardner, H., Phelps, E., & Wolf, D. (1990). The roots of adult creativity in children's symbolic products. In C. N. Alexander & E. J. Langer (Eds.), *Higher stages of human development: Perspectives on adult growth.* New York: Oxford University Press.

Getzels, J. W., & Jackson, P. W. (1962). *Creativity and intelligence: Explorations with gifted children.* New York: Wiley.

Golomb, C. (1992). Eytan: The early development of a gifted child artist. *Creativity Research Journal, 5,* 265–279.

Gottfredson, L. S. (1986). Societal consequences of the g factor in employment. *Journal of Vocational Behavior, 29,* 379–410.

Gottfried, A. W. (1984). Home environment and early cognitive development: Integration, meta-analyses, and conclusions. In A. W. Gottfried (Ed.), *Home environment and early cognitive development: Longitudinal research.* Orlando, FL: Academic Press.

Gottfried, A. W., & Gottfried, A. E. (1984). Home environment and cognitive development in young children of middle-socioeconomic-status families. In A. W. Gottfried (Ed.), *Home environment and early cognitive development: Longitudinal research.* Orlando, FL: Academic Press.

Gottfried, A. W., Gottfried, A. E., Bathurst, K., & Guerin, D. W. (1994). *Gifted IQ: Early developmental aspects: The Fullerton Longitudinal Study.* New York: Plenum.

Gray, S. W., Ramsey, B. K., & Klaus, R. A. (1982). *From 3 to 20: The early training project.* Baltimore: University Park Press.

Gruber-Baldini, A. L., Schaie, K. W., & Willis, S. L. (1995). Similarity in married couples: A longitudinal study of mental abilities and rigidity-flexibility. *Journal of Personality and Social Psychology, 69,* 191–203.

Guilford, J. P. (1967). *The nature of human intelligence.* New York: McGraw-Hill.

Guilford, J. P. (1988). Some changes in the structure-of-the-intellect model. *Educational and Psychological Measurement, 40,* 1–4.

Harrell, T. W., & Harrell, M. S. (1945). Army General Classification Test scores for civilian occupations. *Educational and Psychological Measurement, 5,* 229–239.

Harrington, D. M., Block, J. H., & Block, J. (1987). Testing aspects of Carl Rogers's theory of creative environments: Child-rearing antecedents of creative potential in young adolescents. *Journal of Personality and Social Psychology, 52,* 851–856.

Helms, J. E. (1992). Why is there no study of cultural equivalence in standardized cognitive-ability testing? *American Psychologist, 47,* 1083–1101.

Helms, J. E. (1997). The triple quandary of race, culture, and social class in standardized cognitive ability testing. In D. P. Flanagan, J. Genshaft, & P. L. Harrison (Eds.), *Contemporary intellectual assessment: Theories, tests, and issues.* New York: Guilford.

Herrnstein, R. J., & Murray, C. (1994). *The bell curve: Intelligence and class structure in American life.* New York: Free Press.

Holahan, C. K., & Sears, R. R. (1995). *The gifted group in later maturity.* Stanford, CA: Stanford University Press.

Holliday, S. G. , & Chandler, M. J. (1986). *Wisdom: Explorations in adult competence.* Basel, Switzerland: Karger.

Honzik, M. P. (1983). Measuring mental abilities in infancy: The value and limitations. In M. Lewis (Ed.), *Origins of intelligence: Infancy and early childhood* (2nd ed.). New York: Plenum.

Honzik, M. P., Macfarlane, J. W., & Allen, L. (1948). The stability of mental test performance between two and eighteen years. *Journal of Experimental Education, 17,* 309–324.

Horn, J. L., & Cattell, R. B. (1967). Age differences in fluid and crystallized intelligence. *Acta Psychologica, 26,* 107–129.

Horn, J. L., & Noll, J. (1997). Human cognitive capabilities: Gf-Gc theory. In D. P. Flanagan, J. Genshaft, & P. L. Harrison (Eds.), *Contemporary intellectual assessment: Theories, tests, and issues.* New York: Guilford.

Howieson, N. (1981). A longitudinal study of creativity: 1965-1975. *Journal of Creative Behavior, 15,* 117–134.

Hunt, J. M., & Paraskevopoulos, J. (1980). Children's psychological development as a function of the inaccuracy of their mothers' knowledge of their abilities. *Journal of Genetic Psychology, 136,* 285–298.

Hunter, J. E., & Hunter, R. F. (1984). Validity and utility of alternative predictors of job performance. *Psychological Bulletin, 96,* 72–98.

Jaquish, G. A., & Ripple, R. E. (1981). Cognitive creative abilities and self-esteem across the adult life-span. *Human Development, 24,* 110–119.

Jarvik, L. F., & Bank, L. (1983). Aging twins: Longitudinal psychometric data. In K. W. Schaie (Ed.), *Longitudinal studies of adult psychological development.* New York: Guilford.

Jensen, A. R. (1969). How much can we boost IQ and scholastic achievement? *Harvard Educational Review, 39,* 1-123.

Jensen, A. R. (1977). Cumulative deficit in the IQ of blacks in the rural South. *Developmental Psychology, 13,* 184–191.

Jensen, A. R. (1980). *Bias in mental testing.* New York: Free Press.

Jensen, A. R. (1993). Why is reaction time correlated with psychometric g? *Current Directions in Psychological Science, 2,* 53–56.

Johansson, B., Zarit, S. H., & Berg, S. (1992). Changes in cognitive functioning of the oldest old. *Journal of Gerontology: Psychological Sciences, 47,* P75–P80.

Kail, R., & Salthouse, T. A. (1994). Processing speed as a mental capacity. *Acta Psychologica, 86,* 199–225.

Kaufman, A. S., Kamphaus, R. W., & Kaufman, N. L. (1985). New directions in intelligence testing: The Kaufman Assessment Battery for Children (K-ABC). In B. B. Wolman (Ed.), *Handbook of intelligence.* New York: Wiley.

Kaufman, A. S., & Kaufman, N. L. (1997). The Kaufman Adolescent and Adult Intelligence Test. In D. P. Flanagan, J. L. Genshaft, & P. L. Harrison (Eds.), *Contemporary intellectual assessment: Theories, tests, and issues.* New York: Guilford.

Kleemeier, R. W. (1962). Intellectual change in the senium. *Proceedings of the Social Statistics Section of the American Statistical Association,* 290–295.

Klineberg, O. (1963). Negro-white differences in intelligence test performance: A new look at an old problem. *American Psychologist, 18,* 198–203.

Kogan, N. (1983). Stylistic variation in childhood and adolescence: Creativity, metaphor, and cognitive styles. In J. H. Flavell & E. H. Markman (Eds.), *Handbook of child psychology: Vol. 3. Cognitive development* (4th ed.). New York: Wiley.

Labouvie-Vief, G. (1985). Intelligence and cognition. In J. E. Birren & K. W.

Schaie (Eds.), *Handbook of the psychology of aging* (2nd ed.). New York: Van Nostrand Reinhold.

Lazar, I., & Darlington, R. (1982). Lasting effects of early education: A report from the Consortium for Longitudinal Studies. *Monographs of the Society for Research in Child Development, 47* (2–3, Serial No. 195).

Lehman, H. C. (1953). *Age and achievement.* Princeton, NJ: Princeton University Press.

Lewontin, R. C. (1976). Race and intelligence. In N. J. Block & G. Dworkin (Eds.), *The IQ controversy.* New York: Pantheon.

Lidz, C. S. (1997). Dynamic assessment approaches. In D. P. Flanagan, J. Genshaft, & P. L. Harrison (Eds.), *Contemporary intellectual assessment: Theories, tests, and issues.* New York: Guilford.

Loehlin, J. C., Horn, J. M., & Willerman, L. (1997). Heredity, environment, and IQ in the Texas Adoption Project. In R. J. Sternberg & E. L. Grigorenko (Eds.), *Intelligence, heredity, and environment.* New York: Cambridge University Press.

Lopez, E. C. (1997). The cognitive assessment of limited English proficient and bilingual children. In D. P. Flanagan, J. Genshaft, & P. L. Harrison (Eds.), *Contemporary intellectual assessment: Theories, tests, and issues.* New York: Guilford.

Luckasson, R., Coulter, D. L., Polloway, E. A., Reiss, S., Schalock, R. L., Snell, M. E., Spitalnik, D. M., & Stark, J. A. (1992). *Mental retardation: Definition, classification, and systems of supports.* Washington, DC: American Association on Mental Retardation.

Luster, T., & Dubow, E. (1992). Home environment and maternal intelligence as predictors of verbal intelligence: A comparison of preschool and school-age children. *Merrill-Palmer Quarterly, 38,* 151–175.

MacPhee, D., Ramey, C. T., & Yeates, K. O. (1984). Home environmental and early cognitive development: Implications for intervention. In A. W. Gottfried (Ed.), *Home environment and early cognitive development: Longitudinal research.* Orlando, FL: Academic.

McCall, R. B. (1981). Nature-nurture and the two realms of development: A proposed integration with respect to mental development. *Child Development, 55,* 1–12.

McCall, R. B. (1983). A conceptual approach to early mental development. In M. Lewis (Ed.), *Origins of intelligence: Infancy and early childhood* (2nd ed.). New York: Plenum.

McCall, R. B., Applebaum, M. I., & Hogarty, P. S. (1973). Developmental changes in mental test performance. *Monographs of the Society for Research in Child Development, 38* (3, Serial No. 150).

McCall, R. B., & Carriger, M. S. (1993). A meta-analysis of infant habituation and recognition memory performance as predictors of later IQ. *Child Development, 64,* 57–79.

McCall, R. B., Eichorn, D. H., & Hogarty, P. S. (1977). Transitions in early mental development. *Monographs of the Society for Research in Child Development, 42* (3, Serial No. 171).

McCrae, R. R., Arenberg, D., & Costa, P. T., Jr. (1987). Declines in divergent thinking with age: Cross-sectional, longitudinal, and cross-sequential analyses. *Psychology and Aging, 2,* 130–137.

McGue, M., Bouchard, T. J., Jr., Iacono, W. G., & Lykken, D. T. (1993). Behavioral genetics of cognitive ability: A life span perspective. In R. Plomin & G. E. McClearn (Eds.), *Nature, nurture, and psychology.* Washington, DC: American Psychological Association.

Miller, J. G. (1997). A cultural-psychology perspective on intelligence. In R. J. Sternberg & E. L. Grigorenko (Eds.), *Intelligence, heredity, and environment.* New York: Cambridge University Press.

Miller, S. A. (1986). Parents' beliefs about their children's cognitive abilities. *Developmental Psychology, 22,* 276–284.

Monty, S. (1981). *May's boy: An incredible story of love.* Nashville: T. Nelson.

Moore, E. G. J. (1986). Family socialization and the IQ test performance of traditionally and transracially adopted black children. *Developmental Psychology, 22,* 317–326.

Morse, C. K. (1993). Does variability increase with age? An archival study of cognitive measures. *Psychology and Aging, 8,* 156–164.

Neisser, U., Boodoo, G., Bouchard, T. J., Jr., Boykin, A. W., Brody, N., Ceci, S. J., Halpern, D. F., Loehlin, J. C., Perloff, R., Sternberg, R. J., & Urbina, S. (1996). Intelligence: Knowns and unknowns. *American Psychologist, 51,* 77–101.

Nettelbeck, T., & Young, R. (1996). Intelligence and savant syndrome: Is the whole greater than the sum of the fragments? *Intelligence, 22,* 49–68.

Noble, K. D., Robinson, N. M., & Gunderson, S. A. (1993). All rivers lead to the sea: A follow-up study of gifted young adults. *Roeper Review, 15,* 124–130.

Ochse, R. (1990). *Before the gates of excellence: The determinants of creative genius.* Cambridge: Cambridge University Press.

O'Connor, N., & Hermelin, B. (1991). Talents and preoccupations in idiot-savants. *Psychological Medicine, 21,* 959–964.

Oden, M. H. (1968). The fulfillment of promise: 40-year follow-up of the Terman gifted group. *Genetic Psychology Monographs, 77,* 3–93.

Ogbu, J. U. (1994). From cultural differences to differences in cultural frames of reference. In P. M. Greenfield & R. R. Cocking (Eds.), *Cross-cultural roots of minority child development.* Hillsdale, NJ: Erlbaum.

Okagaki, L., & Sternberg, R. J. (1993). Parental beliefs and children's school performance. *Child Development, 64,* 36–56.

Owens, W. A., Jr. (1953). Age and mental abilities: A longitudinal study. *Genetic Psychology Monographs, 48,* 3–54.

Page, T. (1996, December 22). 'Shine,' brief candle. *Washington Post,* pp. G1, G10–G11.

Patterson, C. J., Kupersmidt, J. B., & Vaden, N. A. (1990). Income level, gender, ethnicity, and household composition as predictors of children's school-based competence. *Child Development, 61,* 485–494.

Perkins, D. (1996). *Outsmarting IQ: The emerging science of learnable intelligence.* New York: Free Press.

Piaget, J. (1950). *The psychology of intelligence.* New York: Harcourt, Brace & World.

Plomin, R. (1990). *Nature and nurture: An introduction to behavior genetics.* Pacific Grove, CA: Brooks/Cole.

Ramey, C. T., & Ramey, S. L. (1992). Effective early intervention. *Mental Retardation, 30,* 337–345.

Reiss, S. (1994). Issues in defining mental retardation. *American Journal of Mental Retardation, 99,* 1–7.

Reznikoff, M., Domino, G., Bridges, C., & Honeyman, M. (1973). Creative abilities in identical and fraternal twins. *Behavior Genetics, 3,* 365–377.

Richards, R. (1996). Beyond Piaget: Accepting divergent, chaotic, and creative thought. In M. A. Runco (Ed.), *Creativity from childhood through adulthood: The developmental issues.* San Francisco: Jossey-Bass.

Robinson, N. M., & Janos, P. M. (1986). Psychological adjustment in a college-level program of marked academic acceleration. *Journal of Youth and Adolescence, 15,* 51–60.

Roeleveld, N., Zielhuis, G. A., & Gabreels, F. (1997). The prevalence of mental retardation: A critical review of recent literature. *Developmental Medicine and Child Neurology, 39,* 125–132.

Rose, S. A., & Feldman, J. F. (1995). Prediction of IQ and specific cognitive abilities at 11 years from infancy measures. *Developmental Psychology, 31,* 685–696.

Rose, S. A., Feldman, J. F., Wallace, I. F., & McCarton, C. (1989). Infant visual attention: Relation to birth status and developmental outcome during the first 5 years. *Developmental Psychology, 25,* 560–576.

Ross, R. T., Begab, M. J., Dondis, E. H., Giampiccolo, J. S., Jr., & Meyers, C. E. (1985). *Lives of the mentally retarded. A forty-year follow-up study.* Stanford, CA: Stanford University Press.

Runco, M. A. (1992). Children's divergent thinking and creative ideation. *Developmental Review, 12,* 233–264.

Russ, S. W. (1996). Development of creative processes in children. In M. A. Runco (Ed.), *Creativity from childhood through adulthood: The developmental issues.* San Francisco: Jossey-Bass.

Sacks, E. L. (1952). Intelligence scores as a function of experimentally established social relationships between child and examiner. *Journal of Abnormal and Social Psychology, 47,* 354–358.

Sameroff, A. J., Seifer, R., Baldwin, A., & Baldwin, C. (1993). Stability of intelligence from preschool to adolescence: The influence of social and family risk factors. *Child Development, 64,* 80–97.

Scarr, S., & Weinberg, R. A. (1983). The Minnesota adoption studies: Genetic differences and malleability. *Child Development, 54,* 260–267.

Schaie, K. W. (1983). The Seattle longitudinal study: A 21-year exploration of psychometric intelligence in adulthood. In K. W. Schaie (Ed.), *Longitudinal studies of adult psychological development.* New York: Guilford.

Schaie, K. W. (1989). The hazards of cognitive aging. *The Gerontologist, 29,* 484–493.

Schaie, K. W. (1990). Intellectual development in adulthood. In J. E. Birren & K. W. Schaie (Eds.), *The handbook of the psychology of aging* (3rd ed.). San Diego: Academic Press.

Schaie, K. W. (1996). *Intellectual development in adulthood. The Seattle Longitudinal Study.* New York: Cambridge University Press.

Schaie, K. W., & Willis, S. L. (1986). Can decline in adult intellectual functioning be reversed? *Developmental Psychology, 22,* 223–232.

Schalock, R. L., Holl, C., Elliott, B., & Ross, I. (1992). A longitudinal follow-up of graduates from a rural special education program. *Learning Disability Quarterly, 15,* 29–38.

Shurkin, J. N. (1992). *Terman's kids: The groundbreaking study of how the gifted grow up.* Boston: Little, Brown.

Simonoff, E., Bolton, P., & Rutter, M. (1996). Mental retardation: Genetic findings, clinical implications, and research agenda. *Journal of Child Psychology and Psychiatry and Allied Disciplines, 37,* 259–280.

Simonton, D. K. (1984). *Genius, creativity, and leadership: Historiometric inquiries.* Cambridge, MA: Harvard University Press.

Simonton, D. K. (1990). Creativity in the later years: Optimistic prospects for achievement. *Gerontologist, 30,* 626–631.

Simonton, D. K. (1991). Career landmarks in science: Individual differences and interdisciplinary contrasts. *Developmental Psychology, 27,* 119–130.

Smith, J., & Baltes, P. B. (1990). Wisdom-related knowledge: Age/cohort differences in response to life-planning problems. *Developmental Psychology, 26,* 494–505.

Spearman, C. (1927). *The abilities of man.* New York: Macmillan.

Staudinger, U. M., & Baltes, P. B. (1996). Interactive minds: A facilitative setting for wisdom-related performance? *Journal of Personality and Social Psychology, 71,* 746–762.

Staudinger, U. M., Smith, J., & Baltes, P. B. (1992). Wisdom-related knowledge in a life review task: Age differences and the role of professional specialization. *Psychology and Aging, 7,* 271–281.

Steele, C. M. (1997). A threat in the air: How stereotypes shape intellectual identity and performance. *American Psychologist, 52,* 613–629.

Steele, C. M., & Aronson, J. (1995). Stereotype threat and the intellectual test performance of African Americans. *Journal of Personality and Social Psychology, 69,* 797–811.

Sternberg, R. J. (1985). *Beyond IQ: A triarchic theory of human intelligence.* Cambridge: Cambridge University Press.

Sternberg, R. J. (1988). *The triarchic mind. A new theory of human intelligence.* New York: Viking.

Sternberg, R. J. (Ed.). (1990). *Wisdom: Its nature, origins, and development.* Cambridge: Cambridge University Press.

Sternberg, R. J. (1991). Theory-based testing of intellectual abilities: Rationale for the triarchic abilities test. In H. A. H. Rowe (Ed.), *Intelligence: Reconceptualization and measurement.* Hillsdale, NJ: Erlbaum.

Sternberg, R. J. (1992). Ability tests, measurements, and markets. *Journal of Educational Psychology, 84,* 134–140.

Sternberg, R. J. (1997). Educating intelligence: Infusing the triarchic theory into school instruction. In R. J. Sternberg & E. L. Grigorenko (Eds.), *Intelligence, heredity, and environment.* New York: Cambridge University Press.

Sternberg, R. J., & Berg, C. A. (1986). Quantitative integration: Definitions of intelligence: A comparison of the 1921 and 1986 symposia. In R. J. Sternberg & D. K. Detterman (Eds.), *What Is intelligence? Contemporary viewpoints on its nature and definition.* Norwood, NJ: Ablex.

Sternberg, R. J., & Lubart, T. I. (1996). Investing in creativity. *American Psychologist, 51,* 677–688.

Sternberg, R. J., Wagner, R. K., Williams, W. M., & Horvath, J. A. (1995). Testing common sense. *American Psychologist, 50,* 912–927.

Taylor, R. E., & Richards, S. B. (1991). Patterns of intellectual differences of black, Hispanic, and white children. *Psychology in the Schools, 28,* 5–9.

Terman, L. M. (1954). The discovery and encouragement of exceptional talent. *American Psychologist, 9,* 221–238.

Thorndike, R. L., Hagen, E. P., & Sattler, J. M. (1986). *The Stanford-Binet Intelligence Scale* (4th ed.). Chicago: Riverside Publishing.

Thorndike, R. M. (1997). The early history of intelligence testing. In D. P.

Flanagan, J. L. Genshaft, & P. L. Harrison (Eds.), *Contemporary intellectual assessment: Theories, tests, and issues.* New York: Guilford.

Thurstone, L. L. (1938). *Primary mental abilities.* Chicago: University of Chicago Press.

Thurstone, L. L., & Thurstone, T. G. (1941). Factorial studies of intelligence. *Psychometric Monographs,* No. 2.

Thurstone, L. L., & Thurstone, T. G. (1948). *SRA Primary Mental Abilities, Ages 11–17, Form AM.* Chicago: Science Research Associates.

Tomlinson-Keasey, C., & Little, T. D. (1990). Predicting educational attainment, occupational achievement, intellectual skill, and personal adjustment among gifted men and women. *Journal of Educational Psychology, 82,* 442–455.

Torrance, E. P. (1969). *Creativity.* San Rafael, CA: Dimensions.

Torrance, E. P. (1975). Creativity research in education: Still alive. In I. A. Taylor & J. W. Getzels (Eds.), *Perspectives in creativity.* Chicago: Aldine-Atherton.

Torrance, E. P. (1988). The nature of creativity as manifest in its testing. In R. J. Sternberg (Ed.), *The nature of creativity: Contemporary psychological perspectives.* Cambridge, England: Cambridge University Press.

Turkheimer, E. (1991). Individual and group differences in adoption studies of IQ. *Psychological Bulletin, 110,* 392–405.

Vincent, K. R. (1991). Black/white IQ differences: Does age make the difference? *Journal of Clinical Psychology, 47,* 266–270.

Wallace, A. (1986). *The prodigy: A biography of William Sidis.* New York: Dutton.

Wallach, M. A. (1971). *The intelligence-creativity distinction.* Morristown, NJ: General Learning Press.

Wallach, M. A., & Kogan, N. (1965). *Thinking in young children.* New York: Holt, Rinehart & Winston.

Weakliem, D., McQuillan, J., & Schauer, T. (1995). Toward meritocracy? Changing social-class differences in intellectual ability. *Sociology of Education, 68,* 271–286.

Wechsler, D. (1981). *Wechsler Adult Intelligence Scale—Revised.* New York: Psychological Corporation.

Wechsler, D. (1989). *WPPSI-R manual: Wechsler Preschool and Primary Scale of Intelligence—Revised.* San Antonio, TX: Psychological Corporation.

Wechsler, D. (1991). *Manual, WISC-III: Wechsler Intelligence Scale for Children—Third Edition.* San Antonio, TX: Psychological Corporation.

Weinberg, R. A., Scarr, S., & Waldman, I. D. (1992). The Minnesota transracial adoption study: A follow-up of IQ test performance at adolescence. *Intelligence, 16,* 117–135.

Winner, E. (1996). *Gifted children: Myths and realities.* New York: Basic Books.

Yeates, K. O., MacPhee, D., Campbell, F. A., & Ramey, C. T. (1983). Maternal IQ and home environment as determinants of early childhood intellectual competence: A developmental analysis. *Developmental Psychology, 19,* 731–739.

Yerkes, R. M. (1921). Psychological examining in the U.S. Army. *Memoirs: National Academy of Science, 15,* 1–890.

Zigler, E. (1995). Can we "cure" mild mental retardation among individuals in the lower socioeconomic stratum? *American Journal of Public Health, 85,* 302–304.

Zigler, E., Abelson, W. D., Trickett, P. K., & Seitz, V. (1982). Is an intervention program necessary to improve economically disadvantaged children's IQ scores? *Child Development, 53,* 340–348.

Zigler, E., & Hodapp, R. M. (1991). Behavioral functioning in individuals with mental retardation. *Annual Review of Psychology, 42,* 29–50.

Zigler, E., & Styfco, S. J. (1994). Head Start: Criticisms in a constructive context. *American Psychologist, 49,* 127–132.

CHAPTER 10: Self-Conceptions and Personality

Adams, G. R., & Archer, S. L. (1994). Identity: A precursor to intimacy. In S. L. Archer (Ed.), *Interventions for adolescent identity development.* Thousand Oaks, CA: Sage.

Archer, S. L. (1982). The lower age boundaries of identity development. *Child Development, 53,* 1551–1556.

Archer, S. L. (1992). A feminist's approach to identity research. In G. R. Adams, T. P. Gullotta, & R. Montemayor (Eds.), *Adolescent identity formation* (Advances in Adolescent Development, Vol. 4). Newbury Park, CA: Sage.

Asendorpf, J. B., & Van Aken, M. A. G. (1991). Correlates of the temporal consistency of personality patterns in childhood. *Journal of Personality, 59,* 689–703.

Asendorpf, J. B., Warkentin, V., & Baudonnière, P. M. (1996). Self-awareness and other-awareness: 2. Mirror self-recognition, social contingency awareness, and synchronic imitation. *Developmental Psychology, 32,* 313–321.

Bandura, A. (1986). *Social foundations of thought and action: A social cognitive theory.* Englewood Cliffs, NJ: Prentice-Hall.

Bengtson, V. L., Reedy, M. N., & Gordon, C. (1985). Aging and self-conceptions: Personality processes and social contexts. In J. E. Birren & K. W. Schaie (Eds.), *Handbook of the psychology of aging* (2nd ed.). New York: Van Nostrand Reinhold.

Bernal, M. E., & Knight, G. P. (1997). Ethnic identity of Latino children. In J. G. Garcia & M. C. Zea (Eds.), *Psychological interventions and research with Latino populations.* Boston: Allyn and Bacon.

Bertenthal, B. I., & Fischer, K. W. (1978). Development of self-recognition in the infant. *Developmental Psychology, 14,* 44–50.

Berzonsky, M. D., & Neimeyer, G. J. (1994). Ego identity status and identity processing orientation: The moderating role of commitment. *Journal of Research in Personality, 28,* 425–435.

Blasi, A., & Glodis, K. (1995). The development of identity: A critical analysis from the perspective of the self as subject. *Developmental Review, 15,* 404–433.

Block, J., & Robins, R. W. (1993). A longitudinal study of consistency and change in self-esteem from early adolescence to early adulthood. *Child Development, 64,* 909–923.

Bodily, C. L. (1991). "I have no opinions. I'm 73 years old": Rethinking ageism. *Journal of Aging Studies, 5,* 245–264.

Brandtstädter, J., & Greve, W. (1994). The aging self: Stabilizing and protective processes. *Developmental Review, 14,* 52–80.

Braungart, J. M., Plomin, R., DeFries, J. C., & Fulker, D. W. (1992). Genetic influence on tester-rated infant temperament as assessed by Bayley's Infant Behavior Record: Nonadoptive and adoptive siblings and twins. *Developmental Psychology, 28,* 40–47.

Brooks-Gunn, J., & Lewis, M. (1981). Infant social perception: Responses to pictures of parents and strangers. *Developmental Psychology, 17*, 647–649.

Brownell, C. A., & Carriger, M. S. (1990). Changes in cooperation and self/other differentiation during the second year. *Child Development, 61*, 1164–1174.

Buss, A. H., & Plomin, R. (1984). *Temperament: Early developing personality traits.* Hillsdale, NJ: Erlbaum.

Butler, R. (1990). The effects of mastery and competitive conditions on self-assessment at different ages. *Child Development, 61*, 201–210.

Butler, R., & Ruzany, N. (1993). Age and socialization effects on the development of social comparison motives and normative ability assessment in kibbutz and urban children. *Child Development, 64*, 532–543.

Butler, R. N. (1963). The life review: An interpretation of reminiscence in the aged. *Psychiatry, 26*, 65–76.

Butler, R. N. (1975). *Why survive? Being old in America.* New York: Harper & Row.

Campbell, E., Adams, G. R., & Dobson, W. R. (1984). Familial correlates of identity formation in late adolescence: A study of the predictive utility of connectedness and individuality in family relations. *Journal of Youth and Adolescence, 13*, 509–525.

Carmichael, C. M., & McGue, M. (1994). A longitudinal family study of personality change and stability. *Journal of Personality, 62*, 1–20.

Carstensen, L. L., & Freund, A. M. (1994). Commentary: The resilience of the aging self. *Developmental Review, 14*, 81–92.

Caspi, A. (1993). Why some maladaptive behaviors persist: Sources of continuity and change across the life course. In D. C. Funder, R. D. Parke, C. Tomlinson-Keasey, & K. Widaman (Eds.), *Studying lives through time: Personality and development.* Washington, DC: American Psychological Association.

Caspi, A., Elder, G. H., Jr., & Bem, D. J. (1987). Moving against the world: Life-course patterns of explosive children. *Developmental Psychology, 23*, 308–313.

Caspi, A., Elder, G. H., Jr., & Bem, D. J. (1988). Moving away from the world: Life-course patterns of shy children. *Developmental Psychology, 24*, 824–831.

Caspi, A., & Silva, P. A. (1995). Temperamental qualities at age three predict personality traits in young childhood: Longitudinal evidence from a birth cohort. *Child Development, 66*, 486–498.

Chess, S., & Thomas, A. (1984). *Origins and evolution of behavior disorders: From infancy to early adult life.* New York: Brunner/Mazel.

Cohler, B. J., & Musick, J. S. (1996). Adolescent parenthood and the transition to adulthood. In J. A. Graber, J. Brooks-Gunn, & A. C. Petersen (Eds.), *Transitions through adolescence: Interpersonal domains and context.* Mahwah, NJ: Erlbaum.

Coles, R. (1970). *Erik H. Erikson: The growth of his work.* Boston: Little, Brown.

Connolly, J. A., & Konarski, R. (1994). Peer self-concept in adolescence: Analysis of factor structure and of associations with peer experience. *Journal of Research on Adolescence, 4*, 385–403.

Connolly, J. J. (1991). Longitudinal studies of personality, psychopathology, and social behavior. In D. G. Gilbert & J. J. Connolly (Eds.), *Personality, social skills, and psychopathology. An individual differences approach.* New York: Plenum.

Cooley, C. H. (1902). *Human nature and the social order.* New York: Scribner's.

Coopersmith, S. (1967). *The antecedents of self-esteem.* San Francisco: W. H. Freeman.

Costa, P. T., Jr., & McCrae, R. R. (1988). Personality in adulthood: A six-year longitudinal study of self-reports and spouse ratings on the NEO Personality Inventory. *Journal of Personality and Social Psychology, 54*, 853–863.

Costa, P. T., Jr., & McCrae, R. R. (1992). Trait psychology comes of age. In T. B. Sonderegger (Ed.). *Nebraska symposium on motivation: Vol. 39. Psychology and aging.* Lincoln, NB: University of Nebraska Press.

Costa, P. T., Jr., & McCrae, R. R. (1994). Stability and change in personality from adolescence through adulthood. In C. F. Halverson, Jr., G. A. Kohnstamm, & R. P. Martin (Eds.), *The developing structure of temperament and personality from infancy to adulthood.* Hillsdale, NJ: Erlbaum.

Cote, J. E., & Levine, C. (1988). A critical examination of the ego identity status paradigm. *Developmental Review, 8*, 147–184.

Crain, R. M. (1996). The influence of age, race, and gender on child and adolescent multidimensional self-concept. In B. A. Bracken (Ed.), *Handbook of self-concept: Developmental, social, and clinical considerations.* New York: Wiley.

Damon, W. (1994). *Greater expectations: Overcoming the culture of indulgence in America's homes and schools.* New York: Free Press.

Damon, W., & Hart, D. (1982). The development of self-understanding from infancy through adolescence. *Child Development, 53*, 841–864.

Damon, W., & Hart, D. (1988). *Self-understanding in childhood and adolescence.* New York: Cambridge University Press.

DeBerry, K. M., Scarr, S., & Weinberg, R. (1996). Family racial socialization and ecological competence: Longitudinal assessments of African-American transracial adoptees. *Child Development, 67*, 2375–2399.

DeVries, M. W. (1984). Temperament and infant mortality among the Masai of East Africa. *American Journal of Psychiatry, 141*, 1189–1194.

Digman, J. M. (1990). Personality structure: Emergence of the 5-factor model. *Annual Review of Psychology, 41*, 417–440.

DiLalla, L. F., Kagan, J., Reznick, S. J. (1994). Genetic etiology of behavioral inhibition among 2-year-old children. *Infant Behavior and Development, 17*, 405–412.

Douglas, K., & Arenberg, D. (1978). Age changes, cohort differences, and cultural change on the Guilford-Zimmerman Temperament Survey. *Journal of Gerontology, 33*, 737–747.

Dyk, P. H., & Adams, G. R. (1990). Identity and intimacy: An initial investigation of three theoretical models using cross-lag panel correlations. *Journal of Youth and Adolescence, 19*, 91–110.

Eccles, J., Wigfield, A., Harold, R. D., & Blumefeld, P. (1993). Age and gender differences in children's self- and task perceptions during elementary school. *Child Development, 64*, 830–847.

Eder, R. A. (1989). The emergent personologist: The structure and content of 3½-, 5½-, and 7½-year-olds' concepts of themselves and other persons. *Child Development, 60*, 1218–1228.

Eder, R. A. (1990). Uncovering young children's psychological selves: Individual and developmental differences. *Child Development, 61,* 849–863.

Erikson, E. H. (1963). *Childhood and society* (2nd ed.). New York: Norton.

Erikson, E. H. (1968). *Identity: Youth and crisis.* New York: Norton.

Erikson, E. H. (1982). *The life cycle completed: A review.* New York: Norton.

Erikson, E. H., Erikson, J. M., & Kivnick, H. Q. (1986). *Vital involvement in old age.* New York: Norton.

Felson, R. B. (1990). Comparison processes in parents' and children's appraisals of academic performance. *Social Psychology Quarterly, 53,* 264–273.

Field, D., & Millsap, R. E. (1991). Personality in advanced old age: Continuity or change? *Journal of Gerontology: Psychological Sciences, 46,* P299–308.

Finn, S. E. (1986). Stability of personality self-ratings over 30 years: Evidence for an age/cohort interaction. *Journal of Personality and Social Psychology, 50,* 813–818.

Fleeson, W., & Heckhausen, J. (1997). More or less 'me' in past, present, and future: Perceived lifetime personality during adulthood. *Psychology and Aging, 12,* 125–136.

Floderus-Myrhed, B., Pedersen, N., & Rasmuson, I. (1980). Assessment of heritability for personality, based on a short-form of the Eysenck Personality Inventory: A study of 12,898 twin pairs. *Behavior Genetics, 10,* 153–162.

Fordham, S., & Ogbu, J. (1986). Black students' school success: Coping with the "burden of 'acting white.'" *Urban Review, 18,* 176–206.

Frey, K. S., & Ruble, D. N. (1985). What children say when the teacher is not around: Conflicting goals in social comparison and performance assessment in the classroom. *Journal of Personality and Social Psychology, 48,* 550–562.

Gallup, G. G., Jr. (1979). Self-recognition in chimpanzees and man: A developmental and comparative perspective. In M. Lewis & L. A. Rosenblum (Eds.), *Genesis of behavior: Vol. 2. The child and its family.* New York: Plenum.

Gambria, L. M. (1979–1980). Sex differences in daydreaming and related mental activity from the late teens to the early nineties. *International Journal of Aging and Human Development, 10,* 1–34.

Glick, M., & Zigler, E. (1985). Self-image: A cognitive-developmental approach. In R. L. Leahy (Ed.), *The development of the self.* Orlando, FL: Academic.

Grotevant, H. D., & Cooper, C. R. (1986). Individuation in family relations. A perspective on individual differences in the development of identity and role-taking skills in adolescence. *Human Development, 29,* 82–100.

Guerin, D., & Gottfried, A. W. (1994). Developmental stability and change in parent reports of temperament: A 10-year longitudinal investigation from infancy through preadolescence. *Merrill-Palmer Quarterly, 40,* 334–355.

Haan, N. (1981). Common dimensions of personality development: Early adolescence to middle life. In D. H. Eichorn, J. A. Clausen, N. Haan, M. P. Honzik, & P. H. Mussen (Eds.), *Present and past in middle life.* New York: Academic Press.

Haight, B. K. (1988). The therapeutic role of a structured life review process in homebound elderly subjects. *Journal of Gerontology: Psychological Sciences, 43,* P40–P44.

Haight, B. K. (1992). Long-term effects of a structured life review process. *Journal of Gerontology: Psychological Sciences, 47,* P312–P315.

Halverson, C. F., Jr., Kohnstamm, G. A., & Martin, R. P. (Eds.). (1994). *The developing structure of temperament and personality from infancy to adulthood.* Hillsdale, NJ: Erlbaum.

Harter, S. (1982). The perceived competence scale for children. *Child Development, 53,* 87–97.

Harter, S. (1986). Cognitive-developmental processes in the integration of concepts about emotions and the self. *Social Cognition, 4,* 119–151.

Harter, S. (1990). Processes underlying adolescent self-concept formation. In R. Montemayor, G. R. Adams, & T. P. Gullotta (Eds.), *From childhood to adolescence: A transitional period?* Newbury Park, CA: Sage.

Harter, S. (1996). Historical roots of contemporary issues involving self-concept. In B. A. Bracken (Ed.), *Handbook of self-concept: Developmental, social, and clinical considerations.* New York: Wiley.

Harter, S., Marold, D. B., Whitesell, N. R., & Cobbs, G. (1996). A model of the effects of perceived parent and peer support on adolescent false self-behavior. *Child Development, 67,* 360–374.

Harter, S., & Monsour, A. (1992). Development analysis of conflict caused by opposing attributes in the adolescent self-portrait. *Developmental Psychology, 28,* 251–260.

Harter, S., & Pike, R. (1984). The pictorial scale of perceived competence and social acceptance for young children. *Child Development, 55,* 1969–1982.

Hartup, W. W., & van Lieshout, C. F. M. (1995). Personality development in social context. *Annual Review of Psychology, 46,* 655–687.

Hattie, J. (1992). *Self-concept.* Hillsdale, NJ: Erlbaum.

Heckhausen, J., & Krueger, J. (1993). Developmental expectations for the self and most other people: Age grading in three functions of social comparison. *Developmental Psychology, 29,* 539–548.

Helson, R., & Wink, P. (1992). Personality change in women from the early 40s to the early 50s. *Psychology and Aging, 7,* 46–55.

Hill, S. D., & Tomlin, C. (1981). Self-recognition in retarded children. *Child Development, 52,* 145–150.

Hodgson, J. W., & Fischer, J. L. (1979). Sex differences in identity and intimacy development in college youth. *Journal of Youth and Adolescence, 8,* 37–50.

Hoffman, M., Levy-Shiff, R., & Malinsky, D. (1996). Stress and adjustment in the transition to adolescence: Moderating effects of neuroticism and extroversion. *Journal of Youth and Adolescence, 25,* 161–175.

Kagan, J. (1989). Temperamental contributions to social behavior. *American Psychologist, 44,* 668–674.

Kagan, J. (1994). *Galen's prophecy: Temperament in human nature.* New York: Basic Books.

Kagan, J., & Moss, H. A. (1962). *Birth to maturity.* New York: Wiley.

Keller, A., Ford, L. H., Jr., & Meachum, J. A. (1978). Dimensions of self-concept in preschool children. *Developmental Psychology, 14,* 483–489.

Kerr, M., Lambert, W. W., Stattin, H., & Klackenberg-Larsson, I. (1994). Stability of inhibition in a Swedish longitudinal sample. *Child Development, 10,* 443–458.

Kerwin, C., Ponterotto, J. G., Jackson, B. L., & Harris, A. (1993). Racial identity in biracial children: A qualitative investigation. *Journal of Counseling Psychology, 40,* 221–231.

Korn, S. J. (1984). Continuities and discontinuities in difficult/easy temperament: Infancy to young adulthood. *Merrill-Palmer Quarterly, 30,* 189–199.

Kroger, J. (1996). Identity, regression, and development. *Journal of Adolescence, 19,* 203–222.

Kroger, J. (1997). Gender and identity: The intersection of structure, content, and context. *Sex Roles, 36,* 747–770.

Labouvie-Vief, G., Chiodo, L. M., Goguen, L. A., Diehl, M., & Orwoll, L. (1995). Representations of self across the life span. *Psychology and Aging, 10,* 404–415.

Lamborn, S. D., Mounts, N. S., Steinberg, L., & Dornbusch, S. M. (1991). Patterns of competence and adjustment among adolescents from authoritative, authoritarian, indulgent, and neglectful families. *Child Development, 62,* 1049–1065.

Leon, G. R., Gillum, B., Gillum, R., & Gouze, M. (1979). Personality stability and change over a 30-year period—middle age to old age. *Journal of Consulting and Clinical Psychology, 47,* 517–524.

Lerner, J. V., Nitz, K., Talwar, R., & Lerner, R. M. (1989). On the functional significance of temperamental individuality: A developmental contextual view of the concept of goodness of fit. In G. A. Kohnstamm, J. E. Bates, & M. K. Rothbart (Eds.), *Temperament in childhood.* Chichester, England: Wiley.

Lewis, M., Alessandri, S. M., & Sullivan, M. W. (1990). Violation of expectancy, loss of control, and anger expressions in young infants. *Developmental Psychology, 26,* 745–751.

Lewis, M., & Brooks-Gunn, J. (1979). *Social cognition and the acquisition of self.* New York: Plenum.

Lewis, M., Sullivan, M. W., Stanger, C., & Weiss, M. (1989). Self-development and self-conscious emotions. *Child Development, 60,* 146–156.

Livesley, W. J., & Bromley, D. B. (1973). *Person perception in childhood and adolescence.* London: Wiley.

Livson, F. B. (1976). Patterns of personality in middle-aged women: A longitudinal study. *International Journal of Aging and Human Development, 7,* 107–115.

Livson, F. B. (1981). Paths to psychological health in the middle years: Sex differences. In D. H. Eichorn, J. A. Clausen, N. Haan, M. P. Honzik, & P. H. Mussen (Eds.), *Present and past in middle life.* New York: Academic Press.

Luster, T., & McAdoo, H. P. (1995). Factors related to self-esteem among African American youths: A secondary analysis of the High/Scope Perry Preschool data. *Journal of Research on Adolescence, 5,* 451–467.

Magnus, K., Diener, E., Fujita, F., & Payot, W. (1993). Extraversion and neuroticism as predictors of objective life events: A longitudinal analysis. *Journal of Personality and Social Psychology, 65,* 1046–1053.

Mahler, M. S., Pine, F., & Bergman, A. (1975). *The psychological birth of the infant.* New York: Basic Books.

Marcia, J. E. (1966). Development and validation of ego identity status. *Journal of Personality and Social Psychology, 3,* 551–558.

Markstrom-Adams, C. (1992). A consideration of intervening factors in adolescent identity formation. In G. R. Adams, T. P. Gullotta, & R. Montemayor (Eds.), *Adolescent identity formation* (Advances in Adolescent Development, Vol. 4). Newbury Park, CA: Sage.

Markstrom-Adams, C., & Adams, G. R. (1995). Gender, ethnic group, and grade differences in psychosocial functioning during middle adolescence. *Journal of Youth and Adolescence, 24,* 397–417.

Marsh, H. W., & Hattie, J. (1996). Theoretical perspectives on the structure of self-concept. In B. A. Bracken (Ed.), *Handbook of self-concept: Developmental, social, and clinical considerations.* New York: Wiley.

Marshall, S. (1995). Ethnic socialization of African American children: Implications for parenting, identity development, and academic achievement. *Journal of Youth and Adolescence, 24,* 377–396.

Maziade, M., Caron, C., Côté, R., Merette, C., Bernier, H., Laplante, B., Boutin, P., & Thivierge, J. (1990). Psychiatric status of adolescents who had extreme temperaments at age 7. *American Journal of Psychiatry, 147,* 1531–1536.

McAdams, D. P. (1993). *The stories we live by: Personal myths and the making of the self.* New York: Morrow.

McClelland, D. C. (1981). Is personality consistent? In A. I. Rabin, J. Aronoff, A. M. Barclay, & R. A. Zucker (Eds.), *Further explorations in personality.* New York: Wiley.

McCrae, R. R., & Costa, P. T., Jr. (1990). *Personality in adulthood.* New York: Guilford.

McCrae, R. R., & Costa, P. T., Jr. (1997). Personality trait structure as a human universal. *American Psychologist, 52,* 509–516.

McGue, M., Hirsch, B., & Lykken, D. T. (1993). Age and the self-perception of ability: A twin study analysis. *Psychology and Aging, 8,* 72–80.

McGuire, W. J., McGuire, C. V., Child, P., & Fujioka, T. (1978). Salience of ethnicity in the spontaneous self-concept as a function of one's ethnic distinctiveness in the social environment. *Journal of Personality and Social Psychology, 36,* 511–520.

Mead, G. H. (1934). *Mind, self, and society.* Chicago: University of Chicago Press.

Meilman, P. W. (1979). Cross-sectional age changes in ego identity status during adolescence. *Developmental Psychology, 15,* 230–231.

Mischel, W. (1973). Toward a cognitive social learning reconceptualization of personality. *Psychological Review, 80,* 252–283.

Mischel, W., & Shoda, Y. (1995). A cognitive-affective system theory of personality: Reconceptualizing situations, dispositions, dynamics, and invariance in personality structure. *Psychological Review, 102,* 246–268.

Molinari, V., & Reichlin, R. E. (1984–1985). Life review reminiscence in the elderly: A review of the literature. *International Journal of Aging and Human Development, 20,* 81–92.

Montemayor, R., & Eisen, M. (1977). The development of self-conceptions from childhood to adolescence. *Developmental Psychology, 13,* 314–319.

Mortimer, J. T., Finch, M. D., & Kumka, D. (1982). Persistence and change in development: The multidimensional self-concept. In P. B. Baltes & O. G. Brim, Jr. (Eds.), *Life-span development and behavior* (Vol. 4). New York: Academic.

Moss, H. A., & Susman, E. J. (1980). Longitudinal study of personality development. In O. G. Brim, Jr., & J. Kagan (Eds.), *Constancy and change in human development.* Cambridge, MA: Harvard University Press.

Munro, G., & Adams, G. R. (1977). Ego-identity formation in college students and working youth. *Developmental Psychology, 13,* 523–524.

Neugarten, B. L. (1977). Personality and aging. In J. E. Birren & K. W. Schaie (Eds.), *Handbook of the psychology of aging.* New York: Van Nostrand Reinhold.

Offer, D., & Schonert-Reichl, K. A. (1992). Debunking the myths of adolescence: Findings from recent research. *Journal of the American Academy of Child and Adolescent Psychiatry, 31,* 1003–1013.

Oosterwegel, A., & Oppenheimer, L. (1993). *The self-system: Developmental changes between and within self-concepts.* Hillsdale, NJ: Erlbaum.

Orlofsky, J. L. (1993). Intimacy status: Theory and research. In J. E. Marcia, A. S. Waterman, D. R. Matteson, S. L. Archer, & J. L. Orlofsky (Eds.), *Ego identity: A handbook for psychosocial research.* New York: Springer-Verlag.

Patterson, S. J., Sochting, I., & Marcia, J. E. (1992). The inner space and beyond: Women and identity. In G. R. Adams, T. P. Gullotta, & R. Montemayor (Eds.), *Adolescent identity formation* (Advances in Adolescent Development, Vol. 4). Newbury Park, CA: Sage.

Peterson, B. E., & Klohnen, E. C. (1995). Realization of generativity in two samples of women at midlife. *Psychology and Aging, 10,* 20–29.

Phinney, J. S. (1993). A three-stage model of ethnic identity development in adolescence. In M. E. Bernal & G. P. Knight (Eds.), *Ethnic identity: Formation and transmission among Hispanics and other minorities.* Albany: State University of New York Press.

Phinney, J. S. (1996). When we talk about American ethnic groups, what do we mean? *American Psychologist, 51,* 918–927.

Pipp, S., Easterbrooks, M. A., & Harmon, R. J. (1992). The relation between attachment and knowledge of self and mother in one-year-old infants to three-year-old infants. *Child Development, 63,* 738–750.

Pipp-Siegel, S., & Foltz, C. (1997). Toddlers' acquisition of self/other knowledge: Ecological and interpersonal aspects of self and other. *Child Development, 68,* 69–79.

Plomin, R., Pedersen, N. L., McClearn, G. E., Nesselroade, J. R., & Bergeman, C. (1988). EAS temperaments during the last half of the life span: Twins reared apart and twins reared together. *Psychology and Aging, 3,* 43–50.

Pomerantz, E. M., Ruble, D. N., Frey, K. S., & Grenlich, F. (1995). Meeting goals and confronting conflict: Children's changing perceptions of social comparison. *Child Development, 66,* 723–738.

Reznick, J. S., Kagan, J., Snidman, N., Gersten, M., Baak, K., & Rosenberg, A. (1986). Inhibited and uninhibited children: A follow-up study. *Child Development, 57,* 660–680.

Rochat, P., & Morgan, R. (1995). Spatial determinants of the perception of self-produced leg movements by 3- to 5-month-old infants. *Developmental Psychology, 31,* 626–636.

Rodin, J., & Langer, E. (1980). Aging labels: The decline of control and the fall of self-esteem. *Journal of Social Issues, 36,* 12–29.

Rogers, C. R. (1951). *Client-centered therapy: Its current practice, implications, and theory.* Boston: Houghton-Mifflin.

Rothbart, M. K., Derryberry, D., & Posner, M. I. (1994). A psychobiological approach to the development of temperament. In J. E. Bates & T. D. Wachs (Eds.), *Temperament: Individual differences at the interface of biology and behavior.* Washington, DC: American Psychological Association.

Rowe, D. C. (1994). *The limits of family influence: Genes, experience, and behavior.* New York: Guilford.

Ruble, D. N. (1983). The development of comparison processes and their role in achievement-related self-socialization. In E. T. Higgins, D. N. Ruble, & W. W. Hartup (Eds.), *Social cognition and social development: A sociocultural perspective.* New York: Cambridge University Press.

Ruth, J. E., & Coleman, P. (1996). Personality and aging: Coping and management of the self in later life. In J. E. Birren, K. W. Schaie, R. P. Abeles, M. Gatz, & T. A. Salthouse (Eds.), *Handbook of the psychology of aging* (4th ed.). San Diego, CA: Academic.

Ryff, C. D. (1991). Possible selves in adulthood and old age: A tale of shifting horizons. *Psychology and Aging, 6,* 286–295.

Samuels, C. (1986). Bases for the infant's development of self-awareness. *Human Development, 29,* 36–48.

Schaie, K. W., & Parham, I. A. (1976). Stability of adult personality traits: Fact or fable? *Journal of Personality and Social Psychology, 34,* 146–158.

Schiedel, D. G., & Marcia, J. E. (1985). Ego identity, intimacy, sex role orientation, and gender. *Developmental Psychology, 21,* 149–160.

Schmitz, S., Saudino, K. J., Plomin, R., Fulker, D. W., & DeFries, J. C. (1996). Genetic and environmental influences on temperament in middle childhood: Analyses of teacher and tester ratings. *Child Development, 67,* 409–422.

Scott, W. A., Scott, R., & McCabe, M. (1991). Family relationships and children's personality: A cross-cultural, cross-source comparison. *British Journal of Social Psychology, 30,* 1–20.

Secord, P. F., & Peevers, B. H. (1974). The development and attribution of person concepts. In T. Mischel (Ed.), *Understanding other persons.* Totowa, NJ: Rowman & Littlefield.

Seidman, E., Allen, L. R., Aber, J. L., Mitchell, C., & Feinman, J. (1994). The impact of school transitions in early adolescence on the self-system and perceived social context of poor urban youth. *Child Development, 65,* 507–522.

Selman, R. L. (1980). *The growth of interpersonal understanding.* New York: Academic Press.

Shirk, S., & Harter, S. (1996). Treatment of low self-esteem. In M. A. Reineke, F. M. Dattilio, & A. Freeman (Eds.), *Cognitive therapy with children and adolescents: A casebook for clinical practice.* New York: Guilford.

Simmons, R. G., Burgeson, R., Carlton-Ford, S., & Blyth, D. A. (1987). The impact of cumulative change in early adolescence. *Child Development, 58,* 1220–1234.

Simmons, R. G., Rosenberg, F., & Rosenberg, M. (1973). Disturbance in self-image at adolescence. *American Sociological Review, 38,* 553–568.

Spencer, M. B., & Markstrom-Adams, C. (1990). Identity processes among racial and ethnic minority children in America. *Child Development, 61,* 290–310.

Steinberg, L., Dornbusch, S. M., & Brown, B. B. (1992). Ethnic differences in adolescent achievement: An ecological perspective. *American Psychologist, 47,* 723–729.

Stern, D. N. (1983). The early development of schemas of self, other, and "self with other." In J. D. Lictenberg & S. Kaplan (Eds.), *Reflections on self psychology.* Hillsdale, NJ: Erlbaum.

Stevens, D. P., & Truss, C. V. (1985). Stability and change in adult personality over 12 and 20 years. *Developmental Psychology, 21,* 568–584.

Stipek, D., Gralinski, H., & Kopp, C. (1990). Self-concept development in the toddler years. *Developmental Psychology, 26,* 972–977.

Taft, L. B., & Nehrke, M. F. (1990). Reminiscence, life review, and ego integrity in nursing home residents. *International Journal of Aging and Human Development, 30,* 189–196.

Thomas, A., & Chess, S. (1977). *Temperament and development.* New York: Brunner/Mazel.

Thomas, A., & Chess, S. (1986). The New York longitudinal study: From infancy to early adult life. In R. Plomin & J. Dunn (Eds.), *The study of temperament: Changes, continuities, and challenges.* Hillsdale, NJ: Erlbaum.

Thomas, A., Chess, S., & Birch, H. G. (1970). The origin of personality. *Scientific American, 223,* 102–109.

Thorne, A., & Michaelieu, Q. (1996). Situating adolescent gender and self-esteem with personal memories. *Child Development, 67,* 1374–1390.

Tran, T. V., Wright, R., & Chatters, L. (1991). Health, stress, psychological resources, and subjective well-being among older blacks. *Psychology and Aging, 6,* 100–108.

Vaillant, G. E. (1977). *Adaptation to life.* Boston: Little, Brown.

Vaillant, G. E. (1983). Childhood environment and maturity of defense mechanisms. In D. Magnusson & V. L. Allen (Eds.), *Human development: An interactional perspective.* New York: Academic Press.

Vaillant, G. E., & Milofsky, E. (1980). Natural history of male psychological health. IX: Empirical evidence for Erikson's model of the life cycle. *American Journal of Psychiatry, 137,* 1348–1359.

van der Velde, M. E. G., Feij, J. A., & Taris, T. W. (1995). Stability and change of person characteristics among young adults: The effect of the transition from school to work. *Personality and Individual Differences, 18,* 89–99.

Verschueren, K., Marcoen, A., & Schoefs, V. (1996). The internal working model of self, attachment, and competence in five-year-olds. *Child Development, 67,* 2493–2511.

Vikem, R. J., Rose, R. J., Kaprio, J., & Koskenvuo, M. (1994). A developmental genetic analysis of adult personality: Extraversion and neuroticism from 18 to 59 years of age. *Journal of Personality and Social Psychology, 66,* 722–730.

Waterman, A. S. (1982). Identity development from adolescence to adulthood: An extension of theory and a review of research. *Developmental Psychology, 18,* 341–358.

Waterman, A. S. (1992). Identity as an aspect of optimal psychological functioning. In G. R. Adams, T. P. Gullotta, & R. Montemayor (Eds.), *Adolescent identity formation* (Advances in Adolescent Development, Vol. 4). Newbury Park, CA: Sage.

Webster, J. D., & Cappeliez, P. (1993). Reminiscence and autobiographical memory: Complimentary contexts for cognitive aging research. *Developmental Review, 13,* 54–91.

Whitbourne, S. K., & Tesch, S. A. (1985). A comparison of identity and intimacy statuses in college students and alumni. *Developmental Psychology, 21,* 1039–1044.

Wigfield, A., Eccles, J. S., Mac Iver, D., Reuman, D. A., & Midgley, C. (1991). Transitions during early adolescence: Changes in children's domain-specific self-perceptions and general self-esteem across the transition to junior high school. *Developmental Psychology, 27,* 552–565.

Wink, P. (1996). Transition from the early 40s to the early 50s in self-directed women. *Journal of Personality, 64,* 49–69.

Wong, P. T. P., & Watt, L. M. (1991). What types of reminiscence are associated with successful aging? *Psychology and Aging, 6,* 272–279.

Wrightsman, L. S. (1994). *Adult personality development: Vol. 1. Theories and concepts.* Thousand Oaks, CA: Sage.

CHAPTER 11: Gender Roles and Sexuality

Abrahams, B., Feldman, S. S., & Nash, S. C. (1978). Sex role self-concept and sex role attitudes: Enduring personality characteristics or adaptations to changing life situations? *Developmental Psychology, 14,* 393–400.

Alfieri, T., Ruble, D. N., Higgins, E. T. (1996). Gender stereotypes during adolescence: Developmental changes and the transition to junior high school. *Developmental Psychology, 32,* 1129–1137.

Arber, S., & Ginn, J. (1991). *Gender and later life: A sociological analysis of resources and constraints.* London, England: Sage.

Archer, J. (1991). The influence of testosterone on human aggression. *British Journal of Psychology, 82,* 1–28.

Archer, J. (1996). Sex differences in social behavior: Are the social role and evolutionary explanations compatible? *American Psychologist, 51,* 909–917.

Atkinson, J., & Huston, T. L. (1984). Sex role orientation and division of labor early in marriage. *Journal of Personality and Social Psychology, 46,* 330–345.

Baier, J. L., Rosenzweig, M. G., & Whipple, E. G. (1991). Patterns of sexual behavior, coercion, and victimization of university students. *Journal of College Student Development, 32,* 310–322.

Bailey, J. M., & Pillard, R. C. (1991). A genetic study of male sexual orientation. *Archives of General Psychiatry, 48,* 1089–1096.

Bailey, J. M., Pillard, R. C., Neale, M. C., & Agyei, Y. (1993). Heritable factors influence sexual orientation in women. *Archives of General Psychiatry, 50,* 217–223.

Bailey, J. M., & Zucker, K. J. (1995). Childhood sex-typed behavior and sexual orientation: A conceptual analysis and quantitative review. *Developmental Psychology, 31,* 43–55.

Baker, D. P., & Jones, D. P. (1992). Opportunity and performance: A sociological explanation for gender differences in academic mathematics. In J. Wrigley (Ed.), *Education and gender equality.* London: The Falmer Press.

Bakwin, H. (1973). Erotic feelings in infants and young children. *American Journal of Diseases of Children, 126,* 52–54.

Bandura, A. (1986). *Social foundations of thought and action: A social cognitive theory.* Englewood Cliffs, NJ: Prentice-Hall.

Baruch, G. K., & Barnett, R. C. (1986). Father's participation in family work and children's sex-role attitudes. *Child Development, 57,* 1210–1223.

Beal, C. R. (1994). *Boys and girls: The development of gender roles.* New York: McGraw-Hill.

Beitchman, J. H., Zucker, K. J., Hood, J. E., daCosta, G. A., & Akman, D. (1991). A review of the short-term effects of child sexual abuse. *Child Abuse and Neglect, 15,* pp. 537–556.

Bem, S. L. (1974). The measurement of psychological androgyny. *Journal of Consulting and Clinical Psychology, 42,* 155–162.

Bem, S. L. (1975). Sex-role adaptability: One consequence of psychological androgyny. *Journal of Personality and Social Psychology, 31,* 634–643.

Bem, S. L. (1978). Beyond androgyny: Some presumptuous prescriptions for a liberated sexual identity. In J. A. Sherman & F. L. Denmark (Eds.), *The psychology of women: Future directions in research.* New York: Psychological Dimensions.

Bem, S. L. (1979). Theory and measurement of androgyny: A reply to the Podhazer-Tetenbaum and Locksley-Colten critiques. *Journal of Personality and Social Psychology, 37,* 1047–1054.

Bem, S. L. (1989). Genital knowledge and gender constancy in preschool children. *Child Development, 60,* 649–662.

Benbow, C. P., & Arjmand, O. (1990). Predictors of high academic achievement in mathematics and science by mathematically talented students: A longitudinal study. *Journal of Educational Psychology, 82,* 430–441.

Berenbaum, S. A., & Hines, M. (1992). Early androgens are related to childhood sex-typed toy preferences. *Psychological Science, 3,* 203–206.

Bergen, D. J., & Williams, J. E. (1991). Sex stereotypes in the United States revisited: 1972–1988. *Sex Roles, 24,* 413–424.

Bernstein, A. C., & Cowan, P. A. (1975). Children's concepts of how people get babies. *Child Development, 46,* 77–91.

Best, D. L., Williams, J. E., Cloud, J. M., Davis, S. W., Robertson, L. S., Edwards, J. R., Giles, H., & Fowles, J.

(1977). Development of sex-trait stereotypes among young children in the United States, England, and Ireland. *Child Development, 48,* 1375–1384.

Bigler, R. S., & Liben, L. S. (1990). The role of attitudes and interventions in gender-schematic processing. *Child Development, 61,* 1440–1452.

Bjorkqvist, K. (1994). Sex differences in physical, verbal, and indirect aggression: A review of recent research. *Sex Roles, 30,* 177–188.

Blakemore, J. E. O., LaRue, A. A., & Olejnik, A. B. (1979). Sex-appropriate toy preference and the ability to conceptualize toys as sex-role related. *Developmental Psychology, 15,* 339–340.

Boldizar, J. P. (1991). Assessing sex-typing and androgyny in children: The Children's Sex-role Inventory. *Developmental Psychology, 27,* 505–515.

Bradbard, M. R., Martin, C. L., Endsley, R. C., & Halverson, C. F. (1986). Influence of sex stereotypes on children's exploration and memory: A competence versus performance distinction. *Developmental Psychology, 22,* 481–486.

Breedlove, S. M. (1994). Sexual differentiation of the human nervous system. *Annual Review of Psychology, 45,* 389–418.

Brody, N. (1985). The validity of tests of intelligence. In B. B. Wolman (Ed.), *Handbook of intelligence.* New York: Wiley.

Brooks-Gunn, J., & Furstenberg, F. F., Jr. (1989). Long-term implications of fertility-related behavior and family formation on adolescent mothers and their children. In K. Kreppner & R. M. Lerner (Eds.), *Family systems and life-span development.* Hillsdale, NJ: Erlbaum.

Broverman, I. K., Vogel, S. R., Broverman, D. M., Clarkson, F. E., & Rosenkrantz, P. S. (1972). Sex-role stereotypes: A current appraisal. *Journal of Social Issues, 28,* 59–78.

Burn, S., O'Neil, A. K., & Nederend, S. (1996). Childhood tomboyishness and adult androgyny. *Sex Roles, 34,* 419–428.

Burnham, D. K., & Harris, M. B. (1992). Effects of real gender and labeled gender on adults' perceptions of infants. *Journal of Genetic Psychology, 153,* 165–183.

Buss, D. M. (1995). Psychological sex

differences: Origins through sexual selection. *American Psychologist, 50,* 164–168.

Bussey, K., & Bandura, A. (1992). Self-regulatory mechanisms governing gender development. *Child Development, 63,* 1236–1250.

Byne, W. (1994). The biological evidence challenged. *Scientific American, 270,* 50–55.

Cahan, S., & Ganor, Y. (1995). Cognitive gender differences among Israeli children. *Sex Roles, 32,* 469–484.

Caldera, Y. M., Huston, A. C., & O'Brien, M. (1989). Social interactions and play patterns of parents and toddlers with feminine, masculine, and neutral toys. *Child Development, 60,* 70–76.

Carter, D. B., & Patterson, C. J. (1982). Sex roles as social conventions: The development of children's conceptions of sex-role stereotypes. *Developmental Psychology, 18,* 812–824.

Centers for Disease Control. (1992). Sexual behavior among high school students—United States, 1990. *Morbidity and Mortality Weekly Reports, 40,* 885–888.

Centers for Disease Control. (1997). Youth risk behavior surveillance: National College Health Risk Behavior Survey—United States, 1995. *Morbidity and Mortality Weekly Reports, 46,* 1–56.

Clements, M. (1996, March 17). Sex after 65. *Parade Magazine,* 4–6.

Coats, P. B., & Overman, S. J. (1992). Childhood play experiences of women in traditional and nontraditional professions. *Sex Roles, 26,* 261–271.

Colapinto, J. (1997, December 11). The true story of John Joan. *Rolling Stone,* 54–97.

Cole, P. M., & Putnam, F. W. (1992). Effect of incest on self and social functioning: A developmental psychopathology perspective. *Journal of Consulting and Clinical Psychology, 60,* 174–184.

Colley, A., Griffiths, D., Hugh, M., Landers, K., & Jaggli, N. (1996). Childhood play and adolescent leisure preferences: Associations with gender typing and the presence of siblings. *Sex Roles, 35,* 233–245.

Comfort, A. (1974). Sexuality in old age. *Journal of the American Geriatrics Society, 22,* 440–442.

Condry, J., & Condry, S. (1976). Sex differences: A study in the eye of the beholder. *Child Development, 47,* 812–819.

Cowan, C. P., Cowan, P. A., Heming, G., & Miller, N. B. (1991). Becoming a family: Marriage, parenting, and child development. In P. A. Cowan & M. Hetherington (Eds.), *Family transitions.* Hillsdale, NJ: Erlbaum.

Cowan, G., & Avants, S. K. (1988). Children's influence strategies: Structure, sex differences, and bilateral mother-child influences. *Child Development, 53,* 984–990.

Crick, N. R. (1996). The role of overt aggression, relational aggression, and prosocial behavior in the prediction of children's future social adjustment. *Child Development, 67,* 2317–2327.

Crockett, L. J., Bingham, C. R., Chopak, J. S., & Vicary, J. R. (1996). Timing of first sexual intercourse: The role of social control, social learning, and problem behavior. *Journal of Youth and Adolescence, 25,* 89–111.

Crouter, A. C., Manke, B. A., & McHale, S. M. (1995). The family context of gender intensification in early adolescence. *Child Development, 66* 317–329.

Dabbs, J. M., & Morris, R. (1990). Testosterone, social class, and antisocial behavior in a sample of 4,462 men. *Psychological Science, 1,* 209–211.

Damon, W. (1977). *The social world of the child.* San Francisco: Jossey-Bass.

Darling, C. A., Davidson, J. K., & Passarello, L. C. (1992). The mystique of first intercourse among college youth: The role of partners, contraceptive practices, and psychological reactions. *Journal of Youth and Adolescence, 21,* 97–117.

Darling, C. A., & Hicks, M. W. (1982). Parental influence on adolescent sexuality: Implications for parents and educators. *Journal of Youth and Adolescence, 11,* 231–245.

Deaux, K., & Major, B. (1990). A social-psychological model of gender. In D. L. Rhode (Ed.), *Theoretical perspectives on sexual difference.* New Haven, CT: Yale University Press.

de Gaston, J. P., Jensen, L., & Weed, S. (1995). A closer look at adolescent sexual activity. *Journal of Youth and Adolescence, 24,* 465–479.

Diamond, M., & Sigmundson, H. K. (1997). Sex reassignment at birth: Long-term review and clinical implications. *Archives of Pediatric and Adolescent Medicine, 151,* 298–304.

DiPietro, J. A., Hodgson, D. M., Costigan, K. A., Hilton, S. C., & Johnson, T. R. B. (1996). Fetal neurobehavioral development. *Child Development, 67,* 2553–2567.

Dittman, R. W., Kappes, M. E., & Kappes, M. H. (1992). Sexual behavior in adolescent and adult females with congenital adrenal hyperplasia. *Psychoneuroendocrinology, 17,* 153–170.

Dreyer, P. H. (1982). Sexuality during adolescence. In B. B. Wolman (Ed.), *Handbook of developmental psychology.* New York: Wiley.

Dunne, M. P., Martin, N. G., Statham, D. J., Slutske, W. S., Dinwiddie, S. H., Bucholz, K. K., Madden, P. A. F., & Heath, A. C. (1997). Genetic and environmental contributions to variance in age at first sexual intercourse. *Psychological Science, 8,* 211–216.

Eagly, A. H. (1995). The science and politics of comparing women and men. *American Psychologist, 50,* 145–158.

Eagly, A. H. (1987). *Sex differences in social behavior: A social-role interpretation.* Hillsdale, NJ: Erlbaum.

Eaton, W. O., & Enns, L. R. (1986). Sex differences in human motor activity level. *Psychological Bulletin, 100,* 19–28.

Eaton, W. O., & Yu, A. P. (1989). Are sex differences in child motor activity level a function of sex differences in maturational status? *Child Development, 60,* 1005–1011.

Eccles, J. S., Jacobs, J. E., & Harold, R. D. (1990). Gender role stereotypes, expectancy effects, and parents' socialization of gender differences. *Journal of Social Issues, 46,* 183–201.

Ehrhardt, A. A. (1985). The psychobiology of gender. In A. S. Rossi (Ed.), *Gender and the life course.* New York: Aldine.

Ehrhardt, A. A., & Baker, S. W. (1974). Fetal androgens, human central nervous system differentiation, and behavioral sex differences. In R. C. Friedman, R. M. Rickard, & R. L. Van de Wiele (Eds.), *Sex differences in behavior.* New York: Wiley.

Elias, J., & Gebhard, P. (1969). Sexuality and sexual learning in childhood. *Phi Delta Kappan, 50,* 401–405.

Ellis, L., Ames, M. A., Peckham, W., & Burke, D. M. (1988). Sexual orientation in human offspring may be altered by severe emotional distress during pregnancy. *Journal of Sex Research, 25,* 152–157.

Fabes, R. A., Eisenberg, N., & Miller, P. A. (1990). Maternal correlates of children's vicarious emotional responsiveness. *Developmental Psychology, 26,* 639–648.

Fagot, B. I. (1978). The influence of sex of child on parental reactions to toddler children. *Child Development, 49,* 459–465.

Fagot, B. I. (1985). Beyond the reinforcement principle: Another step toward understanding sex-role development. *Developmental Psychology, 21,* 1097–1104.

Fagot, B. I., & Leinbach, M. D. (1989). The young child's gender schema: Environmental input, internal organization. *Child Development, 60,* 663–672.

Fagot, B. I., & Leinbach, M. D. (1993). Gender-role development in young children: From discrimination to labeling. *Developmental Review, 13,* 205–224.

Fagot, B. I., Leinbach, M. D., & Hagan, R. (1986). Gender labeling and the adoption of sex-typed behaviors. *Developmental Psychology, 22,* 440–443.

Fagot, B. I., Leinbach, M. D., & O'Boyle, C. (1992). Gender labeling, gender stereotyping, and parenting behaviors. *Developmental Psychology, 28,* 225–230.

Feingold, A. (1988). Cognitive gender differences are disappearing. *American Psychologist, 43,* 95–103.

Feingold, A. (1992). Sex differences in variability in intellectual abilities: A new look at an old controversy. *Review of Educational Research, 62,* 61–84.

Feingold, A. (1994a). Gender differences in personality: A meta-analysis. *Psychological Bulletin, 116,* 429–456.

Feingold, A. (1994b). Gender differences in intellectual abilities: A cross-cultural perspective. *Sex Roles, 30,* 81–92.

Feldman, S. S., Biringen, Z. C., & Nash, S. C. (1981). Fluctuations of sex-related self-attributions as a function of stage of family life cycle. *Developmental Psychology, 17,* 24–35.

Felstein, I. (1983). Dysfunction: Origins and therapeutic approaches. In R. B. Weg (Ed.), *Sexuality in the later years: Roles and behavior.* New York: Academic Press.

Finkelhor, D., & Berliner, L. (1995). Research on the treatment of sexually abused children: A review and recommendations. *Journal of the American Academy of Child and Adolescent Psychiatry, 34,* 1408–1423.

Finkelhor, D., Hotaling, G. T., Lewis, I. A., & Smith, C. (1989). Sexual abuse and its relationship to later sexual satisfaction, marital status, religion, and attitudes. *Journal of Interpersonal Violence, 4,* 379–399.

Ford, C. S., & Beach, F. A. (1951). *Patterns of sexual behavior.* New York: Harper & Row.

Forrest, J. D., & Singh, S. (1990). The sexual and reproductive behavior of American women, 1982–1988. *Family Planning Perspectives, 22,* 206–214.

Frey, K. S., & Ruble, D. N. (1992). Gender constancy and the cost of sex-typed behavior: A test of the conflict hypothesis. *Developmental Psychology, 28,* 714–721.

Furstenberg, F. F., Jr., Brooks-Gunn, J., & Morgan, S. P. (1987). *Adolescent mothers in later life.* New York: Cambridge University Press.

Furstenberg, F. F., Jr., Lincoln, R., & Menken, J. (Eds.). (1981). *Teenage sexuality, pregnancy, and childbearing.* Philadelphia: University of Pennsylvania Press.

Galambos, N. L., Almeida, D. M., & Petersen, A. C. (1990). Masculinity, femininity, and sex role attitudes in early adolescence: Exploring gender intensification. *Child Development, 61,* 1905–1914.

Gandelman, R. (1992). *Psychobiology of behavioral development.* New York: Oxford University Press.

Garnets, L., & Kimmel, D. (1991). Lesbian and gay male dimensions of the psychological study of human diversity. In J. D. Goodchilds (Ed.), *Psychological perspectives on human diversity in America.* Washington, DC: American Psychological Association.

Goldman, R., & Goldman, J. (1982). *Children's sexual thinking: A comparative study of children aged 5 to 15 years in Australia, North America, Britain, and Sweden.* London: Routledge and Kegan Paul.

Golombok, S., & Tasker, F. (1996). Do parents influence the sexual orientation of their children? Findings from a longitudinal study of lesbian families. *Developmental Psychology, 32,* 3–11.

Gordon, B. N., Schroeder, C. S., & Abrams, J. M. (1990). Children's knowledge of sexuality: A comparison of sexually abused and non-abused children. *American Journal of Orthopsychiatry, 60,* 250–257.

Green, R. (1987). *The "sissy boy syndrome" and the development of homosexuality.* New Haven, CT: Yale University Press.

Gutmann, D. (1987). *Reclaimed powers: Toward a new psychology of men and women in later life.* New York: Basic Books.

Gutmann, D. (1997). *The human elder in nature, culture, and society.* Boulder, CO: Westview Press.

Hall, J. A., & Halberstadt, A. G. (1980). Masculinity and femininity in children: Development of the Children's Personal Attributes Questionnaire. *Developmental Psychology, 16,* 270–280.

Hamer, D. H., Hu, S., Magnuson, V. L., Hu, N., & Pattatucci, A. M. L. (1993). A linkage between DNA markers on the X chromosome and male sexual orientation. *Science, 261,* 321–327.

Hamilton, V. L., Blumenfeld, P. C., Akoh, H., & Miura, K. (1991). Group and gender in Japanese and American elementary classrooms. *Journal of Cross-Cultural Psychology, 22,* 317–346.

Henker, B., & Whalen, C. K. (1989). Hyperactivity and attention deficits. *American Psychologist, 44,* 216–223.

Herdt, G. H., & Davidson, J. (1988). The Sambia "turnim-man": Sociocultural and clinical aspects of gender formation in male pseudohermaphrodites with 5-alpha-reductase deficiency in Papua New Guinea. *Archives of Sexual Behavior, 17,* 33–56.

Hetherington, E. M., & Frankie, G. (1967). Effect of parental dominance, warmth, and conflict on imitation in children. *Journal of Personality and Social Psychology, 6,* 119–125.

Hill, J. P., & Lynch, M. E. (1983). The intensification of gender-related role expectations during early adolescence. In J. Brooks-Gunn & A. C. Petersen (Eds.), *Girls at puberty: Biological and psychosocial perspectives.* New York: Plenum.

Huston, A. C. (1983). Sex-typing. In E. M. Hetherington (Vol. Ed.; P. H. Mussen, General Ed.), *Handbook of child psychology: Vol. 4. Socialization, personality, and social development.* New York: Wiley.

Huston, A. C. (1985). The development of sex typing: Themes from recent research. *Developmental Review, 5,* 1–17.

Hyde, J. S. (1984). How large are sex differences in aggression? A developmental meta-analysis. *Developmental Psychology, 20,* 722–736.

Hyde, J. S., Fennema, E., & Lamon, S. J. (1990). Gender differences in mathematics performance: A meta-analysis. *Psychological Bulletin, 107,* 139–155.

Hyde, J. S., & Linn, M. C. (1988). Gender differences in verbal ability: A meta-analysis. *Psychological Bulletin, 104,* 53–69.

Hyde, J. S., & Plant, E. A. (1995). Magnitude of psychological gender differences: Another side to the story. *American Psychologist, 50,* 159–161.

Imperato-McGinley, J., Peterson, R. E., Gautier, T., & Sturla, E. (1979). Androgens and the evolution of male gender identity among male pseudohermaphrodites with 5a-reductase deficiency. *New England Journal of Medicine, 300,* 1233–1237.

Intons-Peterson, M. J., & Reddel, M. (1984). What do people ask about a neonate? *Developmental Psychology, 20,* 358–359.

Jacklin, C. N. (1989). Male and female: Issues of gender. *American Psychologist, 44,* 127–133.

Jacklin, C. N., & Maccoby, E. E. (1978). Social behavior at 33 months in same-sex and mixed-sex dyads. *Child Development, 49,* 557–569.

Jacobs, J. E., & Eccles, J. S. (1992). The impact of mothers' gender-role stereotypic beliefs on mothers' and children's ability perceptions. *Journal of Personality and Social Psychology, 63,* 932–944.

Jung, C. G. (1933). *Modern man in search of a soul* (W. S. Dell & C. F. Baynes, Trans.). New York: Harcourt, Brace and Company.

Jussim, L., & Eccles, J. S. (1992). Teacher expectations II: Construction and reflection of student achievement. *Journal of Personality and Social Psychology, 63,* 947–961.

Katcher, A. (1955). The discrimination of sex differences by young children. *Journal of Genetic Psychology, 87,* 131–143.

Katz, P. A. (1986). Modification of children's gender-stereotyped behavior: General issues and research considerations. *Sex Roles, 14,* 591–602.

Katz, P. A., & Walsh, P. V. (1991). Modification of children's gender-stereotyped behavior. *Child Development, 62,* 338–351.

Kaye, R. A. (1993). Sexuality in the later years. *Aging and Society, 13,* 415–426.

Kendall-Tackett, K. A., Williams, L. M., & Finkelhor, D. (1993). Impact of sexual abuse on children: A review and synthesis of recent empirical studies. *Psychological Bulletin, 113,* 164–180.

Kerns, K. A., & Berenbaum, S. A. (1991). Sex differences in spatial ability in children. *Behavior Genetics, 21,* 383–396.

Kimura, D. (1992). Sex differences in the brain. *Scientific American, 267,* 119–125.

Knight, G. P., Fabes, R. A., & Higgins, D. A. (1996). Concerns about drawing causal inferences from meta-analyses: An example in the study of gender differences in aggression. *Psychological Bulletin, 119,* 410–421.

Kohlberg, L. (1966). A cognitive-developmental analysis of children's sex-role concepts and attitudes. In E. E. Maccoby (Ed.), *The development of sex differences.* Stanford, CA: Stanford University Press.

Konker, C. (1992). Rethinking child sexual abuse: An anthropological perspective. *American Journal of Orthopsychiatry, 62,* 147–153.

Kortenhaus, C. M., & Demarest, J. (1993). Gender role stereotyping in children's literature: An update. *Sex Roles, 28,* 219–232.

Kovacs, D. M., Parker, J. G., & Hoffman, L. W. (1996). Behavioral, affective, and social correlates of involvement in cross-sex friendships in elementary school. *Child Development, 67,* 2269–2286.

Kuhn, D., Nash, S. C., & Brucken, L. (1978). Sex-role concepts of two- and three-year-olds. *Child Development, 49,* 445–451.

Laumann, E. O., Gagnon, J. H., Michael, R. T., & Michaels, S. (1994). *The social organization of sexuality: Sexual practices in the United States.* Chicago: University of Chicago Press.

Leaper, C. (1994). *Childhood gender segregation: Causes and consequences* (New Directions for Child Development, Vol. 65). San Francisco: Jossey-Bass.

Lee, V. E., & Bryk, A. S. (1986). Effects of single-sex secondary schools on student achievement and attitudes. *Journal of Educational Psychology, 78,* 381–395.

Lee, V. E., Marks, H. M., & Byrd, T. (1994). Sexism in single-sex and co-educational independent secondary school classrooms. *Sociology of Education, 67,* 92–120.

Leigh, B. C., Morrison, D. M., Trocki, K., & Temple, M. T. (1994). Sexual behavior of American adolescents: Results from a U.S. national survey. *Journal of Adolescent Health, 15,* 117–125.

LePore, P. C., & Warren, J. R. (1997). A comparison of single-sex and co-educational Catholic secondary schooling: Evidence from the National Educational Longitudinal Study of 1988. *American Educational Research Journal, 34,* 485–511.

Leung, A. K. C., & Robson, W. L. M. (1993). Childhood masturbation. *Clinical Pediatrics, 32,* 238–241.

LeVay, S. (1996). *Queer science: The use and abuse of research into homosexuality.* Cambridge, MA: The MIT Press.

Leve, L. D., & Fagot, B. I. (1997). Gender-role socialization and discipline processes in one- and two-parent families. *Sex Roles, 36,* 1–21.

Lewis, M., & Weinraub, M. (1979). Origins of early sex-role development. *Sex Roles, 5,* 135–153.

Liben, L. S., & Signorella, M. L. (1993). Gender-schematic processing in children: The role of initial interpretations of stimuli. *Developmental Psychology, 29,* 141–149.

Liebert, R. M., & Sprafkin, J. (1988). *The early window: Effects of television on children and youth* (3rd ed.). New York: Pergamon.

Linn, M. C., & Petersen, A. C. (1985). Emergence and characterization of sex differences in spatial ability: A meta-analysis. *Child Development, 56,* 1479–1498.

Lobel, T., Slone, M., & Winch, G. (1997). Masculinity, popularity, and self-esteem among Israeli preadolescent girls. *Sex Roles, 36,* 395–408.

Lockheed, M. E. (1986). Reshaping the social order: The case of gender segregation. *Sex Roles, 14,* 617–628.

Loehlin, J. C. (1992). *Genes and environment in personality development* (Individual Differences and Development Series, Vol. 2). Newbury Park, CA: Sage.

Loewenstein, G., & Furstenburg, F. (1991). Is teenage sexual behavior rational? *Journal of Applied Social Psychology, 21,* 957–986.

Lorber, J. (1986). Dismantling Noah's ark. *Sex Roles, 14,* 567–580.

Luecke-Aleksa, D., Anderson, D. R., Collins, P. A., & Schmitt, K. L. (1995). Gender constancy and television viewing. *Developmental Psychology, 31,* 773–780.

Lytton, H., & Romney, D. M. (1991). Parents' differential socialization of boys and girls: A meta-analysis. *Psychological Bulletin, 109,* 267–296.

Maccoby, E. E. (1980). *Social development.* New York: Harcourt Brace Jovanovich.

Maccoby, E. E. (1990). Gender and relationships: A developmental account. *American Psychologist, 45,* 513–520.

Maccoby, E. E., & Jacklin, C. N. (1974). *The psychology of sex differences.* Stanford, CA: Stanford University Press.

Maccoby, E. E., & Jacklin, C. N. (1987). Gender segregation in childhood. In H. W. Reese (Ed.), *Advances in child development and behavior* (Vol. 20). Orlando, FL: Academic Press.

MacFarlane, A. (1977). *The psychology of childbirth.* Cambridge, MA: Harvard University Press.

Marcus, D. E., & Overton, W. F. (1978). The development of cognitive gender constancy and sex-role preferences. *Child Development, 49,* 434–444.

Marsh, H. W. (1989). Effects of attending single-sex and coeducational high schools on achievement, attitudes, behaviors, and sex differences. *Journal of Educational Psychology, 81,* 70–85.

Marsiglio, W., & Donnelly, D. (1991). Sexual relations in later life: A national study of married persons. *Journal of Gerontology: Social Sciences, 46,* S338–S344.

Martin, C. L. (1990). Attitudes and expectations about children with non-traditional gender roles. *Sex Roles, 22,* 151–165.

Martin, C. L., & Halverson, C. F., Jr. (1981). A schematic processing model of sex typing and stereotyping in children. *Child Development, 52,* 1119–1134.

Martin, C. L., & Halverson, C. F., Jr. (1983). The effects of sex-typing schemas on young children's memory. *Child Development, 54,* 563–574.

Martin, C. L., & Halverson, C. F., Jr. (1987). The roles of cognition in sex-roles and sex-typing. In D. B. Carter (Ed.), *Current conceptions of sex roles and sex-typing: Theory and research.* New York: Praeger.

Masters, W. H., & Johnson, V. E. (1966). *Human sexual response.* Boston: Little, Brown.

Masters, W. H., & Johnson, V. E. (1970). *Human sexual inadequacy.* Boston: Little, Brown.

McClintock, M. K., & Herdt, G. (1996). Rethinking puberty: The development of sexual attraction. *Current Directions in Psychological Science, 5,* 178–183.

McGhee, P. E., & Frueh, T. (1980). Television viewing and the learning of sex-role stereotypes. *Sex Roles, 6,* 179–188.

Meyer-Bahlburg, H. F. L., Ehrhardt, A. A., Rosen, L. R., Gruen, R. S. (1995). Prenatal estrogens and the development of homosexual orientation. *Developmental Psychology, 31,* 12–21.

Mischel, W. (1970). Sex-typing and socialization. In P. H. Mussen (Ed.), *Carmichael's manual of child psychology* (Vol. 2). New York: Wiley.

Mitchell, J. E., Baker, L. A., & Jacklin, C. N. (1989). Masculinity and femininity in twin children: Genetic and environmental factors. *Child Development, 60,* 1475–1485.

Moller, L. C., & Serbin, L. A. (1996). Antecedents of toddler gender segregation: Cognitive consonance, gender-typed toy preferences, and behavioral compatibility. *Sex Roles, 35,* 445–460.

Money, J. (1985). Pediatric sexology and hermaphroditism. *Journal of Sex and Marital Therapy, 11,* 139–156.

Money, J. (1988). *Gay, straight, and in-between: The sexology of erotic orientation.* New York: Oxford University Press.

Money, J., & Ehrhardt, A. (1972). *Man and woman, boy and girl.* Baltimore: Johns Hopkins University Press.

Money, J., & Tucker, P. (1975). *Sexual signatures: On being a man or a woman.* Boston: Little, Brown.

Morrison, D. M. (1985). Adolescent contraceptive behavior: A review. *Psychological Bulletin, 98,* 538–568.

Munroe, R. H., Shimmin, H. S., & Munroe, R. L. (1984). Gender understanding and sex-role preferences in four cultures. *Developmental Psychology, 20,* 673–682.

Mussen, P. H., & Rutherford, E. (1963). Parent-child relations and parental personality in relation to young children's sex-role preferences. *Child Development, 34,* 589–607.

Myers, J. K., Weissman, M. M., Tischler, G. L., Holzer, C. E., III, Leaf, P. J., & Orvaschel, H. (1984). Six-month prevalence of psychiatric disorders in three communities. *Archives of General Psychiatry, 41,* 959–967.

Oliver, M. B., & Hyde, J. S. (1993). Gender differences in sexuality: A meta-analysis. *Psychological Bulletin, 114,* 29–51.

Parsons, J. E., Adler, T. F., & Kaczala, C. M. (1982). Socialization of achievement attitudes and beliefs: Parental influences. *Child Development, 53,* 310–321.

Parsons, T. (1955). Family structure and the socialization of the child. In T. Parsons & R. F. Bales (Eds.), *Family socialization and interaction processes.* Glencoe, IL: Free Press.

Patterson, C. J. (1992). Children of lesbian and gay parents. *Child Development, 63,* 1025–1042.

Paul, J. P. (1993). Childhood cross-gender behavior and adult homosexuality: The resurgence of biological models of sexuality. *Journal of Homosexuality, 24,* 41–54.

Persson, G., & Svanborg, A. (1992). Marital coital activity in men at the age of 75: Relation to somatic, psychiatric, and social factors at the age of 70. *Journal of the American Geriatrics Society, 40,* 439–444.

Pleck, J. H. (1981). *The myth of masculinity.* Cambridge, MA: MIT Press.

Pleck, J. H. (1985). *Working wives/working husbands.* Beverly Hills, CA: Sage.

Pomerleau, A., Bolduc, D., Malcuit, G., & Cossette, L. (1990). Pink or blue: Environmental gender stereotypes in the first two years of life. *Sex Roles, 22,* 359–367.

Poulin-Dubois, D., Serbin, L. A., Kenyon, B., & Derbyshire, A. (1994). Infants' intermodal knowledge about gender. *Developmental Psychology, 30,* 436–442.

Purifoy, F. E., Grodsky, A., & Giambra, L. M. (1992). The relationship of sexual daydreaming to sexual activity, sexual drive, and sexual attitudes for women across the life-span. *Archives of Sexual Behavior, 21,* 369–385.

Raz, S., Goldstein, R., Hopkins, T. L., Lauterbach, M. D., Shah, F., Porter, C. L., Riggs, W. W., Magill, L. H., & Sander, C. J. (1994). Sex differences in early vulnerability to cerebral injury and their neurobehavioral implications. *Psychobiology, 22,* 244–253.

Reid, P. T., & Trotter, K. H. (1993). Children's self-presentations with infants: Gender and ethnic comparisons. *Sex Roles, 29,* 171–181.

Reinisch, J. M., Sanders, S. A., Hill, C. A., & Ziemba-Davis, M. (1992). High-risk sexual behavior among heterosexual undergraduates at a midwestern university. *Family Planning Perspectives, 24,* 116.

Resnick, S. M., Berenbaum, S. A., Gottesman, I. I., & Bouchard, T. J. (1986). Early hormonal influences on cognitive functioning in congenital adrenal hyperplasia. *Developmental Psychology, 22,* 191–198.

Rheingold, H. L., & Cook, K. V. (1975). The contents of boys' and girls' rooms as an index of parents' behavior. *Child Development, 46,* 459–463.

Roberts, L. R., Sarigiani, P. A., Petersen, A. C., & Newman, J. L. (1990). Gender differences in the relationship between achievement and self image during early adolescence. *Journal of Early Adolescence, 10,* 159–175.

Robinson, C. C., & Morris, J. T. (1986). The gender-stereotyped nature of Christmas toys received by 36-, 48-, and 60-month-old children: A comparison between nonrequested vs. requested toys. *Sex Roles, 15,* 21–32.

Robinson, I., Ziss, K., Ganza, B., Katz, S., & Robinson, E. (1991). Twenty years of sexual revolution, 1965–1985: An update. *Journal of Marriage and the Family, 53,* 216–220.

Robinson, P. K. (1983). The sociological perspective. In R. B. Weg (Ed.), *Sexuality in the later years: Roles and behavior.* New York: Academic Press.

Rosenwasser, S. M., Lingenfelter, M., & Harrington, A. F. (1989). Nontraditional gender role portrayals on television and children's gender role perceptions. *Journal of Applied Developmental Psychology, 10,* 97–105.

Ross, C. A., Miler, S. D., Bjornson, L., Reagor, P., Fraser, G. A., & Anderson, G. (1991). Abuse histories in 102 cases of multiple personality disorder. *Canadian Journal of Psychiatry, 36,* 97–101.

Rubin, J. Z., Provenzano, F. J., & Luria, Z. (1974). The eye of the beholder: Parents' views on sex of newborns. *American Journal of Orthopsychiatry, 44,* 512–519.

Rubinow, D. R., & Schmidt, P. J. (1996). Androgens, brain, and behavior. *American Journal of Psychiatry, 153,* 974–984.

Sadker, M., & Sadker, D. (1994). *Failing at fairness: How America's schools cheat girls.* New York: Charles Scribner's Sons.

Savin-Williams, R. C. (1995). An exploratory study of pubertal maturation timing and self-esteem among gay and bisexual male youths. *Developmental Psychology, 31,* 56–64.

Schiavi, R. C., Schreiner-Engel, P., White, D., & Mandeli, J. (1991). The relationship between pituitary-gonadal function and sexual behavior in healthy aging men. *Psychosomatic Medicine, 53,* 363–374.

Shaffer, D. R., Pegalis, L. J., & Cornell, D. P. (1992). Gender and self-disclosure revisited: Personal and contextual variations in self-disclosure to same-sex acquaintances. *Journal of Social Psychology, 132,* 307–315.

Serbin, L. A., Powlishta, K. K., & Gulko, J. (1993). The development of sex typing in middle childhood. *Monographs of the Society for Research in Child Development, 58* (2, Serial No. 232).

Serbin, L. A., Tonick, I. J., & Sternglanz, S. H. (1977). Shaping cooperative cross-sex play. *Child Development, 48,* 924–929.

Shepard, R. N., & Metzler, J. (1971). Mental rotation of three-dimensional objects. *Science, 171,* 701–703.

Sigelman, C. K., Carr, M. B., & Begley, N. L. (1986). Developmental changes in the influence of sex-role stereotypes on person perception. *Child Study Journal, 16,* 191–205.

Signorella, M. L., Bigler, R. S., & Liben, L. S. (1993). Developmental differences in children's gender schemata about others: A meta-analytic review. *Developmental Review, 13,* 147–183.

Signorella, M. L., Frieze, I. H., & Hershey, S. W. (1996). Single-sex versus mixed-sex classes and gender schemata in children and adolescents. *Psychology of Women Quarterly, 20,* 599–607.

Signorielli, N., & Lears, M. (1992). Children, television, and conceptions about chores: Attitudes and behaviors. *Sex Roles, 27,* 157–170.

Slaby, R. G., & Frey, K. S. (1975). Development of gender constancy and selective attention to same-sex models. *Child Development, 46,* 849–856.

Smith, P. K., & Daglish, L. (1977). Sex differences in parent and infant behavior in the home. *Child Development, 48,* 1250–1254.

Smith, T. W. (1991). Adult sexual behavior in 1989: Number of partners, frequency of intercourse and risk of AIDS. *Family Planning Perspectives, 23,* 102–107.

Spence, J. T., & Hall, S. K. (1996). Children's gender-related self-perceptions, activity preferences, and occupational stereotypes: A test of three models of gender constructs. *Sex Roles, 35,* 659–691.

Spence, J. T., & Helmreich, R. L. (1978). *Masculinity and femininity: Their psychological dimensions, correlates, and antecedents.* Austin: University of Texas Press.

Sroufe, L. A., Bennett, C., Englund, M., Urban, J., & Shulman, S. (1993). The significance of gender boundaries in preadolescence: Contemporary correlates and antecedents of boundary violation and maintenance. *Child Development, 64,* 455–466.

Starr, B. D., & Weiner, M. B. (1981). *The Starr-Weiner report on sex and sexuality in the mature years.* New York: Stein & Day.

Stern, M., & Karraker, K. H. (1989). Sex stereotyping of infants: A review of gender labeling studies. *Sex Roles, 20,* 501–522.

Stevenson, M. R., & Black, K. N. (1988). Paternal absence and sex-role development: A meta-analysis. *Child Development, 59,* 793–814.

Stoddart, T., & Turiel, E. (1985). Children's concepts of cross-gender activities. *Child Development, 56,* 1241–1252.

Stumpf, H., & Stanley, J. C. (1996). Gender-related differences on the College Board's Advanced Placement and Achievement Tests, 1982–1992. *Journal of Educational Psychology, 88,* 353–364.

Taylor, M. G. (1996). The development of children's beliefs about social and biological aspects of gender differences. *Child Development, 67,* 1555–1571.

Tharinger, D. (1990). Impact of child sexual abuse on developing sexuality. *Professional Psychology: Research and Practice, 21,* 331–337.

Thompson, S. K. (1975). Gender labels and early sex-role development. *Child Development, 46,* 339–347.

Thorne, B. (1993). *Gender play: Girls and boys in school.* New Brunswick, NJ: Rutgers University Press.

Trickett, P. K., & Putnam, F. W. (1993). Impact of child sexual abuse on females: Toward a developmental, psychobiological integration. *Psychological Science, 4,* 81–87.

Turner, P. J., & Gervai, J. (1995). A multidimensional study of gender typing in preschool children and their parents: Personality, attitudes, preferences, behavior, and cultural differences. *Developmental Psychology, 31,* 759–772.

Turner-Bowker, D. M. (1996). Gender stereotyped descriptors in children's picture books: Does "Curious Jane" exist in the literature? *Sex Roles, 35,* 461–488.

Twenge, J. M. (1997). Changes in masculine and feminine traits over time: A meta-analysis. *Sex Roles, 36,* 305–325.

Updegraff, K., & McHale, S. M., & Crouter, A. C. (1996). Gender roles in marriage: What do they mean for girls' and boys' school achievement? *Journal of Youth and Adolescence, 25,* 73–88.

Urberg, K. A. (1979). Sex-role conceptualization in adolescents and adults. *Developmental Psychology, 15,* 90–92.

U.S. Bureau of the Census. (1997). *Statistical abstract of the United States* (117th ed.). Washington, DC: U.S. Government Printing Office.

Vobejda, B., & Havemann, J. (1997, May 2). Teenagers less sexually active in U.S. *The Washington Post,* A1, A12.

Voyer, D., Voyer, S., & Bryden, M. P. (1995). Magnitude of sex differences in spatial abilities: A meta-analysis and consideration of critical variables. *Psychological Bulletin, 117,* 250–270.

Wallen, K. (1996). Nature needs nurture: The interaction of hormonal and social influences on the development of behavioral sex differences in rhesus monkeys. *Hormones and Behavior, 30,* 364–378.

Welch-Ross, M. K., & Schmidt, C. R. (1996). Gender-schema development and children's constructive story memory: Evidence for a developmental model. *Child Development, 67,* 820–835.

Whiting, B. B., & Edwards, C. P. (1988). *Children of different worlds: The formation of social behavior.* Cambridge, MA: Harvard University Press.

Williams, J. E., & Best, D. L. (1990). *Measuring sex stereotypes: A multination study* (rev. ed.). Newbury Park, CA: Sage.

Wink, P., & Helson, R. (1993). Personality change in women and their partners. *Journal of Personality and Social Psychology, 65,* 597–605.

Young, W. C., Goy, R. W., & Phoenix, C. H. (1964). Hormones and sexual behavior. *Science, 143,* 212–218.

Zick, C. D., & McCullough, J. L. (1991). Trends in married couples' time use: Evidence from 1977–78 and 1987–88. *Sex Roles, 24,* 459–487.

CHAPTER 12: Social Cognition and Moral Development

Ainlay, S. C., & Smith, D. R. (1984). Aging and religious participation. *Journal of Gerontology, 39,* 357–363.

Anderson, K. E., Lytton, H., & Romney, D. M. (1986). Mothers' interactions with normal and conduct-disordered boys: Who affects whom? *Developmental Psychology, 22,* 604–609.

Bailey, A., Phillips, W., & Rutter, M. (1996). Autism: Towards an integration of clinical, genetic, neuropsychological, and neurobiological perspectives. *Journal of Child Psychology and Psychiatry and Allied Disciplines, 37,* 89–126.

Bandura, A. (1986). *Social foundations of thought and action: A social cognitive theory.* Englewood Cliffs, NJ: Prentice-Hall.

Bandura, A. (1991). Social cognitive theory of moral thought and action. In W. M. Kurtines & J. L. Gewirtz (Eds.), *Handbook of moral behavior and development: Vol. 1. Theory.* Hillsdale, NJ: Erlbaum.

Bank, L., Marlowe, J., Reid, J., Patterson, G., & Weinrott, M. (1991). A comparative evaluation of parent-training interventions for families of chronic delinquents. *Journal of Abnormal Child Psychology, 19,* 15–33.

Barenboim, C. (1981). The development of person perception in childhood and adolescence: From behavioral comparisons to psychological constructs to psychological comparisons. *Child Development, 52,* 129–144.

Baron-Cohen, S. (1995). *Mindblindness: An essay on autism and theory of mind.* Cambridge, MA: MIT Press.

Baron-Cohen, S., Leslie, A. M., & Frith, U. (1985). Does the autistic child have a "theory of mind"? *Cognition, 21,* 37–46.

Berkowitz, M. W., & Gibbs, J. C. (1983). Measuring the developmental features of moral discussion. *Merrill-Palmer Quarterly, 29,* 399–410.

Blanchard-Fields, F. (1986). Reasoning on social dilemmas varying in emotional saliency: An adult developmental perspective. *Psychology and Aging, 1,* 325–333.

Blanchard-Fields, F. (1996). Social cognitive development in adulthood and aging. In F. Blanchard-Fields & T. M. Hess (Eds.), *Perspectives on cognitive change in adulthood and aging.* New York: McGraw-Hill.

Blasi, A. (1980). Bridging moral cognition and moral action: A critical review of the literature. *Psychological Bulletin, 88,* 1–45.

Blazer, D., & Palmore, E. (1976). Religion and aging in a longitudinal panel. *Gerontologist, 16,* 82–85.

Brabeck, M. (1983). Moral judgment: Theory and research on differences between males and females. *Developmental Review, 3,* 274–291.

Bretherton, I., & Beeghly, M. (1982). Talking about internal states: The acquisition of an explicit theory of mind. *Developmental Psychology, 18,* 906–921.

Brody, G. H., & Shaffer, D. R. (1982). Contributions of parents and peers to children's moral socialization. *Developmental Review, 2,* 31–75.

Bruggeman, E. L., & Hart, K. J. (1996). Cheating, lying, and moral reasoning by religious and secular high school students. *Journal of Educational Research, 89,* 340–344.

Burton, R. V. (1963). The generality of honesty reconsidered. *Psychological Review, 70,* 481–499.

Burton, R. V. (1976). Honesty and dishonesty. In T. Lickona (Ed.), *Moral development and behavior.* New York: Holt, Rinehart & Winston.

Burton, R. V. (1984). A paradox in theories and research in moral development. In W. M. Kurtines & J. L. Gewirtz (Eds.), *Morality, moral behavior, and moral development.* New York: Wiley.

Bussey, K. (1992). Lying and truthfulness: Children's definitions, standards, and evaluative reactions. *Child Development, 63,* 129–137.

Chandler, M., Fritz, A. S., & Hala, S. (1989). Small-scale deceit: Deception as a marker of two-, three-, and four-year-olds' early theories of mind. *Child Development, 60,* 1263–1277.

Chandler, M., & Hala, S. (1994). The role of personal involvement in the assessment of early false belief skills. In C. Lewis & P. Mitchell (Eds.), *Children's early understanding of mind.* Hove, England: Lawrence Erlbaum.

Chap, J. B. (1985–1986). Moral judgment in middle and late adulthood: The effects of age-appropriate moral dilemmas and spontaneous role taking. *International Journal of Aging and Human Development, 22,* 161–171.

Coie, J. D., Dodge, K. A., Terry, R., & Wright, V. (1991). The role of aggression in peer relations: An analysis of aggression episodes in boys' play groups. *Child Development, 62,* 812–826.

Coke, M. M. (1992). Correlates of life satisfaction among elderly African Americans. *Journal of Gerontology: Psychological Sciences, 47,* P316–P320.

Colby, A., & Damon, W. (1992). *Pathways to commitment: Moral leaders in our time.* New York: Free Press.

Colby, A., & Kohlberg, L. (1987). *The measurement of moral judgment. Vol. 1: Theoretical foundations and research validation.* Cambridge: Cambridge University Press.

Colby, A., Kohlberg, L., Gibbs, J., & Lieberman, M. (1983). A longitudinal study of moral judgment. *Monographs of the Society for Research in Child Development, 48* (1–2, Serial No. 200).

Cole, P. M., Barrett, K. C., & Zahn-Waxler, C. (1992). Emotion displays in two-year-olds during mishaps. *Child Development, 63,* 314–324.

Crick, N. R., & Dodge, K. A. (1994). A review and reformulation of social information-processing mechanisms in children's social adjustment. *Psychological Bulletin, 115,* 74–101.

Crick, N. R., & Dodge, K. A. (1996). Social information-processing mechanisms in reactive and proactive aggression. *Child Development, 67,* 993–1002.

Crockenberg, S., & Litman, C. (1990). Autonomy as competence in 2-year-olds: Maternal correlates of child defiance, compliance, and self-assertion. *Developmental Psychology, 26,* 961–971.

Custer, W. L. (1996). A comparison of young children's understanding of contradictory representations in pretense, memory, and belief. *Child Development, 67,* 678–688.

Damon, W., & Hart, D. (1992). Self-understanding and its role in social and moral development. In M. H. Bornstein & M. E. Lamb (Eds.), *Developmental psychology: An advanced textbook.* Hillsdale, NJ: Erlbaum.

Deater-Deckard, K., Dodge, K. A., Bates, J. E., & Pettit, G. S. (1996). Physical discipline among African American and European American mothers: Links to children's externalizing behaviors. *Developmental Psychology, 32,* 1065–1072.

de Vries, B., & Walker, L. J. (1986). Moral reasoning and attitudes toward capital punishment. *Developmental Psychology, 22,* 509–513.

Dishion, T. J., Andrews, D. W., & Crosby, L. (1995). Antisocial boys and their friends in adolescence: Relationship characteristics, quality, and interactional process. *Child Development, 66,* 139–151.

Dishion, T. J., Patterson, G. R., Stoolmiller, M., & Skinner, M. L. (1991). Family, school, and behavioral antecedents to early adolescent involvement with antisocial peers. *Developmental Psychology, 27,* 172–180.

Dodge, K. A. (1986). A social information processing model of social competence in children. In M. Perlmutter (Ed.), *Minnesota symposia on child psychology* (Vol. 18). Hillsdale, NJ: Erlbaum.

Dodge, K. A. (1993). Social-cognitive mechanisms in the development of conduct disorder and depression. *Annual Review of Psychology, 44,* 559–584.

Dodge, K. A., Lochman, J. E., Harnish, J. E., Bates, J. E., & Pettit, G. S. (1997). Reactive and proactive aggression in school children and psychiatrically impaired chronically assaultive youth. *Journal of Abnormal Psychology, 106,* 37–51.

Dodge, K. A., & Price, J. M. (1994). On the relation between social information processing and socially competent behavior in early school-aged children. *Child Development, 65,* 1385–1397.

Dolen, L. S., & Bearison, D. J. (1982). Social interaction and social cognition in aging. *Human Development, 25,* 430–442.

Droege, K. L., & Stipek, D J. (1993). Children's use of dispositions to predict classmates' behavior. *Developmental Psychology, 29,* 646–654.

Dunn, J., Brown, J., Slomkowski, C., Tesla, C., & Youngblade, L. (1991). Young children's understanding of other people's feelings and beliefs: Individual differences and their antecedents. *Child Development, 62,* 1352–1366.

Eisenberg, N., Miller, P. A., Shell, R., McNalley, S., & Shea, C. (1991). Prosocial development in adolescence: A longitudinal study. *Developmental Psychology, 27,* 849–857.

Elliott, D. S., & Ageton, S. S. (1980). Reconciling race and class differences in self-reported and official estimates of delinquency. *American Sociological Review, 45,* 95–110.

Emde, R. N., Biringen, Z., Clyman, R. B., & Oppenheim, D. (1991). The moral self of infancy: Affective core and procedural knowledge. *Developmental Review, 11,* 251–270.

Fischer, W. F. (1963). Sharing in preschool children as a function of the amount and type of reinforcement. *Genetic Psychology Monographs, 68,* 215–245.

Flavell, J. H. (1985). *Cognitive development* (2nd ed.). Englewood Cliffs, NJ: Prentice Hall.

Fowler, J. W. (1981). *Stages of faith: The psychology of human development and the quest for meaning.* San Francisco: Harper & Row.

Fowler, J. W. (1991). The vocation of faith developmental theory. In J. W. Fowler, K. E. Nipkow, & F. Schweitzer (Eds.), *Stages of faith and religious development.* New York: Crossroad Publishing Company.

Freud, S. (1960). *A general introduction to psychoanalysis.* New York: Washington Square Press. (Original work published 1935)

Garmon, L. C., Basinger, K. S., Gregg, V. R., & Gibbs, J. C. (1996). Gender differences in stage and expression of moral judgment. *Merrill-Palmer Quarterly, 42,* 418–437.

Gibbs, J., Arnold, K., Cheesman, F. L., & Ahlborn, H. (1984). Facilitation of sociomoral reasoning in delinquents. *Journal of Consulting and Clinical Psychology, 52,* 37–45.

Gibbs, J. C., & Schnell, S. V. (1985). Moral development "versus" socialization: A critique. *American Psychologist, 40,* 1071–1080.

Gilligan, C. (1977). In a different voice: Women's conceptions of self and morality. *Harvard Educational Review, 47,* 481–517.

Gilligan, C. (1982). *In a different voice: Psychological theory and women's development.* Cambridge, MA: Harvard University Press.

Gilligan, C. (1993). Adolescent development reconsidered. In A. Garrod (Ed.), *Approaches to moral development: New research and emerging themes.* New York: Teachers College Press.

Gnepp, J. (1989). Personalized inferences of emotions and appraisals: Component processes and correlates. *Developmental Psychology, 25,* 277–288.

Gnepp, J., & Chilamkurti, C. (1988). Children's use of personality attributions to predict other people's emotional and behavioral reactions. *Child Development, 59,* 743–754.

Gopnik, A., Slaughter, V., & Meltzoff, A. (1994). Changing your views: How understanding visual perception can lead to a new theory of mind. In C. Lewis & P. Mitchell (Eds.), *Children's early understanding of mind: Origins and development.* Hove, England: Erlbaum.

Gralinski, J. H., & Kopp, C. B. (1993). Everyday rules for behavior: Mothers' requests to young children. *Developmental Psychology, 29,* 573–584.

Green, M. (1989). *Theories of human development: A comparative approach.* Englewood Cliffs, NJ: Prentice-Hall.

Gregg, V., Gibbs, J. C., & Basinger, K. S. (1994). Patterns of developmental delay in moral judgment by male and female delinquents. *Merrill-Palmer Quarterly, 40,* 538–553.

Grusec, J. E., & Goodnow, J. J. (1994). Impact of parental discipline methods on the child's internalization of values: A reconceptualization of current points of view. *Developmental Psychology, 30,* 4–19.

Grusec, J. E., Kuczynski, L., Rushton, J. P., Simutis, Z. (1979). Learning resistance to temptation through observation. *Developmental Psychology, 15,* 233–240.

Guerra, N. G., & Slaby, R. G. (1990). Cognitive mediators of aggression in adolescent offenders: 2. Intervention. *Developmental Psychology, 26,* 269–277.

Haan, N., Aerts, E., & Cooper, B. A. B. (1985). *On moral grounds: The search for practical morality.* New York: New York University Press.

Haidt, J., Koller, S. H., & Dias, M. G. (1993). Affect, culture, and morality, or is it wrong to eat your dog? *Journal of Personality and Social Psychology, 65,* 613–628.

Harris, P. L. (1989). *Children and emotion: The development of psychological understanding.* Oxford, England: Basil Blackwell.

Hart, D., & Chmiel, S. (1992). Influence of defense mechanisms on moral judgment development: A longitudinal study. *Developmental Psychology, 28,* 722–730.

Hartshorne, H., & May, M. S. (1928–1930). *Studies in the nature of character: Vol. 1. Studies in deceit. Vol. 2.*

Studies in self-control. Vol. 3. Studies in the organization of character. New York: Macmillan.

Hatch, L. R. (1991). Informal support patterns of older African-American and white women: Examining effects of family, paid work, and religious participation. *Research on Aging, 13,* 144–170.

Hess, T. M. (1994). Social cognition in adulthood: Age-related changes in knowledge and processing mechanisms. *Developmental Review, 14,* 373–412.

Hoffman, M. L. (1970). Moral development. In P. H. Mussen (Ed.), *Carmichael's manual of child psychology* (Vol. 2). New York: Wiley.

Hoffman, M. L. (1981). Is altruism part of human nature? *Journal of Personality and Social Psychology, 40,* 121–137.

Hoffman, M. L. (1983). Affective and cognitive processes in moral internalization. In E. T. Higgins, D. N. Ruble, & W. W. Hartup (Eds.), *Social cognition and social development: A sociocultural perspective.* Cambridge: Cambridge University Press.

Hoffman, M. L. (1988). Moral development. In M. H. Bornstein & M. E. Lamb (Eds.), *Developmental psychology: An advanced textbook* (2nd ed.). Hillsdale, NJ: Erlbaum.

Hoffman, M. L. (1993). Empathy, social cognition, and moral education. In A. Garrod (Ed.), *Approaches to moral development: New research and emerging themes.* New York: Teachers College Press.

Hudley, C., & Graham, S. (1993). An attributional intervention to reduce peer-directed aggression among African-American boys. *Child Development, 64,* 124–138.

Hudson, L. M., Forman, E. R., & Brion-Meisels, S. (1982). Role-taking as a predictor of prosocial behavior in cross-age tutors. *Child Development, 53,* 1320–1329.

Huesmann, L. R., Eron, L. D., Lefkowitz, M. M., & Walder, L. O. (1984). Stability of aggression over time and generations. *Developmental Psychology, 20,* 1120–1134.

Ingrassia, M. (1993, July 19). "Life means nothing." *Newsweek, 122,* 16–17.

Jagers, R. J., Bingham, K., & Hans, S. L. (1996). Socialization and social judgments among inner-city African-American kindergartners. *Child Development, 67,* 140–150.

Jenkins, J. M., & Astington, J. W. (1996). Cognitive factors and family structure associated with theory of mind development in young children. *Developmental Psychology, 32,* 70–78.

Kagan, J. (1981). *The second year: The emergence of self-awareness.* Cambridge, MA: Harvard University Press.

Kazdin, A. (1995). *Conduct disorders in childhood and adolescence.* Thousand Oaks, CA: Sage.

Keller, B. B., & Bell, R. Q. (1979). Child effects on adult's method of eliciting altruistic behavior. *Child Development, 50,* 1004–1009.

Kochanska, G. (1993). Toward a synthesis of parental socialization and child temperament in early development of conscience. *Child Development, 64,* 325–347.

Kochanska, G. (1995). Children's temperament, mothers' discipline, and security of attachment: Multiple pathways to emerging internalization. *Child Development, 66,* 597–615.

Kochanska, G. (1997a). Multiple pathways to conscience for children with different temperaments: From toddlerhood to age 5. *Developmental Psychology, 33,* 228–240.

Kochanska, G. (1997b). Mutually responsive orientation between mothers and their young children: Implications for early socialization. *Child Development, 68,* 94–112.

Kochanska, G., Casey, R. J., & Fukumoto, A. (1995). Toddlers' sensitivity to standard violations. *Child Development, 66,* 643–656.

Kochanska, G., Murray, K., & Coy, K. C. (1997). Inhibitory control as a contributor to conscience in childhood: From toddler to early school age. *Child Development, 68,* 263–277.

Kohlberg, L. (1963). The development of children's orientations toward a moral order: I. Sequence in the development of moral thought. *Vita Humana, 6,* 11–33.

Kohlberg, L. (1973). Continuities in childhood and adult moral development revisited. In P. B. Baltes & K. W. Schaie (Eds.), *Life-span developmental psychology: Personality and socialization.* New York: Academic Press.

Kohlberg, L. (1975, June). The cognitive-developmental approach to moral education. *Phi Delta Kappan,* pp. 670–677.

Kohlberg, L. (1981). *Essays on moral development: Vol. 1. The philosophy of moral development.* San Francisco: Harper & Row.

Kohlberg, L. (1984). *Essays on moral development: Vol. 2. The psychology of moral development.* San Francisco: Harper & Row.

Kohlberg, L. (1985). The just community approach to moral education in theory and practice. In M. W. Berkowitz & F. Oser (Eds.), *Moral education: Theory and application.* Hillsdale, NJ: Erlbaum.

Kreutz, D. (1991, May 1). Tucsonan who saved drowning man honored for act transcending heroism. *Arizona Daily Star,* pp. 1B–2B.

Kruger, A. C. (1992). The effect of peer and adult-child transductive discussions on moral reasoning. *Merrill-Palmer Quarterly, 38,* 191–211.

Kruger, A. C., & Tomasello, M. (1986). Transactive discussions with peers and adults. *Developmental Psychology, 22,* 681–685.

Kupersmidt, J. B., Griesler, P. C., DeRosier, M. E., Patterson, C. J., & Davis, P. W. (1995). Childhood aggression and peer relations in the context of family and neighborhood factors. *Child Development, 66,* 360–375.

Kurdek, L. A., & Krile, D. (1982). A developmental analysis of the relation between peer acceptance and both interpersonal understanding and perceived social self-competence. *Child Development, 53,* 1485–1491.

Kurtines, W. M. (1986). Moral behavior as rule-governed behavior: Person and situation effects on moral decision making. *Journal of Personality and Social Psychology, 50,* 784–791.

Lapsley, D. K. (1996). *Moral psychology.* Boulder, CO: Westview.

Lapsley, D. K., Harwell, M. R., Olson, L. M., Flannery, D., & Quintana, S. M. (1984). Moral judgment, personality, and attitude toward authority in early and late adolescence. *Journal of Youth and Adolescence, 13,* 527–542.

Leekam, S. (1993). Children's understanding of mind. In M. Bennett (Ed.), *The development of social cognition: The child as psychologist.* New York: Guilford.

LeMare, L. J., & Rubin, K. H. (1987). Perspective taking and peer interaction: Structural and developmental analyses. *Child Development, 58,* 306–315.

Lewis, C., Freeman, N. H., Kyriakidou, C., Maridaki-Kassotaki, K., & Berridge, D. M. (1996). Social influences on false belief access: Specific sibling influences or general apprenticeship? *Child Development, 67*, 2930–2947.

Livesley, W. J., & Bromley, D. B. (1973). *Person perception in childhood and adolescence.* London: Wiley.

Lollis, S., Ross, H., & Leroux, L. (1996). An observational study of parents' socialization of moral orientation during sibling conflicts. *Merrill-Palmer Quarterly, 42*, 475–494.

Lytton, H. (1990). Child and parent effects in boys' conduct disorder: A reinterpretation. *Developmental Psychology, 26*, 683–697.

Martin, G. B., & Clark, R. D., III. (1982). Distress crying in neonates: Species and peer specificity. *Developmental Psychology, 18*, 3–9.

McFadden, S. H. (1996). Religion, spirituality, and aging. In J. E. Birren & K. W. Schaie (Eds.), *Handbook of the psychology of aging* (4th ed.). San Diego: Academic Press.

McFadyen-Ketchum, S. A., Bates, J. E., Dodge, K. A., & Pettit, G. S. (1996). Patterns of change in early childhood aggressive-disruptive behavior: Gender differences in predictions from early coercive and affectionate mother-child interactions. *Child Development, 67*, 2417–2433.

McGuire, K. D., & Weisz, J. R. (1982). Social cognition and behavior correlates of preadolescent chumship. *Child Development, 53*, 1478–1484.

McLoyd, V. C. (1990). The impact of economic hardship on black families and children: Psychological distress, parenting, and socioemotional development. *Child Development, 61*, 311–346.

Miles, D. R., & Carey, G. (1997). Genetic and environmental architecture on human aggression. *Journal of Personality and Social Psychology, 72*, 207–217.

Miller, P. A., Eisenberg, N., Fabes, R. A., & Shell, R. (1996). Relations of moral reasoning and vicarious emotion to young children's prosocial behavior toward peers and adults. *Developmental Psychology, 32*, 210–219.

Mischel, W. (1974). Processes in the delay of gratification. In L. Berkowitz (Ed.), *Advances in experimental social psychology* (Vol. 7). New York: Academic Press.

Mitchell, P. (1997). *Introduction to theory of mind: Children, autism, and apes.* London: Arnold.

Nelson, E. A., Grinder, R. E., & Biaggio, A. M. B. (1969). Relationships between behavioral, cognitive-developmental, and self-report measures of morality and personality. *Multivariate Behavioral Research, 4*, 483–500.

Nelson, E. A., Grinder, R. E., & Mutterer, M. L. (1969). Sources of variance in behavioral measures of honesty in temptation situations: Methodological analyses. *Developmental Psychology, 1*, 265–279.

Nelson, S. A. (1980). Factors influencing young children's use of motives and outcomes as moral criteria. *Child Development, 51*, 823–829.

Newman, D. L., Caspi, A., Moffitt, T. E., & Silva, P. A. (1997). Antecedents of adult interpersonal functioning: Effects of individual differences in age 3 temperament. *Developmental Psychology, 33*, 206–217.

Newstead, S. E., Franklyn-Stokes, A., & Armstead, P. (1996). Individual differences in student cheating. *Journal of Educational Psychology, 88*, 229–241.

Niles, W. (1986). Effects of a moral development discussion group on delinquent and predelinquent boys. *Journal of Counseling Psychology, 33*, 45–51.

Nucci, L. P., & Nucci, M. S. (1982). Children's responses to moral and social conventional transgressions in free-play settings. *Child Development, 53*, 1337–1342.

Nucci, L. P., & Turiel, E. (1993). God's word, religious rules, and their relation to Christian and Jewish children's concepts of morality. *Child Development, 64*, 1475–1491.

O'Mahony, J. F. (1986). Development of person description over adolescence. *Journal of Youth and Adolescence, 15*, 389–403.

Palmore, E. (1981). *Social patterns in normal aging: Findings from the Duke Longitudinal Study.* Durham, NC: Duke University Press.

Patterson, G. (1974). Interventions for boys with conduct problems: Multiple settings, treatments, and criteria. *Journal of Consulting and Clinical Psychology, 42*, 471–481.

Patterson, G. R., DeBaryshe, B. D., & Ramsey, E. (1989). A developmental perspective on antisocial behavior. *American Psychologist, 44*, 329–335.

Perner, J., Ruffman, T., & Leekam, S. R. (1994). Theory of mind is contagious: You catch it from your siblings. *Child Development, 65*, 1228–1238.

Perry, D. G., & Parke, R. D. (1975). Punishment and alternative response training as determinants of response inhibition in children. *Genetic Psychology Monographs, 91*, 257–279.

Piaget, J. (1965). *The moral judgment of the child.* New York: Free Press. (Original work published 1932)

Power, F. C., Higgins, A., & Kohlberg, L. (1989). *Lawrence Kohlberg's approach to moral education.* New York: Columbia University Press.

Pratt, M. W., Diessner, R., Hunsberger, B., Pancer, S. M., & Savoy, K. (1991). Four pathways in the analysis of adult development and aging: Comparing analyses of reasoning about personal-life dilemmas. *Psychology and Aging, 4*, 666–675.

Pratt, M. W., Diessner, R., Pratt, A., Hunsberger, B., & Pancer, S. M. (1996). Moral and social reasoning and perspective taking in later life: A longitudinal study. *Psychology and Aging, 11*, 66–73.

Quiggle, N. L., Garber, J., Panak, W. F., & Dodge, K. A. (1992). Social information processing in aggressive and depressed children. *Child Development, 63*, 1305–1320.

Reker, G. T., Peacock, E. J., & Wong, P. T. P. (1987). Meaning and purpose in life and well-being: A life-span perspective. *Journal of Gerontology, 42*, 44–49.

Repacholi, B. M., & Gopnik, A. (1997). Early reasoning about desires: Evidence from 14- and 18-month-olds. *Developmental Psychology, 33*, 12–21.

Rest, J., Thoma, S., & Edwards, L. (1997). Designing and validating a measure of moral judgment: Stage preference and stage consistency approaches. *Journal of Educational Psychology, 89*, 5–28.

Rholes, W. S., Newman, L. S., & Ruble, D. N. (1990). Understanding self and other: Developmental and motivational aspects of perceiving persons in terms of invariant dispositions. In E. T. Higgins & R. M. Sorrentino (Eds.), *Handbook of motivation and cognition: Vol. 2. Foundations of Social Behavior.* New York: Guilford.

Rholes, W. S., & Ruble, D. N. (1984). Children's understanding of dispositional characteristics of others. *Child Development, 55,* 550–560.

Ruble, D. N., & Dweck, C. S. (1995). Self-conceptions, person conceptions, and their development. In N. Eisenberg (Ed.), *Social development.* Thousand Oaks, CA: Sage.

Rushton, J. P. (1980). *Altruism, socialization, and society.* Englewood Cliffs, NJ: Prentice-Hall.

Sacks, O. (1993, December 27). A neurologist's notebook: An anthropologist on Mars. *The New Yorker,* pp. 106–125.

Selman, R. L. (1976). Social-cognitive understanding: A guide to educational and clinical experience. In T. Lickona (Ed.), *Moral development and behavior: Theory, research and social issues.* New York: Holt, Rinehart & Winston.

Selman, R. L. (1980). *The growth of interpersonal understanding.* New York: Academic Press.

Selman, R. L., Beardslee, W., Schultz, L. H., Krupa, M., & Podorefsky, D. (1986). Assessing adolescent interpersonal negotiation strategies: Toward the integration of structural and functional models. *Developmental Psychology, 22,* 450–459.

Shweder, R. A., Mahapatra, M., & Miller, J. G. (1990). Culture and moral development. In J. W. Stigler, R. A. Shweder, & G. Herdt (Eds.), *Cultural psychology: Essays on comparative human development.* Cambridge: Cambridge University Press.

Skoe, E. E., Pratt, M. W., Matthews, M., & Curror, S. E. (1996). The ethic of care: Stability over time, gender differences, and correlates in mid- to late adulthood. *Psychology and Aging, 11,* 280–292.

Slaby, R. G., & Guerra, N. G. (1988). Cognitive mediators of aggression in adolescent offenders: 1. Assessment. *Developmental Psychology, 24,* 580–588.

Smetana, J. G. (1981). Preschool children's conceptions of moral and social rules. *Child Development, 52,* 1333–1336.

Smetana, J. G., Schlagman, N., & Adams, P. W. (1993). Preschool children's judgments about hypothetical and actual transgressions. *Child Development, 64,* 202–214.

Snarey, J. R. (1985). Cross-cultural universality of social-moral development: A critical review of Kohlber-

gian research. *Psychological Bulletin, 97,* 202–232.

Sodian, B. (1994). Early deception and the conceptual continuity claim. In C. Lewis & P. Mitchell (Eds.), *Children's early understanding of mind: Origins and development.* Hove, England: Erlbaum.

Speicher, B. (1994). Family patterns of moral judgment during adolescence and early adulthood. *Developmental Psychology, 30,* 624–632.

Stouthamer-Loeber, M. (1991). Young children's verbal misrepresentations of reality. In K. J. Rotenberg (Ed.), *Children's interpersonal trust.* New York: Springer-Verlag.

Taylor, M., & Carlson, S. M. (1997). The relation between individual differences in fantasy and theory of mind. *Child Development, 68,* 436–455.

Thoma, S. J., Rest, J. R., & Davison, M. L. (1991). Describing and testing a moderator of the moral judgment and action relationship. *Journal of Personality and Social Psychology, 61,* 659–669.

Tietjen, A. M., & Walker, L. J. (1985). Moral reasoning and leadership among men in a Papua New Guinea society. *Developmental Psychology, 21,* 982–992.

Tisak, M. S., & Tisak, J. (1990). Children's conceptions of parental authority, friendship, and sibling relations. *Merrill-Palmer Quarterly, 36,* 347–368.

Tolan, P. H., Guerra, N. G., & Kendall, P. C. (1995). A developmental-ecological perspective on antisocial behavior in children and adolescents: Toward a unified risk and intervention framework. *Journal of Consulting and Clinical Psychology, 63,* 579–584.

Tomlinson-Keasey, C., & Keasey, C. B. (1974). The mediating role of cognitive development in moral judgment. *Child Development, 45,* 291–298.

Toner, I. J., Parke, R. D., & Yussen, S. R. (1978). The effect of observation of model behavior on the establishment and stability of resistance to deviation in children. *Journal of Genetic Psychology, 132,* 283–290.

Toner, I. J., & Potts, R. (1981). Effect of modeled rationales on moral behavior, moral choice, and level of moral judgment in children. *Journal of Psychology, 107,* 153–162.

Trevethan, S. D., & Walker, L. J. (1989). Hypothetical versus real-life moral

reasoning among psychopathic and delinquent youth. *Development and Psychopathology, 1,* 91–103.

Turiel, E. (1978). The development of concepts of social structure: Social convention. In J. Glick & A. Clarke-Stewart (Eds.), *The development of social understanding.* New York: Gardner Press.

Turiel, E. (1983). *The development of social knowledge. Morality and convention.* Cambridge: Cambridge University Press.

Vinden, P. G. (1996). Junin Quechua children's understanding of mind. *Child Development, 67,* 1707–1716.

Waldman, I. D. (1996). Aggressive boys' hostile perceptual and response biases: The role of attention and impulsivity. *Child Development, 67,* 1015–1033.

Walker, L. J. (1980). Cognitive and perspective-taking prerequisites of moral development. *Child Development, 51,* 131–139.

Walker, L. J. (1989). A longitudinal study of moral reasoning. *Child Development, 60,* 157–166.

Walker, L. J. (1995). Sexism in Kohlberg's moral psychology? In W. M. Kurtines & J. L. Gewirtz (Eds.), *Moral development: An introduction.* Boston: Allyn and Bacon.

Walker, L. J. (1997). Is morality gendered in early parent-child relationships? A commentary on the Lollis, Ross, and Leroux study. *Merrill-Palmer Quarterly, 43,* 148–159.

Walker, L. J., & Taylor, J. H. (1991). Family interactions and the development of moral reasoning. *Child Development, 62,* 264–283.

Wark, G. R., & Krebs, D. L. (1996). Gender and dilemma differences in real-life moral judgment. *Developmental Psychology, 32,* 220–230.

Wellman, H. M. (1990). *The child's theory of mind.* Cambridge, MA: MIT Press.

Wellman, H. M., & Banerjee, M. (1991). Mind and emotion: Children's understanding of the emotional consequences of beliefs and desires. *British Journal of Developmental Psychology, 9,* 191–214.

Wellman, H. M., & Bartsch, K. (1994). Before belief: Children's early psychological theory. In C. Lewis & P. Mitchell (Eds.), *Children's early understanding of mind: Origins and development.* Hove, England: Erlbaum.

Wolff, M., Rutten, P., & Bayer, A. F., III. (1992). *Where we stand: Can America make it in the race for health, wealth, and happiness?* New York: Bantam Books.

Yeates, K. O., & Selman, R. L. (1989). Social competence in the schools: Toward an integrative developmental model for intervention. *Developmental Review, 9,* 64–100.

Young, G., & Dowling, W. (1987). Dimensions of religiosity in old age: Accounting for variation in types of participation. *Journal of Gerontology, 42,* 376–380.

Youngblade, L. M., & Dunn, J. (1995). Individual differences in young children's pretend play with mother and sibling: Links to relationships and understanding of other people's feelings and beliefs. *Child Development, 66,* 1472–1492.

Yuill, N. (1993). Understanding of personality and dispositions. In M. Bennett (Ed.), *The development of social cognition: The child as psychologist.* New York: Guilford.

Zahn-Waxler, C., Friedman, R. J., Cole, P. M., Mizuta, I., & Himura, N. (1996). Japanese and United States preschool children's responses to conflict and distress. *Child Development, 67,* 2462–2477.

Zahn-Waxler, C., Radke-Yarrow, M., & King, R. A. (1979). Child rearing and children's prosocial initiations toward victims of distress. *Child Development, 50,* 319–330.

Zahn-Waxler, C., Radke-Yarrow, M., Wagner, E., & Chapman, M. (1992). Development of concern for others. *Developmental Psychology, 28,* 126–136.

Zelazo, P. D., Helwig, C. C., & Lau, A. (1996). Intention, act, and outcome in behavioral prediction and moral judgment. *Child Development, 67,* 2478–2492.

CHAPTER 13: Attachment and Social Relationships

Aboud, F. E., & Mendelson, M. J. (1996). Determinants of friendship selection and quality: Developmental perspectives. In W. M. Bukowski, A. F. Newcomb, & W. W. Hartup (Eds.), *The company they keep: Friendship in childhood and adolescence.* New York: Cambridge University Press.

Adams, R. G. (1985–1986). Emotional closeness and physical distance between friends: Implications for el-derly women living in age-segregated and age-integrated settings. *International Journal of Aging and Human Development, 22,* 55–76.

Ainsworth, M. D. S. (1973). The development of infant-mother attachment. In B. M. Caldwell & H. N. Ricciuti (Eds.), *Review of child development research* (Vol. 3). Chicago: University of Chicago Press.

Ainsworth, M. D. S. (1979). Attachment as related to mother-infant interaction. In J. G. Rosenblatt, R. A. Hinde, C. Beer, & M. Busnel (Eds.), *Advances in the study of behavior* (Vol. 9). New York: Academic Press.

Ainsworth, M. D. S. (1989). Attachments beyond infancy. *American Psychologist, 44,* 709–716.

Ainsworth, M. D. S., Blehar, M., Waters, E., & Wall, S. (1978). *Patterns of attachment.* Hillsdale, NJ: Erlbaum.

Alley, T. R. (1981). Head shape and the perception of cuteness. *Developmental Psychology, 17,* 650–654.

Anisfeld, E., Casper, V., Nozyce, M., & Cunningham, N. (1990). Does infant carrying promote attachment? An experimental study of the effects of increased physical contact on the development of attachment. *Child Development, 61,* 1617–1627.

Antonucci, T. C. (1985). Personal characteristics, social support, and social behavior. In R. H. Binstock & E. Shanas (Eds.), *Handbook of aging and the social sciences* (2nd ed.). New York: Van Nostrand Reinhold.

Antonucci, T. C., & Akiyama, H. (1991). Social relationships and aging well. *Generations, 15,* 39–44.

Antonucci, T. C., Fuhrer, R., & Jackson, J. S. (1990). Social support and reciprocity: A cross-ethnic and cross-national perspective. *Journal of Social and Personal Relationships, 7,* 519–530.

Athey, I. (1984). Contributions of play to development. In T. D. Yawkey & A. D. Pelligrini (Eds.), *Child's play: Developmental and applied.* Hillsdale, NJ: Erlbaum.

Barnas, M. V., Pollina, L., & Cummings, E. M. (1991). Life-span attachment: Relations between attachment and socioemotional functioning in adult women. *Genetic, Social, and General Psychology Monographs, 117,* 175–202.

Barnes, K. E. (1971). Preschool play norms: A replication. *Developmental Psychology, 5,* 99–103.

Bartholomew, K., & Horowitz, L. M. (1991). Attachment styles among young adults: A test of a four-category model. *Journal of Personality and Social Psychology, 61,* 226–244.

Baydar, N., & Brooks-Gunn, J. (1991). Effects of maternal employment and child-care arrangements on preschoolers' cognitive and behavioral outcomes: Evidence from the children of the National Longitudinal Survey of Youth. *Developmental Psychology, 27,* 932–945.

Belsky, J., Campbell, S. B., Cohn, J. F., & Moore, G. (1996). Instability of infant-parent attachment security. *Developmental Psychology, 32,* 921–924.

Belsky, J., & Rovine, M. J. (1988). Nonmaternal care in the first year of life and the security of infant-parent attachment. *Child Development, 59,* 157–167.

Belsky, J., Rovine, M. J., & Taylor, D. G. (1984). The Pennsylvania infant and family development project, III: The origins of individual differences in infant-mother attachment: Maternal and infant contributions. *Child Development, 55,* 718–728.

Belsky, J., Spritz, B., & Crnic, K. (1996). Infant attachment security and affective-cognitive information processing at age 3. *Psychological Science, 7,* 111–114.

Belsky, J., Woodworth, S., & Crnic, K. (1996). Trouble in the second year: Three questions about family interaction. *Child Development, 67,* 556–578.

Benenson, J. F., Apostoleris, N. H., & Parnass, J. (1997). Age and sex differences in dyadic and group interaction. *Developmental Psychology, 33,* 538–543.

Benoit, D., & Parker, K. C. (1994). Stability and transmission of attachment across three generations. *Child Development, 65,* 1444–1456.

Berman, W. H., & Sperling, M. B. (1991). Parental attachment and emotional distress in the transition to college. *Journal of Youth and Adolescence, 20,* 427–440.

Berndt, T. J. (1979). Developmental changes in conforming to peers and parents. *Developmental Psychology, 15,* 608–616.

Berndt, T. J. (1982). The features and effects of friendship in early adolescence. *Child Development, 53,* 1447–1460.

Berndt, T. J., & Hoyle, S. G. (1985). Stability and change in childhood and adolescent friendships. *Developmental Psychology, 21,* 1007–1015.

Berndt, T. J., & Perry, T. B. (1990). Distinctive features and effects of early adolescent friendships. In R. Montemayor, G. R. Adams, & T. P. Gullotta (Eds.), *From childhood to adolescence: A transitional period.* Newbury Park, CA: Sage.

Biller, H. B. (1993). *Fathers and families: Paternal factors in child development.* Westport, CT: Auburn House.

Biringen, A. (1990). Direct observation of maternal sensitivity and dyadic interactions in the home: Relations to maternal thinking. *Developmental Psychology, 26,* 278–284.

Bixenstine, V. C., DeCorte, M. S., & Bixenstine, B. A. (1976). Conformity to peer-sponsored misconduct at four grade levels. *Developmental Psychology, 12,* 226–236.

Black, B., & Logan, A. (1995). Links between communication patterns in mother-child, father-child, and child-peer interactions and children's social status. *Child Development, 66,* 255–271.

Blieszner, R., & Adams, R. G. (1992). *Adult friendship.* Newbury Park, CA: Sage.

Bohlin, G., & Hagekull, B. (1993). Stranger wariness and sociability in the early years. *Infant Behavior and Development, 16,* 53–67.

Bossé, R., Aldwin, C. M., Levenson, M. R., Spiro, A., III, & Mroczek, D. K. (1993). Change in social support after retirement: Longitudinal findings from the Normative Aging Study. *Journal of Gerontology: Psychological Sciences, 48,* P210–P217.

Bowlby, J. (1960). Separation anxiety. *International Journal of Psychoanalysis, 41,* 89–113.

Bowlby, J. (1969). *Attachment and loss: Vol. 1. Attachment.* New York: Basic Books.

Bowlby, J. (1973). *Attachment and loss: Vol. 2. Separation.* New York: Basic Books.

Bowlby, J. (1980). *Attachment and loss: Vol. 3. Loss, sadness, and depression.* New York: Basic Books.

Bowlby, J. (1988). *A secure base: Parent-child attachment and healthy human development.* New York: Basic Books.

Brennan, K. A., & Shaver, P. R. (1995). Dimensions of adult attachment, affect regulation, and romantic relationship functioning. *Personality and Social Psychology Bulletin, 21,* 267–283.

Bretherton, I. (1996). Internal working models of attachment relationships as related to resilient coping. In G. G. Noam & K. W. Fischer (Eds.), *Development and vulnerability in close relationships.* Mahwah, NJ: Erlbaum.

Bretherton, I., Stolberg, U., & Kreye, M. (1981). Engaging strangers in proximal interaction: Infants' social initiative. *Developmental Psychology, 17,* 746–755.

Bridges, L. J., & Grolnick, W. J. (1995). The development of emotional self-regulation in infancy and early childhood. In N. Eisenberg (Ed.), *Social development: Vol. 15. Review of personality and social psychology.* Thousand Oaks, CA: Sage.

Broberg, A. G., Wessels, H., Lamb, M. E., & Hwang, C. P. (1997). Effects of day care on the cognitive development of 8-year-olds: A longitudinal study. *Developmental Psychology, 33,* 62–69.

Brook, J. S., Brook, D. W., Gordon, A. S., Whiteman, M., & Cohen, P. (1990). The psychosocial etiology of adolescent drug use: A family interactional approach. *Genetic, Social, and General Psychology Monographs, 116,* 111–267.

Brown, B. B., & Lohr, M. J. (1987). Peer-group affiliation and adolescent self-esteem: An integration of ego-identity and symbolic-interaction theories. *Journal of Personality and Social Psychology, 52,* 47–55.

Brown, B. B., Mory, M. S., & Kinney, D. (1994). Casting adolescent crowds in a relational perspective: Caricature, channel, and context. In R. Montemayor, G. R. Adams, & T. P. Gulotta (Eds.), *Personal relationships during adolescence.* Thousand Oaks, CA: Sage.

Brown, B. B., Mounts, N., Lamborn, S. D., & Steinberg, L. (1993). Parenting practices and peer group affiliation in adolescence. *Child Development, 64,* 467–482.

Brownell, C. A. (1986). Convergent developments: Cognitive-developmental correlates of growth in infant/toddler peer skills. *Child Development, 57,* 275–286.

Buhrmester, D. (1996). Need fulfillment, interpersonal competence, and the developmental contexts of early adolescent friendship. In W. M. Bukowski, A. F. Newcomb, & W. W. Hartup (Eds.), *The company they keep: Friendship in childhood and adolescence.* Cambridge: Cambridge University Press.

Buhrmester, D., & Furman, W. (1986). The changing functions of friends in childhood: A neo-Sullivanian perspective. In V. J. Derlega & B. A. Winstead (Eds.), *Friendship and social interaction.* New York: Springer-Verlag.

Bukowski, W. M., Gauze, C., Hoza, B., & Newcomb, A. F. (1993). Differences and consistency between same-sex and other-sex peer relationships during early adolescence. *Developmental Psychology, 29,* 253–263.

Cairns, R. B., Leung, M. C., Buchanan, L., & Cairns, B. D. (1995). Friendships and social networks in childhood and adolescence: Fluidity, reliability, and interrelations. *Child Development, 66,* 1330–1345.

Campbell, F. A., & Ramey, C. T. (1994). Effects of early intervention on intellectual and academic achievement: A follow-up study of children from low-income families. *Child Development, 65,* 684–698.

Carlson, V., Cicchetti, D., Barnett, D., & Braunwald, K. (1989). Disorganized/disoriented attachment relationships in maltreated infants. *Developmental Psychology, 25,* 525–531.

Carstensen, L. L. (1992). Social and emotional patterns in adulthood: Support for socioemotional selectivity theory. *Psychology and Aging, 7,* 331–338.

Cassidy, J., Kirsh, S. J., Scolton, K. L., & Parke, R. D. (1996). Attachment and representations of peer relationships. *Developmental Psychology, 32,* 892–904.

Chen, X., Rubin, K. H., & Sun, Y. (1992). Social reputation in Chinese and Canadian children: A cross-cultural study. *Child Development, 63,* 1336–1343.

Christopher, J. S., Nangle, D. W., & Hansen, D. J. (1993). Social-skills interventions with adolescents: Current issues and procedures. *Behavior Modification, 17,* 314–338.

Cillessen, A. H., van IJzendoorn, H. W., Van Lieshout, C. F., & Hartup, W. W. (1992). Heterogeneity among peer-rejected boys: Subtypes and stabilities. *Child Development, 63,* 893–905.

Clarke-Stewart, A. (1993). *Daycare* (rev. ed.). Cambridge, MA: Harvard University Press.

Coie, J. D., Dodge, K. A., & Coppotelli, H. (1982). Dimensions and types of social status: A cross-age perspective. *Developmental Psychology, 18,* 557–570.

Coie, J. D., Dodge, K. A., & Kupersmidt, J. B. (1990). Peer group behavior and social status. In S. R. Asher & J. D. Coie (Eds.), *Peer rejection in childhood.* Cambridge: Cambridge University Press.

Coie, J. D., Lochman, J. E., Terry, R., & Hyman, C. (1992). Predicting early adolescent disorder from childhood aggression and peer rejection. *Journal of Consulting and Clinical Psychology, 60,* 783–792.

Cole, P. M., Michel, M. K., & Teti, L. O. (1994). The development of emotion regulation and dysregulation: A clinical perspective. In N. Fox (Ed.), The development of emotion regulation: Biological and behavioral considerations. *Monographs of the Society for Research in Child Development, 59* (Nos. 2–3, Serial No. 240).

Colin, V. (1996). *Human attachment.* New York: McGraw-Hill.

Connidis, I. A., & Davies, L. (1992). Confidants and companions: Choices in later life. *Journal of Gerontology: Social Sciences, 47,* S115–S122.

Connolly, J. A., & Doyle, A. B. (1984). Relation of social fantasy play to social competence in preschoolers. *Developmental Psychology, 20,* 797–806.

Crockenberg, S., & Litman, C. (1991). Effects of maternal employment on maternal and two-year-old child behavior. *Child Development, 61,* 930–953.

Crowell, J. A., & Feldman, S. S. (1991). Mothers' working models of attachment relationships and mother and child behavior during separation and reunion. *Developmental Psychology, 27,* 597–605.

Curry, N. E., & Arnaud, S. H. (1984). Play in developmental preschool settings. In T. D. Yawkey & A. D. Pelligrini (Eds.), *Child's play: Developmental and applied.* Hillsdale, NJ: Erlbaum.

de Jong-Gierveld, J. (1986). Loneliness and the degree of intimacy in interpersonal relationships. In R. Gilmour & S. Duck (Eds.), *The emerging field of personal relationships.* Hillsdale, NJ: Erlbaum.

Denham, S. A. (1989). Maternal affect and toddlers' social-emotional competence. *American Journal of Orthopsychiatry, 141,* 1189–1194.

Depner, C. E., & Ingersoll-Dayton, B. (1988). Supportive relationships in later life. *Psychology and Aging, 3,* 348–357.

DeRosier, M. E., Kupersmidt, J. B., & Patterson, C. J. (1994). Children's academic and behavioral adjustment as a function of the chronicity and proximity of peer rejection. *Child Development, 65,* 1799–1813.

DeWolff, M. S., & van IJzendoorn, M. H. (1997). Sensitivity and attachment: A meta-analysis on parental antecedents of infant attachment. *Child Development, 68,* 571–591.

Dickens, W. J., & Perlman, D. (1981). Friendship over the life cycle. In S. Duck & R. Gilmour (Eds.), *Personal relationships: Vol. 2. Developing personal relationships.* London: Academic Press.

Dishion, T. J., Patterson, G. R., Stoolmiller, M., & Skinner, M. L. (1991). Family, school, and behavioral antecedents to early adolescent involvement with antisocial peers. *Developmental Psychology, 27,* 172–180.

Dixon, S., Tronick, E., Keefer, C., & Brazelton, T. B. (1981). Mother-infant interaction among the Gusii of Kenya. In T. M. Field, A. M. Sostek, P. Vietze, & P. H. Leiderman (Eds.), *Culture and early interactions.* Hillsdale, NJ: Erlbaum.

Dodge, K. A., Coie, J. D., Pettit, G. S., & Price, J. M. (1990). Peer status and aggression in boys' groups: Developmental and contextual analysis. *Child Development, 61,* 1289–1309.

Douvan, E., & Adelson, J. (1966). *The adolescent experience.* New York: Wiley.

Dunphy, D. C. (1963). The social structure of urban adolescent peer groups. *Sociometry, 26,* 230–246.

Eckerman, C. O., & Didow, S. M. (1996). Nonverbal imitation and toddlers' mastery of verbal means of achieving coordinated action. *Developmental Psychology, 32,* 141–152.

Eckerman, C. O., & Stein, M. R. (1990). How imitation begets imitation and toddlers' generation of games. *Developmental Psychology, 26,* 370–378.

Elicker, J., Englund, M., & Sroufe, L. A. (1992). Predicting peer competence and peer relationships in childhood from early parent-child relationships. In R. D. Parke & G. W. Ladd (Eds.), *Family-peer relationships: Modes of linkage.* Hillsdale, NJ: Erlbaum.

Ellis, S., Rogoff, B., & Cromer, C. C. (1981). Age segregation in children's social interactions. *Developmental Psychology, 17,* 399–407.

Fagot, B. I. (1997). Attachment, parenting, and peer interactions of toddler

children. *Developmental Psychology, 33,* 489–499.

Fallon, B. J., & Bowles, T. V. (1997). The effect of family structure and family functioning on adolescents' perceptions of intimate time spent with parents, siblings, and peers. *Journal of Youth and Adolescence, 26,* 25–43.

Farver, J. A. M., & Shin, Y. L. (1997). Social pretend play in Korean and Anglo-American preschoolers. *Child Development, 68,* 544–556.

Feeney, J. A., & Noller, P. (1996). *Adult attachment.* Thousand Oaks, CA: Sage.

Fein, G. G. (1986). The affective psychology of play. In A. W. Gottfried & C. C. Brown (Eds.), *Play interactions: The contributions of play material and parental involvement to children's development.* Lexington, MA: Lexington Books.

Feinman, S. (1992). *Social referencing and the social construction of reality in infancy.* New York: Plenum.

Feiring, C. (1996). Concepts of romance in 15-year-old adolescents. *Journal of Research on Adolescence, 6,* 181–200.

Felton, B. J., & Berry, C. A. (1992). Do the sources of the urban elderly's social support determine its psychological consequences? *Psychology and Aging, 7,* 89–97.

Field, T. M. (1987). Affective and interactive disturbances in infants. In J. D. Osofsky (Ed.), *Handbook of infant development* (2nd ed.). New York: Wiley.

Fischer, C. S., & Phillips, S. L. (1982). Who is alone? Social characteristics of people with small networks. In L. A. Peplau & D. Perlman (Eds.), *Loneliness. A sourcebook of current theory, research, and therapy.* New York: Wiley-Interscience.

Fischer, J. L., Sollie, D. L., Sorell, G. T., & Green, S. K. (1989). Marital status and career stage influences on social networks of young adults. *Journal of Marriage and the Family, 51,* 521–534.

Fisher, E. P. (1992). The impact of play on development: A meta-analysis. *Play and Culture, 5,* 159–181.

Fisher, L., Ames, E. W., Chisholm, K., & Savoie, L. (1997). Problems reported by parents of Romanian orphans adopted to British Columbia. *International Journal of Behavioral Development, 20,* 67–82.

Fox, N. A., Kimmerly, N. L., & Schafer, W. D. (1991). Attachment to mother/

attachment to father: A meta-analysis. *Child Development, 62,* 210–225.

Fraley, R. C., & Shaver, P. R. (1997). Adult attachment and the suppression of unwanted thoughts. *Journal of Personality and Social Psychology, 73* 1080–1091.

Freud, S. (1930). *Three contributions to the theory of sex.* New York: Nervous and Mental Disease Publishing Company. (Original work published 1905)

Fuligni, A. J., & Eccles, J. S. (1993). Perceived parent-child relationships and early adolescents' orientation toward peers. *Developmental Psychology, 29,* 622–632.

Fuller, B., Holloway, S. D., & Liang, X. (1996). Family selection of child-care centers: The influence of household support, ethnicity, and parental practices. *Child Development, 67,* 3320–3337.

Fullerton, C. S., & Ursano, R. J. (1994). Preadolescent peer friendships: A critical contribution to adult social relatedness? *Journal of Youth and Adolescence, 23,* 43–63.

Furman, W., & Bierman, K. L. (1983). Developmental changes in young children's conceptions of friendship. *Child Development, 54,* 549–556.

Furman, W., & Buhrmester, D. (1992). Age and sex differences in perceptions of networks of personal relationships. *Child Development, 63,* 103–115.

Furman, W., & Wehner, E. A. (1994). Romantic views: Toward a theory of adolescent romantic relationships. In R. Montemayor, G. R. Adams, & T. P. Gullotta (Eds.), *Personal relationships during adolescence: Vol. 6. Advances in adolescent development.* Thousand Oaks, CA: Sage.

Gandelman, R. (1992). *Psychobiology of behavioral development.* New York: Oxford University Press.

Gauvain, M., & Rogoff, B. (1989). Collaborative problem solving and children's planning skills. *Developmental Psychology, 25,* 139–151.

Gauze, C., Bukowski, W. M., Aquanassee, J., & Sippola, L. K. (1996). Interactions between family environment and friendship and associations with self-perceived well-being during early adolescence. *Child Development, 67,* 2301–2316.

George, T. P., & Hartmann, D. P. (1996). Friendship networks of unpopular, average, and popular children. *Child Development, 67,* 2301–2316.

Goldberg, S., Perrotta, M., Minde, K., & Corter, C. (1986). Maternal behavior and attachment in low-birth-weight twins and singletons. *Child Development, 57,* 34–46.

Goldfarb, W. (1943). The effects of early institutional care on adolescent personality. *Journal of Experimental Education, 12,* 107–129.

Goldfarb, W. (1945). Effects of psychological deprivation in infancy and subsequent stimulation. *American Journal of Psychiatry, 102,* 18–33.

Goldfarb, W. (1947). Variations in adolescent adjustment in institutionally reared children. *Journal of Orthopsychiatry, 17,* 449–457.

Goldsmith, H. H., & Alansky, J. A. (1987). Maternal and infant temperamental predictors of attachment: A meta-analytic review. *Journal of Consulting and Clinical Psychology, 55,* 805–816.

Gordon, D. E. (1993). The inhibition of pretend play and its implications for development. *Human Development, 36,* 215–234.

Gottman, J. M. (1983). How children become friends. *Monographs of the Society for Research in Child Development, 48,* (3, Serial No. 201).

Grolnick, W. S., Bridges, L. J., & Connell, J. P. (1996). Emotion regulation in two-year-olds: Strategies and emotional expression in four contexts. *Child Development, 67,* 928–941.

Grossmann, K., Grossmann, K. E., Spangler, S., Suess, G., & Unzner, L. (1985). Maternal sensitivity and newborn responses as related to quality of attachment in Northern Germany. In I. Bretherton & E. Waters, *Growing points of attachment theory. Monographs of the Society for Research in Child Development, 50* (1–2, Serial No. 209).

Halberstadt, A. G. (1991). Toward an ecology of expressiveness: Family socialization in particular and a model in general. In R. S. Feldman & B. Rime (Eds.), *Fundamentals of nonverbal behavior.* New York: Cambridge University Press.

Harlow, H. F., & Zimmerman, R. R. (1959). Affectional responses in the infant monkey. *Science, 130,* 421–432.

Harris, J. R. (1995). Where is the child's environment? A group socialization theory of development. *Psychological Review, 102,* 458–489.

Harris, P. L., & Kavanaugh, R. D. (1993). Young children's understanding of pretense. *Monographs of the Society for Research in Child Development, 58* (1, Serial No. 181).

Harrist, A. W., Zaia, A. F., Bates, J. E., Dodge, K. A., & Pettit, G. S. (1997). Subtypes of social withdrawal in early childhood: Sociometric status and social-cognitive differences across four years. *Child Development, 68,* 278–294.

Hartup, W. W. (1996). The company they keep: Friendships and their developmental significance. *Child Development, 67,* 1–13.

Hartup, W. W., & Stevens, N. (1997). Friendships and adaptation in the life course. *Psychological Bulletin, 121,* 355–370.

Hay, D. F. (1985). Learning to form relationships in infancy: Parallel attainments with parents and peers. *Developmental Review, 5,* 122–161.

Hay, D. F., Nash, A., & Pedersen, J. (1983). Interaction between six-month-old peers. *Child Development, 54,* 557–562.

Hazan, C., & Shaver, P. (1987). Romantic love conceptualized as an attachment process. *Journal of Personality and Social Psychology, 52,* 511–524.

Hazan, C., & Shaver, P. R. (1990). Love and work: An attachment-theoretical perspective. *Journal of Personality and Social Psychology, 59,* 270–280.

Hertsgaard, L., Gunnar, M., Erickson, M. F., & Nachmias, M. (1995). Adrenocortical responses to the Strange Situation in infants with disorganized/disoriented attachment relationships. *Child Development, 66,* 1100–1106.

Hetherington, E. M., Cox, M., & Cox, R. (1979). Play and social interaction in children following divorce. *Journal of Social Issues, 35,* 26–49.

Hodges, J., & Tizard, B. (1989). IQ and behavioural adjustment of ex-institutional adolescents. *Journal of Child Psychology and Psychiatry, 30,* 53–75.

Holden, C. (1996, November 15). Small refugees suffer the effects of early neglect. *Science, 274,* 1076–1077.

Howes, C. (1990). Can the age of entry into child care and the quality of child care predict adjustment in kindergarten? *Developmental Psychology, 26,* 292–303.

Howes, C. (1996). The earliest friendships. In W. M. Bukowski, A. F. Newcomb, & W. W. Hartup (Eds.), *The company they keep: Friendships in childhood and adolescence.* Cambridge: Cambridge University Press.

Howes, C., & Matheson, C. C. (1992). Sequences in the development of competent play with peers: Social and social pretend play. *Developmental Psychology, 28*, 961–974.

Howes, C., Phillips, D. A., & Whitebrook, M. (1992). Thresholds of quality: Implications for the social development of children in center-based child care. *Child Development, 63*, 449–460.

Howes, P., & Markman, H. J. (1989). Marital quality and child functioning: A longitudinal investigation. *Child Development, 60*, 1044–1051.

Ingrassia, M., & Springen, K. (1994, March 21). She's not baby Jessica anymore. *Newsweek, 123*, 60–66.

Isabella, R. A. (1993). Origins of attachment: Maternal interactive behavior across the first year. *Child Development, 64*, 605–621.

Isabella, R. A., & Belsky, J. (1991). Interactional synchrony and the origins of infant-mother attachment: A replication study. *Child Development, 62*, 373–384.

Izard, C. E. (1982). *Measuring emotions in infants and children.* New York: Cambridge University Press.

Izard, C. E. (1993). Four systems for emotion activation: Cognitive and noncognitive processes. *Psychological Review, 100*, 68–90.

Jacobsen, T., & Hofmann, V. (1997). Children's attachment representations: Longitudinal relations to school behavior and academic competency in middle childhood and adolescence. *Developmental Psychology, 33*, 703–710.

Jankowiak, W. R., & Fischer, E. F. (1992). A cross-cultural perspective on romantic love. *Ethnology, 31*, 149–155.

Johnson, C. L., & Troll, L. E. (1994). Constraints and facilitators to friendships in late late life. *Gerontologist, 34*, 79–87.

Johnson, E. P. (1991). Searching for the social and cognitive outcomes of children's play: A selective second look. *Play and Culture, 4*, 201–213.

Johnson, W., Emde, R. N., Pannabecker, B., Stenberg, C., & Davis, M. (1982). Maternal perception of infant emotion from birth through 18 months. *Infant Behavior and Development, 5*, 313–322.

Jones, W. H., Hobbs, S. A., & Hockenbury, D. (1982). Loneliness and social skill deficits. *Journal of Personality and Social Psychology, 42*, 682–689.

Juffer, F., & Rosenboom, L. G. (1997). Infant-mother attachment of internationally adopted children in the Netherlands. *International Journal of Behavioral Development, 20*, 93–107.

Kagan, J. (1972). Do infants think? *Scientific American, 226*, 74–82.

Kagan, J. (1976). Emergent themes in human development. *American Scientist, 64*, 186–196.

Kagan, J., Kearsley, R. B., & Zelazo, P. R. (1978). *Infancy: Its place in human development.* Cambridge, MA: Harvard University Press.

Kahn, R. L., & Antonucci, T. C. (1980). Convoys over the life course: Attachment, roles, and social support. In P. B. Baltes & O. G. Brim, Jr. (Eds.), *Life-span development and behavior* (Vol. 3). New York: Academic Pess.

Keller, H., & Scholmerich, A. (1987). Infant vocalizations and parental reactions during the first four months of life. *Developmental Psychology, 23*, 62–67.

Kendig, H. L., Coles, R., Pittelkow, Y., & Wilson, S. (1988). Confidants and family structure in old age. *Journal of Gerontology: Social Sciences, 43*, S31–S40.

Kenny, M. E. (1987). The extent and function of parental attachment among first-year college students. *Journal of Youth and Adolescence, 16*, 17–29.

Kenny, M. E., & Donaldson, G. A. (1991). Contributions of parental attachment and family structure to the social and psychological functioning of first-year college students. *Journal of Counseling Psychology, 38*, 479–486.

Kenny, M. E., & Rice, K. G. (1995). Attachment to parents and adjustment in late adolescent college students: Current status, applications, and future considerations. *The Counseling Psychologist, 23*, 433–456.

Kerns, K. A. (1996). Individual differences in friendship quality: Links to child-mother attachment. In W. M. Bukowski, A. F. Newcomb, & W. W. Hartup (Eds.), *The company they keep: Friendship in childhood and adolescence.* Cambridge: Cambridge University Press.

Kerns, K. A., Klepac, L., & Cole, A. K. (1996). Peer relationships and preadolescents' perceptions of security in the child-mother relationship. *Developmental Psychology, 32*, 457–466.

Kessen, W. (1975). *Childhood in China.* New Haven, CT: Yale University Press.

Klaus, H. M., & Kennell, J. H. (1976). *Maternal-infant bonding.* St. Louis: Mosby.

Klinnert, M. D., Emde, R. N., Butterfield, P., & Campos, J. J. (1986). Social referencing: The infant's use of emotional signals from a friendly adult with mother present. *Developmental Psychology, 22*, 427–432.

Kobak, R. R., Cole, H. E., Ferenz-Gilles, R., Fleming, W. S., & Gamble, W. (1993). Attachment and emotional regulation during mother-teen problem solving: A control theory analysis. *Child Development, 64*, 231–245.

Kohlberg, L. (1969). Stage and sequence: The cognitive-developmental approach to socialization. In D. A. Goslin (Ed.), *Handbook of socialization theory and research.* Chicago: Rand McNally.

Kopp, C. B. (1989). Regulation of distress and negative emotions: A developmental view. *Developmental Psychology, 25*, 343–354.

Krause, N. (1995). Negative interaction and satisfaction with social support among older adults. *Journal of Gerontology: Psychological Sciences, 50B*, P59–P73.

Ladd, G. W. (1990). Having friends, keeping friends, making friends, and being liked by peers in the classroom: Predictors of children's early school adjustment. *Child Development, 61*, 1081–1100.

Ladd, G. W., Price, J. M., & Hart, C. H. (1990). Preschoolers' behavioral orientations and patterns of peer contact: Predictive of peer status? In S. R. Asher & J. D. Coie (Eds.), *Peer rejection in childhood.* New York: Cambridge University Press.

Lamb, M. E. (1987). Predictive implications of individual differences in attachment. *Journal of Consulting and Clinical Psychology, 55*, 817–824.

Lamb, M. E., Sternberg, K. J., & Prodromidis, M. (1992). Nonmaternal care and the security of infant-mother attachment: A reanalysis of the data. *Infant Behavior and Development, 15*, 71–83.

Lang, F. R., & Carstensen, L. L. (1994). Close emotional relationships in late life: Further support for proactive aging in the social domain. *Psychology and Aging, 9*, 315–324.

Langlois, J. H. (1986). From the eye of the beholder to behavioral reality: Development of social behaviors and social relations as a function of physical attractiveness. In C. P. Herman, M. P. Zanna, & E. T. Higgins (Eds.), *Physical appearance, stigma, and social behavior: The Ontario symposium, volume 3.* Hillsdale, NJ: Erlbaum.

Lapsley, D. K., Rice, K. G., & FitzGerald, D. P. (1990). Adolescent attachment, identity, and adjustment to college: Implications for the continuity of adaptation hypothesis. *Journal of Counseling and Development, 68,* 561–565.

Laursen, B. (1996). Closeness and conflict in adolescent peer relationships: Interdependence with friends and romantic partners. In W. M. Bukowski, A. F. Newcomb, & W. W. Hartup (Eds.), *The company they keep: Friendship in childhood and adolescence.* Cambridge: Cambridge University Press.

Lempers, J. D., & Clark-Lempers, D. S. (1992). Young, middle, and late adolescents' comparisons of the functional importance of five significant relationships. *Journal of Youth and Adolescence, 21,* 53–96.

Lester, B. M., Kotelchuck, M., Spelke, E., Sellers, M. J., & Klein, R. E. (1974). Separation protest in Guatemalan infants: Cross-cultural and cognitive findings. *Developmental Psychology, 10,* 79–85.

Levesque, R. J. R. (1993). The romantic experience of adolescents in satisfying love relationships. *Journal of Youth and Adolescence, 22,* 219–251.

Levitt, M. J. (1991). Attachment and close relationships: A life-span perspective. In J. L. Gewirtz & W. M. Kurtines (Eds.), *Intersections with attachment.* Hillsdale, NJ: Erlbaum.

Levitt, M. J., Guacci-Franco, N., & Levitt, J. L. (1993). Convoys of social support in childhood and early adolescence: Structure and function. *Developmental Psychology, 29,* 811–818.

Levitt, M. J., Weber, R. A., & Guacci, N. (1993). Convoys of social support: An intergenerational analysis. *Psychology and Aging, 8,* 323–326.

Lewis, M., & Rosenblum, M. A. (1975). *Friendship and peer relations.* New York: Wiley.

Lorenz, K. Z. (1937). The companion in the bird's world. *Auk, 54,* 245–273.

Lyons-Ruth, K., Connell, D. B., Grunebaum, H. U., & Botein, S. (1990). Infants at social risk: Maternal depression and family support services as mediators of infant devel-

opment and security of attachment. *Child Development, 61,* 85–98.

Main, M., & Cassidy, J. (1988). Categories of response to reunion with the parent at age 6: Predictable from infant attachment classifications and stable over a 1-month period. *Developmental Psychology, 24,* 415–426.

Main, M., & Solomon, J. (1990). Procedures for identifying infants as disorganized/disoriented during the Ainsworth Strange Situation. In M. T. Greenberg, D. Cicchetti, & E. M. Cummings (Eds.), *Attachment in the preschool years: Theory, research, and intervention.* Chicago: University of Chicago Press.

Main, M., & Weston, D. R. (1981). The quality of the toddler's relationship to mother and to father: Related to conflict and the readiness to establish new relationships. *Child Development, 52,* 932–940.

Malatesta, C. Z., Culver, C., Tesman, J. R., & Shepard, B. (1989). The development of emotion expression during the first two years of life. *Monographs of the Society for Research in Child Development, 54* (1–2, Serial No. 219).

Malatesta, C. Z., Grigoryev, P., Lamb, C., Albin, M., & Culver, C. (1986). Emotional socialization and expressive development in preterm and full-term infants. *Child Development, 57,* 316–330.

Malik, N. M., & Furman, W. (1993). Practitioner review: Problems in children's peer relations: What can the clinician do? *Journal of Child Psychology and Psychiatry, 34,* 1303–1326.

Mangelsdorf, S. C. (1992). Developmental changes in infant-stranger interaction. *Infant Behavior and Development, 15,* 191–208.

Mangelsdorf, S. C., Gunnar, M., Kestenbaum, R., Lang, S., & Andreas, D. (1990). Infant proneness-to-distress temperament, maternal personality, and mother-infant attachment: Associations and goodness of fit. *Child Development, 61,* 820–831.

Mangelsdorf, S. C., Shapiro, J. R., & Marzolf, D. (1995). Developmental and temperamental differences in emotion regulation in infancy. *Child Development, 66,* 1817–1828.

Marcovitch, S., Goldberg, S., Gold, A., Washington, J., Wasson, C., Krekewich, K., & Handley-Derry, M. (1997). Determinants of behavioural problems in Romanian children adopted in Ontario. *International*

Journal of Behavioral Development, 20, 17–31.

Matthews, S. H. (1986). *Friendships through the life course: Oral biographies in old age* (Vol. 161, Sage Library of Social Research). Beverly Hills, CA: Sage.

Mayseless, O., Danieli, R., & Sharabany, R. (1996). Adults' attachment patterns: Coping with separations. *Journal of Youth and Adolescence, 25,* 667–690.

Mize, J., & Pettit, G. S. (1997). Mothers' social coaching, mother-child relationship style, and children's peer competence: Is the medium the message? *Child Development, 68,* 312–332.

Morgan, G. A., & Ricciuti, H. N. (1969). Infants' responses to strangers during the first year. In B. M. Foss (Ed.), *Determinants of infant behavior* (Vol. 4). London: Methuen.

Morison, P., & Masten, A. S. (1991). Peer reputation in middle childhood as a predictor of adaptation in adolescence: A seven-year follow-up. *Child Development, 62,* 991–1007.

Mounts, N. S., & Steinberg, L. (1995). An ecological analysis of peer influence on adolescent grade point average and drug use. *Developmental Psychology, 31,* 915–922.

Mueller, E., & Lucas, T. (1975). A developmental analysis of peer interactions among toddlers. In M. Lewis & L. Rosenblum (Eds.), *Friendship and peer relations.* New York: Wiley.

Mueller, E., & Vandell, D. (1979). Infant-infant interaction. In J. Osofsky (Ed.), *Handbook of infant development.* New York: Wiley.

Murray, L., Fiori-Cowley, A., Hooper, R., & Cooper, P. (1996). The impact of postnatal depression and associated adversity on early mother-infant interactions and later infant outcome. *Child Development, 67,* 2512–2526.

Newcomb, A. F., & Bagwell, C. L. (1995). Children's friendship relations: A meta-analytic review. *Psychological Bulletin, 117,* 306–347.

NICHD Early Child Care Research Network. (1997). The effects of infant child care on infant-mother attachment security: Results of the NICHD Study of Early Child Care. *Child Development, 68,* 860–879.

Nicolich, L. M. (1977). Beyond sensorimotor intelligence: Assessment of symbolic maturity through analysis of pretend play. *Merrill-Palmer Quarterly, 23,* 89–99.

Noam, G. G., & Fischer, K. W. (1996). Introduction: The foundational role of relationships in human development. In G. G. Noam & K. W. Fischer (Eds.), *Development and vulnerability in close relationships.* Mahwah, NJ: Erlbaum.

O'Connor, B. P. (1995). Family and friend relationships among older and younger adults: Interaction motivation, mood, and quality. *International Journal of Aging and Human Development, 40,* 9–29.

Oden, S., & Asher, S. R. (1977). Coaching children in social skills for friendship making. *Child Development, 48,* 495–506.

Oppenheim, D., Sagi, A., & Lamb, M. E. (1988). Infant-adult attachments on the kibbutz and their relation to socioemotional development 4 years later. *Developmental Psychology, 24,* 427–433.

Parker, J. G., & Asher, S. R. (1993). Friendship and friendship quality in middle childhood: Links with peer group acceptance and feelings of loneliness and social dissatisfaction. *Developmental Psychology, 29,* 611–621.

Parkhurst, J. T., & Asher, S. R. (1992). Peer rejection in middle school: Subgroup differences in behavior, loneliness, and interpersonal concerns. *Developmental Psychology, 28,* 231–241.

Parlee, M. B., & the Editors of *Psychology Today* (1979, October). The friendship bond. *Psychology Today,* 42–54, 113.

Parten, M. B. (1932). Social participation among preschool children. *Journal of Abnormal and Social Psychology, 27,* 243–269.

Passman, R. H. (1977). Providing attachment objects to facilitate learning and reduce distress: Effects of mothers and security blankets. *Developmental Psychology, 13,* 25–28.

Pettit, G. S., Clawson, M. A., Dodge, K. A., & Bates, J. E. (1996). Stability and change in peer-rejected status: The role of child behavior, parenting, and family ecology. *Merrill-Palmer Quarterly: Journal of Developmental Psychology, 42,* 267–294.

Piaget, J. (1965). *The moral judgment of the child.* New York: Free Press. (Original work published 1932)

Pilisuk, M., & Minkler, M. (1980). Supportive networks: Life ties for the elderly. *Journal of Social Issues, 36* (2), 95–116.

Provence, S., & Lipton, R. C. (1962). *Infants in institutions.* New York: International Universities Press.

Putallaz, M., & Wasserman, A. (1989). Children's naturalistic entry behavior and sociometric status: A developmental perspective. *Developmental Psychology, 25,* 297–305.

Rabiner, D. L., Keane, S. P., & MacKinnon-Lewis, C. (1993). Children's beliefs about familiar and unfamiliar peers in relation to their sociometric status. *Developmental Psychology, 29,* 236–243.

Reis, H. T., Lin, Y., Bennett, M. E., & Nezlek, J. B. (1993). Change and consistency in social participation during early adulthood. *Developmental Psychology, 29,* 633–645.

Roberto, K. A., & Scott, J. P. (1986). Equity considerations in the friendships of older adults. *Journal of Gerontology, 41,* 241–247.

Rook, K. S. (1984). Promoting social bonding. Strategies for helping the lonely and socially isolated. *American Psychologist, 39,* 1389–1407.

Rook, K. S. (1991). Facilitating friendship formation in late life: Puzzles and challenges. *American Journal of Community Psychology, 19,* 103–110.

Rubin, K. H., Fein, G., & Vandenberg, B. (1983). Play. In E. M. Hetherington (Ed.; P. H. Mussen, General Ed.), *Handbook of child psychology: Vol. 4. Socialization, personality, and social development.* New York: Wiley.

Rutter, M. (1981). *Maternal deprivation revisited* (2nd ed.). New York: Penguin Books.

Scarr, S., & Eisenberg, M. (1993). Child care research: Issues, perspectives, and results. *Annual Review of Psychology, 44,* 613–644.

Scarr, S., Phillips, D., McCartney, K., & Abbot-Shim, M. (1993). Quality of child care as an aspect of family and child care policy in the United States. *Pediatrics, 91,* 182–188.

Schaffer, H. R., & Emerson, P. E. (1964). The development of social attachments in infancy. *Monographs of the Society for Research in Child Development, 29* (3, Serial No. 94).

Sebald, H. (1986). Adolescents' shifting orientation toward parents and peers: A curvilinear trend over recent decades. *Journal of Marriage and the Family, 48,* 5–13.

Selman, R. L. (1980). *The growth of interpersonal understanding.* New York: Academic Press.

Sharabany, R., Gershoni, R., & Hofman, J. E. (1981). Girlfriend, boyfriend: Age and sex differences in intimate friendship. *Developmental Psychology, 17,* 800–808.

Sharpsteen, D. J., & Kirkpatrick, L. A. (1997). Romantic jealousy and adult romantic attachment. *Journal of Personality and Social Psychology, 72,* 627–640.

Shaver, P. R., & Clark, C. L. (1996). Forms of adult romantic attachment and their cognitive and emotional underpinnings. In G. G. Noam & K. W. Fischer (Eds.), *Development and vulnerability in close relationships.* Mahwah, NJ: Erlbaum.

Shea, L., Thompson, L., & Blieszner, R. (1988). Resources in older adults' old and new friendships. *Journal of Social and Personal Relationships, 5,* 83–96.

Silverstein, M., & Waite, L. J. (1993). Are blacks more likely than whites to receive and provide social support in middle and old age?—Yes, no, and maybe so. *Journal of Gerontology: Social Sciences, 48,* S212–S222.

Skolnick, A. (1986). Early attachment and personal relationships across the life course. In P. B. Baltes, D. L. Featherman, & R. M. Lerner (Eds.), *Life-span development and behavior* (Vol. 7). Hillsdale, NJ: Erlbaum.

Smith, P. K. (1978). A longitudinal study of social participation in preschool children: Solitary and parallel play reexamined. *Developmental Psychology, 14,* 517–523.

Sroufe, L. A. (1977). Wariness of strangers and the study of infant development. *Child Development, 48,* 1184–1199.

Sroufe, L. A. (1985). Attachment classification from the perspective of infant-caregiver relationships and infant temperament. *Child Development, 56,* 1–14.

Sroufe, L. A., Bennett, C., Englund, M. Urban, J., & Shulman, S. (1993). The significance of gender boundaries in preadolescence: Contemporary correlates and antecedents of boundary violation and maintenance. *Child Development, 64,* 455–466.

Sroufe, L. A., Waters, E., & Matas, L. (1974). Contextual determinants of infant affectional response. In M. Lewis & L. A. Rosenblum (Eds.), *The origins of fear.* New York: Wiley.

Steele, H., Steele, M., & Fonagy, P. (1996). Associations among attachment classifications of mothers, fathers, and their infants. *Child Development, 67,* 541–555.

Steinberg, L., & Silverberg, S. B. (1986). The vicissitudes of autonomy in early adolescence. *Child Development, 57,* 841–851.

Stern, D. (1977). *The first relationship: Infant and mother.* Cambridge, MA: Harvard University Press.

Stevenson, M. B., VerHoeve, J. N., Roach, M. A., & Leavitt, L. A. (1986). The beginning of conversation: Early patterns of mother-infant vocal responsiveness. *Infant Behavior and Development, 9,* 423–440.

Sullivan, H. S. (1953). *The interpersonal theory of psychiatry.* New York: Norton.

Takahashi, K. (1990). Are the key assumptions of the "Strange Situation" procedure universal? A view from Japanese research. *Human Development, 33,* 23–30.

Terry, R., & Coie, J. D. (1991). A comparison of methods for defining sociometric status among children. *Developmental Psychology, 27,* 867–880.

Thompson, R. A. (1994). Emotion regulation: A theme in search of definition. In N. A. Fox (Ed.), The development of emotion regulation: Biological and behavioral considerations. *Monographs of the Society for Research in Child Development, 59* (2–3, Serial No. 240).

Thorne, B. (1993). *Gender play: Girls and boys in school.* New Brunswick, NJ: Rutgers University Press.

Thurber, C. A. (1995). The experience and expression of homesickness in preadolescent and adolescent boys. *Child Development, 66,* 1162–1178.

Tronick, E. Z. (1989). Emotions and emotional communication in infants. *American Psychologist, 44,* 112–119.

Tronick, E. Z., Morelli, G. A., & Ivey, P. K. (1992). The Efe forager infant and toddler's pattern of social relationships: Multiple and simultaneous. *Developmental Psychology, 28,* 568–577.

Tudge, J. R. H. (1992). Processes and consequences of peer collaboration: A Vygotskian analysis. *Child Development, 63,* 1364–1379.

Uchino, B. N., Cacioppo, J. T., & Keicolt-Glaser, J. K. (1996). The relationship between social support and physiological processes: A review with emphasis on underlying mechanisms and implications for health. *Psychological Bulletin, 119,* 488–531.

Uchino, B. N., Cacioppo, J. T., Malarkey, W., & Glaser, R. (1995). Appraisal support predicts age-related differences in cardiovascular function

in women. *Health Psychology, 14,* 556–562.

Udry, J. R. (1971). *The social context of marriage* (2nd ed.). Philadelphia: J. B. Lippincott.

Vandell, D. L., & Wilson, K. S. (1987). Infants' interactions with mother, sibling, and peer: Contrasts and relations between interaction systems. *Child Development, 58,* 176–186.

Vandell, D. L., Wilson, K. S., & Buchanan, N. R. (1980). Peer interaction in the first year of life: An examination of its structure, content, and sensitivity to toys. *Child Development, 51,* 481–488.

van den Boom, D. C. (1995). Do first-year intervention effects endure? Follow-up during toddlerhood of a sample of Dutch irritable infants. *Child Development, 66,* 1798–1816.

van IJzendoorn, M. H. (1995). Adult attachment representations, parental responsiveness, and infant attachment: A meta-analysis on the predictive validity of the Adult Attachment Interview. *Psychological Bulletin, 117,* 387–403.

van IJzendoorn, M. H., & De Wolff, M. S. (1997). In search of the absent father: Meta-analyses of infant-father attachment: A rejoinder to our discussants. *Child Development, 68,* 604–609.

van IJzendoorn, M. H., Goldberg, S., Kroonenberg, P. M., & Frenkel, O. J. (1992). The relative effects of maternal and child problems on the quality of attachment: A meta-analysis of attachment in clinical samples. *Child Development, 63,* 840–858.

van IJzendoorn, M. H., Juffer, F., & Duyvesteyn, M. G. C. (1995). Breaking the intergenerational cycle of insecure attachment: A review of the effects of attachment-based interventions on maternal sensitivity and infant security. *Journal of Child Psychology and Psychiatry and Allied Disciplines, 36,* 225–248.

van IJzendoorn, M. H., & Kroonenberg, P. M. (1988). Cross-cultural patterns of attachment: A meta-analysis of the Strange Situation. *Child Development, 59,* 147–156.

Vaughn, B. E., Egeland, B. R., Sroufe, L. A., & Waters, E. (1979). Individual differences in infant-mother attachment at twelve and eighteen months: Stability and change in families under stress. *Child Development, 50,* 971–975.

Vaughn, B. E., Lefever, G. B., Seifer, R., & Barglow, P. (1989). Attachment behavior, attachment security, and temperament during infancy. *Child Development, 60,* 728–737.

Vormbrock, J. K. (1993). Attachment theory as applied to wartime and job-related marital separation. *Psychological Bulletin, 114,* 122–144.

Walden, T. A., & Ogan, T. A. (1988). The development of social referencing. *Child Development, 59,* 1230–1240.

Walster, E., Walster, G. W., & Berscheid, E. (1978). *Equity: Theory and research.* Boston: Allyn and Bacon.

Waters, E., Wippman, J., & Sroufe, L. A. (1979). Attachment, positive affect, and competence in the peer group: Two studies in construct validation. *Child Development, 50,* 821–829.

Weinraub, M., & Lewis, M. (1977). The determinants of children's responses to separation. *Monographs of the Society for Research in Child Development* (4, Serial No. 172).

Wilks, J. (1986). The relative importance of parents and friends in adolescent decision making. *Journal of Youth and Adolescence, 15,* 323–334.

Wolff, P. H. (1963). Observations on the early development of smiling. In B. M. Foss (Ed.), *Determinants of infant behavior* (Vol. 2). London: Methuen.

Youniss, J. (1980). *Parents and peers in social development. A Sullivan-Piaget perspective.* Chicago: University of Chicago Press.

Youniss, J., McLellan, J. A., & Strouse, D. (1994). "We're popular, but we're not snobs": Adolescents describe their crowds. In R. Montemayor, G. R. Adams, & T. P. Gullotta (Eds.), *Personal relationships in adolescence: Vol. 6. Advances in adolescent development.* Thousand Oaks, CA: Sage.

Zaslow, M. (1980). Relationships among peers in kibbutz toddler groups. *Child Psychiatry and Human Development, 10,* 178–189.

Zaslow, M. (1991). Variation in child care quality and its implications for children. *Journal of Social Issues, 47,* 125–138.

CHAPTER 14: The Family

Abramovitch, R., Corter, C., Pepler, D. J., & Stanhope, L. (1986). Sibling and peer interaction: A final follow-up and a comparison. *Child Development, 57,* 217–229.

Agnew, R., & Huguley, S. (1989). Adolescent violence toward parents. *Journal of Marriage and the Family, 51,* 699–711.

Amato, P. R. (1989). Family processes and the competence of adolescents and primary school children. *Journal of Youth and Adolescence, 18,* 39–53.

Amato, P. R. (1993). Children's adjustment to divorce: Theories, hypotheses, and empirical support. *Journal of Marriage and the Family, 55,* 23–38.

Amato, P. R. (1996). Explaining the intergenerational transmission of divorce. *Journal of Marriage and the Family, 58,* 628–640.

Amato, P. R., & Booth, A. (1996). A prospective study of divorce and parent-child relationships. *Journal of Marriage and the Family, 58,* 356–365.

Amato, P. R., & Keith, B. (1991). Parental divorce and the well-being of children: A meta-analysis. *Psychological Bulletin, 110,* 26–46.

Amato, P. R., & Rogers, S. J. (1997). A longitudinal study of marital problems and subsequent divorce. *Journal of Marriage and the Family, 59,* 612–624.

Ambert, A. (1992). *The effect of children on parents.* New York: Haworth.

Ambert, A. (1994). An international perspective on parenting: Social change and social constructs. *Journal of Marriage and the Family, 56,* 529–543.

Ammerman, R. T., & Patz, R. J. (1996). Determinants of child abuse potential: Contribution of parent and child factors. *Journal of Clinical Child Psychology, 25,* 300–307.

Anderson, K. E., Lytton, H., & Romney, D. M. (1986). Mothers' interactions with normal and conduct-disordered boys: Who affects whom? *Developmental Psychology, 22,* 604–609.

Aneshensel, C. S., Pearlin, L. I., Mullan, J. T., Zarit, S. H., & Whitlatch, C. J. (1995). *Profiles in caregiving: The unexpected career.* San Diego: Academic Press.

Aquilino, W. S. (1991). Predicting parents' experiences with coresident adult children. *Journal of Family Issues, 12,* 323–342.

Aquilino, W. S. (1997). From adolescent to young adult: A prospective study of parent-child relations during the transition to adulthood. *Journal of Marriage and the Family, 59,* 670–686.

Arnett, J. J. (1995). Broad and narrow socialization: The family in the con-text of a cultural theory. *Journal of Marriage and the Family, 57,* 617–628.

Atkinson, M. P., Kivett, V. R., & Campbell, R. T. (1986). Intergenerational solidarity: An examination of a theoretical model. *Journal of Gerontology, 41,* 408–416.

Axinn, W. G., & Barber, J. S. (1997). Living arrangements and family formation attitudes in early adulthood. *Journal of Marriage and the Family, 59,* 595–611.

Axinn, W. G., & Thornton, A. (1993). Mothers, children, and cohabitation: The intergenerational effects of attitudes and behavior. *American Sociological Review, 58,* 233–246.

Azmitia, M., & Hesser, J. (1993). Why siblings are important agents of cognitive development: A comparison of siblings and peers. *Child Development, 64,* 430–444.

Bagley, C. (1995). *Child sexual abuse and mental health in adolescents and adults.* Aldershot, England: Ashgate Publishing Company.

Bailey, J. M., Bobrow, D., Wolfe, M., & Mikach, S. (1995). Sexual orientation of adult sons of gay fathers. *Developmental Psychology, 31,* 124–129.

Barber, B. L., & Eccles, J. S. (1992). Long-term influence of divorce and single parenting on adolescent family- and work-related values, behaviors, and aspirations. *Psychological Bulletin, 111,* 108–126.

Barnett, R. C., & Baruch, G. K. (1987). Determinants of father's participation in family work. *Journal of Marriage and the Family, 49,* 29–40.

Baskett, L. M., & Johnson, S. M. (1982). The young child's interaction with parents versus siblings: A behavioral analysis. *Child Development, 53,* 643–650.

Baumrind, D. (1967). Child care practices anteceding three patterns of preschool behavior. *Genetic Psychology Monographs, 75,* 43–88.

Baumrind, D. (1977, March). *Socialization determinants of personal agency.* Paper presented at the biennial meeting of the Society for Research in Child Development, New Orleans.

Baumrind, D. (1991). Effective parenting during the early adolescent transition. In P. A. Cowan & M. Hetherington (Eds.), *Family transitions.* Hillsdale, NJ: Erlbaum.

Belsky, J. (1981). Early human experience: A family perspective. *Developmental Psychology, 17,* 3–23.

Belsky, J. (1993). Etiology of child maltreatment: A developmental ecological analysis. *Psychological Bulletin, 114,* 413–434.

Belsky, J., Gilstrap, B., & Rovine, M. (1984). The Pennsylvania infant and family development project, I: Stability and change in mother-infant and father-infant interaction in a family setting at one, three, and nine months. *Child Development, 55,* 692–705.

Belsky, J., & Isabella, R. A. (1985). Marital and parent-child relationships in family of origin and marital change following the birth of a baby: A retrospective analysis. *Child Development, 56,* 342–349.

Belsky, J., Lang, M. E., & Rovine, M. (1985). Stability and change in marriage across the transition to parenthood: A second study. *Journal of Marriage and the Family, 47,* 855–865.

Bengtson, V., Rosenthal, C., & Burton, L. (1990). Families and aging: Diversity and heterogeneity. In R. H. Binstock & L. K. George (Eds.), *Handbook of aging and the social sciences* (3rd ed.). San Diego: Academic Press.

Bengtson, V., Rosenthal, C., & Burton, L. (1996). Paradoxes of families and aging. In R. H. Binstock, L. K. George, V. W. Marshall, G. C. Myers, & J. H. Schulz (Eds.), *Handbook of aging and the social sciences* (4th ed.). San Diego: Academic Press.

Biller, H. B. (1993). *Fathers and families: Paternal factors in child development.* Westport, CT: Auburn House.

Block, J. H., Block, J., & Gjerde, P. F. (1986). The personality of children prior to divorce: A prospective study. *Child Development, 57,* 827–840.

Blumstein, P., & Schwartz, P. (1983). *American couples. Money, work, sex.* New York: Morrow.

Bolger, K. E., Patterson, C. J., Thompson, W. W., & Kupersmidt, J. B. (1995). Psychosocial adjustment among children experiencing persistent and intermittent family economic hardship. *Child Development, 66,* 1107–1129.

Booth, A., & Amato, P. (1991). Divorce and psychological stress. *Journal of Health and Social Behavior, 32,* 396–407.

Booth, A., & Johnson, D. (1988). Premarital cohabitation and marital success. *Journal of Family Issues, 9,* 255–272.

Brayfield, A. (1995). Juggling jobs and kids: The impact of employment schedules on fathers' caring for children. *Journal of Marriage and the Family, 57,* 321–332.

Brody, E. M. (1985). Parent care as a normative family stress. *Gerontologist, 25,* 19–29.

Brody, E. M. (1990). *Women in the middle: Their parent-care years.* New York: Springer.

Brody, E. M., Johnsen, P. T., & Fulcomer, M. C. (1984). What should adult children do for elderly parents? Opinions and preferences of three generations of women. *Journal of Gerontology, 39,* 736–746.

Brody, E. M., Litvin, S. J., Hoffman, C., & Kleban, M. H. (1992). Differential effects of daughters' marital status on their parent care experiences. *Gerontologist, 32,* 58–67.

Brody, G. H., Stoneman, Z., & McCoy, J. K. (1994). Forecasting sibling relationships in early adolescence from child temperaments and family processes in middle adulthood. *Child Development, 65,* 771–784.

Bronfenbrenner, U. (1979). Contexts of child rearing: Problems and prospects. *American Psychologist, 34,* 844–850.

Bronfenbrenner, U. (1995). The bioecological model from a life course perspective: Reflections of a participant observer. In P. Moen, G. H. Elder, Jr., & K. Luscher (Eds.), *Examining lives in context.* Washington, DC: American Psychological Association.

Brown, B. B., Mounts, N., Lamborn, S. D., & Steinberg, L. (1993). Parenting practices and peer group affiliation in adolescence. *Child Development, 64,* 467–482.

Buehler, C. A., Hogan, M. J., Robinson, B. E., & Levy, R. J. (1985–1986). The parental divorce transition: Divorce-related stressors and well-being. *Journal of Divorce, 9,* 61–81.

Bugental, D. B., Blue, J., & Cruzcosa, M. (1989). Perceived control over caregiving outcomes: Implications for child abuse. *Developmental Psychology, 25,* 532–539.

Buhrmester, D., & Furman, W. (1990). Perceptions of sibling relationships during middle childhood and adolescence. *Child Development, 61,* 1387–1398.

Bumpass, L. L. (1990). What's happening to the family? Interactions between demographic and institutional change. *Demography, 27,* 483–498.

Burchinal, M. R., Follmer, A., & Bryant, D. M. (1996). The relations of maternal social support and family structure with maternal responsiveness and child outcomes among African-American families. *Developmental Psychology, 32,* 1073–1083.

Burton, L. M. (1990). Teenage childrearing as an alternative life-course strategy in multigenerational black families. *Human Nature, 1,* 123–143.

Burton, L. M. (1996). The timing of childbearing, family structure, and the role responsibilities of aging black women. In E. M. Hetherington & E. A. Blechman (Eds.), *Stress, coping, and resiliency in children and families.* Mahwah, NJ: Erlbaum.

Carstensen, L. L. (1992). Social and emotional patterns in adulthood: Support for socioemotional selectivity theory. *Psychology and Aging, 7,* 331–338.

Carstensen, L. L., Levenson, R. W., & Gottman, J. M. (1995). Emotional behavior in long-term marriages. *Psychology and Aging, 10,* 140–149.

Caspi, A., Herbener, E. S., & Ozer, D. J. (1992). Shared experiences and the similarity of personalities: A longitudinal study of married couples. *Journal of Personality and Social Psychology, 62,* 281–291.

Chadwick, B. A., & Heaton, T. B. (1992). *Statistical handbook on the American family.* Phoenix: Onyx Press.

Chao, R. K. (1994). Beyond parental control and authoritarian parenting style: Understanding Chinese parenting through the cultural notion of training. *Child Development, 65,* 1111–1119.

Chase-Lansdale, P. L., Cherlin, A. J., & Kiernan, K. E. (1995). The long-term effects of parental divorce on the mental health of young adults: A developmental perspective. *Child Development, 66,* 1614–1634.

Chen, X., Rubin, K. H., & Li, B. (1994). Only children and sibling children in urban China: A reexamination. *International Journal of Behavioral Development, 17,* 413–421.

Cherlin, A. J., & Furstenberg, F. F., Jr. (1986). *The new American grandparent: A place in the family, a life apart.* New York: Basic Books.

Cherlin, A. J., Furstenberg, F. F., Jr., Chase-Lansdale, P. L., Kiernan, K. E., Robins, P. K., Morrison, D. R., &

Teitler, J. O. (1991). Longitudinal studies of effects of divorce on children in Great Britain and the United States. *Science, 252,* 1386–1389.

Cherlin, A. J., Kiernan, K. E., & Chase-Lansdale, P. L. (1995). Parental divorce in childhood and demographic outcomes in young adulthood. *Demography, 32,* 299–318.

Cicchetti, D., & Barnett, D. (1991). Attachment organization in maltreated preschoolers. *Development and Psychopathology, 3,* 397–411.

Cicirelli, V. G. (1982). Sibling influence throughout the life span. In M. E. Lamb & B. Sutton-Smith (Eds.), *Sibling relationships: Their nature and significance across the lifespan.* Hillsdale, NJ: Erlbaum.

Cicirelli, V. G. (1991). Sibling relationships in adulthood. *Marriage and Family Review, 16,* 291–310.

Cicirelli, V. G. (1993). Attachment and obligation as daughters' motives for caregiving behavior and subsequent effect on subjective burden. *Psychology and Aging, 8,* 144–155.

Cicirelli, V. G. (1995). *Sibling relationships across the life span.* New York: Plenum.

Clingempeel, W. G., Colyar, J. J., Brand, E., & Hetherington, E. M. (1992). Children's relationships with maternal grandparents: A longitudinal study of family structure and pubertal status effects. *Child Development, 63,* 1404–1422.

Clingempeel, W. G., & Segal, S. (1986). Stepparent-stepchild relationships and the psychological adjustment of children in stepmother and stepfather families. *Child Development, 57,* 474–484.

Conger, R. D., Conger, K. J., Elder, G. H., Jr., Lorenz, F. O., Simons, R. L., & Whitbeck, L. B. (1992). A family process model of economic hardship and adjustment of early adolescent boys. *Child Development, 63,* 526–541.

Conger, R. D., Patterson, G. R., & Ge, X. (1995). It takes two to replicate: A mediational model for the impact of parents' stress on adolescent adjustment. *Child Development, 66,* 80–97.

Connidis, I. A. (1994). Sibling support in older age. *Journal of Gerontology: Social Sciences, 49,* S309–S317.

Coohey, C., & Braun, N. (1997). Toward an integrated framework for understanding child physical abuse. *Child Abuse and Neglect, 21,* 1081–1094.

Cooksey, E. C., & Fondell, M. M. (1996). Spending time with his kids: Effects of family structure on fathers' and children's lives. *Journal of Marriage and the Family, 58,* 693–707.

Cooney, T. M., & Smith, L. A. (1996). Young adults' relations with grandparents following recent parental divorce. *Journal of Gerontology: Social Sciences, 51,* S91–S95.

Coulton, C. J., Korbin, J. E., Su, M., & Chow, J. (1995). Community level factors and child maltreatment rates. *Child Development, 66,* 1262–1276.

Cowan, C. P., Cowan, P. A., Heming, G., & Miller, N. B. (1991). Becoming a family: Marriage, parenting, and child development. In P. A. Cowan & M. Hetherington (Eds.), *Family transitions.* Hillsdale, NJ: Erlbaum.

Cox, M. J., Owen, M. T., Henderson, V. K., & Margand, N. A. (1992). Prediction of infant-father and infant-mother attachment. *Developmental Psychology, 28,* 474–483.

Crnic, K., & Booth, C. (1991). Mothers' and fathers' perceptions of daily hassles of parenting across early childhood. *Journal of Marriage and the Family, 53,* 1042–1050.

Crockenberg, S., & Litman, C. (1990). Autonomy as competence in 2-year-olds: Maternal correlates of child defiance, compliance, and self-assertion. *Developmental Psychology, 26,* 961–971.

Culp, R. E., Little, V., Letts, D., & Lawrence, H. (1991). Maltreated children's self-concept: Effects of a comprehensive treatment program. *American Journal of Orthopsychiatry, 61,* 114–121.

Darling, N., & Steinberg, L. (1993). Parenting style as context: An integrative model. *Psychological Bulletin, 113,* 487–496.

Deater-Deckard, K., Dodge, K. A., Bates, J. E., & Pettit, G. S. (1996). Physical discipline among African-American and European American mothers: Links to children's externalizing behaviors. *Developmental Psychology, 32,* 1065–1072.

DeMaris, A., & MacDonald, W. (1993). Premarital cohabitation and marital instability: A test of the unconventionality hypothesis. *Journal of Marriage and the Family, 55,* 399–407.

DeMaris, A., & Rao, K. V. (1992). Premarital cohabitation and subsequent marital stability in the United States: A reassessment. *Journal of Marriage and the Family, 54,* 178–190.

Demo, D. H., & Allen, K. R. (1996). Diversity within lesbian and gay families: Challenges and implications for family theory and research. *Journal of Social and Personal Relationships, 13,* 415–434.

Dickson, F. C. (1995). The best is yet to be: Research on long-lasting marriages. In J. T. Wood & S. Duck (Eds.), *Understudied relationships: Off the beaten track.* Thousand Oaks, CA: Sage.

Dilworth-Anderson, P., & Burton, L. M. (1996). Rethinking family development: Critical conceptual issues in the study of diverse groups. *Journal of Social and Personality Relationships, 13,* 325–334.

Dishion, T. J., Patterson, G. R., Stoolmiller, M., & Skinner, M. L. (1991). Family, school, and behavioral antecedents to early adolescent involvement with antisocial peers. *Developmental Psychology, 27,* 172–180.

Dornbusch, S. M., Carlsmith, J. M., Bushwall, S. J., Ritter, P. L., Leiderman, H., Hastorf, A. H., & Gross, R. T. (1985). Single parents, extended households, and the control of adolescents. *Child Development, 56,* 326–341.

Dunn, J. (1993). *Young children's close relationships. Beyond attachment.* Newbury Park, CA: Sage.

Dunn, J., & Kendrick, C. (1981). Interaction between young siblings: Association with the interaction between mother and firstborn child. *Developmental Psychology, 17,* 336–343.

Dunn, J., & Kendrick, C. (1982). *Siblings: Love, envy, and understanding.* Cambridge, MA: Harvard University Press.

Dunn, J., Slomkowski, C., & Beardsall, L. (1994). Sibling relationships from the preschool period through middle childhood and early adolescence. *Developmental Psychology, 30,* 315–324.

Duvall, E. M. (1977). *Marriage and family development* (5th ed.). Philadelphia: J. B. Lippincott.

Dwyer, J. W., & Coward, R. T. (1991). A multivariate comparison of the involvement of adult sons versus daughters in the care of impaired parents. *Journal of Gerontology: Social Sciences, 46,* S259–S269.

East, P. L., & Rook, K. S. (1992). Compensatory patterns of support among children's peer relationships: A test using school friends, non-school friends, and siblings. *Developmental Psychology, 28,* 163–172.

Eckenrode, J., Laird, M., & Doris, J. (1993). School performance and disciplinary problems among abused and neglected children. *Developmental Psychology, 29,* 53–62.

Egeland, B. (1979). Preliminary results of a prospective study of the antecedents of child abuse. *International Journal of Child Abuse and Neglect, 3,* 269–278.

Egeland, B., Jacobvitz, D., & Sroufe, L. A. (1988). Breaking the cycle of abuse. *Child Development, 59,* 1080–1088.

Egeland, B., Sroufe, L. A., & Erickson, M. (1983). The developmental consequences of different patterns of maltreatment. *International Journal of Child Abuse and Neglect, 7,* 459–469.

Egerton, J. (1983). *Generations: An American family.* Lexington: University Press of Kentucky.

Eggebeen, D. J., & Lichter, D. T. (1991). Race, family structure, and changing poverty among American children. *American Sociological Review, 56,* 801–817.

El-Khorazaty, M. N. (1996). Twentieth-century family life cycle and its determinants in the United States. *Journal of Family History, 22,* 70–109.

Emery, R. E. (1989). Family violence. *American Psychologist, 44,* 321–328.

Emery, R. E., & Tuer, M. (1993). Parenting and the marital relationship. In T. Luster & L. Okagaki (Eds.), *Parenting: An ecological perspective.* Hillsdale, NJ: Erlbaum.

Erel, O., & Burman, B. (1995). Interrelatedness of marital relations and parent-child relations: A meta-analytic review. *Psychological Bulletin, 118,* 108–132.

Fagot, B. I., & Kavanaugh, K. (1993). Parenting during the second year: Effects of children's age, sex, and attachment classification. *Child Development, 64,* 258–271.

Falbo, T. (1991). The impact of grandparents on children's outcomes in China. *Marriage and Family Review, 16,* 369–376.

Falbo, T., & Poston, D. L., Jr. (1993). The academic, personality, and physical outcomes of only children in China. *Child Development, 64,* 18–35.

Field, D., Minkler, M., Falk, R. F., & Leino, E. V. (1993). The influence of health on family contacts and family feelings in advanced old age: A longitudinal study. *Journal of Gerontology: Psychological Sciences, 48,* P18–P28.

Fingerman, K. L. (1996). Sources of tension in the aging mother and adult daughter relationship. *Psychology and Aging, 11,* 591–606.

Finkelhor, D., & Dziuba-Leatherman, J. (1994). Victimization of children. *American Psychologist, 49,* 173–183.

Flaks, D. K., Ficher, I., Masterpasqua, F., & Joseph, G. (1995). Lesbians choosing motherhood: A comparative study of lesbian and heterosexual parents and their children. *Developmental Psychology, 31,* 105–114.

Frodi, A. M., & Lamb, M. E. (1980). Child abusers' responses to infant smiles and cries. *Child Development, 51,* 238–241.

Furman, W., & Buhrmester, D. (1985a). Children's perceptions of the personal relationships in their social networks. *Developmental Psychology, 21,* 1016–1024.

Furman, W., & Buhrmester, D. (1985b). Children's perceptions of the qualities of sibling relationships. *Child Development, 56,* 448–461.

Furman, W., & Buhrmester, D. (1992). Age and sex differences in perceptions of networks of personal relationships. *Child Development, 63,* 103–115.

Galambos, N. L. (1992). Parent-adolescent relations. *Current Directions in Psychological Science, 1,* 146–149.

Galambos, N. L., & Maggs, J. L. (1991). Out-of-school care of young adolescents and self-reported behavior. *Developmental Psychology, 27,* 644–655.

Garbarino, J. (1992). *Children and families in the social environment* (2nd ed.). New York: Aldine de Gruyter.

Garbarino, J., & Sherman, D. (1980). High-risk neighborhoods and high-risk families: The human ecology of child maltreatment. *Child Development, 51,* 188–198.

Ge, X., Best, K. M., Conger, R. D., & Simons, R. L. (1996). Parenting behaviors and the occurrence and co-occurrence of adolescent depressive symptoms and conduct problems. *Developmental Psychology, 32,* 717–731.

Gigy, L., & Kelly, J. B. (1992). Reasons for divorce: Perspectives of divorcing men and women. *Journal of Divorce and Remarriage, 18,* 169–187.

Gil, D. G. (1970). *Violence against children.* Cambridge, MA: Harvard University Press.

Gilbert, N. (1997). *Combatting child abuse: International perspectives and trends.* New York: Oxford University Press.

Glasgow, K. L., Dornbusch, S. M., Troyer, L., Steinberg, L., & Ritter, P. L. (1997). Parenting styles, adolescents' attributions, and educational outcomes in nine heterogeneous high schools. *Child Development, 68,* 507–529.

Glenn, N. D., & McLanahan, S. (1981). The effects of offspring on the psychological well-being of older adults. *Journal of Marriage and the Family, 43,* 409–421.

Glenn, N. D., & Weaver, C. N. (1988). The changing relationship of marital status to reported happiness. *Journal of Marriage and the Family, 50,* 317–324.

Glick, P. C. (1989). Remarried families, stepfamilies, and stepchildren: A brief demographic profile. *Family Relations, 38,* 24–47.

Golombok, S., & Tasker, F. (1996). Do parents influence the sexual orientation of their children: Findings from a longitudinal study of lesbian families. *Developmental Psychology, 32,* 3–11.

Gottman, J., & Levenson, R. (1992). Marital processes predictive of later dissolution: Behavior, physiology, and health. *Journal of Personality and Social Psychology, 63,* 221–233.

Greenberger, A., & Chen, C. (1996). Perceived family relationships and depressed mood in early and late adolescence: A comparison of European and Asian Americans. *Developmental Psychology, 32,* 707–716.

Greene, A. L., & Boxer, A. M. (1986). Daughters and sons as young adults: Restructuring the ties that bind. In N. Datan, A. L. Greene, & H. W. Reese (Eds.), *Life-span developmental psychology. Intergenerational relations.* Hillsdale, NJ: Erlbaum.

Grossman, F. K., Eichler, L. S., Winickoff, S. A., & Associates (1980). *Pregnancy, birth, and parenthood: Adaptations of mothers, fathers, and infants.* San Francisco: Jossey-Bass.

Grotevant, H. D., & Cooper, C. R. (1986). Individuation in family relations: A perspective on individual differences in the development of identity and role-taking skills in adolescence. *Human Development, 29,* 82–100.

Gruber-Baldini, A. L., Schaie, K. W., & Willis, S. L. (1995). Similarity in married couples: A longitudinal study of mental abilities and rigidity-flexibility. *Journal of Personality and Social Psychology, 69,* 191–203.

Grych, J. H., & Fincham, F. D. (1992). Interventions for children of divorce: Toward greater integration of research and action. *Psychological Bulletin, 111,* 434–454.

Hagestad, G. O. (1985). Continuity and connectedness. In V. L. Bengtson & J. F. Robertson (Eds.), *Grandparenthood.* Beverly Hills, CA: Sage.

Haley, W. E., West, C. A. C., Wadley, V. G., Ford, G. R., White, F. A., Barrett, J. J., Harrell, L. E., & Roth, D. L. (1995). Psychological, social, and health impact of caregiving: A comparison of Black and White dementia family caregivers and noncaregivers. *Psychology and Aging, 10,* 540–552.

Harkins, E. B. (1978). Effects of empty nest transition on self-report of psychological and physical well-being. *Journal of Marriage and the Family, 40,* 549–556.

Harold, G. T., Fincham, F. D., Osborne, L. M., & Conger, R. D. (1997). Mom and dad are at it again: Adolescent perceptions of marital conflict and adolescent psychological distress. *Developmental Psychology, 33,* 333–350.

Hashima, P. Y., & Amato, P. R. (1994). Poverty, social support, and parental behavior. *Child Development, 65,* 394–403.

Haskett, M. E., Johnson, C. A., & Miller, J. W. (1994). Individual differences in risk of child abuse by adolescent mothers: Assessment in the perinatal period. *Journal of Child Psychology and Psychiatry, and Allied Disciplines, 35,* 461–476.

Haskett, M. E., & Kistner, J. A. (1991). Social interactions and peer perceptions of young physically abused children. *Child Development, 62,* 979–990.

Heath, D. T. (1995). Parents' socialization of children. In B. B. Ingoldsby & S. Smith (Eds.), *Families in multicultural perspective.* New York: Guilford.

Hernandez, D. J. (1997). Child development and the social demography of childhood. *Child Development, 68,* 149–169.

Hetherington, E. M. (1981). Children and divorce. In R. W. Henderson (Ed.), *Parent-child interaction: Theory, research and prospects.* New York: Academic Press.

Hetherington, E. M. (1989). Coping with family transitions: Winners, losers, and survivors. *Child Development, 60,* 1–14.

Hetherington, E. M., & Camara, K. A. (1984). Families in transition: The processes of dissolution and reconstitution. In R. D. Parke (Ed.),

Review of child development research: Vol. 7. The family. Chicago: University of Chicago Press.

Hetherington, E. M., Clingempeel, W. G., & Associates. (1992). Coping with marital transitions. *Monographs of the Society for Research in Child Development, 57* (2–3, Serial No. 227).

Hetherington, E. M., Cox, M., & Cox, R. (1982). Effects of divorce on parents and children. In M. E. Lamb (Ed.), *Nontraditional families.* Hillsdale, NJ: Erlbaum.

Hetherington, E. M., & Jodl, K. M. (1994). Stepfamilies as settings for child development. In A. Booth & J. Dunn (Eds.), *Stepfamilies: Who benefits? Who does not?* Hillsdale, NJ: Erlbaum.

Hewlett, B. S. (1992). Introduction. In B. S. Hewlett (Ed.), *Father-child relations. Cultural and biosocial contexts.* New York: Aldine de Gruyter.

Hill, R., & Rodgers, R. H. (1964). The developmental approach. In H. Christensen (Ed.), *Handbook of marriage and the family.* Chicago: Rand-McNally.

Hobbs, F. B. (with B. L. Damon). (1996). *65+ in the United States.* Washington, DC: U.S. Bureau of the Census.

Hoffman, L. W., & Manis, J. D. (1979). The value of children in the United States: A new approach to the study of fertility. *Journal of Marriage and the Family, 41,* 583–596.

Holmbeck, G. N., & Hill, J. P. (1991). Conflictive engagement, positive affect, and menarche in families with seventh-grade girls. *Child Development, 62,* 1030–1048.

Howe, N., & Ross, H. S. (1990). Socialization, perspective-taking, and the sibling relationship. *Developmental Psychology, 26,* 160–165.

Howes, P., & Markman, H. J. (1989). Marital quality and child functioning: A longitudinal investigation. *Child Development, 60,* 1044–1051.

Hudson, M. F. (1986). Elder mistreatment: Current research. In K. A. Pillemer & R. S. Wolf (Eds.), *Elder abuse: Conflict in the family.* Dover, MA: Auburn House.

Huston, M., & Schwartz, P. (1995). The relationships of lesbians and gay men. In J. T. Wood & S. Duck (Eds.), *Under-studied relationships: Off the beaten track.* Thousand Oaks, CA: Sage.

Huston, T. L., McHale, S. M., & Crouter, A. C. (1986). When the honeymoon's over: Changes in the marriage relationship over the first year. In R. Gilmour & S. Duck (Eds.), *The emerging field of personal relationships.* Hillsdale, NJ: Erlbaum.

Huston, T. L., & Vangelisti, A. L. (1991). Socioemotional behavior and satisfaction in marital relationships: A longitudinal study. *Journal of Personality and Social Psychology, 6,* 721–733.

Ingoldsby, B. B., & Smith, S. (1995). *Families in multicultural perspective.* New York: Guilford.

Jacobson, C. K., & Heaton, T. B. (1991). Voluntary childlessness among American men and women in the late 1980's. *Social Biology, 38,* 79–93.

Jiao, S., Ji, G., & Jing, Q. (1996). Cognitive development of Chinese urban only children and children with siblings. *Child Development, 67,* 387–395.

Johnson, C. L., & Troll, L. (1996). Family structure and the timing of transitions from 70 to 103 years of age. *Journal of Marriage and the Family, 58,*178–187.

Johnson, D. R., Amoloza, T. O., & Booth, A. (1992). Stability and developmental change in marital quality: A three-wave panel analysis. *Journal of Marriage and the Family, 54,* 582–594.

Jonsson, J. O., & Gahler, M. (1997). Family dissolution, family reconstitution, and children's educational careers: Recent evidence for Sweden. *Demography, 34,* 277–293.

Julian, T. W., McKenry, P. C., & McKelvey, M. W. (1991). Mediators of relationship stress between middle-aged fathers and their adolescent children. *Journal of Genetic Psychology, 152,* 381–386.

Kalmuss, D., Davidson, A., & Cushman, L. (1992). Parenting expectancies, experiences, and adjustment to parenthood: A test of the violated expectations framework. *Journal of Marriage and the Family, 54,* 516–526.

Kaufman, J., & Zigler, E. (1989). The intergenerational transmission of child abuse. In D. Cicchetti & V. Carlson (Eds.), *Child maltreatment: Theory and research on the causes and consequences of child abuse and neglect.* New York: Cambridge University Press.

Keith, J. (1992). Care-taking in cultural context: Anthropological queries. In H. L. Kendig, A. Hashimoto, & L. C. Coppard (Eds.), *Family support for the elderly. The international experience.* Oxford: Oxford University Press.

Keller, B. B., & Bell, R. Q. (1979). Child effects on adult's method of eliciting altruistic behavior. *Child Development, 50,* 1004–1009.

Kempe, R. S., & Kempe, C. H. (1978). *Child abuse.* Cambridge, MA: Harvard University Press.

Kendler, K. S. (1996). Parenting: A genetic-epidemiologic perspective. *American Journal of Psychiatry, 153,* 11–20.

Kiernan, K. E. (1989). Who remains childless? *Journal of Biosocial Science, 21,* 387–398.

King, V., & Elder, G. H., Jr. (1997). The legacy of grandparenting: Childhood experiences with grandparents and current involvement with grandchildren. *Journal of Marriage and the Family, 59,* 848–859.

Kitson, G. C. (1992). *Portrait of divorce: Adjustment to marital breakdown.* New York: Guilford.

Kitson, G. C., Babri, K. B., & Roach, M. J. (1985). Who divorces and why: A review. *Journal of Family Issues, 6,* 255–293.

Klein, D. M., & White, J. M. (1996). *Family theories: An introduction.* Thousand Oaks, CA: Sage.

Klimes-Dougan, B., & Kistner, J. (1990). Physically abused preschoolers' responses to peers' distress. *Developmental Psychology, 26,* 599–602.

Kline, M., Tschann, J. M., Johnston, J. R., & Wallerstein, J. S. (1989). Children's adjustment in joint and sole physical custody families. *Developmental Psychology, 25,* 430–438.

Kobak, R. R., Cole, H. E., Ferenz-Gilles, R., Fleming, W. S., & Gamble, W. (1993). Attachment and emotional regulation during mother-teen problem solving: A control theory analysis. *Child Development, 64,* 231–245.

Koestner, R., Zuroff, D. C., & Powers, T. A. (1991). Family origins of adolescent self-criticism and its continuity into adulthood. *Journal of Abnormal Psychology, 100,*191–197.

Kohn, M. L. (1969). *Class and conformity: A study of values.* Homewood, IL: Dorsey Press.

Kosberg, J. I., & Garcia, J. L. (Eds.). (1995). *Elder abuse: International and cross-cultural perspectives.* New York: Haworth.

Kuczynski, L., & Kochanska, G. (1995). Function and content of maternal demands: Developmental significance of early demands for competent action. *Child Development, 66,* 616–628.

Kurdek, L. A. (1991a). Correlates of relationship satisfaction in cohabiting gay and lesbian couples: Integration of contextual investment, and problem-solving models. *Journal of Personality and Social Psychology, 61,* 910–922.

Kurdek, L. A. (1991b). The relations between reported well-being and divorce history, availability of a proximate adult, and gender. *Journal of Marriage and the Family, 53,* 71–78.

Kurdek, L. A. (1995). Lesbian and gay couples. In A. R. Augelli & C. J. Patterson (Eds.), *Lesbian and gay identities over the life span: Psychological perspectives on personal, relational, and community processes.* New York: Oxford University Press.

Kurdek, L. A., Fine, M. A., & Sinclair, R. J. (1995). School adjustment in sixth graders: Parenting transitions, peer climate, and peer norm effects. *Child Development, 66,* 430–445.

Lachs, M. S., Williams, C., O'Brien, S., Hurst, L., & Horwitz, R. (1997). Risk factors for reported elder abuse and neglect: A nine-year observational cohort study. *Gerontologist, 37,* 469–474.

Laird, J. (1993). Lesbian and gay families. In F. Walsh (Ed.), *Normal family processes* (2nd ed.). New York: Guilford.

Lamb, M. E. (1981). *The role of the father in child development.* New York: Wiley.

Lamborn, S. D., Mounts, N. S., Steinberg, L., & Dornbusch, S. M. (1991). Patterns of competence and adjustment among adolescents from authoritative, authoritarian, indulgent, and neglectful families. *Child Development, 62,* 1049–1065.

Lamborn, S. D., & Steinberg, L. (1993). Emotional autonomy redux: Revisiting Ryan and Lynch. *Child Development, 64,* 483–499.

Larson, R. W., Richards, M. H., Moneta, G., Holmbeck, G., & Duckett, E. (1996). Changes in adolescents' daily interactions with their families from ages 10 to 18: Disengagement and transformation. *Developmental Psychology, 32,* 744–753.

Lauer, R. H., & Lauer, J. C. (1986). Factors in long-term marriages. *Journal of Family Issues, 7,* 382–390.

Lee, G. R. (1988). Marital satisfaction in later life: The effects of nonmarital roles. *Journal of Marriage and the Family, 50,* 775–783.

Lee, G. R., Netzer, J. K., & Coward, R. T. (1995). Depression among older parents: The role of intergenerational exchange. *Journal of Marriage and the Family, 57,* 823–833.

Lempers, J. D., & Clark-Lempers, D. S. (1992). Young, middle, and late adolescents' comparisons of the functional importance of five significant relationships. *Journal of Youth and Adolescence, 21,* 53–96.

Lerner, J. V. (1993). The influence of child temperamental characteristics on parent behaviors. In T. Luster & L. Okagaki (Eds.), *Parenting: An ecological perspective.* Hillsdale, NJ: Erlbaum.

Lerner, M. J., Somers, D. G., Reid, D., Chiriboga, D., & Tierney, M. (1991). Adult children as caregivers: Egocentric biases in judgments of sibling contributions. *Gerontologist, 31,* 746–755.

Levinson, D. (1989). *Family violence in cross-cultural perspective.* Newbury Park, CA: Sage.

Levy-Shiff, R. (1994). Individual and contextual correlates of marital change across the transition to parenthood. *Developmental Psychology, 30,* 591–601.

Lewis, R. A., Freneau, P. J., & Roberts, C. L. (1979). Fathers and the post-parental transition. *Family Coordinator, 28,* 514–520.

Lillard, L. A., & Panis, C. W. A. (1996). Marital status and mortality: The role of health. *Demography, 33,* 313–327.

Litwak, E. (1960). Geographic mobility and extended family cohesion. *American Sociological Review, 25,* 385–394.

Lorenz, F. O., Simons, R. L., Conger, R. D., Elder, G. H., Jr., Johnson, C., & Chao, W. (1997). Married and recently divorced mothers' stressful events and distress: Tracing change across time. *Journal of Marriage and the Family, 59,* 219–232.

Lustig, J. L., Wolchik, S. A., & Braver, S. L. (1992). Social support in chumships and adjustment in children of divorce. *American Journal of Community Psychology, 20,* 393–399.

Lye, D. N. (1996). Adult child-parent relationships. *Annual Review of Sociology, 22,* 79–102.

Lytton, H. (1990). Child and parent effects in boys' conduct disorder: A reinterpretation. *Developmental Psychology, 26,* 683–697.

Lytton, H., & Romney, D. M. (1991). Parents' differential socialization of boys and girls: A meta-analysis. *Psychological Bulletin, 109,* 267–296.

Maccoby, E. E. (1980). *Social development.* San Diego: Harcourt Brace Jovanovich.

Maccoby, E. E., & Martin, J. A. (1983). Socialization in the context of the family: Parent-child interaction. In E. M. Hetherington (Ed.; P. H. Mussen, General Ed.), *Handbook of child psychology: Vol. 4. Socialization, personality, and social development* (4th ed.). New York: Wiley.

MacDonald, K. (1992). Warmth as a developmental construct: An evolutionary analysis. *Child Development, 63,* 753–773.

Mackey, R. A., & O'Brien, B. A. (1995). *Lasting marriages: Men and women growing together.* Westport, CT: Praeger.

MacKinnon, C. E. (1989). An observational investigation of sibling interactions in married and divorced families. *Developmental Psychology, 25,* 36–44.

MacPhee, D., Fritz, J., & Miller-Heyl, J. (1996). Ethnic variations in personal social networks and parenting. *Child Development, 67,* 3278–3295.

Main, M., & George, C. (1985). Responses of abused and disadvantaged toddlers to distress in agemates: A study in the day-care setting. *Developmental Psychology, 21,* 407–412.

Main, M., & Weston, D. R. (1981). The quality of the toddler's relationship to mother and to father: Related to conflict and the readiness to establish new relationships. *Child Development, 52,* 932–940.

Malinosky-Rummell, R., & Hansen, D. J. (1993). Long-term consequences of childhood physical abuse. *Psychological Bulletin, 114,* 68–79.

Markides, K. S., Boldt, J. S., & Ray, L. A. (1986). Sources of helping and intergenerational solidarity: A three-generations study of Mexican Americans. *Journal of Gerontology, 41,* 506–511.

Marshall, N. L., Coll, C. G., Marx, F., McCartney, K., Keefe, N., & Ruh, J. (1997). After-school time and children's behavioral adjustment. *Merrill-Palmer Quarterly, 43,* 497–514.

Matthews, S. H., & Sprey, J. (1985). Adolescents' relationships with grandparents: An empirical contribution to conceptual clarification. *Journal of Gerontology, 40,* 621–626.

McCloskey, L. A., Figueredo, A. J., & Koss, M. P. (1995). The effects of systemic family violence on children's mental health. *Child Development, 66,* 1239–1261.

McHale, S. M., Crouter, A. C., McGuire, S. A., & Updegraff, K. A. (1995). Congruence between mothers' and fathers' differential treatment of siblings: Links with family relations and children's well-being. *Child Development, 66,* 116–128.

McHale, S. M., & Gamble, W. C. (1989). Sibling relationships of children with disabled and nondisabled brothers and sisters. *Developmental Psychology, 25,* 421–429.

McLanahan, S. S., & Sorensen, A. B. (1985). Life events and psychological well-being over the life course. In G. H. Elder, Jr. (Ed.), *Life course dynamics: Trajectories and transitions, 1968–1980.* Ithaca, NY: Cornell University Press.

McLoyd, V. C. (1990). The impact of economic hardship on Black families and children: Psychological distress, parenting, and socioemotional development. *Child Development, 61,* 311–346.

McLoyd, V. C., Jayaratne, T. E., Ceballo, R., & Borquez, J. (1994). Unemployment and work interruption among African-American single mothers: Effects on parenting and adolescent socioemotional functioning. *Child Development, 65,* 562–589.

Mekos, D., Hetherington, E. M., & Reiss, D. (1996). Sibling differences in problem behavior and parental treatment in nondivorced and remarried families. *Child Development, 67,* 2148–2165.

Menaghan, E. (1983). Marital stress and family transitions: A panel analysis. *Journal of Marriage and the Family, 45,* 371–386.

Menaghan, E. G., & Lieberman, M. A. (1986). Changes in depression following divorce: A panel study. *Journal of Marriage and the Family, 48,* 319–328.

Miller, N. B., Cowan, P. A., Cowan, C. P., Hetherington, E. M., & Clingempeel, W. G. (1993). Externalizing in preschoolers and early adolescents: A cross-study replication of a family model. *Developmental Psychology, 29,* 3–18.

Monk, T. H., Essex, M. J., Smider, N. A., Klein, M. H., Lowe, K. K., & Kupfer, D. (1996). The impact of the birth of a baby on the time structure and social mixture of a couple's daily life and its consequences for well-being. *Journal of Applied Social Psychology, 26,* 1237–1258.

Mylod, D. E., Whitman, T. L., & Borkowski, J. G. (1997). Predicting adolescent mothers' transition to adulthood. *Journal of Research on Adolescence, 7,* 457–478.

Neville, B., & Parke, R. D. (1997). Waiting for paternity: Interpersonal and contextual implications of the timing of fatherhood. *Sex Roles, 37,* 45–59.

Newcomb, P. R. (1979). Cohabitation in America: An assessment of consequences. *Journal of Marriage and the Family, 41,* 597–603.

Norman-Jackson, J. (1982). Family interactions, language development, and primary reading achievement of Black children in families of low income. *Child Development, 53,* 349–358.

Nydegger, C. N. (1986). Asymmetrical kin and the problematic son-in-law. In N. Datan, A. L. Greene, & H. W. Reese (Eds.), *Life-span developmental psychology: Intergenerational relations.* Hillsdale, NJ: Erlbaum.

Oates, R. K., & Bross, D. C. (1995). What have we learned about treating child physical abuse? A literature review of the last decade. *Child Abuse and Neglect, 19,* 463–473.

O'Brien, M. (1996). Child-rearing difficulties reported by parents of infants and toddlers. *Journal of Pediatric Psychology, 21,* 433–446.

Offer, D., Ostrov, E., & Howard, K. I. (1981). *The adolescent. A psychological self-portrait.* New York: Basic Books.

Ogbu, J. U. (1981). Origins of human competence: A cultural-ethological perspective. *Child Development, 52,* 413–429.

Ogbu, J. U. (1994). From cultural differences to differences in cultural frames of reference. In P. M. Greenfield & R. R. Cocking (Eds.), *Cross-cultural roots of minority child development.* Hillsdale, NJ: Erlbaum.

Oyserman, D., Radin, N., & Benn, R. (1993). Dynamics in a three-generational family: Teens, grandparents, and babies. *Developmental Psychology, 29,* 564–572.

Padilla, M. L., & Landreth, G. L. (1989). Latchkey children: A review of the literature. *Child Welfare, 68,* 445–454.

Paikoff, R. L., & Brooks-Gunn, J. (1991). Do parent-child relationships change during puberty? *Psychological Bulletin, 110,* 47–66.

Palkovitz, R. (1984). Parental attitudes and fathers' interactions with their 5-month-old infants. *Developmental Psychology, 20,* 1054–1060.

Palkovitz, R. (1996). Parenting as a generator of adult development: Conceptual issues and implications. *Journal of Social and Personal Relationships, 13,* 571–592.

Parke, R. D. (1996). *Fatherhood.* Cambridge, MA: Harvard University Press.

Parke, R. D., & Sawin, D. B. (1976). The father's role in infancy: A re-evaluation. *Family Coordinator, 25,* 365–371.

Patterson, C. J. (1995). Lesbian and gay parenthood. In M. H. Bornstein (Ed.), *Handbook of parenting: Vol. 3. Status and social conditions of parenting.* Mahwah, NJ: Erlbaum.

Paulhus, D., & Shaffer, D. R. (1981). Sex differences in the impact of number of older and number of younger siblings on scholastic aptitude. *Social Psychology Quarterly, 44,* 363–368.

Paveza, G. J., Cohen, D., Eisdorfer, C., Freels, S., Semla, T., Ashford, J. W., Gorelick, P., Hirschman, R., Luchins, D., & Levy, P. (1992). Severe family violence and Alzheimer's disease: Prevalence and risk factors. *Gerontologist, 32,* 493–497.

Pearson, J. L., Hunter, A. G., Ensminger, M. E., & Kellam, S. G. (1990). Black grandmothers in multigenerational households: Diversity in family structure and parenting involvement in the Woodlawn community. *Child Development, 61,* 434–442.

Perez-Granados, D. R., & Callanan, M. A. (1997). Conversations with mothers and siblings: Young children's semantic and conceptual development. *Developmental Psychology, 33,* 120–134.

Peters, A., & Liefbroer, A. C. (1997). Beyond marital status: Partner history and well-being in old age. *Journal of Marriage and the Family, 55,* 687–699.

Peterson, J. W. (1990). Age of wisdom: Elderly black women in family and church. In J. Sokolovsky (Ed.), *The cultural context of aging: Worldwide perspectives.* New York: Bergin and Garvey Publishers.

Pettit, G. S., Laird, R. D., Bates, J. E., & Dodge, K. A. (1997). Patterns of after-school care in middle childhood: Risk factors and developmental outcomes. *Merrill-Palmer Quarterly, 43,* 515–538.

Phares, V. (1996). *Fathers and developmental psychopathology.* New York: Wiley.

Pianta, R., Egeland, B., & Erickson, M. F. (1989). The antecedents of maltreatment: Results of the Mother-Child Interaction Research Project. In D. Ciccetti & V. Carlson (Eds.), *Child maltreatment: Theory and research on the causes and consequences of child abuse and neglect.* Cambridge: Cambridge University Press.

Pinto, A., Folkers, E., & Sines, J. O. (1991). Dimensions of behavior and home environment in school-age children: India and the United States. *Journal of Cross-Cultural Psychology, 22,* 491–508.

Posner, J. K., & Vandell, D. L. (1994). Low-income children's after-school care: Are there beneficial effects of after-school programs? *Child Development, 65,* 440–456.

Reiss, D. (1995). Genetic influence on family systems: Implications for development. *Journal of Marriage and the Family, 57,* 543–560.

Rempel, J. (1985). Childless elderly: What are they missing? *Journal of Marriage and the Family, 47,* 343–348.

Roberto, K. A., & Stroes, J. (1992). Grandchildren and grandparents: Roles, influences, and relationships. *International Journal of Aging and Human Development, 34,* 227–239.

Rollins, B. C., & Feldman, H. (1970). Marital satisfaction over the family life cycle. *Journal of Marriage and the Family, 32,* 20–28.

Rosenthal, R., & Vandell, D. L. (1996). Quality of care at school-aged child-care programs: Regulatable features, observed experiences, child perspectives, and parent perspectives. *Child Development, 67,* 2434–2445.

Ross, H. G., & Milgram, J. I. (1982). Important variables in adult sibling relationships: A qualitative study. In M. E. Lamb & B. Sutton-Smith (Eds.), *Sibling relationships: Their nature and significance across the lifespan.* Hillsdale, NJ: Erlbaum.

Rossi, A. S., & Rossi, P. H. (1990). *Of human bonding: Parent-child relations across the life course.* New York: Aldine de Gruyter.

Rowe, D. C. (1994). *The limits of family influence: Genes, experience, and behavior.* New York: Guilford.

Rowland, D. T. (1991). Family diversity and the life cycle. *Journal of Comparative Family Studies, 22,* 1–14.

Rubinstein, R. L., Alexander, R. B., Goodman, M., & Luborsky, M. (1991). Key relationships of never married, childless older women: A cultural analysis. *Journal of Gerontology: Social Sciences, 46,* S270–S277.

Ruggles, S. (1994). The origins of African-American family structure. *American Sociological Review, 59,* 136–151.

Russell, R. J., & Wells, P. A. (1991). Personality similarity and quality of marriage. *Personality and Individual Differences, 12,* 407–412.

Salzinger, S., Feldman, R. S., Hammer, M., & Rosario, M. (1993). The effects of physical abuse on children's social relationships. *Child Development, 64,* 169–187.

Sameroff, A. (1975). Early influences on development: Fact or fancy? *Merrill-Palmer Quarterly, 21,* 263–294.

Scarr, S., & McCartney, K. (1983). How people make their own environments: A theory of genotype → environment effects. *Child Development, 54,* 424–435.

Schaefer, E. S. (1959). A circumplex model for maternal behavior. *Journal of Abnormal and Social Psychology, 59,* 226–235.

Schinke, S. P., Schilling, R. F., II, Barth, R. P., Gilchrist, L. D., & Maxwell, J. S. (1986). Stress-management intervention to prevent family violence. *Journal of Family Violence, 1,* 13–26.

Scott, W. A., Scott, R., & McCabe, M. (1991). Family relationships and children's personality: A cross-cultural, cross-source comparison. *British Journal of Social Psychology, 30,* 1–20.

Seltzer, J. A., & Bianchi, S. M. (1988). Children's contact with absent parents. *Journal of Marriage and the Family, 50,* 663–677.

Shanas, E. (1980). Older people and their families: The new pioneers. *Journal of Marriage and the Family, 42,* 9–15.

Sherrod, K. B., O'Connor, S., Vietze, P. M., & Altemeier, W. A., III. (1984). Child health and maltreatment. *Child Development, 55,* 1174–1183.

Silverberg, S. B., & Steinberg, L. (1987). Adolescent autonomy, parent-adolescent conflict, and parental well-being. *Journal of Youth and Adolescence, 16,* 293–312.

Silverberg, S. B., & Steinberg, L. (1990). Psychological well-being of parents with early adolescent children. *Developmental Psychology, 26,* 658–666.

Silverstein, M., Chen, X., & Heller, K. (1996). Too much of a good thing? Intergenerational social support and the psychological well-being of older parents. *Journal of Marriage and the Family, 58,* 970–982.

Simons, R. L., Beaman, J., Conger, R. D., & Chao, W. (1993). Stress, support, and antisocial behavior trait as determinants of emotional well-being and parenting practices among single mothers. *Journal of Marriage and the Family, 55,* 385–398.

Simons, R. L., Robertson, J. F., & Downs, W. R. (1989). The nature of the association between parental rejection and delinquent behavior. *Journal of Youth and Adolescence, 18,* 297–310.

Simons, R. L., Whitbeck, L. B., Beaman, J., & Conger, R. D. (1994). The impact of mothers' parenting, involvement by nonresidential fathers, and parental conflict on the adjustment of adolescent children. *Journal of Marriage and the Family, 56,* 356–374.

Simons, R. L., Whitbeck, L. B., Conger, R. D., & Wu, C. (1991). Intergenerational transmission of harsh parenting. *Developmental Psychology, 27,* 159–171.

Sirignano, S. W., & Lachman, M. E. (1985). Personality change during the transition to parenthood: The role of perceived infant temperament. *Developmental Psychology, 21,* 558–567.

Skolnick, A. (1981). Married lives: Longitudinal perspectives on marriage. In D. H. Eichorn, J. A. Clausen, N. Haan, M. P. Honzik, & P. H. Mussen (Eds.), *Present and past in middle life.* New York: Academic Press.

Smith, T. W. (1990). Academic achievement and teaching younger siblings. *Social Psychology Quarterly, 53,* 352–363.

Smock, P. J. (1993). The economic costs of marital disruption for young women over the past two decades. *Demography, 30,* 353–371.

Snow, M. E., Jacklin, C. N., & Maccoby, E. E. (1983). Sex-of-child differences in father-child interaction at one year of age. *Child Development, 54,* 227–232.

Somers, M. D. (1993). A comparison of voluntarily childfree adults and parents. *Journal of Marriage and the Family, 55,* 643–650.

Sorensen, E. (1997). A national profile of nonresident fathers and their ability to pay child support. *Journal of Marriage and the Family, 59,* 785–797.

Starrels, M. E., Ingersoll-Dayton, B., Dowler, D. W., & Neal, M. B. (1997). The stress of caring for a parent: Effects of the elder's impairment on an employed adult child. *Journal of Marriage and the Family, 59,* 860–872.

Steinberg, L. (1986). Latchkey children and susceptibility to peer pressure: An ecological analysis. *Developmental Psychology, 22,* 433–439.

Steinberg, L. D. (1996). *Adolescence* (4th ed.). New York: McGraw-Hill.

Steinberg, L., Darling, N. E., & Fletcher, A. C., in collaboration with B. B. Brown & S. M. Dornbusch. (1995). Authoritative parenting and adolescent adjustment: An ecological journey. In P. Moen, G. H. Elder, Jr., & K. Luscher (Eds.), *Examining lives in context: Perspectives on the ecology of human development.* Washington, DC: American Psychological Association.

Stemp, P. S., Turner, J., & Noh, S. (1986). Psychological distress in the postpartum period: The significance of social support. *Journal of Marriage and the Family, 48,* 271–277.

Stephens, M. A. P., & Franks, M. M. (1995). Spillover between daughters' roles as caregiver and wife: Interference or enhancement? *Journal of Gerontology: Psychological Sciences, 50,* P9–P17.

Stevenson, M. R., & Black, K. N. (1988). Paternal absence and sex-role development: A meta-analysis. *Child Development, 59,* 793–814.

Stewart, R. B., & Marvin, R. S. (1984). Sibling relations: The role of conceptual perspective-taking in the ontogeny of sibling caregiving. *Child Development, 55,* 1322–1332.

Stoneman, Z., & Brody, G. H. (1993). Sibling temperaments, conflict, warmth, and role asymmetry. *Child Development, 64,* 1786–1800.

Stormshak, E. A., Bellanti, C. J., Bierman, K. L., & the Conduct Problems Prevention Research Group. (1996). The quality of sibling relationships and the development of social competence and behavioral control in aggressive children. *Developmental Psychology, 32,* 79–89.

Straus, M. A. (1980). A sociological perspective on the causes of family violence. In M. R. Green (Ed.), *Violence and the family* (AAAS Selected Symposium No. 47). Boulder, CO: Westview.

Straus, M. A., & Gelles, R. J. (1986). Societal change and change in family violence from 1975 to 1985 as revealed by two national surveys. *Journal of Marriage and the Family, 48,* 465–479.

Straus, M. A., & Gelles, R. J. (Eds.). (with C. Smith). (1990). *Physical violence in American families: Risk factors and adaptations to violence in 8,145 families.* New Brunswick, NJ: Transaction Publishers.

Stull, D. E., & Scarisbrick-Hauser, A. (1989). Never-married elderly: A reassessment with implications for long-term care policy. *Research on Aging, 11,* 124–139.

Suitor, J. J. (1991). Marital quality and satisfaction with the division of household labor across the family life cycle. *Journal of Marriage and the Family, 53,* 221–230.

Sweet, J. A., & Bumpass, L. L. (1987). *American families and households.* New York: Russell Sage Foundation.

Taeuber, C. (1990). Diversity: The dramatic reality. In S. A. Bass, E. A. Kutza, & F. M. Torres-Gil (Eds.), *Diversity in aging.* Glenview, IL: Scott, Foresman.

Taylor, R. D. (1996). Adolescents' perceptions of kinship support and family management practices: Association with adolescent adjustment in African-American families. *Developmental Psychology, 32,* 687–695.

Taylor, R. D., & Roberts, D. (1995). Kinship support and maternal and adolescent well-being in economically disadvantaged African-American families. *Child Development, 66,* 1585–1597.

Teti, D. M., Sakin, J. W., Kucera, E., & Corns, K. M. (1996). And baby makes four: Predictors of attachment security among preschool-age firstborns during the transition to siblinghood. *Child Development, 67,* 579–596.

Thomson, E., & Colella, U. (1992). Cohabitation and marital stability: Quality or commitment. *Journal of Marriage and the Family, 54,* 259–267.

Tietjen, A. M., & Bradley, C. F. (1985). Social support and maternal psychosocial adjustment during the transition to parenthood. *Canadian Journal of Behavioral Science, 17,* 109–121.

Trickett, P. K., Aber, J. L., Carlson, V., & Cicchetti, D. (1991). Relationship of socioeconomic status to the etiology and developmental sequelae of physical child abuse. *Developmental Psychology, 27,* 148–158.

Trickett, P. K., & McBride-Chang, C. (1995). The developmental impact of different forms of child abuse and neglect. *Developmental Review, 15,* 311–337.

Umberson, D. (1992). Relationships between adult children and their parents: Psychological consequences for both generations. *Journal of Marriage and the Family, 54,* 664–674.

U.S. Bureau of the Census. (1997). *Statistical abstract of the United States* (117th ed.). Washington, DC: U.S. Government Printing Office.

Vandell, D. L., & Ramanan, J. (1991). Children of the National Longitudinal Survey of Youth: Choices in after-school care and child development. *Developmental Psychology, 27,* 637–643.

van IJzendoorn, M. H. (1992). Intergenerational transmission of parenting: A review of studies in nonclinical populations. *Developmental Review, 12,* 76–99.

van IJzendoorn, M. H., Goldberg, S., Kroonenberg, P. M., & Frenkel, O. J. (1992). The relative effects of maternal and child problems on the quality of attachment: A meta-analysis of attachment in clinical samples. *Child Development, 63,* 840–858.

Volling, B. L., & Belsky, J. (1992). The contribution of mother-child and father-child relationships to the quality of sibling interaction: A longitudinal study. *Child Development, 63,* 1209–1222.

Vondra, J., & Belsky, J. (1993). Developmental origins of parenting: Personality and relationship factors. In T. Luster & L. Okagaki (Eds.), *Parenting: An ecological perspective.* Hillsdale, NJ: Erlbaum.

Waldron-Hennessey, R., & Sabatelli, R. M. (1997). The parental comparison level index: A measure for assessing parental rewards and costs relative to expectations. *Journal of Marriage and the Family, 59,* 824–833.

Wallerstein, J. S. (1984). Children of divorce: Preliminary report of a ten-year follow-up of young children. *American Journal of Orthopsychiatry, 54,* 444–458.

Wallerstein, J. S., & Blakeslee, S. (1989). *Second chances: Men, women, and children a decade after divorce.* New York: Ticknor & Fields.

Ward, R., Logan, J., & Spitze, G. (1992). The influence of parent and child needs on coresidence in middle and later life. *Journal of Marriage and the Family, 54,* 209–221.

Ward, R., & Spitze, G. (1992). Consequences of parent-adult child coresidence. *Journal of Family Issues, 13,* 533–572.

Weibel-Orlando, J. (1990). Grandparenting styles: Native American perspectives. In J. Sokolovsky (Ed.), *The cultural context of aging: Worldwide perspectives.* New York: Bergin and Garvey Publishers.

Weisner, T. S., & Gallimore, R. (1977). My brother's keeper: Child and sibling caretaking. *Current Anthropology, 18,* 169–190.

Weiss, L. H., & Schwarz, J. C. (1996). The relationship between parenting types and older adolescents' personality, academic achievement, adjustment, and substance use. *Child Development, 67,* 2101–2114.

Whipple, E. E., & Richey, C. A. (1997). Crossing the line from physical discipline to child abuse: How much is too much? *Child Abuse and Neglect, 21,* 431–444.

Whitbeck, L. B., Hoyt, D. R., & Huck, S. M. (1994). Early family relationships, intergenerational solidarity, and support provided to parents by their adult children. *Journal of Gerontology: Social Sciences, 49,* S85–S94.

White, K., Speisman, J. C., & Costos, D. (1983). Young adults and their parents: Individuation to mutuality. In H. D. Grotevant & C. R. Cooper (Eds.), *Adolescent development in the family* (New Directions for Child Development, No. 22). San Francisco: Jossey-Bass.

White, L., & Edwards, J. N. (1990). Emptying the nest and parental well-being: An analysis of national panel data. *American Sociological Review, 55,* 235–242.

White, L. K., & Rogers, S. J. (1997). Strong support but uneasy relationships: Coresidence and adult children's relationships with their parents. *Journal of Marriage and the Family, 59,* 62–76.

Widmayer, S., & Field, T. (1980). Effects of Brazelton demonstrations on early interactions of preterm infants and their teen-age mothers. *Infant Behavior and Development, 3,* 79–89.

Wiehe, V. R. (1996). *Working with child abuse and neglect.* Thousand Oaks, CA: Sage.

Wilson, M. N. (1986). The black extended family: An analytical consideration. *Developmental Psychology, 22,* 246–258.

Wolf, R. S., & Pillemer, K. A. (1989). *Helping elderly victims: The reality of elder abuse.* New York: Columbia University Press.

Wolfner, G. D., & Gelles, R. J. (1993). A profile of violence toward children: A national study. *Child Abuse and Neglect, 17,* 197–212.

Yau, J., & Smetana, J. G. (1996). Adolescent-parent conflict among Chinese adolescents in Hong Kong. *Child Development, 67,* 1262–1275.

Zaslow, M. J. (1989). Sex differences in children's response to parental divorce: 2. Samples, variables, ages, and sources. *American Journal of Orthopsychiatry, 59,* 118–141.

Zeiss, A. M., Zeiss, R. A., & Johnson, S. M. (1980). Sex differences in initiation of and adjustment to divorce. *Journal of Divorce, 4,* 21–33.

Zigler, E., & Finn Stevenson, M. F. (1993). *Children in a changing world: Developmental and social issues.* Pacific Grove, CA: Brooks/Cole.

Zimmerman, M. A., Salem, D. A., & Maton, K. I. (1995). Family structure and psychosocial correlates among urban African-American adolescent males. *Child Development, 66,* 1598–1613.

CHAPTER 15: Achievement

Ablard, K. E., & Mills, C. J. (1996). Implicit theories of intelligence and self-perceptions of academically talented adolescents and children. *Journal of Youth and Adolescence, 25,* 137–148.

Abraham, J. D., & Hansson, R. O. (1995). Successful aging at work: An applied study of selection, optimization, and compensation through impression management. *Journal of Gerontology: Psychological Sciences, 50,* P94–P103.

Achenbaum, W. A., & Bengtson, V. L. (1994). Re-engaging the disengagement theory of aging: On the history and assessment of theory development in gerontology. *Gerontologist, 34,* 756–763.

Alessandri, S. M., Sullivan, M. W., & Lewis, M. (1990). Violation of expectancy and frustration in early infancy. *Developmental Psychology, 26,* 738–744.

Anderman, E. M., & Midgley, C. (1997). Changes in achievement goal orientations, perceived academic competence, and grades across the transition to middle-level schools. *Contemporary Educational Psychology, 22,* 269–298.

Aneshensel, C. S., & Rosen, B. C. (1980). Domestic roles and sex differences in occupational expectations. *Journal of Marriage and the Family, 42,* 121–131.

Arber, S., & Ginn, J. (1991). *Gender and later life: A sociological analysis of resources and constraints.* London: Sage.

Aronson, E., Blaney, N., Stephan, C., Sikes, J., & Snapp, M. (1978). *The jigsaw classroom.* Beverly Hills, CA: Sage.

Arroyo, C. G., & Zigler, E. (1995). Racial identity, academic achievement, and the psychological well-being of economically disadvantaged adolescents. *Journal of Personality and Social Psychology, 69,* 903–914.

Atchley, R. C. (1976). *The sociology of retirement.* Cambridge, MA: Schenkman.

Atkinson, J. W. (1964). *An introduction to motivation.* Princeton, NJ: Van Nostrand.

Bachman, J. G., & Schulenberg, J. (1993). How part-time work intensity relates to drug use, problem behavior, time use, and satisfaction among high school seniors: Are these consequences or merely correlates? *Developmental Psychology, 29,* 220–235.

Baltes, P. B., & Baltes, M. M. (1990). Psychological perspectives on successful aging: The model of selective optimization with compensation. In P. B. Baltes & M. M. Baltes (Eds.), *Successful aging: Perspectives from the behavioral sciences.* New York: Cambridge University Press.

Barling, J., Rogers, K. A., & Kelloway, E. K. (1995). Some effects of teenagers' part-time employment: The quantity and quality of work make the difference. *Journal of Organizational Behavior, 16,* 143–154.

Barnett, R. C. (1994). Home-to-work spillover revisited: A study of full-time employed women in dual-earner couples. *Journal of Marriage and the Family, 56,* 647–656.

Barnett, R. C., Raudenbush, S. W., Brennan, R. T., Pleck, J. H., & Marshall, N. L. (1995). Change in job and marital experiences and change in psychological distress:

A longitudinal study of dual-earner couples. *Journal of Personality and Social Psychology, 69,* 839–850.

Barrett, K. C., & Morgan, G. A. (1995). Continuities and discontinuities in mastery motivation during infancy and toddlerhood: A conceptualization and review. In R. H. MacTurk & G. A. Morgan (Eds.), *Mastery motivation: Origins, conceptualizations, and applications.* Norwood, NJ: Ablex.

Baruch, G. K., & Barnett, R. (1986). Role quality, multiple role involvement, and psychological well-being in midlife women. *Journal of Personality and Social Psychology, 51,* 578–585.

Baruch, R. (1967). The achievement motive in women: Implications for career development. *Journal of Personality and Social Psychology, 5,* 260–267.

Battle, E. S. (1966). Motivational determinants of academic competence. *Journal of Personality and Social Psychology, 4,* 634–642.

Belsky, J., & Most, R. (1981). From exploration to play: A cross-sectional study of infant free-play behavior. *Developmental Psychology, 17,* 630–639.

Bernhardt, A., Morris, M., & Handcock, M. S. (1995). Women's gains or men's losses? A closer look at the shrinking gender gap in earnings. *American Journal of Sociology, 101,* 302–328.

Beyer, S. (1995). Maternal employment and children's academic achievement: Parenting styles as mediating variable. *Developmental Review, 15,* 212–253.

Bizot, E. B., & Goldman, S. H. (1993). Prediction of satisfactoriness and satisfaction: An 8-year follow-up. *Journal of Vocational Behavior, 43,* 19–29.

Bogenschneider, K. (1997). Parental involvement in adolescent schooling: A proximal process with transcontextual validity. *Journal of Marriage and the Family, 59,* 718–733.

Boggiano, A. K., & Katz, P. (1991). Maladaptive achievement patterns in students: The role of teachers' controlling strategies. *Journal of Social Issues, 47* (4), 35–51.

Bossé, R., Aldwin, C. M., Levenson, M. R., Spiro, A., III, & Mroczek, D. K. (1993). Change in social support after retirement: Longitudinal findings from the Normative Aging Study. *Journal of Gerontology: Psychological Sciences, 48,* P210–P217.

Braddock, J. H., II, & McPartland, J. M. (1993). Education of early adolescents. *Review of Educational Research, 19,* 135–170.

Bretz, R. D., & Judge, T. A. (1994). Person-organization fit and the theory of work adjustment: Implications for satisfaction, tenure, and career success. *Journal of Vocational Behavior, 44,* 32–54.

Brookover, W., Beady, C., Flood, P., Schweitzer, J., & Wisenbaker, J. (1979). *School social systems and student achievement: Schools can make a difference.* New York: Praeger.

Brown, B. B., Mounts, N., Lamborn, S. D., & Steinberg, L. (1993). Parenting practices and peer group affiliation in adolescence. *Child Development, 64,* 467–482.

Brownell, C. A. (1988). Combinatorial skills: Converging developments over the second year. *Child Development, 59,* 675–685.

Bryant, W. K., & Zick, C. D. (1996). An examination of parent-child shared time. *Journal of Marriage and the Family, 58,* 227–237.

Burhans, K. K., & Dweck, C. S. (1995). Helplessness in early childhood: The role of contingent worth. *Child Development, 66,* 1719–1738.

Busch-Rossnagel, N. A. (1997). Mastery motivation in toddlers. *Infants and Young Children, 9,* 1–11.

Butler, R. (1990). The effects of mastery and competitive conditions on self-assessment at different ages. *Child Development, 61,* 201–210.

Buysse, V., & Bailey, D. B. (1993). Behavioral and developmental outcomes in young children with disabilities in integrated and segregated settings: A review of comparative studies. *Journal of Special Education, 26,* 434–461.

Call, K. T., Mortimer, J. T., & Shanahan, M. (1995). Helpfulness and the development of competence in adolescence. *Child Development, 66,* 129–138.

Campbell, F. A., & Ramey, C. T. (1995). Cognitive and school outcomes for high-risk African-American students at middle adolescence: Positive effects of early intervention. *American Educational Research Journal, 32,* 743–772.

Carstensen, L. L. (1993). Motivation for school contact across the life span: A theory of socioemotional selectivity. In R. Dienstbier & J. E. Jacobs (Eds.), *Nebraska symposium on motivation: Vol. 40. Developmental perspectives on motivation.* Lincoln: University of Nebraska Press.

Cassidy, J. (1986). The ability to negotiate the environment: An aspect of infant competence as related to quality of attachment. *Child Development, 57,* 331–337.

Ceci, S. J., & Williams, W. M. (1997). Schooling, intelligence, and income. *American Psychologist, 52,* 1051–1058.

Chen, C., & Stevenson, H. W. (1989). Homework: A cross-cultural examination. *Child Development, 60,* 551–561.

Chen, C., & Stevenson, H. W. (1995). Motivation and mathematics achievement: A comparative study of Asian-American, Caucasian-American, and East Asian high school students. *Child Development, 66,* 1214–1234.

Clark, D. O., & Maddox, G. L. (1992). Racial and social correlates of age-related changes in functioning. *Journal of Gerontology: Social Sciences, 47,* S222–S223.

Clarke-Stewart, A. (1993). *Daycare* (rev. ed.) Cambridge, MA: Harvard University Press.

Clausen, J. A., & Gilens, M. (1990). Personality and labor force participation across the life course: A longitudinal study of women's careers. *Sociological Forum, 5,* 595–618.

Coleman, J. (1961). *The adolescent society.* New York: Free Press.

Comer, J. (1993). *School power* (rev. ed.). New York: Free Press.

Corrigan, R. (1987). A developmental sequence of actor-object pretend play in young children. *Merrill-Palmer Quarterly, 33,* 87–106.

Cox, T. H., & Harquail, C. V. (1991). Career paths and career success in the early career stages of male and female MBAs. *Journal of Vocational Behavior, 39,* 54–75.

Crandall, V. C. (1967). Achievement behavior in young children. In *The young child: Reviews of research.* Washington, DC: National Association for the Education of Young Children.

Crandall, V. C. (1969). Sex differences in expectancy of intellectual and academic reinforcement. In C. P. Smith (Ed.), *Achievement-related motives in children.* New York: Russell Sage Foundation.

Cronbach, L. J., & Snow, R. E. (1977). *Aptitudes and instructional methods: A* handbook for research on interactions. New York: Irvington.

Crouter, A. C., & McHale, S. M. (1993). The long arm of the job: Influences of parental work on childrearing. In T. Luster & L. Okagaki (Eds.), *Parenting: An ecological perspective* Hillsdale, NJ: Erlbaum.

Crystal, D. S., Chen, C., Fuligni, A. J., & Stevenson, H. W. (1994). Psychological maladjustment and academic achievement: A cross-cultural study of Japanese, Chinese, and American high school students. *Child Development, 65,* 738–753.

Cumming, E., & Henry, W. E. (1961). *Growing old: The process of disengagement.* New York: Basic Books.

Damast, A. M., Tamis-LeMonda, C. S., & Bornstein, M. H. (1996). Mother-child play: Sequential interactions and the relation between maternal beliefs and behaviors. *Child Development, 67,* 1752–1766.

Dancer, L. S., & Gilbert, L. A. (1993). Spouses' family work participation and its relation to wives' occupational level. *Sex Roles, 28,* 127–145.

Drebing, C. E., & Gooden, W. E. (1991). The impact of the dream on mental health functioning in the male midlife transition. *International Journal of Aging and Human Development, 32,* 277–287.

Drebing, C. E., Gooden, W. E., Drebing, S. M., Van de Kamp, H., & Malony, H. N. (1995). The dream in midlife women: Its impact on mental health. *International Journal of Aging and Human Development, 40,* 73–87.

Dunn, T. R., & Merriam, S. B. (1995). Levinson's age thirty transition: Does it exist? *Journal of Adult Development, 2,* 113–124.

Dweck, C. S. (1975). The role of expectations and attributions in the alleviation of learned helplessness. *Journal of Personality and Social Psychology, 31,* 674–685.

Dweck, C. S., & Elliott, E. S. (1983). Achievement motivation. In E. M. Hetherington (Vol. Ed.; P. H. Mussen, General Ed.), *Handbook of child psychology: Vol. 4. Socialization, personality, and social development* (4th ed.). New York: Wiley.

Dweck, C. S., & Leggett, E. L. (1988). A social-cognitive approach to motivation and personality. *Psychological Review, 95,* 256–273.

Eccles, J. S., Lord, S., & Midgley, C. (1991). What are we doing to early adolescents? The impact of educational contexts on early adolescents. *American Journal of Education, 99,* 521–542.

Eccles, J. S., Midgley, C., Wigfield, A., Buchanan, C. M., Reuman, D., Flanagan, C., & Mac Iver, D. (1993). Development during adolescence. The impact of stage-environment fit on young adolescents' experiences in schools and in families. *American Psychologist, 48,* 90–101.

Ekerdt, D. J., Bossé, R., & Levkoff, S. (1985). Empirical test for phases of retirement: Findings from the Normative Aging Study. *Journal of Gerontology, 40,* 95–101.

Ekerdt, D. J., & Vinick, B. H. (1991). Marital complaints in husband-working and husband-retired couples. *Research on Aging, 13,* 364–382.

Elkind, D. (1981). *The hurried child: Growing up too fast too soon.* Reading, MA: Addison-Wesley.

Elliott, E. S., & Dweck, C. S. (1988). Goals: An approach to motivation and achievement. *Journal of Personality and Social Psychology, 54,* 5–12.

England, P., Reid, L. L., & Kilbourne, B. S. (1996). The effect of the sex composition of jobs on starting wages in an organization: Findings from the NLSY. *Demography, 33,* 511–521.

Ensminger, M. E., & Slusarcick, A. L. (1992). Paths to high school graduation or dropout: A longitudinal study of a first-grade cohort. *Sociology of Education, 65,* 95–113.

Entwisle, D. R., & Alexander, K. L. (1992). Summer setback: Race, poverty, school composition, and mathematics achievement in the first two years of school. *American Sociological Review, 57,* 72–84.

Erdley, C. A., Loomis, C. C., Cain, K. M., & Dumas-Hines, F. (1997). Relations among children's social goals, implicit personality theories, and responses to social failure. *Developmental Psychology, 33,* 263–272.

Etaugh, C., & Liss, M. B. (1992). Home, school, and playroom: Training grounds for adult gender roles. *Sex Roles, 26,* 129–147.

Evans, L., Ekerdt, D. J., & Bossé, R. (1985). Proximity to retirement and anticipatory involvement: Findings from the Normative Aging Study. *Journal of Gerontology, 40,* 368–374.

Farrell, M. P., & Rosenberg, S. D. (1981). *Men at midlife.* Dover, MA: Auburn House.

Featherman, D. L. (1980). Schooling and occupational careers: Constancy and change in worldly success. In O. G. Brim, Jr., & J. Kagan (Eds.), *Constancy and change in human development.* Cambridge, MA: Harvard University Press.

Filipp, S. H. (1996). Motivation and emotion. In J. E. Birren, K. W. Schaie, R. P. Abeles, M. Gatz, & T. A. Salthouse (Eds.), *Handbook of the psychology of the aging* (4th ed.). San Diego: Academic Press.

Findley, M. J., & Cooper, H. M. (1983). Locus of control and academic achievement: A literature review. *Journal of Personality and Social Psychology, 44,* 419–427.

Ford, M. E., & Thompson, R. A. (1985). Perceptions of personal agency and infant attachment: Toward a life-span perspective on competence development. *International Journal of Behavioral Development, 8,* 377–406.

Fordham, S., & Ogbu, J. U. (1986). Black students' school success: Coping with the "burden of 'acting white.'" *Urban Review, 18,* 176–206.

Frankel, K. A., & Bates, J. E. (1990). Mother-toddler problem-solving: Antecedents in attachment, home behavior, and temperament. *Child Development, 61,* 810–819.

Fraser, B. J., Walberg, H. J., Welch, W. W., & Hattie, J. A. (1987). Synthesis of educational productivity research. *International Journal of Educational Research, 11,* 145–252.

Fry, P. S. (1992). Major social theories of aging and their implications for counseling concepts and practice: A critical review. *Counseling Psychologist, 20,* 246–329.

Fuligni, A. J., & Stevenson, H. W. (1995). Time use and mathematics achievement among American, Chinese, and Japanese high school students. *Child Development, 66,* 830–842.

Gall, T. L., Evans, D. R., & Howard, J. (1997). The retirement adjustment process: Changes in the well-being of male retirees across time. *Journal of Gerontology: Psychological Sciences, 52,* P110–P117.

Gendell, M., & Siegel, J. S. (1996). Trends in retirement age in the

United States, 1955–1993, by sex and race. *Journal of Gerontology: Social Sciences, 51,* S132–S139.

Ginsburg, G. S., & Bronstein, P. (1993). Family factors related to children's intrinsic/extrinsic motivational orientation and academic performance. *Child Development, 64,* 1461–1474.

Ginzberg, E. (1972). Toward a theory of occupational choice: A restatement. *Vocational Guidance Quarterly, 20,* 169–176.

Ginzberg, E. (1984). Career development. In D. Brown, L. Brooks, & Associates (Eds.), *Career choice and development.* San Francisco: Jossey-Bass.

Glasgow, K. L., Dornbusch, S. M., Troyer, L., Steinberg, L., & Ritter, P. L. (1997). Parenting styles, adolescents' attributions, and educational outcomes in nine heterogeneous high schools. *Child Development, 68,* 507–529.

Goldberg, W. A., Greenberger, E., & Nagel, S. K. (1996). Employment and achievement: Mothers' work involvement in relation to children's achievement behaviors and mothers' parenting behaviors. *Child Development, 67,* 1512–1527.

Gottfredson, L. S. (1996). Gottfredson's theory of circumscription and compromise. In D. Brown, L. Brooks, & Associates (Eds.), *Career choice and development* (3rd ed.). San Francisco: Jossey-Bass.

Gottfried, A. E., Gottfried, A. W., & Bathurst, K. (1995). Maternal and dual-earner employment status and parenting. In M. H. Bornstein (Ed.), *Handbook of parenting: Vol. 2. Biology and ecology of parenting.* Mahwah, NJ: Erlbaum.

Gray-Little, B., & Carels, R. A. (1997). The effect of racial dissonance on academic self-esteem and achievement in elementary, junior high, and high school students. *Journal of Research on Adolescence, 7,* 109–131.

Greenberger, E., O'Neil, R., & Nagel, S. K. (1994). Linking workplace and homeplace: Relations between the nature of adults' work and their parenting behaviors. *Developmental Psychology, 30,* 990–1002.

Greenberger, E., & Steinberg, L. (1986). *When teenagers work: The psychological and social costs of adolescent employment.* New York: Basic Books.

Greenwald, R., Hedges, L. V., & Laine, R. D. (1996). The effect of school resources on student achievement. *Review of Educational Research, 66,* 361–396.

Grolnick, W. S., & Ryan, R. M. (1989). Parent styles associated with children's self-regulation and competence in school. *Journal of Educational Psychology, 81,* 143–154.

Grotevant, H. D., Cooper, C. R., & Kramer, K. (1986). Exploration as a predictor of congruence in adolescents' career choices. *Journal of Vocational Behavior, 29,* 201–215.

Gutek, B. A., Searle, S., & Klepa, L. (1991). Rational versus gender role explanations for work-family conflict. *Journal of Applied Psychology, 76,* 560–568.

Hanson, K., & Wapner, S. (1994). Transition to retirement: Gender differences. *International Journal of Aging and Human Development, 39,* 189–208.

Hanson, S. L. (1994). Lost talent: Unrealized educational aspirations and expectations among U.S. youths. *Sociology of Education, 67,* 159–183.

Hansson, R. O., DeKoekkoek, P. D., Neece, W. M., & Patterson, D. W. (1997). Successful aging at work: Annual review, 1992–1996: The older worker and transitions to retirement. *Journal of Vocational Behavior, 51,* 202–233.

Hanushek, E. A. (1997). Assessing the effects of school resources on student performance: An update. *Educational Evaluation and Policy Analysis, 19,* 141–164.

Harlow, R. E., & Cantor, N. (1996). Still participating after all these years: A study of life task participation in later life. *Journal of Personality and Social Psychology, 71,* 1235–1249.

Harter, S. (1981). A new self-report scale of intrinsic versus extrinsic orientation in the classroom: Motivational and informational components. *Developmental Psychology, 17,* 300–312.

Havighurst, R. J. (1982). The world of work. In B. B. Wolman (Ed.), *Handbook of developmental psychology.* Englewood Cliffs, NJ: Prentice-Hall.

Havighurst, R. J., Neugarten, B. L., & Tobin, S. S. (1968). Disengagement and patterns of aging. In B. L. Neugarten (Ed.), *Middle age and aging.* Chicago: University of Chicago Press.

Hedges, L. V., Laine, R. D., & Greenwald, R. (1994). Does money matter? A meta-analysis of studies of the effects of differential school inputs on student outcomes. *Educational Researcher, 23,* 5–14.

Hedlund, B., & Ebersole, P. (1983). A test of Levinson's mid-life reevaluation. *Journal of Genetic Psychology, 143,* 189–192.

Helmreich, R. L., Sawin, L. L., & Carsrud, A. L. (1986). The honeymoon effect in job performance: Temporal increases in the predictive power of achievement motivation. *Journal of Applied Psychology, 71,* 185–188.

Herring, C., & Wilson-Sadberry, K. R. (1993). Preference or necessity? Changing work roles of black and white women, 1973–1990. *Journal of Marriage and the Family, 55,* 314–325.

Herzog, A. R., Kahn, R. L., Morgan, J. N., Jackson, J. S., & Antonucci, T. C. (1989). Age differences in productive activities. *Journal of Gerontology: Social Sciences, 44,* S129–S138.

Hoffman, L. W. (1989). Effects of maternal employment in the two-parent family. *American Psychologist, 44,* 283–292.

Hokoda, A., & Fincham, F. D. (1995). Origins of children's helpless and mastery achievement patterns in the family. *Journal of Educational Psychology, 87,* 375–385.

Holland, J. L. (1985). *Making vocational choices: A theory of vocational personalities and work environments* (2nd ed.). Englewood Cliffs, NJ: Prentice-Hall.

Hooker, K., & Siegler, I. C. (1993). Life goals, satisfaction, and self-rated health: Preliminary findings. *Experimental Aging Research, 19,* 97–110.

Hunt, P., & Goetz, L. (1997). Research on inclusive educational programs, practices, and outcomes for students with severe disabilities. *Journal of Special Education, 31,* 3–29.

Hyson, M. C., Hirsch-Pasek, K., & Rescorla, L. (1989). *Academic environments in early childhood: Challenge or pressure?* Summary report to the Spencer Foundation.

Jenkins, S. R. (1989). Longitudinal prediction of women's careers: Psychological, behavioral, and social-structural influences. *Journal of Vocational Behavior, 34,* 204–235.

Johnson, D. W., Johnson, R. T., & Maruyama, G. (1983). Interdependence and interpersonal attraction among heterogeneous and homogeneous individuals: A theoretical formulation and a meta-analysis of the research. *Review of Educational Research, 53,* 5–54.

Kagan, J., & Moss, H. A. (1962). *Birth to maturity.* New York: Wiley.

Kaplan, D. S., Damphousse, K. R., & Kaplan, H. B. (1994). Mental health implications of not graduating from high school. *Journal of Experimental Education, 62,* 105–123.

Kelso, G. I. (1977). The relation of school grade to ages and stages in vocational development. *Journal of Vocational Behavior, 10,* 287–301.

Kohn, M. L., & Schooler, C. (1982). Job conditions and personality: A longitudinal assessment of their reciprocal effects. *American Journal of Sociology, 87,* 1257–1286.

Kohn, M. L., & Schooler, C. (in collaboration with J. Miller, K. A. Miller, C. Schoenbach, & R. Schoenberg). (1983). *Work and personality: An inquiry into the impact of social stratification.* Norwood, NJ: Ablex.

Krogh, K. M. (1985). Women's motives to achieve and to nurture in different life stages. *Sex Roles, 12,* 75–90.

Kulik, J. A., & Kulik, C. C. (1992). Meta-analytic findings on grouping programs. *Gifted Child Quarterly, 36,* 73–77.

Lamborn, S. D., Mounts, N. S., Steinberg, L., & Dornbusch, S. M. (1991). Patterns of competence and adjustment among adolescents from authoritative, authoritarian, indulgent, and neglectful families. *Child Development, 62,* 1049–1065.

Langer, E. J., & Rodin, J. (1976). The effects of choice and enhanced personal responsibility for the aged: A field experiment in an institutional setting. *Journal of Personality and Social Psychology, 34,* 191–198.

Lauver, P. J., & Jones, R. M. (1991). Factors associated with perceived career options in American Indian, white, and Hispanic rural high school students. *Journal of Counseling Psychology, 38,* 159–166.

Levinson, D. J. (1986). A conception of adult development. *American Psychologist, 41,* 3–13.

Levinson, D. J., with Darrow, C. N., Klein, E. B., Levinson, M. H., & McKee, B. (1978). *The seasons of a man's life.* New York: Ballantine Books.

Levinson, D. J. (in collaboration with J. D. Levinson). (1996). *The seasons of a woman's life.* New York: Alfred A. Knopf.

Lewis, M., Alessandri, S. M., & Sullivan, M. W. (1990). Violation of expectancy, loss of control, and anger expressions in young infants. *Developmental Psychology, 26,* 745–751.

Linney, J. A., & Seidman, E. (1989). The future of schooling. *American Psychologist, 44,* 336–340.

Lloyd, D. N. (1978). Prediction of school failure from third-grade data. *Educational and Psychological Measurement, 38,* 1193–1200.

Mac Iver, D. J., & Reuman, D. A. (1988, April). *Decision-making in the classroom and early adolescents' valuing of mathematics.* Paper presented at the annual meeting of the American Educational Research Association, New Orleans, LA.

Mac Iver, D. J., Reuman, D. A., & Main, S. R. (1995). Social structuring of the school: Studying what is, illuminating what could be. *Annual Review of Psychology, 46,* 375–400.

Mac Iver, D. J., Stipek, D. J., & Daniels, D. H. (1991). Explaining within-semester changes in student effort in junior high school and senior high school courses. *Journal of Educational Psychology, 83,* 201–211.

MacTurk, R. H., McCarthy, M. E., Vietze, P. M., & Yarrow, L. J. (1987). Sequential analysis of mastery behavior in 6- and 12-month-old infants. *Developmental Psychology, 23,* 199–203.

Malatesta, C. Z., & Culver, L. C. (1984). Thematic and affective content in the lives of adult women. In C. Z. Malatesta & C. E. Izard (Eds.), *Emotion in adult development.* Beverly Hills, CA: Sage.

Manset, G., & Semmel, M. I. (1997). Are inclusive programs for students with mild disabilities effective? A comparative review of model programs. *Journal of Special Education, 31,* 155–180.

Mayes, L. C., & Zigler, E. (1992). An observational study of the affective concomitants of mastery in infants. *Journal of Psychology and Psychiatry, 4,* 659–667.

McAdams, P. P., de St. Aubin, E., & Logan, R. L. (1993). Generativity among young, middle, and older adults. *Psychology and Aging, 8,* 221–230.

McCaul, E. J., Donaldson, G. A., Coladarci, T., & Davis, W. E. (1992). Consequences of dropping out of school: Findings from high school and beyond. *Journal of Educational Research, 85,* 198–207.

McClelland, D. C. (1985). How motives, skills, and values determine what people do. *American Psychologist, 40,* 812–825.

McClelland, D. C., Atkinson, J. W., Clark, R. A., & Lowell, E. L. (1953). *The achievement motive.* New York: Appleton-Century-Crofts.

McCrae, R. R., & Costa, P. T., Jr. (1990). *Personality in adulthood.* New York: Guilford.

McCune, L. (1995). A normative study of representational play in the transition to language. *Developmental Psychology, 31,* 198–206.

Mehan, H., Villanueva, I., Hubbard, L., & Lintz, A. (1996). *Constructing school success: The consequences of untracking low-achieving students.* New York: Cambridge University Press.

Mellinger, J. C., & Erdwins, C. J. (1985). Personality correlates of age and life roles in adult women. *Psychology of Women Quarterly, 9,* 503–514.

Menaghan, E. G., & Parcel, T. L. (1991). Transitions in work and family arrangements: Mothers' employment conditions, children's experiences, and child outcomes. In K. Pillemer & K. McCartney (Eds.), *Parent-child relations throughout life.* Hillsdale, NJ: Erlbaum.

Mercer, R. T., Nichols, E. G., & Doyle, G. C. (1989). *Transitions in a woman's life: Major life events in developmental context.* New York: Springer.

Messer, D. J., McCarthy, M. E., McQuiston, S., MacTurk, R. H., Yarrow, L. J., & Vietze, P. M. (1986). Relation between mastery behavior in infancy and competence in early childhood. *Developmental Psychology, 22,* 366–372.

Midgley, C., Feldlaufer, H., & Eccles, J. S. (1989). Student/teacher relations and attitudes toward mathematics before and after the transition to junior high school. *Child Development, 60,* 981–992.

Miller, A. (1985). A developmental study of the cognitive basis of performance impairment after failure. *Journal of Personality and Social Psychology, 49,* 529–538.

Moen, P. (1992). *Women's two roles: A contemporary dilemma.* New York: Auburn House.

Moorehouse, M. J. (1991). Linking maternal employment patterns to mother-child activities and children's school competence. *Developmental Psychology, 27,* 295–303.

Morgan, G. A., MacTurk, R. H., & Hrncir, E. J. (1995). Mastery motivation: Overview, definitions, and conceptual issues. In R. H. MacTurk & G. A. Morgan (Eds.), *Mastery motivation: Origins, conceptualizations, and applications.* Norwood, NJ: Ablex.

Morinaga, Y., Frieze, I. H., & Ferligoj, A. (1993). Career plans and gender-role attitudes of college students in the United States, Japan, and Slovenia. *Sex Roles, 29,* 317–334.

Mortimer, J. T., Finch, M. D., Ryu, S., Shanahan, M. J., & Call, K. T. (1996). The effects of work intensity on adolescent mental health, achievement, and behavioral adjustment: New evidence from a prospective study. *Child Development, 67,* 1243–1261.

Nicholls, J. G., & Miller, A. T. (1984). Reasoning about the ability of self and others: A developmental study. *Child Development, 55,* 1990–1999.

Nicolich, L. M. (1977). Beyond sensorimotor intelligence: Assessment of symbolic maturity through analysis of pretend play. *Merrill-Palmer Quarterly, 23,* 89–99.

Nock, S. L., & Kingston, P. W. (1988). Time with children: The impact of couples' work-time commitment. *Social Forces, 67,* 59–85.

O'Connor, B. P., & Vallerand, R. J. (1994). Motivation, self-determination, and person-environment fit as predictors of psychological adjustment among nursing home residents. *Psychology and Aging, 9,* 189–194.

Odden, A. (1990). Class size and student achievement: Research-based policy alternatives. *Educational Evaluation and Policy Analysis, 12,* 213–227.

O'Donnell, A. M., & O'Kelly, J. (1994). Learning from peers: Beyond the rhetoric of positive results. *Educational Psychology Review, 6,* 321–349.

Ornstein, S., & Isabella, L. A. (1990). Age vs. stage models of career attitudes of women: A partial replication and extension. *Journal of Vocational Behavior, 36,* 1–19.

Orth, L. C., & Martin, R. P. (1994). Interactive effects of student temperament and instruction method on classroom behavior and achievement. *Journal of School Psychology, 32,* 149–166.

Palmore, E. B., Burchett, B. M., Fillenbaum, G. G., George, L. K., & Wallman, L. M. (1985). *Retirement: Causes and consequences.* New York: Springer.

Parasuraman, S., & Greenhaus, J. H. (1997). The changing world of work and family. In S. Parasuraman & J. H. Greenhaus (Eds.), *Integrating work and family.* Westport, CT: Quorum Books.

Parnes, H. S., & Less, L. (1985). Variation in selected forms of leisure activity among elderly males. In Z. S. Blau (Ed.), *Current perspectives on aging and the life cycle: Vol. 1. Work, retirement, and social policy.* Greenwich, CT: JAI Press.

Peisner-Feinberg, E. S., & Burchinal, M. R. (1997). Relations between preschool children's child-care experiences and concurrent development: The cost, quality, and outcomes study. *Merrill-Palmer Quarterly, 43,* 451–477.

Peterson, P. L. (1977). Interactive effects of student anxiety, achievement orientation, and teacher behavior on student achievement and attitude. *Journal of Educational Psychology, 69,* 779–792.

Phelan, P., Yu, H. C., & Davidson, A. L. (1994). Navigating the psychosocial pressures of adolescence: The voices and experiences of high school youth. *American Educational Research Journal, 31,* 415–447.

Phillips, M. (1997). What makes schools effective? A comparison of the relationships of communitarian climate and academic climate to mathematics achievement and attendance during middle school. *American Educational Research Journal, 34,* 633–662.

Phillips, S. D. (1982). Career exploration in adulthood. *Journal of Vocational Behavior, 20,* 129–140.

Phipps, B. J. (1995). Career dreams of preadolescent students. *Journal of Career Development, 22,* 19–32.

Piaget, J. (1962). *Play, dreams, and imitation in childhood.* New York: Norton. (Original work published 1951)

Pomerantz, E. M., & Ruble, D. N. (1997). Distinguishing multiple dimensions of conceptions of ability: Implications for self-evaluation. *Child Development, 68,* 1165–1180.

Portes, A., & MacLeod, D. (1996). Educational progress of children of immigrants: The roles of class, ethnicity, and school context. *Sociology of Education, 69,* 255–275.

Rapkin, B. D., & Fischer, K. (1992). Personal goals of older adults: Issues in assessment and prediction. *Psychology and Aging, 7,* 127–137.

Raynor, J. O. (1970). Relationships between achievement-related motives, future orientation, and academic performance. *Journal of Personality and Social Psychology, 15,* 28–33.

Redding, R. E., Harmon, R. J., & Morgan, G. A. (1990). Maternal depression and infants' mastery behaviors. *Infant Behavior and Development, 13,* 391–395.

Reich, J. W., & Zautra, A. J. (1989). A perceived control intervention for at-risk older adults. *Psychology and Aging, 4,* 415–424.

Reich, J. W., & Zautra, A. J. (1990). Dispositional control beliefs and the consequences of a control-enhancing intervention. *Journal of Gerontology: Psychological Sciences, 45,* P46–P51.

Reker, G. T., Peacock, E. J., & Wong, P. T. P. (1987). Meaning and purpose in life and well-being: A life-span perspective. *Journal of Gerontology, 42,* 44–49.

Reynolds, A. J., Mavrogenes, N. A., Bezruczko, N., & Hagemann, M. (1996). Cognitive and family-support mediators of preschool effectiveness: A confirmatory analysis. *Child Development, 67,* 1119–1140.

Reynolds, D. (1992). School effectiveness and school improvement: An updated review of the British literature. In D. Reynolds & P. Cuttance (Eds.), *School effectiveness: Research, policy, and practice.* London: Cassell.

Rhodes, S. R. (1983). Age-related differences in work attitudes and behavior: A review and conceptual analysis. *Psychological Bulletin, 93,* 328–367.

Roberts, P., & Newton, P. M. (1987). Levinsonian studies of women's adult development. *Psychology and Aging, 2,* 154–163.

Rodin, J., & Langer, E. J. (1977). Long-term effects of a control-relevant intervention with the institutionalized aged. *Journal of Personality and Social Psychology, 35,* 897–902.

Roeser, R. W., & Eccles, J. S. (1998). Adolescents' perceptions of middle school: Relation to longitudinal changes in academic and psychological adjustment. *Journal of Research on Adolescence, 8,* 123–158.

Rogoff, B. (1990). *Apprenticeship in thinking: Cognitive development in social context*. New York: Oxford University Press.

Rogoff, B., Mistry, J., Goncu, A., & Mosier, C. (1991). Cultural variation in the role relations of toddlers and their families. In M. H. Bornstein (Ed.), *Cultural approaches to parenting*. Hillsdale, NJ: Erlbaum.

Rojewski, J. W., & Yang, B. (1997). Longitudinal analysis of select influences on adolescents' occupational aspirations. *Journal of Vocational Behavior, 51*, 375–410.

Rosen, B. C., & D'Andrade, R. (1959). The psychosocial origins of achievement motivation. *Sociometry, 22*, 185–218.

Rosenholtz, S. J., & Simpson, C. (1984). The formation of ability conceptions: Developmental trend or social construction? *Review of Educational Research, 54*, 31–63.

Roth, P. L., Bevier, C. A., Switzer, F. S., & Schippmann, J. S. (1996). Meta-analyzing the relationship between grades and job performance. *Journal of Applied Psychology, 81*, 548–556.

Ruble, D. N., Eisenberg, R., & Higgins, E. T. (1994). Developmental changes in achievement evaluation: Motivational implications of self-other differences. *Child Development, 65*, 1095–1110.

Ruff, H. A., & Saltarelli, L. M. (1993). Exploratory play with objects: Basic cognitive processes and individual differences. In M. H. Bornstein & A. W. O'Reilly (Eds.), *The role of play in the development of thought* (New Directions for Child Development, No. 59). San Francisco: Jossey-Bass.

Rutter, M. (1983). School effects on pupil progress: Research findings and policy implications. *Child Development, 54*, 1–29.

Rutter, M., Maughan, B., Mortimore, P., Ouston, J., & Smith, A. (1979). *Fifteen thousand hours: Secondary schools and their effects on children*. Cambridge, MA: Harvard University Press.

Sacks, C. H., & Mergendoller, J. R. (1997). The relationship between teachers' theoretical orientation toward reading and student outcomes in kindergarten children with different initial reading abilities. *American Educational Research Journal, 34*, 721–739.

Schulz, R., & Heckhausen, J. (1996). A life span model of successful aging. *American Psychologist, 51*, 702–714.

Seidman, E., Allen, L. R., Aber, J. L., Mitchell, C., & Feinman, J. (1994). The impact of school transitions in early adolescence on the self-system and perceived social context of poor urban youth. *Child Development, 65*, 507–522.

Seleen, D. R. (1982). The congruence between actual and desired use of time by older adults: A predictor of life satisfaction. *Gerontologist, 22*, 95–99.

Seligman, M. E. P. (1975). *Helplessness: On depression, development, and death*. San Francisco: W. H. Freeman.

Shanahan, M. J., Finch, M. D., Mortimer, J. T., & Ryu, S. (1991). Adolescent work experience and depressive affect. *Social Psychology Quarterly, 54*, 299–317.

Shelton, B. A. (1992). *Women, men, and time: Gender differences in paid work, housework, and leisure*. Westport, CT: Greenwood Press.

Sigman, M., & Sena, R. (1993). Pretend play in high-risk and developmentally delayed children. In M. H. Bornstein & A. W. O'Reilly (Eds.), *The role of play in the development of thought*. (New Directions for Child Development, No. 59). San Francisco: Jossey-Bass.

Simmons, R. G., & Blyth, D. A. (1987). *Moving into adolescence: The impact of pubertal change in school context*. New York: Aldine de Gruyter.

Slavin, R. E. (1986). Cooperative learning: Engineering social psychology in the classroom. In R. S. Feldman (Ed.), *The social psychology of education: Current research and theory*. Cambridge: Cambridge University Press.

Slavin, R. E. (1989). Class size and student achievement: Small effects of small classes. *Educational Psychologist, 24*, 99–110.

Smart, R., & Peterson, C. (1997). Super's career stages and the decision to change careers. *Journal of Vocational Behavior, 51*, 358–374.

Smith, J. B. (1997). Effects of eighth-grade transition programs on high school retention and experiences. *Journal of Educational Research, 90*, 144–152.

Sorensen, A. (1983). Women's employment patterns after marriage. *Journal of Marriage and the Family, 45*, 311–321.

Sorensen, E. (1991). *Exploring the reasons behind the narrowing gender gap in earnings* (Urban Institute Report 1991-1992). Washington, DC: Urban Institute Press.

Spence, J. T. (1985). Achievement American style: The rewards and costs of individualism. *American Psychologist, 40*, 1285–1295.

Spokane, A. (1996). Holland's theory. In D. Brown, L. Brooks, & Associates (Eds.), *Career choice and development* (3rd ed.). San Francisco: Jossey-Bass.

Steinberg, L. (1984). The varieties and effects of work during adolescence. In M. E. Lamb, A. L. Brown, & B. Rogoff (Eds.), *Advances in developmental psychology* (Vol. 3). Hillsdale, NJ: Erlbaum.

Steinberg, L., & Dornbusch, S. M. (1991). Negative correlates of part-time employment during adolescence: Replication and elaboration. *Developmental Psychology, 27*, 304–313.

Steinberg, L., Dornbusch, S. M., & Brown, B. B. (1992). Ethnic differences in adolescent achievement. An ecological perspective. *American Psychologist, 47*, 723–729.

Steinberg, L., Elmen, J. D., & Mounts, N. S. (1989). Authoritative parenting, psychosocial maturity, and academic success among adolescents. *Child Development, 60*, 1424–1436.

Steinberg, L., Fegley, S., & Dornbusch, S. M. (1993). Negative impact of part-time work on adolescent adjustment: Evidence from a longitudinal study. *Developmental Psycholgy, 29*, 171–180.

Stephan, W. G. (1978). School desegregation: An evaluation of the predictions made in *Brown v. Board of Education*. *Psychological Bulletin, 85*, 217–238.

Stevens, D. P., & Truss, C. V. (1985). Stability and change in adult personality over 12 and 20 years. *Developmental Psychology, 21*, 568–584.

Stevens, R. J., & Slavin, R. E. (1995). The cooperative elementary school: Effects on students' achievement, attitudes, and social relations. *American Educational Research Journal, 32*, 321–351.

Stevenson, H. W., Chen, C., & Lee, S. (1993). Mathematics achievement of Chinese, Japanese, and American children: Ten years later. *Science, 259*, 53–58.

Stevenson, H. W., & Lee, S. Y. (1990). Contexts of achievement: A study of American, Chinese, and Japanese children. *Monographs of the Society for Research in Child Development, 55* (1–2, Serial No. 221).

Stevenson, H. W., Lee, S. Y., & Stigler, J. W. (1986). Mathematics achievement of Chinese, Japanese, and American children. *Science, 231,* 693–699.

Stevenson, H. W., Stigler, J. W., Lee, S. Y., Lucker, G. W., Litamura, S., & Hsu, C. (1985). Cognitive performance and academic achievement of Japanese, Chinese, and American children. *Child Development, 56,* 718–734.

Stewart, W., & Barling, J. (1996). Fathers' work experiences affect children's behaviors via job-related affect and parenting behaviors. *Journal of Organizational Behavior, 17,* 221–232.

Stigler, J. W., Lee, S. Y., & Stevenson, H. W. (1987). Mathematics classrooms in Japan, Taiwan, and the United States. *Child Development, 58,* 1272–1285.

Stipek, D. J. (1984). The development of achievement motivation. In R. Ames & C. Ames (Eds.), *Research on motivation in education* (Vol. 1). Orlando, FL: Academic Press.

Stipek, D. J., Feiler, R., Daniels, D., & Milburn, S. (1995). Effects of different instructional approaches on young children's achievement and motivation. *Child Development, 66,* 209–223.

Stipek, D. J., & Gralinski, J. H. (1996). Children's beliefs about intelligence and school performance. *Journal of Educational Psychology, 88,* 397–407.

Stipek, D. J., & MacIver, D. (1989). Developmental change in children's assessment of intellectual competence. *Child Development, 60,* 521–538.

Stipek, D. J., Recchia, A., & McClintic, S. (1992). Self-evaluation in young children. *Monographs of the Society for Research in Child Development, 57* (1, Serial No. 226).

St. John, N. H. (1975). *School desegregation: Outcomes for children.* New York: Wiley.

Sui-Chu, E. H., & Willms, J. D. (1996). Effects of parental involvement on eighth-grade achievement. *Sociology of Education, 69,* 126–141.

Suitor, J. J., & Reavis, R. (1995). Football, fast cars, and cheerleading: Adolescent gender norms, 1978–1989. *Adolescence, 30,* 265–272.

Super, D. E. (1991). A life-span life-space approach to career development. In D. Brown, L. Brooks, & Associ-ates (Eds.), *Career choice and development: Applying contemporary theories to practice* (2nd ed.). San Francisco: Jossey-Bass.

Super, D. E., Savickas, M. L., & Super, C. M. (1996). The life-span, life-space approach to careers. In D. Brown, L. Brooks, & Associates (Eds.), *Career choice and development* (3rd ed.). San Francisco: Jossey-Bass.

Szinovacz, M., & Ekerdt, D. J. (1995). Families and retirement. In R. Blieszner & V. H. Bedford (Eds.), *Handbook of aging and the family.* Westport, CT: Greenwood.

Taylor, R. D., Casten, R., Flickinger, S. M., & Roberts, D. (1994). Explaining the school performance of African-American adolescents. *Journal of Research on Adolescence, 4,* 21–44.

Toch, T., & Streisand, B. (1997, October 13). Does class size matter? *U.S. News & World Report, 123,* 22–29.

Trice, A. D., & McClellan, N. (1993). Do children's career aspirations predict adult occupations? An answer from a secondary analysis of a longitudinal study. *Psychological Reports, 72,* 368–370.

U.S. Bureau of the Census. (1997). *Statistical abstract of the United States* (117th ed.). Washington, DC: U.S. Government Printing Office.

Vaillant, G. E. (1977). *Adaptation to life.* Boston: Little, Brown.

van den Boom, D. C. (1994). The influence of temperament and mothering on attachment and exploration: An experimental manipulation of sensitive responsiveness among lower-class mothers with irritable infants. *Child Development, 65,* 1457–1477.

Vandewater, E. A., Ostrove, J. M., & Stewart, A. J. (1997). Predicting women's well-being in midlife: The importance of personality development and social role involvements. *Journal of Personality and Social Psychology, 72,* 1147–1160.

Van Velsor, E., & O'Rand, A. M. (1984). Family life cycle, work career patterns, and women's wages at midlife. *Journal of Marriage and the Family, 46,* 365–373.

Veroff, J., Reuman, D., & Feld, S. (1984). Motives in American men and women across the adult life span. *Developmental Psychology, 20,* 1142–1158.

Waite, L. J., Haggstrom, G., & Kanouse, D. E. (1986). The effects of parenthood on the career orientation and job characteristics of young adults. *Social Forces, 65,* 43–73.

Waldman, D. A., & Avolio, B. J. (1986). A meta-analysis of age differences in job performance. *Journal of Applied Psychology, 71,* 33–38.

Waldman, E. (1985). Today's girls in tomorrow's labor force: Projecting their participation and occupations. *Youth and Society, 16,* 375–392.

Wang, M. C., Haertel, G. D., & Walberg, H. J. (1993). Toward a knowledge base for school learning. *Review of Educational Research, 63,* 249–294.

Warr, P. (1992). Age and occupational well-being. *Psychology and Aging, 7,* 37–45.

Weiner, B. (1974). *Achievement and attribution theory.* Morristown, NJ: General Learning Press.

Weiner, B. (1986). *An attributional theory of motivation and emotion.* New York: Springer-Verlag.

Weisner, T. S. (1984). Ecocultural niches of middle childhood: A cross-cultural perspective. In W. A. Collins (Ed.), *Development during middle childhood: The years from six to twelve.* Washington, DC: National Academy Press.

Welch, D. C., & West, R. L. (1995). Self-efficacy and mastery: Its application to issues of environmental control, cognition, and aging. *Developmental Review, 15,* 150–171.

White, R. W. (1959). Motivation reconsidered: The concept of competence. *Psychological Review, 66,* 297–333.

Wigfield, A., & Eccles, J. S. (1992). The development of achievement task values: A theoretical analysis. *Developmental Review, 12,* 265–310.

Wigfield, A., Eccles, J. S., Yoon, K. S., & Harold, R. D. (1997). Change in children's competence beliefs and subjective task values across the elementary school years: A 3-year study. *Journal of Educational Psychology, 89,* 451–469.

Winterbottom, M. (1958). The relation of need for achievement to learning experiences in independence and mastery. In J. Atkinson (Ed.), *Motives in fantasy, action, and society.* Princeton, NJ: Van Nostrand.

Yarrow, L. J., Klein, R., Lomonaco, S., & Morgan, G. A. (1975). Cognitive and motivational development in early childhood. In B. Z. Friedlander, G. M. Sterritt, & G. E. Kirk (Eds.), *Exceptional infant: Assessment and intervention.* New York: Bruner/Mazel.

Yarrow, L. J., MacTurk, R. H., Vietze, P. M., McCarthy, M. E., Klein, R. P., & McQuiston, S. (1984). Developmental course of parental stimulation and its relationship to mastery motivation during infancy. *Developmental Psychology, 20,* 492–503.

Zigler, E., & Finn-Stevenson, M. (1993). *Children in a changing world: Developmental and social issues.* Pacific Grove, CA: Brooks/Cole.

Zigler, E., Finn-Stevenson, M., & Stern, B. M. (1997). Supporting children and families in the schools: The school of the 21st century. *American Journal of Orthopsychiatry, 67,* 396–407.

CHAPTER 16: Psychological Disorders Throughout the Life Span

Achenbach, T. M. (1982). *Developmental psychopathology* (2nd ed.). New York: Wiley.

Achenbach, T. M., & Edelbrock, C. S. (1978). The classification of child psychopathology: A review and analysis of empirical efforts. *Psychological Bulletin, 85,* 1275–1301.

Aldwin, C. M. (1994). *Stress, coping, and development.* New York: Guilford.

American Psychiatric Association. (1994). *Diagnostic and statistical manual of mental disorders DSM-IV* (4th ed.). Washington, DC: Author.

Angold, A., & Rutter, M. (1992). Effects of age and pubertal status on depression in a large clinical sample. *Development and Psychopathology, 4,* 5–28.

Bailey, A., Phillips, W., & Rutter, M. (1996). Autism: Towards an integration of clinical, genetic, neuropsychological, and neurobiological perspectives. *Journal of Child Psychology and Psychiatry and Allied Disciplines, 37,* 89–126.

Barkley, R. A. (1997). Behavioral inhibition, sustained attention, and executive functions: Constructing a unifying theory of ADHD. *Psychological Bulletin, 121,* 65–94.

Barkley, R. A., Fischer, M., Edelbrock, C., & Smallish, L. (1991). The adolescent outcome of hyperactive children diagnosed by research criteria: Mother-child interactions, family conflicts, and maternal psychopathology. *Journal of Child Psychology and Psychiatry and Allied Disciplines, 32,* 233–255.

Bauchner, H. (1996). Failure to thrive.

In R. E. Behrman, R. M. Kliegman, & A. M. Arvin (Eds.), *Nelson textbook of pediatrics* (15th ed.). Philadelphia: W. B. Saunders.

Baumrind, D. (1985). Familial antecedents of adolescent drug use: A developmental perspective. In C. L. Jones & R. J. Battjes, *Etiology of drug abuse: Implications for prevention* (NIDA Research Monograph No. 56, DHHS Pub. No. [ADM] 85–1335). Washington, DC: U.S. Government Printing Office.

Beautrais, A. L., Joyce, P. R., & Mulder, R. T. (1997). Precipitating factors and life events in serious suicide attempts among youths aged 13 through 24 years. *Journal of the American Academy of Child and Adolescent Psychiatry, 36,* 1543–1551.

Beck, D., Casper, R., & Andersen, A. (1996). Truly late onset of eating disorders: A study of 11 cases averaging 60 years of age at presentation. *International Journal of Eating Disorders, 20,* 389–395.

Bemporad, J. R. (1979). Adult recollections of a formerly autistic child. *Journal of Autism and Developmental Disorders, 9,* 179–197.

Bergem, A. L. M., Engedal, K., & Kringlen, E. (1997). The role of heredity in late-onset Alzheimer disease and vascular dementia: A twin study. *Archives of General Psychiatry, 54,* 264–270.

Berman, A. L., & Jobes, D. A. (1991). *Adolescent suicide: Assessment and intervention.* Washington, DC: American Psychological Association.

Biederman, J., Faraone, S., Milberger, S., Guite, J., Mick, E., Chen, L., Mennin, D., Marrs, A., Oullette, C., Moore, P., Spencer, T., Norman, D., Wilens, T., Kraus, I., & Perrin, J. (1996). A prospective 4-year follow-up study of attention-deficit hyperactivity and related disorders. *Archives of General Psychiatry, 53,* 437–446.

Biederman, J., Milberger, S., Faraone, S. V., Kiely, K., Guite, J., Mick, E., Ablon, S., Warburton, R., & Reed, E. (1995). Family-environment risk factors for attention-deficit hyperactivity disorder: A test of Rutter's indicators of adversity. *Archives of General Psychiatry, 52,* 464–470.

Birmaher, B., Ryan, N. D., Williamson, D. E., Brent, D. A., & Kaufman, J. (1996). Childhood and adolescent depression: A review of the past 10 years. Part II. *Journal of the American Academy of Child and Adolescent Psychiatry, 35,* 1575–1583.

Black, M. M., Hutcheson, J. J., Dubowitz, H., & Berenson-Howard, J. (1994). Parenting style and developmental status among children with nonorganic failure to thrive. *Journal of Pediatric Psychology, 19,* 689–707.

Blanchard-Fields, F., Jahnke, H. C., & Camp, C. (1995). Age differences in problem-solving style: The role of emotional salience. *Psychology and Aging, 10,* 173–180.

Blazer, D. G. (1993). *Depression in late life.* St. Louis: Mosby.

Blazer, D. G. (1996). Epidemiology of psychiatric disorders in late life. In E. W. Busse & D. G. Blazer (Eds.), *Textbook of geriatric psychiatry* (2nd ed.). Washington, DC: American Psychiatric Press.

Blazer, D. G., & Koenig, H. G. (1996). Mood disorders. In E. W. Busse & D. G. Blazer (Eds.), *Textbook of geriatric psychiatry* (2nd ed.). Washington, DC: American Psychiatric Press.

Borchardt, C. M., & Meller, W. H. (1996). Symptoms of affective disorder in pre-adolescent vs. adolescent inpatients. *Journal of Adolescence, 19,* 155–161.

Bowers, W. A., Evans, K., & Van Cleve, L. (1996). Treatment of adolescent eating disorders. In M. A. Reineke, F. M. Dattilio, & A. Freeman (Eds.), *Cognitive therapy with children and adolescents: A casebook for clinical practice.* New York: Guilford.

Brandtstädter, J., & Renner, G. (1990). Tenacious goal pursuit and flexible goal adjustment: Explication and age-related analysis of assimilative and accommodative strategies of coping. *Psychology and Aging, 5,* 58–67.

Breitner, J. C. S. (1997). Onset of Alzheimer's disease: Influence of genes and environmental factors, including anti-inflammatory drugs. In L. L. Heston (Ed.), *Progress in Alzheimer's disease and similar conditions.* Washington, DC: American Psychiatric Press.

Bristol, M. M., Cohen, D. J., Costello, E. J., Denckla, M., Eckberg, T. J., Kallen, R., Kraemer, H. C., Lord, C., Maurer, R., Mcilvane, W. J., Minshew, N., Sigman, M., & Spence, M. A. (1996). State of the science in autism: Report to the National Institutes of Health. *Journal of Autism and Developmental Disorders, 26,* 121–154.

Brook, J. S., Brook, D. W., Gordon, A. S., Whiteman, M., & Cohen, P. (1990). The psychosocial etiology of adolescent drug use: A family interactional approach. *Genetic, Social, and General Psychology Monographs, 116,* 111–267.

Brownell, K. D., & Napolitano, M. A. (1995). Distorting reality for children: Body size proportions of Barbie and Ken dolls. *International Journal of Eating Disorders, 18,* 295–298.

Buhrmester, D., Camparo, L., Christensen, A., Gonzales, L. S., & Hinshaw, S. P. (1992). Mothers and fathers interacting in dyads and triads with normal and hyperactive sons. *Developmental Psychology, 28,* 500–509.

Bukstein, O., & the Work Group on Quality Issues. (1997). Practice parameters for the assessment and treatment of children and adolescents with substance use disorders. *Journal of the American Academy of Child and Adolescent Psychiatry, 36,* 140S–156S.

Campbell, M., Schopler, E., Cueva, J. E., & Hallin, A. (1996). Treatment of autistic disorder. *Journal of the American Academy of Child and Adolescent Psychiatry, 35,* 134–135.

Cantwell, D. P. (1996). Attention deficit disorder: A review of the past 10 years. *Journal of the American Academy of Child and Adolescent Psychiatry, 35,* 978–987.

Capps, L., Sigman, M., & Mundy, P. (1994). Attachment security in children with autism. *Development and Psychopathology, 6,* 249–261.

Cash, T. F., & Deagle, E. A. (1997). The nature and extent of body-image disturbances in anorexia nervosa and bulimia nervosa: A meta-analysis. *International Journal of Eating Disorders, 22,* 107–125.

Caspi, A., Moffitt, T. E., Newman, D. L., & Silva, P. A. (1996). Behavioral observations at age 3 years predict adult psychiatric disorders: Longitudinal evidence from a birth cohort. *Archives of General Psychiatry, 53,* 1033–1039.

Cauffman, E., & Steinberg, L. (1996). Interactive effects of menarcheal status and dating on dieting and disordered eating among adolescent girls. *Developmental Psychology, 32,* 631–635.

Charman, T. (1997). The relationship between joint attention and pretend play in autism. *Development and Psychopathology, 9,* 1–16.

Cicchetti, D., & Toth, S. L. (1998). The development of depression in children and adolescents. *American Psychologist, 53,* 221–241.

Clark, L. A., Watson, D., & Reynolds, S. (1995). Diagnosis and classification of psychopathology: Challenges to the current system and future directions. *Annual Review of Psychology, 46,* 121–153.

Cohen, D., Eisdorfer, C., Gorelick, P., Paveza, G., Luchins, D. J., Freels, S., Ashford, J. W., Semla, T., Levy, P., & Hirschman, R. (1993). Psychopathology associated with Alzheimer's disease and related disorders. *Journal of Gerontology: Medical Sciences, 48,* M255–M260.

Cohen, P., Cohen, J., Kasen, S., Velez, C. N., Hartmark, C., Johnson, J., Rojas, M., Brook, J., & Streuning, E. L. (1993). An epidemiological study of disorders in late childhood and adolescence: I. Age- and gender-specific prevalence. *Journal of Child Psychology and Psychiatry and Allied Disciplines, 34,* 851–867.

Cole, P. M., & Putnam, F. W. (1992). Effect of incest on self and social functioning: A developmental psychopathology perspective. *Journal of Counseling and Clincial Psychology, 60,* 174–184.

Committee on Adolescence. (1996). *Adolescent suicide* (Group for the Advancement of Psychiatry, Report No. 140). Washington, DC: American Psychiatric Press.

Costa, P. T., Jr., Zonderman, A. B., & McCrae, R. R. (1991). Personality, defense, coping, and adaptation in older adulthood. In E. M. Cummings, A. L. Greene, & K. H. Karraker (Eds.), *Life-span developmental psychology: Perspectives on stress and coping.* Hillsdale, NJ: Erlbaum.

Coyne, J. C., & Whiffen, V. E. (1995). Issues in personality as diathesis for depression: The case of sociotropy-dependency and autonomy-self-criticism. *Psychological Bulletin, 118,* 358–378.

Crago, M., Shisslak, C. M., & Estes, L. S. (1996). Eating disturbances among American minority groups: A review. *International Journal of Eating Disorders, 19,* 239–248.

Crijnen, A. A. M., Achenbach, T. M., & Verhulst, F. C. (1997). Comparisons of problems reported by parents of children in 12 cultures: Total problems, externalizing, and internalizing. *Journal of the American Academy of Child and Adolescent Psychiatry, 36,* 1269–1277.

Crook, W. G. (1980). Can what a child eats make him dull, stupid, or hyperactive? *Journal of Learning Disabilities, 13,* 53–58.

Crowley, M. (1997, October 20). Do kids need Prozac? *Newsweek,* 73–74.

Cytryn, L., & McKnew, D. H., Jr. (1996). *Growing up sad: Childhood depression and its treatment.* New York: Norton.

Deutsch, C. K., & Kinsbourne, M. (1990). Genetics and biochemistry in attention deficit disorder. In M. Lewis and S. M. Miller (Eds.), *Handbook of developmental psychopathology.* New York: Plenum Press.

DiBattista, D., & Shepherd, M. (1993). Primary school teachers' beliefs and advice to parents concerning sugar consumption and activity in children. *Psychological Reports, 72,* 47–55.

Diehl, M., Coyle, N., & Labouvie-Vief, G. (1996). Age and sex differences in strategies of coping and defense across the life span. *Psychology and Aging, 11,* 127–139.

Donenberg, G., & Baker, B. L. (1993). The impact of young children with externalizing behaviors on their families. *Journal of Abnormal Child Psychology, 21,* 179–198.

Dulcan, M., & the Work Group on Quality Issues. (1997). Practice parameters for the assessment and treatment of children, adolescents, and adults with attention-deficit/hyperactivity disorder. *Journal of the American Academy of Child and Adolescent Psychiatry, 36,* 85S–121S.

Eckert, E. D., Halmi, K. A., Marchi, P., Grove, W., & Crosby, R. (1995). Ten-year follow-up of anorexia nervosa: Clinical course and outcome. *Psychological Medicine, 25,* 143–156.

Emslie, G. J., Rush, J., Weinberg, W. A., Guillion, C. M., Rintelmann, J., & Hughes, C. W. (1997). Recurrence of major depressive disorder in hospitalized children and adolescents. *Journal of the American Academy of Child and Adolescent Psychiatry, 36,* 785–792.

Feingold, B. F. (1975). Why your child is hyperactive. New York: Random House.

Felton, B. J., & Revenson, T. A. (1987). Age differences in coping with chronic illness. *Psychology and Aging, 2,* 164–170.

Field, T. (1995). Infants of depressed mothers. *Infant Behavior and Development, 18,* 1–13.

Fischer, K. W., Ayoub, C., Singh, I., Noam, G., Maraganore, A., & Raya, P. (1997). Psychopathology as adaptive development along distinctive pathways. *Development and Psychopathology, 9,* 749–779.

Fischer, M., Barkley, R. A., Edelbrock, C. S., & Smallish, L. (1990). The adolescent outcome of hyperactive children diagnosed by research criteria: II. Academic, attentional, and neuropsychological status. *Journal of Consulting and Clinical Psychology, 58,* 580–588.

Folkman, S., Lazarus, R. S., Pimley, S., & Novacek, J. (1987). Age differences in stress and coping processes. *Psychology and Aging, 2,* 171–184.

Frauenglass, S., Routh, D. K., Pantin, H. M., & Mason, C. A. (1997). Family support decreases influence of deviant peers on Hispanic adolescents' substance use. *Journal of Clinical Child Psychology, 26,* 15–23.

Frith, U. (1989). Autism and "theory of mind." In C. Gillberg (Ed.), *Diagnosis and treatment of autism.* New York: Plenum.

Gallo, J. J., Anthony, J. C., & Muthen, B. O. (1994). Age differences in the symptoms of depression: A latent trait analysis. *Journals of Gerontology, 49,* P251–P264.

Garber, J. (1984). The developmental progression of depression in female children. In D. Cicchetti & K. Schneider-Rosen (Eds.), *Childhood depression* (New Directions for Child Development, No. 26). San Francisco: Jossey-Bass.

Garber, J., Weiss, B., & Shanley, N. (1993). Cognitions, depressive symptoms, and development in adolescents. *Journal of Abnormal Psychology, 102,* 47–57.

Gard, M. C. E., & Freeman, C. P. (1996). The dismantling of a myth: A review of eating disorders and socioeconomic status. *International Journal of Eating Disorders, 20,* 1–12.

Gardner, L. J. (1972). Deprivation dwarfism. *Scientific American, 227,* 76–82.

Gardner, R. A. (1993). *Psychotherapy with children.* Northvale, NJ: Jason Aronson.

Garland, A., & Zigler, E. (1993). Adolescent suicide prevention: Current research and social policy implications. *American Psychologist, 48,* 169–182.

Garmezy, N. (1994). Reflections and commentary on risk, resilience, and development. In R. J. Haggerty, L. R. Sherrod, N. Garmezy, & M. Rutter (Eds.), *Stress, risk, and resilience in children and adolescents: Processes, mechanisms, and interventions.* Cambridge: Cambridge University Press.

Gatz, M., Pedersen, N. L., Berg, S., Johansson, B., Johansson, K., Mortimer, J. A., Posner, S. F., Viitanen, M., Winblad, B., & Ahlbom, A. (1997). Heritability for Alzheimer's disease: The study of dementia in Swedish twins. *Journal of Gerontology: Medical Sciences, 52,* M117–M125.

Gatz, M., Popkin, S. J., Pino, C. D., & VandenBos, G. R. (1985). Psychological interventions in older adults. In J. E. Birren & K. W. Schaie (Eds.), *Handbook of the psychology of aging* (2nd ed.). New York: Van Nostrand Reinhold.

Gatz, M., & Smyer, M. (1992). The mental health system and older adults in the 1990s. *American Psychologist, 47,* 741–751.

Ge, X. J., Conger, R. D., Cadoret, R. J., Neiderhiser, J. M., Yates, W., Troughton, E., & Stewart, M. A. (1996). The developmental interface between nature and nurture: A mutual influence model of child antisocial behavior and parent behaviors. *Developmental Psychology, 32,* 574–589.

Ge, X. J., Lorenz, F. O., Conger, R. D., Elder, G. H., & Simons, R. L. (1994). Trajectories of stressful life events and depressive symptoms during adolescence. *Developmental Psychology, 30,* 467–483.

Gelfand, D. M., & Peterson, L. (1985). *Child development and psychopathology.* Beverly Hills, CA: Sage.

Gelfand, D. M., Teti, D. M., Seiner, S. A., & Jameson, P. B. (1996). Helping mothers fight depression: Evaluation of a home-based intervention program for depressed mothers and their infants. *Journal of Clinical Child Psychology, 25,* 406–422.

Gillberg, C., Melander, H., von Knorring, A. L., Janols, L.-O., Thernlund, G., Hägglöf, B., Eidevall-Wallin, L., Gustafsson, P., & Kopp, S. (1997). Long-term stimulant treatment of children with attention-deficit hyperactivity disorder symptoms: A randomized, double-blind, placebo-controlled trial. *Archives of General Psychiatry, 54,* 857–864.

Gillberg, C., & Steffenburg, S. (1987). Outcome and prognostic factors in infantile autism and similar conditions: A population-based study of 46 cases followed through puberty. *Journal of Autism and Developmental Disorders, 17,* 273–287.

Girard, C. (1993). Age, gender, and suicide: A cross-national analysis. *American Sociological Review, 58,* 553–574.

Gordon, R. A. (1990). *Anorexia and bulimia: Anatomy of a social epidemic.* Cambridge, MA: Basil Blackwell.

Gorman, J., Leifer, M., & Grossman, G. (1993). Nonorganic failure to thrive: Maternal history and current maternal functioning. *Journal of Clinical Child Psychology, 22,* 327–336.

Gotlib, I. H., & Hammen, C. L. (1992). *Psychological aspects of depression: Toward a cognitive-interpersonal integration.* Chichester, England: John Wiley & Sons.

Graber, J. A., Brooks-Gunn, J., Paikoff, R. L., & Warren, M. P. (1994). Prediction of eating problems: An 8-year study of adolescent girls. *Developmental Psychology, 30,* 823–834.

Grant, B. F., & Dawson, D. A. (1997). Age at onset of alcohol use and its association with DSM-IV alcohol abuse and dependence: Results from the National Longitudinal Alcohol Epidemiologic Survey. *Journal of Substance Abuse, 9,* 103–110.

Green, W. H. (1986). Psychosocial dwarfism: Psychological and etiological considerations. In B. B. Lahey & A. E. Kazdin (Eds.), *Advances in clinical child psychology* (Vol. 9). New York: Plenum.

Greene, R. W., Biederman, J., Faraone, S. V., Sienna, M., & Garcia-Jetton, J. (1997). Adolescent outcome of boys with attention-deficit/hyperactivity disorder and social disability: Results from a 4-year longitudinal follow-up study. *Journal of Consulting and Clinical Psychology, 65,* 758–767.

Grober, E., & Kawas, C. (1997). Learning and retention in preclinical and early Alzheimer's disease. *Psychology and Aging, 12,* 183–188.

Gross, M. D., Tofanelli, R. A., Butzirus, S. M., & Snodgrass, E. W. (1987). The effect of diets rich in and free from additives on the behavior of children with hyperkinetic and learning disorders. *Journal of the American Academy of Child and Adolescent Psychiatry, 26,* 53–55.

Gurland, B. (1991). Epidemiology of psychiatric disorders. In J. Sadavoy, L. W. Lazarus, and L. F. Jarvik (Eds.), *Comprehensive review of geriatric psychiatry.* Washington, DC: American Psychiatric Press.

Hall, G. S. (1904). *Adolescence* (2 vols). New York: Appleton.

Hammen, C., & Compas, B. E. (1994). Unmasking masked depression in children and adolescents: The problem of comorbidity. *Clinical Psychology Review, 14,* 585–603.

Happé, F. G. E. (1994). Current psychological theories of autism: The "theory of mind" account and rival theories. *Journal of Child Psychology and Psychiatry and Allied Disciplines, 35,* 215–229.

Harley, J. P., Ray, R. S., Tomasi, L., Eichman, P. L., Matthews, C. G., & Chun, R. (1978). Hyperkinesis and food additives: Testing the Feingold hypothesis. *Pediatrics, 61,* 818–828.

Harrington, R., Rutter, M., & Fombonne, E. (1996). Developmental pathways in depression: Multiple meanings, antecedents, and endpoints. *Development and Psychopathology, 8,* 601–616.

Hart, E. L., Lahey, B. B., Loeber, R., Applegate, B., & Frick, P. J. (1995). Developmental change in attention-deficit hyperactivity disorder in boys: A four-year longitudinal study. *Journal of Abnormal Child Psychology, 23,* 729–749.

Haxby, J. V., & Schapiro, M. B. (1992). Longitudinal study of neuropsychological function in older adults with Down syndrome. In L. Nadel & C. J. Epstein (Eds.), *Down syndrome and Alzheimer's disease.* New York: Wiley-Liss.

Heffer, R. W., & Kelley, M. L. (1994). Nonorganic failure to thrive: Developmental outcomes and psychosocial assessment and intervention issues. *Research in Developmental Disabilities, 15,* 247–268.

Heston, L. L. (1997). The future is now (provided we recognize it). In L. L. Heston (Ed.), *Progress in Alzheimer's disease and similar conditions.* Washington, DC: American Psychiatric Press.

Heston, L. L., & White, J. A. (1991). *The vanishing mind: A practical guide to Alzheimer's disease and other dementias.* New York: W. H. Freeman.

Hill, J. C., & Schoener, E. P. (1996). Age-dependent decline of attention deficit hyperactivity disorder. *American Journal of Psychiatry, 153,* 1143–1146.

Hill, P. (1993). Recent advances in selected aspects of adolescent development. *Journal of Child Psychology and Psychiatry and Allied Disciplines, 34,* 69–99.

Hilsman, R., & Garber, J. (1995). A test of the cognitive diathesis-stress model of depression in children: Academic stressors, attributional style, perceived competence, and control. *Journal of Personality and Social Psychology, 69,* 370–380.

Hinshaw, S. P. (1991). Stimulant medication and the treatment of aggression in children with attention deficits. *Journal of Clinical Child Psychology, 20,* 301–312.

Hinz, L. D., & Williamson, D. A. (1987). Bulimia and depression: A review of the affective variant hypothesis. *Psychological Bulletin, 102,* 150–158.

Holahan, C. J., & Moos, R. H. (1986). Personality, coping, and family resources in stress resistance: A longitudinal analysis. *Journal of Personality and Social Psychology, 51,* 389–395.

Holahan, C. J., & Moos, R. H. (1987). Personal and contextual determinants of coping strategies. *Journal of Personality and Social Psychology, 52,* 946–955.

Holroyd, S., & Baron-Cohen, S. (1993). How far can people with autism go in developing a theory of mind? *Journal of Autism and Developmental Disorders, 23,* 379–385.

Hooper, S. R., & Tramontana, M. G. (1997). Advances in the neuropsychological bases of child and adolescent psychopathology: Proposed models, findings, and ongoing issues. In T. H. Ollendick & R. J. Prinz (Eds.), *Handbook of adolescent health risk behavior.* New York: Plenum.

Horwitz, A. V., & White, H. R. (1987). Gender role orientations and styles of pathology among adolescents. *Journal of Health and Social Behavior, 28,* 158–170.

Howieson, D. B., Dame, A., Camicioli, R., Sexton, G., Payami, H., & Kaye, J. A. (1997, May). Cognitive markers preceding Alzheimer's dementia in the healthy oldest old. *Journal of the American Geriatrics Society, 45,* 584–589.

Hsu, L. K. G. (1990). *Eating disorders.* New York: Guilford.

Hutcheson, J. J., Black, M. M., & Starr, R. H., Jr. (1993). Developmental differences in interactional characteristics of mothers and their children with failure to thrive. *Journal of Pediatric Psychology, 18,* 453–466.

Igra, V., & Irwin, C. E., Jr. (1996). Theories of adolescent risk-taking behavior. In R. DiClemente, W. B. Hansen, & L. E. Ponton (Eds.), *Handbook of adolescent health risk behavior.* New York: Plenum.

Irion, J. C., & Blanchard-Fields, F. (1987). A cross-sectional comparison of adaptive coping in adulthood. *Journal of Gerontology, 42,* 502–504.

Jacobvitz, D., & Sroufe, L. A. (1987). The early caregiver-child relationship and attention-deficit disorder with hyperactivity in kindergarten: A prospective study. *Child Development, 58,* 1496–1504.

Jensen, P. S., & Hoagwood, K. (1997). The book of names: DSM-IV in context. *Development and Psychopathology, 9,* 231–249.

Jensen, P. S., Mrazek, D., Knapp, P. K., Steinberg, L., Pfeffer, C., Sehowalter, J., & Shapiro, T. (1997). Evolution and revolution in child psychiatry: ADHD as a disorder of adaptation. *Journal of the American Academy of Child and Adolescent Psychiatry, 36,* 1672–1679.

Jessor, R. (1987). Problem-behavior theory, psychosocial development, and adolescent problem drinking. *British Journal of Addiction, 82,* 331–342.

Jessor, R., Donovan, J. E., & Costa, F. M. (1991). *Beyond adolescence. Problem behavior and young adult development.* Cambridge: Cambridge University Press.

Johnson, C. L., Stuckey, M. K., Lewis, L. D., & Schwartz, D. M. (1982). Bulimia: A descriptive survey of 316 cases. *International Journal of Eating Disorders, 2,* 3–16.

Johnson, J. H., Rasbury, W. C., & Siegel, L. J. (1986). *Approaches to child treatment: Introduction to theory, research, and practice.* New York: Pergamon.

Johnston, L. D., O'Malley, P. M., & Bachman, J. G. (1995). *National survey results on drug use from the Monitoring the Future Study, 1975–1994.* Rockville, MD: National Institute on Drug Abuse.

Kandel, D. B., & Davies, M. (1991). Decline in use of illicit drugs by high school students in New York State: A comparison with national data.

American Journal of Public Health, 81, 1064–1067.

Kandel, D. B., Johnson, J. G., Bird, H. R., Canino, G., Goodman, S. H., Lahey, B. B., Regier, D. A., & Schwab-Stone, M. (1997). Psychiatric disorders associated with substance use among children and adolescents: Findings from the Methods for the Epidemiology of Child and Adolescent Mental Disorders (MECA) study. *Journal of Abnormal Child Psychology, 25,* 121–132.

Kanner, A. D., Coyne, J. C., Schaefer, C., & Lazarus, R. S. (1981). Comparison of two modes of stress measurement: Daily hassles and uplifts versus major life events. *Journal of Behavioral Medicine, 4,* 1–39.

Kanner, L. (1943). Autistic disturbances of affective contact. *Nervous Child, 2,* 217–250.

Kaplan, H. I., & Sadock, B. J. (1998). *Synopsis of psychiatry: Behavioral sciences/ clinical psychiatry* (8th ed.). Baltimore: Williams & Wilkens.

Kashani, J. H., Orvaschel, H., Rosenberg, T. K., & Reid, J. C. (1989). Psychopathology in a community sample of children and adolescents: A developmental perspective. *Journal of the American Academy of Child and Adolescent Psychiatry, 28,* 701–706.

Kaszniak, A. W. (1990). Psychological assessment of the aging individual. In J. E. Birren and K. W. Schaie (Eds.), *The handbook of the psychology of aging* (3rd ed.). San Diego: Academic Press.

Keel, P. K., & Mitchell, J. E. (1997). Outcome in bulimia nervosa. *American Journal of Psychiatry, 154,* 313–321.

Kendler, K. S., Kessler, R. C., Neale, M. C., Heath, A. C., & Eaves, L. J. (1993). The prediction of major depression in women: Toward an integrated etiologic model. *American Journal of Psychiatry, 150,* 1139–1148.

Kendler, K. S., MacLean, C., Neale, M., Kessler, R. C., Heath, A., & Eaves, L. (1991). The genetic epidemiology of bulimia nervosa. *American Journal of Psychiatry, 148,* 1627–1637.

Kendler, K. S., Neale, M. C., Kessler, R. C., Heath, A. C., & Eaves, L. J. (1992). A population-based twin study of major depression in women: The impact of varying definitions of illness. *Archives of General Psychiatry, 49,* 257–266.

Kessler, R. C., McGonagle, K. A., Zhao, S., Nelson, C. B., Hughes, M., Eshleman, S., Wittchen, H. U., &

Kendler, K. S. (1994). Lifetime and 12-month prevalence of DSM-III-R psychiatric disorders in the United States: Results from the National Comorbidity Study. *Archives of General Psychiatry, 51,* 8–19.

Kosky, R. (1983). Childhood suicidal behavior. *Journal of Child Psychology and Psychiatry and Allied Disciplines, 24,* 457–468.

Kovacs, M. (1996). Presentation and course of major depressive disorder during childhood and later years of the life span. *Journal of the American Academy of Child and Adolescent Psychiatry, 35,* 705–715.

Kovacs, M., & Goldston, D. (1991). Cognitive and social cognitive development of depressed children and adolescents. *Journal of the American Academy of Child and Adolescent Psychiatry, 30,* 388–392.

Larson, R., & Ham, M. (1993). Stress and "storm and stress" in early adolescence: The relationship of negative events with dysphoric affect. *Developmental Psychology, 29,* 130–140.

Larson, R., & Lampman-Petraitis, C. (1989). Daily emotional states as reported by children and adolescents. *Child Development, 60,* 1250–1260.

La Rue, A., Dessonville, C., & Jarvik, L. F. (1985). Aging and mental disorders. In J. E. Birren & K. W. Schaie (Eds.), *Handbook of the psychology of aging* (2nd ed.). New York: Van Nostrand Reinhold.

Lazarus, R. S. (1993). From psychological stress to the emotions: A history of changing outlooks. *Annual Review of Psychology, 44,* 1–21.

Lazarus, R. S., & Folkman, S. (1984). *Stress, appraisal, and coping.* New York: Springer.

Le Couteur, A., Bailey, A., Goode, S., Pickles, A., Robertson, S., Gottesman, I., & Rutter, M. (1996). A broader phenotype of autism: The clinical spectrum in twins. *Journal of Child Psychology and Psychiatry, 37,* 785–801.

Leslie, A. M. (1992). Pretense, autism, and theory-of-mind module. *Current Directions in Psychological Science, 1,* 18–21.

Lester, D. (1994). Are there unique features of suicide in adults of different ages and developmental stages? *Omega, 29,* 337–348.

Leung, F., Geller, J., & Katzman, M. (1996). Issues and concerns associated with different risk models for

eating disorders. *International Journal of Eating Disorders, 19,* 249–256.

Levy, F., Hay, D. A., Mcstephen, M., Wood, C., & Waldman, I. (1997). Attention-deficit hyperactivity disorder: A category or a continuum? Genetic analysis of a large-scale twin study. *Journal of the American Academy of Child and Adolescent Psychiatry, 36,* 737–744.

Li, G., Silverman, J. M., Smith, C. J., Zaccario, M. L., Schmeidler, J., Mohs, R. C., & Davis, K. L. (1995). Age at onset and familial risk in Alzheimer's disease. *American Journal of Psychiatry, 152,* 424–430.

Lieberman, M. A. (1983). Social contexts of depression. In L. D. Breslau & M. R. Haug (Eds.), *Depression and aging: Causes, care, and consequences* New York: Springer.

Lovaas, O. I. (1987). Behavioral treatment and normal educational and intellectual functioning in young autistic children. *Journal of Consulting and Clinical Psychology, 55,* 3–9.

Lovaas, O. I., Smith, T., & McEachin, J. J. (1989). Clarifying comments on the young autism study: Reply to Schopler, Short, and Mesibov. *Journal of Consulting and Clinical Psychology, 57,* 165–167.

Lowe, M. R., Gleaves, D. H., DiSimone-Weiss, R. T., Furgueson, C., McKinney, S., Gayda, C. A., Kolsky, P. A., Neal-Walden, T., Nelsen, L. A., & McKinney, S. (1996). Restraint, dieting, and the continuum model of bulimia nervosa. *Journal of Abnormal Psychology, 105,* 508–517.

Luk, S. L. (1996). Cross-cultural aspects. In S. Sandberg (Ed.), *Hyperactivity disorders of childhood.* Cambridge: Cambridge University Press.

Lyness, J. M., Cox, C., Curry, J., Conwell, Y., King, D. A., & Caine, E. D. (1995). Older age and the underreporting of depressive symptoms. *Journal of the American Geriatrics Society, 43,* 216–221.

Lynskey, M. T., & Fergusson, D. M. (1995). Childhood conduct problems, attention deficit behaviors, and adolescent alcohol, tobacco, and illicit drug use. *Journal of Abnormal Child Psychology, 23,* 281–302.

Mannuzza, S., Klein, R. G., Bessler, A., Malloy, P., & LaPadula, M. (1993). Adult outcome of hyperactive boys: Educational achievement, occupational rank, and psychiatric status. *Archives of General Psychiatry, 50,* 565–576.

Marin, D. B., Green, C. R., Schmeidler, J., Harvey, P. D., Lawlor, B. A., Ryan, T. M., Aryan, M., Davis, K. L., & Mohs, R. C. (1997). Noncognitive disturbances in Alzheimer's disease: Frequency, longitudinal course, and relationship to cognitive symptoms. *Journal of the American Geriatrics Society, 45,* 1331–1338.

McCall, P. L. (1991). Adolescent and elderly white male suicide trends: Evidence of changing well-being? *Journal of Gerontology: Social Sciences, 46,* S43–S51.

McCrae, R. R. (1982). Age differences in the use of coping mechanisms. *Journal of Gerontology, 37,* 454–460.

McLanahan, S. S., & Sorensen, A. B. (1985). Life events and psychological well-being over the life course. In G. H. Elder, Jr. (Ed.), *Life course dynamics: Trajectories and transitions, 1968–1980.* Ithaca, NY: Cornell University Press.

Meador, K. G., & Davis, C. D. (1996). Psychotherapy. In E. W. Busse & D. G. Blazer (Eds.), *Textbook of geriatric psychiatry* (2nd ed.). Washington, DC: American Psychiatric Press.

Milberger, S., Biederman, J., Faraone, S. V., Chen, L., & Jones, J. (1996). Is maternal smoking during pregnancy a risk factor for attention deficit hyperactivity disorder in children? *American Journal of Psychiatry, 153,* 1138–1142.

Milich, R., & Pelham, W. E. (1986). Effects of sugar ingestion on the classroom and playgroup behavior of attention deficit disordered boys. *Journal of Consulting and Clinical Psychology, 54,* 714–718.

Miller, E., & Morris, R. (1993). *The psychology of dementia.* Chichester, England: Wiley.

Minuchin, S., Rosman, B. L., & Baker, L. (1978). *Psychosomatic families: Anorexia nervosa in context.* Cambridge, MA: Harvard University Press.

Mittelman, M. S., Ferris, S. H., Steinberg, G., Shulman, E., Mackell, J. A., Ambinder, A., & Cohen, J. (1993). An intervention that delays institutionalization of Alzheimer's disease patients: Treatment of spouse-caregivers. *Gerontologist, 33,* 730–740.

Monroe, S. M., & Simons, A. D. (1991). Diathesis-stress theories in the context of life stress research: Implications for the depressive disorders. *Psychological Bulletin, 110,* 406–425.

Murnen, S. K., & Smolak, L. (1997). Femininity, masculinity, and disordered eating: A meta-analytic review. *International Journal of Eating Disorders, 22,* 231–242.

Musten, L. M., Firestone, P., Pisterman, S., Bennett, S., & Mercer, J. (1997). Effects of methylphenidate on preschool children with ADHD: Cognitive and behavioral functions. *Journal of the American Academy of Child and Adolescent Psychiatry, 36,* 1407–1415.

Myers, J. K., Weissman, M. M., Tischler, G. L., Holzer, C. E., III, Leaf, P. J., & Orvaschel, H. (1984). Six-month prevalence of psychiatric disorders in three communities. *Archives of General Psychiatry, 41,* 959–967.

Nolen-Hoeksema, S. (1990). *Sex differences in depression.* Stanford, CA: Stanford University Press.

Nolen-Hoeksema, S., & Girgus, J. S. (1994). The emergence of gender differences in depression during adolescence. *Psychological Bulletin, 115,* 424–443.

Nolen-Hoeksema, S., Morrow, J., & Fredrickson, B. L. (1993). Response styles and the duration of episodes of depressed mood. *Journal of Abnormal Psychology, 102,* 20–28.

Offer, D., & Schonert-Reichl, K. A. (1992). Debunking the myths of adolescence: Findings from recent research. *Journal of the American Academy of Child and Adolescent Psychiatry, 31,* 1003–1013.

Pataki, C. S., & Carlson, G. A. (1990). Major depression in childhood. In M. Hersen and C. G. Last (Eds.), *Handbook of child and adult psychopathology: A longitudinal perspective.* New York: Pergamon.

Pearlin, L. I. (1980). Life strains and psychological distress among adults. In N. J. Smelser & E. H. Erikson (Eds.), *Themes of work and love in adulthood.* Cambridge, MA: Harvard University Press.

Pelham, W. E., Jr., Carlson, C., Sams, S. E., Vallano, G., Dixon, M. J., & Hoza, B. (1993). Separate and combined effects of methylphenidate and behavior modification on boys with attention deficit-hyperactivity disorder in the classroom. *Journal of Consulting and Clinical Psychology, 61,* 506–515.

Peskind, E. R., & Raskind, M. A. (1996). Cognitive disorders. In E. W. Busse & D. G. Blazer (Eds.), *Textbook of geriatric psychiatry* (2nd ed.). Washington, DC: American Psychiatric Press.

Petersen, A. C., Compas, B. E., Brooks-Gunn, J., Stemmler, M., Ey, S., & Grant, K. E. (1993). Depression in adolescence. *American Psychologist, 48,* 155–168.

Pfeffer, C. R., Hurt, S. W., Kakuma, T., Peskin, J. R., Siefker, C. A., & Nagabhairava, S. (1994). Suicidal children grow up: Suicidal episodes and effects of treatment during follow-up. *Journal of the American Academy of Child and Adolescent Psychiatry, 33,* 225–230.

Pfeiffer, E. (1977). Psychopathology and social pathology. In J. E. Birren & K. W. Schaie (Eds.), *Handbook of the psychology of aging.* New York: Van Nostrand Reinhold.

Phares, V. (1996). *Fathers and developmental psychopathology.* New York: Wiley.

Phillips, M. A., & Murrell, S. A. (1994). Impact of psychological and physical health, stressful events, and social support on subsequent mental health help seeking among older adults. *Journal of Consulting and Clinical Psychology, 62,* 270–275.

Piven, J., Harper, J., Palmer, P., & Arndt, S. (1996). Course of behavioral change in autism: A retrospective study of high-IQ adolescents and adults. *Journal of the American Academy of Child and Adolescent Psychiatry, 35,* 523–529.

Plassman, B. L., & Breitner, J. C. S. (1996). Recent advances in the genetics of Alzheimer's disease and vascular dementia with an emphasis on gene-environment interactions. *Journal of the American Geriatrics Society, 44,* 1242–1250.

Polivy, J., & Herman, C. P. (1985). Dieting and binging: A causal analysis. *American Psychologist, 40,* 193–201.

Polivy, J., Zeitlin, S. B., Herman, C. P., & Beal, A. L. (1994). Food restriction and binge eating: A study of former prisoners of war. *Journal of Abnormal Psychology, 103,* 409–411.

Pollen, D. A. (1996). *Hannah's heirs: The quest for the genetic origins of Alzheimer's disease* (expanded ed.). New York: Oxford University Press.

Quay, H. C., Routh, D. K., & Shapiro, S. K. (1987). Psychopathology of childhood: From description to validation. *Annual Review of Psychology, 38,* 491–532.

Raskind, M. A., & Peskind, E. R. (1997). Neurotransmitter abnormalities and the psychopharmacology of Alzheimer's disease. In L. L. Heston (Ed.), *Progress in Alzheimer's disease and similar conditions*. Washington, DC: American Psychiatric Press.

Regier, D. A., Boyd, J. H., Burke, J. D., Rae, D. F., Myers, J. K., Kramer, M., Robins, L. N., George, L. K., Karno, M., & Locke, B. Z. (1988). One-month prevalence of mental disorders in the United States. *Archives of General Psychiatry, 45,* 977–986.

Rende, R. (1996). Liability to psychopathology: A quantitative genetic perspective. In L. Smolak, M. P. Levine, & R. Striegel-Moore (Eds.), *The developmental psychopathology of eating disorders: Implications for research, prevention, and treatment.* Mahwah, NJ: Erlbaum.

Roberts, R. E., Kaplan, G. A., Shema, S. J., & Strawbridge, W. J. (1997). Does growing old increase the risk for depression? *American Journal of Psychiatry, 154,* 1384–1390.

Robins, L. N., & Regier, D. A. (Eds.). (1991). *Psychiatric disorders in America: The Epidemiologic Catchment Area Study.* New York: The Free Press.

Rodin, J., Striegel-Moore, R. H., & Silberstein, L. R. (1990). Vulnerability and resilience in the age of eating disorders: Risk and protective factors for bulimia nervosa. In J. Rolf, A. S. Masten, D. Cicchetti, K. H. Nuechterlein, & S. Weintraub (Eds.), *Risk and protective factors in the development of psychopathology.* Cambridge: Cambridge University Press.

Rook, K., Dooley, D., & Catalano, R. (1991). Age differences in workers' efforts to cope with economic distress. In J. Eckenrode (Ed.), *The social context of coping.* New York: Plenum.

Rosenthal, P. A., & Rosenthal, S. (1984). Suicidal behavior by preschool children. *American Journal of Psychiatry, 141,* 520–525.

Rovner, S. (1994, March 29). An Alzheimer's journal. *Washington Post Health,* 12–15.

Rutter, M. (1996). Developmental psychopathology: Concepts and prospects. In M. Lenzenweger & J. Havgaard (Eds.), *Frontiers of developmental psychopathology.* New York: Oxford University Press.

Rutter, M., Dunn, J., Plomin, R., Simonoff, E., Pickles, A., Maughan, B., Ormel, J., Meyer, J., & Eaves, L. (1997). Integrating nature and nurture: Implications of person-environment correlations and interactions for developmental psychopathology. *Development and Psychopathology, 9,* 335–364.

Rutter, M., & Schopler, E. (1987). Autism and pervasive developmental disorders: Concepts and diagnostic issues. *Journal of Autism and Developmental Disorders, 17,* 159–186.

Sampson, R. J., & Laub, J. H. (1993). *Crime in the making: Pathways and turning points through life.* Cambridge, MA: Harvard University Press.

Schachar, R. J., Tannock, R., Cunningham, C., & Corkum, P. V. (1997). Behavioral, situational, and temporal effects of treatment of ADHD with methylphenidate. *Journal of the American Academy of Child and Adolescent Psychiatry, 36,* 754–763.

Scogin, F., & McElreath, L. (1994). Efficacy of psychosocial treatments for geriatric depression: A quantitative review. *Journal of Consulting and Clinical Psychology, 62,* 69–74.

Seidman, L. J., Biederman, J., Faraone, S. V., Weber, W., & Ouellette, C. (1997). Toward defining a neuropsychology of attention-deficit hyperactivity disorder: Performance of children and adolescents from a large clinically referred sample. *Journal of Consulting and Clinical Psychology, 65,* 150–160.

Selkoe, D. J. (1997). Alzheimer's disease: From genes to pathogenesis. *American Journal of Psychiatry, 154,* 1198.

Shapiro, S., Newcomb, M., & Loeb, T. B. (1997). Fear of fat, disregulated-restrained eating, and body-esteem: Prevalence and gender differences among eight- to ten-year-old children. *Journal of Clinical Child Psychology, 26,* 358–365.

Sharpe, T. M., Killen, J. D., Bryson, S. W., Shisslak, C. M., Estes, L. S., Gray, N., Crago, M., & Taylor, C. G. (1998). Attachment style and weight concerns in preadolescent and adolescent girls. *International Journal of Eating Disorders, 23,* 39–44.

Silver, L. B. (1992). *Attention-deficit hyperactivity disorder: A clinical guide to diagnosis and treatment.* Washington, DC: American Psychiatric Press.

Sines, J. O. (1987). Influence of the home and family environment on childhood dysfunction. In B. B. Lahey & A. E. Kazdin (Eds.), *Advances in clinical child psychology* (Vol. 10). New York & London: Plenum.

Smith, I. M., & Bryson, S. E. (1994). Imitation and action in autism: A critical review. *Psychological Bulletin, 116,* 259–273.

Smith, T., & Lovaas, O. I. (1998). Intensive and early behavioral intervention with autism: The UCLA Young Autism Project. *Infants and Young Children, 10,* 67–78.

Smolak, L., & Levine, M. P. (1993). Separation-individuation difficulties and the distinction between bulimia nervosa and anorexia nervosa in college women. *International Journal of Eating Disorders, 14,* 33–41.

Smolak, L., & Levine, M. P. (1996). Adolescent transitions and the development of eating problems. In L. Smolak, M. P. Levine, & R. Striegel-Moore (Eds.), *The developmental psychopathology of eating disorders: Implications for research, prevention, and treatment.* Mahwah, NJ: Erlbaum.

Smolak, L., & Striegel-Moore, R. (1996). The implications of developmental research for eating disorders. In L. Smolak, M. P. Levine, & R. Striegel-Moore (Eds.), *The developmental psychopathology of eating disorders: Implications for research, prevention, and treatment.* Mahwah, NJ: Erlbaum.

Smoller, J. W. (1986). The etiology and treatment of childhood. In G. C. Ellenbogen (Ed.), *Oral sadism and the vegetarian personality: Readings from the Journal of Polymorphous Perversity.* New York: Brunner/Mazel. (Originally published by Wry-Bred Press)

Snowdon, D. A. (1997). Aging and Alzheimer's disease: Lessons from the Nun Study. *Gerontologist, 37,* 150–156.

Spencer, T. J., Biederman, J., Harding, M., O'Donnell, D., Faraone, S. V., & Wilens, T. E. (1996). Growth deficits in ADHD children revisited: Evidence for disorder-associated growth delays? *Journal of the American Academy of Child and Adolescent Psychiatry, 35,* 1460–1469.

Spitz, R. A. (1946). Anaclitic depression: An inquiry into the genesis of psychiatric conditions in early childhood, II. *Psychoanalytic Study of the Child, 2,* 313–342.

Sprock, J., & Yoder, C. Y. (1997). Women and depression: An update on the report of the APA Task Force. *Sex Roles, 36,* 269-303.

Sroufe, L. A. (1997). Psychopathology as an outcome of development. *Development and Psychopathology, 9,* 251-268.

Sroufe, L. A., & Rutter, M. (1984). The domain of developmental psychopathology. *Child Development, 55,* 17-29.

Stapley, J. C., & Haviland, J. M. (1989). Beyond depression: Gender differences in normal adolescents' emotional experiences. *Sex Roles, 20,* 295-308.

Steffenburg, S., Gillberg, C., Hellgren, L., Andersson, L., Gillberg, I. C., Jakobsson, G., & Bohman, M. (1989). A twin study of autism in Denmark, Finland, Iceland, Norway, and Sweden. *Journal of Child Psychology and Psychiatry and Allied Disciplines, 30,* 405-416.

Stewart, M. A., Pitts, F. N., Craig, A. G., & Dieruf, W. (1966). The hyperactive child syndrome. *American Journal of Orthopsychiatry, 36,* 861-867.

Stice, E., & Barrera, M. (1995). A longitudinal examination of the reciprocal relations between perceived parenting and adolescents' substance use and externalizing behaviors. *Developmental Psychology, 31,* 322-334.

Strauss, J., Muday, T., McNall, K., & Wong, M. (1997). Response style theory revisited: Gender differences and stereotypes in rumination and distraction. *Sex Roles, 36,* 771-792.

Strober, M. (1986). Psychopathology in adolescence revisited. *Clinical Psychology Review, 6,* 199-209.

Strober, M., Freeman, R., & Morrell, W. (1997). The long-term course of severe anorexia nervosa in adolescents: Survival analysis of recovery, relapse, and outcome predictors over 10-15 years in a prospective study. *International Journal of Eating Disorders, 22,* 339-360.

Strober, M., & Humphrey, L. L. (1987). Familial contributions to the etiology and course of anorexia nervosa and bulimia. *Journal of Consulting and Clinical Psychology, 55,* 654-659.

Study Group on Anorexia Nervosa. (1995). Anorexia nervosa: Directions for future research. *International Journal of Eating Disorders, 17,* 235-241.

Sullivan, P. F. (1995). Mortality in anorexia nervosa. *American Journal of Psychiatry, 152,* 1073-1074.

Swarr, A. E., & Richards, M. H. (1996). Longitudinal effects of adolescent girls' pubertal development, perceptions of pubertal timing, and parental reactions on eating problems. *Developmental Psychology, 32,* 636-646.

Teri, L., McCurry, S. M., Edland, S. D., Kukull, W. A., & Larson, E. B. (1995). Cognitive decline in Alzheimer's disease: A longitudinal investigation of risk factors for accelerated decline. *Journal of Gerontology: Medical Sciences, 50,* M49-M55.

Thase, M. E., & Kupfer, D. J. (1996). Recent developments in the pharmacotherapy of mood disorders. *Journal of Consulting and Clinical Psychology, 64,* 646-659.

Thelen, M. H., Powell, A. L., Lawrence, C., and Kuhnert, M. E. (1992). Eating and body image concerns among children. *Journal of Clinical Child Psychology, 21,* 41-46.

U.S. Bureau of the Census. (1996). *Statistical abstract of the United States* (116th ed.). Washington, DC: U.S. Government Printing Office.

U.S. Bureau of the Census. (1997). *Statistical abstract of the United States* (117th ed.). Washington, DC: U.S. Government Printing Office.

Vaillant, G. E. (1977). *Adaptation to life.* Boston: Little, Brown.

van IJzendoorn, M. H., & Bakermans-Kranenburg, M. J. (1996). Attachment representations in mothers, fathers, adolescents, and clinical groups: A meta-analytic search for normative data. *Journal of Consulting and Clinical Psychology, 64,* 8-21.

Vannatta, R. A. (1996). Risk factors related to suicidal behavior among male and female adolescents. *Journal of Youth and Adolescence, 25,* 149-160.

von Knorring, A., Andersson, O., & Magnusson, D. (1987). Psychiatric care and course of psychiatric disorders from childhood to early adulthood in a representative sample. *Journal of Child Psychology and Psychiatry and Allied Disciplines, 28,* 329-341.

Wagner, B. M. (1997). Family risk factors for child and adolescent suicidal behavior. *Psychological Bulletin, 121,* 246-298.

Wallander, J. L., & Hubert, N. C. (1985). Long-term prognosis for children with attention deficit disorder with hyperactivity (ADD/H). In B. B. Lahey & A. E. Kazdin (Eds.), *Advances in clinical child psychology* (Vol. 8). New York: Plenum.

Wallis, C. (1994, July 18). Life in overdrive. *Newsweek,* 42-50.

Wampler, K. S., Halverson, C. F., Jr., & Deal, J. (1996). Risk and resiliency in nonclinical young children: The Georgia Longitudinal Study. In E. M. Hetherington & E. A. Blechman (Eds.), *Stress, coping, and resiliency in children and families.* Mahwah, NJ: Erlbaum.

Ward, M. J., Kessler, D. B., & Altman, S. C. (1993). Infant-mother attachment in children with failure to thrive. *Infant Mental Health Journal, 14,* 208-220.

Weiss, G., & Hechtman, L. T. (1993). *Hyperactive children grown up* (2nd ed.). New York: Guilford.

Weissman, M. M., Warner, V., Wickramaratne, P., Moreau, D., & Olfson, M. (1997). Offspring of depressed parents: 10 years later. *Archives of General Psychiatry, 54,* 932-940.

Weisz, J. R., Sigman, M., Weiss, B., & Mosk, J. (1993). Parent reports of behavioral and emotional problems among children in Kenya, Thailand, and the United States. *Child Development, 64,* 98-109.

Weisz, J. R., & Weiss, B. (1993). *Effects of psychotherapy with children and adolescents* (Vol. 27, Developmental Clinical Psychology and Psychiatry Series). Newbury Park, CA: Sage.

Weisz, J. R., Weiss, B., Alicke, M. D., & Klotz, M. L. (1987). Effectiveness of psychotherapy with children and adolescents: A meta-analysis for clinicians. *Journal of Consulting and Clinical Psychology, 55,* 542-549.

Wender, P. H. (1995). *Attention-deficit hyperactivity disorder in adults.* New York: Oxford University Press.

Whalen, C. K., Henker, B., Buhrmester, D., Hinshaw, S. P., Huber, A., & Laski, K. (1989). Does stimulant medication improve the peer status of hyperactive children? *Journal of Consulting and Clinical Psychology, 57,* 545-549.

Whitbeck, L. B., Hoyt, D. R., Simons, R. L., Conger, R. D., Elder, G. H., Jr., Lorenz, F. O., & Huck, S. (1992). Intergenerational continuity of parental rejection and depressed affect. *Journal of Personality and Social Psychology, 63,* 1036-1045.

Wilens, T. E., & Biederman, J. (1992). The stimulants. *Psychiatric Clinics of North America, 15,* 191-222.

Williams, G. J., Power, K. G., Millar, H. R., Freeman, C. P., Yellowlees, A.,

Dowds, T., Walker, M., Campsie, L., MacPherson, F., & Jackson, M. A. (1993). Comparison of eating disorders and other dietary/weight groups on measures of perceived control, assertiveness, self-esteem, and self-directed hostility. *International Journal of Eating Disorders, 14,* 27–32.

Williams, M. E. (1995). *The American Geriatrics Society's complete guide to aging and health.* New York: Harmony Books.

Williamson, D. A., Davis, C. J., Goreczny, A. J., & Blouin, D. C. (1989). Body-image disturbances in bulimia nervosa: Influences of actual body size. *Journal of Abnormal Psychology, 98,* 97–99.

Windle, M., Shope, J. T., & Bukstein, O. (1996). Alcohol use. In R. DiClemente, W. B. Hansen, & L. E. Ponton (Eds.), *Handbook of adolescent health risk behavior.* New York: Plenum.

Windle, R. C., & Windle, M. (1997). An investigation of adolescents' substance use behaviors, depressed affect, and suicidal behaviors. *Journal of Child Psychology and Psychiatry and Allied Disciplines, 38,* 921–929.

Wolfe, R., Morrow, J., & Fredrickson, B. L. (1996). Mood disorders in older adults. In L. L. Carstensen, B. A. Edelstein, & L. Dornbrand (Eds.), *The practical handbook of clinical gerontology.* Thousand Oaks, CA: Sage.

Wonderlich, S., Klein, M. H., & Council, J. R. (1996). Relationship of social perceptions and self-concept in bulimia nervosa. *Journal of Consulting and Clinical Psychology, 64,* 1231–1237.

Wrightsman, L. S., Sigelman, C. K., & Sanford, F. H. (1979). *Psychology. A scientific study of human behavior.* Pacific Grove, CA: Brooks/Cole.

Wu, X., & DeMaris, A. (1996). Gender and marital status differences in depression: The effects of chronic strains. *Sex Roles, 34,* 299–319.

Yamaguchi, K., & Kandel, D. B. (1984). Patterns of drug use from adolescence to young adulthood: II. Sequences of progression. *American Journal of Public Health, 74,* 668–672.

Yang, B., & Clum, G. A. (1996). Effects of early negative life experiences on cognitive functioning and risk for suicide: A review. *Clinical Psychology Review, 16,* 177–195.

Yeung-Courchesne, R., & Courchesne, E. (1997). From impasse to insight in autism research: From behavioral symptoms to biological explanations. *Development and Psychopathology, 9,* 389–419.

Yirmiya, N., & Sigman, M. (1991). High functioning individuals with autism—Diagnosis, empirical findings, and theoretical issues. *Clinical Psychology Review, 11,* 669–683.

Yirmiya, N., Solomonica-Levy, D., Shulman, C., & Pilowsky, T. (1996). Theory of mind abilities in individuals with autism, Down syndrome, and mental retardation of unknown etiology: The role of age and intelligence. *Journal of Child Psychology and Psychiatry and Allied Disciplines, 37,* 1003–1014.

Zarit, S. H., Eiler, J., & Hassinger, M. (1985). Clinical assessment. In J. E. Birren & K. W. Schaie (Eds.), *Handbook of the psychology of aging* (2nd ed.). New York: Van Nostrand Reinhold.

Zeanah, C. H., Boris, N. W., & Scheeringa, M. S. (1997). Psychopathology in infancy. *Journal of Child Psychology and Psychiatry and Allied Disciplines, 38,* 81–99.

CHAPTER 17: The Final Challenge: Death and Dying

Adams, D. W., & Deveau, E. J. (1986). Helping dying adolescents: Needs and responses. In C. A. Corr & J. N. McNeil (Eds.), *Adolescence and death.* New York: Springer.

Adams, D. W., & Deveau, E. J. (1987). When a brother or sister is dying of cancer: The vulnerability of the adolescent sibling. *Death Studies, 11,* 279–295.

Alvarado, K. A., Templer, D. I., Bresler, C., & Thomas-Dobson, S. (1995). The relationship of religious variables to death depression and death anxiety. *Journal of Clinical Psychology, 51,* 202–204.

Applebaum, D. R., & Burns, G. L. (1991). Unexpected childhood death: Posttraumatic stress disorder in surviving siblings and parents. *Journal of Clinical Child Psychology, 20,* 114–120.

Arbuckle, N. W., & de Vries, B. (1995). The long-term effects of later life spousal and parental bereavement on personal functioning. *Gerontologist, 35,* 637–647.

Ariès, P. (1981). *The hour of our death* (H. Weaver, Trans.). New York: Knopf. (Original work published 1977)

Aspinall, S. Y. (1996). Educating children to cope with death: A preventive model. *Psychology in the schools, 33,* 341–349.

Baker, S. R. (1991). Utilizing art and imagery in death and dying counseling. In D. Papadatou & C. Papadatos (Eds.), *Children and death.* New York: Hemisphere.

Bankoff, E. A. (1983). Aged parents and their widowed daughters: A support relationship. *Journal of Gerontology, 38,* 226–230.

Berger, A. S. (1993). *Dying and death in law and medicine: A forensic primer for health and legal professionals.* Westport, CT: Praeger.

Bertman, S. L. (1991). Children and death: Insights, hindsights, and illuminations. In D. Papadatou & C. Papadatos (Eds.), *Children and death.* New York: Hemisphere.

Bluebond-Langner, M. (1977). Meanings of death to children. In H. Feifel (Ed.), *New meanings of death.* New York: McGraw-Hill.

Bodnar, J. C., & Kiecolt-Glaser, J. K. (1994). Caregiver depression after bereavement: Chronic stress isn't over when it's over. *Psychology and Aging, 9,* 372–380.

Bohannon, J. R. (1990–1991). Grief responses of spouses following the death of a child: A longitudinal study. *Omega, 22,* 109–121.

Bohannon, J. R. (1991). Religiosity related to grief levels of bereaved mothers and fathers. *Omega, 23,* 153–159.

Bonanno, G. A., Holen, A., Keltner, D., & Horowitz, M. J. (1995). When avoiding unpleasant emotions might not be such a bad thing: Verbal-autonomic response dissociation and midlife conjugal bereavement. *Journal of Personality and Social Psychology, 69,* 975–989.

Bower, A. R. (1997). The adult child's acceptance of parent death. *Omega, 35,* 67–96.

Bowlby, J. (1980). *Attachment and loss: Vol. 3. Loss, sadness, and depression.* New York: Basic Books.

Brent, S. B., Speece, M. W., Lin, C. G., Dong, Q., & Yang, C. M. (1996). The development of the concept of death among Chinese and U.S. children 3–17 years of age: From binary to "fuzzy" concepts? *Omega, 33,* 67–83.

Caddell, D. P., & Newton, R. R. (1995). Euthanasia: American attitudes toward the physician's role. *Social Science and Medicine, 40,* 1671–1681.

Cesario, T. C., & Hollander, D. (1991).

Life span extension by means other than control of disease. In F. C. Ludwig (Ed.), *Life span extension: Consequences and open questions.* New York: Springer.

Clark, D. C., Pynoos, R. S., & Goebel, A. E. (1994). Mechanisms and processes of adolescent bereavement. In R. J. Haggerty, L. R. Sherrod, N. Garmezy, & M. Rutter (Eds.), *Stress, risk, and resilience in children and adolescents: Processes, mechanisms, and interventions.* Cambridge: Cambridge University Press.

Cleiren, M. P. H. D. (1993). *Bereavement and adaptation: A comparative study of the aftermath of death.* Washington, DC: Hemisphere.

Colburn, D. (1994, May 10). Debate on assisted suicide gains steam. *Washington Post Health,* p. 8.

Colburn, D. (1995, December 5). The grace of a "good death" escapes many. *Washington Post Health,* p. 7.

Cook, A. S., & Dworkin, D. S. (1992). *Helping the bereaved: Therapeutic interventions for children, adolescents, and adults.* New York: Basic Books.

Corr, C. A. (1993). Coping with dying: Lessons that we should and should not learn from the work of Elisabeth Kübler-Ross. *Death Studies, 17,* 69–83.

Corr, C. A. (1995). Entering into adolescent understanding of death. In E. A. Grollman (Ed.), *Bereaved children and teens.* Boston: Beacon Press.

Corr, C. A., & Corr, D. M. (1992). Children's hospice care. *Death Studies, 16,* 431–449.

Cristofalo, V. J. (1996). Ten years later: What have we learned about human aging from studies of cell cultures? *Gerontologist, 36,* 737–741.

Cutter, J. (1998, March 29). On death and dying. *The State-Journal Register,* p. 15.

Cytron, B. D. (1993). To honor the dead and comfort the mourners: Traditions in Judaism. In D. P. Irish, K. F. Lundquist, & V. J. Nelson (Eds.), *Ethnic variations in dying, death, and grief: Diversity in universality.* Washington, DC: Taylor and Francis.

Davies, B. (1995). Toward siblings' understanding and perspectives of death. In E. A. Grollman (Ed.), *Bereaved children and teens.* Boston: Beacon Press.

DeFrain, J. D., Jakub, D. K., & Mendoza, B. L. (1991–1992). The psychological effects of sudden infant death on grandmothers and grandfathers. *Omega, 24,* 165–182.

DeFrain, J., Taylor, J., & Ernst, L. (1982). *Coping with sudden infant death.* Lexington, MA: Lexington Books.

DeGarmo, D. S., & Kitson, G. C. (1996). Identity relevance and disruption as predictors of psychological distress for widowed and divorced women. *Journal of Marriage and the Family, 58,* 983–997.

de Vries, B. (1997). Kinship bereavement in later life: Understanding variations in cause, course, and consequence. *Omega, 35,* 141–157.

de Vries, B., Lana, R. D., & Falck, V. T. (1994). Parental bereavement over the life course: A theoretical intersection and empirical review. *Omega, 29,* 47–69.

Dickinson, G. E. (1992). First childhood death experiences. *Omega, 25,* 169–182.

Elizur, E., & Kaffman, M. (1983). Factors influencing the severity of childhood bereavement reactions. *American Journal of Orthopsychiatry, 53,* 668–676.

Essa, E. L., & Murray, C. I. (1994). Young children's understanding and experience with death. *Young Children, 49,* 74–81.

Faulkner, K. W. (1997). Talking about death with a dying child. *American Journal of Nursing, 97,* 64, 66, 68–69.

Florian, V., & Kravetz, S. (1985). Children's concepts of death: A cross-cultural comparison among Muslims, Druze, Christians, and Jews in Israel. *Journal of Cross-Cultural Psychology, 16,* 174–189.

Fry, P. S. (1997). Grandparents' reactions to the death of a grandchild: An exploratory factor analytic study. *Omega, 35,* 119–140.

Furman, E. (1984). Children's patterns in mourning the death of a loved one. In H. Wass & C. A. Corr (Eds.), *Childhood and death.* Washington, DC: Hemisphere.

Gilewski, M. J., Farberow, N. L., Gallagher, D. E., & Thompson, L. W. (1991). Interaction of depression and bereavement on mental health in the elderly. *Psychology and Aging, 6,* 67–75.

Glaser, B. G., & Strauss, A. L. (1968). *Time for dying.* Chicago: Aldine.

Gordon, J. (1995). Grieving together: Helping family members share their grief. In S. C. Smith & M. Pennells (Eds.), *Interventions with bereaved children.* London: Jessica Kingsley.

Gottlieb, L. N., Lang, A., & Amsel, R. (1996). The long-term effects of grief on marital intimacy following an infant's death. *Omega, 33,* 1–19.

Graham-Pole, J., Wass, H., Eyberg, S., Chu, L., & Olejnik, S. (1989). Communicating with dying children and their siblings: A retrospective analysis. *Death Studies, 13,* 463–483.

Grollman, E. A. (1995). Explaining death to young children: Some questions and answers. In E. A. Grollman (Ed.), *Bereaved children and teens.* Boston: Beacon Press.

Haas-Hawkings, G., Sangster, S., Ziegler, M., & Reid, D. (1985). A study of relatively immediate adjustment to widowhood in later life. *International Journal of Women's Studies, 8,* 158–166.

Harlow, S. D., Goldberg, E. L., & Comstock, G. W. (1991). A longitudinal study of the prevalence of depressive symptomatology in elderly widowed and married women. *Archives of General Psychiatry, 48,* 1065–1068.

Harris, J. R., Pederson, N. L., McClearn, G. E., Plomin, R., & Nesselroade, J. R. (1992). Age differences in genetic and environmental influences for health from the Swedish Adoption/Twin Study of Aging. *Journal of Gerontology: Psychological Sciences, 47,* P213–P220.

Harris, T., & Bifulco, A. (1991). Loss of parent in childhood, attachment style, and depression in adulthood. In C. M. Parkes, J. Stevenson-Hinde, & P. Marris (Eds.), *Attachment across the life cycle.* London: Tavistock/Routledge.

Hayflick, L. (1976). The cell biology of human aging. *New England Journal of Medicine, 295,* 1302–1308.

Hays, J. C., Kasl, S. V., & Jacobs, S. C. (1994). The course of psychological distress following threatened and actual conjugal bereavement. *Psychological Medicine, 24,* 917–927.

Hickson, J., Housley, W. F., & Boyle, C. (1988). The relationship of locus of control, age, and sex to life satisfaction and death anxiety in older persons. *International Journal of Aging and Human Development, 26,* 191–199.

Hinton, J. (1975). The influence of previous personality on reactions to having terminal cancer. *Omega, 6,* 95–111.

Hodes, R. J., McCormick, A. M., & Pruzan, M. (1996). Longevity assurance genes: How do they influence aging and life span? *Journal of the American Geriatrics Society, 44,* 988–991.

Hoffman, S. I., & Strauss, S. (1985). The development of children's concepts of death. *Death Studies, 9,* 469–482.

Hutti, M. H. (1992). Parents' perceptions of the miscarriage experience. *Death Studies, 16,* 401–415.

Irish, D. P., Lundquist, K. F., & Nelson, V. J. (1993). *Ethnic variations in dying, death, and grief: Diversity in universality.* Washington, DC: Taylor amd Francis.

Jacobs, S. (1993). *Pathological grief: Maladaptation to loss.* Washington, DC: American Psychiatric Press.

Jacobs, S. C., Kosten, T. R., Kasl, S. V., Ostfeld, A. M., Berkman, L., & Charpentier, P. (1987–1988). Attachment theory and multiple dimensions of grief. *Omega, 18,* 41–52.

Janssen, H. J. E. M., Cuisinier, M. C. J., & Hoogduin, K. A. L. (1996). A critical review of the concept of pathological grief following pregnancy loss. *Omega, 33,* 21–42.

Jazwinski, S. M., Howard, B. H., & Nayak, R. K. (1995). Cell cycle progression, aging, and cell death. *Journal of Gerontology: Biological Sciences, 50,* B1–B8.

Kalish, R. A. (1981). *Death, grief, and caring relationships.* Pacific Grove, CA: Brooks/Cole.

Kalish, R. A., & Reynolds, D. K. (1977). The role of age in death attitudes. *Death Education, 1,* 205–230.

Kallmann, F. J., & Sander, G. (1949). Twin studies on senescence. *American Journal of Psychiatry, 106,* 29–36.

Kaminer, H., & Lavie, P. (1993). Sleep and dreams in well-adjusted and less adjusted Holocaust survivors. In M. S. Stroebe, W. Stroebe, & R. O. Hansson (Eds.), *Handbook of bereavement. Theory, research, and intervention.* Cambridge: Cambridge University Press.

Kastenbaum, R. (1985). Dying and death: A life-span approach. In J. E. Birren & K. W. Schaie (Eds.), *Handbook of the psychology of aging* (2nd ed.). New York: Van Nostrand Reinhold.

Kastenbaum, R. J. (1998). *Death, society, and human experience* (6th ed.). Boston: Allyn and Bacon.

Kinsella, K., & Tauber, C. M. (1993). *An aging world, II* (International Population Reports, P25, 92-3). Washington, DC: U.S. Bureau of the Census.

Kissane, D. W., Bloch, S., Onghena, P., McKenzie, D. P., Snyder, R. D., & Dowe, D. L. (1996). The Melbourne Family Grief Study, II: Psychosocial morbidity and grief in bereaved families. *American Journal of Psychiatry, 153,* 659–666.

Klass, D. (1993). Solace and immortality: Bereaved parents' continuing bond with their children. *Death Studies, 17,* 343–368.

Koocher, G. P. (1973). Childhood, death, and cognitive development. *Developmental Psychology, 9,* 369–375.

Koocher, G. P. (1974). Talking with children about death. *American Journal of Orthopsychiatry, 44,* 404–411.

Kristal, B. S., & Yu, B. P. (1992). An emerging hypothesis: Synergistic induction of aging by free radicals and maillard reactions. *Journal of Gerontology: Biological Sciences, 47,* B107–B114.

Kübler-Ross, E. (1969). *On death and dying.* New York: Macmillan.

Kübler-Ross, E. (1974). *Questions and answers on death and dying.* New York: Macmillan.

Lamberti, J. W., & Detmer, C. M. (1993). Model of family grief assessment and treatment. *Death Studies, 17,* 55–67.

Lang, A., & Gottlieb, L. (1993). Parental grief reactions and marital intimacy following infant death. *Death Studies, 17,* 233–255.

Leahy, J. M. (1992–1993). A comparison of depression in women bereaved of a spouse, child, or a parent. *Omega, 26,* 207–217.

Lehman, D. R., Davis, C. G., DeLongis, A., Wortman, C. B., Bluck, S., Mandel, D. R., & Ellard, J. H. (1993). Positive and negative life changes following bereavement and their relations to adjustment. *Journal of Social and Clinical Psychology, 12,* 90–112.

Lehman, D. R., Ellard, J. H., & Wortman, C. B. (1986). Social support for the bereaved: Recipients' and providers' perspectives on what is helpful. *Journal of Consulting and Clinical Psychology, 54,* 438–446.

Lehman, D. R., Wortman, C. B., & Williams, A. F. (1987). Long-term effects of losing a spouse or child in a motor vehicle crash. *Journal of Personality and Social Psychology, 52,* 218–231.

Lesher, E. L., & Bergey, K. J. (1988). Bereaved elderly mothers: Changes in health, functional activities, family cohesion, and psychological well-being. *International Journal of Aging and Human Development, 26,* 81–90.

Lester, D., & Templer, D. (1992–1993). Death anxiety scales: A dialogue. *Omega, 26,* 239–253.

Levy, L. H., Martinkowski, K. S., & Derby, J. F. (1994). Differences in patterns of adaptation in conjugal bereavement: Their sources and potential significance. *Omega, 29,* 71–87.

Lieberman, M. (1993). Bereavement self-help groups: A review of conceptual and methodological issues. In M. S. Stroebe, W. Stroebe, & R. O. Hansson (Eds.), *Handbook of bereavement. Theory, research, and intervention.* Cambridge: Cambridge University Press.

Lieberman, M. A., & Videka-Sherman, L. (1986). The impact of self-help groups on the mental health of widows and widowers. *American Journal of Orthopsychiatry, 56,* 435–449.

Lillard, L. A., & Waite, L. J. (1995). 'Til death do us part: Marital disruption and mortality. *American Journal of Sociology, 100,* 1131–1156.

Littlefield, C. H., & Rushton, J. P. (1986). When a child dies: The sociobiology of bereavement. *Journal of Personality and Social Psychology, 51,* 797–802.

Lohnes, K. L., & Kalter, N. (1994). Preventive intervention groups for parentally bereaved children. *American Journal of Orthopsychiatry, 64,* 594–603.

Lonetto, R., & Templer, D. I. (1986). *Death anxiety.* Washington, DC: Hemisphere.

Lopata, H. Z. (1996). *Current widowhood: Myths and realities.* Thousand Oaks, CA: Sage.

Lund, D. A., Caserta, M. S. (1992). Older bereaved spouses' participation in self-help groups. *Omega, 25,* 47–61.

Lund, D. A., Dimond, M. F., Caserta, M. S., Johnson, R. J., Poulton, J. L., & Connelly, J. R. (1985–1986). Identifying elderly with coping difficulties after two years of bereavement. *Omega, 16,* 213–224.

Martikainen, P., & Valkonen, T. (1996). Mortality after the death of a spouse: Rates and causes of death in a large Finnish cohort. *American Journal of Public Health, 86,* 1087–1093.

Masoro, E. J. (1988). Minireview: Food restriction in rodents—An evaluation of its role in the study of aging. *Journal of Gerontology: Biological Sciences, 43,* B59–B64.

Maurer, A. (1961). The child's knowledge of non-existence. *Journal of Existential Psychiatry, 2,*193–212.

McGoldrick, M., Almeida, R., Hines, P. M., Garcia-Preto, N., Rosen, E., & Lee, E. (1991). Mourning in different cultures. In F. Walsh & M. McGoldrick (Eds.), *Living beyond loss: Death in the family.* New York: Norton.

McGue, M., Vaupel, J. W., Holm, N., & Harvald, B. (1993). Longevity is moderately heritable in a sample of Danish twins born 1870–1880. *Journals of Gerontology, 48,* B237–B244.

McIntosh, D. N., Silver, R. C., & Wortman, C. B. (1993). Religion's role in adjustment to a negative life event: Coping with the loss of a child. *Journal of Personality and Social Psychology, 65,* 812–821.

McWhirter, L., Young, V., & Majury, J. (1983). Belfast children's awareness of violent death. *British Journal of Social Psychology, 22,* 81–92.

Medina, J. J. (1996). *The clock of ages: Why we age—how we age—winding back the clock.* Cambridge: Cambridge University Press.

Medvedev, Z. A. (1991). The structural basis of aging. In F. C. Ludwig (Ed.), *Life span extension: Consequences and open questions.* New York: Springer.

Metcalf, P., & Huntington, R. (1991). *Celebrations of death. The anthropology of mortuary ritual* (2nd ed.). Cambridge: Cambridge University Press.

Moss, M. S., Moss, S. Z., Rubinstein, R., & Resch, N. (1993). Impact of elderly mother's death on middle age daughters. *International Journal of Aging and Human Development, 37,* 1–22.

Najman, J. M., Vance, J. C., Boyle, F., Embleton, G., Foster, B., & Thearle, J. (1993). The impact of a child death on marital adjustment. *Social Science and Medicine, 37,* 1005–1010.

Neimeyer, R. A. (Ed.). (1994). *Death anxiety handbook: Research, instrumentation, and application.* Washington, DC: Taylor and Francis.

Nolen-Hoeksema, S., McBride, A., & Larson, J. (1997). Rumination and psychological distress among bereaved partners. *Journal of Personality and Social Psychology, 72,* 855–862.

Noppe, I. C., & Noppe, L. D. (1997). Evolving meanings of death during early, middle, and later adolescence. *Death Studies, 21,* 253–275.

Noppe, L. D., & Noppe, I. C. (1996). Ambiguity in adolescent understandings of death. In C. A. Corr & D. E. Balk (Eds.), *Handbook of adolescent death and bereavement.* New York: Springer.

Norris, F. H., & Murrell, S. A. (1990). Social support, life events, and stress as modifiers of adjustment to bereavement by older adults. *Psychology and Aging, 5,* 429–436.

O'Halloran, C. M., & Altmaier, E. M. (1996). Awareness of death among children: Does a life-threatening illness alter the process of discovery? *Journal of Counseling and Development, 74,* 259–262.

Osterweis, M., Solomon, F., & Green, M. (Eds.). (1984). *Bereavement: Reactions, consequences, and care.* Washington, DC: National Academy Press.

Parkes, C. M. (1986). *Bereavement: Studies of grief in adult life* (2nd ed.). London: Tavistock.

Parkes, C. M. (1991). Attachment, bonding, and psychiatric problems after bereavement in adult life. In C. M. Parkes, J. Stevenson-Hinde, & P. Marris (Eds.), *Attachment across the life cycle.* London: Tavistock/Routledge.

Parkes, C. M., & Weiss, R. S. (1983). *Recovery from bereavement.* New York: Basic Books.

Pennebaker, J. W., & O'Heeron, R. C. (1984). Confiding in others and illness rate among spouses of suicide and accidental-death victims. *Journal of Abnormal Psychology, 93,* 473–476.

Perry, H. L. (1993). Mourning and funeral customs of African Americans. In D. P. Irish, K. F. Lundquist, & V. J. Nelson (Eds.), *Ethnic variations in dying, death, and grief: Diversity in universality.* Washington, DC: Taylor and Francis.

Piper, W. E., McCallum, M., & Azim, H. F. A. (1992). *Adaptation to loss through short-term group psychotherapy.* New York: Guilford.

Ponzetti, J. J. (1992). Bereaved families: A comparison of parents' and grandparents' reactions to the death of a child. *Omega, 25,* 63–71.

Quill, T. E. (1993). *Death and dignity: Making choices and taking charge.* New York: Norton.

Rando, T. A. (1986). A comprehensive analysis of anticipatory grief: Perspectives, processes, promises, and problems. In T. A. Rando (Ed.), *Loss and anticipatory grief.* Lexington, MA: Lexington Books.

Rando, T. A. (1991). Parental adjustment to the loss of a child. In D. Papadatou & C. Papadatos (Eds.), *Children and death.* New York: Hemisphere.

Raphael, B. (1983). *The anatomy of bereavement.* New York: Basic Books.

Rappaport, H., Fossler, R. J., Bross, L. S., & Gilden, D. (1993). Future time, death anxiety, and life purpose among older adults. *Death Studies, 17,* 369–379.

Rasmussen, C. A., & Brems, C. (1996). The relationship of death anxiety with age and psychosocial maturity. *Journal of Psychology, 130,* 141–144.

Rosen, H. (1986). *Unspoken grief: Coping with childhood sibling loss.* Lexington, MA: Lexington Books.

Rosenblatt, P. C. (1993). Cross-cultural variation in the experience, expression, and understanding of grief. In D. P. Irish, K. F. Lundquist, & V. J. Nelson (Eds.), *Ethnic variations in dying, death, and grief: Diversity in universality.* Washington, DC: Taylor and Francis.

Rubin, S. S. (1993). The death of a child is forever: The life course impact of child loss. In M. S. Stroebe, W. Stroebe, & R. O. Hansson (Eds.), *Handbook of bereavement. Theory, research, and intervention.* Cambridge: Cambridge University Press.

Salahu-Din, S. N. (1996). A comparison of coping strategies of African American and Caucasian widows. *Omega, 33,* 103–120.

Sanchez, L., Fristad, M., Weller, R. A., Weller, E. B., & Moye, J. (1994). Anxiety in acutely bereaved prepubertal children. *Annals of Clinical Psychiatry, 6,* 39–43.

Sanders, C. M. (1979–1980). A comparison of adult bereavement in the death of a spouse, child, and parent. *Omega, 10,* 303–322.

Sanders, C. M. (1993). Risk factors in bereavement outcome. In M. S. Stroebe, W. Stroebe, & R. O. Hansson (Eds.), *Handbook of bereavement: Theory, research, and intervention.* Cambridge: Cambridge University Press.

Sandler, I. N., West, S. G., Baca, L., Pillow, D. R., Gersten, J. C., Rogosch, F., Virdin, L., Beals, J., Reynolds,

K. D., Kallgren, C., Tein, J., Kriege, G., Cole, E., & Ramirez, R. (1992). Linking empirically based theory and evaluation: The family bereavement program. *American Journal of Community Psychology, 20,* 491–521.

Saunders, C. (1977). Dying they live: St. Christopher's Hospice. In H. Feifel (Ed.), *New meanings of death.* New York: McGraw-Hill.

Schachter, S. (1991–1992). Adolescent experiences with the death of a peer. *Omega, 24,* 1–11.

Scharlach, A. E., & Fredriksen, K. I. (1993). Reactions to the death of a parent during midlife. *Omega, 27,* 307–319.

Schonfeld, D. J., & Kappelman, M. (1990). The impact of school-based education on the young child's understanding of death. *Developmental and Behavioral Pediatrics, 11,* 247–252.

Schreder, M. (1995). Special needs of bereaved children: Effective tools for helping. In E. A. Grollman (Ed.), *Bereaved children and teens.* Boston: Beacon Press.

Schulz, R., & Aderman, D. (1974). Clinical research and the stages of dying. *Omega, 5,* 137–143.

Schulz, R., & Schlarb, J. (1987–1988). Two decades of research on dying: What do we know about the patient? *Omega, 18,* 299–317.

Schwab, R. (1992). Effects of a child's death on the marital relationship: A preliminary study. *Death Studies, 16,* 141–154.

Seale, C. F. (1989). What happens in hospices: A review of research evidence. *Social Science and Medicine, 28,* 551–559.

Seale, C. F. (1991). A comparison of hospice and conventional care. *Social Science and Medicine, 32,* 147–152.

Shneidman, E. S. (1973). *Deaths of man.* New York: Quadrangle.

Shneidman, E. S. (1980). *Voices of death.* New York: Harper & Row.

Shuchter, S. R., & Zisook, S. (1993). The course of normal grief. In M. S. Stroebe, W. Stroebe, & R. O. Hansson (Eds.), *Handbook of bereavement: Theory, research, and intervention.* Cambridge: Cambridge University Press.

Siebold, C. (1992). *The hospice movement: Easing death's pains.* New York: Twayne Publishers.

Siegel, K., Karus, D., & Raveis, V. H. (1996). Adjustment of children fac-ing the death of a parent due to cancer. *Journal of the American Academy of Child and Adolescent Psychiatry, 35,* 442–450.

Silverman, P. R. (1981). *Helping women cope with grief* (Sage Human Services Guide No. 25). Beverly Hills, CA: Sage.

Silverman, P. R., & Worden, J. W. (1993). Children's reactions to the death of a parent. In M. S. Stroebe, W. Stroebe, & R. O. Hansson (Eds.), *Handbook of bereavement: Theory, research, and intervention.* Cambridge: Cambridge University Press.

Smith, D. W. E. (1997). Centenarians: Human longevity outliers. *Gerontologist, 37,* 200–206.

Speece, M. W., & Brent, S. B. (1984). Children's understanding of death: A review of three components of a death concept. *Child Development, 55,* 1671–1686.

Speece, M. W., & Brent, S. B. (1992). The acquisition of a mature understanding of three components of the concept of death. *Death Studies, 16,* 211–229.

Sprang, G., & McNeil, J. (1995). *The many faces of bereavement.* New York: Brunner/Mazel.

Stambrook, M., & Parker, K. C. H. (1987). The development of the concept of death in childhood: A review of the literature. *Merrill-Palmer Quarterly, 33,* 133–157.

Stein, S., Linn, M. W., & Stein, E. M. (1989). Psychological correlates of survival in nursing home cancer patients. *Gerontologist, 29,* 224–228.

Stevens, M. M., & Dunsmore, J. C. (1996). Adolescents who are living with a life-threatening illness. In C. A. Corr & D. E. Balk (Eds.), *Handbook of adolescent death and bereavement.* New York: Springer.

Stillion, J. M., & McDowell, E. E. (1996). *Suicide across the life span: Premature exits* (2nd ed.). Washington, DC: Taylor and Francis.

Stroebe, M. S., Gergen, M. M., Gergen, K. J., & Stroebe, W. (1992). Broken hearts or broken bonds. *American Psychologist, 47,* 1205–1212.

Stroebe, M. S., & Stroebe, W. (1993). The mortality of bereavement: A review. In M. S. Stroebe, W. Stroebe, & R. O. Hansson (Eds.), *Handbook of bereavement: Theory, research, and intervention.* Cambridge: Cambridge University Press.

Stroebe, W., & Stroebe, M. S. (1993). Determinants of adjustment to bereavement in younger widows and widowers. In M. S. Stroebe, W. Stroebe, & R. O. Hansson (Eds.), *Handbook of bereavement: Theory, research, and intervention.* Cambridge: Cambridge University Press.

Thompson, L. W., Gallagher-Thompson, D., Futterman, A., Gilewski, M. J., & Peterson, J. (1991). The effects of late-life spousal bereavement over a 30-month interval. *Psychology and Aging, 6,* 434–441.

Trueheart, C. (1997, August 5). Champion of longevity ends her reign at 122. *Washington Post,* pp. A1, A12.

Tyson-Rawson, K. J. (1996). Adolescent responses to the death of a parent. In C. A. Corr & D. E. Balk (Eds.), *Handbook of adolescent death and bereavement.* New York: Springer.

Umberson, D., & Chen, M. D. (1994). Effects of a parent's death on adult children: Relationship salience and reaction to loss. *American Sociological Review, 59,* 152–168.

Umberson, D., Wortman, C. B., & Kessler, R. C. (1992). Widowhood and depression: Explaining long-term gender differences in vulnerability. *Journal of Health and Social Behavior, 33,* 10–24.

Urofsky, M. I. (1993). *Letting go. Death, dying, and the law.* New York: Charles Scribner's Sons.

U.S. Bureau of the Census. (1997). *Statistical abstracts of the United States* (117th ed.). Washington, DC: U.S. Government Printing Office.

Van Eerdewegh, M. M., Clayton, P. J., & Van Eerdewegh, P. (1985). The bereaved children: Variables influencing early psychopathology. *British Journal of Psychiatry, 147,* 188–194.

Waechter, E. H. (1984). Dying children: Patterns of coping. In H. Wass & C. A. Corr (Eds.), *Childhood and death.* Washington, DC: Hemisphere.

Walford, R. L. (1983). *Maximum life span.* New York: Norton.

Wass, H. (1991). Helping children cope with death. In D. Papadatou & C. Papadatos (Eds.), *Children and death.* New York: Hemisphere.

Wenestam, C., & Wass, H. (1987). Swedish and U.S. children's thinking about death: A qualitative study and cross-cultural comparison. *Death Studies, 11,* 99–121.

Wikan, U. (1988). Bereavement and loss in two Muslim communities: Egypt and Bali compared. *Social Science and Medicine, 27,* 451–460.

Wikan, U. (1991). *Managing turbulent hearts.* Chicago: University of Chicago Press.

Worchel, F. F., Copeland, D. R., & Barker, D. G. (1987). Control-related coping strategies in pediatric oncology patients. *Journal of Pediatric Psychology, 12,* 25–38.

Worden, J. W. (1991). *Grief counseling and grief therapy. A handbook for the mental health practitioner* (2nd ed.). New York: Springer.

Worden, J. W., & Silverman, P. R. (1993). Grief and depression in newly widowed parents with school-age children. *Omega, 27,* 251–261.

Worden, J. W., & Silverman, P. R. (1996). Parental death and the adjustment of school-age children. *Omega, 33,* 91–102.

Wortman, C. B., & Silver, R. C. (1989). The myths of coping with loss. *Journal of Consulting and Clinical Psychology, 57,* 349–357.

Zisook, S., & Shuchter, S. R. (1991). Depression through the first year after the death of a spouse. *American Journal of Psychiatry, 148,* 1346–1352.

EPILOGUE: Fitting the Pieces Together

Baltes, P. B. (1987). Theoretical propositions of life-span developmental psychology: On the dynamics between growth and decline. *Developmental Psychology, 23,* 611–626.

Baltes, P. B., Smith, J., & Staudinger, U. M. (1992). Wisdom and successful aging. In T. B. Sonderegger (Ed.), *Nebraska symposium on motivation: Vol. 39. Psychology and aging.* Lincoln: University of Nebraska Press.

Bronfenbrenner, U. (1995). Developmental ecology through space and time: A future perspective. In P. Moen, G. H. Elder, Jr., & K. Luscher (Eds.), *Examining lives in context: Perspectives on the ecology of human development.* Washington, DC: American Psychological Association.

Eccles, J. S., Midgley, C., Wigfield, A., Buchanan, C. M., Reuman, D., Flanagan, C., & Mac Iver, D. (1993). Development during adolescence: The impact of stage-environment fit on young adolescents' experiences in schools and in families. *American Psychologist, 48,* 90–101.

Flavell, J. H., Miller, P. H., & Miller, S. A. (1993). *Cognitive development.* Englewood Cliffs, NJ: Prentice Hall.

Harris, J. R., Pedersen, N. L., McClearn, G. E., Plomin, R., & Nesselroade, J. R. (1992). Age differences in genetic and environmental influences for health from the Swedish Adoption/Twin Study of Aging. *Journal of Gerontology: Psychological Sciences, 47,* P213–P220.

Lerner, R. M., & Kauffman, M. B. (1985). The concept of development in contextualism. *Developmental Review, 5,* 309–333.

Morse, C. K. (1993). Does variability increase with age? An archival study of cognitive measures. *Psychology and Aging, 8,* 156–164.

Schaie, K. W. (1996). *Intellectual development in adulthood. The Seattle Longitudinal Study.* New York: Cambridge University Press.

Thomas, A., & Chess, S. (1986). The New York longitudinal study: From infancy to early adult life. In R. Plomin & J. Dunn (Eds.), *The study of temperament: Changes, continuities, and challenges.* Hillsdale, NJ: Erlbaum.

Werner, H. (1957). The concept of development from a comparative and organismic point of view. In D. B. Harris (Ed.), *The concept of development: An issue in the study of human behavior.* Minneapolis: University of Minnesota Press.

Author Index

Abel, E. L., 89, 92, 94
Ablard, K. E., 435
Aboud, F. E., 382
Abraham, J. D., 449
Abrahams, B., 316
Abramov, I., 145, 146, 147, 153
Abramovitch, R., 407
Abrams, J. M., 317
Abrams, L., 196
Abravanel, E., 211
Achenbach, T. M., 467, 469, 471
Achenbaum, W. A., 454
Achter, J. A., 256
Ackermann-Liebrich, U., 105
Acredolo, L., 192
Adams, C., 224
Adams, D. W., 510, 514
Adams, G. R., 283, 284, 290
Adams, M. J., 159
Adams, P., 130
Adams, P. W., 343
Adams, Rebecca G., 389
Adelson, J., 383
Aderman, D., 503
Adey, P. S., 201
Adkinson, C. D., 119
Adler, Alfred, 34
Adler, J., 82
Adler, T. F., 309
Aerts, E., 354
Ageton, S. S., 348
Agnew, R., 423
Ainlay, S. C., 350
Ainscough, C. E., 132
Ainsworth, Mary D. S., 362, 367, 369, 371, 373, 387
Akiyama, H., 390
Alansky, J. A., 372
Albert, M. L., 196
Albert, R. S., 261
Aldridge, S., 59, 73, 76, 84
Aldwin, C. M., 483
Alessandri, S. M., 93, 434
Alexander, J. L., 12
Alexander, K. L., 440
Alfieri, T., 304
Allen, K. R., 418
Allen, L., 244

Allen, M. C., 85
Alley, T. R., 366
Allison, S., 124, 134
Almeida, D. M., 304
Alpert, Richard, 268
Altmaier, E. M., 508
Altman, S. C., 469
Alvarado, K. A., 511
Amato, Paul R., 397, 405, 419, 420, 421, 422
Ambert, A., 396, 405, 407
American Humane Association, 424
American Psychiatric Association, 463–464, 464, 465, 466, 470, 473, 477, 485, 488
American Psychological Association, 21
Amini, S. B., 88
Ammerman, R. T., 424
Amoloza, T. O., 409
Amsel, R., 514
Anand, K. J., 153
Anastasi, Ann, 71
Anderman, E. M., 442
Andersen, A., 477
Anderson, D. R., 156
Anderson, Kathleen E., 345, 405
Anderson, T. W., 89
Andersson, O., 476
Andres, R., 111
Andrich, D., 245
Aneshensel, C. S., 416, 444
Angold, A., 481
Anisfeld, E., 370
Anisfield, M., 211
Anthony, J. C., 485
Antonucci, Toni C., 361, 387, 389, 390
Apgar, V., 84, 92, 94, 97
Apostoleris, N. H., 378
Applebaum, D. R., 515
Applebaum, M. I., 244
Appollonio, I., 166
Aquilino, W. S., 412, 415
Arana-Ward, M., 166
Arber, S., 324, 454
Arbuckle, N. W., 518
Archer, J., 56, 57, 131, 306, 307
Archer, Sally L., 281, 290
Ardelt, M., 249
Arenberg, D., 261, 287
Ariès, Phillippe, 5, 496

Arjmand, O., 309
Arlin, P. K., 185
Armon, C., 185
Arnaud, S. H., 380
Arnett, J. J., 404
Aronson, E., 441
Aronson, J., 254
Arroyo, C. G., 442
Asendorpf, J. B., 271, 272, 277
Asher, Steven R., 381, 382, 390
Aslin, R. N., 145, 146, 149, 198
Aspinall, S. Y., 508, 510
Astington, J. W., 331
Atchley, Robert, 452–453
Athey, I., 379
Atkinson, J., 314
Atkinson, J. W., 431
Atkinson, Richard, 213
Au, R., 196
Avants, S. K., 300
Avolio, B. J., 449
Axinn, W. G., 416, 418
Azim, H. F. A., 519
Azmitia, M., 202, 407

Bachman, J. G., 444, 479
Baer, D. M., 38
Bafitis, H., 131
Bagley, C., 425
Bagwell, C. L., 382
Bahrick, H. P., 225
Bahrick, P. O., 225
Baier, J. R., 321
Bailey, A., 331, 466, 467
Bailey, D. B., 440
Bailey, J. M., 66, 320, 418
Baillargeon, Renee, 174
Baird, P. A., 89
Baker, B. L., 467
Baker, D. P., 300
Baker, L., 222, 478
Baker, L. A., 69, 306
Baker, R. L., 88, 102, 103
Baker, S. R., 509
Baker, S. W., 306
Bakermans-Kranenburg, M. J., 474
Baker-Ward, L., 218
Bakwin, H., 317

643

Balassone, M. L., 50
Baldwin, G., 194
Baltes, Margaret M., 449
Baltes, Paul B., 3, 8, 10, 135, 165, 225, 229,
    230, 231, 249, 250, 449, 529
Bandura, Albert, 38–39, 40, 48, 49, 50, 196,
    210, 213, 230, 270, 303, 308–309, 339
Banerjee, M., 331
Bank, L., 68, 247, 356, 357, 360
Bankoff, E. A., 520
Banks, M. S., 145, 146
Barber, B. L., 421
Barber, J. S., 418
Barenboim, C., 332
Barglow, P. D., 106
Barker, D. G., 509
Barker, D. J. P., 89
Barkley, R. A., 470, 471
Barling, J., 444, 452
Barnas, M. V., 390
Barnes, K. E., 378, 379
Barnett, D., 425
Barnett, R. C., 314, 400, 451
Baron, N. S., 197
Baron-Cohen, Simon, 329, 330, 466
Barr, H. M., 94
Barr, R., 211
Barrera, M., 474
Barrett, D. E., 96
Barrett, K. C., 340, 433, 434
Barrett, T. R., 224
Barron, K. L., 225
Barry, Dave, 110, 132
Barry, H., III, 127
Bartholomew, K., 388
Barton, M. E., 199
Bartoshuk, L. M., 163
Bartsch, K., 331
Baruch, G. K., 314, 400, 451
Baruch, R., 446
Basinger, K. S., 346
Baskett, L. M., 407
Basseches, M., 186
Bates, E., 192, 198
Bates, J. E., 209, 433
Battaglia, F., 92
Battle, E. S., 431
Bauchner, H., 468, 469
Baudonnière, P. M., 271
Bauer, Patricia J., 211, 216
Baum, B. J., 163
Baumeister, A. A., 119
Baumrind, Diana, 402, 406, 479
Baydar, N., 374
Bayer, A. F., 348
Bayley, N., 128, 243
Beach, D. R., 218
Beach, Frank A., 317, 318
Beal, C. R., 195, 297, 309, 310
Beard, 261
Beardsall, L., 407
Beardsley, T., 75
Bearison, D. J., 334
Beauchamp, G. K., 163
Beautrais, A. L., 482
Beck, D., 477
Beck, J., 84, 92, 94
Beck, M., 83

Becker, J. B., 127
Beckwith, L., 103
Beeghly, M., 331
Begley, N. L., 304
Begley, S., 76, 83, 114
Behrend, D. A., 190
Behrman, R. E., 96
Beidelman, T. O., 127
Beilin, Harry, 43, 187
Beitchman, J. H., 319
Bell, Richard Q., 345, 405
Bellinger, D., 94
Bellugi, Ursula, 196, 200
Belsky, Jay, 13, 57, 367, 371, 374, 375, 376,
    396, 397, 401, 406, 410, 411, 424, 434
Bem, D. J., 277
Bem, Sandra L., 33, 307, 315, 316
Bemporad, J. R., 466
Benbow, C. P., 256, 309
Benedict, H., 192
Benenson, J. F., 378
Benes, F. M., 115
Bengtson, Vern L., 12, 286, 399, 415, 416, 417,
    454
Benn, R., 413
Bennett, E. L., 114
Benoit, D., 389
Benson, P., 69
Berenbaum, S. A., 299, 306
Berg, C. A., 222, 229, 236
Berg, S., 248
Berg, W. K., 119, 150
Bergem, A. L. M., 487, 488
Bergeman, C. S., 73
Bergen, D. J., 299
Berger, A. S., 495, 496, 497
Bergey, K. J., 514
Bergholz, T., 88
Bergman, A., 271
Bergman, M., 163
Berk, L. E., 189, 190, 201
Berkowitz, M. W., 356
Berliner, L., 319
Berman, A. L., 481, 482
Berman, W. H., 383
Bernal, M. E., 283
Berndt, T. J., 382, 383, 384, 385
Bernhardt, A., 450
Bernieri, F., 67
Bernstein, Anne C., 317
Berry, C. A., 389
Berry, J. W., 155, 156
Berscheid, E., 127, 389
Bertenthal, B. I., 121, 148, 272
Bertman, S. L., 513
Berzonsky, M. D., 282
Bess, F. H., 166
Best, Deborah L., 231, 298, 299, 302
Beyer, S., 452
Biaggio, A. M. B., 355
Bianchi, S. M., 422
Bidell, T., 150
Biederman, I., 223
Biederman, J., 470, 471, 472
Bierman, K. L., 382
Biesele, M., 8
Bifulco, A., 510, 517
Biggs, J., 230

Bigler, Rebecca S., 303, 325
Bijou, S. W., 38
Biller, H. B., 376, 399, 400, 401
Billing, L., 94
Binet, Alfred, 240
Bingham, K., 348
Birch, H. G., 273
Biringen, A., 367
Birmaher, B., 474
Birren, James E., 3, 134, 135, 162, 249
Bisanz, J., 213
Bishop, J. A., 56
Bishop, J. E., 74
Bishop, S. J., 100
Bivens, J. A., 190
Bixenstine, B. A., 385
Bixenstine, V. C., 385
Bizot, E. B., 448
Bjorklund, D. F., 177, 211, 214, 217, 218, 219,
    220, 222
Bjorkqvist, K., 299
Black, B., 381
Black, J. E., 114, 116, 136, 154
Black, K. N., 307, 400
Black, M. M., 469
Blackburn, J., 201
Blackburn, J. A., 184, 186
Blagg, N., 263
Blakemore, C., 154
Blakemore, J. E. O., 303
Blakeslee, S., 421
Blanchard-Fields, Fredda, 334, 483
Blasi, A., 280, 343, 346
Blass, E. M., 152
Blazer, D. G., 350, 485, 486
Blieszner, R., 389
Block, J., 259, 279, 421
Block, J. H., 259, 421
Bloom, Lois, 194
Blue, J., 424
Bluebond-Langner, Myra, 509
Blumstein, P., 418
Blyth, Dale A., 129, 442
Bodily, C. L., 292
Bodnar, J. C., 517
Bodrova, E., 188, 189, 201
Bogenschneider, K., 439, 440
Boggiano, A. K., 437
Bohannon, J. N., III, 196, 198
Bohannon, J. R., 511, 514
Bohlin, G., 368
Bohrnstedt, G., 127
Boismier, J. D., 119
Boldizar, J. P., 304, 315, 317
Boldt, J. S., 416
Bolger, K. E., 403
Bolh, Y., 195
Bolton, P., 255
Bonanno, G. A., 516
Bondareff, W., 115, 116
Bonvillian, J. D., 196, 198
Boodman, S. G., 137
Booth, A., 409, 418, 419, 421
Booth, C., 411
Borchardt, C. M., 473
Boris, N. W., 468
Borkowski, J. G., 411

Bornstein, Marc H., 145, 154, 243, 434
Borton, R. W., 153
Bosman, E. A., 135
Bossé, R., 387, 452, 453
Bottino, P. J., 61, 63
Botuck, S., 153
Botwinick, J., 224
Bouchard, Thomas J., Jr., 55, 67, 69
Bowen, R., 183
Bower, A. R., 515
Bower, T. G. R., 122, 149, 153
Bowers, W. A., 479
Bowlby, John, 362, 363, 364, 366, 367, 372,
    373, 376, 377, 388, 504–505, 506, 517
Bowles, T. V., 382
Boxer, A. M., 415
Boyle, C., 511
Brabeck, M., 354
Brackbill, Yvonne, 97
Brackett, D., 166
Bradbard, M. R., 312
Braddock, J. H., III, 442
Braden, J. P., 263
Bradley, C. F., 411
Bradley, Robert H., 106, 250, 251, 252
Braine, Martin D. S., 194, 195
Brambilla, D. J., 132
Brandtstädter, J., 285, 483
Braun, N., 424
Braungart, J. M., 272
Braver, S. L., 422
Bray, N. W., 218, 222
Brayfield, A., 400
Brazelton, T. Berry, 105
Breedlove, S. M., 305, 306, 307
Breitner, J. C. S., 488
Bremner, W. J., 130, 133
Brems, C., 511
Brennan, K. A., 388
Brent, S. B., 507, 508
Bretherton, I., 331, 363, 368
Bretz, R. D., 448
Bridges, L. J., 365, 366, 371
Brion-Meisels, S., 334
Bristol, M. M., 466, 467
Britt, G. C., 105
Broberg, A. G., 252, 374, 375
Brody, E. B., 245
Brody, Elaine M., 416
Brody, G. H., 344, 345, 407
Brody, N., 245, 310
Bromley, D. B., 275, 278, 332
Bronfenbrenner, Urie, 18, 44–47, 46, 48, 49,
    50, 76, 81, 100, 397, 532
Bronstein, P., 436
Brook, J. S., 386, 480
Brookover, W., 439
Brooks-Gunn, Jeanne, 26, 50, 103, 106, 127,
    255, 271, 275, 321, 322, 374, 409
Bross, D. C., 426
Broughton, J. M., 153
Broverman, I. K., 299
Brown, A. L., 218, 219, 222
Brown, Ann E., 222
Brown, B. B., 384, 385, 386, 409, 442, 445
Brown, E., 147
Brown, J. L., 119
Brown, R., 194, 197

Brown, Roger, 196
Brownell, C. A., 272, 377
Brownell, K. D., 478
Browning, Robert, 528
Bruck, M., 158
Brucken, L., 302
Bruggeman, E. L., 355
Bruner, Jerome, 188, 189, 198
Bryan, J., 228
Bryant, D. M., 397
Bryant, W. K., 452
Bryden, M. P., 299
Bryk, A. S., 310
Bryson, S. E., 467
Buchanan, C. M., 127
Buchanan, N. R., 377
Buehler, C. A., 422
Buell, S. J., 116
Bugental, D. B., 424
Buhrmester, D., 364, 378, 382, 383, 384, 385,
    407, 408, 414, 415, 470
Bukowski, W. M., 381
Bukstein, O., 479
Bulterys, M. G., 92
Bumpass, L. L., 398, 417
Burchinal, M. R., 397, 437
Burhans, K. K., 435
Burlingham, 506
Burman, B., 401
Burnham, D. K., 301
Burns, G. L., 515
Burns, G. W., 61, 63
Burton, Linda M., 8, 397, 398, 399, 413, 416,
    417
Burton, Roger V., 340, 343, 344
Busch-Rossnagel, N. A., 433
Buskirk, E. R., 129
Buss, Arnold, 69, 272
Buss, David M., 57, 306
Busse, E. W., 247
Bussey, K., 303, 342
Butler, R., 437
Butler, R. N., 162, 275, 276, 291, 292
Butterfield, E. C., 152
Buysse, V., 440
Byne, W., 321
Byrd, J. E., 89, 91
Byrd, T., 310
Byrnes, J. P., 213, 223

Cabaniss, M. L., 75
Cacioppo, J. T., 390
Caddell, D. P., 497
Cahan, S., 299
Cairns, R. B., 382
Caldera, Y. M., 302
Caldwell, Bettye M., 250, 251
Caldwell, P., 98
Call, K. T., 444
Callanan, M. A., 408
Camara, K. A., 419
Camp, C., 483
Camp, Cameron J., 225, 231
Campbell, E., 284
Campbell, F. A., 252, 262, 374, 437
Campbell, Keith, 83
Campbell, M., 467, 468
Campbell, S. B., 100, 376

Campione, J. C., 241
Campos, J. J., 121
Campos, Joseph J., 148
Canfield, R. L., 150
Cantor, N., 454
Cantwell, D. P., 471, 472
Capelli, C. A., 181
Cappeliez, P., 291
Capps, L., 466
Capute, A. J., 85
Carels, R. A., 440
Carey, G., 348
Carey, J., 82
Carey, S., 195
Carlson, G. A., 474
Carlson, S. M., 175, 331
Carlson, V., 371
Carmichael, C. M., 286
Carper, R., 112
Carr, M. B., 304
Carriger, M. S., 243, 272
Carroll, J. B., 238
Carsrud, A. L., 446
Carsten, O., 161
Carstensen, Laura L., 285, 387, 414, 417, 455
Carter, D. B., 303
Cartwright, B. S., 175
Case, Robbie, 115, 217, 218, 245
Caserta, M. S., 520
Casey, R. J., 340
Cash, T. F., 478
Casper, R., 477
Caspi, Avshalom, 187, 277, 287, 288, 414, 475
Cassidy, D. J., 219
Cassidy, J., 375, 376, 433
Castle, J. M., 159
Catalano, R., 483
Cattell, Raymond B., 238
Catz, C. S., 103
Cauffman, E., 478
Cavanaugh, J. C., 224, 226, 227
Cazden, Courtney, 196
Ceci, S. J., 44, 76, 438, 445
Cefalo, R. C., 75
Centers for Disease Control, 322
Cernoch, J. M., 153
Cesario, T. C., 501, 502
Chadwick, B. A., 398, 399, 417
Chaisson, R., 91
Chalmers, B., 98
Champaud, C., 195
Chance, G., 149
Chandler, M., 331
Chandler, M. J., 88, 96, 249
Chandler, S., 100
Chao, Ruth K., 404
Chap, J. B., 349
Chapman, A. J., 181
Chapman, M., 179
Chapman, R. S., 193
Charlesworth, W. R., 9, 56
Charman, T., 467
Charness, Neil, 260
Chase, W. G., 223
Chase-Lansdale, P. L., 420
Chassin, L., 127
Chatters, L., 285
Chen, C., 409, 455, 456

Chen, D., 166
Chen, J. Q., 238
Chen, M. D., 515, 517
Chen, X., 381, 408, 416
Cherlin, Andrew J., 413, 420, 421
Cherry, K. E., 136
Chescheir, N. C., 75
Chess, Stella, 273, 274, 532
Chi, Michelene T. H., 219, 223
Chilamkurti, C., 332
Chinsky, J. M., 218
Chmiel, S., 354
Chomsky, Noam, 195, 197
Christopher, J. S., 391
Cicchetti, D., 425, 480, 485
Cicirelli, Victor, 415, 417, 423
Cillessen, A. H., 381
Clark, C. L., 388
Clark, D. C., 511
Clark, D. O., 131, 454
Clark, E. V., 193, 194
Clark, H. H., 193, 194
Clark, J. L., 155
Clark, L. A., 464, 470
Clark, R. A., 431
Clark, R. D., III, 341
Clarke, A. S., 88
Clarke, S. C., 97
Clarke-Stewart, A., 374, 375, 436, 438
Clark-Lempers, D. S., 383, 408
Clarkson, B. H., 134
Clarkson, M. G., 150
Clausen, J. A., 452
Clavien, H., 136
Clayton, P. J., 510
Clayton, V. P., 249
Cleiren, M. P. H. D., 506, 512, 513, 515, 516, 517
Clements, M., 323
Clifton, R. K., 215
Clingempeel, W. G., 413, 420, 421
Clum, G. A., 482
Coates, B., 211
Coats, P. B., 309
Cohen, D., 487
Cohen, P., 480
Cohler, B. J., 284
Cohn, J. F., 376
Coie, J. D., 347, 380, 381, 382
Coke, M. M., 350
Col, N. F., 133
Colapinto, J., 308
Colbert, K. K., 186
Colburn, D., 92, 105, 497, 518
Colby, A., 336, 337, 341, 345, 346, 349, 350, 355
Cole, A. K., 373
Cole, P. M., 319, 340, 365, 490
Cole, T. R., 7
Colella, U., 418
Coleman, James, 442
Coleman, L. J., 256
Coleman, P., 285, 286
Coleman, P. D., 116
Coles, R., 283
Colin, V., 372, 387, 388
Colley, A., 310
Comer, James, 438, 439, 456–457

Comfort, Alex, 324
Committee on Adolescence, 462, 481, 482
Commons, M. L., 185, 186
Compas, B. E., 473
Comstock, G. W., 512
Condon, J. T., 132
Condry, J., 301
Condry, S., 301
Conger, Rand D., 403–404
Connell, J. P., 365
Connidis, I. A., 387, 390, 415
Connolly, J. A., 279, 380
Connolly, J. J., 286
Connolly, K. J., 155
Connor, J. R., Jr., 116
Coohey, C., 424
Cook, A. S., 498
Cook, K. V., 301
Cook, M. L., 122
Cooke, L. M., 56
Cooksey, E. C., 400
Cooley, Charles, 272
Cooney, T. M., 413
Cooper, B. A. B., 354
Cooper, C. R., 284, 409, 444
Cooper, H. M., 432
Cooper, R. P., 198
Coopersmith, S., 277
Copeland, D. R., 509
Coppotelli, H., 380
Corah, N. L., 96
Corbin, C., 124
Corder, L., 138
Coren, Stanley, 115
Corley, R., 73
Cornelius, S. W., 187, 247
Cornell, D. P., 316
Corns, K. M., 406
Corr, C. A., 503, 510, 519
Corr, D. M., 519
Corrigan, R., 434
Corso, J. F., 167
Corwin, J., 164
Costa, F. M., 479
Costa, Paul T., Jr., 261, 269, 286, 287, 288, 449, 483, 484
Costos, D., 415
Cote, J. E., 284
Cotterell, J. L., 45
Coulton, C. J., 424
Council, J. R., 478
Courage, M. L., 216, 217
Courchesne, E., 467
Coverly, Dave, 415
Cowan, C. P., 314, 410
Cowan, G., 300
Cowan, Philip A., 314, 317
Cowan, W. M., 112
Coward, R. T., 416
Cowart, B. J., 163
Cowley, G., 91
Cox, C. M., 236
Cox, M., 380
Cox, M. J., 400, 401
Cox, R., 380
Cox, T. H., 450
Coyle, N., 483
Coyne, J. C., 485

Crago, M., 477
Crain, R. M., 280, 283
Crandall, V. C., 431, 432
Creehan, P. A., 91, 97
Crews, F., 33
Crick, N. R., 299, 346, 347, 348
Crijnen, A. A. M., 469
Cristofalo, V. J., 130, 499, 500, 501
Crnic, Keith, 13, 374, 375, 411
Crockenberg, S., 251, 340, 375, 406
Crockett, L. J., 321
Croft, K., 177
Cromer, C. C., 378
Cronbach, Lee J., 440
Crook, C. K., 152
Crook, T. H., 225
Crook, W. G., 470
Cross, C. E., 10
Crouter, A. C., 304, 309, 409, 451
Crouter, Ann, 81
Crowell, J. A., 367
Crowley, M., 474
Cruzcosa, M., 424
Crystal, D. S., 455
Cuellar, Jose, 12
Cuisinier, M. C. J., 514
Culp, R. E., 426
Cultice, J. C., 218
Culver, L. C., 446
Cumming, E., 454
Cummings, E. M., 390
Cunningham, D. A., 134
Cunningham, H., 5
Cunningham, W. R., 246
Curry, N. E., 380
Curtiss, S., 81
Cushman, L., 411
Custer, W. L., 331
Cutter, J., 503
Cytron, B. D., 498
Cytryn, L., 468, 473, 474, 486

Dabbs, J. M., 307
Daglish, L., 302
Daher, M., 152
Dale, P. S., 195
Damast, A. M., 434
Damon, William, 275, 276, 278, 293, 302–303, 346
Damphouse, K. R., 445
Dancer, L. S., 451
D'Andrade, R., 436
Daniels, Denise, 69
Daniels, D. H., 431
Dannemiller, James, 147
Darby, B. L., 94
Darling, C. A., 321
Darling, N., 401
Darlington, Richard, 262
Darwin, Charles, 9, 56
Davidson, A., 411
Davidson, A. L., 442
Davidson, J., 308
Davidson, J. K., 321
Davies, B., 514
Davies, G. T., 130
Davies, L., 387, 390
Davies, Mark, 479

Davis, A. C., 162
Davis, C. D., 490
Davis, M. A., 137
Davison, M. L., 355
Dawson, D. A., 479
Day, J. D., 241, 256
Deagle, E. A., 478
Deal, J., 474
Deater-Deckard, K., 344, 404
Deaux, K., 300
DeBaryshe, B. D., 349
DeBerry, K. M., 283
De Boysson-Bardies, B., 191
DeCasper, Anthony, 151, 152
DeCorte, M. S., 385
DeFrain, J. D., 515, 518
DeFries, J. C., 59, 72, 73
DeGarmo, D. S., 512, 517
De Gaston, J. P., 322
Dehaene, P., 93
De Jong-Gierveld, J., 390
De Lisi, Richard, 184
DeLoache, J. S., 219
Demarest, J., 310
DeMaris, A., 418, 485
DeMause, L., 5
Dement, W. C., 119
Demo, D. H., 418
Dempster, F. N., 218
Denham, S. A., 365
Denney, Nancy W., 186–187, 224, 229, 230
Dennis, Wayne, 261
Depner, C. E., 387
Derby, J. F., 513
DeRosier, M. E., 382
Derryberry, D., 272
Dery, G. K., 132
Descartes, Rene, 143
Desjardins, R. N., 150, 151, 191
Dessonville, C., 485
Detmer, C. M., 512
Deutsch, C. K., 471
Deveau, E. J., 510, 514
Devenny, D. A., 256
De Villiers, J. G., 193
De Villiers, P. A., 193
DeVos, J., 174
De Vries, B., 352, 506, 514, 517, 518
DeVries, M. W., 274
De Wolff, M. S., 371, 372, 376
Dews, S., 181
Diamond, A., 174
Diamond, M. C., 116
Diamond, Milton, 308
Dias, M. G., 353
Diaz, J., 85, 92, 93, 94
DiBattista, D., 472
Dickens, W. J., 382
Dickinson, G. E., 507
Dick-Read, Grantly, 104
Dickson, F. C., 414
Didow, S. M., 377
Diehl, M., 483
Digman, J. M., 269
DiLalla, L. F., 273
Dilworth-Anderson, P., 398, 417
DiMatteo, M. R., 97
DiPietro, Janet A., 85, 300

Dishion, T. J., 349, 386, 409
Disney, E. R., 93
Dittman, R. W., 306, 321
Dixon, R. A., 47, 227, 228, 230, 248
Dixon, S., 365
Dobson, W. R., 284
Dodge, Kenneth A., 209, 346–348, 356, 380, 381
Dolen, L. S., 334
Dollberg, S., 88
Domjan, M. J., 209
Donaldson, G. A., 383
Donenberg, G., 467
Donnelly, D., 324
Donovan, J. E., 479
Dooley, D., 483
Doris, John, 425
Dornbusch, S. M., 422, 442, 444
Doty, R. L., 163
Dougherty, T. M., 243
Douglas, K., 287
Douvan, E., 383
Dowden, A., 211
Dowling, W., 350
Downey, J., 64
Doyle, A. B., 380
Doyle, G. C., 448
Draper, P., 57
Drebing, C. E., 447, 448, 450
Dreyer, Philip, 321, 322
Droege, K. L., 332
Dubas, J. S., 128, 129
Dublin, L. I., 6
Dubow, E., 252
Dulcan, M., 469, 471
Duncan, Greg, 255
Duncan, Pam, 115
Duncan, P. D., 127
Dunn, Judy, 68, 69, 331, 332, 406, 407
Dunn, T. R., 448
Dunphy, Dexter, 384, 385
Dunsmore, J. C., 510
Durand, C., 191
Dustman, Robert E., 134, 138
Duvall, Evelyn M., 397, 398
Duyvesteyn, M. G. C., 390
Dweck, Carol S., 332, 435, 437
Dworkin, D. S., 498
Dwyer, J. W., 416
Dyer, K. F., 130
Dyk, P. H., 290
Dywan, J., 115, 162
Dziuba-Leatherman, J., 422, 424

Eagly, A. H., 299, 300, 316
Earles, J. L., 134
Earles, J. L. K., 224, 226, 228
Easley, J. A., Jr., 201
East, P. L., 407
Easterbrooks, M. A., 272
Eaton, W. O., 300
Ebersole, P., 448
Eccles, Jacquelynne S., 127, 276, 301, 309, 310, 386, 421, 431, 441, 442, 443, 532
Eckenrode, John, 425
Eckerman, C. O., 377
Eckert, E. D., 479
Ecklund-Flores, L., 151

Edelbrock, C. S., 469
Edelman, C. L., 91
Eder, R. A., 275
Edgell, D., 85, 112
Edwards, C. P., 298, 303
Edwards, J. N., 412
Edwards, L., 349
Edwards, M., 96, 105
Egeland, Byron, 424, 425
Egerton, J., 396
Eggebeen, D. J., 399
Ehrhardt, Anke A., 305, 306, 307, 308, 313
Eichen, E. B., 166
Eichorn, D. H., 124, 243, 245
Eiler, J., 485
Eimas, Peter D., 149–150, 191
Eisen, Marvin, 278
Eisenberg, M., 374
Eisenberg, N., 300, 346
Eisenberg, R., 435
Ekerdt, David J., 452, 453, 454
Elder, Glen H., Jr., 10, 277, 413
Eldred, L., 91
Elias, James, 318
Elicker, J., 373
Elizur, E., 517
El-Khorazaty, M. N., 398
Elkind, David, 5, 182–183, 436
Ellard, J. H., 518
Elliott, D. S., 348
Elliott, Elaine S., 435, 437
Ellis, L., 320
Ellis, Sharri, 378
Elmen, J. D., 436
Ely, R., 181, 195
Emde, R. N., 33, 34, 336, 340
Emerson, Peggy E., 367, 368, 370
Emery, R. E., 410, 414, 418, 422
Emory, E. K., 97
Emslie, G. J., 474
Engedal, K., 487
England, P., 450
Englander-Golden, P., 132
Englund, M., 373
Enns, L. R., 300
Enright, R., 183
Ensminger, M. E., 445
Entwisle, D. R., 440
Eppler, M. A., 155
Erdley, C. A., 435
Erdwins, C. J., 446
Erel, O., 401
Erickson, M. F., 424
Ericsson, K. Anders, 223, 260
Erikson, Erik, 34–36, 49, 249, 269, 270, 280, 281, 283, 284, 288–292, 371, 387, 412, 447, 511, 524, 526, 528
Erikson, J. M., 291
Ernst, L., 518
Escalona, S., 243
Essa, E. L., 507, 508, 509
Estes, L. S., 477
Etaugh, C., 443
Evans, D. R., 453
Evans, K., 479
Evans, L., 452
Evans, S., 75
Everett, B. H., 177

Fabes, R. A., 299, 300
Fagan, J. F., 146
Fagan, J. F., Jr., 215
Fagot, Beverly I., 301, 303, 309, 377, 405
Falbo, T., 408, 414
Falck, V. T., 514
Falek, A., 74
Fallon, B. J., 382
Faloon, S., 223
Fantz, Robert L., 145, 146
Farkas, K., 93
Farkas, M. S., 162
Farrell, M. P., 448
Farver, Jo Ann, 379
Faulkner, K. W., 509
Faust, M. S., 129
Featherman, D. L., 445
Feeney, J. A., 387, 388
Fegley, S., 444
Feij, J. A., 288
Fein, G. G., 93, 94, 380
Feingold, A., 299, 300
Feingold, Benjamin, 472
Feinman, S., 365
Feld, Sheila, 446
Feldlaufer, H., 442
Feldman, David, 260
Feldman, Harold, 412, 414
Feldman, J. F., 243
Feldman, R. D., 257
Feldman, Shirley S., 316, 367
Felson, R. B., 277
Felstein, I., 324
Felton, B. J., 389
Fentress, J. C., 118
Fenwick, K. D., 149
Fergusson, D. M., 471
Ferligoj, A., 444
Fernald, A., 198
Feuerstein, Reuven, 241
Fiano, K., 97
Field, D., 201, 287, 291, 415
Field, J., 118, 149
Field, P. A., 100
Field, T., 100, 105, 153, 426, 468
Field, T. M., 367
Fifer, William, 151
Figueredo, A. J., 423
Filipp, S. H., 446
Finch, M. D., 285
Fincham, F. D., 422, 437
Fincher, J., 256
Findlay, I., 75
Findley, M. J., 432
Fine, M. A., 421
Fingerman, K. L., 415
Finitzo, T., 155
Finkelhor, David, 209, 319, 422, 424
Finlay, B. L., 113
Finn, S. E., 286
Finn-Stevenson, M. F., 403, 426, 437, 457
Fischer, C. S., 387
Fischer, E. F., 388
Fischer, J. L., 290
Fischer, K., 446, 455
Fischer, Kurt W., 150, 174, 184, 186, 188, 272, 389, 490

Fischer, M., 471
Fischer, W. F., 344
Fisher, C., 191
Fisher, E. P., 380
Fisher, L., 373
Fisher, L. M., 134
Fisher, M. A., 256
Fisher, S., 33
FitzGerald, D. P., 383
Fivush, R., 217
Flaks, D. K., 418
Flavell, E. R., 177
Flavell, John H., 171, 177, 187, 217, 218, 219, 329, 530
Fleeson, W., 285
Fletcher, K. L., 218
Flint, Marcia, 133
Floderus-Myrhed, B., 287
Flood, D. G., 116
Florian, V., 508
Floyd, M., 231
Flynn, C. P., 209
Flynn, James, 252
Foege, W. H., 138
Foley, H. J., 145, 149
Folkers, E., 404
Folkman, S., 482, 483
Follmer, A., 397
Foltz, C., 272
Fombonne, E., 473
Fonagy, P., 389
Fondell, M. M., 400
Foorman, B. R., 159
Ford, Clellan S., 317, 318
Ford, L. H., 275
Ford, M. E., 433
Fordham, Signithia, 283, 442
Forman, E. R., 334
Forrest, J. D., 321, 322
Fortin, M., 163
Fowler, 438
Fowler, James, 350
Fox, N. A., 375
Fozard, J. L., 160, 163
Fraley, R. C., 388
Francis, D. J., 158
Frankel, K. A., 433
Frankie, G., 308
Franklin, C., 50
Franklin, M. B., 130
Franks, M. M., 417
Fraser, B. J., 438
Frauenglass, S., 480
Fredrickson, B. L., 485
Fredriksen, K. I., 515
Freedland, R. L., 121
Freedle, R., 192
Freeman, C. P., 477
Freeman, R., 479
Freier, K., 93
French, K. E., 128, 129
Freneau, P. J., 412
Freud, 506
Freud, Anna, 34
Freud, Sigmund, 30–34, 49, 217, 268–269, 307, 317, 335–336, 362, 364, 376, 490, 531, 533
Freund, Alexandra, 285

Freund, Lisa, 201
Frey, K. S., 275, 276, 309, 312
Friberg, L., 67
Fried, P. A., 92, 94
Friedman, J. M., 89, 91, 94
Friedman, S. B., 215
Friedrich, Lynette, 17–18
Frieze, I. H., 310, 444
Frisby, C. L., 263
Frisch, R. E., 127
Frith, Uta, 329, 466
Fritz, A. S., 331
Fritz, J., 404
Frodi, A. M., 424
Fromhoff, F. A., 217
Frueh, T., 311
Fry, A. F., 227
Fry, Christine, 7, 8
Fry, P. S., 454, 515
Fryauf-Bertschy, H., 165, 166
Fuhrer, R., 389
Fukumoto, A., 340
Fulcomer, M. C., 416
Fuligni, A. J., 386, 456
Fulker, D. W., 73
Fuller, B., 375
Fullerton, C. S., 384
Fullerton, J. T., 105
Furman, E., 506
Furman, W., 364, 378, 381, 382, 383, 385, 390, 407, 408, 414, 415
Furstenberg, Frank F., Jr., 26, 49, 50, 321, 322, 413

Gabiano, C., 91
Gabreels, F., 256
Gaddis, A., 127
Gahler, M., 420
Galambos, N. L., 304, 403, 408
Gall, T. L., 453, 454
Gallagher, J. D., 125
Gallagher, J. M., 201
Gallimore, R., 407
Gallo, J. J., 485
Gallup, G. G., Jr., 272
Galuska, D. A., 137
Gamble, W. C., 407
Gambria, L. M., 291
Ganchrow, J. R., 152
Gandelman, R., 57, 306, 380
Ganor, Y., 299
Garbarino, James, 396, 424
Garber, J., 468, 473, 481, 486
Garcia, J. L., 423
Gard, M. C. E., 477
Gardner, Howard, 213, 238–239, 259, 260
Gardner, Lytt, 468–469
Gardner, R. A., 489
Garland, A., 481
Garmezy, Norman, 103, 476
Garmon, L. C., 354
Garnets, L., 320
Gatz, M., 487, 490
Gautier, T., 308
Gauvain, M., 202, 382
Gauze, C., 382
Ge, X. J., 402, 405, 406, 474, 481
Gebhard, Paul, 318

Gelfand, D. M., 468, 489
Geller, J., 478
Gelles, Richard J., 422, 424, 425
Gelman, J., 150
Gelman, Rochel, 177, 179, 198
Gelman, S. A., 149, 177, 193
Gendell, M., 452
Genetics Working Group, 58, 76
George, Carol, 425
George, T. P., 382, 384
Gershoni, R., 384
Gervai, J., 310
Getzels, J. W., 258, 259
Gewirtz, J. L., 39, 208
Giambra, L. M., 324
Gibbs, J., 337
Gibbs, J. C., 346, 352, 354, 356
Gibson, Eleanor J., 147–148, 155, 157, 158
Gibson, J. J., 158
Gigy, L., 419, 420
Gil, D. G., 424
Gilbert, A. N., 164
Gilbert, L. A., 451
Gilbert, N., 424
Gilens, M., 452
Gilewski, M. J., 517
Gillberg, C., 467, 471
Gilligan, Carol, 354
Gilmore, R. O., 147
Gilstrap, B., 401
Ginn, J., 324, 454
Ginsburg, A. P., 146
Ginsburg, G. S., 436
Ginzberg, Eli, 443
Girard, C., 481
Girgus, J. S., 481
Gjerde, P. F., 421
Glantz, L. H., 21
Glaser, B. G., 503
Glaser, R., 223
Glasgow, K. L., 404, 436
Glassman, M., 189
Gleason, J. K., 192, 193
Glenn, N. D., 418
Glick, J. C., 187
Glick, M., 276
Glick, P. C., 399
Glicksman, A., 165
Glodis, K., 280
Gnepp, J., 332, 334
Goebel, A. E., 511
Goetz, L., 440
Goffiner, J. M., 166
Goldberg, A. P., 131, 135, 136
Goldberg, E. L., 512
Goldberg, G. R., 89
Goldberg, S., 99, 372
Goldberg, W. A., 452
Goldfarb, William, 372, 373
Goldfield, B., 193
Goldfield, Eugene, 123
Goldman, J., 317
Goldman, R., 317
Goldman, S. H., 448
Goldsmith, D., 101
Goldsmith, H. H., 372
Goldston, D., 474
Golombok, Susan, 83, 320, 418

Golub, M., 89
Gooden, W. E., 447, 448
Goodman, M., 75
Goodnow, J. J., 344, 345
Goodwyn, S., 192
Goossens, L., 230
Gopnik, A., 187, 331
Gordon, B. N., 317
Gordon, D. E., 380
Gordon, J., 519
Gordon, P., 198
Gordon, R. A., 477
Gorman, J., 469
Gortmaker, S. L., 137
Gotlib, I. H., 99, 468, 473, 486
Gottesman, I. I., 69
Gottfredson, Linda S., 245, 443, 444
Gottfried, A. E., 252, 451
Gottfried, A. W., 244, 251, 252, 256, 277
Gottlieb, Gilbert, 57, 59, 76, 106
Gottlieb, L. N., 513, 514
Gottlieb, S. E., 96
Gottman, J., 419
Gottman, J. M., 382, 414
Goy, R. W., 307
Graber, J. A., 128, 478
Graber, Marcia, 174
Grady, J. G., 224
Graf, P., 225, 250
Graham, S., 356
Graham-Pole, J., 515
Gralinski, H., 275
Gralinski, J. H., 340, 435
Grandin, Temple, 330
Grant, B. F., 479
Grave, G. D., 103
Gray, J. T., 217
Gray, S. W., 262
Gray, W. M., 183
Gray-Little, B., 440
Green, M., 336, 510
Green, Richard, 320
Green, S. K., 387
Green, W. H., 468
Greenberg, M., 99, 100
Greenberg, R. P., 33
Greenberger, A., 409
Greenberger, E., 444, 451, 452
Greene, A. L., 415
Greene, J. G., 132
Greene, K., 183
Greene, R. W., 471
Greenfield, P. M., 192, 197
Greenhaus, J. H., 450
Greenland, S., 92
Greenough, William T., 114, 116, 154
Greenwald, R., 438
Gregg, V., 346
Greif, E. B., 127
Greve, W., 285
Grilo, C. M., 70, 137
Grinder, R. E., 343, 355
Grober, E., 487
Grodin, M., 21
Grodsky, A., 324
Grodstein, F., 133
Grollman, E. A., 507
Grolnick, W. J., 365, 366, 371, 436

Gross, M. D., 472
Gross, S., 241
Grossman, F. K., 410
Grossman, G., 469
Grossman, K., 367
Grotevant, H. D., 284, 409, 444
Gruber, H. E., 41
Gruber-Baldini, A. L., 248, 414
Grusec, J. E., 39, 344, 345
Grych, J. H., 422
Guacci, N., 361
Guacci-Franco, N., 361
Guerin, D., 277
Guerra, Nancy G., 347, 356, 357
Guilford, J. P., 237, 258
Gulko, J., 302
Gunderson, S. A., 257
Gunnarson, A. D., 155
Guralnik, J. M., 137, 138
Gurland, B., 488
Gusella, James, 74
Gutek, B. A., 450
Gutmann, David, 315, 316
Guttentag, R. E., 224, 227
Guyer, B., 92

Haan, Norma, 3, 287, 354
Haas-Hawkings, G., 517
Haber, D., 130, 136, 137, 138
Haertel, G. D., 438
Hagan, R., 303
Hagberg, J. M., 131, 135, 136
Hagekull, B., 368
Hagen, E. P., 241
Hagestad, Gunhild, 413
Haggstrom, G., 451
Haidt, J., 353, 354
Haight, B. K., 291
Hainline, L., 145, 146, 147, 153
Haith, Marshall M., 118, 148, 150, 243
Hala, S., 331
Halberstadt, A. G., 315, 365
Hale, S., 134, 227
Haley, W. E., 416
Hall, C. S., 30
Hall, G. Stanley, 9–10, 279–280, 476
Hall, J. A., 315
Hall, L. K., 225
Hall, S. K., 317
Halpern, L. F., 119
Halverson, Charles F., Jr., 269, 300, 311, 312, 313, 315, 474
Halverson, H. M., 122
Ham, M., 481
Hamer, Dean, 320
Hamilton, V. L., 310
Hamm, A. C., 94
Hammen, C. L., 468, 473, 486
Hampson, J., 192
Handcock, M. S., 450
Hanlon, C., 197
Hans, S. L., 348
Hansen, D. J., 391, 425
Hanson, K., 444, 453
Hansson, R. O., 449, 450, 453
Hanushek, E. A., 438, 439
Happé, F. G. E., 467
Harkins, E. B., 412

Harkins, S. W., 134
Harkness, Sara, 101–102
Harley, J. P., 472
Harlow, Harry F., 370
Harlow, R. E., 454
Harlow, S. D., 512
Harman, S. M., 131, 133
Harmon, R. J., 272, 433
Harmon, T. M., 105
Harold, G. T., 421
Harold, R. D., 301
Harquail, C. V., 450
Harrell, M. S., 246
Harrell, T. W., 246
Harrington, A. F., 311
Harrington, D. M., 259
Harrington, R., 473
Harris, J. R., 131, 363, 500, 532
Harris, Judith, 382
Harris, M., 198
Harris, M. B., 301
Harris, M. J., 67
Harris, P. L., 331, 379
Harris, T., 510, 517
Harrist, A. W., 381
Hart, C. H., 381
Hart, D., 275, 276, 278, 346, 354
Hart, E. L., 472
Hart, K. J., 355
Harter, Susan, 276, 277, 278, 279, 280, 292, 441
Hartley, A. A., 162
Hartman, B. T., 163
Hartmann, D. P., 382, 384
Hartshorne, Hugh, 343
Hartup, W. W., 211, 277, 382, 385, 389
Harvey, S., 105
Hasher, L., 162
Hashima, P. Y., 397
Haskett, M. E., 424, 425
Hassinger, M., 485
Hatch, L. R., 350
Hatch, Thomas, 177–178
Hatcher, R. P., 106
Hattie, J., 230, 276, 293
Hauspie, R. C., 119
Havemann, J., 321, 322
Havighurst, R. J., 452, 454
Haviland, J. M., 485
Hawley, T. L., 93
Haxby, J. V., 488
Hay, D. F., 377
Hay, W. W., Jr., 103
Hayflick, Leonard, 500
Hayne, H., 211
Hays, J. C., 517
Hayward, C., 129
Haywood, K. M., 124
Hazan, Cindy, 388
Heath, D. T., 404
Heath, G. W., 138
Heaton, T. B., 398, 417
Hebb, D. O., 71
Hechtman, L. T., 471
Heckhausen, J., 285, 292, 430, 456
Hedges, L. V., 438
Hedlund, B., 448
Heffer, R. W., 469

Heinonen, O. P., 89, 94
Heller, K., 416
Helmreich, R. L., 315, 446
Helms, J. E., 8, 253
Helson, R., 287, 316
Helwig, C. C., 342
Heming, G., 314
Hencke, R. W., 174
Henderson, C. R., Jr., 104
Henderson, V. W., 133
Henker, B., 300
Henry, W. E., 454
Henshaw, S. K., 26
Herbener, E. S., 414
Herdt, G. H., 111, 308, 318
Herkowitz, J., 124, 130
Herman, C. P., 478
Herman-Giddens, Marcia, 125
Hermelin, B., 239
Hermer, L., 148
Hernandez, D. J., 398, 399
Herrera, M. G., 89
Herring, C., 450
Herrnstein, Richard J., 253, 254
Hersh, R. E., 222
Hershey, S. W., 310
Hertsgaard, L., 370
Hertzog, C., 226
Herzog, A. R., 452, 453
Hespos, Susan, 150
Hess, T. M., 225, 229, 334
Hesser, J., 407
Heston, L. L., 69, 486, 487, 488
Hetherington, E. M., 73, 308, 380, 399, 419, 420, 421, 422
Hetu, R., 163
Hewlett, B. S., 400
Hickey, P. R., 153
Hicks, M. W., 321
Hickson, J., 511
Higgins, A., 356
Higgins, D. A., 299
Higgins, E. T., 304, 435
Hildebrandt, K. A., 103
Hill, J. C., 470
Hill, J. P., 304, 305, 409
Hill, P., 476
Hill, R., 397
Hill, S. D., 272
Hilsman, R., 486
Hinde, R. A., 56
Hines, M., 306
Hingson, R., 26
Hinshaw, S. P., 471
Hinton, John, 504
Hinz, L. D., 477
Hirsch, B., 285
Hirsch-Pasek, K., 436
Hjertholm, E., 190
Hoagwood, K., 490
Hobbes, Thomas, 28
Hobbs, F. B., 131, 398, 414
Hodapp, R. M., 255, 256
Hodes, R. J., 500
Hodges, J., 373
Hodgson, J. W., 290
Hodnett, E. D., 98
Hoff-Ginsberg, E., 191, 192, 194, 195, 200

Hoffman, L. W., 69, 303, 410, 452
Hoffman, M., 286
Hoffman, Martin L., 341, 344, 345
Hoffman, S. I., 507
Hofman, J. E., 384
Hofmann, V., 373
Hogarty, P. S., 243, 244
Hokoda, A., 437
Holahan, C. J., 486
Holahan, C. K., 258
Holden, C., 372
Holden, D. J., 218
Holland, John, 443, 444
Hollander, D., 501
Holliday, S. G., 249
Holloway, S. D., 375
Holmbeck, G. N., 183, 409
Holroyd, S., 466
Honzik, M. P., 243, 244, 245
Hoogduin, K. A. L., 514
Hooker, K., 446
Hooper, F. H., 186
Hooper, J. O., 186
Hooper, S. R., 467, 471
Hopkins, Brian, 122–123
Hopkins, J. R., 34
Hopwood, N. J., 127
Horn, J. M., 250
Horn, John L., 238, 247
Horney, Karen, 34
Horowitz, L. M., 388
Horwitz, A. V., 485
House, B. J., 217
Housley, W. F., 511
Houx, P. J., 136, 227
Howard, B. H., 501
Howard, D. V., 225
Howard, J., 453
Howard, K. I., 408
Howe, C., 92
Howe, G. W., 73
Howe, M. L., 216, 217
Howe, N., 406
Howell, N., 8
Howes, C., 374, 377, 378, 379, 382
Howes, P., 367, 401
Howieson, D. B., 487
Howieson, N., 259
Hoyer, William J., 162
Hoyle, S. G., 382
Hoyt, D. R., 417
Hrncir, E. J., 433
Hsu, L. K. G., 477, 478
Hubel, David H., 114, 154
Hubert, N. C., 471
Huck, S. M., 417
Hudley, C., 356
Hudson, L. M., 183, 334
Hudson, Margaret F., 423
Huesmann, L. R., 348
Huguley, S., 423
Hulicka, I. M., 228
Hultsch, D. F., 226
Humphrey, H. E., 95
Humphrey, Laura L., 478
Hunt, J. M., 252
Hunt, J. V., 245
Hunt, K. W., 195

Hunt, P., 440
Hunter, J. E., 245
Hunter, R. F., 245
Huntington, R., 496, 497
Huston, A. C., 301, 302
Huston, M., 418
Huston, Ted L., 314, 409
Hutcheson, J. J., 469
Hutchinson, J. E., 220
Hutt, S. J., 119
Huttenlocher, J., 150
Huttenlocher, P. R., 113
Hutti, M. H., 514
Hutton, N., 91
Hyde, Janet S., 299, 300, 321
Hynan, M. T., 105
Hyson, M. C., 436

Iacono, W. G., 70
Igra, V., 479, 480
Imperato-McGinley, J., 308
Ingersoll-Dayton, B., 387
Ingoldsby, B. B., 409
Ingrassia, M., 329, 361
Inhelder, Barbel, 42, 177, 184, 221
Intons-Peterson, M. J., 297
Irion, J. C., 483
Irish, D. P., 498
Irwin, C. E., Jr., 479, 480
Irwin, R. R., 186
Isaacs, K. R., 116
Isabella, L. A., 448
Isabella, R. A., 367, 371, 411
Ito, M., 115
Ivey, P. K., 8, 373
Izard, Carroll, 364

Jacklin, Carol N., 299, 300, 301, 303, 306,
    308, 400
Jackson, J. S., 389
Jackson, P. W., 258, 259
Jacobs, J. E., 301, 309
Jacobs, S. C., 505, 506, 515, 517, 519
Jacobsen, T., 373
Jacobson, C. K., 398
Jacobson, Joseph L., 93–94, 95
Jacobson, S. W., 93–94, 95
Jacobvitz, D., 424, 471
Jagers, R. J., 348
Jahnke, H. C., 483
James, Alice, 529
James, L. S., 97
James, William, 144, 153
Jancar, J., 256
Jankowiak, W. R., 388
Janos, P. M., 257
Janowsky, J. S., 112, 113
Janssen, H. J. E. M., 514
Jaquish, G. A., 262
Jarvik, J. F., 485
Jarvik, L. F., 68, 247
Jazwinski, S. M., 501
Jeffery, P. M., 98
Jeffery, R., 98
Jenkins, J. M., 331
Jenkins, S. R., 448, 451
Jensen, Arthur R., 223, 244, 247, 254, 262
Jensen, L., 322

Jensen, P. S., 490
Jessor, Richard, 479, 480
Jette, A. M., 131, 135
Ji, G., 408
Jiao, S., 408
Jing, Q., 408
Jobes, D. A., 481, 482
Jockin, V., 73
Jodl, K. M., 399
Johansson, B., 248
Johnsen, P. T., 416
Johnson, C. A., 424
Johnson, C. L., 389, 399, 418, 477
Johnson, D., 418
Johnson, D. R., 409, 414
Johnson, D. W., 441
Johnson, E. P., 380
Johnson, J., 199
Johnson, J. H., 489
Johnson, K. E., 194
Johnson, M. H., 112, 114, 116, 146, 147, 154
Johnson, M. L., 119
Johnson, R. E., 116
Johnson, R. T., 441
Johnson, S. M., 407, 419
Johnson, S. P., 146
Johnson, Virginia E., 136, 323, 324
Johnson, W., 364
Johnson, W. R., 129
John-Steiner, V., 190
Johnston, C. C., Jr., 130
Johnston, L. D., 479
Jolles, J., 136, 227
Jones, D. P., 300
Jones, K. L., 92
Jones, Mary Cover, 128, 129, 206
Jones, R. M., 444
Jones, Susan, 211
Jones, Warren H., 391
Jonsson, J. O., 420
Judge, T. A., 448
Juffer, F., 373, 390
Julian, T. W., 412
Jung, Carl, 34, 315–316
Jusczyk, P. W., 149, 152
Jussim, L., 310
Justice, E. M., 219

Kaczala, C. M., 309
Kaffman, M., 517
Kagan, Jerome, 3, 147, 272–273, 274, 277,
    278, 340, 367, 374, 446
Kahler, S. R., 102
Kahn, H. A., 160
Kahn, Robert, 361
Kail, R., 115, 125, 213, 217, 218, 222, 227, 245
Kalish, Richard A., 511–512
Källen, K., 92
Kallmann, Franz J., 500
Kalmuss, D., 411
Kalter, N., 516
Kaminer, H., 516
Kamphaus, R. W., 253
Kandel, Denise B., 479
Kanner, A. D., 482
Kanner, Leo, 465
Kanouse, D. E., 451
Kant, Immanuel, 143

Kaplan, B., 26
Kaplan, D. J., 445
Kaplan, G. A., 137, 138
Kaplan, H. B., 445
Kaplan, H. I., 488
Kappas, A., 208
Kappelman, M., 508
Kappes, M. E., 306
Kappes, M. H., 306
Karraker, K. H., 301, 307
Karus, D., 510
Kashani, J. H., 476
Kasl, S. V., 517
Kastenbaum, R. J., 503, 506, 507, 511, 519
Kasworth, C. E., 230
Kaszniak, A. W., 488
Katcher, A., 33, 307
Katz, D. B., 144
Katz, P., 437
Katz, P. A., 325
Katz, V. L., 91
Katzman, M., 478
Kauffman, M. B., 43, 47, 533
Kaufman, A. S., 247, 253
Kaufman, J., 424
Kaufman, N. L., 247, 253
Kausler, D. H., 212
Kavanaugh, K., 405
Kavanaugh, R. D., 379
Kawas, C., 487
Kay, Bruce, 123
Kaye, Herbert, 211
Kaye, R. A., 323, 324
Kazdin, A., 349, 356
Kean, A. W. G., 5
Keane, S. P., 381
Kearsley, R. B., 374
Keasey, C. B., 351
Keating, D. P., 179
Keel, P. K., 479
Keicholt-Glaser, J. K., 390
Keith, B., 420
Keith, Jennie, 7, 8, 416
Keith-Spiegel, P., 22
Keller, A., 275
Keller, Barbara B., 345, 405
Keller, H. H., 366
Kelley, M. L., 469
Kelley-Buchanan, C., 90, 91, 94
Kellman, P. J., 148
Kelly, J. B., 419, 420
Kelsall, D. C., 167
Kelso, G. I., 443
Kempe, C. H., 424
Kempe, R. S., 424
Kempen, G. I.-J. M., 131
Kemper, S., 196
Kemtes, K. A., 196
Kendall, P. C., 357
Kendall-Tackett, Kathleen A., 319
Kendig, H. L., 389
Kendler, K. S., 73, 132, 405, 474, 478, 485, 486
Kendrick, Carol, 406, 407
Keniston, K., 6
Kennell, J. H., 98, 99, 366
Kenny, M. E., 383
Kenny, S. L., 184
Kenshalo, D. R., 164

Kent, P., 228
Keough, J., 124, 129
Kermoian, R., 121, 148
Kerns, K. A., 299, 373, 381, 382
Kerr, M., 277
Kerwin, C., 283
Kessen, W., 145, 373
Kessler, D. B., 469
Kessler, R. C., 484, 490, 518
Kett, J. F., 6
Kettlewell, H. B. D., 56
Khoury, M. J., 58, 76
Kidd, K. K., 56
Kieley, J. M., 162
Kiernan, K. E., 418, 420
Kilbourne, B. S., 450
Kim, K., 149
Kimmel, D., 320
Kimmerly, N. L., 375
Kimura, D., 306
King, A. C., 138
King, R. A., 341
King, V., 413
Kingston, P. W., 452
Kinney, D., 384
Kinsbourne, M., 115, 471
Kinsella, K., 499
Kintsch, W., 223
Kirby, Douglas, 50
Kirkpatrick, L. A., 388
Kisilevsky, B. S., 153
Kissane, D. W., 518
Kistner, J. A., 425
Kitchener, K. S., 185
Kitson, Gay C., 419, 517
Kitson, G. S., 512
Kivnick, H. Q., 291
Klaczynski, P. A., 229
Klass, D., 506, 516
Klaus, H. M., 366
Klaus, Marshall, 98–99
Klaus, R. A., 262
Klebanov, Pamela, 255
Klecolt-Glaser, J. K., 517
Klee, L., 105
Kleemeier, R. W., 248
Klein, D. M., 396, 397, 398, 417
Klein, M. H., 478
Klein, W., 195
Klepa, L., 450
Klepac, L., 373
Kliegl, R., 230, 231
Kliegman, R., 93
Klimes-Dougan, B., 425
Kline, D. W., 160, 161, 162, 163
Kline, M., 422
Klineberg, Otto, 244
Klinnert, M. D., 365
Klohnen, E. C., 291
Knight, G. P., 283, 299
Knopf, Irwin, 159
Kobak, R. R., 383, 409
Kobayashi, L., 98
Kochanevich-Wallace, P. M., 96
Kochanska, Grazyna, 336, 340–341, 345, 406
Koenig, H. G., 485
Koestner, R., 409
Koff, E., 127

Kogan, N., 259
Kohlberg, Lawrence, 29, 190, 311–312, 313, 336–339, 341–342, 343, 350, 351, 355, 356, 371
Kohn, Melvin L., 404, 452
Kolb, S., 122
Koller, S. H., 353
Konarski, R., 279
Konker, C., 319
Konner, M. J., 101
Koocher, G. P., 22, 507, 510
Kopp, C. B., 45, 102, 103, 275, 340, 365
Korbutt, Olga, 260
Korn, S. J., 273
Kortenhaus, C. M., 310
Kory, R. C., 134
Kosberg, J. I., 423
Kosky, R., 473
Kosnik, W., 160, 161
Koss, M. P., 423
Kovacs, D. M., 303
Kovacs, M., 473, 474
Kozma, Albert, 136
Krakow, J. B., 45
Kramer, K., 444
Kraus, J. F., 92
Kraus, M. A., 99
Krause, N., 390
Kravetz, S., 508
Krebs, D. L., 350, 354
Kremenitzer, J. P., 146
Kreutz, D., 329
Kreutzer, M. A., 219
Kreye, M., 368
Krile, D., 334
Kringlen, E., 487
Kristal, B. S., 501
Kroger, J., 281, 282
Krogh, K. M., 446
Kron, R. E., 118, 211
Kroonenberg, P. M., 367
Krowitz, A., 148
Krueger, J., 292
Kruger, A. C., 351
Krumhansl, C. L., 152
Kübler-Ross, Elisabeth, 502–504, 518
Kubota, K., 115
Kucera, E., 406
Kuczkkowski, R., 183
Kuczynski, L., 344, 406
Kuhl, P. K., 150
Kuhn, Deanna, 227, 302
Kulik, C. C., 439
Kulik, J. A., 439
Kuller, J. A., 63, 73, 75
Kumka, D., 285
Kupersmidt, J. B., 254, 349, 381, 382
Kupfer, D. J., 474
Kurdek, L. A., 334, 409, 414, 418, 421
Kurtines, W. M., 355

Labouvie-Vief, Gisela, 185, 186, 247, 291, 483
Lachman, M. E., 411
Lachs, M. S., 423
Ladd, G. W., 10, 381, 382
LaGasse, L., 93
Laine, R. D., 438
Laird, J., 418

Laird, Molly, 425
Lakatta, E. G., 131
Lamaze, Fernand, 104
Lamb, M. E., 373, 374, 376, 400, 424
Lamberti, J. W., 512
Lamborn, S. D., 277, 402, 409, 436
Lamphiear, D. E., 130
Lampl, M., 119, 125
Lampman-Petraitis, C., 476
Lamy, P. P., 136
Lana, R. D., 514
Landau, S., 190
Landreth, G. L., 403
Lang, A., 513, 514
Lang, F. R., 387
Lang, M. E., 410
Lange, Garrett, 230
Langer, A., 148
Langer, Ellen J., 226, 292, 456
Langlois, J. A., 134
Langlois, J. H., 381
Lapsley, D. K., 183, 336, 342, 352, 354, 356, 383
Larson, L., 516
Larson, R., 476, 481
Larson, R. W., 407
La Rue, A., 485
LaRue, A. A., 303
Latchford, S. A., 88
Lau, A., 342
Laub, J. H., 476
Lauer, J. C., 414
Lauer, R. H., 414
Laumann, E. O., 323
Laursen, B., 385
Lauver, P. J., 444
Lavie, P., 516
Lawson, K. R., 156
Lawton, M. P., 165
Lazar, Irving, 262
Lazarus, Richard S., 482, 483
Leadbeater, B. J., 100
Leahy, J. M., 515
Leaper, C., 303
Le Couteur, A., 467
Lee, G. R., 412, 416
Lee, S. Y., 455, 456
Lee, V. E., 310
Leekam, S., 330
Leekam, S. R., 331
Lefkowitz, M. M., 102
Leggett, E. L., 435
Lehman, Darrin R., 513, 518
Lehman, Harvey, 261
Leifer, M., 469
Leigh, B., 321, 322
Leinbach, Mary D., 301, 303, 309
LeMare, L. J., 334
Lempers, J. D., 383, 408
Lenard, H. G., 119
Lenhardt, M. L., 134
Lenneberg, Eric, 199
Leonard, C., 219
Leong, D. J., 188, 189, 201
LePore, P. C., 310
Lerner, J. V., 274, 405
Lerner, M. J., 415
Lerner, R. M., 43, 47, 533

Leroux, L., 354
Leroy, M., 88
Lesher, E. L., 514
Leslie, Alan M., 329
Leslie, A. M., 466
Less, L., 453
Lester, B. M., 93, 371
Lester, D., 481, 511
Leung, A. K. C., 317
Leung, F., 478
LeVay, S., 320, 321
Leve, L. D., 309
Levenson, R. W., 414, 419
Levesque, R. J. R., 385
Levin, Harry, 157
Levin, J. R., 219
Levine, C., 284
Levine, M. P., 478
LeVine, R. A., 100–101, 197
Levine, S. C., 150
Levinson, Daniel J., 446–447, 448, 450
Levinson, David, 423, 424
Levinson, Judy D., 447
Levitt, J. L., 361
Levitt, M. J., 361, 387, 390
Levy, Becca, 226
Levy, F., 471
Levy, L. H., 513, 514
Levy, V. M., 219
Levy-Shiff, R., 286, 401, 410, 411
Lewis, B. A., 197
Lewis, C., 331, 332
Lewis, M. I., 162
Lewis, Michael, 192, 271, 272, 275, 301, 302, 363, 367, 434
Lewis, R. A., 412
Lewontin, Richard, 254
Li, B., 408
Li, G., 488
Liang, X., 375
Liben, Lynn S., 303, 313, 325
Lichter, D. T., 399
Lidz, C. S., 241
Lieberman, M., 337, 519
Lieberman, M. A., 422, 486, 520
Lieberman, Morton, 482
Liebert, R. M., 310
Liederman, P. H., 99
Liefbroer, A. C., 418
Lieven, E. V. M., 194, 198
Light, L. L., 196, 225, 226, 227
Liker, J. K., 10
Lillard, L. A., 419, 513
Lima, S. D., 134
Lincoln, R., 26, 322
Lindenberger, U., 165, 179
Lindsey, D. T., 145
Lingenfelter, M., 311
Linn, M. C., 299
Linn, M. W., 504
Linney, J. A., 438
Lipsitt, Lewis P., 8, 118, 211
Lipton, R. C., 372
Liss, M. B., 443
Litman, C., 340, 375, 406
Lits, B., 89
Little, T. D., 258
Littlefield, C. H., 514

Litwak, E., 416
Livesley, W. J., 275, 278, 332
Livson, Florine, 288
Livson, N., 128, 129
Lloyd, D. N., 445
Lobel, M., 88
Lobel, T., 317
Localio, A. R., 97
Lock, M., 133
Locke, J. L., 198, 199, 200
Locke, John, 28, 37, 143
Lockheed, M. E., 325
Loeb, T. B., 478
Loehlin, J. C., 65, 69, 73, 250, 306
Loewenstein, G., 322
Logan, A., 381
Logan, J., 412
Logan, R. L., 446
Lohnes, K. L., 516
Lohr, M. J., 384, 385
Lollis, Susan, 354
Lonetto, R., 511
Lopata, H. Z., 512, 516, 517, 518, 519
Lopez, E. C., 253
Lorber, J., 325
Lord, S., 441, 442
Lorenz, F. O., 419
Lorenz, Konrad, 56, 362, 363
Lorsbach, T. C., 222
Lotka, A. J., 6
Lourenco, O., 43, 187
Loury, M., 164
Lovaas, O. Ivar, 467, 468
Loveless, M. K., 224
Lowe, C. R., 82
Lowe, J. C., 4
Lowe, M. R., 478
Lowell, E. L., 431
Lowry, R. B., 89
Lubart, T. I., 260
Lubinski, D., 256
Lucas, T., 377
Luckasson, R., 255
Luecke-Aleksa, D., 312
Luk, S.-L., 470
Lund, D. A., 517, 520
Lundquist, K. F., 498
Luria, Z., 301
Luster, T., 252, 276
Lustig, J. L., 422
Luszcz, M. A., 228
Lye, D. N., 413, 415
Lykken, D. T., 70, 73, 285
Lynch, M. E., 304, 305
Lynch, Michael, 155
Lyness, J. M., 485
Lynskey, M. T., 471
Lyons-Ruth, K., 367
Lytton, H., 65, 309, 345, 400, 405

Ma, Yo-Yo, 260
Maccoby, Eleanor E., 157, 299, 300, 301, 303, 308, 400, 401, 402, 403
MacDonald, Kevin, 402
MacDonald, W., 418
MacFarlane, A., 85, 301
Machado, A., 43, 187
Mac Iver, D. J., 431, 435, 438, 439, 441

MacKay, D. G., 196
Mackey, R. A., 414
MacKinnon, C. E., 407
MacKinnon-Lewis, C., 381
MacLean, W. E., 119
MacLeod, D., 439
Macmillan, M., 33
MacPhee, D., 252, 404
MacRae, P. G., 134
MacTurk, R. H., 433
Madden, C. M., 181
Maddox, G. L., 131, 247, 454, 455
Maggs, J. L., 403
Magnus, K., 286
Magnusson, D., 127, 128, 129, 476
Mahapatra, Manamohan, 352, 353
Mahler, Margaret S., 271
Maier-Bruckner, W., 220
Main, Mary, 370, 376, 400, 425
Main, S. R., 438
Major, B., 300
Majury, J., 508
Maki, B. E., 134
Malatesta, C. Z., 364, 365, 446
Malik, N. M., 381, 390
Malinosky-Rummell, R., 425
Malinski, D., 286
Mandle, C. L., 91
Mandler, G., 225
Mandoki, M. W., 64
Mangelsdorf, S. C., 365, 368, 372
Manis, J. D., 410
Manke, B. A., 66, 69, 304
Mannuzza, S., 471
Manset, G., 440
Manton, Kenneth G., 4, 7, 138
Marcia, James E., 281, 282, 284, 290
Marcoen, A., 230, 231, 277
Marcovitch, S., 373
Marcus, D. E., 312
Marean, G. C., 150
Marentette, P. F., 200
Margolis, L. H., 136, 138
Marin, D. B., 487
Marini, Z., 217
Markides, K. S., 416
Markman, E. M., 177, 193
Markman, H. J., 367, 401
Marks, H. M., 310
Markstrom-Adams, C., 282, 283
Marschark, M., 166
Marsh, H. W., 276, 310
Marshall, N. L., 403
Marshall, R. E., 153
Marshall, S., 283
Marsiglio, W., 324
Marsiske, M., 229
Martikainen, P., 513
Martin, Carol L., 300, 304, 311, 312, 313, 315
Martin, C. E., 133
Martin, F. N., 163
Martin, G. B., 341
Martin, J. A., 401, 402
Martin, John, 224
Martin, N. G., 70
Martin, R. P., 440
Martinkowski, K. S., 513

Martlew, M., 155
Martorano, Suzanne, 182
Maruyama, G., 441
Marvin, R. S., 407
Marzolf, D., 365
Masataka, N., 200
Masoro, E. J., 502
Massie, R. K., 63
Massie, S., 63
Masson, J. M., 33
Masten, A. S., 382
Masters, William H., 136, 323, 324
Matas, L., 368
Matheson, C. C., 377, 378, 379
Mathew, A., 122
Matlin, M. W., 145, 149
Maton, K. I., 397
Matsuzawa, T., 115
Matthews, Karen A., 132, 133
Matthews, S. H., 389, 413
Mattock, A., 147
Maurer, A., 506
Maxon, A. B., 166
May, Mark, 343
Mayberry, Rachel I., 166, 199, 200
Mayes, L. C., 433
Mayseless, Ofra, 383
Maziade, M., 274
McAdams, Dan, 291
McAdams, P. P., 446
McAdoo, H. P., 276
McBride, A., 516
McBride-Chang, C., 425
McCabe, M., 404
McCable, M., 277
McCall, P. L., 481
McCall, Robert B., 18, 67, 243, 244
McCallum, M., 519
McCartney, Kathleen, 67, 71, 72–73, 405
McCarton, C. M., 106
McCaul, E. J., 445
McClearn, G. E., 59, 67
McClellan, N., 443
McClelland, David C., 268, 431
McClintic, S., 434
McClintock, Martha, 318
McClintock, M. K., 111
McCloskey, L. A., 423, 424, 425
McConnell, F. E., 166
McCormick, A. M., 500
McCoy, J. K., 407
McCrae, Robert R., 261, 269, 270, 286, 287, 288, 449, 483
McCubbin, J. A., 88
McCullough, J. L., 301, 314
McCune, L., 434
McDonald-Miszczak, L., 226
McDowd, J. M., 162
McDowell, E. E., 496, 497, 517
McEachin, J. J., 468
McElreath, L., 490
McFadden, S. H., 350
McFadyen-Ketchum, S. A., 349
McFarlane, J. A., 132, 244
McGhee, P. E., 181, 311
McGhee-Bidlack, B., 195
McGinnis, J. M., 138
McGoldrick, M., 498

McGue, Matthew, 67, 69, 71, 73, 285, 286, 500
McGuire, K. D., 334
McGuire, W. J., 276
McHale, S. M., 304, 309, 407, 409, 451
McIntosh, D. N., 511
McKay, J. R., 96
McKay, K. E., 159
McKelvey, M. W., 412
McKenry, P. C., 412
McKinlay, S. M., 132
McKnew, D. H., Jr., 468, 473, 474, 486
McKusick, V. A., 61
McLanahan, S. S., 5, 412, 418, 483
McLellan, J. A., 363
McLeod, P. J., 118, 198
McLoyd, V. C., 348, 403, 424
McMahon, M. J., 91
McNeil, J., 514
McNeill, D., 197
McPartland, J. M., 442
McQuillan, J., 245
McWhirter, L., 508
Meachum, J. A., 275
Mead, George Herbert, 272
Meador, K. G., 490
Meadows-Orlans, K. P., 166
Medina, John J., 495, 499, 501–502
Medina, R. A., 230
Mednick, B. R., 88, 102, 103
Medvedev, Z. A., 500
Mehan, Hugh, 439
Mehl, L. E., 99
Meier, R. P., 200
Meilman, Philip W., 281, 282
Mekos, D., 421
Meller, W. H., 473
Mellinger, J. C., 446
Meltzoff, A. N., 153, 211, 216, 331
Menaghan, E. G., 412, 422, 452
Mendel, Gregor, 60
Mendelson, M. J., 382
Menken, J., 26, 322
Mercer, R. T., 448, 449
Mergendoller, J. R., 440
Merriam, S. B., 448
Mervis, C. B., 194
Merzenich, M. M., 159
Messer, D. J., 433
Metcalf, P., 496, 497
Metsala, J. L., 158
Metzler, J., 299
Meyer-Bahlburg, H. F. L., 320
Michaelieu, Q., 277
Michel, G. F., 115
Michel, M. K., 365
Midgley, C., 441, 442
Milberger, S., 471
Miles, D. R., 348
Milgram, J. I., 415
Milich, Richard, 472
Miller, A., 132, 435
Miller, A. T., 435
Miller, E., 488
Miller, J. A., 75
Miller, J. L., 150
Miller, Joan G., 239, 352, 353
Miller, J. W., 424

Miller, N. B., 314, 402
Miller, P. A., 300, 355
Miller, Patricia H., 159, 187, 219, 222, 530
Miller, P. M., 101, 197
Miller, R. H., 153
Miller, S. A., 187, 219, 252, 530
Miller-Heyl, J., 404
Mills, C. J., 435
Millsap, R. E., 287, 291
Milofsky, E., 290
Minkler, Meredith, 391
Minois, Georges, 7
Minuchin, S., 478
Mischel, Walter, 270, 308–309, 339
Mitchell, D. E., 155
Mitchell, J. E., 306, 479
Mitchell, J. J., 74
Mitchell, P., 330, 331
Mittelman, M. S., 488
Mix, K. S., 150
Miyawaki, K., 151
Mize, J., 10, 381
Moerk, E. L., 197
Molfese, D. L., 115
Molfese, V. J., 97
Molina, B. S. G., 127
Molinari, V., 291
Moller, L. C., 303
Mollnow, E., 92, 94
Money, John, 305, 306, 307, 308, 313, 321
Monk, T. H., 410
Monroe, S. M., 485
Monsour, Ann, 279
Montelpare, W., 135
Montemayor, Raymond, 278
Montgomery, A., 132
Montoye, H. J., 130
Monty, S., 239
Moore, E. G. J., 254, 255
Moore, G., 376
Moore, J. W., 4
Moore, K. L., 90
Moore, M. K., 153, 211, 212
Moore, S. M., 127
Moorehouse, Martha J., 452
Moos, R. H., 486
Mora, J. O., 89
Morelli, G. A., 8, 101, 373
Morgan, G. A., 368, 433, 434
Morgan, M., 134
Morgan, R., 271
Morgan, S. P., 50, 322
Morinaga, Y., 444
Morison, P., 382
Morrell, R. W., 231
Morrell, W., 479
Morris, J. T., 311
Morris, M., 450
Morris, N., 99, 100
Morris, R., 307, 488
Morrison, D. M., 322
Morrison, F. J., 157
Morrongiello, B. A., 149
Morrow, D., 223, 225
Morrow, D. G., 196
Morrow, J., 485
Morse, C. K., 10, 116, 248, 532
Mortimer, Jeylen T., 285, 288, 444, 445

Morton, M. R., 136
Mory, M. S., 384
Moss, H. A., 277, 446
Moss, Howard, 277
Moss, M. S., 165
Most, A., 132
Most, R., 434
Mounts, N. S., 386, 436
Mueller, E., 377
Muir, D. W., 149, 153
Mundy, P., 466
Munro, G., 284
Munroe, R. H., 312
Munroe, R. L., 312
Murnen, S. K., 478
Murphy, Claire, 164
Murphy, S. P., 137
Murphy, W. E., 162
Murray, Charles, 253, 254
Murray, C. I., 507, 508, 509
Murray, I., 98
Murray, K., 340
Murray, L., 100, 367, 371
Murray, M. P., 130, 134
Murrell, S. A., 490, 517
Musick, J. S., 284
Mussen, P. H., 129, 308
Must, A., 137
Muthen, B. O., 485
Mutryn, C. S., 97
Mutterer, M. L., 343
Muzio, J. W., 119
Myers, B. J., 105
Myers, J., 191
Myers, J. K., 300, 484
Myers, R. E., 97
Myers, S. E., 97
Myerson, J., 134
Mylod, D. E., 411

Nagel, S. K., 451, 452
Nahak, R. K., 501
Nahom, A., 134
Naigles, L. G., 193
Najman, J. M., 514
Nakagawa, N., 181
Nanez, J. E., 147
Nangle, D. W., 391
Napolitano, M. A., 478
Nash, A., 377
Nash, S. C., 302, 316
Nashner, L. M., 134
National Institute on Aging, 167
National Institute on Deafness and Other
    Communication Disorders, 167
National Institutes of Health, 165
Neale, M. C., 70
Nederend, S., 304
Nehrke, M. F., 291
Neimark, E. D., 184
Neimeyer, G. J., 282
Neimeyer, R. A., 511
Neisser, Ulric, 216, 245, 250, 253, 254
Nelson, C. A., 216, 225
Nelson, E. A., 343
Nelson, Katherine, 192, 193, 216
Nelson, Sharon A., 342, 355
Nelson, V. J., 498

Nettelbeck, T., 239
Netzer, J. K., 416
Neugarten, Bernice L., 4, 5, 7, 132, 286, 454
Neugarten, D. A., 7
Neuhaus, J. M., 137
Neville, B., 400
Neville, Helen, 200
Newberger, J. J., 154
Newberry, J., 134
Newcomb, A. F., 382
Newcomb, M., 478
Newcomb, P. R., 418
Newcombe, H. B., 89
Newell, A., 213
Newman, D. L., 348
Newport, Elissa L., 199
Newton, P. M., 449, 450
Newton, R. R., 497
NICHD Early Child Care Research Network,
    374, 375
Nicholls, J. G., 435
Nichols, E. G., 448
Nicholson, T., 159
Nicolich, L. M., 379, 434
Nightingale, E. O., 75
Nikolic, J., 183
Niles, William, 356
Noam, G. G., 389
Noble, K. D., 257
Nock, S. L., 452
Noh, S., 411
Nolen-Hoeksema, S., 481, 485, 516
Noll, J., 238, 247
Noller, P., 387, 388
Noppe, I. C., 510
Noppe, L. D., 510
Norman-Jackson, J., 408
Norris, F. H., 517
Northern, J. L., 162
Nsamenang, A. B., 101
Nucci, L. P., 343
Nucci, M. S., 343
Nydegger, Corinne, 409

Oates, R. K., 426
Obler, L. K., 196
O'Boyle, C., 309
O'Brien, B. A., 414
O'Brien, M., 302, 411
O'Brien, W. H., 133
Ochs, A. L., 134
Ochs, E., 197, 198
Ochse, R., 259
O'Connell, B., 192
O'Connell, C. M., 94
O'Connor, B., 183
O'Connor, B. P., 389, 390
O'Connor, Brian, 457
O'Connor, N., 239
Odden, A., 439
O'Dempsey, T. J. D., 98
Oden, M. H., 257, 258
Oden, Sherrie, 390
O'Donnell, A. M., 441
Offer, D., 279, 408, 476
Ogan, Tamra, 365
Ogbu, John U., 8, 254, 283, 401, 442
O'Halloran, C. M., 508

O'Hara, M. W., 99
O'Heeron, R. C., 518
Okagaki, L., 239
O'Kelly, J., 441
Olds, D. L., 104
Olejnik, A. B., 303
Oliver, E. I., 195
Oliver, M. B., 321
Oller, D. K., 192
Olson, D. R., 177
Olson, P. L., 161
O'Mahony, J. F., 332
O'Malley, P. M., 479
O'Neil, A. K., 304
O'Neil, R., 451
Oosterwegel, A., 276
Oppenheim, D., 101, 373
Oppenheimer, L., 276
O'Rand, A. M., 451
Orlans, H., 166
Orlofsky, J. L., 290
Ornstein, P. A., 9, 28, 218
Ornstein, S., 448
Orth, L. C., 440
Osborn, R. W., 98
Osser, H. A., 158
Osterweis, M., 510, 511, 514, 515, 517
Ostri, B., 162
Ostrov, E., 408
Ostrove, J. M., 451
O'Sullivan, J. T., 219
Overman, S. J., 309
Overton, W. F., 47, 312
Owens, W. A., Jr., 246
Owsley, C., 161
Oyserman, D., 413
Ozer, D. J., 414

Paarlberg, K. M., 88
Padilla, M. L., 403
Paganini-Hill, A., 133
Page, T., 260
Paikoff, R. L., 127, 409
Palkovitz, R., 100, 401, 412
Palmore, E. B., 350, 452, 453, 454
Pan, B. A., 192, 193
Panis, C. W. A., 419
Papalia, D. E., 184, 186, 201
Papousek, H., 211
Paraskevopoulos, J., 252
Parasuraman, S., 450
Parazzini, F., 94
Parcel, T. L., 452
Parham, I. A., 286
Park, Denise C., 231
Parke, R. D., 9, 28, 49, 209, 307, 344, 399,
    400
Parker, J. G., 303, 382
Parker, K. C., 389
Parker, K. C. H., 507, 508
Parkes, Colin Murray, 504–505, 512, 513, 517,
    518
Parkhurst, J. T., 381
Parlee, M. B., 387
Parmelee, A. H., 103
Parnass, J., 378
Parnes, H. S., 453
Parsons, J. E., 309

Parsons, T., 298
Parten, Mildred, 378
Parving, A., 162
Pasaro Mendez, E. J., 64
Pascalis, O., 146
Passarello, L. C., 321
Passman, R. H., 368
Pastalan, L. A., 161
Pataki, C. S., 474
Pate, R. T., 138
Patterson, C. J., 254, 303, 382, 418, 419
Patterson, Gerald R., 349, 356
Patterson, S. J., 282
Patz, R. J., 424
Paul, J. P., 320
Paulhus, D., 408
Paveza, G. J., 423
Peacock, E. J., 350
Pearce, Kathy, 186–187, 229
Pearlin, L. I., 482, 483
Pearson, J., 397
Pearson, J. D., 163
Pecheux, M., 153
Pedersen, J., 377
Pedersen, N. L., 67, 287
Peeples, D. R., 145
Peevers, B. H., 275
Pegalis, L. J., 316
Pegg, J. E., 198
Peisner-Feinberg, E. S., 437
Pelaez-Nogueras, M., 39, 208
Pelham, W. E., Jr., 471, 472
Pellegrini, A. D., 12
Pennebaker, J. W., 518
Penner, S. G., 199
Pepper, S. C., 47
Perez-Granados, D. R., 408
Perkins, D., 236
Perlman, D., 382
Perlmutter, M., 190, 217, 224, 230
Perner, J., 331
Perry, D. G., 344
Perry, H. L., 498
Perry, T. B., 383
Perry, William, 185
Persson, G., 324
Peskin, H., 128, 129
Peskind, E. R., 487, 488
Peters, A., 418
Petersen, A. C., 128, 299, 304, 481
Peterson, B. E., 291
Peterson, C., 448
Peterson, G. H., 99
Peterson, J. W., 413
Peterson, L., 489
Peterson, P. L., 440
Peterson, R. E., 308
Petitto, L. A., 200
Pettit, Gregory S., 209, 381, 403
Pfeffer, C. R., 473
Pfeiffer, E., 483
Phares, V., 399, 400, 411, 474
Phelan, P., 442
Phelps, E., 259
Phillips, D. A., 374
Phillips, M. A., 490
Phillips, S. L., 387
Phillips, Susan D., 448

Phillips, W., 331, 467
Phinney, J. S., 283
Phipps, B. J., 443
Phoenix, C. H., 307
Piaget, Jean, 40–43, 44, 47, 49, 115, 171–187,
     189, 198, 201, 217, 220, 221, 236, 278,
     311, 332–333, 336, 339, 342, 343, 355,
     363–364, 372, 379, 433–434, 506, 510,
     523, 524, 529, 533
Pianta, R., 424
Pick, A. D., 158
Pickens, J., 153
Pierce, Sarah, 230
Pike, R., 276
Pilisuk, Marc, 391
Pillard, R. C., 66, 320
Pillemer, D. B., 217
Pillemer, K. A., 423
Pine, F., 271
Pine, J. M., 194, 196, 198
Pinto, A., 404
Piper, W. E., 519
Pipp, S., 272
Pipp, S. L., 184
Pipp-Siegel, S., 272
Pisoni, D. B., 149
Pitts, D. G., 160, 161
Piven, J., 467
Plant, E. A., 300
Plassman, B. L., 488
Pleck, J. H., 298, 314
Plomin, Robert, 58, 59, 62, 63, 64, 66, 67, 68,
     69, 70, 71, 72, 73, 197, 259, 272, 287
Plude, Dana J., 162
Pogue-Geile, M. F., 70, 137
Polifka, J. E., 89, 91, 94
Polivy, J., 478
Pollen, D. A., 486, 487
Pollina, L., 390
Pomerantz, E. M., 275, 276, 435
Pomerleau, A., 301
Ponzetti, J. J., 515
Poon, L. W., 225, 231
Porac, Clare, 115
Porter, F. L., 153
Porter, R. H., 153
Portes, A., 439
Posner, B. M., 136–137
Posner, J. G., 132
Posner, Jill K., 403
Posner, M. I., 272
Post, T., 98
Poston, D. L., Jr., 408
Potts, R., 355
Poulin-Dubois, D., 301
Power, F. C., 356
Powlishta, K. K., 183, 302
Pratt, K. C., 153
Pratt, M. W., 334, 349, 350, 351, 354
Prechtl, H. F. R., 117, 119, 120
Prentice, A. M., 89
Pressley, M., 218, 219, 222, 231
Price, D. J., 154
Price, J. M., 347, 381
Prodromidis, M., 374
Provence, S., 372
Provenzano, F. J., 301
Pruzan, M., 500

Pullen, S. M., 225, 229
Purdie, N., 230
Purifoy, F. E., 324
Purvis, G. J., 125
Putallaz, M., 381
Putnam, F. W., 319, 490
Pynoos, R. S., 511

Quay, H. C., 473
Quiggle, N. L., 347
Quill, T. E., 497

Rabiner, D. L., 381
Radin, N., 413
Radke-Yarrow, M., 100, 341
Ragan, Pauline, 12
Rakic, P., 114
Ramanan, J., 403
Ram Dass, Baba, 268
Ramey, Craig T., 89, 244, 252, 262, 374, 437
Ramey, S. L., 244, 262
Ramsey, B. K., 262
Randels, S. P., 92
Rando, T. A., 504, 514
Rango, N., 164
Rao, K. V., 418
Raphael, B., 495, 506, 510, 511, 515, 516
Rapkin, B. D., 446, 455
Rappaport, H., 511
Rasbury, W. C., 489
Raskind, M. A., 487, 488
Rasmuson, I., 287
Rasmussen, C. A., 511
Ratcliffe, S. D., 89, 91
Raveis, V. H., 510
Raver, C. C., 100
Ray, L. A., 416
Raynor, J. O., 431
Raynor, Rosalie, 206
Raz, S., 300
Reavis, R., 442
Recchia, A., 434
Reddel, M., 297
Redding, R. E., 433
Reder, Lynne, 224
Redman, E. S., 99
Reese, H. W., 8, 47
Regier, D. A., 484, 486
Reich, J. W., 457
Reichlin, R. E., 291
Reid, L. L., 450
Reid, P. T., 300
Reid, T. R., 7
Reimer, J. F., 222
Reinisch, J. M., 321
Reis, Harry T., 383, 386–387
Reiser, L. W., 127
Reiss, D., 73, 405, 421
Reiss, S., 255
Reker, G. T., 350, 446
Remley, A., 6
Rende, R., 478
Renner, G., 483
Repacholi, B. M., 331
Rescorla, L., 436
Resnick, S. M., 306
Rest, J., 349, 350
Rest, J. R., 355, 356

Reuman, D. A., 438
Reuman, David, 446
Reynolds, A. J., 437
Reynolds, D., 438, 439
Reynolds, David K., 511–512
Reynolds, S., 464
Reznick, J. S., 193, 273
Reznikoff, M., 71, 259
Rheingold, H. L., 301
Rhodes, S. R., 449
Rholes, W. S., 332
Riach, J., 159
Ricciuti, H. N., 368
Rice, K. G., 383
Rice, M. L., 196
Richards, F. A., 185, 186
Richards, M. H., 127, 478
Richards, R., 258
Richards, S. E., 253
Richey, C. A., 424
Richman, Amy L., 101, 197
Riegel, K. F., 43, 186
Rierdan, J., 127
Riesen, Austin H., 154
Rieser, J. J., 9, 28, 152
Ripple, R. E., 262
Risser, A. H., 85, 112
Roberto, Karen A., 389, 413, 414
Roberts, C. J., 82
Roberts, C. L., 412
Roberts, D., 397
Roberts, L. R., 305
Roberts, P., 449, 450
Roberts, R. E., 485
Robertson, N. R. C., 110
Robin, A. F., 220
Robins, L. N., 484
Robins, R. W., 280
Robinson, C. C., 311
Robinson, G., 132, 133
Robinson, I., 321
Robinson, N. M., 257
Robinson, Pauline K., 324
Robinson, S. R., 82, 84, 85, 105
Robson, W. L. M., 317
Rochat, Philippe, 150, 271
Roche, M. I., 73
Rodgers, R. H., 397
Rodin, Judith, 292, 456, 478
Roediger, H. L., 225
Roeleveld, N., 256
Roeser, R. W., 442, 443
Roffwarg, H. P., 119
Rogers, Carl, 280
Rogers, S. J., 412, 419
Rogoff, Barbara, 101, 189, 202, 228, 378, 382, 430, 438
Rojewski, J. W., 444
Rollins, Boyd C., 412, 414
Romney, D. M., 309, 345, 400, 405
Rook, K. S., 391, 407, 483
Rose, R. J., 67
Rose, S. A., 243
Rosen, B. C., 436, 444
Rosen, H., 518
Rosenberg, F., 279
Rosenberg, M., 279
Rosenberg, S. D., 448

Rosenblatt, P. C., 496, 497, 498
Rosenbloom, L. G., 373
Rosenblum, M. A., 363
Rosenfeld, R. G., 110
Rosengren, K., 190
Rosenholtz, S. J., 442
Rosenthal, C., 399
Rosenthal, P. A., 473
Rosenthal, R., 403
Rosenthal, S., 473
Rosenwasser, S. M., 311
Rosenzweig, M. G., 321
Rosman, B. L., 478
Ross, H., 354
Ross, H. G., 415
Ross, H. S., 406
Ross, R. T., 256
Rosser, R., 144, 145
Rossi, A. S., 415, 416
Rossi, P. H., 415, 416
Roth, P. L., 445
Rothbart, M. K., 155, 156, 157, 272
Rothberg, A. D., 89
Rousseau, Jean Jacques, 28
Rovee-Collier, Carolyn, 211, 215–216, 217, 225
Rovine, M. J., 371, 374, 375, 401, 410
Rovner, S., 487
Rowe, D. C., 66, 67, 69, 70, 73, 171, 269, 272, 405
Rowland, D. T., 421
Rubin, D. H., 92
Rubin, J. Z., 301
Rubin, K. H., 334, 379, 381, 408
Rubin, S. S., 506, 514
Rubinow, D. R., 306, 307
Rubinstein, R. L., 418
Ruble, D. N., 275, 276, 304, 309, 312, 332, 435
Rudin, Rose, 110
Ruff, H. A., 155, 156, 157, 434
Ruffman, T., 331
Ruffman, T. K., 177
Ruggles, S., 397
Runco, M. A., 258, 260
Rushton, J. P., 343, 344, 514
Russ, S. W., 261
Russell, C., 102
Russell, R. J., 414
Russo, R., 225
Ruth, J. E., 285, 286
Rutherford, E., 308
Rutten, P., 348
Rutter, Michael, 59, 255, 331, 372, 438, 439, 445, 464, 466, 467, 473, 474, 475, 476, 481
Ruzany, N., 276
Ryan, R. M., 183, 436
Ryff, Carol, 285
Rymer, R., 81

Sabatelli, R. M., 411
Sacks, C. H., 440
Sacks, E. L., 254
Sacks, O., 330
Sadker, D., 310
Sadker, M., 310
Sadler, T. W., 82, 84
Sadock, B. J., 488
Sagart, L., 191

Sagi, A., 373
Sakin, J. W., 406
Sakornbut, E. L., 89, 91
Salahu-Din, S. N., 518
Salapatek, P., 145, 147
Salatas, H., 219
Salem, D. A., 397
Saltarelli, L. M., 434
Salthouse, T. A., 134, 135, 165, 184, 186, 187, 217, 225, 227, 245
Salzinger, S., 425
Sameroff, Arnold J., 43, 88, 96, 244, 250, 251, 405
Sampson, P. D., 94
Sampson, R. J., 476
Samuels, S. M., 271
Sanchez, L., 510
Sander, Gerhard, 500
Sanders, C. M., 514, 517
Sandler, I. N., 519
Sanford, F. H., 462
Sargent, F., III, 131
Sattler, J. M., 241
Saul, S., 110
Saunders, Cicely, 519
Savage-Rumbaugh, E. S., 197
Savickas, M. L., 444
Savin-Williams, R. C., 320
Sawin, D. B., 399
Sawin, L. L., 446
Saxton, M., 198
Scafidi, Frank, 106
Scarisbrick-Hauser, A., 418
Scarr, Sandra, 56, 68, 72–73, 252, 255, 283, 374, 375, 405
Schachar, R. J., 472
Schachter, S., 510
Schacter, D. L., 225
Schaefer, M., 106
Schaer, T., 245
Schafer, W. D., 375
Schaffer, H. Rudolph, 367, 368, 370
Schaie, K. Warner, 16, 196, 228, 246–247, 248, 263, 264, 286, 414, 532
Schalock, R. L., 256
Schalrb, J., 504
Schapiro, M. B., 488
Schardein, J. L., 94
Scharlach, A. E., 515
Scheeringa, M. S., 468
Schellenberg, E. G., 152
Scherr, P. A., 138
Schiavi, R. C., 131, 133, 323
Schieber, F., 161
Schiedel, D. G., 290
Schieffelin, B. B., 197
Schiff, Andrew, 159
Schiffman, Susan S., 164
Schinke, Steven, 426
Schlackman, L. J., 97
Schlagman, N., 343
Schlegel, A., 127
Schmidt, C. R., 302
Schmidt, P. J., 306, 307
Schmitz, S., 272
Schneider, M. L., 88
Schneider, W., 220
Schnell, S. V., 352, 354

Schnoll, S. H., 91
Schoefs, V., 277
Schoener, E. P., 470
Scholmerich, A., 366
Schonert-Reichl, K. A., 279, 476
Schonfeld, D. J., 508
Schooler, Carmi, 452
Schopler, E., 466
Schroeder, C. S., 317
Schulenberg, J., 444
Schulz, R., 430, 456, 503, 504
Schutz, R. W., 130
Schwab, R., 514
Schwartz, P., 418
Scialfa, C. T., 160, 161, 162, 163
Scogin, F., 231, 490
Scott, Jean, 389
Scott, R., 277, 404
Scott, W. A., 277, 404
Seale, Clive F., 519
Searle, S., 450
Sears, R. R., 258
Sebald, H., 386
Secord, P. F., 275
Segal, S., 421
Segalowitz, S. J., 115
Seidman, E., 279, 438, 441
Seidman, L. J., 471
Seleen, D. R., 455
Seligman, Martin E. P., 435
Selkoe, D. J., 115, 488
Selman, R. L., 279, 333, 334, 339, 382
Seltzer, J. A., 422
Semmel, M. I., 440
Sena, R., 434
Serbin, L. A., 302, 303, 313, 325
Severino, R., 105
Shaefer, E. S., 401
Shafer, J. H., 63
Shaffer, D. R., 316, 344, 345, 408
Shakespeare, William, 528
Shama, A., 69
Shanahan, M. J., 444
Shanas, E., 415
Shanley, N., 481
Shannon, E., 145, 146
Shapiro, J. R., 365
Shapiro, S., 89, 478
Sharabany, Ruth, 384
Sharpe, P. A., 138
Sharpe, T. M., 478
Sharpsteen, D. J., 388
Shatz, M., 198
Shaver, Phillip R., 388
Shaw, L. K., 192
Shayer, M., 201
Shea, L., 389
Shelton, B. A., 451
Shepard, R. N., 299
Shephard, R. J., 135, 138
Shepherd, M., 472
Sherman, D., 424
Shiffrin, Richard, 213
Shiloh, S., 73
Shimamura, A. P., 228
Shimmin, H. S., 312
Shin, Yoolim, 379
Ship, J. A., 163, 164

Shirk, Stephen, 276, 292
Shisslak, C. M., 477
Shneidman, Edwin, 503, 504
Shoda, Y., 270
Shope, J. T., 479
Shore, C., 192
Shreder, M., 514
Shuchter, S. R., 505, 506, 512, 517
Shukla, D., 183
Shumway-Cook, A., 134
Shurkin, Joel, 257
Shweder, Richard A., 352, 353
Sidis, William, 257
Siebold, C., 519
Siegel, J. S., 452
Siegel, L., 510
Siegel, L. J., 489
Siegler, I. C., 446
Siegler, Robert, 221
Sigafoos, E., 211
Sigelman, C. K., 304, 462
Sigman, Marian, 136, 434, 462, 466, 467
Sigman, M. D., 243
Sigmundson, H. Keith, 308
Signorella, M. L., 303, 310, 311, 313
Silberstein, L. R., 478
Silva, P. A., 127, 277
Silver, L. B., 470, 471, 472
Silver, Roxane C., 506, 511, 516
Silverberg, Susan B., 385, 411–412
Silverman, P. R., 510, 517, 518
Silverstein, M., 389, 416
Simmons, Roberta G., 129, 279, 442
Simon, Theodore, 240
Simon, Tony, 150
Simonoff, E., 255
Simons, A. D., 485
Simons, H. A., 213
Simons, R. L., 406, 422, 424
Simons-Morton, B. G., 138
Simonton, Dean, 261
Simpson, C., 442
Simpson, K. R., 91, 97
Simutis, Z., 344
Sinclair, R. J., 421
Sines, J. O., 404, 474
Singer, Dorothy G., 19, 20, 175
Singer, J. E., 104
Singer, Jerome L., 19, 20, 175
Singer, L., 93
Singh, S., 321, 322
Sinnott, J., 185, 186
Siperstein, G. N., 152
Sirignano, S. W., 411
Sivak, M., 161
Sjogren, B., 75
Skinner, B. F., 37–38, 46, 47–48, 50, 144, 196,
    207, 209, 211, 213, 224, 230
Skoe, E. E., 354
Skolnick, Arlene, 376, 414
Slaby, Ronald G., 312, 347, 356
Slater, A., 146, 147
Slaughter, V., 331
Slavin, Robert E., 439, 441
Sliwinski, M., 134
Slomkowski, C., 407
Slone, D., 89
Slone, M., 317

Slusarcick, A. L., 445
Smart, R., 448
Smetana, Judith G., 343, 409
Smiley, Sandra, 222
Smith, A. D., 224, 226, 228
Smith, B., 152
Smith, D. R., 350
Smith, D. W., 92
Smith, D. W. E., 500
Smith, E. G., 150
Smith, G. E., 224
Smith, I. M., 467
Smith, J., 3, 135, 225, 529
Smith, Jacqui, 249
Smith, J. B., 443
Smith, J. H., 192
Smith, L. A., 413
Smith, L. B., 123, 144
Smith, P. K., 302, 379
Smith, R. S., 102, 103
Smith, S., 409
Smith, T., 467, 468
Smith, T. W., 320, 323, 408
Smock, P. J., 419
Smolak, L., 477, 478
Smoll, F. L., 130
Smoller, Jordan W., 463
Smotherman, W. P., 82, 84, 85, 105
Smyer, M., 490
Snarey, J. R., 350, 351, 352
Snow, Catherine, 198
Snow, M. E., 400
Snow, Richard E., 440
Snowdon, D. A., 487
Sochting, I., 282
Society for Research in Child Development, 21
Socolar, R. R., 209
Sodian, B., 331
Soederberg, L. M., 196, 224
Sollie, D. L., 387
Solomon, F., 510
Solomon, J., 370
Solomon, P. R., 212
Somers, M. D., 418
Somerville, S. C., 218
Sommers, M. S., 163, 196
Somsen, R. J. M., 115
Sophian, C., 216
Sorell, G. T., 387
Sorensen, A., 451
Sorensen, A. B., 5, 412, 483
Sorensen, E., 422
Soto, A., 88
Soules, M. R., 130, 133
Sparrow, A. W., 136
Spearman, Charles, 237
Speece, M. W., 507, 508
Speicher, B., 351
Speisman, J. C., 415
Spelke, Elizabeth S., 144, 148, 149, 150
Spence, J. T., 315, 317, 446
Spence, Melanie, 152
Spencer, M. B., 283
Spencer, P. E., 200
Spencer, T. J., 471
Sperling, M. B., 383
Spilich, George, 223
Spirduso, W. W., 134

Spitz, R. A., 468
Spitze, G., 412
Spokane, A., 444
Sprafkin, J., 310
Sprang, G., 513, 514
Spreen, O., 85, 89, 112, 115
Sprey, J., 413
Springen, K., 361
Spritz, Becky, 374
Sprock, J., 485
Squire, L. R., 225
Sroufe, L. Alan, 368, 372, 373, 381, 424, 464,
    471, 475
Stallard, E., 138
Stambrook, M., 507, 508
Stanley, J. C., 299, 300
Stanwicz, L., 198
Stapley, J. C., 485
Starkey, P., 150
Starr, Bernard D., 323
Starr, R. H., Jr., 469
Starrels, M. E., 416
Stattin, H., 129
St. Aubin, E., 446
Staudinger, Ursula M., 3, 135, 225, 249, 529
Staudt, Joanne, 184
Steele, Claude M., 254
Steele, H., 389
Steele, M., 389
Steffenburg, S., 467
Stein, Aletha, 17–18
Stein, E. M., 504
Stein, J. H., 127
Stein, M. R., 377
Stein, R. E., 209
Stein, S., 504
Stein, Z. A., 89, 102
Steinberg, Laurence, 57, 127, 385, 386, 401,
    403, 404, 409, 411–412, 436, 442, 444,
    445, 478
Steinberg, S., 83, 98
Steiner, Jacob E., 152
Stelmach, G. E., 134
Stemp, P. S., 411
Stephan, W. G., 440
Stephens, Benjamin, 147
Stephens, M. A. P., 416–417
Stern, B. M., 457
Stern, D., 366
Stern, M., 103, 301, 307
Sternberg, K. J., 374
Sternberg, Robert J., 239–240, 241, 249, 250,
    260
Sternglanz, S. H., 325
Stevens, B., 153
Stevens, D. P., 287, 446
Stevens, J. C., 163
Stevens, M. M., 510
Stevens, N., 382, 385, 389
Stevens, R. J., 441
Stevenson, Harold W., 455, 456
Stevenson, M. B., 366
Stevenson, M. R., 307, 400
Stewart, A. J., 451
Stewart, M. A., 470
Stewart, R. B., 407
Stewart, W., 452
St. George, I. M., 127

Stice, E., 474
Stigler, J. W., 455
Stillion, J. M., 496, 497, 517
Stine, E. A. L., 196
Stine-Morrow, E. A. L., 224
Stipek, Deborah J., 275, 332, 431, 434, 435, 441
St. John, N. H., 440
Stoddart, Trish, 304
Stolberg, U., 368
Stone, R., 95
Stoneman, Z., 407
Stones, Michael J., 136
Storandt, M., 231
Stormshak, E. A., 407
Stott, D. H., 88
Stouthamer-Loeber, M., 331
Stratton, K., 92, 93
Straus, Murray A., 209, 423
Strauss, A. L., 503
Strauss, S., 507
Strayer, F. F., 57
Streisand, B., 438, 439
Streri, A., 153
Striegel-Moore, R., 477, 478
Strigini, P., 64, 95
Strober, Michael, 476, 478, 479
Strock, B. D., 119
Stroebe, M. S., 506, 513, 516
Stroebe, W., 506, 513
Stroes, J., 413, 414
Strouse, D., 363
Strunin, L., 26
Strutt, G. F., 157
Stryker, M. P., 155
Study Group on Anorexia Nervosa, 478
Stull, D. E., 418
Stumpf, H., 299, 300
Sturla, E., 308
Stuss, D. T., 115
Styfco, S. J., 262
Styles, I., 245
Sudhalter, V., 195
Sugden, D., 124, 129
Sui-Chu, E. H., 439
Suitor, J. J., 410, 412, 442
Sullivan, Harry Stack, 34, 364, 382, 384
Sullivan, M. W., 271, 434
Sullivan, P. F., 477
Sun, Y., 381
Super, Charles M., 89, 101–102, 444
Super, Donald E., 443, 444, 448
Suro, M. D., 161
Susman, E. J., 277
Susser, M. W., 89, 102
Suzman, R. M., 4
Svanborg, A., 324
Sveistrup, H., 123, 124
Swain, I. U., 215
Swanson, G. M., 136
Swarr, A. E., 127, 478
Swavely, S. M., 74
Sweet, J. A., 417
Sweetnam, P., 130
Szinovacz, M., 453, 454

Taeuber, C. M., 415, 499
Taffel, S. M., 97

Taft, L. B., 291
Takahashi, K., 367
Talbert, G. B., 131
Tallal, P., 159
Tamis-LeMonda, C. S., 434
Tanner, J. M., 110, 111, 115, 125, 126, 136, 159
Tarabulsy, G. M., 208
Taris, T. W., 288
Tasker, F., 320, 418
Tatelbaum, R., 104
Taylor, D. G., 371
Taylor, J., 518
Taylor, John H., 351
Taylor, M., 175, 177, 193, 331
Taylor, Marianne G., 305
Taylor, R. D., 397, 444
Taylor, R. E., 253
Tellegen, A., 70
Teller, D. Y., 145
Templer, D. I., 511
Teri, L., 487
Terman, Lewis, 240–241, 256–257, 258
Terry, R., 380
Tesch, Stephanie A., 289
Tessier, R., 208
Teti, D. M., 406
Teti, L. O., 365
Tharinger, D., 319
Thase, M. E., 474
Thelen, Esther, 121–122, 123, 124
Thelen, M. H., 478
Thoma, S. J., 349, 355
Thoman, E. B., 119
Thomas, Alexander, 273, 274, 532
Thomas, D., 192
Thomas, J. R., 125, 128, 129
Thompson, 85
Thompson, J. R., 193
Thompson, L., 389
Thompson, L. A., 197
Thompson, L. W., 513
Thompson, R. A., 365, 433
Thompson, Richard F., 61, 112, 113–114, 154,
    197
Thompson, S. K., 301
Thomson, E., 418
Thorndike, R. L., 241
Thorndike, R. M., 236, 240, 245
Thorne, A., 277
Thorne, Barrie, 303, 319, 384
Thornton, A., 416
Thurber, C. A., 367
Thurstone, Louis L., 237
Thurstone, T. G., 237
Tietjen, A. M., 352, 411
Tinbergen, Niko, 56
Tisak, J., 343
Tisak, M. S., 343
Tizard, B., 373
Tobin, J. D., 111
Tobin, S. S., 454
Toch, T., 438, 439
Tokura, H., 191
Tolan, P. H., 357, 360
Tomasello, M., 199, 351
Tomlin, C., 272
Tomlinson-Keasey, C., 258, 351
Toner, I. J., 344, 355

Tonick, I. J., 325
Torrance, E. P., 258, 259, 260
Toth, S. L., 480, 485
Tousignant, M., 2
Trabasso, T., 179
Trafford, A., 7
Tramontana, M. G., 467, 471
Tran, T. V., 285
Trehub, S. E., 149, 152
Treiber, F., 146
Treloar, A. E., 132
Trevethan, S. O., 346
Trice, A. D., 443
Trickett, P. K., 319, 425
Troll, L. E., 389, 418
Tronick, Edward Z., 8, 366–367, 373
Trotter, K. H., 300
Trueheart, C., 500
Truss, C. V., 287, 446
Tryon, R. C., 65
Tschann, J. M., 128, 129
Tsitouras, P. D., 133
Tucker, P., 308
Tudge, J. R. H., 49, 382
Tuer, M., 410, 414, 418, 422
Tulviste, P., 189
Turiel, Elliot, 304, 342–343
Turkewitz, G., 151, 153
Turkheimer, E., 252
Turner, H. A., 209
Turner, J., 411
Turner, L. A., 222
Turner, P. J., 310
Turner-Bowker, D. M., 310
Twenge, Jean, 299
Tye-Murray, N., 165
Tyre, T. E., 105
Tyson-Rawson, K. J., 510

Uchino, B. N., 390
Uddenberg, N., 75
Udry, Richard, 387
Ulleland, C. N., 92
Ulman, K. J., 127
Umberson, D., 412, 515, 517, 518
U.S. Bureau of the Census, 6, 131, 301, 398, 409, 418, 445, 450, 481, 498, 499
Unsal, A., 115
Updegraff, K., 309
Urberg, K. A., 305
Urofsky, M. I., 496, 497
Ursano, R. J., 384
Usher, JoNell A., 216

Vaden, N. A., 254
Vaillant, George E., 290–291, 448, 483
Valdez-Menchaca, M. C., 196
Valenza, E., 147
Valkonen, T., 513
Vallerand, Robert, 457
Van Aken, M. A. G., 277
Van Balen, F., 83
Van Cleve, L., 479
Vandell, Deborah L., 377, 403
Van den Boom, D. C., 390, 433
Van der Velde, M. E. G., 288
Vandewater, E. A., 451
Van Eerdewegh, M. M., 510, 517

Van Eerdewegh, P., 510
Van Galen, G. P., 124, 125
Vangelisti, A. L., 409
Van Gennep, A., 127
Van Giffen, Katherine, 148
Van IJzendoorn, M. H., 367, 371, 372, 376, 389, 390, 399, 411, 424, 474
Van Lieshout, C. F. M., 277
Vannatta, R. A., 482
Van Velsor, E., 451
Vartanian, L. R., 183
Vaughn, B. E., 88, 372, 376
Vaughn, V. C., 96
Veldhuis, J. D., 119
Vellutino, F. R., 158
Verhaeghen, P., 230, 231
Verhulst, F. C., 469
Verna, G. B., 209
Veroff, Joseph, 446
Verrillo, R. T., 164
Verrillo, V., 164
Verschueren, K., 277
Videka-Sherman, L., 520
Vikem, R. J., 269
Vincent, K. R., 255
Vincent, L., 127
Vinden, P. G., 332
Vinick, B. H., 453
Vinovskis, M. A., 5
Vinter, A., 211
Vobejda, B., 321, 322
Voda, A. M., 132, 133
Volling, B. L., 406
Vondra, J., 424
Voneche, J. J., 41
Von Hofsten, C., 121, 122
Von Knorring, A., 476
Voos, D. K., 99
Vorhees, C. V., 92, 94
Vormbrock, J. K., 387
Voyer, D., 299
Voyer, S., 299
Vreeling, F. W., 136, 227
Vurpillor, Elaine, 157
Vygotsky, Lev, 188–190, 191, 198, 201, 263

Waddell, Kathryn J., 228
Waechter, E. H., 509
Wagner, B. M., 482
Wagner, D. A., 227
Wagner, E. H., 136
Waite, L. J., 389, 451, 513
Walberg, 438
Walberg, H. J., 438
Walden, Tedra, 365
Waldenström, U., 98
Waldholz, M., 74
Waldman, D. A., 449
Waldman, E., 450
Waldman, I. D., 68, 347, 252
Waldorf, M., 96, 105
Waldron-Hennessey, R., 411
Walford, R. L., 136, 138, 499, 500
Walk, Richard D., 147–148, 154
Walker, Lawrence J., 346, 349, 351, 352, 354
Walker-Andrews, A. S., 153
Wallace, Amy, 257
Wallace, C. S., 114, 154

Wallach, M. A., 258
Wallander, J. L., 471
Wallen, K., 307
Wallerstein, J. S., 421
Wallis, C., 469
Walsh, A., 56
Walsh, P. V., 325
Walster, E., 127, 389
Walster, G. W., 389
Wampler, K. S., 474
Wang, M. C., 438, 439
Wapner, S., 453
Ward, M. J., 469
Ward, R., 412
Ward, S. A., 130
Wark, G. R., 350, 354
Warkentin, V., 271
Warr, P., 449
Warren, J. R., 310
Warren, M. P., 127
Warren, William, 123
Warwick, Z. S., 164
Wass, H., 508, 510, 511, 515
Wasserman, A., 381
Waterman, A. S., 282, 284
Waters, Everett, 368, 373
Watkinson, B., 94
Watson, D., 464
Watson, John B., 37, 47–48, 206, 211, 213, 533
Watt, L. M., 291
Waxman, Sandra, 177–178
Weakliem, D., 245
Weaver, C. N., 418
Weber, R. A., 361
Webster, J. D., 291
Wechsler, David, 241
Weed, S., 322
Weg, R. B., 137
Wehner, E. A., 385
Weibel-Orlando, J., 413
Weiffenbach, J. M., 163, 164
Weinberg, Richard A., 68, 252, 255, 283
Weiner, Bernard, 431–432
Weiner, Marcella B., 323
Weinraub, M., 301, 302, 367
Weisberg, Paul, 40
Weiskopf, S., 145
Weisner, T. S., 407, 430
Weiss, Bahr, 209, 481, 489, 490
Weiss, G., 471
Weiss, L. H., 402
Weiss, Michael G., 159, 222
Weiss, R., 74
Weiss, R. S., 504, 513
Weissman, M. M., 485
Weisz, John R., 334, 462, 463, 489, 490
Welch, D. C., 457
Welch-Ross, M. K., 302
Wellman, Henry M., 149, 217, 218, 219, 331
Wells, P. A., 414
Wender, P. H., 471
Wenestam, C., 508, 511
Werker, J. F., 150, 151, 191, 198
Werner, E. E., 102, 103
Werner, Heinz, 120, 529
Werner, L. A., 150
Wertsch, J. V., 189

West, R. L., 225, 227, 457
Weston, D. R., 376, 400
Wexler, Nancy, 74
Whalen, C. K., 300, 470, 471
Whiffen, Valerie E., 99, 100, 485
Whipp, B. J., 130
Whipple, E. E., 424
Whipple, E. G., 321
Whitbeck, L. B., 417, 468
Whitbourne, S. K., 116, 130, 131, 162, 164, 289
White, H. R., 485
White, J. A., 486, 487, 488
White, J. M., 396, 397, 398, 417
White, K., 415
White, L., 412
White, L. K., 412
White, Robert W., 432–433
White, S. H., 217
Whitebook, M., 374
Whitehurst, G. J., 196
Whiting, B. B., 298, 303
Whitman, T. L., 411
Whitney, M. P., 119
Wible, Cynthia, 224
Wideman, M. V., 104
Widmayer, S., 105, 426
Wiehe, V. R., 422, 423, 424, 426
Wiesel, Torsten N., 114, 154
Wigfield, A., 279, 431, 435
Wiggins, S., 74
Wikan, U., 516
Wilbur, J., 132
Wilcock, A., 98
Wilcox, S., 146
Wilens, T. E., 471, 472
Wilkinson, R. T., 124, 134
Wilkner, K., 152
Wilks, J., 386
Willems, E. P., 12
Willemsen, E., 215
Willerman, L., 250
Williams, Allan F., 161, 513
Williams, G. J., 478
Williams, J. E., 298, 299
Williams, K. C., 201
Williams, Linda M., 319
Williams, M. E., 487, 488
Williams, P. T., 138
Williams, S., 127
Williams, T. M., 132
Williams, W. M., 438, 445

Williamson, D. A., 477
Willis, D. P., 4
Willis, S. L., 228, 230, 248, 414
Willms, J. D., 439
Wilson, E. O., 56
Wilson, G. T., 137
Wilson, K. S., 377
Wilson, M. N., 8, 414
Wilson, Ronald, 67, 103
Wilson-Sadberry, K. R., 450
Winch, G., 317
Windle, M., 479, 481, 482
Windle, R. C., 481, 482
Wingfield, A., 163
Wink, P., 287, 316
Winner, E., 256, 257, 260
Winsler, A., 201
Winterhoff, P. A., 49
Wippman, J., 373
Wittlinger, R. P., 225
Wolchik, S. A., 422
Wolf, O., 259
Wolf, R. S., 423
Wolfe, R., 485, 490
Wolfe, W. S., 137
Wolff, M., 348
Wolff, P. H., 119, 192, 366
Wolfner, G. D., 422, 424, 425
Wonderlich, S., 478
Wong, P. T. P., 291, 350
Woodruff-Pak, D. S., 212
Woods, N. F., 132
Woodsmall, L., 196
Woodworth, S., 375
Woodworth, Sharon, 13
Woollacott, M. H., 134
Woollacott, M. J., 123, 124
Worchel, F. F., 509
Worden, J. W., 510, 517, 518, 519
Wortman, Camille B., 506, 511, 513, 516, 518
Wright, L., 55
Wright, M., 224
Wright, R., 285
Wrightsman, L. S., 288, 462
Wu, X., 485
Wynn, Karen, 150
Wyshak, G., 127

Yaeger, J., 190
Yaffe, S. J., 103
Yalisove, D., 181

Yamaguchi, K., 479
Yamaura, H., 115
Yan, B., 185
Yang, B., 444, 482
Yarrow, L. J., 433
Yau, J., 409
Yeates, Keith O., 243, 252, 333, 334
Yendovitskaya, T. V., 156
Yerkes, R. M., 246
Yeung-Courchesne, R., 467
Yirmiya, N., 467
Yoder, C. Y., 485
Yonas, A., 147, 152
Young, G., 350
Young, R., 239
Young, V., 508
Young, W. C., 307
Youngblade, L. M., 331
Youniss, J., 363, 364
Yu, A. P., 300
Yu, B. P., 501
Yu, H. C., 442
Yuill, N., 332
Yussen, S. R., 219, 344

Zahn-Waxler, Carolyn, 9, 28, 340, 341, 348
Zani, B., 127
Zaporozhets, A. V., 157
Zarit, M., 3
Zarit, S. H., 248, 485
Zaslow, Martha J., 374, 377, 420, 421
Zautra, A. J., 457
Zeaman, D., 256
Zeanah, C. H., 468
Zeilhuis, G. A., 256
Zeiss, A. M., 419
Zeiss, R. A., 419
Zelazo, N. A., 122
Zelazo, P. D., 342
Zelazo, P. R., 122, 215, 374
Zelizer, 6
Zeskind, P. S., 89
Zick, C. D., 301, 314, 452
Zigler, E., 254, 255, 256, 262, 276, 403, 424, 426, 433, 437, 442, 457, 481
Zimmerman, M. A., 397
Zimmerman, Robert R., 370
Zisook, S., 505, 506, 512, 517
Zonderman, A. B., 483
Zucker, K. J., 320
Zweifel, J. E., 133

Subject Index

A, not B, error, 174
Ability, incremental vs. entity views of, 435
Ability tracking, 439
Absence/inhibition/delay of grief, 515–516
Abstract thinking, 179–180
Academic achievement. *See* School achievement
Acceptance/responsiveness dimension of parenting, 401, 402
Acceptance stage of dying, 503
Accommodation, 172
Achievement motivation, 430–457
   adolescence, 441–445
   adulthood, 445–452
   attribution theory, 431–432, 435, 437
   childhood, 434–441
   infancy, 432–434
   need for achievement, 431
   old age, 446, 454–455, 456–457
   retirement, 452–454
Acquired immune deficiency syndrome. *See* AIDS
Active self, 275
Activity dimension of temperament, 272
Activity/passivity issue, 28, 533
Activity theory of aging, 454
Adaptation, 172
ADHD. *See* Attention-deficit hyperactivity disorder
Adolescence
   achievement motivation, 441–445
   ADHD, 471
   brain development, 115
   contextual theories, 45, 46, 50
   creativity, 259–260
   and death, 510–511
   and divorce, 420–421, 422
   egocentrism, 182–183
   employment, 444–445
   Eriksonian psychoanalytic theory, 35, 36, 49, 280–281, 526
   Freudian psychoanalytic theory, 32, 33, 34, 49
   gender roles, 304–305
   historical perspective, 6
   hormones, 111
   information processing, 222

intelligence, 245, 263
language development, 195
learning theories, 40, 50
moral development, 345–349, 355–357, 526
mortality, 499
nutrition, 136
parent/child relationships, 127, 383, 408–409, 411–412
perceptual development, 159–160
physical development, 125–130, 136, 442
Piagetian theory, 43, 44, 49–50, 179–183, 526
psychological disorders, 476–482
relationships, 382–386
self-concept, 278–284
sexuality, 319–322
sibling relationships, 415
social cognition, 332, 333–334
vocational development, 443–444
whole-person perspective, 526
Adolescence (Hall), 9
Adoption studies, 65, 68
Adrenal glands, 111
Adulthood. *See also* Aging; Old age
   achievement motivation, 445–452
   coping skills, 483–484
   creativity, 260–262
   and death, 511–518
   Eriksonian psychoanalytic theory, 35–36, 528
   family transitions, 414–417
   Freudian psychoanalytic theory, 32, 33
   gender roles, 314–317
   historical perspective, 6–7
   information processing, 222–224
   intelligence, 245–247
   language development, 195–196
   moral development, 349–350, 526
   mortality, 499
   new marriages, 409–410
   personality, 286–288, 289–292
   Piagetian theory, 183–186
   psychological disorders, 482–486, 513
   relationships, 386–390
   self-concept, 285
   sexuality, 322–323

social cognition, 334–335
stress, 483
whole-person perspective, 526, 528
Afterbirth, 95
Age effects, 14, 16
Age grades, 4
Ageism, 292, 490
Age norms, 4–5, 463, 516
Aggression
   and moral development, 346–349
   prevention, 355–357
   sex differences, 299, 306–307
Aging. *See also* Adulthood; Old age
   and coping skills, 483–484
   defined, 2, 3
   and employment, 449–450
   and intelligence, 245–250
   and perceptual development, 160–165
   and physical development, 130–136
   theories of, 454–455, 499–502
AIDS, 90–91, 322, 488
Alcohol
   adolescent use, 479–480
   and health, 136, 138
   and prenatal development, 92–93
Alpert, Richard, 268
Alternative birth centers, 105
Alzheimer's disease, 115, 116, 133, 231, 486–488
American Sign Language (ASL), 166, 199, 200
Amino acids, 59
Amniocentesis, 75
Amnion, 82
Amorality, 340, 341
Anal stage of psychosexual development, 32
Androgenized females, 306
Androgens, 111
Androgyny, 315–317
Anger stage of dying, 503
Anorexia nervosa, 127, 477
Anoxia, 95–96
Anticipatory grief, 504
Antisocial behavior, 346–349, 385, 386, 480, 481
Anxiety, sex differences, 300
Apgar test, 97–98

Aptitude-treatment interaction (ATI), 440
Army Alpha Test, 246
Artificial insemination, 83
ASL. *See* American Sign Language
Assimilation, 172
Assisted suicide, 497
Associative play, 378
ATI. *See* Aptitude-treatment interaction
"At risk" infants, 102–104, 105–106, 300
Attachment theory, 362–363. *See also* Infant
    attachment
    and achievement motivation, 433
    and bereavement, 504–505, 506, 517
    and romantic relationships, 387–389
Attention, 156–157, 159, 161–162
Attention-deficit hyperactivity disorder
    (ADHD), 92, 469–473
Attribution theory, 431–432, 435, 437
Authoritarian parenting, 401
Authoritative parenting, 401–402, 436
Autism, 329–330, 465–468
Automatization, 218, 240
Autonomy, 408–409
    vs. shame/doubt, 35, 289, 524
Autosomes, 58
Avoidant attachment, 369, 371
Axons, 111

Babbling, 192
Babinski reflex, 117, 118
Baby biographies, 9
Baby boom generation, 6
Baby Jessica, 361
Bargaining stage of dying, 503
Bayley Scales of Infant Development, 243, 244
Beanpole families, 399
Beginning of thought stage, 173
Behavioral genetics, 64–71, 73, 76
    on intelligence, 67–68
    on personality, 68–69, 272
Behavioral inhibition, 272–273, 340–341
Behaviorism, 37. *See also* Learning theories;
    Operant conditioning
Belief-desire psychology, 331
Bell Curve, The (Herrnstein & Murray), 253
Bereavement, 504–506, 509–510, 512–515
    coping skills, 517–518
    pathological grief, 515–517
    support, 519–520
Big five dimensions of personality, 269–270,
    286
Binge/purge syndrome. *See* Bulimia nervosa
Bioecological approach. *See* Ecological
    approach
Biological/environmental interaction, 43–44,
    71–73. *See also* Biological vs.
    environmental influences
    achievement motivation, 440, 442–443
    aging, 455, 501–502
    brain development, 114
    and cloning, 83
    diathesis/stress model, 485–486
    dynamic systems approach, 123–124
    ecological approach, 44–47, 50, 397,
        424–425
    Eriksonian psychoanalytic theory, 36
    evolutionary theory, 56, 57
    gender roles, 313–314

gene/environment correlations, 72–73,
    252, 287–288, 405–406, 474–475
gene/environment interactions, 59, 71–72
infant attachment, 372
information processing, 227–228
intelligence, 239–240
language development, 198–199
moral development, 341, 348
parent/child relationships, 405–406
and parenting style, 102
personality, 272, 274, 287–288
Piagetian theory, 41, 43, 172, 188
psychological disorders, 474–475, 478, 482
reciprocal influence, 39, 81–82, 396,
    405–406, 408, 474–475
sexual maturation, 126–127, 128
sexual orientation, 321
Biological influences. *See also* Attachment
    theory; Hormones; Infant attachment
    ADHD, 471
    aging, 500–501
    autism, 467
    dementia, 487
    ethology, 56–57, 362–363
    gender roles, 305–307, 306
    intelligence, 250, 254
    language development, 197–198
    personality, 269
    psychological disorders, 474–475
    relationships, 362–363
    sexuality, 318
    weight, 137
Biological vs. environmental influences,
    531–532. *See also*
    Biological/environmental interaction;
    Biological influences; Environmental
    influences
    gender roles, 308
    gene/environment correlations, 72–73,
        252, 287–288, 405–406, 474–475
    and heritability, 70–71
    intelligence, 67–68, 250–255
    perceptual development, 143–144, 147
    personality, 68–69, 269, 270, 272, 274,
        287–288
    psychological disorders, 69–70, 471
    reproductive system, 132
    research methods, 64–67
    sexual orientation, 320–321
    weight, 137
Biosocial theory of gender-role development,
    305–307
Birth. *See* Perinatal environment
Birth defects. *See* Chromosome
    abnormalities; Teratogens
Bisexuality, 320–321
Blastula, 82
Bodily kinesthetic intelligence, 238
Body image, 478
Bonding, 98–99, 366
Boredom, 144
Brain
    and ADHD, 471
    development of, 112–115, 134, 245
    and endocrine system, 110
Brain growth spurt, 113–114
Brazelton Neonatal Behavioral Assessment Scale
    (Brazelton), 105

Breathing reflex, 117
Breech presentation, 96
Brown v. Board of Education of Topeka, 440
Bulimia nervosa, 477

Cancer, 133
Caregiver burden, 416
Care, morality of, 354
Carriers, 61
Cataracts, 161
Catch-up growth, 136
Categorical self, 271, 275
Centenarians, 1, 500
Centration, 175, 217
Cephalocaudal principle, 119–120, 121
Cerebral cortex, 112
Cerebral palsy, 96
Cesarean section, 96–97
Child abuse, 422–426. *See also* Child sexual
    abuse
    effects of, 425
    historical perspective, 5
    and infant attachment, 363, 371
    and moral development, 348
    solutions, 425–426
Child-directed speech, 198
Child effects model, 405–406
Childhood. *See also* Childhood psychological
    disorders; Family; Infancy; Parent/child
    relationships; Parenting style
    achievement motivation, 434–441
    brain development, 114–115
    cognitive development, 42, 125, 175–179,
        180–181, 220, 333, 524
    creativity, 259–260
    and death, 507–510
    Eriksonian psychoanalytic theory, 35, 289,
        524
    and family, 401–408, 411–412
    Freudian psychoanalytic theory, 30–32, 33
    gender roles, 302–304
    historical perspective, 5–6
    information processing, 217–222, 230
    intelligence, 244, 262
    language development, 193–195
    moral development, 341–345, 355–357,
        524, 526
    perceptual development, 156–160
    personality, 277–278
    physical development, 124–125, 136
    Piagetian theory, 42, 175–179, 180–181,
        220, 333, 524, 526
    relationships, 363–364, 377–382
    self-concept, 275–277
    sexuality, 317–319
    social cognition, 331–334
    whole-person perspective, 524, 526
Childhood psychological disorders, 469–476
    attention-deficit hyperactivity disorder,
        469–473
    causes of, 475–476
    depression, 473–474
    persistence of, 475–476
    treatment, 489–490
Childless couples, 418
Childrearing practices. *See* Parental
    influences
Child sexual abuse, 33–34, 319, 422

Child support, 422
Chorion, 82
Chorionic villus biopsy (CVS), 75
Chromosome abnormalities, 63–64, 88
Chromosomes, 58
Chronic grief, 515
Chumships, 364, 382, 383–384
Cigarettes. *See* Tobacco
Class differences
    and divorce, 422
    and health, 131
    and intelligence, 252
    and moral development, 348–349
    and parenting, 402–404
    poverty, 398–399
    and vocational development, 444
Classical conditioning, 206–207, 211
Classification, 177–178
Class inclusion, 179
Climacteric, 133
Clinical method, 171
Cliques, 384–385
Cloning, 83
Cocaine, 93
Cochlear implants, 165–166
Codominance, 62
Coercive family environment, 349, 356
Cognitive development. *See also* Intelligence;
    Learning; Memory; Piagetian theory
    and achievement motivation, 441
    adolescence, 43, 44, 49–50, 179–183
    adulthood, 183–186
    and autism, 467
    and brain development, 115
    childhood, 42, 125, 175–179, 180–181,
        220, 333, 524
    defined, 1
    genetic factors, 3
    and identity formation, 282
    infancy, 42, 172–175, 523
    and moral development, 351
    old age, 186–187
    optimization of, 201–202
    and physical development, 125
    and relationships, 362
    and self-concept, 272
    sociocultural perspective, 188–190,
        201–202
    and understanding of death, 506,
        507–508, 510
Cognitive-developmental theory. *See*
    Piagetian theory
Cohabitation, 417–418
Cohort effects, 14–15, 20–21, 246
College, 284, 289–290
Coming-of-age rituals, 7, 127
Companionate grandparenting style, 413
Compensation for decline, 135
Complementary interactive stage of
    sociability, 377
Compliance, 300
Computers, 213
Conception, 57–58, 82, 83
Concordance rates, 65–67
Concrete operations stage of cognitive
    development, 42, 178–179, 180–181,
    333, 524
Conditioned response (CR), 206

Conditioned stimulus (CS), 206
Conduct disorders, 405
Confidants, 390
Confidentiality, 22
Conformity, 385–386
Consent, informed, 21–22
Conservation, 175–177, 178–179
Constraint-seeking questions, 229
Constructivism, 41
Contact comfort, 370
Contextual component of intelligence,
    239–240
Contextual theories, 43–47, 50, 532. *See also*
    Biological/environmental interaction;
    Environmental influences
    ecological approach, 44–47, 50, 397,
        424–425
    personality, 270
Contextual world view, 48–49
Continuity/discontinuity issue, 28–29, 39,
    529–530. *See also* Stage theories
Continuous reinforcement, 208
Contour, 146–147
Contraception, 322
Contractions, 95
Control, experimental, 18
Conventional morality, 337, 338, 345–346,
    526
Convergent thinking, 258
Cooing, 192
Cooperation, 300
Cooperative learning methods, 441
Cooperative play, 378
Coping skills, 483–484, 517–518
Correlational method, 18–20
Correlation coefficients, 19, 66
Counterconditioning, 206
CR. *See* Conditioned response
Crawling, 121
Creativity, 258–262. *See also* Intelligence
Critical period, 89, 90
    brain development, 114
    gender identity, 308
    language development, 199–201
    relationships, 362, 363
Crossing over, 58
Cross-modal perception, 153
Cross-sectional research designs, 14–16, 17,
    20–21, 246
Crowds, 384–385
Crystallized intelligence, 238, 247, 252
CS. *See* Conditioned stimulus
Cued recall memory, 214
Cultural differences, 7–8. *See also* Racial
    differences
    achievement motivation, 442
    birth experience, 98
    child abuse, 424
    cognitive development, 187, 188, 189
    death, 496–498, 508, 516
    emotional development, 365
    grandparenthood, 413
    and identity formation, 284
    infant attachment, 367
    infant perceptual development, 155–156
    infant socialization, 101–102
    and intelligence, 239, 253–254
    menopause, 132–133

moral development, 348–349, 351–352,
    353
old age, 8, 226
parent/child relationships, 415–416
parenting, 100–102, 401, 404–405
physical development, 122–123
psychological disorders, 462–463, 464
school achievement, 455–456
self-concept, 276
sexuality, 317, 318–319
Cultural-familial retardation, 255
Culture bias, 240, 253–254
Culture-fair IQ tests, 253–254
Cumulative-deficit hypothesis, 244
CVS. *See* Chorionic villus biopsy

Daily hassles, 482
Damage theories of aging, 499, 501
Dark adaptation, 161
Data collection, 11–13
Dating, 384–385
Day care, 374–375
Deafness, 165–166, 199, 200
Death, 495–520. *See also* Aging; Bereavement
    and adolescence, 510–511
    and adulthood, 511–518
    anxiety about, 511–512
    care of dying person, 518–519
    and childhood, 507–510
    coping skills, 517–518
    and family life cycles, 512–515
    and infancy, 506–507
    Kübler-Ross's stages, 502–504
    life expectancy, 6, 498–499, 500
    meanings of, 495–498
    pathological grief, 515–517
    suicide, 473, 481–448, 497, 517
    theories of, 500–502
Death anxiety, 511–512
Death instincts, 30
Debriefing, 22
Decentration, 175, 178
Defense mechanisms, 31
Deferred imitation, 211–212
Delirium, 488
Delivery, 95
Demandingness/control dimension of
    parenting, 401, 402
Dementia, 486–488
Dendrites, 111, 116
Denial stage of dying, 502
Dependent variable, 17–18
Depression, 464
    adolescence, 480–482
    adulthood, 484–486, 513
    childhood, 473–474
    and dementia, 488
    and dying, 503
    infancy, 468–469
    postpartum, 99–100
    and sexuality, 324
Depression stage of dying, 503
Depth perception, 147–148
Desire psychology, 331
Development
    defined, 2–3
    as lifelong process, 3, 533
Developmental norms, 120–121

Developmental psychology, 8–11
  goals of, 8–9
Developmental psychology (continued)
  origins of, 9–10
  research, 11–22
Developmental psychopathology, 464–465
Developmental quotients (DQ), 242–243
Developmental research designs, 13–16, 17, 20–21, 246
Developmental stages, 29. See also specific stage theories
Developmental theories, 11, 26–30, 47–51, 533
  application example, 34, 36, 40, 44, 46, 49–50
  basic issues, 28–30, 529–534
  nature of, 26–27
  and world views, 47–49
Deviant behavior. See Antisocial behavior
Diagnostic and Statistical Manual of Mental Disorders (DSM-IV) (American Psychiatric Association), 463–464, 469, 484
Diathesis/stress model of psychopathology, 485–486
Dietary restriction, 502
Differential reinforcement, 308–309
Differentiation of neurons, 112
Difficult temperament, 273
Diffusion identity status, 281
Disabilities, children with, 440–441
Disease. See also Health
  maternal, 89–91
  and memory, 227
  old age, 130–131, 135, 227
  and personality, 288
Disenchantment phase of retirement, 453
Disengagement theory of aging, 454–455
Dismissing working model, 388
Disorganization/despair phase of grieving, 505
Disorganized/disoriented attachment, 370, 371
Distinctive features, 158
Distorted grief, 515
Distraction strategies, 485
Distribution of IQ scores, 241, 243
Divergent thinking, 258
Divorce, 398, 413, 418, 419–421, 422
Domestic violence, 422–426
Dominance hierarchies, 57
Dominant genes, 60–61
Double standard, 321
Dowager's hump, 130, 131
Down syndrome, 63, 255, 487
DQ. See Developmental quotients
Drugs
  for ADHD, 471–472
  adolescent use, 479
  for Alzheimer's disease, 487
  and health, 136
  in perinatal environment, 97
  and prenatal development, 91–94
DSM-IV. See Diagnostic and Statistical Manual of Mental Disorders
Dynamic assessment, 241, 263
Dynamic systems approach, 123–124
Dyslexia, 158, 159

Easy temperament, 273
Eating disorders, 477–479
Echolalia, 466
Eclectics, 50, 533
Ecological approach, 44–47, 50, 397, 424–425
Education. See also School achievement
  and gender roles, 310
  improving, 455–457
  and memory, 230–231
  and moral development, 351
Education for All Handicapped Children Act, 440
Effectance motivation, 433
Ego, 30–31
Egocentrism, 42, 177
  adolescent, 182–183, 526
  and friendships, 382
  and language development, 195
  and moral development, 341
  and self-concept, 276
  and social cognition, 332–333
Elaboration, creative, 261
Elaboration strategy, 218
Elderly people. See Old age
Electra complex, 33, 34, 307, 336
Embryonic period, 82, 84
Emotional development. See Emotions
Emotionality dimension of temperament, 272, 273, 345
Emotion-focused coping, 483
Emotions. See also Depression; Grief
  Freudian psychoanalytic theory, 34
  infancy, 364–366
  maternal, 88–89
  and moral development, 335, 354–355
  and Piagetian theory, 43
  and play, 380
  postpartum depression, 99–100
  regulation, 365–366
Empathy, 300, 335, 425
Empiricists, 143
Employment, 447–448. See also Achievement motivation
  adolescence, 444–445
  and aging, 449–450
  and intelligence, 245
  Levinson's development theory, 446–447
  and midlife crisis, 448–449
  and parenting style, 404
  retirement, 452–454
  substantive complexity, 452
  vocational development, 443–444
  women, 398, 450–452
Empty nest, 412
Encoding, 213
Endocrine glands, 110
Endocrine system, 110–111
Enmeshed families, 478
Entity view of ability, 435
Environmental influences, 81–107. See also
  Biological/environmental interaction;
  Biological vs. environmental influences;
  Cultural differences; Learning theories;
  Parental influences; Prenatal
  development
  "at risk" infants, 102–104, 105–106
  and behavioral genetics, 66
  child abuse, 424–425

defined, 3, 81
dementia, 488
early infancy, 105–106
emotional development, 364–365
gender roles, 304–306, 307, 308–311
and infant perceptual development, 154–155
intelligence, 250–252, 254–255
language development, 196–197
learning theories, 37, 38–39, 40, 50, 196, 209–211, 309–311
moral development, 339, 344, 351–352
perinatal, 95–100
personality, 269, 270, 272
and self-concept, 272, 276–277, 292
sex differences, 300–301
sexuality, 318–319
social cognition, 331–332
socialization, 100–102, 340, 364–365, 382, 438
teratogens in, 94–95
Epilepsy, and autism, 467
Equity, 389–390
Eriksonian psychoanalytic theory, 34–36
  and achievement motivation, 447
  adolescence, 35, 36, 49, 280–281, 526
  adulthood, 35–36, 528
  and death, 511
  and empty nest, 412
  vs. Freudian psychoanalytic theory, 32
  infant attachment, 371
  personality, 269, 288–292
  relationships, 35, 289–290, 362, 387
  and whole-person perspective, 524, 526, 528
Error accummulation theory of aging, 501
Estrogen, 111
Ethics, 18, 21–22, 76–77
Ethnic differences. See Racial differences
Ethnic identity, 283
Ethology, 56–57, 362–363
Eugenics, 76
Euthanasia, 496, 497
Evolutionary psychology, 56, 57, 306, 490
Evolutionary theory, 9, 55–57. See also
  Evolutionary psychology
Executive control processes, 214, 467
Exercise, 127, 137–138
Exosystem, 45
Expansion, 198–199
Experience. See Biological/environmental
  interaction; Environmental influences;
  Learning
Experiential component of intelligence, 240
Experimental control, 18
Experimental method, 17–18, 20
Explicit memory, 225
Expressive role, 298
Extended family households, 397
Externalizing problems, 469, 489–490
Extinction, 208
Eyeblink reflex, 117

Factor analysis, 236–237, 238, 269
Failure to thrive, 468–469
False belief task, 329
False self behavior, 280

Family, 396–426. *See also* Marriage; Parental influences; Parenting experience; Parenting style
  and adolescence, 408–409, 411–412
  adult transitions, 414–417
  and childhood, 401–408, 411–412
  childless couples, 418
  and contextual theories, 44–45
  and death, 512–515
  diversity of, 399, 417–422
  divorce, 398, 413, 418, 419–421, 422
  dual-career, 451
  and eating disorders, 478
  gay/lesbian, 418–419
  and gender roles, 314
  grandparenthood, 412–414
  and infancy, 399–401, 410–411
  influence models, 405–406
  life cycles, 397, 398, 418, 512–515
  and moral development, 349, 356–357
  and recent demographic trends, 398–399
  reconstituted, 399, 421–422
  sibling relationships, 331–332, 406–408, 415, 514–515
  single adults, 398, 417–418
  systems theory, 396–398
  violence, 422–426
Family development theories, 397
Family influences. *See* Parental influences
Family life cycles, 397, 398, 418
  and death, 512–515
Family therapy, 489
Family violence, 422–426
Fantasy stage of employment, 443
FAS. *See* Fetal alcohol syndrome
Father/infant relationships, 399–400
Fathers. *See also* Parental influences; Parent/child relationships; Parenting experience; Parenting style
  birth experience, 100
  and infant attachment, 375–376
Fearfulness/fearlessness. *See* Behavioral inhibition
Fearful working model, 388
Feingold diet, 472
Fetal alcohol syndrome (FAS), 92–93
Fetal period, 84–85
Fine motor skills, 121
Fixation, 31–32
Fluid intelligence, 238, 247, 252
Flynn effect, 252
Forceps, 96
Foreclosure identity status, 281, 284
Formal operations stage of cognitive development, 42, 43, 526
Frames of Mind (Gardner), 238–239
Fraternal twins, 58
Free radicals, 501, 502
Freudian psychoanalytic theory, 30–34
  adolescence, 32, 33, 34, 49
  ageism in, 490
  gender roles, 33, 307–308
  and infant attachment, 370–371, 376
  infantile amnesia, 217
  moral development, 31, 34, 335–336
  personality, 268–269
  and plasticity, 531

relationships, 362, 364
sexuality, 31–33, 317
and world view, 47, 49
Friendships, 382, 383–384, 389–390. *See also* Relationships
Full-scale IQ, 241
Functional grammar, 194
Functional play, 434

Gay/lesbian people, 320–321, 418–419
Gender consistency, 312
Gender identity, 301–302, 303, 308
Gender intensification, 304
Gender-role norms, 298–299, 301
Gender roles. *See also* Sex differences
  adolescence, 304–305
  adulthood, 314–317
  biosocial theory, 305–307
  as cause of sex differences, 300–301
  changing, 325
  childhood, 302–304
  cognitive theory, 311–313
  defined, 298
  double standard, 321
  and eating disorders, 477–478
  and employment, 450, 451
  and father/infant relationships, 399
  Freudian psychoanalytic theory, 33, 307–308
  and gay/lesbian families, 418
  and gifted women, 258
  and grandparenthood, 413
  and identity formation, 282
  infancy, 301–302
  and moral development, 354
  and motor development, 130
  norms, 298–299, 301
  parental influences, 307–308, 309, 400
  and personality, 277–278, 288
  and sexual orientation, 320
  social learning theory, 308–311
  social-role hypothesis, 300
  and vocational development, 443, 444
Gender-role stereotypes, 298, 302–303. *See also* Gender roles
Gender schemata, 312–313
Gender segregation, 303–304, 378, 381
Gender stability, 312
Gender typing, 298. *See also* Gender roles
Gene/environment correlations, 72–73
  and family, 405–406
  intelligence, 252
  personality, 287–288
  psychological disorders, 474–475
Gene/environment interaction, 59, 71–72
Generalized other, 333
Generativity vs. stagnation, 35, 290–291, 528
Genetic code, 57–60
Genetic counseling, 73–74, 75
Genetic engineering, 76–77
Genetic epistemology, 171
Genetic factors, 55–64, 73–77. *See also* Biological/environmental interaction; Biological influences; Biological vs. environmental influences
  chromosome abnormalities, 63–64, 88
  defined, 3
  disorder prevention/treatment, 74–77

evolutionary theory, 9, 55–57
genetic code, 57–60
genetic counseling, 73–74, 75
inheritance mechanisms, 60–63
mutations, 63
Genital stage of psychosexual development, 32, 33
Genotype, 60
Germinal period, 82
Gerontology, 10
Giftedness, 256–258
Glaucoma, 161
Goodness of fit, 532
  and achievement motivation, 440, 442–443
  infancy, 102, 274, 372
  and moral development, 341
  old age, 455
  and personality, 288
  and temperament, 274
Grammar, 194–195
Grandparenthood, 412–414, 515
Grasping reflex, 117, 118
Grief, 504. *See also* Bereavement
Gross motor skills, 121
Growth
  adolescence, 125
  childhood, 124
  defined, 3
  infancy, 119–120
Growth hormone, 110
Growth hypothesis of coping skills, 483
Guided participation, 189

Habituation, 144, 215, 243
Hand preferences, 114–115
Harm, protection from, 22
Hayflick limit, 500–501
Head Start, 262
Health, 130–131, 135–136. *See also* Physical development
  and intelligence decline, 248
  and physical behavior, 134
  risks, 138–139
Hearing
  and aging, 162–163
  impairments, 165–167, 199, 200
  infancy, 149–152
Heredity. *See* Genetic factors
Heritability, 64–65, 70–71. *See also* Genetic factors
Heterosexuality, 320–321
Hierarchy of abilities, 238
Historical perspective, 5–7, 240
HIV. *See* AIDS
Holophrases, 192
HOME inventory, 250–251, 252
Home Observation for Measurement of the Environment. *See* HOME inventory
Homosexuality, 320–321. *See also* Gay/lesbian people
Honeymoon phase of retirement, 453
Horizontal décalage, 179
Hormone replacement therapy (HRT), 133
Hormones, 110–111
  and gender roles, 305, 306–307
  and maternal condition, 88
  and menopause, 132, 133

Hormones (continued)
  and menstrual cycle, 131–132
  and postpartum depression, 99
  and sexuality, 111, 318, 323
  and sexual orientation, 320–321
Hospices, 518–519
Hot flashes, 132
HRT. See Hormone replacement therapy
Human growth hormone, 110
Human nature, 28
Humor, 181
Huntington's disease, 74, 288, 488
Hurried Child, The (Elkind), 436
Hyperactivity. See Attention-deficit
    hyperactivity disorder
Hypothalamus, 110, 501
Hypotheses, 11
Hypothetical-deductive reasoning, 181–182

Id, 30
Ideation, 261
Ideational fluency, 258
Identical twins, 58
Identity achievement status, 281, 284
Identity formation, 280–284, 346, 478
Identity vs. role confusion, 35, 36, 280–281,
    289
Imaginary audience phenomenon, 182, 183
Imagination, 379
Implicit memory, 225
Imprinting, 362, 363
Impulsivity, 345, 347
Inclusion, 440–441
Incomplete dominance, 61
Incremental view of ability, 435
Independent variable, 17–18
Indirect effects, 400–401
Individuality. See Universality/particularity
    issue
Induction, 344–345, 405
Industry vs. inferiority, 35, 289, 524
Infancy. See also Infant perceptual
    development; Infant physical
    development; Perinatal environment
  achievement motivation, 432–434
  ADHD, 470
  "at risk" infants, 102–104, 105–106, 300
  attention, 156
  bonding, 98–99
  brain development, 112–114
  contextual theories, 44–45
  and death, 506–507
  early, 105–106, 116–119
  emotions, 364–366
  Eriksonian psychoanalytic theory, 35,
      288–289, 371, 524
  and family, 399–401, 410–411
  Freudian psychoanalytic theory, 30, 32,
      217, 370–371, 376
  gender roles, 301–302
  information processing, 215–217
  intelligence, 242–244
  language development, 191–193, 217
  moral development, 339–341
  mortality, 98, 101, 499
  Piagetian theory, 42, 172–175, 523
  and prenatal development, 85
  psychological disorders, 465–469

self-concept, 271–272
sexuality, 317
social cognition, 331
socialization, 100–102, 364–365
temperament, 68–69, 102, 119, 272–274,
    340–341, 345, 372
whole-person perspective, 523–524
Infant attachment, 362–363, 364–377
  and achievement motivation, 433
  and caregiver attachment, 366–367
  and day care, 374–375
  and depression, 468
  and emotional development, 364–366
  and exploratory behavior, 369
  and fathers, 375–376
  and fears, 367–369
  influences on, 370–372
  and later development, 372–376, 390
  peers, 376–377
  phases of, 367
  types of, 369–370
Infantile amnesia, 216–217
Infantile autism, 329–330, 465–468
Infant mortality, 98, 101, 499
Infant perceptual development, 118, 144–156
  cultural differences, 155–156
  hearing, 149–152
  influences on, 154–156
  mathematics, 150–151
  research methods, 144–145
  sensory integration, 153–154
  taste/smell, 152–153
  touch, 153
  vision, 145–149, 154–155
Infant physical development, 116–124
  growth, 119–120
  motor development, 120–124
  newborns, 116–119
  and nutrition, 136
Infant states, 85, 118–119
Infertility, 83, 418
Informal curriculum, 438
Information processing, 43, 212–230
  adolescence, 222
  adulthood, 222–224
  childhood, 217–222, 230
  and gender roles, 312–313
  and identity formation, 282
  infancy, 215–217
  and intelligence, 236, 240, 243
  moral development, 346–348, 349, 356
  old age, 224–230
Informed consent, 21–22
In-group/out-group schema, 312
Inheritance mechanisms, 60–63
Initiative vs. guilt, 35, 289, 524
Inner speech, 189–190
Instincts, 30
Instrumental conditioning. See Operant
    conditioning
Instrumental role, 298
Integrity vs. despair, 36, 291, 511, 528
Intelligence, 236–258. See also Creativity
  adolescence, 245, 263
  adulthood, 245–247
  and autism, 466
  biological vs. environmental influences,
      67–68, 250–255

childhood, 244, 262
and cultural differences, 239, 253–254
defined, 236
and fetal alcohol syndrome, 92
giftedness, 256–258
infancy, 242–244
measurement, 240–242
mental retardation, 74–76, 96, 255–256,
    466
and motivation, 254
multiple intelligences theory, 238–239
old age, 246, 247–250, 263–264
optimization, 262–264
and Piagetian theory, 41, 171–172, 236, 243
psychometric approach, 236–238
and race, 252–255
and social class, 252
triarchic theory, 239–240
Intelligence quotient (IQ), 41, 241
Internalization, 336
Internalizing problems, 469, 490
Internal working models, 363, 388–389, 478
Interpersonal intelligence, 238
Intimacy, adolescence, 383–384
Intimacy vs. isolation, 35, 289–290, 528. See
    also Relationships
Intonation, 191
Intrapersonal intelligence, 239
Intuitive theories, 149
In vitro fertilization (IVF), 83
Involved grandparenting style, 413
IQ. See Intelligence quotient
IQ tests. See Intelligence
IVF. See In vitro fertilization

Jessica, Baby, 361
Jobs. See Employment
Joint attention, 330–331
Junior high school, 442–443
Justice, morality of, 354

Karyotype, 59
Klinefelter syndrome, 64, 76
Knowledge base, 217, 219–220, 222, 223–224,
    225, 249
Kohlberg's theory of moral development,
    336–339. See also Moral development
  evaluation of, 350–352, 354–355
  and violence prevention, 356–357
  and whole-person perspective, 524, 526
Kübler-Ross's stages of dying, 502–504

LAD. See Language acquisition device
Lamaze method, 104
Language. See also Language development
  defined, 191
  and hearing impairments, 165–166
  infancy, 149–151, 155
  and intelligence, 253
  and play, 434
  reading, 157–159
Language acquisition device (LAD), 197
Language development, 190–201. See also
    Language
  adulthood, 195–196
  and autism, 466
  childhood, 193–195
  critical period, 199–201

cultural differences, 101
definitions, 191
and humor, 181
infancy, 191–193, 217
interactionist perspective, 198–199
learning theories, 196–197
and memory, 217
nativist perspective, 197–198
Piagetian theory, 42, 198
and self-concept, 275
sociocultural perspective, 189–190, 201–202
Latchkey children, 402, 403
Latency period of psychosexual development, 32, 33, 318
Lateralization, 114–115
Learned helplessness orientation, 435, 436, 437
Learning, 206–215. *See also* Learning theories; Memory; Operant conditioning
adolescence, 222
childhood, 217
classical conditioning, 206–207, 211
defined, 3
infancy, 118, 210–211
and information processing, 212–215
observational, 38–39, 196, 209–211, 309–301
old age, 212
operant conditioning, 37–38, 207–209
Learning goals, 437, 442
Learning Potential Assessment Device (Feuerstein), 241
Learning theories, 37–40. *See also* Learning; Observational learning
adolescence, 40, 50
language development, 196–197
and world view, 47–48, 49
Lesbian/gay people, 320–321, 418–419
Levinson's adult development theory, 446–447
Liberal bias, and moral development, 352, 354
Libido, 31–33
Life expectancy, 6, 498–499, 500
Life extension, 502
Life instincts, 30
Life review, 291
Life-span perspective, 10–11, 46–47
Life structure, 447
Linguistic intelligence, 238
Living Will, 497
Loci, method of, 230–231
Locus of control, 432
Logical-mathematical intelligence, 238
Longitudinal research designs, 14, 16, 17, 246
Long-term memory, 213
Looking-glass self, 272, 277, 292
Love withdrawal, 344
Low-birth-weight babies, 103, 105–106

MA. *See* Mental age
Macrosystems, 45, 100
Mainstreaming. *See* Inclusion
Major depressive disorder, 464
Maladaptiveness criteria, 462
Male climacteric, 133

Marriage, 322, 387. *See also* Divorce; Family; Romantic relationships
change in, 414
and death of child, 514
establishing, 409–410
and intelligence, 248
and parent caregiving, 416–417
and parenting experience, 410, 412
postponement of, 398
remarriage, 399, 421–422
widowhood, 414, 512–513, 518, 519–520
Masked depression, 473
Mastery motivation. *See* Effectance motivation
Mastery orientation, 435, 436
Masturbation, 318
Maternal age, 63–64, 88
Maternity blues, 99
Mate selection, 57, 387
Mathematical ability, 299, 309
Maturation, 3, 31, 41, 243. *See also* Biological/environmental interaction; Biological vs. environmental influences
Maximum life span, 500
Measurement, intelligence, 240–242
Mechanistic world view, 47–48
Meiosis, 58
Memory, 213–215. *See also* Information processing; Savant syndrome
adolescence, 222
childhood, 217–220
infancy, 215–217
old age, 196, 224–225, 226, 227, 228–229, 488
optimization, 230–231
Men. *See* Gender roles; Sex differences
Menarche, 125, 127, 132
Menopause, 130, 132–133, 324
Mental age (MA), 240–241
Mental health. *See* Psychological disorders
Mental retardation, 74–76, 96, 255–256, 466
Mentors, 447, 450
Mesosystem, 45
Metacognition, 219, 222
Metamemory, 219, 222, 226
Method of loci, 230–231
Methylphenidate (Ritalin), 471
Microsystems, 44–45
Middle age. *See also* Adulthood; Aging
Eriksonian psychoanalytic theory, 35, 290–291
gender roles, 315–316
grandparenthood, 412–414
historical perspective, 7
identity, 290–291
midlife crisis, 448–449
parent/child relationships, 415–416
relationships, 387
Middle generation squeeze, 416
Middle school, 442–443
Midlife crisis, 448–449
Migration of neurons, 112
Mind, theory of, 329–332, 466–467
Minnesota Twin Study, 70
Mitosis, 58
Models, 38, 210, 344
Modified extended family, 416
Moral affects, 335, 354

Moral behavior, 343–345, 354–355
Moral development, 335–355
adolescence, 345–349, 355–357, 526
adulthood, 349–350, 526
childhood, 341–345, 355–357, 524, 526
cultural differences, 348–349, 351–352, 353
Freudian psychoanalytic theory, 31, 34, 335–336
infancy, 339–341
Piagetian theory, 336–339, 342–343, 350–352, 354–357
and sexuality, 321
social learning theory, 339, 344
Morality of care, 354
Morality of justice, 354
Moral reasoning, 336–339, 345–346, 355–356
Moral rules, 343
Moratorium identity status, 281
Moro reflex, 117
Morphology, 191
Mortality, 98, 101, 499. *See also* Death
Motherese. *See* Child-directed speech
Mothers. *See* Parental influences; Parent/child relationships; Parenting experience; Parenting style
Motivation. *See also* Achievement motivation
and creativity, 260
and Freudian psychoanalytic theory, 30, 34
and information processing, 228
and intelligence, 254
and Piagetian theory, 43
Motor development. *See also* Physical development
adolescence, 128, 129, 130
and brain development, 114
childhood, 124–125
dynamic systems approach to, 123–124
infancy, 120–124
old age, 134–135
Mourning, 504. *See also* Bereavement
Multigeneration families, 399
Multiple intelligences theory, 238–239
Music, and perception, 155
Musical intelligence, 238
Mutations, 63
Mutual support self-help groups, 519–520
Myelin, 85, 112, 114, 115, 159

N Ach. *See* Need for achievement
National Institute of Mental Health, 484
Nativist perspective, 143, 197–198
Natural childbirth, 104
Naturalistic observation, 12, 13
Natural selection, 56, 221
Nature/nurture issue, 28, 531–532. *See also* Biological/environmental interaction; Biological vs. environmental influences; Environmental influences; Genetic factors
Need for achievement (n Ach), 431
Negative punishment, 208
Negative reinforcement, 207
Neglectful parenting, 402
Neo-Freudians, 34. *See also* Eriksonian psychoanalytic theory
Nervous system, 111–116
old age, 115–116, 134
plasticity, 114, 116, 248

Neurofibrillary tangles, 487
Neurons, 111–114, 115–116
Neurotransmitters, 111–112, 116
Newborns, 105–106, 116–119. *See also* Infancy
Nonshared environmental influences, 66, 407
Normal distribution, 241
Novelty, preference for, 243
Nuclear family, 396–397
Numbness phase of grieving, 505
Nurturance, 300
Nutrition, 136–137, 138
   and ADHD, 471, 472
   and life extension, 502
   and prenatal development, 89, 136
   and secular trend, 126–127

Obesity, 137
Object-centered stage of sociability, 377
Object manipulation, 122
Object permanence, 173–174, 371–372, 506
Observation, 12–13
Observational learning, 38–39, 196, 209–211
   gender roles, 309–311
Oedipus complex, 33, 34, 307, 335–336
Old age. *See also* Adulthood; Aging
   achievement motivation, 446, 454–455, 456–457
   coping skills, 483
   cultural differences, 8, 226
   and death, 511–512
   Eriksonian psychoanalytic theory, 36, 291, 511, 528
   gender roles, 316
   grandparenthood, 412–414
   health, 130–131, 134, 135–136, 138–139, 248
   historical perspective, 7
   identity, 291
   information processing, 224–230
   intelligence, 246, 247–250, 263–264
   learning, 212
   memory, 196, 224–225, 226, 227, 228–229, 488
   nervous system development, 115–116, 134
   nutrition, 136–137
   parent/child relationships, 415–417
   physical development, 130–136
   Piagetian theory, 186–187
   psychological disorders, 484–485, 486–488, 490
   relationships, 389
   retirement, 452–454
   self-concept, 285
   sexuality, 323–324
   social cognition, 334–335
   stereotypes, 110, 130, 226, 292, 293, 324
   whole-person perspective, 528
Oldest-old people, 4
Old-old people, 4, 418
Olfaction. *See* Smell
Onlooker play, 378
Operant conditioning, 37–38, 207–209, 211, 230. *See also* Learning theories
   and autism, 467–468
   and perceptual development, 144–145
Oral stage of psychosexual development, 32, 317, 370–371

Organic retardation, 255
Organismic world view, 47, 49
Organization strategy, 172, 218, 222, 231
Organogenesis, 82, 89
Orthogenetic principle, 120, 121, 529
Osteoarthritis, 130
Osteoporosis, 130, 131
Overbenefited friends, 389
Overcontrolled disorders. *See* Internalizing problems
Overextension, 193
Overregularization, 194
Own-sex schema, 312

Pain, 153, 164–165
Parallel play, 378
Parental imperative, 315
Parental influences. *See also* Learning theories; Parent/child relationships; Parenting style; Prenatal development
   achievement motivation, 433, 435–436
   adolescent relationships, 385–386
   autism, 467
   cultural differences, 100–102
   emotional development, 364–365
   failure to thrive, 468–469
   and female employment, 451–452
   Freudian psychoanalytic theory, 33, 34
   gay/lesbian families, 418–419
   gender roles, 307–308, 309, 400
   goodness of fit, 102, 274, 277, 341, 372
   and infant attachment, 370–371, 372, 375
   infant socialization, 100–102, 364–365
   and intelligence, 250–252
   language development, 196–197, 198–199
   and moral development, 340, 344–345, 348, 349, 351, 356–357
   and operant conditioning, 208–209
   psychological disorders, 474–475
   and self-concept, 277
   and sexual orientation, 320
   sibling relationships, 407
   and temperament, 69, 274
   understanding of death, 508
Parent/child relationships. *See also* Infant attachment; Parenting style
   adolescence, 127, 383, 408–409, 411–412
   adulthood, 415–417
   bonding, 98–99, 366
   childhood, 377–378
   contextual theories, 44–45, 48
   cultural differences, 415–416
   and divorce, 419–420, 422
   and eating disorder, 478
   and identity formation, 282, 284
   parent effects model, 405–406
   and reproductive technologies, 83
Parent effects model, 405–406
Parenting experience
   bereavement, 513–515
   birth, 98–100
   and gender roles, 314, 315
   new parenthood, 410–411
Parenting style. *See also* Parental influences; Parent/child relationships
   and achievement motivation, 436
   and ADHD, 471
   and child abuse, 424

   class differences, 402–404
   cultural differences, 100–102, 401, 404–405
   dimensions of, 401–402
   and divorce, 419–420
   and infant attachment, 371
   sex differences, 400
Parents Anonymous, 426
Parkes-Bowlby attachment model of grieving, 504–505, 506
Parkinson's disease, 488
Partial reinforcement, 208
Passivity/activity. *See* Activity/passivity issue
Pathological grief, 515–517
Pattern perception, 145–146
PCBs. *See* Polychlorinated biphenyls
Peer influences
   and achievement motivation, 442
   adolescence, 351, 355–356, 382–383, 385–386, 510
   childhood, 378–382
   and gender roles, 304–305
   and infant attachment, 376–377
   relationships, 363–364
Penis envy, 33
Perception, 143. *See also* Perceptual development
Perceptual development, 143–167. *See also* Infant perceptual development
   adolescence, 159–160
   and aging, 160–165
   childhood, 156–160
   old age, 134
Performance goals, 435, 437, 442
Performance IQ, 241, 247
Perinatal environment, 95–100
   hazards in, 95–98
   maternal experience, 98–100
   optimizing, 105
Permissive parenting, 402
Permissive societies, 318
Personal distress criteria, 462
Personal fable, 182–183
Personality. *See also* Goodness of fit; Temperament
   adulthood, 286–288, 289–292
   androgyny, 315–317
   biological vs. environmental influences, 68–69, 269, 270, 272, 274, 287–288
   childhood, 277–278
   and death, 504, 511, 517
   defined, 268
   infancy, 272–274
   and marital happiness, 414
   psychoanalytic theory, 268–269, 288–292
   psychometric theory, 269–270
   social learning theory, 270
Person perception, 332
Person permanence, 371–372
Phallic stage of psychosexual development, 32, 33, 318, 335–336
Phenotype, 60
Phenylketonuria (PKU), 74–76, 255
Phonemes, 158, 191
Phonics approach to reading, 158, 159
Phonological awareness, 158, 159
Phonology, 191, 196
Physical attractiveness, and popularity, 381

Physical behavior
    adolescence, 128, 129, 130
    childhood, 124–125
    infancy, 120–124
    old age, 134–135
    sex differences, 300
Physical development, 110–139. *See also*
        Infant physical development
    adolescence, 125–130, 136, 442
    and aging, 130–136
    childhood, 124–125, 136
    defined, 2
    endocrine system, 110–111
    and exercise, 137–138
    infancy, 116–124
    nervous system, 111–116, 134, 248
    and nutrition, 136–137
    and simple model, 3
Physical growth. *See* Growth
Piagetian theory, 40–43, 171–188. *See also*
        Cognitive development
    and achievement motivation, 433
    adolescence, 43, 44, 49–50, 179–183, 526
    adulthood, 183–186
    childhood, 42, 175–179, 180–181, 220,
        333, 524, 526
    and cognitive optimization, 201
    criticisms of, 187–188
    and gender roles, 311–312
    infancy, 42, 172–175, 523
    and intelligence, 41, 171–172, 236, 243
    and memory, 217–218
    moral development, 336–339, 342–343,
        350–352, 354–357
    old age, 186–187
    and problem solving, 220
    and self-concept, 278
    social cognition, 332–333
    and whole-person perspective, 523, 524,
        526
    and world view, 47, 49
Pincer grasp, 122
Pituitary gland, 110
PKU. *See* Phenylketonuria
Placenta, 82, 95
Placental barrier, 82
Plasticity, 10, 114, 116, 248, 530–531
Play, 378–380, 433–434
Play therapy, 489
PMS. *See* Premenstrual syndrome
Pollutants, 94–95
Polychlorinated biphenyls (PCBs), 94–95
Polygenic traits, 62–63
Popularity, 380–382
Populations, 20
Positive punishment, 208
Positive reinforcement, 207
Postconventional morality, 337–338, 346,
        349, 526
Postformal thought, 185–186
Postpartum depression, 99–100
Postpartum psychosis, 99
Posttraumatic stress disorder, 319
Poverty, 398–399
Power assertion, 344
Pragmatics, 191, 192, 195
Preconventional morality, 337, 338, 343–344,
        345, 526

Preference for novelty, 243
Preferential looking, 144
Premenstrual syndrome (PMS), 132
Prenatal development, 82–95
    brain development, 112–114
    conception, 57–58, 82, 83
    embryonic period, 82, 84
    fetal period, 84–85
    genetic counseling, 73–74, 75
    genetic engineering, 76–77
    maternal condition, 63–64, 88–89, 136
    optimizing, 104–105
    perceptual development, 152
    teratogens, 89–95
Preoccupied working model, 388
Preoperational stage of cognitive
        development, 42, 175–178
Preretirement phase, 452–453
Presbycusis, 162
Presbyopia, 160
Preschool, 436–437
Pretend play, 379, 434, 467
Primary mental abilities, 237, 247
Primitive reflexes, 117, 118
Private speech, 189
Proactive aggression, 348
Problem-focused coping, 483
Problem solving, 180–181
    childhood, 220–222
    and information processing, 214
    old age, 229–230
    sociocultural perspective, 190
Progesterone, 111
Programmed theories of aging, 499, 500–501
Project Head Start, 262
Proliferation of neurons, 112
Prosocial behavior, 335, 341
Protective factors, 103
Proximal development, zone of, 189
Proximodistal principle, 120, 121, 125
Psychoanalytic theory. *See* Eriksonian
        psychoanalytic theory; Freudian
        psychoanalytic theory
Psycholinguistics, 194
Psychological disorders, 462–490. *See also*
        Childhood psychological disorders
    adaptive functions of, 490
    adolescence, 476–482
    adulthood, 482–486, 513
    biological vs. environmental influences,
        69–70, 471, 474–475, 478, 482
    and child abuse, 423–424
    and child effects model, 405
    developmental psychopathology, 464–465
    diagnosis criteria, 462–464
    infancy, 465–469
    old age, 484–485, 486–488, 490
    and sexuality, 324
    treatment, 488–490
Psychometric approach to intelligence,
        236–238
Psychometric theory of personality, 269–270
Psychopathology. *See* Psychological disorders
Psychosexual development, 31–33. *See also*
        Freudian psychoanalytic theory;
        Sexuality
Psychosocial development, 3. *See also*
        Eriksonian psychoanalytic theory

Psychotherapy, 30, 40, 319, 489–490
Puberty, 125–127, 128, 442
Punishment, 37, 207–208, 209, 344
Puns, 181
Pupillary reflex, 117
Puritans, 5

Qualitative vs. quantitative changes, 29
Quasi-experiments, 18, 19

Racial differences. *See also* Cultural
        differences
    and eating disorders, 477
    and identity formation, 283
    and intelligence, 252–253
    and life expectancy, 499
    and school achievement, 440–441
    and sexual maturation, 125
Radiation, 94
Ram Dass, Baba. *See* Alpert, Richard
Random assignment, 18
Random samples, 20
Reaction time, 124–125
Reactive aggression, 348
Reading, 157–159
Realistic stage of employment, 443
Recall memory, 214, 224–225, 487
Recessive genes, 60–61
Reciprocal determinism, 39. *See also*
        Reciprocal influence
Reciprocal influence, 39, 44, 81–82, 396,
        405–406, 408, 474–475
Recognition memory, 214, 224–225
Reconstituted families, 399, 421–422
Reflexes, 117–118, 367
Regression, 32–33
Regression hypothesis of coping skills, 483
Rehearsal strategy, 218
Reinforcement programs. *See* Operant
        conditioning
Reinforcers, 37
Relationships, 361–391. *See also* Infant
        attachment; Marriage; Parent/child
        relationships
    adolescence, 382–386
    adulthood, 386–390
    attachment theory, 362–363, 387–389,
        433, 504–505, 506, 517
    childhood, 363–364, 377–382
    Eriksonian psychoanalytic theory, 35,
        289–290, 362, 387
    Freudian psychoanalytic theory, 362, 364
    importance of, 361–362
    mate selection, 57, 387
    optimization, 390–391
    peers, 363–364
Relativistic thinking, 185
Religion, 350
Remarriage, 399, 421–422
Remote grandparenting style, 413
REM sleep, 119
Reorganization phase of grieving, 505
Reorientation phase of retirement, 453
Reproductive system, 131–133. *See also*
        Genetic factors; Prenatal development
Reproductive technologies, 83
Research, 11–22
    behavioral genetics, 64–67

Research (continued)
  correlational method, 18–20
  data collection, 11–13
  developmental designs, 13–16, 17, 20–21, 246
  experimental method, 17–18, 20
  infant perceptual development, 144–145
  problems in, 20–22
  scientific method, 11
Research ethics, 18, 21–22
Reserve capactiy, 131
Resilience, 103
Resistant attachment, 369, 371
Responsiveness, 371, 433
Restrictive societies, 318
Retirement, 7, 452–454
Retrieval strategies, 214, 218–219
Reversibility, 175, 178
"Right to die" cases, 496
Risk-taking, 183
Ritalin, 471
Rites of passage, 7, 127
Role conflict, 450–451
Role overload, 450–451
Role reversal, 416
Romantic relationships. See also
    Relationships; Sexuality
  adolescence, 384–385
  adulthood, 387–389
Rooting reflex, 117
Rubella, 89–90
"Rule assessment" approach, 221
Rules, 342–343, 379
Rumination strategies, 485

Samples, 20–21
Sandwich generation, 416
Savant syndrome, 239, 466
Scaffolding, 189
Schemes, 171
Schizophrenia, 69–70
School achievement, 245, 436–441, 470. See
    also Achievement motivation;
    Education
School segregation, 440
Scientific method, 11
Secondary circular reactions, 173
Secular trend, 126–127, 130, 132
Secure attachment, 369, 373–374, 376, 433
Secure base, 369
Secure working model, 388
Selective breeding, 65
Selective optimization with compensation,
    449–450
Self-concept. See also Self-esteem
  adolescence, 278–284
  adulthood, 285
  childhood, 275–277
  defined, 268
  infancy, 271–272
  and vocational development, 443
Self-esteem
  adolescence, 279–280, 283
  childhood, 276–277
  defined, 268
  optimization, 292–293
Self-recognition, 271–272
Self-reports, 12

Self-talk, 189–190
Semantics, 191, 192, 194, 195
  learning theories, 196–197
Semirestrictive societies, 318
Senile plaques, 116, 487
Sensation, 143
Sensorimotor stage of cognitive
    development, 42, 172–175, 506, 523. See
    also Infancy
Sensory integration, 153–154
Sensory register, 213
Sensory stimulation, 433
Sensory stimulation programs, 106
Sensory thresholds, 160
Separation anxiety, 367, 505
Sequential research designs, 16, 17, 246
Seriation, 179
Sex differences, 297–298, 299–301. See also
    Gender roles
  achievement motivation, 448–449
  ADHD, 469–470
  adolescent growth spurt, 125
  aggression, 299, 306–307
  death anxiety, 511
  divorce, 420
  family transitions, 414
  friendships, 383–384
  genetic inheritance, 62
  giftedness, 258
  identity formation, 281–282, 290
  life expectancy, 498
  motor development, 128, 129
  parenting experience, 410
  parenting style, 400
  play, 378
  psychological disorders, 466, 481, 484, 485
  reconstituted families, 421
  sexuality, 321–323
  sexual maturation, 125
Sexism, 34, 450. See also Gender roles;
    Gender-role stereotypes
Sex-linked characteristics, 62
Sexual differentiation, 58–59, 84, 110–111
Sexuality, 317–325. See also Romantic
    relationships
  adolescence, 319–322
  adulthood, 322–323
  childhood, 317–319
  Freudian psychoanalytic theory, 31–33, 317
  and hormones, 111, 318, 323
  infancy, 317
  old age, 323–324
Sexually transmitted diseases (STDs), 83,
    90–91. See also AIDS
Sexual maturation, 125–126, 128
Sexual orientation, 320–321
Shared environmental influences, 66
Short-term memory, 213
Sibling rivalry, 406, 415
Siblings, 406–408
  adult transitions, 415
  and death of child, 514–515
  and social cognition, 331–332
Sickle-cell disease, 61, 63, 76
SIDS. See Sudden infant death syndrome
Sign language, 166, 199, 200
Simple interactive stage of sociability, 377
Single adults, 398, 417–418

Single gene-pair inheritance, 60–62
Single parents, 398
Size constancy, 147
Sleep, infancy, 119
Slow-to-warm-up temperament, 273
Smell, 152–153, 163–164
Smoking. See Tobacco
Sociability dimension of temperament, 272,
    273
Social class. See Class differences
Social clock, 5
Social cognition, 329–335
  adulthood, 334–335
  childhood, 331–334
  person perception, 332
  role-taking skills, 332–334
  theory of mind, 329–332
Social comparisons, 275–276, 332
Social competence, 381, 390–391
Social-conventional rules, 343
Social convoys, 361–362
Social deprivation, 372–373
Social influences. See Environmental
    influences
Social information-processing model,
    346–348, 356
Socialization, 277, 382, 438. See also
    Environmental influences; Parental
    influences
  infancy, 100–102, 340, 364–365
Social learning theory, 38–39, 50, 196, 230.
    See also Observational learning
  gender roles, 308–311
  moral development, 339, 344
  personality, 270
Social networks, 361–362, 384–385, 386–387,
    390
Social norms, 462–463
Social pretend play, 379
Social referencing, 365, 368
Social relationships. See Relationships
Social-role hypothesis, 300
Social speech, 189
Social support, 361, 397, 422, 517–518
Societal norms. See Age norms; Gender roles
Sociobiology, 56
Sociocultural perspective, 188–190,
    201–202
Socioeconomic status, 8. See also Class
    differences
Socioemotional selectivity hypothesis, 387
Sociometric status, 380–381
Solitary play, 378
Somatic symptoms, 468
Spatial ability, 299
Spatial intelligence, 238
Species heredity, 55–57
Speed of habitation, 243
Spillover, 451
Spouse abuse, 423. See also Family violence
Stage theories, 28–29. See also
    Continuity/discontinuity issue
Standardization, 12
Stanford-Binet Scale, 240–241, 243
Statistical deviance criteria, 462
STDs. See Sexually transmitted diseases
Stepfamilies. See Reconstituted families
Stepping reflex, 117, 121–122

Stereotypes. *See also* Gender-role stereotypes
  menopause, 132
  old age, 110, 130, 226, 292, 293, 324
  physical attractiveness, 381
Storage, 213–214
Storm and stress, 279, 476
Stranger anxiety, 367–369
Strange Situation test, 369
Stress, 482–484
  and bereavement, 518
  and eating disorders, 478
  and infant attachment, 367
  maternal, 88
  and new parenthood, 410–411
  and parenting style, 403–404
  and sexuality, 324
Structured observation, 12–13
Structure-of-intellect model, 237
Subcultural differences, 8
Substantive complexity, 452
Sucking reflex, 117
Sudden infant death syndrome (SIDS), and
  tobacco, 92
Sugar, 472
Suicide
  adolescence, 481–448
  assisted, 497
  childhood, 473
  coping skills, 517
Superego, 31, 335, 336
Surfactant, 103
Survival reflexes, 117–118
Swallowing reflex, 117
Swimming reflex, 117
Symbolic capacity, 173, 434, 523
Symbolic play. *See* Pretend play
Synapses, 111–112
Synaptogenesis, 112–113
Synchronized routines, 366–367
Syntax, 191, 196–197
Syphilis, 90

Tabula rasa, 28, 37, 143
Tact, 300
Talent. *See* Creativity; Giftedness
Taste, 152–153, 163–164
Tay-Sachs disease, 73–74
Telegraphic speech, 193–194
Television, 310–311, 348, 403
Telomeres, 501
Temperament, 102, 119, 272–274
  biological vs. environmental influences,
    68–69
  and infant attachment, 372
  and moral development, 340–341, 345
Temperature, 153, 165

Tentative stage of employment, 443
Teratogens, 89–95
Terman's Kids (Shurkin), 257
Terminally ill children/adolescents, 508–509,
  510
Tertiary circular reactions, 173
Testing, intelligence, 236–238, 239, 240–243,
  244, 253–254
Test norms, 241
Testosterone, 84, 111, 305, 306–307
Thalidomide, 91–92
Theories. *See* Developmental theories
Theory of mind, 329–332, 466–467
Therapy. *See* Psychotherapy
Thyroid gland, 110
Time of measurement effects, 15, 16
Time out, 209
Tobacco, 92, 136, 138
Total brain death, 495
Touch, 153, 164–165
Tracking, 146
Trait theories of personality, 269–270, 286
Transactional model of family influence,
  405–406. *See also*
    Biological/environmental interaction
Transformational grammar, 195
Transformational thought, 175, 178
Transitivity, 179
Trial-and-error approach, 42, 180–181
Triarchic theory of intelligence, 239–240
Trisomy 21. *See* Down syndrome
Trust vs. mistrust, 35, 288–289, 371, 524
Turner syndrome, 64, 76
Twin studies, 55, 65–66, 69, 70
  intelligence, 67–68, 250
  sexual orientation, 320

UCR. *See* Unconditioned response
UCS. *See* Unconditioned stimulus
Ultrasound, 75
Umbilical cord, 82
Unconditioned response (UCR), 206
Unconditioned stimulus (UCS), 206
Unconscious motivation, 30, 34
Undercontrolled disorders. *See* Externalizing
  problems
Underextension, 193
Universalistic moral thinking, 353
Universality/particularity issue, 29, 39, 43,
  45, 47, 532
Unoccupied play, 378

Vaginal dryness, 132
Variables, 17–18, 19
Vascular dementia, 488
Verbal ability, 299

Verbal IQ, 241
Viability, age of, 85
Vicarious reinforcement, 210
Violence. *See* Aggression; Family violence
Vision
  adulthood, 160–162
  and brain development, 114
  infancy, 145–149, 154–155
Visual accommodation, 145
Visual acuity, 145
Visual cliff, 147–148
Vocabulary spurt, 193
Vocational development, 443–444
Vygotsky's theory. *See* Sociocultural
  perspective

WAIS-R. *See* Wechsler Adult Intelligence
  Scale
Walking, 121–122
Wechsler Adult Intelligence Scale (WAIS-R),
  241, 247
Wechsler Intelligence Scale for Children
  (WISC-III), 241, 242, 243
Wechsler Preschool and Primary Scale of
  Intelligence (WPPSI), 241
Weight, 130, 137, 138, 477, 478
Whole-language approach to reading,
  158–159
Whole-person perspective, 523–529
  adolescence, 526
  adulthood, 526, 528
  childhood, 524, 526
  infancy, 523–524
  old age, 528
Widowhood, 415, 512–513, 518, 519–520
WISC-III. *See* Wechsler Intelligence Scale for
  Children
Wisdom, 249, 334
Women. *See* Gender roles; Sex differences;
  Women's employment
Women's employment, 398, 450–452
Working memory, 213, 227
Workplace. *See* Employment
World views, 47–49
WPPSI. *See* Wechsler Preschool and Primary
  Scale of Intelligence

X chromosome, 58–59

Y chromosome, 58–59
Yearning phase of grieving, 505
Young-old people, 4

Zone of proximal development, 189
Zygote, 58, 82

Credits

These pages constitute an extension of the copyright page. We have made every effort to trace the ownership of all copyrighted material and to secure permission from copyright holders. In the event of any question arising as to the use of any material, we will be pleased to make the necessary corrections in future printings. Thanks are due to the following authors, publishers, and agents for permission to use the material indicated.

Tables and Figures

Chapter 1: **p. 12:** Figure 1.2 from "Stratum Contrasts and Similarities in Attitudes Toward Death" by V. L. Bengtson, J. B. Cuellar, and P. K. Ragan, 1977, *Journal of Gerontology,* 32. Reprinted by permission.

Chapter 3: **p. 66:** Table 3.2 from "EAS Temperaments during the Last Half of the Life Span: Twins Reared Apart and Twins Reared Together" by R. Plomin et al. from *Psychology and Aging,* 3, 1988. Copyright © 1988 by The American Psychological Association. Reprinted by permission. **p. 68:** Figure 3.7 from "Behavioral Genetics of Cognitive Ability: A Life-Span Perspective" by M. McGue et al. in *Nature, Nurture, and Psychology,* edited by R. Plomin & G. E. McClearn. Copyright © 1993 by American Psychological Association. Reprinted by permission.

Chapter 4: **p. 88:** Figure 4.3 from "Fetal Neurobehavioral Development" by J. A. DiPietro et al. from *Child Development,* 67. © 1996 Society for Research in Child Development, Inc. Reprinted by permission. **p. 90:** Figure 4.4 adapted from *The Developing Human,* by K. L. Moore, 1988 (4th ed.). Philadelphia, W. B. Saunders. Reprinted by permission. **p. 95:** Figure 4.7 adapted with permission from "Longitudinal analyses of prenatal and postnatal lead exposure and early cognitive development" by D. Bellinger et al. from *The New England Journal of Medicine,* 316, 1987. Copyright © 1987 by Massachusetts Medical Society. All rights reserved.

Chapter 5: **p. 112:** Figure 5.1 from *The Five to Seven Year Shift: The Age of Reason and Responsibility* by J. S. Janowsky and R. Carper, 1996. Reprinted by permission of the University of Chicago Press. **p. 113:** Figure 5.2 from *The Brain: A Neuroscience Primer, 2E* by Thompson. © 1993 by W. H. Freeman and Company. Used with permission. **p. 121:** Table 5.3 adapted from "The Denver Development Screening Test" by W. K. Frankenburg and J. B. Dodds, 1967, *Journal of Pediatrics,* 71, pp. 181–191. Reprinted by permission. **p. 126:** Figure 5.5 from "Variations in the Pattern of Pubertal Changes in Boys" by W. A. Marshall and J. M. Tanner, 1970, *Archives of Disease in Childhood,* 45, pp. 13–23. Reprinted by permission of the BMJ Publishing Group, London. **p. 129:** Figure 5.6 from *Science and Medicine of Exercise and Sport, 2E,* edited by Warren K. Johnson and Elsworth R. Buskirk. Reprinted by permission of Harper and Row, Publishers, Inc.

Chapter 6: **p. 146:** Figure 6.1 from *Handbook of Child Psychology: Vol. 2 Infancy and Developmental Psychobiology, 4E,* edited by Paul Henry Mussen. Copyright © 1983 by John Wiley and Sons, Inc. Reprinted by permission. **p. 147:** Figure 6.2 adapted from "Pattern Perception in Infancy" by P. Salapatek from *Infant Perception: From Sensation to Cognition, Vol. 1* edited by L. B. Cohen and P. Salapatek. Copyright © 1975 by Academic Press, Inc. Reprinted by permission. **p. 151:** Box 6.1 reprinted with permission from *Nature,* 358, "Addition and Subtraction by Human Infants" by K. Wynn, 1992, pp. 749–750. Copyright 1992 Macmillan Magazines Limited. **p. 156:** Figure 6.4 from "Human Figure Drawings by Schooled and Unschooled Children in Papua New Guinea" by M. Martlew and K. J. Connolly from *Child Development,* 67. © 1996 Society for Research in Child Development, Inc. Reprinted by permission. **p. 158:** Figure 6.6 from "A Developmental Study of the Discrimination of Letter-Like Forms" by E. J. Gibson, J. J. Gibson, A. D. Pick, and H. A. Osser, 1962, *Journal of Comparative and Physiological Psychology,* 55, pp. 897–906. Copyright © 1962 by the American Psychological Association. Reprinted by permission. **p. 164:** Table 6.1 from "Food Recognition by the Elderly" by S. Schiffman, 1977, *Journal of Gerontology,* 32. Reprinted by permission.

Chapter 7: **p. 184:** Figure 7.5 data from "Individual Differences in College Students' Performance on Formal Operations Tasks," by R. De Lisi and J. Straudt, 1980, *Journal of Applied Developmental Psychology,* 1, pp. 163–174. **p. 193:** Table 7.3 from *Development of Language, 4E* by Jean Berko Gleason. Copyright © 1997 by Allyn & Bacon. Reprinted by permission. **p. 194:** Figure 7.4 from *Psycholinguistics, 2nd Edition* by Dan I. Slobin. Copyright © 1979, 1974 by Scott, Foresman and Company. Reprinted by permission of Addison Wesley Longman, Inc.

Chapter 8: **p. 214:** Figure 8.4 adapted from "Human Memory: A Proposed System and Its Control Processes" by R. C. Atkinson and R. M. Shiffrin from *The Psychology of Learning and Motivation: Advances in Research and Theory* edited by K. W. Spence and J. T. Spence, Vol. 2, 1968. Copyright © 1968 by Academic Press. Reprinted by permission. **p. 216:** Figure 8.6 from "Childhood Amnesia and the Beginnings of Memory for Four Early Life Events" by J. A. Usher and U. Neisser, 1993, *Journal of Experimental Psychology: General,* 122, pp. 155–165. Copyright 1993 by the American Psychological Association. Reprinted by permission. **p. 220:** Figure 8.8 adapted from "Knowledge Structures and Memory Development" by M. T. H. Chi from *Children's Thinking: What Develops?* edited by R. Siegler. Copyright 1978 by Lawrence Erlbaum Associates, Inc. Reprinted by permission. **p. 221:** Figure 8.10 from *Emerging Minds: The Process of Change in Children's Thinking* by Robert S. Siegler. Copyright © 1996 by Oxford University Press, Inc. Used by permission of Oxford University Press, Inc. **p. 227:** Figure 8.12 from "Aging free from negative stereotypes: Successful memory in China and among the American deaf" by B. Levy and E. Langer, *Journal of Personality* and *Social Psychology, 66,* 1994. Copyright © 1994 by the American Psychological Association. Reprinted by permission. **p. 229:** Figure 8.13 from "Effect of Contextual Organization on Spatial Memory of Middle-Aged and Older Women" by K. J. Waddell and B. Rogoff, 1981, *Developmental Psychology, 17,* pp. 878–885. Copyright 1981 by the American Psychological Association. Reprinted by permission. **p. 231:** Figure 8.15 adapted from "Further Testing of Limits of Cognitive Plasticity: Negative Age Differences in a Mnemonic Skill Are Robust" by P. B. Baltes and R. Kliegl, 1992 *Developmental Psychology, 28,* pp. 121–125. Copyright 1992 by the American Psychological Association. Reprinted by permission.

Chapter 9: **p. 237:** Figure 9.1 from *The Nature of Human Intelligence* by J. P. Guilford, 1967. Reprinted by permission of The McGraw-Hill Companies as publisher. **p. 242:** Figure 9.3 from *Developmental Psychology: Childhood and Adolescence, 4E* by D. R. Shaffer, p. 334, Brooks/Cole Publishing Company, 1996. Reprinted by permission. **p. 244:** Table 9.1 from "The Stability of Mental Test Performance between Two and Eighteen Years," by P. Honzik, J. W. Macfarlane, and L. Allen, 1948, *Journal of Experimental Education, 17,* pp. 309–324. **p. 246:** Table 9.2 from "Army General Classification Test Scores for Civilian Populations" by T. W. Harrell and M. S. Harrell, 1945, *Educational and Psychological Measurement, 5,* pp. 229–239. Reprinted by permission. **p. 248:** Figure 9.5 from *Intellectual Development in Adulthood. The Seattle Longitudinal Study* by K. W. Schaie, 1996. Reprinted by permission of Cambridge University Press. **p. 251:** Table 9.4 adapted from B. M. Caldwell and R. H. Bradley, *Manual for the HOME Observation for Measurement of the Environment,* 1984. Little Rock: University of Arkansas Press. Adapted by permission of the authors. **p. 254:** Figure 9.6 from "Stereotype Threat and the Intellectual Test Performance of African Americans" by C. M. Steele and J. Aronson, *Journal of Personality and Social Psychology, 69,* 1995. Copyright © 1995 by the American Psychological Association. Reprinted by permission. **p. 259:** Figure 9.7 adapted from *Modes of Thinking in Young Children* by Michael A. Wallach and Nathan Kogan, copyright © 1965 by Holt, Rinehart and Winston and renewed 1993 by Michael A. Wallach and Nathan Kogan, reproduced by permission of the publisher. **p. 260:** Figure 9.8 from "Eytan: The Early Development of a Gifted Child Artist" by C. Golomb, *Creativity Research Journal, 5,* 1992. Reprinted by permission of Lawrence Erlbaum Associates. **p. 261:** Figure 9.9 data from "Creative Productivity between the Ages of 20 and 80 Years" by W. Dennis, 1966, *Journal of Gerontology, 21,* p. 2. Reprinted by permission.

Chapter 10: **p. 278:** Figure 10.2 adapted from *Birth to Maturity* by K. Kagan and H. A. Moss, 1962. Copyright © 1962 by John Wiley and Sons, Inc. Reprinted by permission of the author. **p. 282:** Figure 10.3 adapted from "Cross-Sectional Age Changes in Ego Identity Status during Adolescence" by P. W. Meilman, 1979, *Developmental Psychology, 15,* pp. 230–231. Copyright 1979 by the American Psychological Association. Reprinted by permission. **p. 285:** Figure 10.4 from "Possible Selves in Adulthood and Old Age: A Tale of Shifting Horizons" by C. D. Ryff, 1991, *Psychology and Aging,* pp. 286–295. Copyright by the American Psychological Association. Reprinted by permission.

Chapter 11: **p. 299:** Figure 11.1 from "Mental Rotation of Three-Dimensional Objects" by R. N. Shepard, and J. Metzler, 1971, *Science, 17,* pp. 701–703. Copyright 1971 by the American Association for the Advancement of Science. **p. 300:** Figure 11.2 adapted from "Gender Differences in Mathematics Performance: A Meta-Analysis" by J. S. Hyde, E. Fennema, and S. J. Lamon, 1990, *Psychological Bulletin, 107,* pp. 139–155. Copyright 1990 by the American Psychological Association. Reprinted by permission. **p. 303:** Figure 11.3 based on "Social Behavior at 33 Months in Same-Sex and Mixed-Sex Dyads" by C. N. Jacklin and E. E. Maccoby, 1978, *Child Development, 49,* pp. 557–559. © 1978 by The Society for Research in Child Development, Inc. Reprinted by permission. **p. 304:** Figure 11.4 adapted from "Children's Concepts of Cross-Gender Activities" by T. Stoddart and E. Turiel, 1985, *Child Development, 56,* pp. 1241–1252. © 1985 by The Society for Research in Child Development, Inc. Reprinted by permission. **p. 306:**

Figure 11.5 from *Man and Woman, Boy and Girls,* by J. Money and A. Ehrhardt, 1972, Johns Hopkins University Press. Reprinted by permission. **p. 313:** Figure 11.6 adapted from "The Roles of Cognition in Sex-Roles and Sex Typing" by C. L. Martin and C. F. Halverson, Jr. in *Current Conceptions of Sex Roles and Sex-Typing: Theory and Research* edited by D. B. Carter. Copyright © 1987 by Bruce Carter. Reprinted by permission.

Chapter 12: **p. 330:** Figure 12.1 from "Factors Influencing Young Children's Use of Motives and Outcomes as Moral Criteria" by S. A. Nelson, 1980, *Child Development, 51,* pp. 823–829. © 1980 by The Society for Research in Child Development, Inc. Reprinted by permission. **p. 334:** Figure 12.2 adapted from "Reasoning on Social Dilemmas Varying in Emotional Saliency: An Adult Developmental Perspective" by F. Blanchard-Fields, 1986, *Psychology and Aging, 1,* pp. 325–333. Copyright 1986 by the American Psychological Association. Reprinted by permission. **p. 342:** Figure 12.3 adapted from "Factors Influencing Young Children's Use of Motives and Outcomes as Moral Criteria" by S. A. Nelson, 1980, *Child Development, 51,* pp. 823–829. © by The Society for Research in Child Development, Inc. Reprinted by permission. **p. 342:** Figure 12.4 adapted from "Factors Influencing Young Children's Use of Motives and Outcomes as Moral Criteria" by S. A. Nelson, 1980, *Child Development, 51,* pp. 823–829. © by The Society for Research in Child Development, Inc. Reprinted by permission. **p. 345:** Table 12.1 adapted from "Contributions of Parents and Peers to Children's Moral Socialization" by G. H. Brody and D. R. Shaffer, 1982, *Developmental Review, 2,* pp. 31–75. Reprinted by permission of Academic Press, Inc. **p. 346:** Figure 12.5 from "A Longitudinal Study of Moral Judgment" by A. Colby, L. Kohlberg, J. Gibbs, and M. Lieberman, 1983, *Monographs of the Society for Research in Child Development, 48* (Nos. 1–2 serial No. 200). © 1983 by The Society for Research in Child Development, Inc. Reprinted by permission. **p. 353:** Box 12.3 from "Culture and Moral Development" by R. A. Shweder, M. Mahapatra, and J. G. Miller in *Cultural Psychology Essays on Comparative Human Development* edited by J. W. Stigler, R. A. Shweder, and G. Herdt. Reprinted by permission of Cambridge University Press.

Chapter 13: **p. 378:** Figure 13.4 from "Age Segregation in Children's Social Interactions" by S. Ellis, B. Rogoff, and C. C. Cromer, 1981, *Developmental Psychology, 17,* pp. 299–407. Copyright 1981 by the American Psychological Association. Reprinted by permission. **p. 379:** Figure 13.5 adapted from "Preschool Play Norms: A Replication" by K. E. Barnes, 1971, *Developmental Psychology, 5,* pp. 99–103. Copyright 1971 by the American Psychological Association. Reprinted by permission. **p. 384:** Figure 13.6 from "Girlfriend, Boyfriend: Age and Sex Differences in Intimate Friendship" by R. Sharabany, R. Gershoni, and J. E. Hofman, 1981, *Developmental Psychology, 17,* pp. 800–808. Copyright 1981 by the American Psychological Association. Reprinted by permission. **p. 385:** Figure 13.7 from "The Social Structure of Urban Adolescent Peer Groups" by D. C. Dunphy, 1963, *Sociometry, 26,* pp. 230–246. Reprinted by permission.

Chapter 14: **p. 397:** Figure 14.1 from "Early Human Experience: A Family Perspective" by J. Belsky, 1981, *Developmental Psychology, 17,* pp. 3–23. Copyright 1981 by the American Psychological Association. Reprinted by permission. **p. 398:** Table 14.1 from E. M. Duvall, *Marriage and Family Development,* 1978. Copyright © 1978 by J. B. Lippincott Company. Reprinted by permission of Harper and Row, Publishers, Inc. **p. 404:** Figure 14.3 from "A Family Process Model of Economic Hardship and Adjustment of Early Adolescent Boys" by R. D. Conger, K. J. Conger, G. H. Elder, Jr., F. O. Lorenz, R. L. Simons, and L. B. Whitbeck, 1992, *Child Development, 63,* pp. 526–541. Copyright © 1992 by The Society for Research in Child Development, Inc. Adapted by permission. **p. 408:** Table 14.2 from *The Adolescent: A Psychological Self-Portrait,* by Daniel Offer, Eric Ostrov, and Kenneth I. Howard. Copyright © 1981 by Basic Books, Inc. Reprinted by permission of Basic Books, Publishers, New York. **p. 414:** Figure 14.5 from "Marital Satisfaction over the Family Life Cycle" by B. C. Rollins and H. Feldman, 1970, *Journal of Marriage and the Family, 32,* pp. 20–28. Copyrighted 1970 by the National Council on Family Relations. Reprinted by permission. **p. 420:** Table 14.3 adapted from "Reasons for Divorce: Perspectives of Divorcing Men and Women" by L. Gigy and J. B. Kelly, *Journal of Divorce and Remarriage,* Vol. 18, 1992. Copyright © 1992 The Haworth Press, Inc. Reprinted by permission. **p. 425:** Figure 14.6 adapted from "Responses of Abused and Disadvantaged Toddlers to Distress in Age-mates: A Study in the Day-Care Setting" by M. Main and C. George, 1985, *Developmental Psychology,* 21, pp. 407–412. Copyright 1985 by the American Psychological Association. Reprinted by permission.

Chapter 16: **p. 465** Figure 16.1 from "Psychopathology as an Outcome of Development" by L. A. Sroufe, *Development and Psychopathology,* Vol. 9, 1997. Reprinted by permission of Cambridge University Press. **p. 488:** Figure 16.6 adapted from *The Vanishing Mind* by Heston and White. Copyright © 1991 by W. H. Freeman and Company. Reprinted by permission.

Chapter 17: **p. 506:** Figure 17.2 reprinted from *Omega* 18, S. C. Jacobs et al., "Attachment Theory and Multiple Dimensions of Grief," pp. 41–52. Copyright 1987–1988, with permission from Elsevier Science. **p. 512:** Table 17.2 from "The Role of Age in Death Attitudes," by R. A. Kalish and D. K. Reynolds, *Death Education,* 1, (2), p. 225. Copyright 1977 by Hemisphere Publishing Corp. Reprinted by permission. **p. 513:** Table 17.3 adapted from C. M. Parkes, *Bereavement: Studies of Grief in Adult Life (*2nd ed.*),* 1986, Tavistock Publications. Reprinted by permission. **p. 514:** Figure 17.6 reprinted from *Omega* 29, L. H. Levy et al., "Differences in Patterns of Adaptation in Conjugal Bereavement," pp. 71–87. Copyright 1994, with permission from Elsevier Science.

Photographs

Chapter 1: **p. 2:** James A. Parcell/*The Washington Post.* **p. 4:** Charles Gupton/Stock Boston. **p. 6:** Henry Lillie Pierce Fund, Courtesy, Museum of Fine Arts, Boston. **p. 7:** Corbis-Bettmann. **p. 9:** Corbis-Bettmann. **p. 13:** Arlene Collins/Monkmeyer. **p. 15:** Lewis Heine/SuperStock. **p. 21:** Marc Pokempner/Tony Stone Images.

Chapter 2: **p. 26:** Spencer Grant/Monkmeyer. **p. 30:** UPI/Corbis-Bettmann. **p. 35:** UPI/Corbis-Bettmann. **p. 37:** Underwood and Underwood/Corbis-Bettmann. **p. 38 (top):** AP/Wide World Photos. **p. 38 (bottom):** L. A. Cicero/ Stanford University News Service. **p. 39:** Tony Freeman/Photo Edit. **p. 41:** Bill Anderson/Monkmeyer. **p. 43:** Stock Boston. **p. 45:** Cornell University.

Chapter 3: **p. 55:** Thomas S. England/Photo Researchers, Inc. **p. 59:** Biophoto Association/Photo-Researchers, Inc. **p. 61:** Omikron/Photo Researchers, Inc. **p. 63:** Gale Zucker. **p. 72:** Donna Jernigan/Monkmeyer. **p. 75:** SuperStock. **p. 76:** Courtesy of Prof. Karl Fredga, Uppsala University.

Chapter 4: **p. 81:** Stephanie Maze/Woodfin Camp & Associates, Inc. **p. 86 (top left):** CC Studio/Science Photo Library/Photo Researchers, Inc. **p. 86 (top right):** SuperStock. **p. 86 (bottom left):** Petit Format/Nestle/Science Source/Photo Researchers, Inc. **p. 86 (bottom right):** Nestle/Petit Format/Photo Researchers, Inc. **p. 87 (top):** Petit Format/Nestle/Science Source/Photo Researchers, Inc. **p. 87: (middle):** Petit Format/Nestle/Science Source/Photo Researchers, Inc. **p. 87 (bottom):** NIH/Science Source/Photo Researchers, Inc. **p. 92:** Heggemann/Stern/Black Star. **p. 93:** Streissguth, Ann P., Ph.D.; Aase, Jon M., M.D.; Clarren Sterling K., M.D.; Randels, Sandra P., RN; LaDue, Robin A., Ph.D.; and Smith, David F., M.D. (1991). Fetal Alcohol Syndrome in Adolescents and Adults. *The Journal of the American Medical Association* 265(15), 1961–1967. **p. 96:** Byron/Monkmeyer. **p. 99:** Laura Dwight/Photo Edit. **p. 101:** P. Amranand/SuperStock, Inc. **p. 106:** SuperStock.

Chapter 5: **p. 116:** Nathan Benn/Woodfin Camp & Associates Inc. **p. 118 (left):** Ellis Herwig/Stock Boston. **p. 118 (right):** Myrleen Ferguson Cate/Photo Edit. **p. 122:** T. Rosenhthal/SuperStock, Inc.

p. 123: Michael Newman/Photo Edit. **p. 124:** Dennis MacDonald/Photo Edit. **p. 129:** Tony Freeman/Photo Edit. **p. 131:** Robert Brenner/Photo Edit. **p. 133:** Mimi Forsyth/Monkmeyer. **p. 135:** David W. Hamilton/The Image Bank. **p. 137:** Camerapix/Gamma. **p. 138:** Robert E. Daemmrich/Tony Stone Images.

Chapter 6: **p. 143:** Al Cook/Stock Boston. **p. 145:** Suzanne Szasz/Photo Researchers, Inc. **p. 148:** Mark Richards/Photo Edit. **p. 149:** Myrleen Ferguson/Photo Edit. **p. 152:** Cathy Watterson/Meese Photo Research. **p. 154:** Mary Kate Dennis/Photo Edit. **p. 159:** Shackman/Monkmeyer. **p. 162:** Gail Meese/Meese Photo Research. **p. 166:** HMS Images/The Image Bank.

Chapter 7: **p. 172:** Gale Zucker Photography. **p. 174:** Rivera Collection/SuperStock, Inc. **p. 178:** Joel Gordon. **p. 181:** Richard Heinzen/Superstock. **p. 183:** Phyllis Picordi/Stock Boston. **p. 185:** Gale Zucker Photography. **p. 186:** Gianni Cigolini/The Image Bank. **p. 189:** Peter Buckley/Photo Researchers, Inc. **p. 196:** Gale Zucker Photography. **p. 199:** Gale Meese/Meese Photo Research. **p. 200:** Stephen McBrady/Photo Edit.

Chapter 8: **p. 209:** David Strickler/Meese Photo Research. **p. 210:** Kopstein/Monkmeyer. **p. 212:** A. N. Meltzoff & A. K. Moore/University of Washington. **p. 215:** Carolyn Rovee-Collier/Rutgers University. **p. 220:** Marianne Gontarz. **p. 223:** Tim Davis/Photo Researchers, Inc. **p. 226:** Joel Gordon.

Chapter 9: **p. 236:** Austin MacRae. **p. 239:** Jim Whitmer/Stock Boston. **p. 249:** Audrey Topping/Photo Researchers, Inc. **p. 253:** Spencer Grant/Monkmeyer/Grantpix. **p. 256:** AP/Wide World Photos. **p. 257:** Harvard University Archives. **p. 260:** Lawrence Erlbaum Associates, Inc. *Creativity Research Journal,* Vol 5, p. 270. **p. 263:** Joel Gordon.

Chapter 10: **p. 268 (left):** AP/Wide World Photos. **p. 268 (right):** Peter Simon/Stock Boston. **p. 271:** Paul Damien/Tony Stone Images. **p. 275:** Randy Schulze/Design Conceptions. **p. 283:** David Young-Wolff/Photo Edit. **p. 284:** Ulrike Welsch. **p. 289:** Photo Researchers, Inc. **p. 290:** SuperStock, Inc. **p. 291:** E. J. Camp/Outline Press Syndicate.

Chapter 11: **p. 297:** John Running/Black Star. **p. 310:** Cassy Cohen/Photo Edit. **p. 311:** Andy Sacks/Tony Stone Images. **p. 316:** Robert Morfey/Tony Stone Images. **p. 318:** Gail Meese/Meese Photo Research. **p. 323:** Doug Mason/Woodfin Camp & Associates, Inc. **p. 324:** Marianne Gontarz.

Chapter 12: **p. 331:** SuperStock. **p. 333:** Jim Whitmer/Stock Boston. **p. 335:** Elizabeth Crews/Stock Boston. **p. 340:** Felicia Martinez/Photo Edit. **p. 344:** Bruce Kliewe/Jeroboam. **p. 352:** Kal Muller/Woodfin Camp & Associates, Inc. **p. 355:** David R. Frazier.

Chapter 13: **p. 361:** AP/Wide World Photos. **p. 363 (left):** Nina Leen/*Life Magazine.* **p. 363 (right):** Myrleen Ferguson/Photo Edit. **p. 365:** Izard/University of Delaware. **p. 366:** Michael Newman/Photo Edit. **p. 368:** Michael Newman/Photo Edit. **p. 371:** Harlow Primate Laboratory, University of Wisconsin. **p. 373:** Corbis-Bettmann. **p. 375:** Joseph Schuyler/Stock Boston. **p. 377:** Gail Meese/Meese Photo Research. **p. 380:** Laura Dwight/ Photo Edit. **p. 381:** Mary Kate Denny/Photo Edit. **p. 382:** Terry Wild Studio. **p. 386:** Joel Gordon. **p. 389:** Cleo Freelance Photography. **p. 391:** Donna Day/Tony Stone Images.

Chapter 14: **p. 396:** Myrleen Ferguson/Photo Edit. **p. 400:** T. Rosenthal/SuperStock, Inc. **p. 403:** Renee Lynn/Photo Researchers. **p. 407:** Pennie Tweedie/Tony Stone Images. **p. 410:** Superstock. **p. 411:** SuperStock. **p. 413:** John Kelly/The Image Bank. **p. 417:** Spencer Grant/Stock Boston. **p. 423:** Grant Le Duc/Monkmeyer.

Chapter 15: **p. 430:** C. Blankenhorn/The Picture Cube. **p. 431:** David Shaffer. **p. 433:** Ray Ellis/Photo Researchers, Inc. **p. 438:** Meese Photo Research. **p. 439:** Gail Meese/Meese Photo Research. **p. 433:** Alexander Lowery/Photo Researchers, Inc. **p. 444:** Sarah Putnam/The Picture Cube. **p. 446:** Keren Su/Tony Stone Images.

p. 450: Andy Sachs/Tony Stone Images.   p. 454: Terry Vine/Tony Stone Images.   p. 457: Gale Zucker Photography.

TO THE OWNER OF THIS BOOK:

I hope that you have found *Life-Span Human Development*, Third Edition, useful. So that this book can be improved in a future edition, would you take the time to complete this sheet and return it? Thank you.

School and address: _____

Department: _____

Instructor's name: _____

1. What I like most about this book is: _____

_____

_____

2. What I like least about this book is: _____

_____

_____

3. My general reaction to this book is: _____

_____

4. The name of the course in which I used this book is: _____

_____

5. Were all of the chapters of the book assigned for you to read? _____

   If not, which ones weren't? _____

 6. In the space below, or on a separate sheet of paper, please write specific suggestions for improving this book and anything else you'd care to share about your experience in using the book.

_____

_____

_____

_____

_____

_____

Optional:

Your name: _____ Date: _____

May Brooks/Cole quote you, either in promotion for *Life-Span Human Development*, Third Edition, or in future publishing ventures?

Yes: _____ No: _____

Sincerely,

Carol K. Sigelman